A Political

(States drawn in proportion to number of electora...

(Electo... be reassigned after the 1960 census.)

A NEW AMERICA

3000 miles of unfortified border

St. Lawrence Seaway

FRENCH-CANADIAN- -AMERICANS

VT. 3 — GOOD VOTING RECORD

N.H. 4

ME. 5 — FATHER, WHAT'S A DEMOCRAT?

N.Y. 45 — HAS MOST ELECTORAL VOTES

L. Ontario

Erie

Boston — MELTING POT OF YANKEELAND

MASS. 16

GOVERNOR HERE IS LIKELY CANDIDATE FOR PRESIDENCY

F.D.R. LIVED HERE

SHAYS' REBELLION, 1787

CONN. 8

R.I. 4 — STAYED AWAY FROM CONSTITUTIONAL CONVENTION

FIRST STATE TO REQUIRE LITERACY TEST

New York City
THE MELTING POT —HAS OVER 3 MILLION VOTERS

Dems. Reps.

LONG ISLAND

PA. 32

COAL

CONSTITUTIONAL CONVENTION—1787

Philadelphia

1ST PRESIDENTIAL CONVENTION

N.J. 16

INTERSTATE COOPERATION IN RUNNING PORT OF N.Y.

TIME FOR A CHANGE

W.VA. 8 COAL

VA. 12

Baltimore MD 9

DEL. 3 — HOME OF CORPORATIONS

BIRTHPLACE OF 8 PRESIDENTS

Washington, D.C. — NO ELECTORS NO VOTERS

N.C. 14

S.C. 8

TOBACCO POLITICS

FATHER, WHAT'S A REPUBLICAN?

COUNTY-UNIT SYSTEM FOR ELECTION OF GOVERNORS

STORMY DEMOCRATIC POLITICS

TURN THE RASCALS OUT

A FULL DINNER PAIL

Key:

1 — NUMBER OF ELECTORAL VOTES

THE PIVOTAL STATES

TOTAL NUMBER OF ELECTORAL VOTES 537 FOR 1960 ELECTION

Outline of the above proportional map, super-imposed on an actual map of the United States

GOVERNMENT BY THE PEOPLE

The dynamics of American national government

James MacGregor Burns

Williams College

Jack Walter Peltason

University of Illinois

b y

The dynamics of American

PRENTICE-HALL, INC.

Englewood Cliffs, N. J.

FOURTH EDITION

Government

the

People

national government

Fourth Edition

GOVERNMENT BY THE PEOPLE

The dynamics of American national government

Burns and Peltason

Designed by Walter Behnke

Third printing . . . . June, 1961

36080—C

To the memory of
John Calyer Ranney, *1915-1950*
Teacher, scholar, friend

Preface

The meaning and challenge of American government are in the spotlight. The meaning goes beyond the headlines, and the challenge transcends the latest crises. In this fourth edition of *Government by the People,* the authors have tried to clarify, relate, and integrate the facts about American government and political institutions in order to encourage conceptual and critical thinking. Training for citizenship and cultivating a basic interest in liberal and general education both remain as related aims of this edition.

The chief method of trying to reach these goals continues to be an emphasis on *problems.* Because the problems as well as the facts of the American political system are extremely varied and wide-ranging, a special effort has been made to organize these problems in terms of *five basic questions* that the authors consider fundamental in understanding and evaluating American democratic government. These five questions are listed in the introduction to Part One, and the introductions to the remaining parts serve as guides to places where aspects of these basic problems are treated.

For invaluable assistance in preparing the fourth edition we wish to thank Lee F. Anderson, who helped revise and modernize the state and local chapters, who assumed the chief responsibility for the revision of the bibliography, and who prepared the Index; Valentine Jobst III, of the University of Illinois, who checked the galleys once again against his wide knowledge of American government; Ruth Silva of the Pennsylvania State University and Warren Miller of the Survey Research Center, University of Michigan, who advised us on matters in their special fields of competence; Theodore Mitau of Macalester College, Melvin P. Straus of San Jose State University, and Howard White of Miami University, who made suggestions for improving the previous edition; and David J. Danelski and Denis Sullivan of the University of Illinois. Ruth Greene and Gretel Clark kindly read galley and page proofs for a final check. We especially wish to thank Everett Sims of Prentice-Hall, Inc. for one of the most detailed, exacting, and constructive sets of editorial suggestions we have ever encountered. Any errors, of course, are the authors' alone—and we would greatly appreciate being notified of them.

For invaluable help on the previous edition we wish to thank Hollis W. Barber, University of Illinois (Navy Pier); Clarence A. Berdahl, University of Illinois; Donald C. Blaisdell, City College of New York; Gordon B. Cleveland, University of North Carolina; Samuel J. Eldersveld, University of Michigan; George Harvey, University of Missouri; Robert F. Karsch, University of Missouri; Mahmut N. Lacin, Sacramento State; Frederic D. Ogden, University of Alabama; Thomas Page, J. Austin Ranney, Robert E. Scott, and Clyde F. Snider, all of University of Illinois; Gustav R. Serino, Edward Sofen, and J. Ben Stalvey, all of University of Miami; and Pauline Yelderman, University of Houston. We are also grateful to Henry Holt, Inc. for permission to quote from occasional sentences in previous publications.

Those who have contributed to earlier editions ideas and criticisms meriting special appreciation are: Professors S. S. Aichele, Temple; Charles Aikin, University of California (Berkeley); Charles R. Cherington, Harvard; Thomas I. Cook, Johns Hopkins; U. G. Dubach, Lewis and Clark; Charles D. Goff, University of Wisconsin (Milwaukee Extension); Fred Greene, Williams; Cecilia Kenyon, Smith; Robert E. Lane, Yale; Donald R. Larson, University of Miami; Clay P. Malick, University of Colorado; Alpheus T. Mason, Princeton; James W. Prothro, Florida State University; Landon G. Rockwell, Hamilton; Victor G. Rosenblum, University of California (Berkeley); Wallace Sayre, Columbia University; Carl O. Smith, Wayne State University; and Joseph R. Starr, University of Maryland. Colleagues at the University of Illinois and at Williams were most generous in their advice and assistance. Professors Charles M. Kneier, University of Illinois; Rollin B. Posey, Northwestern; and Paul N. Ylvisaker, Swarthmore, gave informed advice on the state and local chapters.

The names and dates of court decisions are given in the body of the text, but full citations of all cases mentioned can be found in the Index.

A final note: Both the National and the National-State-Local editions have been so organized that they can be adapted for use in several different types of course. For those who want the minimum essentials of American national government, chapters 2-21, numbering 526 pages, provide a self-contained core coverage for the standard shorter course. For courses covering the basic materials of state and local government also, Part Seven of the larger edition can be included. Governmental functions are described in Part Six. Part One and Epilogue cover materials directly related to the study of American government and permit more extended coverage, either by themselves or in conjunction with any of the excellent problem or reading texts now available. Further suggestions on use of the text are available in the teaching manual for this edition prepared by Lucius J. Barker of the University of Wisconsin—Milwaukee.

J.W.P.
J.M.B.

Contents

Epilogue,   *page 729*

Democratic Government in America

A PROBLEM GUIDE

The American system of government is probably the most complicated on earth. It is also one of the most interesting, and—since the United States exerts world leadership—one of the most important. Because our system is so complex, however, it is easy to get bogged down in details and to lose perspective. The purpose of these "problem guides" at the opening of each part of this book is to help you gain an overview of the main problems that lie behind the details of government.

The book as a whole will emphasize five sets of problems:

First, *the challenge to democratic government:* How can we answer the claim of communists and other antidemocrats that democratic government is just a cloak for rule by a few selfish interests, that "government by the people" is a luxury to be enjoyed by only a few peoples, that for most of mankind it is ineffective and inappropriate, and that democratic government as we know it in America cannot compete with other types of government throughout the world? Part One poses this problem.

Second, *the problem of constitutional government:* How can we maintain a constitutional government largely shaped in 1787 in the face of the vast and urgent demands of the 1960's? For example, how can we give our leaders enough power to do their jobs well and still prevent them from misusing that power? How can we create genuine teamwork within Washington and between Washington and the state capitals, and at the same time maintain a constitutional system that divides power

1

among a host of officials? Part Two emphasizes this set of problems.

Third, *the problem of individual rights:* How can democratic government maintain a balance between liberty and order, between uniformity and diversity, between individual rights and collective needs? The philosopher Bertrand Russell has stated this problem well: "How can we combine that degree of individual initiative which is necessary for progress with the degree of social cohesion that is necessary for survival?" This set of problems is treated chiefly in Part Three.

Fourth, *the problem of popular representation:* Do our interest groups, opinion agencies, political parties, and elections fairly reflect the interests and needs of the American people? For example, how much influence should a popular majority (exerted perhaps through a political party) have as compared with the major interest groups, such as labor and business (exerted perhaps through publicity and lobbying organizations)? How can we meet the demands of organized groups without sacrificing the welfare of the people as a whole? Part Four focuses on this set of problems.

Fifth, *the problem of responsible leadership:* How can we give our leaders enough governmental authority to cope with present and emerging problems and still keep them accountable to the people? For example, should the President have more leeway, at least in foreign affairs? Should we create more unity between President and Congress, or do we want them to check each other? How responsible is Congress to the people—and to what groups of people? Should we make our leaders—executive and legislative and even judicial—more responsible to the majority of the people? If so, how could this be done? What is the case against leadership responsible mainly to a majority of the voters? Part Five is largely concerned with this set of problems.

But here is an important reminder: Since American government is a "seamless web," it is impossible (and undesirable) to separate one problem sharply from another. Hence every one of the major problems that we have mentioned is bound to spill over into every part of this book. The guides above simply suggest the part of the book in which certain sets of problems are *emphasized.* Most of these problems are closely interrelated—for example: constitutionalism in Part Two is related to individual liberty in Part Three, representation in Part Four is related to responsible leadership in Part Five.

CHAPTER 1

Democratic Government
in America

The place is Anytown, U.S.A. The time is immediately before an election. For months, candidates for office, high and low, have been viewing with alarm and pointing with pride. The papers have been carrying big headlines.

SENATOR SMITH ACCUSES JONES OF RED LINKS

Jones Says Nation's Main Threat is Smithism

Jones Tool of Labor Bosses, Smith Charges

DEFEAT JONES TO SAVE AMERICAN WAY OF LIFE, URGES SENATOR SMITH

SMITH AGENT OF WALL STREET, JONES SAYS

OPPOSITION DESPERATE, WILL GO TO ANY LENGTHS — JONES SAYS

The day after the election, the count is Jones, 1,511,000; Smith, 1,403,000. At eleven in the morning Smith wires Jones: "YOU HAVE BEEN ENTRUSTED BY THE PEOPLE WITH GREAT RESPONSIBILITY. MY CONGRATULATIONS AND COMMISERATIONS TO YOU."

All is calm. The factories are open, people at work, stores crowded, students in their classrooms. On Main Street there are no barricades, no angry mobs, no protesting parades. The people of a large country, after months of vigorous campaigning and bitter argument, have chosen the men who are to run their school systems, direct their cities, legislate in their state capitols, and

3

guide the nation in Washington. These decisions will closely affect their lives and their fortunes. Yet they were made without bloodshed. When the votes were all counted, the Smithites shook their heads in disgust, but it never entered their minds not to accept the verdict of the ballot box. The "College Students for Smith" did not meet to discuss whether to take up arms in defense of the American way of life—the very way of life that they had insisted before the election would be destroyed if Jones were elected. Nor did the Jonesites, now that they had power, proceed to round up their political enemies and throw them into jail.

Is this not a remarkable thing? So deeply ingrained are the habits of democracy that Americans sometimes forget that in relatively few places in the world could such an event take place. In many other countries, brute force is the accustomed way of deciding who shall hold power. Even where no open clash occurs, a small group of self-appointed bosses, by stifling criticism and manipulating propaganda, can make decisions without consulting anyone else. Such are the tactics of the totalitarians.

To Americans, the workings of democratic government are a common and rather dull matter. We tend to take democratic government for granted; even worse, we seem to consider it inevitable. We take pride in our ability to make it work, and rightly so. But we must remember that we have inherited a going system—a system established by others, not by ourselves. Our job is to keep it going, and to keep it going we must understand it.

In this introductory chapter we shall first discuss the social, psychological, and economic forces that help shape American government. Next we shall look briefly at the nature of government as a whole. We shall then turn to democratic *government,* the democratic essentials embodied in it, and the necessary conditions for its existence. The chapter will conclude with the challenge to democratic government from without and within, and with the resulting challenge to the student of American government.

Dynamic America

When we study American government we study certain aspects of the behavior of the American people. That is all there is to it—the people with their ideas and customs and the things they inherit and create. Sometimes we forget this simple but fundamental fact. We become so involved in talking about federalism, or separation of powers, or constitutions, or laws, that we lose sight of the fact that all these things are merely descriptions of *people* and the things *people* produce, that they are shorthand ways to describe how *people* behave, what they believe, what they do.

Now the way Americans behave politically and the operation of their governmental institutions are obviously related to how they make a living, their fears and anxieties, where they live—in fact, with everything important to them and about them. Since we shall spend most of our time concentrating on the political and governmental aspects of American people, let us first set the stage so that we shall not forget the social, psychological and economic forces that shape politics. What are the salient aspects of American society that condition and influence the nature of American democratic government?

First of all, the United States is a land of infinite diversity. Consider our climate and geography. The continental sweep of our nation embraces burning deserts, thousand-mile-long mountain ranges, humid areas drenched with rain, immense prairies, dust bowls, lake regions, vast forests, and many thousands of miles of coastline. We are a nation of regions vast enough to be called subnations, and each subnation is bound by ties of history, politics, economics, and language. Each is a nation in itself, containing nearly as much diversity as France, Spain, or England.

Ours is a nation of nations in an even more literal sense. America is the fabled "melting pot." We are a nation of Italian-Americans, Irish-Americans, Polish-Americans, Swedish-Americans, German-Americans, Latin-Americans, and many other "hyphenated" groups, along with Negroes, old Yankee groups, Indians, and others. The millions of immigrants brought the old country with them; they introduced not only differences in languages and customs but also

EVOLUTION

From the infinite variety of Nature to the universal pudd'nhead.

David Low for *Survey Graphic.* Copyright Low all countries. Reprinted by permission of Low.

Unity is not uniformity.

clashing religious and political attitudes. They did not discard their old beliefs and languages and customs overnight; on the contrary, they often clung to their separate ways as long as they could. In short, the melting pot did not melt everyone into the same dull gray.

Put these two elements together—sectionalism and a variety of national origins—and the checkered, polyglot nature of America begins to emerge. Add to these the religious diversity—the scores of Protestant sects, the powerful Catholic and Jewish groups; add also the divisive impact of political doctrines that have swept the country, some from Europe, some home-grown; add finally the influence of the competitiveness and individualism that Americans have long praised and practiced—and the heterogeneity of America becomes even clearer.

Yet there is an underlying homogeneity too. Americans have a common language and pay homage to national heroes like George Washington and Thomas Jefferson. Wherever we live we listen to the same song hits, read the same comic strips, watch the same movies. Great corporations, labor unions, farm organizations span the nation and affect the lives of people everywhere. To walk down Main Street in our home town, with its bright lights, chain stores, parking meters, traffic jams, is to walk down *any* Main Street in America.

The homogeneity of Americans stems from the fact that regardless of our religion, place of birth, or national origin, we share a common culture, a common language, common heroes, common ideals, a common nationality. On the other hand, no single religion or industry, no single class or profession, is overpowering. We have social checks and balances, a pluralistic outlook, that in many ways are more important than our form of government itself in creating a climate of democracy.

Other social trends, too, have had an effect on government. The movement of our people—first from country to city, and now from city to suburb—has forced politicians to change their campaign appeals. The aging of our population has directed attention to pensions and programs for the elderly, whose numbers have increased their political power. The incorporation of minorities into the mainstream of American life has led to a keener concern for civil liberties. All these social trends make clear that what happens to Americans happens to American government. Let us look briefly at some of these trends.

SOCIAL TRENDS

1. *Population changes.* There were about 180 million Americans in 1960. Our population has doubled in the last fifty years. Not long ago the demographers, who study vital statistics such as births, marriages, and deaths were predicting that our population curve would soon flatten out and that the proportion of young people in the total population would decline at a rapid rate. The tremendous increase in population during recent years of prosperity,

however, has led to a revision of these estimates. It has been predicted that, barring catastrophic wars or depressions, our population will reach 240 million by 1975.

Our population is also changing in character. For many decades there has been an increase in urban population, as compared with rural, and this trend is continuing. Almost two-thirds of the people live in urban areas as defined by the Census Bureau. Suburban communities are growing at a much faster rate than the central, built-up areas of our cities. The rise of "Suburbia" is having a variety of social and political effects. Population increase is also uneven in different areas of the country. During the 1950's the population of the West, for example, grew much faster than that of the South. During the 1940's several agricultural states declined in population.

Our population is *aging* as well as growing. The median age in 1900 was 23 years; in 1960 it reached 30. The proportion of people over 65 was 4 per cent in 1900 and is about twice that today. Such changes have important implications for government—for example, in the scope of old-age assistance.

2. *The class system.* In certain ways American society is stratified. Study after study of American communities has revealed a social-economic class system based largely on wealth. People with similar incomes, occupations, or social positions tend to associate and to form relatively distinct classes. In the typical community at least three basic classes are found—upper, middle, and lower—but usually there are gradations within classes, such as the upper-middle class (wealthy business and professional groups) and the lower-middle class (clerical workers and highly skilled labor).

The important question is not whether classes exist but whether America is becoming more or less stratified. The day when an individual could rise rapidly from class to class seems to be passing. The "rags to riches" feats of Horatio Alger heroes were always exaggerated, but they happen even less often today. Increasingly, people seem to follow the occupational and social paths of their parents. On the other hand, there is considerable mobility and flexibility in the largest and most dynamic strata, the middle classes. Here people move "down" or "up" much more freely than in the more stratified upper and lower classes. There are tendencies toward *caste,* too, in American life, especially in the case of minority groups; but the caste system also is in a state of flux, owing to pressures from inside the caste and from outside. Our class system contains within itself the seeds of change.

3. *Mass culture.* The United States, as we have noted, is a medley of diverse groups and subcultures. But the nation and its people have a sense of unity too, and underlying this sense of unity is a mass culture that is common to all the subcultures. Our mass culture is the result of many things—common traditions, folklore, a common language, past and present wars and crises, and the like. It is produced also by our mass media of communications—films that

---

[1] J. W. Bennett and M. M. Tumin, *Social Life* (Knopf, 1948), pp. 570-600. See also C. Wright Mills, *White Collar* (Oxford Univ. Press, 1952).

are shown in every community in the land, magazines that sell millions of copies an issue, and radio and television programs that blanket the nation.

What happens when a mass culture exists along with many subcultures? The mass culture serves as a bridge linking one group to another. But can the mass culture go very deep? According to some sociologists, it lacks roots, consisting of a shifting set of attitudes and values that tend to be simple and fleeting in nature: the fads of teen-agers, the cult of actor worshipers, food

THE AMERICAN CLASS SYSTEM

(Tendency toward rigidity of this UPPER stratum through hereditary wealth and social position.)

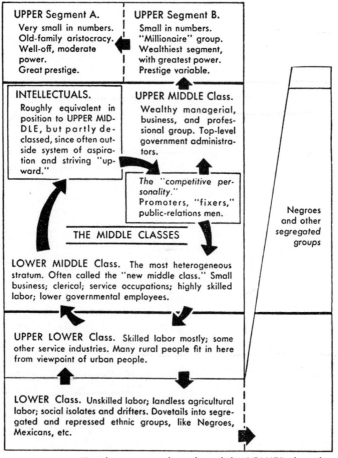

UPPER Segment A. Very small in numbers. Old-family aristocracy. Well-off, moderate power. Great prestige.

UPPER Segment B. Small in numbers. "Millionaire" group. Wealthiest segment, with greatest power. Prestige variable.

INTELLECTUALS. Roughly equivalent in position to UPPER MIDDLE, but partly declassed, since often outside system of aspiration and striving "upward."

UPPER MIDDLE Class. Wealthy managerial, business, and professional group. Top-level government administrators.

The "competitive personality." Promoters, "fixers," public-relations men.

THE MIDDLE CLASSES

LOWER MIDDLE Class. The most heterogeneous stratum. Often called the "new middle class." Small business; clerical; service occupations; highly skilled labor; lower governmental employees.

UPPER LOWER Class. Skilled labor mostly; some other service industries. Many rural people fit in here from viewpoint of urban people.

LOWER Class. Unskilled labor; landless agricultural labor; social isolates and drifters. Dovetails into segregated and repressed ethnic groups, like Negroes, Mexicans, etc.

Negroes and other segregated groups

(Tendency toward rigidity of this LOWER class through constant economic underprivilege and unemployment.)

From John W. Bennett and Melvin M. Tumin, *Social Life*, by permission of Alfred A. Knopf, Inc. Copyright 1948 by Alfred A. Knopf, Inc.

fetishes, and self-improvement formulas for everything from hair styles to hypnosis. Such common patterns do not provide a core of common fixed meaning and values.

4. *War.* Fourteen million Americans donned military uniforms in World War II, and countless other millions worked in the war program at home. Almost six million served in the three-year-long Korean war, and we are still involved in a gigantic defense effort. In a sense, we have a whole new sub-culture—that of millions of men, and some women, working and training in camps and other military installations at home and abroad. It is too early to estimate the impact of continued war crises upon Americans, but surely it will leave its mark on our attitudes, customs, behavior, and way of life.

PSYCHOLOGICAL TRENDS

All these social trends, though at times contradictory and conflicting, reveal a common trend: the trend toward *bigness.* Ours is a civilization of big cities, big machines, big labor, big business, big bombs, big government. In the shadow of this bigness, the individual stands a tiny and puny figure. To be sure, he created this bigness, but in doing so he may have built a Franken-stein's monster that in turn will destroy him, or at least destroy his power to fashion his life as he wishes.

Little man, big world—this is the nub of the problem. But the problem shows itself in several ways. One is the individual's feeling of *helplessness.* The world is swept by gigantic forces over which he has little sense of control. A second is his feeling of *rootlessness.* Millions of men, living in cities, have little of the feeling of belonging and permanence that their grandfathers experienced in more stable, rural areas. A third aspect, closely related to the other two, is the feeling of *impersonality.* Our social relationships often lack depth and meaning; in the fast pace of urban life our contacts with others may be fleeting and shallow. Individual personality is ignored or crushed.

These feelings of helplessness, rootlessness, and impersonality have influenced our literature and art. Think of Charlie Chaplin in the movie *Modern Times*—the little man controlled by the great machine. Or Franz Kafka's famous novel *The Trial,* in which the hero, accused of a crime he did not commit and even the nature of which he knows not, becomes entangled in a vast nightmarish bureaucracy and is finally destroyed. Social scientists have become increasingly interested in the fate of the little man in the big society. Psychologists have identified three important forces relating to government:

1. *The quest for security.* Man has freed himself from many old bonds, such as slavery and feudalism, and has won for himself certain individual rights and liberties. But in gaining freedom from the old controls, he has failed to gain the positive freedom of realizing his intellectual and artistic potentialities. Instead, freedom has posed new problems that he feels unable to meet.

Living amid modern industrial civilization—with its large-scale organization, its mobility and competitiveness, its impersonality, its sheer bigness—he feels isolated, insecure, and lonely. Gone is the old framework of custom and authority, of life in small groups and stable communities. The machine age has made man rich in material things, but he feels insecure, helpless, isolated, powerless, and lost.

What is the result? Modern man has tried, in the words of the psychoanalyst Erich Fromm, to *escape* from freedom. Faced with impossible situations and decisions, he may turn away from freedom and individuality and try to fuse himself with some outside person or thing to gain a sense of security.[2] He may submit to some self-confident person who has all the "answers" and issues all the orders. One reason Hitler took power in the early 1930's was the feeling of millions of Germans that they were in the grip of giant economic and social forces that they could not control.

2. *The quest for conformity*. Another current tendency, some social scientists feel, is that people are increasingly eager to conform to the standards of men and women around them. In bringing up children, David Riesman has noted, parents want their children to be *popular* with *other* children.[3] Mother becomes a chauffeur and a booking agent. The teen-ager's most important possession is a "popularity kit" composed of set types of clothes, a knowledge of the latest gadgets, of movie and TV stars, of popular tunes, plus an amazing storehouse of small talk on all sorts of subjects. One must conform and adjust. Being high-hat or "different" is forbidden.

Many adults also seek to conform. Consider, for example, life in some of our bigger organizations, such as government agencies, universities, and especially business corporations. According to one study, success in these organizations forces one to become an "organization man" who conforms to the "system."[4] In a big corporation the trainees, the executives, and even their wives are not supposed to exhibit too much individuality; they are expected to adjust themselves to the needs and life of the corporation, even when they are back home in Suburbia. The pressure to conform is not tyrannical; it is subtle, continuous, and all-pervasive, and, for that reason, all the more effective. The organization man gains security and "togetherness" but suffers some loss in individual responsibility and the freedom to be an *un*common man.

The implications for democratic government are important. (Adjusting to others is not the same as individual freedom) The person whose greatest need in life is the approval of his neighbors, whose driving aim is to get along with others at almost any price—such a person may yet feel lonely in the great crowd) There is a need for autonomy as well as for adjustment, for individuality as well as for conformity. Democratic government cannot last in a homog-

---

2 Erich Fromm, *Escape from Freedom* (Farrar & Rinehart, 1941).
3 David Riesman, *The Lonely Crowd* (Yale Univ. Press, 1950).
4 W. H. Whyte, Jr., *The Organization Man* (Doubleday, 1957).

enized society; civil liberties perish in a society where men will not tolerate political opinions other than their own.

3. *The quest for community.* Closely related to these forces is man's desire for some sense of *direction,* of *belonging,* of *community* with his neighbors. Just as children grow anxious when separated from their parents, says Sebastian de Grazia, adults become anxious when separated from their political and religious "fathers"—from their tribal chiefs, priests, gods, kings, and presidents.[5] People *need* such rulers, for the rulers personify the moral codes that help bind citizens together and give them a sense of purpose and direction.

Trouble may result when our moral codes conflict. Our religion, de Grazia says, teaches us the need for brotherly love, while our economic philosophy teaches the need for competitiveness. Modern Western culture, with its stress on individual liberty, tends to leave people confused, insecure, and lacking in purpose. *Men must believe in something or somebody.* They must have leaders who symbolize and help realize men's highest aspirations and who can give them a sense of community.

What of the impact of these psychological trends on American government? War and fear of war have led to huge government bureaucracies for defense and for veterans' welfare. The quest for security is often cited as one of the factors lying behind the rise of "big government." The psychological insecurity of some Americans, it is said, has led to the success of politicians who play on these fears by manufacturing conspiracies and by exaggerating threats of internal subversion in an attempt to win mass followings.

Yet a word of caution: it is difficult to generalize with confidence about psychological trends. Many social scientists disagree that the trends outlined here are so clear or the situation so serious as some of the above views seem to indicate. Other and even contradictory generalizations could be made. It is not certain, for example, that life in the rural communities of a hundred years ago was psychologically secure or that modern urban man feels less rooted than did some of his isolated and culturally poverty-stricken forefathers. Generalizations about psychological trends often depend on which evidence is emphasized. Usually there are many forces working in many directions.

ECONOMIC TRENDS

Perhaps nothing has such a direct impact upon American government as the economic needs and satisfactions of Americans. What trends characterize our economy?

1. *Technological progress.* From the Stone Age and the Iron Age, man has passed into an age of glass, plastic fibers, alloys, an age of crop genetics,

---

[5] Sebastian de Grazia, *The Political Community* (Univ. of Chicago Press, 1948), p. ix.

agrobiology, and mechanized farming, an age of speed and the invasion of outer space. A century ago a commissioner of patents asked Congress to abolish his office because everything had been invented. And yet inventions have come at a faster and faster rate; twice as many patents were granted between 1940 and 1950 as between 1890 and 1900. Less dramatic than these technological strides, but perhaps as important, has been our advance in understanding the human problems of our industrial civilization, such as employer-employee relations.

Two recent developments indicate that more industrial revolutions lie ahead. One of these, of course, is atomic energy, a source of vast power that can be harnessed to peacetime as well as wartime uses. The second is automation. Fantastically complicated but reliable machines can do certain kinds of work, including "thinking work," now done by skilled and white-collar people—and do that work much more economically.[6] Such machines, unlike a human operator, do not become bored, unhappy, distracted, bed-ridden, or rebellious.

2. *Mass production and consumption.* As a result of advanced technology, rich resources, and varied skills, Americans produce and consume more goods than any other people. Physical output has increased at least five-fold in the last fifty years, while the number of employees has only doubled and the length of the work-day has actually dropped by a third. Output per man-hour is still increasing. In 1944, at the peak of our war effort, 63 million persons working 47 hours a week produced in terms of 1954 dollars a gross national product of $318 billion. It has been estimated that our gross product in 1960 (in terms of 1954 dollars) will be over $450 billion.[7]

Our capacity to consume goods and services is equally gigantic. In the past fifty years the proportion of our income spent on food, liquor, and tobacco has decreased slightly, and the proportion spent on clothing and personal care has stayed about the same. The proportion spent on personal transportation (notably automobiles) and on medical care and insurance, however, has doubled.

3. *Interdependence.* Years ago, the members of a family made most of what they needed with their own hands; today the average urban family produces only a tiny fraction of its needs. We have become increasingly *specialized* in our work. Specialization promotes greater efficiency, but it also allows disturbances in one sector of the economy to move quickly to other areas. We sink or swim together.

Related to this interdependence is the concentration of industrial and financial strength in fewer and larger corporations. Despite antitrust laws, the process of consolidation goes on. Today we have scores of "supermonopolies" in basic industries such as banking, railroads, automobiles, insurance, and

---

6 Norbert Wiener, *The Human Use of Human Beings* (Houghton Mifflin, 1950).
7 U.S. Dept. of Commerce, *Survey of Current Business* (July 1959) p. 7, and (August 1959) pp. 1-7.

public utilities; and widespread consolidation in textiles, foods, and the distributive trades. Labor organizations, too, have tended to become more and more centralized and integrated nationally.

4. *A mature or expanding economy?* Dynamic though it is, our economy is showing some signs of old age. We no longer have a western frontier offering limitless opportunities for economic expansion. Immigration today is small compared to what it was fifty or seventy-five years ago. Certain areas of the country are declining economically and some investment outlets have dwindled sharply.

But there are also signs of youthful vigor. Our power to produce continues to increase. Population and national income have soared in the last fifteen years. Some sections of the country—notably the West and Southwest—are expanding at an explosive rate. Even older areas, such as the South and Northeast, have shown amazing powers of economic growth since the end of World War II. Instead of a western frontier, we have a sort of internal frontier that offers tremendous possibilities for the investment of money and manpower.

Indeed, Americans live in grand style. Never before have so many people "had it so good." Ours has been described as an "affluent society" in which our economic problems stem not from scarcities but surpluses.[8] We have a labor force of over 73 million. Our productivity is high, our technological advances are great, and our natural resources are still immense.

But amid these superlatives, two cautious comments are in order. Although the United States can boast of a wider sharing of wealth than most other nations, certain Americans do not benefit from our high standard of living. Amidst our wealth there is still poverty. Tenant farmers, migratory workers, low-paid factory workers, and especially members of certain minority groups, have little of the material goods of life. Second, despite our wealth we are still in need of more hospitals, schools, roads, and houses. We spend billions for new and shiny automobiles to drive along dirty, congested city streets. We cheerfully support gigantic football stadiums but continue to crowd the mentally ill into dilapidated institutions. How we use our wealth is one of the great political questions facing Americans.

5. *Economic instability.* Our economy continues to be unstable. For over a century our business cycle has climbed and dipped like a roller coaster. We suffered long and severe depressions in the late 1830's, the 1870's, the 1890's, and the 1930's. In between were sharp but minor slumps, in 1884, 1904, 1914, 1920, 1937, and 1958. We have also had periods of sustained prosperity, however, as during the 1880's and recent years.

Is there a trend toward economic stability? Nobody knows. We have acquired a good deal of economic understanding in recent years and we have established rudimentary machinery for evening out the peaks and canyons in

---

[8] J. K. Galbraith, *The Affluent Society* (Houghton Mifflin, 1958).

the business cycle. The 1958 recession was one of the shortest and mildest of our history. Some economists, however, have grave doubts that we have yet learned how to achieve long-term stability. And persistent fear of tomorrow's depressions directly affects the way our governments operate.

The Stuff of Government

One freshman, after reading a book about government, laid it down, threw up his hands, and exclaimed, "It's just a big, buzzing confusion to me!" He was right. Government *is* immensely complex, especially in a large, industrialized society. Veteran reporters in Washington sometimes describe the nation's capital as a jungle, criss-crossed by a tangled network of trails. But let us see if we can find some kind of order and sense in all this complexity.

To begin with, it is well to remember that "government" is not just the national government, or city government, or British, or Russian government. Government is all around us, for in its broadest sense government is the *ordering* of human relations. Hence, it takes many forms. The most common government—in this broad use of the term—is the *family,* where rules are laid down and decisions are made by the head of the family. Other examples are student government, church government, fraternity government, the government of professional groups.

Political scientists, however, are primarily concerned with the *more formal government* operating amid the informal governments. They are con-

"When you say that it's all about government, do you mean it doesn't make sense?"

cerned, that is, with *centralized organizations* that maintain *systems of order* over communities large and small.[9] Unlike the family or many other informal governments, these organizations usually have constitutions, legislatures, elections, bureaucracies. Such a formal government—that of the United States— is the subject of this book. But remember that a big formal government such as that of the United States cannot be understood as something isolated from the thousands of informal governments that cluster throughout our society, and with which formal government continually interacts.

So much for government in general. What are the ingredients of formal

---

[9] R. M. MacIver, *The Web of Government* (Macmillan, 1947).

government? How can we begin to make our path through the "big buzzing confusion"?

Glance through the Table of Contents of this book and you will get a sense of the component parts of the great machine that is the American political system—parts such as the Constitution, federalism, civil liberties, political parties and groups, elections, Congress, President, and so on. These are described one by one because each is a big subject in itself. Yet there is bound to be something artificial about such a description. It is like describing a baseball game by telling first about the catcher, pitcher, first baseman, and so on, then the players on the other side, then the rules, the ball, the gloves, and all the rest, without saying anything about the players in *action*. And yet it is this very interaction, this give-and-take among the players, that makes up the essence of the ball game.

So it is with government. All its component parts—constitutions, legislatures, political parties, and so on—affect one another. What we need, then, is some way of cutting across all these component parts to reveal the totality of the political system. One way of doing this is to concentrate on the "Four I's" of government: institutions, interests, ideas, and individuals.[10]

1. *Institutions.* A political institution is any organized pattern of behavior that is well established as a continuing part of a political system: secret ballots, government agencies, courts, press conferences, congressional committees. They have a strong element of permanence; they are often embedded in law or tradition. They are somewhat predictable: we know that a presidential election will be held in 1964 and a new Congress elected, even though we do not know who the President will be or what bills the new Congress will pass.

2. *Interests.* Government operates amid a tangle of interests, with millions of men pushing and hauling in their efforts to reach private and public goals. Workers want more pay; farmers seek higher prices; businessmen demand less government interference; veterans ask higher pensions. Other interests are less economic, as in the case of religious or temperance groups. Groups tend to grow out of interests and to create new interests in turn. Interest groups affect, and are affected by, the operations of government. The American system would look very different without the business, labor, professional, and hundreds of other groups that exert political pressure.

3. *Ideas.* Men possess thoughts, it is said, but ideas possess men. Ideas come in all shapes and sizes. They may be strong and durable, such as the general American belief in "government by the people," or they may be

---

[10] After Pendleton Herring; for an excellent example of how this method of analysis can be used to illuminate the policy-making process, see Stephen K. Bailey, *Congress Makes a Law* (Columbia Univ. Press, 1950).

superficial or short-lived. They may be rational or irrational. An example of the latter was the fervent belief of millions of Germans that the "Aryan" race was superior to others. They may relate closely to people's economic interests, as in the case of trade-union support of social welfare laws, or they may run directly counter to the material welfare of those holding the belief. Ideas, in short, are forces that in themselves have an impact on politics.

4. *Individuals.* All the above forces operate through, and are transformed by, the people and their leaders. Obviously, America would be a different kind of country had it not been for great Presidents such as Washington and Lincoln, potent senators such as Henry Clay and Robert A. Taft, famous Supreme Court justices such as John Marshall and Oliver Wendell Holmes—and hundreds of industrialists, warriors, inventors, scholars, financiers, and writers who have left their imprint on American history. America would also be a much different place were it not for the millions of "plain" or "common" men and women—the Smiths, Cohens, Murphys, Muellers, and all the rest—who have elected the Presidents and congressmen, fought the wars, built the railroads and dams, and paid the taxes.

These, then, are four basic forces that interact with one another, like the players in a baseball game, and produce the political system that will be described in the following chapters.

THE ROLE OF GOVERNMENT

What is the purpose of government? Government is often damned as an evil or, at best, as a necessary evil. Some philosophers have believed that man in his most exalted state might live best without government, in a state of anarchy. But hard experience teaches that, man being what he is, the absence of government means the absence of peace and liberty. Without government, private individuals and groups would seize power and set up a narrow "private" government of their own; injustice, chaos, and conflict would then be the order of the day. Without government, as Hobbes wrote long ago, "the life of man would be solitary, poor, nasty, brutish, and short." Because ultimately it monopolizes force, government can establish the framework within which groups and individuals can live and work together peacefully.

The most essential tasks of government, then, might be summed up as:

1. *"Insuring Domestic Tranquillity."* This, incidentally, is one of the historic purposes of the new American government as set forth in the Preamble of the Constitution. Four other purposes described in that Preamble ably define the role of government, especially democratic government.

2. *"Provide for the Common Defense."* This is probably the oldest task of government, and today it makes the most pressing demands on our resources and physical energies. In the absence of international tranquillity, nations must be ready to protect themselves through military strength and

alliances. Under Jefferson, the national government spent only a few millions a year for defense. In President Eisenhower's budget for the fiscal year 1961, $46,500,000,000 was requested for national security, 54 per cent of the whole budget. *Our main economic stays out*

3. *"Establish Justice."* Another vital task of government is to regulate and order the lives of men fairly and humanely, with a quality called "justice." In a legal sense, justice calls for impartial judges and juries and for laws that are clear and explicit, that reflect the settled attitudes of the great mass of fair-minded people, that apply alike to rich and poor, white and Negro, Catholic and Protestant, and to all other human beings. In a broader sense, "justice" means that government serves as one agent that helps to distribute the good things of life as widely and fully as possible. Securing legal justice is an accepted function of government; to what extent government should assume the function of assuring "social justice" is one of the great questions of our time.

4. *"Promote the General Welfare."* Like "social justice," promoting the general welfare is a controversial problem. Most people, of course, believe that government should protect the welfare of those who cannot take care of themselves—the infirm, aged, blind. But how far should government go in helping farmers, workers, businessmen, consumers? Lincoln's answer was that government should "do for the community of people whatever they need to have done, but cannot do so well for themselves in their separate and individual capacities."

5. *"Secure the Blessings of Liberty."* To many, the noblest role of government is to enlarge the liberties and opportunities of the individual. This means in part *limiting* the role of government to prevent the heavy hand of law and police from stifling rightful individual activity. But it may mean—and this is another key issue of our time—*expanding* the role of government to enable it to protect individual liberties against encroachment. The power of government to prevent a lynching is an example of the use of government to protect an elementary right, the right to life and to a fair trial. The government's far-reaching control over highways through traffic laws and hordes of "state cops" is a way of expanding another freedom, that of travelling freely and securely.

We have been discussing government in general. But what are the distinctive features of *democracy* and *democratic government?*

The Nature of Democratic Government

Democracy—like liberty, equality, and justice—is hard to define. The term has come to mean so many different things and has won such great popularity that even the communists have tried to take it over; communist-controlled eastern Germany, for example, is called the German Democratic Republic. The word itself is made up of two Greek roots—*demos,* the people, and *kratos,* authority—and was used by the Greeks to mean government by the many, as contrasted with government by the few (oligarchy), or by one (autocracy). The word came into English usage in the seventeenth century to denote direct democracy, the kind of government that existed in Athens and other Greek city-states, where all enfranchised citizens came together to discuss and pass laws.

The term democratic government, like the term democracy, can be ambiguous and confusing. Some writers distinguish between *democratic* and *republican* governments, the former meaning governments in which decisions are made *directly* by a majority of the people—as in a New England town meeting—and the latter meaning governments in which the people's wishes are filtered through a series of *representative bodies,* such as Congress. But in this book we shall use the terms democratic and republican governments interchangeably to mean any government in which those who do the actual governing acquire their power to do so by means of a *fair, free, and competitive contest for the people's votes.* Or to paraphrase a definition by Madison, a government in which the persons making and carrying out public policies are chosen directly or indirectly by the voters at free and periodic elections.

So much, then, for what we mean generally by "government by the people." What we mean by democratic government will be discussed more concretely in the next few pages. But first we should note that democracy in itself is merely an expression of qualities that are deeply rooted in a people. What are the essential ideas that buttress democratic government?

THREE BASIC IDEAS OF DEMOCRACY

Democracy rests on a belief in the fundamental dignity and importance of the *individual,* in the essential *equality* of human beings, and in the need for *freedom.*

The emphasis on the supreme worth of the individual has run like an unbroken thread through democratic thought. It is woven into the writings of Thomas Jefferson, especially in the Declaration of Independence, where he eloquently proclaimed that all men have been endowed by their Creator with certain inalienable rights and that men create governments to secure these rights. It recurs in the speeches of present-day democrats such as David E. Lilienthal, former chairman of the TVA and of the Atomic Energy Commission, who said: "All government and all private institutions must be designed to promote and protect and defend the integrity and dignity of the individual." [11]

This doctrine of *individualism* (not to be confused with the doctrine of laissez faire) rests on the conviction that there is something of supreme worth in every human being. It demands that we should, in the words of a great

---

[11] David E. Lilienthal, *This I Do Believe* (Harper, 1949), p. x.

philosopher, Immanuel Kant, "so act as to treat humanity, whether in thine own person or in that of any other, in every case as an end withal, never as means only." Individualism makes the individual the central measure of value. The state, the union, and the corporation are valued solely in terms of their usefulness for individuals.

The doctrine of *statism*, on the other hand, makes the state the measure of value, and holds that public policies and governmental forms are good if they promote the well-being of the state. But democratic political theory has refused to glorify the state or to shroud it in metaphysical abstractions. The state is nothing more than the organized political society that operates through government. And the government is a group of men called congressmen, members of parliament, presidents, prime ministers, judges, and bureaucrats who, as agents of society, are granted certain powers and perform certain public functions. The welfare of the state has no meaning except in terms of the welfare of the individuals who comprise it.

II. The second basic premise of democracy is the right of *each* individual to be treated as a unique and inviolable person. The democrat does not insist, as his critics sometimes imply, that all men are equal in talents, virtues, or capabilities. He does insist that the claims of one individual to his life, liberty, and happiness must be treated as just as important as those of any other individual. He insists that "the poorest he that is in England has a life to live as the richest he," [12] as Colonel Rainboro said back in 1647.

III. The third basic premise of democracy is the belief that liberty is desirable, that freedom is good. "Liberty" and "freedom" are slippery words, but as we are using them here they mean that each individual should have the maximum opportunity to select his own purposes in life and to choose the means to accomplish those purposes. The core of liberty is self-determination. "Positive freedom consists," writes Erich Fromm, "in the spontaneous activity of the total, integrated personality." Liberty and freedom mean more than the absence of external restraints; they connote the "power" to act positively toward the goals one has chosen.

Why is freedom desirable? Briefly, and of course oversimply, because the freedom *to make choices* and *to act upon them* is essential to the development of those faculties that make one a human being. Denied this freedom, the individual becomes something less than a man. It is this quality of being able to make rational choices, to select the good from the bad and to decide whether to seek the good, that distinguishes men from other animals. It is only through the use of his freedom that the individual develops a sense of responsibility and self-restraint. It is only by acting as free and responsible individuals that men are able to exploit their full capacity for growth.

From the viewpoint of society, freedom is desirable because both history and logic suggest that liberty is the key to social progress. The greater the area

---

[12] Col. Thomas Rainboro, "Debates on the Putney Project, 1647," from A. T. Mason, *Free Government in the Making* (Oxford Univ. Press, 1949), p. 12.

of freedom, the greater the probability of discovering better ways of living. Where men enjoy freedom of inquiry and expression, they are more likely to detect error and uncover truth. Progress is stifled wherever an authoritarian group or even social custom imposes an orthodoxy that none may question. Denial of freedom, moreover, generates personal frustration, which in turn may erupt into aggressive, antisocial behavior.

There is nothing new about these basic principles of democracy. They express ancient ideals of brotherhood, compassion, justice, and the dignity of man—ideals that have deep roots in the religions of the world.

WHAT WE MEAN BY DEMOCRATIC GOVERNMENT

Since in all but the most simple societies the day-by-day operation of government must be in the hands of a small group of people, democratic government is essentially a device to determine which of the several competing groups shall run the government. In a democracy the electorate chooses the major policy officials in *free* and *relatively frequent elections*. Here we pass over the important question of just what proportion of the adult population must be given a voice in the political affairs of the community in order to conform to democratic ground rules. The proportion must be large enough, however, so that the electorate will represent the interests of all and all the interests.

The elections must be free. There is no meaning to sham elections in which no criticism is permitted and no opposition party allowed to bid for votes. In the Soviet Union it may well be that a large number of Soviet citizens actually support their leaders and consent to their rule. But it is a consent of ignorance, since the ruling elite secures the citizens' support through a complete monopoly of all the sources of information. The only way the rulers of the Soviet Union may be removed by office is by revolution or assassination. In a democratic government the choice of rulers is a matter of routine.

In order for the elections to be free, the citizens must enjoy the right to *criticize,* to have *access* to the facts, to *participate* in political deliberations, and to *organize* for political purposes. This last is of especial importance in modern societies where the units of politics are organized groups. Individuals can become politically effective only by joining with others. Those who hold power can be checked only when the people are free to form pressure groups and political parties, and to use all methods of peaceful persuasion.

A democratic government operates in accord with the *decisions of majorities;* the decisions about who is to run the government and what policies are to become the law of the land are determined by voting. He who gets the most votes wins the election. There is no magic in numerical majorities; but some practical means is needed to determine the outcome of elections and to make decisions. The people do not speak with a united voice; they are divided about candidates and public policies. We do what the majority wants. The majority is not necessarily right, but it is right to do what the majority wishes.

Finally, a democratic government is one in which all citizens have *equal voting power*. This does not mean that all must or will have equal political influence. Some men, by virtue of wealth, talent, or position, will have much greater political power than their fellow citizens. A newspaper publisher undoubtedly has considerably more influence in determining who gets elected to public office and what policies are enacted into law than does an ordinary citizen, but when the votes are counted the publisher has no more nor less voting power than the ordinary citizen. To give one side more votes than the other would negate the very idea of majority rule.

From our analysis of democratic government we can see that the crucial factor determining whether or not we shall consider a government democratic is not how much power the public officials have *but how public officials secure and retain their offices*. The President of the United States wields great power, but this in no way makes our government less democratic—the key point is that the man who is President had to win a free election.

Although the extent of power of public officials is not the crucial test of whether or not the government is democratic, those who hold public power must proceed in accordance with the basic rules of democracy. If they suppress the right of their opponents to engage in peaceful political activity, or if they deprive part of the electorate of the opportunity to vote, or if they suppress vital information that the electorate needs in order to decide how to vote, they are staying in power by undemocratic methods. The vanquished in a political election are required by the rules of democracy to allow the victorious to govern, but the same rules require the victorious to allow today's minorities to try to become tomorrow's political majorities. You can win a tennis match by jumping over the net and hitting your opponent over the head with the racket, but then you are no longer playing tennis. You can win an election by throwing your opponents in jail, but then you are no longer operating democratically.

So much for the meaning of democratic government. What do we mean by *constitutional* government?

CONSTITUTIONALISM—LIMITED GOVERNMENT

Constitutionalism has to do with the *limits* set on the power of public officials. A constitutional government is one in which there are recognized and generally accepted *limits to the power of those who govern*. In a constitutional government officials have only the authority that the constitution has delegated to them, and any official who exceeds the scope of this authority surrenders his claim to obedience.

Our American government is both democratic *and* constitutional, for there are recognized limits to what government may do, even a government that speaks for a majority. The individual has certain basic rights that he enjoys merely because he is a human being, and not at the pleasure of the government, or even at the pleasure of the majority. Not everyone agrees on the concrete content of these rights, but it is agreed that there are certain things that no government may do and other things that it may do only according to proper and fair procedure. At a minimum, the government may not deprive any person of his life, liberty, or property except by just and fair procedures of law.

Although there have been in the past, under rather unusual circumstances, constitutional governments that were not democratic, it is unlikely that a constitutional government could be maintained in any industrialized modern nation unless it was also democratic. The primary sanction for insuring that those who hold public power do not exceed the limits of their authority are the rights of unfettered criticism joined with the necessity of those in office periodically to win elections in order to retain their power. Constitutionalism, with its emphasis on *limited* government, and democracy, with its emphasis on the right of the people to decide who shall wield governmental power, are not exclusive categories but mutually supporting institutions.

WHAT DEMOCRATIC GOVERNMENT IS NOT

Democratic governments come in many varieties, of which the American is only one. Yet some Americans assume that only governments exactly like our own are democratic. They confuse the essentials with the nonessentials. Separation of powers, written constitutions, federalism, and judicial review—to mention just a few of the basic features of American government that will be taken up in this book—are generally supported by Americans as desirable ways of limiting government and making it responsible to the people. But these do not in themselves make our government democratic. The government of England has virtually none of these features; the Canadian, Australian, French, and Swedish governments have them only in part. But in all these countries the majority rule and minority rights are secure. On the other hand, the Soviet Union has a written constitution and, at least formally, federalism; but the government is in the hands of a self-appointed elite, and those who differ with the rulers have the choice of silence or Siberia.

Some Americans assume also that only countries that have our kind of mixed, free-enterprise, competitive economy can have democratic governments. Can free government be maintained, they ask, when the economy is controlled by the government? Democracy has in the past been closely associated with capitalism. It developed along with the rise of the middle class and the growth of the private-enterprise system. Because of this historical connection, many argue that capitalism is necessary to democratic government and that the end of capitalism would mean the end of free government. Others are equally convinced, however, that democratic government does not depend on capitalism. They believe, on the contrary, that effective democracy cannot be achieved until economic power is made subject to governmental control. Political democracy, they say, is impossible without "economic democracy."

In a like manner, some believe that a planned economy is the "road to serfdom," while others consider it to be the road to freedom. Some believe that the welfare state will undermine democratic government, while to others such a program is essential for the preservation of republican government. These positions, and all those in between, are tenable. Plausible arguments can be made and evidence marshaled to support any of them.

But democracy is not capitalism, socialism, the welfare state, planning, the absence of planning, or any other particular economic system, nor does democratic government require any of these. At times our government has followed the favorite policies of business, at times those of labor. In our country the coal industry is privately owned and operated; in England it is owned and operated by the government. But we and the British both have democratic governments because policy is made after free discussion and free elections, and the government does not jeopardize the right of the opposition to oppose. Within limits it is not the *content* of the economic policies that makes a government democratic as much as it is the *procedures* by which they are adopted. A free people have the right to choose socialism, laissez faire, the welfare state, or any mixture they want.

Democratic government, then, is not an economic system but a *way of governing and of being governed.* This does not mean that an economic system is unrelated to the amount of democracy in a country. The point is that democratic government allows the people to discuss different economic arrangements, to test them in terms of democratic ideals, and to change them if they are found wanting. Wise economic policies will help democratic government survive, but democratic government, in turn, enables us to develop wise economic policies.

CONDITIONS OF DEMOCRATIC GOVERNMENT

Why does democratic government exist in so few places in the world? In part, because democratic government depends for success upon certain conditions.

Educational conditions. Before democratic government can operate effectively for any length of time in a large nation, most of the people must at least be able to read and write. A recent study shows that in the more democratic European and English-speaking nations most of the people are literate, in contrast with the high rate of illiteracy in the dictatorial Latin-American nations. Moreover, the Latin-American democracies have a significantly higher percentage of literacy than do the Latin-American dictatorships.[13] Other studies show a high correlation between education and such democratic ideas as belief

---

[13] Seymour M. Lipset, "Some Social Requisites of Democracy: Economic Development and Political Legitimacy," *The American Political Science Review* (March 1959), pp. 76-77, 96.

in tolerance for the opposition. But a word of caution: a high level of education does not "cause" or "guarantee" democratic government, as the examples of Nazi Germany and Soviet Russia readily illustrate, and some relatively less-educated peoples such as the Indians have democratic governments. Nonetheless, a high level of education contributes to the stability of democracy.

ß Economic conditions. A relatively prosperous nation, with security and an equitable distribution of wealth, provides the best milieu for democracy. Starving men are more interested in food than in the franchise. Where economic power is concentrated, political power is likely to be concentrated too. The same study confirms the long-held generalization of political theorists that the more well-to-do nations have a greater chance of sustaining democratic governments than do those with widespread poverty.[14] In modern times wealthy nations have been the urban and industrial ones. And though the evidence is by no means conclusive, modern social scientists tend to question Jefferson's belief that democratic stability is best preserved by preventing the growth of cities. Not only do urbanization and industrialization lead to economic well-being; they also bring a breakdown of isolation and homogeneity, and promote a cosmopolitan outlook.[15]

Social conditions. In a society fragmented into large, solid, warring groups that differ on fundamental questions, government by discussion and compromise becomes difficult. When the issues at stake between ideologically separated groups are vital, men may prefer to fight than to accept the verdict of the ballot box. But when society consists of many overlapping associations and groupings, individuals are not as likely to identify themselves completely with a single group and to give their total allegiance to it. Joe Brown, for example, is a Methodist, Legionnaire, Rotarian, southerner, Democrat, electrician, and a member of the $6000-a-year economic bracket. On some issues Joe thinks as a Methodist, on others as a southerner, and on still others as an electrician. Bill Jones is a Methodist, Legionnaire, and Rotarian—but he is also a Republican, an auto dealer, and a member of the $12,000-a-year bracket. Sometimes he acts more like a Republican, sometimes more like a Legionnaire. Jones and Brown differ on some issues but agree on many others. Certainly the differences between them are not likely to be greater than their common interest in maintaining democracy.

Democracy is also more likely to survive where other social institutions reinforce democratic habits. The family, the church, the lodge, the union, the school, for example, are institutions regulating important areas of life affected by and affecting government. If these institutions support and reinforce the idea of government by democratic procedures, then the habits of discussion,

---

14 *Ibid.*, p. 76.
15 *Ibid.*, p. 96.

compromise, respect for differences are developed and strengthened by constant use. In the family, for example, there appears to be a close reciprocal connection (not necessarily causal) between the authoritarian family and authoritarian political attitudes.[16]

Ideological conditions. Out of these educational, economic, and social conditions there must also develop widespread acceptance of the ideals of democracy, the willingness of an overwhelming proportion of the people to agree to proceed democratically. This quality is *democratic consensus.* A perceptive discussion of democratic theory states: "Prior to politics, beneath it, enveloping it, restricting it, conditioning it, is the underlying consensus on policy that usually exists in the society among a predominant portion of the politically active members. Without such a consensus no democratic system would long survive the endless irritations and frustrations of elections and party competition." [17]

To sum up: a society that offers the best chances for democratic success is one with an educated and fairly prosperous electorate without concentrated wealth, with relative freedom from bitter class, religious, or sectional antagonisms, with many private loyalties and associations, with other social institutions that buttress the principles and practices of democracy, all tending to produce a democratic consensus. But no one of these conditions—nor even all of them—guarantees democracy. There is no foolproof double-your-money-back guarantee for freedom.

Democratic Government under Fire

Today democracy is under fire from many directions. Some critics of democratic government are the brutalitarians of fascism and communism who wish to discredit democracy and destroy our freedom. They question the desirability of liberty, deny the primacy of the individual, and consider human inequality inevitable. Other critics of democracy are men of good will. They accept some of the basic democratic values but maintain that democratic government, as we know it, destroys those values and that other forms of government are better designed to protect them.

It is dangerous to brush aside such critics of democracy; they must be understood and answered. This entire volume, in a sense, is an answer to the fascists, communists, and others who reject government by the people. The following sections, in particular, deal with direct threats to democracy, both external and internal, and with arguments advanced by believers in aristocracy (government by an elite) and by communist totalitarians.

---

16 T. W. Adorno and others, *The Authoritarian Personality* (Harper, 1950), p. 971.
17 Robert A. Dahl, *A Preface to Democratic Theory* (Univ. of Chicago Press, 1956), p. 132.

THE CHALLENGE FROM OUTSIDE

Over a hundred years ago, in 1848, Karl Marx and Friedrich Engels published *The Communist Manifesto*. Today, one-third of the world's population is governed by men who claim to have answered that call to action. Modern communists attack not merely capitalism, but the whole democratic system of government. They insist that behind our democratic exterior, a small group of capitalists dominate public affairs. They urge members of the working class to believe that their real interests are identical with those of the Soviet Union, which, they argue, speaks for workers everywhere against the capitalists who dominate nations outside the Soviet orbit.

Marxism is shot through with errors and contradictions. It grossly overestimates the power and unity of the working class; it underestimates the size and influence of the middle class under capitalism. The class structure of any modern industrial nation is far more complex than the simple capitalistic-proletarian division that Marx foresaw. Capitalism has shown considerable adaptability and flexibility, and a modified form of capitalism, at least in the United States, has shown the capacity to distribute goods and services rather widely. Contrary to Marx, it has not been the capitalistic nations in which communists have seized power, but precapitalistic countries like Russia and China.

But whatever the errors of Marxism, we must recognize its powerful grip on the minds of millions who live in hunger and despair. Democracy's best answer to communism is less in the realm of debate than in the realm of action—in raising the living standards of the mass of people, in making civil liberties and civil rights tangible things for all citizens, in acting fairly and responsibly in international affairs. In the same way, the communist philosophy is less revealing than communist action. Wherever the communists have taken power they have set up an elite that felt it knew what was best for the people. They have ruthlessly destroyed those who differed with them. They have crushed the individual to make him conform to the totalitarian pattern. Doubtless some of these evils result from international and domestic tensions as well as from communism itself. But if a doctrine is known by its works, communism can be understood best by the trail of brutal purges, slave-labor camps, fake elections, and party-line art, music, science, and thought that it has left in its wake.

The antidemocratic communists should not be confused with the democratic socialists of England, Australia, Scandinavia, the United States, or elsewhere. These socialists, though they draw many insights from Karl Marx and are critical of many aspects of capitalistic economics, are democrats. They reject revolutionary tactics and are dedicated to working within the democratic framework in attempting to achieve their goals. Many Americans are critical of their programs and fear that they would endanger or destroy democratic government, but both democratic socialists and democratic capitalists agree

**"I've been away.
Who's inside?"**

Drawing by Dedini, Copr.
© 1955 *The New Yorker
Magazine,* Inc.

that democracy, not the dictatorship of workers or any other group, is the best form of government.

THE CHALLENGE FROM WITHIN

1. *The communist threat.* The communist attack on democracy proceeds on many fronts. Communism has developed to a high degree the tactics of infiltration and propaganda. Even so, it is very doubtful that communists could win a free election in any established democracy (see Chapter 6). Certainly in the United States communists pose no serious threat at the polls. But communists, whose first loyalty is to the Soviet Union and who are working for the destruction of our democratic system, present a genuine danger when they get into positions of influence. At critical times they can use these positions to aid our enemies. The danger from these subversives must be recognized, and, as enemies of democracy, they must be fought. But a danger no less real is that self-government will be lost in the very process of meeting the threat of foreign attack from without and of subversives from within.

2. *The garrison state.* It is more than coincidence that democracy has been most firmly established in countries that did not have to maintain large standing armies and that, for one reason or another, did not live in constant fear of attack. A nation at war or in constant fear of war does not provide a very satisfactory milieu for the toleration and encouragement of difference and discussion. Concern with security matters, fear of disloyal persons, demand for swift action, and an atmosphere of fear are not conducive to free and open debate, protection of individual liberty, and careful deliberation.[18]

The internal conditions and the geographic position of the United States have, in the past, created an ideal environment for the development of democratic government. Wars were rare, and the nation was relatively secure.

with our Cold war we use all

---

[18] H. D. Lasswell, *National Security and Individual Freedom* (McGraw-Hill, 1950).

*our economy and social
being — that what is meant by a
garrison state —*

Unfortunately, this environment has been destroyed. Peace did not follow World War II. For the first time, Americans must expect a long period when the economy will have to be geared to defense production. Large armed forces, civilian defense preparation, sizable defense expenditures, and the military's great prominence in public affairs will be normal features of the American republic for some time to come. The security of the United States is, and will continue to be, in imminent danger.

Modern warfare has so expanded the scope of military affairs that there is no longer a clear separation between military and civilian spheres of activity. All aspects of society—labor relations, science, the press, education—affect the nation's military power. As military aspects of problems are brought to the fore, the generals, often reluctantly, are called upon to pass judgment on issues that in the past have been regarded as outside their competence. At the same time, their civilian superiors find it more difficult to secure the information needed to exercise control, for often it is the military who decide what information must remain top secret.

A continuing emphasis on security matters enhances the military method of doing things. The armed services are organized for fast action. Authority is concentrated at the top, and unquestioning obedience to orders is essential. Civilian government, at the other extreme, gives to the "privates" the constitutionally protected right of telling the "generals" where they get off. The principal agent of democracy is the politician, the man of talk and compromise. But when people become frightened, they are likely to turn to the man of action. The general's prestige rises; the politician's falls.

3. *Authoritarianism*. The instability of democracy is one of the oldest themes of political science. Some writers have always insisted that if the people are given power, they will hand it over to the demagogue who makes the most appealing promises. Authoritarians of all kinds—caesars, demagogues, fascists, communists, anti-Semites—exist in all democracies, creating confusion and spreading hate. In normal times, their appeals have little attraction except to the lunatic fringe. But in times of crisis and tension, when people are groping for emotional security, simple authoritarian panaceas become a real threat to democracy.

The appeal of an antidemocratic leader is less the *cause* than the *result* of social maladjustments. He becomes dangerous only when the democratic leaders fail to respond to the demands of the people. It is when responsible government is too weak, not when it is too strong, that it is most likely to be destroyed. When peaceful change is thwarted, violent change erupts.

Where does the demagogue find his audience? Mainly among the helpless and the hopeless, among those who have genuine and deep-seated grievances. He plays on peoples' fears and hopes. He promises to make the sharecropper a king. He is a great simplifier. He has an answer for the confused clerk thrown out of a job, for the frustrated student, for the underpaid worker: it is all the fault of Wall Street, the communists, the Jews, or the international bankers. His appeal, however, is not only to the poor and downtrodden. Social crises create frustrations and lead to aggressive feelings among the wealthy as well as among the poverty-stricken.

Courtesy *The Saturday Review* and Mirachi

"That's the trouble with a monarchy—they can't vote you out of office."

In the Great Depression of the 1930's, millions of people were cut loose from their traditional moorings. They were at the mercy of forces they could not understand. They were bitter because they had lost their jobs, had been forced out of their homes, had been deprived of rights to which they felt entitled. In Germany, Hitler had scapegoats and panaceas, and in the United States so did Gerald L. K. Smith, Father Coughlin, and Huey Long. But in the United States democratic government responded to the needs of the times, gave hope to millions, and acted to maintain their faith in democracy. Through peaceful change, the threat of social revolution was put down.

THE CASE AGAINST DEMOCRATIC GOVERNMENT

Aside from tangible threats to democracy from outside and from within, there is an intellectual case against democratic government. Democrats who are worth their salt must recognize and answer this case rather than evade it. From Plato's day to the present, men of thought and men of action have argued against democracy both in practice and in theory. Here is how a forthright antidemocrat might argue his case:

"You democrats have an overoptimistic view of human nature. You think that men are rational, inherently good, and have an infinite capacity for self-improvement. How foolish you are! Haven't you heard of Freud? Don't you know that modern psychology proves that man is a *rationalizing* as well as a rational animal? Can you deny that man sees the public interest in terms of his own *self*-interest?

"You have a false concept of people and politics. Politics is not a struggle among *rational individuals.* It is a contest among a few powerful *leaders* and *groups* who compete for the support of a bored public—so bored that many people don't even vote. As for your naïve belief in the goodness of man, need I do more than point to today's paper for many examples of man's inhumanity to man?

"Most people are ignorant. They haven't had much schooling; they don't know what's going on in the world; they can't even tell you the name of their senator or congressman. They are not competent to govern themselves. Indeed, they often sell their 'birthright' by voting for the demagogue who promises the most. They become the corrupt tools of selfish leaders.

"Rule by the many—'government by the people,' as you so hopefully call it—means government by the great mass, rule by the common, the coarse, the vulgar. Culture—music, the arts, literature—is transmitted by the educated and cultivated few, or else it disappears. So democracy means a general lowering of standards; it leads to stagnation and incompetence.

"Even if you democrats could demolish all these arguments, I have one final unanswerable point. Democracy is a luxury for the few, not the necessity of the many. It exists in only a small part of the world, and some so-called democratic governments are merely masks for rule by an elite. Democracy is a luxury because it can exist only in a certain type of environment—as even some of you democrats admit."

There is the intellectual challenge to democracy, put as forcefully as possible. The authors of this book would deny most of these arguments: those that the authors would accept do not, in their opinion, necessarily prove a case against democracy. But what is your response to this intellectual challenge to democracy? Perhaps, like the authors, you are impatient to answer. But since this whole book is a description of the workings, problems, and accomplishments of democratic government in one great nation, the authors will provide their answers in the last chapter, after the whole terrain has been surveyed. You are invited to formulate *your* own answer to the case against democracy as you study American government.

PART **2**

The Rules
and How They Grew

A PROBLEM GUIDE

How did Americans create a constitutional system in the 1780's to meet the needs of that day, and how do we maintain constitutional government in the face of the urgent demands of the 1960's? This is the general problem that we will be exploring in Part Two.

Forty men gathered in Philadelphia in 1787 to write the Constitution under which we are still governed today. They faced the problem of building a national government strong enough to perform its tasks but not too strong to suit the people. They also faced the problem of compromising among many different ideas of government and many different interests and sections. Chapter 2 describes how the Framers met these problems.

The Constitution posed further prob-

lems, however, that have challenged Americans ever since 1787. Basically a constitution both grants and controls power. Ideally it gives the leaders—in our country, the President, congressmen, and so on—enough power to meet the nation's needs, but it also prevents them from abusing this power. It sets up certain "rules of the game" that determine how leaders must win office (for example, through fair elections) and how they must exercise power once they are in office.

Now the Framers—and most other Americans in 1787—feared government, especially a *national* government, even though they knew that some government was necessary. So they designed a national government that could handle the tasks facing the nation but that would not be able to seize or wield *too much*

31

power. To check national power the Framers depended on two devices: (1) *free and fair elections,* so that nobody could take elective office unless he was acceptable to a majority of the voters; and (2) an elaborate system of *balancing power.*

This system of balancing power is the heart of our constitutional system. It rests in turn on two other devices: (1) a *distribution of governmental power* among the several branches of the national government (for example, between President and Congress); and a *system of checks and balances* which makes the branches of government independent of one another and responsive to different sources of popular support (for example, election of senators by states and of representatives by population). This system has stood the test of time and is still very much with us.

But this arrangement creates a set of difficult problems: Is a system of checks and balances that was adequate for the "horse-and-buggy age" good enough for the space age? Does it allow the people direct and strong control over their leaders? By dividing up national power among a great variety of officials, responding to different groups of voters, does it make teamwork and efficiency difficult to achieve? Does it allow leaders to evade responsibility and "pass the buck," so that the voters have trouble finding out who does what, when, and how well? Chapter 3 takes up this set of problems.

A closely related problem is: How flexible and adaptable should our Constitution be? After all, it was drawn up almost 175 years ago, and the demands on government are much greater now than they were then. Is the Constitution a timeless charter whose principles and methods are as sound today as ever? Or should it be possible to amend it easily

to keep it attuned to new demands? Chapter 3 discusses this problem too.

Finally, there are the problems created by *federalism*—the division of power between the national and state governments. Our country has undergone vast economic, social, and military changes, and the national government has taken on heavier and heavier burdens. Relatively, the states have lost ground. Is federalism obsolete? Does it deprive the government of the power and teamwork it needs to handle its huge tasks? Or is federalism as valid as ever? In either case, who should decide what powers the states should have, and what powers the national government should have? Of course the Constitution itself divides power between the two, but it does so in general terms. Who should make the specific division? Congress? The Supreme Court? What devices have been worked out to foster cooperation among the states, and between the national and state governments, despite the division of power under the Constitution? Chapters 4 and 5 deal with these and related problems.

Taking up these specific problems will help us to think more concretely about the basic problem of Part Two—how can we maintain a constitutional system largely shaped in 1787 in the face of the urgent demands of the 1960's? The answer turns partly on what we mean by "constitutional." Do we mean all the detailed provisions and requirements in the Constitution of 1787? Or do we mean the essential idea of *all* constitutions—free elections, civil liberties, and fair procedures in government? Or do we mean the *main* general feature of *our* Constitution, namely the system of balanced powers? Part Two sets these problems forth, but of course they will crop up time and again throughout the book.

CHAPTER **2**

The Birth of a Nation

n a bright Sunday afternoon in May 1787, George Washington, escorted by three generals and a troop of light horse, arrived in Philadelphia to the sound of chiming bells and cheering citizens. After depositing his baggage at the fine house where he was to stay, Washington went around the corner to call on an old friend, Benjamin Franklin. It was no coincidence that these two world-famous Americans should meet on this day in Philadelphia. They had much to talk about. For Washington, as a delegate from Virginia, and Franklin, as a delegate from Pennsylvania, were in the vanguard of a group of illustrious men who were to spend the hot summer of 1787 writing a new constitution for the thirteen American states.

A constitution that is to endure must reflect the hard experience and high hopes of the people for whom it is written. It cannot emerge merely from the inspiration of a few leaders. Our Constitution is no exception. Those who framed it built with the institutions and ideas that they knew. But they did build; their creative feat can hardly be exaggerated. They did not, of course, complete the job of constitution-making, for it is a process that never can be completed. It began long before the constitutional convention met and it continues today. Constitutions—even written ones—are *growing* and *evolving* organisms rather than documents that are "struck off, at a given time, by the brain and purpose of man" (as Gladstone once described our Constitution). So we shall leave Washington and Franklin for a moment and look at the materials out of which our Constitution has grown.

Toward Independence and Self-Government

To trace the Constitution back to its ultimate sources would be to write an intellectual history of western civilization. For our purposes it is enough to note that the first immigrants to this continent brought with them English political ideas and institutions. For the next hundred and fifty years these English ideas and institutions were adapted to fit the conditions of the New World. (Sometimes we forget that this nation was part of the British Empire for almost as long as it has been independent.) By July 4, 1776, the colonists had shaped the basic framework of government that still serves us today.

THIRTEEN SCHOOLS OF GOVERNMENT

It was in the colonies that early Americans first learned something of the difficult art of government. There were three kinds of colonial governments: *royal, proprietary,* and *charter,* but in practice the differences were slight. All the colonies had written charters that established the form of government and set forth the rights of colonists. These charters were not subject, so the colonists argued, to change by ordinary law. The charters of the eight *royal* colonies had been granted to them by the king and gave the Crown considerable power of supervision. The three *proprietary* colonies—Maryland, Pennsylvania, and Delaware—were each governed in accordance with a charter issued by their respective proprietors, who in turn had received a patent from the king granting the proprietor the right to establish a colony. But by the middle of the eighteenth century the Crown exerted almost the same control over proprietary colonies as it did over royal ones.

The two *charter* colonies—Rhode Island and Connecticut—operated under charters issued by the king confirming the governmental compacts that the colonists themselves had drawn up. These two colonies had the greatest measure of local autonomy. They were required to conform to the laws of England and to recognize the right of the Privy Council in London to review decisions of their courts, but unlike the other colonies they did not have to send their own laws to England for review, and their legislatures elected the colonial governor.

In all the colonies governmental authority was divided among the legislative, executive, and judicial branches. All but one (Pennsylvania) had a *bicameral* (two-house) legislature. The upper house, composed of a dozen or so landed gentlemen and wealthy merchants, advised the governor, heard appeals from colonial courts, and reviewed legislation submitted by the lower chamber. The members of the upper house were appointed by the Crown or the proprietor on the recommendation of the governor.

The lower house of the colonial legislature consisted of *elected* representatives; the suffrage varied from colony to colony, but in all it was limited to property-owning adult males; some colonies even had religious requirements. The lower chambers insisted that they alone had authority to raise taxes from the colonists and to appropriate funds. Since they staunchly refused to pass permanent revenue measures, the royal authorities were often forced to make concessions in order to secure the money needed to run the government. The lower houses used this control over the purse to gain further powers; over the years, they gradually assumed power to pass general laws, subject to veto by the upper house, the governor, and imperial authorities in England.

In the royal colonies the governors were appointed by the king and served as his representatives; it was through the governors that instructions from London were transmitted. In proprietary colonies the proprietor selected the governor, but his appointments were subject to confirmation by the Crown, and the governors were pledged to execute the laws of Parliament relating to America. Governors of the charter colonies, Rhode Island and Connecticut, were named by the colonial assemblies.

The royal and proprietary governors were very powerful. They could exercise an absolute veto over legislation, they could dissolve the legislatures, they appointed administrative subordinates, they commanded the colonial militia, and they presided over religious and social activities. Despite their great authority, however, these governors had a difficult job. They had to please both the colonists and the British government, and often ended up pleasing neither.

The judicial system grew more slowly than the other two branches, but eventually both lower and higher courts were established. The judges were appointed by the Crown, although in some colonies they depended on the legislatures for their salaries. In most cases appeals could be taken from colonial courts to the Privy Council in London, an important device of British control to insure that colonial legislation conformed to the laws of England.

Thus it was during the colonial period that the basic pattern of American government was laid down. Relations between the colonies and England familiarized Americans with the division of powers between a central and constituent governments and made federalism a natural development. The role of the Privy Council in enforcing English law as superior to colonial legislation was a forerunner of the Supreme Court's task of deciding whether state acts violate the Constitution or national law. The familiar separation of powers and the bicameral legislatures also were developing during this time.

Early Americans became experts at operating, or at times evading, this governmental machinery. By the latter part of the eighteenth century it was becoming clear that there might soon be a heightened demand for such experts.

THE KINDLING OF NATIONALISM

Despite all this experience with government within the several colonies, the colonists had little training in *inter*colonial problems. Under a divide-and-rule policy, London tried to keep the colonies separate and dependent on England. The colonists themselves developed little sense of real unity until the events leading to the Revolutionary War stirred American patriotism. Until a few years before the Revolution, the colonists considered themselves Englishmen, and their national loyalty was to the British Crown. The local loyalty of each was to his own colony, not to America. Beyond this there was some sectional feeling based on familiarity and identity of interests, so that New England, the South, and, to a lesser extent, the Middle Colonies became identifiable communities.

Yet even during the colonial period, the demands of war and the need for common defense forced the colonies on occasion to think of problems beyond their own boundaries. The origins of American federalism and the roots of American patriotism reach back into this period. As early as 1643 the New England Confederation was organized to provide unified action against the threats of the Indians, Dutch, and French. The Confederation lasted as an effective organization until 1664. Not for almost a hundred years was there another important proposal for intercolonial cooperation. Then, in 1754, the British Ministry called the seven northern colonies into conference at Albany to discuss Indian affairs. Benjamin Franklin, aware of an underlying cultural and political identity among the colonies, seized the opportunity to propose a scheme of continental government. Franklin's proposals, known as the Albany Plan, called for the creation of a Grand Council composed of delegates elected by the colonial assemblies and a President General appointed by the king. This central government was to be given the power to regulate trade with the Indians, make war and peace, and to *levy taxes* and collect customs duties in order to raise military and naval forces.

Meeting under the threat of attack by the French and Indians, the delegates to the Albany Conference avowed that some form of union was necessary to preserve the colonies. They recommended proposals for unity to the colonial assemblies, but not a single assembly approved. Those who controlled colonial affairs saw no need to subordinate their authority to an intercolonial government. Among the people themselves, there were no common American loyalties, no consciously shared experiences, no universally revered ideas. It was to take another thirty years and two wars before a strong central government would be acceptable to the colonists.

But the groundwork was being laid. During the French and Indian War, known in Europe as the Seven Years' War, American war heroes began to emerge. Gradually the colonists became aware of American, as distinct from English or purely local, interests. And persistent trouble with the mother country served to intensify this sense of American unity.

Prior to the end of the French and Indian War, the imperial authorities had allowed the colonists to handle their own affairs with relatively little interference from London. They had supervised American affairs in a lax and haphazard manner. But one thing the British had done—at considerable expense, they had driven the French from the North American continent and had made new territories available for settlement. The British ministers decided it would only be fair to ask the colonists to pay some of the cost of defending their own frontiers. Steps were taken to raise revenue among the Americans, to enforce trade regulations more rigorously, and generally to tighten English control over colonial affairs. But what seemed logical and just to the English authorities was viewed differently on this side of the Atlantic. Colonial businessmen wanting to develop their own industries, merchants and shippers wishing to trade with nations other than England, planters believing they could get better prices from the Dutch and French than from the English, speculators wishing to buy western land—all these and others chafed under the heavier taxes and harsher restrictions.

What did these restless colonists want? Not very much. They had hardly a thought of independence. They merely wanted Parliament to repeal the onerous laws and to leave the colonists alone as much as possible. Their protests were couched in legal and constitutional phraseology.

But to make their protests more effective, these essentially conservative men stirred up the feelings of other elements in the colonies. Many of the small artisans, lesser merchants, and farmers were not directly affected by the tax and trade laws, and many of them did not have the right to vote; nevertheless, the actions of the English government affronted their developing national feeling. Leadership of the protest movement began to pass from the hands of the more restrained group to those who were asking for more radical action, men like Sam and John Adams in Massachusetts and Patrick Henry and Thomas Jefferson in Virginia. These leaders gave more stress to the concepts of the natural rights of men and of government resting on the consent of the governed, and less stress to constitutional and legal arguments. They started to talk about individual liberty and human rights.[1]

These arguments had a double edge. They could be used against the dominant groups *within* the colonies as well as against the British.[2] Gradually some of the conservatives began to lose their enthusiasm for protest, fearing that revolution might lead not merely to changes in Empire relations but also to domestic reform. Feeling against England, however, did become sharper. The colonists were forced, first for political and then for military purposes, to join together in defense of their common cause. Colonial leaders began to get in closer touch with one another. The Committees of Correspondence, the Stamp Act Congress, and the First Continental Congress stimulated awareness of the common bond and gave the colonists experience in intercolonial cooperation. Finally, in 1775, the Second Continental Congress began to speak for *Americans*.

THE SURGE TOWARD INDEPENDENCE

Even after minutemen began fighting with redcoats in 1775, many Americans found the idea of independence quite unacceptable and still hoped for reconciliation with England. But the fighting continued through the months, and the English government refused to make concessions to American de-

---

[1] Cf. J. F. Jameson, *The American Revolution Considered as a Social Movement* (Princeton Univ. Press, 1926).

[2] See Elisha P. Douglas, *Rebels and Democrats: The Struggle for Equal Political Rights and Majority Rule during the American Revolution* (Univ. of North Carolina Press, 1955).

mands. In August 1775, the king issued a proclamation declaring the colonies to be in a state of rebellion, and in December 1775, Parliament forbade all trade with the colonies. These actions played into the hands of the radicals and strengthened their cause. Then in January 1776, Thomas Paine issued his pamphlet, *Common Sense,* calling on Americans to proclaim their independence. Seldom in history has a single pamphlet had so much influence. "It rallied the undecided and the wavering, and proved a trumpet call to the radicals." [3]

Those clamoring for independence became stronger. In Pennsylvania the struggle was especially bitter; there the radicals finally gained control, established a new government, drew up a new constitution, and instructed their delegation in Congress to work for independence. On June 7, Richard Henry Lee, following instructions from the Virginia Assembly, moved in Congress "that these United Colonies are, and of right ought to be, Free and Independent States." After bitter debate, Lee's motion was adopted on July 2. The Congress had already appointed a committee, consisting of Thomas Jefferson, John Adams, Benjamin Franklin, Roger Sherman, and Robert Livingston, to prepare a formal declaration of "the causes which impelled us to this mighty resolution." This Declaration of Independence was adopted on July 4, 1776.

The Declaration is more than a justification of rebellion. It is also a statement of the American democratic creed, "designed to justify the past and chart the future." [4] This creed is set forth in succinct and eloquent language:

> We hold these Truths to be self-evident, that all Men are created equal, that they are endowed by their Creator with certain unalienable Rights, that among these are Life, Liberty, and the Pursuit of Happiness.—That to secure these Rights, Governments are instituted among Men, deriving their just powers from the Consent of the Governed, that whenever any Form of Government becomes destructive of these Ends, it is the Right of the People to alter or to abolish it, and to institute new Government, laying its Foundation on such Principles, and organizing its Powers in such Form, as to them shall seem most likely to effect their Safety and Happiness. . . .

Here we find the democratic beliefs in man's *natural rights,* in *popular consent* as the only just basis for political obligations, in *limited government,* and in the right of the people to *revolt* against *tyrannical government.*

SOME INTELLECTUAL LUGGAGE

To most American patriots in 1776, these doctrines were just plain common sense. Jefferson, who wrote the Declaration, stated in a letter to Henry Lee that he did not feel it his duty to set out "new principles . . . never

---

[3] S. E. Morison and H. S. Commager, *The Growth of the American Republic* (Oxford Univ. Press, 1950), 4th ed., p. 194.

[4] Ralph Barton Perry, *Puritanism and Democracy* (Vanguard, 1944), pp. 124-125.

before thought of," but to "place before mankind the common sense of the subject, in terms so plain and firm as to command their assent, and to justify ourselves in the independent stand we are compelled to take." These ideas had come to a white heat in the crucible of America. But in essence they were part of the intellectual luggage that the colonists had brought with them, or later imported, from the Old World.

The man most responsible for popularizing these doctrines was *John Locke,* who had written his famous *Second Treatise of Civil Government* a century before to justify the English Revolution of 1688. Locke's arguments were tailor-made for the defense of the American cause. He profoundly influenced the patriot leaders, and his ideas, along with some of his phraseology, found their way into the Declaration.

Prior to the establishment of organized society and government, Locke had written, man lived in a state of nature. This was not a lawless condition, however, because the natural law was known to all men through the use of reason and was binding on all. (The real nature of natural law has been argued by philosophers for centuries; for our purposes it is enough to think of the laws of nature as inherent, inescapable rules of human behavior—laws, in Cicero's words, that are in accordance with nature, apply to all men, and are unchangeable and eternal.) According to the natural law, each individual has a basic, inalienable right to his life, liberty, and that property with which he has mixed his own labor. Whoever deprives another of his natural rights violates the natural law and can justly be punished.

Most men obeyed the natural law, but living in a state of nature was inconvenient. There were always a few lawless souls; and whenever a person's natural rights were violated, he had to enforce the law himself. Furthermore, when people had differences, there was no impartial judge to whom they could turn for a decision. Therefore, being endowed with reason, men decided to end this inconvenience by *contracting* among themselves to form a society and to establish a government for the purpose of protecting each man's natural rights. By the terms of this social contract, each individual promised to abide by the decisions of the majority and to surrender to society his private right to enforce the law.

Government was thus limited by the purpose for which it was established. It had only the authority to enforce the natural law. *When government becomes destructive of man's inalienable rights,* it ceases to have a claim on his allegiance. The people then have the duty to revolt and to create a government better designed to promote their natural rights.

Does this sound like pretty radical doctrine? It must be remembered that while Locke's ideas would give power to the people, they also put checks on that power. In effect, depending on one's interpretation of natural rights, these theories could be used either to strengthen or to weaken the right of the people to control their relations with one another through the agency of government.

Moreover, early Americans were also influenced by other thinkers in the Old World. One of the most prominent of these was *Montesquieu, who,* in the time of Louis XIV and Louis XV, believed that liberty must be secured *against* government. Montesquieu's importance lies in the fact that he had a very practical scheme to keep government from violating man's natural right to liberty. This was the *separation of powers.* The way to prevent the abuse of power is to check power with power, said Montesquieu, by giving some authority to the legislative branch, some to the executive, and some to the judicial. This kind of built-in mechanism safeguards liberty against government.

These were the ideas that set the intellectual tone during the period when Americans were replacing English authority with their own governments. Broadly speaking, our forefathers leaned more heavily on Locke in setting up government under the Articles of Confederation, more heavily on Montesquieu in framing the Constitution of 1787.

Experiment in Confederation

The American Revolution was primarily a rebellion of colonies against an empire; "in the modern European sense of the word, it was hardly a revolution at all." [5] There were no sharp breaks with the past. The government remained in the hands of a relatively small governing class, the same class that had dominated colonial affairs. There were no great social, economic, or political upheavals.

And yet in significant ways the new governments were different from those existing before the Revolution. The English had tried to regulate the colonists from London; now power was to be held firmly in the hands of state governments. The imperial authorities had trampled on men's liberties; now the new state constitutions incorporated bills of rights, abolished most religious qualifications for voting, and liberalized property and tax-paying requirements.

The most glaring difference between the old colonial charters and the new state constitutions was the *concentration of power* in the *legislatures.* The legislative branches had enhanced their prestige as champions of popular causes. The current emphasis on the consent of the governed, borrowed from Locke and others, also stressed the legislature as the repository of that consent. The governorship, on the other hand, savored of royalty and stirred unpleasant memories. In most of the states the governors were made dependent on the legislature for election, their terms of office were shortened, their veto power reduced, their power to appoint officials curbed. Judges, too, carried overtones of royalty. The new state legislatures saw no reason why they should not override judicial decisions and scold judges whose

---

[5] Daniel J. Boorstin, *The Genius of American Politics* (Univ. of Chicago Press, 1953), p. 68.

rulings were unpopular. The legislative branch, complained Madison later in *Federalist No. 48*, was "drawing all power into its impetuous vortex."

THE ARTICLES OF CONFEDERATION

What about the central government? The Continental Congress, like the colonial legislatures, had assumed governmental powers at the outbreak of hostilities. Although the Congress appointed General Washington commander in chief of the Continental Army, carried on negotiations with foreign countries, raised and supported troops, and borrowed and printed money, its powers were based only on a revolutionary act. A more permanent constitutional arrangement was needed. Accordingly, in June 1776, the Congress created a committee to draft a constitution. A few days after the Declaration was adopted, this committee submitted a plan for a "league of friendship and perpetual Union," but not until a year later, after months of interrupted debate, did Congress finally submit the Articles of Confederation to the states for their approval. Within two years all the states except Maryland had ratified the Articles; but since unanimous consent was required, the Articles did not go into effect until 1781, when Maryland finally ratified.

The Articles more or less constitutionalized existing arrangements. They frankly established only a league of friendship and cooperation—not a national government. Each state retained its "sovereignty, freedom, and independence, and every power, jurisdiction, and right" that was not *expressly* delegated to "the United States, in Congress assembled." The states had jointly declared their independence of the king and had jointly fought against him, but they considered themselves free and independent sovereignties. They were loath to part with any of their newly won powers. After fighting a war against centralized authority, they did not want to create another central government, even though it would be American rather than English. Most of the patriots shared the belief that republican governments could exist only in small states. They feared that a strong central government would fall into the hands of those who would nullify the work of the Revolution.

There was, nevertheless, a universal recognition of the need for "the more convenient management of the general interests of the United States," and for this purpose a Congress was established in which each state was to be represented by not fewer than two nor more than seven delegates. The voting in Congress was by states, each state having one vote regardless of size or contributions to the general treasury. Delegates were chosen by the state legislatures, and their salaries were paid from their respective state treasuries. Since the delegates were state representatives rather than national legislators, they were subject to recall by their state legislatures.

Under the Articles, Congress was given the power to determine peace and war, to make treaties and alliances, to coin money, to regulate trade with the Indians, to borrow money, to issue bills of credit, to build and equip a navy, to establish a postal system, and to appoint senior officers of the United States army (composed of state militias). In short, Congress was given substantially the same powers that the Continental Congress had already been exercising. Approval of nine of the thirteen states was required to make important decisions.

The two most important powers *denied* to Congress were the power to levy taxes and the power to regulate commerce. It was the British government's abuse of these two powers that had precipitated the Revolutionary War. Naturally enough, there was little desire to grant them to another central government. All that Congress could do was to ask the states for funds, and then hope that the state governments would collect taxes and turn the money over to the central treasury. And though the states promised to refrain from discriminating against one another's trade, Congress had no power to prevent such discrimination or to pass positive measures to promote national commerce. Only through treaties could Congress regulate foreign commerce, but here, too, it had no enforcement powers.

Clearly Congress under the Confederation was a feeble body. Furthermore, neither a federal executive nor a federal judiciary existed to enforce what decisions the Congress did make. There was simply the promise of each state to observe the Articles and abide by the decisions of Congress. The Articles were ratified by the several state legislatures, not by the voters. The Articles could be amended, but—more like a treaty than a constitution—the approval of all thirteen state legislatures was needed. In many respects the national government was like the United Nations today—although the similarity has often been exaggerated.

Nevertheless, the government created by the Articles of Confederation, however weak, was what most people wanted. They believed that the goals of the Revolution could be achieved only through strong local governments and that centralized authority was dangerous. A truly national government at this time could have been established only by the sword and probably would have been destroyed by the sword. The Articles reflected public sentiment and rested on political reality. A unified national government cannot be created by documents; it must have the support of diverse interests and individuals within the community.

POSTWAR PROBLEMS

The war was over and independence won. Could the new nation survive —a nation just becoming conscious of its own nationality? The practical difficulties confronting the infant republic would have tested the strongest and best-entrenched government. Within the limits of its powers, the government of the Confederation did an excellent job: it adopted a program for governing and developing western lands, it established diplomatic relations with other nations, it laid the foundations of a central bureaucracy, and it met the financial problems growing out of the war. By the time the Constitutional Convention assembled, the postwar depression was giving way to a period of business and commercial expansion.

Yet the problems were great and the central government was unable to provide strong leadership. Newly won independence deprived Americans of some of the special trading and commercial privileges they had enjoyed as members of the British Empire. The profitable trade with the English West Indies was prohibited. Congress found it difficult to negotiate favorable trade treaties with other nations because of a general belief in Europe that the states would not comply with the treaties even if they were ratified. The Spanish closed the mouth of the Mississippi at New Orleans to all American goods, and Barbary pirates freely looted American shipping in the Mediterranean. There was no uniform medium of exchange, because each state provided its own money, which fluctuated greatly in value. Paper money issued by Congress to finance the war was circulating at about one-thousandth of its face value. Lacking confidence in the ability of Congress to redeem its pledges, creditors were reluctant to lend money to the central government except at high interest rates. Public securities sold at a fraction of their face value. The states themselves began to default in their payments into the federal treasury. Each state regulated commerce, some discriminating against their neighbors, and the lack of uniformity of trade regulations made it difficult to develop interstate commerce. The end of the war reduced the sense of urgency that had helped to unite the several states, and conflicts among the states were frequent.

Within the states affairs went badly too. Delinquent debtors, primarily farmers, who faced the loss of their property and the prospect of debtor's prison, began to exert pressure on the state legislatures for relief. In several of the states they were successful, and the legislatures extended the period for the payment of mortgages, issued legal-tender paper money for the payment of debts, and scaled down the taxes. Creditors resented these interferences. Throughout the nation the conflicts grew bitter between debtor and creditor, between poor and rich, between manufacturer and shipper.

To add to the difficulties, neither the English nor the states would live up to the terms of the treaty of peace. The English refused to withdraw their troops from the western frontier until American debtors had paid their English creditors and until the states had repaid the Loyalists for confiscated property. Congress lacked the power to force either the English or the states to comply. To the English on the west and the Spanish and French in the south, the new nation, internally divided and lacking a strong central government, made a tempting prize.

MOVEMENT FOR REVISION

Was it surprising that, in the face of postwar problems of demobilization, economic changes and expansion, foreign relations, and conflicts among the various sectional and economic interests, some of the democratic ardor of the revolutionary days began to wane? The radicals, who had engineered the Revolution, began to lose power. Most of the conservatives—the property-owners, the creditors, the shippers, the "better people"—had never been satisfied with the Articles of Confederation, considering them too democratic and too feeble. The inability of the Confederation to provide a strong union, to prevent the states from interfering with business, to pay its creditors, added to the conviction of the conservatives that the central government must be strengthened and that checks must be placed on the state governments. They undoubtedly did, for partisan purposes, "paint dark the picture of the times and blame the supposed woes of the country on the Articles of Confederation," [6] but they were genuinely alarmed. It was, after all, *their* contracts that the state legislatures were interfering with, *their* bonds that the central government was unable to pay, *their* businesses that needed uniform commercial regulations and national protective tariffs, *their* manufacturing for which they wanted bounties. But beyond this they were concerned about the dangers of disunion, anarchy, and tyranny.

These fears were sharpened by the growth of a small but dangerous group, composed chiefly of men who had never believed in government by the people. These men began to argue publicly that republican government was a failure—that a strong monarchical government was needed to protect persons and property. Washington, who, fortunately for the nation, would have nothing to do with the persistent attempts to make him a king or dictator of the United States, wrote in alarm in August 1786, to John Jay, Director of Foreign Affairs:

> What astonishing changes a few years are capable of producing! I am told that even respectable characters speak of a monarchical form of Government without horror. But how irrevocable and tremendous! What a triumph for our enemies to verify their predictions. What a triumph for the advocates of despotism to find that we are incapable of governing ourselves, and that systems founded on the basis of equal liberty are merely ideal and fallacious. Would to God that wise measures be taken in time to avert the consequences we have but too much reason to apprehend. [7]

The politicians, creditors, speculators, merchants, manufacturers, army officers, and others who believed that wise measures should be taken to avert disaster felt that the situation was so critical that it would not be enough merely to amend the Articles of Confederation. They wanted to alter the basic nature of the Union and to create a strong national government with coercive powers. They wanted to place checks on the state legislatures to prevent interference with property rights.

---

[6] Merrill Jensen, *The Articles of Confederation* (Univ. of Wisconsin Press, 1940), p. 245.
[7] John D. Fitzpatrick (ed.), *The Writings of George Washington* (Government Printing Office), XXVIII, 503.

How could all this be done? The nationalists had to move carefully. Although there was growing recognition of the need to amend the Articles in order to give Congress the power to collect taxes and to regulate commerce among the states, many Americans were still suspicious of a central government with coercive powers. Many of the people did not think things were so bad, certainly not bad enough to call for any basic alterations in the governmental structure. Debtor laws and paper currency were not to them abuses of republican liberty, and whatever evils existed, they felt, could not be attributed to the venality of the state legislators or to the weakness of the central government. John Fiske, a noted nineteenth-century historian, stated, "At no time in this distressed period would a frank and abrupt proposal for a convention to remodel the government have found favour."

Nevertheless, knotty practical problems—problems of boundaries, navigation, tariffs, and so on—continued to arise, and often these problems were common to most or all of the states. In the fall of 1786 the Virginia legislature, guided by James Madison, invited the states to send delegates to Annapolis to discuss uniform trade regulation. This was the ostensible purpose of the convention, but, as Madison wrote Jefferson, "Many gentlemen both within and without Congress wish to make this meeting subservient to a plenipotentiary Convention for amending the Confederation." [8] Only five states sent delegates. Many who wanted action lost hope. But Alexander Hamilton seized the opportunity to push through the Annapolis Convention a discreetly worded resolution. Congress was requested to ask the states to send commissioners to Philadelphia to "devise such further provisions as shall appear to them necessary to render the Constitution of the Federal Government adequate to the exigencies of the Union." But Congress, apathetic and perhaps suspicious that Hamilton had more in mind than amending the Articles, was loath to act. Some state legislatures appointed delegates, but throughout the states not much more than polite interest was shown. It seemed likely that little would come of the project.

INCIDENT IN MASSACHUSETTS

In the fall and winter of 1786-1787, however, events in western Massachusetts seemed to justify the dire predictions that the country was on the verge of anarchy. The farmers were in a desperate plight. Many faced imprisonment through inability to meet their mortgages or their taxes. They had unsuccessfully petitioned the Massachusetts legislature for relief. Finally, the angry farmers rallied around Daniel Shays, a Revolutionary War captain, and marched into Northampton, where they blocked the entrance to the courthouse and forcibly restrained the judges from foreclosing mortgages on their farms.

---

[8] Quoted by Charles Warren, *The Making of the Constitution* (Little, Brown, 1937), p. 22.

The militia readily put down the uprising, but the revolt sent a shudder down the spines of the more substantial citizens. The outraged General Knox, Secretary of War, wrote to Washington:

> This dreadful situation has alarmed every man of principle and property in New England. They start as from a dream and ask what has been the cause of our delusion? What is to afford us security against the violence of lawless men? Our government must be braced, changed or altered to secure our lives and property. . . .[9]

During the winter, as the story of this open rebellion spread through the nation, it took on lurid overtones and, in the minds of many, became a threat to each person's life and fortune. Some reacted by abandoning any pretense of support for republican principles. Madison warned that the "turbulent scenes" in Massachusetts had done inexpressible injury to the republican cause and even had caused a "propensity toward Monarchy" in the minds of some leaders.[10] A letter widely circulated throughout the states argued that it would be "preferable to distribute the United States into Three Republics, who should enter into a perpetual league and alliance for mutual defence." [11]

What could be done? The more respectable leaders were not ready to plunge into either monarchy or disunion. Fortunately, an instrument was at hand that promised a better way to deal with the crisis—the proposed Philadelphia Convention. Shays' Rebellion served as a catalyst, and the movement toward revision of the Articles, which had been brewing for a long time, began to boil. Throughout the states there was a quickening of interest in the recommendation of the Annapolis Convention. Seven states appointed delegates without waiting for Congress to act. Finally Congress jumped on the convention band wagon with a cautiously worded request to the states to appoint delegates for the "sole and express purpose of revising the Articles of Confederation . . . to render the Federal Constitution adequate to the exigencies of Government, and the preservation of the Union." The careful congressmen specified that no recommendation would be effective unless approved by Congress and confirmed by all the state legislatures as provided by the Articles.

Eventually every state except Rhode Island appointed delegates. (The debtors and farmers who controlled the Rhode Island legislature suspected that the very purpose of the convention was to place limits on their power.) Many of the delegations were bound by instructions only to consider amendments to the Articles of Confederation. Delaware went so far as to forbid her representatives to consider any proposal that would deny any state equal representation in Congress. Few people were aware of the portentous changes that were in store.

---

[9] *Ibid.*, p. 31.
[10] Madison to Edmund Pendleton, February 28, 1787. Cited by Warren, *ibid.*, p. 45.
[11] *Ibid.*, p. 29.

The Philadelphia Story   The Constitutional Convention was the third step in the birth of the new nation. The first step was the destruction of English governmental authority. The next step was the creation of new state governments to replace the colonial governments. But after fighting against foreign despotism under banners of liberty and local self-government, the patriots had failed to establish a system capable of providing the order and unity in which liberty and diversity could thrive. The third step began in Philadelphia in the summer of 1787. The delegates to the convention were presented with a condition, not a theory. They had to establish a national government with enough power to prevent the nation from degenerating into anarchy or despotism.

Although seventy-four delegates were appointed by the various states, only fifty-five put in an appearance in Philadelphia, of whom approximately forty took a real part in the work of the convention. But it was a distinguished gathering. Many of the most important men of the nation were there—successful merchants, planters, bankers, and lawyers, former and present governors and congressional representatives. As theorists, they had read Locke, Montesquieu, and other philosophers. As men of affairs, they were interested in the intensely practical job of constructing a national government. Theory played its part, but experience was to be their main guide.

THE CAST

Although most of the Revolutionary leaders eventually supported the Constitution in the ratification debate, only eight of the fifty-six signers of the Declaration of Independence were present at the Constitutional Convention. Among the Revolutionary leaders absent (for various reasons) were Jefferson, Paine, Henry, Richard Henry Lee, Sam and John Adams, and John Hancock. The delegates to the convention were mainly aristocrats. There were no small farmers or working artisans among them. But in the 1780's the common men were not expected to participate in politics, and the Constitutional Convention was as representative as most meetings of the time. Of the forty active participants, the following stand out as the prime movers of the convention:

Alexander Hamilton was, as we have already noted, one of the most impassioned proponents of a strong national government. He had been the engineer at the Annapolis Convention, and as early as 1778 he had been urging upon his wealthy and aristocratic friends the necessity for invigorating the national government. Born in the West Indies, he lacked strong local attachments and was dedicated to the vision of a unified and powerful United States. He had come to the United States when only 16, and while still a student at Kings College (now Columbia University) had won national attention by his brilliant pamphlets in defense of the colonial cause. He married Elizabeth Schuyler, daughter of one of New York's most important gentlemen, and soon became a member of the governing group in that state. During the war he served as General Washington's aide, and his war experiences confirmed his distaste for a Congress so weak that it could not even supply its troops with enough food or arms. Although highly influential in the movement leading to the convention and afterwards in securing ratification of the Constitution, he did not play as important a role during the deliberation as might have been expected. Behind the closed doors of the convention he freely expressed his views, but they were much too nationalistic and aristocratic—his advocacy of a central government patterned after that of England was unacceptable. The two other delegates from New York, Robert Lansing and John Yates, were, ideologically, at the opposite pole from Hamilton. They had little desire to strengthen the national government. Since the voting was by states, Yates and Lansing, when present, controlled the vote of New York. They went home early and Hamilton followed. He returned only at the end of the summer, so New York was unrepresented most of the time.

From Virginia came three of the leading delegates, General George Washington, James Madison, and Edmund Randolph. *Washington* was even at that time "first in war, first in peace, and first in the hearts of his countrymen." Although active in the movement to revise the Articles of Confederation, he had been extremely reluctant to attend the convention. He accepted only when persuaded that his prestige was needed for its success. When the Virginia legislature placed his name at the top of their list of delegates, the importance of the convention was made manifest. After Franklin withdrew his name from consideration, Washington was unanimously selected to preside over the meetings. According to the records, he spoke only twice during the deliberations, but his influence was felt in the informal gatherings as well as during the sessions. His views were well known, and he was counted among those who were convinced of the necessity for a drastic revision of the Articles. The universal assumption that Washington would become the first President under the new Constitution inspired confidence in it.

James Madison, slight of build and small in voice, was only 36 at the time of the convention, but he was one of the most learned members present. Despite his youth, he had helped frame Virginia's first constitution and had served in both the Virginia Assembly and in the Congress. Realizing the importance of the convention, Madison had spent months in preparation by studying the history of Greek confederacies and Italian republics. During the deliberations, he sat in the front of the room and kept full notes on what was said and done. These notes are the major source of information about the convention. Madison was also a member of the group who favored the establishment of a real national government.

Of less importance than either Washington or Madison, but still a man of front rank, was *Edmund Randolph,* the 34-year-old governor of Virginia, and, as such, the titular head of the Virginia delegation. His political views were ambiguous and erratic, but he usually voted with Madison. Although he refused to sign the Constitution, he later worked actively for its ratification in Virginia. *George Mason* was another influential Virginia delegate who refused to sign the Constitution. Mason, a close friend of Jefferson, was the author of the Virginia Declaration of Rights in 1776 and worked unsuccessfully to get the delegates to include a bill of rights in the proposed Constitution.

The Pennsylvania delegation rivaled that of Virginia. Its membership included Benjamin Franklin, James Wilson, and Gouverneur Morris. *Franklin,* at 81, was the convention's oldest member and, as one of his fellow delegates said, "He is well known to be the greatest philosopher of the present age." Second only to Washington in the esteem of his countrymen, he enjoyed a world reputation unrivaled by that of any other American. He was one of the first to hold a vision of a strong and united America. Because of his age and because his opinions were too democratic for most of the delegates, his views were usually given polite attention and then ignored. But at critical moments his sage and humorous remarks served to break the tension and prevent bitterness.

Gouverneur Morris, "a very handsome, bold, and—the ladies say—a very impudent man," was more eloquent than brilliant. He addressed the convention more often than any other person. His views were those of an aristocrat with disdain for both the rabble and the uncouth moneymakers. The elegance of the language of the Constitution is proof of his facility with the pen, for he was responsible for the final draft. Another Pennsylvanian of importance was *James Wilson,* a tall, Scottish-born and Scottish-trained lawyer. He was one of the eight delegates who had signed the Declaration of Independence. His keen mind was an important asset to those working for a strong central government.

Of course there were many other distinguished delegates present. Luther Martin of Maryland, John Dickinson of Delaware, and William Paterson of New Jersey were not in agreement with a majority of the delegates, but they ably defended the position of those who insisted on equal representation for the smaller states.

The proceedings of the convention were kept secret, and delegates were forbidden to discuss any of the debates with outsiders. This rule was adopted to encourage the delegates to speak freely. It was feared that if a member publicly took a firm stand on an issue, it would be harder for him to change his mind after debate and discussion. Looking ahead to the ratification struggle, the members knew that if word of the inevitable disagreements got out it would provide ammunition for the many enemies of the convention. There were critics of this secrecy rule, but probably it was a wise move. Without it agreement might have been impossible.

CONSENSUS

The Constitutional Convention is usually discussed in terms of the three famous compromises: the compromise between large and small states over representation in Congress; the compromise between North and South over the counting of slaves for taxation and representation; and the compromise between North and South over the regulation and taxation of foreign commerce. But this emphasis obscures the facts that there were many other important compromises and that on many of the more significant issues most of the delegates were in substantial agreement. While it is impossible to make neat generalizations about the ideas of some forty-odd men, it is clear that certain basic ideas were part of the operating assumptions of the leading delegates. Underlying all the compromises was a general concurrence on certain basic principles.

A few delegates personally favored a limited monarchy, but almost all were convinced supporters of republican government, and this was the only form of government seriously considered at the convention. It was obvious that no other form would be acceptable to the nation. Most important, all the delegates, including those few who favored a monarch, were *constitutionalists* who opposed arbitrary and unrestrained government, whether monarchical, aristocratic, or democratic.

All agreed that society is divided along class lines and that "the most common and durable source of factions" was "the various and unequal distribution of property," as Madison wrote in *Federalist No. 10*. The common philosophy accepted by most of the delegates was that of *balanced government*. They wanted to construct a national government in which no single interest would dominate the others. Since the men in Philadelphia represented groups alarmed by the tendencies of the agrarian interests to interfere with property, they were primarily concerned with balancing the government in the direction of protection for property and business. George Mason and Benjamin Franklin warned of the danger of going too far in this direction, but there was an almost universal concurrence in the remarks of Elbridge Gerry (delegate from Massachusetts), "The evils we experience flow from the excess of democracy. The people do not want virtue, but are dupes of pretended patriots."

Likewise there was substantial agreement with Gouverneur Morris' statement that *property* was the *"principal object of government."* John Rutledge of South Carolina not only agreed, but went one step further and stated that "property was the sole end of government." Nor was there dissent from Madison's statement that the meddling by state legislatures with the rights of property had, more than anything else, made the convention necessary.

Benjamin Franklin favored extending the right to vote to nonproperty-owners, but most of the delegates agreed in general with the sentiments expressed by John Dickinson, James Madison, and Gouverneur Morris. Dickinson argued that property-holders were the best guardians of liberty and that only they could be counted on to resist the "dangerous influence of those multitudes without property and without principle." James Madison voiced the fear that those without property would soon become the largest part of the population and, if given the right to vote, would either combine to deprive the property-owners of their rights or would become the "tools of opulence and ambition." Gouverneur Morris, too, was inclined to the view that the masses would sell their votes to the rich. The delegates agreed in principle on restricted suffrage, but they differed over the kind and amount of property that one must own in order to vote. As a result, each state was left to determine the qualifications for electing members to the House of Representatives, the only branch of the national government in which the electorate was given a direct voice.

Within five days of its opening, the convention ("with more boldness than legality"), only Connecticut dissenting, voted to approve the Fourth Virginia Resolve that "a national government ought to be established consisting of a supreme legislative, executive, and judiciary." All the delegates were bound by the instructions from Congress merely to suggest amendments to the Articles of Confederation, and some were bound by even more strict instructions from their state legislatures. Yet this decision, approved by a majority of the delegates, to establish *a national government resting on and exercising power over individuals* proposed profoundly to alter the nature of the central government—changing it from a league of states to a national government. Later on, delegates from the smaller states contended that the convention had no authority to establish a national government operating over individuals through its own agents. But these objections were primarily tactical maneuvers to force the large states to make concessions.

At no time was there serious consideration of constructing the national government in any way except by *a distribution of powers among the three branches of government.* A strong executive would provide the energy and direction for the general government that had been lacking under the Articles, and, with an independent judiciary, would provide a practical check on the excesses of democracy. Here the delegates borrowed from Montesquieu. There was little dissent from the proposal to grant the new Congress all the powers of the old Congress, and all other powers in which the separate states were incompetent or in which the harmony of the United States might be interrupted by the exercise of individual legislation. Bicameralism was also accepted without much debate, with only Franklin favoring a single-house national legislature. Almost all the states had had two-chamber legislatures since colonial times, and the delegates were used to the system. Bicameralism also conformed to their belief in the need for balanced government, the upper house representing the aristocracy to offset the more democratic lower house.

CONFLICT

There were serious differences among the various groups, especially between the representatives of the large states who favored a strong national government and the delegates from the small states who were anxious to preserve the confederate character of the Union.

The nationalists took the initiative. The Virginia delegation had caucused during the delay before the convention, and, as soon as the convention was organized, was ready with fifteen resolutions. These resolutions, known as the *Virginia Plan,* called for a strong central government. The legislature was to be composed of two chambers. The members of the lower house were to be elected by the people, those of the upper house to be chosen by the lower chamber from nominees submitted by the state legislatures. Representation in both branches was to be on the basis of either wealth or numbers, thus giving the more populous and wealthy states—Virginia, Massachusetts, and Pennsylvania—a majority in the legislature.

The Congress thus created was to be given all the legislative power of its predecessor under the Articles of Confederation and the right "to legislate in all cases in which the separate States are incompetent." Furthermore, it was to have the authority to disallow state legislation in conflict with the proposed constitution. The Virginia Plan also called for a national executive to be chosen by the legislature and a national judiciary with rather extensive jurisdiction. The national supreme court, along with the executive, was to have a qualified veto over acts of Congress.

For the first few weeks the nationalists were in control. But by June 15 additional delegates from the small states had arrived and they began to counterattack. They rallied around William Paterson of New Jersey, who presented a series of resolutions known as the *New Jersey Plan.* This plan struck at the heart of the convention's earlier basic decision to set aside the Articles of Confederation and to establish a national government, for Paterson merely proposed a series of amendments to the existing Articles. He would give Congress the right to tax and regulate commerce and to coerce recalcitrant states, but he would retain a single-house legislature in which all states would have the *same vote, regardless of size.* The New Jersey Plan called for a plural national executive with little power. A national supreme court was to hear appeals from state judges, who were to have the authority to interpret the constitution. These judges were to be instructed to treat the laws of the national Congress and the treaties of the United States as superior to the laws of their own states.

For a time the convention was deadlocked. The small states argued that states should be represented equally in Congress, at least in the upper house. The large states were adamant, insisting that representation in both houses be based on population or wealth, and that national legislators be elected by the electorate rather than by the state legislatures. Finally a Committee of Eleven was elected to devise a compromise, and on July 5 it presented its proposals. Because of the prominent role of the Connecticut delegation, this plan has since been known as the *Connecticut Compromise.* It called for: a lower house in which representation would be on the basis of population, the origination in the lower house of all bills raising or appropriating money, and an upper house in which each state would have an equal vote. This was a setback to the large states, who gave way only when the small states made it clear that this was their price for union. After equality of representation for the states in the Senate was accepted, most objections to the establishment of a strong national government dissolved.

The problem of representation was complicated by the existence of slavery. Looking back today, we are apt to exaggerate the differences that existed between the North and South over slavery. At that time the question was not one that divided the nation along sectional lines. Slavery was already dying in the North, and there were signs of its demise in the South. Southerners and northerners generally agreed that it was an unfortunate system, that eventually it would have to be removed. There was neither the intense opposition to slavery in the North nor the impassioned defense of it in the South that later developed. States with large numbers of slaves, nevertheless, wanted them to be counted in determining representation in the House of Representatives. At the same time, they did not want to count them as property for tax purposes. A compromise was agreed on: that a slave should count as three-fifths of a free person, both in determining representation in the House of Representatives and in apportionment of direct taxes.

Perhaps more important to the southerners was the fear that a northern majority in Congress might discriminate against southern trade. They had some basis for this concern. John Jay, Director of Foreign Affairs for the Confederation, had proposed a treaty with Great Britain that would have given advantages to northern merchants at the expense of southern exporters. To protect themselves, the southern delegates insisted on requiring a two-thirds majority for Senate consent to the ratification of treaties. This sectional check on treaties was supplemented by a provision denying to Congress the power to levy taxes on exports. Another dispute involved the slave trade. To meet the demands of South Carolina and Georgia, Congress was denied until 1808 the right to prohibit the importing of slaves. By that time, it was thought, there would be enough slaves within the United States to supply all demands.

The delegates found other issues, of course, to argue about. Should the national government have lower courts, or would one federal Supreme Court be enough? This issue was resolved by postponing the decision. The Constitution merely states that there *shall* be one Supreme Court and that Congress *may* establish inferior courts. How should the President be selected? For a long time the convention accepted the idea that the President should be elected by the Congress. But it was feared that either the Congress would dominate the President or vice versa. Election by the state legislatures was rejected because of distrust of these bodies. Some of the nationalistic delegates favored election by qualified voters, but others believed that the voters would not be sufficiently informed or dispassionate to make the selection. Finally, after much discussion, the electoral-college system was decided upon. This was perhaps the most original contribution of the delegates, although it was patterned after procedures used by Maryland to select state senators. It is also one of the most criticized provisions in the Constitution (see Chapter 14).

Finally, after three months, the delegates ceased their debating. On September 17, 1787, they assembled for the impressive ceremony of placing their names on the document they were recommending to the nation. All but three of those still present signed; others who opposed the general drift of the convention had already left. Their work over, the delegates adjourned to the City Tavern to relax and celebrate a job well done.

WHAT MANNER OF MEN?

Were the delegates an inspired group of men who cast aside all thoughts of self-interest? Were they motivated by the desire to save the Union or by the desire to save themselves? Was the convention the inevitable result of the weaknesses of the Articles? Was it a carefully maneuvered *coup d'état* on the part of wealthy aristocrats? Was the difference between those who favored and those who opposed the Constitution mainly economic? Or was the difference mainly regional?

All these interpretations—and a few others—have been put forward by students of history and government. During the early part of our history, the members of the convention were the object of uncritical adulation; the Constitution was the object of universal reverence. Early in the twentieth century a more critical attitude was inspired by the scholarship of J. Allen Smith and Charles A. Beard. Smith, in his *The Spirit of American Government* (1911), painted the Constitution as the outgrowth of an antidemocratic reaction, almost a conspiracy, against the rule of majorities. Beard's thesis was that the Constitution represented the platform of the propertied groups who wanted to limit state legislatures and strengthen the national government as a means of protecting property. In his influential book, *An Economic Interpretation of the Constitution* (1913), Beard described the economic holdings of the delegates and argued that their support or opposition to the Constitution could best be explained in terms of their financial interests. Beard explicitly denied that he was charging the Founding Fathers with writing the Constitution for their personal benefit. Rather, he contended that men's political behavior reflects their economic interests.

Recently historians, especially Professors Robert E. Brown and Forrest McDonald, have questioned the soundness of Beard's scholarship and challenged his interpretation of the data. Brown points out that there was no great propertyless mass in the United States and that "practically everybody was interested in the protection of property." [12] "We would be doing a grave injustice to the political sagacity of the Founding Fathers," Brown has written, "if we assumed that property or personal gain was their only motive." [13] Professor McDonald after looking into Beard's data has concluded that the

---

[12] Robert E. Brown, *Charles Beard and the Constitution* (Princeton Univ. Press, 1956), p. 198.

[13] *Ibid.*, p. 197.

"economic interpretation of the Constitution does not work," although he concedes "economic interpretation renders intelligible many of the forces at work in the making of the Constitution." [14]

Probably no interpretation ascribing an exclusive role to any one facet of human life can be satisfactory. Beard himself recognized that men are motivated by a complex of factors, conscious and unconscious. Self-interests, economic or otherwise, and principle are inextricably mixed in human behavior. The Founding Fathers were neither minor gods for whom self-interests or economic considerations were of no importance, nor men who thought only in terms of their own pocketbooks. They were concerned with the state of the Union and they wanted to protect the nation from aggression abroad and dissension at home. Fortunately, their own interests coincided with the long-run interests of the nation. Stability and strength were needed to protect property—but also to secure the unity and order indispensable for the operation of a democracy.

To Adopt or Not to Adopt

The delegates had gone far. After exceeding their authority by completely setting aside the Articles of Confederation, they had not hesitated to contravene Congress' instructions about ratification, or to ignore Article XIII of the Articles of Confederation. This article declared the Union to be *perpetual* and prohibited any alteration in the Articles unless agreed to by the Congress and by *every one of the state legislatures*—a provision that had made it impossible to amend the Articles. The delegates, aware that there was little chance of securing approval of the new Constitution in all the state legislatures, boldly declared that the Constitution should go into effect for those states that approved as soon as ratified by *conventions* in *nine* states.

But even this method was not going to be easy. Any political pollsters around in the fall of 1787 would probably have predicted defeat for the Constitution. Certainly the nation was not ready to adopt without a full-dress debate, and the country was soon divided into two camps. The supporters of the new government, by cleverly appropriating the name of Federalists, took some of the sting out of the charges that they were trying to destroy the states and establish an all-powerful central government. By dubbing their opponents Antifederalists, they pointed up the essentially negative character of the arguments of those who opposed ratification.

The split was in part geographical. The seaboard and city regions tended to be Federalist strongholds. The vast back-country regions from Maine through Georgia, inhabited by farmers and lesser folk, were the areas in which the Antifederalists were most strongly entrenched. But, as in all political contests, no single factor, geographical or economic or ideological, completely

---

[14] Forrest McDonald, *We the People: The Economic Origins of the Constitution* (Univ. of Chicago Press, 1958), pp. vii and 415.

accounts for the division between Federalist and Antifederalist. For example, in Virginia the leaders of both sides came from the same general social and economic class. In Massachusetts the delegates from the "Dan Shays" territory in the western part of the state voted for ratification. New York City and Philadelphia strongly supported the Constitution, but so did predominantly rural New Jersey.

From our present vantage point, many of the criticisms raised by the Antifederalists obviously were unfounded, and many of their fears unjustified. It used to be the fashion among historians and political scientists to picture these opponents of our Constitution as small-minded, selfish men who could not see beyond their own local interests. With the introduction of a more critical attitude toward the Founding Fathers, there was a swing to the other extreme; the Antifederalists were then described as the true defenders of liberty and democracy, fighting the economically motivated aristocratic Federalists. Quite obviously both these characterizations are overdrawn. Each side included able and enlightened men as well as those with less admirable motives. Furthermore, it is of questionable profit to try to give twentieth-century labels to eighteenth-century political debates or to engage in retrospective "loyalty" investigations using current political standards to determine whether or not the Federalists were democrats or antidemocrats. Certainly, judged within the context of the eighteenth century, both Federalists and Antifederalists were confirmed defenders of republican government.

The great debate was conducted with pamphlets, papers, letters to the editors, and speeches. Interest was intense and the issue important. But the argument was, in the main, carried on in a temperate manner. This great debate stands even today as an outstanding example of a free people using the techniques of free discussion to determine the nature of their fundamental laws.

THE GREAT DEBATE

In general, the Antifederalist argument developed along these lines: There is much of merit in the proposed Constitution, but it contains many provisions that show the aristocratic bias of its authors. It lacks many guarantees of the people's fundamental rights. Present conditions are not as bad as the Federalists make out: we are at peace, and there is no danger of internal dissension. What we need is a correction of the Articles of Confederation, but a correction that preserves, as the Constitution does not, the power of the states and the freedom of the people. We should not ratify the proposed Constitution; but after it has been fully discussed and its defects made apparent, another convention should be called to revise the Articles in the light of these discussions.

This summary cannot, of course, give a complete catalogue of all the objections raised to the Constitution, for almost all its articles and provisions were criticized. The Antifederalists were suspicious of the intentions of the delegates to the convention—delegates who had exceeded their instructions, deliberated in secret, and presented a Constitution that established a powerful national government. Something of this suspicion can be gained from the remarks of Amos Singletary, delegate from a western town in the Massachusetts ratifying convention. Singletary was a veteran member of the Massachusetts legislature and had served in the Revolutionary army. He said:

> Mr. President, if any body had proposed such a constitution as this in that day [Revolutionary period], it would have been thrown away at once. . . . These lawyers, and men of learning, and moneyed men, that talk so finely, and gloss over matters so smoothly, to make us poor illiterate people swallow down the pill, expect to get into Congress themselves; they expect to be the managers of this Constitution, and get all the power and all the money into their own hands, and then they will swallow up all of us little folks, like the great *Leviathan,* Mr. President; yes, just as the whale swallowed up *Jonah.*

The Federalists, on the other side, argued that there were just two alternatives: adoption of the Constitution or disunion. They insisted that the Confederation was hopelessly defective and, unless it was quickly altered, the Union would be lost. Arguing that union was indispensable to liberty and security, they defended the Constitution as conforming to the true principles of republican government. They admitted that it was not perfect, but held that it was the best that could be obtained, and that the way was open to correct such deficiencies as were uncovered through time and experience.

FEDERAL FARMER VERSUS PUBLIUS

One of the best attacks produced by the Antifederalists was a series of articles written by Richard Henry Lee, the man who had introduced the resolution in the Second Continental Congress calling for independence. Lee's *Letters of the Federal Farmer,* published in the fall of 1787, were widely circulated throughout the nation. *The Federalist,* on the other hand, is without doubt the best defense of the Constitution produced by the Federalists. Charles and Mary Beard have written, "From that day to this *The Federalist* has been widely regarded as the most profound single treatise on the Constitution ever written and as among the few masterly works on political science produced in all the centuries of history.[15] These essays were written by Alexander Hamilton, James Madison, and John Jay. Over the name of Publius, they were published serially in the New York papers during the winter of 1787. Taking historic license, let us rearrange and paraphrase this great debate in order to get the feel of the times, and to understand better the fears and hopes of the Federal Farmer and Publius.

---

[15] Charles and Mary Beard, *A Basic History of the United States* (New Home Library, 1944), p. 136.

Lee opened the argument by admitting that the Articles of Confederation were defective, but he said, in effect: [16]

> Ought we to precipitate the adoption of the proposed constitution? We are in no immediate danger of any commotion; we are in a state of perfect peace, and in no danger of invasion. We have hardly recovered from a long and distressing war, and we impute to the defects in our government many evils and embarrassments which are most clearly the result of the late war. It is natural for men who wish to hasten the adoption of a measure to tell us, "now is the crisis."

Publius spoke up: [17]

> I acknowledge that I cannot entertain an equal tranquillity with those who affect to treat the dangers of a longer continuance in our present situation as imaginary. A nation without a national government is, in my view, an awful spectacle. Nothing can be more evident, to those who are able to take an enlarged view of the subject, than the alternatives of an adoption of the new Constitution or a dismemberment of the Union.

Lee pressed his point:

> Probably not one man in ten thousand in the United States, till within these last few days, had an idea that the old ship was to be destroyed. The states universally supposed the convention would report alterations in the confederation. But when Virginia made a very respectable appointment, and placed at the head of it the first man in America, Pennsylvania appointed principally those men who are esteemed aristocratic. We shall view the convention with proper respect—and, at the same time, we must recollect how disproportionately the democratic and aristocratic parts of the community were represented.

Publius retorted:

> A dangerous ambition more often lurks behind the specious mask of zeal for the rights of the people than under the forbidding appearance of zeal for the firmness and efficiency of government. While our opponents admit that the government of the United States is destitute of energy, they contend against conferring upon it those powers which are requisite to supply that energy. They seem still to aim at things repugnant and irreconcilable; at an augmentation of federal authority, without a diminution of State authority; at sovereignty in the Union, and complete independence of the members. They fail to see that the evils we experience proceed not from minute or partial imperfections, but from fundamental errors in the structure of the building, which cannot be amended otherwise than by an alteration in the first principles and main pillars of the fabric.

---

16 See P. L. Ford, *Pamphlets on the Constitution of the United States* (1888), pp. 260-325.
17 *The Federalist* is available in several editions. One of the best is that edited by Max Beloff, *The Federalist* (Macmillan, 1948).

Still unsatisfied, Lee returned to the attack:

> The plan of government now proposed is clearly designed to make us one consolidated government. The general government will possess all essential powers, the states a mere shadow of power. The general government, far removed from the people, will find either that its laws are neglected or that it must use military force to execute them; either will lead to a revolution, and to the destruction of freedom.

Publius answered:

> It will always be far more easy for the state governments to encroach upon the national authority than for the national government to encroach upon the state authorities. The people of each state would be apt to feel a stronger bias towards their local government than towards the government of the Union. Nor will the government of the Union have to use the sword to execute its laws. The great and radical vice in the construction of the existing Confederation is in the principle of *legislation for states* or governments, in their corporate or collective capacities, as contradistinguished from the individuals of which they consist.

Lee summed up his arguments:

> An examination of the proposed constitution opens to my mind a new scene; instead of seeing powers lodged cautiously in the hands of numerous legislators, and many magistrates, we see all important powers collecting in one center, where a few men can use them almost at discretion. There are many good things in the proposed system. It is founded on elective principles, and the deposit of powers in different hands is essentially right. But the value of every feature is vastly lessened for the want of that one important feature in a free government, a representation of the people. Because we have sometimes abused democracy, I am not among those who think a democratic branch a nuisance.

Perhaps the most telling criticism of the proposed Constitution made by Lee and others was its failure to include a bill of rights.[18] The Federalists' explanations did not sound highly convincing. They argued that a bill of rights would be superfluous. The general government had only delegated powers, and there was no need to specify that Congress could not, for example, abridge freedom of the press. It had no power to regulate the press. Moreover, the Federalists argued, to guarantee *some* rights might be dangerous because it would then be thought that rights *not* listed could be denied. Contradictorily, they then pointed out that the Constitution protected some of the most important rights—trial by jury in federal criminal cases, for example. Hamilton and others also insisted that paper guarantees were weak reeds on which to depend for protection against governmental tyranny.

---

[18] See Robert A. Rutland, *The Birth of the Bill of Rights* (Univ. of North Carolina Press, 1955).

The Antifederalists, as well as many who were otherwise generally favorable to ratification, were unconvinced. If some rights were protected, what could be the objection to providing constitutional protection for others? Without a bill of rights, what was to prevent Congress from using one of its delegated powers in such a manner that free speech would be abridged? If bills of rights were needed in state constitutions to limit state governments, why was one not needed in the national constitution to limit the national government—a government more distant from the people and more likely to subvert natural rights? The Federalists, forced to concede, agreed to add a bill of rights if and when the new Constitution was approved.

THE POLITICS OF RATIFICATION

Despite the great debate, many people remained apathetic. The only direct voice the electorate had in the writing and adopting of our Constitution was in choosing delegates to the state ratifying conventions. In most of the states suffrage requirements were liberalized and from 80 to 85 per cent of the adult white males (but only about 20 per cent of the whole adult population) were eligible to vote for delegates; yet only a fraction of those qualified to vote actually did so. "The Constitution was adopted with a great show of indifference." [19]

The political strategy of the Federalists was to secure ratification in as many states as possible before the opposition had time to organize. The Antifederalists were handicapped because their main strength was in the rural areas, which were underrepresented in some state legislatures and which were the most difficult to arouse to political action. They needed time to perfect their organization and collect their strength. But the Federalists, composed of a more closely knit group of leaders throughout the colonies, moved in a hurry. "Unless the Federalists had been shrewd in manipulation as they were sound in theory, their arguments could not have prevailed." [20]

Delaware was the first state to ratify; in most of the small states, now propitiated by equal representation in the Senate, ratification was gained without difficulty. The first large state to take action was Pennsylvania. The Federalists presented the Constitution to the state legislature immediately after the Philadelphia Convention adjourned in September 1787, urging the legislators to issue the call for the ratifying convention to consider adoption of the new Constitution. But the legislature was about to adjourn, and the Antifederalist minority felt that this was moving with unseemly haste (especially since Congress had not even formally transmitted the document to the legislature for its consideration!). They wanted to postpone action until after the

---

[19] Brown, *op. cit.*, pp. 69, 197. See also A. C. McLaughlin, *A Constitutional History of the United States* (Appleton-Century, 1935), pp. 220-221.

[20] S. E. Morison and H. S. Commager, *The Growth of the American Republic* (Oxford Univ. Press, 4th ed., 1950), p. 296.

coming state elections, when they hoped to win a legislative majority, in which event they would not call a ratifying convention. When it became clear that the Federalists were going to move ahead, the Antifederalists left the legislative chamber. With three short of a quorum, business was brought to a standstill. Philadelphia, the seat of the legislature, was a Federalist stronghold. The next morning three Antifederalists were roused from their taverns, forcibly carried into the legislative chamber, sat on, and with a quorum thus obtained, the resolution calling for election of delegates to a ratifying convention was adopted. Under the astute generalship of James Wilson, the Pennsylvania Convention ratified by a vote of 46 to 23, the opposition coming from the western districts.

By the middle of January, New Jersey, Connecticut, and Georgia had ratified. The scene of battle then shifted to Massachusetts, a key state and a doubtful one. John Hancock and Samuel Adams had not declared themselves, and these gentlemen, with their great popular following, held the balance of power. The Federalists cleverly pointed out to Hancock that Washington would be the first President, and that therefore the Vice-President would undoubtedly be a New Englander. What citizen of New England was more distinguished than John Hancock? Whether or not this hint was the cause, Hancock eventually came out for ratification, and Adams was persuaded to vote for approval after securing a promise that a bill of rights would be forthcoming after adoption. Even so, Massachusetts ratified by the narrow margin of 187 to 168.

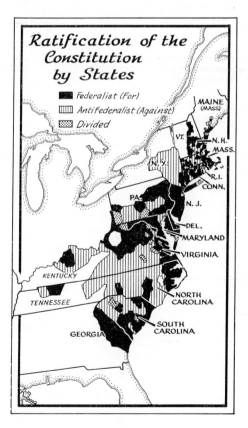

Ratification of the
Constitution
by States

■ *Federalist (For)*
▥ *Antifederalist (Against)*
▨ *Divided*

By June, Maryland, South Carolina, and New Hampshire had ratified, so the nine states required to bring the Constitution into effect had been obtained. But neither Virginia nor New York had taken action, and without them the new Union would have little chance of success. Virginia was the most populous state and the home of many of the nation's outstanding leaders, and New York's geographical position split the ratifying states in two.

The Virginia ratifying convention rivaled the Constitutional Convention in the caliber of its delegates. James Madison was the captain of the Federalist forces, and he had able lieutenants in Governor Randolph and young John Marshall. Patrick Henry, George Mason, and James Monroe within the convention, and Richard Henry Lee outside, led the opposition. Henry attacked the proposed government, point by point, with great eloquence; Madison turned back each attack quietly but cogently—sometimes in a voice so low that the recorder of the debates was unable to hear him. At the critical juncture Washington sent a letter to the convention urging unqualified ratification. This tipped the scale, and Virginia ratified. News was rushed to New York.

The great landowners along the Hudson, unlike their southern planter friends, were opposed to the Constitution. They feared federal taxation of their holdings, and they did not want to abolish the profitable tax that New York had been levying on the trade and commerce of other states. When the convention assembled, the Federalists were greatly outnumbered, but they were aided by the strategy and skill of Hamilton, and by word of Virginia's ratification. New York approved by a margin of three votes.

Although North Carolina and Rhode Island still remained outside the Union (the former ratified in November 1789 and the latter six months later), the new ship of state was launched. In New York, a few members of the old Congress assembled to issue the call for elections under the new Constitution, and then Congress adjourned *sine die*. Throughout the nation citizens paraded and drank toasts to the new ship, *The Constitution*.

The Living Constitution

F or a time, some people remained skeptical of the new Constitution. After watching merchants and mechanics march side by side in a parade celebrating ratification, a Bostonian remarked sourly that "it may serve to please children, but freemen will not be so easily gulled out of their liberties." On the other hand, a Philadelphian said that the procession in his city had "made such an impression on the minds of our young people that 'federal' and 'union' have now become part of the household words of every family in the city." This effect on the youth was significant, for it was on the younger generation that hopes for the new government depended.

The new ship of state was launched in favorable seas. The adoption of the Constitution coincided with the return of prosperity; markets for American goods were opening in Europe; and business was pulling out of its postwar slump. Such events seemed to justify Federalist claims that adoption of the Constitution would correct the nation's ills. Within a surprisingly short time the Constitution lost its partisan character. Antifederalists vied with Federalists in honoring it—so much so, said one cynic, that "whenever its eulogium is pronounced, I feel an involuntary apprehension of mischief." Politicians differed less and less over whether the Constitution was good. More and more they argued over what it meant.

As the Constitution won the support of Americans, it began to take on the aura of the higher natural law itself. "Here was the document," it has been said, "into which the Founding Fathers had poured their wisdom as into a vessel; the Fathers themselves grew ever larger in stature as they receded from view; the era in which they lived and fought became a Golden Age; in that age there had been a fresh dawn for the world, and its men were giants against the sky; what they had fought for was abstracted from its living context and became a set of 'principles,' eternally true and universally applicable." [1] This

---

[1] Max Lerner, *Ideas for the Ice Age* (Viking, 1941), pp. 241-242.

adoration of the Constitution—sometimes called the "cult of the Constitution" —was important as a means of bringing unity into the diversity of the new nation. Like the Crown in Britain, the Constitution became a symbol of national loyalty, a unifying symbol that evoked both emotional and rational support from all Americans regardless of their differences. The framers' work became part of the American creed; it stood for liberty, equality before the law, limited government—indeed, for whatever anyone wanted to build into it.

The new Constitution was thus a *symbol*. It was also an *instrument*, a supreme and binding law that both *grants* and *limits* powers. "In framing a government which is to be administered by men over men," wrote Madison in *The Federalist*, "the great difficulty lies in this: you must first enable the government to control the governed; and in the next place oblige it to control itself." As an instrument, the Constitution serves a dual function. It is a *positive* instrument of government, enabling the governors to control the governed. It is also a *restraint* on government, enabling the ruled to check the rulers.

In what ways does the Constitution *limit* the power of the national government? In what way does it *create* national power? How has it managed to serve both as a great symbol of national unity and at the same time as a somewhat adaptable and changing instrument?

Checking Power with Power

It is strange, perhaps, to begin by stressing the ways in which the Constitution *limits* national power. Yet we must keep in mind the dilemma that the framers faced. They wanted a more effective national government, but at the same time they were keenly aware that the people would not accept too strong a national government. Accordingly, they allotted certain powers to the *national* government, and reserved the rest for the *states*. In short, they established a system of *federalism* (the nature and problems of which will be taken up in Chapters 4 and 5). But this distribution of powers between the national and state governments, they felt, was not enough. Other ways of limiting the national government were needed.

The most important device to make public officials observe the constitutional limits on their powers is the right of voters to go to the polls and defeat those who abuse power. Why were the framers not willing to depend solely on such *political* controls? The answer is simple: They did not fully trust the people's judgment. The people might be misled and vote a demagogue into power. Even more important, the framers feared that a majority faction might use the new central government to deprive minorities of their rights. "A dependence on the people is, no doubt, the primary control on the government," Madison admitted, "but experience has taught mankind the necessity of auxiliary precautions."

What were these "auxiliary precautions"? The framers hoped that two different but related arrangements—*separation of powers* and *checks and balances*—would achieve their supreme goal of preventing public officials from abusing their power and of preventing any one group of people, even a majority, from capturing control of the government and tyrannizing the rest of the people.

DIVIDING NATIONAL POWER

The first step was the *separation of powers*—that is, dividing power among the three branches of the national government. As we have seen, the idea of parceling out power is an old one. Locke had discussed the need for separating powers, and Montesquieu had argued that liberty could last only where powers were distributed among different departments of government. American leaders were familiar with the arguments of both. In *Federalist No. 47* James Madison wrote:

> No political truth is certainly of greater intrinsic value, or is stamped with the authority of more enlightened patrons of liberty, than that ... the accumulation of all powers, legislative, executive, and judiciary, in the same hands ... may justly be pronounced the very definition of tyranny.

But the power of Locke's and Montesquieu's logic alone does not account for the incorporation of the doctrine of separation of powers in our basic document. It was, as we have seen, no novelty, and had been the operating practice in the colonies for over a hundred years. Only during the Revolutionary period was the doctrine compromised and power concentrated in the hands of the legislature. This experience merely confirmed the belief in the merits of separation of powers. Many of the framers attributed the evils of state government and the want of energy of the central government to the lack of a strong executive who could both check legislative abuses and give energy and direction to administration.

But dividing up power in itself was not enough. For there was always the danger—from the framers' point of view—that different officials with different powers might pool their authority and act together. Two modern examples may make this situation clear. In a football team, power is divided up—the quarterback has one job, the center another, the guards still another. But all players act in harmony in their efforts to score. In Britain today there are executive, legislative, and judicial officials, but they act together in response to directions from the Cabinet. Separation of powers by itself would not prevent governmental branches and officials from responding to the same pressures—for example, an overwhelming majority of the voters. If dividing up power by itself was not enough, what further could be done?

CHECKS AND BALANCES

The framers' answer was to make these branches and officials responsive to *different* pressures. This is the system of *checks and balances*. The framers deliberately designed a system in which President, legislators, and judges would not be dependent on one another or on the same source of popular support. The President was to be chosen by a group of *electors,* so that he would have different loyalties and interests from senators chosen by state legislators, from representatives directly elected by local constituencies, from judges holding office for life and appointed by the President with the consent of the Senate.

The framers were also careful to arrange matters so that a majority could win control over only part of the government at one time. A popular majority might take control of the House of Representatives in an off-year election, but the President, representing previous popular sentiment, would still have two years to go. That majority might win the Presidency (difficult, however, because of the electoral-college system, the framers hoped), but other forces might still control the Senate.

Moreover, each branch of our national government is given some responsibilities in performing the functions of the other, and each is given some authority to control the operations of the other. Congress enacts laws, the President can veto them, and Congress can repass them over his veto. The Supreme Court can invalidate laws passed by Congress and signed by the President, but the Chief Executive and the Senate appoint the judges. The President administers the laws, but Congress provides the money for him and his agencies. Senate and House of Representatives have an absolute veto on each other. These are the essential features of the checks-and-balances system, but it has almost endless ramifications.

It was the legislative branch that the framers felt was most likely to take over the whole government. "In republican government," Madison wrote, "the legislative authority necessarily predominates." It was in part to meet this problem that the framers chopped the legislature in two and made the two branches responsible to different constituencies. Thus, said Madison, the two branches were rendered "by different modes of election and different principles of action, as little connected with each other as the nature of their common functions and their common dependence on the society will admit."

Finally, if this did not work, there were the judges. It was not for some years after the Constitution was in operation that the judges obtained the power of *judicial review*—the right to be the official interpreters of the Constitution and to refuse to enforce those laws of Congress that in the judges' opinion were unconstitutional (see Chapter 20). But from the beginning, the judges were expected to check the legislature and the groups that the Congressional majority might represent. "Independent judges," wrote Alexander Hamilton in *Federalist No. 78,* would be "an essential safeguard against the effects of occasional ill humors in society. These sometimes extend no farther than to the injury of the private rights of particular classes of citizens, by unjust and partial laws." Independent judges, Hamilton pointed out, were in a monarchy "an excellent barrier to the despotism of the prince," and, in a republic, they were a "no less excellent barrier to the encroachments and oppressions of the representative body."

AMBITION TO COUNTERACT AMBITION

The doctrine of separation of powers, at least as it is combined with checks and balances in American practice, is one of *interdependence* rather than *independence*. It is, as Madison pointed out, merely the principle that the accumulation of *all* powers in the *same* hands is to be avoided. Governmental power cannot be divided neatly into three separate categories, nor can the three departments be kept separate and distinct. That is not the intent of the principle of separation of powers. What is required is a *blending* and *mingling* of powers. "The great security against a gradual concentration of the several powers in the same department," wrote Madison, "consists in giving to those who administer each department the necessary constitutional means and personal motives to resist encroachment on the others. . . . Ambition must be made to counteract ambition."

Could such a system really work? What if a majority of the people should get control of all branches of government and force through radical and impulsive measures? The framers were realists. They knew that if, over a period of years, the great majority of the voters wanted to take a certain step, nothing could stop them. Nothing, that is, except despotic government, and they did not want that. The men of 1787 reasoned that all they could do—and this was quite a lot—was to stave off, temporarily, full control by the popular majority.

It may seem surprising that the people—or at least the large number of them who were suspicious of the new Constitution—did not object to these "auxiliary precautions," which were barriers to action by a popular majority. But most early Americans, like many Americans today, had an innate distrust of government, especially a national government. They did not look on government as an instrument they could seize with their votes and use for their own purposes. (Of course, in the eighteenth century, only a small percentage of the population had the right to participate in selecting the governors.) They looked on government as something to be handcuffed, hemmed in, and rendered harmless. Thus separation of powers and checks and balances have come to serve two roles: to *make it difficult for a majority to control the government,* and to *restrain all government.*

A STUDY IN CONTRASTS

Most Americans now take this system for granted. To them the separating and checking of power seem to be the very essence of constitutional government. Like Madison, they view the amassing of power in the hands of any one branch of government as the essence of tyranny. Yet it is quite possible for a government to be constitutional without such an apparatus. Consider the British system. The voters elect members of Parliament from districts throughout the nation (much as we elect members of the House of Representatives). The members of the House of Commons have almost complete constitutional power. The House of Lords once could check the Commons, but today the Lords are almost powerless. There is no High Court with power to void acts of Parliament: the Prime Minister cannot veto them. If, tomorrow, Parliament decided to outlaw mustaches or make everyone wear green clothes, it could do so constitutionally through a majority vote. Its decisions would be carried out by the Cabinet, which constitutionally is simply the organ of Parliament (although *politically* Parliament is largely controlled by the Prime Minister and the Cabinet). And, of course, good Englishmen take their system for granted, too.

The British system is strict majority rule—that is, a majority of the voters can elect a majority of the legislators, who can put through the majority's program without hindrance, at least until the next election rolls around. Ours is something else; it usually depends for action on the agreement of many elements of the society, comprising much more than a mere majority. The British system *concentrates* control and responsibility in the legislature; ours *diffuses* control and responsibility among the several organs of government.

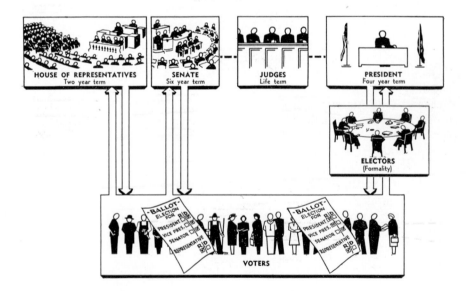

AMERICAN SYSTEM OF SEPARATION OF POWERS

But both systems may be described as constitutional government. In both, the rulers are subjected to regular restraints—in Britain to free elections and constant open criticism; in the United States to these *plus* the "auxiliary precautions" Madison mentioned. In both, the constitutional limitations are binding on all those who exercise governmental power—on President and Prime Minister, congressmen and members of Parliament, judges, sheriffs, the London bobby and the corner cop. Both systems are constitutional in the basic sense that the rulers are subject to regular restraints. In contrast, an arbitrary government is checked only by the rulers' fear that if the people are pushed around too much they might revolt. But revolution today is a small threat when the rulers control modern arms and communications and the people are unarmed.

Which system is better, British or American? Each has its supporters, and some very able Americans have been among the sternest critics of our system of checks and balances. Some Englishmen have admired certain aspects of our system—or at least they believed that they well suited a nation as safe and prosperous as ours. James Bryce, writing in 1893, pointed out: "Social convulsions from within, warlike assaults from without, seem now as

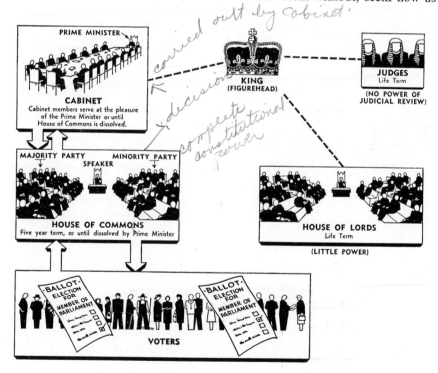

BRITISH SYSTEM OF CONCENTRATION OF RESPONSIBILITY

unlikely to try the fabric of the American Constitution, as an earthquake to rend the walls of the Capitol. This is why Americans submit, not merely patiently but hopefully, to the defects of their government. The vessel may not be any better built, or found, or rigged than are those which carry the fortunes of the great nations of Europe. She is certainly not better navigated. But for the present at least—it may not always be so—she sails upon a summer sea." [2] Today, of course, the seas are somewhat more wintry. Today the ship must be navigated with more precision, for the government's responsibilities are much greater.

The attack on our system of checks and balances, and the defense of it, will be described in Chapter 21. It is important to note here, however, that several developments have modified the system: *of checks & balance*

① The rise of national political parties. Political parties have served to some extent as unifying factors, drawing together the President, senators, representatives, and even judges behind a common program. But the parties, in turn, have been divided and weakened by the workings of the checks-and-balances system.

② Changes in electoral methods. The framers wanted the President to be chosen by wise, independent-minded men free from popular passions and hero worship. Almost from the beginning, however, the presidential electors have acted as automata, pledged prior to elections to cast their electoral vote for their party's presidential candidate. And senators, who were originally elected by state legislatures, are today directly chosen by the people.

③ The establishment of agencies exercising all three functions: legislative, executive, and judicial. When the government began to regulate the economy, it became clear that agencies had to have some legislative and judicial as well as administrative power. It was difficult, if not impossible, to grant an agency only administrative powers when detailed rules had to be made and judgments rendered on highly complex matters, such as policing air waves or checking the purity of food and drugs.

④ The rise of the President as the dominating, unifying element in national government. Drawing on his constitutional, political, and emergency powers, the President has overcome some of the divisive effects of checks and balances.

Despite these developments, however, the fragmentation of governmental power remains a basic factor in American government and politics, as almost every page of this book will testify.

---

2 James Bryce, *The American Commonwealth* (Macmillan, 1911), I, 310. This classic study remains one of the most perceptive interpretations of American government and society.

The Constitution
as Instrument of Government

As careful as the Founding Fathers were to limit the powers they conferred on the national government, the main reason they assembled in Philadelphia, after all, was to create a strong national government. They had learned that weak government, incapable of governing, is as great a danger to liberty as overly powerful government. They wished to create a national government within the framework of a federal system and endow that government with enough authority to meet the exigencies of all times. But how much power would be needed and how should it be distributed?

The Founding Fathers were wise and humble men who doubted they had either the right or the wisdom to prescribe for future generations the details of how the nation should be governed. They knew that to endure, the government must be capable of meeting the needs of future generations whose problems could not be anticipated. Hence they did not try to put down all the rules in black and white. Instead they painted in broad strokes, made their grants of power general, leaving the way open for succeeding generations to fill in the details and organize the structure of government in accordance with experience.

Consequently, our formal, written Constitution is only the skeleton of our system and is supplemented by a number of fundamental rules that must be considered part of our constitutional system in its larger sense. Without an understanding of these rules, often referred to as the "unwritten Constitution," we would have an incomplete and even misleading picture of our government.

It is primarily through changes in our "unwritten Constitution" that our constitutional system is kept up to date. These features of our "unwritten Constitution," many of which are not unwritten at all, are to be found in certain basic statutes of Congress, decisions of the Supreme Court, actions of the President, and customs and usages of the nation.

KEEPING THE CONSTITUTION UP TO DATE

Congressional elaboration is one of the most important ways of adapting our constitutional system to new problems. Since the framers left to Congress authority to prescribe the details of the structure of the national government, it is unnecessary to amend the formal Constitution every time a change is needed. Examples of congressional elaboration appear in such fundamental legislation as the Judiciary Act of 1789, which laid the foundations of our national judicial system; in the laws establishing the organization and functions of all federal executive officials subordinate to the President; in the Presidential Succession Act of 1947, which determines the succession in the event of the death or disability of the President and Vice President; and in the rules of procedure and internal organization and practices of the Congress itself.

B   *Judicial interpretation* of the Constitution, especially by the Supreme Court, has played an important part in the continuous process of modernizing the constitutional system. As we shall note in fuller detail in Chapter 20, American judges have the power of *judicial review*—that is, the power to prevent those practices and to refuse to enforce those laws that the judges think are in conflict with the Constitution. The power of judicial review makes the Supreme Court the authoritative interpreter of the Constitution. The words of the Constitution are sufficiently broad and ambiguous to allow divergent interpretations; as conditions have changed and new national demands have developed, so too the Supreme Court's interpretation of the Constitution has changed to accommodate these new conditions and demands. In the words of Woodrow Wilson, "The Supreme Court is a constitutional convention in continuous session." The establishment of judicial review itself is a classic example of the importance of judicial interpretation in the adaptation of our constitutional system. The Constitution does not specifically give the judges the power of judicial review. Rather, the Supreme Court in the famous case of *Marbury v. Madison* interpreted the Constitution to mean that judges should interpret the Constitution.

C.   *Presidential practices* have had much to do with the development of our constitutional system. There has been no change in the formal Constitution in this respect, but the constitutional position of the President is different today from what it was in 1789. The Presidency has become the pivotal office of our national government and the President has become Chief Legislator as well as Chief Executive. This fundamental change in the American constitutional system has come about because of the willingness of several Presidents, especially Jackson, Lincoln, Wilson, and both Roosevelts, to respond to national crises by a vigorous use of presidential power to provide the leadership the people wanted. Other examples of how our Presidents have contributed to the building of our constitutional system are the establishment of the Cabinet, which rests upon traditions going back to President Washington; the precedent established by John Tyler in 1841 that the Vice President when he accedes to the Presidency on the death on the incumbent becomes President and not merely Acting President; and the precedent established by Wilson that the President may leave the United States and retain the full powers of his office.

D.   *Customs and usages* of the nation have rounded out our governmental system. Presidential nominating conventions and other party activities, and the residence requirement for congressmen—all to be described in later chapters—are examples of constitutional usages. We can search the written Constitution in vain for any specific mention of these practices, but they are fundamental to an understanding of our constitutional system. In fact, it has been primarily through the *extra*constitutional development of national political parties and the extension of the suffrage within the states that our Constitution was democratized. A broader electorate began to exercise control over the national government. The presidential office was made more responsive to the people, and the relationship between Congress and the President was altered. Through the growth of political parties some of the Constitution's blocks to majority rule were overcome.

Because the Constitution is so flexible and because it allows for easy adaptation to changing times, it does not require frequent formal amendment. The advantages of this flexibility may be appreciated when the national Constitution is compared with the rigid and over-specific state constitutions. Many state constitutions, more like legal codes than basic charters, are so long, complex, and detailed that the hands of public officials are tied. State constitutions leave so little discretion to those who govern that in order to adapt state governments to changing conditions the constitutions must be amended frequently or replaced every generation or so.

A RIGID OR FLEXIBLE CONSTITUTION?

This picture of a constantly changing national constitutional system disturbs many people. They would prefer a fixed Constitution that establishes precise rules alterable only by formal amendment. How, they argue, can you have a constitutional government when the Constitution is constantly being twisted by interpretation and changed by informal methods? This view fails to distinguish between two aspects of the Constitution. As an expression of basic and almost timeless personal liberties, the Constitution does not and should not change. For example, no government can today, any more than it could yesterday or can tomorrow, destroy the right to free speech and remain a constitutional government. In this sense—the civil liberties expressed in the Bill of Rights in our Constitution—the Constitution *is* timeless and essentially unchanging.

But in another sense the Constitution can and must change. When we consider it as an *instrument of government* and a *positive grant of power,* we realize that if it does not grow with the nation it serves, it soon will be pushed aside. The purposes of government remain the same: to establish liberty, promote justice, ensure domestic tranquillity, and provide for the common defense. But the powers of government adequate to accomplish these purposes in 1787 are no longer adequate in the 1960's. A constitution suitable to promote justice, let us say, for a small agricultural nation may not be suitable for a large industrial nation. No constitution can long deny to the government the right to do what its people want done.

"We the people"—the people of today and tomorrow, not just the people of 1787—ordain and establish the Constitution. "The Constitution," wrote Jefferson, "belongs to the living and not to the dead." So firmly did he believe this that he advocated a new constitution for every generation. New constitutions have not been necessary, because in a less formal way each generation has taken part in the never-ending process of developing the Constitution.

Because of its remarkable adaptability, the Constitution has survived the rigors of democratic and industrial revolutions, the turmoil of civil war, the tensions of major depressions, and the dislocations of world wars.

The problem is, then, to preserve the Constitution in its role, as a protector of fundamental liberties, to preserve the essentials of justice and democracy upon which our system is based, and at the same time to permit government to operate in accordance with the wishes of the people and to adapt itself to new conditions.

Changing the Letter of the Constitution   The framers of the Constitution knew that future experience would call for changes in the text of the Constitution itself and that some means of formal amendment would be necessary. Accordingly, they set forth two ways to *propose* amendments to the Constitution and two ways to *ratify* them. Furthermore, they carefully saw to it that amendments could not be made by simple majorities.

PROPOSING AND RATIFYING

The first method of *proposing* amendments, and the only one that has ever been used, is by a two-thirds vote of both houses of Congress. The second method is by a national convention called by Congress at the request of the legislatures of two-thirds of the states. Shortly before the Civil War there was some discussion about holding a national convention, but nothing came of it. Several scholars have advocated the calling of such a convention to revise the Constitution in the light of modern conditions, and from time to time several states have petitioned Congress with respect to specific amendments. During the last decade or so over half the state legislatures asked Congress either to propose or to call a convention to propose an amendment limiting the power of the national government to tax incomes, gifts, and estates. But the state legislatures by themselves, no matter how many of them act, cannot officially propose amendments, all they can do is petition. There is no legal way to force Congress to call a national convention even if the necessary two-thirds of the state legislatures petition for it. In the past, Congress has preferred to propose amendments itself instead of calling a convention to do so. Perhaps Congress remembers the fate of its predecessor at the hands of the convention it called into being in 1787!

After an amendment has been proposed, it must be *ratified*. Again two methods are provided: by approval of the legislatures in three-fourths of the states, or by approval of specially called ratifying conventions in three-fourths of the states. Congress determines which method of ratification shall be used.

A state may ratify an amendment after it has once voted against ratification, but once it approves it cannot change its mind and "unratify." States must ratify within a "reasonable time" in order for their action to be effective. Congress determines what is a reasonable time either by including within the proposed amendment a specific time limit for ratification or by determining the effectiveness of state ratifications at a later date. For example, in the child labor amendment proposed by Congress in 1924 no time limit was set. To date, only twenty-eight states have ratified; the last was Kansas, in 1937. If ten more states should ratify, would the amendment become part of the Constitution? Congress would have to decide if the necessary three-fourths of the states had ratified within a "reasonable time."

FOUR METHODS OF AMENDING THE CONSTITUTION

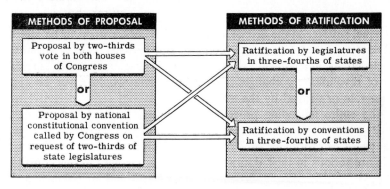

The submission of amendments to legislatures instead of to ratifying conventions has been criticized because it permits the Constitution to be changed without any clear expression of the electorate's desires. State legislators who do the ratifying may even have been elected before the proposed amendment was submitted to the states. In any event, state legislators are chosen because of their views on schools, taxation, bond issues, and other matters, or because of their personal popularity—they are almost never elected because of their stand on a proposed constitutional amendment.

Despite these objections to ratification by legislatures, the only amendment to be submitted to ratifying conventions was the Twenty-first (to repeal the Eighteenth or Prohibition Amendment). The "wets" rightly believed that repeal had a better chance of success with conventions than with the rural-dominated state legislatures. These strategic considerations rather than any desire to submit the question to the electorate was the important factor, but many commentators mistakenly thought a new precedent had been set and that in the future Congress would choose the more democratic ratification method.

The major obstacle to the adoption of constitutional amendments has not been ratification but getting Congress to propose amendments in the first place. Although dozens of resolutions proposing amendments are introduced in every session, few make any headway. But what Congress proposes is usually ratified. Of twenty-seven amendments proposed, twenty-two have been ratified. Four of the five unratified amendments were proposed prior to the Civil War; since then, the only amendment that has failed to win the necessary state approval is the child labor amendment.

The President has no formal authority over constitutional amendments: his veto power does not extend to them, although his political influence in getting amendments through Congress is often crucial. Nor may governors veto approval of amendments by their respective legislatures, since the Constitution vests ratification in the legislatures alone.

Are there any changes in the Constitution that cannot be made by amendment? Not if Congress and enough state legislatures or state conventions can agree on a change. The Constitution does say that no state shall be deprived of its equal suffrage in the Senate, or be deprived of territory, or be joined with another state except with its own consent. But perhaps these provisions could be repealed by amendment. However, this is essentially trivial speculation. Short of revolutionary changes such amendments would never be approved by Congress or ratified by the states.

The entire amending procedure has been criticized because neither a majority of the voters at large nor even a majority of the voters in a majority of the states can formally alter the Constitution. But when a majority of the people are serious in their desire to bring about changes in our constitutional system, their wishes are implemented either by formal amendment or by the more subtle methods of interpretation and adaptation.

As we have mentioned, the flexibility of our federal Constitution has reduced the need for formal amendments. If we disregard the Bill of Rights, which for all practical purposes may be considered as part of the original document, the Constitution has been amended only twelve times, and two of these, the Eighteenth and Twenty-first, involving Prohibition, cancel each other out. The twelve amendments adopted since the Bill of Rights are difficult to classify, but they may be grouped somewhat arbitrarily into the following categories: (1) Those whose chief importance is to add to or subtract from the power of the national government; (2) those whose main effect is to limit the power of the state governments; (3) those whose chief impact has been to add to or subtract from the role of the electorate; and (4) those making structural changes in governmental machinery.

CHANGES IN NATIONAL POWER

The Eleventh Amendment. When the Constitution was adopted, it was generally assumed that no private individual could sue a state in federal courts, at least without the consent of the state. But in 1793, when the Supreme Court ruled otherwise in the case of *Chisholm v. Georgia,* there was immediate alarm lest citizens flood the federal courts with suits against states defaulting on their debts. The Eleventh Amendment, which became part of the Constitution in 1798, took from federal courts any authority to hear suits *commenced* or *prosecuted* by individuals against the states.

The Sixteenth Amendment. This amendment was also adopted to reverse a Supreme Court decision. In 1895 the Supreme Court, overruling a long line of precedents, for all practical purposes denied to the federal government the power to levy a graduated income tax.[3] The Sixteenth Amendment, which was adopted in 1913, empowers the national government to collect such a tax.

The Eighteenth Amendment. This amendment, adopted in 1919, was the culmination of a long struggle of the prohibitionists against the use of alcoholic beverages. The amendment gave Congress power to enforce the prohibitions of the amendment against the manufacture, sale, or transportation of liquors. Although the amendment was ratified by all but two state legislatures, prohibition did not have the support of large groups of people, especially in urban areas. During the 1920's public indifference made it impossible to enforce prohibition without adopting police-state methods and spending vast sums of money. A thriving bootlegging industry developed, and prohibition, instead of cutting down the consumption of alcohol, served mainly to enrich criminals and to foster a callous attitude toward the law. After thirteen years of disappointment, and the outbreak of the Great Depression (which made new taxes desirable), the *Twenty-first Amendment* was adopted in 1933, repealing the Eighteenth.

The Thirteenth Amendment. Although this amendment by its own force freed the slaves, its chief significance today is that it gives to Congress power to prevent any attempt to hold a human being in slavery or involuntary servitude (see Chapter 7).

Formal amendments, it is clear, have not been very important in adding to or detracting from the power of the federal government. One amendment took away power that the national government was not thought to have had; one added power that it was believed to have had; one grant of power was subsequently repealed; and one gave it power which it has never chosen to exercise vigorously and which has been narrowed by judicial interpretation (see Chapter 7).

LIMITING STATE POWER

The Fourteenth and Fifteenth Amendments. Along with the Thirteenth Amendment, these two were adopted following, and as a result of, the Civil War. As we have noted, the major purpose of the Thirteenth was to free the slaves; the major purpose of the Fourteenth was to make them citizens and to protect their civil rights, and that of the Fifteenth was to protect their right to vote. Only the objectives of freedom and citizenship were immediately

---

[3] *Pollock* v. *Farmers' Loan and Trust Co.*

accomplished. But the amendments had other consequences not generally anticipated, the most important being that the Supreme Court for a time used the Fourteenth Amendment to give constitutional sanction to the gospel of laissez faire (see Chapter 8).

These amendments substantially increased the power of the Supreme Court to review actions of the state governments and might well be placed among those that add to the power of the national government—or at least to the judicial branch of that government.

The Nineteenth Amendment. This amendment, adopted in 1920, deprives the states (and the national government) of the right to deny any citizen the right to vote because of sex. Although women were voting in many states prior to its adoption, the amendment was the final step in providing the constitutional framework for universal suffrage (see Chapter 9).

CHANGING THE POWER OF THE VOTERS

The Seventeenth Amendment. This amendment, adopted in 1913, provides that United States senators be chosen directly by the electorate instead of being selected by the state legislatures. When the Constitution came from the hands of its framers, the House of Representatives was the only branch of the national government that the electorate chose directly. The rise of political parties and the extension of the suffrage within the states brought the

The United States Senate was called the "Millionaires' Club" before the adoption of the 17th Amendment.

From *Puck*, January 23, 1889. Courtesy Roger Butterfield

presidential office under the control of the voters by the 1830's. From then on it was a matter of time before the people would demand the right to choose their senators as well.

As the twentieth century opened, the people in many of the states were, in effect, choosing their senators, because the legislatures were simply ratifying the results of popular referendums. But the demand for constitutional change became insistent. It was charged that great sums of money were being used to bribe state legislators to choose men of wealth and conservative outlook. The Senate came to be dubbed the "Millionaires' Club," and individual senators were tagged as representatives, not of the people, but of the Steel Trust, the Sugar Trust, the Railroad Trust, and so on. Several times the House of Representatives approved an amendment that would require direct election, but the Senate resisted. Finally, in 1912, the Senate capitulated. The Seventeenth Amendment rounded out the process by which the political branches of the national government were made more directly responsive to the voters.

The Twenty-second Amendment bans presidential third terms.

B *The Twenty-second Amendment.* This, the most recent amendment, was adopted in 1951. It prevents anyone from being elected to the office of President more than twice (except the incumbent at that time, Harry S. Truman). A man succeeding to the Presidency and serving more than two years may be elected President in his own right only once. The chief significance of the amendment, however, is that it limits the electorate. Prior to the third-term election of Franklin D. Roosevelt in 1940, one of the unwritten usages of the American Constitution was that a man should not run and the voters should not elect a man to this high office for more than two terms. In 1940 and again in 1944, a majority of the voters, aided by Roosevelt, "amended" this unwritten rule. But with the adoption of the Twenty-second Amendment, the restriction on the political majority was made absolute.

IV CHANGING THE CONSTITUTIONAL STRUCTURE

A *The Twelfth Amendment.* This amendment was adopted in 1804 to correct a deficiency in the original Constitution. The original provisions for the selection of President and Vice President were that electors should be chosen in each state according to the method prescribed by the state legislature. Each elector, without consultation with others, was to vote for the two men he deemed best qualified to serve as President. The person with the most votes, provided the number of votes represented a majority of the electors, was to be President, and the person with the next highest number of votes was to be Vice President. It was generally expected that the electors in the several states would normally cast their votes for the leading members of their own states and that no one would receive a majority. In such cases the House of Representatives, voting by states, was to choose the President from among the five men with the most votes. In the event that two men received the same number of votes, each representing a majority of the number of electors, the House was to choose between them.

The rise of national political parties made this system unworkable. By the time the presidential election of 1800 took place, the electors had become party functionaries pledged to vote for the candidates of their own parties. In that year the Republicans, whose candidates were Jefferson for President and Aaron Burr for Vice President, elected a majority of the electors. Each Republican elector, as pledged, cast one of his ballots for Jefferson and one for Burr, so that each man had the same number of electoral votes. As a result, the election was thrown into the House of Representatives, still controlled by the Federalists. For a while the Federalists toyed with the idea of making Burr President; from their point of view this would have been the lesser of two evils. It was only with the greatest difficulty that Jefferson was finally installed in the White House. Immediately thereafter, the Twelfth Amendment was adopted. Each elector now votes separately for President and for Vice President, and the candidate with the majority of the votes in each case is elected. In the event no candidate receives a majority of the votes for President, the House, voting by states, chooses from among the three men with the most electoral votes. If no man receives a majority of the votes cast for Vice President, the Senate chooses between the two men with the most votes.

The Twentieth Amendment. Popularly known as the "lame-duck amendment," this measure was largely inspired by the late Senator George Norris of Nebraska. Before it was adopted, a President elected in November did not take office until the following March, and congressmen chosen at the same time did not begin to legislate for thirteen months after their election. Meanwhile, congressmen who had been defeated in the elections continued to represent—or misrepresent—their constituents in the short and ineffective December-to-March session. The Twentieth Amendment rearranged the schedule of congressional and presidential terms so that congressmen elected in November now begin their duties on January 3, and the President takes office on January 20. This also does away with the short December-to-March session of Congress, which used to specialize in filibusters.

THE CHANGING CONSTITUTION—A CASE STUDY

The history of national regulation of child labor offers an interesting example of constitutional change by a combination of all the methods previously discussed. At the beginning of the twentieth century, people were becoming alarmed over the widespread employment of children in heavy and dangerous industries at an age when they should have been in school. In some places the conditions were so deplorable, the hours so long, that young children of eight and ten were slowly dying of undernourishment, disease, or overwork. Wages were so low that those who exploited child labor were able to undersell their competitors. To meet the competition, other employers, in turn, were forced to hire children.

Here was an admitted evil; yet, individually, the states were unable to act. If the more progressive states outlawed child labor, they could not prevent the sale within their boundaries of cheap goods produced elsewhere by children, and they could not attract industries seeking cheap labor. Finally, in 1916, after years of agitation, Congress closed the channels of interstate commerce to goods manufactured by, or with the help of, child labor. But the Supreme Court, by a close decision and—it now seems fair to say—by a tortured construction of the Constitution, in *Hammer* v. *Dagenhart* (1918), struck down the law as an interference with the reserved powers of the states. Congress tried to overcome the constitutional block by placing a tax on goods produced by or with the help of children. In 1922, in *Bailey* v. *Drexel Furniture Company,* the Court ruled this law unconstitutional.

Apparently nothing could be done without a constitutional amendment. In 1924 Congress proposed an amendment that would give to the national government the power to "limit, regulate, and prohibit the labor of persons under 18 years of age." The amendment specifically stated that "the power of the several States is unimpaired by this Article except that the operations of State laws shall be suspended to the extent necessary to give effect to legislation enacted by Congress." But the opponents of the measure, behind the mask of states' rights, were able to prevent ratification by the necessary three-fourths of the states.

By 1937, although the country had experienced a major depression and a marked change in political climate, the Supreme Court was still dominated by judges who represented the views of the 1920's. Congress in 1935 had enacted a law that, if upheld, would indicate that Congress could use its power over interstate commerce to limit child labor. Would the Court approve? After much agitation by the President (see Chapter 20), including a proposal to pack the Supreme Court with judges more responsive to the political majorities of the 1930's, the Supreme Court reversed its ruling on the extent of the power of Congress over interstate commerce.[4] The following year, 1938, Con-

---

[4] *National Labor Relations Board* v. *Jones & Laughlin Steel Corporation.*

gress once again enacted a law closing the channels of interstate commerce to goods produced by child labor. This time the Supreme Court upheld the law, specifically overruling its decision of 1918.[5] It had taken twenty years, but congressional, judicial, and presidential action had at last succeeded in bringing the Constitution into line with the desires of the people. Since 1937 no state has ratified the child labor amendment, for it is no longer so vitally needed. The Constitution had been "amended" by other means.

Summary Read over

Before we leave the unfinished story of our living Constitution, a summary of the chapter is in order:

1. The Constitution is a symbol of national unity.
2. The Constitution both limits and grants governmental powers.
3. Powers are limited in order to preserve the federal system, and to protect rights reserved for the people that are necessary in order to operate a free government and to live a free life.
4. These limitations on governmental power are enforced by the ballot box, by the power of independent judges to void laws that encroach upon constitutional limitations, by a general distribution of authority between the national and the state governments, and, most important of all, by scattering power among President, House, Senate, and judges and by making the different branches of government responsible to different combinations of voters.
5. While the Constitution limits and restricts the power of the rulers, it also checks the power of popular majorities.
6. The Constitution is an instrument designed to provide the government with sufficient powers to meet national problems.
7. As an instrument of government, the Constitution must grow and be adapted to changing conditions, but at the same time the basic liberties of the people must be protected.
8. The Constitution is kept alive by adaptation and amendment.
9. The problem of the Constitution is to create a government that "enables the government to control the governed," and, at the same time, one that permits the governed to control the government.

The one principal feature of our constitutional system that remains to be examined is *federalism,* one of the most important "auxiliary precautions" against the abuse of power. The United States is not the only or even the oldest federal union, but it was the first to operate successfully a federal system on a continental scale. This has been one of America's major contributions to the science and art of government.

---

[5] *United States* v. *Darby* (1941).

CHAPTER 4

The Dynamics
of American Federalism

ederalism 1787-style and federalism of the 1960's are as different as a stage coach and a jet airliner. Since 1787 our federal system has been molded by a dynamic society and altered by the thoughts and actions of millions of men. This chapter will explore the nature of American federalism and its constitutional structure. But first we must define our terms.

A *federal system of government* is one in which a constitution divides governmental powers between the central, or national, government, and the constituent governments (called "states" in the United States), giving substantial functions to each. Neither the central nor the constituent government receives its powers from the other; both derive them from a common source, the constitution. This constitutional distribution of powers cannot be altered by the ordinary process of legislation—for example, by an act of the national legislature or by act of the several constituent governments. Finally, both levels of government operate through their own agents and exercise power directly over individuals.[1] Among the modern governments that have a federal system are the United States, Canada, Switzerland, India, Mexico, and Australia.

A *unitary,* as opposed to a federal, system of government is one in which a constitution vests all governmental power in the central government, and in which constituent units exercise only the authority given to them by the central government. What the central government gives it can take away. Britain and France are examples of unitary government. The unitary form should not seem strange to Americans for the relation between states and their subdivisional governments, such as counties and cities, is ordinarily of this sort.

Some students distinguish a *confederation* from a federation by defining the former as a government in which the constituent governments by constitu-

---

[1] Based on discussion of A. W. Macmahon (ed.), "The Problems of Federalism," *Federalism Mature and Emergent* (Doubleday, 1955), pp. 4-5.

tional compact create a central government but give it no power to regulate the conduct of individuals. The central government makes regulations for the constituent governments but it exists and operates only by their sufferance. The thirteen states operating under the Articles of Confederation fit this definition.

Unless we get the concept of federalism clearly in mind at the outset, we shall fall into confusion when we try to understand how it operates in practice. To add to our difficulties, in the last century the term "federal" was often used to describe what we would now call a confederate form of government. And if

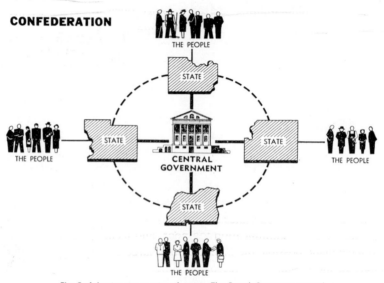

CONFEDERATION

The Confederation was a union of states. The Central Government received power from the states and had no direct authority over the people.

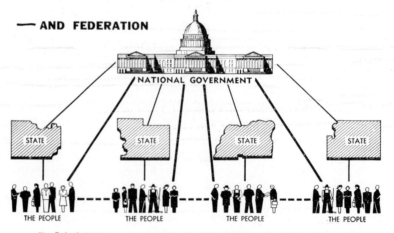

— AND FEDERATION

The Federal Union is a union of people. The National Government and State Governments receive power from the people and exercise authority directly over them.

this were not enough, today "federal" is frequently used as a synonym for "national"—that is, people often refer to the government in Washington as "the federal government." In an exact sense, of course, the states *and* the national government make up our federal system.

Why Federalism?

Why do we have a federal form of government? In part, because in 1787 there was no other practical choice. After confederation had been tried and found wanting, the only choice open to those who wanted a more closely knit union was federation. "No political dreamer was wild enough," said John Marshall in *McCulloch* v. *Maryland,* "to think of breaking down the lines which separate the States and of compounding the American people into one common mass." Perhaps Marshall's statement is too extreme. Hamilton, for one, is on record as favoring such a policy, and at least one scholar believes that the framers did intend to establish a national government with full power over affairs that affected the whole nation.[2] At any rate Hamilton knew, as did all the leaders, that the overwhelming majority of the people were too deeply attached to the state governments to permit the states to be subordinated to a central government. Many were even reluctant, as we have seen, to substitute federation for confederation.

Today, a unitary system may be operated democratically even in a large country. But in the United States of 1787 distances were too great, methods of transportation and communication too poor, and techniques of democracy too new to have made possible the operation of a large unitary state by democratic methods. In the absence of widespread cohesion and nationally shared sentiments, such a union could have been held together only by force. Federalism, 1787-style, went as far in the direction of union as public opinion and the technology of the time permitted.

Federalism also has had the great advantage of being the ideal system for "the great enterprise of appropriating the North American Continent to western civilization."[3] It has enabled the Union to expand from thirteen states to fifty without any disruption or revision of the governmental structure. As people moved into a new territory, they drew up state constitutions which were then approved by the Congress and the President. Each new state became a member of the Union with the same powers and responsibilities as the original thirteen; the only changes required were the addition of new desks in the Senate and House of Representatives in Washington and new stars on the flag.

---

2 W. W. Crosskey, *Politics and the Constitution in the History of the United States* (Univ. of Chicago Press, 1953), 2 vols. Most students of constitutional history remain convinced, despite Mr. Crosskey's impressive work, that it was not the intention of the framers to create a consolidated national government.

3 Edward S. Corwin, "American Federalism—Past, Present, and Future," Princeton University Bicentennial Address, October 7, 1946.

UNITY WITHOUT UNIFORMITY

Even if a unitary state had been politically possible in 1787, it would not have been preferred. For federalism was and still is regarded as the appropriate form of government for the people of the United States. It is ideally suited to the needs of a relatively heterogeneous people who are spread over a large continent, who are suspicious of concentrated power, and who desire unity but not uniformity.

Federalism institutionalizes the American suspicion of concentrated powers. The distribution of governmental authority on a geographical basis throws another block in the path of would-be dictators and adds another whole dimension to the checks-and-balances system. Tyrannical action by national officials can be checked by those who control the state governments. Conversely, if, as Madison pointed out in *Federalist No. 10,* "factious leaders . . . kindle a flame within their particular states," national leaders can check the spread of the "conflagration into the other states. . . ."

This diffusion of power, of course, has the defects of its virtues—it makes it difficult for a popular majority to carry into effect a national program of action. To control the three branches of the national government sometimes is not enough; power must be won at the state level too. Whether this is an advantage or a disadvantage depends on one's political outlook. To the Founding Fathers it was an advantage. As we know, they did not favor majority rule and they feared that the mass of people "without property or principle" would seize control of the government. Federalism, they hoped, would make such a seizure less probable, since *national* majorities could be checked by *local* majorities. Of course—and this is a point often overlooked—the extent of the nation and the multiplicity of interests within it are the greatest obstacles to the formation of an arbitrary, single-interest majority. But even if such a majority should ever be formed, the fact that it would have to work through a federal system would serve to restrain its powers.

Federalism also provides an arrangement under which all local issues need not be thrust into the national arena, thereby making it easier to reach national compromise on truly national problems. Instead of one big struggle, there are many little struggles for power, and national politicians and parties do not have to iron out every difference on every issue between citizens in each of the states. As a result, many issues that might prove irreconcilable in Congress are readily disposed of in the state legislatures. If Congress were the nation's only legislative body, it would be forced to solve all the issues that divide people along religious, racial, and social lines. The continental dimensions of the United States, embracing many diverse cultures, make it difficult to set national norms for ticklish local issues.

Suppose, for example, that Congress had to establish national policy on morals or education. The problem of securing agreement would be infinitely complicated. Or take the control of alcoholic beverages. Many persons living in large cities feel that the moderate use of alcohol is one of the amenities of life and that prohibition of its manufacture or sale is an infringement on their personal liberty. Many people in rural areas, on the other hand, are convinced that alcohol harms morals and health, causes many social problems, and should be outlawed. Our federal system permits these battles to be fought out in the state legislatures. There is no need to try to enforce an inflexible national standard on divergent areas and cultures.

THE STATES AS PROVING GROUND

Federalism also encourages experimentation. Fifty-one governments give us more latitude to try out new methods and to compare results. By experimenting with governmental procedures, police administration, budgetary and personnel services, the states provide a wealth of experience from which the best can be adopted. The national government benefited from this experimentation, for example, when it adopted modern budgetary methods in 1921. Unfortunately, although in recent decades there has been a much greater exchange of information among the states, neither the states nor the national government has taken full advantage of the opportunities of federalism's "many laboratories of political science."

The states also serve as training grounds for Presidents, congressmen, federal judges, and, to a lesser extent, federal administrators. Generally, more than half of the members of Congress have had prior service in their own state legislatures, and many of our Presidents served their apprenticeship as state governors.

Finally, through its decentralization of power, federalism keeps the governed and the governors in close and continuing contact. Few people can serve the national government as President, congressman, Cabinet member, or even as administrator, but many thousands can participate in the operation of their state and local governments and by so doing strengthen democratic habits.

This, then, is why we have federalism. Clearly, it offers many advantages. It also creates some difficult problems and exaggerates others. These we shall discuss in the following chapter. Now we turn to the constitutional basis of American federalism and to the ways in which it has been adapted to changing conditions.

The Constitutional Structure of American Federalism

The constitutional framework of federalism may be stated simply: the national government, with one important exception, has only those powers *delegated* to it by the Constitution; the states have all the powers that are not delegated to the United States except those *denied* to them by the Constitution; but within the scope of its operation, the national government is supreme. Furthermore, some powers are specifically denied to both national and state governments; others are specifically denied only to the states; still others only to the national government. Here in outline form is the constitutional structure of our federal system.

1. *Powers of the national government.* The Constitution, chiefly in the first three Articles, *delegates* certain specifically *enumerated* legislative, execu-

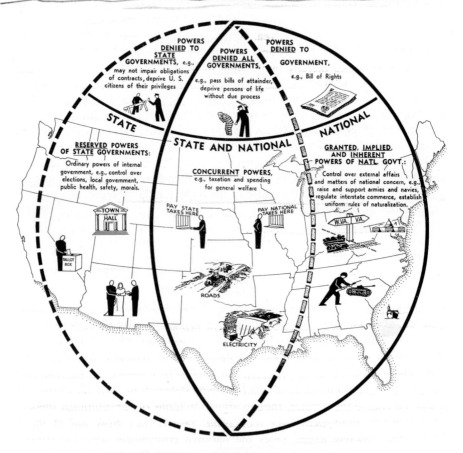

CONSTITUTIONAL DISTRIBUTION OF POWERS

tive, and judicial powers to the national government. In addition to these *express* or enumerated powers, the Constitution delegates to Congress *implied* powers, those powers that may be reasonably inferred from the express powers. Furthermore, in the field of foreign affairs the national government has *inherent* powers which do not depend on specific constitutional grants, but grow out of the very existence of the national government.

2. *Powers of the states.* The Constitution *reserves* to the states (see the

Tenth Amendment) all the powers not exclusively granted to the national government nor denied in the Constitution to the states. Powers that have not by express provision of the Constitution or by judicial interpretation been exclusively conferred on the national government, may be *concurrently* exercised by the states so long as there is no conflict with national law.

3. *National supremacy.* Although the national government can operate only within limited areas, within these areas it is supreme. Article VI states: "This Constitution, and the Laws of the United States which shall be made in Pursuance thereof; and all Treaties made . . . under the Authority of the United States, shall be the supreme Law of the Land; and the Judges in every state shall be bound thereby; any Thing in the Constitution or Laws of any State to the Contrary notwithstanding." Moreover, all officials, state as well as national, are bound by constitutional oath to support the Constitution. The national government may exercise its full powers over every square inch of the United States, and the states may not interfere with the constitutional activities of national officials.

4. *Constitutional limits.* The Constitution imposes certain restraints on the national or state governments or both, not only to preserve the federal system, but also to protect various individual freedoms. Most of these restraints are set forth in Article I; the Bill of Rights; and the Thirteenth, Fourteenth, and Fifteenth Amendments.

CONFLICTING INTERPRETATIONS
OF AMERICAN FEDERALISM

This outline oversimplifies and leaves unanswered some important questions. Is ours a union of *states* or a union of *people?* Should the powers of the national government be narrowly or broadly construed? Does the reservation of powers to the state determine the limits of how national power may be used? These questions do not concern just lawyers or scholars. Throughout our history they have been constantly and heatedly debated; in 1861 they even led to war. Of course the debates, though argued in terms of constitutional theory, are not merely differences over federalism; rather, they grow out of more specific and concrete issues. Does the national government have the constitutional power to outlaw slavery in the territories? Do the states have the reserved power to operate racially segregated schools? Can the national government use its power to regulate interstate commerce in such a way as to control relations between employers and employees? Fights over lofty constitutional issues often involve struggles over very practical matters.

As the issues and times have changed, so have the details of the arguments. However, it is a useful oversimplification to classify the approaches to federalism into two broad schools—the states-rights and the nationalist.

Among those who have championed the *states-rights* interpretation, albeit with varying emphasis, are Thomas Jefferson, John C. Calhoun, the Supreme

Court from the 1920's to 1937, and, today, many white southerners. The states-righters' basic premise is that the Constitution is an intergovernmental compact among the states which thereby created the central government and gave it carefully limited authority. Since the national government is nothing more than the agent of the states, each and every one of its powers should be narrowly construed. In case of doubt whether the states gave a particular function to the general government or reserved it for themselves, the doubt should be resolved in favor of the states.

The states-righters argue that the national government should not be permitted to exercise its delegated powers in such a way as to interfere with activities reserved to the states. The Tenth Amendment, it is claimed, makes this emphatic: "The powers not delegated to the United States by the Constitution, nor prohibited by it to the States, are reserved to the states respectively, or to the people." This amendment, it is contended, means, for example, that Congress' power to regulate commerce among the states cannot be used to regulate agriculture or to curtail child labor since the Constitution reserves the regulation of agriculture and child labor to the states. Some of the more extreme states-righters have even gone so far as to contend that the states as sovereign entities may exercise their reserved powers to the fullest extent even if they conflict with programs of the national government.[4]

Underlying the states-righters' position is their insistence that the state governments are closer to the people and more accurately reflect their wishes than does the national government, which they view as a distant and essentially external authority. They argue that the national government is inherently heavy-handed and bureaucratic, and that to preserve our federal system and our liberties it must be carefully contained.

The *nationalist* position, supported, again with varying emphasis, by Chief Justice John Marshall, Abraham Lincoln, Theodore and Franklin Roosevelt, and throughout most of our history by the Supreme Court, rejects the whole concept of the Constitution as an interstate compact. Rather, the Constitution is a supreme law ordained and established by the people. The national government is an agent of the *people*, not of the states, for it was the people who drew up the Constitution and created the national government. The sovereign people gave the national government sufficient power to accomplish the great objectives listed in the Preamble. They intended that the central government's powers should be liberally construed and that it not be denied authority unless there is a clear conflict with express constitutional limits or a clear absence of constitutional sanction.

The nationalists contend that the national government is not a foreign entity but a government of all the people; each state speaks for only some of the people. Of course the Tenth Amendment reserves powers to the states, but as Chief Justice Stone said, "The Tenth Amendment states but a truism that all

---

4 For an able statement of the states-rights interpretation see James Jackson Kilpatrick, *The Sovereign States* (Regnery, 1957).

is retained which has not been surrendered." The amendment does not deny the national government the right to exercise to the fullest extent all the powers given to it by the Constitution. The supremacy of the national government does restrict the states, for a government representing part of the people cannot be allowed to interfere with a government representing all of them.

McCULLOCH v. MARYLAND—A NATIONALIST VICTORY

In 1819 the Supreme Court had the first of many occasions to choose among these two interpretations of our federal system, in the great case of *McCulloch* v. *Maryland*. Maryland had levied a tax against the Baltimore branch of the Bank of the United States, which had been established in accordance with a law of Congress. McCulloch, the cashier, refused to pay on the ground that a state could not tax an instrumentality of the national government. Maryland's attorneys argued that the national government did not have the power in the first place to incorporate a bank, but even if it did, the state could tax it.

Maryland was represented before the Court by some of the most distinguished men of the bar, including Luther Martin, a delegate to the Constitutional Convention who had left early in the deliberations when it became apparent that a strong national government was in the making. Martin, basing his argument against the constitutionality of the bank on the states-rights view of federalism, pointed out that the power to incorporate a bank is not one of the powers expressly delegated to the national government. He contended that Article I, Section 8, Clause 18, which gives Congress the right to choose whatever means are necessary and proper to carry out its delegated powers, should, like all grants of national power, be narrowly construed. So interpreted, the clause gives Congress only the power to choose those means and to pass those laws absolutely essential to the execution of its expressly granted powers. Since a bank is not absolutely necessary to the exercise of any of its delegated powers, Congress has no authority to establish it.

What about Maryland's right to tax the bank? Martin's position was simply stated: the power to tax is one of the powers reserved to the states which they may use as they see fit.

The national government was represented by equally distinguished counsel, chief of whom was Daniel Webster. Webster conceded that the power to create a bank is not one of the express powers of the national government. But the power to pass laws necessary and proper to carry out enumerated powers is expressly delegated to Congress, and this power should be interpreted generously to mean that Congress has authority to enact any legislation convenient and useful in carrying out delegated national powers. Therefore, Congress may incorporate a bank as an appropriate, convenient, and useful means of exercising the granted powers of collecting taxes, borrowing money, and caring for the property of the United States.

As to Maryland's attempt to tax the bank, Webster contended that though the power to tax is reserved to the states, states cannot use their reserved powers to interfere with the operations of the national government. The Constitution leaves no room for doubt that in case of conflict between the national and state governments the former is supreme.

THE SUPREME COURT'S DECISION

In 1819 the Supreme Court was presided over by Chief Justice John Marshall, a nationalist and an advocate of the liberal interpretation of the central government's constitutional authority. Speaking for a unanimous Court, Marshall rejected every one of Maryland's contentions. In his usual forceful style, he wrote: "We must never forget that it is a *constitution* we are expounding. . . . [A] constitution intended to endure for ages to come, and consequently, to be adapted to the various crises of human affairs." "The government of the Union," he continued, "is emphatically and truly a government of the people. In form and substance it emanates from them, its powers are granted by them, and are to be exercised directly on them. . . . It can never be to their interest and cannot be presumed to have been their intention, to clog and embarrass its execution, by withholding the most appropriate means." Marshall summarized his views on how the powers of the national government should be broadly construed in these now-famous words:

> Let the end be legitimate, let it be within the scope of the Constitution, and all means which are appropriate, which are plainly adapted to that end, which are not prohibited, but consist with the letter and spirit of the Constitution, are constitutional.

Having thus established the doctrine of implied national powers, Marshall set forth the doctrine of national supremacy. No state, he said, can use its reserved taxing powers to tax a national instrumentality. "The power to tax involves the power to destroy. . . . If the right of the states to tax the means employed by the general government be conceded, the declaration that the Constitution, and the laws made in pursuance thereof, shall be the supreme law of the land, is empty and unmeaning declamation."

The significance of *McCulloch v. Maryland* can hardly be overstated. Although many persons still support the states-rights interpretation, this case went far to establish the doctrines of liberal construction and national supremacy. The arguments of the states-righters, if accepted, would have strapped the national government in a constitutional strait jacket and denied it the powers needed to handle the problems of an expanding nation. In all probability, the Constitution would have been replaced many years ago as succeeding generations were forced, once again, to render the central government adequate to the needs of each new age. Marshall's vision accounts in part for the longevity of our Constitution, today the oldest written constitution in the world—and truly a living constitution.

NATIONAL POWERS AND FOREIGN AFFAIRS

Even the states-rights theory of federalism recognizes that in the field of *foreign relations* the national government is not restricted to powers expressly granted or even to those that may be implied. So far as the external relations of the United States are concerned, the national government has inherent powers derived only indirectly from the Constitution. It has the same authority in dealing with other nations as it would if it were a unitary government. International law, not constitutional law, determines the limits of the national government's powers in its relations with the other members of the society of nations. For example, the government of the United States may acquire territory by discovery and occupation even though there is no specific constitutional basis for such acquisition, and may make agreements other than constitutionally defined treaties. Even if the Constitution were silent about foreign affairs—which it is not—the national government would have as "necessary concomitants of its nationality" [5] the right to declare war, make treaties, and appoint and receive ambassadors.

Not only does the national government have inherent power over external relations, but this power "is not shared by the states; it is vested in the national government exclusively." [6] In short, federalism stops at the water's edge. Of course, the fact that ours is a federal system does have an impact on our foreign relations. Relations between the United States and other nations have been embarrassed by the failure of some states to prosecute persons who have injured foreign nationals, by state laws that discriminate against aliens, and by critical speeches made by public officials. And national officials are often cautious in making agreements with other nations that cover subjects normally handled by states. Still, the Constitution does bestow on the national government *ample* and *exclusive* authority to conduct our foreign affairs.

TREATIES AND THE FEDERAL SYSTEM

The national government's power to make treaties, vested in the President with the advice and consent of two-thirds of the Senate, is *not unlimited*. The Supreme Court has "regularly and uniformly recognized the supremacy of the Constitution over a treaty." [7] The national government cannot, by treaty, abridge rights guaranteed by the Constitution. It could not, for example, deprive a person of his First Amendment rights by treaty or by a law to implement a treaty any more than it could do so by any other law. Treaties and the laws passed to implement treaties, like all other laws, must conform to the

---

[5] *United States* v. *Curtiss-Wright Export Corporation* (1936).
[6] *United States* v. *Pink* (1942).
[7] *Reid* v. *Covert* (1956).

Constitution. Furthermore, Congress may, at any time, as far as its application within the United States is concerned, abrogate a treaty.

The reserved powers of the states, however, do not set bounds to the national government's treaty power. Treaties made under the authority of the United States, and laws passed by Congress to carry treaties into effect, are *superior* to state constitutions and state laws. A *self-executing treaty,* one that operates of itself and goes into effect without the need of any further action by Congress, is regarded by the courts on the same (but not higher) level as any other national law. The framers felt that the national interest was superior to the interest of any state and that if a conflict arose between a national treaty and state policy, the state policy should give way.

In short, so long as treaties do not abridge a specific provision of the Constitution, the President and the Senate may make agreements with foreign nations regulating subjects, or giving Congress the power to regulate them even though the regulations are not within the lawmaking power directly granted by the Constitution to the national government. This doctrine had been familiar for many years, but in 1920 the Supreme Court's decisions in *Missouri v. Holland* made its implications clear. The story of this important case is as follows:

In 1914 Congress had passed a law dealing with the hunting of birds migrating between the United States and Canada. Two federal district courts held this law unconstitutional on the ground that Congress had no authority, express or implied, to regulate wildlife. The Supreme Court did not review these decisions, but a few years later Congress enacted an even more stringent law governing the hunting of such birds. This measure, however, was passed in order to comply with a treaty between the United States and Great Britain. This time the Supreme Court did review the law and upheld its constitutionality. Justice Holmes, speaking for the Court, said that assuming Congress could not in the absence of the treaty have enacted this legislation, it did not follow that the same law to implement a treaty would also be unconstitutional. The treaty did not contravene any prohibitory words in the Constitution. It could not be declared unconstitutional because of some "invisible radiation from the general terms of the Tenth Amendment." Since the treaty was constitutional, Congress had power to pass whatever laws were necessary and proper to implement it.

After World War II, when the United States became increasingly active in foreign affairs, some people expressed alarm that the doctrine of *Missouri v. Holland* would permit the national government to use the treaty power to authorize the regulation of matters normally handled by state governments. They have urged, so far unsuccessfully, that the Constitution be amended to limit the national government's power to make agreements with foreign nations and international agencies. Opponents of such an amendment, generally referred to as "the Bricker Amendment" since it was actively sponsored by former Senator John Bricker of Ohio, have argued that it would severely

as long as treaty not unconstitutional this gives the national gov. a lot of leeway —

restrict America's role as the leader of the free world and that fears that the treaty-power would be used to alter our constitutional structure are without historical or political justification.

The Constitutional Position of the States

The powers of the states are also derived from the Constitution, which reserves to them all powers not granted to the national government subject only to the limitations of the Constitution. Of course, states may not use their reserved powers to frustrate national policies. (It should be recognized that local units of government are merely agents of the states exercising powers given to them by the states. What states cannot constitutionally do, local units cannot do. In our discussion of national-state relations and the constitutional structure of federalism, the local units are subsumed in all references to states.)

The Constitution, as we have noted, contains certain explicit limitations upon state power in behalf of individual liberties. In addition, the Constitution forbids the states to make treaties, impair the obligation of contracts, coin money, and pass bills of attainder and ex post facto laws (see Chapter 8). States may not, except with the consent of Congress, collect duties on exports or imports or make compacts with another state.

What if the Constitution does not specifically vest a particular power exclusively in the national government or specially limit state power? Does the mere vesting of a particular power in the national government by itself withdraw that power from the states? There is no general answer to this question. The Supreme Court has ruled that the very nature of some powers granted to the national government is such that they are exclusive powers—to determine the rules of naturalization, for example. On the other hand, granting to the national government the power to tax does not preclude state taxation even of the same item. Both national and state governments have *concurrent* powers to tax, and as long as a state tax measure does not conflict with a national law or treaty or unduly burden a function of the federal government, it is constitutional.

The commerce clause granting to Congress the power to regulate interstate and foreign commerce illustrates the complexities of the situation. Some of the most difficult questions of constitutional law arise over the extent to which this clause limits the reserved powers of the state. Obviously, congressional regulations of this commerce take precedence over any state enactments. But what if Congress has said nothing? May the states regulate interstate commerce? The answer would be simpler if the Supreme Court had adopted the position that the commerce clause totally excludes any state regulation. But the Court has ruled that the states may—when Congress has not acted—regulate those local aspects of interstate commerce that do not require uniform national treatment, and they may apply their laws, designed to protect the public, to interstate commerce, if those laws do not unduly burden, obstruct, or discriminate against such commerce.

Who is to say whether a particular measure discriminates against interstate commerce or that the subject in question requires uniform national treatment? When Congress has not acted, the Supreme Court is the "arbiter of the competing demands of state and national interest." In each case, the Court must make the decision, after weighing state and national considerations. Proceeding by this method, the Court in 1946 declared that a Virginia statute requiring segregation of Negroes and whites on interstate buses was an unconstitutional attempt by a state to regulate an aspect of interstate commerce requiring uniformity of treatment.[8] State laws imposing speed limits on trains within city limits and requiring the elimination of grade crossings have been upheld, but laws requiring trains to stop at every crossing have been invalidated.[9] The Court has upheld the right of a state to refuse a permit to an interstate motor carrier because the resulting congestion on the highways would create a hazard.[10] On the other hand, it has held that a state unconstitutionally interfered with interstate commerce when it refused to grant a permit to an interstate motor carrier because of fear of excessive competition.[11]

Does all this sound complicated? It is. But complications are inevitable under federalism. For federalism means that someone—mainly legislators and judges—must apportion duties to different governments in an increasingly unified country.

OBLIGATIONS OF THE NATIONAL GOVERNMENT

TO THE STATES

The Constitution obliges the national government to guarantee to each state a *republican form of government*. It does not define what is meant by a republican form—the framers undoubtedly used the term to distinguish it from a monarchy on the one hand and a pure direct democracy on the other —and the Supreme Court has consistently held that the enforcement of this constitutional clause is a congressional obligation.[12] Congress determines whether a state has a republican form of government when it decides whether or not to permit the congressional representatives of that state to take their seats in Congress.

In addition to guaranteeing to each state a republican form of government, the national government is obliged by the Constitution to protect the states against domestic insurrection. Congress has delegated to the President

---

[8] *Morgan v. Virginia.*

[9] *Erb* v. *Morasch* (1900); *Erie R. Co.* v. *Board of Public Utility Commissioners* (1921); *Seaboard Air Line Ry. Co.* v. *Blackwell* (1917).

[10] *Bradley* v. *Public Utilities Commission of Ohio* (1933).

[11] *Buck* v. *Kuykendall* (1925); see also *Southern Pacific* v. *Arizona* (1945) and cases mentioned therein.

[12] *Pacific States Telephone and Telegraph Co.* v. *Oregon* (1912).

the authority to send troops to quell such insurrections on the request of the proper state authorities. This gives the President the power to determine which of contending factions is the proper authority in a state. President Tyler's decision was binding on the courts when in effect he threatened to send federal troops to protect the Rhode Island government against the "domestic insurrection" of a rival government contending for the right to speak for the state.[13]

HORIZONTAL FEDERALISM— INTERSTATE CONSTITUTIONAL RELATIONS

What obligations does the Constitution impose on the states in their *dealings with one another?* Three clauses of the Constitution, taken from the Articles of Confederation, require the states to give full faith and credit to one another's public acts, records, and judicial proceedings; to extend to one another's citizens the privileges and immunities of their own citizens; and to return persons who are fleeing from justice in sister states.

Full faith and credit. The full-faith-and-credit clause is one of the most technical provisions of the Constitution. Speaking in general terms, it requires each state to enforce civil judgments of other states and to accept their public records and acts as valid documents. (It does not require states to enforce the criminal laws of sister states; in fact, in most cases for one state to enforce the criminal laws of another would be unconstitutional.) The clause applies especially to noncriminal judicial proceedings. Suppose Smith obtains a $5000 judgment against Jones from the Pennsylvania courts. But then Jones moves to California and refuses to pay up. Thanks to the full-faith-and-credit clause, Smith does not have to start a new suit against Jones in California. The California courts will give full faith and credit to the Pennsylvania judgment and will enforce it just as they would a similar judgment of the California courts.

Some idea of the complexity of the problems growing out of the full-faith-and-credit clause is suggested by the question, "How much faith and credit must a state give to a divorce decree, a civil judgment, granted by another state?" Clearly a divorce granted by a state to two bona-fide residents must be given full faith and credit by all the other states, even though they might not themselves have granted the divorce for the grounds alleged. On the other hand, what if Mrs. A, a citizen of North Carolina, goes to Reno, Nevada, in order to avoid the divorce laws of her own state, stays just the six weeks necessary to establish residence in Nevada, obtains a divorce, and returns to North Carolina? Must North Carolina give full faith and credit to the divorce? Not necessarily, for the Supreme Court has held that under certain circumstances it is permissible for the courts of other states to rule that the divorce-granting state lacked jurisdiction over the parties; hence, there would be no validly obtained divorce decree to which full faith and credit must be given. In our

[13] *Luther* v. *Borden* (1849).

example, North Carolina would not be required by the Constitution to recognize Mrs. A's divorce, though in Nevada it would be unquestioned.

2 Interstate privileges and immunities. States may not deny to citizens of other states the full protection of the law, the right to engage in peaceful occupations, or access to the courts. States may not tax citizens of other states at a discriminatory rate or otherwise arbitrarily interfere with the use of their property within the state. In short, states must extend to citizens of other states the privileges and immunities of their own citizens. However, this does not extend to political rights such as voting, serving on juries, or admission to publicly supported institutions such as schools or hospitals.

3. Extradition. The Constitution asserts that a state shall, when requested by the governor of the state from which a criminal has fled, deliver him to the proper officials. Congress has supplemented this provision by making the governor of the state to which the fugitive has fled responsible for returning him. Despite the use of the word "shall," the federal courts will not order governors to extradite (return) persons wanted in other states. A few years ago the Governor of New Jersey, horrified at the conditions under which men lived in a chain gang, refused to hand over a fugitive to Georgia officials. There was nothing that Georgia could do about it. An 1861 decision of the Supreme Court, *Kentucky* v. *Dennison,* held that Congress could not, even if it wanted to, establish procedures to force states to comply with the extradition clause of the Constitution. This decision rested on a theory of the federal union as a compact among sovereign states depending primarily for its enforcement on the good will of the states who were parties to the contract. The theory of federalism on which this decision is based has been rejected, but the decision itself has never been reversed. Although there are some spectacular examples of governors' refusing to deliver persons wanted in other states, extradition is normally handled in a routine fashion. Furthermore, Congress has closed this "gap" in part by making it a federal crime to flee from one state to another for the purpose of avoiding prosecution for certain felonies. Trial for this federal crime is held in the state from which the fugitive has fled, thus making it possible for federal authorities to turn him over to the state officials to prosecute him for state crimes.

In addition to these three obligations, the Constitution also requires the states to settle their disputes with one another without the use of force. States may carry their legal arguments to the Supreme Court or may negotiate *interstate compacts.* Compacts may also be used to establish interstate agencies and to solve joint problems (see Chapter 5). Before interstate compacts become effective, the approval of Congress is required, an approval that is sometimes given in advance. After a compact has been signed and approved by Congress, it becomes binding on all signatory states, and its terms are enforceable by the Supreme Court. Not all agreements among states, however, require congressional approval—only those, the Supreme Court held in 1893, "tending to increase the political power of the States, which may encroach upon or interfere with the just supremacy of the United States." [14]

This discussion of the constitutional relations between the national and state governments shows the important role of the Supreme Court as the umpire of the federal system. The Court is not the only umpire. Congress has much to say about the distribution of functions and the extent to which state regulations will be permitted.[15] The courts, however—ultimately the Supreme Court—determine whether the national government is going to be called to task for invading the sphere left to the states or whether the states have usurped national duties.

The Supreme Court, itself a branch of the national government, has often been accused of bias. "The States," it has been charged, "have had to play against the umpire as well as against the national government itself." [16] Though the states have had their innings, over the long pull the Court's decisions have favored national powers. Especially in recent years, Congress has shown more of a tendency than the Supreme Court to respond to local pressures and to favor local regulations. And the local majorities that control the state governments have been severe in their criticism of the Court for its decisions curtailing their authority.

Despite the frequent criticism of the Supreme Court by some outraged groups who control the machinery of state government, not many would deny the Supreme Court the power to review state actions. Support for Supreme Court review of actions of state and local governments rests upon a different basis than does the argument for Supreme Court review of acts of Congress or the President. As Justice Holmes once remarked, "I do not think the United States would come to an end if we lost our power to declare an Act of Congress void. I do think the Union would be imperiled if we could not make that declaration as to the laws of the several states." [17] Or, as Justice Story wrote many years earlier, such a review is necessary to maintain "uniformity of decisions throughout the whole United States, upon all subjects within the purview of the constitution. . . . Judges of equal learning and integrity, in different states, might differently interpret a statute, or a treaty of the United States, or even the constitution itself: If there were no revising authority to control these jarring and discordant judgments, and harmonize them into uniformity, the

---

14 *Virginia* v. *Tennessee* (1893).

15 See Paul A. Freund, "Umpiring the Federal System," in A. W. Macmahon (ed.), *Federalism Mature and Emergent* (Doubleday, 1955), p. 160.

16 O. P. Field, "State versus Nation, and the Supreme Court," *The American Political Science Review*, April 1934, p. 233.

17 O. W. Holmes, *Collected Legal Papers* (Harcourt, Brace, 1920), pp. 295-296.

laws, the treaties and the constitution of the United States would be different in different states and might, perhaps, never have precisely the same construction, obligation or efficacy, in any two states." [18]

This review of the formal constitutional structure of American federalism contains little that would have startled the generation of 1787, for the *structure* of our federalism is little changed. Its actual *operation,* however, has been drastically altered.

Growth of the National Government

The words of the Constitution, wrote Justice Holmes in *Missouri* v. *Holland,* called into life a being whose development "could not have been foreseen completely by the most gifted of its begetters. It was enough for them to realize or to hope that they had created an organism; it has taken a century and has cost their successors much sweat and blood to prove that they created a nation." [19] The Constitution established a framework in which a national government could develop, but it was some time before a viable national community to support this national government actually existed.

As we saw in the case of *McCulloch* v. *Maryland,* John Marshall argued that ours is a union of *people,* that the central government is both in theory and in fact a national government resting directly on the people. But there were many, foremost of whom was John C. Calhoun, who dissented. These dissenters argued that the central government was only a *federal,* not a national, government, created by the states and receiving all its powers from the states acting in their organized sovereign capacities. When the Constitution of the Southern Confederacy was written, its Preamble pointedly declared, "We, the People of the Confederate States, each State acting in its sovereign and independent character do ordain and establish this Constitution. . . ."

The question was ultimately decided at Appomattox Court House, but from the beginning the logic of events vindicated the nationalists. It has made no difference whether the party in power has been Federalist, Jeffersonian, Whig, Republican, or Democratic—the national government's sphere has constantly expanded. The platforms of both major parties today reflect the wishes of the major interest groups and continue to call for programs that require greater activity by the central government. The political pressures calling for an expansion of national functions are so powerful that even President Eisenhower, who was pledged to return functions to the states, was unable to do so. A special Joint Federal-State Action Committee, consisting of men appointed by the President and by ten governors chosen by the Chairman of the Governor's Conference, after hard work was able to designate only two rather

---

[18] *Martin* v. *Hunter's Lessee* (1816).
[19] *Missouri* v. *Holland* (1920).

trivial federal functions that might be returned to the states.[20] Even these rec-, ommendations—cessation of federal aid for vocational education and for building municipal waste-treatment plants—ran into heavy opposition. It seems a safe bet that the domain of the federal government will continue to grow, no matter which party is in power.

BASIS OF THE GROWTH

How has this expansion taken place? Not by amendment: the formal constitutional powers of the national government are essentially the same today as they were in 1789. But the Supreme Court (building on Marshall's work in *McCulloch* v. *Maryland*), the Congress, the President, and—ultimately— the people, have taken advantage of the Constitution's flexibility to permit the national government to exercise the powers needed to fight wars and depressions and to serve the needs of a modern industrial nation. The full scope of the central government's constitutional powers has been used to support this expansion of functions, but there are three major constitutional pillars on which the expansion has taken place.

The war power. The national government traditionally has been responsible for protecting the nation from external aggression, and, when necessary, for waging war. In a world community that knows total war, the power needed to provide for the common defense is of a scope hardly dreamed of in 1787. With the possibility of attack always present, the national government cannot wait until war is declared. It must keep the nation strong enough to prevent wars if possible and to win them if they break out. Military strength no longer depends primarily on troops in the field, but on the ability to mobilize the nation's industrial might and to apply its scientific knowledge to the tasks of defense. Everything from the physics courses taught in the schools to the conservation of natural resources and the maintenance of a prosperous economy affects the nation's war-making potential (see Chapter 24).

In wartime, the national government has to organize, coordinate, and channel all human and natural resources to the end of destroying the war-making power of the enemy. It then becomes not only proper, but absolutely necessary, to conscript men, requisition property, control prices, encourage scientific studies, allocate resources, maintain the supporting economy, and bolster public morale. And when the fighting ceases, the government must cope with the problems of demobilization and reconversion. After disrupting national life by converting manpower, materials, and machines to war, it is responsible for achieving the return to peacetime living as smoothly as possible. It must give aid to veterans and correct the many war-caused or war-aggravated maladjustments in the economy, such as housing shortages.

In brief, the national government has the power to wage war and to do

---

[20] *Report* of the Joint Federal-State Action Committee (Government Printing Office, 1957).

what is necessary and proper to wage it successfully. In total war this means almost total power. As long as we live in a world where war is an ever-present possibility, the defense activities of the government will be many and varied, and they will impinge on all aspects of our lives.

The power to regulate interstate and foreign commerce. This is the second constitutional pillar supporting the expansion of the national government's functions. Congressional authority extends to all commerce *that affects more states than one*—to those activities, wherever they exist or whatever their nature, whose control is necessary and proper to regulate interstate and foreign commerce. The term "commerce" includes all commercial intercourse, the production, buying, selling, and transporting of goods. The power to regulate is the power to prescribe the rules by which this commerce is governed—that is, the right to foster, promote, protect, defend all commerce that affects more states than one. Hence, the short constitutional clause giving Congress the power to regulate commerce among the states and with foreign nations carries a tremendous constitutional punch. In these few words the national government has been able to find constitutional justification for regulating persons and property in the public interest. The national government, unlike the states, has no inherent police power (the power to regulate persons and property for the general welfare), but it can and does use its power to regulate interstate commerce in order to promote the general welfare. For example, it is now a federal crime to use the channels of interstate commerce to sell adulterated goods, to steal automobiles, to rob a bank, to kidnap, and to transport women for immoral purposes. Moreover, Congress has forbidden the *production* of goods intended for the interstate market by persons who receive less than a federally established minimum wage.

Today there are few aspects of our economy that do not affect commerce in more states than one. When Farmer Filburn plants wheat in his own back yard to feed his own children and chickens, his actions affect the price of wheat in the interstate market, and therefore his activities are within the scope of congressional authority. When a large steel company fires men because they belong to a labor union, it enhances the danger of industrial strife and threatens the flow of goods in interstate commerce. Thus, national laws regulating employer-employee relations in industries that affect interstate commerce have been upheld as necessary and proper means to protect the free flow of this commerce.

Some people have accused the Supreme Court of making strained and unrealistic interpretations of the commerce clause in order to find constitutional justification for national regulation. But the Court has simply recognized the obvious facts of our economic life and has refused to make its decisions in an "intellectual vacuum." Wheat planted in people's back yards does, as a matter of economic fact, affect the interstate commerce in wheat. A strike in Pittsburgh or Detroit does affect commerce in California and New York. To deny Congress the power to deal with homegrown wheat or Pittsburgh strikes would leave the nation defenseless in the face of pressing economic problems.

③ *The power to tax and spend for the general welfare.* Congress lacks constitutional authority to pass laws solely on the ground that the laws will promote the general welfare, but it may raise taxes and spend money to promote the general welfare. This distinction between legislating and appropriating frequently makes little practical difference; the distinction is primarily of legal significance. For example, if Congress tried directly to regulate education or agriculture it would be unconstitutional, but Congress has the power to appropriate money to support education or to pay farmers subsidies, and by attaching conditions to its grants of money it may regulate what it could not constitutionally control by legal fiat.

Congress may appropriate the money directly to the states by what are known as *grants-in-aid*. These grants are generally conditional—that is, the states must match with their own money some of the federal funds, create an agency to supervise the spending, and submit to federal inspection. Or Congress may bypass the states and give the money to individuals, local governments, or private organizations. For example, the G.I. Bill of Rights made funds directly available to millions of veterans to support their education, and in 1958 Congress appropriated money directly to colleges for student loans and graduate fellowships.

Since Congress puts up the money, it has a strong voice in determining how it shall be spent. By withholding or threatening to withhold funds, the national government can influence state operations or regulate individual conduct. Unless farmers agree to certain restrictions, they are not eligible for federal loans or other subsidy programs. Unless students sign a loyalty affidavit, they are not eligible for federally supported scholarships. Unless states agree to build highways that meet federal standards, they are not eligible for federal grants.

In addition to using its power to appropriate for regulatory purposes, Congress may use its power to tax. For example, Congress has laid heavy taxes on white-phosphorus matches, on the sale of sawed-off shotguns, on the sale of narcotics, not to raise money but to regulate specific activities. Similarly, Congress requires professional gamblers to secure an annual federal license and to pay a federal tax on their gross receipts. Since gambling is illegal in forty-nine states, gamblers have a choice of paying the federal tax and thereby alerting state and local officers to their illegal activities or not paying the federal taxes and thereby running the risk of federal prosecution for tax evasion.

Congress has also used its taxing powers "to induce" states to adopt certain kinds of programs. For example, Congress has levied a tax on employers but allows them to deduct from the amount they owe the national government the state taxes they pay to support state unemployment compensation. Since the employer has to pay the taxes anyhow, all the states have been induced to establish unemployment compensation programs.

These three constitutional powers—the war power, the power over interstate commerce, and the power to tax and spend for the general welfare—have supported a tremendous expansion of federal functions. If all the laws Congress has passed in pursuance of these powers were wiped off the statute books, the size of the federal government and the scope of its functions would shrink drastically.

REASON FOR THE GROWTH

Why has this expansion of federal functions taken place? Certainly not because of the superior logic of the affirmative side in the age-old debate: "Resolved: that the powers of the federal government should be increased." Nor has it come about because of the desire of "that man" or "those men" to consolidate power in Washington. Such glib explanations, so prevalent in political campaigns, overlook many fundamental factors. Rather, "big government" has come about because of deep-seated changes in our society and as the result of the pushing and hauling of interest groups.

Since 1789 we have grown from a poor, sparsely populated agricultural society to a rich, densely populated industrial nation. Our meager and slow transportation and communication network has been replaced by one that is vast and rapid. The farmer who used to eat what he raised now produces for people who live thousands of miles away. The small, local businessman who owned, organized, and operated his business has been joined by large-scale business owned by thousands of persons throughout the nation and operated by a nationally organized corporation. Our labor force has grown from unorganized artisans to nationally organized, mass-production workers. The United States has grown from a weak, isolated debtor nation to a powerful creditor that plays a central role in the world community.

Clearly, such profound alterations in any society would have a powerful impact on the government of that society. People's attitudes toward the national government have changed, too. While the government of the Union was viewed in the 1780's as a distant, even foreign government, today most people identify their fortunes much more closely with Washington than they do with their own state governments.[21] The railroad, telegraph, telephone, radio, airplane, and television have made the activities of federal officials familiar to all. Most people do not even know when their state legislature is in session, but what goes on in Washington is known throughout the land in a matter of minutes. The President, his family, their troubles and habits—even the Presi-

---

[21] See George M. Belknap and Ralph Smuckler, "Political Power Relations in a Mid-West City," *The Public Opinion Quarterly*, Spring 1956, p. 80.

dent's golf score—are objects of dinner-table conversations. Likewise, citizens of other states are no longer considered strange. The highway, automobile, and house on wheels have made us a nation on the move. This mobility and inter-mixture of people from all parts of the nation are not conducive to the building of strong local attachments and deep sectional ties. Almost two hundred years of common experiences, especially the fighting of two major wars, have ce-mented the Union and made Washington the focus of attention.

An urban-industrial society, moreover, requires greater *social control* than does an agricultural-rural one. A thousand people in the country might need only one policeman, since informal pressures can be counted on to keep them in line. The same number of people living in the city, with its impersonal and diversified make-up, might require five policemen to enforce social sanctions. The states have also had to expand their functions, but because many of our problems have become national in scope, even greater responsibilities have devolved on the national government. In recent decades the national govern-ment has gradually taken over a greater role in business regulation, law en-forcement, conservation, education, housing, and civil rights, among others. Much of what was local in 1789, or even in 1860, is now national. It is axio-matic that the unit of government dealing with a problem should be coextensive in area with the problem. States could most efficiently and democratically supervise the relations between a small merchant, who bought and sold his products within the local market, and his few employees. In fact, little super-vision was needed, as the employer was undoubtedly well acquainted with his workers, knowing their names, their families, and their problems. But only the national government can supervise the relations between a nationally organized industry that buys and sells its materials all over the world and its thousands of employees organized into national unions.

With the industrialization of the United States there also came about a concentration of economic power, first in the form of business units and later in the form of labor unions. These units, along with professional organizations, are private governments exercising *political* as well as *economic* power. The concentration of economic power required a corresponding concentration of political power; if the unit of public government is not as powerful as the unit of private government it is meant to regulate, the regulated often regulates the regulator. The activities of a John L. Lewis or an American Telephone and Telegraph Company are too far-flung and their power too formidable to enable the states to provide the needed social control. Big business, big agriculture, big labor, all add up to big government. As can be seen from the table on page 106, many private governments—financial corporations—are larger than the states.

As industrialization progressed, various powerful interests began to make demands on the national government. First the business groups, who were largely responsible for building industrial America, called on the government for aid in the form of tariffs, a national banking system, a uniform and stable

Corporation or State	1958 gross revenue (in millions)	Employees
General Motors Corporation	$ 9,522	521,000
Standard Oil Company (New Jersey)	7,544	154,000
United States Steel Corporation	3,472	223,000
California	2,965	111,000
New York State	2,558	115,000
Du Pont (E.I.) de Nemours	1,829	86,000
Michigan	1,421	56,000
Illinois	1,111	52,000
Oregon	387	19,000
Wyoming	99	4,000
Vermont	70	5,000

Compiled from *Fortune*, July 1959, p. 126; *Compendium of State Government Finances in 1958*, p. 9, Bureau of Census; *State Distribution of Public Employment in 1958*, March 16, 1959, p. 10, Bureau of Census.

currency, and subsidies to railroads, airlines, and the merchant marine. Once the business groups had got what they wanted, however, and generally felt strong enough to take care of themselves, they began to oppose governmental aid to other groups. But then the farmers learned that the national government could give them much more aid in solving their economic problems than could their states, and they too began to demand help. The farm groups used their powers to secure such laws as regulation of the railroads, antitrust legislation, paper currency, parcel post, and finally government support for farm prices. Industrialization did not diminish the influence of the farmers; on the contrary, it gave them a balance-of-power position. By the beginning of the present century, the urban groups in general, and organized labor in particular, began to press their demands. Workers found that they could not organize unions with a hostile government issuing injunctions and calling out troops. They began to work for restrictions on injunctions and for friendly administrations. Finally, with increased industrialization and urbanization, the working groups and city dwellers found that, for political reasons, they normally received more help from the national government than from the states.

How has the new world role of the United States contributed to the growth of the national government? Until recently, the United States played a small part in maintaining order in the world community. Because of our isolated geographic position, a favorable balance of power in Europe, and a relatively stable world in Asia, we easily maintained our security without the need for a positive foreign policy. All this, of course, has changed. Today the United States has to work at the job of maintaining order and stability in the world; we no longer get a free ride. The defense of the free democratic world requires a great deal of effort and money on the part of the national government. The funds spent for direct military expenditures, aid to allies, to veterans, and for interest on a debt largely acquired fighting past wars, account for approximately 80 per cent of the central government's annual budget, and the activities of well over half of its employees.

FAILURES OF THE STATES

Finally, in order to account for the growth of the national government, we must turn to what have to be called the failures of the states. Many of our fifty states were arbitrarily blocked out on the map, with little reference to underlying geographic, social, or historical realities. With the passage of time, growing discrepancies have developed between these artificial state boundaries and new conditions. Many natural regions, such as river valleys, are cut in half by the surveyor's line. Many large cities have grown up along state boundaries, which means that a cohesive metropolitan area is fragmented between two or three states—New York City, Kansas City, and Washington, D.C., for example. When the people of a river valley or a metropolitan region want to act through their governments to conserve human and natural resources, they often find that no one state has jurisdiction to deal with the problems of the entire area. A few states are too large; most are too small. They vary in size from Alaska to Rhode Island and in population from New York to Alaska. Regardless of size or population, however, they all support the same elaborate governmental organization.

Some states lack the resources to satisfy even minimum public needs. Worse, many of the problems that affect citizens most directly are of such scope that only the national government can handle them. Faced with the Great Depression of the 1930's, when there were over twelve million unemployed out of a labor force of fifty million, and many more millions destitute, the states had neither the financial resources for relief nor the power over a wide enough area to stimulate recovery. The national government, with its much greater tax resources and almost unlimited borrowing power, was literally forced to act. It was the only government capable of dealing with a national— a world-wide—depression.

The increased confidence of Americans in the national government has been paralleled by a diminishing sense of loyalty to the respective states. This is due in part, as we have noted, to the greater mobility of our population. Also, most states had no independent existence prior to becoming members of the Union. There developed no strong feeling of local pride, and the original settlers long looked to the central government for protection and advancement.

But even within the limits of their jurisdiction and their resources, many of our state governments, through their failure to provide the programs desired by the public, have failed to keep the loyalty of large numbers of their citizens. Over a half-century ago Elihu Root warned, "It may be that [governmental] control would be better exercised in particular instances by the governments of the states, but the people will have the control they need, either from the states or from the national government; and if the states fail to furnish it in due measure sooner or later constructions of the constitution will be found to vest the power where it will be exercised—in the national government." [22] And more recently J. Melville Broughton, a former governor of North Carolina, wrote: "Those of us who believe in the fundamental principles of states' rights and local self-government may as well concede frankly that much of the almost terrifying expansion of federal encroachment upon the original domain of the States has come about because state governments failed to meet the challenge of the new day. Inadequate educational opportunities, archaic labor laws and regulations, unrelieved hardships and inequities suffered by the working people, low-pitched politics and unjust class and race discriminations have, all too frequently, caused the people to lift their eyes beyond the horizon of state lines and call for relief from the Federal Government. . . ." [23]

Although we hear much about the waste and extravagance of the national government, Washington is almost a model of perfection when compared to *some* state capitals which are graft-ridden, inefficient, and unable to provide the services that the people expect. Generally speaking, "the most critically defective part of our present system is the state government." [24] Some states, of course, are doing an excellent job of providing a high level of public service. But there are others that reflect the interest, not of the majority, but of political bosses or powerful economic interests.

Even if we had ideal state governments throughout the country, the national government's functions would continue to expand in response to national needs. But, as a result of the less-than-ideal state governments, the central government has acquired some functions by default. The people demand that certain things be done, and if the states cannot or do not act, the people inevitably turn to Washington. President Eisenhower, who was strongly committed to doctrines of states rights, testified to these pressures when he said, "Opposed though I am to needless Federal expansion, since 1953 I have found it necessary to urge Federal action in some areas traditionally reserved to the States. In each instance state inaction, or inadequate action, coupled with undeniable national need, has forced emergency Federal action." [25]

The primary reasons, then, for the expansion of federal functions are the industrialization and urbanization of the United States, the consequent concentration of economic power, the resulting national problems that require action by a national government with sufficient resources and extensive jurisdiction, and the deficiencies of the states. Governments, like men, can survive only by adapting themselves to their changing environment. It is not surprising

---

[22] Elihu Root, Address before the Pennsylvania Society, September 1906, quoted in The Commission on Intergovernmental Relations, *A Report to the President* (Government Printing Office, 1956), p. 56.

[23] "The Future of the States," *State Government*, March 1943, pp. 142-143.

[24] G. C. S. Benson, *The New Centralization* (Farrar & Rinehart, 1941), p. 157.

[25] Text of Address by Dwight D. Eisenhower at the State Dinner of the 1957 Governors' Conference, June 25, 1957, in *Report of the Joint Federal-State Action Committee* (Government Printing Office, 1957), p. 19.

that a central government adequate for the days of the stage coach is not suitable in an era of television and hydrogen bombs.

Up to this point we have been talking about the constitutional relations between national and state governments and the dynamic character of our federal system. This dynamic quality is also illustrated by the ability of the federal system to incorporate without interruptions new units and to grow from thirteen states to fifty. But what about the relations between the national government and our territories and possessions and the District of Columbia?

The American "Empire"

For all practical purposes, to over three million people the United States is a unitary and not a federal government. These three million live in the District of Columbia or in the several territories under the control of the United States. Over these people the national government has full governmental power, though in most cases it has established local governments and has given the people a voice in their local affairs.

With the admission of Hawaii and Alaska, there are no longer any incorporated territories—that is, territories which Congress has determined should be groomed for statehood. "Dominion status" rather than statehood is the goal of most of the inhabitants of our largest remaining territory, the Commonwealth of Puerto Rico.

THE COMMONWEALTH OF PUERTO RICO

Puerto Rico, an island only 95 by 35 miles but inhabited by over two million people, was acquired from Spain as a result of the Spanish-American War. Although it has many of the characteristics of an incorporated territory, it does not actually fall into that category. Puerto Ricans are American citizens, but they are governed under their own constitution and through their own elected representatives. Most of the people have a Latin culture and lack any strong affinity for American ways. But proximity, historical attachment to the United States, and a need for help in overcoming economic problems will sustain Puerto Rico's close ties with the United States.

Its present relation to the United States is ambiguous. In 1950 Congress authorized the Puerto Ricans to draw up their own constitution. After Congress deleted a provision dealing with economic and social rights, this constitution was approved, signed by the President, and became the basic charter of the Commonwealth of Puerto Rico.[26] This constitution establishes a form of government much like that of our states. Although Puerto Ricans may amend their constitution without submitting the changes to Congress, and are considered by the United Nations to be self-governing, their constitution and

---

[26] Gordon K. Lewis, "Puerto Rico: A New Constitution in American Government," *The Journal of Politics*, February 1953, pp. 42-66.

laws are subordinate to the Constitution of the United States and to certain federal laws. Most of our federal laws do not apply to Puerto Rico—the income tax, for example—but Congress sometimes passes laws that apply specifically to the Island Commonwealth.

Many Puerto Ricans live in poverty, their death rate is high, and their educational standards are woefully below average. Within recent years modern sanitation and health programs have lowered the death rate somewhat, but the resultant speed-up in population growth is now straining the island's limited resources. Despite improvement, the economy is still not diversified and depends primarily upon the sugar industry. Until the recent movement of many Puerto Ricans to the United States, Americans on the mainland paid little attention to their depressed fellow citizens. Often settling in conditions as squalid as those they left, their plight is now arousing increasing public concern. As these citizens begin to exercise their political power, more attention will undoubtedly be paid to attempting to solve the social and economic problems of Puerto Rican American citizens.

OTHER TERRITORIES

The United States domain also includes other territories in various categories of development. The most important of these are the Virgin Islands, Samoa, Guam, the Panama Canal Zone, and the trust territories. Full American citizenship has been given to the residents of the Virgin Islands and Guam, but the residents of Samoa are classified as American *nationals*. Nationality is a condition of less than full citizenship, but it involves allegiance to the United States and the obligation of protection by the national government. The people of the Virgin Islands and Guam have a large measure of self-government. The trust territories in the Pacific—the Marianas, Marshalls, and Carolines—are strategic trusteeships acquired by the United States by conquest. Most of these islands were formerly Japanese mandates under the League of Nations. They are now held by the United States under limited supervision of the United Nations. The United States also controls, with Great Britain, the Canton and Enderbury Islands in the Central Pacific.

Although the Republic of the Philippines became a completely independent and sovereign nation on July 4, 1946, the United States still maintains close ties with its former dependency. The Commonwealth receives special tariff concessions, and the United States maintains naval bases there. Because the Philippines are important links in the American defense system and because of their former relations, the United States exercises what is tantamount to a protectorate over the Islands.

THE DISTRICT OF COLUMBIA

Although almost all our territories enjoy a large measure of home rule, our nation's capital enjoys none at all. Congress itself serves as the city council of Washington, D.C.; most of the work, however, is done by the House and

23 Amendment, allows citizens to vote in of col. vote

Senate Committees on District Affairs. Three commissioners appointed by the President with the consent of the Senate administer the laws. Local judges are chosen by the President with approval of the Senate. In addition, there are the regular federal courts.

Except for those who maintain a legal residence elsewhere, citizens in the District of Columbia have no voice in electing either national or local officials. It would take a constitutional amendment to give them the right to participate in federal elections, but it would require only an ordinary law to empower them to run their own local affairs. Prior to 1874 Washington did have home rule, but because of corruption and inefficiency —evils not confined to Washington, especially in 1874—the present system was adopted that year. Since that time residents in the District have agitated for a return to home rule. Within recent years the pressures for a change have grown stronger.

From *The Herblock Book* (Beacon Press)

"Honestly, I'd Rather Walk"

The advocates of home rule have many impressive complaints. In addition to the obvious injustice of being denied the right to govern themselves, they argue, most congressmen are little concerned about District affairs. Housing, hospital, and educational conditions in Washington, it is argued, are deplorable. Home rule would relieve Congress of attending to petty details and enable it to spend its time on more important responsibilities. But the rest of the nation has not been sufficiently aroused to press for reform. Furthermore, some people believe that since the District is the capital of all the people, it should be governed by the national legislature. Undoubtedly, Congress will always exercise more authority in Washington than in other cities, but it is questionable if this requires the denial of local self-government.

Summary *read*

1. A federal system of government is one in which power is divided constitutionally among the general (national) and constituent (state) governments; both sets of governments have substantial powers, and both exercise power directly over individuals.

2. American federalism in practice provides a compromise between excessively centralized and dangerously decentralized government, permits the states to serve as proving grounds for new ideas, and keeps leaders close to the people.

3. Simply put, the Constitution delegates certain powers to the national government and reserves the rest for the states. The Constitution places some limits on the powers of both the national and state governments. When acting within the scope of its constitutional powers, the national government is supreme. In foreign affairs, the national government is not only supreme, but it has inherent, complete, and exclusive powers. In domestic matters, there is considerable controversy over the precise division of power between the national and state governments.

4. Questions concerning this division of power are decided by the Supreme Court, itself a branch of the national government and indirectly responsive to national political trends and forces.

5. Constitutional powers that have helped create the expansion of the national government include the powers to wage war, to regulate interstate and foreign commerce, to tax and spend for the general welfare. Responding to popular needs and demands, the national government has often exercised these powers vigorously in dealing with economic and social problems.

6. Congress has granted varying degrees of self-government to United States territories but not to the District of Columbia.

CHAPTER 5

Problems
of American Federalism

In talking about federalism, we must beware of the "billiard-ball" concept of the state and national governments as hard, solid objects that collide with sharp impact.

Actually all these governments *mesh* with one another, for they are made up of people who govern, and are governed by, other people. To talk of states rights is but a shorthand way of referring to the rights of people who live in states and to the authority of officials elected by them. It is not Texas that has rights, but Texans.

To put it another way, national and state governments are merely arenas in which differing groups engage in political combat over public policies. Congressmen and state legislators often respond to the same groups and express the same ideas, and we have "national-state cooperation." At other times, congressmen and state legislators represent sharply different combinations of interests, and we have "national-state conflict." But this conflict between the two levels of government is just one facet of the continuing struggle among groups that makes up our politics.

The Politics   From the day the colonists first
of Federalism   set foot on the soil of the New
World, Americans have been arguing about the "proper" division of powers between central and local governments. But from then to the present it has been impossible to disentangle substantive issues of politics from these discussions. In 1953 President Eisenhower sponsored a Commission on Intergovernmental Relations, composed of members of both political parties, with instructions to make an impartial and objective study to determine the "proper" distribution of functions between the national and state governments. In 1957 a Joint Federal-State Action Com-

mittee appointed by the President and the Governors' Conference made another such attempt. Apparently it was thought that these experts could find some nonpolitical scientific standards to distinguish between national and state functions. But these commissions, like all others of their kind, soon realized that there are no such objective standards and that the "propriety" of the division is a political judgment.

"To locate a governmental function, or a certain portion of the decisional process . . . , at one level of government rather than another," it has been pointed out, "weights the scales in favor of the interest which has better access to that particular level." [1] Hence national action is favored by those who anticipate that national officials will be responsive to what they conceive to be in the general interest. But those who believe that state officials will be most likely to support their goals are the champions of states rights. The attachments of groups to one or the other level of government change over time; and they change not because of conversions on philosophical issues but because of changed estimates of ability to influence one or the other level of decision.

At one time or another northerners, southerners, businessmen, farmers, workers, Federalists, Democrats, Whigs, and Republicans have thought it "improper" to vest a particular function in the national government. They opposed "control by Washington" in the name of maintaining the federal system. But underlying the debates were such issues as slavery, labor-management relations, government regulation of business, civil rights.

When the Federalists were in control of the central government and, in behalf of merchants and creditors, established a national bank, assumed state debts in full, proclaimed the neutrality of the United States in the French-English struggles, and passed the Alien and Sedition laws, the Jeffersonian agrarians and debtors protested each move as a violation of "states rights." But when these same Jeffersonians captured the national government and placed embargoes on shipping, purchased Louisiana, and fought the War of 1812, it was the New England Federalists who picked up the cry of "states rights." When the Republican party threatened the slave economy in 1861, the South arose to defend "states rights." When the industrial interests used their influence with the national government to raise the tariff, secure land grants for railroads, and tax state bank notes out of existence, the exporters and agrarians championed "states rights."

The agility with which groups rush to the defense of states one year and leave them to their fate the next is demonstrated by the railroaders who protested, when the states started to regulate their activities in the 1870's, that Congress alone should regulate interstate commerce. But when Congress started to move in this direction in the 1880's, these same railroad men charged that Congress was subverting the reserved power of the states.

With the advent of the New Deal and the growth of organized labor's

---

[1] York Willburn, "The States as Components in an Areal Division of Powers," in Arthur Maass (ed.), *Area and Power* (The Free Press, 1959), p. 78.

influence at the national level, most business groups became devotees of the rights of states. The national government was controlled by persons in whom many businessmen had little confidence and over whom they had less influence. They discovered that state legislatures and state courts were more likely than their national counterparts to make decisions favored by businessmen. On the other hand, labor leaders found national agencies more responsive to their claims. It is not suprising that businessmen's organizations were quick to defend the states against what they characterized as the "federal octopus," while labor leaders emphasized the need for national action and charged the states with being dominated by "special interests."

In recent years those who favor segregation have rightly recognized that those who control southern state and local governments are also likely to favor segregation. They fear that national officials, responding to different political majorities, will favor integration. Naturally, segregationists sing of the virtues of local governments close "to the people," they are quick to emphasize the dangers of "overcentralization," and they argue at length that the regulation of civil rights is not a "proper" function of the national government. On the other side, those who want legal segregation abolished emphasize the "propriety" of national power being used because they recognize that state governments controlled by segregationists will never on their own work against segregation.

Although the debates are frequently couched in constitutional language, and appeals are often made to the great principles of federalism, the words are symbols used to debate more immediate and specific policy goals. "It behooves us . . . to take thought before drenching our handkerchiefs when the National Association of Manufacturers and the American Bar Association bewail the prostrate position of the states before the federal colossus. These mourners are not shedding tears over the lamentable conditions of New Hampshire and North Carolina and Montana and Texas but over the enterprise caught in the grip of the federal regulatory hand. . . ." [2]

So it is that political issues are involved in discussions of national-state relations. Nevertheless, almost all observers, however sharply they differ on particular issues, agree that a country the size of the United States needs strong and active state governments and that maintaining a balance between national and state governments is a major problem of federalism.

The Problem of Maintaining the Balance

The awful spectacle that disturbed Hamilton—"a nation without a national government" —need frighten us no longer. The national government's activities have greatly expanded, and they probably will continue to do so. What can be done to pre-

---

2 Carl B. Swisher, *The Growth of Constitutional Power in the United States* (Univ. of Chicago Press, 1946), p. 33.

vent the rise of a colossus in Washington that can be neither efficiently operated nor democratically controlled?

MODERNIZED STATE AND LOCAL GOVERNMENTS

We hear so much about the growth of national governmental functions that we sometimes overlook the growth of state activities. State and national power is not a seesaw on which one side has to be up and the other down. An increase in the authority of one does not necessarily detract from the authority of the other. On the contrary, the entrance of the national government into new fields has in many cases strengthened the states and helped them to improve their services. Despite the lamented "weakening of states" and the constant cries about national interference, states are today, measured by the amount of money spent and the number of functions performed, stronger units of government than they were in 1787. Indeed, since the end of World War II activities of states and their subdivisions have been increasing at a faster rate than the nondefense activities of the national government.[3] Nonetheless, the demands for increased assumption of functions by national authorities continues.

As we noted in Chapter 4, one reason for the expansion of the national government has been the failure of the states themselves to provide satisfactory services. Clearly, then, one of the most promising approaches to keeping the national government within reasonable bounds is to improve, simplify, and modernize the state governments. Many reforms designed to vitalize state governments have long been advocated—such as reorganizing administrative machinery, streamlining legislative procedures, keeping up to date the basis of representation in state legislatures to reflect the growing urban population, shortening the ballot, and making officials responsive to wider segments of the electorate. Although recommendations for reform are often filed and forgotten, several states—New Jersey, New York, and Virginia, for example—have made considerable progress. But much remains to be done.

REGIONAL ADMINISTRATION OF FEDERAL FUNCTIONS

Centralization of policy-making need not lead to centralization of administration. Policies and programs can be adopted at the national level, but their administration can be decentralized. Today only 11 per cent of all federal employees work in the Washington metropolitan area. This decentralization permits greater local participation in national programs and encourages adjustment of policies to local conditions.

Hitherto, each agency in Washington tended to set up its own field headquarters in accordance with the demands of its own activities and with little thought to the established field units already created by other federal agencies.

---

[3] The Commission on Intergovernmental Relations, *Report to the President* (Government Printing Office, 1955), p. 36.

The United States is now blanketed by approximately 110 different federal administrative regions, but there is a growing tendency for one agency to use the regional divisions created by another. Perhaps in time we shall have regional national capitals throughout the United States.

Another kind of federal decentralization is represented by the Tennessee Valley Authority, which Congress established in 1933 to develop the resources of the Tennessee Valley. Instead of having the Army Corps of Engineers deal with flood control and navigation, the Bureau of Reclamation with irrigation, the Department of Agriculture with conservation, the Federal Power Commission with power, and so on, one federal corporation was established to deal with the problems of the valley as a unit. Working closely with the states, cities, and private organizations in the valley, the TVA has done an effective job of preventing floods, providing cheap power, controlling the soil, improving navigation, providing irrigation, preventing stream pollution, and developing recreational facilities.

Originally, many people within the Tennessee Valley, along with government officials in the area, opposed the creation of the Authority for fear that it would dwarf and dominate state governments. But from the outset, the TVA has championed "grass-roots" administration and has cooperated closely with state and local officials. Wherever possible it has even delegated responsibility to state and local agencies. State departments of health, conservation, education, highways, and other agencies have joined with the TVA to raise the level of government throughout the valley.

Some federal administrators object to the idea of too great a parceling

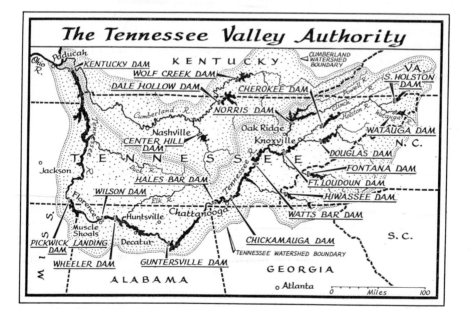

out of federal powers to regional authorities. If there were four or five TVA's, these administrators insist, the problems of securing national action on national problems would be most difficult. There is also the very real difficulty of ensuring public control of river valley authorities. Despite the TVA's solicitude toward local and state governments, it is responsible to the people of the valley only through Congress and the President. Certainly, the TVA method is not the solution to all problems, but it is one of the best examples of creative statesmanship and social innovation developed by the American people to meet some of the difficulties that grow out of our federal system.

The TVA idea does not exhaust the possibilities of federal regional development. The Missouri River Valley, for example, is not subject to the authority of a single federal agency. Instead, an Interagency Committee on Water Resources is maintained by the Departments of Interior, Agriculture, Commerce, Labor, and Health, Education and Welfare, along with the Army and the Federal Power Commission. This group, joined by the governors of the five states in the region, forms the Missouri Basin Interagency Committee, which tries to coordinate the efforts of all the federal and state agencies operating in the valley. The Committee has met with some success, though the proponents of a comprehensive regional authority insist that it has been unable to work out unified programs. Each federal agency and state is free to go its own way. Moreover, no one agency can coordinate the operations of the various completed projects.

Thus the pattern of federalism is constantly being altered. We have a variety of regional organizations across the nation, some the result of federal action, others of federal-state cooperation, and, as we shall presently note, still others the result of action by individual states. These regional organizations supplement the constitutional division between the central government and the states. At present, they are mainly concerned with the administration of single programs; but conceivably in the future, as they assume more functions of national, state, and local governments, they could be given representative institutions—legislatures, executives, and courts—and a new dimension would be added to our federal union.

"FEDERALISM WITHOUT WASHINGTON"—
INTERSTATE COOPERATION

The states do not have to wait for the national government to take the initiative in dealing with problems that require regional action. Several states together can deal with problems too large for any one to handle alone. If the states were more effective in solving their own regional problems, there would be less need for the national government to step in (aside, perhaps, from giving financial aid). One instrument they can use is the *interstate compact*.

Until the twentieth century interstate compacts were used only to settle boundary disputes between states, but since 1900 over twenty interstate agencies have been established by compact.[4] One of the more successful of these is the Port of New York Authority, established by New Jersey and New York. This agency develops and operates the harbor as a unit, and recently it has been given the job of coordinating the operation of airports in the area. Other promising interstate compact agencies are those created to deal with education, abatement of water pollution, conservation of oil and gas, parole and probation, and conservation of fish.

In addition to these more formal interstate compact agencies, state officials often get together to handle a particular problem: for example, to establish joint operations of police radio broadcasting nets or to coordinate plans for highway safety. These efforts have on occasion given rise to regular organizations, such as the Interstate Commission on the Delaware River Basin, composed of representatives from New York, New Jersey, Pennsylvania, and Delaware, or the Conference of Southern Governors. In addition to these regional conferences, state officials have joined together in various nationwide organizations—the American Legislators' Association, the National Associations of Attorneys General, of Secretaries of State, of State Budget Officers, of State Purchasing Officials, and others. Each state now has a Commission on Interstate Cooperation. Most of the interstate agencies are coordinated through the Council of State Governments, which serves as a secretariat, collects data, sponsors research, and publicizes results. This kind of cooperation is bringing about greater uniformity among the states and higher standards in the administration of laws within the states.

Genuine interstate cooperation could lead ultimately to greater uniformity of laws throughout the country. Although diversity is a virtue of federalism, it can also be a fault. For example, the wide diversity in traffic rules, even in neighboring states, makes it virtually impossible to drive across the nation without violating some law along the way. The story of Harry Harper, an Iowa farmer, is not unusual. Harper "started out for St. Louis, Missouri, to sell a load of melons he had grown. During his journey he was stopped by the Iowa Highway Patrol at night and required to put three green lights on his truck. After driving across the state line into Missouri, the Missouri police stopped him and told him it was illegal in Missouri to have three green lights on his truck, so he had to take them off." [5]

Diversity of state laws on insurance, contracts, negotiable instruments, judicial procedures—in fact, on the whole scope of business transactions—increases operating costs and makes it difficult to do business on a national basis. Labeling laws designed to protect consumers against fraud, for example, are so diverse that manufacturers often have to use special labels in order to sell their products in certain states.

---

[4] Richard H. Leach and Reading S. Sugg, Jr., *The Administration of Interstate Compacts* (Louisiana State Univ. Press, 1959), p. 6.

[5] Related by Frank Bane and reported in W. Brooke Graves, *American State Government* (Heath, 1946, 3rd ed.), p. 914. Used by permission of D. C. Heath and Company.

The application and interpretation of all these laws by the fifty-one court systems in the United States create another level of confusion. What law applies to a contract signed in California, delivered in New York, between citizens of Wisconsin and Minnesota, about property located in New Jersey? This is not a fanciful question, but an example of the actual problems confronting judges in their everyday decisions.

How can we create some measure of uniformity among state laws? Members of the American Bar Association in 1892 organized the Conference of Commissioners on Uniform State Laws. Under the guidance of this conference, composed of commissioners appointed by the state governors, committees have been established to recommend uniform laws to the state legislatures. All the states have adopted the Negotiable Instrument Law and the Warehouse Receipt Act, and some states have adopted other uniform laws including those dealing with stock transfers, narcotics, and criminal extradition. The most ambitious project of the conference has been the attempt to secure adoption of a Uniform Commercial Code. These attempts to bring about uniformity of the laws also have the desirable effect of raising standards as the best practices are spread throughout the states. But despite occasional successes, over sixty years' work has not significantly decreased the diversity of state laws. Furthermore, even after all the states adopt a particular code, there is no guarantee that uniformity will in fact result. The fifty separate state court systems are likely to interpret their codes in their fifty separate ways, and before long wide differences in interpretation and application have sprung up once again.

How successful, then, have the states been in their efforts to cooperate? On balance, "Federalism without Washington" has not brought about the results that its sponsors had hoped for. One of the difficulties has been too much emphasis on simply forestalling centralization. Horizontal cooperation —that is, cooperation at the state level—has perhaps made its greatest contribution "in providing central staff research and educational facilities to strengthen the competence with which the governments at a particular level do their job, so that governmental bankruptcy alone cannot justify the transference of authority to higher levels of government." [6] Horizontal federalism, then, has brought only marginal results. What about cooperation between national and state governments?

Cooperative Federalism

Cooperative federalism is a general approach rather than a specific program. It visualizes the national and state governments as partners in the common function of serving the people. It rejects the concept of two governments as antagonistic sovereigns jealously competing with each other for power. Cooperative federalism is the search for a middle ground between the

---

[6] James W. Fesler, *Area and Administration* (Univ. of Alabama Press, 1949), p. 40.

either-or attitude typified by discussions of national government versus the states or the advantages of centralization versus decentralization. Joint action of federal and state governments, it is hoped, will gradually produce the advantages of a unitary state without destroying the essential values of federalism.

TYPES OF JOINT ACTION

Cooperation among national and state governments takes many forms. When a secret service agent is helped by state and local police to nab a counterfeiter, we are benefiting from cooperative federalism. A public health official tracking down carriers of disease uses both federal and state services. Many federal agencies, such as the United States Public Health Service, the United States Office of Education, and the Bureau of the Census, conduct surveys and gather statistics for state officials. Others train local employees and help enforce state laws. This kind of cooperation avoids duplication and provides better services at less cost.

In some cases, the administration of federal programs is delegated to state governments. The TVA, as we have noted, encouraged state and local officials to help run parts of the TVA program. The administration of the selective service system is primarily a responsibility of state and local officials. Some people favor a broad extension of state administration of national programs, arguing that the national government should lay down general policies but delegate administration to state and local governments. It is doubtful, however, if this can be done except on a limited scale. "State administrations that are not in sympathy with the National Government will cause considerable difficulty; and it is doubtful whether United States Senators will favor administrative methods that give their potential or actual rivals, the state Governors, the power of patronage over national programs in their States." [7]

In addition, when national programs are turned over to state governments, there is the risk that they will not be administered in accordance with national purposes. Philip Selzick, in his discerning study, *TVA and the Grass Roots* (1949), has presented evidence that TVA's policy of working with local governments often amounts to handing over the TVA to powerful local interests. And Paul H. Appleby, an experienced administrator, says: "If a program is Federal and if the responsibility is Federal, the authority should be Federal and the administering bureaucracy should almost always be Federal." [8]

Conversely, some oppose state administration of national policies on the grounds that it turns the states into administrative districts of the federal government. Nevertheless, where responsibility for programs is only partly national, delegation of administration to the states would seem feasible, especially if the

---

[7] William Anderson, "Federalism—Then and Now," *State Government,* May 1943, pp. 107-111.

[8] Paul H. Appleby, *Big Democracy* (Knopf, 1945), p. 87.

states were to modernize their practices so that they could better handle the jobs given to them.

GRANTS-IN-AID

More promising than turning over complete administration of federal policies to the states is the joint operation of programs through the grant-in-aid (see p. 103). There are some programs for which the states have chief constitutional responsibility, but in which the entire nation has an interest. By an accident of geography, for example, some children are deprived of an adequate education, and many people are denied good health services, for states in which they live either lack adequate resources to provide minimum essential services, or else the dominant groups within the state lack the desire to do so. These problems can no longer be considered of only local concern. Children and bacteria travel everywhere these days. Young people who have been deprived of educational opportunities, or whose health has been impaired, are national liabilities.

Much of our national wealth is concentrated in the industrialized areas—the northeastern, midwestern, and far-western states. As a result, other areas, especially the rural South, find it difficult to raise funds for public services. Moreover, since many southern industries are owned by persons living elsewhere, the profits are drained away from the South, leaving the states without funds to support adequate facilities for education, welfare, and highways, for example. This is only one reason why public services in some states are below the national level, but it is an important reason.

What can be done? The national government could take over the entire responsibility for the programs. (In some fields where the states have authority there are constitutional limitations that prevent national action, although the number of such cases is no longer so important in view of the Supreme Court's liberal interpretation of national powers.) But as an alternative to complete national control, Congress, through the grant-in-aid, has tried to secure a national minimum level and to encourage the states to take action on their own. With its broader tax base, it taxes the wealth where it is located and turns the money over to the states for programs that Congress feels should be more adequately supported. This system of federal grants-in-aid goes back at least as far as 1802, but it got its real start in 1916 when Congress gave money to the states for the construction of "rural post roads." During the depression of the 1930's the number of federal grants greatly increased; today the national government gives money to the states for agricultural extension work, forest preservation, land-grant colleges, wildlife restoration, highways, old-age assistance, aid to dependent children, aid to the blind, maternal and child health services, and aid to crippled children, to mention only some of the more important. On the average, the states now receive from the national government about one-sixth of the money they spend.

Most of these grants are *conditional,* however—that is, the states must match the federal funds with state funds, establish agencies to expend the funds, submit their plans for advance approval, permit inspection by national officials of the work done, and place the employees who administer the grant under a merit system.

Since most grants require the states to match the federal dollars, the poor states, even with federal assistance, are often unable to provide the same services as their richer sisters. For example, an aged indigent in recent years might receive as much as $109.85 a month in Connecticut or as little as $29.81 in Mississippi. To help correct these inequalities, formulas for the distribution of federal funds have been proposed that take the relative needs of the several states into account. Quite naturally, the wealthy states that contribute most of the money to the federal treasury are not happy when much of it goes to the less fortunate areas.

One of the dangers of federal grants is that states may be tempted to match federal money for prescribed purposes even when they could better spend their limited resources for something else. States can now receive federal dollars for the dollars they spend on highway construction, but in many states, perhaps, the money could be better spent for schools or mental hospitals. The lure of federal funds tends to destroy the flexibility of state programs, and makes the states take a back seat in planning their own expenditures. Is there a way out of this dilemma?

MORE FLEXIBLE GRANTS?

The first Hoover Commission (a group of distinguished men headed by former President Herbert Hoover who directed an exhaustive study of the national administrative system in 1948-1949) recommended to Congress that grants be established on the basis of broad *categories,* such as highways, education, public assistance, and public health. Pointing out that under the "present system of extensive fragmentation" there are at least ten separate and distinct federal grants in the field of public health, the Commission stated that grants for broader purposes would return the initiative to the states and make them responsible for working out their own programs.[9] But the Commission on Intergovernmental Relations, though agreeing that the broadening of some grants might be desirable, has opposed more general grants because of the fear that they would lead to more extensive federal control.[10]

Some students have urged that we go even further and substitute *unconditional* federal subsidies to the states. This approach has been taken by central governments in other federal systems—Canada and Australia, for example. It is argued that under such a system the national government could use its greater

---

[9] Commission on Organization of the Executive Branch of the Government, *Overseas Administration, Federal-State Relations, Federal Research* (Government Printing Office, 1949), p. 36.
[10] *Report* of The Commission on Intergovernmental Relations, pp. 132-133.

tax resources to give the states funds, but that each state would be able to use the money as it wished. But again the Commission on Intergovernmental Relations has advised against such subsidies, arguing that they might not be used to provide necessary services, and warning that the states might continue to press for additional grants for specific programs. Furthermore, the Commission predicted, "A policy of unconditional subsidies with no matching requirements would be likely to undermine the sense of financial responsibility. The tendency would be for states and localities to look more and more to the national government to perform the disagreeable task of extracting money from the taxpayer." [11] Whatever case might be made for changing the nature of the federal grants to the states, it seems unlikely that there will be any fundamental change in the system.

GRANTS-IN-AID: A TRIAL BALANCE

After a careful study of the federal grant system, one expert came to the conclusion that it

> strengthens the states and thereby strengthens but profoundly modifies the federal system. . . . The achievements of direct federal administration are not so striking as to make federal assumption an inviting alternative to the grant system. The governance of a nation of continental proportions is a matter for which no simple blueprint and specifications are available. The grant system builds on and utilizes existing institutions to cope with national problems. Under it the states are welded into a national machinery of sorts and the establishment of costly, parallel, direct federal services is made unnecessary. A virtue of no mean importance is that the administrators in actual charge of operations remain amenable to local control. In that way the supposed formality, the regularity, and the cold-blooded efficiency of a national hierarchy are avoided. [12]

The Commission on Intergovernmental Relations confirms Key's judgment. The grant system is here to stay. Its constitutionality is beyond question, in more senses than one. The Supreme Court has ruled that neither a state nor a taxpayer has the right to contest the constitutionality of a grant. [13] Today, discussion centers around more specific questions: Just what functions should be supported by federal money? What conditions should be tied to the grant? How should grants be administered?

The federal grant is not the solution to all problems, of course. And certainly the system is subject to abuse. Federal money is not "free"; all services must be paid for by the taxpayers. Nevertheless, an intelligently administered program of grants-in-aid can bring greater strength to the states and better services to the people.

---

[11] The Commission on Intergovernmental Relations, *op. cit.,* pp. 132-133.

[12] V. O. Key, Jr., *The Administration of Federal Grants to States* (Public Administration Service, 1937), pp. 375, 383.

[13] *Massachusetts* v. *Mellon* (1923).

BYPASSING THE STATES—
NATIONAL-LOCAL COOPERATION

A more controversial example of cooperative federalism involves relations between national and local governments that bypass the states. According to the traditional theory of American federalism, the national government should deal with local governments only through the states. It is true that in a constitutional sense local governments are creatures of the states. But to "refer to Chicago as but an arm of Illinois or to New York City as but an arm of New York is as unrevealing as to call the General Motors Corporation an instrument of Delaware or the Southern Pacific Company an instrument of Kentucky, under whose laws it is organized." [14]

Although sooner or later everything the national government does affects the operations of local governments, it was not until the Great Depression that the national government began to deal directly with city officials. Today cities receive federal aid for building streets and airports, for civil defense, for slum clearance and housing, urban renewal, and other projects.

State officials have sharply criticized this bypassing of the states; on the other hand, of course, city officials favor direct federal help. Many large cities —actually "city-states" in many respects—fail to receive sympathetic treatment from state legislatures dominated by rural representatives who not only have little sympathy or understanding for city problems but are often downright hostile to city politicians. As a result, as President Eisenhower told the Conference of State Governors, "Today, for help in urban problems, committees of Mayors are far more likely to journey to Washington than to their own state capitals." [15] Mayor Richard Daley of Chicago told a congressional committee, "I think a city the size of Chicago should be able to go directly to its Federal Government with its programs, because we find in many instances the greater responsiveness and greater understanding." [16] Another mayor, Charles P. Taft of Cincinnati, agreed, stating simply, "I would rather do business with Washington." [17]

This difference of opinion between state and city officials over federal assistance reflects a more general conflict. City people often contribute most of the tax money to support state activities, but because they are underrepresented in the state legislatures they have a proportionately small voice in its allotment. Since urban populations are likely to have more influence with the national than with their own state governments, it is not surprising that states sometimes get caught in the squeeze between national and city officials. Prob-

---

[14] C. B. Swisher, *American National Government* (Houghton Mifflin, 1951), p. 908.

[15] Text of Address by the President at the State Dinner of the 1957 Governors' Conference, June 24, 1957, in *Report of the Joint Federal-State Action Committee* (Government Printing Office, 1957), p. 20.

[16] Hearings on "Federal-State-Local Relations" before a Subcommittee of the Committee on Government Operations, House of Representatives, 85th Cong., 1st Sess., October 16-22, 1957, p. 391.

[17] *Ibid.*, p. 641.

ably the best way to correct this situation, if correction appears to be called for, would be to reorganize state governments to improve their operations, and thus give city people a greater voice in state affairs so that the states could serve as more effective intermediaries between national and local governments.[18]

Clearly, intergovernmental relations can be cooperative as well as competitive, and cooperative federalism is a going business. And yet cooperative federalism means all things to all men. To some it is a midway station on the road to greater power for the national government; to others it is a way of strengthening the states; but above all it is an example of what de Tocqueville noticed over a hundred years ago: "I have never been more struck by the good sense and the practical judgment of the Americans than in the manner in which they elude the numberless difficulties resulting from their Federal Constitution." [19]

Trouble Spots **T**he truck driver who is stopped
of Federalism at the state boundary because his
vehicle is six inches too long, the governor who would like to sign a new tax measure but is warned that industry may move out of the state if he does so, the woman who discovers that she is legally divorced in one state but not in another, the businessman who discovers that he cannot lawfully segregate his employees in one state but is required to do so in another—these people, like the rest of us, face problems of federalism. What are some of these problems and what steps have been taken to solve them?

LAW ENFORCEMENT

Not many years ago the local constabulary had little difficulty in dealing with crime. Everybody knew everybody else and detection of the guilty ones required little skill. Whenever help was needed in capturing a fugitive, the sheriff could rally law-respecting citizens by raising the "hue and cry." Today, in our mobile society where anonymity makes discovery difficult, criminals move swiftly across the nation by automobile or airplane, cutting across one jurisdictional boundary after another. Our multitude of police agencies, all with overlapping responsibilities, give criminals an advantage that they are quick to exploit. On the national level, postal inspectors, "T" men, "G" men, and other specialized federal police have limited authority to enforce specified federal laws. State police operate within the boundaries of their own states and, within the state, city police, county sheriffs, and township constables often spend as much time competing for glory as they do in crime detection.

---

[18] See *Report* of Commission on Intergovernmental Relations, p. 40.
[19] Alexis de Tocqueville, *Democracy in America,* ed., Phillips Bradley (Knopf, 1946), I, p. 167.

What happens outside their jurisdiction is often of little interest to police officers. Frequently, troublemakers are simply chased out of town. Some cities have even gone so far as to agree not to bother criminals who promise not to make trouble within the city limits.

In 1951 a Senate committee investigating crime uncovered many instances of the failure of police agencies to cooperate even in the most obvious ways. The committee pointed to a case of a gambling house that straddled the Missouri-Kansas border. Whenever the Missouri police staged a raid, the gamblers merely moved to the back of the house, which was located in Kansas. Whenever the Kansas police knocked on the back door, the gamblers returned to the front of the house, which was located in Missouri. The fact that the Missouri police never picked up the phone and arranged a simultaneous raid with Kansas police officers suggests either stupidity or corruption.

Failures of state and local police to cope with criminals have led to demands for national action. Congress has already made it a federal offense to use the channels of interstate commerce to steal property valued over $5,000, to kidnap, or to transport women for immoral purposes. The recent terroristic bombings of schools and churches—violence that the states and local police appear to be unable to prevent—have stimulated additional demands for further extension of the police duties of the national government.

The constant expansion of federal police jurisdiction, if carried far enough, could be dangerous. The concentration of control over the police in a central agency is a characteristic of totalitarian police states. However, there is much that can be done short of giving complete authority over law enforcement to the national government. Something could be done, for example, about the hundreds of inadequate, overlapping police agencies. Here again, cooperative federalism is needed. Already progress is being made. The FBI Police Academy has been opened to state and local law-enforcement officers, and the FBI fingerprint file, with over 21 million prints, is available to all law-enforcement officers, who in turn record their own collection of prints with the FBI. Federal officers enforcing national law turn over to state officials any evidence of the violation of state laws. Some states have coordinated their police radio networks, and neighboring states often grant reciprocal arrest privileges to out-of-state officers who are in "hot pursuit" of offenders.

Of course, even with the best state and local police forces, the role of the national government will expand. Crime is a national problem. Criminals are organized in national syndicates and they use two-way radios, airplanes, and telegraph systems for flashing information. But this traditional state activity need not be abandoned if the states clean their own houses and provide, in cooperation with the national government, the protection people demand.

LAW AVOIDANCE

Federalism also helps people who can hardly be called criminals to evade state laws. State sales taxes on cigarettes, liquor, and gasoline, for example, can often be avoided simply by crossing the state line. "Last-chance" gasoline stations that dot the highways just before one enters a state with higher taxes are evidence of this everyday tax evasion. Cigarette dealers in low-tax states did a thriving business by sending their wares to people all over the nation until 1949, when the national government required all persons who regularly ship cigarettes by mail or through the channels of interstate commerce to report sales to officials in the receiving states. When metropolitan cities are located near state boundaries, persons who earn their living in one state and benefit from its public services can in certain cases avoid paying city and state taxes by commuting to work from an adjoining low-tax state.

A more spectacular form of law avoidance is carried on by those who have the money and time to go to Reno for six weeks to avoid their own state divorce laws. As we have seen, the validity of some of these divorces has been questioned, but Nevada still does a thriving divorce business and, in a sense, sets the divorce standards for the wealthy members of the entire nation. Moreover, despite the efforts of the Supreme Court to protect each state's right to control the matrimonial affairs of its own citizens and at the same time to accommodate the national interest in seeing that states respect the full-faith-and-credit clause, there is greater confusion than ever about the validity of divorces. Some observers favor uniform divorce standards throughout the nation. But since all fifty state legislatures could probably never agree on the same standards, federal action would be required. Congress has no power to pass laws regulating marriage and divorce, but the Supreme Court may have left the way open under the full-faith-and-credit clause for Congress to determine the type of divorce judgment that must be recognized by all states.

Evasion of business laws is another problem. New Jersey, in earlier years, and Delaware today have been the Renos of the world of corporation charters. Many corporations that do most of their business and sell most of their securities in other states have responded to advertisements such as this:

> Charters—Delaware Best, Quickest, Cheapest, Most Liberal. Nothing needs to be paid in. Do business and hold meetings anywhere. Free forms. Colonial Charter Company, Wilmington, Delaware.[20]

Corporations gaining such charters in Wilmington maintain nominal one-room-one-desk headquarters there simply to evade the stricter charter laws (designed to protect stockholders, consumers, and the public) of the states in which they do business. Periodically, it is proposed that all corporations carrying on an interstate business be required to incorporate under national law, but so far nothing has come of these proposals. Congress also could require all corporations using interstate commerce or the mails to incorporate in the state in which they maintain their real headquarters or do the bulk of their business. But until such action is taken, the most lax state will be permitted to set the standards for the entire nation.

---

[20] W. Z. Ripley, *Main Street and Wall Street* (Little, Brown, 1927), p. 29, cited by George C. S. Benson, *The New Centralization* (Farrar & Rinehart, 1941), p. 28.

INTERSTATE COMPETITION

In their zeal to attract business, some states and cities offer free factory sites, tax exemptions, free water, and laws that make it difficult for labor to organize unions. Often these concessions to business are made at the public expense. Many states hesitate to levy taxes to pay for better schools or to increase aid to the needy for fear that the higher taxes may drive industries away to states with lower rates. There is no conclusive evidence that the tax rate is a cause of business migrations, but the fear that taxes will drive businesses out of the state is often a factor leading to the defeat of tax measures. Similarly, states are often reluctant to enact minimum-wage laws or to extend welfare programs because the additional cost may place their industries at a competitive disadvantage to those in states without such provisions.

Competition among the states has also retarded the development of state conservation programs. Each state hesitates to require industries to follow conservation procedures—for example, preventing water pollution—for fear that the resulting expenses will cause local business firms to lose out to those operating in states with a "get-rich-quick-and-never-mind-the-future" philosophy. Although interstate agreements, especially in the oil and gas industry, have led to some conservation programs, such agreements have been made only when conservation coincides with more immediate economic interests— for example, controlling the supply of a commodity to prevent the depressing of prices.

MAINTAINING THE NATIONAL MARKET

One of the major goals of the Constitution was to create a free trade area within the United States. To a large extent this goal has been achieved. Certainly one of the major reasons for the remarkable economic development of this nation has been the absence of state barriers to trade and commerce. Throughout the years, however, some state regulations have imposed restraints on the free flow of commerce. Some of these regulations are designed to protect consumers from fraud, some are in the form of health and quarantine regulations, and others are attempts to collect a fair share of taxes from those who use the roads or other tax-supported facilities. However, many laws passed ostensibly to protect persons from disease or fraud, or to protect animals and crops from infection, are actually designed to give home industries the advantage of the home market. And almost all states favor their own workers, contractors, or manufacturers in making official purchases of goods and services, sometimes at great expense to the taxpayer.

The interstate-commerce clause of the Constitution deprives states of any power to tax interstate commerce as such, but they may levy fees for the use of their highways and require out-of-state trucks to secure licenses, permits, and registration tickets. So long as the fee bears some reasonable relation to the use of the highways, it is not forbidden by the commerce clause. Although no state has yet tried to collect fees from nonresident passenger vehicles, they all have some form of charge for out-of-state trucks. The most common forms are: registration fees, mileage taxes, consumption-of-gasoline taxes, and levies on the receipts received for hauling goods. One survey reports that a trucker traveling from Alabama to South Carolina in a five-to-six ton truck would have to pay fees totaling several hundred dollars.

These burdens are to some extent lightened by reciprocity agreements, but only nine states grant complete freedom from fees by such agreements. States are rightly entitled to receive some payment for the use of their highways by those who do not pay the normal state taxes. But many state highways are in part financed by federal grants drawn from federal tax funds, and the burdens placed on the free movement of goods are ultimately paid through increased costs by all the people of the nation.

True to the traditions of John Marshall, the Supreme Court has struck down some laws whose purpose is to discriminate against the commerce of other states. Many discriminatory practices, however, are never brought to the Court. Moreover, the Supreme Court has a difficult task. For, while it must protect interstate commerce from discriminatory treatment and must prevent the "Balkanization" of our national economy, it cannot permit business firms to hide behind the commerce clause in order to avoid paying their fair share of taxes or to escape compliance with regulations necessary to protect the public health, welfare, safety, and morals.

LEGALISM AND CONFUSION

"Federalism means legalism." Certainly much time and energy are spent on the "legalistic" and "constitutional" aspects of public problems. We have already noted how issues such as "states rights" versus "national action" can be used to confuse issues of policy. The constitutional aspects of federalism are important, but they should not be permitted to exclude or confuse the real merits of an issue. "Is it *constitutional?*" is an important question to ask, but so is the question, "Is it *desirable?*"

The division of powers is a valuable safeguard, but it also encourages buck-passing. As late as 1960, for example, long after the need for taking action on a civil defense program was apparent, nothing of consequence had been done. The states blamed the central government, the central government blamed the states.

By way of summary, many of the problems of federalism are offset by corresponding advantages. Other problems are unavoidable in that they represent the price we gladly pay for federalism. And yet a good many of the difficulties that spring from federalism could be corrected, or at least minimized, if we understood that we must sink or swim together. Through the intelligent use of regional organizations, interstate compacts, grants-in-aid, and closer cooperation among federal-state-local officials, much can be done to create a "more perfect union." This optimism, however, is by no means shared by all.

The Future of Federalism There are many who consider federalism as only a midway station between a confederation and a unitary state. These critics point out that various federal systems of the past were ultimately transformed into unitary systems, and that modern techniques of transportation and communication have destroyed the barriers of time and distance that originally gave rise to federalism. In short, they insist that federalism has become obsolete.

IS FEDERALISM OBSOLETE?

Harold J. Laski, the late British political scientist, socialist writer, and critic of American federalism, argued that federalism

> is insufficiently positive in character; it does not provide for sufficient rapidity of action; it inhibits the emergence of necessary standards of uniformity; it relies upon compacts and compromises which take insufficient account of the urgent category of time; it leaves the backward areas a restraint, at once parasitic and poisonous, on those which seek to move forward. . . .

Here is the crux of his argument:

> Giant capitalism has . . . concentrated the control of economic power in a small proportion of the American people. . . . For forty-eight separate units to seek to compete with the integrated power of giant capitalism is to invite defeat in every element of social life where approximate uniformity of conditions is the test of the good life.[21]

Laski charged that our national government lacks the constitutional authority to control vested business interests, and that the state governments are reluctant to regulate them lest these business interests withdraw their patronage and go elsewhere. He predicted that public pressures would force positive national action, eventually leading to the abandonment of federalism. But Laski was not so much predicting the end of our federal system as he was arguing for its abolition. Favoring more vigorous national regulation of business and more positive government management of the economy, he believed that the federal system stood in the way of achieving these goals.

Perhaps those who believe American federalism is obsolete fail to give enough credit to its dynamic character. It has been, and is being, adapted to changing conditions, as so many of the preceding pages attest. Today the *national government has sufficient constitutional power to dispose of virtually any problem of national extent.*

Laski, like many other critics, attributed to federalism difficulties for which it is only partly responsible. Many of the problems we have discussed

---

21 H. J. Laski, "The Obsolescence of Federalism," *The New Republic*, May 3, 1939, pp. 367-369.

arise not from our federal system but from the fact that we are a nation of continental proportions with a rich variety of sections and groups. Even if the federal system were abolished tomorrow, there would still be a South and a New England, with all their differences. The giant capitalists and trade unionists would remain strong, and positive national regulation would not necessarily be forthcoming.

Constitutional forms such as federalism are only a part of the picture. England has a unitary form of government, and the English Parliament, it is often said, in contrast to Congress, has power to deal with any problem unencumbered by limitations of federalism. But Parliament is effectively restrained by strong English traditions of local government, while Congress is not wholly powerless, as we have seen, to influence the operations of local governments. Many of the advantages of federalism, moreover, can be secured within the unitary framework—experimentation and decentralization of power, for example, are not unknown in England or France. On the other hand, many of the problems of federalism—such as sectionalism and overlapping governmental jurisdictions—also plague unitary states. True, federalism accentuates both the positive and negative problems of the geographical distribution of governmental power, but comparisons between federal and unitary states are comparisons of degree rather than kind.

Whether or not federalism is obsolete, there is little chance that it will be replaced in the United States by the unitary form. Federalism is the system under which we will have to solve the urgent problems that confront us. If we fail to solve those problems, the fault will lie with us more than with federalism. Moreover, as long as we want union without uniformity, federalism, adapted to our changing society, remains our best bet.

Summary

1. Federalism is a political issue as well as a mechanical or structural arrangement. People differ over federalism not just as an abstract issue but largely because they differ over particular programs.
2. A balance between national and state power can be achieved by improving state and local governments and also by regional administration of federal functions and interstate cooperation.
3. Cooperative federalism between Washington and the states through grants-in-aid is an important method of national-state cooperation, but it raises difficult problems—especially that of allowing proper national supervision without too much national control.
4. Other problems complicated by American federalism are law enforcement, interstate competition, and confusion as to which level of government is responsible for what.
5. Some believe that federalism is an obsolescent system that thwarts national action, but others hold that federalism is a flexible system adaptable to changing national and state needs.

PART **3**

Civil Liberties
and Citizenship

A PROBLEM GUIDE

How can we maintain the proper balance between liberty and order, between diversity and uniformity, between individual rights and collective needs? This is the main problem of Part Three. To many Americans the safeguarding and broadening of individual freedom—of civil liberties and civil rights—is the most important task of a democratic society. These are the lofty and historic rights of the Western tradition—freedom of religion, freedom of speech, freedom of assembly, freedom of the press.

When we think of protecting these freedoms of the individual, we usually think of protecting them against *government.* This is only natural, for government historically has often been the great "engine of tyranny." We are all familiar with the struggles of oppressed peoples and individuals against government—Americans in 1776, Hungarians (in a far worse context) against communist tyranny only a few years ago. But in a democracy the protection of the rights of the individual against the government is only part of the problem (though probably the major part). The other part of the problem concerns the rightful power of government *over the individual.* A person's freedom from governmental oppression is of little use, after all, except in a peaceful, orderly society. And government must have some power over individuals if it is to maintain peace and order.

Motorists meet this problem whenever they go out for a drive. Every minute they face the heavy hand of government—GO SLOW, 25-MILE ZONE, STOP, NO U-TURN. But few drivers complain,

133

because they know that without these restrictions driving would be so suicidal that they would lose a greater freedom —the freedom to drive safely. In effect, the motorist is willing to swap some freedoms for other freedoms.

The problem, then, is how to balance individual rights against collective needs, remembering always that individual freedom and social order are necessary to each other. Chapter 6 describes how Americans have tried to achieve this balance in several important areas —freedom of religion and of speech and of the press, for example. Which goals —individual liberties or collective needs —should receive priority if they come into conflict with each other? When and under what conditions should one or the other receive priority? Who should decide—judges, legislators, or someone else? Achieving this balance is especially difficult today, for our chief collective need is national survival, which means, among other things, emphasis on military strength and internal security. How much individual liberty can we allow in face of our need for military security? How much, in a *democracy,* can we afford to let military security threaten individual freedom? This problem is the focus of the second half of Chapter 6.

We have been talking about individual liberties, such as freedom of speech; there is also the matter of *civil rights,* such as the right to equal opportunity in education and voting. Chapter 7 takes up the constitutional guarantees and political battles behind the idea that no man should suffer pains and penalties because of his race, religion, national origin, or other qualities irrelevant to his individual merit. Chapter 8 describes a different but equally important type of right—the right not to be deprived arbitrarily of life, liberty, and property—for example, freedom from arbitrary arrest. Both sets of rights

—*civil* rights and (mainly) *procedural* rights—raise the problem of balancing individual rights against collective needs.

There is a final basic problem in this Part—*which government,* state or federal, should determine the balance between individual rights and collective needs? What if one government—say, the state government—should fail to protect a man's individual liberties or his civil rights as fully as most Americans would wish. Should the national government step in and protect those liberties and rights? Hence the problem of *federalism* is crucial to the problem of freedom in America. This problem— the relation of *governments* to one another in protecting individual freedom —is emphasized in the last two sections of Chapter 7 and the last section of Chapter 8.

Implicit in this discussion is one very important point: individual freedom may be threatened directly by *other individuals* as well as by government. For example, a man trying to speak from a soapbox may be knocked down by a mob, just as he may be arrested by a policeman. It is also possible that the policeman might protect him *against* the mob—a case of *government* guarding the liberty of one individual against other individuals. Hence it is always advisable, when considering a problem of individual freedom, to ask the question: *Whose* civil liberties are to be protected, against *what,* by *whom* (for example, what agency of government), and *how?*

Chapter 9 turns to a related problem: the status and rights of immigrants, aliens, and citizens. The Constitution guarantees to no one the right to be admitted to the United States from abroad, and aliens do not enjoy all the privileges of American citizens. But important problems of individual liberty are involved in our treatment of noncitizens.

CHAPTER 6

The First Amendment
and the First Freedoms

"Congress shall make no law," declares the First Amendment, "respecting an establishment of religion, or prohibiting the free exercise thereof; or abridging the freedom of speech, or of the press; or the right of the people peaceably to assemble, and to petition the Government for a redress of grievances." Here in bold and absolute terms are set forth the fundamental supports of a free society—freedom of conscience and freedom of expression.

Although the framers drafted the Constitution, in a sense it was the *people* who drafted our basic charter of liberties. The Constitution drawn up at Philadelphia included no specific guarantee of freedom of speech and religion and other basic freedoms—an omission that aroused suspicion and distrust among the people at large. In order to win ratification, the Federalists promised to correct this oversight, and in the very first session of the new Congress they lived up to their promise. Congress proposed amendments that were ratified by the end of 1791 and became part of the Constitution. These Ten Amendments, or more precisely the first eight of them, are known as the Bill of Rights.

Note that the Bill of Rights is addressed to the *national* government. As John Marshall held long ago, in *Barron* v. *Baltimore* (1833), the Bill of Rights limits the national but not the state governments. Why not the states? In the 1790's the people were confident they could control their own state officials. Furthermore, most of the state constitutions already had a bill of rights. It was the new and distant central government the people feared.

But as it turned out, those popular fears of 1790 were largely misplaced. The national government, responsive to tens of millions of voters from a variety of races, creeds, religions, and economic groups, has shown less tendency to curtail civil liberties than have state and local governments. It was not long after the Bill of Rights had been adopted that people began to recognize the mistake of exempting state governments from the prohibitions of the national Bill of Rights and thereby allowing state regulation of our liberties. True, each state constitution includes a bill of rights, but for the most part state judges have not been inclined to apply these bills of rights to protect civil liberties.

How to plug the gap created by the exemption of the states from the Bill of Rights? With the adoption of the due-process clause of the Fourteenth Amendment in 1868, which *does* apply to the states, litigants tried to persuade the Supreme Court to construe this clause to mean that the *states* are limited in the same way that the Bill of Rights limits the *national* government. At a minimum, they contended, freedom of speech should be brought within the confines of the Fourteenth Amendment.

For decades the Supreme Court refused to interpret the Fourteenth Amendment in this way. Then in 1925, in a historic decision, *Gitlow* v. *New York,* the Supreme Court announced:

> For present purposes we may and do assume that freedom of speech and of press—which are protected from abridgment by Congress—are among the fundamental personal rights and liberties protected by the due process clause of the Fourteenth Amendment from impairment by the states.

Gitlow v. *New York* was a decision of major, almost revolutionary, significance. Since that date the Fourteenth Amendment has placed the same restraints in behalf of free speech on states (in a constitutional sense, all subdivisional units of a state, such as cities, counties, and school districts, are part of the state) that the First Amendment places on the national government. By 1947 the Supreme Court had brought all the other liberties of the First Amendment under the protection of the Fourteenth. But note that it is only the *First* Amendment that has been completely incorporated into the Fourteenth. Most of the other provisions of the Bill of Rights have not thus been made applicable to the states (see pp. 208-210).

Although Congress is governed by the absolute language of the First Amendment to pass no law abridging free speech and press, whereas states are limited by the relative language of the Fourteenth not to deprive a person of speech or press without due process of law, this difference in constitutional language has had no significance. For all practical purposes the Fourteenth imposes on the states the same restrictions that the First Amendment imposes on the national government.

Today virtually all Americans agree that governmental power should not be used to interfere with free speech and freedom of conscience. Yet the country seems to be almost constantly involved in quarrels about specific application of these restraints. It is all very well to venerate our liberties in general. The trouble arises when we move from generalities to specifics. And in few areas are the problems more difficult to resolve than those concerning religious freedom.

Each May Worship　　Since a society is composed of
in His Own Way　　many people with conflicting
needs, very few rights can be ab-
solute. But the right to hold any religious view is one of these few. One's
religious beliefs are inviolable, and no government in the United States has
any authority whatsoever to compel the acceptance of, or to censor, any creed.
Furthermore, the right to advocate one's religion by speech or writing—like
the right to use speech or writing for any other purpose—can be curbed only
when there is danger of substantial injury to others. In fact, the Supreme
Court has shown greater concern for religious advocacy than for political
advocacy, perhaps because Congress is specifically enjoined by the First
Amendment (and the states through interpretation by the Fourteenth) to make
no law "prohibiting the free exercise" of religion.

The *practice* of one's religion has less protection than its *advocacy*. As
the Supreme Court has said, "It was never intended that the First Amendment . . . could be invoked as a protection against legislation for the punishment of acts inimical to the peace, good order and morals of society." One
cannot claim exemption from payment of taxes on the grounds of religious
scruples. And if one's religious practices interfere with the peace, health, safety,
or morals of the public, these practices may be regulated by state laws.

"ESTABLISHMENT OF RELIGION"

The First Amendment not only forbids Congress and the states (via the
Fourteenth) to prohibit the free exercise of religion; it also forbids them to
pass laws respecting an establishment of religion. But what does "an establishment of religion" mean? When the First Amendment was adopted, this phrase
meant, according to James Madison, that "Congress should not establish a
religion, and enforce the legal observation of it by law, nor compel men to
worship God in any manner contrary to their conscience." The Supreme Court
has, however, considerably expanded the scope of the clause to include the
doctrine of *separation of church and state*. In an opinion that sustained the
right of New Jersey to reimburse parents for their children's bus fares to
private or parochial schools (*Everson* v. *Board of Education,* 1947), the
Court, speaking through Justice Black, uttered the following sweeping dicta:

> Neither a state nor the Federal Government can set up a church. Neither
> can pass laws that aid one religion, aid all religions, or prefer one religion
> over another. Neither can force nor influence a person to go to or to remain
> away from church . . . or force him to profess a belief or a disbelief in any
> religion. . . . No tax in any amount, large or small, can be levied to support
> any religious activities or institutions, whatever they may be called, or what-
> ever form they may adopt to teach or practice religion. Neither a state nor
> the Federal Government can, openly or secretly, participate in the affairs

of any religious organizations or groups and vice versa. In the words of Jefferson, the clause against establishment of religion by law was intended to erect "a wall of separation between Church and State."

In view of these statements, how did the Supreme Court sustain the payment of tax money for transportation of children to church schools? A bare majority of the Court reasoned that these funds were being used to aid *school children* and not to aid *religion*. The Court has made similar distinctions in upholding state expenditures for school books and hot lunches for children attending parochial schools. Nor has anyone seriously challenged the constitutionality of granting tax exemptions to property owned and used by a church or of providing chaplains for Congress, the state legislatures, or the armed forces.

Does the establishment-of-religion clause forbid public schools to release school children to attend religious classes? Few questions have caused more difficulty than this one. In 1947, Illinois, acting through the Champaign Board of Education, ran afoul of the clause when it allowed privately chosen instructors to teach religion during school hours and in public school rooms to students whose parents approved such instruction. Children who chose not to attend these religious classes were required to remain in study hall. By an eight-to-one majority, the Supreme Court struck this program down, saying, "Here not only are the State's tax-supported public school buildings used for the dissemination of religious doctrines. The State also affords sectarian groups an invaluable aid in that it helps to provide pupils for their religious classes through the use of the State's compulsory school machinery. This is not separation of Church and State." [1]

People have strong emotions on this kind of question, some holding that a high, strong wall must separate church and state, others that government must simply treat all religious groups equally. The dicta in the New Jersey case and the decision in the Illinois case appeared to place the Supreme Court on the side of those who believe that the Constitution forbids any form of state encouragement to religion.

Then in 1952 the Supreme Court reconsidered its position. The issue before the justices was the constitutionality of New York City's released-time program, which was essentially like that of Champaign. The only substantial difference was that in New York the religion classes were held outside the school buildings in classrooms provided by the various religious bodies. Six justices, though refusing to overrule the Champaign decision, thought that this difference saved New York's program from being unconstitutional. The dissenting justices pointed out that New York, like Champaign, was helping sectarian groups secure pupils for their religious classes through the use of the state's compulsory school machinery. Justice Douglas' opinion for the majority

---

[1] *Illinois ex rel McCollum* v. *Board of Education* (1948).

was also at odds in other respects with the doctrines previously supported by the Court. He wrote:

> The First Amendment ... does not say that in every and all respects there shall be a separation of Church and State. ... We are a religious people. ... When the state encourages religious instruction or cooperates with religious authorities by adjusting the schedule of public events to sectarian needs, it follows the best of our traditions.[2]

How much of a retreat from the doctrines of the New Jersey and Illinois cases this decision foreshadows remains to be seen. One thing is sure: If the Supreme Court continues to hold to the views expressed in the New York case, it will be sharply criticized. If it changes its views, it will be just as sharply criticized.

Free Speech and Free Men

Government by the people is based on the individual's right to speak freely, to organize in groups, to question the decisions of the government, and to campaign openly against it. Only through free and uncensored expression of opinion can the government be kept responsive to the electorate and can governmental power be transferred peacefully. Elections, separation of powers, and constitutional guarantees are meaningless unless each person has the right to speak frankly and to hear and judge for himself the worth of what others have to say.

Despite the fundamental importance of free speech in a democracy, some seem to believe that speech should be free only for those who agree with them. A recent national poll indicated that one American in three did not seem truly to believe in free speech, feeling, for example, that the newspapers should not be permitted to criticize the government, even in peacetime.

Why, one might well ask, should evil or ignorant men be permitted to spread falsehoods and confuse the minds of others? Why should they be allowed to utter dangerous ideas that subvert the very foundations of our democratic society? These are challenging questions. How can they be answered?

THE BEST TEST OF TRUTH

Believers in democracy insist on free debate and the unlimited exchange of ideas because they hold that no group has a monopoly on truth, that no group has the right to establish in the field of politics absolute standards of what is true and what is false. A man may be convinced that he is right, that truth is on his side, but in the midst of debate he appeals to no philosopher-king, commissar, or oracle of wisdom, but to the power of his reason. As

---

[2] *Zorach v. Clauson.*

Justice Holmes wrote: "The best test of truth is the power of the thought to get itself accepted in the competition of the market." The insistence upon free speech for others stems from the recognition that men are not infallible, that perhaps the other person is right, or at least, that "I might be wrong."

Free speech is not simply the personal right of an individual to have his say: *it is also the right of the rest of us to hear him.* When John Smith out in California is denied the right to speak, the Bill Browns all over the United States are denied the right to hear what he had to say and to judge its worth for themselves. John Stuart Mill, whose *Essay on Liberty* is an illuminating defense of free speech, put it this way: "The peculiar evil of silencing the expression of opinion, is that it is robbing the human race: . . . If the opinion is right, they are deprived of the opportunity for exchanging error for truth; if wrong, they lose, what is almost as great a benefit, the clearer perception and livelier impression of truth, produced by the collision with error." [3]

Freedom of speech is not merely freedom to express ideas that differ from ours only slightly; it is, as the late Justice Jackson said, "freedom to differ on things that go to the heart of the matter." Some people profess to believe in free speech, but they draw the line at ideas they consider abhorrent or dangerous. But what is a dangerous idea? Who decides? Socrates was forced to drink the cup of hemlock for expressing dangerous ideas. Christians were persecuted for holding "dangerous ideas." The heresies of yesterday are often the orthodoxies of today. In the realm of political ideas who can find an objective, eternally valid standard of right? The search for truth is an endless one. It involves the possibility—even the inevitability—of error. The search cannot go on unless it proceeds unfettered in the minds and speech of men. This means, in the words of Justice Holmes, not only free thought for those who agree with us "but freedom for the thought that we hate."

In short, to forbid the expression of ideas on the ground that they are dangerous is to set oneself up as an infallible judge of what speech should be permitted. Such presumptuousness stifles the fearless exchange of opinions and short-circuits the procedures of democratic government that are protected by the First Amendment.

CONSTITUTIONAL GUARANTEES

Despite the fact that the First Amendment emphatically and absolutely denies the national government the power to pass *any* law abridging freedom of speech, the amendment has never been interpreted in such sweeping terms. Liberty of expression is important—but it is not absolute. Like almost all rights, the right to freedom of speech and press is limited by the fact that its free exercise "implies the existence of an organized society maintaining public order without which liberty itself would be lost in the excess of unrestrained

---

[3] John Stuart Mill, *Essay on Liberty, The English Philosophers from Bacon to Mill,* ed. Edwin A. Burtt (Modern Library, 1939), p. 961.

abuses." [4] How is the line to be drawn between permissible and unconstitutional restraint on freedom of expression?

In discussing the constitutional power of government to regulate speech, it is useful to distinguish among belief, speech, and action. At one extreme is the right to *believe* as one wishes, a right about as absolute as any can be for men living in organized societies. Despite occasional deviations in practice, the traditional American view is that *thoughts* are inviolable, and no government has the right to punish a man for his beliefs or to interfere in any way with his freedom of conscience.

At the other extreme from belief is *action,* which is constantly constrained. We may *believe* it perfectly all right to go sixty miles an hour through an intersection, but if we do so we will be punished. We may *believe* that it is proper to build glue factories in residential districts, but government will probably stop us from doing so. Since one man's action directly affects the liberty and property of others, "his right to swing his arm ends where the other fellow's nose begins."

Speech stands somewhere between belief and action; it is not an absolute, or almost absolute, right like belief, but it is not so exposed to governmental restraint as is action. There are certain narrowly limited classes of speech that "by their very utterance inflict injury or tend to incite an immediate breach of peace" which government may clearly prevent or punish; these are the obscene, the libelous, the fighting words. What about speech outside these narrow categories?

THE HOLMES-BRANDEIS

CLEAR-AND-PRESENT-DANGER TEST

The first test adopted by the Supreme Court to distinguish between protected speech and that which could be regulated was announced by Justice Holmes in *Schenck* v. *United States* (1919): "The question in every case is whether the words are used in circumstances and are of such a nature as to create a clear and present danger that they will bring about substantive evils that Congress has a right to prevent." Furthermore, "no danger flowing from speech can be deemed clear and present," wrote Justice Brandeis (concurring in *Whitney* v. *California,* 1927), "unless the incidence of the evil is so imminent that it may befall before there is opportunity for full discussion."

Holmes and Brandeis, although conceding that speech is not an absolute right, felt it to be so fundamental that under our Constitution no government has authority to suppress speech or punish a man for what he has said unless the connection between the speech and illegal action is so close that the speech itself takes on the character of the action. The Holmes-Brandeis clear-and-present-danger formula is primarily a rule to determine the sufficiency of the evidence. It requires that before being allowed to punish a man for what he

---

[4] *Cox* v. *New Hampshire* (1941).

has said or written, a government must prove clearly that his speech presents an imminent danger of a major substantive evil. Note, it is not *any* clear and present danger that justifies conviction, but only danger of a substantive evil the government has a right to prevent—for example, rioting and destruction of property, or forceful overthrow of the government.

Let us see how the clear-and-present-danger test might be applied. Suppose, for example, a legislature has made it illegal to utter scurrilous and abusive remarks about members of another race. Under the clear-and-present-danger doctrine, a man could be punished for making such remarks only if at his trial the government has convincing evidence that his particular scurrilous remarks *clearly* and *presently* might have led to a riot or some other serious substantive evil that the government had the right to prevent.

DANGEROUS-TENDENCY DOCTRINE

Although the clear-and-present-danger doctrine was the first to receive formal Supreme Court support, the *dangerous- or bad-tendency doctrine* stemming from the common law is the older, and it too at various times has been the official doctrine of the Court, most notably in *Gitlow* v. *New York* (1925). According to adherents of the dangerous-tendency doctrine, the Constitution does not require government to stay its hand until there is a clear and present danger flowing from a particular speech, but it may outlaw speech that has a *tendency* to lead to a substantive evil. Furthermore, those who espouse this view contend that it is primarily a legislative and not a judicial responsibility to determine what kinds of speech have a dangerous tendency. Once the legislature has made it a crime to say or write certain things that have a dangerous tendency, persons may be punished who have used the forbidden words, even if there is no immediate danger flowing from their particular speech. For the legislature has already decided that such words are dangerous.

Now let us take the same example as above and apply to it the dangerous-tendency doctrine. The legislature has already determined that scurrilous and abusive remarks about members of another race are dangerous, and since it is not unreasonable to conclude that such comments have a *tendency* to stir up riots, all that is necessary in this case to convict a person is to show that he in fact made such comments.

THE PREFERRED-POSITION DOCTRINE

Another test, the *preferred-position* doctrine, was the official view of the Supreme Court during the 1940's, but is today supported by only a minority of the Court. This doctrine is an extension of the clear-and-present-danger formula—indeed, some of its supporters come close to the position that freedom of expression is an absolute right. Those who espouse the preferred-position interpretation believe that First Amendment freedoms occupy a preferred position in our constitutional hierarchy and that courts have a special responsibility to scrutinize with extra care laws trespassing on these freedoms. Whereas legislative majorities are free to experiment and adopt various schemes regulating our *economic* lives, *when they tamper with freedom of speech they close the channels of the political process by which error can be corrected.* The majority is free via the legislature to adopt any policies it wishes, provided it leaves untouched the procedures by which new majorities may be formed. Hence, any law that on its face limits the First Amendment freedoms is presumed to be unconstitutional. Only if the government can show that limitations on speech are absolutely necessary to avoid extremely imminent and extremely serious substantive evils are they to be tolerated.

If the preferred-position doctrine were applied to our example above, of a law against abusive racial remarks, the law would be declared unconstitutional. Restraints on such abusive speech are not absolutely necessary to prevent riots, according to this doctrine, and whatever danger may flow from such abusive remarks does not justify a restriction on free comment. Moreover, supporters of the preferred-position doctrine contend that it is not merely the application of this law to a particular speaker that is unconstitutional, but that the law itself violates the Constitution.

These three doctrines are subject to many different interpretations and applications. Even these three, while the most important, are not the only formulas the Supreme Court has used to measure the constitutionality of laws regulating speech. And whether the test is clear and present danger, dangerous tendency, or preferred position, or any other, there is no pat rule, no easy answer in deciding cases. Behind the formulas stand a host of considerations. *What* was said? Obscene speech, libelous statements, fighting words are not in the same category as political disputations. *Where* was it said? On the street corner, in a man's living room, over the radio? *How* was it said? In an inflammatory manner? What was the *intent* of the person who said it? To encourage people to violate the laws, to stir them to violence, or merely to cause them to think? What were the *circumstances* in which it was said? During time of war, in front of a hostile audience? *Which* government is attempting to regulate the speech? The city council that speaks for a few people, or the Congress that speaks for a wide variety of people? (No *congressional* enactment has ever been struck down because of conflict with the First Amendment.) *How* is the government attempting to regulate the speech? By prior censorship, by punishment after the speech, by administrative procedures? *Why* is the government attempting to regulate the speech? To protect the national security, to keep the streets clean, to protect the rights of unpopular religious minorities, to prevent criticism of those in power? These and scores of other considerations are involved. The social interests must be weighed in each case. And there is the further question of how much deference judges should show to the legislature's attempt to adjust these social interests. In short, no test has been devised that will automatically weigh all the factors.

FREEDOM OF THE PRESS

"Upon what meat doth this our democracy feed?" asks Herbert Brucker, a noted newspaper editor. "It feeds upon facts brought into the minds of its citizens by the press, the radio, and the supplementary media of information." [5] So important is this system of disseminating information, says Brucker, that it constitutes the indispensable "fourth branch" of the national government. Today, information is seldom spread through street-corner meetings or public assemblies, the historic centers of debate. Rather, it is broadcast wholesale by the press, television, radio, movies, and other media.

On the whole, the Supreme Court has been zealous in guarding freedom of the press from government restriction in peacetime. In general, it has followed a basic rule of the English constitution described almost two centuries ago by Blackstone, the great legal thinker: "The liberty of the press is indeed essential to the nature of a free state; but this consists in laying no *previous* restraints upon publications, and not in freedom from censure for criminal matter when published." This is a useful general rule, since it suggests that freedom of the press while important is not absolute. But how broad is this freedom?

The case of *Near* v. *Minnesota* (1931) provided a partial answer to this question. A Minneapolis newspaper charged, among other things, that a known gangster controlled racketeering in the city and that the chief of police was receiving graft. Under a Minnesota law authorizing injunctions against "malicious, scandalous, and defamatory" action, the newspaper was permanently enjoined from being published. The editor appealed ultimately to the Supreme Court. "The question," said Chief Justice Hughes, speaking for a closely divided court, "is whether a statute authorizing such proceedings in restraint of publication is consistent with the conception of the liberty of the press as historically conceived and guaranteed. . . . The fact that the liberty of the press may be abused by miscreant purveyors of scandal does not make any the less necessary the immunity of the press from previous restraint in dealing with official misconduct." The Court held the Minnesota law to be an infringement of the liberty of the press. This case made clear that government may not set up advance censorship except in extraordinary circumstances.

Sometimes freedom of the press comes into conflict with another basic right, trial by an impartial judge and jury in a calm and judicious atmosphere. When newspapers and other mass media report in vivid detail the facts of a lurid crime and secure press releases from the prosecutor, it may be impossible to hold a trial in an atmosphere free from hysteria or to secure a jury that can decide in an impartial manner. In England the weight is on the side of fair trial. British courts do not hesitate to hold in contempt newspapers that comment on pending criminal proceedings. In the United States the weight is on the

[5] Herbert Brucker, *Freedom of Information* (Macmillan, 1949), p. 10.

side of free comment. The Court has sustained the right of the press to criticize judges, even to the point of allowing editors to threaten judges with political reprisals unless they deal with defendants in a certain fashion. As Justice Douglas put it, "Judges are supposed to be men of fortitude, able to thrive in a hardy climate" (*Craig* v. *Harney,* 1947).

Juries, on the other hand, are more susceptible to inflammatory comments and events. In 1952, for example, a defendant was given a new trial because, after his indictment, a congressional investigating committee held open hearings that the judges believed so inflamed public opinion that a fair trial was impossible.[6]

Is there a freedom of the press to *obtain* news as well as to print it? Recently threats to freedom of the press arising out of so-called "censorship at the source" have aroused public concern. Governments have always withheld information, especially during time of war. But as the "cold war" has reached into more and more sectors of life—education, for example—public officials have classified all sorts of information as "restricted" or "secret," so that it becomes a crime to divulge it. Too, federal agencies have used a 1789 statute authorizing executive officials to conceal government documents from newsmen, sometimes even from congressmen. This "housekeeping statute" has been used even where information is not classified as military or secret. For example, the Department of Defense at one time ordered officials not to release information unless it would "constitute a constructive contribution to the primary mission of the Department of Defense."

In 1958 Congress amended the 1789 statute by stipulating that it is not to be construed as authorizing the withholding of information from the public or limiting the availability of records. The President signed the 1958 act, but only after saying that he did not interpret it to alter the President's inherent constitutional power to withhold information whose release he considered not in the public interest. Despite the 1958 law, the President still has the upper hand.

OTHER MEANS OF COMMUNICATION

Does the right of free expression extend to books and magazines, motion pictures, radio and television, picket lines, and sound trucks? No general answer can be given. Each of these media presents special problems.

Books and magazines. If one publishes false and malicious comments about another, he may be forced to pay damages, but through a progressive relaxation of the restraints of the law of libel, the danger of prosecution no longer constitutes a serious threat to free comunication.

But what about group libel statutes making it a criminal offense to publish materials defaming races, religions, or other such groups? A closely divided

---

[6] *Delaney* v. *United States,* U.S.C.A. (1952).

Supreme Court sustained such an Illinois law (*Beauharnais* v. *Illinois,* 1952), the majority arguing that it was a reasonable measure to avoid race riots and that libelous comments are not within the protection of the Constitution. The dissenting justices contended that since there was no evidence of any danger of disorder arising from the publication in question, the state had exceeded its constitutional authority. Group libel laws, the minority charged, restrain public discussion because they make people afraid of expressing adverse judgments about members of other races or religions.

Obscene publications, like libelous ones, are not entitled to constitutional protection. But what is the test of obscenity and who is to apply it? Obscenity has often been broadly interpreted; books by such distinguished writers as Edmund Wilson, Lillian Smith, D. H. Lawrence, James Joyce, and even Aristophanes, have been held obscene.

In 1957 the Supreme Court, though holding that obscene publications are not entitled to constitutional protection, insisted upon a narrow definition of the term. The Court warned that sex and obscenity are not synonymous and that only materials "which deal with sex in a manner appealing to prurient interest" could properly be judged obscene. The Court stated further that books and other materials should be judged as a whole rather than on the basis of a few scattered passages, and their impact on normal adults should be assessed on the basis of "contemporary community standards." [7]

States are primarily responsible for regulating obscene literature and those who publish, or knowingly sell such materials run the risk of state prosecution. The national government, through its control over customs and postal matters, also attempts to prevent the circulation of obscene materials. In 1958 Congress amended the criminal code to make it easier to convict persons for sending obscene publications through the mails by allowing trial in any judicial district through which the offending publication was sent from point of origin to point of delivery. Until the law was so amended, the government could prosecute only in the district from which the mail originated, chiefly urban centers where juries are likely to be more tolerant of reading matter than in some rural communities. Under the new amendment, the government can choose the district where convictions are most likely. In effect, the judicial districts with the most puritanical standards may set the national standards.

In addition to federal criminal prosecutions, the Postmaster General has been authorized to exclude obscene publications from the mails, revoke second-class mailing privileges of publications alleged to be obscene, and cut off all incoming mail to a person sending obscene matters through the mails. The basic assumption underlying these delegations of authority to the Postmaster General is that the use of the mails is a privilege that the government may terminate at its discretion. But this assumption has been questioned by the courts in the last several years, and judges have been clamping down on

---

[7] *Roth* v. *United States* and *Smith* v. *California* (1959).

the Postmaster General's discretion.[8] In 1959 an attempt by the Postmaster General to bar from the mails the unexpurgated version of D. H. Lawrence's famous novel, *Lady Chatterley's Lover,* was checked by the courts; and earlier the Post Office Department in the face of threatened judicial action backed down from its proposed ban on the mailing of Aristophanes' *Lysistrata.* The Post Office Department also contends it has authority from Congress to refuse to carry seditious publications or to deliver printed matter from behind the Iron Curtain. These assertions of censoring powers are likely to be challenged in the courts.

Motion pictures. In 1915 the Supreme Court (*Mutual Film Corporation* v. *Ohio Industrial Commission*) concluded that motion pictures were a form of entertainment and not a method of communication, and therefore not protected by the free speech and press guarantees of the Constitution. Taking advantage of this opening, censors in seven states and over a hundred cities prohibited the showing of pictures violating their sense of propriety. Unlike the general laws against obscenity, these motion-picture regulations were *prior* censorship. Then in 1951 (*Joseph Burstyn, Inc.* v. *Wilson*) the Supreme Court brought the movies under the protection of the Constitution and held that New York authorities lacked power to prevent the showing of a film called "The Miracle" because it was "sacrilegious." Not only does "sacrilegious" lack precise meaning, the Court held, but government has no right to censor movies solely because they may offend some people's religious sensibilities.

Although the Supreme Court has not held that all prior licensing of motion pictures is in itself unconstitutional, since 1951 it has ruled in case after case against the censors. The Court has upset attempts to ban motion pictures on the grounds that they "tend to corrupt morals," or "on account of being harmful," or because they "present acts of sexual immorality as desirable, acceptable or proper patterns of behavior." [9] The Court has even set aside bans against motion pictures alleged to be "obscene." [10] Since the Court did not explain its rulings in the cases where obscenity has been the grounds of refusal to license, we do not know for sure whether the justices decided that a state may not generally ban obscene motion pictures or merely that they did not think the particular motion pictures in question were obscene. The latter appears to be the explanation most consistent with other Court opinions. A carefully drawn statute requiring the submission of motion pictures to prior censorship but limiting the authority to withhold a license only for obscenity narrowly defined is likely to be sustained by the Court. But the justices will readily reverse the ruling of a licensing board against a motion picture if they consider the picture in question to be in fact not obscene.

---

[8] See, for example, *Hannegan* v. *Esquire, Inc.,* 1946, and *Summerfield* v. *Sunshine Book Company,* 1954.

[9] *Kingsley Pictures Corp.* v. *Regents* (1959).

[10] *Holmby Products* v. *Vaughn* (1956); *Times Film Corp.* v. *Chicago* (1957).

As a result of the Supreme Court's hostility toward pre-showing censorship of motion pictures, today only four states and a few cities continue to require licensing. More troublesome are the attempts by local police to threaten exhibitors with criminal prosecution if they persist in showing pictures of which the local police disapprove. The threat is frequently sufficient to compel exhibitors to stop showing the picture. Of course any group is free to stay away from pictures that they dislike, even to try to persuade others to stay away. What the Constitution forbids is the use of the coercive powers of government.

Radio and television. The number of frequencies that can be used for broadcasting and telecasting is limited. Chaos would result if the national government could not use its power over interstate commerce to allocate the airways and to issue licenses for broadcasting and television. The regulating agency, the Federal Communications Commission, has not tried to exercise direct power of censorship over political views or ideas presented over the airways, and doubtless it would be stopped by the courts if it did. But the First Amendment does not include "the right to use the facilities of a radio without a license" (*National Broadcasting Co.* v. *United States,* 1943). Nor does the First Amendment prevent the Federal Communications Commission from refusing or canceling a license if, in its opinion, the broadcasting station is not serving the public interest, convenience, or necessity. Federal regulation of radio and television does, however, protect these media from *state* regulation. When Philadelphia officials tried to censor motion pictures shown on television, a United States Court of Appeals ruled that the federal regulation was exclusive (*Dumont Laboratories* v. *Carroll,* 1950).

Picketing. This is a means of speech traditionally used by workers to convey their messages to the public. At the same time it is an economic weapon in the struggle between labor and capital. In 1940 the Supreme Court ruled in *Thornhill* v. *Alabama* that picketing was a form of communication protected by the First and Fourteenth amendments; therefore, a state law forbidding all peaceful picketing carried on for any purpose was an unconstitutional invasion of freedom of speech. However, the Court has held that even peaceful picketing can be restricted if it is conducted for a purpose that is against public policy as declared either by the state legislatures or by state judges.[11]

Sound trucks. Which is more important—the right to an undisturbed Sunday afternoon nap or the right to use a sound truck to publicize a message? In 1948, by a five-to-four decision, the Supreme Court held in *Saia* v. *New York* that the Fourteenth Amendment was violated by a city ordinance requiring an official permit from the chief of police before one could use a sound truck. Justice Douglas, speaking for the majority, said that sound trucks are

---

[11] *Building Service Employees* v. *Gazzam* and cases cited therein (1950).

"indispensable instruments of effective public speech, and . . . such abuses as they create can be controlled only by statutes narrowly drawn." The very next year, however, the authority of this ruling was thrown in doubt by another five-to-four ruling in *Kovacs* v. *Cooper* upholding a municipal ordinance forbidding any sound truck that emitted "loud and raucous noises." The Court majority believed that this ordinance provided a definite enough standard to guide administrators, and that it was a justifiable exercise of the police power "to protect the well-being and tranquility of a community." These two cases are an excellent example of the narrow and delicate balance between civil liberties and the needs of an ordered community.

FREEDOM OF ASSEMBLY

The right to assemble peaceably applies not only to meetings in private homes and meeting halls, but also to meetings held in public streets and parks, which, the Supreme Court has said, "time out of mind have been used for purposes of assembly . . . and discussing public questions" (*Hague* v. *C.I.O.,* 1939). The government has the duty to protect persons who wish to sound off on public questions. But people are not free to incite riots, to block traffic, to hold parades, or to make speeches in public places during rush hours, and the government may make reasonable regulations to preserve order. The Court, however, has struck down licensing laws that give administrative officials unlimited discretion to decide who can speak in a public park or on the street corner. Such laws involve *prior* censorship, to which the Supreme Court has been especially opposed (*Kunz* v. *New York,* 1951), although a law providing precise and reasonable standards to guide officials might get by the Court.

Laws regulating uses of streets have won judicial support when they do not involve prior censorship. Some years ago Feiner, a university student, stood on a large box in a predominantly Negro residential section of Syracuse and spoke over a loud speaker to an audience of about seventy-five people, Negro and white. He was publicizing a meeting to be held that evening by the Young Progressives of America and was protesting the revocation of a permit to use the public school auditorium so that the meeting had to be transferred to a local hotel. In the course of his speech he made derogatory remarks about public officials and exhorted the Negroes to "rise up in arms and fight for their rights." His speech stirred up a little excitement in the crowd, and one man threatened to haul him from his platform. Two police officers on the scene asked Feiner to stop his speech in order to avoid a fight. He refused, and finally the officers arrested him. Feiner was tried and convicted of disorderly conduct. The Supreme Court (*Feiner* v. *New York,* 1951) upheld the conviction on the ground that a clear danger of disorder was threatened and the state had the right to preserve peace on the streets.

Justices Douglas, Black, and Minton dissented. They argued that the record showed only an unsympathetic audience, that there was no danger of a riot, and that if the police were really interested in preserving public order they should have arrested those who were threatening to break up the meeting, instead of arresting Feiner, who was exercising his right to speak. Justice Black said, "I think this conviction makes a mockery of the free speech guarantees of the First and Fourteenth Amendments. . . . I will have no part or parcel in this holding which I view as a long step toward totalitarian authority."

FREEDOM OF PETITION AND ASSOCIATION

The right to petition the government is specifically listed among the liberties protected by the First Amendment, but the right to associate with others for the peaceful promotion of political causes is not mentioned. However, in 1958 the Supreme Court made specific what has long been implied, namely, "It is beyond debate that freedom to engage in association for the advancement of beliefs and ideas is an inseparable aspect of the 'liberty' protected by the Constitution." [12]

The recent attempts by southern states to illegalize the operations of the National Association for the Advancement of Colored People and to place obstacles in the way of a person's joining this association appear to impair the freedom of association guaranteed by the Constitution. One device to curtail the NAACP's activities has already been declared unconstitutional. The NAACP, which proceeds mainly by pressing cases before the courts, has by its successful sponsorship of civil-rights suits aroused considerable public hostility among white citizens in areas where segregation traditions are strong. In these areas persons who are known to belong to the NAACP run the risk of economic reprisal, loss of employment, even physical coercion. For this reason the NAACP refused to hand over to an Alabama court the names of its rank-and-file members, and was fined $100,000. The Supreme Court set the fine aside, holding that this attempt by the state to force publication of the names of members would serve no public purpose and would seriously interfere with freedom of association. The Court said, "State action which may have the effect of curtailing the freedom to associate is subject to closest scrutiny," [13] thus suggesting that many of the other anti-NAACP regulations are likely to be held unconstitutional in the near future.

Subversive Conduct and Seditious Speech

If there is any fixed star in our constitutional constellation," Justice Jackson has said, "it is that no official, high or petty, can prescribe what shall be orthodox in politics, nationalism, religion, or other matters of opinion. . . ." Any group that abides by the basic rules of democracy can champion whatever position it wishes, whether

---

[12] *NAACP* v. *Alabama* (1958).
[13] *Ibid.*

vegetarianism, socialism, or even communism. But what about the American Communist party? Its leaders are unwilling to abide by democratic methods.

"Fire!"

Courtesy of Herblock

They use force and deceit. Their organization is an instrument of a foreign power whose aggressive policies threaten the free world.[14] Yet they claim the right under the Constitution to carry on their propaganda and other activities.

Here is a perplexing problem for American democratic government. How can the United States protect itself against communists and other antidemocrats and at the same time preserve traditional American freedoms? The weapons in the battle against disloyalty are hazardous—there is a constant risk that they will backfire. If used clumsily, they may do more to undermine individual freedom and the security of the United States than can the communists themselves. Let us look first at the least dangerous weapons—those aimed at disloyal *actions*.

TRAITORS, SPIES, SABOTEURS, REVOLUTIONARIES

Laws punishing disloyal *actions* raise no constitutional questions nor do they infringe on civil liberties, except when they are loosely drawn or indiscriminately administered. The framers of the Constitution—themselves considered traitors by the English government—knew the dangers of loose definitions of treason. Accordingly, they carefully inserted a constitutional definition of the crime of treason by stating that it consists only of the overt acts of giving aid and comfort to the enemies of the United States or levying war against the United States. Furthermore, in order to convict a person of treason, the Constitution requires the testimony of two witnesses to the overt treasonable acts or else confession in open court.

Against what other forms of disloyal action does the national govern-

---

14 See decision of Subversive Activities Control Board, which after fourteen months of hearings concluded that the Communist party is dominated by the Soviet Union and ordered it to register as a "communist-action organization" (see page 164). F.R. Vol. 18, No. 83, p. 2513, April 30, 1953. The communists have appealed this decision to the courts.

ment have constitutional power to protect itself? It has the power to make it a crime to engage in espionage or sabotage, to overthrow the government by force, or to conspire to do any of these things.

This power to proceed against disloyal action, however, is not unlimited. Some constitutional lawyers suggest that perhaps Congress went too far in the Internal Security Act of 1950, which outlaws any conspiratorial action, peaceful or violent (except proposals for constitutional amendments), designed to contribute substantially to the establishment of a foreign-controlled dictatorship in the United States. So far the Department of Justice has made no attempt to prosecute any person under this provision, which, unlike other antisubversive laws, is not aimed at specific acts or merely at the use of violence or other unlawful means, but attempts to outlaw political goals.

SEDITIOUS SPEECH

It is one thing to punish men for what they *do;* it is quite another to punish them for what they *say.* The story of the development of free government is in large measure the story of making clear this distinction between speech and other kinds of activity, and of restricting the power of government to define and punish seditious speech. Until recent centuries seditious speech was so broadly defined that all criticism of those in power was suppressed. As late as the eighteenth century in England, seditious speech was defined to cover any publication intended to bring the king into hatred or to incite disaffection against him or the government or to raise discontent among the people or to promote feelings of ill will between different classes.[15] And it did not make any difference if what was said was true. On the contrary, "the greater the truth the greater the libel." For if one charged the king's ministers with being corrupt and in fact they were corrupt, such a charge would more likely cause discontent among the people than if it were false.

The adoption of the Constitution and the Bill of Rights did not result in a quick, easy victory for those who wished to establish free speech in the United States. In 1798, only seven years after the First Amendment had been ratified, Congress passed the first national sedition law. These were perilous times for the young Republic, for war with France seemed imminent. The Federalists, in control of both Congress and the Presidency, were so stung by the criticisms of the Jeffersonian Republicans that they persuaded themselves that national safety required a little suppression of speech. The Sedition Act made it a crime to utter false, scandalous, or malicious statements intended to bring the government or any of its officers into disrepute or "to incite against them the hatred of the good people of the United States."[16]

---

[15] Zechariah Chafee, Jr., "The Great Liberty: Freedom of Speech and Press," in Alfred H. Kelly (ed.), *Foundations of Freedom in the American Constitution* (Harper, 1958), p. 79.
[16] See James Morton Smith, *Freedom's Fetters: The Alien and Sedition Laws and American Civil Liberties* (Cornell Univ. Press, 1956).

The Sedition Act of 1798 marked a definite advance over the English common law, for it made truth a defense and allowed the jury to determine the seditious character of the utterances. (At about this same time in England these same procedural reforms were also being adopted.) But Federalists, like most officials wielding the power to suppress, regarded all criticism of their actions as scandalous, malicious, and false, and they used the law to punish their political opponents for criticizing the policies of the Federalist administration.

The popular reaction to the Sedition Act helped defeat the Federalists in the elections of 1800. They had failed to grasp the core of the democratic idea that a man may criticize the *government of the day,* he may work for its downfall, he may oppose its policies, and still be loyal to the *nation.* If the Sedition Act had been left on the statute books and applied in its full measure, neither a "loyal opposition" nor a free government would have been possible.

THE SEDITION ACT OF 1918

Not until World War I did such a severe measure again become the law of the land. In 1918 Congress made it a crime to print, write, or publish any "disloyal, profane, scurrilous, or abusive language about the form of government of the United States or the Constitution . . . or any language intended to bring the form of government of the United States, or the Constitution of the United States, or the military forces . . . or the flag . . . or the uniform of the Army and Navy . . . into contempt, scorn, contumely, or disrepute."

This drastic measure was not aimed at talk that might lead to specific kinds of illegal activity. Rather, it made *the speech itself* illegal. Like the Sedition Act of 1798, this law made it a crime not only to advocate illegal activities, but even to criticize the government. Loosely drawn and poorly administered, it was applied at a time when many people, emotionally aroused by the war, were willing to restrict the liberties of their fellow citizens. As a result of the combined effort of state laws against anarchy and sedition and federal laws against interfering with drafting men for the army, it became a crime "to advocate heavier taxation instead of bond issues, to state that conscription was unconstitutional . . . to say that the sinking of merchant vessels was legal, to urge that a referendum should have preceded our declaration of war, to say that war was contrary to the teachings of Christ." [17] A twenty-one-year-old girl was sentenced to fifteen years in jail for taking part in the scattering of pamphlets attacking President Wilson and opposing American intervention in Russia.[18] During the "red scare" that followed the war, judges and juries punished hundreds of people who expressed ideas to which their neighbors objected.

---

[17] Zechariah Chafee, Jr., *Free Speech in the United States* (Harvard Univ. Press, 1942), p. 51.

[18] *Abrams v. United States* (1919).

THE SMITH ACT OF 1940

The next sedition law, the first to apply in peacetime since the Sedition Act of 1798, was the Smith Act of 1940. Unlike earlier sedition laws, it does not make mere criticism of the government a crime, nor does it contain such loose language as "bring into contempt" or "cause discontent." The central core of the offense to which this law applies is to advocate the overthrow of the government by force with the intent to bring about this overthrow. It forbids persons to advocate forceful overthrow; to distribute, with disloyal intent, matter teaching or advising the overthrow of government by violence; and to organize knowingly or to help organize any group having such purposes. According to Zechariah Chafee, Jr., a leading authority on the problems of free speech, the act introduces for the first time into federal criminal law the concept of *guilt by association,* by making it a crime for an individual to be a member of any organization that advocates forceful overthrow of the government when the individual *knows* that this is its purpose (even though he himself does not so advocate).

Although some anti-Soviet Trotskyites were punished under the Smith Act, its constitutionality was not tested before the Supreme Court until 1951, in *Dennis* v. *United States.* This important case arose out of the conviction of the leaders of the Communist party for violating the Smith Act by *conspiring to advocate* the overthrow of the government by force.

The attorneys for the communist leaders pointed out that the charge was not attempting to overthrow, conspiring to overthrow, or even advocating the overthrow of the government, but solely of *conspiring to advocate.* They argued that, unless the government could prove (which they held it had not done) a clear and present danger that the conspiracy to advocate was about to ripen into action, the First Amendment forbade conviction.

Chief Justice Vinson, speaking for the Court, rejected this contention. In distinguishing previous applications of the clear-and-present-danger doctrine from this case, he said, "the interest which the State was attempting to protect [in earlier cases] was itself too insubstantial to warrant restriction of speech." But in this case the government was protecting its *right to existence.* Therefore the probability of success of the speech in question was not to serve as the criterion. Quoting from Circuit Judge Learned Hand, the Chief Justice said the question was "whether the gravity of the evil, discounted by its improbability," justified such invasion of free speech as was necessary to avoid the danger. The evil was grave. Moreover, the danger presented by the communists could not be discounted. The Court gave great weight to the fact that this was not a case of an isolated socialist scattering a few insignificant pamphlets, or of a zealot on the street corner, but of rigidly disciplined members of a world-wide conspiratorial group whose purpose was to destroy democracy. This group existed in the context of world crisis. Thus invasion of their freedom to conspire to advocate the overthrow of the government by force could be sustained.

Justices Douglas and Black dissented. Justice Douglas insisted that no evidence had been introduced to indicate that the communists were teaching the techniques of sabotage, advising the desirability of assassinating the President, or giving instructions on the filching of documents from public files. "The teaching of methods of terror and seditious conduct should be beyond the pale along with obscenity and immorality." But, he argued, the evidence presented by the government indicated only that the communists had organized people to teach them Marxist-Leninist doctrines. Moreover, the evidence did not show that this teaching presented any danger to the government. The communists in America, he wrote, are "miserable merchants of unwanted ideas; their wares remain unsold. The fact that their ideas are abhorrent does not make them powerful. . . . The invisible army of petitioners is the best known, the most beset, and the least thriving of any fifth column in history. Only those held by fear and panic could think otherwise. . . . Unless and until extreme and necessitous circumstances are shown our aim should be to keep speech unfettered and to allow the process of law to be invoked only when the provocateurs among us move from speech to action."

The Dennis decision was widely construed as an abandonment by the Supreme Court of the clear-and-present-danger approach to the First Amendment. The Department of Justice proceeded to prosecute the second-string communist leaders, approximately a hundred of whom were jailed. Until 1956, when the Supreme Court in *Pennsylvania* v. *Nelson* interpreted the Smith Act as precluding state prosecutions for seditious advocacy against the *national* government, many state prosecutors also moved against these same communists. Although technically it was not illegal to be a member of the Communist party, the fact remained that holding party office involved grave risk of conviction for violating the Smith Act.

THE YATES CASE—DENNIS MODIFIED

In June 1957, in *Yates* v. *United States,* the Supreme Court by drastically modifying its Dennis dictum called a halt to the easy conviction of communist leaders. The Court, speaking through Justice Harlan, held that its Dennis decision had been misunderstood. The Smith Act does not outlaw the advocacy of the abstract doctrine of violent overthrow. "That sort of advocacy," Justice Harlan explained, "even though uttered with the hope that it may ultimately lead to violent revolution, is too remote from concrete action to be regarded as the kind of indoctrination preparatory to action which was condemned in Dennis. The essential distinction is that those to whom the advocacy is addressed must be urged *to do* something, now or in the future, rather than merely *to believe* in something."

What is the significance of the Yates decision? The Supreme Court denied that it was reversing the Dennis case, but certainly it severely restricted the sweep of that decision. Furthermore, although the Court deliberately refused to decide whether Congress could make it a crime to advocate the abstract doctrine of violent overthrow, it strongly hinted that officials so interpreting the Smith Act would be invading the constitutional danger zone.

Does the Yates decision mark a return to the clear-and-present-danger doctrine? Clearly the Court moved closer to the position that advocacy must have some immediate relationship to an unlawful act. Nonetheless, Harlan was careful to note that if persons urge others to act violently *now or in the future,* they violate the Smith Act, apparently even if there is no danger that violent acts will result.

From this brief survey of laws aimed at seditious advocacy it seems clear that *seditious speech if narrowly defined to cover only the advocacy of concrete acts of violence is, like libel and obscenity, not constitutionally protected.* Such narrowly construed anti-sedition acts leave communists and other totalitarians free to work for their political objectives so long as they abandon force or its advocacy.

THE INTERNAL SECURITY ACT OF 1950

With steadily increasing tension between the United States and the Soviet world, many have pressed for even more stringent restrictions on communist political activity than the Smith Act. When the "cold war" turned into a hot one in Korea, Congress responded with the Internal Security Act of 1950, popularly known as the McCarran Act. In addition to the so far ineffective provision mentioned on page 152, which outlaws conspiratorial action designed to establish a totalitarian dictatorship in the United States, the Internal Security Act also tries to strip the veil of secrecy from communist political activity and to impose certain disabilities on communists.

The act creates a Subversive Activities Control Board, which is to determine on the request of the Attorney General whether a particular organization is a communist action, front, or infiltrated organization. A communist *action* organization is defined as one that is substantially directed by the U.S.S.R. or operates primarily to advance the objectives of world communism. A communist *front* organization is one that is dominated by a communist action organization or that is operated for the purpose of giving aid to a communist organization or communist government. A communist-*infiltrated* organization is a group—a labor union, for example—that is substantially dominated by persons who are giving aid, actively and knowingly, to a communist action organization or a communist foreign government or who knowingly work to impair the military or industrial capacity of the United States. (Labor unions affiliated with national unions that have acted to expel communists are presumed by the law not to be communist-infiltrated.)

After the Subversive Activities Control Board issues a final order declaring an organization to be a communist organization and this order has been sustained by the courts, the following disabilities are imposed:

1. Action and front organizations must *register* annually with the Attorney General, giving names of officers and an account of all money spent and received, including its sources.
2. Action organizations must *report* the names of all their members. Members aware that their names are not registered must inform the Attorney General on pain of criminal punishment.
3. Action and front organizations must submit to the Attorney General full *information* on printing equipment under their control.
4. Action, front, and infiltrated organizations must *label* as communist propaganda all their publications sent through the mails or across state boundaries.
5. Infiltrated organizations *lose all rights* accorded to unions under national laws, and employers no longer have to bargain with them.
6. No member of an action, front, or infiltrated organization may apply for or use a *passport,* hold any nonelective federal *position,* or serve as an officer or employee of a labor *union.*
7. No member of an action organization may work in a *defense plant* listed by the Secretary of Defense as a defense facility; members of front and infiltrated organizations working in a defense plant must make known their membership.

The Internal Security Act also strengthens existing laws against espionage and sedition, adds to alien registration requirements, makes it more difficult for communist aliens to enter or remain in the United States, and establishes procedures for detaining, in the event of a national emergency, any person who can "reasonably" be expected to engage in acts of sabotage or espionage.

By 1960 the Attorney General had instituted proceedings before the Subversive Activities Control Board against some twenty organizations. The Board has declared the Communist party to be a communist action organization, has ordered five organizations to register as communist fronts, and has designated two unions as communist-infiltrated. But these organizations promptly appealed to the courts, where the cases are still pending. "In view of the constitutional doubts which spring from every cranny of the Internal Security Act, there will be a luxuriant growth of issues to be hacked away before the validity of this measure is clarified." [19]

THE COMMUNIST CONTROL ACT OF 1954

The purpose of the Internal Security Act of 1950 was to bring communists out into the open. But even before this act could be applied, Congress decided to take more drastic action. Although for some time there had been

---

[19] Ralph S. Brown, Jr., *Loyalty and Security* (Yale Univ. Press, 1958), p. 472. For more comprehensive discussion of the several laws discussed above, see Harold W. Chase, *Security and Liberty: The Problem of Native Communists, 1947-1955* (Random House, 1955).

agitation to outlaw the Communist party and its successors, no action was taken until 1954, partly because of doubts about the constitutionality of such a measure, partly because of doubts about its effectiveness.

In that year Congress declared that even the overt political activities of the Communist party serve as a front behind which the party can seduce individuals into the service of world communism and work toward the violent overthrow of the government of the United States. (Such a conspiracy, of course, is illegal; and evidence to support this finding, if properly presented in court proceedings, would be sufficient under existing law to throw the conspirators into jail.) The party's very existence, declared Congress, renders it a "clear, present, and continuing danger to the security of the United States." Therefore, in the Communist Control Act of 1954, Congress deprived the Communist party and its successors of "any of the rights, privileges, and immunities attendant upon legal bodies created under the laws of the United States" or any of the states.

The act does not make it a crime to be a communist (although members of the party may be subjected to the penalties that the Internal Security Act imposes on members of communist action organizations). The major effect of the law has been to deprive the Communist party of the right to seek places on election ballots for its candidates. For the first time in our history, a political party has been outlawed by the national government, and a group has been denied the opportunity to use the traditional instruments of democracy.

Disloyalty and the Public Service

Spies, saboteurs, and those who advocate the forceful overthrow of the government may be tried and punished under existing laws. But what about persons who commit no crimes and yet are sympathetic to the cause of communism, or who have joined organizations that the Attorney General believes to be subversive? Should they be permitted to work for the government, serve in the armed forces, work in defense plants, secure passports? Apparently most Americans believe that they should not, and a whole host of disabilities has been imposed upon such persons.

J. Edgar Hoover has estimated that there are about 5,000 hard-core communists in this country and perhaps ten times that many who are sympathetic to their cause. In order to forestall this group from securing public employment, receiving government-financed fellowships, joining the merchant marine, or working in defense plants, about twenty million Americans have been subjected to some kind of federal loyalty check. They may be questioned about their views on foreign policy, their reading, their friends, and the organizations to which they belong. In addition, Congress and at least six state legislatures have established committees to investigate un-American activities. These committees have checked into the loyalty of public employees, newspaper men, teachers, scientists, and others, and have "exposed" those whom the committee members believe to be un-American.

Employees of the executive branch of the national government have been particularly vulnerable to investigation. Until 1939 their private political life was of no concern to the government unless it intruded on their ability to perform their jobs. In that year, however, political tests were imposed, and persons who advocated the overthrow of the government, or who belonged to communist, Nazi, or fascist organizations, were disqualified from government service. During World War II, all applicants for government jobs were carefully investigated, and access to classified and secret information was denied to all except those who had been cleared. Persons suspected of disloyalty were either fired or transferred to nonsensitive positions—that is, positions not directly concerned with national security.

THE TRUMAN LOYALTY PROGRAM

In 1947, President Truman, responding to public concern over disclosures of communist espionage, stepped up the program of loyalty investigations and ordered all employees of the executive branch and all future applicants to be removed or denied employment if there was "reasonable grounds for belief that the person was disloyal." Then in 1951 the President made the standards more stringent by calling for dismissal "if there were reasonable doubt as to loyalty." Among the factors to be taken into account in determing loyalty was membership in an organization judged by the Attorney General to be totalitarian, fascist, communist, or subversive. (The Attorney General's list of such organizations is not to be confused with organizations declared communistic by the Subversive Activities Control Board; see p. 156.) An employee charged with disloyalty had a right to a hearing before a loyalty board in his own agency with an appeal to a central loyalty review board. Employees were entitled to engage counsel, to present evidence, and to be informed of the charges against them. However, the investigative agency did not have to disclose the names of confidential informants, not even to the boards that were judging the case.

This loyalty program applied to all members of the executive branch, from grounds-keepers to cabinet members. In addition there were, and are, various *security* programs for sensitive positions, those directly concerned with national security. Persons holding sensitive positions can be suspended *immediately* not only for doubts about their loyalty but for other reasons, such as untrustworthiness, liability to blackmail, and drunkenness.

In 1950 Congress supplemented the President's executive orders and specifically authorized the heads of eleven sensitive agencies and departments, including Defense, State, and the Atomic Energy Commission, to suspend immediately without pay any employee whose dismissal is essential to national security. Permanent employees, however, were entitled to a hearing and a written statement of the final decision. The President was also authorized to apply these provisions to other agencies whenever he deems it necessary "in the best interests of national security."

THE EISENHOWER SECURITY PROGRAM

In 1953, President Eisenhower abolished the Truman loyalty program and, citing the 1950 Act of Congress as his authority, extended the security program to all executive employees. Through executive order, he directed that the head of an agency should immediately dismiss any employee regarded as a security risk because of disloyalty, character faults such as drug addiction or general untrustworthiness, or refusal to testify before a congressional committee. Under the revised program, loyalty boards were abolished, but permanent employees could request hearings before panels drawn from outside their agencies. The head of the agency, however, was to make the final decision in each case. As before, the government was not required to disclose the names of its informants.

Then in 1956 the Supreme Court, without ruling directly on the constitutionality of the security program, held in *Cole* v. *Young* that the President had unlawfully extended the security programs to nonsensitive agencies. A majority ruled that Congress had intended to authorize summary dismissal only for employees who held positions immediately involving the nation's safety.

It may be that Congress will revive the *status quo ante* and extend the security programs again to all employees. Even if it does not, existing civil service regulations make it unlawful for members of communist organizations to work for the government. These regulations also permit dismissal of all employees "for the good of the service," a category broad enough to cover most persons thought to be security risks. At any rate, some kind of check on the loyalty of employees will be with us for a long time.

In addition to these investigations into the political activities of its own employees, the national government has operated an Industrial Security Program covering employees of defense contractors and a Port Security Clearance Program covering the maritime labor force, and the military services look into the political background of members of the armed forces. Moreover, in the Taft-Hartley Act the government imposed a loyalty oath on union officials as a condition of their unions' being permitted to file complaints before the National Labor Relations Board; [20] and the National Defense Education Act of 1958 requires applicants for loans or fellowships to sign loyalty affidavits. Both the Taft-Hartley and Defense Education oaths even go so far as to include provisions designed to determine whether the affiviant *believes* in the doctrines of violent overthrow of government.

---

[20] This provision was repealed in 1959, but members of the Communist Party are prohibited from serving as union officers.

STATE LOYALTY PROGRAMS

Although few positions occupied by state and local officials can be thought to affect directly our national security, almost all our states today require loyalty oaths from public employees, and some even require oaths from attorneys, students in the state university, public accountants, occupants of public housing projects, and persons applying for unemployment compensation. One state includes wrestlers and fighters, on the grounds, according to the executive secretary of the state athletic commission, that "we didn't want to license a professional boxer and wrestler who might become a hero in the eyes of youthful fans and then discover he was a Communist." [21]

Few object to oaths requiring one to swear or to affirm loyalty to the United States. But state loyalty oaths reverse the normal presumption of loyalty and proceed on the assumption that one is disloyal unless he swears to the contrary.[22] Of the several kinds of loyalty oaths required by the states, the more carefully drawn are limited to statements that the person does not advocate the overthrow of government by unlawful means or knowingly belong to any organization that does. But some of the oaths range much further and lack precision.

THE CONSTITUTIONALITY OF LOYALTY OATHS
AND SECURITY INVESTIGATIONS

The Supreme Court has ruled that loyalty oaths may be required as a condition of public employment, provided they require only that the individual swear he does not advocate overthrow by unlawful means or *knowingly* belong to organizations that so advocate. The oaths cannot be used, however, to disqualify persons who innocently join subversive organizations.[23] Moreover, the Supreme Court and other courts generally have been hostile to attempts to demand loyalty oaths of individuals as a condition of receiving general public benefits and services. The lower courts have thrown out oath requirements for occupants of public housing projects,[24] and the Supreme Court invalidated a California requirement that church organizations and veterans sign loyalty affidavits in order to receive tax exemptions normally given to religious institutions and veterans.[25] The Taft-Hartley oath is the only one the Court has so far sustained for nonpublic employees.[26] The oath requirement of the Defense Education Act has not as yet been challenged before the courts.

---

[21] See testimony before Subcommittee on Constitutional Rights of the Senate Committee on the Judiciary, Hearings, *Security and Constitutional Rights,* 84 Cong., 2 Sess., November 17, 1955, p. 350.

[22] See Milton Greenberg, "Loyalty Oaths: An Appraisal of the Legal Issues," *The Journal of Politics,* Vol. 20, 1958, pp. 487-514.

[23] *Wieman* v. *Updegraff* (1952).

[24] *Rudder* v. *United States,* U.S.C.A. for D.C. (1955).

[25] *Speiser* v. *Randall* (1958) and *First Unitarian Church of Los Angeles* v. *County of Los Angeles* (1958).

[26] *American Communications Association* v. *Douds* (1955).

What about loyalty-security programs that go beyond oaths? Obviously a government has the constitutional power to fire its own employees. The constitutional problems are not presented by the dismissal of public employees but rather by the government's charging an employee with being "of doubtful loyalty" or "a bad security risk." There are two facets to be considered—first, the substantive power of government officials to make such declarations; second, the procedures that are used to do so.

The Supreme Court has not ruled directly on these questions, but by a four-to-four vote it left undisturbed a decision of the Court of Appeals for the District of Columbia sustaining the Truman loyalty program.[27] The Court of Appeals held that the government could establish reasonable qualifications for its employees and that it was reasonable to require that they be persons of unquestionable loyalty. Moreover, the Court of Appeals held that since employment is a privilege and not a right no employee has a right to a hearing or to be confronted by his accusers but may be dismissed summarily. Circuit Judge Henry Edgerton dissented, arguing that though employees have no right to their jobs, they do have the right to be treated fairly and that they are denied such treatment when branded as disloyal on the basis of charges brought by "faceless informers." He argued that at least in non-sensitive positions the government could not punish employees merely for having peacefully exercised their political rights.

Despite its avoidance of direct rulings on the underlying constitutional questions presented by the loyalty-security programs, the Supreme Court did rule that organizations listed by the Attorney General as being subversive are entitled to a formal hearing,[28] and at every opportunity the Court has narrowly construed the loyalty-security regulations. In addition to limiting the Eisenhower security program to security-sensitive positions, it has ruled that the Department of Defense had not been authorized either by Congress or the President to establish security regulations for employees of defense contractors that could result in denial of security clearance without the employees' having the opportunity to confront and cross-examine adverse witnesses.[29] The Defense Department was also called to task for using the pre-service record of soldiers as a basis for giving them less than honorable discharges.[30] Furthermore, a court of appeals required the Coast Guard to observe more careful procedures in its administration of the Port Security Clearance Program,[31] a decision that the Supreme Court would so obviously have approved that the government did not even bother to appeal.

---

[27] *Bailey* v. *Richardson* (1951).
[28] *Joint-Anti-Fascist Refugee Committee* v. *McGrath* (1951)
[29] *Greene* v. *McElroy* (1959).
[30] *Harmon* v. *Brucker* (1958).
[31] *Parker* v. *Lester* (1955).

THE OPERATION AND IMPACT
OF LOYALTY-SECURITY HEARINGS

Many of the objections to the loyalty-security programs have to do with the procedures used. The government is allowed to judge loyalty on the basis of hearsay evidence. Frequently neither the "accused" nor the board sifting the evidence knows where the charges came from or who the informants are. Frequently the hearings go far afield. Not untypically, in one security hearing a witness was asked, "Do you consider Dr. V— as a religious man?" and "Was he an extremist on equality?" At another hearing, one of the charges against the person under investigation was that years ago he had attended a dinner of an organization that had since been cited as a communist front, a dinner also attended by many Washington notables.[32]

One of the most frequently criticized aspects of loyalty-security hearings has been the government's use of unidentified informants. Although many critics concede that the government may be justified in refusing to disclose the names of regularly established informants because disclosure would destroy their usefulness in counterespionage work, they see no reason why the government should be allowed to use derogatory information supplied by casual informants—next-door neighbors, fellow employees, former classmates, and so on—unless they are willing to disclose their identities and be subject to cross-examination. Such was the recommendation of the Commission on Government Security, created by Congress in 1955 and composed of men appointed by the President, the President of the Senate, and the Speaker of the House of Representatives.[33]

But no matter how fairly they are administered, programs calling for a check on the political activities of millions of Americans may create an atmosphere of suspicion that does more harm, some fear, than could be done by communists in positions not involving national security. Unquestionably the morale of civil servants has suffered, especially in the early 1950's. A task force of the Second Hoover Commission reported, "There is fear that honest and loyal employees can be destroyed by unsupported or trivial derogatory charges; there is fear that security authorities can be stampeded; and there is fear that security charges are at times a means of making 'political' removals."[34]

Are the various security-loyalty programs necessary? Most citizens seem to believe that the tactics of communists and the necessities of the cold war require unusual precautions in sensitive agencies such as the Federal Bureau of Investigation, Atomic Energy Commission, State Department, Defense Depart-

---

[32] See *Vitarelli* v. *Seaton* (1959) and *Greene* v. *McElroy* (1959).

[33] *Report of the Commission on Government Security* (Government Printing Office, 1957), pp. 669-671.

[34] Commission on Organization of the Executive Branch of the Government, *Task Force Report on Personnel and Civil Service* (Government Printing Office, 1955), p. 121.

ment, and other vital departments exposed to internal subversion and foreign influence. But there is far less agreement on the need for intensive investigations into the beliefs and political actions of thousands of persons in non-sensitive positions.

Justice Clark, dissenting in *Cole* v. *Young,* argued, "It is unrealistic to say that the Government can be protected merely by applying [the security program] to sensitive jobs. One never knows just which job is sensitive. The janitor might prove to be in as important a spot security-wise as the top employee in the building." The Commission on Government Security also recommended full loyalty investigations for all government employees and continuation and extension of existing programs. However, many others who have studied our entire security system want detailed investigations into political associations to be limited to those in sensitive positions.[35] Loyalty-security programs, they argue, are inherently dangerous; the gains in security they achieve do not balance the resulting losses in liberty and pressures to conform. They favor placing more reliance on the old-fashioned procedures of police work and counterespionage and less on the new-fangled techniques of security hearings.

WHERE WE STAND
IN THE BATTLE AGAINST DISLOYALTY

As a result of the security programs, loyalty oaths, the Smith Act, Internal Security Act, the Communist Control Act, and similar state laws, communists and those suspected of communistic sympathies are now subject to many restrictions. A communist alien may not enter the United States, may be deported from the United States, and cannot become an American citizen. Communists cannot work for the federal government, for most state and local governments, or for defense industries. They cannot teach in most school systems, cannot serve as labor union officials, cannot travel abroad. They face prosecution for advocating the overthrow of the government by force and contributing to the establishment of totalitarian dictatorships. They are denied the right to run for elective office. In addition to these governmental restrictions, they must cope with the many serious limitations that grow out of public abhorrence of their ideas and activities.

Some feel that certain of these restrictions are unjustified. Although they would use every resource to ferret out and punish anyone guilty of espionage or conspiracy to overthrow the government by force, they would not penalize

---

[35] See, for example, *Report of the Special Committee on the Federal-Loyalty-Security Program* of the Association of the Bar of the City of New York (Dodd, Mead, 1956); Ralph S. Brown, Jr., *Loyalty and Security* (Yale Univ. Press, 1958), pp. 463-485; Adam Yarmolinsky, *Case Studies in Personnel Security* (The Bureau of National Affairs, Inc., 1955); Subcommittee on Constitutional Rights of Senate Committee on the Judiciary, *Hearings on Security and Constitutional Rights,* November 14-18, 21-23, 25, 28-29, 1956, 84 Cong., 2 Sess.; Subcommittee on Reorganization of the Senate Committee on Government Operations, *Hearings on Commission on Government Security,* March 8-11, 14-18, 1955, 84 Cong., 1 Sess.

persons who have combined for political action nor deny antidemocrats the right to use the regular methods of democratic government. They would place no restrictions on communists except those absolutely necessary to protect national safety. These critics of governmental restrictions are moved, not by love for communists, but by the conviction that democracy itself is endangered when any group is punished because its ideas are abhorrent to the majority. As Justice Jackson stated it, "the right of every American to equal treatment before the law is wrapped up in the same constitutional bundle with those of the communists."

Those who support governmental limitations on communist activity argue that the communists are not entitled to any rights, since they are at war with our whole democratic system. They insist that the communists, unless they are carefully controlled, will take advantage of their status as a legitimate political party to camouflage their underground activities. Only by denying communists their veil of secrecy can innocent persons be protected. Democratic government, it is contended, must curtail the freedom of those who would destroy freedom.

All recognize that we must act to protect ourselves against those who are conspiring to destroy our democratic system. On the other hand, all recognize that we must be careful not to jeopardize the rights that we have developed to prevent the growth of tyranny. An undemocratic but relatively insignificant minority does not justify panic. In fact, it is in times of national peril that our traditional liberties must be most steadfastly strengthened and protected.

Summary

The Constitution protects the rights of freedom of conscience and expression from infringement by either national or state governments. These basic liberties are threatened by enemies of democracy. But in protecting freedom from totalitarians, the resort—either from malice or ignorance—to totalitarian patterns of thought control is a danger that cannot be overlooked.

Head-on assaults on freedom are relatively rare. The real threat comes from flanking attacks. Liberty can be lost by erosion as well as by flood. A little impairment here, a little there—never enough at one time to alert the lethargic—this is the danger. That eternal vigilance is the price of liberty is more than a Fourth of July truism; it is a statement of profound truth.

Equality under the Law

Certain liberties are essential to the operation of democratic government. But these liberties are not merely means of attaining self-government; they are ends in themselves. They exist not for the government; rather, the government exists to protect them. Our forefathers called them natural rights—today we speak of human rights—but the belief is still the same, the belief in the moral primacy of men over government and in the dignity and fundamental worth of *each* individual.

The Declaration of Independence proclaims in ringing terms, "We hold these truths to be self-evident, that all men are created equal, that they are endowed by their Creator with certain unalienable rights, that among these are life, liberty, and the pursuit of happiness. That to secure these rights, governments are instituted among men. . . ." The Declaration does not talk about the equality of white, Christian, or Anglo-Saxon men, but of *all* men. This creed of individual dignity and equality is older than the Declaration of Independence; its roots go back at least as far as the teachings of Judaism and Christianity. To act by this creed, to bring practice into conformity with principles, has long been a central preoccupation of Americans.

Today no problem is more compelling than that of insuring to every American his basic *civil rights,* his right to enjoy his life and liberty, and to pursue his happiness without discrimination because of his race, religion, national origin, or any other irrelevant characteristic. American democracy, despite its many triumphs, has not extended civil rights to all people, especially not to Negroes. From the time he is born until he dies a Negro suffers handicaps that no other American has to face—handicaps imposed on him by other Americans. Because we know this and feel it deeply, the lack of racial equality is an injury that every American must live with day by day.

What should we do to protect civil rights? This question has been of significance in our presidential elections; it gives rise each year to battles in Congress and to debates in state legislatures and city councils. What we do, or fail to do, has significance beyond our national borders. Our attacks on communist totalitarianism throughout the world lose some of their force in the light of the obvious chinks in our democratic armor. Colored peoples in Asia and Africa, our potential allies, follow the treatment of American Negroes with more than casual interest. And it is not only the colored people who are concerned, for all who hear us talk of democracy may lose faith in a government that denies in fact the very rights that it promises in theory. As Justice Douglas has said, "If we are truly to be an arsenal of democratic faith, we must first inspire and justify that faith by our own performance." [1]

Our denial of equal rights not only negates the equality that the Declaration of Independence champions—it is also contrary to the commands of the Constitution. For under the Constitution each person has the right to live and work and participate in public affairs, free of discriminatory laws. The Constitution provides two ways of protecting these civil rights: first, by seeing to it that *government* itself imposes no discriminatory barriers; second, by granting the national and state governments authority to act positively to protect civil rights against interference by *private individuals*. In this chapter we shall be concerned with both these aspects, government as a *threat* to civil rights and government as the *protector* of civil rights.

The Life— and Death?—of Jim Crow

Laws requiring the segregation of Negroes and whites date only from the end of the nineteenth century.[2] Prior to that time it was social custom and economic status, rather than law, that kept the two races apart. Then toward the end of the nineteenth century segregationists insisted that laws were needed to maintain racial segregation. Before long, southern states and cities had made it a crime for whites and Negroes to ride in the same car on a train, attend the same theater, or go to the same schools. "Jim Crow" laws, as they came to be called, soon blanketed southern life.

How could these segregation laws be adopted and enforced in the face of the Fourteenth Amendment, which declares: "No state [including any subdivision thereof] shall deny to any person within its jurisdiction the equal protection of the laws. . . ."? Supporters of Jim Crow argue that the Constitution simply forbids discriminatory classification and that classification on the basis of race is not discriminatory so long as *equal facilites* are made available to Negroes. Furthermore, they insist, segregation laws are needed to preserve public order.

Before turning to the question of the constitutionality of segregation laws, let us look briefly at this more general problem of the power of government

---

[1] "Freedom Train Address, 1949" in A. T. Mason, *Free Government in the Making* (Oxford Univ. Press, 1949), p. 843.

[2] C. Vann Woodward, *The Strange Career of Jim Crow* (Oxford Univ. Press, 1955).

to classify. Most laws classify, but what the Constitution forbids is *unreasonable* classification. (Although there is no equal-protection clause limiting the national government, unreasonable classification on its part is made unconstitutional by the due-process clause of the Fifth Amendment.) A classification is unreasonable when there is no relation between the classes it creates and permissible governmental goals. For example, a law prohibiting redheads from voting would be unreasonable, because there is no relation between red hair and the ability to vote. On the other hand, laws denying to persons under 21 the right to vote, to marry without the permission of their parents, or to drive a car are reasonable because (to most adults, at least) there seems to be a relationship between maturity and voting, marrying, and driving. Similarly, the Supreme Court has held the following classifications to be reasonable: classification of persons on the basis of income for tax purposes, classification of property according to its use for zoning purposes, classification of employers by the number of their employees for purposes of collecting social security taxes, classification of persons by sex for purposes of regulating hours and conditions of employment.

Classifications based on religion, national origin, or race, especially the last, however, have caused great controversy. The courts have always been particularly suspicious of these classifications, allowing them only in the most unusual cases—for example, when the government can demonstrate some exceptional justification and show some relation between race or religion or national origin and the permissible goal. Since the end of World War II the Supreme Court has come pretty close to the view that *all* racial classifications are inherently arbitrary and unconstitutional. But that gets ahead of our story.

IS SEGREGATION DISCRIMINATION?

Since the ratification of the Fourteenth Amendment and the abolition of slavery, it has been unconstitutional for governments to discriminate against Negroes or any other racial or religious groups. But in 1896 the Supreme Court in *Plessy* v. *Ferguson* endorsed the view that racial *segregation* did not constitute discrimination, and that states could by law require the separation of races in public places so long as *equal accommodations* for all were provided. Even equal accommodations were not required except in the case of services provided out of public funds or in a limited category of public utilities, such as trains and buses. Under this celebrated *separate-but-equal* formula, several states, most of them in the South, enforced segregation in transportation, places of public accommodation such as inns, restaurants, and theaters, and in schools and colleges.

For many years the "equal" part of the formula was meaningless in actual practice. The Supreme Court itself required only a slight nod on the part of the states in the direction of equality. In 1899, for example, the Court found no denial of equal protection in the fact that a county provided a high school for white children, but none for the sixty colored children of the district.[3] By the 1950's, despite much improvement, educational facilities available for Negroes in segregated states were frequently not equal in fact to those provided for whites. A report of the United States Office of Education, for example, stated that to equalize Negro and white schools, Negro teachers' salaries would have to be advanced by 44 per cent, current expenses by 80 per cent, and plant and equipment by 400 per cent. In 1950 in all the segregated states there were fourteen medical schools for whites, none for Negroes; sixteen law schools for whites, five for Negroes; fifteen engineering schools for whites, none for Negroes; five dentistry schools for whites, none for Negroes.

Beginning in the late 1930's Negroes started to file law suits challenging the separate-but-equal doctrine as a sham. They cited facts to show that in practice separate-but-equal always resulted in discrimination against Negroes. However, the Supreme Court justices were not yet willing to upset the doctrine directly. Rather, they began to undermine it. No longer satisfied with mere token equality, the courts began first to scrutinize each situation and in case after case to order facilities to be equalized.

Then in 1950, the Supreme Court, though specifically refusing either to affirm or reject the doctrine of *Plessy* v. *Ferguson,* ruled (*Sweatt* v. *Painter*) that Negroes otherwise qualified could not be denied admission to state law schools. A segregated legal education, said the Court, was not in fact equal to a non-segregated one and could never be made equal. To segregate Negroes into schools from which the state excluded members of the white race, which numbered 85 per cent of the population—including most of the lawyers, witnesses, jurors, judges, and other officials with whom Negroes would be dealing when they became members of the bar—in itself discriminated against Negroes.

On the same day it handed down the decision in the Sweatt case, the Supreme Court held that once a state admitted a Negro to a graduate school, it could not segregate him within the school (*McLaurin* v. *Oklahoma*). Clearly the legal underpinnings of segregation were getting shaky. If a state could not segregate within a school, could it do so between schools? If segregated legal education is always discriminatory, why would this not be the case for *all* kinds of education? Although for a while the Court continued to avoid a specific overruling of the separate-but-equal doctrine, no one could doubt the direction of its decisions. But how far would it go?

THE END OF SEPARATE-BUT-EQUAL:
BROWN v. *BOARD OF EDUCATION*

Finally, in 1952, the Supreme Court agreed to consider five cases involving elementary and secondary schools that squarely challenged the sep--

---

[3] *Cumming* v. *County Board of Education.*

arate-but-equal doctrine. For two years the Court carefully considered the issues. By Monday, May 17, 1954, the last decision day before the end of the Court's term, no decision had been forthcoming. No one except the Supreme Court justices themselves knew for sure if this would be the day the decision would be announced. But by 9 A.M., when the doors opened to the great main hall, a capacity crowd had already formed.

The people stood quietly for another two hours until the doors to the courtroom itself were opened. At 11:45 the lawyers came in and took the front benches. The high-ceilinged, marbled-columned courtroom awed the audience into silence. Promptly at high noon the red velvet curtains parted behind the nine chairs on the dais, the audience rose, and the Chief Justice and his eight black-robed associates took their seats. The more knowledgeable of the spectators pointed out to their neighbors that Associate Justice Robert Jackson, who was recovering from a heart attack, had left his hospital room in order to be present. This must be the day.

For fifty-two minutes three justices took turns reading decisions, but they were not the ones that had drawn the crowd to the courtroom. Then at 12:52 P.M. the Chief Justice picked up a printed document and began to read in a clear voice: "Does segregation of children in public schools solely on the basis of race, even though the physical facilities and other tangible factors may be equal, deprive the children of the minority group of equal educational opportunity? *We believe it does.*" Citing psychological findings as well as legal sources, the Chief Justice continued:

> In these days it is doubtful that any child may reasonably be expected to succeed in life if he is denied the opportunity of an education. . . . To separate [children] from others of similar age and qualifications solely because of their race generates a feeling of inferiority as to their status in the community that may affect their hearts and minds in a way unlikely ever to be undone.

The Supreme Court justices, knowing their decision conflicted with long-established southern customs and recognizing the formidable problems involved, postponed for a year any final decree. Then in May 1955, after hearing suggestions from state attorney generals, the High Court issued its implementation decree. The Supreme Court directed local school authorities to proceed "with all deliberate speed" to make a prompt and reasonable start toward admitting Negroes to public schools on a racially nondiscriminatory basis. The Court stated, however, that local officials could take time to make necessary administrative adjustments and need not immediately desegregate schools under their jurisdiction. The Supreme Court did not itself formulate precise instructions, but rather returned the cases to the federal district judges (who could best take into account the great variety of local conditions) to supervise the implementation of desegregation by local school authorities.[4]

---

4 *Brown* v. *Board of Education* (1955).

Following its decisions in the Brown Case, also known as the *School Segregation Cases,* the Supreme Court made it clear that the time allowed to desegregate the elementary and secondary schools was not to be granted for the desegregation of public professional or graduate schools; at this level no delay was to be allowed in admitting otherwise qualified Negroes.[5] The Court also moved from school segregation into other areas and has ruled that laws requiring the segregated use of public recreational facilities (parks, golf courses, and so forth) and public transportation are also unconstitutional.[6] Clearly, the separate-but-equal formula is dead, and government action at any level to require racial segregation is unconstitutional.

"A GENERATION OF LITIGATION"

The school segregation decisions have spawned what is likely to be a "generation of litigation." There have already been over 150 court cases as those favoring and those opposing desegregation fight out the issues before the judges. From this mass of litigation the following legal doctrines have been reasonably clearly established:

1. The Supreme Court's school segregation decisions do not require states to force Negroes and whites to attend the same schools, but states may not use legal compulsion to keep them from doing so. The Constitution requires that school authorities ignore race as a factor in assigning pupils to particular schools or school rooms.

2. School authorities may delay the complete desegregation of schools under their jurisdiction, but they are constitutionally obligated to make an immediate start.

3. Community opposition to desegregation, even violent protests, does not justify a delay in the desegregation programs. If there is violence, the duty of public officials is to proceed against those who are acting unlawfully; they may not use the possibility of violence to deprive Negro children of their right to attend nonsegregated schools. In the Little Rock case, *Cooper* v. *Aaron* (1958), in an opinion signed by all members of the Court individually—an unprecedented move to indicate their unanimity and strength of conviction—the Court stated: "Law and order are not here to be preserved by depriving the Negro children of their constitutional rights."

4. A state or school district may not close only the public schools to which Negroes have been assigned, for such action discriminates not only against Negroes but also the white students who have been assigned to these schools. Although no state has any national constitutional obligation to maintain public schools, if it does operate public schools it may not operate them just for students in segregated institutions.

---

[5] *Hawkins* v. *Florida Board of Control* (1956).
[6] *Baltimore* v. *Dawson* (1955); *Holmes* v. *Atlanta* (1955); and *Gayle* v. *Browder* (1956).

5. Evasive schemes designed to keep public schools segregated—for example, pretending to make public schools private, or assigning Negro children to segregated schools but doing so ostensibly for some reason other than race—are unconstitutional. Nor may states provide financial or other assistance to private schools that do segregate. As the Supreme Court phrased it in *Cooper v. Aaron,* "The Constitutional rights of children not to be discriminated against in school admission on grounds of race or color declared by this Court in the Brown case can neither be nullified openly and directly by state legislators or state executives or judicial officers, nor nullified indirectly by them through evasive schemes for segregation whether attempted 'ingeniously or ingenuously.' "

Desegregation— Problem and Promise

The Supreme Court has spoken. But it is one thing for the justices to declare segregation unconstitutional, another thing to abolish segregation in practice. Six years, 150 federal court cases, two acts of Congress, over 200 state laws, a dozen or so state court rulings, a brace of books, thousands of articles, millions of speeches, and two score "incidents" after the Brown case, it is still too soon to know precisely what the consequence of this famous decision will be. Short of revolutionary developments, segregation imposed by government will be abolished, but no one knows how, or when, for the decision has provoked an intense controversy, has led to action, reaction, and inaction at every level of government, and has called forth a states-rights resistance movement rivaled only by that preceding the Civil War.

Clearly the problems presented by desegregation are not to be solved by judges alone. For the abolition of legally required segregation presents to the American people—to the President and Congress, to state officials, to school administrators, ultimately to all of us—a problem and a challenge of enormous complexity and importance. What has been the public response in the years since the Court declared segregation unconstitutional?

PROGRESS TO DATE

In 1954, at the time of the Brown case, segregation was required in the District of Columbia and in seventeen states stretching from Texas to the Atlantic coast, from the Gulf of Mexico to Missouri, Kentucky, and West Virginia. Six years later the picture was this: full compliance had been achieved, or almost achieved, in the District of Columbia, Missouri, Maryland, Kentucky, West Virginia, Oklahoma, and Delaware. In Virginia, North Carolina, Tennessee, Texas, Arkansas, and Florida, token compliance had been achieved in a few cities. Although in some of these states desegregation had been resisted by violent demonstrations, except in Arkansas and Texas governors supported by local authorities had used their executive powers to back up school boards and to maintain order. In Little Rock, Arkansas, the governor had sided with the segregationists to oppose local officials, but after the intervention of national authorities and a year's delay, token desegregation was reestablished there in 1959.

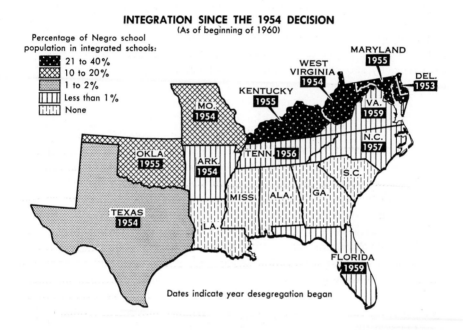

INTEGRATION SINCE THE 1954 DECISION
(As of beginning of 1960)

Percentage of Negro school population in integrated schools:
- 21 to 40%
- 10 to 20%
- 1 to 2%
- Less than 1%
- None

Dates indicate year desegregation began

In Louisiana, the state-supported colleges and universities were desegregated, but as schools opened in 1959 all public schools were still segregated, though action in New Orleans could not be delayed much longer. In Alabama, Georgia, Mississippi, and South Carolina all schools still operated on a segregated basis, but court action in Atlanta and Birmingham promised (or threatened, depending on one's point of view) to lead to desegregation in these cities in the not-too-distant future.

RESPONSE IN THE SOUTH

Many white southerners are openly defiant. The Supreme Court, they argue, is ignoring strongly held racial attitudes, the relationship between the two races that has been worked out over the years, the traditional way of life in the South. According to their views, Negroes are not ready for integration because of deficiencies in culture, health, and even in innate capacities. Integration, they charge, is a step toward "race mongrelization." Many southerners also disagree strongly with the Supreme Court's interpretation of the Constitution. To them the decision is bad law and bad policy. "No decision of the

Supreme Court," said former Governor (now Senator) Herman Talmadge of Georgia, "is entitled to any greater moral weight than its content merits." [7]

In Congress, representatives of the Deep South have attacked the Supreme Court justices and have supported moves to "curb the Court." Southern state legislatures, reaching back to pre-Civil War precedents, have asserted the right to "interpose" and resist the Supreme Court mandates; some have even claimed the right to declare the Court's decisions null and void. They have taken steps to thwart the Court's decrees, primarily by giving officials power to assign Negro pupils to segregated schools but ostensibly for reasons other than race, by subsidizing private education or denying state money to local authorities who allow mixed schools, or by using the pretext of violence to close desegregated institutions. Although many of these measures have been and others will eventually be declared unconstitutional, they will allow years of delay.

A host of organizations have sprung up in the South to fight for continued school segregation. The most important of these, the White Citizens Councils, have claimed a membership of half a million persons. Among the members are some political leaders who, either out of genuine conviction or a desire to survive politically, though decrying force, have urged parents to barricade and boycott schools—even at the risk of creating riots—in order to prevent Negro children from attending schools formerly reserved for whites.

Some white southerners are wholeheartedly in favor of integration. They regard the Supreme Court decision as a milestone in the long struggle to achieve equal treatment and to bring into reality the promise of the American Revolution.

Outside the South, the decision has been applauded by church leaders, labor organizations, newspaper editors, teachers, and by many others, including, of course, Negroes in both North and South. Those who approve the decision, however, differ on how to proceed. Some, such as the leaders of the National Association for the Advancement of Colored People (see p. 297), argue that too much delay will play into the hands of the segregationists and make integration much harder to achieve in the long run. The Supreme Court decision, they hold, calls for a drastic but necessary surgical operation, and prolonging the operation will only make matters worse. They point out that delay and obstruction help to create incidents of violence and extremism. They are concerned, moreover, about the millions of Negro children now in school who will miss their right to a first-class education if integration is delayed. Negro children, they insist, do not need a good primary or high-school education in ten years; they need it now.

Finally, there is the "moderate" position. In both the North and the South the moderates feel that history is on the side of eventual desegregation. They point out that the South is changing economically and socially as it

---

[7] Herman E. Talmadge, "Schools Systems, Segregation and the Supreme Court," *Mercer Law Review*, Vol. VI, 1954-55.

becomes increasingly industrialized and urbanized. Every year, it attracts thousands of people from the North and West, who bring with them new social and political attitudes. Many southern Negroes are still moving north; those who stay in the South are winning the right to vote (see pp. 180-181). "All in all," says an Arkansas editor, "the cultural, political, and economic isolation which is necessary to the preservation of the region's special identity is breaking down—and southerners themselves are speeding the process in many ways. . . ." [8]

IT'S AN AMERICAN, NOT A SOUTHERN PROBLEM.

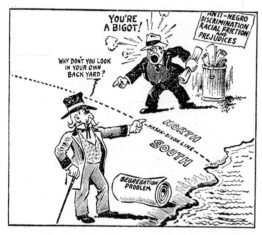

Courtesy *The Richmond Times-Dispatch* and Seibel

THE GREAT GAME OF HOW-NOT-TO.

Courtesy *St. Louis Post-Dispatch* and Fitzpatrick

Two views of desegregation.

Moderates in the South, however, find it difficult to express their opinions or develop programs of action. Those favoring cautious but deliberate steps toward integration are subjected to intense pressures. Public officials taking a moderate stand have often been defeated at the polls. Teachers who favor integration risk losing their jobs. In some localities advocacy of integration is considered almost a criminal offense. Negroes, barred from the ballot boxes in many areas, are unable to use democratic techniques to defend their rights. Some states have banned legal action by the NAACP and other groups working to enforce the Supreme Court's decisions. Clearly, such responses have served to sharpen rather than resolve the issues involved and have minimized, at least for the moment, the role and voice of the moderates.

[8] Harry S. Ashmore, *The Negro and the Schools* (Univ. of North Carolina Press, 1954), pp. 138-139.

The challenge presented by the Supreme Court's decisions is national, not just southern. Many communities in the North face the same problems as those in the South. Although for many years segregation has not been required by law in the North, a condition of virtual segregation in the schools has been created in many communities by residential segregation, social pressures, gerrymandering of school districts, and other devices. Northern Negroes face other kinds of discrimination as well. In some cities their homes have been bombed and their lives threatened. They face discrimination in housing, jobs, and public places. Well-meaning northerners and southerners, white and Negro alike, have a great deal to learn from one another in their continuing effort to make the promise of the American Dream a reality to all its citizens.

Color Bar at the Polls

Equality at the polls is one of the most important civil rights still denied to many Negroes, for their social, economic, and legal rights depend largely on their success in gaining—and exercising—the right to vote.

After the Civil War the Radical Republicans gained control first of Congress and then of the White House. They were determined to protect the hard-won freedom of the newly liberated Negroes, and, even more, to secure the supremacy of the North and of the Republican party. To accomplish both ends, they decided to establish *constitutionally* through the Fourteenth and Fifteenth amendments the Negro's citizenship and his right to vote.

The Fourteenth Amendment, after granting citizenship to Negroes (see p. 224), forbids states to deprive any person of the equal protection of the laws. Hence, a state law is unconstitutional if it gives whites the right to vote but denies it to Negroes who are otherwise qualified. The Fourteenth Amendment further declares that if, in any state, for any reason other than participation in rebellion or other crime, male citizens 21 years and over are denied the right to vote, the state is to suffer a proportionate loss of representation in the House of Representatives.

The Fourteenth Amendment implicitly denies states the right to deprive Negroes of the suffrage because of their race. The Fifteenth Amendment makes this denial explicit: "The right of citizens of the United States to vote shall not be denied or abridged by the United States or by any State on account of race, color, or previous condition of servitude."

For over a decade after the Civil War, the provisions of the Fourteenth and Fifteenth amendments were backed up by federal troops. Negroes, in alliance with northern Radical Republicans ("carpetbaggers") and certain white southerners ("scalawags"), assumed full control of some state governments. The new regimes passed good laws as well as bad, but they were loathed and feared by all "patriotic" white southerners.

Then came the counterrevolution. Even before federal troops were withdrawn from the South in 1877, white Democrats had begun to regain power.

Organizing secret societies like the Knights of the White Camelia and the Ku Klux Klan, the aroused southerners set out to restore southern government to white rule. Often they resorted to threats, force, and fraud, to midnight shootings, burnings, and whippings. Many Negroes concluded that it would be healthier to stay away from the polls than to insist on their vote, and the carpetbaggers began to retreat north.

CIRCUMVENTING THE FOURTEENTH AND FIFTEENTH AMENDMENTS "LEGALLY"

Once they had regained control of southern state governments, southern Democrats resolved to continue to keep the Negro from voting. At first they continued to rely only on social pressures and threats of violence. But toward the end of the nineteenth century, for the first time since the Civil War there were in many parts of the South two strong parties, the Democrats and the Populists. White supremacists were fearful that the competing political parties might bid for the Negro's vote and the Negro might come to have a balance-of-power role. They searched for "legal" ways to disfranchise the Negro. To continue to rely on extralegal and illegal means had other disadvantages: it undermined the moral fabric of the society, and for many years southerners feared that a too flagrant use of force and fraud might cause a Republican President and Congress to intervene.[9]

The Constitution forbids denying the right to vote because of race or color. Southern leaders reasoned that if laws could be passed which, while ostensibly not denying the vote on those grounds, in effect deprived the Negro of the vote on other grounds, it would be difficult for Negroes to challenge the laws in the courts. Some whites protested, saying that such laws could be used against whites as well as Negroes. But the likelihood that the laws would keep poor whites from voting did not disturb the conservative leaders of the Democratic party in control of some southern states, for they were often just as anxious to undermine white support for the Populist party as they were to disfranchise Negroes. Leaders in the Black Belt, where Negroes constituted a large minority and sometimes even a majority, skillfully played on memories of Negro rule and northern intervention. "The disfranchisement movement of the 'nineties,'" says V. O. Key, "gave the southern states the most impressive systems of obstacles between the voter and the ballot box known to the democratic world."[10] By the end of the century the machinery for disfranchisement included:

Good-character tests. Some southern state constitutions deny the ballot to persons who have been convicted of crimes, including minor offenses such

---

[9] Frederic D. Ogden, *The Poll Tax in the South* (Univ. of Alabama Press, 1958), pp. 30-31.
[10] V. O. Key, Jr., *Southern Politics* (Knopf, 1949), p. 555.

as vagrancy. These provisions were adopted on the assumption that the poor, uneducated, and destitute Negroes would more often run afoul of the law than whites.

Literacy tests. Most states in the South and some elsewhere require that citizens wishing to vote must correctly read or write sections of the state constitution. The ability to read is an important safeguard against fraud and uninformed voting, and a literacy test as such is perfectly constitutional.[11] It is always possible, however, to administer the requirement in such a manner as to discriminate against Negroes by disqualifying them for trivial errors that go unnoticed in the case of whites.

Understanding tests. Some states require voters to demonstrate to the satisfaction of election officials that they understand the meaning of the national and state constitutions. These tests give wide discretion to officials, who may ask Negroes impossibly difficult questions.

Poll tax. The best-known though not the most important disfranchising device is a tax that must be paid only by those who want to vote. Thus it puts a price tag on the ballot. The price is not high—one to two dollars a year— but in Alabama, Mississippi, and Virginia it is cumulative (in order to vote, one must make up past payments he has missed). The poll tax probably keeps the ballot from more whites than Negroes. Since 1920, North Carolina, Louisiana, Florida, Georgia, South Carolina, and Tennessee have abolished the poll tax as a prerequisite to voting; it still exists in Alabama, Arkansas, Mississippi, Texas, and Virginia. (Poll taxes are required by many other states, but they are levied whether one votes or not and are not a prerequisite for voting.)

The true significance of all these laws lies in the manner in which they are administered. In the South they are applied by white election officers. White policemen stand guard at the polls. White judges hear appeals—if any— from decisions of local officials. It is easy also for registration officers to seize on the smallest error in an application blank as an excuse to disqualify a hopeful voter. Whites may be asked simple questions about the Constitution; Negroes may be asked questions that would baffle a Supreme Court justice— perhaps while a critical crowd looks on. Or whites may be excused from the tests altogether. In Louisiana, for example, where illiterates may qualify to vote if they pass an understanding test, 49,603 white voters made their marks instead of writing their names in a recent election, but only two Negroes did so. Many southerners, convinced of the rightness of their cause, make no attempt to conceal the purpose of these laws. Asked whether a proposed state constitutional provision was intended to discriminate against the Negro, Carter Glass, later a United States senator, exclaimed: "Discrimination! Why, that is precisely what we propose; that, exactly, is what this convention was elected for—

---

[11] *Lassiter* v. *Northampton County Board* (1959).

to discriminate to the very extremity of permissible action under the limitations of the Federal Constitution, with a view to the elimination of every Negro voter who can be gotten rid of, legally. . . ." [12]

To facilitate discrimination, various *exemptions* to the disfranchising laws were devised to enable whites to vote but not Negroes. The most notorious was the "grandfather" clause, which exempted from literacy and property tests anyone who had voted before the Civil War or whose parents or grandparents had voted. This was a way of saying "whites only." Grandfather clauses were outlawed by the Supreme Court in 1915, but other methods of discrimination persist, especially in the handling of understanding tests.

THE WHITE PRIMARY

"The southern states show a kind of defense in depth against the would-be Negro voter," says Dayton McKean; "if one barrier falls before courts or legislatures there is another behind it." [13] The white primary is an excellent example of this defense in depth. In the South, for most offices the decisive political contests are the *primary* elections within the Democratic party (see Chapter 14); in most sections, Republicans are so scarce that the Democratic nominee is an easy winner in the fall elections. Obviously, exclusion of the Negro from the Democratic primary would deprive him of much influence in politics. Hence it is not surprising that the Democratic party in the South for many years barred Negroes from its primaries.

The Fourteenth and Fifteenth amendments forbid the *states* to deprive Negroes of the right to vote. For many years the white primary seemed to be constitutional because, the argument ran, it was set up privately by a political *party* and not by the *state*. The theory was that a political party, as a voluntary association, had as much right to exclude people from its activities as did the Elks, or the Daughters of the American Revolution, or any other social group. The problem seemed to be merely to avoid any connection between the Democratic party and the state government. For a short period in Texas, the white primary ran afoul of the Constitution when, first, the state legislature barred Negroes from the Democratic primary, and then authorized the executive committee of the party to prescribe qualifications for participation. Since in both these cases the discrimination against Negroes was authorized by *law*, the Supreme Court ruled that this was state action contrary to the Fourteenth Amendment. [14] But when the state legislature said nothing and the state convention of the Democratic party ruled that only whites could vote, the Supreme Court (in *Grovey v. Townsend*, 1935) decided that the exclusion rule was the work of the party itself, as a voluntary association, and that state action was not involved either directly or indirectly.

[12] Quoted by Paul Lewinson, *Race, Class, and Party* (Oxford Univ. Press, 1932), p. 86.
[13] Dayton McKean, *Party and Pressure Politics* (Houghton Mifflin, 1949), p. 66.
[14] *Nixon* v. *Herndon* (1927) and *Nixon* v. *Condon* (1932).

A few years later, however, a revamped Supreme Court looked squarely at the facts and ruled in a Louisiana case (*United States* v. *Classic,* 1941) that a primary is really an election. Soon after this, the Supreme Court, flatly overruling its *Grovey* decision, held in the important case of *Smith* v. *Allwright,* 1944, that the Texas primary was a basic part of the governmental machinery for choosing officials, and that discrimination by the *party* was as unconstitutional as discrimination by the state.

Constitutionally the white primary was dead. But the white southerners did not take this decision lying down. The white primary, after all, was the simplest and most efficient of all the methods of disfranchisement. South Carolina, trying to make party primaries completely private, repealed all its laws—147 of them—controlling political nominations. But the maneuver failed. A federal district judge, an old South Carolinian himself, held that it was an obvious subterfuge to circumvent the Supreme Court's rulings, that if the state turned over to a political party the control of elections in which public officials were chosen, the party was no longer a private club, and that it was "time for South Carolina to rejoin the Union." [15]

One county in Texas responded to the 1944 Supreme Court ruling by trying to employ a "pre-primary primary." An organization known as the Jaybird Association, insisting that it was a private club, held elections from which Negroes were excluded. Only the winner of that election filed in the Democratic primary; consequently, Negroes had no voice in selecting public officials. Again the Court vetoed this as violating the Fifteenth Amendment.[16]

With the demise of the white primary in some areas of the Deep South, white citizens have fallen back on tried-and-true good-character and understanding tests. How successful some of these devices will be, in the face of hostility from courts and from many whites as well as Negroes, only the future will tell. But since 1957 Negroes have not had to depend on their own resources alone to win the right to vote, for Congress has authorized the Department of Justice to initiate suits for injunctions against illegal interferences with the suffrage (see pp. 190-191).

Is the Negro winning his long fight for the ballot? He is, though very slowly. Outside the South neither social pressures nor legal barriers discriminate against the Negro's exercising his right to vote. In most southern cities there are no external obstacles to Negro voting. But Negro voting is still suppressed in many areas of the rural South. The rate of increase in Negro voting in the South as a whole, after increasing sharply in the 1940's, has slowed considerably in the face of the intensified white hostility resulting from reaction to the Supreme Court's school desegregation decisions. But over the long pull, the significance of Negro voting is increasing.[17] It is already important in

---

[15] *Brown* v. *Baskin* (1948).

[16] *Terry* v. *Adams* (1953).

[17] See H. D. Price, *The Negro and Southern Politics* (New York Univ. Press, 1957); Margaret Price, *The Negro and the Ballot in the South* (Southern Regional Council, 1959); U.S. Commission on Civil Rights, *Report* (Government Printing Office, 1959).

southern cities. In at least a dozen southern cities Negroes are serving on city councils or boards of education, and in many others public officials no longer find it so politically profitable to be identified with the more extreme white supremacists.

Many southern whites want the Negro to have the ballot, but not too soon. Hodding Carter, editor of a Mississippi newspaper, has said that Negroes must have more education before they vote, so that they will learn to vote, not "by color and for color," but in terms of enlightened self-interest. He wants more schools for Negroes, decent housing, better health facilities. "We want all this too," say Negro leaders, "but how can we get it unless we can vote for it at the polls?" Increased voting by Negroes and better education for Negroes must go hand in hand, the one fortifying the other. But full Negro voting will not come automatically even after all external barriers have been destroyed. Negro voters—like voters everywhere—stay away from the polls also because of ignorance and inertia. For even in the North and in southern cities where Negroes are free to vote if they wish, many do not. Negro political apathy is much like that of white voters, but it is perhaps more pronounced because of a sense of inferiority and of the importance of "staying out of trouble," products of decades of deference and subordination. In the last analysis, the solution is both to insure the Negro the right to vote, and also to help him, like any other citizen, to see that he has a duty to participate in democratic politics.

Government as Protector of Civil Rights

When a "government" does something, it usually acts because a considerable number of people living under that government have wanted that thing done. Some citizens, for example, who believe that Negroes and whites should be compelled to sit apart in buses, may seek to use governmental power to achieve their goals and so ask the city council or state legislature to make it illegal for whites and Negroes to ride on buses except in separate sections. Or they may take direct action to achieve their wishes without any such assistance from government. They may try to persuade the bus-company managers to segregate passengers. Indeed, they may threaten the company with a boycott unless segregation is imposed. They may use various pressures and threats against the Negroes themselves to induce them to sit apart in buses. In short, civil rights may be threatened not only by governmental action but also by *private* action. In the United States, for example, the right to life is jeopardized more often by lawless individuals than by the government.

Bills of rights in constitutions are designed to restrain *governments* from unreasonable interferences with civil rights. But what is to restrain *individuals* from interfering with such rights of other individuals? What about the use, in other words, of governmental power to protect civil rights?

THE STATES AND PRIVATE DISCRIMINATION

The Fourteenth Amendment forbids discrimination by states, including, of course, all subdivisional units of states. However, unless the discrimination is sanctioned or supported by the state, the Fourteenth Amendment offers the victim no protection at all. But what, precisely, constitutes state sanction or support of discrimination? This is currently one of the "hot" issues of public law. In recent decades the Supreme Court has significantly expanded the concept of "state action." In 1948 the Court held that though there is nothing unconstitutional about making and signing racial restrictive covenants (provisions attached to deeds restricting the sale or use of property to certain groups), court *enforcement* of such covenants is state action and therefore unconstitutional.[18] In another line of cases the Supreme Court has said trade unions whose right to engage in collective bargaining is protected by the government may not discriminate.[19] And, as we have seen, the Supreme Court has come very close to the position that the holding and operation of elections in which public officials are nominated or elected is a governmental function and that whoever discharges these functions is therefore restrained by the Constitution.

Can a state deny equal protection by acts of *omission* as well as by acts of commission? Is the equal-protection clause violated when a state permits private mobs to keep Negroes out of public schools? The Supreme Court has ruled that there is a denial of equal protection when state officials participate or willfully stand aside in order to permit others to deprive persons of their civil rights. But the Supreme Court has refused to accept the view that the equal protection clause requires states to take *positive* action to protect individuals against discrimination by other *private individuals.*

STATE CIVIL-RIGHTS POWERS AND PROGRAMS

Although private acts of discrimination are not unconstitutional, states have ample authority to make these acts *illegal.* Just as the states have the authority to protect a person's property rights against infringement by others, so they have the authority to protect civil rights. The Constitution, in fact, places the primary responsibility for protecting civil rights on the states and, as we shall shortly note, gives the national government only limited power in this respect.

Should states use their police powers to make it illegal for landlords, employers, trade unions, private schools, and others to discriminate against persons because of their race or religion? "No," say some people. Prejudice cannot be eradicated by laws. Others respond that if laws cannot eradicate prejudice itself, they *can* eliminate the *product*—actual overt discriminatory

---

[18] *Shelly* v. *Kraemer* (1948); and *Barrows* v. *Jackson* (1953).
[19] *Conley* v. *Gibson* (1957).

action that deprives people of their right to be treated as human beings and American citizens.

In the South, as we have noted, state laws require segregation, and they are still being enforced despite their unconstitutionality. But other states *outlaw* segregation and other kinds of racial or religious discrimination. Discrimination by owners and operators of places of public recreation and accommodation has long been a tort (civil wrong) under the common law, and twenty-five states have special statutes making it a criminal or civil offense for places of public accommodation to refuse to serve patrons because of their race, religion, or place of national origin. Eighteen states apply these civil-rights statutes to private employers, and the same number prohibit unions from controlling membership on the basis of race or religion. Some states have made it illegal for university authorities to discriminate racially or religiously against students seeking to enter colleges or universities, except, of course, religious schools. New York City forbids landlords to discriminate. Almost all northern states forbid discrimination in public employment.

The weakness of some of these civil-rights statutes is that they make no special provision for enforcement other than by regular court action instituted by public prosecutors or through the initiation of law suits by the person being discriminated against. Frequently, the persons who are denied a job or service have neither the knowledge to bring the matter to the attention of prosecutors nor the money to undertake a civil suit. Moreover, many prosecutors have been something less than eager to take action.

The ineffectiveness of criminal laws against discrimination and of dependence on damage suits brought by the aggrieved persons has led to a new development in the enforcement of civil rights.[20] New York in 1945 created a five-member commission charged with investigating and hearing complaints in instances of alleged discrimination, and since then eighteen states and numerous cities containing 40 per cent of the total population of the United States have established such special civil-rights commissions with the exclusive duty of acting against discrimination.

The New York procedures are typical. The Commission Against Discrimination is responsible for enforcing the state laws forbidding racial, religious, and national-origin discrimination by employers, labor unions, places of public accommodation, and governmentally aided housing projects. (Laws covering discrimination in educational institutions are enforced by the Commissioner of Education and Board of Regents.) Any person suffering such discrimination may file a complaint with the commission. If, after investigation, the commission finds the complaint is justified, it first tries to remove the cause through "conference, conciliation and persuasion." If these efforts fail, a formal hearing takes place before at least three members of the commission.

---

[20] "Anti-Discrimination Commissions," *Race Relations Law Reporter*, October, 1958, pp. 1085-1108 (Vanderbilt Univ. School of Law).

If the commission discovers evidence of violation of the law, it orders the offender to cease and desist from such practices. Violation of a commission order is punishable by imprisonment for not more than one year or by a fine of not more than $500 or both. The courts may review decisions of the commission on questions of law. The commission has seldom had to resort to its coercive powers, and through a program of education and publicity it has done much to improve human relations in this most difficult of all fields.

Other states and cities have made similar progress. Although the Missouri and Maryland commissions operate in border states with many southern traditions, as yet none has been established in southern areas. In some cases the commissions have advisory rather than regulatory powers and cannot punish offenders. Their efforts are being watched with interest, and each year another state or two is added to the list. More and more the people seem to be concluding that civil rights are at least as worthy of state legal protection as property rights.

National Protection of Civil Rights: Quest for a Sword [21]   One of the most hotly debated topics of contemporary politics is whether the *national* government should provide positive protection for civil rights. Some contend that federal civil-rights laws upset the federal system and lead to dangerous centralization of power. They insist that national legislation is ineffective and creates more problems than it solves. A national program cannot be enforced contrary to local public opinion, it is contended. Let the states do the job, it is argued, for they can protect civil rights by laws adapted to the attitudes of the local citizenry.

In answer, defenders of national action point out that not only have most states failed to protect civil rights effectively, but in some areas they have actually been instruments of discrimination. Furthermore, the denial of civil rights is not merely a local matter, for it has national and international implications. The national Constitution promises to every person who lives in the United States that he will receive equal treatment before the law without respect to his race, religion, or national origin, and it is up to the national government to see that this promise is kept. Whatever the speculative merits of local rather than national action, as a matter of practical political fact respect for civil rights will be extended only by the national majority using the power of the national government. For as one southerner has noted, "not one concrete step toward full rights for the southern Negro—whether in voting or education—has been achieved without the intervention of the national government." [22]

---

[21] This is the title of an excellent volume by Robert K. Carr published by Cornell Univ. Press, 1947.

[22] James W. Prothro, "A Southerner's View of a Southerner's Book," *The Reporter,* September 20, 1956, p. 46.

FEDERAL POWER TO PROTECT CIVIL RIGHTS

Although the Constitution reserves to the states the major responsibility for protecting civil rights, it also vests in the national government ample power to support civil-rights legislation. The *Thirteenth* Amendment gives Congress power to protect the basic right of personal freedom. By its own force it freed the slaves of 1865 and prevents all forms of involuntary servitude. This amendment, along with Section II of the Twenty-first, is unique in that by its own terms it directly and immediately applies to private individuals as well as to public officials. The power of Congress to enforce this amendment extends to legislating against slavery no matter who tries to impose it. However, the Supreme Court has narrowly construed the prohibitions of the Thirteenth so that they do not apply to racial discrimination and has limited the national legislature's authority under it to legislating only against slavery and peonage (peonage is a condition of compulsory servitude based on the indebtedness of the worker to the employer).

The *Fifth* and *Fourteenth* amendments give Congress the power to legislate against discrimination that is in any fashion effected through the use of the power of national or state *governments.*

The *Fifteenth* Amendment authorizes Congress to legislate against racial discrimination by *any public officials* in *any election,* including primary elections.

What about discrimination by private individuals unsupported by government action? It was the hope of many of the congressmen who proposed the Fourteenth Amendment that its ratification would authorize federal action against nongovernmental discrimination, but this hope was quickly dashed by the Supreme Court. In 1875 Congress had made it a federal crime for any owner or operator of a public conveyance, hotel, or theater to deny accommodations to any person because of his race or color. In the *Civil Rights Cases* (1881) the Supreme Court invalidated this law on the ground that the Fourteenth Amendment applies only to state action and does not give Congress authority to forbid discrimination by private individuals.

But the Civil War amendments are not the only sources of Congress' civil-rights powers. Congress has the implied power to protect all the rights that arise out of the relationship between the national government and its own citizens and that are essential for the effective operation of the national government; Congress can protect these rights against encroachment by private individuals as well as by national, state, or local officials. The Supreme Court has never given a complete listing of the rights that are thus subject to comprehensive national protection, but here are some that have been defined in various decisions: the right of a qualified voter to vote in an election (including primaries) in which national officials are to be chosen, and to have this vote properly counted; the right to be protected from mob violence while being held by federal officials; the right to petition Congress; the right to travel freely throughout the United States; the right to the full enjoyment of all benefits conferred by national laws.

There are many other constitutional provisions that Congress could use to enact civil-rights legislation. For example, Congress could use its authority over interstate commerce to forbid any employer or trade union whose activities affect such commerce to refuse to hire or admit to membership any person because of his race, color, or religion. In making grants-in-aid to the states, Congress could stipulate that the money could not be used to maintain segregated facilities or to deprive persons of constitutional rights. Congress could make it a federal offense for any person to refuse service because of race or religion to any person wearing the uniform of the United States military services. In short, Congress has plenty of constitutional power. The big question is: how has the power been used?

FEDERAL CIVIL-RIGHTS LAWS

From the end of Reconstruction until 1957, Congress refused to pass any civil-rights laws. Furthermore, in the last half of the nineteenth century the wide range of civil-rights measures enacted during Reconstruction were either declared unconstitutional or narrowly construed by a Supreme Court dominated by justices who did not look with favor upon federal civil-rights protection. This left available only a few federal civil-rights statutes, the most important of which are the following:

1. *The Civil Rights Act of 1866* makes it a federal crime, punishable by a fine of not more than $1000 and imprisonment for not more than one year, for any person *acting under color of law* to deprive any person of rights secured or protected by the Constitution or laws of the United States. This act protects those rights that the Constitution secures only against abridgment by public officials. For example, any person acting under color of law who willfully deprives a person of a fair trial, or discriminates against a person because of his race, or who uses force to obtain a confession would be liable to prosecution under this act.[23]

2. *The Civil Rights Act of 1871,* unlike the above act, provides for civil and not criminal remedies. It authorizes persons whose constitutional rights are being abridged by state or local officials to sue them for damages in federal courts or seek federal court injunctions ordering the officials to cease their discriminatory conduct.

3. *The Civil Rights Act of 1957,* the first post-Reconstruction civil-rights act, provides additional civil remedies. Its most important provision authorizes the Department of Justice on its own motion to seek injunctions in federal courts in behalf of persons who are being illegally deprived of their right to vote (see pp. 189-191).

---

[23] *Williams* v. *United States* (1951) and cases cited therein.

PROBLEMS OF ENFORCEMENT
OF FEDERAL CIVIL-RIGHTS ACTS

Although Negroes, working mainly through the National Association for the Advancement of Colored People (NAACP), have had some spectacular success using the Act of 1871 to secure injunctions against discrimination in elections and public education, private litigants often meet difficulty in gathering evidence to challenge the more subtle forms of discrimination. On the other hand, the Department of Justice, which has the resources to obtain the evidence, had no authority until 1957, and since then only in the area of the right to vote, to take any action against those who violate civil rights except by criminal prosecution—a difficult, time-consuming, and often inappropriate procedure.

Despite the difficulties, the Department of Justice has since 1938 taken an active role in the enforcement of the federal civil-rights criminal laws. Here is a revolting episode to illustrate the problems it has encountered.

Late one night in 1944, a car stopped in front of the home of Robert Hall, a citizen of the United States and of Georgia. Three men got out of the car: Screws, the county sheriff; Jones, a policeman; and Kelly, a special deputy. The men had been drinking. A few days before, Screws had threatened Hall that he was going to get him, and Hall was terrified. Screws flashed a warrant charging Hall with the theft of a tire. Hall resisted, but the three men pushed him into the waiting car. The car pulled up in the courthouse square, Hall got out, and immediately the three men "began beating him with their fists and with a solid-bar blackjack about eight inches long and weighing two pounds." [24] Hall was handcuffed and defenseless, and the three men continued to beat him for fifteen to thirty minutes. Then the unconscious Hall was dragged feet first through the courthouse into the jail and thrown on the floor. He died within an hour.

Here was a clear case of murder, but as the days went by no action by state authorities was taken against the three men. Hall was a Negro. The matter was brought to the attention of the civil-rights section, but it waited for the state to punish the guilty men. Still no action. Finally, the Department of Justice started to move. Under the Civil Rights Act of 1866, the penalty for willfully subjecting any inhabitant, under color of any law, to the deprivation of any rights, privileges, or immunities secured or protected by the Constitution and laws of the United States is a fine of not more than $1000 and prison sentence for not more than one year. Admittedly this was puny punishment for such a heinous crime, puny even when combined with the possible two-year imprisonment for conspiring to violate a federal law. But at least it would serve notice that the federal government was not powerless to protect rights guaranteed by the Constitution against abuse by state officials.

---

[24] *Screws* v. *United States* (1945).

The federal officials, careful lest they arouse local resistance to outside interference, assigned only southern attorneys to the case. An indictment was secured against Screws and his companions for willfully causing Hall to be deprived of rights secured to him or protected by the Fourteenth Amendment, specifically the right not to be deprived of life without due process of law; the right to be tried by due process upon the charge on which he was arrested; and, if found guilty, the right to be punished in accordance with the laws.

The case proceeded. In his charge to the jury, the judge said that if the jurors believed that the facts were established, then the "defendants would be depriving Hall of certain constitutional rights guaranteed to him by the Constitution of the United States and consented to by the State of Georgia."

The jury's verdict, "Guilty." But the case was not over. Screws turned to the court of appeals, which affirmed the decision of the trial court. The case then went to the Supreme Court. A majority of the justices felt (there were five separate opinions) that the trial judge had erred in failing to instruct the jury that Screws and his companions could be held guilty of the crime only if they had "willfully" intended to deprive Hall of his constitutional rights, that it was not sufficient that Screws had a generally bad intent.

The case was returned to the district courts for a retrial. Screws and his friends were duly retried. This time they were acquitted.

The Department of Justice has been more successful in other cases. In 1947, for example, Crews, a Florida town marshal, arrested a Negro and, after beating him with a heavy whip, forced him to jump from a high bridge into a river. The Negro drowned. Crews was successfully convicted of violating the civil-rights statute, and this time the conviction was sustained.[25] In another case, a private detective (but authorized by law to act as a special police officer) was convicted of extracting a confession from a prisoner by physical brutality.[26]

Thus the civil-rights section has been instrumental in alerting local police officers to the fact that they violate at their own peril rights and privileges protected by the Constitution and federal laws.

TO SECURE THESE RIGHTS—THE PRESIDENTS ACT

By the 1930's, as a result of the northern migration of Negroes, industrialization and urbanization, the Great Depression, and the New Deal, Negroes began to emerge as a significant political group. From then on the man in the White House and all those who aspire to live there could no longer afford to ignore the political demands of Negro voters. Perhaps because the impact of Negro political activity has been felt less in Congress, the executive power of

---

[25] *Crews* v. *United States* (1947).
[26] *Williams* v. *United States* (1951).

the President has been used with more vigor to protect civil rights than has the legislative power of Congress.

Presidents Truman and Eisenhower used their authority as Chief Administrator of the executive branch and as Commander in Chief of the armed forces to issue directives against discrimination in federal employment and within the armed services. Today segregation is virtually nonexistent in the Army, Navy, and Air Force, and employment in the various agencies of the federal government is progressively being opened to all persons without regard to their race, religion, or national origin.

Our Chief Executives have also fought discrimination in employment by contractors of the federal government. As a result of a presidential executive order in 1941, substantially all the six million contracts made annually by the government contain a provision that states: "In connection with the performance of work under this contract, the contractor agrees not to discriminate against any employee or applicant for employment because of race, religion, color or national origin." [27]

Congress has refused to appropriate funds to enforce these nondiscrimination clauses, but Presidents have moved ahead by establishing on their own a Committee on Government Contracts. This committee, presently presided over by the Vice President and consisting of six government officials and nine public members, cannot terminate contracts for noncompliance, but it carefully investigates all complaints and brings offenders to the attention of government contracting officials. Through education, mediation, and persuasion it has brought about affirmative action by many employers, especially in the oil-refining, meatpacking, aircraft-manufacturing, and airline industries.

CONGRESS FINALLY ACTS—THE CIVIL-RIGHTS LAW OF 1957

The hostile reaction to the Supreme Court's school segregation decisions made it even more difficult for Negroes to defend their civil rights by law suits. Southern states tried to suppress the NAACP, which sponsors most civil-rights suits. In the tense atmosphere of the South, Negroes who sued to secure civil rights ran a serious risk of losing their jobs, even of incurring personal injury.

Civil-rights advocates urged the Department of Justice to lend Negroes a helping hand to bring about faster school desegregation and to prevent abridgments of the right to vote. But prior to 1957 the only procedure open to the Department was to initiate criminal proceedings. Southern juries were often reluctant to convict public officials for discriminating against Negro voters because the jurors themselves approved of discrimination. Moreover, the goal was not to throw men into jail but to secure to Negroes their rights.

---

[27] John F. Cushman, "Mediation and Education for Equal Economic Opportunity," in *Aspects of Liberty: Essays Presented to Robert E. Cushman,* Milton R. Konvitz and Clinton Rossiter (eds.) (Cornell Univ. Press, 1958), pp. 115-126.

[handwritten marginalia: up to 1957 Department of Justice had no power — only to bring to courts which ner... wor... becau... south... would not Conur other south]

Under these circumstances many supporters of civil rights contended that, if the burden of enforcing civil-rights laws was left to Negroes themselves, it would be tantamount to conceding victory to those who favor racial discrimination. They argued that if Negroes were not to be deprived of their right to vote and if schools were to be desegregated, Congress would have to enact new laws authorizing the Department of Justice to enter the fray.

But would Congress act? Until 1957, although the House frequently passed civil-rights bills, the intense opposition of southern Democrats and the indifference of many conservative Republicans kept the Senate from approving any changes in civil-rights statutes. When Congress assembled in 1957, however, the political situation had changed. For in the 1956 elections there had been a substantial movement of Negro voters into the Republican column, especially in the cities. For the first time in our history neither party could consider the "Negro vote" safe and neither party wanted to be tagged as being opposed to civil rights. The southern Democrats, although still powerful enough to force concessions, were no longer able to block all civil-rights legislation. They no longer could count on the support of border-state senators and they were losing their Republican allies, who had much to gain by supporting civil rights legislation.

Hence in 1957 Congress adopted and the President signed into law the first civil-rights law since Reconstruction. This law did the following:

1. Made the civil-rights section of the Department of Justice a separate division in charge of an Assistant Attorney General.

2. Created for two years a bipartisan six-man Civil Rights Commission to investigate alleged civil-rights violations and to make recommendations to Congress for corrective legislation.

3. Authorized the Department of Justice on its own motion to initiate suits for injunctions in behalf of persons being denied the right to vote in any election in violation of the Fifteenth Amendment or otherwise being illegally kept from voting in a federal election. Federal courts were instructed to hear voting cases even if state administrative remedies had not been exhausted. (This technical change is of importance because it makes it impossible for states to construct elaborate administrative procedures in order to frustrate federal suits.) In the event of criminal prosecutions for violating injunctions issued under this section, the accused are to be tried before a jury if a fine of more than $300 or imprisonment for more than forty-five days is sought.

The most drastic modification made by the Senate in the Civil Rights Act as originally passed by the House and as recommended by the President was to delete what has come to be known as Part III. Part III would have authorized the Department of Justice on its own motion to initiate suits for injunctions in behalf of persons being denied rights secured by the Fourteenth Amendment. Or in less technical language, the Department could have taken an active role in school desegregation suits.

THE CIVIL RIGHTS ACT OF 1957 IN ACTION

It is still too early to know how the new Civil Rights Act will work. The Civil Rights Commission, which was given two more years of life in 1959 by Congress, held public hearings focusing national and congressional attention on some of the more flagrant violations of the Constitution. The Commission in its first *Report* made strong recommendations for additional national civil-rights laws. It stated that existing remedies under the Civil Rights Act of 1957 are insufficient and recommended, among other things, that a method be found to create temporary federal registrars to serve in localities where state officials are refusing to register otherwise qualified Negroes to vote in elections in which national officials are chosen.[28] The Department of Justice has just started to use the Civil Rights Act of 1957 to seek injunctions in behalf of voters whose rights are being abridged and has run into some adverse rulings by federal judges sitting in southern districts. This development was not unexpected and in time the Supreme Court probably will reverse most of these decisions. But not until the new procedures have been thoroughly challenged will they be fully available and their significance determined.

Both Republican and Democratic national leaders have called on Congress to enact additional civil-rights legislation, though there is considerable difference of opinion as to what kind of law is called for. Which of the several proposals will be enacted may depend on events in the South. If southern cities start to desegregate their public schools peacefully, their action would undoubtedly undermine the sense of urgency and reduce the pressures for national action. On the other hand, if there are more "Little Rock" episodes or increased violence against Negroes, the likelihood of strong federal civil-rights laws will be greatly enhanced, and Part III, deleted from the 1957 Act, might be adopted.

Summary

1. The Constitution asserts the equal right of all men to life, liberty, and property.
2. The Constitution denies to both national and state governments the right to discriminate against people because of race or religion, and specifically deprives government of the authority to deny any person the right to vote because of race or color.
3. In the South there are still barriers to voting by Negroes, but the Supreme Court has tended to scrutinize more carefully measures that in effect deprive Negroes of the right to vote. In recent years, it has declared the white primary unconstitutional.
4. The Supreme Court has held public school segregation unconstitutional and has ordered school districts to take action in good faith toward the desegregation of

---

[28] United States Commission on Civil Rights, *Report* (Government Printing Office, 1959), p. 141.

public schools. The High Court has also gone far toward the position that the Constitution is "color-blind" and that racial classifications are unconstitutional.

5. Considerable resistance has arisen to the desegregation of public schools, especially in the Deep South.

6. States have the constitutional power to make laws prohibiting racial or religious discrimination by employers, trade unions, and operators of public places. Some states have done so.

7. The national government's constitutional authority to protect persons against discrimination is more restricted. It may legislate to protect against discrimination or denial of due process by those who act under the color of law. It also could use its other grants of power to protect civil rights, but until 1957 the southern bloc in the Senate was able to block civil-rights legislation.

8. The executive power of the President to protect civil rights has been used more vigorously.

9. The struggle to achieve equality under the law is far from over.

CHAPTER 8

Rights to Life, Liberty, and Property

Public officials have great power. Under certain conditions they can seize our property, throw us into jail and, in extreme circumstances, even take our lives. It is necessary to vest great power in those who govern; it is also dangerous. It is so dangerous that to keep officials from becoming tyrants we are unwilling to depend on the ballot box alone. For we know that political controls do little good when a hysterical majority uses governmental power to deprive unpopular minorities of their rights.

Because governmental power can be dangerous, we parcel it out in small chunks and surround it with elaborate restraints. No single official can by himself decide to take our life, liberty, or property. And officials must proceed according to established forms. If they act outside the scope of their authority or contrary to the law, be they the President or policeman, they have no claim to obedience. The *restraints* on government designed to protect our lives, liberties, and properties are the subject of this chapter.

The Constitution Protects Property

By "property rights" we mean the rights of the individual to own, use, rent, invest, or contract for property. Property has no rights; it is the individual's right in property to which we refer. From Aristotle, through the English philosopher Harrington, to the Founding Fathers, there had run a persistent emphasis on the close connection between liberty and private ownership of property, between property and power. This emphasis has been clearly reflected in American political thinking and in American political institutions. A major purpose of the framers of our Constitution was to establish a government strong enough to protect each person's right to use and enjoy his property, and, at the same time, a government so limited that it could not encroach upon that right. For example, they were disturbed by the efforts of some state legislatures in behalf of debtors at the expense of creditors (see Chapter 2). So in the Constitution they forbade states to make anything except gold or silver legal tender for the payment of debts or to pass any law "impairing the obligation of contracts."

THE CONTRACT CLAUSE

The obligation-of-contracts clause of Article I, Section 10, was aimed at state laws extending the period during which debtors could meet their payments or otherwise relieving them of their contractual obligations. The framers had in mind an ordinary contract between private persons. But in characteristic fashion Chief Justice Marshall later expanded the meaning of this clause to cover transactions to which the state government itself was a party. So, when the Georgia legislature annulled a grant of a large tract of land fraudulently made by an earlier legislature, the Supreme Court declared that the annulling act was an unconstitutional impairment of the obligation of contract.[1] Then in 1819 the Supreme Court ruled that charters creating corporations are contracts. Thus whatever privileges a charter conferred on a corporation appeared to be irrevocable and untouchable by any subsequent law.[2]

In effect, the contract clause was being used to protect vested property at the expense of the power of the states to guard the public welfare. State regulations of business enterprises ran a serious risk of being declared unconstitutional. Gradually, however, the Court began to restrict the coverage of the contract clause. Finally, in 1880, in the case of *Stone v. Mississippi,* the Supreme Court ruled that all contracts are subject to the states' *police power* and could be regulated when necessary to protect the public health, safety, welfare, or morals. In 1934 the Supreme Court declared that even contracts between individuals—the very ones the contract clause was intended to protect—could be reasonably modified by state law in order to avert social and economic catastrophe resulting from the depression.[3]

But in the 1880's just as the contract clause ceased to be an important block to state regulation of property, the due process clause took over.

DUE PROCESS OF LAW

Perhaps the hardest parts of the Constitution to understand are those clauses in the Fifth and Fourteenth amendments that forbid the national and state governments, respectively, to deny any person his life, liberty, or property without due process of law. These due process clauses have resulted in

---

[1] *Fletcher v. Peck* (1810).
[2] *Dartmouth College v. Woodward* (1819).
[3] *Home Building and Loan Association v. Blaisdell.*

procedural — criminal case — fair trial

substantive — content - law must be reasonable and fair

more Supreme Court decisions than has any other clause in the Constitution. Even so, it is impossible to give due process any exact and completely satisfactory explanation. Indeed, the Supreme Court itself has refused to give it precise definition.

There are two types of due process: *procedural* and *substantive*. The *procedural* kind is the older, for it grew out of Magna Carta and embodies the ancient notion that no man should be deprived of his life, liberty, or property unless he has violated the law and has had a fair trial. It requires, to paraphrase Daniel Webster's famous definition, that government render judgment against a man only after he has had a hearing in which the essentials of justice have been preserved. For the most part, procedural due process has its application in the administration of *criminal justice,* as we shall see below.

Substantive due process has to do not with the procedures but the *content* of law, which it requires to be reasonable and fair. Whereas procedural due process primarily restrains the executive and judicial branches, substantive due process mainly limits the lawmaking branch. Substantive due process means that even if a law has been legally passed and is being properly applied, nonetheless if the law itself is unreasonable it is unconstitutional. Or to put it still another way, procedural due process places limits on the *manner* in which governmental power may be exercised, but substantive due process withdraws certain *subjects* from the reach of public regulation regardless of the procedures used.

For an extreme example of denial of substantive due process, suppose that a state legislature should adopt a law requiring employers to pay all their employees precisely the same salary that is paid to the president of the firm. An employer being prosecuted for violating this law might well object that the law is unreasonable, that even though he is being given a fair trial, to make him comply with the law would be to deprive him of his property without due process. He would be raising the substantive interpretation of due process.

Substantive due process dates from the 1880's. The Supreme Court from about 1880 to 1937 was composed for the most part of conservative gentlemen who considered almost all social welfare legislation unreasonable and hence contrary to substantive due process. They used the due process clause to strike down laws regulating hours of labor, establishing minimum wages, regulating prices, forbidding employers to discharge workers for union membership, and many other laws the legislatures thought were needed. The Supreme Court, elevating the doctrine of laissez faire into a constitutional principle, vetoed laws adversely affecting property rights unless the judges could be persuaded that such laws were absolutely necessary to protect public health or safety.

But what is "reasonable"? What is "necessary"? The trouble with the substantive interpretation of due process is that the view of the reasonableness of a law depends on a man's economic, social, and political views rather than on his legal training. In democracies, *elected* officials are supposed to be responsible for accommodating the clashing notions of "reasonableness" and for deciding what regulations of liberty and property are needed to promote the public welfare. When the Supreme Court substituted its own idea of "reasonableness" for the legislature's, it was acting like a superlegislature. But how competent were *judges* to say what the nation's economic policies should be?

Under the impact of this criticism the Supreme Court since 1937 has largely abandoned substantive due process as a check on legislative regulation of the economy (but not as a check on legislative regulations of civil liberties). The Court now consists of justices who believe that determining the reasonableness of laws regulating the uses of property is a legislative and not a judicial duty. As long as it sees some connection between such a law and the promotion of the public welfare, the Supreme Court will not interfere, even if the justices personally believe the law to be unwise.

EMINENT DOMAIN

Many government regulations affect the value of the property we own, sometimes making it worth more, sometimes less. For example, a zoning law restricting a particular area to residential uses may decrease the immediate value of a particular individual's property. Maybe he was about to use his land for a gas station, but now he cannot do so. The government does not have to remunerate the owner for such losses, so he loses money—but the rest of the community gains.

What if the government goes beyond reasonable regulation and *takes* property? Both the national and state governments have a constitutional right to do so, to exercise what is known as the power of eminent domain. But the Constitution requires that property be seized only for public purposes—for example, to build a highway or school or military installation—and that the owner must be paid a fair price. If there is any dispute about what price is fair, the final decision is made by the courts.

To sum up, where do we stand today in terms of constitutional protection of property? The obligation-of-contracts clause no longer is a major barrier to state regulations of property, and substantive due process has been abandoned as a judicially enforced limit on legislative regulation of our economy. The constitutional limits to the power of eminent domain remain as important as ever. But our right to use our property is not above regulation in the public interest. What regulations are needed is determined by the legislatures; the courts will intervene only if the laws are outrageously arbitrary and outrageously unreasonable or are being applied without procedural due process.

Freedom from Arbitrary Arrest, Questioning, and Imprisonment

James Otis' address in 1761 protesting arbitrary searches and seizures by English customs officials was the opening salvo of the

American Revolution; as John Adams later said, "American independence was then and there born." It is not surprising to find that the Fourth Amendment states:

> The right of the people to be secure in their persons, houses, papers, and effects, against unreasonable searches and seizures, shall not be violated, and no Warrants shall issue, but upon probable cause, supported by Oath or affirmation, and particularly describing the place to be searched, and the persons or things to be seized.

Despite what one might think from looking at television police dramas, police may search homes without warrants only under certain narrowly defined conditions. If a person is otherwise lawfully arrested, he may be searched, but a search warrant is needed if the police wish to search beyond his immediate person or the area under his immediate control.[4] When there is probable cause to believe that an automobile contains contraband or incriminating evidence, police do not need warrants, for the obvious reason that the automobile might not be there when the police return.

Some observers believe the Supreme Court has diluted the right of privacy, for in 1959 it held in a five-to-four decision that a person could be fined for refusing to allow a health inspector to make a daytime house search even though the inspector had no warrant.[5] The Supreme Court made it clear, however, that its decision was not to be construed as authorizing health inspectors to make forcible entry without warrants. This distinction between fining a householder unless he lets inspectors enter, but not allowing the inspectors to make forcible entry without warrant was to the dissenting justices of little significance. To them the entire procedure was unconstitutional.

Combining the Fourth Amendment prohibition against unreasonable searches and seizures with the Fifth Amendment injunction that no person shall be compelled to be a witness against himself, the Supreme Court has come up with the rule that evidence unconstitutionally or illegally obtained cannot be used in a *federal* court against persons from whom it was seized. To allow the use of this evidence would be in effect to force persons to testify against themselves. Nor does it make any difference if the evidence was obtained by illegal methods by persons other than federal officers—it still cannot be used in federal courts.[6] Further, federal officers may be enjoined from testifying in state courts about evidence they secured by illegal methods.[7]

In the famous 1928 case of *Olmstead* v. *United States*, the Supreme Court, over the dissent of four justices, narrowly construed the Fourth Amendment to cover only physical, tangible objects and not police seizure of evidence by tapping telephone wires. Subsequent to the decision, however, Congress made

---

[4] *Jones* v. *United States* (1958).
[5] *Frank* v. *Maryland.*
[6] *Benati* v. *United States* (1957).
[7] *Rea* v. *United States* (1956).

it illegal to tap telephone wires. Since it is illegal to do so, evidence thus obtained cannot be used in federal proceedings. The Attorney General of the United States has tried unsuccessfully to persuade Congress to authorize federal police to tap telephone wires so that they may introduce in federal courts the evidence thus uncovered.

As long as police make no unconstitutional entry or tap no wires, they may use evidence (even in federal courts) obtained by various amplification devices such as detectaphones. A Mr. On Lee discovered this when the Supreme Court permitted the introduction into his trial of evidence obtained when an informer entered Lee's shop with a concealed radio transmitter in his pocket.[8] Lee, thinking he was talking to a friend, made damaging admissions that were transmitted to a government agent.

The Fourth Amendment, like all the first ten amendments, does not apply to state governments. However, the Supreme Court has ruled that the due process clause of the Fourteenth Amendment, which does apply to states, makes unconstitutional unreasonable searches and seizures by *state* officers (and of course by local officers, since in a constitutional sense officials of all local units of government are covered by the term state officers).[9]

Although state officers may not engage in unreasonable searches and seizures, the Supreme Court has ruled that states need not follow the federal practice of excluding from criminal prosecutions unconstitutionally secured evidence. In other words, it is a denial of due process for state officers to make unreasonable searches and seizures, but it is not a denial of due process for a state court to convict a person on the basis of evidence unconstitutionally obtained. As far as the national Constitution is concerned, states are free to adopt their own rules governing the admission of evidence, except that they cannot use evidence obtained by third-degree methods.

THE THIRD DEGREE

The questioning of suspects by the police is a key procedure for solving crimes—and also one that can easily be abused. Police sometimes forget or ignore the constitutional rights of suspects, especially of those who are frightened and ignorant. Torture, detention incommunicado, and sustained interrogation to wring confessions from suspects are commonly used by police states. Unfortunately such tactics are not unknown in the United States.

Judges, especially those on the Supreme Court, have used their power to try to stamp out police brutality. The Supreme Court has ruled that even though there may be sufficient evidence to support a conviction apart from a coerced confession, the admission in evidence of a coerced confession violates the due process clause and vitiates the entire proceeding. Hence any conviction by either *national* or *state* courts on the basis of a trial in which a confession

[8] *On Lee* v. *United States* (1952).
[9] *Wolf* v. *Colorado* (1949).

secured by physical torture or psychological coercion has been introduced is unconstitutional.[10]

The federal rules of criminal procedure and the laws of all our states require officers promptly to take those whom they have arrested before a magistrate. Police have no lawful right to hold a person for questioning prior to this hearing before a magistrate. The magistrate informs the person in custody of his constitutional rights, and allows him to get in touch with friends and to seek legal advice. However, police are often tempted to question first. Sometimes they lack evidence to make an arrest stick but feel that if they can interrogate the suspect before he knows of his constitutional rights they can frighten him into confessing.

The Supreme Court has adopted a rule against the use in national courts of any confession, whether voluntary or involuntary, made while a person was being illegally detained by national officers. In 1957 the Supreme Court reaffirmed this doctrine in the *Mallory case,* a case that made front-page head-lines because it involved an especially heinous crime, and because the application of the exclusion rule resulted in the release of a confessed criminal. The decision provoked a storm of public protest and in 1958 Congress came close to changing the federal rules of evidence in order to modify the ruling.

It should be noted that the ruling is not constitutionally required but is an attempt by the Supreme Court to elevate the administration of justice by national courts. Most state courts do not subscribe to this practice and are not required by the Fourteenth Amendment due process clause to do so. So long as a confession is secured without the use of coercion, it may be used in state courts—as far as the Fourteenth Amendment is concerned—even if it is obtained while the police are illegally detaining the suspect.

THE RIGHT TO REMAIN SILENT

During the seventeenth century in England, Star Chamber and High Commission courts were used to force confessions of heresy and sedition from religious dissenters. The judges of these courts assumed that unless suspects brought before them would take expurgatory oaths they were guilty. It was in response to these practices that the British privilege against self-incrimination developed, and it was because the framers of the Bill of Rights were familiar with the history of these odious oaths that they included within the Fifth Amendment the provision that no person shall be compelled to testify against himself in criminal prosecutions.

The provision against self-incrimination is designed to strengthen the fundamental principle of Anglo-American justice that no man has any obligation to prove he is innocent—rather, the burden is on the government to prove him guilty. Under the Fifth Amendment the defendant in a federal criminal

---

[10] *Payne* v. *Arkansas* (1958).

prosecution may refuse to take the stand and the judge must warn the jury not to draw any adverse inferences from the defendant's silence. However, if a defendant elects to take the stand he cannot claim the Fifth Amendment to prevent cross examination by the prosecutor.

Literally read, the privilege against self-incrimination applies only in criminal prosecutions, but it has always been interpreted to protect any person subject to questioning by any agency of the national government. Hence a witness before a congressional committee or before the Interstate Commerce Commission or before the Immigration and Naturalization Service, for example, may claim the Fifth Amendment and refuse to answer incriminating questions. But to invoke the Fifth Amendment, it is not enough that the witness' answers might be embarrassing or lead to public disapproval or to loss of job or might incriminate others; there must be a reasonable fear that the answers might support a federal prosecution or "furnish a link in the chain of evidence needed to prosecute" him for a federal crime.[11] A witness may refuse to answer even if his responses would not indicate guilt, for the right covers answers that might lead to *prosecution* even if the witness knows the prosecution would not lead to conviction.

Does the Fifth Amendment protect one against questioning by *state* officials? No—a witness may not claim the Fifth Amendment before a state agency even if his answers might lead to his prosecution by the national government.[12] Conversely, before a national agency a person may not claim the Fifth Amendment because his answers might lead to a state prosecution.[13]

Although the Fifth Amendment does not apply to the states, in 1956 in *Slochower* v. *Board of Education* the Supreme Court held that New York City could not automatically dismiss a public school teacher from his position merely because he had claimed the Fifth Amendment. Such automatic dismissal denied the teacher due process and thus violated the Fourteenth Amendment. However, in 1959 the Belian Case undermined the significance of this ruling.[14] The Supreme Court sustained Philadelphia's dismissal of Belian from his post as a teacher after he had claimed the Fifth Amendment before the House Un-American Activities Committee. Philadelphia officials had been careful to base their dismissal on the grounds of Belian's "incompetency," which they had inferred from his refusal to answer questions about his political affiliations put to him by school authorities. Although Belian's refusal to answer these questions of school authorities, rather than his recourse to the Fifth Amendment before a Congressional investigating Committee, was the ostensible reason for his dismissal, the questioning by school authorities had taken

---

11 *Blau* v. *United States* (1950).

12 *Knapp* v. *Schweitzer* (1957).

13 See J. A. C. Grant, "Federalism and Self-Incrimination," *University of California at Los Angeles Law Review*, June, 1957, and January, 1958, pp. 549-582 and pp. 1-25 for persuasive evidence against these interpretations of the self-incrimination clause.

14 *Belian* v. *Board of Education*.

place some thirteen months earlier and it was not until immediately after Belian had pleaded the Fifth Amendment that he was dismissed.

In 1954 Congress passed an Immunity Act in order to force witnesses to testify on matters involving national security. Under the Immunity Act, whenever a majority of either house of Congress, two-thirds of the members of a congressional committee, or a United States district attorney deems such action necessary, they may petition a federal district judge to grant the witness immunity. After a witness has been given this immunity, he is guaranteed immunity against *federal* or *state* prosecution for crimes uncovered by his compelled testimony, and he may no longer use the Fifth Amendment to refuse to answer.[15]

THE WRIT OF HABEAS CORPUS

Even though the framers did not think a Bill of Rights necessary, they considered certain rights important enough to be included in the original Constitution. Foremost is the guarantee that the *writ of habeas corpus will be available unless suspended in time of rebellion or invasion,* Since permission to suspend the writ of habeas corpus is found in the article setting forth the powers and organization of Congress, presumably only Congress has the right to suspend it. When President Lincoln assumed this privilege on his own during the Civil War, Congress subsequently and retroactively authorized him to do so.

There are several kinds of writ of habeas corpus and, as developed in the United States, the device has several uses. Simply stated, it is a court order to any official having a person in his custody, directing him to produce the prisoner in court and explain to the court the reasons for confining him. A person held in custody applies under oath (usually through his attorney) stating why he believes that he is being held unlawfully. The judge then orders the jailer to show cause why the writ should not be issued. Testimony can be taken if there is a dispute over the facts. If the judge finds that the prisoner is being unlawfully detained, he orders the prisoner's release.

The case of Messrs. Duncan and White is a good example of one use of the writ. Duncan and White were civilians who had been convicted by military tribunals and were being held by military authorities in Hawaii during World War II. They filed petitions for writs of habeas corpus in the District Court of Hawaii, citing both statutory and constitutional reasons to prove that the military had no right to keep them in prison. The court then asked the military officers to show cause why the petition should not be granted. The military replied that Hawaii had become part of an active theater of war, that the writ of habeas corpus had been suspended, that martial law had been established, and that consequently the District Court had no jurisdiction to issue the writs.

---

[15] *Ullman* v. *United States* (1956).

Moreover, the military answered, even if the writ of habeas corpus had not been suspended, it should not be issued in this case because the military trials of Duncan and White were valid. After hearing both sides, the District Court, in an action eventually approved by the Supreme Court, agreed with Duncan and White, and issued writs ordering their release.[16]

State courts do not have the power to issue writs to federal officials. But a federal judge may issue writs to *state* officers whenever it appears that a person is being held in violation of a federal law, treaty, or the Constitution. The applicant must first show that he has exhausted his remedies at state law, and persons are released only in the most unusual circumstances. Even so, a good many habeas corpus cases come before federal judges. Recently, protest has been growing against the habeas corpus jurisdiction of federal district judges. Some state officials have asked that the federal district courts be denied the power to nullify state court judgments in criminal cases. On the other hand, many oppose any action to restrict the full use of this important procedure, which gives to all persons within the United States easy access to the courts and protection against arbitrary arrest and imprisonment.

EX POST FACTO LAWS AND BILLS OF ATTAINDER

The Constitution in express terms forbids both the national and state governments to pass ex post facto laws or enact bills of attainder (Article I, Sections 9 and 10).

An *ex post facto law is a retroactive criminal law that works to the detriment of an individual*—for example, a law making a particular act a crime that was not a crime when committed, or a law increasing the punishment for a crime after it was committed. The prohibition of ex post facto laws does not prevent the passage of retroactive civil laws—for example, increasing income tax rates as applied to income already earned—nor does it prevent the passage of retroactive penal laws that work to the *benefit* of an accused—for example, a law decreasing a punishment or changing the rules of evidence to make conviction more difficult.

A *bill of attainder is a legislative act inflicting punishment on specified individuals without judicial trial*. Bills of attainder have been rare in American history. Perhaps the most famous was one enacted by Congress less than two decades ago.

In 1943 Representative Martin Dies, then chairman of the House Committee on Un-American Activities, denounced from the floor of Congress thirty-nine officials as "crackpot, radical bureaucrats." He singled out three of these men for special abuse. Shortly afterward, Congress attached a rider to an appropriation bill naming these three employees and ordering that they should receive no salary from the federal government until the President had reap-

---

[16] *Duncan* v. *Kahanamoku* (1946).

pointed them and the Senate had confirmed their nominations. President Roosevelt, convinced that Congress had acted unconstitutionally, refused to resubmit their names. The three men kept on working and sued for their salaries in the Court of Claims, which upheld their claim. The Supreme Court, affirming that decision, ruled (in *United States* v. *Lovett,* 1948) that by accusing the men of disloyalty and denying them their pay Congress had punished them without a trial and thus had violated the constitutional prohibition against bills of attainder.

Rights of Persons Accused of Crime

That the innocent will go free and that the guilty will be punished, that rich and poor, educated and ignorant will secure justice under law—these are among the most ancient and honorable goals of free nations.[17] Some feel that the rights of persons accused of crime are less important that other civil liberties, but, as Justice Frankfurter has written, "The history of liberty has largely been the history of observance of procedural safeguards." These safeguards, moreover, have frequently "been forged in controversies involving not very nice people." Their purpose is not "to convenience the guilty but to protect the innocent."

JOHN T. CROOK AND THE FEDERAL COURTS

The rights of persons accused of crime by the national government can be found in the Fourth, Fifth, Sixth, and Eighth Amendments. In order to get some idea of the application of these constitutional safeguards, let's follow the fortunes and misfortunes of John T. Crook. (This is a purely fictitious name.)

Crook sent circulars through the mails soliciting purchases of stock in a nonexistent gold mine. This action is contrary to at least three federal laws. When postal officers uncovered these activities, they went to the district court and secured warrants to arrest Crook and to search his house for copies of the circulars. They found Crook at home, arrested him for using the mails to defraud, and seized some of the circulars. Crook was promptly brought before a federal district judge, who set bail at $1500 and ordered him held over until the convening of the next federal grand jury in the district. After posting bond, Crook was permitted his freedom so long as he remained within the limits of the judicial district.

When the next grand jury was convened, the United States district attorney brought before the twenty-three jurors evidence to indicate that Crook had committed a federal crime. Grand jurors are concerned not with a man's guilt or innocence, but merely with whether there seems to be enough evidence to

---

[17] For a comprehensive treatment of the rights of persons accused of crime, see David Fellman, *The Defendant's Rights* (Rinehart, 1958).

warrant bringing him to trial. No person has a *right* to appear before a grand jury, but he may be *invited* or *ordered* to do so. If a majority of the grand jurors agree that a trial is justified, they return what is known as a "true bill" or "indictment." Except in cases arising in the military forces, the national government cannot force any person to stand trial for any serious crime except on grand jury indictment. In our particular case, the grand jury agreed with the United States district attorney and returned a true bill against Crook.

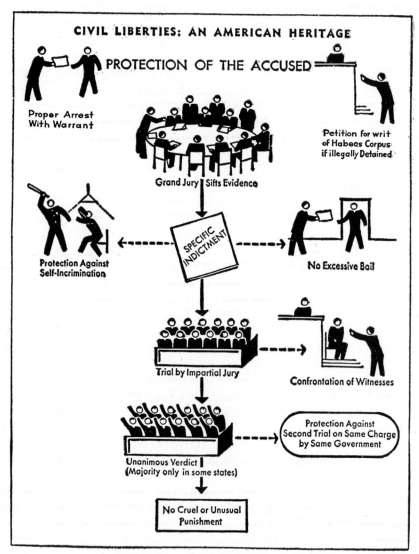

From *Our Constitutional Freedoms* by Robert E. Cushman, published by the Public Affairs Committee, Inc., and the National Foundation for Education in American Citizenship

A copy of the indictment was served on Crook and he was again ordered before a federal district judge. A poor and ignorant man, Crook did not know that he had a constitutional right to the *assistance of counsel,* and that even if he could not afford to pay for an attorney the national government could not bring him to trial without legal assistance. The judge saw to it that he was informed of his right and after being told that Crook had no money, the judge appointed a lawyer to undertake his defense. The Constitution also guarantees to the accused the right to be *informed of the nature and cause of the accusation* so that he can prepare his defense; consequently, the federal prosecuting officers had seen to it that the indictment clearly stated the nature of the offense, and they had given copies to Crook and his lawyer. After consulting with his lawyer, Crook entered the plea of "not guilty."

After indictment, Crook's bail was raised to $3000. Now the federal government was obliged to give him a *speedy and public trial;* the word "speedy" should not be taken too literally, however, especially since Crook had to be given time to prepare his defense. His lawyer pointed out that he had the right to a *trial by an impartial jury* selected from the state and district where the alleged crime was committed, but that his right could be waived and the trial could be held before a judge alone. After some thought, however, the attorney advised him to take his chances with a jury.

Crook told his lawyer that he had had dinner with George X. Witness on the night on which he was charged with sending the damaging circulars. But when Witness was approached, he said that he was unwilling to testify at the trial. The attorney took advantage of Crook's constitutional right to *obtain witnesses in his favor,* and had the judge subpoena Witness to appear at the trial and testify. Witness could have refused to testify on the grounds that his testimony would tend to incriminate him, but he agreed to testify. Crook himself, however, chose to use his constitutional right not to be a witness against himself and refused to take the witness stand. He knew that if he did so, the prosecution would have a right to cross-examination, and he was fearful of what might be uncovered. The federal judge conducting the trial cautioned the jury against drawing any conclusions from Crook's reluctance to testify—although nothing could prevent the jurors from being affected. All prosecution witnesses appeared in court and were available to defense cross-examination, since the Constitution insists that the accused has the right to *be confronted with the witnesses against him.*

At the conclusion of the trial, the jury rendered a verdict of "guilty." The judge then raised Crook's bail to $5000 and announced that he would hand down a sentence on the following Monday. The Eighth Amendment forbids *excessive bail,* the levying of *excessive fines,* and the *inflicting of cruel and unusual punishments.* But in view of Crook's past record and the nature of the offense, the bail could not be considered excessive; nor when the judge, in accordance with the law, gave Crook the maximum punishment of $5000 fine and five years in jail, could it be considered cruel and unusual punishment.

Since the Constitution forbids the federal government to place anyone *twice in jeopardy for the same offense,* Crook could not be tried again by federal courts for this crime. But double jeopardy does not apply to actions initiated by the defendant. Crook's lawyer appealed to the court of appeals on the ground that the judge had improperly instructed the jury. If the court of appeals had sustained the appeal, which it did not, and ordered a new trial, no double jeopardy would have been involved. Finally, the Supreme Court refused to review the case and Crook went to jail.

In addition to the protection of the specific provisions of the Constitution, Crook was entitled to certain safeguards insured by the more general terms of the *due process clause.* Due process, which requires that persons receive fair treatment, goes beyond mere forms of procedure. Even if all the specific provisions of the Constitution are scrupulously followed, a trial might be unfair if, for example, the judge were, in his words and manner, obviously antagonistic and biased against the accused. Or suppose the jury returned a verdict of guilty on the basis of perjured testimony. Although there would be no specific procedural error in these cases, the trial would not have been fair, justice would not have been done, and the due process clause would have been violated.

The State Courts and the National Constitution

After three years in the federal penitentiary, Crook was paroled. But his freedom was short-lived. The next day he was arrested by state officers, brought before a state judge, and charged with violating the state statutes against fraud. He protested that he had already been tried and punished by the federal government for using the mails for fraudulent purposes, and he pointed to the Fifth Amendment provision that no person shall "be subject for the same offense to be twice put in jeopardy of life or limb."

The judge answered that the double jeopardy provision is contained in the Fifth Amendment and the Fifth Amendment does not apply to the states. Anyway, the judge told Crook, "the Supreme Court of the United States has said that double jeopardy prevents only two trials by the *same* government for the *same* offense." [18] Crook, who had learned something about constitutional rights while serving in the federal penitentiary, then argued that the Fourteenth Amendment, which *does* apply to the states, forbids them to prosecute persons for offenses for which the persons have already been tried by the federal government. But the judge pointed to a 1959 Supreme Court decision in which the Court had even sustained a state conviction of a man for robbing a bank after he had previously been *acquitted* by a federal court of robbing the same bank. [19]

What constitutional rights can Crook claim in the state courts? In the

---

[18] *United States* v. *Lanza* (1922).
[19] *Bartkus* v. *Illinois.*

first place, every state constitution contains a bill of rights listing practically the same guarantees against state abridgment that the Bill of Rights in the national Constitution contains against national abridgment. By and large, however, state judges have been less inclined than federal judges to construe constitutional guarantees of their own state constitutions liberally in favor of those accused of crime.

To what extent does the national Constitution protect courtroom freedoms from state abridgment? The Bill of Rights does not apply to the states, but the Fourteenth Amendment does, and it contains two clauses of great importance in courtroom procedures—the *due process* and the *equal protection* clauses.

The equal-protection-of-the-laws clause protects persons accused of crime against discriminatory state action. Hence, in those cases where the state provides trial by jury, it must be a fair and impartial jury. A jury, either grand or petit (trial), from which Negroes have been barred because of their race would not be able constitutionally to try a Negro, for this would deny him equal protection of the laws. (Such action would also violate the civil rights of Negroes denied the opportunity to serve on juries.) Nor could a state provide different punishments for persons of different races or religions.

THE FOURTEENTH AMENDMENT, DUE PROCESS, AND THE BILL OF RIGHTS

It is clear that states do not have to follow in criminal prosecutions the same procedures specified in the Bill of Rights for the national government. This does not mean that states can act arbitrarily, for the due process clause of the Fourteenth Amendment requires the states to proceed in a just fashion. As the Supreme Court has put it, states may use any procedures they wish provided they do not act in a manner "shocking to the sense of justice of the civilized world." Just what is shocking, the Supreme Court finally decides as cases are brought before its bar.

Some Supreme Court justices, but always in a minority, have argued that instead of using the subjective, vague test of "fundamental fairness" to determine whether state procedures violate due process, the due process clause should be construed to apply to the states precisely the same restrictions that the Bill of Rights applies to the national government. These justices contend that what the *national* government cannot do because of the *Bill of Rights,* the *state* governments should not be permitted to do because of the Fourteenth Amendment.

The Supreme Court majority, however, has steadfastly refused to accept the view that the Fourteenth Amendment incorporates *all* the guarantees of the Bill of Rights. But the Court has recognized that *some* of the rights secured against abridgment by federal authorities by the Bill of Rights are protected against state abridgment by the Fourteenth Amendment. The test to determine which rights are, so to speak, automatically incorporated into the Fourteenth was laid down by Justice Cardozo for the Court in *Palko* v. *Connecticut* (1937): the rights automatically covered by the Fourteenth are those "implicit in the concept of ordered liberty" which are so important that neither "liberty nor justice would exist if they were sacrificed," and every denial of which would be "shocking to the sense of justice of the civilized world." For example, freedom of thought and speech are rights so fundamental that there could be no liberty or justice if they were lost, they are the "matrix, the indispensable condition, of nearly every other form of freedom." Hence, freedom of speech is automatically protected by the Fourteenth Amendment. On the other hand, the right to be indicted only by a grand jury or the right to be tried only by a jury of twelve are not rights inherent in the concept of ordered liberty; their replacement by other procedures would not necessarily be a denial of justice or "shocking to the sense of justice of the civilized world." In England, for example, many persons are tried by judges without juries, yet we cannot say that this is a denial of justice. Hence, states may if they wish try persons only before judges without violating the Fourteenth Amendment.

Using the Palko test, the Supreme Court has brought within the scope of the Fourteenth Amendment all provisions of the First Amendment, the prohibition against unreasonable searches and seizures of the Fourth, that part of the Sixth Amendment guaranteeing a public trial, and that part of the Eighth Amendment forbidding cruel and unusual punishment.[20] The Court has also ruled that the following procedures are so unjust, so shocking that they are under all circumstances contrary to due process: conviction based on coerced confession; trial in an atmosphere so hostile that calm deliberation is impossible; trial without the assistance of counsel in cases involving possible capital punishment.[21]

On the other hand, the Court has held that the following do not *necessarily* violate due process: indictment by means other than grand jury; compelling a witness to testify against himself (in the absence of physical or psychological coercion); placing a man twice in jeopardy; trial without a jury; and trial without assistance of counsel in other than capital cases. Whether or not such procedures are unconstitutional depends on the circumstances. For example, suppose a state brings to trial for armed robbery a young, frightened, and ignorant boy who is without legal assistance. Under these conditions his trial would be so unfair that it would violate due process. On the other hand, trial of a mature and knowledgeable adult without assistance of counsel is not so shocking—at least to a Supreme Court majority—that the states are required to provide legal assistance in all trials in order to comply with the due process requirement.

---

[20] *Wolf* v. *Colorado* (1949); *In re Oliver* (1948); *Louisiana ex rel Francis* v. *Resweber* (1947). For more detailed coverage see Richard A. Edwards, *The Fourteenth Amendment and Civil Liberty* (Carrie Chapman Catt Memorial Fund, Inc., 1955).

[21] *Adamson* v. *California* (1947) and cases cited therein.

RELATION BETWEEN BILL OF RIGHTS

AND THE FOURTEENTH AMENDMENT DUE PROCESS CLAUSE

Provisions of National Bill of Rights which apply to states because included within the Fourteenth Amendment

FIRST AMENDMENT

No law establishing a religion.	*Applies to states.*
Freedom of religion.	*Applies to states.*
Freedom of speech and press.	*Applies to states.*
Freedom of assembly and petition.	*Applies to states.*

SECOND AMENDMENT

Right to keep and bear arms not to be denied.	*Does not apply to states.*

THIRD AMENDMENT

No soldiers to be quartered in private homes during time of peace, and in time of war only as the law allows.	*Does not apply to states except where the taking of private property is involved (see Fifth Amendment below).*

FOURTH AMENDMENT

No unreasonable searches and seizures.	*Applies to states; however, without violating the Constitution, states may use evidence obtained by an unreasonable search and seizure, provided no force was used to obtain the evidence.*

FIFTH AMENDMENT

No indictments for serious offenses except by a grand jury. (Does not apply to members of armed forces.)	*Does not apply to states.*
No person shall be twice placed in jeopardy for the same offense.	*Does not apply to states. No specific Supreme Court ruling, but probably the Court would declare unconstitutional several trials of person for same offense if no errors of law were committed in the first trial.*
No person shall be compelled to be a witness against himself in criminal prosecution.	*Does not apply to states; however, no state may coerce confessions by physical or mental torture or use such confessions against the defendant himself.*
No witness may be compelled to answer questions which will incriminate him (by interpretation from provisions mentioned just above).	*Does not apply to states, but torture may not be used.*
No person shall be denied life, liberty, or property without due process of law.	*Same provision specifically applied to states by Fourteenth Amendment.*
Private property may not be taken except for public use and with just compensation.	*Applies to states.*

SIXTH AMENDMENT

Accused persons to have speedy and public trial.

Applies to states.

Trial by impartial jury.

Jury trial not required; but if there is one, the jury must be impartial and states may not exclude members of defendant's race or national origin because of their race or national origin.

Trial in district where crime committed.

Does not apply to states.

Accused must be informed of nature and cause of accusation.

Applies to states; essential for a fair trial; criminal statutes must not be vague or ambiguous.

Accused must be confronted with witnesses against him.

No specific Supreme Court ruling, but probably necessary in order to have a fair trial.

Accused must have compulsory process for obtaining witnesses in his favor.

Does not apply to states.

Accused must have right to the assistance of counsel in criminal prosecutions.

States must permit defendants to have counsel, but not required to secure legal assistance for indigent defendants except in cases involving capital punishment or where special circumstances such as youth or ignorance make legal assistance necessary to a fair trial.

SEVENTH AMENDMENT

Jury trials in suits of common law.

Does not apply to states.

EIGHTH AMENDMENT

Excessive bail shall not be required.

Does not apply to states; however, denial of bail or imposition of excessive bail under some circumstances could result in denial of due process.

Excessive fines shall not be imposed, nor cruel and unusual punishments exacted.

Applies to states.

NINTH AMENDMENT

Listing of some rights not to disparage existence of others.

Does not apply to states.

TENTH AMENDMENT

Powers not given to national government and not denied to states are reserved to states or to the people.

Not applicable to states.

NOTE: The fact that the Fourteenth Amendment may not deny a state the right to do certain things does not automatically mean the state is free to do those things. The bill of rights in a *state* constitution frequently denies a state the power to do what the *national* Constitution would permit.

How Just Is Our System of Justice?

What are the major criticisms of the American system of justice? How have they been answered?

Too many loopholes. In our zeal to protect the innocent and to place the burden of proof upon the government, it is argued, we have established so many elaborate procedures that justice is delayed, disrespect for the law is encouraged, and guilty men are allowed to go unpunished. Justice should be swift and sure without being arbitrary. But under our procedures a criminal may go unpunished because (1) the police decide not to arrest him, (2) the judge decides not to hold him, (3) the prosecutor decides not to prosecute him, (4) the grand jury decides not to indict him, (5) the jury decides not to convict him, (6) the judge decides not to sentence him, (7) an appeals court decides to reverse the conviction, or (8) the executive decides to pardon, reprieve, or parole him.

As a result, some complain, the public never knows whom to hold responsible when laws are not enforced. The police can blame the prosecutor, the prosecutor can blame the police, and they can all blame the grand jury.

And yet there is more to justice than simply securing convictions. We must remember that all steps in the administration of criminal laws developed out of centuries of trial and error and that each of them has been constructed to provide protection against particular abuses. History warns against entrusting the awful instruments of the criminal law to a single functionary. For this reason responsibility is vested in many officials. And as long as all these safeguards are maintained, no one need fear for his life or liberty because of the overzealous or despotic action of another.

The most debated step in the administration of justice is the grand jury. Many students feel that the grand jury is unnecessary. W. F. Willoughby has summarized these criticisms of the grand jury as follows: that it

> is in the nature of a fifth wheel; that real responsibility for the bringing of criminal charges is in fact exercised by the prosecuting attorney, the grand jury doing little or nothing more than follow his suggestions; that it entails delay . . . ; that it renders prosecution more difficult through important witnesses getting beyond the jurisdiction . . . or through memory of facts becoming weakened by lapse of time; that it entails unnecessary expense to the government; and that it imposes a great burden on the citizen called upon to render jury service.[22]

As a result of such criticisms the grand jury has been largely replaced in England. And in this country twenty-eight of our states allow the prosecuting attorney to dispense with grand jury indictments for all but the most serious

---

[22] W. F. Willoughby, *Principles of Judicial Administration* (Brookings Institution, 1929), p. 186.

crimes. The prosecutor simply files an *information* affidavit that he has evidence in his possession to justify a trial.

But the grand jury has its defenders, who see it as necessary to protect innocent persons against arbitrary prosecutors. Although in a formal sense a man is still presumed to be innocent even after he has been charged with committing a crime, in actual practice indictment injures a person's reputation and subjects him to the expense and strain of defending himself. On the other hand, grand juries have the power—and there are many instances where they have used it—to carry out their own independent investigations and to act when a lax prosecutor is permitting crimes to go unpunished. The grand jury is one of the few agencies with the power to limit the almost unfettered discretion of the prosecuting officers.

Too unreliable. Critics who complain that our system of justice is unreliable point to trial by jury as the chief source of trouble. Trial by jury, they argue, leads to a theatrical combat between lawyers who base their appeals on the prejudice and sentiments of the jurors. "Mr. Prejudice and Miss Sympathy are the names of witnesses whose testimony is never recorded but must nevertheless be reckoned with in trials by jury." [23] Too often verdicts are influenced by the jurors' dislike for an attorney's personality or for a defendant's appearance. In addition, because of mass circulation of newspapers, untrained jurors are easily swayed by the prejudices and sentiments of the community and lack the training to distinguish between fact and fiction. No other country relies as much as does the United States on trial by jury. In short, according to this argument, the jury system is an unreliable method of sorting the guilty from the innocent.

Defenders of the system reply that trial by jury provides an invaluable check by nonprofessionals over the actions of judges and prosecutors. Justice is too important to be left to the professionals. True, juries are sometimes swayed by their feelings, but the record of judges is not substantially better. The jury system, moreover, helps to educate citizens and enables them to participate in the application of their own laws. The jury trial, said Justice Murphy, has the beneficial effect of "leavening justice with the spirit of the times." Abuses in the system call for improvement, not abolishment.

Too inflexible. The elaborate and detailed procedures of our system of justice, some critics complain, stem from the day when people wanted to limit the behavior of royal officials over whom they had no other control. But now there are better methods of preventing abuse. Modern newspapers and other media of information also reduce the danger that officials will act despotically. Then, too, hemming in the administrators of criminal laws with detailed procedures denies them the discretion that modern criminology calls for. Each criminal should be dealt with as an individual, and the findings of sociology, psychology, and criminology should be applied to protect the community and

---

[23] Jerome Frank, *Courts on Trial* (Princeton Univ. Press, 1949), p. 122.

to rehabilitate the criminal. More attention should be paid to selecting better prosecutors and judges, and to insuring them the discretion they need to administer justice.

Again, defenders of the system reply that the day of arbitrary officials has not passed. They cite cases in which prosecutors, judges, and juries have deprived individuals of justice or have failed to prosecute the guilty. So long as we have to deal with men as they are, rather than as they should be, we must limit the discretion of those who apply criminal law and trust to the Constitution itself to provide the system with the necessary flexibility.

4. *Too undemocratic.* There are two parts to this indictment. First, it is argued that the high cost of justice gives an advantage to the man who can afford the best legal advice and who can pay for the appeals and other expenses connected with preparing his defense. True, the Sixth Amendment requires federal judges to assign counsel to all impoverished persons accused of serious federal crimes. But the Fourteenth Amendment requires *state* judges to do so only in cases involving capital punishment or in cases where peculiar circumstances—youth or ignorance of the defendant, for example—make the assignment of counsel necessary for a fair trial. The second part of the indictment is that Negroes and other minority groups do not receive equal treatment before the law.

Undeniably there is much evidence to back up both these accusations. But a poor man or a Negro is more likely to get fair treatment before a court of justice than before any other agency in our society. The ideal of equal justice for all is generally honored in American criminal procedures, although courts are inevitably composed of men who reflect the prejudices and values of society. Judges and juries, even when surrounded by elaborate safeguards, cannot be expected to shed their personal attitudes and sentiments when they enter the courtroom. Where poverty and prejudice exist in the community, they will affect all institutions of the community. And yet there are few agencies that do as much as the courts to isolate prejudice and to compensate for poverty.

In summary, some observers believe that our system of justice could be improved without sacrificing the essential safeguards. But others believe along with the late Justice Rutledge that "the old time-tried 'principles and institutions of the common law' perpetuated for us in the Bill of Rights" are a "basic charter of personal liberty, and there should be no experimentation with them under the guise of improving the administration of justice." [24]

The Supreme Court and Civil Liberties

In our discussion of civil liberties in the last three chapters, it has become clear that the judges, espe-

---

[24] Concurring opinion, *In re Oliver* (1948).

cially those on the Supreme Court, play a significant role in enforcing constitutional guarantees. In fact, this combination of judicial enforcement and written guarantees of enumerated liberties is one of the basic features of the American system of government. The full significance of this combination has only recently been recognized (though at times exaggerated). Many of the framers, for example, thought of the Bill of Rights merely as a statement of general principles to guide government officials. But the Bill of Rights is now regarded as a *judicially enforceable limitation* on legislative and executive powers.

This emphasis on constitutional limitations and judicial enforcement is an example of the "auxiliary precautions" that James Madison felt were necessary to prevent arbitrary governmental action. Other free nations tend to rely more on free elections and political checks to protect their rights. But in the United States we look to judges to hear appeals from people who feel that their freedoms are being jeopardized. All judges, not only those on the Supreme Court, have taken an oath to measure the actions of public officials against the appropriate *constitutional,* as well as legislative, provisions.

English judges have authority to restrain executive officials from depriving people of their legal rights, but they do not have the power to declare legislative acts unconstitutional. Moreover, Englishmen place primary reliance on an alert and aroused public opinion, operating through elected officials, to safeguard their liberty. The late Justice Jackson once commented: "I have been repeatedly impressed with the speed and certainty with which the slightest invasion of British individual freedom or minority rights by officials of the government is picked up in Parliament, not merely by the opposition but by the party in power, and made the subject of persistent questioning, criticism, and sometimes rebuke. There is no waiting on the theory that the judges will take care of it. . . . In Great Britain, to observe civil liberties is good politics and to transgress the rights of the individual or minority is bad politics. In the United States, I cannot say this is so." [25]

In the United States, our emphasis on the judicial protection of civil liberties focuses attention on the Supreme Court. The High Court gets the headlines, but it is the judges of lower courts, both national and state, policemen, prosecutors, newspaper reporters, and other citizens who are on the firing lines. Only a small number of controversies get to the Supreme Court. It is the inferior court judge and the policeman on the beat who have to translate the doctrines of the Supreme Court and apply them to hundreds of cases. It is the police officer who, acting for his local community, has to decide on the spot whether a particular speaker is inciting people to riot or merely exercising his freedom of speech.

To focus attention on constitutionality of laws is to risk ignoring consideration of their merits. Much that is constitutional may still be unwise, and it is often more important to ask *should* it be done rather than ask *may* it

---

[25] Robert H. Jackson, *The Supreme Court in the American System of Government* (Harvard Univ. Press, 1955), pp. 81-82.

constitutionally be done. Moreover, to consider civil liberties only in the context of constitutionality may cause us to ignore other factors of critical significance in determining the extent of our liberties. We cannot protect freedom merely through law suits and legal decisions. A society plagued by depression, hysteria, and fifth columnists offers a poor prospect for keeping freedom, no matter what is set down in the Constitution or what the judges may decide. Efforts to prevent poverty and insecurity, to preserve order and stability, may have more to do with maintaining our constitutional freedoms than the actions of our judges.

We must not, of course, underestimate the contribution of the nine justices of the Supreme Court in defending civil liberties. Even aside from their decision-making power, their opinions are influential in clarifying the law and determining people's attitudes. But judges by themselves cannot guarantee anything. Neither can the First Amendment. As the late Justice Jackson once asked: "Must we first maintain a system of free political government to assure a free judiciary, or can we rely on an aggressive, activist judiciary to guarantee free government? . . . [It] is my belief that the attitude of a society and of its organized political forces, rather than its legal machinery, is the controlling force in the character of free institutions. . . . [Any] court which undertakes by its legal processes to enforce civil liberties needs the support of an enlightened and vigorous public opinion. . . ." [26] In short, only so long as we desire liberty for ourselves and are willing to restrict our own actions in order to preserve the liberty of others can freedom be maintained.

Summary

1. Property rights were built by the Supreme Court into a powerful restraint on governmental regulation of business, with the help of the doctrine of *substantive* due process. Today property rights, like all rights, are subject to regulation by the legislature, but fair procedures must be used.
2. The Bill of Rights guarantees a host of *procedural* rights against *federal* interference. *All* basic rights (such as freedom of speech and religion), but only *some* procedural rights, are protected against *state* interference by the Fourteenth Amendment. State and local governments, however, are also restrained by their respective state constitutions, which are interpreted and enforced by state courts.
3. The American system of justice is criticized on several scores, but its defenders insist that in this country it provides the best means of protecting the innocent and punishing the guilty.
4. Judges have a major responsibility to enforce the constitutional guarantees of civil liberties, but they cannot do the job without the support of the people. Civil liberties are everybody's business.

---

[26] *Ibid.*

CHAPTER **9**

Immigrants, Aliens, and Citizens

Remember, remember always that all of us, and you and I especially," President Franklin D. Roosevelt once said to a convention of the Daughters of the American Revolution, "are descended from immigrants and revolutionists." Beginning with a trickle, rising to a flood tide, and recently subsiding to a small stream, the flow of immigration has persisted since the first colonists touched the shores of the New World. After their long and arduous journey across the sea most of the early arrivals moved on to the rich farmlands of the continent; later immigrants, often lacking money and skills to cultivate the soil, tended to cluster in seaports and inland cities.

Once here, most of the immigrants were anxious to throw off their alien status and become full members of the body politic. This chapter describes the rules that determine who may come to the United States, the rights that aliens enjoy when they get here, and how an immigrant is transformed into a citizen of the United States.

The Land of Immigrants   **C**ongress has complete constitutional power to decide who shall be admitted to the United States and under what conditions. Ironically, some Americans, themselves immigrants or descendants of immigrants, have urged Congress ever since the days of the Alien Acts of 1798 to use its powers to keep others from entering the land of the free. After each generation of immigrants became integrated into American life, some of them displayed toward newer arrivals the same hostility and criticism that they themselves had encountered. At every stage some have insisted that the quality of persons seeking admission is not as high as it was when they or their ancestors came. First the English looked down on the Irish, then the Irish on the Germans, then the

216

Germans on the Italians, Poles, Russians, and others from southern and eastern Europe. But, although there was considerable agitation against the admission of the Irish, especially during the 1830's and 1840's, it was not until 1875 that Congress began to impose restrictions on immigration.

In 1875 Congress established the first of the so-called "qualitative" limitations by excluding certain types of criminals and prostitutes. A few years later convicts, lunatics, and idiots were added to the list. In 1882 Congress completely barred entry by the Chinese. Toward the end of the century Congress closed the door to paupers, polygamists, and persons suffering from certain "dangerous and loathsome diseases." In 1903 the first political test was established, excluding anarchists and advocates of the forceful overthrow of government. In 1907 Japan, by a "Gentlemen's Agreement," promised to prevent the emigration of Japanese laborers to the United States. In 1917, over President Wilson's veto, Congress made illiteracy grounds for exclusion and added further racial restrictions to bar most Asiatics. But despite these restrictions, until World War I the land of opportunity remained open to the "tired and huddled masses" of Europe.

Courtesy Library of Congress

"The Last Yankee"—A cartoon attacking unrestricted immigration, 1888.

Just before the war, over a million people were entering the United States every year. Then during the war the gates were closed.

CLOSING THE GATES

After World War I, organized labor began to fear that the resumption of immigration by European workers would undercut the American wage scale and prevent the organization of unions. Pressures against a liberal immigration policy were strengthened by the growing fear of un-American ideas, and by pseudo-biological claims that the population of the United States was being "mongrelized." Hence, in 1924 the wartime-imposed "quantitative" limits on immigration were made permanent.

The 1924 Immigration Act barred Asiatics entirely, and immigration from Europe was limited to not more than 154,000 a year. *Quotas* were allotted to each nationality in proportion to the number of people of that national background who were living in the United States in 1920. The purpose of these quotas was to curtail immigration from southern and southeastern Europe, whence the greatest proportion of immigrants had come during the early years of the twentieth century. These people, primarily Catholics and Jews, had aroused the prejudices of the earlier immigrants.

LEADING SOURCES OF IMMIGRATION TO THE UNITED STATES AT DIFFERENT PERIODS

Period	County and area*	Period of largest volume of immigration of each region
Colonial	Great Britain and Northern Ireland	
1820-60	Ireland	1851-55
	Germany (mainly west and southwest)	
	Palatinate-Rhine hinterland (1820-30)	
	Weser hinterland (1830-40)	
	Elbe hinterland (Westphalia, etc.) (1840-50)	
1861-90	Germany (mainly east)	1881-85
	Ireland	
	Scandinavia	1886-90
1891-1920	Italy	1906-10
	North (up to 1890)	
	South (after 1890)	
	Austria-Hungary	1906-10
	Bohemia, Carinthia, Tyrol (up to 1900)	
	Galicia, Hungary (after 1900)	
	Russia (chiefly nonethnic Russians: Jews, Baltic peoples, Poles, Ukrainians)	1911-15
1921-30	Canada	1921-25
	Mexico	1921-25
	Italy (1921-24)	
	Germany	
1931-51	Germany (primarily refugees)	
	Canada	
1952-59	Canada	
	Mexico	
	Germany	

* Within each period listed in order of relative volume.

Source: Report of the President's Commission on Immmigration and Naturalization, *Whom We Shall Welcome* (Government Printing Office, 1952), p. 26, and *Statistical Abstract, 1959* (Government Printing Office, 1958), p. 26.

Although people from independent nations in the Western Hemisphere could still enter the United States without quota restrictions—subject only to the general laws excluding illiterates, criminals, anarchists, and the like—the combined effect of the restrictive laws and the depression was to reduce immigration in the 1930's to the smallest number in our history. In fact, between 1931 and 1935 more people left the United States than came in.

THE IMMIGRATION AND NATIONALITY ACT OF 1952

Although Congress has since the end of World War II enacted two temporary emergency measures to admit without quotas 650,000 persons who were displaced and uprooted from their homes by war and political upheavals, there been no general reversal of the restrictive immigration policy established in 1924. The most recent immigration act, the Immigration and Nationality Act of 1952, also known as the McCarran-Walter Act, did abolish race as a bar to immigration, but it fixed the over-all annual limit at 154,657 and retained the national-origin system for allotting quotas. Hence, our immigration laws continue to discriminate against Asiatics and southern and eastern Europeans. Since quotas are still based on the 1920 white population, only a few nationals of eastern and southern European countries are permitted entry each year. Japan, China, and India have an allotment of only a hundred each. Furthermore, any person, no matter where he was born, "attributable by as much as one-half of his ancestry" to peoples native to the Asia-Pacific zones, is charged against the limited Asiatic quotas. Thus a child born in England to a Chinese mother and an English father is classified as an Asiatic. The act also discriminates against colored people of the colonial regions in the Western Hemisphere by giving them a limited quota within the allotment of the mother country.

Since the largest annual allotments go to countries from which few people want to emigrate, and the smallest to those where there are large numbers waiting, considerably less than the permissible 154,657 *quota immigrants* come to the United States each year. National-origin limitations do not apply to natives of independent countries of the Western Hemisphere; husbands, wives, and minor children of American citizens; re-entering alien residents; ministers; and a few others. (These *nonquota* immigrants, however, must meet all the other requirements of the law.) And *nonimmigrant aliens* who come to the United States just for a visit do not have to secure a quota assignment.

The 1952 act retains the "qualitative" requirements of earlier laws and adds a few new ones. Thus, all immigrants, quota and otherwise, are excluded if they are illiterate, immoral, have contagious diseases, are likely to become public charges, are subversives, or are or have been members of totalitarian parties. A totalitarian party is defined to include communist organizations but not fascist organizations. The law also distinguishes between those who voluntarily joined a totalitarian party and those who were compelled to do so.

Persons who joined such parties because of compulsion or in order to obtain the necessities of life, and those whose membership terminated prior to their sixteenth birthday, may be admitted. Reformed totalitarians may also enter if they have for at least the past five years been actively opposed to the subversive organization of which they were a member, provided both the consular officials and the Attorney General believe that their admission would be in the public interest. Furthermore, Congress has given the President the power to refuse entry to any alien if he feels that it would be detrimental to the interests of the United States. The President's decisions on such matters are not subject to review by any court.

ANNUAL IMMIGRATION QUOTAS, BY COUNTRY

	1952 Immigration and Nationality Act
Total	154,657
Asia	2,990
Africa and Oceania	2,000
Europe	149,667
Northern and western Europe:	
Belgium	1,297
Denmark	1,175
France	3,069
Germany	25,814
Great Britain and Northern Ireland	65,361
Irish Free State	17,756
Netherlands	3,136
Norway	2,364
Sweden	3,295
Switzerland	1,698
Total northern and western Europe	126,131
Southern and eastern Europe:	
Austria	1,405
Czechoslovakia	2,859
Greece	308
Hungary	865
Italy	5,645
Poland	6,488
Portugal	438
Rumania	289
Union of Soviet Socialist Republics	2,697
Turkey	225
Yugoslavia	933
Total southern and eastern Europe	23,536

Source: Report of the President's Commission on Immigration and Naturalization. (Washington: Government Printing Office, 1952), pp. 75, 76.

A rounded description of our immigration laws has to take into account the hundreds of private bills adopted each year by Congress. A typical example is the case of Mr. J., who came as a student to the United States from Yugoslavia in 1951 on a nonimmigrant visa (a permit to enter). While at Northwestern University he met and married an American citizen. Although his marriage to an American citizen made him eligible for a nonquota visa for permanent residence, without special legislation he would have had to return to Yugoslavia to obtain such a visa. This would have been costly and dangerous, since Mr. J. had been outspoken in his criticism of the communist regime in his native country. So Mr. J. talked with a congressman who induced Congress to enact a law, applicable just to Mr. J., exempting him from the requirements of the general law. By passing special legislation in this and hundreds of other cases, Congress attempts to mitigate some of the harsher features of our immigration laws.

ADMISSION OF VISITORS

No quota restrictions are applied to students, businessmen, vacationers, or other aliens who wish to visit the United States. But, with certain exceptions, these nonimmigrants have to comply with the same detailed regulations as do those who intend to reside here permanently. Many visitors—scientists coming for a week to attend a scholarly conference, musicians to perform a concert, businessmen to trade—have complained of the red tape. They tell of the many days that are required to secure a visa, of being asked insulting questions, and of the indignity of being treated with suspicion by American officials. For a time all visitors even had to be fingerprinted, a procedure reserved in most countries for those suspected of being criminals. These restrictive regulations were embarrassing to the United States, especially in view of our criticism of the communist nations for their "iron curtains." At the urging of the Secretary of State, in 1957 Congress gave the Secretary, with the concurrence of the Attorney General, permission to waive fingerprinting requirements. Furthermore, by the end of 1957 the Immigration and Naturalization Service had streamlined its procedures, cut out much red tape, abolished visa fees for nationals of seventy-five countries, and instructed officials to welcome visitors as guests rather than to greet them as potential felons. But the law continues to require close inspection of all applicants for nonimmigrant visas.

ADMINISTRATION OF THE IMMIGRATION LAWS

Aliens seeking entrance have few, if any, constitutional rights. Congress has delegated to immigration officials almost absolute discretion and has deliberately created a system of dual administration. Applicants are screened both by consular officials of the Department of State and by the Immigration and Naturalization Service of the Department of Justice, each independent of the other.

Applicants for admission must first apply for a visa at a United States consulate abroad, where they are registered, fingerprinted, and made to take a physical and mental examination. They must furnish information about past activities, present status, and future intentions. They must have a passport or a travel document and copies of birth, military, and other records. If the consular official knows or has *reason to believe* that the applicant is ineligible for admission to the United States, he is instructed to deny the visa, a decision that cannot be reviewed, not even by the consul's superiors in the Department.

The granting of the visa, however, does not ensure entry. When the applicant arrives at an American port of entry, Public Health Service officers make another physical and mental examination, and Immigration officials make another check of admissibility. Decisions of these officers are reviewable within the Department of Justice, but only in unusual circumstances by a court. Finally, when this hurdle is cleared, the alien is allowed to enter.

Rights of Aliens

Once here, aliens remain in this country only at the sufferance of the national government. Aliens who enter illegally may be expelled without much ado. Even those who have been legally admitted may be deported for a variety of reasons, such as two convictions for crimes involving moral turpitude, joining an organization that advocates revolutionary doctrines, or if the Attorney General believes they intend, or have intended, to engage in activities "subversive to the national security." The Attorney General may even hold aliens without bail while he determines whether they are to be deported. His discretion is subject only to very narrow court review.

Since the Supreme Court has ruled that deportation, despite its drastic consequences, is a civil rather than a criminal proceeding, the constitutional prohibition against ex post facto laws does not apply. Aliens may be deported for acts that were not grounds for banishment when they were performed. In 1940 and 1950, for example, Congress changed the rules to require the expulsion of aliens who "at any time" after entering the United States became members of or affiliated with the Communist party, however brief such affiliation might have been or whatever their present political position. As a result, many aliens faced deportation, including some who had briefly joined the party years ago at a time when membership was not grounds for deportation and when the party was a legal institution appearing on many election ballots. For a time the Supreme Court interpreted the acts of Congress to require expulsion even of those aliens whose membership in the Communist party seemed to be devoid of any political implications.[1] But in 1957 by a five-to-four vote the Court ruled that Congress had not intended to banish these "innocents"; that before an alien can be deported, the government must have solid proof that he joined the party conscious of it as a distinct and active political organization and aware of its character.[2]

---

[1] *Galvan* v. *Press* (1954).
[2] *Rowaldt* v. *Perfetto* (1957).

CONSTITUTIONAL AND TREATY RIGHTS OF ALIENS

Aliens resident in the United States are subject to all general laws and, like citizens, they must pay taxes. Congress may, if it chooses, subject them to the draft. Under present laws, if an alien raises his foreign nationality as an objection to being drafted, he may be excused, but he loses all right ever to become a citizen.

Many constitutional provisions protect the rights not merely of citizens but of *persons*. For example, aliens accused of crimes enjoy the protection of the Fifth, Sixth, Eighth, and Fourteenth amendments. Moreover, the government has no more power to regulate the speech and religion of aliens than of citizens. Although aliens may be deported for political reasons, they have the same protection as citizens against criminal prosecution for their speech.

The equal protection and due process clauses protect aliens against arbitrary and unreasonable deprivation of life, liberty, or property by the states. State laws interfering with an alien's right to engage in normal businesses, or requiring employers to hire only citizens, have been declared unconstitutional. On the other hand, the Supreme Court has held that states may constitutionally reserve certain privileges for citizens, such as the right to own firearms, to enjoy the benefits of workmen's compensation, to practice law or medicine or other licensed professions, to be employed on public works, and to own real estate. And there is no question that states may deny aliens the right to vote or hold public office. The Supreme Court and some state courts, however, have tended recently to look askance at state laws that discriminate against aliens, although the basic doctrine that states may exclude aliens from certain privileges still stands.

According to various treaties, Americans living abroad are given certain rights in return for rights granted to other countries' nationals living here. Like all treaties, these are the supreme law of the land and take precedence over state enactments. The states, subject to Supreme Court review, are responsible for enforcing these treaties.

ALIEN REGISTRATION AND NATIONAL CONTROL

The national government requires resident aliens to register every year, giving their name, address, occupation, and other data, and to inform the Attorney General of any changes. In wartime, the liberty and property of resident nationals of enemy countries are further restricted. During World War II, for example, enemy aliens were not permitted to move from place to place without official permission, they were denied the right to own short-wave radios, and to some extent they lost control over their property. (Property located in the United States and owned by *non*resident enemy aliens was taken over by the national government.)

Above all, an alien does not have a legal right to reside in the United

States. In our war-torn and dictator-ridden world, the right of an American citizen to reside in the United States takes on additional value. But how is this citizenship acquired?

Citizenship   It was not until 1868, with the adoption of the Fourteenth Amendment, that the basic right to membership in the body politic was given constitutional protection. This amendment makes "all persons *born or naturalized* in the United States and subject to the jurisdiction thereof . . . citizens of the United States and of the State wherein they reside." Thus, with the minor exception, for example, of children born to foreign ambassadors and ministers (but not consuls), all persons born in the United States are citizens of this country regardless of the citizenship of their parents. (Congress has defined "the United States" to include Puerto Rico, Guam, and the Virgin Islands.) Members of Indian tribes were not made citizens of the United States by the Fourteenth Amendment, but Congress has by law conferred citizenship on persons born in the United States to members of Indian tribes.

The Fourteenth Amendment confers citizenship according to the principle of *jus soli*—that is, by place of birth. In addition, Congress has granted under certain conditions citizenship at birth according to the principle of *jus sanguinis*—that is, by blood. Thus a child born of American parents living abroad becomes an American citizen at birth provided at least one of his citizen parents had been physically present in the United States or one of its possessions prior to the child's birth. If only one parent is an American citizen and the other an alien, the child becomes a citizen at birth provided that parent had lived in the United States or one of its possessions for at least ten years, five of them after the age of fourteen. In order, however, to *retain* citizenship derived through only one citizen parent, a person must come to the United States before he is twenty-three and must live here for at least five years between his fourteenth and twenty-eighth birthday.

Citizenship may also be acquired by naturalization, collective or individual. The granting of citizenship to Puerto Ricans in 1917 by an act of Congress is an example of collective naturalization. Individual naturalization requirements are determined by Congress.

Today any nonenemy alien over 18 years of age who has been lawfully admitted for permanent residence (except a military deserter, draft dodger, or alien who has refused to serve in our armed forces because of allegiance to another country) can be naturalized if:

1. He has lawfully resided in the United States for at least five years, and for at least six months in the state or territory in which he files his petition for naturalization. (This time is reduced for spouses and children of citizens, persons who have served in the military or maritime service, former citizens, and persons performing religious duties abroad.)

2. He can read, write, and speak words in ordinary usage in the English language. (This requirement is waived for persons who were over fifty years of age on December 24, 1952, and who have lived in the United States for twenty years.)

3. He is and always has been of good moral character while a resident of the United States.

4. He understands and is attached to the fundamentals of the history, the principles, and the form of government of the United States and is well disposed toward the good order and happiness of this country.

5. He does not now (nor did he within ten years immediately prior to his application for citizenship) believe in, advocate, or belong to an organization that supports opposition to organized government, the overthrow of government by violence, the illegal destruction of property, or the doctrines of world communism or any other form of totalitarianism. If a petitioner establishes, however, that he joined a subversive organization involuntarily in order to obtain food or a job or other essentials, or that his membership occurred and terminated before he was sixteen, he may nevertheless be naturalized.

6. He takes an oath in open court to renounce all allegiance to his former country, to support and defend the Constitution and laws of the United States against all enemies, and to bear arms in behalf of the United States when required by law. A person who is opposed to bearing arms or serving in the armed forces *because of religious belief* may, however, be naturalized if he will take an oath to serve in the armed forces as a noncombatant or perform work of national importance under civilian direction.

A person who wants to be naturalized goes to the office of the clerk of a court of record—federal or state—and files a petition for naturalization, verified by two witnesses and including all required information. An examiner of the Immigration and Naturalization Service then conducts an investigation, examines the petitioner to insure that he meets all the requirements of the law, and makes a report of his finding to the court. The final step is a hearing in open court before a judge who, if he is satisfied that the petitioner is qualified, administers the oath of allegiance and grants a certificate of naturalization. The petitioner is then a citizen of the United States.

What about the citizenship of minor children? As is true of most phases of the naturalization laws, there are so many exceptions that it is difficult to make any blanket statements. In general, however, children under sixteen years of age who are lawfully resident in the United States become citizens when their parents become citizens.

Until 1922 a married woman took on the citizenship of her husband. Hence, an alien woman who married an American became an American citizen herself. On the other hand, a woman who married an alien lost her American citizenship. Today, women acquire and lose citizenship on the same terms as men, except for a shortening of the residence requirement for naturalization,

a married woman's citizenship status is not affected by that of her husband.
American women may marry foreigners and still retain their citizenship.

LOSS OF CITIZENSHIP BY EXPATRIATION

American citizenship may be lost by expatriation or by denaturalization.
Expatriation applies to both natural-born and naturalized citizens. The law
now specifies nine types of conduct that result in the loss of citizenship. They
include such actions as becoming naturalized in a foreign state, taking an oath
of allegiance to another country, accepting a job in a foreign state that is open
only to citizens of that state, voting in the election of a foreign state, serving
in the armed forces of another state without the approval of the Secretaries of
State and Defense, and departing from the United States in time of war or
emergency for the purpose of evading military service. Furthermore, citizenship is lost when a person is convicted of treason, of attempting by force to
overthrow, or conspiring to advocate forceful overthrow, of the government
of the United States. It is not true, as it is sometimes assumed, however, that
a convicted felon automatically loses his American citizenship. He does lose
some of his political rights, such as the right to vote, but unless his crime is one
of those mentioned above he does not cease to be an American citizen.

A person outside the United States may formally renounce his citizenship
before an American diplomatic or consular officer. But a person living within
the United States may formally renounce his citizenship only during time of
war and only with the approval of the Attorney General.

Only conduct voluntarily performed can lead to expatriation. Still, if a
person voluntarily commits what Congress has stipulated as an act of expatriation, he loses citizenship even if it is contrary to his intentions and wishes.

In 1958 the Supreme Court in *Trop* v. *Dulles* declared unconstitutional
a provision taking citizenship away from servicemen dishonorably discharged
by a court martial for war-time desertion. Desertion does not necessarily indicate allegiance to another country, and, according to the Chief Justice, use of
denationalization as punishment is barred by the Eighth Amendment. Although the Court in *Perez* v. *Brownell* ruled that Congress could make voting
in foreign political elections ground for expatriation, it strongly hinted that
the provision denationalizing persons for remaining outside the United States
for the purpose of avoiding military service is unconstitutional. Constitutional
questions are also raised by the fact that Congress had stipulated that if naturalized, but not natural-born, citizens live abroad for five continuous years
(three years if in the country of their former nationality), they should be considered to have abandoned their American citizenship.

LOSS OF CITIZENSHIP BY DENATURALIZATION

Naturalized citizenship may be revoked at any time by a court order if
the government proves that it was procured by concealment of a material fact

or by willful misrepresentation. The Supreme Court requires the government to demonstrate by overwhelming evidence that naturalization was illegally received before it permits court revocation. However, certain acts by the naturalized citizen result in a presumption of fraud and largely shift the burden of proof from the government's shoulders.

The law has long provided that a naturalized citizen who within five years after naturalization establishes a foreign residence is to be presumed to have obtained naturalization fraudulently; unless he can overcome this presumption, a court can revoke his citizenship. In 1950 and 1952, Congress added other grounds of presumptive fraud. If within five years after naturalization a person joins or affiliates with a subversive organization, it is now presumed in the absence of contrary evidence that such a person was not at the time of naturalization attached to the principles of the Constitution. A similar presumption, of doubtful constitutionality, is to be made if within ten years after naturalization a person is convicted of contempt of Congress for refusing to testify as a witness before a congressional committee concerning subversive activities.

DUAL NATIONALS

Each nation determines for itself who shall be considered a citizen. Consequently, persons frequently acquire the nationality of both the United States and of a foreign state. A person born in the United States of Greek parents, for example, is, according to the Fourteenth Amendment, an American citizen and, according to Greek law, a Greek citizen. Similarly, a person born of American parents abroad may be an American citizen and also acquire the nationality of the country in which he is born. A dual national who, after reaching 22, resides in the foreign state of which he is a national by birth, loses his American citizenship if he voluntarily claims the benefits of his foreign nationality—by making an application for a foreign passport, for example—unless he takes an oath of allegiance to the United States before a diplomatic or consular official.

PRIVILEGES AND IMMUNITIES
OF UNITED STATES CITIZENS

States may establish residence requirements before they permit citizens to vote, attend the state university, practice law, and so on. But the Fourteenth Amendment automatically confers state citizenship upon all American citizens who reside in that state. (*Residence,* as used in the Fourteenth Amendment, means "domicile," the place one calls "home." The legal status of domicile should not be confused with the fact of physical presence. A person may be living in Washington, D.C. but be a citizen of California—that is, he may consider California "home." *Domicile* or *residence* as used in the Fourteenth Amendment is a question primarily of intent.)

Most American citizens are also state citizens, but some—for example, those who reside in Puerto Rico, Washington, D.C., or in England—have only national citizenship. The Fourteenth Amendment, among other things, protects this national citizenship by denying states the right to abridge privileges and immunities of United States citizens. What are these privileges and immunities? The Supreme Court, in the *Slaughter House Cases* (1873), carefully distinguished between privileges of *United States* citizens and of *state* citizens, holding that the only privileges attaching to national citizenship are those that "owe their existence to the Federal Government, its National character, its Constitution, or its laws." The Supreme Court's narrow construction of the privileges and immunities clause has made it of little value as a restraint on state regulation.

Although the privileges of United States citizenship have never been completely enumerated, they include the right to use the navigable waters of the United States, to assemble peaceably and petition the national government for redress of grievances, to be protected by the national government on the high seas, to travel throughout the United States, and—if qualified to do so under state laws—to vote in national elections and to have one's vote counted properly.

In recent years there has been a good bit of discussion about an American citizen's right to travel. Except for persons under legal restraint—committed to jail, subject to the draft, out on bail, and so forth—all American citizens may travel throughout the nation. During World War II, however, American citizens who had committed no crime, but were of Japanese ancestry, were forced to move from their homes to relocation centers. The Supreme Court reluctantly approved this denial of their liberty, accepting as reasonable the decision of military commanders that such measures were necessary. But the Supreme Court insisted that after the loyalty of these people was established, restrictions that were not legally imposed upon all other persons could not be placed on their freedom to travel.[3]

Do American citizens have a right to travel abroad, or is that a privilege that the government may limit at its discretion? Until World War I no passports were required, though one could be obtained as a convenience if wanted. Other nations then began to demand passports before they would grant visas to our citizens. Under present law and presidential directives, when the United States is at war or during the existence of a national emergency proclaimed by the President, it is unlawful, except as otherwise provided by the President, for any citizen to depart from or enter the United States unless he bears a valid passport. Since 1941 Presidential proclamations have brought these provisions into effect and, except for departure for a few nations—Mexico and Canada, for example—no citizen can lawfully leave the United States without a passport.

For many years the Secretary of State refused to give passports to citizens if he believed they were going abroad "to further the Communist cause" or if

---

[3] *Korematsu* v. *United States* (1944) and *Ex parte Endo* (1944).

he determined their travel "would be contrary to the interest of the United States." Before a passport application would even be considered, a noncommunist affidavit was required. Then in 1958 (*Kent* v. *Dulles* and *Dayton v. Dulles*), the Supreme Court ruled that Congress had not given the Secretary authority to withhold a passport because of a citizen's political beliefs or associations.

The Department of State has asked Congress to authorize it to deny passports to communists and those the Department determines are traveling abroad to work against the United States. If Congress should do so, the Supreme Court might be forced to deal with the underlying constitutional issue it avoided in the Kent and Dayton cases. Since the Internal Security Act of 1950 makes it a crime for a person belonging to organizations determined to be communist-action organizations by the Subversive Activities Control Board to apply for a passport, a similar constitutional question will be presented if the Board's order against the Communist party becomes final and one of its members applies for a passport.

The Department of State still contends that it may grant passports valid only for travel in certain nations, and it continues to refuse to permit citizens to go to certain "iron curtain" countries, the most prominent being Communist China. After strong pressure the Department agreed to permit a select few journalists to go to China, but its basic position is unaltered. This stand, combined with the Communist Chinese unwillingness to let American newsmen into their country, means that we have to depend on journalists of other countries for news from these critical areas. The Department's ban on travel thus raises issues not only about the constitutional right of American citizens to travel, but also questions about the government's power to control news-gathering.

Summary

1. Under current restrictions on immigration, only a limited number of persons from outside the Western Hemisphere may enter this country each year for permanent residence. They must meet health, moral, and political qualifications. There is no limitation upon the number of nonimmigrant aliens who wish to enter, but they must meet other qualifications.
2. Aliens reside in the United States under terms established by Congress, and they have no constitutional right to remain. While here, however, they are entitled to certain protections under the Constitution and under various treaties.
3. Citizenship may be acquired by birth in the United States, birth abroad to American parents, and by naturalization. It may be lost by expatriation and denaturalization.
4. American citizens enjoy certain rights denied to aliens. These rights flow directly from national citizenship and indirectly from state citizenship. The latter is acquired whenever American citizens reside in a state.

PART **4**

The People in Politics

A PROBLEM GUIDE

The main problem raised in Part Four is *popular representation.* We speak of "government by the people"—but what do we really mean when we say that the "people" run the government? Do *all* the people take part? Do some people have more political influence than others? How are the people organized to take part in "government by the people"? Through what instruments—pressure groups, newspapers, parties—do they express themselves? And how do these different types of political organization and representation square with our ideals of democratic government?

One problem is that of voting and non-voting. Millions of Americans do not vote because they are barred from the polls; other millions do not vote because going to the polls does not seem worth the trouble. Hence right away we must qualify our phrase "government by the people"—it is usually government by *some* of the people. How serious a problem is this in a democracy? How was the right to vote broadened historically? Should we *make* people vote? These problems all relate to the central problem of Chapter 10: how much equality of political influence do we have in America?

The next two chapters, 11 and 12, develop this problem further. Some people—businessmen, workers, and farmers, for example—by organizing into strong interest groups can greatly increase their influence over "who gets what, when, and how" in government. Other persons—for example, publishers, TV news commentators, columnists—occupy strong points along the channels of news and opinion dissemination. How much influence do such men have over voting? Do group leaders and opinion leaders fully express the interests and reflect the needs of the people as a whole? Or do some people get less, and others more, than their fair share of representation?

The next chapter (13), on political parties, deals with this same problem of *fair representation* but in connection with another part of our political system. Under a two-party system, in theory at least, the party that wins a majority of the votes then proceeds to represent the interests of that popular majority in government. How effectively does the winning party speak for the majority of voters that elected it? Not very effectively. But that raises another question: *Can* the parties be strengthened so that they may represent their supporters more effectively? (Whether or not the parties *should* be strengthened is taken up in Part Five.) And what about the minority party—can it do the job of *opposing* the majority as well as it should?

A final problem of Part Four is the fairness and efficiency of the electoral system. We might think that electoral machinery would be neutral, but it is not. Some election arrangements make it difficult for people to vote. Others—for example, the electoral college—give some voters more weight than others in the election of office-seekers. How fair is our system of nominating candidates —especially the President? Chapter 14 raises such problems, which all relate to the basic question in Part Four of equality of political influence for the sake of fair representation.

Sometimes this problem of fair representation is described in terms of "special interests versus the general interest." The "special interests" are often pictured as small, selfish groups that "gang up" on the rest of the people, who represent the "general interest." Actually, the problem is more complex. A special interest may be selfish, or it may represent the real interest of the great majority. As used here, the term "special interest" means merely the interest (the goal or attitude) of considerably less than the whole. It is special in the sense that it immediately and directly favors the part rather than the totality. The "general interest" simply means the interest of all, or most, of the people, at least in the short run.

CHAPTER 10

Political Behavior

Politics is sometimes called "the great American game." Thousands of politicians take part in it; millions of people follow the election fights, and decide who will win and who will lose. Yet the real nature of the game remains a mystery. Why does one candidate win and another lose? What causes some people to go to the polls and vote when others do not? How do we decide to vote the way we do? Why do the voting returns from some areas shift crazily from year to year, while other areas seem to be stable? Man is a political animal, yet man knows very little about his own political behavior—or misbehavior.

Of course, there are a lot of pet theories—theories that are resurrected in every election by the newspapers and by the politicians themselves. Experience often deals harshly with these theories, but they live on. Take the old saying, "As Maine goes, so goes the nation." This has been disproved in election after election. (In 1936, Jim Farley said, "As goes Maine so goes Vermont.") But it was years before the old adage died. Again, it has long been political gospel that mid-term congressional elections foreshadow the results of the next presidential election, but the 1948 and 1956 results upset this theory—at least for a while.

We are still groping for some understanding of our own political behavior. Recent years, however, have seen a more systematic approach to the study. Political scientists, social psychologists, cultural anthropologists, sociologists, and others are making new studies that in time may throw a flood of light on the political process. Their tools—questionnaires, voting statistics, polls, interviews, intensive studies of particular campaigns, and so on—are still crude, but they are slowly being improved. We are gaining new insights into the way relations among members of groups, between leaders and followers, and among members of families affect political activity. We are probing into the dark forces that fight for supremacy within the individual.

One crucial fact, however, is crystal clear: political power in the Ameri-

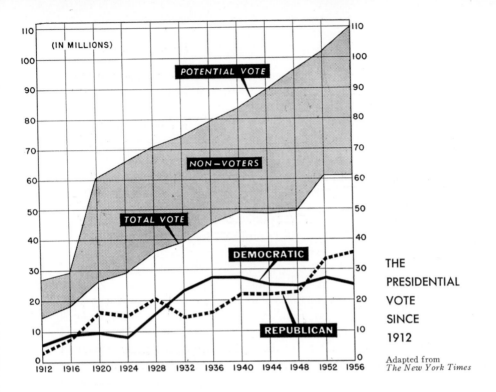

Adapted from
The New York Times

THE
PRESIDENTIAL
VOTE
SINCE
1912

can democracy is not spread evenly among all the voters. We talk about "one man, one vote"—but in practice millions of Americans have no part in the political game, sometimes not even as spectators, while a few Americans may call the signals. First we shall look at those who do and those who do not take part in the great American game of politics.

Who Shall Vote?—
The Fight for the Ballot

In modern society, government by the people means government elected by and responsive to the wishes of the voters. Today we have universal adult suffrage in *form,* though the struggle to extend the right to all adults in *fact* is not over (as we saw in Chapter 7). The history of the suffrage in the United States has been a continuing struggle to extend the right to vote from a small group of property-owning white males to the great bulk of adults. The issue of Negro suffrage, as described in Chapter 7, is only one phase—though an important one—of this struggle.

The Declaration of Independence states that all men are created equal, but it says nothing about the right to vote. Evidently our Revolutionary forefathers were not primarily concerned about this right. They would not have dreamed of giving the ballot to Negro slaves, or women, or people under 21, and they were dubious about giving the ballot to people without property.

They were acting in accordance with custom, for the colonies had restrictions on voting based on property. A few of the framers of the Constitution in 1787 argued for easing up on the property requirement for voting, but, as we saw in Chapter 2, most of them stood firm for it. "Give the votes to people who have no property," Gouverneur Morris warned, "and they will sell them to the rich. . . ." The safest procedure, the Founding Fathers decided, was to leave it to the *states* to set the voting requirements for both national and state elections.

Surely this was a faltering start. About one American in every thirty voted in the first election held under the new Constitution. But the situation was to change radically. By the 1850's the property restriction had become almost extinct. By 1870 the right of the states to deprive Negroes of the vote because of their race had been terminated. And by 1920 women had been given the ballot. Indeed, the United States has the distinction of being the first of the great nations to attain universal adult suffrage. What caused this vast widening of the right to vote?

ONE MAN, ONE VOTE

Economic and social changes helped broaden the suffrage. Property restrictions on voting had come to be accepted in the cities and towns of the East, where most people had a sense of position and rank. Social distinctions did not mean so much along the western frontier. There the settlers lived on a more equal basis; they tended to share and share alike. Why should one man have the vote and another not? State after state joined the Union with no property restrictions at all.

The impact of this kind of democracy was also felt in the East. Most of the states there had their own "western" counties where the settlers often looked on property restrictions as a way for the easterners to protect their commercial interests. In urban areas, too, new ideas were taking root. In the great cities, "mechanics" and other workingmen were eager to express themselves politically, and immigrants were already flowing in from abroad at an increasing rate. Here was a tremendous pool of votes that competing parties wanted to draw on. Shrewd politicians figured that they could tighten their hold on office by giving the ballot to groups likely to vote "right."

Conservatives like Chancellor Kent of New York could argue—as he did at the New York constitutional convention of 1821—that universal male suffrage would "jeopardize the rights of property and the principles of liberty." But the rising groups could not be held down. They appealed to the names of Thomas Jefferson and other popular heroes to back up their demands. A delegate to the Massachusetts convention of 1853 ridiculed property qualifications with a story that Tom Paine, the great pamphleteer of the Revolution, used to tell:

> You require that a man shall have sixty dollars' worth of property, or he shall not vote. Very well, take an illustration. Here is a man who today owns a jackass, and the jackass is worth sixty dollars. Today the man is a

voter and goes to the polls and deposits his vote. Tomorrow the jackass dies. The next day the man comes to vote without his jackass and he cannot vote at all. Now tell me, which was the voter, the man or the jackass?

If such common sense was not enough to bring about a change in qualifications, men were ready to fight for the right to vote. The Rhode Islanders made this clear. For years they had protested against control of their government by a small landed oligarchy. In 1841 a convention representing the voteless met and drew up a "People's Constitution" that greatly broadened the right to vote. Now uneasy, the old-time leaders offered a new constitution that was almost equally liberal on voting. But the rebels, headed by Thomas Dorr, were too aroused to compromise. After a struggle the landowners won out and Dorr fled the state, but the victors were wise enough to provide broadened suffrage provisions in the new constitution of 1843.

The forces of unrest and protest worked slowly but surely. First, the states substituted a taxpaying requirement for the property-owning requirement. Then they did away with the taxpaying provision too. By the mid-nineteenth century manhood suffrage had been established almost everywhere. North Carolina—the last of the states to yield—finally abandoned its property test for voting in 1856.

Thus one phase of a long struggle came to a happy end. But only one phase. While men were still fighting for their right to vote, women were beginning to fight for theirs. The agitation over slavery during the mid-nineteenth century gave a great impetus to the idea of women's suffrage. Why agitate over the Negro's wrongs, women asked their husbands, and ignore those of your own mothers, wives, and sisters? Indeed, in their legal rights women were little more than a step or two above slaves. What was the men's reply? They argued loftily that woman's sacred duty was in the bosom of the family and that she could leave the stern and exacting job of politics to the males. But the argument had a hollow ring.

SUFFRAGETTES IN ACTION

Only grudgingly did men give in to the protests of the opposite sex. As early as 1838 Kentucky allowed widows and unmarried women to vote in school elections, provided they held property taxable for school purposes; by 1890 all women in fourteen states and territories had gained the right to vote on school matters. Naturally women were not content with this; many of them were doing men's work in professions, in factories and fields, and they pressed for full suffrage. Oddly enough, their first victories came in western states popularly known for their high percentage of tough hombres. Wyoming led the way. As a territory, Wyoming had given women equal rights with men; when congressmen in Washington grumbled about this "petticoat provision," the Wyoming legislators replied that they would stay out of the Union a hundred years rather than come in without women's suffrage. Congress gave in.

By the end of World War I, over half the states had granted women the right to vote in some or all elections.

To many suffragettes, however, this state-by-state approach seemed very slow and uncertain. Some of them had set their hearts on nothing less than a constitutional amendment that would at one blow force all the states to allow women to vote. In fighting for this amendment the women taught their fathers and husbands a lesson in dynamic political tactics. Under the leadership of Alice Paul, Carrie Chapman Catt, and others, they organized pressure groups, Washington lobbies, and even a National Woman's party. They held noisy parades, drew up petitions, printed militant propaganda, put mass pressure on Congress. Women who had already won the vote stole a leaf from labor's book by trying to help their friends and defeat their enemies.

The struggle came to a head during the war years when President Wilson and congressional leaders were trying—like good politicians—to dodge the issue. Women, impatient with such straddling, began to picket the White House. Carrying banners and singing lustily, the suffragettes marched month after month around the executive mansion. Then the authorities made the mistake of using force and had the police arrest some of the demonstrators for "obstructing traffic." This was just the kind of heavy-handed treatment on which agitators thrive. New picketers snatched up the banners; when patrol wagons carted them off, more took over. In jail, treated like common criminals, the women went on hunger strikes. Some of them—including prominent women of wealth and high social standing—had to be forcibly fed. By this time the whole nation was aroused. Protests poured in on Washington. The militant suffragettes were looked on as martyrs.

Many women, including supporters of suffrage, scorned the hot-headed tactics of their sisters. But the agitators retorted that lacking the *legal* right to vote, they had the *moral* right to resort to direct action, even violence, just as their forefathers had. In any event, their hard-hitting tactics, along with organization and propaganda, turned the trick. In 1919 the Nineteenth Amendment granting women the suffrage passed Congress by the needed two-thirds vote in each chamber. So well were the women organized in the states that by August, 1920, the amendment had been passed by the necessary three-fourths of the state legislatures.

The battle of the sexes was over—and women had written a notable chapter in the struggle to extend the suffrage. Although, as we found in Chapter 7, Negroes are still seeking full access to the ballot, we now have universal adult suffrage—in constitutional form, at least. This does not mean that all adults have the right to vote. Some are not likely ever to be given the ballot: criminals and the insane, for example.

Subject to the limitations set by the Fourteenth, Fifteenth, and Nineteenth amendments, each state determines qualifications for voting, not only for state officials but also for congressmen and President. The Constitution merely stipulates that those who are qualified under state law to vote for the most

State or other jurisdiction	Minimum age	U. S. citizen	Residence in			Property	Literacy test	Poll tax(a)
			State	County	District			
Alabama	21	★	2 yrs.	1 yr.	3 mo.	....	....	(b)
Alaska	19	★	12 mo.	......	30 da.(ad)	....	★	....
Arizona	21	★	1 yr.	30 da.	30 da.	....	★	....
Arkansas	21	★	12 mo.	6 mo.	1 mo.	....	....	★
California	21	(f)	1 yr.	90 da.	54 da.	....	★	....
Colorado	21	★	1 yr.	90 da.	15 da.(g)	....	....	....
Connecticut ...	21	(i)	1 yr.	......	6 mo.	....	★	....
Delaware	21	★	1 yr.	3 mo.	30 da.	....	★	....
Florida	21	★	1 yr.	6 mo.	......	....	....	....
Georgia	18	★	1 yr.	6 mo.	......	....	(j)	....
Hawaii........	20	★	1 yr.	......	......	....	(af)	....
Idaho	21	★	6 mo.	30 da.	......	....	....	....
Illinois	21	★	1 yr.	90 da.	30 da.	....	....	....
Indiana	21	★	6 mo.	60 da.(l)	30 da.	....	....	....
Iowa	21	★	6 mo.	60 da.	10 da.	....	....	....
Kansas	21	★	6 mo.	30 da.(l)	30 da.	....	....	....
Kentucky	18	★	1 yr.	6 mo.	60 da.	....	....	...,.
Louisiana	21	★	1 yr.	1 yr.	3 mo.(m)	....	(n)	....
Maine	21	★	6 mo.	3 mo.	3 mo.	....	★	....
Maryland	21	★	1 yr.	6 mo.	6 mo.	....	....	....
Massachusetts..	21	★	1 yr.	......	6 mo.(o)	....	★	....
Michigan	21	★	6 mo.	......	30 da.	(p)	....	....
Minnesota	21	(f)	6 mo.	......	30 da.	....	....	....
Mississippi	21	★	2 yrs.	......	1 yr.(q)	....	★	(r)
Missouri	21	★	1 yr.	60 da.	60 da.	....	....	....
Montana	21	★	1 yr.	30 da.	......	(p)	....	....
Nebraska	21	★	6 mo.	40 da.	10 da.	....	....	....
Nevada	21	★	6 mo.	30 da.	10 da.	(p)	....	....
New Hampshire	21	★	6 mo.	......	6 mo.	....	★	....
New Jersey ...	21	★	1 yr.	5 mo.	......	....	....	....
New Mexico...	21	★	12 mo.	90 da.	30 da.	(p)	....	....
New York.....	21	(f)	1 yr.	4 mo.	30 da.	....	(t)	....
North Carolina.	21	★	1 yr.	......	30 da.	....	★	....
North Dakota..	21	★	1 yr.	90 da.	30 da.	....	....	....
Ohio	21	★	1 yr.(ah)	40 da.	40 da.	....	....	....
Oklahoma.....	21	★	1 yr.	6 mo.	30 da.	....	....	....
Oregon	21	★	6 mo.	......	30 da.	....	★	....
Pennsylvania ..	21	★	1 yr.(w)	......	2 mo.	....	....	....
Rhode Island ..	21	★	1 yr.	......	6 mo.	....	....	....
South Carolina.	21	★	2 yrs.(x)	1 yr.	4 mo.	(y)	(y)	....
South Dakota..	21	★	1 yr.	90 da.	30 da.	....	....	....
Tennessee	21	★	12 mo.	6 mo.	......	....	....	(r)
Texas	21	★	1 yr.	6 mo.	6 mo.	(p)	....	(r)
Utah	21	(f)	1 yr.	4 mo.	60 da.	(p)	....	....
Vermont	21	★	1 yr.	......	3 mo.(l)	....	....	....
Virginia	21	★	1 yr.	6 mo.	30 da.	....	★	(aa)
Washington ...	21	★	1 yr.	90 da.	30 da.	....	★	....
West Virginia..	21	★	1 yr.	60 da.	......	....	....	....
Wisconsin	21	★	1 yr.	......	10 da.	....	....	....
Wyoming	21	★	1 yr.	60 da.	10 da.	....	★	....
Guam	18	★	2 yrs.	......	90 da.(ad)	....	....	....
Puerto Rico ...	21	★	1 yr.	......	1 yr.	....	....	....
Virgin Islands..	21	★	1 yr.	......	60 da.	....	★	...

(a) Poll or head taxes are levied in many other states. Those listed here, however, provide that payment of the poll tax is a prerequisite for voting.

(b) Must pay all poll taxes owed for the two years next preceding election at which person offers to vote. Persons who have honorably served in the military service of the United States while the United States is engaged in hostilities, whether war is declared or not, are exempt from payment of poll taxes.

(d) Conditioned upon voting and continued residence.

(f) Must have been citizen ninety days.

(g) City or town, thirty days.

(h) All except certain minor elections.

(i) Must have been citizen five years.

(j) Under 1949 act, all voters must re-register and pass literacy test. Those failing test may qualify by answering 10 of 30 oral questions.

(l) Township.

(m) Municipality, four months.

(n) Literacy test required but exception allowed if person can pass certain specified requirements.

(o) In city or town.

(p) For vote on bond issues or special assessments only.

(q) Ministers of the Gospel and their wives may vote after six months' residence.

(r) Assessed upon citizens 21 to 60 years of age except those specifically exempted.

(t) A person who became entitled to vote after January 1, 1922 must be able, except for physical disability, to read and write English.

(w) Six months if previously an elector or native of U. S.

(x) Ministers of the Gospel and teachers in public schools may vote after six months' residence.

(y) Property ownership alternative to literacy.

(aa) Must owe no past due taxes.

(ad) Precinct.

(af) English or Hawaiian language.

From *The Book of the States*, 1958-1959. Courtesy Council of State Governments. Information on Alaska and Hawaii taken from respective constitutions.

numerous branch of the state legislature are qualified to vote for congressmen and leaves it up to the state legislatures to set qualifications for voting for presidential electors. Thus the suffrage requirements—citizenship, age, residence, literacy, and so on—vary from state to state as indicated in the chart on page 238.

Who Votes?

On the average, the proportion of Americans who vote is smaller than that of the British, French, Italians—or Russians. Talk as we will about the right to vote, the hard fact remains that millions of Americans do not want to vote or somehow fail to get to the polls on election day. They disfranchise themselves. In the most democratic of nations, of course, there will always be some nonvoters. But the startling feature of nonvoting in America is its extent. In recent presidential elections only about three-fifths of the potential voters showed up at the polls. Participation in state and local elections is usually even less than that. Voting for President in the 1952 and 1956 presidential elections rose to between 60 and 65 per cent of the potential vote, but this figure is still not very impressive.

MILLIONS OF NONVOTERS

Why do people fail to vote? Some years ago investigators asked several thousand Chicagoans why they had not voted in a recent mayoralty election.[1] The answers were illuminating. About one in every eight said that they were ill at the time; about the same number said that they were away from their voting district. Only 10 per cent simply disbelieved in voting for one reason or another—they were "disgusted with politics," or they thought that women should not vote, or something of the sort. Some found it inconvenient to vote; a few—mostly women—did not want to disclose their ages. Some persons were afraid that they would lose business or wages while they went to the polls. But one factor stood out above all others—simple lack of interest in elections. Over one-third of the nonvoters gave this as their reason. A salesman said he was more concerned with his business than with politics. A housewife said she did her washing that day. A mother explained simply, "Got a lot of children." A young musician confessed that he had had one of his temperamental spells on election day. Some nonvoters said that they had intended to vote, but had forgotten all about it until too late.

This high rate of indifference, ignorance, and even downright opposition to voting shows that much nonvoting is deliberate and intentional, not a result of chance factors like illness or absence. Other studies of voting underline the situation even more sharply: almost two-thirds of those who failed to vote stated to interviewers shortly before one presidential election that they did not

---

[1] C. E. Merriam and H. F. Gosnell, *Non-Voting* (Univ. of Chicago Press, 1924).

intend to vote.[2] One conclusion is clear. An important reason for nonvoting—perhaps the most important reason—lies in peoples' *attitudes,* not in external factors beyond their control.

Why then do people *vote?* Investigators have found many causes. One is sheer habit—people go to the polls because it's "the thing to do," or because their parents always did, or because their neighbors do. Another reason people vote is that they see a relationship between what government does and their own lives. Another is their concern over issues, a concern sharpened by their exposure to radio and television programs and magazines and newspapers that play up political events. Another is psychological—people's sense of political *efficacy,* their feeling as to whether their vote will make any difference. It seems clear from voting studies, for example, that a close contest will usually bring out more voters than one whose results seem a foregone conclusion.

The extent to which people turn out to vote has, of course, an enormous effect on politics. The big job for a politician is not merely to induce people to vote for him or his party; it is to get the vote out in the first place. Often the outcome of elections will turn largely on this factor. Both parties work hard to register their supporters—that is, to see that the voters get their names on registration lists (see Chapter 14) at the required time before election. The campaign itself not only influences the decisions of potential voters. The hullabaloo that goes with it—the parades and posters, the politicians' grim warnings and bright promises—helps activate people so that they will vote on election day.

Nevertheless, in most elections turnout is relatively small. A study of voting in Ann Arbor, Michigan, for example, revealed that, on the average, barely more than one-fourth of eligible voters actually went to the polls in a series of elections, national, state, and local.[3] Politicians know that this low turnout plays into the hands of party or interest-group machines, for it gives the organization vote much more weight in the final count.

WHO FAILS TO VOTE?

The discerning politician knows something even more important—that the extent of voting varies with different types of persons, different areas,[4] different elections. Observation of voting habits suggests the following:

1. *Men tend to vote more than women.* This variation between the sexes —not very great in most elections—exists in many foreign countries as well

---

[2] P. F. Lazarsfeld and Associates, *The People's Choice* (Duell, Sloan, and Pearce, 1944), pp. 45-46. See also S. M. Lipset, "The Psychology of Voting: An Analysis of Political Behavior," in Gardner Lindzey (ed.), *Handbook of Social Psychology* (Addison-Wesley, 1954), II, pp. 1124-1175.

[3] J. K. Pollock, *Voting Behavior: A Case Study* (Univ. of Michigan Press, 1939).

[4] For a useful tabular summary of conclusions about voting behavior produced by recent studies, see Bernard R. Berelson, Paul F. Lazarsfeld, and William N. McPhee, *Voting* (Univ. of Chicago Press, 1954), pp. 331-347.

as in the United States. In recent presidential elections about 61 in every 100 women have voted, about 75 in every 100 men. Women seem to feel less social pressure to vote than men.[5] Perhaps the difference will lessen as women become more used to voting.

2. *The higher a person's income and educational level, the more likely he is to vote.* In the 1940 presidential election, according to the National Opinion Research Center, 85 per cent of the top fourth of the income scale went to the polls, 69 per cent of the middle half, and only 54 per cent of the lowest quarter. A study of the 1952 election by the Survey Research Center of the University of Michigan showed that of persons earning less than $2000 a year, only 53 per cent voted; of those earning between $2000 and $3000 a year, 68 per cent voted; of those earning over $5000 a year, 88 per cent voted.[6]

3. *Younger and older people tend to vote less than middle-aged.* Voting seems to be highest in the middle-age groups, and then falls off in the sixties and seventies owing partly to the infirmities of old age. In Ann Arbor, voting by persons in their twenties was about half that by persons in their fifties. Why do so many younger people fail to vote? And does that failure cause American politics to lack a measure of vitality?

4. *Republicans tend to vote more than Democrats.* Of the people who show a marked preference for one or the other of our major parties, those who prefer the Republicans turn out in larger proportions than do those who prefer the Democrats. The Michigan study of the 1952 election, for example, showed that only 8 per cent of the people who regarded themselves as "strong Republicans" failed to vote, while 24 per cent of those who regarded themselves as "strong Democrats" stayed at home. This is probably because the Republicans tend to draw their strength from the better-educated and higher-income groups (the groups with the largest turnout), and the Democrats draw from the less-educated and lower-income groups (the groups with the smallest turnout).

5. *More people vote in national elections than in state or local elections.* In most states presidential elections attract the greatest number of voters. Off-year congressional elections almost invariably draw fewer persons to the polls. City elections tend to attract the fewest voters. And participation is lowest, of course, in party primaries. Even when voters are marking a ballot that offers a variety of national and local contests, many voters will check their presidential choice but not bother with the others. This is one reason that our governmental officials are chosen by somewhat different electorates. Does this fact intensify disunity in government?

6. *Voting varies according to party competition.* Voting turnout is lowest in areas in which there is little two-party competition and is highest where strong competition exists. Thus the lowest voting figures are to be found in

---

[5] Lazarsfeld, *The People's Choice*, pp. 48-49.
[6] Angus Campbell, Gerald Gurin, and Warren E. Miller, *The Voter Decides* (Row, Peterson, 1954), pp. 70-73.

states such as Vermont and Mississippi, and the highest figures in states such as New York and ·Pennsylvania. Voting in the "modified one-party states," such as Oklahoma, the Dakotas, and Nebraska, is usually somewhere in between the one-party and two-party states. The number of southern nonvoters is a crucial factor in southern politics. V. O. Key, Jr., estimates that if southerners had voted in 1940 to the same degree as Americans as a whole voted in the presidential election of that year, over *six million* more ballots would have been cast in the South.[7]

To sum up, if you are a southern woman, poor, in your twenties, and faced with a local election, the chances, *on the average,* of your going to the polls are far less than if you are a wealthy man, in your fifties, voting for a presidential candidate in the North.

Nonvoting is a sign of political apathy. To be sure, it is only one sign, and a person may have a significant effect on politics even if he fails to vote. There are other ways of "voting" besides formally casting a ballot. "Citizens . . . vote by adding their names and energies to membership rolls," says Paul H. Appleby. "They vote by swelling, or failing to swell, the circulations of particular newspapers or periodicals. They vote by contributing to the popularity of particular radio or newspaper commentators. They vote by writing 'letters to the editor.' . . ." [8] Still, nonvoting and nonparticipation generally go hand in hand. Political pollsters regularly discover the existence of a "hard core of chronic know-nothings"—people who know almost nothing about public affairs. These "know-nothings" do not read the newspapers, do not join organizations, do not write to the editor, and they do not vote.[9]

What causes such political apathy or inactivity? Some of the causes have been described as a feeling that political activity may alienate one's friends or employer, that political activity is futile because "the politicians run everything anyway," that the "little man" does not know enough to act intelligently, that politics is remote and does not affect people very much. Another cause is the lack of political leadership strong enough to arouse people to vote.

SHOULD WE MAKE PEOPLE VOTE?

Nonvoting has serious implications. It suggests that many Americans have no interest in taking part in our system of self-government. Somehow our democracy has failed to kindle their sense of participation. Moreover, it suggests that the *less protected* groups economically and socially tend to be the very groups that are less active politically. In other words, the people who most

---

[7] V. O. Key, Jr., *Southern Politics* (Knopf, 1949), p. 506. Southern voting figures are based on voting in primaries.

[8] Paul H. Appleby, *Policy and Administration* (Univ. of Alabama Press, 1949), p. 168.

[9] See Morris Rosenberg, "Some Determinants of Political Apathy," *Public Opinion Quarterly,* Winter 1954, pp. 349-366.

need to enlist governmental protection in their own support are the very ones who have least weight in making governmental decisions. Failure to vote may mean less public housing, fewer roads, even less police protection, for the nonvoters.

Disturbed by these implications, some Americans would solve the problem of nonvoting through a drastic step. They would make voting compulsory for all those eligible. This idea has been tried in several foreign countries with mixed results. Australia makes both registration (see Chapter 14) and voting compulsory. Thus the government takes the responsibility of mobilizing the voters at the polls, and voting becomes a legal duty as well as a legal right. The delinquent voter is fined or reprimanded.

What about compulsory voting for the United States? There are obvious practical difficulties, but probably these could be overcome through simplifying and standardizing election laws. A big question is whether we could expect enlightened voting from people who had to be herded to the polls, perhaps against their will. And indeed, some students of politics feel that a measure of nonvoting is a sign of a healthy society, an indication of widespread satisfaction with the existing state of affairs. They look on nonvoters as a sort of cushion or shock-absorber; when social tensions increase and political rivalries grow sharp, the result is simply to draw more voters to the polls, rather than to set off a revolution or civil war.

Perhaps so. Perhaps, on the other hand, excess political steam can always be blown off through participating in political campaigns or even by running for office or starting a new political party or cause. At any rate, Americans can do a great deal about the problem of nonvoting without resorting to methods of compulsion. We can open the polls to every adult who is willing and able to vote. We can shorten the ballot, cutting down the number of unimportant elective positions, so that the bewildered voter does not face quite so many meaningless choices at the polls. We can simplify burdensome registration and residence requirements. (One study showed that six million Americans did not vote in 1956 because they had moved across state or county lines and were therefore unable to meet residence requirements.) Above all, we can try to strengthen our political processes—especially in the areas where one party seems to have a monopoly of power—so that more Americans would look on the polling booth as a place where they can help shape their future.

So much for the nonvoters. What about the people who *do* vote?

How We Vote

Sometimes Americans are called fickle voters who switch from party to party as blithely and as often as women change fashions. Actually, however, the great majority of Americans stick to one party year after year, and their sons and grandsons vote for the same party long after that. Politically these voters are "set in their ways." As a result, both parties can count on the support of an almost irreducible minimum of voters who will go Republican or Democratic almost by habit.

Of course, there are still millions of so-called independent voters who tack back and forth from party to party. They help make our elections the unpredictable and breathless affairs that they so often are. Still, even in the variations from year to year one finds certain persistent elements. Looking closely at the complex mosaic of American politics, we can see *patterns* of voting habits that help us understand *how* we vote, and a little about *why* we vote as we do.

We find:

1. A pattern of *state* voting. Since the Civil War, Vermont has never given its electoral votes to the Democrats, and Maine has done so only once since 1912. Mississippians and South Carolinians, on the other hand, have given as much as a fifth of their popular votes to Republicans only once, and usually much less. Between these extremes some states have tended to be Republican in national elections, as in the case of Oregon, Kansas, Pennsylvania, and New Hampshire, or to be Democratic, as with several Rocky Mountain states, some border states, and of course the Solid South. Most states, however, are doubtful; they cannot be considered safe by either party. Indeed, some doubtful states are consistent only in their inconsistency.

2. A pattern of *sectional* voting. The South is the most famous example. The Democratic solidarity of the states that formed the Confederacy has been breached in only four presidential races: in 1928, when Al Smith, a Catholic, headed the Democratic national ticket; in 1948, when President Truman was campaigning on a civil-rights platform; in 1952, when Stevenson lost some southern states; and in 1956, when Eisenhower carried all but seven states in the nation. North of the Solid South lies a band of border states that lean toward the Democrats. Republican sectionalism is not so clear-cut. New England was firmly Republican for many years, but recently Massachusetts and Rhode Island have tended to go Democratic in presidential elections, and Maine and Vermont elected statewide Democratic candidates in 1958. The states of the upper Midwest, and those of the Far West, once seemed to be normally Republican, but since the Democratic victories of the 1930's and 1940's they can no longer be considered safe Republican territory.

3. A pattern of *national voting*. In most states party popularity rises and falls with the national popularity of the party. National trends, in other words, are reflected in trends in most of the states. States and sections are subject to a variety of local influences, but they cannot resist the great tides that sweep the nation. This is especially true of changes in economic conditions. Our national economy is so integrated that people in every state tend to feel the effects of highs and lows in the business cycle. As a result, the percentage of the vote for

SIX PRESIDENTIAL ELECTIONS, 1928-1956

☐ Democratic　■ Republican

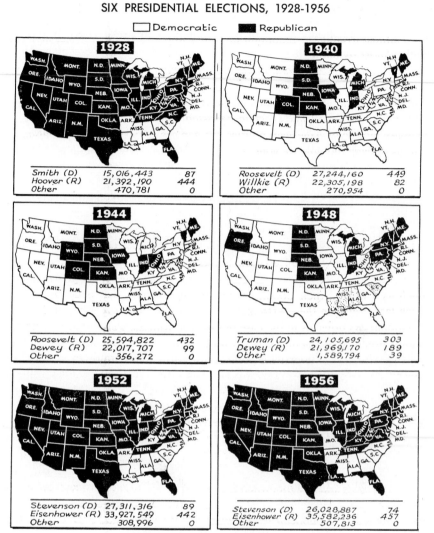

1928		
Smith (D)	15,016,443	87
Hoover (R)	21,392,190	444
Other	470,781	0

1940		
Roosevelt (D)	27,244,160	449
Willkie (R)	22,305,198	82
Other	270,954	0

1944		
Roosevelt (D)	25,594,822	432
Dewey (R)	22,017,707	99
Other	356,272	0

1948		
Truman (D)	24,105,695	303
Dewey (R)	21,969,170	189
Other	1,589,794	39

1952		
Stevenson (D)	27,311,316	89
Eisenhower (R)	33,927,549	442
Other	308,996	0

1956		
Stevenson (D)	26,028,887	74
Eisenhower (R)	35,582,236	457
Other	507,813	0

Adapted from Dayton D. McKean, *Party and Pressure Politics*
(Boston: Houghton Mifflin, 1949)

Patterns of voting.

a party in many states is a gauge of national voting behavior. "As the nation goes," says Louis H. Bean, "so goes Massachusetts ... New York ... Pennsylvania ... Illinois ... Ohio ... Michigan ... Wisconsin ... Minnesota ... California ... and so goes almost any state outside the South." [10] In other words, the relation between the Democratic vote in these states and the national Democratic vote tends to remain constant. In the case of Illinois, for

---

[10] Louis H. Bean, *How to Predict Elections* (Knopf, 1948), pp. 105-106.

example, one need only add 3 or 4 percentage points to its Democratic percentage to get a rough gauge of the national Democratic percentage. Iowa usually stays about 7 percentage points below the national Democratic level.

4. A pattern of voting for candidates for *different offices* in the same election. Well over half the voters usually vote a straight ticket—that is, they throw their support to every one of their party's candidates. If one candidate is an especially able vote-getter—as Roosevelt was in 1936, for example—the party's whole slate may gain. Thus it is said that weaker candidates ride into office on the coattails of stronger ones. The pulling power of a presidential candidate's coattails seems to help elect members of his own party to office during presidential election years; Democrats, for example, won many more seats in Congress in 1936, 1940, and 1944 than in the off-year elections in between, as did Republicans clinging to Eisenhower's coattails in 1952. It is not easy to tell, however, which candidate rides on whose coattails, or just how important the relation may be.[11]

5. Finally, a pattern of voting *over time*. There seem to be great political tides that flow back and forth as decade follows decade. The general mood of the nation for the past century has seemed to alternate broadly between liberalism and conservatism; it has been suggested by one historian, for example, that the periods 1841-1861, 1869-1901, and 1918-1931 were marked by a general emphasis on property rights, and the other periods by a stress on human rights. Another historian has predicted that the 1960's will be a liberal period following the relative conservatism of the 1950's.[12] Moreover, the Republican and Democratic parties have alternated in power (especially in their control of the House of Representatives) with a fair degree of regularity.

BEHIND THE TIDES

What causes the political tides to rise and fall? The business cycle, for one thing. A drop in business activity has often preceded a loss of congressional seats by the party in power; the latest case was in 1958. But we cannot be sure that business cycles *cause* political cycles. Sometimes the two cycles diverge from each other in erratic fashion. Psychological, political, traditional, sectional, international, and other forces may muddle the effect of economic forces.

Clearly, then, there are patterns in American politics. Yet these patterns are rough, and they are often blurred by capricious and unexplainable variations. Indeed, the patterns may exist for many years and then disappear. For example, before the 1948 election a change in party control of Congress in

---

[11] D. B. Truman, "Political Behavior and Voting," *The Pre-Election Polls of 1948* (Social Science Research Council, 1949), pp. 239-244. See also Malcolm Moos, *Politics, Presidents, and Coattails* (The Johns Hopkins Press, 1952).

[12] A. M. Schlesinger, "Tides of American Politics," *Yale Review*, Vol. 29 (1939), pp. 217-230; A. M. Schlesinger, Jr., "The Shape of National Politics to Come" (privately circulated memorandum, 1959).

an off-year election had regularly preceded a change in party fortunes in the following presidential election. But the Democrats, who lost control of Congress in 1946, won both houses of Congress and the Presidency in 1948; and despite 1954 Democratic congressional victories, the Republicans captured the White House, though not Congress, in 1956. So perhaps we will hear less of this "pattern" in the future.

Perhaps this murkiness in American politics is a good thing. Perhaps it shows that we are not caught up in inevitable and relentless forces beyond our control. Unfathomable factors of chance and human nature still have their place. Even the opinion polls, with all their careful scientific techniques, must reckon with these factors. As someone said following Truman's startling victory in 1948, no one can expect to deliver the American people, neatly packaged, tied, and ticketed. Men of determination in either party, campaigning skillfully and energetically, can overcome "inevitable" political trends.

Why We Vote as We Do

Suppose we were able to find ten voters who represented a tiny but fairly accurate cross section of the American electorate. Suppose—shortly after an exciting and close presidential election—we asked them to tell us in a few words why they voted as they did. And suppose they gave us the *real* reason they voted as they did. What kind of answer would we get? Studies of voting indicate that their answers might go something like this:

> MR. ANDERSON (*a fruitgrower*): "I voted Republican. I always do. I'm a businessman, you see, and the Republicans have a sound, businesslike point of view. All the fruitgrowers around here voted that way."

> MRS. SMITH (*a housewife*): "I supported the Democratic candidate. My husband said he was going to vote that way. He doesn't tell me how to vote, but I leave the politics to him. He always seems to vote Democratic anyway."

> MARY BROWN (*a stenographer*): "Well, I didn't know what to do. I wasn't much interested, frankly, but all the girls at the office seemed to think the Democrats are doing a good job, so that's the way I decided to go."

> JOE VENUTI (*a young barber*): "Me? Democratic. The Venutis always vote Democratic. We go along with Tom Murphy—he's a big wheel in the party here, and he's a nice fellow too. He's done us some good turns."

> DR. WHITE (*local surgeon*): "I voted Republican. I don't like these medical programs the Democrats keep talking about. They'll hurt all us doctors if they go through."

> JOHNNY BLACK (*factory worker*): "Democratic. That's the way the boys in the plant were talking. Besides, one of the boys on the union committee gave us a pep talk about supporting the Democrats."

> MRS. MURPHY (*housewife*): "I was on the fence a long time. I read the speeches in the paper, and listened to the radio, and finally I went Democratic."

MR. GREEN (*industrialist*): "Republican, of course. We can't take these high taxes much longer."

BILL JOHNSON (*unemployed*): "I didn't know what to do. The family's Republican, but the Democrats seem to want to do something to get more jobs. Well, the paper we get seemed to think the Democratic candidate is on the wrong track, so I voted Republican."

SALLY GREY (*salesgirl*): "Well, I didn't even plan to vote. I'm not much interested in politics. But I was so mad after some people booed the Republican candidate at the movies the night before that I went out and voted for him."

VOTING BEHAVIOR

In what ways are these ten persons representative of Americans as a whole in the manner in which they made up their minds? For one thing, at least half of the ten supported their party almost automatically, and this voting by *habit* is true of most American voters. No matter what the candidates or issues, no matter whether wars or depressions are taking place, millions of voters in both parties can be relied on to put their X's in the same party column election after election. This traditional voting is not necessarily blind or irrational. In many cases voting for the same party over the years may represent a person's rational view of his self-interest, as in the case of Mr. Anderson above, or Joe Venuti. In any case, habitual party voting is one of the decisive facts that a politician must accept in laying his campaign plans.

In the second place, most of the ten voted the same way as their *families* or *friends* or *workmates* were going to vote. On election day Americans mark their ballots in private, yet voting is essentially a *group* experience. We tend to vote as applegrowers, union members, Legionnaires, prohibitionists, Catholics, Constitution reverers, isolationists, or as members of other existing or potential groups. The most homogeneous of all groups in molding the opinions of its members is probably the family. In Erie County it was discovered that among husbands and wives, both of whom planned to vote, twenty-one couples out of every twenty-two agreed on their choice. Parents and children tended to vote the same way too; only one pair in twelve divided. As might be expected, in-laws were less in agreement, but even here four out of five agreed in their party choice.[13] The reasons for this uniformity are twofold: members of the family shape one another's attitudes (often unintentionally); and members of the same family are usually exposed to similar economic, religious, class, and geographical influences. The husband seems to be head of the house

---

[13] Lazarsfeld, *The People's Choice*, p. 141. See also T. M. Newcomb, *Social Psychology* (Dryden, 1950), pp. 531-534. For some interesting exceptions to this tendency, see E. E. Maccoby, R. E. Matthews, and A. S. Morton, "Youth and Political Change," *Public Opinion Quarterly*, Vol. 18 (1954), pp. 23-29; and Campbell and others, *The Voter Decides*, pp. 109-206.

politically as well as otherwise. Most wives talk the election over with their husbands. Men, on the other hand, "do not feel that they are discussing politics with their wives; they feel they are telling them." [14]

A third influence, as in the cases of Mr. Anderson and Johnny Black, was *economic*. When people break away from their traditional party ties, the reason may be that they have come to look on another party as more responsive to their material needs. Doubtless this factor was central in the swing away from the Republicans in 1932. There seems to be a relationship—albeit a rough one—between income and voting. Most recent studies of voting behavior confirm what everyday observation has already indicated: the highest proportions of persons who prefer the Republican party are in the upper-income brackets, especially those with incomes of over $5000 a year.[15]

But we cannot make too much of this economic motivation, or of any other single motivation. For although we can isolate economic influences that affect voting, we cannot tell just how they affect it, or to what extent. Voting is the product of many factors besides the economic. Religion, for example, or geographical location, may cut across the lines of economic interest. Or voters of all types may respond in the same way to national or international developments. Studies suggest, for example, that the shift from Republicans to Democrats between 1928 to 1932 and from Democrats to Republicans between 1948 and 1952, was not peculiar to one or two groups, but was in fact common to all economic classes.

To generalize briefly, if Mr. Jones is a wealthy businessman, Protestant, living in rural Ohio, married to a Protestant, and the son of a Republican, the chances are very good that Jones will vote Republican. Unless radical alterations occur in our party structure or in our society generally, we can predict that such a person as Jones will vote Republican in a future election before we know either the candidates or the issues. Does this mean that people's political behavior can be predicted with certainty, or that voting is a simple mechanical addition of set factors? Not at all. Some men, like Jones, vote Democratic—or even socialist. It merely means that voting behavior, like all other behavior, is the outcome of a complex interrelationship of a number of significant factors. *On the average* the Joneses will vote Republican.

ALL KINDS OF INDEPENDENTS

Then there are the independent voters. Some are like our Mrs. Murphy, who made a conscientious effort to hear all sides of the argument before

---

[14] Lazarsfeld, *The People's Choice*, p. 141. For some recent studies in this area, see articles by H. W. Riecken, C. W. Wahl, and R. D. Luce in the provocative collection of essays, Eugene Burdick and A. J. Brodbeck (eds.), *American Voting Behavior* (The Free Press, 1959); and Herbert McClosky and H. E. Dahlgren, "Primary Group Influence on Party Loyalty," *American Political Science Review* (September 1959), pp. 757-776.

[15] See Berelson, Lazarsfeld, and McPhee, *Voting*, p. 333.

WHO PLAYS POLITICS? *

POLITICAL ACTIVITY SCORE
OF THE AMERICAN PEOPLE

	Per cent
Very active	10
Active	17
Inactive	35
Very inactive	38

AFFILIATIONS OF POLITICALLY ACTIVE

	Politically Very Active 100%	Population as a Whole 100%
Democrats	39.8	48.9
Republicans	43.8	32.7
Independents	16.4	18.4

PERCENTAGE OF VOTERS WHO VOTED ONCE IN THE PAST FOUR YEARS

	Per cent
Total Population	52
By Occupation	
Housewife	44
Professional	74
Executive	75
White-collar	63
Labor	47
Farmer	52
By Sex	
Men	57
Women	45
By Age	
21-34 years old	40
35-49	59
50 and over	60

	Per cent
By Economic Status	
Prosperous	77
Upper middle income	63
Lower middle income	56
Poor	37
By Education	
Grade school or less	43
High school	52
College	66
By Size of Place	
Over 100,000	52
2500 to 100,000	57
Under 2500	48
By Region	
Northeast	62
Midwest	56
South	39
Far West	48

VOTING TURNOUT OF SOURCES OF
REPUBLICAN PARTY STRENGTH

	Per cent
Prosperous	77
Executive	75
Professional	74
College educated	66
Upper middle income	63
Northeast	62
50 and over	60
2500-100,000 (size of place)	57

VOTING TURNOUT OF SOURCES OF
DEMOCRATIC PARTY STRENGTH

	Per cent
Far West	48
Labor	47
Women	45
Housewives	44
Grade school or less educated	43
21-34 years old	40
South	39
Poor	37

* Elmo Roper and Louis Harris, "Crime, Reform & the Voter," *The Saturday Review of Literature*, April 7, 1951, pp. 8, 9, 34, 35. By permission.

voting. Others resemble Sally Grey, who voted almost by whim. Unable to identify themselves consistently with one party or candidate, some independents cross and recross party lines from election to election. Some "split" their ticket and vote for some candidates from one party and other candidates from another party. Some people call themselves independents because they think it is socially more respectable, but actually they vote with the same degree of regularity for one party as do others who are not so hesitant to admit party loyalty.[16] So there are all kinds of independent voters. A recent study indicates that younger voters who live in middle-size cities, with over $3000 income, and with a college education, tend to be more independent than other groups, but that the independent vote is rather evenly distributed throughout the population.[17] On the average, about one out of every five voters calls himself independent, and twelve million independent-minded voters are a fact for any politician to reckon with.

Copyright 1956, Crowell Collier Publishing Company by Bill Mauldin

"Me, I vote the man, not the party. Harding, Coolidge, Hoover, Landon, Dewey . . ."

Variations in party strength may be due less to voters' shifting from one party to another than to the acquisition of new voters from the ranks of nonvoters or of younger people voting for the first time. In 1952, however, voters shifting their allegiance from one party to another were of crucial importance. According to a careful study, former Democrats who voted for Dwight D. Eisenhower held the balance of power in the 1952 election. "While sizable numbers of 1948 nonvoters were coming into the ranks of 1952 voters, dividing their favors rather equally between the two presidential aspirants, smaller numbers of people who had voted in 1948 were withdrawing from the political arena to become nonvoters in 1952. The net result of these additions and subtractions left the Republicans with an added 6 per cent of the population supporting their cause. In the same way, the Democrats picked up slightly more than 2 per cent of the population. As these sizable, but to some extent compensating, shifts were occurring, some 11 per cent of the citizens were deciding to change their votes from 1948 Democratic to 1952 Republican. . . ."[18] All told, the study concludes, some 25 per cent of the final Republican vote came from 1948 Democrats.

---

[16] Samuel J. Eldersveld, "The Independent Vote: Measurement, Characteristics, and Implications for Party Strategy," *The American Political Science Review* (September 1952), p. 737. In one study reported by Eldersveld one-half of those who claimed to be independents were *not*, by objective criteria.

[17] *Ibid.*, pp. 743, 751.

[18] Angus Campbell, Gerald Gurin, and Warren E. Miller, "Political Issues and the Vote: November, 1952," *The American Political Science Review* (June 1953), p. 369. This study was based on data gathered through nationwide sample surveys (conducted in October and November 1952) of over 2000 persons.

DOES CAMPAIGNING CHANGE VOTES?

From our discussion of voting behavior, we might conclude that all the speeches of vote-seekers, all the hullabaloo of their campaigns, had little effect compared to the other forces at work. In part this conclusion would be true. A campaign usually *converts* only a small fraction of the electorate. But it has other important effects. It *reinforces* the convictions of those already tending one way or another. And it *activates* people—that is, it arouses their interest,

TWO-PARTY DIVISION OF ENTIRE POPULATION
VS. DIVISION OF THE VOTING POPULATION*

	Among the Population Over 21 Claiming to Be		Among Those Who Turn Out to Vote	
	Democratic	Republican	Democratic	Republican
Total	60%	40%	53%	47%
By Occupation				
Housewife	60	40	51	49
Professional	53	47	49	51
Executive	36	64	32	68
White-collar	52	48	47	53
Labor	70	30	66	34
Farmer	67	33	64	36
By Sex				
Men	59	41	55	45
Women	60	40	51	49
By Age				
21-34	66	34	61	39
35-49	59	41	51	46
50 and over	54	46	45	55
By Economic Status				
Prosperous	31	69	27	73
Upper middle income	47	53	41	59
Lower middle	60	40	55	45
Poor	70	30	64	36
By Education				
Grade school	66	34	60	40
High school	61	39	54	46
College	46	54	43	57
By Size of Place				
Over 100,000	63	37	55	45
2500 to 100,000	58	42	49	51
Under 2500	62	38	55	45
By Region				
Northeast	46	54	40	60
Midwest	52	48	46	54
South	80	20	80	20
Far West	64	36	61	39

* Elmo Roper and Louis Harris, "Crime, Reform & the Voter."

exposes them to particular candidates and ideas, shapes their attitudes, and stimulates them to vote on election day.[19]

Even television may not influence voting as much as some have thought. In 1952 two students of politics took advantage of a "happy accident"—a government freeze on the construction of new television stations—to study voting in comparable Iowa counties, some of which received television clearly and others poorly. They found no significant differences between the two sets of counties either in voting turnout or in the division of the vote between the parties.[20]

Still, events between elections, and underlying attitudes, traditions, and pressures, are far more important than the campaign. Does this situation discourage the vote-seeking politician? Not at all. He knows that he is dealing in margins, often in close margins. He knows that a hundred unknown intangibles will shape the final outcome. Great political forces are delicately balanced—perhaps a good push by his party and himself will tip them in the right direction.

To summarize briefly this discussion of voting behavior:

1. The rate of nonvoting is very high in the United States. The main cause is apathy. A number of remedies for nonvoting have been proposed, including compulsory voting.

2. Voting falls into rough patterns, mainly geographical. The somewhat regular swing of the political pendulum over time is caused by a variety of economic and other factors.

3. The way we vote stems in large part from tradition, the groups we belong to (including family groups), our economic and social status. Independent voting also results from a variety of factors.

As a statistical summary the data on pp. 250 and 252, gathered in a 1950 study, underscore some of the major points offered in this chapter.

Changing Patterns of Politics   **A** century ago, American politics was still essentially "rustic." Then, as people crowded into the great cities, rustic politics came to be overshadowed by the rise of an urban politics. Currently we are witnessing the development of a suburban politics. Of course no stage in this series of transitions has wholly obliterated the preceding one. Today, in the fabulous breadth and diversity of American political life, rural, urban, and suburban politics exist comfortably side by side. Each deserves attention.

---

[19] Lazarsfeld, *The People's Choice,* Chapters 7-11.

[20] H. A. Simon and Frederick Stern, "The Effect of Television Upon Voting Behavior in Iowa in the 1952 Presidential Election," *The American Political Science Review* (June 1955), pp. 470-477.

Jonesville is a prairie town of several thousand people in the Midwest. It is of interest to us because it is a rather "typical" small town in an agricultural area, and because a group of sociologists made a careful study of the town and its people following World War II.[21] What did they discover about the political life of Jonesville?

In the first place, Jonesville, like so many country towns in the United States, is strongly Republican. For half a century, no Democratic President had carried the county in which Jonesville is located, except Franklin D. Roosevelt by a narrow margin in 1932. Social pressure seems to keep the town Republican, even when the nation goes Democratic. "People around here," says a leading Democrat, "are scared to admit they're Democrats." Even voters with definite Democratic tendencies dislike to vote in the Democratic primaries, where they must openly display their party allegiance: they prefer to vote Democratic in the privacy of the polling booth at the general election.

The fact that Jonesville is a Republican stronghold does not mean that it is a bustle of partisan activity. Less than 20 per cent of the people voted Republican faithfully enough in a number of primary and general elections to be classified as "solid Republican voters." (The proportion of Democratic voters was much less—barely 2 per cent.) Significantly, voting in Jonesville tends to follow class lines—at least on the Republican side—much as it does in the country as a whole. The percentage of persons who are "solid Republican voters" is 24 per cent in the upper-middle class and 7 per cent in the lowest social class.[22] The Republican strength in Jonesville is important for our two-party system; it indicates how a major party can survive at the grass-roots level during long years of being in the minority nationally.

The Republicans are relatively well organized in Jonesville. There are six precinct committeemen and a number of other party workers and miscellaneous hangers-on. Their main job is to get the vote out in primary and general elections. To do this they rely chiefly on the most important means of influence in grass-roots democracy: face-to-face contact with voters. Some of the party wheel-horses work at politics throughout the year; others are active only at election time. For the most part, the precinct committeemen deal in small political currency: "fixing" traffic tickets, arranging tax adjustments, and the like. By way of reward, the committeeman can expect an invitation to the governor's inaugural, some control of patronage, and perhaps a state job for himself.

Behind these minor politicos in Jonesville are a few "big shots" who have considerable influence over the Republican organization. Their power depends

---

[21] W. L. Warner and Associates, *Democracy in Jonesville* (Harper, 1949). All the material in this section is drawn from this provocative and significant study.
[22] *Ibid.*, p. 219.

on their ability to maintain two sets of relationships, "outward" and "local." They must deal outwardly with county and state politicians, the governor, and leaders of interest groups; locally they must deal with the party workers and town officials. The "goods" they deal in consist of patronage, favors, legislative influence, campaign funds—and votes on election day. An important factor in maintaining both sets of relationships is "the class position of the individuals involved: the ability to circulate socially in 'important' circles at the state capital, the educational requirements of certain positions, practice in management and the exercise of initiative demand a middle-class social position as a sort of minimum if the outward connections are to be established and maintained." [23] Such connections are also important in raising campaign funds.

The Democratic party in Jonesville is a feeble organization. It lacks money, patronage, party workers, and voting support. It is split by petty factionalism. The basic fact is that Jonesville is Republican by tradition, ideology, and perhaps interest. In Jonesville, "Democrats are made, not born." In big-city politics, the reverse is generally true.

STREET-CORNER POLITICS

American politics, big-city style, has long been a matter of powerful bosses, elaborate organizations, myriad party workers, systematic patronage on the grand scale, considerable party discipline over national, state, and local legislators, and hundreds of thousands of Democratic votes for national, state, and local candidates (except in Philadelphia and a few other cities that were traditionally Republican).

But remember that inside these large organizations there is a pattern of political organization and influence on a block and street-corner basis. Here we find the "wheels within wheels" of urban political life, the crisscrossing relationships among families, neighborhoods, religious and ethnic groups, places of business, criminal groups, athletic clubs. An important "building-block" of political organization is the street-corner gang of young men. Some years ago, a young social scientist, William F. Whyte, spent many months with such a gang in a slum district inhabited mainly by Italian immigrant families, in the heart of a large city, and later reported on his observations. [24]

In "Cornerville," as Whyte calls it, there are a number of political clubs started by politicians and organized around them. These clubs supply votes that the politician can use either to elect himself to local office or to deliver to bosses farther up in the machine hierarchy. Corner gangs are usually an active part of these clubs. The boss who runs the club maintains close working relationships with the gang leader, consulting him on policy questions and doing favors for him. The gang leader, in turn, learns the political trade by serving as apprentice to the politician. In Cornerville politics, the gangs are

---

[23] *Ibid.*, p. 230.
[24] W. F. Whyte, *Street Corner Society* (Univ. of Chicago Press, 1943).

perhaps even more important than families, for the latter have tended to be weakened by divisions between first and second generations.

The economic and social stresses of the 1930's tended to undermine some of these local organizations. A former boss, speaking nostalgically about earlier times, said, "In those days we really controlled. We could tell within fifty votes how the ward would go in any election. One time we changed the ward from Democratic to Republican overnight. That was in the mayoralty contest of 1905. There was a meeting in the club till three in the morning right before the election. We printed the slate we were backing and circulated it around as much as we had time for. When the people came to the polls, the captain would ask them, 'Do you have the slate?' If they didn't he would give it to them, and they would go in and vote it. . . .

"Today everything has changed. We've got a floating population in the South Side now. People are moving out all the time. You can't expect a precinct captain to know everybody any more. . . ." [25]

Cornerville politics can best be described, according to Whyte, as a "system of reciprocal personal obligations." People do favors for one another, and mutual loyalty is an indispensable part of the political code. Affecting all these interpersonal relationships, however, are two broader influences. One is national origin. In an area heavily populated by foreign-born Americans, the politician must know how to play on their national sympathies, their sense of being the "underdog," their feelings against other groups. The other is class appeal. While the Cornerville politician talks little about specific national or state policy questions, he speaks often of "God's own poor" and of the lot of working people. "The most important qualification a politician can claim is that he has been and will always be loyal to his old friends, to his class, and to his race." This is the hallmark of politicians everywhere, but it takes on special importance in the politics of the melting pot.

THE NEW POLITICS OF SUBURBIA

The old boss quoted above complained that people were moving out all the time. Where are they going? Many of them to suburban areas outside the large and medium-sized cities. In the past decade, Americans have been flooding into Suburbia. City growth since 1940 has averaged less than 10 per cent, and the relative number of people on farms is declining. But the suburban population has shot up by 50 to 100 per cent throughout the country. New York's Nassau County alone, for example, has shown a gain of over 60 per cent. Suburbs of Boston, Chicago, Philadelphia, Los Angeles, and other metropolises—along with those of middle-sized cities—have shown startling increases. Today one out of every four Americans is a suburbanite.

Are we finding a new suburban complexion in the pattern of American

---

[25] *Ibid.,* p. 195.

politics? Who will reap the millions of votes in Suburbia? What role will the suburban masses have in national politics? How will they line up on issues? Will they mark the supremacy of the middle classes in American politics? What, in short, will be the impact of Suburbia on American political life?

When a city Democrat settles down in the midst of suburban Republicans, he must adjust to a different political world as well as to a different social one. He often finds that the Republicans have as tight a grip on local government as the Democrats had on the politics of his old neighborhood. From the standpoint of business contacts, it may seem expedient to register Republican. Often people moving into the suburbs are also moving into higher income brackets, and changing parties seems all the more logical. But the influence is by no means all in one direction. The "immigrants" from the city have some impact too. They bring with them different ideas and often a flair for political action. They speak up at the meetings of the League of Women Voters and the Civic Association. Many of them continue to vote Democratic as they have in the past.

Nevertheless, the Republicans are dominant in Suburbia, and they probably will continue to be so for some time. Here they will harvest the hundreds of thousands of votes they badly need to offset the two- or three-million vote edge that the Democrats have gained in the nation as a whole. Election night in most large states has usually seen huge urban majorities washing out the Republican votes from small towns and rural areas. In future elections, we may see suburban majorities tipping the balance back toward the Republicans.[26] "The suburbs beat us!" exclaimed a Democratic city boss following a recent Republican victory in his state.

A recent study of politics in Suburbia, however, questions the likelihood of any strong political trends there. After all, it points out, suburbs vary enormously in make-up just as other areas of the country do. But one trend does seem clear, according to this study—there seems to be a decline in the importance of partisan association as such. In St. Louis suburbs, for example, a strikingly high proportion of the residents thought of themselves as "independents." Such a trend may result in de-emphasizing not only partisanship but politics as a whole.[27]

Still, for the moment, most suburban areas outside the South are heavily Republican. Does this mean that Suburbia will be a conservative force in American politics? Perhaps. But the situation is a bit more complicated than this. There is reason to expect that Suburbia will be a liberalizing and broadening force in both parties. Engaged as they are in hundreds of different sectors of the economy, the new suburban masses have a variety of economic interests. One suburban commuter works in a great insurance firm; his neighbor

---

[26] Louis Harris, *Is There a Republican Majority?* (Harper, 1954), Chapter 8; and Samuel Lubell, *Revolt of the Moderates* (Harper, 1956), Chapter 5.

[27] R. C. Wood, *Suburbia: Its People and Politics* (Houghton Mifflin, 1959), especially Chapter 5.

next door is in the steel-fabricating business; Mr. Jones across the street plans advertising campaigns in the headquarters of a giant food chain. Their political attitudes tend to reflect these diverse economic interests.

This situation is a far cry from the style of political life in areas domiinated by a single economic interest, as in one-crop sections of the South or mining areas in Pennsylvania or cattle districts of the West. Involved in the economics of the whole nation, Suburbia is concerned more with a politics of broad national and international programs than with a politics of narrow sectional interest. It is not surprising that polls show a marked support for internationalist foreign policies in many middle-class, suburban areas. Suburbia will be more cosmopolitan and sophisticated in political outlook than rural or urban areas have been. Its representatives in Washington and the state capitals will not get far on the easy formula of "Everything for the folks back home." To act for his suburban constituents, each legislator must mediate among interests almost as diverse as those of the whole nation.

Suburbia, in short, may tend to be less concerned with pork-barrel politics, trivial favors, patronage, and errand-running, and more concerned with matters of broad policy, such as taxes, labor, foreign affairs, Cold War strategy, farm subsidies, prices. This concern may have a wholesome influence on American politics.

Leaders and Followers

Not long ago an interviewer from the Survey Research Center of the University of Michigan asked some questions of the wife of a machinist in Kentucky.[28] The dialogue went like this:

> "What do you like about the Democrats?"
> "That's Stevenson, ain't it?"
> "Yes, that's his party."
> "No, I don't know anything about Stevenson but I do like the party."
> "What is it that you like about the Democratic party?"
> "There's always been more Democrats running for President than there has been for the other party, and they've got in more."
> "Is there anything else you like about the Democratic party?"
> "No."
> "What do you dislike about the Democrats?"
> "I don't know anything about the Democratic party. . . . Well, for one thing, they were hard on the farmers. . . . No, I always liked the Democratic party until Truman was in. He said that he was going to do things for the farmers and he backed out."
> "What do you like about the Republicans?"
> "That's Stevenson, ain't it? I get them mixed up."

---

[28] Angus Campbell, W. E. Miller, and Donald Stokes, *The American Voter* (Wiley, 1960).

"No, that's Eisenhower's party."

"Well, one thing, I heard he lowered taxes."

"Is there anything else you like about the Republican party?"

"And he's a good man—I hope he gets in this time."

"Anything else you dislike about the Republicans?"

"No, I can't think of anything."

"Anything you like about Stevenson?"

"No, there's no faults. I just don't like him."

"Anything you like about Eisenhower?"

"I don't know of any."

Obviously this woman knows little about national affairs. She thought Stevenson was a Republican and was hazy about why she felt as she did about the candidates and the parties. Yet we cannot dismiss her as an ignoramus. She had some idea about the relation of politics and economic problems—note her reference to farmers and to taxes. She may be inarticulate about why she liked Eisenhower, but the feeling was there and was perhaps important to her. She probably votes, at least occasionally.

In any event, this housewife is typical of millions of Americans, who, lacking solid information and clear views, usually vote under the influence of other people—their parents, the newspaper editor, the local party boss, or someone else. In their voting they tend to be *followers*—if they vote at all.

At the other extreme are the leaders who influence the followers. These we might call "multivoters"—persons whose influence over other voters is so great that they in effect control more than one voter. This influence may or may not be intended. The head of a family may be a multivoter simply because he holds the respect and confidence of his wife and children. The party worker, on the other hand, deliberately sets out to win votes from friends and neighbors in his ward. In either case the personal, face-to-face contact is highly effective.

Is there any way to measure the varying extent to which people take part in politics? Some years ago pollsters asked a series of questions of a cross section of adult Americans: [29] Do you discuss public issues, like taxes or foreign policy, with your friends? Do you belong to an organization that sometimes takes positions on such issues? Have you ever told your Representative about your views? How often have you voted? Have you taken part in political campaigns? The answers were graded; the highest score possible was twelve, the lowest zero. How well did these typical people do?

The results were disappointing to anyone wishing Americans to be politically active. Hardly more than 10 per cent scored six or more points— these were labeled "very active." Another 17 per cent scored four to five points—these were called politically "active." At the extreme were the "very inactive," scoring one point or none—over 38 per cent flunked the test this

---

[29] J. L. Woodward and Elmo Roper, "Political Activity of American Citizens," *The American Political Science Review* (December 1950), pp. 872-885.

badly. About 35 per cent were only a bit away from the bottom, scoring two to three points, and these were labeled "inactive."

The results, in short, indicate that almost three-quarters of American adults are politically inactive. Who are these people? They are much like the nonvoters described above—more women than men, less educated, with lower income, more Democrats than Republicans, younger in years. The top tenth of very active people includes a far more than average number of executives, professional people, and persons with college educations. Another study of political participation in a small country town has confirmed these findings and suggests also that the inactive people are less likely to feel themselves members of, or affected by, the community they live in.[30] Political inactivity, in short, reflects psychological as well as economic and social forces.

Is leadership, then, restricted entirely to a small "elite"—the 10 per cent at the top? Not entirely, by any means. There is still some role for local "grass-roots" leadership. If our country were made up of a few leaders at the top and a hundred million followers at the bottom, our democracy might not be as solid and resilient as we like to think it is. Actually, leaders are found at all levels. The leader in the local community may be a follower in the county or state. The head of a local labor or business organization is perhaps a follower of a state or national labor or business leader. Thus there are *overlapping hierarchies* of leaders and followers.

LOCAL LEADERS

Through their face-to-face contacts, local opinion leaders have an influence that national leaders, with their less personal relationship, cannot always match. Many voters, moreover, pay more attention to local opinion leaders than to the radio or newspaper. "In comparison with the formal media of communication," says Lazarsfeld, "personal relationships are potentially more influential for two reasons: their coverage is greater and they have certain psychological advantages over the formal media," such as the newspaper.[31] Opinion leaders can get through to persons who rarely expose themselves to the radio or printed page. And their technique—consciously or not—is far more effective. Listening to a candidate or reading a campaign poster, the follower may suspect that someone is trying to sell him a bill of goods. But the seemingly casual remarks of the opinion leader may catch him off guard. The leader can talk in terms that the follower understands, can find the right time to deliver his opinions, can tailor his argument to suit the follower's personality or beliefs. In politics, just as in business, face-to-face contact lowers sales resistance.

---

[30] R. E. Agger and Vincent Ostrom, "Political Participation in a Small Community," in Heinz Eulau, S. J. Eldersveld, and Morris Janowitz, *Political Behavior* (The Free Press, 1956). This volume of readings is excellent both for substance and as a guide to recent research in the "frontiers of theory."

[31] Lazarsfeld, *The People's Choice*, p. 150.

Successful political leaders understand all this. Half a century ago Boss Plunkitt, a Tammany district leader, was quoted as saying:

> There's only one way to hold a district; you must study human nature and act accordin'. You can't study human nature in books. Books is a hindrance more than anything else. If you have been to college, so much the worse for you. You'll have to unlearn all you learned before you can get right down to human nature, and unlearnin' takes a lot of time. Some men can never forget what they learned at college. Such men may get to be district leaders by a fluke, but they never last.
>
> To learn real human nature you have to go among the people, see them and be seen. I know every man, woman, and child in the Fifteenth District, except them that's been born this summer—and I know some of them, too. I know what they like and what they don't like, what they are strong at and what they are weak in, and I reach them by approachin' at the right side.
>
> For instance, here's how I gather in the young men. I hear of a young feller that's proud of his voice, thinks that he can sing fine. I ask him to come around to Washington Hall and join our Glee Club. He comes and sings, and he's a follower of Plunkitt for life. Another young feller gains a reputation as a baseball player in a vacant lot. I bring him into our baseball club. That fixes him. . . . I don't trouble them with political arguments. I just study human nature and act accordin'. . . .
>
> As to the older voters, I reach them, too. No, I don't send campaign literature. That's rot. People can get all the political stuff they want to read— and a good deal more, too—in the papers. Who reads speeches, nowadays, anyhow? It's bad enough to listen to them. You ain't goin' to gain any votes by stuffin' the letter boxes with campaign documents. . . .[32]

We need not accept all Boss Plunkitt's arguments to appreciate the role of direct personal leadership.

ALL KINDS OF LEADERS

Do certain people have innate qualities of leadership and others not? Some social scientists used to believe that leadership was restricted to people possessing certain traits, such as imagination, foresight, versatility, good health, courage—or even well-functioning endocrine glands! Elaborate lists were drawn up of so-called leadership qualities.[33] Investigators had trouble, however, in agreeing what were the key, universal qualities of leadership. More recently expert opinion has shifted somewhat. Careful experiments indicate that leadership is *related to a given situation.* A baseball team, a religious club, and a corrupt political machine will produce different types of leaders. Since America, as we noted in Chapter 1, is composed of a fabulous diversity of groups, inevitably there will be a variety of leaders.[34] A person who is a

---

[32] W. L. Riordan, *Plunkitt of Tammany Hall* (McClure, Phillips, 1905), pp. 33-34.

[33] See E. S. Bogardus, *Fundamentals of Social Psychology* (Appleton-Century, 1942), Chapter 12.

[34] See A. W. Gouldner (ed.), *Studies in Leadership* (Harper, 1950), pp. 14-44.

follower in one group or situation may be a leader in the next. We all know of the football captain who inspires his team on the field but who is a wallflower at the school dance, or the store manager who never opens his mouth at town meeting.

All this means that political leadership is not restricted to a chosen few but can be—and is—exercised by millions of average citizens throughout the land. It means that anyone can wield influence in his own circle, for investigations show that opinion leaders are found at all economic levels and in all social groups. It means, above all, that the right to vote is only the simplest, most elementary privilege available to a citizen of a democracy. He has a further right to seek to influence other voters, and if he exercises that right he can multiply his strength manyfold. One of the hallmarks of a vigorous democracy is that *everyone* can play politics.

What, then, can be said in summary about the political behavior—especially the political participation—of Americans? On the one hand, it is clear, by every test, that political activity and influence tend to increase, on the average, the farther up people are located on the economic and educational ladder. On the other hand, at almost all levels local opinion-leaders talk directly with others in their neighborhood or work group, influencing their ideas and being a bit influenced by them. The great mass of people may be inactive politically, but they are not a herd of sheep to be led hither and thither as some leader may wish. They have some leadership of their own. Still, they do not have the influence that their numbers deserve in a democracy, and one of the great tasks is to draw more people at all economic and social levels into the exciting enterprise of running a government by the people.

CHAPTER 11

Public Opinion:
The Voices of the People

Government by the people is supposed to be government in accordance with the will of the people. So it is, but what *is* the will of the people? What does government do when people disagree? What does it do when opinions change? What does it do when most of the people are indifferent about some issue, while a minority is active and noisy? Should government itself try to influence opinion? If so, how far should it go?

Let us look at these questions from the vantage point of, say, a senator in Washington. He wants to be the servant of the people. But he is not sure what people want. He cannot really tell from his mail, because he is not sure that the letter-writers actually reflect opinion back home. He is suspicious of public opinion polls. He is not sure just what issues he was elected on, since he argued for and against so many propositions in his last campaign. Besides, it is five years since he was elected, and many important events have taken place in that time. He listens for the voice of the people, but the people do not speak with a single voice. No wonder he straddles the fence. From his point of view, the *people* are straddling the fence.

But governments must act. Decisions must be made. Somehow, out of the confusion of raucous voices and dead silences, politicians must shape fairly precise and positive policies. To see the relation between political opinions and governmental actions, we must look first at the variety of people involved.

Millions of Publics   Imagine that the following incident takes place: A group of college students at a state university decides—all in a spirit of frivolity—to announce to the press that they are forming a local chapter of the League of the Militant Godless. The story appears in a newspaper. Immediately a variety of responses takes place. The other students merely smile. They know a joke when they see one. The president and dean of the college do not smile. They know that this is meant as a joke, but they are afraid of the effect it may have on the "public." Local church groups are indignant. Religion is not a matter for pranks, says one minister in a sermon. Local townspeople are divided; some see the incident as a joke, but others feel that the students have gone too far. Several legislators at the state capital denounce the affair as another sign of communist influence in the colleges. Some people read about the incident in the newspapers, shake their heads, and forget about it. Others hear about it indirectly, and perhaps complain that there are too many reds at the state college. A few parents of undergraduates write letters of protest to the college president. But most people, even in the state, never hear about the incident at all. At any rate, after a few weeks have gone by the incident is all but forgotten.

NO MASS MIND

Now it would be wrong to say that one general public opinion, or a single mass mind, was involved here. Actually there were a number of *different public opinions* simply because there were a number of *different publics*. These publics reacted in several ways, largely in accordance with their physical nearness to the incident, the extent of their understanding of the incident, their own occupational position or social group, their stake or interest in the incident, and, above all, their basic attitudes. The other students, for example, were close to the incident and understood its frivolous nature. The college administration, the ministers, and the legislators had an actual or assumed stake in the incident. The townspeople reacted largely as a close-knit group with set attitudes toward student activities. Most people remote from the incident remained uninformed and uninterested.

Translate all this into a real live national issue, and one sees the tremendous complexity of public opinion and the many publics involved. The President makes a speech about labor legislation, and his words fall differently on the ears of union members, businessmen, union leaders, farmers, Democrats, Republicans, and so on. The Secretary of Agriculture announces a new farm program, and he gets mixed reactions not only from the large nonfarming public, but also from the farm public itself—that is, from cotton farmers as against wheat farmers, from large farmers as against small farmers. A senator calls for the end of government subsidies; many businessmen applaud because they want lower taxes, but businessmen who are receiving subsidies, as in the case of ship operators, do not applaud. These are examples merely of different *interests*—but the whole process is immensely complicated by the different attitudes that people have by reason of their economic and social status, their group loyalties, their occupation, their degree of understanding or information.

What, then, are some of the important aspects of public opinions—and of the various publics that hold them?

SOME ASPECTS OF PUBLIC OPINIONS

Basic political attitudes may be fairly stable. People's views on their own political party preference, for example, vary little over the years, as this table on party preference suggests:

PARTY SELF-IDENTIFICATION: 1952-1958

Party preference	1952	1954	1956	1958
Strong Democrat	22%	22%	21%	23%
Weak Democrat	25	25	23	24
Independent Democrat	10	9	6	7
Independent	5	7	9	8
Independent Republican	7	6	8	4
Weak Republican	14	14	14	16
Strong Republican	13	13	15	13
Apolitical	4	4	4	5
	100%	100%	100%	100%

Source: Survey Research Center, University of Michigan.

Public opinions on some issues are sometimes fluid and changeable. Foreign policy is a good example. During the past 15 years Gallup poll-takers have asked a sample of the public: "What do you regard as the most important problem before the American people today?" Over the years the response has varied widely. In 1935 only 11 per cent of the respondents answered, "Foreign policy issues." By 1941, that answer was given by 81 per cent. In 1945 the figure was down to 7 per cent, but by April 1948 it had risen to 73 per cent. The public mood seems to shift quickly and strongly in response to events, even while people's basic party allegiance stays the same.[1]

The interested public is always changing. This is one reason for instability of opinions. Different issues attract different active publics; even the same issue over a period of time may attract a changing public. People get bored with causes or issues just as they get tired of clothing styles or movie stars. Or the objective situation may change. For example, when they are out of office, Democrats may view the issue of governmental economy quite differently from the way they view it when they are in. On the other hand, people informed on one issue tend to be informed on others.

People holding an opinion vary greatly in intensity of belief. Some people hold a belief passively; others are fanatics on the matter. Such variations in intensity have important results in politics. The attitudes of the passive can

[1] Gabriel Almond, *The American People and Foreign Policy* (Harcourt, Brace, 1950), p. 66. See also K. P. Adler, "Interest and Influence in Foreign Affairs," *Public Opinion Quarterly* (Spring 1956), pp. 89-101.

probably be changed more easily than the attitudes of those who have strong feelings. And the latter can be expected to act more positively on their beliefs. They may try to convert others to their cause, to organize in groups, to win votes for a politician.

Public opinion may be latent. Even though public attitudes on a particular issue have not crystallized, they are potentially important, for they can be evoked and converted into action if certain things are done. Indeed, we can often predict how certain persons will react to an incident even though they have never indicated their views on the matter. In the incident with which this chapter opened, for example, the ministers and state legislators had never expressed attitudes toward the League of the Militant Godless, but anyone could have predicted what their views would be. A good politician must be able to assess latent or potential public opinion, so that he can face (or evade) new issues with some knowledge of how public opinion will shape up.[2]

Finally, *the public is made up of numberless subpublics, differentiated in many ways.* This is simply another way of stating what we found in the reaction to our college prank—that different publics were uncovered or created. These subpublics vary in their interest in a given issue, their level of understanding, their basic attitudes, their religion, their section or locality, their economic or social position, their national origin, their cultural inheritance, their education, and in a host of other ways. Moreover, these thousands of subpublics cut across one another in a thousand different ways, in turn creating literally millions of "subsubpublics."

No wonder public opinion seems so illusive and intangible, that the politician treads warily, that opinion polls go wrong. The picture becomes even more complicated when we consider that there can be a difference between opinions privately held and opinions publicly expressed, and that some opinions have high "competence"—that is, are directly related to the person's factual knowledge—while other opinions are uninformed and superficial. But the picture is not one of complete confusion. There is some order, some pattern in the infinite variety of political opinions in our democracy. In part, this order stems from certain basic ideas held by a great number of Americans.

THE AMERICAN IDEA-SYSTEM

What is basic in our own political idea-system? One eminent sociologist, Gunnar Myrdal, has found that the American people, despite their diversity, have a common set of beliefs. This American creed he calls "the cement in the

---

[2] L. W. Doob, *Public Opinion and Propaganda* (Holt, 1948), p. 40. For a study stressing political aspects of public opinion, see M. B. Ogle, Jr., *Public Opinion and Political Dynamics* (Houghton Mifflin, 1950).

structure of this great and disparate nation." [3] It has its roots in the era of "Enlightenment" when early Americans were absorbing the new philosophy of liberty, equality, and fraternity. It also has roots in Christianity—in the biblical teachings about man's need for freedom and equality, for justice and dignity. Americans, in short, believe in democracy.

Americans actually order their lives, however, according to a more specific set of beliefs which somehow they square with their basic creed. These particular beliefs are extremely numerous and complex, but we can list a few of them. After making an exhaustive study of a typical American city (Muncie, Indiana) in the 1930's, two investigators found that most of the citizens of "Middletown," as they called it, shared such beliefs as the following: [4]

That, when in doubt, people should act like other people.

That America is a land of progress, and that increasing size is a sign of progress.

That progress should not be speeded up artificially.

That the middle way is the best way.

That good will and sincerity will solve most problems.

That a man should try to get ahead of his fellows, but not in an unfair way.

That if a man does not get on, it is his own fault.

That people should place *their* family, *their* community, *their* state, *their* nation first.

That American ways are better than foreign ways, and Americans superior to foreigners.

That the small businessman is the backbone of the American economic system.

That capital and labor have basically the same interests.

That such problems as corruption in government can be solved mainly by electing better men to office.

Notice that some of these ideas may contradict one another. The reason is partly that ideas arising in one era are carried over uncritically into new situations. "Men's ideas, beliefs, and loyalties—their nonmaterial culture—are frequently slower to be changed than are their material tools," it has been said. "It is precisely in this matter of trying to live by contrasting rules of the game that one of the most characteristic aspects of our American culture is to be seen." [5]

---

[3] Gunnar Myrdal, *An American Dilemma* (Harper, 1944), Vol. I, p. 3. For a recent astute view of America from abroad, see the volume by the French Dominican priest, Father R. L. Bruckberger, *Image of America* (Viking, 1959).

[4] R. S. Lynd and H. M. Lynd, *Middletown in Transition* (Harcourt, Brace, 1937), pp. 402-486.

[5] R. S. Lynd, *Knowledge for What?* (Princeton Univ. Press, 1939), p. 59.

Here are some of our contrasting rules:

Everyone should try to be successful. *But:* The kind of person you are is more important than how successful you are.

The family is our basic institution and the sacred core of our national life. *But:* Business is our most important institution, and, since national welfare depends upon it, other institutions must conform to its needs.

Religion and the finer things of life are our ultimate values and the things all of us are really working for. *But:* A man owes it to himself and his family to make as much money as he can.

Life would not be tolerable if we did not believe in progress and know that things are getting better. We should, therefore, welcome new things. *But:* The old, tried fundamentals are best; and it is a mistake for busybodies to try to change things too fast or to upset the fundamentals.

Honesty is the best policy. *But:* Business is business, and a businessman would be a fool if he didn't cover his hand.

Education is a fine thing. *But:* It is the practical man who gets things done.

The American judicial system insures justice to every man, rich or poor. *But:* A man is a fool not to hire the best lawyer he can afford.

No man deserves to have what he hasn't worked for. It demoralizes him to do so. *But:* You can't let people starve.[6]

Where Do Our Opinions Come from?

Living in a democracy can be a pretty confusing business. Everyone seems to be trying to get our ear or catch our eye so that he can press on us his point of view. Under a dictatorship life is much simpler. There is officially one public opinion—the Word that comes down from the head man. Some of the lesser citizenry growl and mutter under their breath, but they are in no position to take a public stand. In a democracy we sometimes complain about the babel of voices that shriek at us in the newspaper and over the air waves, but we sense, too, that this babel is a sign of a free society, and one of its foundation posts.

If we look sharply, however, we can see a pattern even in the complex workings of public opinion in a democracy. Along with the basic ideas described above, there are certain forces that have a massive part in the shaping of men's ideas. There are certain methods of persuasion and propaganda common to all opinion-molders.

OPINION-SHAPERS

First of all, our opinions are molded by the *culture* we live in—by the over-all beliefs and behavior that characterize American society. Chapter 1 described the shifting economic and social foundations of our society, the im-

---

[6] Lynd, *Knowledge for What?* pp. 60-61. For a more recent analysis of the American system of values, see R. M. Williams, *American Society* (Knopf, 1951).

pact of these changes on individual and group attitudes and behavior, and certain psychological factors. It will be useful to keep these factors in mind in considering the nature of public opinion. Our society is vast and highly diverse. What influences produce a pattern of opinion within our complex culture?

Probably the most important opinion-molder of all is the *family*. We begin to form our picture of the world at our Mother's knee, or listening to Father talk at breakfast, or hearing the tales that our older brothers and sisters bring back from school. What we learn in the family are not simply political opinions, but the basic attitudes that will shape our future opinions— attitudes toward our neighbors, toward other classes or types of people, toward local rules or customs, toward society in general. "The family is bound up with all the great crises and transitions of life," says MacIver. "It is the primary agent in the molding of the life-habits and the life-attitudes of human beings." [7] Some of us may rebel against the ways of the close little group that we live with, but most of us conform. Thus the family is a sort of link between the past and the present. It translates the world to us, but it does so in its own terms.

We are scarcely out of diapers when our world begins to expand rapidly. We go to school, we associate with different types of people, we get a more general picture of the world we live in. We probably learn as much outside the classroom as in it, because we are reacting not merely to teachers and books but also to behavior—the manners, dress, talk, attitudes—of other children. The same is true of our church, another opinion-making institution. We are influenced by sermons and symbols, and by the behavior of other members of the congregation. The attitudes we develop from living in our community, through association with family, friends, school, church, are attitudes that will influence us all the rest of our lives, because they are gained from *direct personal contact* with other people.

But other influences are coming to bear. We begin to look at the newspaper—perhaps only at the comics, sports, headlines, and pictures at first, but later we read news stories and possibly the editorial page. Indeed, we can hardly avoid some contact with the newspaper, for it has been estimated that only one out of every twenty families in urban areas reads no daily newspaper. The total circulation of American newspapers is almost 58 million copies a day. There are countless foreign-language newspapers, and thousands of weeklies, ranging from mass-circulation magazines we are all familiar with, such as *Newsweek, Life,* and *The Saturday Evening Post,* to more specialized journals, along with the multitude of slicks and pulps that are sold every day. Walter Lippmann has called the newspaper the "bible of democracy, the book out of which a people determines its conduct." [8]

---

[7] R. M. MacIver, *The Web of Government* (Macmillan, 1947), p. 23.
[8] Walter Lippmann, *Liberty and the News* (Harcourt, Brace, and Howe, 1920), p. 47.

We begin to watch television, another key instrument of mass communication and persuasion. Studies show that pictures are often the most effective means of communication and persuasion. Television, by bringing into the home moving pictures combined with sound, is probably becoming the most effective mass medium.[9]

And we begin to go to the movies. Most weeks at least 45 million people pay admissions to motion-picture theaters. (Television may cut permanently into this figure.) They see not only one or two feature films, but short subjects, newsreels, and perhaps even documentary films. Seventy per cent of the people able to go to the movies attend at least once every three weeks, and many of them go much more often. It is estimated that two-thirds of these movie-goers are under thirty years of age. Thus we tend to be most exposed to the movies at an age when our attitudes are most malleable. The movies, with an eye on the box office, may tend to stress the exceptional rather than the typical, the sensational rather than the significant, but they are probably no more prone to this failing than radio or television.

To name these major opinion-forming agencies is not to exhaust the list of influences that focus on us as we grow into citizenhood. Books, for example, play an important though often intangible role. Nor is it to do justice to the many groups or persons, such as parties, interest groups, governments, politicians, businessmen, bureaucrats, and corporations, that seek to use the media of communication and persuasion for their own ends.

How much influence do all these forces have in molding opinion? Are they as formidable as they seem?

HOW INFLUENTIAL ARE THE EDITORS?

Consider the press. It can be argued that the newspapers really do not influence opinion very much, because the editors often think one way and the people vote the opposite way. The four elections of Franklin D. Roosevelt to the Presidency are often cited to support this view. It has been estimated that Roosevelt was backed by 40 per cent of the press (in terms of total circulation) in 1932, by 36 per cent in 1936, by 20 per cent in 1940, and by 17 per cent in 1944. Yet he won all these elections decisively, and he swept some urban areas where he had little or no newspaper support. Harry Truman's victory in 1948 is another case in point, and city bosses have flourished for years in the face of continued denunciation by local newspapers. It is also pointed out that the vast majority of newspaper readers do not bother to look at the editorial page.

These arguments, however, do not wholly meet the issue. The real ques-

---

[9] Angus Campbell, Gerald Gurin, and Warren E. Miller, "Television and the Election," *Scientific American*, Vol. 188, 1953, pp. 46-48.

tion is not whether the press directly influences our choices at the polls, but whether it gives us a conception of the world about us that indirectly influences our political behavior. Our views are shaped, in Lippman's words, by the "pictures inside our heads." The newspaper, in its front-page make-up, its headlines, its use of pictures, its playing up of some news and playing down of other, its distortion or suppression of important information, helps form those "pictures inside our heads." Thus, while it is significant that Roosevelt won out against the majority of the newspapers, the really central question is the extent to which he had to modify his program and actions in the face of public opinion even before he began campaigning. The press has a long-run, continuous influence on opinions that may not be obvious in a particular election.

Other media, such as radio, television, and movies, can also be effective in molding political attitudes. It is sometimes thought that radio, being ostensibly neutral in politics, and the movies, having no political views as such, cannot be viewed in the same light as the press, which often bears an obvious party label (the *New York Herald Tribune,* for example, identifies itself as an independent Republican newspaper). On the contrary, radio, television, and movies, as part of our eyes and ears, help mold our underlying attitudes and thus our decisions at the polls, just as the daily newspaper does. Indeed, the fact that they have no obvious party ties or open intention of influencing voters may actually increase their effect. An Edward R. Murrow or a Jack Paar, speaking over the radio and television to millions, may tell a story about Washington doings that will influence the votes of many more people than the speech of a leading party politician over another major network. A movie depicting Soviet brutality in dramatic and grisly terms may affect attitudes toward American foreign policy more decisively than a statement by the Secretary of State.

MASS MEDIA AND LOCAL LEADERS

It seems clear, then, that the combined weight of mass media—the press, movies, radio, and television—in opinion-making is very large. Some social scientists believe that these agencies are coming to have more influence than the family itself in shaping attitudes. It is difficult to prove this contention, however, because the particular influence of the home or the press cannot easily be isolated for study. For example, if reading a Democratic newspaper for many years influences a father, and he influences his son, which is the dominant factor, home or newspaper?

We do have a little evidence, however, on the relative roles of newspapers and radio in a particular campaign. In a study of Erie County, Ohio, voters indicated that radio and newspapers had helped them equally in making their final choice of a presidential candidate. But when asked for the most important single source, radio was mentioned half again as frequently as the newspaper. The investigators concluded that "to the extent that the formal media exerted any influence at all on vote intention or actual vote, radio proved more effective than the newspaper." [10] The explanation may be that the radio gives the listener a greater sense of participation than the newspaper. Perhaps the importance of radio helps account for Franklin D. Roosevelt's success in electioneering, for he was master of the art of radio speaking. Or perhaps the situation is quite the reverse—perhaps the radio was especially significant because Roosevelt made such expert use of it, in which case it would not play such a role in an ordinary campaign. It was notable, for example, that Republicans in Erie County seemed more influenced by newspapers.

But whatever the role of press and radio and other media may be, we must not lose sight of the fact that it is above all *direct, face-to-face* contacts that influence people, whether in family, neighborhood, or group. Studies have shown that the more *personal* the means of communication, the more effective it is in changing opinions. For example, it seems clear that (other things being equal) face-to-face conversation has more effect than a radio speech, and a radio speech is more effective than a newspaper account of it.[11] Radio singer Kate Smith once sold almost $40 million of bonds in one day, undoubtedly because her regular listeners felt she was talking directly to each of them.

Does this mean that personal methods of communication have more effect on opinions than institutional methods, such as newspapers? Possibly, but the problem is not that simple. For the local opinion leaders, who influence their friends through face-to-face conversations, may have got their ideas from a newspaper or magazine and may pass those ideas on to other people virtually unchanged. If a friend drops in and sells me on the need for a sales tax, and if he in turn got the idea from a popular magazine, what is the source of the influence on me? The shaping of opinions is not a one-way or even a two-way affair. Opinions are the product of many interrelated forces, each acting on others. It seems safe to say, however, that the mass media of communication, while they may influence local opinion leaders, will never be a substitute for them.

"How to Win Friends and . . ."   **W**e live in the Propaganda Age. Propaganda is, of course, nothing new, but in the twentieth century it has truly come into its own. The reasons are not hard to find. The mass media described above have become enormous enterprises: newspapers with circulations in the millions, air waves spanning the continent, movies showing in almost every city and town in the nation. The techniques of communication

---

10 P. F. Lazarsfeld, *The People's Choice* (Duell, Sloan, and Pearce, 1944), p. 128. See also F. E. Lowe and T. C. McCormick, "A Study of the Influence of Formal and Informal Leaders in an Election Campaign," *Public Opinion Quarterly* (Winter 1956), pp. 651-662.

11 See Wilbur L. Schramm (ed.), *Communications in Modern Society* (Univ. of Illinois Press, 1948), esp. pp. 171-185; and Elihu Katz and Paul F. Lazarsfeld, *Personal Influence* (The Free Press, 1955), p. 176.

have been vastly improved in a few decades, and the art of propaganda itself has been refined in our century. Harold Lasswell has said, "A new skill group has come into existence in modern civilization . . . skill in propaganda has become one of the most effective roads to power in modern states." We need think only of Adolf Hitler to realize the truth of this statement.

WHAT IS PROPAGANDA?

Is propaganda bad? Not necessarily. Indeed, it is difficult to say just where propaganda leaves off and education starts. Effective education may include some propaganda (in favor, let's say, of basic democratic values, the virtues of which must in part be taken on faith). And if propaganda is defined as a "method used for influencing the conduct of others on behalf of predetermined ends," then almost every person who writes or talks with a purpose becomes a propagandist. Lasswell has described propaganda as a technique of social control—"the manipulation of collective attitudes by the use of significant symbols (words, pictures, and tunes) rather than violence, bribery, or boycott." Obviously propaganda in these terms can be used for good causes as well as evil ones.

Americans are almost constantly exposed to propaganda techniques, and advertisers exploit these techniques to the full. (It has been said that Adolf Hitler borrowed some of his propaganda methods from American publicity experts.) Advertisements are cunningly designed by "practical psychologists" to appeal to our basic attitudes, especially to our desire for *recognition* by others (above all, by members of our own group), for *prestige,* and for *security.* Constant repetition is the hallmark of effective propaganda. Malcolm M. Willey writes: "In straight advertising, for example, the morning newspaper will carry the [advertising] copy; it will appear again in the street car (or even in the flip device in the taxicab); at the office a letter or a telegram may supplement what already has been said; the menu and the matches of the restaurant will serve as another medium of transmission; the afternoon paper repeats what the morning issue has already said; billboards are employed to catch a wandering eye; the radio program has its sponsor; the motion picture has not been free of advertising influence; and more recently the neon sign takes the 'message' far into the night." [12] This bombardment of potential buyers from all directions seems to get results.

As with the advertiser, so with the politician. The latter, seeking votes instead of sales, makes use of every agency of communication—ranging from skywriting to automobile stickers—that will influence men's attitudes and actions. Despite the variety of channels employed, however, certain methods are characteristic of propaganda, especially political propaganda.

---

[12] M. M. Willey, "Communications Agencies and the Volume of Propaganda," *Annals* of the American Academy of Political and Social Sciences, 1935, p. 197.

SOME PROPAGANDA TECHNIQUES

Name-calling—giving an idea a bad label—is used to make us reject and condemn the idea without examining the evidence.

Glittering generality—associating an idea with a "virtue word"—is used to make us accept and approve the idea without examining the evidence.

Transfer carries the authority, sanction, and prestige of something respected and revered over to something else in order to make the latter acceptable.

Testimonial consists of having some respected or hated person say that a given idea or program or product or person is good or bad.

Plain folks is the method by which a speaker tries to convince his audience that he and his ideas are good because they are "of the people," the "plain folks."

Card-stacking involves selecting truths or falsehoods, logic or illogic, to give the best or the worst possible case for an idea, program, person, or product.

Band wagon—with this, the propagandist tries to convince us that all members of a group to which we belong accept his program and that we must *therefore* follow our crowd and "jump on the band wagon." [13]

A political talk has been analyzed in the above terms, with the names of the various devices italicized in parentheses:

> Ours (*Plain folks*) must be a moral (*Glittering generality*) platform from which there is preached (*Transfer*) a positive (*Glittering generality*) policy based upon the principles of religion (*Glittering generality, Transfer*) and of patriotism (*Glittering generality*). For God (*Transfer*) and country (*Transfer, Glittering generality*). For Christ (*Transfer*) and the flag (*Transfer, Glittering generality*)—that is our motto as we prepare for action, for Christian American (*Transfer, Glittering generality*) action. . . .

IS PROPAGANDA ALL-POWERFUL?

There are, of course, countless other propaganda devices, such as the use of music, color, and pageantry in staging political rallies, and the expert manipulation of "plus" or "minus" symbols in radio speeches. Some of these devices have been developed to Machiavellian proportions. For example, "card-stacking" looks rather harmless compared to Hitler's technique of the "big lie"—in *Mein Kampf* he said that the "primitive" masses will "more easily fall victims to a great lie than to a small one, since they themselves per-

---

13 Slightly paraphrased from A. M. Lee and E. B. Lee (eds.), *The Fine Art of Propaganda* (Harcourt, Brace, 1939), pp. 23-24. The speech analysis was also taken from this source. For a somewhat different treatment of propaganda techniques, see L. I. Pearlin and Morris Rosenberg, "Propaganda Techniques in Institutional Advertising," *Public Opinion Quarterly*, Vol. 16, 1952, pp. 5-26.

haps also lie sometimes in little things, but would certainly still be too much ashamed of too great lies."

Far more important than the techniques of propaganda is the nature of the propagandist and of the person being propagandized, the "propagandee." What is the intention of the propagandist? What is his social or occupational position? How effective is his organization in dispensing propaganda—does he have a soapbox or a nationwide chain of newspapers?[14] What about the propagandee? How much education has he had? How firmly fixed are his ideas? What class or group position does he occupy? How strong is his resistance or skepticism—is he hard to "sell"? Clearly, propaganda involves more than technique; it involves *personality*. And because of the infinite variety of personality no propaganda "gimmick," however slickly manipulated, will always succeed in persuading people.

Thus propaganda is not an invincible weapon. Moreover, after a time the people—in a democracy, at least—somehow seem to get a picture of things as they are, if only through ordinary, day-to-day experience. Against the propaganda of the *word* is the propaganda of the *deed*. Facts to some extent speak for themselves. And if they are backed up by propaganda, they become doubly potent in shaping men's attitudes and behavior. In the long run, then, well-publicized *truth* is the most telling propaganda.

But how can we get at the truth?

A Free Market Place for Ideas?

In Justice Holmes' classic sentence, "The best test of truth is the power of the thought to get itself accepted in the competition of the market." This is a doctrine that most Americans would heartily endorse. But do we have a free market place for ideas in the United States? Or do monopolistic practices exist in the market of opinion just as they do to some extent in the economic market place? Certainly we have a free market in the sense that the government does not control the main agencies of opinion. But the absence of governmental control does not in itself guarantee an open and competitive market.

TRENDS IN THE OPINION INDUSTRIES

Even in the case of our own justly famed free press there are at least three disturbing tendencies:

Concentration. We live in an era of "dying dailies." Newspaper circulation keeps rising, but the number of newspapers keeps decreasing. From 1920 to 1950 the number of dailies in our 25 largest cities dropped from 126 to 86,

---

[14] Doob, *Public Opinion and Propaganda*, pp. 287 ff; see also Ogle, *Public Opinion and Political Dynamics*, pp. 233 ff.

while the circulation of these dailies increased by almost 10 million. In the same period the number of cities with only one daily newspaper climbed from 724 to 1124. While our population doubled between 1910 and 1958, the number of dailies in the country dropped by a third. What has been the result? Many states have not a single city with competing daily papers. Many others are without Sunday newspaper competition. A dozen companies owning big newspapers control over a quarter of our total daily circulation. One company dominates more than 3000 weeklies.[15]

This concentration of ownership and control has led to a *standardizing* of news and editorial opinion. Newspapers get the bulk of their out-of-town news from great newsgathering organizations like the Associated Press and the United Press-International. The AP, for example, sells news to papers controlling over 95 per cent of the total circulation in the United States. The country newspaper—once considered the citadel of rugged, independent journalism—has often become merely the local distributor of opinion "canned" in New York or Chicago. One great newspaper syndicate, for example, supplies boilerplate—features, editorials, and columns—to thousands of local journals. To 3000 country newspapers it sells an eight-page newspaper ready to go to press, with a few pages left blank for local news and advertising. For fear of offending someone, the boilerplate plays down controversial issues and unorthodox views, resulting in a sterile uniformity in many country newspapers from Maine to California.

Commercialism. A newspaper is a business. To survive it must sell copies, for its income depends on sales and advertising. Many publishers feel, perhaps quite rightly, that they must give the public what it wants. If the readers like screaming headlines, comics, scandal, sex, crime, features, and fiction at the expense of full and balanced news stories and editorial discussion, a newspaper can hardly hold out against its customers. Such a policy, however, means that an editor may cater to the political prejudices of his readers. By giving them what they want, he may deny them the chance to break out of their political bias and apathy. And he may block off the expression of controversial views for fear of alienating influential sections of his public.

Conservatism. Newspaper publishers are businessmen. They are worried by the things that worry every businessman, such as labor demands, costs, sales, taxes, dividends, profits. As businessmen, they tend to take a conservative point of view. It is not surprising that their business attitudes are reflected in their editorial columns, and sometimes in the slanting of news. Nor is it surprising that liberal candidates and proposals so often meet stout resistance from the press. Such a situation leaves a pall of orthodoxy on editorial pages. Yet democracy demands the airing of *competing* views.

---

[15] Morris L. Ernst, *The First Freedom* (Macmillan, 1946), p. xii; and Herbert Brucker, "Is the Press Writing Its Obituary?" *The Saturday Review* (April 25, 1959), pp. 9 ff.

Occasionally, too, advertisers bring pressure to bear on publishers. The story of a strike in a local plant may be suppressed, or the news of the indictment of a large corporation for unfair practices may be buried in the back pages. The real problem, however, is not outright pressure or conspiracy but the *community of interest* that exists between the big businessman who is a publisher and the other big businessmen who advertise. An English poet put this point satirically:

> You cannot hope to bribe or twist,
> Thank God, the British journalist;
> But seeing what the man will do
> Unbribed, there's no occasion to.

"If modern journalism tends to speak the language of corporate business instead of that of the little fellow," says Herbert Brucker, well-known editor, "it does so not because it is corrupt and venal but because it is itself a big business, a powerful institution with its interest vested in conservative economics." [16]

Such criticism of the press is sometimes overdrawn, however. Certain newspapers, such as *The New York Times* and the *Christian Science Monitor,* are noted for their fair and full coverage of controversial events, and for their ability to confine their own opinions to the editorial page. Some editors print columns and features presenting different points of view; it is not unusual to see David Lawrence's conservative views next to Marquis Childs' liberal ones. And most editors and reporters have an honest respect for facts, however they may wish to interpret them.

PROPOSALS FOR REFORM

Nevertheless, the problem of monopolistic tendencies—or at least of imperfect competition—in the market place of ideas remains a serious one. Certain solutions have been put forward. One would be to call on editors and publishers to clean their own houses, to police their own industry. It is urged that the press draw up *codes* of fair conduct binding on all, that working newspapermen be given a greater voice in the management and editorial policy of the newspaper. The difficulty is that such codes would not be enforceable, and the worst offenders would be those least likely to conform to them.

Another proposal calls for the establishment of *competing newspapers* wherever possible. Unfortunately, starting a new journal becomes increasingly difficult as the years go by. Some time ago it was possible for William Allen White to establish a famous newspaper—the Emporia (Kansas) *Gazette*—with a few hundred dollars and a lot of determination. To set up a newspaper today in a middle-sized or large city takes hundreds of thousands, perhaps

---

[16] Herbert Brucker, *Freedom of Information* (Macmillan, 1949), p. 68.

millions, of dollars. Once established, the fledgling newspaper faces all the difficulties that confront any newspaper, only in intensified form.

Finally, *government intervention* has been urged as a means of promoting full competition. In 1947 a Commission on Freedom of the Press, headed by Chancellor Robert M. Hutchins of the University of Chicago, recommended that the federal government, if private agencies failed to do the job, should set up its own communications agencies—a government-owned newspaper, perhaps—to tell the people of its plans and policies. To encourage criticism of the press from within and without, the Commission proposed the creation of a "new and independent agency" to "appraise and report annually upon the performance of the press." Further, it urged that the antitrust laws be used to maintain competition among the larger newspapers. The Commission concluded:

> The urgent and perplexing issues which confront our country, the new dangers which encompass our free society, the new fatefulness attaching to every step in foreign policy and to what the press publishes about it, mean that the preservation of democracy and perhaps of civilization may now depend upon a free and responsible press.[17]

These recommendations raise a vital question: Can government take steps to make the press more competitive and more responsible without imperiling our basic freedoms? There is no easy answer. Yet our experience with another great agency of opinion—radio—may throw some light on the problem.

PROBLEMS OF RADIO AND TELEVISION

Since its early infancy, radio has been under some government regulation. During the early 1920's, hundreds of radio stations were established in the United States. In what was virtually a free-for-all, broadcasters sometimes used the same wave lengths at the same time, deafening the listener with a chaos of raucous and muffled sounds. By 1927, sharp protests from across the country had brought government action. Today, by law, a broadcaster must conduct his station in the public interest. He cannot operate without a license from the Federal Communications Commission, a federal regulatory agency (see Chapter 25). In granting licenses, and in renewing them periodically, the F.C.C. has the power to determine whether the public interest is being met.

In practice, the radio industry operates largely under a code set up by the broadcasters themselves, and under a set of model regulations issued by the F.C.C. in 1945. To prevent monopoly, the Commission discourages newspaper control of radio, and forbids one person from owning more than one station in the same area. A few years ago, the F.C.C. ordered two large networks of the National Broadcasting Company to separate. The F.C.C. also

---

[17] *A Free and Responsible Press* (Univ. of Chicago Press, 1947), pp. 105-106.

enforces a measure of political neutrality, or at least equality. Station owners may speak their own minds politically, but they must make time available on the air to persons or parties on opposite sides of a question, within reasonable limits.

Radio in America thus represents a halfway house between private control and state operation. What have been the results? Few people seem to believe that freedom of speech has been impaired in the world of radio. The F.C.C. is strictly forbidden from interfering with the content of radio programs. At the same time, there are complaints that the cooperation of the government and the radio industry has been sterile and unfruitful. Radio is criticized for its commercialism, its devotion to amusement and trivia, its failure to present controversial and competitive ideas. The government is criticized for being heavy-handed, negative, and restrictive. And yet radio has engineered some magnificent reporting in its on-the-spot coverage of political party conventions, the United Nations, and events abroad.

Great Britain has tried an entirely different approach to the problems of radio. There radio has been a government monopoly for over twenty years, administered by a semi-independent government agency, the British Broadcasting Corporation. Over three main channels, the B.B.C. offers a variety of programs, with stress on culture, education, and broad public questions. There are no commercials. (Recently, however, England has undertaken commercially sponsored television.) The B.B.C. is financed by an annual tax on radio sets. Very rarely is the B.B.C. accused of partisanship; more often listeners complain that its efforts to avoid taking sides have led to cautiousness and timidity. Canada enjoys a mixed system. It has a government enterprise, the Canadian Broadcasting Corporation, but there are a good many private stations operating in local areas, carrying programs broadcast from both Canada and the United States.

Television, the young giant of the opinion industry, has already made it clear that government cannot pursue a simple hands-off attitude toward it. For example, television potentially is a superb vehicle for education. Its roving cameras can spotlight meetings of the United Nations, forums, debates, round tables, good plays, music, and painting. In the classroom, television can effectively supplement (but not substitute for) the teacher, the blackboard, and the textbook. But television channels are limited, and they are greatly in demand for military, police, air, and sea communications, as well as for regular commercial purposes. Should certain channels be reserved for education? If so, who will sponsor educational programs? The government? This raises the problem of governmental interference. Advertisers? It is doubtful that they should be allowed to influence the content of education. Universities and foundations? They may lack the large sums needed. The federal government must solve this problem, for it is the Federal Communications Commission that allots the channels. Whatever it does, it cannot duck the issue.

Another problem of television is its screening of congressional investigations. A Senate committee investigating crime had a sensational impact on public opinion in 1951 when it allowed the hearings to be televised. A succession of shady characters—suspected gamblers, racketeers, gangsters—appeared on television screens throughout the nation. So fascinating were the proceedings that millions of viewers sat glued to their chairs, and taxi drivers and merchants complained of a drop in business. The proceedings raised a number of questions. On the one hand, here was a "window on government" that could bring the citizen into intimate contact with public affairs. On the other hand, television intensified a hundredfold the problem of fairness in dealing with witnesses summoned by investigating committees. If the hearings become a Roman holiday, if the witness wilts under the noise, heat, and light, if the proceedings are edited so that only one side of the case gets through to the television audience—then a man may become unjustly suspect in the eyes of millions of people. At the very least his right to privacy will be almost lost. The market place for ideas must be not only free but *fair.*

It seems, then, that the main fault of democratic governments has been excessive caution in the market place of ideas, rather than undue interference. But this fault is a reflection of great virtues. Dictators have shown that the free market becomes an absurdity when the government clamps down a rigid censorship and establishes its own monopoly over ideas. It is a ticklish task for democratic government to keep the channels of communication clear of obstruction without itself becoming the most perilous obstruction of all.

Taking the Pulse of the People

What I want," Abraham Lincoln once said, "is to get done what the people desire to have done, and the question for me is how to find that out exactly." This perplexing question faces every politician, in office or out. Another President, Woodrow Wilson, once complained to newspapermen that they had no business to say, as they often did, that all the people out their way thought so and so: "You do not know, and the worst of it is, since the responsibility is mine, I do not know, what they are thinking about. I have the most imperfect means of finding out, and yet I have got to act as if I knew. . . ."

WHAT DO THE PEOPLE WANT?

How can the politician find out what the people are thinking? The usual way, of course, is to look at the election results. If John Brown wins over James Smith, presumably the people want what John Brown stands for. Thus if Brown is an out-and-out prohibitionist, and Smith is a 100-per-cent wet, evidently the people support some kind of prohibition.

But we know that in practice things do not work out this way. Elections are rarely fought out on single issues like prohibition, and candidates rarely take clear-cut stands. Elections actually turn on many diverse issues, and candidates are often deliberately vague. It is impossible, moreover, to separate issues from candidates. Take the presidential election of 1956, for example. Was President Eisenhower elected because he stood for tax reduction at home? Or because of his farm and labor policies? Or because of his strong support of the new Republicanism? Or because businessmen generally supported him? Or because he had been a popular general during World War II? Or because people liked his platform manner and his wife Mamie? Or because of his opponents' campaign errors? The answer, of course, is that he won for some of these reasons, and for many others. Which brings us right back to the basic question—what do the people want?

This is where straw votes and public opinion polls come in. It is only natural that people should try to measure the popular mind with tools more exact than election results. In this country public opinion polls are over a century old, but their main development has taken place in the last two or three decades. Some of the techniques were worked out by market research analysts hired by businessmen to estimate potential sales for their products. The techniques were then adapted to measuring opinions on general issues. Today there are a number of polling organizations, the most famous of which are the American Institute of Public Opinion, which puts out the Gallup poll, the Elmo Roper agency, and the Survey Research Center at the University of Michigan. Many newspapers conduct local straw votes, and parties, private associations, and governments have been polling people for many years.

PROBLEMS OF POLLING

The most exact way to measure opinions would be to poll every adult—or at least every voter—in the country. But, since the cost would be prohibitive, the pollsters settle for a sample of the population. The accuracy of their final results turns largely on how *representative* their sample is. It may be drawn from a cross section of the people, carefully based on the distribution of the population according to locality, sex, age, education, occupation, social or economic level, and so on. This is called "quota sampling." One polling organization, in testing opinion that would be affected by income status (for example, views on the income tax), makes up a sample based on 2 wealthy persons, 14 members of the upper class, 52 from the middle class, and 32 from the poor. Another method, more widely used, is "random sampling." The sample is drawn by methods that give any person in the population an equal chance of being interviewed. Very small samples can still give amazingly accurate results. In one case, the percentage of the first 500 persons answering "no" to a question was 54.9, while the percentage of all 30,000 answering "no" was 55.5—a difference of less than 1 per cent. The Gallup poll uses a sample of from 1500 to 60,000, depending on the type of question.

Another difficulty in polling is in phrasing the question itself. As everyone

"Do you, or do you not, favor U.S. participation in some form of world government, under which each nation would forfeit a certain amount of its sovereignty?"

Courtesy *Collier's* and David Huffine

knows, if you ask the question in just the right way, you can get the answer you want. Ask a man if he favors labor unions and he may say "no." Ask him if he favors organized efforts by workers to improve their well-being, and chances are he will answer "yes." Or trouble may arise in the alternatives that a question presents. Clearly, asking a person "Do you favor the United States entering a world government, or do you prefer our traditional independence in determining our own affairs?" is to load the dice. To take an actual case, when people were asked late in June 1941, "So far as you, personally, are concerned, do you think the United States has gone too far in helping Britain, or not far enough?" the answers were:

Too far	15%	About right	46%
Not far enough	32%	No opinion	7%

But when the words "President Roosevelt" were substituted for the words "United States" in this question, the answers were:

Too far	20%	About right	57%
Not far enough	17%	No opinion	6%

Polling organizations go to great efforts to make their questions fair; some of them conduct trial runs with differently worded questions.

One way to avoid this difficulty is to ask the multiple-choice—or "cafeteria"—type of question. Here the respondent has his choice of several answers. For example, a Gallup poll asked "How far do you, yourself, think the federal government should go in requiring employers to hire people without regard to race, religion, color, or nationality?" The respondent could answer: *All the way; None of the way; Depends on type of work; Should be left to state governments;* or *Don't know.* A variation of this type—the "open-end question"—allows the respondent to supply his own answer. He may be asked simply, "How do you think we should deal with the problem of disloyalty in government?" The answers to this type of question are, of course, hard to tabulate accurately.

Interviewing itself is a delicate task. Tests show that the interviewer's appearance, clothes, language, and way of asking questions may influence the replies. Inaccurate findings may result from the bias of the interviewer, or from his failure to do his job fully and carefully. And the persons interviewed may be the source of error. Respondents suspicious of the interviewer's motives may give false or confused answers. Their memories may be poor—for example, how they voted in a past election. To cover up ignorance they may give neutral answers, or appear undecided. Or they may give the answers that they think the interviewer would like them to give.

Polling is subject to other limitations. Since any attempt to gather data through sampling must take account of a "sampling error," polls should never be considered exact. Then too, a sample survey of population dispersed over a wide geographical area is unlikely to represent satisfactorily any highly local characteristic of the population. "It is impossible to analyze adequately the complex fabric of social organization through the survey method alone, because the process of sampling tends to lift the individual respondent out of his social context." [18] Obviously the larger the sample and the more careful the polling, the better the results—but also the more costly the investment in money, manpower, and time.

Despite all these difficulties, polling is so useful a device for sounding out opinion that it is employed by a variety of organizations. During elections parties conduct polls to discover their strong points and weak points. Interest groups run polls to back up their claims that the people—or at least their own members—favor or oppose a certain bill. Advertisers and sales executives have an obvious use for polls.

FORECASTING ELECTIONS

What about the pre-election forecast? To the average American this is the most intriguing form of public opinion polling. Everyone likes to know in advance how an election will turn out, whether it's Uncle Charlie who is laying an election bet, or a national party chairman, or a stockbroker watching the market. During election races the pollsters submit regular "returns" on the position of the candidates. The reports are compiled from interviews conducted throughout the nation, usually on a state or regional basis. On the whole, the record of the leading forecasters has been good, as the table on page 284 shows.

But forecasts can—and do—go wrong. In 1936 a highly unscientific poll, conducted by the *Literary Digest* with ballots sent through the mail, underestimated Franklin D. Roosevelt's percentage by almost 20 per cent. Shortly after the election the magazine closed up shop. The most sensational slip came in 1948. During the Presidential battle between President Truman and Governor Dewey, the polls repeatedly indicated that Mr. Truman was running far

---

[18] A. A. Campbell and George Katona, "The Sample Survey: A Technique for Social Science Research," in Leon Festinger and Daniel Katz (eds.), *Research Methods in the Behavioral Sciences* (Dryden, 1953), pp. 15-55.

SOME RECENT PRESIDENTIAL POLLS

Year	Actual Dem. Vote	Roper Poll	Gallup Poll	Crossley Poll
1936	60.2	61.7	53.8	53.8
1940	54.7	55.2	55.0	. . .
1944	53.8	53.6	53.3	52.0
1948	49.4	37.1	44.5	44.8
1952	45.+	43.0	46.0	47.0
1956	42.0	40.0	40.5	. . .

behind. The President denounced these "sleeping polls," but the pollsters stood pat on their statistics. Early in September one of them actually announced that the race was over. Gallup gave the President 44.5 of the popular vote in his final forecast, and Roper's prediction was 37.1 per cent. Actually, Mr. Truman won 49 per cent of the popular vote, and the pollsters were subjected to general ridicule. In 1952 and 1956 they were more cautious.

Why do polls go wrong? Partly because of subjective factors that distort the results. And partly because of the methods used, such as a faulty choice of samples. The *Literary Digest* made the mistake of basing its survey mainly on persons listed in the telephone directory, who in 1936 turned out to be a poor cross section of American voters. But forecasters face some especially difficult problems. Actually they are not polling results—only elections do that—but *intentions*. Some of the respondents may change their plans at the last minute. Following the election of 1948 a committee of experts decided that probably a last-minute swing to Truman had taken place but had not been reflected in the polls.[19] Some voters may vote contrary to how they say they will vote, or they may simply fail to go to the polls. The forecasts must estimate *which* and *how many* of the people will vote, as well as *how* they will vote. In 1948 voting turned out to be lighter than expected, and an unusually large number of people cast ballots for state and local candidates but not for national ones. The "don't-knows"—the people who are undecided about their voting intentions—are another source of error.

Probably the pollsters learned lessons in 1948 that will make their forecasts more exact in the future. In any event, polls are here to stay, as indicated by the extensive use of them by candidates for the 1960 presidential nominations. But they will continue to be the subject of searching observation and criticism. Some objections to opinion polls have been largely overcome. For example, despite charges to the contrary, polls probably do not have a significant band-wagon effect on voting; the 1948 results would indicate quite the reverse, if anything. And the main pollsters cannot justly be accused of dishonesty or partisanship.

---

[19] *The Pre-Election Polls of 1948* (Social Science Research Council, 1949), pp. 251 ff.

But major questions remain. Polls do not differentiate among people; they give equal weight to a follower and to an opinion leader who may in the end influence other votes. Polls may give a false impression of the firmness and intensity of opinion. As we have seen, opinions may be fleeting and volatile. Sixty per cent of the respondents may answer "yes" to some question, but half of them may merely lean that way, and others may have no real opinion on the subject. It is far easier to measure the surface waves and eddies of public opinion than its depth and density.

Surely the polls at best are no substitute for elections. Faced with his ballot, the voter must translate his opinions into concrete decisions between personalities and parties. He must decide what is important, and what is un-important. Then, out of the welter of views of all the voters, a decision emerges for some candidate who will act in terms of some program, however vague. For democracy is more than the expression of views, more than a simple mir-ror of public opinion. It is also the *choosing* among issues—and the govern-mental action that must follow. Democracy is the thoughtful participation of people in the political process; as Lasswell says, it means *using* heads as well as *counting* them. Elections, with all their failings, at least establish the link between the many voices of the people and the decisions of their leaders.

Politics and Public Opinion

We can sum up our discussion of public opinion with a few thumbnail conclusions:

1. Public opinion has many characteristics. In some respects it tends to be compact and stable; in others fluid and varied. One must speak not merely of public opinion, but of many public opinions.

2. The public itself is many-sided in its make-up. Some people are fickle in their views; others are steady and unmoving. Actually there are millions of publics, divided in a thousand different ways.

3. Despite its diversity, public opinion is given a certain orderliness by the fact that most Americans are subjected to common influences—family, schools, press, radio, television, and so on.

4. Much public opinion is formed by deliberate manipulation of attitudes by people with all sorts of purposes, good and bad. The development of highly efficient means of communication and persuasion has enlarged the role of the propagandist, but his influence is by no means unlimited.

5. In the offering of ideas we do not have a wholly free market. In the press and other media we find tendencies toward concentration, commercial-ization, and conservatism. Most Americans probably want a free market, but there is no easy way to get it. The relation of government to the market is the most difficult problem of all.

6. We have fairly reliable methods for roughly measuring people's atti-tudes at a given time. But these methods cannot take the place of elections.

What is the relation of government to all this? Obviously government is not an innocent bystander in the constant play and interplay of political attitudes. It is closely related to the whole process. It has a stake in the way attitudes are formed, in the methods used to form them, such as television, and in the uses to which propaganda is put. A democratic government is especially interested in the degree of competition in the market place of ideas, and in the ways that polling organizations try to measure public opinion.

Above all, government is concerned with the make-up of public opinion itself. To stay in office, politicians must respond—or at least seem to respond—to changing opinions. They must have some sense of the scope of popular attitudes, their intensity, their stability or instability. Measuring public opinion in its many forms—often by a sort of sixth sense—is the essence of the politician's job. To be successful he must have the knack of peering behind propaganda fronts and gauging the real public opinion, of spotting the areas of ignorance, the areas of apathy, the areas of understanding, the areas of action.

But all politicians do not respond to public opinion in the same way. Government is made up of thousands of different men, with varying attitudes, ambitions, and loyalties. Obviously, a President responsible to the whole nation and a senator elected by a state will often react differently to public opinion. The senator will react differently from a member of the House of Representatives. And perhaps an administrative official will take still another view. Many factors lie behind the diverse attitudes of officials—their position in the government, the people by whom they are elected or appointed, the amount of security they enjoy, the date of the next election or appointment, the balance of forces in their home district or in the office of their superior, their own basic attitudes and expectations.

Nor does government merely *respond* to public opinion; it also *creates* it. Government is not merely the broker for outside pressures or putty in the hands of mighty groups. Our "strong" Presidents and even less dynamic ones like Coolidge and Eisenhower have known the uses of public opinion.[20] Congressional investigation committees have learned how to make headlines with their revelations.[21] The job of the political leader is to guide political attitudes and mediate among them as well as to follow them. Hence there is a reciprocal relationship. Where leadership leaves off and followership starts the political leader cannot say, nor is it important. The important thing is that this dual role enables the politician to provide the great need of modern democracies—responsible leadership. Knowing how to respond to public opinion and how to help shape it is much of the art of democratic leadership.

---

[20] See, for example, E. E. Cornwell, Jr., "Coolidge and Presidential Leadership," *Public Opinion Quarterly* (Summer 1957), pp. 265-278.

[21] For a shrewd report on "making news on the Hill," see Douglass Cater, "Government by Publicity," *The Reporter* (March 19, 1959), esp. pp. 19-23.

The Dynamic Role
of Interest Groups

The United States has been called a nation of joiners. Europeans sometimes make fun of us for setting up all sorts of organizations, from antiprofanity leagues to zoological clubs. We ourselves are often amused by the behavior of our groups—the noisy conventions of veterans' associations, the solemn rites of great fraternal organizations, the oratory of patriotic societies, the gossip of local sewing circles, the pomposity of reform leagues. Yet most of these groups are deadly serious in their aims, and they play an enormous role in politics. Moreover, joining is not an exclusively American trait. It is a common trait of human beings—and of many animals as well.

How many groups are there in America? There is no way of knowing accurately. Families are groups—the most basic and important groups of all—and there are at least forty million families in the United States. We have a quarter of a million local religious congregations, countless athletic teams, tens of thousands of trade unions, over two thousand trade associations. And all these are groups in the broadest senses of the term—that is, the members of each group share some common *outlook* or *attitude,* and *interact* with one another in some way.[1]

Nor can we measure the variety of groups in America, although we know that it is tremendous. One observer has made a list of odd organizations to give a hint of this variety: [2]

The Non-Smokers Protective League of America
Simplified Spelling Board
American Sunbathing Association

---

[1] D. B. Truman, *The Governmental Process* (Knopf, 1951), Chapter 2. The basic approach of this chapter is drawn largely from this volume and from the pioneer work, A. F. Bentley, *The Process of Government* (Univ. of Chicago Press, 1908).

[2] From E. E. Schattschneider, *Party Government* (Farrar & Rinehart, Inc., 1942), p. 26.

Blizzard Men of 1888 (to commemorate a famous storm)
American Hackney Horse Association
Soaring Society of America
Toastmasters International

One person may belong to a great variety of groups and organizations. A typical college student is a member of the college community as a whole. But he may also belong to the sophomore class, the Tau Delta Tau fraternity, the basketball squad, the second floor of his dormitory, the Radio Club, the discipline committee, and classes in English, physics, French, and government. He belongs to other groups at home—his family, neighborhood, religious congregation, and so on. This student is a member of all these groups but he is not *equally* a member of them. His loyalty to his family, his class, or his fraternity may greatly outweigh his loyalty to all the other groups.

His father may be a member of an even greater array of groups—not only his family, congregation, and neighborhood, but perhaps, also, the Rotary Club, a philatelic society, the Masons, a downtown law firm, the American Automobile Association, a taxpayers' association, the Republican party, a bowling league, the American Bar Association, the state bar association. Do the individual's allegiances to a wide variety of groups of this sort ever come into conflict with one another? Indeed yes. The AAA may demand better roads, while the taxpayers' association wants less governmental spending. The neighborhood this person lives in may be largely made up of Democrats, whereas he is a Republican. Even without such conflicts, belonging to a variety of groups puts a great strain on his time and his pocketbook.

The fact that groups are so numerous and varied raises a number of questions that go to the very heart of democratic politics in America: Why are some groups strong and organized, others weak and diffused? What happens when competing groups overlap in membership, as in the cases just mentioned? How are groups organized, led, and governed? How do they gain influence? What is their relation to the party system, to elections, to government as a whole?

Politics is concerned with the workings of all groups, but we can simplify our effort to answer these questions by limiting ourselves to a particular type, the *interest group*. *This is any group whose members, as a result of sharing certain attitudes, make claims on other groups in order to realize aims arising from these attitudes.* Interest groups are of many types. Some are formal associations or organizations. Others have no formal organization at all—a young people's interest group, for example. Various interest groups may even exist *within* a given interest group. Thus inside the American Bar Association there may be several interest groups in conflict over a particular issue. An interest group may be either broader or narrower than a particular organization. The American Federation of Labor and Congress of Industrial Organizations, for example, is opposed to a labor reform measure. But not all

members of the AFL-CIO oppose the labor reform bill, and some people who are *not* members do oppose it. The interest group working to amend or abolish this measure, then, is composed of most members of the AFL-CIO, but not all, along with some people outside the formal labor organization.

Politics is largely a conflict among competing groups with conflicting ideas of what is in the "general interest." In political arguments we inevitably talk about special interests versus the general welfare. But in political analysis it is better to talk about *this* group's idea of the general welfare as compared with *that* group's idea. As political partisans we are all committed to particular ideas and values, but as social scientists we cannot pretend to set up a clearly defined national interest. For this is really the question at issue—"What *is* the general interest?" In a democracy it is the ideas of the many rather than the ideas of the few that prevail in defining the general welfare.

Unions for All— Occupational Groups for All

It is only natural that men working together should combine in some sort of association. They tend to have common attitudes and interests, and directly or indirectly they deal with one another during their working day and after. This is true not only of factory workers, but also of businessmen, farmers, doctors, lawyers, and many others. In a sense we all belong to unions, whether we are presidents of insurance companies, apple-growers, baseball umpires, professors, plumbers, or what not. Such unions come in all shapes and sizes, with all sorts of programs, memberships, and interests.

Men interact and unite on a nationwide and statewide basis as well as in local groups. They can do so easily and effectively because of modern methods of communication and transportation. Milk producers in Vermont and Wisconsin, druggists in Boston and Seattle, and garment workers in New York and Chicago can talk with one another in a matter of minutes, or meet in a matter of hours. In fact, members of each group *must* work together if they are to promote their common interests. They can find strength only in unity, and they can meet common, nationwide problems only by organizing on a nationwide basis. The typical large association comprises a mosaic of local and state bodies, heading up in the national organization. Usually it is the product of decades of slow and painful growth. The labor movement illustrates the rise of many separate groups struggling to national status and influence after a period of trial-and-error organization.

WORKERS

The earliest trade union locals in the United States were founded during Washington's first administration. For several decades "mechanics" and other workers organized local groups in the larger cities, but often these failed in the face of hard times, the hostility of employers, or the indifference of the workers themselves. Yet the urge for closer union remained powerful. As the economy became nationally integrated, the local unions in different states began to join hands with one another. Slowly taking root, the unions began to participate actively in politics. The Working Men's party, the first labor party, was born shortly before Andrew Jackson took office. An ambitious attempt to establish one big union of all types of workers came shortly after the Civil War

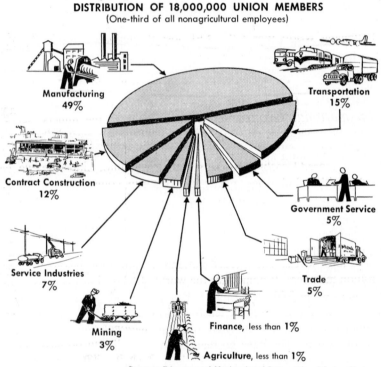

DISTRIBUTION OF 18,000,000 UNION MEMBERS
(One-third of all nonagricultural employees)

Manufacturing
49%

Transportation
15%

Contract Construction
12%

Government Service
5%

Service Industries
7%

Trade
5%

Mining
3%

Finance, less than 1%

Agriculture, less than 1%

Source: *Directory of National and International Labor Unions in U.S. 1957.* Department of Labor.

with the founding of the Knights of Labor, which included in its membership factory workers, farmers, and others—in fact, everyone except gamblers, stockbrokers, lawyers, and bankers! The Knights adopted a progressive platform, lobbied in state capitals, and joined forces in turn with Greenbackers, Populists, and Bryan Democrats. At one point, they claimed 700,000 members. But the experiment failed. Lacking unity, the Knights lost out both in political and economic battles, and had virtually disappeared by the end of the century.

The *American Federation of Labor* was formed in 1886 by skilled workers—carpenters, machinists, and the like—who felt that their particular needs

were overshadowed by the vastness of the Knights of Labor. Organized in tight craft unions, these workers surrendered only limited power to the national AFL, which continued as a true confederation of strong and independent-minded national unions. Headed by the astute Samuel Gompers, an ex-cigar-maker, the AFL stressed the economic weapon of the strike rather than all-out political battles. When compelled to enter politics as a result of hostile governmental action, its method was to reward labor's friends and punish its enemies. Thus it followed a balance-of-power policy, steering shy of any firm party connection. As a result, the Federation was often assailed by socialists and others who felt that labor should take a more aggressive political stand.

Following World War I the AFL lost strength as a result of antiunion drives, unemployment, and its own failure to organize the millions of unskilled workers in the huge mass-production industries of the nation. Under the impact of the New Deal its membership soared, but disunity increased too. Failing to induce the AFL craft leaders to organize the mass-production industries, a group of AFL leaders, led by John L. Lewis of the miners, set up the Committee for Industrial Organization. The AFL soon ejected them as "dual unionists," and the CIO then continued as the *Congress of Industrial Organizations,* composed largely of workers in the steel, auto, rubber, textile, electrical, and maritime industries. Faced with vigorous competition for members, the AFL made stronger organizing attempts, and for a short period won back the miners' union after Lewis deserted the CIO.

In 1955, after long negotiations, the AFL and CIO merged at the top levels. Since that time, their member unions have combined at the national, state, and local levels. The merged national organization has today about fifteen million members. It dominates the world of labor, but there are important groups outside the fold. The miners, teamsters, and one or two other large unions are—at the moment at least—independent. There are thousands of local unions that are not affiliated with any national union. And there are millions of workers who have no regular union at all, but do have some kind of employees' organization. The objectives of all the different organizations, however, are much the same—to improve wages and working conditions, to extend social security, and to stop hostile governmental action.

FARMERS

Farmers, too, have their "unions." Despite their individualism and their physical separation from one another, they have long seen the need for combining to protect their interests. An early farm group—the South Carolina Agricultural Society—was founded even before our Constitution was written. Since then, thousands of local and state associations have sprung up. The oldest nationwide farm group today is the *National Grange* (Patrons of Husbandry). Founded in 1867 by a group of federal employees, the Grange started out as a secret society to promote social and intellectual activities, but it soon become embroiled in the political movements that swept rural areas in the 1870's. Rebelling against low farm prices, railroad monopolies, grasping middlemen, and high taxes, the Grangers turned to political action, such as lobbying. After helping to gain certain reforms, such as railroad regulation and various direct aids to farmers, the Grange declined in influence and membership. Once a fighting organization with 1½ million members, the Grange today has about half that number and is the most conservative farm group in the nation. Strongest in the northeastern states, it works for price-support policies and other governmental protection for its farm members.

The largest farm group today is the *American Farm Bureau Federation,* which claims over a million members, most of them in the corn belt. It is set up on the usual local, state, and national bases, but from its start early in this century it has been organized around the government agents who helped the farmers in rural counties. As experts teaching improved farm methods, the county agents were in close touch with farmers, and they served as the virtual organizers of the local Farm Bureaus.[3] The Federation today is almost a semigovernmental agency, but it retains full freedom to fight for such goals as price supports, conservation measures, and expansion of farm credit facilities.

Herblock in *The Washington Post and Times Herald*

"Nah, that's not a candidate—that's a farmer."

Another important, but far smaller, organization is the *Farmers Union,* founded in 1902, which claims to speak for the family-sized farm. The Farmers Union works for legislation that will protect the small farmer, such as government aid to family-sized farms, the gradual breakup of large farms, and minimum wage laws for farm labor—as well as the usual aims of price supports, rural electrification, easier loan policies, and the like. Largely based on cooperatives of various types, the Farmers Union is centered in the Missouri

---

[3] Wesley McCune, *The Farm Bloc* (Doubleday, Doran, Inc., 1943), p. 165. See also C. M. Hardin, *The Politics of Agriculture* (The Free Press, 1952).

River Valley. It has taken a special interest in the problems of dust-bowl farmers.

A great number of other farm organizations are based on the interests of farmers who produce specific commodities: the National Beet Growers Association, the American Soybean Association, the American Wool Growers Association, and many others. These groups are relatively small, but they wield significant power when they want. After journeying through the states that maintain the sugar bloc in Congress, John Gunther wrote: "Only 3 per cent of American farmers grow sugar beet and cane; the entire processing industry employs no more than twenty-five thousand people. But sugar is spread through many states—beets grow in seventeen, cane in two—which gives it thirty-eight senators out of ninety-six, and they can certainly make a noise." [4]

Most farm organizations profess to be nonpolitical; actually, all of them are in politics. Farmers have exerted influence on government not only through their associations; they have entered politics directly by organizing their own parties. The Greenback party in the 1870's and 1880's fought for currency inflation to ease the distress of farm debtors; at its peak it polled nearly one million votes and sent fifteen congressmen to Washington. The Populist party did even better in the nineties, but the Democratic party under Bryan stole most of its thunder and its support. Farm votes made up much of the strength of Senator Robert La Follette's Progressive movement in 1924. Farm parties have controlled a number of state governments for long intervals.

BUSINESSMEN

Businessmen's "unions" are the most varied and numerous of all. Over 2000 trade associations and other business groups operate on a national or interstate basis, and there are at least 3000 local business groups. The nature of the hundreds of trade associations is almost as varied as the different products and services that are sold. Automobile manufacturers and pin manufacturers both have their national associations; so do canners, cotton manufacturers, retail Kosher butchers, road builders, tobacco merchants. Manufacturers of amusement tickets, clothing tickets, and transit tickets have three separate organizations. The list is almost endless. Businessmen group themselves by size and general function as well as by trade. The National Federation of Small Business, for example, is spokesman for the little businessman. The National Retail Dry Goods Association speaks for a variety of retailers.

Two general, nation-wide organizations of businessmen are especially important. One is the *Chamber of Commerce of the United States,* which was organized in 1912. The Chamber is a federation of federations—it is composed of about 400 trade associations and over 1000 local chambers of commerce. Occupying an impressive office building a block from the White

---

[4] John Gunther, *Inside U.S.A.* (Harper, 1947), p. 221.

House, it calls itself "the Washington office of over 750,000 business people in America." Its members have so many different interests and attitudes that the Chamber must stay aloof from many of the squabbles that divide business internally. It tries to represent business as a whole by opposing antibusiness governmental measures or the demands of other groups, such as labor. A typical set of Chamber of Commerce resolutions might call for lower taxes, a curb on labor excesses, governmental economy, and less centralization of government. The Chamber publicizes its views widely. "As a pipe line for steady, relentless, and timely opinion dissemination," one investigator says, "the Chamber of Commerce is probably unequalled." [5]

Loosely allied with the Chamber on almost all issues is the *National Association of Manufacturers,* a unified organization of about 16,000 manufacturing firms and corporations. Organized in the wake of the depression of 1893, the NAM today speaks for the more conservative elements of American business. Reflecting the attitudes of employers of large numbers of workers, it is more outspoken than the Chamber of Commerce in supporting restrictive labor legislation and opposing certain social legislation. The NAM sponsors an annual convention of industrialists—the Congress of Business—and is run by a large part-time board of directors and by a full-time secretariat. The Association uses a variety of outlets for its "public information," including motion pictures, cartoons, editorials, advertising, and radio speeches.

Traditionally businessmen have shied away from open political activity. But in recent years, partly because of labor's energetic political activity, several big corporations have been experimenting with ways to speak out more effectively on political issues affecting their interests and encouraging their executives and clerical people to become more active in politics. American Can Company, for example, has been mapping a program to educate its employees in practical politics and to urge them to be active in the party of their choice; the Ford Motor Company is intensifying its efforts to educate its managers on political issues, especially major issues before Congress; and General Electric has set up a Government Relations Service to help the company to get a working knowledge of public affairs.

PROFESSIONAL MEN

Alongside the giant groups of farmers, workers, and businessmen, organizations of professional people look small, but still they are important. And they are equally varied in type. About 400 professional organizations with national membership exist in the country today, ranging from accountants to veterinarians, and including architects, beauticians, midwives, optometrists, and undertakers. Large professions are divided into many subgroups; thus teachers are organized in the National Education Association, the American

---

[5] D. C. Blaisdell, "Economic Power and Political Pressures," *T.N.E.C. Monograph 26* (1941), p. 25.

Association of University Professors, and particular subject groups, like the Modern Language Association. Many professions are closely tied in with government, especially on the state level. Lawyers, for example, are licensed by the states, which have set up certain standards of admission to the state bar, often as a result of pressure from lawyers themselves.

Some professions enjoy special influence because of the prestige of their members. Doctors—the "men in white"—are a case in point. Their chief organization, the American Medical Association, has played a notable role in opposing governmental intervention in the field of medicine. It has lobbied before Congress, put out literature, urged its members to talk to their patients, and assessed each of its 140,000 members $25 to build up a war chest for its fight against compulsory health insurance. The doctors are engaged in the political battle—yet somehow they seem to be above politics, perhaps because of their prestige in their communities—and this probably increases their influence. The professional societies do not claim the mass membership of an AFL-CIO or a Farm Bureau Federation, but their prestige and expertness help make up for their lack of numbers.

The Crisscross of Interests

We have been talking about the interaction of individuals within some kind of common occupation. It would be good if we could stop here in our exploration of groups, for these occupational interests are complex enough in themselves. But we have seen only part of the picture. Man does not live by bread alone; he has other interests and attitudes beyond the essentially economic ones, and they can inspire powerful organizations. One of the strongest political forces in American history—the Anti-Saloon League—was aroused not by direct economic motives but simply by a spirit of reform and religion.

Once we look on men as holding nonoccupational as well as occupational interests, the group picture becomes even more complicated and untidy. We have been discussing groups that are somewhat clear-cut and separate from one another; it is a rare person who is at once a farmer, a trade-union member, and a businessman. But most people are members both of occupational and nonoccupational groupings—the businessman who is also a Methodist, for example. Moreover, a person may easily belong to several different nonoccupational groupings, as does a Catholic who is also a Legionnaire, a trade unionist, and a member of the League to Abolish Capital Punishment. Thus we end up with a most elaborate crisscross of interests—a great scrambled collection of attitudes and loyalties working with or across one another in a thousand different ways.

VETERANS

Which is the most important of the nonoccupational interest groups? The answer to this question varies according to the time and the situation. In certain medieval societies the church groups were most important. In a South American country today the military organizations might be dominant. In the jumble of interest groups in the United States no single one is supreme. Since we live, however, in the wake of two world wars in which our country was heavily committed, the veterans are numerous and they are well organized. "In the next generation," said President Truman in the closing days of World War II, "the veterans of this war are going to run this country." [6]

The largest veterans' organization today is the American Legion, claiming over two million members. Founded in Paris at the end of World War I, the Legion gradually became entrenched in thousands of local communities. Thus it was able after World War II to attract many of the recent veterans, despite the efforts of several new outfits, including the American Veterans of World War II (Amvets) and the American Veterans' Committee. The AVC attracted a good deal of attention when it based its program on the principle, "Citizens First, Veterans Second," and adopted a platform intended to benefit lower-income groups generally and not veterans alone. Its failure to attract a large membership suggested that most veterans wanted their own organizations to act essentially for their own interests. The second-largest organization today is the Veterans of Foreign Wars, claiming over a million members. Like most interests the veterans are subdivided into specialized groups—for example, the Disabled American Veterans and organizations of veterans by religion or nationality.

Veterans have many reasons to organize. They share memories of common experiences in wartime, and the local post is a handy place for the boys to get together. Having donned uniform for their country, many veterans feel a right and duty to speak out on governmental matters, especially on matters of patriotism and "Americanism." Above all, they have an economic interest in joining together. Veterans have demanded—and obtained—bonuses, pensions, free education, cheap loans and insurance, and a variety of other favors, even including free hunting licenses, exemptions on certain taxes, and honor guards for veterans' funerals. These favors are not new. "They saved the country, and now they want it," said an exasperated public official about the Grand Army of the Republic, the big post-Civil War veterans' organization. Veterans' lobbies are among the most influential in Washington today.

NATIONAL, RACIAL, AND RELIGIOUS GROUPS

Nationality groups are another important factor in American politics. Today, the American "melting pot" includes over 10 million foreign-born persons and over 23 million native whites of mixed or foreign parentage. Over 150 nationwide organizations of Americans of German, Irish, Italian, Slovak, Polish, Scandinavian, and many other national origins represent several mil-

---

[6] Harry S. Truman, speech in Portland, Oregon, June 25, 1945.

lion members. These groups have put their stamp on American politics. The Irish dominate the politics of many cities, such as Boston; Germans and Scandinavians are especially influential in the north-central states; French Canadians are a cohesive group in many New England areas; New Mexico's state legislators debate in Spanish as well as English. Parties carefully balance their tickets to appeal to all national elements. Party tickets in New York, with their representatives of different nationalities, look like a list of United Nations delegates.[7] Nationality groups take positions on general political issues, but they are concerned especially with such matters as easier naturalization laws and increased immigration quotas.

These nationality groups may gradually lose political leverage as their members become increasingly absorbed into the mainstreams of American life. Our many *racial* groups may have the same experience—but the largest racial group of all may be the last to lose its separate identity. This group consists of the sixteen million American Negroes. Decades of discrimination and segregation—political, economic, and social—forced Negroes to set up an almost separate life of their own on the less agreeable side of the color line. Their most important group is the National Association for the Advancement of Colored People, established in 1910 to fight lynching and peonage, and to press for the right to vote.

Today, with 500 branches, the NAACP works for a variety of economic and social objectives. Its special concern now is to implement the Supreme Court's decision on public school segregation (see pages 169-171). It cooperates with the Urban League, a federation of local groups, which is mainly interested in broadening economic opportunities. In the last twenty years, Negroes have become increasingly active in politics. For decades they tended to back the Republican party, but the depression of the 1930's and the support of New Dealers and Fair Dealers for civil rights brought large numbers of Negroes over to the Democratic party. The anticivil-rights stand of southern Democrats, however, will help maintain the traditional nonpartisanship of Negro organizations. In any event Negroes, like whites, are not agreed on aims or methods. Indeed, their color is perhaps less of a unifying force than a common religious creed is to Irish Americans.

Religion plays a part in American politics. Over half the people in the United States belong to some religious organization; there are more than 59,000,000 Protestants, 36,000,000 Roman Catholics, 5,000,000 Jews. Of these three groups, Protestants are the least united, for they are subdivided into large denominations, such as the Methodists and Baptists, and these denominations are in turn broken up into numerous bodies. The National Council of Churches speaks for some of these groups in its pronouncements on a wide variety of issues. As a result of its unity and discipline, the Roman Catholic Church is probably at least as influential in politics as the Protestants.

---

[7] See Warren Moscow, *Politics in the Empire State* (Knopf, 1948), Chapter 3.

Some of its political activities are conducted by such Catholic groups as the Knights of Columbus (a fraternal order a half-million strong), the Association of Catholic Trade Unionists, and the Catholic War Veterans. The Jews, too, are active politically,[8] as they showed by the influence they mustered in their fight for a national home in Palestine.

Religious bodies are interested in almost every type of legislative matter —especially in education, foreign affairs (for example, our relations with certain other nations, like Spain), social welfare legislation, and various social problems like gambling, child labor, divorce, birth control, euthanasia, vice. The special responsibility of the church in matters of morals gives it considerable influence in a broad range of state and local legislation.

We have now seen something of the shape and size and variety of the larger interest groups in the United States. It would of course be possible to list many other types of association. There are the women's groups, like the League of Women Voters. There are the countless reform groups, such as the Woman's Christian Temperance Union, the Townsend movement, and the National Municipal League. There are groups concerned with particular problems, such as the Foreign Policy Association. A complete list would shade off into thousands of struggling groups that live for a few years, sometimes realize their objectives, and then die. It would include not only existing groups but *potential* groups that would spring into being if certain events took place, such as a new depression.

But our list is long enough. It is time to look more closely at the inner workings of organized groups, to see what makes them behave as they do.

Interest Groups in Ferment

Our picture of interest groups shows a cluster of organizations large and small, old and new, rising and falling, visible and invisible, of endless number and variety. The most important thing about this picture is that it is a *moving* one. There is nothing static about group organization in America. Sometimes the changes within groups and between groups are almost imperceptible; sometimes they are sensational enough to become front-page news. Thus John L. Lewis made headlines when he set up the CIO, when he deserted it, when he joined the AFL, when he left it. On the other hand, the slow gradual effect of religious beliefs on church relationships may be less conspicuous but equally significant over a period of time.

Groups are plastic. In their internal and external relationships they are responsive to the deep economic and social currents that flow through America and the world about it. Successive changes in industrial organization, for

---

8 See Lawrence H. Fuchs, "American Jews and the Presidential Vote," *The American Political Science Review* (June 1955), pp. 385-401.

example, first allowed the AFL to become dominant in labor organization, and then forced it to yield ground to a rival union. Improved agricultural techniques have created new patterns of life on the farm, new relationships among farm groups. The rise of big government has affected the functions of group leaders. The migration of thousands of Negroes from the South to northern cities has brought changes in their economic and social opportunities and in their role in politics.

The relation of groups to other forces is two-way. Thus big government affects interest groups; but the reverse is true, too—interest groups help create and shape big government. Indeed, the process is more than a two-way one; it is multidirectional and many-sided. What we have is a gigantic web of interactions, stretched among interests, associations, governments, beliefs, techniques, and many other elements. A movement anywhere in this web will set the whole elastic network in motion. It is equally certain, however, that in this interrelationship some groups have much more effect than others, just as different politicians have varying influence in government.

THE BASIS OF GROUP POWER

What determines the political effectiveness of an interest group? The main internal elements are two: *size* and *unity*. Obviously numbers are important. An organization with three million members will overshadow one with three thousand. But numbers do not amount to much if the group is so divided internally that the members fail to work together. Just as a small but disciplined army can rout a far larger but disorderly one, so can a compact group make its way against rival organizations, and even against the electorate as a whole.

The question then becomes: What makes a group cohesive? What causes its members to vote the same way? At least three elements are involved here.

By far the most important is the *attitude and make-up of the membership*. If the members of an organization are undivided in their loyalty to it, that group will have an enormous advantage in the political arena. When the leaders can depend absolutely on the full backing of their followers, an organization is able to put its full force into pursuing its aims. Communist groups are said to be made up of people who devote their time and energy single-mindedly to their cause; if this is true, it explains why the communists seem to exercise influence out of proportion to their numbers. But most Americans are not made that way. They cannot possibly give their lives over to one group—not even to their families. Most Americans, in fact, are members of many groups, as we have discovered. Their loyalties are divided. They cannot be depended on to go all-out for any cause.

It is this fact of overlapping membership that largely determines the cohesiveness of a group. Organization leaders run up against the problem time after time. A union official, for example, asks a dozen of his members to come to a meeting the next night. Several say they will show up. But one says that he has to be with his bowling club that night. Two others have to stay home with their families. Another has a church supper. Even those who finally do show up at the union meeting are not "100 per cent supporters." They are asked, perhaps, to vote for a particular candidate in a coming election. Some of them will. But one of them may decide to vote for the other candidate because they are next-door neighbors. Or because they are both Italo-Americans. Or both Republicans. Or both Legionnaires. Or perhaps he will not know what to do, and will not vote at all.

A second factor in the cohesion of a group is its *organizational structure*. Some groups have no formal organization. Others consist of local organizations that have joined together in some sort of loose state or national federation. In such cases the local organizations retain a measure of separate power and independence, just as the states did when they entered the Union. Thus there is a form of federalism in some organizations (like the AFL-CIO and AMA) that may hinder unity.

A sort of separation of powers may be found as well. The national assembly of an organization establishes—or at least ratifies—policy. An executive committee meets more frequently. A president or director is elected to head up and speak for the group. And permanent paid officials form the organization's bureaucracy. Power may be further divided between the organization's main headquarters and its Washington office. An organization of this sort tends to be far less cohesive than a centralized, disciplined group such as the Army or some trade unions.

Closely related to this factor is a third one—the nature of the *leadership* of the group. In a group that embraces many attitudes and interests, the leaders may either weld the various elements together, or else sharpen their disunity. The leader of a national business association, for example, must tread cautiously between big business and little business, between exporters and importers, between chain stores and corner grocery stores, between the makers and sellers of competing products. Yet he must not be a cipher—a mere punching bag for different interests—for above all he must *lead*. He must show how to achieve whatever goals can be agreed on. Thus the group leader is in the same position as a President or a congressman, though his constituency is different. He must act diplomatically in his efforts to patch up differences among the subgroups. He must know when to lead his followers, when to follow them. He is at the head of the parade—but if he gets *too far* ahead the paraders may follow someone else down a side street.

Finally, the power of a group is affected by the nature of the *political* and *governmental system* in which it operates. A system based on centralized governmental power and disciplined parties, like Britain's (see Chapters 3 and 13), may be better able than the American system to withstand pressures from interest groups. Our government, with its decentralized parties, is more responsive to the appeals of well-organized minorities, as later chapters will suggest.

leadership — is money, do
is there to know to psychological fitness of members

THE GROUP LEADER

Leaders of organizations use a variety of methods to hold their followers together. Directing the affairs of every group are a few insiders or old-timers who control the administrative machinery, such as admission to membership, financial affairs, correspondence, and committees. This active minority actually runs the organization. It holds the strings that make the members dance in harmony. In exercising discipline and control, the leaders can withhold certain services (such as lobbying assistance) from rebellious members. Sometimes they can expel members who do not follow the party line; this sanction is important if members lose their jobs when they lose their membership, as with the closed union shop. The leaders may also control the organization's propaganda. The active minority usually puts out the newspaper or magazine that goes to the members. It arranges the meetings and works up the agenda.

The leaders of a group tend to stay in control year after year. Certain union officials such as John L. Lewis of the miners are cases in point, but actually this tendency applies to business, farm, and other organizations as well as to labor. Bossism or oligarchy exists in most groups, including political parties.[9] An organization that is secure in its leadership can confront its enemies and pursue its program with unity and single-mindedness. On the other hand, unchanging leadership may contribute to decay, demoralization, disunity. In order to stay in power it may resort to illegal means, or it may be enthusiastically re-elected or reappointed each year by a rank and file grateful for successes achieved.

Does all this mean that groups are run by little dictatorships? Not necessarily. *If* the members show a blind loyalty to the group, *if* the organization is centralized and compact, *if* the leaders want to be autocratic and have the means to be so—then a kind of dictatorship may result. But, as we have seen, other forces within the groups, such as overlapping membership and interests, and various cross pressures, tend to work against absolutism. These internal forces are crucial, for they help maintain a balance of power both *within* groups and *between* groups.

This balance of power is also upheld by external forces that operate in the whole community. One of these is democracy itself. Americans generally want to have a share in running their government—so naturally they want to have a say in the way their organizations are managed. Actually most groups are little democracies (although they may have their share of undemocratic practices). There are periodic elections; meetings are run in a parliamentary fashion; a member has the right to stand up in a meeting and say what he wants. If an organization violates democratic procedures year after year, it

---

[9] See Robert Michels, *Political Parties: A Sociological Study of the Oligarchical Tendencies of Modern Democracy* (Jarrold, 1915). For a discerning treatment of oligarchic rule within groups, see Grant McConnell, "The Spirit of Private Government," *The American Political Science Review* (September 1958), pp. 754-770.

comes into bad odor. Some of its own members may turn against it. Other organizations become hostile, and may refuse to play ball with it.

Probably the most powerful factor preventing one group from upsetting the balance of power is the existence of other groups. Organization invites counterorganization. The increased influence of one group forces competing groups to strengthen themselves. Decades ago, for example, nationwide corporations helped create nationwide labor unions, which in turn stimulated the organization of national business federations. If tomorrow people over 60 were to form a powerful organization to put over a superbonus plan, people under 60 would organize against it through their existing organizations or through new ones. A sort of organizational arms race takes place, and every member feels that the devil may take the hindmost.

GROUPS IN THE POLITICAL STRUGGLE

Seen in these terms, the power of organized groups does not turn only on internal factors, such as the size and unity and leadership of groups. It also turns on external factors—the nature of the environment, the attitudes of people everywhere, the strength of other groups. Adding up all these factors, what are the main advantages and disadvantages of the major groups in the American political struggle?

Numerically, businessmen are in a minority in the United States, yet they wield great power. This power has several foundations. First, the business community is fairly cohesive. "It is almost as if the business leadership were in a continuous political caucus," says one astute political observer. "Conventions, committee sessions, board meetings, and corporate staff conferences, with their interlocking and overlapping memberships, build a system of face-to-face relations knitting the business community together. The airplane and the corporation expense account bring literally thousands of businessmen into conference every day, and they in turn have their relations back home with the less mobile elements of the business community." [10]

Second, business beliefs are shared by many Americans who are not businessmen. Business values have been stamped on American culture.[11] Many people identify themselves with business. Even after the depression and the New Deal, business leaders enjoyed higher public prestige than labor leaders, according to polls. Given this situation, it becomes easier for people to accept such ideas as "What is good for business is good for you."

Third, businessmen have money, and money means influence. It can be used to pay for propaganda, to support political parties, to finance lobbies, to influence public officials directly or indirectly. Fourth, business has important

---

[10] V. O. Key, Jr., *Politics, Parties, and Pressure Groups,* 4th ed. (Crowell, 1958), p. 102.

[11] The nature and extent of the domination of American thought and practice by business values was vividly described by Thorstein Veblen in a series of pioneering studies, especially in his *The Theory of the Leisure Class* (Macmillan, 1908).

allies who share its community of interest, namely lawyers, editors, and other professional and white-collar people. Finally, businessmen have important skills, such as the ability to explain their case, experience in competition, and the like.

Business suffers certain disadvantages, too. Businessmen are in a numerical minority, and in the long run votes count most in a democracy. The very concentration of business that promotes unity tends to make business a target. Americans tend to be suspicious of bigness and monopoly. Business is also a convenient scapegoat. When business falls off and jobs are scarce, it is easy to blame "Wall Street."

Other groups have their own strengths and weaknesses. Industrial workers are large in numbers, and they are becoming more organizationally and politically conscious. But they are divided into organized and unorganized, white and black, skilled and unskilled. Moreover, many American workers refuse to identify themselves or their interests with an "inferior" class. In 1956, only 2 per cent of American white males considered themselves members of the lower classes; 59 per cent, however, identified themselves as members of the working class, and 36 per cent of the middle class.[12] Further, it is hard for labor to make alliances with farm or business groups, because the latters' views of trade unionism may be somewhat unfavorable.

The farmers' strategic situation is almost the reverse of labor's. They are declining in numerical size relative to the whole population. But their advantages are significant. The geography of American federalism gives them extra political strength, for farmers are spread through all fifty states. Furthermore, farmers enjoy high esteem; in the popular mind they are frugal, hard-working, independent—the backbone of the nation. Like labor, however, the farmers are divided.

These strategic factors are not static. The external factors especially tend to change over time. Business at one time may enjoy enormous prestige, as during the prosperous 1920's, when Calvin Coolidge could say that "the business of America is business." A few years later, it may be relegated to the national doghouse. Labor is usually stronger during a time of ferment and reform than during a period of prosperity.

The Weapons of Group Influence

Groups use a wide range of political techniques to reach their goals. Their capacity to use these techniques is heavily affected by the factors we have just discussed—the size of the group, its cohesion or lack of it, its organizational structure, the skills of its leaders, the external situation. Like a good football team, every group must exploit the particular advantages that its material makes possible. Just as

---

[12] P. E. Converse, "The Shifting Role of Class in Political Attitudes and Behavior," Eleanor Maccoby, *et al.*, *Readings in Social Psychology* (Holt, 1959), p. 288.

a team of lightweights may have to stress deception rather than power drives, so a small but well-organized group will probably rely on skillful lobbying rather than mass election appeals. In plotting their political tactics, most groups use one or more of the following techniques.

PROPAGANDA

All interest groups are propagandistic. They exploit the media described in the preceding chapter—radio, press, film, leaflets, signs, and—above all—word of mouth. Business enjoys a special advantage in this arena, and businessmen have the money to hire propaganda machinery. Being advertisers on a large scale, they know the technique of delivering their message effectively. Most important, they generally have easy access to the means of propaganda, such as the press (see Chapter 11). The NAM spends over $2 million a year in national advertising. It puts out four periodicals—one goes to 36,500 educators, another to 40,000 leaders of women's clubs, another to 30,000 farm leaders, another to clergymen. According to the NAM, during one nine-month period it "turned out 816,110 copies of 45 pamphlets, booklets, leaflets, etc." A speakers' training program, motion pictures (shown to 4620 audiences), and meetings with leaders of the main groups, such as farmers and veterans, are other features of this program of opinion-molding. In any four years, says McKean, the NAM "will spend more for this all-around publicity than any political party. And the material is technically excellent—very

HOW THE INTEREST GROUPS WORK

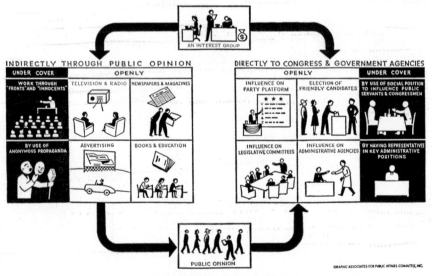

From Donald C. Blaisdell, "Government under Pressure,"
Public Affairs Pamphlet No. 67

shrewdly and carefully prepared—whereas much party propaganda is crude and poorly adapted to its recipients." [13]

Supplementing the NAM's efforts are those of the Chamber of Commerce, trade associations, and individual corporations. An early expert in the propaganda field was the National Electric Light Association, which carried on an elaborate public relations program until it was dissolved in 1933. Its propaganda against public ownership and regulation of the electric utilities reached into churches, schools, clubs, and to the companies' own employees. This campaign cost the companies—and ultimately the public—at least $20 million a year. The Association was especially vigilant in examining textbooks, and even "correcting" them.

Other groups have become increasingly aware of the uses of propaganda. Organized labor is a notable example. When a business organization places full-page messages in newspapers across the nation, unions often find the funds to hire similar space for an answer. Recently the AFL-CIO bought time on national radio networks to present its views, and it put out highly effective pamphlets, especially on political and legislative matters. Although labor has not yet matched the propaganda skills of business, it is devoting more money and attention to this political technique. Other interest groups, such as doctors and teachers, are making effective use of publicity methods. The American Medical Association spent at least one million dollars in 1950 in a highly successful campaign against compulsory health insurance.

ELECTIONEERING

Almost all large organizations avow that they are "nonpolitical." The American Legion's constitution flatly bars political activity. Actually, almost all organized groups are involved in politics in one way or another. What group leaders really mean when they say that they are nonpolitical is that they are *nonpartisan.* A distinguishing feature of organized interest groups is that they try to keep their feet in both camps by working through both parties. Usually this means working for individual candidates in elections. The policy that labor has followed for years—helping friends and defeating enemies—is the policy of almost all organized interest groups.

This policy is put into action in different ways. Occasionally an organization openly endorses a candidate and actively works for his election. Thus in 1924 many labor unions endorsed "Fighting Bob" LaFollette for President; the CIO officially backed President Roosevelt in 1944 and Adlai E. Stevenson in 1952. More often the organization formally stays neutral, but prominent officials take a public stand. In 1944, eleven members of the AFL's executive council worked actively for Roosevelt. Because of such factors as overlapping membership, an organization may set up a front organization to carry on its

---

[13] Dayton McKean, *Party and Pressure Politics* (Houghton Mifflin, 1949), p. 493.

political activities, as in the case of the Committee on Political Education formed by the AFL-CIO.

Individual labor unions, with somewhat homogeneous memberships, sometimes can afford to take a rather firm position on candidates. Other organizations are more handicapped by the diversity of their members. A local retailers' group, for example, might be composed equally of Republicans and Democrats, and many of its members might refuse to take an open position on a candidate for fear of losing business. In such cases more subtle means may be equally effective. At meetings word is passed around that Candidate X is sound from the organization's point of view. Perhaps the hat is passed around, too, and a contribution made to the cause. Members of the organization may serve as local opinion leaders in drumming up support for him. A local organization, such as a Legion post, may be strong enough to serve as a sort of secret caucus. Nationality groups gain much of their effectiveness from using word-of-mouth tactics.

Another method of trying to win elections is to form a separate party. Again and again groups have decided that keeping a foot in the camps of both regular parties often leads to a choice—from their point of view—between Tweedledee and Tweedledum on election day. Third parties in the United States, however, have tended to be self-defeating (see Chapter 13). The strength of interest groups has been siphoned off into minority party politics, while the two old parties have retained control of the government.

Some groups have tried a third method—trying to infiltrate the organization and machinery of the *major parties*. They have placed their members on local, state, and national party committees and have helped send them to party conventions as delegates. For years, one vice president of the AFL was prominent in Republican activities, and another was equally active for the Democrats.

Obviously, boring from within is not a new tactic; but it is being used more and more often, and with increasing success. The AFL-CIO's Committee on Political Education is a good example. Technically, COPE is nonpartisan, assisting prolabor candidates in both parties. Actually, COPE has come to concentrate most of its effort in the Democratic party. Not only does it endorse party candidates, like any organized interest, but in many states it has gone on to exercise electioneering functions that the parties ordinarily monopolize. COPE pays close attention to registration (see Chapter 14) in order to insure a large vote. It takes part in primary campaigns as well as in the later election contests. It puts out posters and leaflets, holds schools on political action techniques, provides automobiles to carry voters to the polls. COPE reported spending over $700,000 in the 1958 elections; most of this went to Democratic candidates.

LOBBYING

Lobbying is a long-used weapon of interest groups. Generations of Americans have been stirred by exposés of the "social lobby" and "invisible government," of bribery and corruption and midnight revels, of invisible agents holding the strings that make politicians dance. Some of this feeling is based on folklore, but much of it on fact. From the time of the Yazoo land frauds 150 years ago, when a whole legislature was bribed and the Postmaster General was put on a private payroll as a lobbyist, to the latest logrolling activity in Congress, Americans have enjoyed denouncing the "unscrupulous" lobbyists.

Over 1000 lobbyists are active in Washington today, but few of them are glamorous, unscrupulous, or very powerful. Most of the organizations maintaining lobbyists are highly specialized outfits such as the National Fertilizer Association, Retired Officers Association, Institute of Shortening and Edible Oils, Associated Tobacco Manufacturers, Texas Water Conservation Association, and a host of others. Lobbyists for these associations are usually hardworking attorneys, with long experience in Washington ways; their job is to watch a handful of bills and to keep in touch with a few administrative officials. Since lawmaking today is a highly technical matter, these lobbyists—or legislative counsel, as they like to be called—play a useful part in modern government. The harried congressman or administrator, threading his way through mountains of paper and seeking to appease conflicting interests, gladly turns to them for their views and information.

Lobbyists for the big groups, such as farmers, labor, and business, operate on a loftier scale. Their specialty is knowing just how to throw their political weight around. These lobbyists are better known throughout the country than some senators, better paid, better staffed, and more secure in their positions. The groups they represent have such broad interests that they must watch a wide variety of bills touching every phase of government. They are expert in raising such a clamor that they seem to be speaking for vast numbers of people. They exert pressure in Congress wherever they can find vulnerable points—regular committees, appropriations committees, individual legislators, even on the floor of the House and Senate (see Chapter 15). They know how to mobilize their organizations back home so that a storm of letters, telegrams, and petitions descends on Washington. They know how to draw up laws, to testify before committees, to help speed a bill through its long legislative journey, or to slow it down. They are experts in the art of influence.

Sometimes lobbyists stay in the background and make use of the legislator's own constituents. The following "Hints on Lobbying" sent by one organization to its members reveal this technique:

1. Interview the legislator at home if you are a constituent. If seeing him at the Capitol, impress on him that you live and vote in his district.
2. Be sure to have read the bill and to know the question with which it deals.
3. Find out main facts about legislator before interviewing him—his party, committee membership, business or profession, etc.
4. Be nonpartisan with legislator of opposite party from your own. In any case make clear our organization's nonpartisanship.

5. Don't pin legislator down to position for or against. Establish friendly relations. We will have to continue working with him in the future.
6. Use good salesmanship techniques. Our organization will be judged by the kind of interview you have.
7. Don't be "superior" even if you know far more about the question than he does. You are not there to score a point but to help get the measure passed!
8. Be patient and keep your temper.
9. Attend House and Senate galleries when bill comes up on the floor.
10. If possible, establish friendly relations with chairman and key members of at least one committee.

Administrative officials are by no means free of the lobbyist's attentions. Many important decisions are made in the executive branch, and these decisions inevitably affect the lobbyist's "constituents." Interest groups claim certain departments as their own, as in the case of farmers and the Department of Agriculture, veterans and the Veterans Administration, businessmen and the Department of Commerce. In some agencies, especially at the state level, the strength of a single interest group is so great that it controls such important administrative actions as licensing of professions, control of examinations, and policing.

How many voters does a particular lobbyist represent? Nobody really knows. For one thing, his strength varies with the issue; on one matter his whole organization will be united, on another it will not be. Moreover, polls and voting studies indicate that the strength an interest group can muster on election day is often exaggerated. But the real question is what the congressman *thinks* the group can do at the polls. Here he is at a disadvantage, for he is always feeling in the dark. As later chapters suggest, he is highly vulnerable to anything that hints of organized power, of purposeful and united action. The administrator, too, is always uncertain about how much congressional strength lobbyists can muster to deprive his agency of funds or even abolish it forever. The great weapon of the lobbyist is that he *seems* to be representing unseen millions of voters. He must remember the old maxim, "Never admit that it is only you who are talking."

OTHER GROUP WEAPONS

Force. We think of force as a weapon used by nation-states (national groups) rather than by internal groups. So it is, for the most part. But clashing groups within the nation have also resorted to force on occasion. In the Whisky Rebellion of 1794, Pennsylvanians refusing to pay excise taxes took up arms against troops directed by President Washington himself. Today race riots and lynchings mark the efforts of one racial group to coerce another. In depression years American farmers sometimes used force—or threats of force —to prevent banks from foreclosing their mortgages. Intimidation is a close cousin to force. In 1941 Negro leaders threatened to march on Washington in protest against discrimination in employment; President Roosevelt headed off the plan by setting up a Committee on Fair Employment Practice.[14] Years ago Mary E. Lease urged farmers to "raise less corn and more hell"—advice that has been followed by a variety of groups.

Strike. We usually think of the strike as a weapon used only by labor. Certainly it is one of the trade union's chief economic methods; there have been hundreds of strikes every year over the past decade. Other groups, however, know how to make strategic use of the withdrawal of their services. Teachers have gone out on strike from time to time. During the depression years, dairymen refused to deliver milk to retailers in protest against low prices; when some dairymen tried to send milk to the cities, their trucks were halted and the milk was spilled in the gutters. Businessmen, too, have withheld their goods for various purposes. Professional people have used an allied weapon, the boycott—when the University of Georgia during Governor Eugene Talmadge's regime failed to meet certain standards of academic freedom, certain graduate schools in the country refused to admit graduates of the university. In Britain the doctors once threatened to go on strike if the Labor government's health scheme was adopted.

Interest Groups and Democratic Government

Almost everyone likes to denounce pressure groups — especially somebody else's pressure group. Editorial columns are filled with protests that big business, or big labor, or the farm bloc, is taking over the country. This viewing with alarm has put organized interest groups under a cloud. Some people even look on them as a perversion of democracy—as a blot on the otherwise fair system of popular representation. Various proposals have been advanced to do away with these allegedly evil interests, or at least to clip their wings.

It is easy enough to answer these gloomy critics. Obviously, organized groups are here to stay. So long as there is a modicum of freedom left in America, men will associate on some basis or other. Life without group activity would be unthinkable. Actually we owe a great deal to the richness and fullness of group life in America. Our progress in technological, cultural, and political areas would have been impossible without it. Yet there are two criticisms of organized interest groups in America that we must consider.

INTEREST GROUPS: ATTACK AND DEFENSE

Certain organizations, it is said, are becoming *too strong*. Once upon a time, big business was the chief target of this criticism, but more recently

[14] L. C. Kesselman, *The Social Politics of FEPC* (Univ. of North Carolina Press, 1948), pp. 13 ff.

farmers and unions have been pictured as the new Goliaths. Are these fears justified? Our discussion above suggests that they are grossly exaggerated. The larger an association becomes, we noticed, the more it includes members of other groups with other allegiances. The stronger a group becomes, the more stimulus there will be for other groups to counterorganize. The real defense against group tyranny in America lies in the groups themselves.[15] So long as we have a great number and a rich diversity of groups, and so long as we preserve our liberties, no single interest or combination of interests can take America over. The competition would simply be too great.

A second criticism is that interest groups are *unrepresentative.* There is a good deal of truth in this charge. In the first place, group leaders often fail to speak fairly for their own members. In the second place, group leaders sometimes ignore the many people with related interests outside their own group, as in the case of agricultural associations acting for a narrow segment of the farm population. In the third place—and most important of all—many elements of the population are not represented in formal organizations at all, or at best are badly underrepresented. Not all groups receive the consideration they deserve in the clash of organized interests. Notable examples of unorganized or underorganized

Fitzpatrick in the *St. Louis Post Dispatch*

"How to curb inflation."

interests are consumers, nonunion laborers, farm workers, and certain professional and white-collar groups. Representative government is bound to suffer under these conditions.

But we must be careful not to push this criticism too far. Our government is still organized on a *territorial* or *geographical* basis; we have made no attempt to build occupational representation into the structure of government. Furthermore, Americans who are underorganized can always resort to the polls, or ultimately they can organize their own associations. Admittedly this is a slow process, but it is a process that has occurred again and again in American history as less organized elements have striven to make up for their weakness by political counterorganization. In the economic sphere, for ex-

---

[15] D. B. Truman, *The Governmental Process,* Chapter 16.

Checks & Balance by count

ample, when business became too strong, unions and consumer groups rose to hold it in check. Or if manufacturers try to raise prices unduly, powerful chain stores threaten to turn to other sources of supply or even to build or buy factories of their own. This doctrine of "countervailing power," [16] operates also in the political sphere, it is said; no one group can become too strong because under a system of private checks and balances among group interests other groups will become politically active and united in opposition. The result is a system of rough justice in the representation of groups.

CONTROL OF LOBBYING—A CASE STUDY

However exaggerated, the criticisms of the activities of organized interest groups cannot be ignored. And they have not been. For years Americans have been trying to curb the excesses of the "pressure groups." The attempt to control lobbying—which, as we have seen, is the primary weapon of interest groups—is a revealing example of the difficulties involved in trying to regulate dynamic groups in a democracy.

Attempts to control lobbying began at least a century ago. In 1877 Georgia wrote into its constitution the simple provision that "lobbying is a crime." Early in this century a number of states passed acts to regulate lobbyists, requiring that legislative counsel or agents officially register as such, and that they file statements of expenses paid or promised in connection with promoting legislation. Under the Federal Regulation of Lobbying Act in 1946 (Title III of the Legislative Reorganization Act of 1946), every person hired to influence or defeat bills in Congress must register and disclose the name and address of his employer, how much he is paid, and who pays him. Every three months he must file a further statement listing the names of publications that have carried his publicity, and the bills he supports or opposes. Organizations whose main purpose is to influence legislation also must furnish information, which is printed regularly in the *Congressional Record*. It seems clear however, that the 1946 act has not diminished the extent of lobbying; its registration provisions, moreover, have been narrowly construed by the courts to apply only to direct pressure on legislators.

Actually, the aim of such legislation is to turn the spotlight of publicity on the expenditures and activities of lobbyists. How successful has the attempt been? The national lobby law has furnished a vast amount of detailed information about lobbyists—who they are, who sponsors and finances them, what bills they seek to pass or block. This information has given the public some idea of the amount of money involved; in the first four years the act was in effect, lobbyists collected about $60 million and spent approximately $30 million. About 500 persons and organizations had filed, but many hundreds of others had not, on one pretext or another.

---

[16] J. K. Galbraith, *American Capitalism* (Houghton Mifflin, 1952).

Some hold that publicity is not enough, that what we need is *actual regulation* of lobbying. Most lobbyists, these critics argue, have no fear of publicity, but on the contrary actually welcome it. There is much doubt, however, that Congress will try to restrict lobbyists. For one thing, such an attempt might drive the lobbyists underground, where their influence might be more insidious and just as effective. Regulation might run into serious constitutional objections based on the rights guaranteed by the First Amendment. But more important, most students of the problem feel that lobbyists serve an important and desirable function, and that nothing more than publicity is needed.

These observers point out that lobbyists are a sort of "third house" of Congress. While Senate and House are set up on a *geographical* basis, lobbyists represent people directly in terms of their *economic* or other interests. The representative speaks for voters as members of, say, the third district of Ohio; the lobbyist speaks for people as manufacturers or steelworkers or veterans or fruitgrowers. Small but important groups, such as bankers, can get representation in this third house that they might not be able to get in the other two. In a nation of large and important interests, this kind of *functional representation*, if not abused, is highly useful as a supplement to geographical representation. The lobbyists pour vitally needed information and ideas into the legislative mill. Some European nations have gone so far as to set up legislative branches to provide functional representation; our informal "third house" is a welcome compromise between such extreme measures and no functional representation at all.

THE REAL PROBLEM

The real problem raised by the activities of interest groups in America is their frequent failure to represent broader segments of the community, organized or not. This problem in turn involves the broader question of *national unity* that we discussed in Part One and that crops up again and again in this book. Somehow Americans must live and work together. To do so they must rise above some of their differences and join hands to work toward more broadly representative goals. To some extent interest groups perform this very function. Especially the great national organizations of farmers, workers, and businessmen tend to reflect broad rather than narrow interests because they must find the beliefs that unite their diverse memberships.

But the process of finding general areas of agreement does not go far enough. Even the strongest organized interests are still minorities—they are not big enough to embrace all the people, or even most of them. Yet they dominate national legislation. A few years ago an influential congressman was quoted as saying, after the late President William Green of the American Federation of Labor had asked him to vote for a food subsidy bill, "I have always followed Mr. Green on labor bills. But this is not a labor bill. This is a farm bill. On this bill I follow the farm leaders." Undoubtedly such a course is good pressure-group politics. But is it good *majority-welfare* politics?

Groups tend to be competitive, and in the noisy clash of special interests the welfare of the great mass of Americans is sometimes drowned out. The dynamic elements of group life that contribute so much to a healthy America give rise at the same time to dangerous stresses and strains. Groups can cement individual *fragments* of the American people, but what will pull together the *people as a whole,* including both the organized and unorganized? Many agencies fulfill this need—our common traditions and ideas, the role of national leaders like the President, and the overlapping character of the groups themselves. On the organizational level, the political party might fill this great function, but it too is often divided and weakened by internal disunities (see Chapter 13). The problem of maintaining internal unity is especially acute in a day when government needs broad and firm support from the people in handling critical problems at home and abroad. We will return to this problem in Chapter 21—but first we must examine the political forces that play upon our government, and the governmental machinery that both reflects and in turn affects these forces.

CHAPTER 13

Party Politics
and Party Problems

The vital feature of our national political system is that it is essentially a two-party system. If we had three or more parties seriously competing for power, our politics would be far different from what it is. If we had a one-party system like the fascist or communist type, our democracy would be far different from what it is—indeed it would be nonexistent. This does not mean that we have only two parties. No less than 135 parties have been able to elect members to Congress in the last 160 years, and there have been countless other local parties. On the other hand, in many areas of the United States only one party dominates local affairs. Recently, in Alabama one lone Republican representative was pitted against 105 Democrats; this state has not elected a Republican governor since Reconstruction. In North Dakota the Senate was composed of one Democrat and 48 Republicans. Even within a state where the two major parties are fairly evenly balanced, many precincts may be dominated by a single party.

Actually we have a series of party systems.[1] In some places one of the major parties may dominate the state government and the state's congressional delegation, but in presidential elections both parties may be strong. Since 1932, for example, Oregon has voted for the Democratic presidential candidate four times, but has normally sent Republican delegations to Congress; the Democrats did not control the Oregon legislature for 78 years. Texas voted for President Eisenhower in 1956, but elected only one Republican congressman, and in the state legislature the Democrats have overwhelming dominance.

Yet when all the qualifications are made, only the Democrats or the Repub-

---

[1] Austin Ranney and Willmoore Kendall, "The American Party Systems," *The American Political Science Review* (June 1954), pp. 477-485. Also Joseph A. Schlesinger, "A Two-Dimensional Scheme for Classifying the States According to Degree of Inter-Party Competition," *The American Political Science Review* (December 1955), pp. 1120-1128.

licans have any real chance to gain power, one of these parties normally can muster the majority to enable it to control Congress or to elect the President without any help from a third party, and over a period of time the two parties alternate in power.

Why do we have a two-party system? Nobody knows for sure. Jefferson thought that men naturally divided into Whigs and Tories. Lord Bryce said they inevitably split into nationalists and states-righters. Some have said that "advanced Anglo-Saxon peoples" sensibly adopted tidy political systems; perhaps the sentry in *Iolanthe* was mocking them when he sang:

> Now let's rejoice
> That Nature wisely does contrive
> That every boy and every gal
> That's born into the world alive
> Is either a little Liberal
> Or else a little Conservative.

Probably the explanation lies largely in the nature of our electoral system. Most of our elections are set up on the basis of single-member districts in which the candidate with the most votes wins.[2] Since only one candidate can win, the largest and second-largest parties monopolize the victories, and the third party, being deprived of the rewards of office, eventually gives up the fight. The system of electing the President, the grand prize of American politics, operates in this fashion on a national scale. In order to win the Presidency, it is necessary for a party to win a majority of the electoral votes; that requires a national organization and party support in more than one region. The two major parties alternate in their possession of the Presidency; deprived of patronage and power, third parties tend to wither away. The ability of some third parties to last for two or three decades has been due largely to their hold on congressional and state offices in certain sections of the country, as in the case of the Wisconsin Progressives in the 1920's and 1930's.

Herblock in *The Washington Post and Times Herald*

"I have the same trouble!"

---

[2] Maurice Klain, "A New Look at the Constituencies: The Need for a Recount and a Reappraisal," *The American Political Science Review* (December 1955), p. 1105. Klain points out that in many states some state legislators are not chosen in single-member elections.

Two important results stem from our two-party system. First, both parties must be broad alliances of many different interests. Parties are the means whereby groups pool their efforts to reach at least some of their goals. Successful party leaders must be group diplomats—they must know how to mediate among more or less hostile groups so that agreement can be reached on general principles. The implications of this tendency are obvious: National unity is not simply a mystical thing—it is the capacity to rise above differences (at least for a while) and pull together. Parties want to *win elections*. In order to win, each of them emphasizes the *common beliefs* that *unite* men, and plays down the issues that divide them. Parties help reconcile unity and diversity.

A second result of the two-party system is that both parties tend to be moderate in their platforms.[3] Under a multiparty system the parties range all the way from extreme conservatism to extreme radicalism. With two big parties, these extremes are normally avoided. Each party must embrace a variety of groups, and above all each must try to attract the crucial middle-of-the-road vote that easily switches from one side to the other. Not only do the parties seek wide support, but the different interest groups try not to alienate either party. This moderating tendency helps unite the country.

Let us glance briefly at the growth of the American party system to see how these two tendencies—toward unity and toward moderation—have worked out in practice over a century and a half of party development.

The Grand Coalitions

The story of American parties is closely bound up with the economic, political, and social history of the whole nation. The full telling of that story would take a four-foot shelf in itself. Here we must oversimplify. Looking at American parties as alliances of interests, we see three great phases. The first, lasting until the Civil War, is the Age of the Democrats. The second, stretching through the first decade of this century, is the Age of the Republicans.[4] The third, beginning in 1930, might be called a New Age of the Democrats. Whether this phase has now ended and a New Age of the Republicans has begun depends on the ability of the GOP to broaden the power it won in the presidential elections of 1952 and 1956.

The peculiar American brand of rough-and-tumble politics did not begin in Revolutionary days. Well before the Revolution there were divisions of interest between economic and sectional groups; there were political clubs and committees; there were meetings, parades, songs, oratory, and fisticuffs, just as today. But the effect of the Revolution and the post-Revolutionary struggles was to crystallize political interests and allegiances into more coherent and lasting form. The great service of George Washington was to give the fledgling government a sense of unity by his ability to rise above faction and

---

[3] E. E. Schattschneider, *Party Government* (Farrar & Rinehart, 1942), pp. 85 ff.

[4] See D. W. Brogan, *Government of the People* (Harper, 1933), Part Two.

party. He had hardly taken the oath of office, however, before there were signs of an emerging party split. On one side was Alexander Hamilton, who was not only Washington's Secretary of the Treasury but the leader of the Federalists. As a supporter of the Constitution, strong central government, and "sound" financial policies, Hamilton was spokesman for the bankers, traders, and manufacturers of the day.

RISE OF THE DEMOCRATS

On the other side was Thomas Jefferson and a motley collection of small farmers, frontiersmen, laborers, debtors, small proprietors, slaveowners—in general, an agrarian group.[5] Jefferson, the first national party leader, resigned as Secretary of State in Washington's second administration to devote full time to the job of welding together a great party following. He accomplished this task by negotiating with local party leaders in New England, New York, Virginia, and other sections, and by expounding a philosophy of equality, agrarianism, and limited government that appealed alike to northern farmer, southern planter, and western frontiersman. By the turn of the century this combination had overcome the Federalists. As President, Jefferson continued to serve as party chief, using the party to put his program through Congress.

Here was the first of the grand coalitions. It started out as the Democratic-Republican party, but soon dropped the "Democratic," later split into Republican and Democratic elements, and ended up as the Democratic party. During this sixty-year period, ending with Lincoln's election, the party changed in many ways. Millions of new voters were casting ballots. Americans were moving westward, and the party had to move with them. Republican leaders in office, like John Quincy Adams, seemed to drift away from the leveling sentiments of Jefferson. The rising democratic elements, led by Andrew Jackson, gave the party a southern and westward cast. Nevertheless, the party retained two of its main features. First, it won elections. The Whigs—who came to be the main opposition party—were able to elect only two Presidents, and only then by nominating war heroes. Second, it continued to play coalition politics. Its following embraced sizable numbers of cotton planters, slaveowners, small farmers in the West, workmen in eastern mills.

How does a major party lose power? In the case of the Democrats, two things happened. The party itself was split by the irrepressible conflict over slavery, and the opposition hammered out a superior combination of voting groups. The 1850's were a time of party upheaval. The Democrats, sharply split between northerners and southerners, broke into fragments. The Whigs' coalition, composed of large sections of the propertied class, big slaveowners and planters, nativists, and antislavery people, had never been stable enough or large enough to turn the tide against the Democrats. But now the conserva-

---

[5] W. E. Binkley, *American Political Parties* (Knopf, 1947), pp. 72-78.

tive elements of the Whig party, especially in the South, went over to the Democrats. Other Whigs looked around for a new party.

The new winning alliance—the Republican party—was founded in 1854 (not by Abraham Lincoln, who was still a Whig). Initially the party was radical in many respects, appealing to farmers, workers, and small business-men. To the revolutionary air of the "Marseillaise" the Republicans sang:

> Arise, arise, ye brave,
> And let your war-cry be
> Free speech, free press, free soil, free men,
> Frémont and victory.

In 1856, the Republicans lost with Frémont to a Democratic coalition still strong enough to win, but four years later Lincoln led the Republicans to victory on a platform that opposed further extension of slavery and favored internal improvements, including a "satisfactory homestead measure" for farmers and "liberal wages for workingmen and mechanics." Lincoln received 40 per cent of the popular vote in 1860, but his common appeal to North and West won him the electoral votes of all the states outside the South.

After the war, the Republican party consolidated and broadened its coalition of interests. Its liberal homestead policies helped solidify the support of farmers, especially in the Midwest, and of immigrants eager for land. Its humanitarian appeal and its high-tariff stand continued to attract many eastern workers. Its aids to business, such as sound money policies and railroad land grants, won the support of financiers, industrialists, and merchants. As the party of Lincoln, it gained a hold on the newly freed Negroes that was long to remain secure. Veterans of the northern armies were part of this coalition; for decades units of the Grand Army of the Republic worked closely with the party machine and reaped their reward in the form of pensions. Above all, the Republicans were the "party of the Union," with a national appeal that seemed to transcend the lines of class, group, or section.

For five decades after 1860 this coalition was to give every presidential race to the Republicans, except for Cleveland's victories in 1884 and 1892. Not that all was smooth sailing for the Grand Old Party. It suffered from the exposure of corruption that marred Grant's administrations. It was shaken by internal divisions between East and West, between conservative businessmen and not-so-conservative farmers and workers, between reform-minded Liberal Republicans and stand-patters, between party regulars (Stalwarts) and party independents (Halfbreeds), and between many different combinations of these interests. Yet the GOP remained a grand coalition. The secret of its success lay in finding, by design or by chance, leaders who could assuage conflicting elements. For example, when important labor and rural elements were on the verge of deserting the party toward the end of the century, it was a group diplomat, William McKinley, who reasserted the party's broad appeal. When the upsurge of reformism and muckraking in the following years presaged a change in political moods, it was a progressive Republican, Theodore Roosevelt, who reoriented the party's appeal.

THE LOYAL OPPOSITION

Meanwhile, what had happened to the Democrats? Discredited—in the minds of many—by the Civil War, this party survived with its hard core in the South. Acting as the loyal opposition after the Civil War, the Democrats capitalized on the mistakes and excesses of the party in power. Along with winning the Presidency twice, and nearly winning it several times, the party occasionally took control of Congress and frequently captured state governments. Its platforms championed the principles of low tariffs, states rights, civil service, currency reform. But the Democrats were not able to consolidate national power. Part of the trouble was their failure to win over dissident groups, like the Greenbackers, that spent their energies in third-party movements in behalf of such "radical" changes as bimetallism and business regulation. But the main difficulty was that the Republicans, riding the wave of a long-term economic boom, were in accord with the main temper of the times. Even in 1896, when the Democrats under William Jennings Bryan finally formed an alliance with the Populists, the GOP re-established control of the White House after one of the most turbulent election fights in American history.

For all their noisy battles during the century, both parties had remained true to the rule that under a two-party system neither side can afford to be extremist. Both parties embraced liberal and conservative elements, both reached out for the support of members of the major interest groups, especially of the dominant business groups. Democrats Tilden and Cleveland shared the major political and economic assumptions of Republicans Hayes and Harrison. Indeed, one of the main complaints of the third parties of the day was that both major parties were in a conspiracy of agreement over policy, disagreeing only over how to split up the spoils of office.[6] Both parties, moreover, were sensitive to shifting public sentiment. Thus during 1896-1912, a period of unrest and protest, the progressive wings of both parties were dominant much of the time.

In 1912 the Republican coalition split as cleanly as the Democratic coalition had in 1860. The conservative wing under President Taft kept a tight grip on the party machinery; the disgruntled progressives deserted the GOP and nominated Theodore Roosevelt on the ticket of a new Progressive party. The Democratic party, led by Woodrow Wilson, won fewer popular votes

---

[6] See Matthew Josephson, *The Politicos* (Harcourt, Brace, 1938).

A SHORT CARTOON HISTORY OF POLITICAL PARTIES

Courtesy *Harper's Weekly*
and Thomas Nast

*1874—The Republican Elephant
appears; the party symbol is
introduced by Thomas Nast in
Harper's Weekly.*

Gillam in *Judge*

*1900—Bryan was bowled over
like Don Quixote by McKinley's
promise to keep the workman's
dinner pail full.*

Little in *The Nashville Tennessean*

*1940—Willkie's new ideas reju-
venated the GOP, but a dynamic challenger succumbed to
F.D.R.'s old mastery.*

Herblock in *The Washington Post
and Times Herald*

*1956—Eisenhower scores another
great triumph but cannot pull his
party to victory.*

than the Republicans and Progressives combined, but it swept the electoral college. As President, Wilson used Jeffersonian precedents in putting through Congress a series of notable measures including a new income tax law, a revised banking system, fair-trade and antimonopoly legislation, and lower tariffs. As party chief, Wilson aimed his "New Freedom" program at the "common man"—labor, farmers, small businessmen—and at the Solid South.

Wilson's coalition was not broad or firm enough, however, to stay in power for long. The Democrats barely won the Presidency in 1916 over a reunited Republican party, with Roosevelt back in the GOP fold. And the 1920's, in the wake of World War I, were years of supremacy for the Republicans as the "party of prosperity." To be sure, the Republicans had during this period no specialist in group diplomacy like McKinley or Roosevelt. Yet Harding, Coolidge, and Hoover triumphed easily over their Democratic opponents, perhaps because the business philosophy of the Republicans was in direct accord with the business mood of the era. The Democrats were an uneasy alliance of urban, Catholic, and "wet" groups with rural, Protestant, and "dry" elements. No matter whether they presented a liberal or a conservative candidate, they could not break the GOP's hold on masses of farmers, businessmen, and even workers.

The Great Depression changed all this. The bleak years of job-hunting and breadlines brought a new political temper and new political alignments. People in all classes and groups turned away from the GOP. The Democrats, under Franklin D. Roosevelt, offered some kind of New Deal to the "forgotten man" and plenty of voters felt themselves forgotten. Roosevelt not only strengthened the farmer-labor-southern alliance that Wilson had led; he put together a grand coalition of these groups plus Negroes, unemployed, middle-class people, national and racial minorities—a coalition that in 1936 gave the Democrats the electoral votes of every state except two. Roosevelt was chief legislator as well as chief executive. Under his generalship Congress enacted a series of laws to provide a new deal for American labor, farmers, small businessmen, old people, and other groups. This grand coalition was strong enough to re-elect Roosevelt three times. That it was not simply F.D.R.'s personal following was indicated when Harry Truman, who lacked some of Roosevelt's superb political skills, led the Democrats to a nationwide triumph in 1948.

A NEW AGE OF THE REPUBLICANS?

The election of 1952 was a sweeping victory for the Republican candidate, Dwight D. Eisenhower, and the Republicans won control of the national House and Senate. Was this the start of a new era of Republican supremacy? Some observers were doubtful. It was an *Eisenhower* victory, they said, resulting from his wartime record and his great popularity.

The 1956 election was both a test of President Eisenhower's personal popularity and a test of the strength of the Republican party. On the first test the results were crystal clear. Running against Adlai E. Stevenson—the same man he had defeated in 1952—Eisenhower boosted his electoral-vote margin to 383 and his popular-vote margin to over nine million, compared with margins of 353 electoral votes and less than seven million popular votes over Stevenson four years before. Moreover, the President unexpectedly won large support in places where the Democrats had been clearly dominant—in northern cities, in the South, among Negroes and many national-origin groups.

Despite Eisenhower's victories, the Republicans did not fare so well as a *party*. They lost control of both houses of Congress in the 1954 midterm elections and failed to regain congressional majorities in 1956 even though Eisenhower won. In 1958 the Republicans suffered a debacle reminiscent of New Deal days. The Democrats won thirteen more Senate seats, forty-seven more House seats, and five more governorships. The congressional trend was almost wholly Democratic, the Republicans picking up no Senate seats and only one House seat. The Grand Old Party was heartened, however, by winning the governorship of New York behind the energetic campaigning of a new figure on the political scene, Nelson Rockefeller. Two weeks later Alaska sent a solid Democratic delegation to Washington, but in 1959 Hawaii elected one Republican senator and a Republican governor, along with a Democratic senator and representative.

As President Eisenhower approached the end of his second term, the Republicans faced serious problems as a party. Their weakness was measured by the fact that not for over a century had a party won the Presidency and failed to win at least one house of Congress. Since the antithird term amendment prevented Eisenhower from running again even if his health permitted, the party faced the prospect (unless the amendment was repealed) of fighting future battles without its popular chief. Many registration and election figures, moreover, indicated that the Democratic party and its position on major issues were somewhat more popular than the Republican party and its stand.

But the Democrats faced perhaps more serious problems. With Stevenson defeated twice in a row, they lacked a party leader who could conduct an energetic and well-publicized opposition. Power in the party shifted to southern Democratic committee leaders in the House and Senate who, as conservatives, showed little interest in carrying out the Democratic national platform of 1956. Since the southern and northern wings of the Democratic party had sharply differing views on most policy issues, the Democrats were a minority party when it came to mustering enough votes in Congress to put across a Democratic program. The Democrats had other sectional troubles. Democratic party leaders in the West—especially California—demanded more influence in the party and set up an informal association to press their views.

Clearly each party would have to grasp a basic factor that had transformed the politics during the previous century. American politics was no longer rustic. Parties were no longer alliances mainly of *sections,* based in turn on agrarian interests. They were coming to be increasingly centered in the urban areas. The new politics would be "less rustic than the old and more urbane." There would be "less sectional politics and more class politics." [7] Unless another world war should totally change the pattern of American politics, it seems likely that both parties will base their coalitions more directly on voters living in urban and suburban areas.

Functions of Political Parties

The foregoing history of the party system, brief though it is, shows that our parties have managed to pull America's warring interest groups into some kind of rough unity. The *unifying* role of the parties was well shown in the years before the Civil War. Most of the other bonds between North and South—for example, between northern and southern members of the same religious denominations, business organizations, reform groups—snapped before the parties broke apart, and the final rending of the parties was the signal for civil war. The *moderating* role of the parties has been demonstrated recently by the Republican party, which in the past two decades has moved from its extreme Old Guard philosophy to a platform only moderately right of center.

The party in power has the formal responsibility of *governing*. It is put into power after presenting its candidates and its platform to the people; once in power it has both the duty and the authority to accept responsibility for the conduct of government. This, at least, is the theory of party government; but in the United States the parties that win elections do not necessarily govern *as parties;* why this is so will be discussed at the end of this chapter and in later chapters.

The party out of power has the job of *opposing* the ins. It tries to play a bright spotlight on any errors the incumbents commit. "The business of the opposition is to oppose" according to an old political phrase; while no party is foolish enough to denounce the party in power for every action it takes, in general the "outs" are supposed to keep before the people an alternative line of action. Our parties usually perform faithfully the basic "watchdog" function of the opposition; they are not so effective in presenting an agreed-on alternative program.

Closely related to these functions are a number of others. In trying to gain votes, parties must *simplify the alternatives*.[8] Usually they present the public with a choice between two relatively understandable solutions to a question, although most controversial matters admit of a variety of solutions. The two main parties have the equally important job of limiting the choice of candidates to two. In framing platforms and choosing candidates, the

---

[7] A. N. Holcombe, *The New Party Politics* (Norton, 1933), p. 11. See also Samuel Lubell, *The Future of American Politics* (Harper, 1951).

[8] Schattschneider, *Party Government,* pp. 50 ff.

parties perform the mammoth function of sifting hundreds of issues to find the right formula. As a result, they make elections meaningful and even exciting to millions of voters who know how to choose between a few alternatives but not among a bewildering variety of men and platforms.

Parties, moreover, play a part in the *shaping of public opinion,* especially at election time. They use all the media—radio, television, press, posters, leaflets, meetings, and the like—in order to saturate the voters with their arguments. After a polite interval following the election, the opposition party maintains a drumfire of faultfinding against the party in power. Sometimes the opposition party, eager for office, has been the most effective source of criticism of an administration. In 1929 the Democrats hired a newspaperman, Charles Michelson, who set about systematically to attack President Hoover almost daily. His attacks, usually issued through the mouths of Democratic congressmen, helped elect Roosevelt in 1932. Today both major parties maintain full-time publicity divisions.

Long ago local party organizations found more direct ways to pick up votes. Almost every political machine in the past has been a *charitable organization,* giving the needy jobs, loans, free coal, picnics, Christmas baskets, and the like. William S. Vare, leader of the Republican machine in Philadelphia, bragged that his organizatin was "one of the greatest welfare organizations in the United States." In every election precinct, he said, his committeemen were at the beck and call of the people day and night, and service was rendered "without red tape, without class, religion, or color distinction." Parties also have played a notable role in helping citizens deal with an often impersonal government on such matters as pensions, unemployment benefits, taxes, and licenses. The creation of the "welfare state" has robbed the parties of most of their charitable activities, but the chance to serve as a bridge between "big government" and the little man may help the machines to carry on operations for a long time to come.

CHOOSING CANDIDATES

Above all, parties are directly concerned with primaries and elections. Their function of *selecting candidates,* whom they try in turn to elect to office, makes the parties virtually semiofficial organs of the government; without parties our election system would be very different, if it existed at all.

Parties have had this task from their beginning. The earliest method of selecting party candidates was the *caucus,* a closed meeting of party leaders. The caucus was used in Massachusetts only a few years after the *Mayflower* landed, and played an important part in pre-Revolutionary politics. John Adams in 1763 described with some distaste a caucus in Tom Dawes' garret:

> There they smoke tobacco till you cannot see from one end of the garret to the other. There they drink flip, I suppose, and there they choose a moderator, who puts questions to the vote regularly; and selectmen, assessors, col-

lectors, wardens, firewards, and representatives are regularly chosen before they are chosen by the town. . . .

After the Union was established, party groups in the national or state legislatures served for several decades as the caucus. The legislators in each party simply met separately to nominate candidates. Our first presidential candidates were chosen by senators and representatives meeting as party delegations.

"King Caucus," however, soon fell into ill repute. Its meetings smacked of secret deals and logrolling; moreover, the caucus could not be fairly representative of the people where the party was in a minority, since only officeholders were members. Andrew Jackson's supporters boycotted the Republican caucus of 1824 because, they argued, the outcome was rigged by the congressional insiders. Although there were efforts to make the caucus more representative, gradually a system of *party conventions* took its place. The convention was made up of delegates usually chosen directly by party members in towns and cities. The conventions served several purposes. They chose the party standard-bearers. They debated and adopted a platform. And they provided a chance to whip up party spirit and perhaps paint the town red.

But the convention method in turn came in for grave criticism. It was charged—and often quite rightly—that the convention was subject to control by the party bosses and their machines. At times delegates were freely bought and sold, instructions from party members were ignored, meetings got completely out of control.

To "democratize" party selections, the *direct primary* was adopted by state after state. This system simply gives every member of the party the right to vote on party candidates in a primary election. The state usually supplies the ballots and supervises the primary election, which takes place some time before the general election in November. The direct primary was hailed by many Americans as a major cure for party corruption but, as we shall see, it did not cure all the existing evils, and it led to new ones.

Today the primary is the main method of making party choices, but the nominating convention remains in one or two states and—grandly—in picking presidential candidates. In either case, the party carries the main burden of activity, although many of its electoral activities are closely regulated by law. In the general election, too, the party has a central role. It campaigns for its candidates, mobilizes its machinery in their behalf, helps finance them, and on election day it produces cars, advice for the voters, and workers at the polls to watch the counting of the ballots.

THE ROLE OF THIRD PARTIES

These are the main functions of the two major parties. What about the minor parties? Obviously they have many of the same electoral and propaganda functions as the big parties, except that they cannot perform the crucial feat of mobilizing a majority of voters at the polls. In one respect, however, minor parties play a special role: They draw public attention to controversial issues that the major parties either ignore or straddle. Such notable minor parties as the Locofocos, the Greenbackers, the Socialists, the Prohibitionists, and the Progressives of 1912 and 1924, in performing this function, have acted as "vehicles for the expression of political discontent." [9]

Disgusted with the conservative policies of both Republicans and Democrats, farmers in the last century organized parties of their own. These parties were short-lived, but they compelled the major parties to modify their programs. In this century some labor groups have repeatedly turned to the third-party technique. In 1912 and 1920 the Socialist party polled over 900,000 votes, but these were its high-water marks. The Liberal party in New York City occasionally has enjoyed some balance-of-power influence. Over the years third parties have been organized by special-interest groups, such as anti-slavery people, Prohibitionists, Christian Nationalists, Vegetarians (who nominated a candidate for President but never got on the ballot), and many others.

In many cases, however, the minor parties have won wide support for their ideas, only to see a major party filch their best planks to adorn its own platform. The Grangers campaigned for regulation of unfair railroad rates. The Greenbackers demanded a graduated income tax. The Populists proposed a constitutional amendment providing for the direct election of United States senators. The Socialists called for an end to child labor, for public works systems, old age and unemployment insurance, the adoption of the initiative and referendum. All these proposals, once they had gained significant popular support, were taken over by the major parties and enacted into law. Minor parties, however, deserve much of the credit for popularizing the ideas.

The failure of third parties has not been due simply to the ability of major parties to steal their thunder. That failure is due in part to the extremism of third parties, their tendency to break up over issues of party dogma, their concentration on propaganda rather than political action at the grass roots. Moreover, the major parties have erected legal barriers against third-party action. For example, in some states the number of signatures on petitions needed to place a third party on the ballot is very high. All these factors, plus the primary role of the single-member district system noted above, explain the fact that no minor party has succeeded in dislodging a major party in national politics at least since the Civil War.

Party Machinery and How It Runs — On paper our parties look like armies. They have the form of a pyramid, with millions of party members and thousands of local party officials at the base, and a few national party heads at the top. Like the army, they have a hierarchy of leaders and

---

[9] M. S. Stedman and S. W. Stedman, *Discontent at the Polls* (Columbia Univ. Press, 1950), p. 168.

followers, running from the national committee at the top down to town and precinct committees at the bottom. Actually, this analogy is false, for the essence of an army is discipline from the top down. And this sort of central discipline is precisely what our parties lack. They have been well described as "loose associations of state and local organizations, with very little national machinery and very little national cohesion." [10]

Why are our parties decentralized and undisciplined? There are many reasons. Perhaps the most important is the *federal* basis of our government. Earlier in the book we suggested that the Constitution has shaped our political system, just as politics in turn has affected the structure of government. Here is an excellent example of this circular relationship. Parties tend to organize around *elections* and *officeholders*. Since our federal system sets up elections and offices on a national-state-local basis, our parties are organized on a similar basis. Just as state and local governments are largely independent of the national government, so the state and local parties are somewhat independent of the national party organizations. Thus the Constitution has given us federalism in our *parties* as well as in our *government*. The nature of our party organization in turn has had a vital impact on the workings of our government, as we shall see in Part Five.

NATIONAL PARTY ORGANIZATION

The supreme authority in both major political parties is the national convention. The convention meets every four years and has four major duties: to nominate the party's candidates for President and Vice President; to write the party's national platform; to adopt the rules of the party; and to go through the formality of electing the national committee. (In Chapter 14 we shall look more closely at the convention.) But the convention is in session only briefly; most of the time party business is handled by party executives.

The Democratic National Committee is composed of something over 100 members—one man and one woman from every state and a few members representing areas like Puerto Rico. The Republican National Committee is also composed of one man and one woman from each state, along with territorial representatives. In addition the Republicans make each Republican state chairman a member of their National Committee if his state cast its electoral vote for the Republican presidential candidate in the preceding election, or if a majority of his state's congressional delegation (House and Senate counted together) are Republican, or if his state has a Republican governor. In form, the committeemen of both parties are elected every four years by their respective national party conventions. Actually, they are chosen by state party conventions or by party committees or by party primaries.

---

[10] "Toward a More Responsible Two-Party System," A Report of the Committee on Political Parties of the American Political Science Association," *Supplement, The American Political Science Review* (September 1950), p. v.

The national committeemen often are influential in their states, but the committee itself is not very important. In fact, it rarely meets. (One of its main jobs is to choose the city where the national convention will meet, a choice usually dictated by the nature of the convention hall and facilities and by the amount of cash offered by cities for the privilege of acting as host to the convention.) The party organization is usually run by the chairman of the committee and by appointed, full-time officials.

The main job of the *chairman* is to manage the presidential campaign. Although in form he is elected by the national committee, actually he is chosen by the party's presidential candidate at the close of the quadrennial convention. It is through him that the presidential candidate—and perhaps later the President—runs the party nationally. By the same token, a defeated presidential candidate may have little control over the national chairman, or the national committeemen may elect a new head who responds to the balance of forces within the committee. Usually the national chairman is the chief dispenser of patronage for the President, using his control of the relatively few but politically important federal jobs that are not covered by civil service to promote zeal and discipline in the party. If a President and a chairman cannot get along with each other, it is the chairman who must go, as with President Franklin D. Roosevelt and Democratic chairman James A. Farley in 1940.

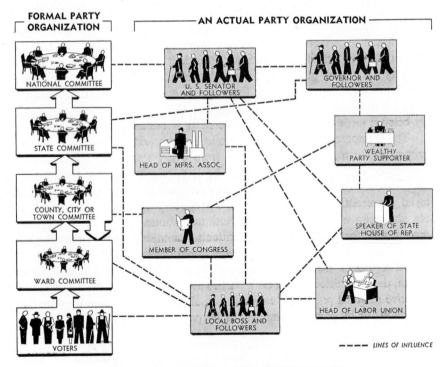

FORMAL AND ACTUAL PARTY ORGANIZATION

Thus the chairman becomes, in V. O. Key's words, "a technician, a specialist in campaign management and machine tending, who exercises his power only so long as he enjoys the confidence of the presidential nominee." [11]

It is the national chairman, backed by the President, who gives the party a measure of unity and direction when the party is in power. When the party loses a presidential race, it often has no real central leadership. The defeated nominee is called the titular leader, but he usually has little real power over the organization, partly because he has no jobs to hand out. As a result, the party out of power nationally may come under the control of influential state and local bosses.

The *Congressional and Senatorial Campaign Committees* aid congressmen in their campaigns for re-election. Today the Republican Senatorial Campaign Committee is composed of seven senators chosen for two-year terms by the Republican senators. The Democrats through their party leader in the Senate normally choose five men for a two-year term. The men selected are usually from states in which there will be no senatorial election. The congressional campaign committees, composed of members chosen by each party group in the House of Representatives, are organized in somewhat similar fashion.

Courtesy *The New York Times Magazine* and Tom Little

One failing of our party system is that the party out of power nationally does not have the kind of leadership that the President can provide for the party in power.

After candidates have been nominated, the committees send them money, provide speakers, supply campaign material, and the like. Normally they concentrate their efforts in doubtful districts and states where an expenditure of money and time can do the most good. During presidential election years, the activities of the national committee tend to overshadow the work of the congressional and senatorial campaign committees. But during off-year elections, these committees often provide the only campaign that is nationally directed.

The *Advisory Council* of the Democratic National Committee is a new and unique national party unit. Set up after the Democrats lost the 1956 presidential election, the Council enunciates the party's position on domestic and foreign policies and thus tries to keep the party platform attuned to changing events. The 25-member Council is composed largely of liberal Democrats such as Harry Truman and Mrs. Franklin D. Roosevelt and hence serves as a

---

[11] V. O. Key, Jr., *Politics, Parties, and Pressure Groups,* 3rd ed. (Crowell, 1952), p. 342.

balancing force against the party's more conservative leadership in Congress. Partly for this reason, partly because they wished to keep their independence from outside party influences, neither Speaker Rayburn nor Majority Leader Johnson joined the Council. As a result, the Council has little influence over Democratic policy in Congress but it raises an eloquent voice for the national party between campaigns. The Republicans have no similar council, but in 1959 they set up a temporary committee on "Program and Progress" that came up with extensive recommendations for party policy.

State Party Organization   At the next lower level in the party hierarchy are the *state committees,* which in general resemble the national committees. They are manned by committeemen chosen locally in counties or other areas. Most state committees are not powerful; they are often dominated by the governor, a United States senator, or a coalition of strong local leaders, just as the President dominates his party's national committee. The state chairman is sometimes the creature of the governor or senator; occasionally, however, he is really the party's boss on the state level and is able to pick—and control— governors, senators, and other key officials. Many state parties are as undisciplined and decentralized as the national party.

Below the fifty state committees each party hierarchy broadens out into countless district and county committees. These, too, vary tremendously in their functions and power. The New York county chairmen are often powerful bosses like the late Ed Flynn of the Bronx, and many county chairmen elsewhere make up the party slates for a host of offices such as county commissioner, sheriff, treasurer, and the like. Some county chairmen, however, are mere figureheads.

It is at the base of the party pyramid—at the city, town, ward, and precinct level—that we find the grass roots of the party in all its richness and profusion. This is the level at which party politics is conducted by thousands of local leaders, not as a free-time diversion but as a round-the-clock, round-the-year occupation. This is where party politics, to quote Mr. Dooley, "ain't bean-bag," but a "professional spoort, like playin' baseball f'r a livin' or wheelin' a truck." The party's sergeants and corporals—the local ward and precinct leaders—are part of the city-wide machine run by the local leader or "boss" who is usually the chairman of the city committee. Their responsibilities are heavy and numerous. Year round they do countless favors for their constituents, from fixing parking tickets and patching up family quarrels to organizing clambakes and supplying free legal help. At election time, when their constituents and their families and friends flock to the polls, the local leaders capitalize on their generosities of the year past. In country areas, the party machinery is usually less tightly organized and disciplined than in the city.

Our party systems are highly complex. For example, the Kansas party organization embraces a state committee, congressional district committees, county committees, state senatorial district committees, state judicial district committees, and precinct committees. The organization of other state parties is hardly less elaborate. Why such complexity? As we have seen in earlier chapters, party politics tends to be highly individualistic and personalized.

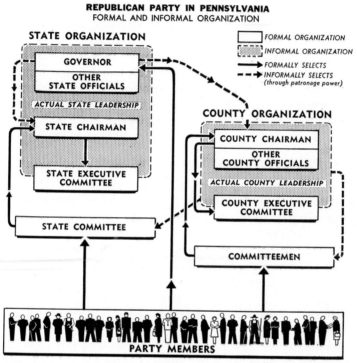

REPUBLICAN PARTY IN PENNSYLVANIA
FORMAL AND INFORMAL ORGANIZATION

Courtesy Samuel Humes

It would be more nearly correct to say that we have *candidate* politics or *office-holder* politics rather than party politics. That is to say, political activity tends to focus on men seeking or holding political power, and on the groups around them, rather than on a unified, hierarchical party system. Since our constitutional arrangements provide for a multiplicity of officeholders at a number of levels of government, our parties are bound to be complicated. The diversity of our country and the absence of strong direction and control by the national party headquarters mean that party systems also vary a good deal from state to state. In Great Britain, one would find about the same party organization and party ideology in Yorkshire, London, Glasgow, and Wales. In our country, the differences between the Democratic party in New York and in Alabama, and between the Republican organizations in Pennsylvania and in California, are quite sharp.

This situation inevitably opens a gulf between national party headquarters and state and local parties. Deepening this gulf is the fact that most election laws are enacted and enforced by the states, not by the national government. "Political parties, as legal entities," says one authority, "are by and large state parties. . . . The national superstructure over the state party organizations, in a sense, derives its power from their consent." [12] Moreover, some states hold their state and local elections in different years from national elections. New York, for example, elects its governors for four-year terms in even-numbered years between presidential elections, and New York City elects its mayors in odd-numbered years.

The gulfs between national and state parties vary from state to state and from year to year. One factor tending to link national and local parties is mutual self-interest; each has a stake in the other's victory. Perhaps more important, most states—especially the more urban ones—are affected by political trends affecting the nation as a whole, as we saw in Chapter 10.

Political Party Trends

In its present form, our two-party system is well over a century old. Attempts have been made to change it: third parties have been formed; the primary system has replaced the convention system in most states; and the early end of one or the other of the major parties is often predicted. Yet, the two parties seem to survive substantially unchanged.

Certain basic forces seem to be at work, however, that may powerfully influence the future shape of our party system.

DECLINE OF THE BOSS?

During the past century local and state bosses have thrived in the American political climate. Men like Boss Crump of Memphis, Ed Kelly of Chicago, Big Bill Thompson of Chicago, and Boss Tweed of New York won nationwide notoriety and put their stamp on American urban politics.

Boss Frank Hague of Jersey City was a good example of the old-time city boss. Raised in Jersey City slums, he worked his way up in local politics, slowly extending his influence through the city. As mayor of the city he consolidated his power by setting up personal organizations in labor, church, business, and veterans groups, stopping newspaper attacks by drastically increasing the hostile newspaper's property-tax assessments, jailing critics, running a huge patronage machine, distributing favors and largesse to the voters, and extending his influence throughout the state. "I am the law," he proclaimed.[13] Hague kept most of his power until his retirement.

---

12 V. O. Key, Jr., *Politics, Parties, and Pressure Groups*, 3rd ed., p. 306.
13 For a full treatment of the Hague machine, see D. D. McKean, *The Boss: The Hague Machine in Action* (Houghton Mifflin, 1940).

A different kind of boss was Edward J. Flynn of the Bronx. An educated and cultivated man, Flynn ran an efficient organization that in certain ways resembled a large business corporation. His machine supported liberal and labor legislation in exchange for union support. Although the Bronx organization was relatively honest, it had the features of most political machines: it dealt in jobs and party spoils; it expected jobholders to contribute to the machine treasury; and it delivered huge Democratic pluralities on election day. Another influential boss was J. Russell Sprague, a Republican leader in Nassau County on Long Island. Disciplined and centralized, his machine ran the county government and helped the Republicans run up heavy pluralities over the Democrats in presidential elections.

Are such bosses and machines on the way out? Perhaps. Few of the old-time city machines are able to deliver the vote as they did in the past. In a recent hard-fought mayoralty contest in New York City, for example, all the Democratic bosses combined could bring hardly a quarter of the registered Democrats to the polls. The boss has far less party patronage today than in the old days. What is left may be more a source of trouble and division to the party leadership [14] than a source of strength. With fewer immigrants arriving in the country, he lacks a reservoir of new citizens. Elections are more closely supervised to prevent old-fashioned ballot-box stuffing. Most important, the welfare functions of modern national, state, and city government have superseded the old charitable activities of the machine.[15]

Yet a funeral service for machine politics would be premature. Bosses may go—but leaders remain. The old-time machine head in command of a whole city or state has given way to the influential governor, senator, or sheriff. These office-holders dominate not as formal *party* leaders but as occupants of important elective posts. For years Governor Dewey was supreme in New York State, Senator Byrd in Virginia, Governor Warren in California, Governor Williams in Michigan. A governor's or senator's office is a far more respectable and efficient place from which to run an organization than the old "back room behind the bar," and today it is more effective in delivering votes and influencing policy.

RISE OF THE INDEPENDENT VOTER?

Some close observers of American politics report that voters are showing a growing disdain for party labels. Most recent presidential elections, it has been estimated, were decided by voters not claiming membership in either of the major parties. Switching back and forth, these voters are said to serve as a balance of power. There is considerable question as to how much inde-

---

[14] F. J. Sorauf, "Patronage and Party," *Midwest Journal of Political Science* (May 1959), pp. 115-126.

[15] For a poignant and amusing picture of an old-fashioned city boss, see the novel *The Last Hurrah* by Edwin O'Connor.

pendent voting has increased. Much depends on the definition of the term, as noted in Chapter 10—for example, whether we mean by an independent someone who "splits his ticket" in favor of candidates of different parties at the same election, or shifts back and forth between parties from election to election, or both.

Is more independent voting desirable? Some argue that it keeps the parties on their toes and prevents either party from holding a monopoly. Others argue that too much independent voting might hurt the major parties by draining away the talent and energy they need to operate efficiently and responsibly. It would be a Pyrrhic victory for the independents themselves, according to this view, if they were to strengthen their power to decide elections, only to discover that they were throwing their weight back and forth between less and less attractive candidates.

In any event, independence and party loyalty are not mutually exclusive. The most valuable partisan may be the man who is independent *within* his party—the man who sits in party councils and presents party regulars with fresh ideas on policies, methods, and candidates. The most valuable independent may be the man who has done what he can within his party and then follows his conscience on election day.

A NATIONWIDE TWO-PARTY SYSTEM?

In the past, most of our states have been dominated by one party. Democratic party control of southern states and Republican party control of northern New England were but extreme examples of the prevailing system. Parties were mainly sectional—Democrats strong in certain states versus Republicans strong in other states—so that real party competition did not exist within the states. In the past fifty years, however, competitive two-party systems have developed within most states. Oregon and Vermont, for example, are no longer guaranteed for the Republicans, nor are all southern states assured for the Democrats.

Political trends in the South are especially interesting. As a result of industrialization, urbanization, migration of northern whites into the South and of Negroes out of it, increased Negro voting, and other economic, social, and political developments, a more competitive two-party system is slowly rising in the South.[16] One southern student distinguishes between the "Inner South" comprising the "black belt" from Georgia to Mississippi, and the "Outer South" composed of the encircling states.[17] The latter, with fewer Negroes and more large cities, is moving faster toward a two-party alignment like that in the rest of the nation. The former will change more slowly but is headed in the same direction. The trend is only a long-term one, however, and

---

[16] Alexander Heard, *A Two Party South?* (Univ. of North Carolina Press, 1952).
[17] William Buchanan, "Cracks in Southern Solidarity," *The Antioch Review* (Fall 1956), pp. 351-364.

the struggle over school integration may impel southerners to veer away from both major parties.

What are the implications of more nationalized parties? Some believe that they will lead to stronger national party organizations than we have had in the past, with less power in the hands of state and local party leaders. Interest groups such as labor and farmers may become even more directly involved in national party politics.[18] Others believe that such a trend might lead to too much centralized party power and to a grave weakening of local and state organizations. They feel that party politics is already becoming too "professionalized," with too much emphasis on campaign management; even party policy, they argue, is being put in the hands of public relations counselors and other experts in the management of modern communications media.[19] This problem of the role of parties will be discussed in more detail in Chapter 21.

American Parties and American Democracy

American political parties are vital to American democracy. They do the jobs that have to be done in any healthy system of representative government. They build a bridge between people and their government. They shore up national unity by bringing warring interests into harmony. They soften the impact of the extremists on both sides. They stimulate and channel public discussion. They find candidates for the voters, and they find voters for the candidates. They help run elections. Parties shoulder much of the hard, day-to-day work of democracy.

Yet today our party system is under attack. The indictment runs somewhat as follows:[20]

Parties are not responsible to their own members. Critics point out that democracy is often conspicuously lacking *within* the party. Bosses control many local parties, urban, suburban, and rural. If there is no single boss, power often falls into the hands of a small oligarchy. The organization of the party—committee piled on committee—obscures the voice of the rank and file. Party committees and conventions, it is argued, often are not representative of party members. Party platforms are drawn up secretly in "smoke-filled rooms." And what does membership mean? Anyone can join a party, no matter where his real sympathies may lie, and can outvote an old party regular who has put in years of service.

---

[18] See the excellent symposium, Sigmund Neumann (ed.), *Modern Political Parties* (Univ. of Chicago Press, 1956), section on United States parties by E. E. Schattschneider, pp. 194-215.

[19] For a vivid treatment of this interesting recent trend, see Stanley Kelley, Jr., *Professional Public Relations and Political Power* (Johns Hopkins Press, 1956).

[20] The following material is drawn in part from "Toward a More Responsible Two-Party System," A Report of the Committee on Political Parties of the American Political Science Association, September 1950, as cited above.

Parties have failed to keep their machinery and organization up to date. These critics allege that formal party organization has changed little in the past century. The parties still have cumbersome committee systems. They fail to make use of modern methods of research and political analysis. The national convention is unwieldy and unrepresentative; it meets only once in four years, and sober discussion is drowned in the uproar and ballyhoo. The parties, it is said, are disorganized. Not only do the national and state organizations operate independently of one another, but even the national organization is divided into a presidential party and a congressional party. Common strategy and common program are lacking.

The parties do not take honest and clear-cut positions. We all know that party platforms are evasive and obscure. Every four years spokesmen of interest groups appear before a bored committee on resolutions, and then a national platform is hastily pieced together. The typical platform seems to be designed to pick up every stray vote rather than to speak out in a forthright manner on the vital questions of the day. The voter often has little choice between party platforms. And they are so vague that candidates can scrap the platform on which they have campaigned and embrace conflicting policies once they have won office. According to an old saying, party platforms are like train platforms—something to get in on, not to stand on.

Parties are irresponsible; they do not deliver on their promises. This is the most important criticism of all. The party in power often shows little responsibility to the majority of voters who put it into power. The President goes in one direction, members of Congress go in others, and state and local organizations act on their own. The party as such is unable to carry out the program on which it was elected. A majority of voters agrees to a party platform at the election; but the party's own members will not agree to that platform when they are in office and presumably able to enact it. The party in power simply is unable to hold its members in line, or to discipline those who fail to live up to party pledges. As for the opposition party, it often fails to criticize the government responsibly or to offer clear alternative policies to the voters.

Yet we must view all these alleged weaknesses in proper perspective. Consider the accusation that our parties lack internal democracy. However true this charge may be, we must remember that the parties are under intense pressure to respond to public opinion as a whole. The party rulers—whether they be local bosses or national leaders—know that the parties must either remain abreast of the times or else lose out to the opposition party or even be displaced by a minor party. Thus the *competition among parties* in a democratic political system in part offsets the lack of democracy *within* them. As for the accusation that our parties straddle issues, it can be said that fence-sitting is part of the *moderating* function of a two-party system, and that some vagueness is inevitable in a country with the economic and geographical diversity of the United States.

TWO BASIC PARTY WEAKNESSES

When all is said and done, two major criticisms of our party system remain. One is that *party machinery* in virtually all the states is *unwieldy and out-of-date*. It is true that the *informal* party structure—for example, the party leadership of the President—in part makes up for the ramshackle nature of the formal organization. But powerful forces are constantly at work dividing and weakening party unity and effectiveness. The national committee, which should do the job of month-to-month governing of the party, is almost powerless. Financially the national party usually exists from hand to mouth. It is often heavily in debt, especially in the years directly following a presidential campaign, and recovers mainly by raising funds from party "fat cats."

A situation underlying this party weakness is indeed curious: *the party has no real rank-and-file membership*. To be sure, individuals may "join" a party by voting in a primary or registering as a party member. But they assume no obligations; they pay no dues; they rarely take part in party discussions of candidates or platforms. A person is usually far more active in his favorite lodge or hobby club than he is in the organization that assumes responsibility for governing the nation—the Democratic or Republican party. Our national parties, in short, have plenty of generals, lieutenants, and sergeants, but practically no privates enlisted in the party cause.

The other major criticism is that of *party irresponsibility*. Indeed, this criticism takes on all the more importance today because of the vital role that parties *could* play in the challenging era in which we live. Today, more than ever before, governmental policies must be coordinated and coherent. One part of the government cannot pursue an inflationary policy, for example, while another is following an anti-inflationary program. Today policies must be *programmatic*—that is, they must fit into a comprehensive and consistent plan. The party—simply because it nominates and elects our chief policy-making officials—is the ideal agency to force these officials in every branch of government to pull together.

But the party does not do this job. It does not even perform the much more elementary task of making politicians live up to whatever hazy and inconsistent promises they make. This basic party weakness affects our whole government. We shall look again at the implications of this weakness (in Chapter 21) after considering how our politicians get into office and how they try to stay in office once they have come to hold power in Washington.

Appeal to the Voters

The preceding four chapters have dealt with the main ingredients of American politics. We have looked at voting behavior—which people vote and fail to vote, how they vote, and why. We have noticed how *opinions* are born and shaped, the various subpublics that hold these opinions, the way opinions can be measured. We have seen something of the role of *interest groups*—their number and complexity, the way they cut across one another and form subgroups, their internal and external relations, their methods of gaining and wielding influence. We have considered parties as grand coalitions of interest groups, doing a variety of important jobs though not always doing them well, sometimes powerful in local activities but poorly coordinated as national agencies.

We have had to consider these factors one at a time, but we must not deceive ourselves into regarding them as separate entities. They are not. Parties, groups, voting behavior, public opinion—all affect one another closely. The forming of political opinions, for example, and the way people vote are largely matters of *group* allegiance and activity, as we have seen. Parties are inseparable from groups, and their role and effectiveness are deeply affected by voting behavior. The close relation between public opinion and voting is obvious. We must see these political processes as a vast network of interrelationships, each process affecting others and in turn being affected by them, all part of a shifting balance of action and counteraction.

The workings of politics seem all the more complex because they so often go on *invisibly*. We cannot actually see Mr. Smith's mind at work as he decides whether or not to vote, or how to vote; we cannot possibly discern the thousands of interrelationships among a number of groups, several political parties, and a maze of political attitudes. But there is one occasion, at least, when some of the labyrinthine attitudes and actions are brought to the surface and exposed to the public view. This occasion is an *election*.

In the election campaign we get some feel for the dominant attitudes of the community, the activities of groups, the role of the party. In the election results we get some idea of the extent of certain attitudes, the power of certain parties and groups, the tendencies of voters, and the number of nonvoters. At least a dim light is thrown on the vast subterranean elements of the political process. In the election itself, the people—who often find it hard to keep their eyes on the many players and the many balls in the great game of politics— finally get the score.

Elections are not merely the showdown for the restless political forces described in the last four chapters. They are also vitally affected by the constitutional and legal factors described earlier in this book. For example, a striking aspect of American elections is that they occur on several levels— local, state, and national. The "federalism" of our elections has an important effect on their outcome and meaning, as we shall see. Again, presidential elections would be different without the electoral college. Constitutional provisions allowing the *states* to administer voting, and the way *states* arrange the balloting, also influence elections. Thus we see again the indivisibility not only of politics in the narrow sense, but of our whole political, legal, and institutional system.

What Every Voter Should Know

It would be pleasant if elections were simple affairs. But they are not. The manner in which they are conducted differs widely from state to state. Their sheer number is amazing —well over a hundred thousand elections a year in all states for all offices, according to the Census Bureau. Voting is a chore as well as a privilege. The Constitution authorizes the state legislatures to regulate the time, place, and manner of congressional elections, but Congress may alter these regulations and may also stipulate the day on which presidential electors shall be chosen and the day on which they should cast their votes. In other respects, Congress has left the regulation of elections almost entirely up to the states. And, of course, each state has control over the election of its own and local officials. The voter who wants to explore the intricacies of voting and registering can talk with election authorities at his local city hall or town office, or consult election law.

Knowing election angles has long been a specialty of political insiders and bosses, but by a little research the interested citizen can also equip himself with the weapon of knowledge. For in elections, too, knowledge is power. Following are merely the ABC's of voting.

REGISTRATION

Almost every state requires that a person must be *registered* if he wants to vote. A registered voter is one who has appeared before election officials during a set period and has established his right to vote. In most states an otherwise qualified voter may register to vote if he has lived in the state for one year; in some states this residence requirement is shorter and in some states (mostly in the South) longer. The would-be voter also must have lived in the election district for a set period, often for six months. Once registered, a person's name appears on registration lists and is checked off when he votes. Residence requirements are designed to give the voter a chance to inform himself about state and local conditions before he votes. Some such requirements, however, are used to deny the ballot to migratory workers or to minority groups, such as Negroes.

Registration is of two types, *permanent* and *periodic*. Under the former system, now used by most states, once the voter is on the list he stays on it as long as he remains in the election district and meets any other requirements established. In a few states a person is dropped from the list if he fails to vote in two successive elections; he must re-register in order to vote again. Permanent registration is easy on the voter, but hard to administer, for election officials must see to it that those who have left the district, have died, or have been committed to an institution, are removed from the list.

The system of periodic registration requires voters to re-register from time to time. This system keeps the registration lists up to date, but it is inconvenient for the voters, expensive, and a deterrent to large voter turn-out.

Al Capp on the importance of registering.

Some states allow absentee registration by persons who must be absent from the state for certain reasons.

Taking part in the selection of party candidates is often as important as voting in the election itself. As we have seen, in almost all the states candidates are chosen in *direct primary elections* rather than in conventions. In almost all states, primaries are financed out of the public treasury, run by the regular election officials, and held in the same polling places as the regular election; moreover, the voters are protected by the same legal safeguards. To get on the primary ballot a candidate usually must file a petition signed by a required number of voters. In practice this means that almost anyone can get on the ballot if he does enough leg work, and the voter may find a large number of names listed on the primary ballot.

Who can vote in a party primary? In most states voters must publicly acknowledge membership in a party in order to help pick that party's nominees. Party membership in the United States is a rather ambiguous matter, and the tests are not very severe. In some states a voter may declare his party allegiance when he registers to vote; in others the voter enrolls as a party member simply by showing up at the party primary to vote. In some states, mainly in the South, voters appearing at the primary must pledge, before receiving the ballot, that they supported the party's nominee at the last election, or will at the next, or both. In any case a voter may change his party affiliation between elections by following prescribed procedures.

All this refers to the *closed* primary, in which the party seeks to close the door of the polling place to all but those who are, in one way or another, party adherents. But a number of states—eight by latest count—have an *open* primary system, under which any qualified voter may participate in the primary of any party he prefers without having to reveal publicly his party affiliation. Except in the state of Washington, however, a voter may participate in only one party's primary. In some open systems the voter receives the ballots of all the parties and then fills out the party ballot he prefers; in others he receives one ballot that lists the candidates of all parties for all offices.

All primary systems allow supporters of one party to enter—or "raid"— the primary of another. The aim may be to nominate the weakest candidate in a rival party's camp. But the *open* primary, exposed to the depredations of one-day Republicans and next-day Democrats, makes raiding particularly easy. For this reason the open primary is deplored by party officials and advocates of more strongly disciplined parties. But it is supported by those who prefer not to reveal their party affiliation or who like to have a free choice on primary day as to the party contest in which they vote.

Several states use a combination convention-primary system. Party conventions—usually called *preprimary conventions*—or committees propose a candidate for each office. The candidate gaining the convention's endorsement then runs in the ensuing primary along with any other aspirants who may wish to compete without that endorsement. This procedure informs the voter of the official party choice of candidates but still leaves him free, if he wishes, to support any other candidate who may enter the race. Two states have *postprimary conventions,* which select party nominees in the event that no candidate polls at least 35 per cent of the vote in the primary.

The *runoff primary* is used in about ten southern or border states. In most of these states the Democratic nomination automatically leads to election, because of the weakness of the Republican opposition. Sometimes so many candidates file in the Democratic primary that the leader may capture only 20 or 30 per cent of the total vote. Under the runoff, if no candidate wins a majority in the first election, the two highest candidates run against each other in a second primary.

In the so-called *nonpartisan primary,* no party designations are permitted; candidates who can qualify simply file and the two candidates who receive the most votes run against each other in the general election. *Crossfiling* also has a nonpartisan or at least a bipartisan tinge. Formerly used most notably in California, it allows a candidate to enter the primaries of more than one party. A candidate may win *both* major party primaries and thus in effect win the election, as former Governor Earl Warren did in California in 1946. California has recently abolished cross-filing, however.

Since the arrangements for party primaries differ greatly from state to state, the voter would do well to inquire at his city hall or town clerk's office about local practices.

BALLOTING

Nowhere are fairness and accuracy more important than in the handling of elections. In balloting, the *Australian ballot system* has long been accepted as a model. Under this system—used in Queensland as early as 1857—the government (rather than the parties or candidates, as had been the earlier practice) prints uniform ballots on good-quality paper, listing the names of all the candidates. Ballots are given to voters only on election day, only at the official polling place, and only by public officials. The ballots are marked secretly, folded, and deposited unopened in a ballot box. We tend to take these arrangements for granted nowadays, but each one was adopted only after hard experience. For example, the use of good-quality paper balks the old trick of issuing tissue-paper ballots that enabled sharp-eyed party workers to see where a voter put his mark after the ballot was folded. Certain aspects of ballots and voting are worth noting:

The *office-group ballot* lists together the names and party designations of all candidates for the same office. Candidates for the highest office, such as President and governor, usually come first and then state and local candidates. Since this type of ballot makes it impossible to vote a straight ticket with a single mark, it encourages independent and split-party voting.[1] It also leads to voter fatigue and to failure to vote for the offices at the bottom of the ballot.

The party-column ballot groups candidates by *party* in columns. A voter can vote for all the candidates of a party, from President to sheriff, simply by making his mark in a large circle or box next to the party's name and emblem. Or he may "scratch his ticket"—that is, go from column to column marking his choice for each office. The party-column ballot encourages straight party voting.

Stickers and write-ins are devices for making last-minute changes in the ballot—for example, when a candidate withdraws or dies after the ballots have been printed. The voter may either paste in a gummed sticker or write in the name of the candidate of his choice. These devices are allowed in some states as a means of voting for some candidate other than the offerings of the parties on the ballot, but write-in or sticker campaigns are rarely successful.

Absentee voting. Almost all the states allow certain persons, such as servicemen, to vote away from home. In order to prevent fraud, however, absentee voting has been made so difficult and cumbersome that often only the most zealous citizen will go to the trouble of sending in an absentee ballot.

Stuffing the ballot box. This is a type of ballot fraud, but the term often is used to denote all methods of fraud. There have been—and still are—so many of these as to defy description; they involve frauds in marking ballots, in collecting them, and in counting them. The "endless chain" or "Tasmanian Dodge" indicates the ingenuity of the corruptionists. A person buying votes will manage somehow (there are various ways) to secure an unmarked ballot. He fills this out, gives it to the bought voter, who enters the polling place, receives a ballot, deposits the *previously* marked one, and brings out the unmarked one for the vote buyer to fill out and hand to his next man. By this method the corruptionist knows that the ballots are being cast just as he wishes.

Voting machines. Originally patented in the United States by Thomas A. Edison, the voting machine is designed to stop ballot frauds and to make vote-counting accurate and speedy. The machines are expensive, and some voters seem to find them difficult to manipulate, but their advantages have led to their use or authorization in over half the states.

THE LONG BALLOT AND THE SHORT

The "long ballot" represents reality, the "short" ballot mainly a hope. In filling out the long ballot, which is used by most of the states, the baffled voter must decide among a fantastic array of candidates for legislative and

---

[1] Angus Campbell and Warren E. Miller, "The Motivational Basis of Straight and Split Ticket Voting," *The American Political Science Review* (June 1957), pp. 293-312.

administrative offices. In one case a ballot was twelve feet long and contained almost five hundred names. Tree warden, coroner, secretary of state, county treasurer, highway inspector—candidates for these and many more offices are crowded onto the ballot, along with lengthy questions or propositions to be accepted or rejected by the voters.

The more insignificant the office, the fewer the voters who know the qualifications of the candidates, and the greater the likelihood that party organizations or interested groups can elect their favorites, good or bad.

There has long been a movement to shorten the ballot by restricting officials popularly elected to those concerned with broad policy determination. But progress has been slow, and the "tablecloth" or "bedsheet" ballot is still common. Many states have, however, adopted the *presidential short ballot,* which, instead of listing the names of all the electors of each party, carries only the names of the presidential and vice-presidential candidates to

Herblock in *The Washington Post and Times Herald*

whom the electors are pledged. By casting one vote for President and Vice President, the voter in effect chooses the entire party slate of electors.

Money and Elections

Elections cost money—often a great deal of it. Reported expenditures by national party organizations in 1956 presidential and congressional campaigns totaled over 13 million. Candidates for the Senate and House of Representatives reported spending over three million in 1958. Many millions more were spent locally on state, county, and city contests. These are the expenditures reported under the law; much—perhaps most—of the spending is never reported. One authority has estimated that $140,000,000 was expended by candidates, their friends, and other interested people (a campaign for governor or senator in a large state can easily cost half a million dollars) in 1952 for nominating and electing all public officials in the United States,[2] and spending in 1956 and 1960 was doubtless at least as much.

---

2 Alexander Heard, *Money and Politics,* Public Affairs Pamphlet No. 242, 1956, p. 2.

Where does the money go? A half-hour program on a coast-to-coast television network costs (depending on the coverage) from $50,000 to $100,000. A one-minute television spot in a medium-sized city may cost $50. A full-page ad in a big-city newspaper costs $2500. Campaign buttons cost three cents each, and candidates distribute tens of thousands of them. One mailing to every voter in a medium-sized state might cost $20,000.[3] Gasoline, telephone, printing, posters, rental of headquarters, hiring paid help—all these and many other items send expenses soaring.

WHERE THE MONEY COMES FROM

Donations to the party treasury come from many sources. In presidential campaigns the national headquarters of the parties take in millions of dollars. Those who have given most to the Republicans in recent presidential elections have been bankers, brokers, manufacturers, utilities, and insurance, mining, and oil interests; to the Democrats, brewers, distillers, contractors, builders, the professions, merchants, amusement and related interests.[4] Wealthy family groups often make big donations. In 1956, the duPonts gave over $248,000 to the Republicans, the Pews $216,000, the Rockefellers, $152,000. Enjoying less support from such big givers, the Democrats run a series of Jackson Day dinners throughout the country, charging from $5 to $100 per plate. Labor usually gives far more to the Democrats than to the Republicans. A little money comes to both parties from small donors, but most of the campaign chest is filled by large contributors. In 1956, for example, both parties together received over $33 million, and well over half of this came in donations of over $1000. Only about 5 per cent of the voters give any money at all to the parties or candidates.

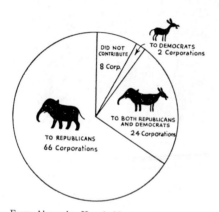

From Alexander Heard, *Money and Politics*, Public Affairs Pamphlet. No. 242, Oct. 1956

How 100 corporations' officers and directors contributed to campaign funds.

State and local parties also receive direct gifts, but much of their money comes from candidates and especially from officeholders. Sometimes candidates give money to local parties in exchange for help from the parties. Assessing appointed officeholders often is a lucrative source of income to the parties.

---

[3] From Ivan Hinderaker, *Party Politics* (Holt, 1956), pp. 579-581.
[4] See analyses by Louise Overacker, *The American Political Science Review*, Vol. 35 (1941), p. 723, and Vol. 39 (1945), p. 916; and Key, *Politics, Parties, and Pressure Groups*.

Although usually kept under cover, the shakedown may be very important. It was revealed in Philadelphia, for example, that 3 to 5 per cent of city workers' salaries was collected by the Republican city committee, and 1 to 2 per cent by the ward committees where the employees lived. Some years ago the Democrats in Indiana ran a notorious "Two Per Cent Club" on the same model.

Why do people give? Mainly because they want something, usually for themselves. City jobholders want to stay in office. Candidates want the party's good will and support. Big donors often want the party's men in office to follow certain policies. Businessmen are concerned about taxes, tariffs, and subsidies. Labor may want the repeal of antiunion legislation. Distillers may hope to get dry laws repealed. Builders want government contracts; suppliers want to sell to government agencies; insurance companies want to write policies covering government property. Some big donors hope to gain prized positions, such as ambassadorships. Often what contributors want is nothing tangible but simply an "entree" or access to those in power in case the need arises.[5]

Herblock in *The Washington Post and Times Herald*

"It's terrible how the big money guys run politics."

The motive for giving is not always direct self-interest, however. Thousands of contributors simply believe the party of their choice will govern best for the whole people. Still, the number of small contributions by the "average citizen" is lamentably low. Most party and campaign contributions come from big donors with an axe to grind.

REGULATIONS ON PARTY FINANCES

The national and state governments have made frequent, but not very successful, attempts to publicize party finances, and to limit contributions and expenditures through *corrupt practices legislation* and other laws. Organiza-

---

5 Alexander Heard, *op. cit.* For excellent material on this general problem, including recommendations from political scientists and others, see "Federal Elections Act of 1955," *Hearings Before the Subcommittee on Privileges and Elections, Committee on Rules and Elections, United States Senate, 84th Congress, 1st Sess.*, on S. 636 (Government Printing Office, 1955).

tions receiving or spending money to influence the election of national officials under certain conditions must file statements with the clerk of the House of Representatives giving the names of all persons contributing over $100, of all persons to whom payments of more than $10 have been made, and a total of all receipts and all expenditures. The national government and most of the states have long prohibited contributions from certain types of corporations, and in 1947 the Taft-Hartley Act barred *any* corporation or labor organization from giving or spending money in connection with elections to national offices or in conventions or primaries choosing candidates for such offices.

Campaign spending is sharply limited. Under federal law, a candidate for representative may not spend more than $2500, a candidate for senator not more than $10,000 or, as an alternative, three cents per vote cast for all candidates for the office at the last general election, but no more than $25,000 for a senator and $5000 for a representative. The Hatch Act of 1939 and later amendments limit spending by any single political committee to $3 million a year and contributions by individuals to each candidate or nationally affiliated party committee to $5000 annually, and it forbids forced contributions from government officeholders to candidates or parties. This act also makes it "unlawful for any person employed in the executive branch of the federal government, or any agency or department thereof, to use his official authority or influence for the purpose of interfering with an election or affecting the result thereof." Such federal employees can vote but they cannot take an active part in party affairs or political campaigns.

How effective are these regulations on campaign finance? The consensus is: not very. Much of the legislation is filled with loopholes and is poorly enforced. Full publicity is often evaded by filing reports after the election is over or by submitting inadequate or even false reports. Corporations make campaign contributions through personal offerings of executives and their families, labor unions through more or less voluntary offerings by their members. The lawmakers, politicians themselves, have made no attempt to pass really rigorous or airtight laws in this field, and it is not certain that such an attempt would be successful, given traditional American attitudes toward such laws.

Senators studying the problem have recently recommended these steps to strengthen the regulation of party finance: 1. Require *all* committees working for a candidate to report contributions and expenditures. 2. Bring all *primary* elections under the law (some are already covered). 3. Prohibit political committees from receiving or spending funds for a candidate without his authorization. 4. Require every person who spends more than $1000 for candidates seeking national office to file a report. 5. Open all reports to public inspection. 6. Raise maximum spending limits to $250,000 for senators and $25,000 for representatives. 7. Limit maximum spending for committees operating in more than one state to $10 million instead of the present $3 million. 8. Restrict individual contributions to candidates or political committees to a total of $10,000, and forbid the present practice whereby one person may give $5000 contributions to any number of candidates. One senator has warned that unless the regulation of party finance is strengthened, such drastic steps as governmental financing of candidates will have to be resorted to.

Mr. Smith Runs for Congress

When we think about elections we usually picture exciting national campaigns, fighting speeches watched by millions of televiewers, political caravans crossing the nation in a blaze of publicity. But not all campaigns for national office are like this. A candidate for Congress often finds that a campaign means a lot of dull legwork and exhausting rounds of speeches to small audiences. "When you get away from the national arena," Pearson and Allen have written, "political campaigning gets right back to the old horse-and-buggy days. . . . What really counts is the all-important ingredient of personal contact." How a member of Congress wins office is important; watching him as a campaigner helps us understand him as a congressman. Let us look at the mythical—but rather typical—case of John Smith, aspirant to Congress.[6]

Why does Mr. Smith want to run for Congress in the first place? Obviously he wants to be a congressman—but so do many other people. In Mr. Smith's case, his decision is not easy. The incumbent, he knows, will be hard to beat. He's not sure that this will be a good year for his party. A campaign will mean practically deserting his law practice for three or four months. It will cost money. On the other hand, he thinks he can win. He has served as district attorney and state senator, and he feels ready for bigger things. And, he reflects, a little campaigning might help advertise his law practice even if he shouldn't win. So Mr. Smith throws his hat into the ring.

First, Mr. Smith must win the party nomination. The party's candidate two years ago lost so badly that he is not making the attempt again, but there are several other candidates in the field. Mr. Smith knows that primary contests usually do not arouse much public attention, involve important public issues, or attract a large vote. He decides on the following strategy: First, to make a special appeal to party officials in the towns and cities throughout the district. Although the party chairmen and committeemen are supposed to stay neutral in the primary contest, actually they are willing to help their friends in an informal way. Second, to establish close relations with organizations that try to induce their members to vote on primary day. So Mr. Smith spends some time talking with leaders of farm and labor organizations in the district. Third, to stress his name and personality rather than issues.

---

[6] For excellent case studies, presented in detail, of the actual campaigns of two candidates for representative, see S. K. Bailey and H. D. Samuel, *Congress at Work* (Holt, 1952), pp. 112-135. See also the illuminating studies of primary and election campaigns, "Case Studies in Practical Politics," sponsored by the Eagleton Foundation Advisory Board at Rutgers University and published by Holt.

In his public talks Mr. Smith must speak cautiously. He must answer the arguments or criticisms of his fellow partisans who are opposing him within his own party primary, but he must not treat them too harshly, because if he wins he will need their support and that of their followers in the general election. He must identify himself with the party in order to gain the backing of the party organization—but not too closely if he hopes to win over support from the opposition party or from independents in the general election. But his main job is to stir up interest. Most people are indifferent toward primary elections. Only a third of the registered voters cast ballots on primary day.

At last the primary rolls around, and Mr. Smith receives more votes than any of his opponents. Even though he lacks a majority of the votes, no runoff election is required in Mr. Smith's state (as it is in some) between the two highest candidates. So Mr. Smith becomes the official candidate of his party.

PLANNING TACTICS

Right away Mr. Smith begins to face a host of new questions: On what issues should he take a stand? Should he adopt the national platform and try to wage his fight on the basis of broad issues such as foreign policy, taxes, labor legislation, housing, and the like? Or should he slant his appeals to the local concerns of the people in the district? Probably Mr. Smith will compromise between the two approaches. What about campaign tactics? Should he devote his time to making party speeches at rallies, touring the district with a public-address system on his car, making as many personal appearances as possible? Or should he operate behind the scenes, building up a personal machine throughout the area, talking with leaders of interest groups, sending out quantities of written material?

What about publicity? Many media are available—local radio and television, newspaper advertisements, outdoor posters, lapel buttons, automobile stickers, booklets with full stories of Mr. Smith and his platform, leaflets that simply play up a few slogans, matchbooks with a thumbnail "blurb," comic books that present Mr. Smith's life dramatically in many colors. And what about the theme of his publicity? Should he play up the fact that he's a family man, with pictures of himself with his wife and three children, or would this seem undignified to the voters?

Then there's the problem of money. An all-out campaign could easily cost $10,000. Of course the federal law is supposed to limit his spending, but Mr. Smith is not worried about that. He knows that it is easy enough to arrange for persons or organizations supporting him to pay for their pro-Smith activities without turning the money over to him. What really worries him is where the money will come from. He has only $1500 of his own to put into the fight. Contributions to his cause are limited by law but, again, he knows that such laws are easily evaded. As it turns out, Mr. Smith gets contributions from a variety of sources. His friends chip in with donations. He receives a few hundred dollars from national and state party headquarters. Being friendly with union labor, he gets a sizable contribution from that source. Some money comes from people who also contribute to Mr. Smith's opponent, on the theory that it is well to have a foot in both doors.

By midsummer—three months before election day—Mr. Smith is running hard. He equips his sedan with sound equipment and a large sign, "VOTE FOR SMITH for Congress." A typical day goes like this:

6:00 A.M. Up early to finish some letters he is sending to local party leaders.

9:00 A.M. Meets at his house with some candidates for local office who want his support.

10:00 A.M. Off in his car for a series of open-air talks. First stop is at crowded street intersection in his home city.

12:00-1:00 P.M. Talks to workers at gates of factories in district's largest industrial area.

1:30 P.M. Lunch with local Smith workers.

2:00-4:00 P.M. Visits party headquarters in the towns; arranges for distribution of leaflets by canvassers.

4:00-6:00 P.M. More talks over the loud-speaker, concentrating on people returning home from work.

6:30 P.M. Ten-minute radio talk over local station.

7:00 P.M. Hurried dinner alone in restaurant. Works on notes for evening rally.

8:00 P.M. Big party rally in city auditorium. Candidates for governor and senator also attend. Mr. Smith is given 15 minutes to explain his platform, but is interrupted halfway through by arrival of gubernatorial candidate, and surrenders floor to him.

11:00 P.M. Home again, and works on some mail before getting to bed.

REACHING THE MAN IN THE STREET

Mr. Smith's biggest problem is simply *getting to* the voters. The crowds on the street seem more curious than really interested. The people who come to party rallies seem to be already committed. How can he establish contact with the thousands of voters who do not go to party rallies or listen to speeches or pay much attention to elections at all? Mr. Smith finds that one way to reach such voters is through the leaders of organized interest groups in his district, which, like most congressional districts, is a complex of economic, religious, nationality, racial, and occupational groups. He makes every effort to gain the support of organization leaders and to induce them to introduce him formally or informally to their members. He speaks before countless groups of veterans, union members, farmers, Polish-Americans, Italo-Americans, and the like.

In appealing for the support of leaders and rank and file, he makes many promises about his future actions as a congressman. To labor he promises repeal of the Taft-Hartley Act, to farmers the continuation of price supports, to businessmen the protection by government of little business, to veterans the safeguarding of ex-servicemen's rights. Yet he never feels sure whether these appeals are striking home. The questions from the audience make him wonder whether his labor audience is concerned more about Taft-Hartley or about taxes, the veterans more about bonuses or foreign policy. In short, he comes up hard against the problem of overlapping membership of groups (see Chapter 12). He finds it difficult to thread his way through the maze of criss-crossing group interests. But at least the groups and group leaders give him a sense of contact with the voters, and for that he is grateful. Otherwise he would feel as though he were campaigning in a vacuum.

Mr. Smith discovers that the local party organization is of little help. Much of the drudgery falls on his own shoulders; little is carried by city and town committees. Mr. Smith himself must supervise much of the work of getting people to register—checking lists and mailing letters reminding people that they must register to vote. He gets most of his help not from the party but from personal friends and leaders of interest groups. He finds that the party organization does not function as a unit but as a collection of people who attach themselves to the fortunes of particular candidates, and that often he himself must activate local party organizations to get them into motion. In effect, Mr. Smith must *build his own machine*. Naturally he develops little

"How does he stand on reciprocal trade agreements? That's what I want to know."

Drawing by Robt. Day, Copr. © 1958, *The New Yorker Magazine, Inc.*

sense of obligation to the party, but a great deal to a number of leaders of other organizations who work zealously in his cause.

Nor does Mr. Smith run on the party platform as such. Rather, he feels his way on issues, trying to gauge the interests and opinions of his audiences as he goes along. Some voters are mainly concerned with local matters, such as a proposed new highway or hospital. Others are more interested in the big issues, but their opinions often show little consistency. In the end he decides that issues as such have not played the most important role in the campaign, but rather his ability to establish personal contact with as many voters as possible. Most of the people, he discovers, are not only ignorant of the record of the incumbent congressman; they do not even know his name. Mr. Smith's biggest job is to drive his own name into the consciousness of the voters so that they will have at least a faint glimmer of recognition when they see "John Smith" among the many names on the ballot.

Election day finds Mr. Smith tired but hopeful. He tours the polling places, where his helpers are bringing people to the polls. By early evening the election returns start to come in over the radio. With pad and pencil Mr. Smith checks his votes against the returns of previous years. It is a seesaw battle, and more than once Mr. Smith thinks the day is lost. But he is ahead when the final returns come in the next morning. Only then does he really start to think about being a congressman.

Mr. Douglas Runs
for Senator   **S**o much for the mythical, but fairly typical, campaign of Mr. Smith for Congress. It is harder to generalize about campaigns for the United States Senate, if only because of the sharp differences in state populations. But the following true-life tale of his race for the Senate in 1948 by Senator Paul H. Douglas, written in the middle of the campaign, suggests some of the problems of campaigning.[7]

RUNNING FOR OFFICE MEANS JUST THAT

The contrast between American and British campaign practices is summed up in the verbs used to describe the activities of candidates. In Great Britain one "stands" for office. In the United States we "run" for it.

As a candidate for the United States Senate from Illinois, I have a vivid sense of that word "run"—and for this reason:

Illinois holds some 8,300,000 people, divided evenly between Chicago and its suburbs on the one hand, and "down-state" on the other. And in both areas the people come from all the world's racial and religious stocks, settled in massive blocks of tens of thousands. The ways in which they make their living are as varied as the people themselves.

---

[7] *The New York Times Magazine,* September 5, 1948, p. 5 ff.; reprinted by permission of *The New York Times Magazine* and of Senator Douglas.

In industry—and moving from north to south—there are giant railroad yards, meat packing plants, steel mills and machine shops, oil fields and coal mines. Farming, on the other hand, and moving from south to north, includes cotton planting in "Little Egypt," where the soil shows signs of exhaustion; the superb corn fields of mid-Illinois, and pedigreed dairy cattle in the northern regions.

Add together the natural variety of interests which comes from such a setting and the task facing a candidate in Illinois can be seen. I have been "running" for office in every corner of the state almost incessantly ever since I was recommended by the state committee for nomination in January. And I have been "sprinting" since I was formally nominated by the Democratic party in April.

Following the state committee's action in January of this year I got hold of a jeep station wagon, had it equipped for sound and took to the road. In the primary campaign during the three months that followed I made 250 speeches and visited eighty out of our 102 counties. Since the primaries last May, I have made approximately 700 speeches in over 300 towns and cities in every county in the state. And the formal campaign doesn't open until Labor Day. A word hasn't been invented yet to describe the form of running that takes place between then and November.

My style of campaigning follows this pattern:

I pull up my sound-equipped jeep wagon at a factory gate during a change in shifts, or on a village street, or somewhere else near the main flow of people. I introduce myself to whatever crowd gathers, and then summarize the main themes of the campaign. Afterward I move among the clusters of people to shake hands and to distribute campaign literature which they can read at leisure. In this way I've spoken to about 225,000 people and have shaken hands with over 100,000 of them. . . .

There is a reason for this direct work. The average voter wants to see the candidates for office and form a visual as well as auditory judgment of them. But the voter is either too busy to go to formal political meetings, or he discounts them as being long winded, hot and blatantly partisan. It becomes necessary, therefore, for the candidate to go direct to the voters.

ON BEING THE OBJECT OF ABUSE

Physical exertion is, however, the least of the burdens a candidate must bear. He must expect in advance to be abused and misrepresented. Indeed, the way the courts have interpreted the libel laws of the nation, political leaders are set up as fair game for any attack short of murder. The whole spirit of those laws says to the candidate for elective office: "Brother, whatever happens to you—you asked for it!" It is only human, of course, for a candidate to be nettled now and then by the bare-faced lies that are spread about him. And in my own case, on being subjected to them, I at first shared the thoughts of young Count Rostov in "War and Peace." As he saw the French lancer come at him in his first engagement, young Rostov asked: "Is it really true that this man wants my life—I whom my mother loves?"

Once the candidate has entered the race he must please everyone . . .

A sore throat and temperature of 102 cannot keep him from the hustings . . .

He must be against the Taft-Hartley Law and a champion of labor . . .

A few ill-chosen words on the golf course can kill the church vote . . .

and at the same time finance his campaign with management's contributions . . .

and a moment of absent-mindedness will cost him the support of the vets . . .

Roy Doty in *The New York Times*

The candidate runs for office.

It was a source of dismay—and also the beginning of wisdom—to discover that not everyone loved me!

Since I aim to be a liberal progressive, I find myself being attacked by both the extreme left and the extreme right. The Communists whisper that I am anti-Semitic, anti-Negro, an advocate of a preventive war against Russia and the tool of bankers and industrialists. The extreme right, on the other hand, calls me a Socialist and a crafty fellow-traveler. It might seem that such mutually contradictory attacks would largely cancel themselves out, but in practice each group aims its propaganda at the circles which are closest to it, with the result that various sections of the population can at the same time believe in conflicting and slanderous reports.

It is this personal abuse which deters most competent men from running for public office. It is as though certain types of politicians tried to make the going so rough that they would shut off competition from all except their own kind, who are protected by the proverbial rhinoceros hide. . . .

He can lose the election by being seen in a non-union barber shop.

Is it all worth it? Only the returns on election day can tell.

PRESSURES ON THE CANDIDATE

In my campaigns I've also been brought face to face with the forces which make politicians "crooked." Though I have no wealth, I have been able to earn enough in private pursuits to support my family. Yet not every politician is so situated. If he has no private means and is not skilled in a trade or profession, then the expenses of campaigning and the demands that are made upon him when he is elected exert a tremendous pressure on him to cut a few corners. . . .

With respect to the "crooked" politician, many voters who are the first to denounce him are also the first to stake out a claim to the fruits of his corruption. The way they do this is an unwitting one. Hundreds of individuals and organizations in a city or state—devoted to the very best of causes—expect the elected politician to contribute to those causes, to buy tickets to their functions or political advertisements in their fund-raising programs. The politician who balks at these demands is met with a veiled or open threat that the voting strength of the organization will be turned against him at election time.

It could be said that the politician should gladly suffer defeat and remain honest. But being human, most politicians want to stay in office, and so some make "deals" with unlawful sources of income in order to meet the demands of lawful organizations performing fine community activities—including the waging of campaigns against "crooked" politicians.

And yet, as between the politicians on the one hand with their genuine "liking for people," and the class of reformers on the other hand who think of good government as being merely a good bookkeeping process, my personal preference, like Lincoln Steffens', runs to the former type—with all their lamentable faults.

ON TAKING AN HONEST STAND

The greatest danger to the functioning of the democratic process comes in the area of ideas and social policies. There is a subtle temptation, which operates on every candidate, to say things he doesn't believe in order to get votes, or for the same reason, to urge contradictory policies before different groups. It is this aspect of political activity which I would call most "crooked." . . .

By the most pragmatic of tests, I have found that a straightforward and consistent approach to any problem brings higher personal rewards than a policy of doubletalk. For instance, I have been a lifelong advocate of unionism and collective bargaining. Yet in this campaign I've reminded union audiences many times about the ways in which their movements could be improved. In every case I found the response of labor to be an approving and hearty one.

Closely related to this danger of being all things to all men is the added danger of treating people as votes and not as persons—as means to the end of winning an election rather than as ends in themselves. As a college student I was thrilled by Immanuel Kant's rule that one "should treat humanity, whether in one's self or in another, always as an end, never as a means." This imperative means that one should really care for people, whether they are partisans for or against you, or in the "no opinion" group. It means a constant view of politics as having one aim—the promotion of justice—justice for all men—and not the mere acquisition of power for one man.

I have dwelt at length on the trials of a campaign without mentioning its rewards. There are many of these rewards—which are independent of how things turn out at the polls. In talking face to face with people you get a renewed personal assurance of the essential decency and fairness of the human race. Most men in fact try to do good and avoid evil. Abundant proofs can be offered, of course, of the many times when community passions have twisted matters so that men in the mass act contrary to their own ultimate interests. Yet the search for truth is not killed off. It reasserts itself as the stronger force in our life and in time bears its fruits.

A second gain from these campaigns is a better appreciation of how vital our democratic process actually is. It is an unending source of joy to see thousands upon thousands of men and women of all ages and in all stations of life lend their efforts to the advancement of political causes. These people are not paid workers. They do not stand to benefit directly from a political victory for their candidate. But they do appreciate the indirect benefits of victory—the creation of an America which better fits their own dreams. . . .

For all its demands, a vigorous "politics" in which everyone takes sides is, paradoxically, the best way to bring about a fuller sense of the community of interest. But underneath all this is needed a sense of the basic unity which should bind men together and should provide a feeling of good-will to all.

Fundamentally men are brothers and the heat and passion of political struggle should not make us forget that fact.

How to Be Nominated for President

To attain the Presidency a man has to run two races and win them both. First he must be nominated at his party's national convention, and this is sometimes the harder of the two jobs. Then he must get a majority of the nation's electoral votes.

The first "national" convention was probably held in 1808, when a few Federalist leaders met secretly in New York to nominate candidates for President and Vice President. In 1831, under Jackson's leadership, the first real national convention was held by a major party. Today the national convention is a famous and unique political institution. Every four years each party convention enjoys—usually for about a week—world attention; covered by batteries of cameras and microphones and by hundreds of newsmen, every incident in the great convention hall is carried to millions in this country and abroad.

Make-up: Each party has the double task of giving convention representation to the states roughly in proportion to their size, and of giving a "bonus" to states that have a heavier concentration of party strength. The *apportionment* of delegates among the states reflects the attempt to do both these things.

The Democratic party allows each state a delegation twice the size of its congressional representation (Michigan, for example, automatically gets 36 delegates, Nebraska 8), plus a bonus of four more delegates if the state went Democratic in the last election. The Republicans also grant a bonus, but they have the special problem that in many southern areas no Republican bothers to run for office, or gets very many votes if he does. So the Republicans have adopted a complex "sliding-scale" system under which a bonus is given for states and districts that have gone Republican at the last election, but if a congressional district cast less than 2000 votes for a Republican presidential or congressional candidate at the last election, it gets no delegate at all. Each party also seats delegates from Puerto Rico, the Virgin Islands, and the District of Columbia, even though those areas cast no electoral votes for President. Under these arrangements the Republicans have about 1300 delegate votes, the Democrats about 1500.

Certain aspects of apportionment arrangements may be confusing. For one thing, in the Democratic convention there are usually more *delegates* than delegate *votes;* to make room for all the party leaders and workers who wish to take part in the convention, some Democratic state parties allow extra-large delegations, in which each delegate may have only half a vote. *Alternate* delegates also attend both conventions and get into the show, if only from a back seat. Second, the rules may change from convention to convention; some of the arrangements for 1960 described above are different from earlier conventions. Third, some delegates are elected for the whole state and are called "delegates at large"; others are elected by congressional districts, and are called "district delegates."

Choosing delegates: The method of selecting delegates is set by *state* law and varies considerably from state to state. In about two-thirds of the states,

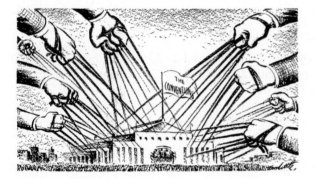

Convention delegates respond to the pulls of many interests.

Courtesy *The New York Times Magazine* and Tom Little

delegates are chosen by party *conventions* or committees. In about one-third, which includes most of the populous states, delegates are picked in state *presidential primaries.* A few states use a combination of the two methods. The *convention* system tends to put selection of the delegation into the hands of a party "inner circle." This may be no problem where the party is vigorous and the leadership representative, but that is often not the case. Most Republican party organizations in the South, for example, have tended to be little "closed corporations" controlled by a few Republican officeholders in Washington with the help of patronage. In such situations the question of who has the right to speak for the rank and file of the party becomes very obscure. This was a main cause of the fierce fight between the Taft and Eisenhower forces in the 1952 Republican convention, culminating in the unseating of the Taft delegations from Georgia, Louisiana, and Texas, and the seating of the Eisenhower forces.

Presidential primaries, the other chief method of choosing delegates, come in many forms. The basic system is for delegates to be elected directly by persons voting in state presidential primaries, which take place variously from March through June of election year. But the primaries vary widely in the extent to which they enable the voter to indicate his preference for the party's presidential nominee by his vote for a candidate for delegate. At one extreme a voter may choose between rival delegate aspirants definitely pledged to specific candidates, and he may also indicate his *personal preference* for President by checking or listing the name of his favorite. At the other extreme a voter may have only the choice of approving a slate of faithful party delegates whose preferences for the presidential nomination are completely unknown to him. Most systems fall between these extremes.

Here are some examples of the main types of presidential primary: [8]

1. *Direct* election of delegates; *no* indication of delegate preference on ballot. *No* presidential preference poll, or inconsequential if held. Examples: West Virginia, Nebraska, New York, Pennsylvania.

2. *Direct* election of delegates; presidential preference *poll;* the presidential *preferences* of *delegates* may appear on the ballot. Examples: New Hampshire, Massachusetts, New Jersey.

3. Combined ballot offering a single-mark opportunity to express a presidential *preference* and to *vote* for a slate of delegates *committed* to the preferred candidate. Examples: California, South Dakota, Wisconsin.

This variety of methods of choosing delegates, combined with the variety of power patterns in state parties, makes it impossible to generalize about the nature of the final delegations. Some may be under the thumb of a powerful state party leader. Others may be "split wide open." Some may be willing to "go down the line" for some presidential candidate. Others may veer from candidate to candidate. Most state delegations mirror the factions in the state party, but sometimes a strong and well-organized group will gain control of the whole delegation.[9]

One thing is clear. The mere adoption of a presidential primary system does not guarantee a delegation that will reflect rank-and-file wishes. Turnout in presidential primaries, as in most primaries, tends to be low. Often presidential candidates simply ignore state primaries, as Adlai E. Stevenson did in 1952, and still win the nomination. Herbert Hoover fared badly in state primaries in 1928 but won both the nomination and the election. Sometimes, on the other hand, success in presidential primaries is decisive, as in the case of Adlai Stevenson's string of state victories in the spring of 1956.

---

[8] Drawn from an analysis by Paul T. David, director of the Cooperative Research Project on Convention Delegations, which, through the participation of political scientists in each state, has made the fullest study ever conducted of the actual methods used to select convention delegates.

[9] For a carefully prepared proposal for state presidential primary improvement, see Manning J. Dauer, William A. F. Stephenson, Harry Macy, and David Temple, "Toward a Model State Presidential Primary Law," *The American Political Science Review* (March 1956), pp. 138-153.

The system is undermined by the tendency of many state delegations, no matter how chosen, to support a "favorite son"—a prominent state leader but often not of "presidential timber"—who is a convenient person to ballot for while the delegation leaders bargain with the main candidates. It can be said for presidential primaries, though, that they have stimulated interest in the early stages of presidential nominations, have opened up the machinery to rank-and-file participation where the voters have been interested enough to use it, and have enabled the country to get some idea—though not a very accurate one—of the popularity of rival candidates in some of the states.

Herblock in *The Washington Post and Times Herald*

"Let's see—four oranges plus three apples, minus one monkey wrench, times two bushels—"

Organizing the convention: The chairman of the national committee presides over the national convention until temporary officers are chosen; these in turn officiate until the convention elects permanent officers. A committee on *credentials* has the power to make recommendations to the convention in the case of disputed seats; a committee on *permanent organization* recommends permanent officers for the convention; a committee on *rules* reports out the rules governing the convention proceedings; a committee on *resolutions* draws up the party platform and recommends that it be adopted by the convention. The actions of each of these committees may be—or at least seem to be—of crucial importance to some one of the contestants. For example, the credentials committee may recommend unseating delegates friendly to a particular candidate and seating his rival's, as in the Republican convention in 1952.

Voting in the national conventions is by simple majority. During most of its existence, the Democratic party had the "two-thirds rule" requiring that fraction of the total vote for the nomination of presidential and vice-presidential candidates. This rule, supported mainly by southern Democrats who feared being outvoted by the northern majority in the party, led to endless deadlocks—in one case a candidate was nominated only after 103 ballots. Finally, in 1936, the Democrats under President Roosevelt's leadership succeeded in abolishing the rule. Under certain circumstances Democratic conventions authorize the *unit rule,* under which the entire vote of a state delegation is cast as the majority of the delegation wishes. Since few state parties now instruct their delegations to act as a unit, the unit rule has become of limited importance. The Republican national convention does not permit the unit rule.

The preconvention campaign usually starts at least a year or two before the convention itself. The candidate—who may be a well-known governor, cabinet member, senator, or perhaps an eminent general—is likely to act the part of a coy maiden for a time, while his scouts are busy sounding out party sentiment from Maine to California. The candidate has his choice of several preconvention strategies, depending on his political position. He can announce his candidacy months before the convention and try openly to capture state delegations, as Senators Hubert Humphrey and John F. Kennedy did prior to the 1960 convention. He can keep silent if he prefers not to show his hand early, especially if it is not a strong one. He can concentrate on gaining a following among the party rank and file and the voters at large through public appearances, television speeches, and the like. He can try to build his strength mainly by lining up delegates through various arrangements or deals. Since the manner of choosing convention delegates varies from state to state, chances are that he will use more than one approach.

As the convention nears, the candidate's search for delegate support becomes more and more intense. In each convention the grand object is to win the support of a simple majority of the votes cast. This job is extremely difficult, however, for the delegates leave for the convention in all stages of commitment, noncommitment, and semicommitment to one candidate or another. Some delegates are pledged to a candidate only on the first ballot; others pledge themselves to one man until "the crack of doom." Some state delegations observe the unit rule; others split their vote according to the position of individual delegates.

As the convention opens, the air is filled with talk of favorite sons; of stalking-horses, who are used as fronts for strong candidates wishing to keep some strength in reserve; and of dark horses, who "stand restively and fully accoutered in their paddocks waiting, watching, and hoping that the favorites will kill each other off, and that the convention in desperation will lead them to the starting post." [10] The big test of a candidate is his *availability,* which turns on whether he has demonstrated vote-getting power, whether he seems to have presidential stature, whether or not he is closely tied to a narrow faction in the party, whether he comes from a politically strategic state or section, and—above all—whether or not he has alienated some vital religious, ethnic, or economic group. Governors have usually met the availability test

---

[10] P. H. Odegard and E. A. Helms, *American Politics,* 2nd ed. (Harper, 1947), p. 532.

better than senators, partly because the former can more easily dodge specific stands on national issues than the latter. But this aspect of availability may be changing, for in 1960 the voters seemed more interested in senatorial candidates who had dealt with international problems.

The doctrine of availability was well illustrated in the choosing of a Democratic nominee for Vice President in 1944. It was generally known that the convention's choice might well succeed President Roosevelt in the White House. According to Bronx leader Edward J. Flynn, he and a number of other Democratic bosses canvassed the field. Vice President Wallace was too liberal, and old-line Democrats did not like him. Speaker Rayburn of Texas would antagonize the crucial Negro vote. "Byrnes, who was the strongest candidate," says Flynn, "wouldn't do because he had been raised a Catholic and had left the church when he married, and the Catholics wouldn't stand for that." Truman, on the other hand, was known to the public and had made few enemies; "he came from a border state, and he had never made any 'racial' remarks. He just dropped into the slot." [11]

CONVENTION BATTLES

Both party conventions follow the same ritual. First there is a keynote speech, which lauds the party and bombards the enemy in equally flamboyant terms. Then come the election of convention officials, the reports of committees, the adoption of a platform. Some of these activities, such as the election of the permanent chairman and the seating of contested delegations, are occasions for tests of strength among leading candidates. After hearing statements from representatives of interested groups, the resolutions committee presents a proposed platform to the convention. Usually the planks are debated by the delegates, although sometimes they are accepted perfunctorily. Though drawn in generalities, negative in tone, and sometimes meaningless in detail, the platform indicates the way the wind is blowing. And on some issues, such as prohibition in the Democrats' 1928 and 1932 conventions and civil rights in their 1948 and 1956 conventions, stormy debate may ensue and planks may be accepted or defeated by close votes.

By the third or fourth day the convention is ready for the main business. Candidates are placed in nomination in fulsome speeches making them out as angels blessed with every virtue—above all, the ability to win elections. In placing Dewey's name before the Republican convention in 1944, a delegate orated:

> We are here to restore the Presidency of the United States to the American people. (Applause.) We are here to bring Washington, D.C., back into the United States. (Applause.) We are here to make the American people masters in their own household. (Applause.) For that job we have the means

[11] Flynn, *You're the Boss,* pp. 180-181.

and we have the man. (Applause.) I give to you the nominee of the Republican party, the spokesman of the future, Thomas E. Dewey!

In the same year Senator Alben W. Barkley nominated Roosevelt in the Democratic convention with these words:

> I present to this Convention for the office of President of these United States the name of one who is endowed with the intellectual boldness of Thomas Jefferson, the indomitable courage of Andrew Jackson, the faith and patience of Abraham Lincoln, the rugged integrity of Grover Cleveland, and the scholarly vision of Woodrow Wilson—Franklin D. Roosevelt.

Pandemonium breaks forth when the name of each candidate is mentioned. Delegates march about singing and cheering in demonstrations that may last half an hour or so. Short seconding speeches come next. Then the balloting begins.

Meantime the candidates have been maneuvering for position. From their headquarters in nearby hotel rooms has emerged a stream of claims of delegate strength, counterclaims, denials, rumors, charges, and countercharges. If one candidate comes to the convention with a big lead in delegate strength, the other candidates will attempt to head him off by combining their forces. For if the convention can be deadlocked, a stampede may start toward even a weak candidate. Anyone controlling delegate votes must make the crucial decision of when to throw his strength to a candidate. If he throws his votes too soon, he may give them to a candidate who loses out in the end. If he waits too long, some candidate may acquire enough strength elsewhere. The trick is to deliver at the right time to the winning man; the reward may be the Vice Presidency or some other prize.

The task of the leading contenders is even more delicate. They must mobilize enough strength in early balloting to prove their power. They must also increase their votes with every new balloting to show that they are gaining. If their total drops on any one ballot, their cause may be lost. Franklin Roosevelt's capture of the Democratic nomination in 1932 shows the intricacies of the process. With Jim Farley's invaluable help, F.D.R. received 666¼ votes in the first balloting (more than a majority, but in 1932 the Democrats still observed the "two-thirds rule"). He gained 11½ votes in the next balloting, but only 5 more in the third. Some observers thought he had reached his peak. But in the next few hours while the weary convention was in adjournment, Farley managed to bring over the Texas and California delegations controlled by John Garner—an objective he had been working toward for months by holding out the Vice Presidency to Garner as bait. This switch brought a break in the opponents' ranks, and a stampede to Roosevelt on the next ballot. Farley said later that if Illinois had come over to Roosevelt after the first or second ballot, the Vice Presidency would have gone to that state.[12]

---

[12] J. A. Farley, *Behind the Ballots* (Harcourt, Brace, 1938), p. 142.

Once a candidate wins a majority, some delegate who has voted against him normally moves that the nomination be made unanimous. This is done, and then another long ovation breaks out. The victorious candidate, who usually has been directing his forces from a nearby hotel suite, may appear before the convention a short while later. Smiling wife by his side, spot-lighted by movie and television cameras, the happy candidate thanks the delegates for their vote of confidence and promises a winning fight.

Nominating a vice-presidential candidate usually comes as an anti-climax. The delegates are tired, broke, and anxious to get home. While the vice-presidential nominee is formally chosen in a rollcall vote, in almost all cases the newly picked presidential nominee and his backers actually make the selection, and the convention is glad to endorse it. An effort is ordinarily made to "balance the ticket" by selecting for Vice President a man who repre-sents a different wing of the party, geographical area, and party faction from the presidential nominee. Sometimes the selection is partly the result of a trade by which a party faction gives its ballots to the man who wins the presi-dential nomination in exchange for the "consolation prize." In 1956 Stevenson set a precedent by "throwing open" the Democratic convention and allowing the delegates to choose his running-mate without any interference on his part.

SHOULD THE NATIONAL CONVENTION BE REFORMED?

One of the most-criticized party institutions is the national convention. It is charged that every party candidate is picked by party bosses in a series of unprincipled deals in "smoke-filled rooms," and that they usually come up with a compromise candidate who represents the dead level of party medi-ocrity. The manner of choosing the delegates is also under attack. Both con-ventions and primaries are rigged and run by state bosses, it is said, and presidential primaries are so complicated that they baffle the voter and dis-courage him from taking part.

The main defense of the convention system is simple: it works. During the last hundred years, it is argued, the convention system has brought before the country men of the caliber of Lincoln, Cleveland, McKinley, Wilson, Smith, Willkie, both Roosevelts, Stevenson, Eisenhower, and others. The genius of the convention system is that it produces a candidate who represents party consensus instead of merely some wing of the party. This is important, it is said, for only such a man can enjoy the united support of the party in the campaign and in the White House. Those who look aghast at convention horse-trades and hijinks often forget that compromise is the very essence of democratic politics. Moreover, it is said, the convention increasingly manages to select the man who is the overwhelming choice of the party rank and file and who is, indeed, a national favorite rather than a "dark horse." [13]

---

[13] W. G. Carleton, "The Revolution in the Presidential Nominating Convention," *Political Science Quarterly* (June 1957), pp. 224-240.

Some opponents of the convention favor a *nationwide direct presidential primary system*. President Woodrow Wilson in 1913 advocated legislation providing for primary elections to take place simultaneously throughout the country, in which the voters in each party would vote directly for their favorite without the intervention of nominating conventions. This system would do away with much of the confusion and inefficiencies of the present system. The proposal, which might require a constitutional amendment, has been criticized, however, by those who feel that one nationwide direct primary would disrupt party solidarity and effectiveness. We need consensus *within* the party, they say, so that all major elements—geographical, economic, ideological—can take part in its affairs. We need division *between* the major parties so that the people will have a more meaningful choice at the polls. A nationwide primary system, critics assert, would give us the reverse.

Both the critics and the supporters of national conventions agree on at least one thing: that methods of *selecting convention delegates* should be improved. The whole system needs to be simplified and clarified. Reform does not necessarily mean that the method of selecting delegates in state party *conventions* must be dropped. Both the primary system and the state convention system can be democratic methods of choosing delegates. Both may become "boss-controlled," however. Whether they become one or the other depends on whether or how the voters use them. Even the most democratic methods will not do the job if they lack the propulsive power of wide participation by the people.

How to Be Elected President

Immediately after nominating the vice-presidential candidate, the convention adjourns. The presidential candidate may choose a new party chairman, who usually serves as his campaign manager. The rest of the summer is spent planning electioneering tactics and arrangements. Campaign headquarters are geared for action. By early fall the presidential race is on.

CAMPAIGN STRATEGY

Grand strategy differs from one election to another, but most campaigns combine certain standard ingredients:

The build-up. The personality of the candidate may be as important as the platform he runs on. If a candidate has serious personality defects, they must either be played down or transformed into virtues. The dour Calvin Coolidge had to be humanized before the presidential campaign of 1924. Franklin Roosevelt in 1936 had been pictured by the opposition as an arrogant dictator; his campaign tour was designed in part to show him as a warm and pleasing personality close to the people.

The candidate's desirable features are played up. In 1944 Dewey was presented as an aggressive young executive, in contrast with the tired old group in power; in 1952 Eisenhower was presented as a man who could unite the American people behind a middle-of-the-road program. In the end, the man offered to the people has become almost a myth. As Boss Penrose once said, "Always after a man is nominated they bring out the royal robe and put it on him, and that covers up all the cracks and nail-holes."

Reproduced by permission. Copyright 1946, *The New Yorker Magazine, Inc.*

Taking the stump. By the end of September both candidates are dashing about the country by train, plane, and automobile. There was a time when candidates conducted front-porch campaigns, receiving friendly delegations at their homes. But that day seems gone forever. Today the campaign must be carried straight to the voters. Presidents Hoover, Franklin Roosevelt, and Eisenhower stayed in the White House until late in their campaigns for re-election to show their devotion to duty, but they took the stump before the end. The candidates' campaign trains and caravans have been seen by too many Americans to need description here. Often overlooked, however, is the planning that goes into the choice of itinerary. Candidates sometimes try to steer clear of areas where they might be embarrassed by a local issue or an intra-party fight.

"The big guy in front is Joseph T. Cochrane. Call him Joe. You met him in Marysville three weeks ago. Talk about hunting. He goes after deer every fall. Man on left is Leo Brown. Sixteenth District in his pocket. Don't ask about his wife. She's ditched him. Fellow with mustache is Jim Cronin. Watch your step with him. He's Cochrane's brother-in-law, and . . ."

Where to stump. The electoral-college system has a strong influence on campaign strategy. Under this system, as we shall see, the presidential contest is not decided by the pooled votes of all those casting ballots throughout the nation, but by the ballots of presidential electors (see pp. 370-373). *All* the electoral votes of a state go to the candidate who gains the most popular votes in that state. As a consequence, candidates concentrate their attention on big, closely divided states. This means that the Democratic candidate writes off

Maine and Vermont and his Republican foe probably does the same with much of the South. Consequently, the candidates make most of their appearances in states like New York, Pennsylvania, Massachusetts, Illinois, and Ohio, for the election outcome may easily be decided by a large bloc of electoral votes from such states as these.

Building group support. The essential strategy of the campaign is to build up a winning alliance of interests—mainly sectional, economic, ideological, national-origin, racial, religious. Some of these interest groups are antagonistic to one another—for example, a Democratic candidate must seek to win the support of northern Negroes without alienating too many southern whites. Since most large organizations, such as the American Legion or the National Grange, will not commit themselves as organizations, the trick is to induce their leaders to take part in special election groups, such as Veterans for Eisenhower or United Farmers for Stevenson. Each party headquarters maintains active bureaus designed to mobilize support from organized groups. Campaign literature is slanted to appeal to housewives, businessmen, farmers, veterans, workers, and so on. The candidate himself must pitch his appeals so that they attract the support of divergent and overlapping groups.

Choosing issues. This is one of the basic arts of campaigning. Issues may not be more important than personalities—but actually the two are inseparable. The candidate has a wide choice of alternatives, for he is not bound by his party's platform; indeed he can openly repudiate or modify planks of the platform if he wishes, as Landon did in 1936. One basic question arises: Should the candidate take a stand on specific issues, or should he speak in generalities? Either way, he is bound both to win and to lose some votes. Traditionally, evasion of issues has been considered an effective tactic, but the success of Roosevelt and Truman in taking fairly definite stands in recent elections may presage a change. Usually the candidate tries to develop a basic theme, which is repeatedly played on, with variations to suit the place and hour. But there is a good deal of improvisation as candidates and campaign managers sense last-minute changes in public feeling from their audiences and from opinion polls. Sometimes developments during campaigns will affect the importance of issues and the outcome of the election, as in 1944, when Dewey's stress on postwar matters lost its appeal in the face of military events that indicated prolonged enemy resistance.

Offensive and defensive tactics. Is it better to concentrate on attacking the enemy and ignoring his charges? Or should the opposition be answered charge for charge? Is it possible to put the opposition on the defensive? How? Do Americans really vote *for* candidates or *against* them? These questions plague any campaign strategist. Of course, a candidate for re-election is often on the defensive, for his public record is on display before the voters. But it is always possible to ignore the opposition's attacks and concentrate on one's own achievements. An effective tactic is to ignore the opposition's most damaging charges and to answer his weakest and wildest ones. In 1940, for example, Roosevelt said nothing about the third-term issue, but he answered at length the reckless statement of a minor Republican official that the President's only supporters were "paupers, those who earn less than $1200 a year and aren't worth that, and the Roosevelt family."

Splitting the opposition. According to an old political maxim, a candidate should always try to separate his opponent from the party rank and file. Willkie in 1940 tried to make a distinction between New Dealers and Democrats. Stevenson in 1956 fired away at Republican "reactionaries" and "isolationists." Campaigners also try to divide the groups that seem to be united behind their opponent; thus Dewey made a point of his support from organized labor, and Roosevelt made use of businessmen's organizations set up to back him. Another splitting device is to focus the attack on a minor figure in the opposition camp, or on the sinister forces that are said to be in command. Republicans play up city bosses, Reds, brain trusters, arrogant bureaucrats; Democrats concentrate on big business, special interests, utilities, Hooverites, and the like. The great weakness of this device is that too much fire directed toward minor figures may leave the candidate himself unscathed.

Auxiliary organizations. While the candidate is parading himself before the voters, he must rely on his national, state, and local party organizations to carry the heavy burden of routine work. His own campaign headquarters must raise money, issue propaganda, coordinate party efforts throughout the nation, and operate special divisions to seek the vote of large groups, such as Negroes, labor, and farmers. An important organizational question is whether to use auxiliary organizations independent of the party. In 1940, for example, Republicans and Independents set up thousands of Willkie Clubs, many of which had somewhat distant relations with the Republican organization. The advantage of auxiliaries is that they can appeal more effectively to independent voters. The disadvantage is that they are likely to duplicate the efforts of the party regulars, and even generate serious friction. In general, a presidential candidate must rely heavily on the party machinery throughout the nation; for he does not have time to build up a nationwide personal organization. The Eisenhower Clubs in 1952 and 1956, however, were probably more effective than most such organizations.

Timing. This is one of the most important and mysterious techniques of all. Candidates try to pace their campaigns to reach a climax just before the election. Eisenhower's promise late in October 1952 to make a personal trip to Korea if elected was perfectly timed for maximum appeal. Although it is doubtful that election climaxes can be planned with complete success, both candidates usually converge on the populous areas of the East shortly before election day. The final campaign speech usually takes place on the Saturday before the Tuesday election; on election eve, however, the candidates make a sober and restrained appeal to the people to do their duty at the polls next day.

An American politician can face no ordeal more exhausting or exacting than a presidential campaign. Adlai E. Stevenson, the unsuccessful Democratic candidate in 1952 and 1956, has told how it feels to campaign.

> You must emerge, bright and bubbling with wisdom and well-being, every morning at 8 o'clock, just in time for a charming and profound breakfast talk, shake hands with hundreds, often literally thousands, of people, make several inspiring, "newsworthy" speeches during the day, confer with political leaders along the way and with your staff all the time, write at every chance, think if possible, read mail and newspapers, talk on the telephone, talk to everybody, dictate, receive delegations, eat, with decorum—and discretion!—and ride through city after city on the back of an open car, smiling until your mouth is dehydrated by the wind, waving until the blood runs out of your arms, and then bounce gaily, confidently, masterfully into great howling halls, shaved and all made up for television with the right color shirt and tie—I always forgot—and a manuscript so defaced with chicken tracks and last-minute jottings that you couldn't follow it, even if the spotlights weren't blinding and even if the still photographers didn't shoot you in the eye every time you looked at them. (I've often wondered what happened to all those pictures.) Then all you have to do is make a great, imperishable speech, get out through the pressing crowds with a few score autographs, your clothes intact, your hands bruised, and back to the hotel—in time to see a few important people.
>
> But the real work has just commenced—two or three, sometimes four hours of frenzied writing and editing of the next day's immortal mouthings so you can get something to the stenographers, so they can get something to the mimeograph machines, so they can get something to the reporters, so they can get something to their papers by deadline time. (And I quickly concluded that all deadlines were yesterday!) Finally sleep, sweet sleep, steals you away, unless you worry—which I do.
>
> The next day is the same.
>
> But I gained weight on it. Somehow the people sustain you, the people and a constant, sobering reminder that you are asking them to entrust to you the most awesome responsibility on earth. It was a glorious, heart-filling, head-filling odyssey for which I shall be forever grateful to my party, to my staff and to my fellow Americans. Their faces are a friendly, smiling sea of memory stretching from coast to coast.[14]

---

[14] Adlai E. Stevenson, *Major Campaign Speeches* (Random House, 1953), pp. xxi-xxiii. Reprinted by permission of Random House, Inc. Copyright 1953 by Random House, Inc.

THE ELECTORAL-COLLEGE SYSTEM—MECHANICS

To win the Presidency, a candidate must put together a combination of electoral votes that will give him a majority in the electoral college. This unique institution has no professors or football team, never meets, and serves only a limited electoral function. Yet it has an importance of its own. Although the framers of the Constitution devised the electoral college system because they wanted the President chosen by *electors* exercising independent judgment, subsequent political changes have transformed the electors into straight party representatives who simply register the electorate's decision.

The system today works as follows: in making his presidential choice on election day, the voter technically does not vote directly for a candidate but chooses between slates of *presidential electors*. Each slate is made up of men selected by the state party (in most states in party conventions) to serve this essentially honorary role. The slate that wins the most *popular* votes throughout the *state* wins, and gets to cast *all* the *electoral* votes for the state (a state has one electoral vote for every senator and representative).

The electors on the winning slate travel to their state capital a few weeks after the election, go through the ceremony of casting their ballots for their party's candidates, perhaps hear some speeches, and go home. The ballots are sent from the state capitals to Washington, where early in January they are formally "counted" by the House and Senate and—to the amazement of nobody—the name of the next President is announced.

The counting of the electoral votes is sometimes, however, more than a formality. In 1876 for example, there was a serious dispute over which slate of electoral votes from several southern states should be counted. The election was so close that the outcome was at stake. The Senate was Republican, the House Democratic. Finally a Commission of Fifteen was elected, composed of eight Republicans and seven Democrats. By a vote of eight to seven, the Commission ruled that the Republican electors in the disputed states had been properly elected; so Hayes became President over Tilden.

The House and Senate also must act when no candidate secures a *majority* of the electoral votes. This is not likely as long as there are only two serious contending parties, but it has happened twice in the case of President and once in the case of Vice President. The House chooses the President from among the top three candidates; each state delegation has one vote, and a majority is necessary for election. If no man receives a majority of the electoral vote in the vice-presidential contest, the Senate picks from among the top two candidates; each senator has one vote, and again a majority is required.

THE ELECTORAL-COLLEGE SYSTEM—POLITICS

The operation of the electoral college, with its statewide electoral slates, sharply influences the Presidency and presidential politics. In order to win a presidential election a candidate must appeal successfully to urban and suburban groups in populous states such as New York, California, Pennsylvania, Illinois, and perhaps a dozen others. A Republican candidate usually enters the fray sure of the backing of rural states such as Vermont, Kansas, Oregon, and the Dakotas. Under ordinary circumstances the Democratic candidate knows that he can depend on the support of the "Solid South" and some of the border states. Under the electoral-college system, as we have seen, a candidate either wins *all* a state's electoral votes or *none;* hence the presidential candidate ordinarily will not waste his time campaigning in states unless he has at least a fighting chance of carrying them; nor will he waste time in states that are assuredly on his side. Consequently, the fight usually narrows down to the big states where the balance between the parties tends to be fairly even.

Obviously the presidential candidate must win over—or at least not antagonize—the masses of voters in industrial centers. He must show sensitivity to their problems—working conditions, housing, wages, social security, and relations with foreign nations, especially nations whose sons and daughters have come by the million to our shores. Moreover, the candidate's appeals must at the same time transcend local and petty matters and dramatize the great national issues. He will, of course, address himself to groups such as farmers, workers, veterans, and the like, but he will try to seize on the issues that unify these groups on a nationwide basis. The candidate, in short, strikes out for a *national majority* rooted in the largest states and sacrifices many narrow issues in order to exploit the broader ones. Candidates for Congress, on the other hand, often win votes by pressing local and sectional claims against those of the rest of the nation.

Presidential elections, with their tremendous publicity, dramatic personalities, and spotlighting of great national issues, draw out a big vote. Off-year congressional elections tend to attract fewer voters than presidential elections, and even in a presidential election more voters at the polls ordinarily will mark their "X" in the box for the presidential race than in those for the House and Senate races. What does all this mean? Simply that the President is usually responsible to a broader constituency than the sum of the constituencies voting for members of Congress.

How the politics of the electoral-college system affects legislation may be seen in the story of veterans' legislation in the House of Representatives. Six times during the 1920's and 1930's Presidents vetoed bills desired by the American Legion. Six times Congress overrode these vetoes. Apparently President and Congress were responding to different alignments of voters. The President did not seem to fear retaliation from the Legion at the polls; both Coolidge and Roosevelt won re-election after vetoing these bills. And the overwhelming majority of congressmen who voted as the Legion wished were also successful in the subsequent elections.[15] In short, it may often be politically

---

15 See V. O. Key, "The Veterans and the House of Representatives: A Study of a Pressure Group and Electoral Mortality," *Journal of Politics,* 5 (1943), pp. 27–40. Key concludes that party affiliation had a more important bearing on a representative's chances for re-election than did his stand on veterans' bills.

expedient to *follow one path of action as President and a contrary one as congressman.*

Almost everyone agrees that the present electoral-college method of electing Presidents is defective. The unit-vote system makes the electoral college inherently unable to give accurate results. For example, Eisenhower won 86 per cent of the electoral vote in 1956 with only 57 per cent of the popular vote. The system is especially unfair to minorities in the various states. No Republican in Georgia, no Democrat in Vermont, is able to make his vote for President count. Far worse, minority party members actually aid the opposition, since the size of a state's electoral vote is related to the size of its population. Although almost three million popular votes were cast for Dewey in New York in 1944, Roosevelt received even more and hence got all that state's electoral votes. In effect, the Dewey popular votes were converted in the electoral college to votes for Roosevelt. This situation helps maintain essentially one-party areas such as the Solid South. Finally, the system could easily break down as a result of mischance or fraud, and lead to violence if people felt that they had been cheated out of a victory by faulty machinery. Like the human appendix, the electoral college is useless, unpredictable, and a possible center of inflammation.

Herblock in *The Washington Post*

"Don't expect me to get this real accurate, Bub."

Many reforms have been suggested. One is to abolish the whole electoral-college arrangement and to elect the President by direct popular vote. But this plan is utopian. It would be opposed by the South and by small states, who could easily muster enough strength to stop a constitutional amendment. Another proposal is more modest. It would abolish the electors but would keep the present distribution of electoral votes among the states. Each candidate would receive the same proportion of the *electoral* votes of a state as he won of its popular vote. For example, if a candidate gained one-third of the popular vote in a state having twelve electoral votes, he would win four of the electoral votes. Minority party votes would have due weight in each state. The electoral and the popular vote would be closely—although not exactly—correlated. Minority parties and candidates would have more incentive to campaign in one-party areas. Some Southerners favored the plan because it would tend to "even up" the electoral totals of the two major parties, might prevent either party from winning a majority, and hence would throw elections into the House of Representatives, where the Southern bloc might play a balance-of-power role in choosing the President.

It might seem that such a modest proposal, compromising as it does with sectional and state interests, might be quickly adopted. But the plan has not got far. An amendment embodying the proposal passed the Senate by the necessary two-thirds majority in the Eighty-first Congress, but it failed in the House. Why? Some Republicans in the House feared that the plan would bring a fairly even division between the two parties in most states in the North, but a strong Democratic electoral vote in the South that would elect the Democratic candidate in a close election. Some southerners feared that the amendment would encourage the Republicans to try to strengthen their party in the South.

Many northern Democrats oppose electoral-college reform, and their reasoning is significant. They argue that the present system compels presidential candidates to fight especially hard to win the support of the big pivotal states such as New York, Illinois, and California, since candidates face the prospect of winning or losing *all* the huge electoral votes in such big states. As a result, presidential candidates will pitch their appeals in these states to the great balance-of-power groups that tend to be composed largely of urban voters, including organized labor, Catholics, nationality groups, Negroes, and other groups that usually give majorities to Democratic candidates. The electoral college therefore forces presidential candidates—and ultimately the President—to be especially responsive to the problems and interests of these groups. If Congress overrepresents conservative, rural areas, they ask, why should not the President overrepresent urban, liberal areas?

Thus the electoral college, even aside from its archaic and unpredictable machinery, involves ultimately the problem of *representation,* which is one of the central problems discussed in Part Five.

Who Won the Election?

The election is over. The victors and the losers exchange gracious messages. Placards and posters blow away in the autumn storms. Soon the successful candidates are taking office in White House, Congress, statehouse, and city hall. These are the winners. But aside from the victorious candidates, can we say who really won the election?

NO TOTAL VICTORS

Did a *party* win it? Only to a limited extent, at best. No party (fortunately) ever sweeps all the national, state, and local elections, nor does any party ever elect all the members of one chamber, like the House of Representatives. And sometimes one party captures one or both chambers of Congress while the opposition party wins or retains the Presidency, leading to divided party rule. Never in the United States does one party seize control of the legislative and executive branches of the national government to the extent that the winning party in Britain takes command in Parliament and Cabinet. Indeed, we cannot speak of party control in any real sense. At most we can speak of control or influence by various factions or individuals in the party. The point is that the elected candidates are not elected by or responsible to a single monolithic party, but rather to groups inside and outside the party. The party as such did not win the election.

Can we say, then, that any particular *group* won the election? Of course, certain groups will say that they were the ones that elected the winning candidates. But these claims are exaggerated. Few organized groups are big enough by themselves to muster enough votes for a majority. And big groups, whether economic, religious, or any other, do not vote as a bloc. The most we can say is that the election was won by a combination of *segments* of groups, or of *subgroups*.

Was the election a victory for a particular *principle* or set of ideas? Here again the answer must be "no." Certainly many persons will make this claim. We will hear over the radio or read in the paper that the election results were a victory for civil rights or for anti-union laws or a repudiation of the bureaucrats or of Wall Street. But an election is rarely if ever a mandate for particular policies. The party platforms are vague catchalls, and the candidates' promises are often obscure and inconsistent. An electoral majority is made up of many different elements with a variety of views. At best the election reflects general attitudes of important segments of the voters.

Who, then, did win the election? What do the election results mean? Of course the winners of the election may have been—at least in the long run— the whole nation, all the people. In a narrower and more immediate sense, the winners were the elected candidates and the voters supporting those candidates —*to the extent that the candidates can follow through on their followers' expectations.* The election results mean simply that the voters have made choices among candidates—choices that give only a rough idea of what the voters are thinking. Election results are not blueprints for future action, but crude guidelines to the general drift of popular feeling. "A vote," says Lippmann, "is a promise of support. It is a way of saying: I am lined up with these men, on this side." [16]

WHAT ELECTIONS ARE

To understand election results, then, we must remember what elections are and what they are not. Elections are not simply a grand rally of the people, who on their own initiative debate issues, produce candidates, and decide

---

[16] Walter Lippmann, *The Phantom Public* (Harcourt, Brace, 1925), pp. 56-57.

among them. Elections are struggles among party and group leaders who go to the voters for support. The voters are of all types, organized and unorganized, active and passive, concerned with world-wide issues and with petty ones. Elections are not the spontaneous acts of a mass of people but the periodic mobilization of voters by leaders at many levels.

Elections are only one of the ways in which the voters can have a say in their government. The people intervene in other ways between elections—by writing to their congressman and to the editor, by signing petitions, by arguing and griping, by organizing in groups. This does not mean that elections are unimportant or uninspiring. Quite the contrary. "A presidential election," William B. Munro once said, "is merely our modern and highly refined substitute for the ancient revolution; a mobilization of opposing forces, a battle of the ins against the outs; with leaders and strategy and campaign chests and all the other paraphernalia of civil war, but without bodily violence to the warriors. This refinement of the struggle for political control, this transition from bullets to ballots, is perhaps the greatest contribution of modern times to the progress of civilization." [17]

Elections set the course of government only in part. Elected officeholders share power with appointed ones, such as judges and administrative officials. All these officials, elected and appointed alike, do not exercise power freely but only within channels set by the forces discussed earlier in this book—the forces of tradition and practice, of laws and institutions, of popular wants and expectations. In the following chapters we turn to our national policy-makers and see how they share and exercise power in the never-ending ferment of ideas, interests, individuals, and institutions.

---

[17] William B. Munro, *The Invisible Government* (Macmillan, 1928), p. 17. For an interesting development of the view that politics is simply the manipulation of rather passive voting groups by elites vying for power, see J. A. Schumpeter, *Capitalism, Socialism, and Democracy* (Harper, 1942), Chapters 21-23.

PART **5**

Policy Makers
for the People

A PROBLEM GUIDE

The main problem posed by Part Five is *responsible leadership.* By "leadership" we mean the readiness and ability of officials to act effectively in meeting the problems that face the country. By "responsible" we mean the ability of voters sooner or later to hold these officials accountable for their actions, and also the accountability of these officials to *one another.*

This problem of responsible leadership arises in the treatment of Congress in Chapters 15 and 16. How quickly and effectively can Congress take the lead in meeting problems? Except in times of crisis, it may be handicapped by the procedures described in Chapter 15, such as the committee system and the power to filibuster. To whom is Congress responsible? Mainly to the voters, of course. But to *what* voters? The prob-

lem here is that individual members of Congress may respond unduly to special and local groups in their states and districts. Should Congress respond more strongly to a broader general interest, such as a majority of the *national* electorate?

The Presidency, discussed in Chapters 17 and 18 poses these twin problems of responsibility and leadership even more sharply. The powers of his office, and his assured rule for at least four years, give the Chief Executive the tools of leadership, and strong Presidents have used these tools boldly. Has the Presidency gained *too much power* for a "government by the people"? These questions in turn raise the problem: To whom is the President responsible? Presumably to the majority of the voters, but the Electoral College, as we saw in

377

Chapter 14, tends to make the President especially sensitive to the big urban states with their balance-of-power voting blocs.

What about civil servants and federal judges? These officials are not directly chosen by the voters and they are not expected to "lead" in the usual sense. In fact, however, bureaucrats and judges, too, must on occasion lead—for example, the official who takes some clearly desirable action when not specifically authorized by law, or the Supreme Court in the famous school desegregation case of 1954. To whom are these officials responsible? To the President? To Congress? To the electorate? To their own professional standards? To all these, of course—but what if officials must choose between different kinds of responsibility? These questions arise in Chapters 19 and 20.

There is one key problem running through all the chapters in this part: the problem of majority rule—that is, whether or not President and Congress should be responsible directly and primarily to the majority of voters that elected them to office. Since our political leaders win power through political parties seeking majority support, this problem in turn raises the further question of how strongly, if at all, the winning party should control the leaders in office. Should we make our leaders, executive and legislative and even judicial, more responsible to the majority of the people? In short, do we want some kind of "party government"? Or do we want a looser, more decentralized political system that gives more power to shifting coalitions of minority groups working through or around our parties? This problem—and its implications for responsible leadership—is explored in Chapter 21.

Clearly *representation*—the focal problem of Part Four—and *responsibility*—the main problem of this part—are closely intertwined. In studying representation we were looking at the problem of how the voters are organized (or *dis*organized or *un*organized) to influence political leaders. In studying responsibility we are trying to discover what voters—in groups, in localities, in parties—the leaders are responsible to, and just how they are responsible. Responsibility and representation are opposite sides of the same coin.

CHAPTER 15

The Houses of Congress

On January 3 every year, 537 men and women meet in the chambers of the Capitol in Washington to inaugurate a new session of Congress. These legislators— 437 representatives and 100 senators—are members of one of the oldest parliaments in the world. They are the symbols of the vigor of representative government in twentieth-century America. They debate and enact laws in the tradition of a legislature that has met every year for almost 170 years despite revolutionary changes in our economic and political life, depressions, wars at home and abroad.[1]

The first important fact about Congress is its *bicameral* structure, its organization as a separate Senate and House of Representatives. As we noticed in Chapters 2 and 3, the framers of the Constitution set up two separate houses partly to settle the fight between the small states and the large, and partly to make the legislators responsible to different groups of voters. The framers planned well and lastingly. Each house has an *absolute veto* over the other in legislation, and each house responds to *different interests*.

Since the two houses of Congress resemble each other in certain ways, we shall first investigate the basic powers and structure common to both. Since the two houses also differ in certain ways, we shall then describe each one separately. The next chapter will stress the personalities, processes, and problems of Congress. Both chapters stress *political* factors affecting Congress.

The Powers of Congress The paramount power of Congress is *legislative*. The first article of the Constitution gives Congress the authority to levy taxes, borrow money, regulate commerce with other nations and among the states, coin

---

[1] Every two years a new Congress comes into being. For example, the Congress that convened in January 1959 was the Eighty-sixth. In each two-year Congress there are two regular sessions, beginning in January of each year, and such other special sessions as may be called by the President. With the admission of Alaska and Hawaii the House has been increased to 437, but under the present law it is to revert to 435 after the next reapportionment.

money, declare war, and to perform a host of other important functions, including passing all laws necessary and proper to execute these powers. Unquestionably the lawmaking function is the main job of Congress. But the legislators have other duties.

Congress has *amendatory powers*. Congress proposes amendments to the Constitution or calls conventions to propose amendments, as we mentioned in Chapter 3. Moreover, Congress determines which *method* of ratification shall be used to approve amendments and it may set the time during which they may be ratified.

Congress has *electoral powers*, as described in the preceding chapter. Congress determines, moreover, who shall be President in the event of the death or disability of the President and Vice President.

Each house is also the judge of the *elections* and *qualifications* of its own members. When election irregularities are charged, each house determines the right of the member-elect to take his seat. Questions about qualifications are also resolved by each chamber. The Constitution stipulates that a member of the House of Representatives must be twenty-five years old, an inhabitant of his state (American political attitudes dictate that he also be a resident of his district), and an American citizen for at least seven years. Senators must be thirty, inhabitants of their states, and citizens for at least nine years. Each House, moreover, may disqualify persons for conduct of which a majority of the members disapprove. Although the constitutionality of this practice has been questioned, ample precedents support it. In 1926, for example, the Senate refused to seat William S. Vare because of excessive campaign expenditures.

The House has the power to *impeach* and the Senate the power to *try* any civil officer of the United States, including the President. If two-thirds of the senators uphold the lower body's impeachment charges, the officer may be removed from his position and disqualified from ever holding an office of profit or trust under the United States.

Each chamber has *disciplinary powers* over both its own members and to a limited extent over private persons. Congressmen are not subject to impeachment (they are not, the Supreme Court has said, civil officers of the United States), and it is up to each chamber to discipline its own members. Once a congressman has been seated, he may be expelled by a two-thirds vote of his own house, though this is a most uncommon proceeding. Each house has inherent power to punish *private* persons whose conduct directly interferes with the exercise of congressional business. If, for example, a witness before a committee refuses to answer a proper question, the chamber may sit as a court, convict him of contempt, and order the sergeant-at-arms to hold him in custody. He may not be held, however, longer than the time Congress remains in session. This inherent power to punish for contempt is not normally used. Rather, Congress turns the matter over to a United States attorney for action.

Congress has *investigatory powers.* Congress may investigate any subjects when necessary to carry out its lawmaking, amendatory, electoral, or other duties. It may subpoena witnesses and documents, subject of course to constitutional limitations.

Congress *admits new states* into the Union, as in the recent cases of Alaska and Hawaii.

Congress has *housekeeping* and *rule-making powers.* The Constitution authorizes Congress to enact the necessary laws to provide for its own maintenance and gives to each house the power to make its own procedural rules.

The Senate *advises* and *consents to treaties* and *confirms most nominations* to offices of the United States (see pp. 394-396).

Great as the powers of Congress are, the framers had, of course, no intention of making it all-powerful. As we have seen, they reserved a great deal of authority to the states, and they gave certain powers to the executive and judicial branches of the national government. As time passed, Congress gained power in some respects and lost it in others. With the expansion of the national government's authority, the scope of the lawmaking power of Congress has also expanded. On the other hand, in its actual exercise of power Congress has lost out to its great rival, the President, who in many respects holds today the commanding place in our national government that the Founding Fathers intended Congress to have.

Congress: Organization and Politics

One of the first things most tourists do in Washington is to watch Congress in session. It is often a disappointing experience. A congressman is shouting into a microphone in the "well" of the House about the needs, say, of the Morumbian valley, but nobody seems to be listening to him. Representatives rush in and out, read newspapers, take catnaps, or talk in small groups in the corridors. When the congressman stops speaking, another is recognized. Does he debate the problems of Morumbians? No, he makes startling revelations about communists in the executive department. The visitor in the gallery, hoping to witness a great forensic battle between two mighty debaters, hears a disconnected string of speeches and questions, partly lost in the buzz and shuffle of the floor. Over in the Senate, the debate may be more coherent, but there, too, only a handful of members may be on hand.

COMMITTEES—THE LITTLE LEGISLATURES

Congress puts its worst foot forward. Formal sessions of Congress, however important, are only a small part of congressional activities. The main legislative work is done in committees. Deluged under several thousand bills a year, Congress could not do its job unless it delegated work to these "little legislatures." There are four types of congressional committee: *standing, special, joint,* and *conference.* These do the main work of framing legislation.

The House of Representatives has twenty standing committees with an average membership of about thirty. Among the most important of these committees are the great spending and taxing committees, namely Appropriations and Ways and Means, and—for a special reason described below—the Rules Committee. Standing committees are divided into subcommittees with jurisdiction over particular subjects. Standing committees have great powers. To them are referred all bills introduced in the House. They can kill bills, pigeonhole them for weeks, amend them beyond recognition, or speed them on their way. They are, as Speaker Reed once said, "the eye, the ear, the hand, and very often the brain of the House."

The House especially depends on the work of its committees. They are important also because of their power to kill a bill merely through inaction. If a committee fails to report a bill, the only way it can be brought to the floor of the House is through a *discharge petition* signed by a majority of the House membership. Many petitions are filed; few gain the necessary number of signatures. Indirectly, however, the threat of a petition sometimes helps move bills out of committee.

The Senate has sixteen standing committees composed of seven to twenty-eight members; each senator normally serves on only two committees. Among the most important Senate committees are Foreign Relations, Finance, and Government Operations; the last supervises and investigates the executive agencies. Senate committees have the same great powers over the framing of legislation as do those of the House.

Committees frequently hold open hearings, where spokesmen from executive departments, representatives of interest-group organizations, experts of various sorts, and mere private citizens testify formally on pending legislation. These hearings may be far more interesting to the visitor than sessions of House or Senate, and the committee proceedings published verbatim by the government afford rich material on the operations of government. The most important work of the committees, however, is done in *executive session,* from which visitors are barred. These sessions are centers of vital decision-making. Their nonpublic character "promotes the free interplay of ideas among committee members. Compromises and alternatives can be shaped in a fluid environment." [2] Committee decisions are made by majority vote.

Standing committees are bipartisan. The chairman and a majority of the members are elected from the majority party, and the minority party is represented roughly in relation to the proportion of its members in the entire chamber. Getting on a politically advantageous committee is important to

---

2 Bertram M. Gross, *The Legislative Struggle* (McGraw-Hill, 1953), pp. 309-310. See also the penetrating analysis, Ralph K. Huitt, "The Congressional Committee: A Case Study," *The American Political Science Review* (June 1954), pp. 340-365.

members of Congress. A representative from Nebraska, for example, would much rather serve on the Agriculture or Public Works Committee than on the District of Columbia Committee. Members usually stay on the same committee from one Congress to the next, but on occasion they jump from one committee to what seems to them a more important one.

How are committee members chosen? At the opening of each Congress, Republican freshmen in the House are given committee assignments by the Committee on Committees of the Republican membership. The Democratic members of the House Committee on Ways and Means handle this job for the Democrats. In the Senate too, committee appointments are decided by small groups of leaders in each party. Committee assignments in both chambers in effect are handled by congressional veterans; this is one of the reasons veterans have more power than newcomers. Each chamber then simply ratifies the decisions that have been made by the party leaders.

To supplement the work of standing committees the House and the Senate occasionally create *special* or *select committees*. Normally the task of these committees is to make a specific investigation rather than to introduce legislation; after submitting their report, they are dissolved. The Speaker—the presiding officer of the House, who is elected to that position by a straight party vote of the membership—chooses members of select (but not of standing) committees. Very occasionally, when problems arise that need joint consideration, House and Senate create *joint committees* composed of members of both chambers. Most of these joint committees, such as the Joint Committee on Atomic Energy, are permanent. Others are temporary, such as the Temporary National Economic Committee, which in the late 1930's conducted an elaborate investigation of economic problems and which included in its membership representatives from several executive agencies. *Conference committees,* a special kind of joint committee, are appointed by the presiding officers of the House and Senate when the two chambers disagree over legislation; their functions are discussed on pp. 410-412.

COMMITTEE LEADERS—THE RULE OF SENIORITY

Although every member of a committee has one vote, the committee chairman is almost always the most influential member, for he has certain formal as well as informal powers. "The chairman is powerful," Roland Young has written, "because he can call committee meetings whenever he wishes, because he has a large amount of freedom in preparing the legislative agenda for the committee, and because he is officially consulted on questions relating to his committee. A chairmanship . . . gives the member a status with Congress, with the bureaucracy, and with the general public." [3] Like the chairman, the other ranking committee members of both parties have the advantage of experi-

---

[3] Roland Young, *This Is Congress* (Knopf, 1943), p. 108.

ence in committee work, legislative and parliamentary know-how, and wide contacts in Congress and outside.

Chairmanships are awarded by the rule of *seniority*. The member of the *majority* party who has had the longest continuous service on the committee becomes chairman. (The member of the minority party with the longest continuous service on the committee is the *ranking minority member*.) The chairman may be at swords' points with his fellow partisans in Congress, he may oppose his party's national program, he may even be incompetent—still, he has the right to the chairmanship under the workings of seniority.

The rule of seniority means that chairmen are not chosen by their own committees, by their party, or by the House or Senate as a whole. They are really picked by the voters in their districts and states, who give them seniority by sending them back to Congress in election after election. Thus the key makers of national policy in Congress are "locally chosen and locally responsible." [4] The seniority rule puts a premium on careful cultivation of the district. It bestows the most influence in Congress on those constituencies that are politically stable or even stagnant—where party competition is low, where a particular interest group or city or rural machine predominates. It stacks the cards against areas where the two parties are more evenly matched, where interest in politics is high, the number of votes large, and competition between groups keen. These are the very areas most likely to reflect quickly and typically the political tides that sweep the nation. In this sense the seniority rule makes Congress more *conservative*.

The effects of the seniority system on party operations are especially devastating. In the words of one student, the system "divides the authority of the party leaders and impairs their practical capacity to carry out consistently a general program of party legislation. It may even defeat the projects to which the majority of a party have been publicly pledged. . . . It makes the party system a less effective instrument than it might and should be in organizing majorities within the House for serving the manifest needs of the people of the country." [5]

THE POLITICS OF THE SENIORITY RULE

What groups does the seniority system benefit? When Democrats control Congress, committee chairmen tend to be mainly southerners from rural areas, along with a few products of city machines. When Republicans are in control of Congress, the midwestern rural areas tend to gain a disproportionate number of chairmanships. President Eisenhower, for example, during his first two

---

[4] *The Reorganization of Congress,* A Report of the Committee on Congress of the American Political Science Association (Public Affairs Press, 1945), p. 69.

[5] A. N. Holcombe, *Our More Perfect Union* (Harvard Univ. Press, 1950), p. 185. For a scholarly treatment of the subject that warns against exaggerating the impact of the system, see George Goodwin, Jr., "The Seniority System in Congress," *The American Political Science Review* (June 1959), pp. 412-436.

years in office had to deal with Republican committee chairmen who had been accumulating seniority during the years of Democratic supremacy and who generally represented different groups in the Republican party than did the Administration. The struggle between Chairman Reed of the Ways and Means committee and the Administration soon after Mr. Eisenhower took office (see pp. 465-466) exemplified this kind of division between the presidential and congressional wings of the party.

The seniority rule, combined with the power of committees and committee chairmen, affects the efficiency of Congress. It tends to divide power among a score of "little legislatures" and their powerful chairmen. The scattering of power is such that it is difficult, for example, for a party majority to unify itself behind a coherent party program.

Seniority is defended on the grounds that it prevents disputes among congressmen and elevates the most experienced members to committee leadership. It is attacked on the grounds that it puts power into the hands of veteran members who may be out of touch with the new needs and problems of the nation. Basically the argument involves political rather than logical matters. Rural interests naturally tend to favor the system. It is opposed by groups such as organized labor, supporters of civil-rights legislation, and other urban-based interests, who feel that it gives the farmers and their conservative representatives too much power in Congress.

The House of Representatives

The framers of the Constitution intended the Senate to represent areas rather than numbers, but this was to be offset by making the House of Representatives roughly reflect population. But even the lower chamber does not represent population accurately. How can this be? The explanation is found in the way congressional districts are set up.

By act of Congress the membership of the House is set at 435. After each ten-year census the Census Bureau submits a report showing the number of representatives each state is entitled to have in the House. (After the 1960 census, for example, California is expected to gain seven new Representatives and Pennsylvania to lose three.) If a state gains or loses one or more representatives as a result of population shifts, alterations in district boundaries must ordinarily be made. The job of laying out the actual boundaries of the new districts falls to the *state legislatures*. At best, districting is a difficult job; districts should be as nearly equal in population as practicable, they should be fairly compact, and boundaries should not cut across unified areas such as cities. In practice, districting is immensely complicated because it is conducted in a *political* atmosphere, influenced by a variety of personal, group, and party forces jockeying for advantage.

THE GERRYMANDER

One result of this jockeying is *gerrymandering*. The term was coined a century and a half ago when Elbridge Gerry of Massachusetts carved out a district that had the shape of a salamander and was quickly dubbed a "Gerrymander." The term now applies to any attempt by a party or faction controlling a state legislature to draw the boundaries of districts in such a way that that party or group enjoys a *close but safe margin of support in many districts,* while the opposition's votes are *concentrated* in a *few districts* and thus wasted. Since both parties freely indulge in this practice, some districts have fantastic shapes. "If you let your imagination go while thumbing through the maps of Congressional districts," Volta Torrey says, "you may readily fancy that you have seen a dumbbell, a tomahawk, a skull, a worm, the M.G.M. lion, and characters from the comic strips." [6]

Another result of the politics of districting is sometimes called the "silent gerrymander." Even though population changes, a state legislature may keep a gerrymander intact simply by refusing to redistrict at all. A state that gains an increase in its quota of representatives may stand pat by electing its new representative "at large"—that is, the whole state becomes his district—and hence keeping its existing districts intact. Also, a legislature may make no effort to adjust its districts to population shifts *within* the state. An urban district may double in population and still have only one representative, while rural districts that have declined in relative population may keep their past representation. Michigan's biggest district, for example, has 525,334 persons, its smallest only 178,251. To be sure, we have nothing as unrepresentative as the famous "rotten boroughs" of England, where one town, half submerged under water and numbering only fourteen voters, had two members in Parliament, while great cities such as Birmingham had none. But Britain long ago cleared up these inequities, while some fear that our own are becoming worse.

Politically, the main effect of gerrymandering is to give extra influence to representatives of rural areas. The reason is twofold: first, since population shifts have been mainly from rural to urban and suburban areas in recent decades, simple failure to redistrict strengthens rural representation at the expense of urban and suburban; second, most state legislatures, themselves reflecting gerrymandered districts, overrepresent rural areas, and hence when they gerrymander congressional districts they draw the boundaries to overrepresent rural voters.

Another feature of the House of Representatives that has important political repercussions is the Rules Committee.

---

[6] Volta Torrey, *You and Your Congress* (Morrow, 1944), p. 31.

GEOGRAPHY IN POLITICS

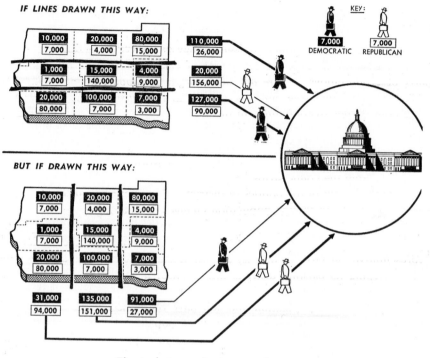

The technique of gerrymandering—

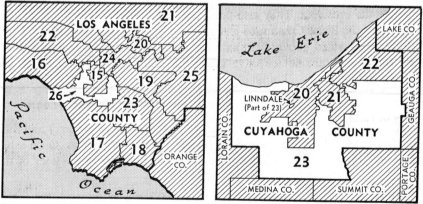

Adapted from *The Reporter*

—and a couple of results.

For most public bills to get onto the floor of the House, a special rule or order must be issued by the Rules Committee. Every large assembly needs a traffic cop to direct the heavy stream of bills and resolutions. The members of the Rules Committee do this job—and many more. They can kill a bill by sitting on it indefinitely. They can insist that a bill be amended as a price of permitting it on the floor. They can substitute a wholly new bill for the one framed by another legislative committee. They receive—and can smother—all proposals for amending the rules of the House. They provide most important bills with a rule that determines the procedure for handling each bill on the floor, and the nature of the rule greatly affects the prospects of the bill. For example, the Rules Committee can give a bill a rule—sometimes called a "wide-open rule"—that opens the bill to crippling amendments from the floor, or it can provide a "gag rule" and prohibit such amendments.

In the words of one authority on Congress, the Rules Committee is "to a large degree the governing committee of the House . . . able to advance directly, or to retard indirectly, any measure which it selects for passage or slaughter." [7] If the Committee were representative of the make-up of the House, such power might be safe in its hands. But it is not. In recent years, at least, it has been dominated by veteran congressmen who have been re-elected time and time again regardless of the ebb and flow of national politics. For example, after the 1958 congressional elections, which were widely viewed as a victory for liberal Democrats, two conservative Democrats (including the chairman) and four conservative Republicans dominated the twelve-man committee and were able to spike many measures.

On the other hand, defenders of the Rules Committee argue that it does just what the framers of the Constitution wanted our system to do—it prevents the House from responding too readily to new popular majorities as represented by the President. They also point out that a *discharge petition* may be used against the Rules Committee just as it can be against regular House committees, as we noted above. Furthermore, the committee can merely recommend rules—they are not effective until approved by the House which can always reject them.

HOUSE PROCEDURE ON THE FLOOR

Usually a bill is drafted by a legislator (with the help of experts) and then submitted to a standing committee for further study and changes. Once a bill has passed through the committee stage, how is it handled on the floor of the

---

[7] George B. Galloway, *Congress at the Crossroads* (Crowell, 1946), p. 61. For a more recent study that views the Rules Committee in its total organizational context, see J. A. Robinson, "Decision Making in the House Rules Committee," *Administrative Science Quarterly* (June 1958), pp. 73-86.

House of Representatives? In contrast to the smaller, more informal Senate, the large membership of the House makes imperative quick and orderly methods. Some of the important procedures are:

Calendars. Bills reported out of committee to the floor of the House are assigned to one of three main calendars, or schedules. Finance measures—tax or appropriations, for example—are put on the *Union* calendar. All bills that are nonfiscal but still of a public character are placed on the *House* calendar. Private bills—bills dealing with individuals' problems, such as a veteran's pension—go on a *Private* calendar. These and other calendars serve as a traffic-directing system designed to give each bill its fair turn. But there are also various means for taking up bills out of their calendar order. For example, House rules may be suspended by a two-thirds vote on certain days; or important bills may be brought up at any time by the Rules Committee; or immediate action on a measure may be won by unanimous consent.

Committee of the Whole. This committee, made up of all members of the House, is another means of expediting business. By sitting as the Committee of the Whole, members are able to operate more informally and quickly than under the regular House rules. For example, a quorum in the Committee of the Whole is 100, compared with a majority of all the members under the

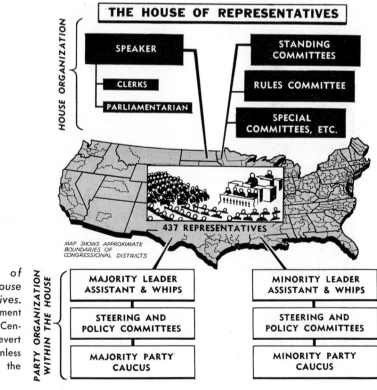

THE HOUSE OF REPRESENTATIVES

HOUSE ORGANIZATION

SPEAKER

STANDING COMMITTEES

CLERKS

RULES COMMITTEE

PARLIAMENTARIAN

SPECIAL COMMITTEES, ETC.

437 REPRESENTATIVES

MAP SHOWS APPROXIMATE BOUNDARIES OF CONGRESSIONAL DISTRICTS

PARTY ORGANIZATION WITHIN THE HOUSE

MAJORITY LEADER ASSISTANT & WHIPS

MINORITY LEADER ASSISTANT & WHIPS

STEERING AND POLICY COMMITTEES

STEERING AND POLICY COMMITTEES

MAJORITY PARTY CAUCUS

MINORITY PARTY CAUCUS

Organization of power in the House of Representatives. (After reapportionment following the 1960 Census the House will revert to 435 members unless Congress changes the law.)

House rules. Very rarely does the whole House reject the recommendations of this committee, though it has the power to do so.

House cloture. In contrast to the smaller upper chamber, the House is too large to let everyone have his full say. Debate may be cut off simply by majority vote. This ready method of cloture (or closure) makes filibusters impossible. Most speakers are allowed only a few minutes, usually by prior agreement between party leaders on both sides.

Voting. Ordinarily voting is conducted quickly in the House either by a viva-voce (voice) vote, or by a standing vote. Occasionally, though, some faction may want to make members go on record as to their stand on a controversial measure; in this case voting is conducted by the slower method of a vote by tellers (the members are checked off as they file past the Speaker's desk), or, upon demand of one-fifth of members present, by the still slower method of a roll call (the clerk calls each member by name).

THE SPEAKER

The most important single leader in the House is the Speaker, who presides over its meetings. His formal authority is not what it was fifty years ago, when such Speakers as Thomas B. (Czar) Reed or Joe Cannon controlled committee assignments and wielded other important powers. Revolts of the rank and file stripped the Speaker of much of his old-time authority. Still, he is important in the work of the House. Without his recognition no person can speak on the House floor. He settles parliamentary disputes (with the help of an expert on parliamentary rules). As noted above, he appoints members of select and conference committees (but not of standing committees), and in general directs the business of the House.

The Speaker's *informal* powers are greater than his formal powers—although much depends on his political talents. As leader of the majority party in the House, he deals with other national leaders in Congress and outside. Unlike the Speaker of the British House of Commons, who is nonpartisan, the Speaker of the House of Representatives is openly a party leader. He is expected, subject to the rules of the game, to use the powers of his office to support the policies of his party. His decisions may be overruled by the House, whose agent he is, but such action is unlikely as long as he keeps the support of his own party. Sam Rayburn, Speaker of the House for years, holds tremendous personal influence over his fellow Democrats.

PARTY OFFICERS AND MEETINGS

Next to the Speaker the most important *party* officer in the House is the *majority floor leader,* who is chosen by the party caucus (see below). He helps plan party strategy, confers with other party leaders, and tries to keep members of his party in line. The minority party elects a *minority floor leader,* who usually steps into the speakership when his party gains a majority in the House. Assisting each floor leader are the *party whips,* who serve as liaison between the leadership and the rank and file.

At the beginning of the session and occasionally thereafter, each party holds a *caucus* (or conference, as the Republicans call it). The caucus, composed of all the party's members in the House, meets privately to elect party officers, approve committee assignments, discuss important legislation, and perhaps try to agree on party policy. Decisions are usually made by simple majority. In theory, the caucus is the directing party agency; in fact, this party group plays a small part in lawmaking. A decision of the Democratic caucus is binding only when approved by two-thirds of the members. When it involves a matter of constitutional interpretation (as do most measures), or when conflicting promises have been made back home (and all sorts of promises have been made), the decision is not binding at all. Republicans are not bound by any conference decision.

Hardly more important than the caucus are the *steering* or *policy committees,* made up of the party leadership, which do little steering but have some influence on party policy and tactics. The Democratic steering committee is composed of fifteen members elected by Democratic representatives from fifteen different geographical areas, and of six ex-officio members. The Republican steering committee is composed of Republican members of the Rules Committee and of other top party and committee leaders. Although individual members of the steering committees are powerful, the committees, as such, are not. It has been observed that they rarely meet and never steer—one more example of the absence of *unified party* control in the House, a matter to which we will return.

The Senate

In many respects the Senate resembles the House. But it is a smaller body of only 100 members with six-year terms. Every state has two senators. Only one-third of the senators face re-election for any Congress. Consequently the Senate, unlike the House, is always organized. It is an ever-continuing body.

The equal representation of the states in the Senate means that Alaska, with 200,000 inhabitants, has the same senatorial strength as New York, with almost ninety times that population. Regionally, it means that the Middle Atlantic states, comprising about one-fifth of the nation's population, hold one-sixteenth of the Senate's seats, while northern New England and the Rocky Mountain states gain at the expense of other sections. Since the sparsely settled areas are largely agricultural, the Senate tends to give special weight to the claims of the nation's farmers. In recent decades, however, the spread of urbanism in many hitherto rural areas has had the effect of making the Senate more reflective of urban opinion.

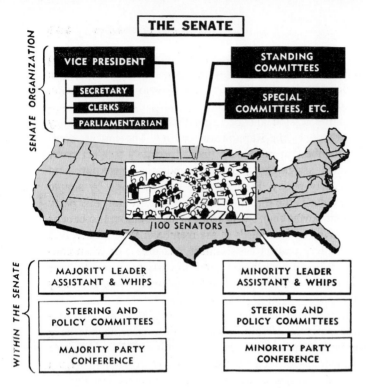

Organization of power in the Senate.

The President of the Senate is the Vice President of the United States. Despite his exalted position, he has much less control over the Senate than the Speaker has over the House. He is not a member of the Senate—not quite a member of the exclusive "senatorial club"—and can vote only in case of a tie. He must recognize members in the order in which they rise. The Senate also elects from among its own membership a *president pro tempore* who presides in the absence of the Vice President. He is of course really chosen by the majority party. As a member of the Senate, he can vote on all issues.

Party machinery in the Senate is somewhat similar to that of the House. There are party conferences (in the Senate, both parties have given up the term "caucus"), majority and minority floor leaders, and party whips. In the Senate each party has a *policy committee,* composed of the leaders of the party, which is theoretically responsible for the party's over-all legislative program. The Democratic policy committeemen are appointed by the Democratic floor leader and serve indefinitely, while their Republican counterparts are elected by the party conference for two-year terms. Unlike the House steering committees, the Senate's policy committees are formally provided for by law and each of them has a regular staff and a significant budget. While the Senate policy committees have some influence on legislation, they have neither asserted strong legislative leadership nor integrated party policy.[8]

---

[8] Hugh A. Bone, "An Introduction to the Senate Policy Committee," *The American Political Science Review* (June 1956), pp. 339-359.

The majority leader, however, is usually a man of great influence in the Senate and of nationwide fame. It was as majority (or floor) leader that Senator Taft became "Mr. Republican" and a strong contender for the presidential nomination. More recently Senator Lyndon Johnson of Texas has made the position of majority leader and chairman of the policy committee more important than ever—amid the grumbling of some Democratic senators who feel that he runs things too much on his own.

Bills are reported to the Senate floor from standing committees in much the same fashion as in the House, but there are important differences in procedure on the two floors. The Senate's Rules Committee has none of the delaying or blocking power of its counterpart in the House. The Senate has only two calendars, and these are usually followed rather closely. It uses its Committee of the Whole only for considering treaties. It has more time for debate and can carry on its business in a more informal manner. Measures in the Senate are normally debated in the order in which they are reported by committees, or else are taken up for discussion by unanimous consent.

THE FILIBUSTER

Another major difference between the two chambers is that debate is sharply limited in the House, and is almost unlimited in the Senate. Once a senator gains the floor, he has the right to go on talking until he relinquishes it voluntarily or through exhaustion. This right to unlimited debate may be used by a small group of senators to *filibuster*—that is, to *delay the proceedings of the Senate in order to prevent a vote*. Debate in the Senate does not have to be germane. A senator may, if he wishes, read the *Congressional Record* at great length or, as the late Senator Long once did, entertain his colleagues with recipes for "Louisiana potlikker."

How can a filibuster be defeated? The majority can keep the Senate in continuous session in the hope that the filibustering senator will have to give up the floor. But if three or four senators cooperate, they can keep going almost indefinitely. They merely ask one another long questions that will permit their partners to take lengthy rests. So long as they keep on their feet, debate can be terminated only by *cloture* (sometimes called *closure*). Under the rule of cloture if sixteen members sign a petition, two days later the question of curtailing debate is put to a vote. If *two-thirds* of the senators on the floor vote for cloture, no senator may speak for more than one hour; then the motion before the Senate must be brought to a vote.

The Senate has acted favorably on cloture petitions only four times since such a procedure was adopted in 1917. The mere threat of a filibuster is normally sufficient to secure the concessions demanded by dissident senators. Filibusters are especially effective near the closing days of a session, when delay can be most injurious. The most spectacular recent filibusters and threats of filibuster have been those of southern senators determined to block civil-rights legislation. The all-time record for holding the floor was achieved in 1957 by Senator Strom Thurmond of South Carolina, who, with little help from "questioners," talked for 24 hours and 18 minutes. But northerners as well as southerners, liberals as well as conservatives, have used this device when it suited their purposes.

POLITICAL ROLE OF THE SENATORS

The two houses of Congress resemble each other in their concern with local and special-interest legislation, their intricate legislative and parliamentary procedure, their tendency toward voting by blocs and interest groups in defiance of party ties. Yet the upper chamber has a character all its own.

Senators are a somewhat different breed of political animal from the average representative. Most of the members of the upper house represent larger and more populous areas than do representatives. They have much more political elbow room. A representative, elected by a smaller constituency both geographically and numerically (in most cases), may feel somewhat cramped by the necessity of devoting himself to the needs of a few interest groups and a handful of local party bosses. A senator, on the other hand, who represents a broader and more varied constituency, has more freedom to maneuver and is less vulnerable to minute shifts in opinion among smaller groups.

Senators tend also to wield greater power in their state political parties. Sometimes they virtually dominate those parties, as in the case of Huey Long of Louisiana, Joseph Guffey of Pennsylvania, Nelson Aldrich of Rhode Island, or, more recently, Robert A. Taft of Ohio and Harry Byrd of Virginia. Their party position often rests partially on their control of federal patronage dispensed to the state, and their patronage power largely rests in turn on the constitutional provision requiring Senate confirmation of major presidential appointments.

This power of the Senate to confirm nominations is important *constitutionally* as a part of our checks-and-balances system. It is even more important *politically,* for under the system of *senatorial courtesy* the individual senator has virtually a veto power over major appointments in his state (provided the President belongs to his party). The arrangement is a simple one. When presidential nominations are received in the Senate, they are referred quietly to the senator or senators from the state involved. The senator may, if he wishes, declare that the nominee is "personally obnoxious" to him, and the Senate almost always respects this declaration and rejects the appointment. Being personally obnoxious does not necessarily mean that the nominee is dishonest, or has insulted the senator on some occasion. It usually means that the nominee has not played ball with the senator *politically,* has been a member of a hostile personal organization in the state—perhaps that of the President. In any event, the upshot is that the President usually makes sure before submitting a nomination to the Senate (especially nominations for appointments located in the state, such as federal judgeships) that the nominee will be acceptable to his party's senator or senators from the state involved. The system of senatorial courtesy has important practical results: it strengthens the senators' role both in national administration and in state politics, and it weakens national party leadership and discipline.

In 1938 President Roosevelt tried to by-pass senatorial courtesy in nominating a federal judge in western Virginia. At the time, Carter Glass, a venerable member of the Senate, and his fellow Virginian, Harry Byrd, were involved in a political battle with Governor Price of Virginia. The governor and his political organization were supporting the President, while both Virginia senators, though Democrats, were hostile to the President's New Deal policies, and maintained a political organization of their own. The President nominated a man who was believed to be in the governor's camp. Senator Byrd called the nomination personally obnoxious to both himself and to Senator Glass, and the Senate rejected it by a vote of 72 to 9. Mr. Roosevelt angrily charged that the Constitution gave only the Senate as a whole, not individual senators, the power of rejecting nominees. Senator Glass, equally aroused, replied that the Constitution gave state governors no power at all over nominations. When the smoke of battle cleared away, senatorial courtesy remained supreme.

THE SENATE'S POWER OVER TREATIES

Another source of the senators' unique position is the fact that *two-thirds of the senators present* must give their consent before the President may ratify a treaty.

The framers of the Constitution probably wanted the President and senators to sit down together and jointly work out treaties. At any rate, George Washington tried this experiment. The story goes that he once visited the Senate to discuss a treaty with the southern Indians; when an obstreperous senator moved to refer the President's proposals to committee, Washington "started up in a violent fret," complaining that "this defeats every purpose of my coming here." No President since has conferred directly with the Senate; nonetheless, the senators help frame treaties as well as ratify them. The voices of influential senators are heard in foreign capitals as well as at home. Some of them can bring a good deal of wisdom and experience to bear on foreign-policy making. Above all, the threat of Senate repudiation of a treaty makes it desirable for the President to solicit their views in advance. As a result, the Secretary of State usually works closely with the Foreign Relations Committee of the Senate and occasionally with the Foreign Affairs Committee of the House. Influential senators often undertake personal missions abroad and serve on delegations to the United Nations and other international bodies.

How important is the Senate's power over treaties? Secretary of State John Hay once complained that "a treaty entering the Senate is like a bull going into the arena; no one can say just how or when the final blow will fall —but one thing is certain—it will never leave the arena alive." The statistics suggest that Mr. Hay's remark was too severe. Even though a two-thirds majority is needed for treaty ratification, the Senate has unconditionally approved about 900 of the approximately 1100 or more submitted to it and many of the remaining 200 were finally passed with amendments or reservations. And yet it is true that some of the rejected treaties were of supreme importance; for example, Senate disapproval of the Taft-Knox arbitration treaties of 1911-1912, of the Treaty of Versailles (involving United States membership in the League of Nations), and of the protocol for participating in the World Court, had a decided effect on the world role of the United States. Moreover, on many occasions Presidents have failed to negotiate treaties, have modified treaty provisions in advance of Senate consideration, or have even recalled treaties already submitted, in the face of opposition from various senators.[9]

The Senate—and to a lesser degree the House—also influences foreign policy through investigations. A widely publicized investigation of munitions-makers by the Nye Committee in 1930 undoubtedly intensified isolationist and pacifist feeling and helped pave the way for neutrality legislation in the 1930's. In 1951 a Senate investigation of the dismissal of General Douglas MacArthur by President Truman raised the whole question of American foreign policy in the Far East and forced the Administration to clarify its position. Occasionally congressional committees or subcommittees make junkets overseas to look into the operations of American agencies.

Until recently, at least, the Senate has been the congressional spokesman on foreign policy, and the House has been decidedly a junior partner. The Senate's superiority stemmed from its treaty-ratifying authority and its veto power over Presidential appointments of ambassadors, ministers, and other important officials. Partly because of the difficulty and unpredictability of the two-thirds treaty rule, however, and partly because of pressure from the House, there has been a marked trend toward joint action by Senate and House. The European Recovery Program, Point Four, the Indian grain program, the Formosa Resolution—to mention but a few—were undertaken by legislation rather than by treaty. Some senators resent this "encroachment," as well as the President's frequent use of *executive agreements* (see Chapter 17), and periodically demands are heard in the Senate that no obligations be made except by formal treaty procedure.

THE SENATE AS A COURT

The Senate also has a *judicial* function. It sits as a court in judgment on officials who have been impeached. The initiative in impeachment proceedings is taken by the House of Representatives, which passes a resolution charging a civil officer (any federal official, including judges but not military officers or

---

[9] For contrasting views of the Senate treaty power see R. J. Dangerfield, *In Defense of the Senate* (Univ. of Oklahoma Press, 1933), and Kenneth Colegrove, *The American Senate and World Peace* (Vanguard, 1944).

members of Congress) with "treason, bribery, or other high crimes and misdemeanors." A committee of House members then prosecutes the impeached official before the Senate. On such an occasion the Senate takes on a judicial character—it issues writs, subpoenas witnesses, and administers oaths. (When a President is on trial, the Chief Justice of the United States presides.) A two-thirds vote is required for conviction; the penalty is removal from office and possible ineligibility for any other office. The Senate has sat as a court of impeachment on twelve occasions and has given a verdict of "Guilty" four times. The most dramatic trial—and the only one involving the Chief Executive—was that of President Andrew Johnson, who in 1868 escaped conviction by only one vote after the Senate had sat for three months.

SENATE SOLIDARITY

In view of the Senate's political and constitutional powers, it is no wonder that the individual member is a person to be reckoned with. Even Presidents at times have had to defer to the wishes of some veteran senator who was entrenched in a state political organization and at the same time headed a powerful legislative committee. Such a man looms large on the Washington scene. His speeches receive nationwide attention, his name comes to stand for a particular public policy, such as economy, military preparedness, social legislation, or a big air force.

In a sense, the Senate is a mutual-protection society. Each member tends to guard the rights and perquisites of his fellow senators—so that his own rights and perquisites will be protected in turn. Any legislative body is a close-knit social and occupational group, and the members must learn to live with one another. This group feeling is especially strong in the Senate, with its small size and hallowed traditions. Senatorial solidarity often cuts across lines of party and issue. Two senators may attack each other in vehement language on the floor, only to be seen a short time later strolling arm in arm in the corridors outside. This sense of solidarity enables the Senate to show a united front against any outside force, such as the President, that seems to be challenging its privileges and powers.

The Senate, in short, is something of a club. Indeed, one veteran Washington reporter contends that there is a club *within* the Senate—an "inner club," without a name or officers, made up of "Senate types" who dominate the politics and procedures of the upper chamber.[10] Republicans Robert A. Taft of Ohio and William Knowland were Senate types, as Democrats Harry Byrd and Lyndon Johnson are today. The "inner club" bolsters the solidarity with which the Senate often acts despite partisan differences.

Two other causes lie behind a senator's sense of authority and independence. One is his six-year term of office. Members who win election four

---

[10] W. S. White, *Citadel* (Harper, 1956).

times—and many of them accomplish this feat—see six presidential terms come and go. No wonder veteran senators exhibit a sense of permanence and position even when dealing with the President. Perhaps more important is the right of unlimited debate. The *filibuster* not only symbolizes the power of the individual senator—it also provides a basis of that power. One senator, moreover, can easily disrupt the bills and business of his fellow members by spiking efforts to expedite action, by the simple means of shouting "I object" every time the presiding officer calls for unanimous consent to a particular motion. "Live and let live" might be the Senate's motto—and might help explain why it has become one of the most powerful and yet unpredictable assemblies in the world.

Summary

1. The main power of Congress is legislative, but it has a number of other functions.
2. The main work of Congress is conducted in committees. Selecting committee chairmen on the basis of seniority puts power in the hands of veteran members of Congress.
3. The two chambers are much the same in general structure and function. Strong central party leadership is lacking in both.
4. Important differences between the two chambers involve their size, electoral districts, length of members' terms, the Rules Committee in the House, and the filibuster in the Senate.

Congressmen at Work

Congress is composed of politicians who have succeeded in winning office. As politicians, the senators and representatives live amid the pulls and pressures of their constituents, powerful interest groups, party leaders in and out out of Congress, and the President. To understand Congress, we must see its institutions and procedures as part of what has been called the "legislative struggle." Let us look at this struggle in terms of the pressures, powers, and problems that affect a typical congressman—Representative Smith—in his work on Capitol Hill.

Mr. Smith Goes to Washington

When Mr. Smith leaves his home for Washington, he carries with him political debts and political hopes. In a way, his biggest debt is to the majority of voters in his district who elected him to office. His chief hope is to keep the support of a majority of the voters and thus to stay in office. How can he do this? It is not just a matter of living up to the platform for which his supporters presumably voted. He does not really know just who his supporters are, or just what policies they favored. He does not really know how to keep their backing. Conditions will change. Some of his supporters will turn against him; others will return to the ranks of the nonvoters.

REPRESENT WHOM?

The chances are that Mr. Smith will work most actively for those who most directly helped him win the election. As we have seen (Chapter 14), his victory in that election did not seem to hinge chiefly on his attitude toward broad national issues, for the voters were not occupied with such issues, or their views were vague and diffused. If they had been interested in national problems, Mr. Smith's job of staying in office might be easier, for he could simply vote "right" on each bill as it came up. As it is, Mr. Smith, like most of his fellow legislators, decides that one way to stay in office is to maintain close and friendly contacts with the leaders of the personal organization that he set up during his campaign.

Some of his most effective support came from *leaders of organized groups* in his district—particularly occupational interest groups. He owes a debt to these persons, and he finds in Washington that he is expected to pay that debt. The associations that he dealt with locally—the labor organizations, or the Farm Bureau Federation, or the American Legion—are well represented in Washington, and their legislative agents are quick to arrange a meeting with Mr. Smith and acquaint him with their programs. Although an organization may have taken positions on broad national issues, such as foreign policy or taxation, it is mainly concerned with specific bills conferring benefits on its members. On these bills—which are little known to his constituents as a whole—Mr. Smith is expected to vote favorably. His support is a means of paying his political debt, and he knows that his actions will be reported to the organization's members back home.

Mr. Smith also enjoyed the support of *local party leaders*. He probably has no great sense of obligation to the party in his district, for an effective local party hardly exists. But he does owe a debt to the individual party leaders back home who worked for him and used their party contacts in his behalf. These local party leaders are not, for the most part, concerned with national legislation, but they are greatly interested in patronage and favors. They look to Mr. Smith for both. As a freshman representative, he does not control much patronage in Washington, but he is permitted to fill certain jobs in the congressional establishment—an elevator operator, perhaps, or messenger—and he probably can find other jobs in the administrative depart-

9:00—"Congressman arrives at office."

9:01—"Telephone rings. Talks, signs mail."

9:58—"Rushes off to committee meeting."

10 to 12—"Hearing. At noon goes to floor."

1:00—"Starts lunch. Call-bell rings."

ments. More important are the federal appointments in his district over which he may have some influence: postmasters, tax collectors, United States mar-

3:00—"Page brings note. Lady outside."

shals, federal attorneys, and other positions not fully covered by nonpartisan civil service laws. Of course, Mr. Smith has little or no patronage if the President belongs to the opposition party. And even if his own party is in power, he may have to share the patronage with one or two senators. Actually, this never-ending scramble for jobs is one of the most trying aspects of his work. Every time he gives out a position, he suspects glumly that he is making nine enemies and one ingrate.

4:00—"At office, sees home-state students."

Mr. Smith's loyalty to local party officials does not necessarily extend to the national party organization. To be sure, he keeps in touch with party leaders *in* Congress, and he must clear his patronage through his national party chairman. Beyond these contacts, however, he sees very little of the party organization in Washington, for the national committee rarely meets or tries to set policy. Occasionally, Mr. Smith hears from the national chairman on a legislative matter that the party considers important. But he feels small sense of obligation. The national party gave him little if any help in the campaign, and he knows that voting as his district seems to want him to vote will probably win him more friends than following the national party line.

4:15—"Call to floor again."

7 to 12—"Does homework."

6:30—"Dinner with wife."   "   12:00—"And so to bed."

Roy Doty in *The New York Times*

A day in the life of a Congressman.

As a congressman,

Mr. Smith keeps all these considerations in mind. This does not mean, however, that he is merely a calculating machine, with various forces punching the keys. For Mr. Smith brings to Congress certain political convictions of his own. He may feel that labor has too much power, that big business should be curbed, that the cost of government should be reduced. No matter what pressures converge on him in Washington, Mr. Smith neither can nor wishes to shake off the ideas that have been part of his environment since birth. In short, Mr. Smith's official acts are not simply a result of the pressures acting *on* him. They are also a result of the pressures acting *within* him.[1]

ERRAND-RUNNING

Mr. Smith knows that one way to win the support of his constituents is by doing countless individual favors. His office is well set up for this task. He has the services of several secretaries and stenographers, as well as a full-time legislative aide. Most important, government agencies are eager to respond to Mr. Smith's requests. Often the people who ask for help are constituents dealing with some agency. A businessman wants to know how to apply for a government contract, or a veteran wants to straighten out his pension. Mr. Smith is glad to help. In order to serve as a sort of Washington representative for his constituents, he must know how to get cooperation from administrative officials. And usually such cooperation is quickly forthcoming, for administrators know that they depend on the good will of congressmen for their annual appropriations.

Mr. Smith finds that he must do much of the errand-running himself. One representative has complained that:

> A congressman has become an expanded messenger boy, an employment agency, getter-out of the Navy, Army, marines, ward heeler, wound healer, trouble shooter, law explainer, bill finder, issue translator, resolution interpreter, controversy oil pourer, gladhand extender, business promoter, convention goer, civic ills skirmisher, veterans' affairs adjuster, ex-serviceman's champion, watchdog for the underdog, sympathizer with the upper dog, namer and kisser of babies, recoverer of lost baggage, soberer of delegates, adjuster for traffic violators, voters straying into Washington and into toils of the law, binder up of broken hearts, financial wet nurse, good samaritan, contributor to good causes—there are so many good causes—cornerstone layer, public building and bridge dedicator, ship christener—to be sure he does get in a little flag waving—and a little constitutional hoisting and spread-eagle work, but it is getting harder every day to find time to properly study legislation—the very business we are primarily here to discharge, and that must be done above all things.[2]

---

[1] See S. K. Bailey, *Congress Makes a Law* (Columbia Univ. Press, 1950), pp. 192-193.
[2] Quoted in Galloway, *Congress at the Crossroads,* p. 61.

There is, of course, a brighter side to the picture. In the era of big government, which often seems cold and impersonal, the congressman can play a vital humanizing role. He can be the mediator between the citizen and the bureaucrats. "One of the things that hold the vast area of the United States together," an English observer has said, "is the belief that the political machinery provides a means whereby local and personal interests and sentiments are really taken into account in Washington." [3] But it is not easy for Mr. Smith to be so philosophical. He has come to Washington to *legislate*—and sometimes he feels that lawmaking is one of the least of his duties.

CONGRESSIONAL PREROGATIVES

Despite all these difficulties, Mr. Smith finds his job a congenial one. He is an important person in his district and an influential politician in his party. The newspapers pay him some attention, although they may often be critical. In Washington he is only one among many legislators, but there are compensations.

Representatives and senators are paid $22,500 a year. (The Speaker and Vice President receive $35,000 and the use of a fancy automobile.) In addition, each member gets an allowance for travel, for stationery, and for help to staff the office which the government also provides. This is not to say that most congressmen have no financial worries. On the contrary, the financial obligations of maintaining two residences and the expenses incurred in doing his job often exceed what he gets from the government. When these expenses are added to those of campaigning and of meeting all the "touches" to which congressmen are exposed, it is a rare member of the legislature who can live on his salary. Congressmen by law determine their own salaries. They have been reluctant to increase their pay; but on the basis of the recommendations of a presidential commission, an increase to the present levels was recently voted. Congress has also established a contributing retirement system, which gives some measure of security to congressmen who retire either voluntarily or at the voters' insistence.

Congressmen also enjoy the *postal frank.* They may use the mails without charge to write to their constituents and to send out literature. This privilege is a decided advantage to incumbent congressmen in their campaigns for re-election.

Congressmen have absolute *immunity* for whatever they say on the floor of the Congress, before a congressional committee, or in connection with congressional business. They may not be sued for libel or slander nor in any way called to question before any court. Here is absolute freedom of speech. Each chamber may, however, discipline members who abuse this privilege. And the voters can always express their disapproval at the polls.

---

[3] D. W. Brogan, *The American Character* (Knopf, 1944), p. 123.

Congressmen are *privileged from arrest* during attendance at Congress and in going to and from Congress, except in cases of treason, felony, and breach of the peace. This privilege does not cover a summons in a civil suit and, since the abolition of imprisonment for debt many years ago, has lost most of its significance. Congressmen are subject to criminal laws in the same manner as other persons.

Congressmen enjoy a good deal of *legislative assistance.* The Legislative Reference Service, consisting of recognized experts in a variety of national problem areas, can supply data to congressmen quickly and authoritatively. Over 50,000 inquiries are handled by the service every year. Legislative counsel provide bill-drafting services to senators and representatives who need such help.

The Smith Bill Runs the Gantlet

The diagram on pp. 406-407 indicates the formal stages a bill must go through to become law. But the *political* as well as the procedural aspects of lawmaking must be kept in view. Let's suppose that Representative Smith decided to sponsor a bill.

It was not until his third term of office that Mr. Smith was able to sponsor legislation on which he had set his heart from the beginning. This was a bill to raise and broaden minimum-wage standards. Usually even a third-termer would not have the chance to sponsor an important piece of legislation requested by the President and party leaders. Mr. Smith, a member of the Education and Labor Committee, got the chance only because the chairman of the committee was a southerner opposed to the bill, the next-ranking member was ill, and two other senior members did not want to commit themselves to specific changes in minimum-wage standards until a later time.[4]

The first step was a meeting with the President. Mr. Smith and several other members of the committee had a 15-minute interview with him in the White House. The President, who did most of the talking, offered no suggestions on the details of the proposed legislation; he simply asked that the coverage of the bill be as broad as possible. He also requested that the committee work closely with the Secretary of Labor to maintain smooth relations between Congress and the executive on this matter. After the exchange of a few pleasantries, the congressmen left.

DRUMMING UP SUPPORT

Mr. Smith was glad to sponsor the bill because minimum wages had been one of his campaign issues. But now that he was ready to champion it, he

---

[4] This description is drawn chiefly from Stephen K. Bailey, *Congress Makes a Law* (Columbia Univ. Press, 1950), and J. M. Burns, *Congress on Trial,* Chapter 5, "The Story of Three Bills." Descriptions of the handling of actual bills will be found in Chapters 17, 25, 26, and below.

found little interest in the matter back home. Local labor leaders and liberal groups endorsed the proposed legislation, of course, but without creating much of a stir. Mr. Smith wanted publicity. He saw that he himself would have to create it. At his suggestion, a committee of liberals, union leaders, and small businessmen began a campaign for the bill in his district. Letters appeared in newspapers. Resolutions were adopted calling on Mr. Smith for action. Hundreds of people signed petitions demanding a raise in minimum standards. At the height of the campaign, Mr. Smith appeared at a mass meeting and promised to fight for the bill. He returned to Washington with cheers still ringing in his ears.

The next step was the difficult one of writing the bill. Mr. Smith took a rough draft over to the Department of Labor—and found that officials there had already drawn up their own bill, complete with preamble and a dozen clauses. Mr. Smith was disturbed to find that the Administration bill, as the Labor Department people called it, went much further than his. For example, Mr. Smith wanted to exempt businesses employing less than seven people; the Administration bill made it five. An inconclusive argument ensued. It was agreed to hold another meeting in a week.

During the next few days Mr. Smith got some telegrams from the union leaders in his district in support of the Administration bill. Surprised and disturbed, Mr. Smith telephoned them to ask why they had changed their positions. They answered that they had talked the matter over with their national headquarters. At the next meeting the Labor Department officials brought with them two national union leaders and a representative from the White House. Mr. Smith was assured by his visitors that the Administration draft was supported by the President and by the national AFL-CIO. He soon gave in on some of the major points. He insisted, however, that the new compromise draft retain one of his provisions exempting fruit-canners (who were fairly strong in his district) from any change in hours standards. He warned that unless this provision was kept in, he would not sponsor the bill. He got his way on this matter. After getting legislative counsel to help him polish up the bill, Mr. Smith introduced the measure into the lower chamber by placing it in the hopper on the clerk's desk which is near the Speaker's rostrum.

The clerk, acting for the Speaker, promptly gave the bill a number— H.R. 2102—and referred it to the Committee on Education and Labor. Then ensued an irritating delay of six weeks. The trouble was—and Mr. Smith knew it—that the committee chairman did not want to act on the bill. First the bill got lost somewhere in the chairman's office. When finally found, the bill had to wait while the chairman held hearings on some minor measures. It was only after Mr. Smith appealed to the Speaker and majority leader, and after the Labor Department asked help from the President, that the chairman finally announced that hearings on the bill would commence.

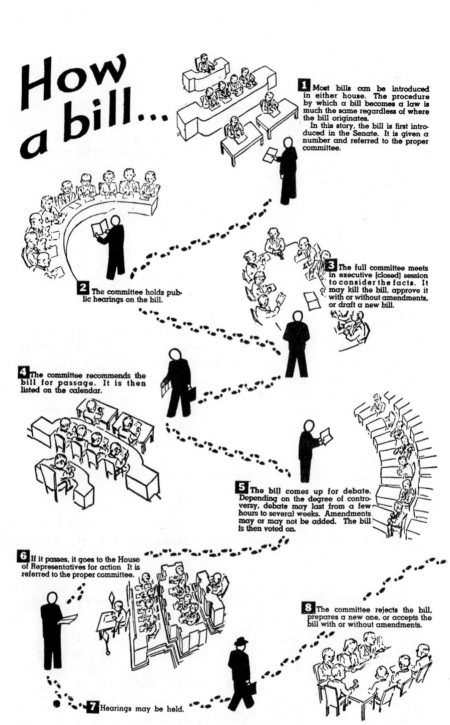

How a bill...

1 Most bills can be introduced in either house. The procedure by which a bill becomes a law is much the same regardless of where the bill originates.
In this story, the bill is first introduced in the Senate. It is given a number and referred to the proper committee.

2 The committee holds public hearings on the bill.

3 The full committee meets in executive [closed] session to consider the facts. It may kill the bill, approve it with or without amendments, or draft a new bill.

4 The committee recommends the bill for passage. It is then listed on the calendar.

5 The bill comes up for debate. Depending on the degree of controversy, debate may last from a few hours to several weeks. Amendments may or may not be added. The bill is then voted on.

6 If it passes, it goes to the House of Representatives for action It is referred to the proper committee.

7 Hearings may be held.

8 The committee rejects the bill, prepares a new one, or accepts the bill with or without amendments.

Adapted from *Journal* of the National Education Association

12 If the bill is passed by the second body but contains major differences, either house may request a conference committee. The conferees meet and try to reconcile their differences. Representing both parties, five conferees are usually appointed from each house.

11 It goes before the entire body, is debated and voted on.

SENATE

HOUSE

13 Generally, they reach an agreement. They report back to their respective houses. The report is accepted or rejected.

10 The Rules Committee is one of the most powerful of the committees in the House of Representatives. After a bill has been recommended for passage by the committee to which it was referred, the Rules Committee can block it or clear it for debate before the entire House.

RULES COMMITTEE

14 If the report is accepted by both houses, the bill is signed by the Speaker of the House, the President of the Senate, and is sent to the President of the United States.

9 The committee recommends the bill for passage. It is listed on the calendar and is sent to the Rules Committee.

...*Becomes a law.*

15 The President may sign or veto the bill within 10 days. If he doesn't sign within 10 days and Congress is still in session, the bill automatically becomes law. If Congress has adjourned before the 10 days have elapsed and the President has not signed the bill, it does not become law. This is known as a "pocket veto." If the President returns the bill with a veto message, it may still become law if passed by a two-thirds majority in each house.

RUNNING INTERFERENCE

Meanwhile Mr. Smith was busy making plans for presenting the case for his bill. (He knew that the committee chairman would see to it that the bill's opponents had a chance to speak.) To lead his parade of witnesses he enlisted the Secretary of Labor, the head of the AFL-CIO, and the senator who had introduced a companion bill to H.R. 2102 in the Senate. A good strategist, Mr. Smith knew that the hearings should not give the impression that labor was for the bill and business and agriculture opposed. So he tried to split the opposition. Fearing that the big organizations of farmers employing hired hands might oppose the bill, he got a promise from the National Farmers Union that it would send an official to endorse H.R. 2102. Knowing that some small manufacturers in his district feared low-wage competition in the South, he asked them to urge their national association of small businessmen to take sides. But the national association had a number of influential members from the South in its ranks, so Mr. Smith was unable to get its support. Instead, some representatives of northern industry agreed to testify.

At first the hearings went splendidly for Mr. Smith and his bill. The "big names" spoke briefly for H.R. 2102, and committee members did not dare to cross-examine them too vigorously. Then trouble developed. After the Farmers Union spokesman endorsed the bill, the chairman called on representatives of the other major farm organizations, who stated that the great majority of farmers did not want an increase in minimum wages because it would raise their labor costs. By asking leading questions, the chairman brought out the fact that his witnesses spoke for many more farmers than did Mr. Smith's. That was bad enough—but then another committee member attacked one of Mr. Smith's liberal businessmen as a former member of two communist-dominated organizations. Mr. Smith was glad that he was able immediately afterward to present the president of a World War II veterans' organization, who spoke in favor of the bill. His hope of gaining business support was further dashed, however, when the National Association of Manufacturers advanced some amendments that—in Mr. Smith's mind at least—would cripple the bill.

The hearings lasted six days. Despite frequent clashes between committeemen and witnesses—and sometimes among committeemen themselves—the hearings played a valuable role. Many useful suggestions were made. A great deal of important economic and statistical material was put into the record. And virtually every interest group involved was able to offer views orally or in writing. True, over half the committee members were absent most of the time, but they could consult the voluminous printed record later on.

Following the open hearings, the committee met in secret *executive session*. Mr. Smith had already begun to count noses. He knew that of the thirteen committeemen of his own (majority) party, eight favored the bill, three opposed it, and two were doubtful. Of the eight members of the minority party, five seemed hostile to the bill, one friendly, and two on the fence. Mr. Smith knew that he needed a majority of at least eleven—and twelve or thirteen would be safer—in reporting out the bill, for Congress rarely approves a bill without a favorable committee report. The first executive session, in which the bill was discussed section by section, gave him a chance to see just where his fellow committeemen stood. Soon afterward he conferred with the majority leader of the House, who then induced the President to invite to lunch two of the doubtful members of the majority party and two of the straddlers—but not the chairman, who was considered beyond hope. At the luncheon table, the President did not try to pressure his guests, but he made his own position clear, described the need for party unity, and incidentally agreed to straighten out some patronage matters that were troubling one or two of the representatives.

Mr. Smith also saw to it—with the help of labor and liberal organizations —that the erring members were deluged with letters and telegrams in behalf of the bill. Most of these communications came from within the members' districts. The combined approach worked. At the next executive session three of the President's four guests were generally in favor of the measure. The real danger now was the adoption of crippling amendments. While announcing their support of the general principles of the bill, member after member demanded amendments that would exempt certain areas, occupations, or classes of workers. Helplessly Mr. Smith watched while his colleagues kept the logs rolling, each supporting another's amendment so that his own amendment would go through in turn. After three such meetings the bill was a tattered remnant of what it had been. Indeed, it had been so weakened that in the final committee vote the bill received the support of half the opposition party members and of all Mr. Smith's fellow party members, including even the chairman.

INTO THE HOUSE

For a time Mr. Smith considered dropping the whole matter. He was reminded, however, that the bill might be strengthened on the floor of the House, and perhaps in the Senate too. He already had a favorable committee report before the House. He decided that the next step was to try to get favorable action from the Rules Committee.

Here Mr. Smith's bill came up against one of its biggest hurdles. The Rules Committee was composed of veteran representatives, a majority of whom were members of the majority party but often sided with the minority. Not only did Mr. Smith need a go-ahead sign from Rules, but he also wanted a rule that would prevent his bill from getting loaded down with amendments during House debate. For three weeks Rules refused to act at all, but when Mr. Smith and other representatives began to talk about prying a rule out by a *discharge petition* (requiring signatures of a majority of the members), the Rules Committee granted a rule. Under the terms of the rule, debate was to take four hours, divided between proponents and opponents of H.R. 2102. The rule also provided, however, that anyone on the floor could offer amendments.

Mr. Smith was floor manager of the bill; with the majority leader he worked out a schedule that allotted thirty minutes to himself and brief five-minute speeches to other supporters of H.R. 2102. The rest of the time was parceled out by minority party leaders to opponents of the bill. The Speaker was to use these two lists in recognizing representatives who wanted to speak on the bill. Meanwhile Mr. Smith was busy lining up support. He arranged with a White House official for a formal message from the President endorsing the objectives of the bill and asking for stronger provisions. Labor organizations set up a nationwide Committee on Social Rights, which issued propaganda for the bill. Lobbyists visited representatives in their offices and buttonholed them in the corridors. Delegations of businessmen and workers arrived in Washington from the lawmakers' districts. A torrent of mail descended on Capitol Hill. The opposition was equally active.

By the time the debate opened, almost all the representatives had made up their minds; the real question was whether the bill would be amended to death and abandoned. The worst threat was an amendment that would have excluded from H.R. 2102 all employees involved in the raising, processing, or delivering of farm or related products. This catchall, which Mr. Smith knew would cut out the heart of the bill, had the backing of a formidable group of representatives from farm states, the opposition party, and low-wage areas. Only by inducing the Speaker to leave the rostrum and make a personal appeal on the floor, and by warning the farm representatives that labor would vote down agricultural legislation unless they supported H.R. 2102, was Mr. Smith able to save the bill. The final threat came on a motion to *recommit* the bill to committee—in effect a motion to kill it. When this attempt narrowly failed, the members voted overwhelmingly in favor of the measure.

When Senate and House Disagree

Mr. Smith's long battle was over —or half over, for H.R. 2102 would still have to clear the Senate. There the bill normally would go through the same steps as in the House —introduction (by a senator who agrees to sponsor the bill jointly with Mr. Smith), long committee hearings, executive committee meetings, debate on the floor, and all amid political conflict throughout the nation. There is no Rules Committee in the Senate to hold up the bill, but a filibuster might stall it on the floor. The Senators, moreover, might be somewhat less responsive to direct pressure from home because of their longer terms.

Let us suppose, however, that Mr. Smith's bill passed the Senate but in substantially different form from the version passed by the House. This is likely, for, as we have seen, the Senate and House were originally set up to represent sharply different interests and attitudes. The upper house was to be a small chamber of men elected indirectly by the people and holding long, over-lapping terms. The House of Representatives, elected *in toto* every two years, was to be the direct, strong organ of the people. Three important changes have brought the two bodies closer together. Senators are now directly elected by the voters. Gerrymandering and the seniority rule have made the House unduly representative of rural and conservative interests. And the spread of urbanism has made the Senate more representative of urban interests. Although the Founding Fathers thought of the Senate as a conservative check on the radical House, it would be hard to say today that the upper chamber tends to be more conservative or more liberal than the lower.

On the other hand, the framers' hope that the two houses would speak for *different* interests has been realized. The differences between the size and nature of the electoral districts in each house, between the length of terms of senators and representatives, between the internal mechanisms in each cham-ber, between the political contexts in which they operate, inevitably bring about sharp disagreements between Senate and House over policy. Such differ-ences, moreover, can create an acute problem, since each chamber has veto power over the other. Only if both houses pass an absolutely identical measure can it become law. How do the legislators resolve their disagreements?

The answer is the *conference committee*. If neither house will accept the other's bill, a special committee of members from each chamber settles the differences. Appointed to the conference committee by their presiding officers, the members are usually the lawmakers who originally handled the bill in their respective chambers. The most senior senator usually serves as chair-man of the conference committee, which has anywhere from three to nine members from each house. Both parties are represented, with the majority party having a larger number. The proceedings of this committee—not open to the public—are usually a shrewd and elaborate bargaining process. Con-cessions must be made not only to each chamber but to the more powerful groups within the chambers. Brought back to the respective chambers, the conference report can be accepted or it can be rejected (often with further negotiations ordered), but it cannot be *amended*. Each set of conferees must convince its colleagues that any concessions made to the other house were on trivialities, and that nothing basic in their own version of the bill was surrendered.

How much leeway does a conference committee have? Ordinarily the conferees are expected to stay somewhere between the alternatives set by the different versions; for example, if the House version of Mr. Smith's bill should set a minimum wage of $1.00 and the Senate bill $1.25, the conference committee would hardly come up with $1.50. But on many matters, where there is no clear middle ground, conferees are sometimes accused of "exceed-ing their instructions" and producing a new measure. Indeed, the conference committee has even been called a "third house of Congress" that arbitrarily revises Senate and House policy in secret session. Despite such criticism, however, some kind of conference committee is indispensable to the workings of a bicameral legislature such as Congress.

Congressmen as Investigators

Both senators and representatives are on a constant quest for facts, ideas, and advice. They need information and opinion in making laws, in publicizing governmental activities, in attacking the other party or other political officials, in overseeing the administrative agencies. They obtain their information from committee hearings, the President, administrative agencies, other congressmen, interest groups, letters from constituents, the Library of Congress and its Legislative Reference Service, and from many other sources.

WHY CONGRESS INVESTIGATES

Hearings by standing committees or by their subcommittees are probably the most important source of information and opinion. Such inquiries provide an arena where experts can submit their views and data, statements and statistics can be entered into the record, and congressmen can quiz a wide variety of witnesses. When an important and controversial bill is under consideration, hearings will last for weeks, and a host of administrative officials, lobbyists, technical experts, interested citizens, and members of Congress will testify. Sometimes the hearings receive front-page billing in newspapers throughout the land; more often they are little publicized unless a well-known person is testifying. Congressmen cannot go to all the hearings, of course, but by means of verbatim records of the hearings they can follow the proceedings as they wish.

Committees investigate not only to collect facts and opinions. Many inquiries are largely *political* in nature—they are designed to help or hinder some bill or party or official. Members of Congress may have information already at hand, but they know that the effective publicizing of those facts before reporters and fellow congressmen may dramatize existing evils and the need for reform. For example, many of the corrupt practices of some labor racketeers "revealed" by Congress in 1959 were well documented in studies and reports; but the "exposés" in Washington helped create the right political climate to allow Congress to act. Hearings, in short, are often directed toward the people in an effort to mobilize public opinion.

Investigations by regular committees have another purpose—the *overseeing* of administration. A committee can summon any administrative official, from Cabinet officer to stenographer, to testify in public or private hearings. Some officials greatly fear these inquiries; they dread the loaded questions of hostile congressmen, and the likelihood that some administrative error in their agency may be uncovered and publicized.

Both the congressman and the administrator suffer certain handicaps in such hearings. The congressman is usually not expert in the field (although some members become highly expert after years of service on a particular committee), and he has a thousand other problems on his mind. The official knows his field, but he may not see the broader problems, and he feels ill at ease among unsympathetic legislators.[5] Despite occasional misunderstandings and abuses, however, the routine investigations of administration are an important means of checking administrative action. In this sense investigations are an important part of the system of checks and balances.

The Constitution gives Congress major investigative powers. Private witnesses can be subpoenaed and required to testify. If the investigation is reasonably connected with matters over which Congress has power, and if the questions asked are pertinent to the purposes of the investigation, witnesses who fail to answer may be punished for contempt of Congress. Still, proceedings are more informal than in a court of law. Since the purpose of an investigation is to gain information, not to prosecute, persons before such committees are not, legally speaking, in jeopardy of life or limb. The elaborate safeguards of the judicial process are not always needed, and if required they might deny essential information to Congress and country.

"GRAND INQUISITIONS"?

We have been talking about the day-to-day inquiries conducted by regular standing committees or their subcommittees. Special investigations made by standing, special, or select committees to probe particular questions present many of the same problems as the more routine inquiries, but in exaggerated form. Special investigations have long been undertaken by Congress. The first one took place in 1793, after General St. Clair's military expedition against the Indians had ended in disaster. Some representatives wanted to let President Washington look into the causes of the failure. But the House, taking matters into its own hands, set up a special investigating committee to act for Congress.

Since then, there have been many famous investigations. Corruption in public office has been repeatedly exposed, infringements of civil liberties uncovered, harmful banking, stock exchange, and utility practices publicized, bureaucratic practices checked, "un-American" practices denounced. A particularly famous investigating committee was the Truman Committee, which, during World War II, probed into waste and inefficiency, made many constructive suggestions, and helped put its chairman into the White House. The number of investigations has also grown; in 1959, for example, Congress authorized over 50 of them at a cost of $8 million. Special investigating committees have all the powers of standing committees except that they normally may not intro-

---

[5] Young, *This Is Congress*, pp. 228-229.

duce legislation. At the same time, they usually enjoy far greater publicity—
and investigations thrive on publicity. These committees operate in the spotlight, and their proceedings are often covered by newsreel and television cameras and reported by a host of newsmen.

Yet right here is where the danger lies. So eager are the investigators for
sensational results that they often permit abuses that bring the congressional
power of investigation into disrepute. This is nothing new. Early in the last
century a committee was criticized for excessive zeal—probing the executive,
it "pointed out little items, sniffed about dark corners, peeped behind curtains
and under beds, and exploited every cupboard of the Executive household with
a mousing alacrity, not so eager to correct abuses as to collect campaign material for damaging some candidate." [6] Recently some investigators have been
so zealous in seeking publicity that they have indulged in defamation of character, bullying and mistreatment of witnesses, and outright partisanship. Sometimes even the better-intentioned have conducted mere fishing expeditions in
the hope that something might turn up.

In 1957 the Supreme Court cautioned Congress (*Watkins* v. *U.S.*) that
the First Amendment limits the power of congressional committees and that
no committee has the power "to expose for the sake of exposure." The Court
continued: "Investigations conducted solely for the personal aggrandizement
of the investigators or to 'punish' those investigated are indefensible. . . . No
inquiry is an end in itself; it must be re-
lated to, and in furtherance of, a legitimate
task of Congress." Thus the Court construed the contempt of Congress power
narrowly to avoid punishment of witnesses
for refusing to answer questions, unless
the questions were clearly pertinent to an
authorized committee function. Many
congressmen attacked the Watkins ruling
as unduly restrictive of the congressional
investigating power. That their fears were
groundless became apparent in 1959 when

Courtesy *The New York Times*
and Tom Little

the High Court, over the strong dissent of four justices, narrowly construed
the Watkins decision and sustained (in *Barenblatt* v. *U.S.*) a conviction for
contempt of a witness who had refused to tell the House Un-American Activities Committee, investigating alleged communist infiltration of education,
whether he had been a communist while a graduate student.

Many members of Congress are disturbed about overzealous investigations. One senator has warned that "unless Congress reforms its methods of
conducting investigations, unless it puts some limits of responsibility both

---

[6] Quoted in Irving M. Ives, "In Place of Congressional 'Circuses,'" *The New York Times
Magazine*, August 27, 1950.

upon the interrogation of witnesses and upon the type of testimony which witnesses are allowed to give—unless, indeed, it adopts a wholly new and more judicious attitude—one of the great and important instruments of the legislative process will be destroyed." [7] Another senator has reminded his colleagues that the investigative function is a valuable but also a "delicate instrument which cannot withstand the jolts and jars, the stress and strain of rude partisan handling." [8]

AN END TO "CONGRESSIONAL CIRCUSES"?

Many reforms have been suggested, some of them involving internal procedure. It has been proposed, for example, that persons attacked before an investigating committee be given the right to appear personally to defend themselves, that the committee be compelled to subpoena witnesses when requested, that accused individuals be permitted to cross-examine witnesses personally or through counsel. Some time ago, Representative Bender of Ohio proposed new rules to regulate the conduct of investigating committees. But Congress has failed to respond to such proposals. Its hesitation is due in part to the fear that investigations might become hedged around by so many rigid restrictions that they would lose their usefulness.

Another proposal would delegate the handling of investigations to bodies outside Congress. It is argued that congressmen are overburdened as it is, and that investigations outside Congress might be more objective and less likely to lead to criticism of the lawmakers. Some Americans have looked enviously on the British royal commissions which, composed both of members of Parliament and outside experts, have led to many governmental reforms and continue to enjoy tremendous prestige in Great Britain. Many congressmen, however, would fear to give the President the power to appoint members of commissions, for they are jealous of their investigative power and are determined to keep it independent of the executive.

Fortunately, we may be slowly perfecting a method of investigation that embodies the best features of royal commissions and congressional inquiries. This is the *mixed* commission or committee, composed both of congressmen and outsiders. The Temporary National Economic Committee, an outstanding investigative body of the 1930's, was made up of six congressmen and six representatives of departments and agencies: its chairman was a senator and its vice-chairman a representative. Equally successful were the two Commissions on Organization of the Executive Branch of the Government, under the chairmanship of former President Herbert Hoover. Each of these commissions had twelve members: four persons (including two representatives) chosen by the Speaker of the House, four (including two senators) chosen by the Presi-

---

[7] Scott W. Lucas, "Congressional Hearing: a Plea for Reform," *The New York Times Magazine,* March 19, 1950.

[8] Ives, *loc. cit.*

dent of the Senate, and four (including two members of the executive department) chosen by the President of the United States.

Such a procedure may come into wider use as the years go by. It provides a balanced group, fairly equally divided between parties, aware of the problems of both Congress and executive, but wholly responsible to neither branch of government, and enjoying great prestige in the nation.

It seems unlikely, however, that investigating bodies will ever be taken wholly out of politics. Politicians in all parties will always make capital out of information that is unearthed. This is the way it should be in a free society. The most we can do is surround the investigative process with proper safeguards to protect the rights of individuals, to cut down as much as possible on abuses and unfairness. In this way the power of vigorous investigation—so indispensable in a democracy—can be given its best expression.

What's the Matter with Congress?

Congress is the nation's whipping boy. Newspaper editors, radio commentators, politicians, and plain citizens seem never to tire of berating individual legislators, blocs, or Congress as a whole. Cartoonists delight in portraying congressmen as timid, ignorant, selfish, and narrow-minded.

Much of this abuse is unjustified. Critics of Congress often seem to forget that our national legislature is particularly exposed to unfair attacks. In the first place, Congress does its work directly under the public eye. Unfortunate incidents—quarrels, name calling, evasive actions, inaccurate statements—that might be hushed up in the executive branch are almost always observed by the alert journalists covering Congress for the whole nation. In the second place, Congress by its very nature is controversial and argumentative. Its members take stands on both sides—sometimes on half a dozen sides—of every important question, and the average citizen holding one opinion is likely to be intolerant of lawmakers holding other views.

Some of the abuse, moreover, stems from confusion *about* Congress and from confusion *in* Congress. There is lack of agreement on what the primary functions of Congress should be. Should it concentrate on making policies, debating them, investigating problems, or curbing the President and bureaucrats—or on something else? Actually Congress can and does do all these things, but not without much waste motion and unnecessary effort. Confusion *in* Congress arises from the different jobs it does, the complexity of the procedure, the sheer number of legislators, the variety of viewpoints, the maze of party and group conflicts. At a baseball game almost anyone can understand the duel between pitcher and batter. In Congress a dozen pitchers throw a dozen balls to a dozen batters. Such confusion, however, is basically not the fault of Congress but the result of a constitutional system that divides up authority and checks power with power.

Granting all this, however, we must admit that some criticism of Congress is justified. Senators and representatives themselves have on many occasions complained about certain features of the legislature and have demanded improvements.

"CONGRESS IS INEFFICIENT"

Critics can cite many facts to support the charge that Congress is woefully inefficient. Procedure in both chambers—especially in the Senate—is often very slow and cumbersome. The many committees, with their scores of subcommittees, operate ponderously. Congressmen spend much of their time on time-wasting activities, such as running errands for individual constituents or making speeches to an almost empty chamber. To take a specific example of inefficiency, calling the roll in the House uses three-quarters of an hour of valuable time.

There is, however, another side to the story. The main reason for slow, cumbersome procedure is the congressional tradition of protecting the rights of minorities and individual legislators. This tradition is an important one. Somewhere in government we must permit opposing and unorthodox views to be presented. By enabling bills to be reconsidered under certain circumstances, by requiring them to be openly read by the clerk, by allowing roll-call votes when the decision is in doubt—to name only a few examples—Congress protects minority rights inside its two houses and outside. To be sure, this protection of minority and individual rights is abused. But abused or not, these rights are basic to the democratic, parliamentary process.

Of course, some of the inefficiencies in Congress have nothing to do with democracy. And some of these inefficiencies Congress has often attempted to correct. To take one important case, in 1945 Congress created a Joint Committee on the Organization of Congress to make recommendations for improving its procedures. After consultation with outstanding authorities and months of study, the committee made its recommendations, some of which were enacted in the Legislative Reorganization Act of 1946. This act "streamlined" the committee system by reducing the number of committees in the House from 48 to 19, in the Senate from 33 to 15, and thus enabled members of Congress to concentrate on a smaller number of policy areas. It strengthened the professional assistance of the committees. It clarified the jurisdiction of committees, and required them to hold regular meetings and to keep a record of votes and proceedings. To prevent delay and obstruction, committee chairmen were required to report promptly any measures approved by their committees.

The 1946 act also tried to streamline legislative procedures by reducing the number of private bills, which take up so much of Congress' time. To strengthen the budgetary process, elaborate provisions were made to supply Congress with an over-all picture of fiscal and budgetary policy. The House Committees on Ways and Means and Appropriations and the Senate Committees on Finance and Appropriations were instructed to hold a joint meeting at the beginning of each session of Congress and, after considering the President's budgetary proposals, to make recommendations for the maximum amount Congress was to appropriate.

Further provisions of the act increased congressmen's salaries, established a retirement system for them, provided for administrative assistants for the Speaker and for the majority and minority leaders of the House, and clarified the powers and responsibilities of conference committees. The Senate amended its rules to make it more difficult to attach *riders* to appropriation bills. A rider is a provision not germane to the rest of the bill. Since the President must sign or veto an entire bill, he cannot veto the rider without losing a whole appropriation measure—a situation that facilitates "raids" on the Treasury.

How well has the Reorganization Act worked out? Some feel that it has been pretty much a failure. It streamlined committees, they point out, but the committees simply spawned scores of subcommittees. Some of the professional staff positions were filled by unqualified persons. The legislative budget provisions failed completely (see Chapter 27). And, critics conclude, nothing was done about the really vital problems of the Rules Committee, seniority, and the filibuster. Others feel happier about the outcome. They point to the progress in clarifying committee duties and jurisdiction, regularizing and publicizing committee procedures, improving staff aids, and raising congressional salaries.[9] But both sides agree that further steps are needed.

What are the next steps? Many observers believe that congressional committees need far better coordination. Some form of electric voting, which has been adopted successfully in a number of state legislatures, would save a great deal of time. Moreover, Congress might delegate such time-consuming functions as running the affairs of the District of Columbia. More use could be made of joint hearings by House and Senate committees. But the basic problem of efficiency "is the integration of Congress itself so that its autonomous and scattered units will act in harmony."[10] This goal, some feel, can best be realized by increased party solidarity and strengthened party machinery in the two houses.

Despite the disappointing results of the 1946 reforms, Congress on the whole must be acquitted of the charge of gross inefficiency. In terms of sheer output alone, its performance is impressive. A recent Congress passed 1625 acts, of which 733 were public and the rest private. In one session alone of that Congress 5995 bills and resolutions were introduced into the House and 2118 in the Senate. Perhaps the quality of all these acts was not what it might be—but considering the time and effort involved in passing legislation, the amount of work done is remarkable.

---

[9] G. B. Galloway, "Next Steps in Congressional Reform," *University of Illinois Bulletin* (December 1952), p. 5.

[10] *Ibid.,* p. 10.

In this sense, then, Congress is not inefficient. If the impression of inadequacy and confusion persists, the cause must lie deeper.

How *representative* Congress is depends on how we define the word. Certainly Congress is not a microcosm of the community. It is not an accurate sample of 180 million Americans. Occupationally, it notoriously overrepresents the "talking" classes of lawyers, businessmen, and teachers (four-fifths of the members of a recent typical Congress had one of these three occupational backgrounds) at the expense of such groups as factory workers and domestic servants.

On the other hand, Congress is highly representative of America in the sense that virtually every important minority group or opinion finds expression there. Just as America is made up of Catholics, Jews, and Protestants, of rich men and poor men, of easterners, westerners, and southerners, of radicals, liberals, middle-of-the-roaders, conservatives, and reactionaries, of prohibitionists, veterans, trade unionists, farmers, so Congress is composed of a similar variety of backgrounds. The fact that certain occupational groups are underrepresented is perhaps not vital; many a congressman who has never worked in a factory speaks eloquently for the millions of Americans who have. The really crucial fact is that Congress provides a forum where scores of groups and ideas can find expression.

We are led to a further question: *"Should* Congress be representative of all the opinions of the people, no matter how faulty or uninformed those opinions may be?" Or should the congressman use his best judgment, instead of slavishly following the wishes of his constituents? Over a century and a half ago the great English legislator, Edmund Burke, speaking to his constituents in Bristol, admitted that a representative should keep in close touch with his constituents, should look after their needs even at the expense of his own. Then he added:

> But his unbiased opinion, his mature judgment, his enlightened conscience, he ought not to sacrifice to you, to any man. . . . Your representative owes you, not his industry only, but his judgment; and he betrays, instead of serving you, if he sacrifices it to your opinion.

Most American congressmen, however, seem to believe that they must vote in accordance with the dominant interests in their own state or district. We have farm senators, silver senators, cotton representatives, textile representatives, and so on. As a result, Congress tends to respond to local pressures, sectional forces, and organized interests. We will return to this problem of representation in Chapter 18 after we have seen how the Presidency and other national offices also involve problems of representation.

An even graver charge is that Congress caters to organized minorities and ignores the needs and aspirations of the people as a whole. There is much evidence to support this charge. The Senate knuckles under to minorities again and again, partly because of two devices for minority rule: the *filibuster* and the *two-thirds vote* required for ratifying treaties. The Senate has not been able to abolish the filibuster; on the contrary, an attempt in 1949 in that direction only strengthened this minority weapon. Before 1949 cloture could be invoked by a two-thirds vote of the senators *on the floor*. In that year cloture was weakened by a new provision that it could be invoked only by two-thirds of the *whole* Senate membership, that is, by 64 senators. As for the two-thirds treaty-ratifying requirement in the Senate, which allows a minority to block treaties, this is not of crucial importance, as we have seen, but it can be troublesome. Finally, both houses of Congress allow minorities to raise havoc with legislation by means of parliamentary gimmicks, such as making frequent points of order and time-consuming motions, introducing irrelevant business, and repeatedly demanding quorum calls.

It may be that Congress will rid itself of some of these obstructionist weapons in time. In 1949, for example, the House of Representatives clipped the wings of its Rules Committee, leaving it power to bottle up a bill for only a limited period, after which the chairman of the committee reporting the bill might call it up before the House. To be sure, the House restored the old power of the Rules Committee in 1951, but the 1949 change showed that the representatives could reform their methods when so minded.

The filibuster, too, has been under sharp attack. At the start of the 1959 session of Congress, liberal Democrats and Republicans proposed a substantial change in the cloture rule. Under their plan, fifteen days after sixteen senators filed a cloture motion, debate could be shut off by a *simple majority* of the whole Senate membership. If a majority (50 senators) voted to shut off debate under this procedure, no senator could speak for more than an hour. It was estimated that the arrangement would still allow several weeks of debate.

The Senate rejected the proposal, however, and instead voted for a compromise plan of Democratic leader Lyndon Johnson. His proposal was to return to the pre-1949 arrangement under which cloture could be invoked by two-thirds of the senators *on the floor*. The difference between two-thirds of the senators on the floor and two-thirds of the whole membership (100 senators) is not just hair-splitting, because a dozen or so senators are often ill, busy in their offices, or out of town. Hence Johnson's plan, which is the present rule, reduced a bit the power to filibuster—at least to the point where it stood before 1949.

Nevertheless, the charge of irresponsibility stands. Some observers feel that minority devices such as the filibuster are mere surface manifestations of political forces deep beneath the surface. Even if these devices were done away with, they warn, minorities could still raise havoc with majority rule because the majority has no cohesiveness or staying power. It is constantly giving way to minorities because its own members defect. Most congressmen may be pledged to social reform—but some will renege on their campaign promises in the face of organized opposition in their district. Or most of them may be in favor of governmental economy, but will still vote for pork-barrel bills in order to get public projects for the home folks.

The trouble does not lie simply with Congress. It lies in part with the residence or locality rule. The Constitution merely requires congressmen to be inhabitants of the state in which they are elected. With few exceptions, however, popular attitudes make it politically impossible for a candidate for the House to come from outside his district. This locality rule contrasts with the practice in Britain, where members of Commons often are elected by districts they have never lived in, and may have visited only a few times. The American system results from the prevailing belief that congressmen are primarily representatives of their own districts, and only secondarily—if at all—representatives of the entire nation. It reinforces the tendency of congressmen to think in local rather than national terms.

What is lacking is a strong party system that could hold together a congressional majority—whether Republican or Democratic—in the face of minorities. Congress, in short, *lacks party responsibility*. Britain, by way of contrast, has parties that manage both to discipline their members in Parliament and to help them win elections in their districts. Our parties, as we have seen, give little aid to members running for office, and have little control of members in office. A close look at Congress reveals not only the Democratic and Republican parties, but a farmers' party, labor party, southern party, veterans' party, and others, all cutting across one another and producing vast confusion.

What are the consequences of this confusion? It creates friction between Congress and the President, who is the national party leader. It helps produce a tangled network of relationships between Congress and the bureaucracy. It even affects the role of judges in our national government. Finally, it gives us a divided government, responsible to shifting and conflicting forces, in a time of domestic and world-wide tension. The next four chapters will consider these and related problems.

CHAPTER **17**

The President

The framers of the Constitution had a hard time deciding how to set up the executive branch. Not that they questioned the need for an executive, for most of the delegates to the Philadelphia Convention were tired of the Articles of Confederation, under which government was carried on by Congress through cumbersome committees and special agents. What the framers wanted was a national executive who could enforce the law and help the states put down such disorders as Shays' Rebellion. But how strong was the new executive to be? And what relation should the executive have to the new Congress?

Day after day the delegates argued. Some, like James Wilson of Pennsylvania, wanted a strong executive, independent of the legislature—an executive who would give "energy, dispatch, and responsibility" to the government. Others, like Roger Sherman of Connecticut, wished to have the "executive magistracy" appointed by Congress and wholly subject to the legislative will. Some delegates favored a one-man executive; others preferred a plural executive composed of two or three men of equal power. Some delegates wanted the executive to be eligible for re-election; others felt that one term was enough.

Two basic considerations dominated the debate. The first was the need for an energetic yet dignified executive who would enforce the national laws firmly, and who would lend a note of stability to the new government. The other was a general fear that the public would protest if the executive was made too strong. The people had rebelled against the king—clearly they would not stomach a new American monarch. So sensitive were the framers to popular reaction that on five separate occasions they voted for *appointment of the chief executive by the legislature*—a move that would have made the President the tool of Congress and probably would have given us a form of parliamentary government something like those in Europe today. But in the end the men of 1787 decided to set up an executive separate from Congress.

The final decision was a compromise, as were so many other decisions in the debate over the Constitution (see Chapter 2). On the one hand, the Presi-

422

dent would be single instead of plural, eligible for re-election, and independent of the legislature. He was to have considerable power over the executive branch. On the other hand, he was hemmed in by the system of checks and balances. His appointments of major officials had to be approved by the Senate. He was given a veto over congressional acts, but Congress could override his veto by a two-thirds vote. His power to appeal directly to the voters was muzzled by an elaborate system of electors, who in choosing a President would act as a sort of screen through which popular passions would be refined and tempered. He could make treaties, but only if two-thirds of the senators present concurred.

As it turned out, the framers accomplished both their objectives. They sufficiently checked presidential power so that the new single chief executive seemed acceptable to the necessary number of voters in 1787-88. At the same time, they set up an office that was to prove a continuing source of energy and power in the new republic. Perhaps they built better than they knew. So powerful has the President become that thoughtful Americans today face precisely the same questions that confronted the framers over 170 years ago. How strong should the executive be? And what should be its relation to Congress? Today we ask also: Why has the President become so powerful? Is this a dangerous trend?

To tackle these questions we must consider the President's vital and many-sided roles—administrative, legislative, political, military, ceremonial, and symbolic. But first let us look at the man himself.

A Day with the President

The President operates at the center of a vast and complex network of governmental and political activity. He has his finger on countless levers that influence the making of public and private policies throughout the land. At the same time he is surrounded by innumerable checks and balances that are inherent in our political as well as our governmental system. To him come men of all kinds, with motives of all types—to advise, beg, urge, consult, exhort, warn, dissuade, even dictate. Watching the President in action for a typical day may suggest the complexity of the job, its scope, and its frustrations. A typical day of a President in recent years might go somewhat as follows: [1]

> 9:00 A.M. *President arrives at his office.*—He has already looked over several Washington and New York newspapers. He discusses the day's agenda with his staff. He reviews an important announcement with his press secretary. He reads some of his mail. (Necessarily he can see only a tiny fraction of the 5000 to 25,000 letters that flood into the White House in a single day.) He signs orders and other documents. He is given a top-secret briefing on the world situation by diplomatic and military assistants.

---

[1] This "typical day" is based on a study of biographical material, journalistic accounts, and documents.

Now a round of appointments with visitors gets under way.

10:00 A.M. *Farm senators.*—Five of these gentlemen, members of both parties, arrive to protest an act of the Secretary of Agriculture involving farm commodities. They indicate that if the Secretary does not rescind or modify his action, they will propose an amendment to new farm legislation that will limit the Secretary's powers. The President listens sympathetically, but makes no promises.

10:15 A.M. *The Secretary of State.*—He tells the President that reports from the United Nations and from our embassies abroad indicate that several neutral countries are planning an action that may leave the United States isolated diplomatically. He has a statement designed to clarify this nation's position. After some discussion the President signs it.

10:40 A.M. *Press conference.*—Over 100 reporters attend. They shower the President with questions. What did the farm senators want? Who will be the new Assistant Secretary of State? What is the President's reaction to yesterday's statement in *Pravda?* Will he veto the pension bill passed by Congress? What will be the government's policy if the United Nations fails to act? The President has to think fast. Some of the questions, he knows, are loaded—he will be embarrassed no matter how he answers them. Others are "iffy"—they are purely speculative in nature, and if he answers them he may unknowingly commit the Administration to a certain policy. Some questions, on the other hand, are planted by the White House itself, so that friendly reporters will ask the President questions he wishes to answer. Sometimes the President takes refuge in the answer, "No comment."

11:10 A.M. *American Legion officials.*—They have come to invite the President to address their next national convention and to put in a word for some pending veterans' legislation. White House photographers take pictures of a smiling President in the midst of the group.

11:20 A.M. *Legislative assistant.*—The President looks over the draft of a veto message, decides it is too severe in its criticism of Congress, asks his assistant to soften it.

11:30 A.M. *Cabinet meeting.*—This is the regular weekly meeting (occasionally the President calls special ones). The President makes a general statement prepared by the Budget Director on the need for economizing in departmental administration, and asks the members to submit reports on economies made. There follow brief reports and comments by the Secretaries of the Treasury, Labor, and Commerce on several different matters. The meeting is informal. Most of the business consists of reporting on departmental problems; there is little discussion of general policy. Several Cabinet members stay on after the meeting to discuss privately with the President matters that they feared to bring up before because of possible opposition or leaks to the press.

12:30 P.M. *Lunch with members of the National Committee of the President's party.*—General talk—no discussion of party or governmental problems.

1:30 P.M. *Key members of the National Committee.*—A few members stay on. They comprise three city bosses, two senators who dominate their state parties, the party chairman, and several others. The President asks their help in keeping a number of congressmen friendly to the Administration. Campaign plans are discussed—also the handling of appointments to a number of federal judgeships that are vacant.

2:30 P.M. *Relaxation.*—Attends baseball game with a delegation of Eagle Scouts. Quietly leaves game at end of sixth inning.

3:45 P.M. *AFL-CIO leaders.*—The labor chiefs, accompanied by the Secretary of Labor, ask about several appointments that are to be made in the Labor Department and in two other agencies.

3:55 P.M. *Ceremony.*—President presses button starting the generators in a new dam in Colorado. Picture taken.

4:00 P.M. *Budget Director.*—He reports that there is trouble in the House of Representatives. A group of western congressmen are trying to boost appropriations for a bureau in the Interior Department. The President and the Secretary of the Interior are both opposed to the increase, but the bureau chief is working closely with the congressmen. The President telephones the Speaker of the House and asks him to look into the situation.

4:30 P.M. *ICA chief.*—Just back from Europe, the director of the International Cooperation Administration is worried about appropriations and a pending amendment that might hurt the program. The President says that he thinks the amendment will be defeated, but certain cuts cannot be averted.

5:00 P.M. *Ceremony.*—Makes contribution to Red Cross, inaugurating drive for funds. Picture taken.

5:05 P.M. *Meeting with National Security Council.*—President discusses a broad range of political, military, and diplomatic problems with other members of the Council. The agenda is carefully prepared. A key decision is made in principle on defensive arrangements with an important ally. A secretariat, which has carefully briefed all members on major problems, records this and other decisions.

6:00 P.M. *Signing of an important act.*—Picture taken with eight senators and representatives who sponsored or supported the act. President signs a score of letters and Army and Navy commissions, looks over reports.

7:00 P.M. *Dinner with family and personal friends.*

9:00 P.M. *Brief talk to a patriotic organization.*

10:00 P.M. *Back in the White House.*—Late reports, then bed.

What does this typical day's schedule reveal about the President and his job?

1. The President faces a ceaseless tide of tough decisions. His staff helps him to decide many questions, but sometimes he alone must make a decision of vital importance.

2. Diplomatic and military problems occupy much of his time.

3. Domestically, he must deal with many legislative and political matters. His greatest concern here is the unpredictable action of Congress. He spends much time dealing with individuals and factions in Congress that are holding up bills and appropriations.

4. Ceremonies take up perhaps an hour or two a day.

5. His purely administrative job (in the sense of management) must be largely delegated to others. The main administrative decisions are made in the Budget Bureau and other staff agencies and in the departments. He must, however, frequently step in when administrative decisions involve important political and legislative relationships.

6. The President has little time for reflection. He must delegate this job, too. Agencies like the Bureau of the Budget, the Council of Economic Advisers, and the National Security Council do most of the long-range planning.

PRESSURE OF THE JOB

Courtesy *The New York Times Magazine* and Tom Little

7. The President is an essentially lonely figure. This is paradoxical, for he sees so many people. But his visitors are usually trying to get something from him. His staff members are his closest associates, but they are also his subordinates. He cannot always turn to the Vice President or Cabinet members, for they have their own responsibilities—and ambitions. The toughest decisions—those that divide the country, his party, and even his own administration—he must make almost alone.

To get a better idea of the size and complexity of the President's job, let us consider the chief executive in each of his six great roles—as chief administrator, party chief, chief legislator, chief foreign-policy maker, commander in chief, and chief of state. Truly "the President is many men." [2] But although we shall explore each of these roles in turn, they must not be viewed as separate or compartmentalized. On the contrary, only in the *interweaving* of these roles can we see the full tapestry of presidential power.

---

[2] L. G. Seligman, "The President Is Many Men," *The Antioch Review* (Fall 1956), pp. 305-318.

Chief Administrator **A** century and a half ago, when Jefferson became President, the federal government employed 2120 persons—Indian commissioners, postmasters, collectors of customs, clerks, tax collectors, marshals, lighthouse keepers, and the like.[3] Today, by latest count, the President heads a colossal establishment of about 2⅓ million federal civilian employees. These employees work in 2072 units of federal administration—2072 departments, services, bureaus, commissions, boards, governmental corporations, and other agencies. They work not only in Washington but throughout the world. Their salaries and wages alone amount to over $8 billion a year.

All this is big government—the result of decades of sporadic expansion of government activities resulting in turn from the attempts of Americans to cope with big problems, such as armed threats at home and abroad, gigantic increases in population, technological changes, depressions, social unrest, and the interdependence and complexity of our national life.

The Constitution charges the President to "take care that the laws be faithfully executed." But the President can be only a part-time administrator, for his other tasks demand most of his attention. Even if he could devote all his time to running the administrative establishment, it would still have to be organized for leadership and control. It is, of course, so organized. These 2072 agencies are set up in great pyramids, each with its own hierarchical structure. Orders—theoretically at least—flow from President to department head to bureau chief down to the offices, services, and smaller units where they are carried out (see Chapter 19). This is the "line," so-called. The President, like all the top brass, is also assisted by a staff, whose job it is to advise and assist him in managing the administration. This *line* and *staff* organization— inherent in any large administrative unit, whether the Army, the General Motors Corporation, or the Veterans Administration—is worth a closer look.

THE PRESIDENT AND HIS CABINET

Directly in line under the President are the executive departments of: State; Treasury; Defense; Interior; Agriculture; Justice; Post Office; Commerce; Labor; Health, Education, and Welfare. The State and Treasury departments were established in 1789, the government's first year of existence. The War Department was also set up that year, but, along with the Navy Department, it was reorganized into the Defense Department in 1947. Health, Education, and Welfare was created in 1953 out of a number of existing agencies.

The heads of these ten departments form the President's Cabinet. It would be hard to find a more unusual or nondescript institution than this one.

---

[3] L. D. White, *The Federalists* (Macmillan, 1948), pp. 255-256.

The Cabinet has existed since early in Washington's administration; yet it is not even mentioned in the Constitution. It is composed—aside from the Vice President—solely of department heads; even the chiefs of the great agencies, such as the Veterans Administration, are not members. However, Presidents often invite high officials—for example, the Budget Director or the chairman of the Civil Service Commission—to attend Cabinet meetings. Cabinet members are often leading figures in the President's party; yet several Presidents have appointed prominent members of the opposition party to their Cabinets, as when Roosevelt chose two prominent Republicans for the secretaryships of War and Navy in 1940. Cabinet membership carries high prestige, and most Presidents meet regularly with their Cabinets; yet the discussions are often casual, perfunctory, and even listless. Presidents turn to their Cabinets for advice on a variety of matters; yet votes are rarely taken and the President can ignore Cabinet sentiment if he wishes. (Lincoln, finding the whole Cabinet opposed to him, could say with impunity, "Seven nays, one aye—the ayes have it.") The President handpicks his Cabinet members with little senatorial interference; yet they are often his worst enemies.

It is also difficult to generalize about how the President chooses his Cabinet members. Political considerations are paramount, and the President usually tries to give representation to various factions of his party—to its liberal and conservative wings, to different sections of the country, to major racial and religious groups. Business, farm, and labor groups must be appeased in the appointment of the Secretaries of Commerce, Agriculture, and Labor, respectively. Most Presidents face a dilemma in Cabinet-making. To choose a weak group may throw the whole Administration into disrepute. To choose strong men with powerful political backing may lead to quarrels within the President's official family. President Eisenhower appointed a Democratic labor leader to his Cabinet, as Secretary of Labor; the experiment came to an end nine months later, when the Secretary of Labor resigned over policy differences with the administration.

Nevertheless, the Cabinet has a character and importance of its own. Membership in it continues to be the ambition of many politicians. On occasion the meetings are devoted to matters of top policy. And the discussions gain from the fact that Cabinet members usually bring lengthy political and policy-making experience to bear on the problems at hand. Most administrative problems—at the White House level—are really legislative and political problems.

The Cabinet may in time become a team that both sustains the President and renders him more responsible to the people. But at present the American Cabinet bears little resemblance to the ideal Cabinet described by Harold J. Laski as a "place where the large outlines of policy can be hammered out in common, where the essential strategy is decided upon, where the President knows that he will hear, both in affirmation and in doubt, even in negation, most of what can be said about the direction he proposes to follow."

What Cabinet unity there is tends to break down as soon as the members leave the Cabinet room. "In matters of prestige, partisan politics, and legislative relations alike," concludes a recent study, "the Cabinet as a collectivity has only a symbolic value, a value which readily disappears when the need for action supersedes the need for a show window. In the day-to-day work of the Cabinet member, each man fends for himself without much consideration for Cabinet unity. His survival, his support, and his success do not depend on his fellow members. His performance is judged separately from theirs. This condition is but another result of the combination of the centrifugal tendencies of our political system with the low degree of institutionalization which characterizes the Cabinet." [4]

If the Cabinet's role is so limited, how does the President direct his far-flung administrative machine? He meets frequently with individual department and agency chiefs. Crucial decisions are sometimes reached in small, informal conferences between the President and the heads of two or three major departments and agencies and with his staff. Another factor in the President's control of administration is his ultimate power—subject to some limitations noted below—to hire and fire his main lieutenants as he deems fit. The Senate must ratify major appointments, but by tradition the President is allowed considerable freedom to pick his immediate subordinates—and to get rid of them.

Of a total federal civil personnel of about 2⅓ million, the President, with the concurrence of the Senate, hires about 16,000. (He can appoint a limited number without Senate assent.) He chooses the department and agency heads who in turn employ other thousands of civil servants. Aside from his power to hire and fire, the President directly or indirectly controls promotions, demotions, and transfers, especially at the top levels. The Supreme Court has upheld (in *Myers* v. *United States,* 1926) the power of the President to remove executive officers at will but has ruled that he has no constitutional power to discharge certain officials with part judicial and part legislative functions (see page 474).

The single most important means of Presidential control, however, is the White House staff.

THE KITCHEN CABINET

Americans hear a great deal about secret, invisible men who are said to control the President. Stories of a palace guard or a White House gang make good feature material for any newspaper columnist, TV or radio commentator. The simple fact is that the President needs help. He must have advisers to help him handle the momentous questions that crowd into the White House. Much of his effectiveness turns on their loyal, disinterested, expert services. So the Washington commentators are right in emphasizing the importance of

---

4 R. F. Fenno, Jr., *The President's Cabinet* (Harvard Univ. Press, 1959), p. 247.

the men who advise the President. But they are wrong when they imply that there is anything sinister or un-American about this practice. Andrew Jackson had his kitchen cabinet; Abraham Lincoln had his personal advisers; Woodrow Wilson had his Colonel House; Franklin Roosevelt had his Harry Hopkins. President Eisenhower, accustomed to the elaborate and powerful staffs found in military organizations, has established a large staff headed by a "staff chief" who works directly under the President. Without a large staff the President today could not possibly do the job that the Constitution—and the people— demand of him.

In recent years the kitchen cabinet has grown in numbers and in importance. Today it comprises a group of perhaps twenty close advisers, assisted by 100 or more experts of all kinds, plus another 1000 clerks, secretaries, and the like. They aid the President in all his roles—administrative, legislative, political, military. They are grouped in a complex agency called the Executive Office of the President. Physically, they work in both the east and west wings of the White House and in an ugly old building near the White House that used to house the State Department.

The President's immediate staff, the *White House Office,* does not have fixed form; indeed, part of its value lies in its flexibility and adaptability. Most Presidents, however, have an appointments secretary, who lets the right people see the President and keeps the others away; a press secretary, who handles presidential publicity and deals with the scores of newsmen and photographers assigned to the White House; a correspondence secretary, who watches the President's mail and often drafts important letters for his chief; a legal counsel, who advises the President on a variety of matters of broad policy (not merely on legal matters); a diplomatic aide, who acts as the President's eyes and ears on the many-sided diplomatic front; military aides, who often have policy as well as ceremonial functions; and several other key legislative, administrative, and political assistants. In his last year in office President Eisenhower had three legal counselors, two deputy assistants, thirteen special assistants, two special consultants, and a dozen other aides of one sort or another. The President's top assistants may have far more influence than the equivalent Cabinet member; for example, the President may lean more heavily on his legal counsel for urgent advice than on his Attorney General.

Outside this inner circle are the heads of a number of staff agencies who advise the President on policy and help him run the administrative leviathan. The most important of these is the Director of the *Bureau of the Budget.* This gentleman is not simply a glorified bookkeeper. He is the person who advises the President almost daily on the real needs of the hundreds of government agencies, how much money they should be allotted in the budget, and what kind of job they are doing. He and his assistants pare down the appropriations requested by the agencies to fit the President's budgetary program. They also try to improve the planning, management, and statistical work of all the bureaucrats. Working under the President, they are able to survey the administration from his broader perspective and to mediate the claims and quarrels of administrators big and small. Seeking to maintain a uniform legislative program for the chief executive, budget officials review the legislative proposals of the departments and advise the President on the bills he should sign or veto.

Several other presidential agencies also have vital functions, especially in the making of economic and military policies. The *Council of Economic Advisers,* a three-man board with a small staff, supplies the President with a broad range of economic information and advice and each year helps him draw up a report on the nation's economic position and prospects. The *National Security Council,* composed of the President, Vice President, Secretaries of State and Defense, and a few others, embraces a small, permanent staff of military and diplomatic experts. The *Office of Civil and Defense Mobilization* advises the chief executive on the coordination of military, industrial, and civilian mobilization, and employs a staff of several hundred to assess the nation's resources of raw materials and manpower in the event of war. The *National Aeronautics and Space Committee* was set up in 1958 to advise the President on policies and development of comprehensive space-age problems. The work of these agencies, all of which are located in the Executive Office, will be described more fully in Part Six.

Why does the President lean so heavily on his staff? Why does he not lean more heavily, for example, on his Cabinet or on the heads of vital departments? The answer is simple. The staff can give the President the help he wants. It can do so because the President can, for the most part, juggle his staff membership and organization in a way that will be most helpful to him. He chooses the men he wants; he chooses them for their experience, their ability to work as part of a team, and above all for their loyalty to himself. Nowhere else—not in Congress, not in his Cabinet, not in his party—can he find the loyalty, the single-mindedness, and the team spirit that he can build, if he is a leader, among his close aides. Such a staff is important to him and to the country—so important that the Hoover Commission urged that the President be given the utmost freedom in organizing his staff as he wishes.[5]

Chief Legislator

Since the national government is divided into the executive, legislative, and judicial branches, many people assume that the President has only administrative functions, the Senate and House only legislative, and the judiciary only judicial. Actually, as we have seen, the essence of the system is an *intermingling* of powers. The President is a prime example. The Constitution grants him certain policy-making power—that is, legislative power. And

---

[5] Commission on Organization of the Executive Branch of the Government, *General Management of the Executive Branch* (Government Printing Office, 1949), p. 15; see also H. M. Somers, "The President as Administrator," *The Annals* (September 1952), pp. 104 ff.

a century and a half of national growth and recurrent crises have vastly increased that power. Today he and his aides ordinarily have more influence over national policy than any single congressman or group of congressmen; truly the President is chief legislator.[6]

The Constitution ordains that the President "shall from time to time give to the Congress Information of the State of the Union, and recommend to their Consideration such Measures as he shall judge necessary and expedient." From the start, strong Presidents have exploited this power. Washington and Adams came in person to Congress to deliver information and recommendations. Jefferson and many Presidents after him sent written messages, but Wilson restored the practice of delivering a personal, and often dramatic, message. Franklin Roosevelt in particular made personal appearances as a means of drawing the attention of the whole nation to his program—with the invaluable help of radio and camera. The President can also dramatize his policies by calling either or both houses of Congress into special session, although the legislators need not act if they do not wish.

Less obvious but perhaps equally important are the frequent written messages dispatched from the White House to Capitol Hill on a vast range of public problems. Often mumbled indistinctly by a clerk, these messages may not create much stir at the moment, but they are important in defining the administration's position and giving a lead to friendly legislators. Moreover, these messages are often accompanied by detailed drafts of legislation that may be put into the hopper with hardly a change. These administration bills, the products of bill-drafting experts on the President's own staff or in the departments and agencies, may be mauled and mutilated by Congress— but many of the original provisions may survive unscathed.

THE POWER TO SAY "NO"

The President can *veto* a bill by returning it with his objections to the house in which it originated. Congress, by a two-thirds vote in each chamber, may then pass it over his veto. If the President does not sign or veto the bill within ten weekdays after he receives it, the bill becomes law without his signature. If Congress adjourns within the ten weekdays, however, the President, by taking no action, can kill the bill. This is known as the *pocket veto*.

The veto is sometimes a strong, sometimes a feeble, weapon. Its essential strength lies in the ordinary failure of Congress to muster a two-thirds majority of both houses in favor of a policy that the President has told the people he dislikes. Yet a Congress that can repeatedly mobilize such a majority against a President can virtually take command of the government. Such was the fate of President Andrew Johnson. Faced after 1866 with a House of Representa-

---

[6] For description of the institutionalization of the President's legislative role see Richard E. Neustadt, "Presidency and Legislation: Planning the President's Program," *The American Political Science Review* (December 1955), pp. 980-1021.

tives almost three to one against his reconstruction policies, he was virtually helpless as bill after bill was passed stripping him of his powers; in fact, he barely escaped being ousted from office.[7] President Eisenhower, on the other hand, had only two vetoes overturned during his eight years in office.

In ordinary times, Congress can manipulate legislation to reduce the likelihood of a presidential veto. For example, it can attach irrelevant but controversial provisions, called *riders,* to vitally needed legislation; the President must either accept or reject the whole bill, for he does not have the power to strike out individual items in the bill—that is, he does not have the *item veto.* Appropriations are a special case in point. The lawmakers may combine in one appropriations bill badly needed funds for the armed forces and a host of costly pork-barrel items, but the President must take or reject the whole bill. Governors of most states do have the power of item veto, and it has long been urged that the President should too. (It is not certain whether a constitutional amendment would be needed or not. Some argue that if the framers had foreseen the legislative use of omnibus bills and riders, they would have given the President specific power to veto items not germane to the main bill.[8]) President Eisenhower and previous chief executives requested Congress to pass legislation providing for the item veto.

For his part, the President can use the veto power in a positive as well as a negative way. He can announce openly, or let it be known quietly, that a bill under consideration by Congress will be turned back at the White House door unless certain changes have been made. He can use the *threat* of a veto against some bill Congress badly wants in exchange for another bill that he wants. But the veto is essentially a negative weapon, of limited use to a President who has a positive program. For it is the President who usually is pressing for action. It is Congress that has the real power to say "no."

FILLING IN THE DETAILS

Most federal legislation today deals with highly complex situations. A labor law, for example, may affect a great variety of industries, a number of different unions, all kinds of labor-management relationships, and diverse attitudes and traditions in different parts of the country. Agricultural legislation may deal with certain farm problems in general, but in practice the law involves big farmers and small ones, prosperous ones and marginal ones, cotton farmers, wheat farmers, applegrowers, and so on. No matter how wise Congress might be, it could not write a law that would automatically adapt itself to such different situations. Indeed, to try to do so would be to put the administrator into a strait jacket and to make the law unworkable. Hence Congress often must content itself with prescribing general standards and

[7] W. E. Binkley, *President and Congress* (Knopf, 1947), pp. 128-144.
[8] See C. J. Zinn, *The Veto Power of the President,* Committee Print, Committee on the Judiciary, House of Representatives (Government Printing Office, 1951).

delegating to the President and administrators the job of *filling in the details of the laws*. Such subordinate legislation is usually issued in the President's executive orders and in circulars, orders, rules, regulations, directives, and so on, issued by departments, regulatory boards, and other agencies.

Much of this delegation of legislative power involves making decisions within rather narrow limits. For example, a law may permit the President to alter tariff or minimum-wage standards to some extent, but only in terms of a standard laid down by Congress. Yet such standards vary greatly in precision. The Trade Agreement Act of 1934 and its extensions empower the President to make trade agreements with foreign nations lowering existing tariff rates by as much as 50 per cent. Other acts authorize him to suspend the eight-hour day for federal employees, to issue civil service rules, to prevent the export of certain raw materials.

An even more radical delegation of legislative power was contained in the Reorganization Act of 1939. By its terms the President could reduce and rearrange certain federal agencies through plans that would come into effect sixty days after being sent to Congress unless turned down by both chambers before that time. Here was a delegation of power that amounted almost to a reversal of the usual relation between Congress and the chief executive. Subsequent reorganization acts have delegated somewhat similar power to the President (see page 496).

Thus Congress, while setting objectives and standards, in practice allows the President not only to fill in the details but even to decide when action shall be taken. It is one thing to delegate the carrying out of specific provisions; it is something else to delegate the power to say when and whether a law will be invoked or applied. Why has Congress seen fit to delegate such sweeping powers? The reason is partly the willingness of the legislators to face the facts of modern life and to allow the President to do quickly and effectively what they could do, at best, haltingly and ineffectively. The reason is also that Congress is often so dominated by warring factions that it cannot find common ground on which to act. It defers to the President because he can act. The Constitution, it is true, prevents Congress from giving away its "essential" legislative powers. This is one of the reasons why the Supreme Court invalidated the National Industrial Recovery Act (*Schechter* v. *United States,* 1935). But so long as Congress lays down some kind of standard, the Supreme Court has been willing to approve extensive delegation of power.

THOUSANDS OF LEGISLATORS

It should be clear by now that policy-making power is not monopolized by Congress. Nor is it monopolized jointly by Congress and President. Just as Congress must delegate legislative power to the President, so he must *re-*delegate policy-making power to hosts of administrators down the line. Obviously the Secretary of State has a decided influence on policy, as do other department heads, along with bureau, division, and section chiefs. In a sense, there is no level in the administrative hierarchy at which discretion really ends. Even a secretary may make policy decisions on what matters or visitors her superior should turn to first—or at all. A sort of settling-down process takes place. Routine, noncontroversial decisions are made at the lower levels, vital and difficult ones at the top echelons. But at any time the most routine matter may be called to the public's attention, perhaps by a newspaper columnist or a congressman. Then the matter will be pulled out of the lower echelon and given consideration by a bureau or department chief—perhaps it will even go to the White House.[9]

In short, there are thousands of legislators throughout the government— and millions more outside, such as editors, lobbyists, and ordinary citizens, who exert pressure on a democratic government. Control of legislation cannot be diagramed neatly, with Congress on top, the President in the middle, and a pyramid of department, bureau, and division heads below. Rather, it is a *circular* system, with President and congressmen cooperating on some matters, fighting over others, and both influencing—and being influenced by—the administrators throughout the administration and by political forces outside.

Moreover, history and politics have bestowed on certain agencies a degree of independence from the White House. The Federal Bureau of Investigation in the Department of Justice, the Bureau of Reclamation in the Interior Department, and the Corps of Engineers in the Department of the Army are agencies somewhat insulated from the White House because of the prestige of their chiefs or the closeness of the agencies to blocs in Congress and to interest groups outside. The independent regulatory commissions (see Chapter 19) are a special case. Congress has delegated legislative (and judicial) powers to agencies like the Interstate Commerce Commission, the Federal Trade Commission, and the National Labor Relations Board in an attempt to keep partisan Presidents from interfering with their decisions. The President hires the commissioners, with the consent of the Senate, but his power to discharge them is limited to that which Congress is willing to authorize. Hence they are often at liberty to make policies at variance with those of the administration. Here is one more set of little legislators in the Washington scene.

Thus the President shares his legislative power not only with Congress but also with administrators in the executive branch that he himself heads. The extent to which he wields legislative power turns not only on his formal constitutional position and powers, but also on his political position and powers. His political powers turn on many factors. How effective is he in appealing to the public? To what extent can he dramatize official business? How magnetic is he on radio or television? How good is his timing? How active and articulate are his lieutenants—his Cabinet members and key agency heads? How close are his relations with congressional leaders? Can he mobi-

---

[9] Appleby, *Policy and Administration*, p. 82.

lize public opinion on crucial issues? Does his influence reach into states and districts throughout the country so that he can "build fires" under recalcitrant legislators?

Beyond the constitutional grants of authority, then, the President's power rests on the extent to which he commands organized, durable, and dependable support in his political party—in short, on his effectiveness as party chief.

Party Chief   **T**he Constitution says nothing about parties or about the President as party chief. Indeed, the framers were determined that the chief executive should *not* act as leader of a party or faction. They planned for a President who would rise above political divisions, who would stand for the nation as a whole, who as chief magistrate would mediate between Senate and House, between rich and poor, between North and South. They planned a system of electing Presidents—the electoral college—that would elevate statesmen to the office, not politicians.

Washington fitted this picture perfectly. He gave the country a form of nonpartisan government, and in his famous Farewell Address he warned the people against the spirit of party. But in a democracy some kind of factional or party politics is inevitable. Even during Washington's Administration, party leaders and party politics began to emerge. Thomas Jefferson actually resigned from Washington's Cabinet as Secretary of State in 1793 in order to travel around the country visiting local politicians and laying the groundwork for a national party.

Jefferson himself became the boss of his new Republican party. When he became President, he showed his power by using party machinery to dominate Congress: he and his aides pushed legislation through House and Senate, stopped bills they disliked, and even influenced committee actions. Clearly, the antiparty plans of the Founding Fathers were not working out. Moreover, the provision for a nonpartisan method of picking Presidents also came to naught. Washington's own successor, John Adams, was nominated in a party caucus made up of Federalist members of the national House and Senate. Jefferson and the next three Presidents were nominated by the Republican members of Congress meeting in a similar legislative caucus. Andrew Jackson's followers attacked "King Caucus" as undemocratic; they replaced it with an even more partisan method of nominating the President— the national convention. Meanwhile the electoral college, as we have seen, was radically transformed. Instead of exercising independent judgment, the presidential electors became merely automatic (though inaccurate) ratifiers of the popular, partisan will.

All Presidents since Washington have been party leaders, and the stronger the President, the greater his power over party has been. Men like McKinley, Wilson, and the two Roosevelts have fortified their executive and legislative influence by resort to their supremacy in the party. Yet no President has fully dominated his party, and the story of all Presidents, including the most famous, revolves largely around their party failures as well as their party triumphs.

How does the President direct his party? Where does his influence stop —and why?

The President is master of the party organization at the national level. Oddly, though, he has no position in the party structure. He stands above the party, and the national organization revolves around him. His vast influence as President over vital national policies and over thousands of appointments commands respect from politicians throughout the party machinery, and especially at the national level. Even aside from this, he is the party's national leader and spokesman, formally chosen at the party convention. President and party need each other. He needs the party's backing throughout the government in order to enact his program. The party needs his direction, his prestige, and the political "gravy" that flows from the White House.

The strings of the national organization are all held in the President's hands. Formally, the national committee picks the national chairman; actually, the President tells the committeemen whom to pick. He hires and fires national party chairmen much as he shifts department heads or, indeed, his own staff. Ordinarily his pronouncements on national party policy are more authoritative than any other party member's, even more significant than the party program itself. The great test of the President's influence in the party is his power to gain renomination if he wishes it, and all recent Presidents have met this test. Taft won renomination in 1912 despite the opposition of Theodore Roosevelt and the Progressives, as did Hoover in 1932 despite the Depression, and Truman in 1948 despite deep divisions in his party.

The President also has some influence over his party's state and local organizations. Two factors, aside from the prestige and power of his office, stand back of this influence. One is patronage. Many party machines live off the jobs that are thrown their way, including judgeships, postmasterships, and the like. The second is the President's power over the Department of Justice and the enforcement of federal criminal law. Some machine practices are illegal; others are questionable; and any political boss would prefer not to have the G-men or T-men poking into his affairs. The President can disrupt a machine whose members are vulnerable under income-tax laws, laws concerning the proper use of the mails, financial regulations, and the like. It was by this means that Huey Long's machine was attacked during the 1930's.[10]

Yet the President's power over his party has limits. He *controls* the

---

[10] D. D. McKean, *Party and Pressure Politics* (Houghton Mifflin, 1949), p. 35.

national organization; he *influences* the state and local organizations—but his power comes to an end precisely where he needs it most. He has little control of the selection of party candidates for Congress and for state and local office, and even less control of their actions once they gain power. The reason is in part his *limited control of state and local organizations;* even more, it is that the *party organizations themselves do not control their candidates*. They do not control them because most candidates, as we have seen, win office not through party action but through their own individual campaigning in both the primary and general elections.

The situation of course varies from place to place. In a boss-controlled center like Chicago or Brooklyn, the President may have great influence over the choice of candidates for Congress because (1) he has power over the machine, and (2) the machine picks faithful men, elects them to office, and holds them responsible. But most party organizations are not of this type. Because they are largely dominated by state and local leaders, because they may receive patronage from state and local governments (or from congressmen), they can operate independently of the national party leadership even if the President cuts them off. And most local party organizations are not strong enough to put their own men into office or control them when they get there, because these organizations lack the leadership and discipline of boss-controlled machines.

Thus the President cannot use his party leadership to strengthen his legislative leadership decisively, much though he might want to. How powerless even a strong President may be to control his party's choices was dramatically shown in Franklin Roosevelt's attempt to discipline the Democratic party in 1938.

F.D.R.'s PURGE

Despite his own victory in the 1936 election and the lopsided Democratic majorities in Congress, President Roosevelt ran into heavy opposition from many Democratic senators and representatives in 1937 and 1938. Aroused and angry at this opposition within his own party, Mr. Roosevelt decided to take a hand in the selection of Democratic candidates in the 1938 congressional primaries. He announced that not as a President but as "head of the Democratic party, charged with the responsibility of carrying out the definitely liberal declaration of principles set forth in the 1936 Democratic platform," he felt that he had "every right to speak in those few instances where there may be a clear issue between candidates for a Democratic nomination involving principles or involving a clear misuse of my own name."

In New York City, Mr. Roosevelt was successful. There he openly repudiated the Democratic chairman of the House Rules Committee, and helped a pro-Administration Democrat win the nomination against the incumbent. The President also bestowed his blessings on a number of incumbent Democratic senators, who gained renomination (as they might have done in any event). But in Maryland and the South Mr. Roosevelt met his Waterloo. Speaking in Georgia, he said in the presence of Senator Walter George, who was seeking renomination for United States senator in the Democratic primary in that state:

> To carry out my responsibility as President, it is clear that if there is to be success in our Government there ought to be cooperation between members of my own party and myself—cooperation, in other words, within the majority party, between one branch of Government, the Legislative branch, and the head of the other branch, the Executive. That is one of the essentials of a party form of government. . . . The test is not measured, in the case of an individual, by his every vote on every bill—of course not. The test lies rather in the answers to two questions: first, has the record of the candidate shown, while differing perhaps in details, a constant active fighting attitude in favor of the broad objectives of the party and of the Government as they are constituted today; and, secondly, does the candidate really, in his heart, deep down in his heart, believe in those objectives? I regret that in the case of my friend, Senator George, I cannot honestly answer either of these questions in the affirmative." [11]

Senator George replied that he "accepted the challenge," and he easily won renomination against the candidate backed by the President. Mr. Roosevelt was no more successful in efforts to oust conservative Democratic senators elsewhere.

The moral is plain. The President's control over his party has limits, no matter how strong and skillful he is. He cannot, under most circumstances, reach into the local party organizations and control their nominations or the policies of their nominees or officeholders. It has been said that Mr. Roosevelt might have dislodged Senator George & Co. had he carefully fostered a rival Democratic party organization. But such an effort would have run head-on into local pride, personal followings, conservatism, and fear of outside control. In practice, the President must negotiate with state and local party chiefs, just as he negotiates with envoys from foreign nations. He cannot dictate.

The President's limited control of the party affects his power not only as chief legislator but also as chief executive. If the President had a tight rein on his whole party, it might be easier for him to control the vast and sprawling executive establishment. In other countries unified parties help provide unified administration. In Britain, for example, a minister is ordinarily subject to party authority and discipline to the same degree as rank-and-file members of Parliament, and he is kept in line by party pressures as well as administrative ones. In the United States an important agency head can use his own backing in a section of the party—or even outside the party

---

[11] *The Public Papers and Addresses of Franklin R. Roosevelt,* 1938 Volume (Macmillan, 1941), pp. 469-470.

—to undertake veiled opposition to the President, provided that he does not go too far.[12]

Chief
Foreign-Policy Maker

The framers of the Constitution foresaw a special need for speed and single-mindedness in our dealings with other nations. The Constitution makes the President the exclusive spokesman for the United States. It gives him control over relations with foreign powers. It vests in him command of the two major instruments of foreign policy, the diplomatic corps and the armed services. It gives him responsibility for negotiating with foreign powers. It permits him to make commitments in behalf of the United States. The Constitution specifically assigns to the President the authority to appoint with the consent of the Senate all United States representatives to foreign nations, and to "receive ambassadors and other public ministers."

The power to appoint ambassadors and to receive them involves the vital power of *recognition*. The President has *complete discretion* to recognize or not to recognize new governments or states. In 1902 Theodore Roosevelt recognized the new state of Panama a few hours after a revolt had been staged with the help of United States forces. President Wilson withheld recognition from Mexican governments of which he disapproved, and President Hoover tried to restrain Japan by refusing to recognize its puppet Manchukuo. In 1933 President Roosevelt recognized the government of the Soviet Union, whose existence the United States had officially ignored for sixteen years. President Truman and Eisenhower withheld recognition from Red China.

EXECUTIVE AGREEMENTS

The chief executive shares his treaty-making power with the Senate, as we found in Chapter 16. Presidents have found an easy way, however, to bypass the Senate under certain conditions. This is the *executive agreement*. Well over half the international agreements signed by the United States have been achieved by this procedure, which involves simply an act by the President without any participation whatsoever by Senate or House. Some executive agreements have signalized famous events, such as the Boxer Protocol of 1901, the Atlantic Charter, and the "destroyer-bases" agreement. In addition to executive agreements, which are based on the President's own constitutional powers, Congress often confers authority on the chief executive to make agreements with other nations. The reciprocal trade program is an important example. Of course executive agreements, like treaties, may be set aside by

---

12 For a useful review of aspects of Presidential party leadership see L. S. Seligman, "The Presidential Office and the President as Party Leader," *Law and Contemporary Problems* (Autumn 1956), pp. 724-734.

the legislature. But unless they are, they seem to have much the same legal validity as treaties in the eyes of the courts. To be sure, treaties possess a "constitutional and moral control over the conscience and conduct of the American people," [13] but agreements made by Presidents with the prestige of a Woodrow Wilson or a Roosevelt or a Dwight Eisenhower have an authority all their own. In the last twenty years Presidents have concluded about 2000 executive agreements, compared to fewer than 300 treaties.

The famous destroyer deal with Britain was a striking example of the uses of executive agreements. In 1940 Britain urgently needed destroyers to protect her shores and convoys. President Roosevelt and his advisers, convinced that prompt action was vital, feared that the Senate might not act fast enough in ratifying a treaty, or might not act at all. By executive agreement the President traded fifty over-age American destroyers to the British in return

---

[13] George B. Galloway, *Congress at the Crossroads* (Crowell, 1946), p. 269.

POWERS OF THE PRESIDENT

HE CAN FORMULATE FOREIGN POLICY INDEPENDENTLY — PRES. MONROE PROCLAIMED MONROE DOCTRINE IN 1823

EUROPE

WESTERN HEMISPHERE

HE IS COMMANDER IN CHIEF OF ARMED FORCES — PRES. WILSON SENT MARINES TO HAITI IN 1915

HE ALONE CAN RECOGNIZE OR NOT REC- OGNIZE A NEW FOREIGN GOVERNMENT — PRES. COOLIDGE AND HOOVER REFUSED TO RECOGNIZE SOVIET GOVERNMENT

USSR

HE CAN CONCLUDE EXECUTIVE AGREE- MENTS — F.D.R. TRADED BASES FOR DESTROYERS IN 1940

HE APPOINTS U. S. AMBASSADORS AND RECEIVES REPRESENTATIVES OF OTHER NATIONS

AS CHIEF OF STATE HE REPRESENTS THE AMERICAN PEOPLE AT SUMMIT MEETINGS

GRAPHIC ASSOCIATES

Powers of the President as chief foreign-policy maker.

Adapted from Blair Bolles, *Who Makes Foreign Policy?* By permission of the Foreign Policy Association

for long-term leases on military and naval bases in the Western Hemisphere. The move won a good deal of popular support; presented with a *fait accompli,* Congress made no attempt to repudiate the agreement.

How much power does the chief executive have over foreign relations? The Supreme Court has repeatedly upheld strong presidential authority in this area. In the *Curtiss-Wright* case in 1936 the Court referred to the "exclusive power of the President as the sole organ of the Federal Government in the field of international relations—a power which does not require as a basis for its exercise an act of Congress, but which of course, like every other governmental power, must be exercised in subordination to the applicable provisions of the Constitution." These are sweeping words. Yet Congress itself does have significant power in foreign relations. It controls the funds to back up our policies abroad. It is a forum of debate and criticism. And it can "take back" powers that it has delegated the President in the realm of foreign affairs.[14]

The President has not only the authority but the *capacity* to act. For example, he has at his command unmatched sources of information. To his desk facts are channeled from all over the world. Diplomatic missions, military observers, undercover agents, personal agents, technical experts gather tons of material which are analyzed by experts in the State Department and elsewhere. Since the President draws on the informed thinking of hundreds of specialists, his pronouncements have a tone of authority. The President and his experts are sometimes wrong, and many gaps appear in their information, but his sources of information give him a clear advantage over Congress.

Diplomacy, moreover, frequently requires quick action. The President can act swiftly; Congress cannot. Diplomacy often has to be secret; as Harold Laski has said, diplomatic negotiations, like a proposal of marriage, must be made in private even if the engagement is later discussed in public. The President can act secretly; Congress cannot. For these and other reasons, Congress has granted the President wide discretion on matters affecting foreign policy and military security. Today the President has leeway in such matters as controlling foreign trade and exchange, in restricting imports and exports, in barring the transfer of ships to foreign registry, in buying military supplies without bids, in restricting immigration—not to mention his vast constitutional powers as commander in chief in time of crisis (see next section). Congress thus has given up tremendous amounts of its power to make foreign policy. It has done so not only because of the advantages the President enjoys in this sphere—the *unity* of his office, its capacity for *secrecy* and *dispatch,* and its superior sources of *information.* It has done so also because it has recognized that the United States must present a united front in dealing with other powers. It is hardly surprising, then, that the President looms large in

---

[14] For a penetrating analysis of presidential-congressional relations in foreign relations, see D. S. Cheever and H. F. Haviland, Jr., *American Foreign Policy and the Separation of Powers* (Harvard Univ. Press, 1952).

world politics. A foreign observer has said that, in the capitals of other nations, "What is the United States going to do?" usually means "What is the President going to do?" Foreign offices throughout the world search the President's words for meaning.

But the limits to presidential power should not be overlooked. Checks and balances operate in foreign-policy making and cannot be ignored. For example, Congress must *finance* the President's policies—a power of special importance when so much of our foreign policy consists of economic and military aid to other countries.

Commander in Chief   **T**he President shall be Commander in Chief of the Army and Navy of the United States," reads Section 2 of Article II of the Constitution. Even though this is the first of the President's powers listed in the Constitution, the framers intended that his military role be a limited one. As Hamilton pointed out in *The Federalist,* the President as commander in chief would be far less powerful than a king. The President's authority, Hamilton said, "would amount to nothing more than the supreme command and direction of the military and naval forces"; he would be a sort of first general and first admiral of the new nation. As things have turned out, however, the President has become far more powerful, as both the custodian and wielder of the nation's armed forces, than Hamilton foresaw.[15]

Today the President has wide powers as commander in chief during peacetime; in wartime his authority increases sharply.

IN PEACETIME

The President is supreme military commander. He appoints, with the consent of the Senate, all officers of the armed forces, from ensigns and second lieutenants to five-star generals. This is a vitally important function; it means that largely on the President's shoulders rests the job of determining whether the Grants, Pershings, and Marshalls will boss our military forces and plan the over-all strategy, or whether mediocre men will rise to the top. He can also dismiss the "top brass," as when President Truman relieved General Mac-Arthur of his Far Eastern command in 1952. The President has charge also of such matters as defense plans and the disposition of forces, but these military decisions he generally leaves to the chiefs of staff and other commanders.

The President's peacetime powers are limited by the same factors that restrict him as chief administrator and chief legislator—the checks and balances within government and the strength of the opposition. Congress has the power to raise armies, to enact military regulations, and to appropriate money,

---

[15] E. S. Corwin, *The President: Office and Powers,* p. 283.

In practice Congress delegates a good deal of military rule-making to the commander in chief, but the legislators can revoke such grants if they wish. Congressmen also make full use of their right to investigate, to question, and to criticize, especially when the military chiefs come around hat in hand to request funds. Occasionally members of Congress try to take a hand in strategic and diplomatic activities, often with unhappy results.

The Constitution delegates to Congress the authority to *declare* war (with the consent of the President), but the commander in chief in practice *precipitates* war. This supreme power of war*making* has been used by the chief executive time and time again. President Polk in 1846 ordered American forces to advance into disputed territory; when Mexico resisted, Polk informed Congress that war existed by act of Mexico, and a formal declaration of war was soon forthcoming. President McKinley's dispatch of a battleship to Havana, where it was blown up, helped precipitate war with Spain. In 1918, when no state of war existed between the United States and Russia, President Wilson sent American forces to Siberia to join Allied troops fighting the Bolsheviks. The United States was not formally at war with Germany until late 1941, but prior to Pearl Harbor President Roosevelt ordered the Navy to guard convoys to Great Britain and to open fire on submarines threatening the convoys. President Truman had no specific authorization from Congress in 1950 when he ordered American forces to resist aggression in Korea, nor did President Eisenhower when he dispatched forces to Lebanon in 1958.

Thus, in a tense situation, the President is able to engage the country in war. And an all-out war in turn means a tremendous enhancement of Presidential power.

THE PRESIDENT'S WAR POWER

When war comes, the central need in a democracy is for unity, teamwork, discipline—plus the preservation of our basic liberties. The people want leadership. Instinctively they turn to the President. He can tap a vast reservoir of power in planning broad strategy, raising military and industrial manpower, mobilizing the nation's economy.

In wartime the White House becomes GHQ for *governmental* as well as for military and industrial mobilization. Political power, which is ordinarily dispersed throughout the national government, is largely centered in the President. He becomes a sort of constitutional dictator. For example, he makes secret diplomatic agreements with foreign powers, far surpassing in importance many treaties that in peacetime would require senatorial consent. He authorizes the allotment of billions of dollars of funds appropriated by Congress. He takes final responsibility for crucial military decisions—as in the case of Roosevelt's decision in World War II to concentrate our armed might against Hitler before finishing off Japan. Constitutional forms are not abandoned, of course. They still exist—at least on paper. But in wartime the people become unified behind one goal—victory—and the solidarity of the people compels a unity in the government behind the President. Opposition congressmen may continue to snipe at the commander in chief's nonmilitary plans or policies, such as domestic economic policy or postwar peace goals, but they will not ordinarily obstruct his war program, even though they may lack confidence in it.

These vast powers of the President in wartime are not a recent development. It was Lincoln himself, struggling to overcome the crisis of civil war, who set the vital precedents for presidential quasi-dictatorship. Congress was not in session when Lincoln was inaugurated in March 1861; despite the emergency (or perhaps because of it) the new President did not even call Congress into session for four months. Meanwhile Lincoln raised and spent money, built up the armed forces beyond the limits set by law, blockaded southern ports—all without the consent of Congress, all without clear authority under the Constitution. Lincoln had a simple defense for his assumption of dictatorial powers. "Was it possible," he asked later, "to lose the nation and yet preserve the Constitution? By general law, life and limb must be protected, yet often a limb must be amputated to save a life, but a life is never wisely given to save a limb."

Congress in wartime has handed the President great chunks of authority. In World War I, President Wilson was given power to control the production, purchase, and sale of various fuels and foods, and to requisition them if he wished. He had power to take over factories, mines, pipelines, and the like, and he had a number of blanket controls under the Selective Service Act and the Espionage Act. In World War II, Congress again delegated vast authority to the President, who redelegated it to price, production, manpower, and transportation czars, who in turn were coordinated by superczars. Mr. Roosevelt used Lincolnian as well as Wilsonian precedents. In 1942, when Congress refused to repeal a provision in the price control act that protected the farmers, the President demanded that Congress act within a month—or he would. This action of Roosevelt's has been called "a claim of power on the part of the President to suspend the Constitution in a situation deemed by him to make such a step necessary." [16] In any event, Mr. Roosevelt's maneuver worked; Congress meekly repealed the provision.

Under the Constitution, a wartime President can direct military operations (taking the field himself if he wishes), establish military government in conquered lands, and end hostilities by means of an armistice. Under authority likely to be granted by Congress, he can raise armies, lend or give money or goods to other countries, take over strikebound plants, requisition property needed for defense, ration goods and set prices, shift military functions from one agency to another, censor mail and radio, control vital imports and exports, and so on. The list is long—and a compliant Congress will delegate even more emergency powers if the President requests them.

Certain forms of the Constitution may seem to be suspended. But two

---

[16] E. S. Corwin, *Total War and the Constitution* (Knopf, 1947), p. 64.

basic constitutional rights remain—or at least have remained in all our wars so far. One is the ultimate control of the President by the people. In no war so far—not in the Civil War when Lincoln had to campaign for re-election, nor in World War II, when Roosevelt had to do the same—have elections been suspended. And so far, despite certain restrictions, our basic liberties of free speech and free press have survived the hard test of war.

Chief of State   **A**s commander in chief the President represents the whole nation. He is not directing the war for the benefit of Republicans or Democrats, of businessmen, farmers, or workers, of easterners, northerners, or southerners. He is acting for all the people. This is only one of several ways in which the President serves as national leader. His military role, his ceremonial function, and his national responsibilities combine to make him a powerful chief of state representing *the whole nation and rising above the claims of majority or minority groups.*

Such was the role the framers of the Constitution hoped the President would fulfill. Looking on him as a sort of chief magistrate, they gave him judicial duties as well. These duties stem from the "power to grant reprieves and pardons for offenses against the United States, except in cases of impeachment." This *pardoning power* leaves the President a good deal of discretion. He can withhold a pardon altogether, or simply grant a reprieve (a delay in executing sentence), or lighten the sentence, such as by substituting life imprisonment for the death penalty, or grant a pardon subject to certain qualifications, or give a full pardon, which makes the offender, in the eyes of the law, as innocent as if he had never committed the offense. Neither Congress nor the courts can overrule a pardon. Since a President receives about 1600 applications for pardons a year, he must lean heavily on advice from the Department of Justice. The pardoning power also includes *amnesty,* a device for pardoning a specific group of persons at one stroke. In the 1860's Presidents Lincoln and Johnson granted amnesties to southerners who had taken part in secession.

Even the Founding Fathers could hardly have foreseen the extent to which the President would become the *ceremonial* head of the nation. No doubt they expected him to receive ambassadors in the manner of a king, and to issue proclamations on matters of national, nonpartisan concern. But today his ritualistic role surpasses all this. He pitches out the first baseball of the season, buys Christmas seals, gets his Red Cross membership card, presses buttons that start big power projects, attends the Army-Navy football game, hurries to the scene of national catastrophes, speaks on the Fourth of July and other patriotic occasions, reviews parades, and receives delegations of Boy Scouts, veterans, 4-H members, students, and the like.

Often these actions may be part of a deliberate effort to humanize the man and the job, a reaching for popular support. But there is also the tendency of people to turn to him. Even in a democracy—perhaps *especially* in a democracy—the people need a leader. They need someone who will personalize government and authority, who will simplify politics, who will symbolize the protective role of the state, who will seem to be concerned with them. How else explain the gifts they shower on him, the tens of thousands of letters that pour into the White House, especially in time of crisis, the sense of private grief felt by masses of people when a President dies? The President is head of the political family; as a sort of father image he sustains a deep-seated longing for a leader and protector.

The role of the *national* leader, then, is vital in the United States. American acceptance of leadership does not rest essentially on blind worship, as in the case of fascists or communists, but on an awareness that in a competitive society the exceptional leader should be allowed to emerge from the mass, take a commanding position, and receive a vote of confidence (at least at the outset). Gunnar Myrdal, a brilliant Swedish social scientist who studied American society, has remarked on the "patterns of strong and competitive personal leadership and weak followership" in the United States. He sees our type of "individual leadership as a great strength of this nation, but the passivity of the masses as a weakness." [17]

All these factors, constitutional, political, and psychological, serve to accentuate the President's role as chief of state, as leader of the nation. Yet under ordinary conditions the President as leader of *all* the people keeps running headlong into the President trying to act for *part* of the people.

THE DOUBLE ROLE

The point is that the President's functions are fundamentally inconsistent with one another. On the one hand he is a party leader, the spokesman and representative of a popular majority more or less organized in the party that he heads. As party chief he not only directs the national party organization; he also uses his powers as chief legislator to put through the party's program. On the other hand, as commander in chief and chief of state he must act for *all* the people, regardless of group or faction. As chief administrator he must faithfully administer the laws, whether these laws were passed by Democratic or Republican majorities in Congress; yet in choosing his subordinates and in applying the law he tends to think first of the interests of his popular majority.

How do the two Presidents live with each other? Sometimes the relationship is an uneasy one. For example, the President may wish to address the nation on an important problem. As *President* he is entitled to free time on the radio and TV networks. But if an election is in the offing, the opposition often charges that the President is really acting in his capacity as *party chief* and that his party should pay for the radio or TV time. The same question

---

[17] Gunnar Myrdal, *An American Dilemma* (Harper, 1944), pp. 709–719. See also Eric Hoffer, *The True Believer* (Harper, 1951).

comes up in connection with the President's inspection trips, especially when he uses them as occasions for political talks and general politicking. The President is often accused, too, of executing laws in a partisan manner, of putting party regulars into administrative offices, of issuing executive orders favorable to the interests of the majority he leads.

During normal times, however, the President manages to combine his roles of chief of state and party leader without too much difficulty. The people expect him to hold both roles, and he moves from one to the other as conditions demand. We are accustomed to seeing the President operate as national leader in conferring with a foreign envoy, only to don partisan clothing an hour later in conferring with party leaders.

During times of emergency the problem tends to solve itself. A crisis at home or abroad demands leadership. People in both parties instinctively turn to the White House for decision and action. The President doffs his party robes and emerges as national leader or chief of state. Two basic changes take place. First, as we have seen, the President assumes extraordinary powers. A serious crisis invariably results in an "increase in the prestige and competence of the President." [18] The President's hold on the people is so strong, his responsibility for action is so great, that Congress almost always follows where he wishes to lead. To meet the crisis he is given wide freedom of action. The normal checks and balances in government are largely suspended.

Even more significant, the normal opposition to the President vanishes— or at least breaks into fragments. To be sure, critics remain. But most of the criticism involves relatively petty matters—problems of mechanics, of methods, of procedures. There remains little organized opposition to the broad goals and programs that the chief of state champions. If any party or group opposes him, it may be suspected of seeking to sap the solidarity of the great majority. Such an opposition element may even be accused of lacking in Americanism. Under such conditions the opposition is likely to vanish.

All this may be inevitable. But is it healthy in a democracy? As chief of state, the President is responsible to the nation as a whole. Consequently, he has wide latitude in making his decisions and shaping his program. In a sense, his freedom is so great that it embarrasses him. He lacks the guidelines that help chart the course of the "party President." Some decisions he must make virtually alone. Being responsible to his majority is one thing. Being responsible to the whole people as chief of state is something else. This plight leads us straight into the general problems and prospects of the Presidency.

---

[18] C. L. Rossiter, *Constitutional Dictatorship* (Princeton Univ. Press, 1948), p. 217.

CHAPTER 18

The Presidency:
Powers and Problems

What, currently, is the American Presidency? "A cat on a hot tin roof." So a student of the executive office sums up the plight of the presidential office as we move deeper into the second half of the twentieth century.[1] The President, according to his view, has not one constituency that he must satisfy but *four:* his "governmental constituency," made up of officials and congressmen who depend on him for leadership and help; his "partisan" constituency, comprising the party leaders, party workers, and voters who helped elect him to office and who have a stake in his success; his "national" constituency, embracing all Americans who look upon him, especially in crisis times, as the symbol and embodiment of national unity; and his "overseas" constituency, made up of the leaders and citizens of other free countries dependent on America for leadership in the Free World.

No wonder the Presidency has been called the toughest job in the world. This relentlessly exacting office takes the best a man can offer. Another student of the Presidency has listed the personal qualifications demanded by the job: [2]

Bounce. The President must have that "extra elasticity" that enables him to thrive on a harsh diet of work and responsibility.

Affability. "The President's heart must be not only stout but warm. . . . The Presidency is a people's office. . . ."

Political skill. The President must be able to win popular support for his programs, to deal with powerful rivals in Congress, with party and interest-group leaders.

[1] R. E. Neustadt, "The Presidency at Mid-Century," *Law and Contemporary Problems* (Autumn 1956), pp. 609-645.

[2] Clinton Rossiter, *The American Presidency* (Harcourt, Brace, 1956), pp. 135-137. The quoted material is taken direct from this excellent volume, the other comment is condensed or adapted from it.

Cunning. The President must know the arts of politics—how to dodge and maneuver, when to be silent and when to speak out, when to lead the people and when to follow them.

Sense of history. The President must feel responsible to the generations who bequeathed us a great nation and to the generations still to come.

The newspaper habit. If the President does not want to be isolated from the outside world, he must have direct lines to information and ideas beyond his immediate staff. A secretary's briefing is no substitute for reading several newspapers with different outlooks, and even glancing at the feature columns and cartoons.

A sense of humor. At least two recent Presidents have said that they "could not have survived in office if they had been unable to laugh at the world and themselves."

If the President's job is the toughest in the world, it is certainly the most powerful position in the Free World. In this chapter, we shall take a close look at three central problems of Presidential power: (1) presidential disability and succession; (2) the President's relation with Congress; (3) the question of whether the President's authority, great though it is, is equal to his heavy responsibilities. We shall conclude with an account of how the Eisenhower Administration dealt with these and other problems.

PRESIDENTIAL DISABILITY AND SUCCESSION

What happens when the President dies, or for some other reason is unable to do his job? The Constitution provides that in the event of the President's removal from office, death, resignation, or inability to discharge the duties of his office, the same shall devolve upon the Vice President, and it gives Congress the power to determine who shall act as President if there is no Vice President. The framers were wise to provide for a Vice President, for seven Presidents have died in office or have been assassinated. Never yet has the nation been without both a President and a Vice President at any one time, but Congress has guarded against such an exigency. For a long time the law provided that the Vice President would be succeeded by the Secretary of State —and he by other Cabinet officers in a prescribed order. In 1947, however, Congress provided that the Vice President would be succeeded first by the Speaker of the House, then by the president pro tempore of the Senate, and only then by the Cabinet members. In no event would persons who lack the constitutional qualifications be eligible to serve, and before acting as President those who are eligible would first have to resign from their respective offices. Moreover, a Cabinet member is to serve only until a Speaker of the House or president pro tempore of the Senate is available and qualifies to supersede him in the office.

If the President dies, the Vice President becomes not merely Acting

President but President. What about the situation when the President is too ill to discharge his duties? Should the Vice President take over? This is not an academic question, for Garfield was disabled for almost three months before he died, Wilson for long periods during the last sixteen months of his second term, and Eisenhower on three separate occasions. But in no case did the Vice President take over.

Although a Vice President never has assumed the powers of the office because of a President's illness, most students of the Constitution agree that the Vice President would become merely Acting President and that the ailing President would resume the duties if and when he recovered. But who is to judge whether or not the President can discharge his duties? The Vice President? Congress? The courts? Congress has recently studied this question and has considered several suggestions; for example, that a group of Cabinet members and congressional leaders be authorized by law to decide on the President's disability after consulting with a panel of doctors. But no procedure has yet been determined on.[3]

Courtesy Fitzpatrick in the *St. Louis Post-Dispatch*

THE VICE PRESIDENT'S JOB

Under the Constitution, the Vice President serves as President of the Senate, voting only to break a tie vote. Since he often temporarily delegates the job of presiding to some senator, however, his legislative duties are not very arduous. Hence at first sight the Vice President might seem to be an ideal officer both to take some of the burdens off the President's shoulders and to serve as liaison with Congress, or at least with the Senate.

In practice, however, the office of Vice President has been something of a joke—and the occupants themselves have often ridiculed it. One of them described the Vice President's predicament as that of "a man in a cataleptic fit. He is conscious of all that goes on but has no part in it." [4] At best the Vice President is a sort of administration handy-man; at worst he is an intriguer who undermines the President's position. The trouble is that a party's candi-

---

[3] For an authoritative study of the problem and of proposals for reform, see Ruth C. Silva, "Presidential Inability," *University of Detroit Law Journal,* Vol. 35, No. 2, pp. 139-173.

[4] Corwin, *The President: Office and Powers,* p. 73.

date for Vice President is usually chosen to balance the ticket—if the Presidential candidate is a party conservative, the vice-presidential candidate is a party liberal; if the head of the ticket has a special appeal to labor, the number-two man will have to possess strong farm support. Hence he usually represents a wing of the party that is not too friendly to the President. In the face of this political fact, attempts to make the Vice President something more than a Throttlebottom (for example, by making him a kind of general manager) have usually come to naught.

Recently, however, the Vice Presidency has taken on important duties. Vice President Richard Nixon, for example, served on the National Security Council, chaired Cabinet committees, and took highly publicized "goodwill trips" abroad; President Eisenhower's illness dramatized the importance of the office. In the 1956 Democratic convention Adlai Stevenson further highlighted its potential role by allowing the delegates to choose the vice-presidential nominee rather than making the choice himself. The office

Holland in the *Chicago Tribune*

"To insure happy landings."

seems destined to become increasingly influential, but of course a Vice President could, if he wished, use his increased power to undermine a President's authority.

President and Congress: Teamwork or Deadlock?

There is a story that Theodore Roosevelt, vexed by opposition in the Senate, exclaimed that he would like to turn sixteen lions loose on the Senate floor. What if the lions ate the wrong senator, he was asked. "They couldn't if they stayed long enough," Roosevelt snorted.

Many another President would have echoed Roosevelt—and thrown in a few representatives to boot. Many a member of Congress has turned a cold and bitter face toward the White House. Physically the Executive Mansion and the Capitol Building are located on the same avenue, hardly more than a dozen long blocks from each other. Yet relations between President and Congress often seem to be marked by misunderstanding, deadlock, and open warfare.

Is this hostility a recent development? Why does it arise? Should anything be done about it? Can anything be done about it?

The first question may be answered easily. Stress and strain have marked relations between President and Congress from the outset. The new government had hardly got under way in 1789 when Hamilton, Jefferson, and other members of Washington's Cabinet were antagonizing members of Congress by drafting bills in their own offices and sending them along to Congress to be passed. In his earlier years Jefferson had feared that the President would be too powerful; after he became President he found that he had to take firm command of Congress if he wanted his program to go through. Jefferson used his party leaders to block bills, to oust committee chairmen, to steer measures through Congress.

The first serious split between President and Congress came a generation later, with Andrew Jackson's Administration. In trying to make the Presidency the "people's office," a rallying point for popular movements, Jackson ran head on into powerful men in the Senate like Daniel Webster and Henry Clay. In his famous struggle with Nicholas Biddle and Biddle's supporters in Congress over the United States Bank, the President freely used patronage, the veto power, and appeals to the people. Jackson, complained Clay, "swept over the Government like a tropical tornado."

Presidential-congressional harmony has ebbed and flowed.[5] During Andrew Johnson's Presidency following the Civil War, as we have seen, Congress virtually took over the government by repassing bills over Johnson's vetoes, and in the end impeached and almost convicted him. Grant maintained close relations with the legislators, but only at the expense of traditional presidential power. Cleveland at the start was willing to let Congress exert full legislative authority in order to maintain harmony. "I did not come here to legislate," he said bluntly. But in the end he was forced to change his mind and resort to patronage and other methods to enact his policies. Both Woodrow Wilson and Franklin D. Roosevelt had dramatic conflicts with Congress; both used the power and prestige of their high office to promote their legislative programs.

BEHIND THE CONFLICT

Why do President and Congress come to loggerheads? The causes are several. Inevitably a kind of jealousy springs up among politicians seeking the national limelight. Sometimes trouble stems from a simple lack of understanding or failure of communication between White House and Capitol Hill. Occasionally a key member of Congress is a "loner" unable to play as a member of a team, or a President may be too stubborn to make the necessary compromises. Then, too, power is so dispersed throughout the legislative branch, and

---

[5] For an excellent history of presidential-congressional relations, see W. E. Binkley, *President and Congress* (Knopf, 1947).

to some extent throughout the executive branch, that a great deal of confusion arises over the question of who has power to do what.

The main reason for conflict, however, lies far deeper: *President and Congress are elected by different alignments of voters and hence have differing loyalties and respond to different pressures.*

As we have seen, Congress tends to reflect sectional, local, and special interests and to overrepresent rural areas and minority groups in general, because of the sectional nature of senators' constituencies, gerrymandering of Representatives' districts, and procedures in Congress such as the seniority rule. The President, on the other hand, tends to represent *national* alignments of voters because his constituency is the whole nation, and to overrepresent urban groups because of the electoral-college system. To gain and keep office, President and congressmen must simply play different kinds of politics. The resulting gap between them goes right back to Madison's old idea that "ambition must be made to counteract ambition."

CAN THE GAP BE BRIDGED?

Some Americans are not disturbed by this conflict between President and Congress. They reason that the nation has successfully survived it for over a century and a half. Lack of harmony between the executive and legislative branches, while troublesome and tending toward inefficiency, has not seriously endangered effective government. In moments of peril—for example, during war and depression—Congress and the President have pulled together for the nation's good. Occasional deadlock, the argument continues, is a good thing. By subjecting bills to the scrutiny of both President and Congress, our system prevents foolish legislation. It may, unfortunately, also prevent good legislation, but in the last analysis national progress is based not on governmental statutes but on the free and unhampered actions of businessmen, farmers, workers, and others. Even if the system leads to negative government, the advantages outweigh the disadvantages.

Justice Brandeis once put the point well: "The doctrine of separation of powers was adopted," he said, "not to promote efficiency but to preclude the exercise of arbitrary power ... not to prevent friction, but, by means of the inevitable friction ... to save the people from autocracy." [6]

Other Americans disagree. They point to the eternal confusion, the wasted time and effort, the irresponsibility, and the frequent deadlock that are inherent in the semi-independence of the executive and legislative branches from each other. The price is often bad legislation, or no legislation at all. Government inaction might have been endurable during most of our history, they concede. But with the United States acting as leader of the free world, and with the national government committed to maintaining economic stability and

---

[6] *Myers* v. *United States* (1926).

well-being at home, the gap between the executive and legislative branches must be closed.

What can be done? Some propose that we forge some permanent link between the two branches. They recognize, of course, that many informal methods of liaison exist—for example, the President's meetings with the congressional Big Four (Vice President, Speaker, and majority leaders of House and Senate), and the thousands of daily contacts that occur between legislators and administrators at conferences, over the telephone, in committee sessions, and even at cocktail parties. But these are highly informal arrangements, dependent on the personal relations between President and congressional leaders, between rank-and-file legislators and bureaucrats. Many observers urge that the ties between the two branches be formalized and institutionalized.

One proposal calls for a *joint cabinet* or council. Advocated by the late Senator Robert M. La Follette, Jr., among others, this plan would set up a permanent group of congressional leaders and key Cabinet officers who together would rough out the broad outlines of national policy. Meeting regularly, the members would come to know one another well and to build a team spirit. Doubtless the President would preside over the meetings. This plan has received wide support. It was recommended in 1946 by the Joint Committee on the Organization of Congress, but Congress did not adopt it.

Another plan, at least a century old, is to give *Cabinet members seats in Congress.* The department secretaries—originally appointed, of course, by the President—could debate matters and answer questions, but they would not vote. This scheme would require no change in the Constitution. Indeed, in the early years of the government certain Cabinet members did speak in Congress, but the practice soon fell into disuse. Today its sponsors feel that it would create more understanding—or at least better communication—between Cabinet and Congress. In a variation of this plan, Senator Estes Kefauver of Tennessee has called for a *question and answer* period during which Cabinet members and other key administrators could report in person to House and Senate, and there answer questions from any and all members.[7]

A final proposal would require that the President choose advisers from among *leading members of Congress,* possibly to serve along with the more important members of the present Cabinet. Such a body would be something of an extension of the present Big Four system, but it would be larger, stronger, and more institutionalized. Here again, no constitutional problems need arise, so long as members of Congress are not made heads of departments. To be sure, the new Cabinet would still be a body of advisers. But as Professor Corwin, a supporter of the plan, has said, there are advisers *and* advisers.

---

[7] Estes Kefauver and Jack Levin, *A Twentieth-Century Congress* (Duell, Sloan & Pearce, 1947), pp. 65-79.

Such a Cabinet, in his view, "would comprise men whose daily political salt did not come from the presidential table, whose political fortunes were not identical with his, who could bring presidential whim under an independent scrutiny which today is lacking." [8]

CRITICISMS OF PROPOSALS

How feasible are these proposals to bring Congress and the President together through some sort of joint cabinet or council? Some observers are highly skeptical. If a joint cabinet is designed simply to acquaint President and Congress with one another's views, they argue, it is completely unnecessary. Each side knows the other's views only too well. The problem, critics emphasize, is not one of simple communication or exchange of views, but of each side speaking for a different combination of voters. No council or cabinet would change the basic power situation.

If a joint cabinet had real power, the critics continue, it might be effective. But would Congress ever grant real power to such a body? They fear not. In fact, Congress carefully promotes the *dispersion of power* among dozens of committee chairmen and other influential party and bloc leaders. The joint council might work out satisfactory agreements with the President only to fail to get backing from other leaders and from the rank and file. It is hard enough to get unity in the Cabinet even now, according to these skeptics—how much worse would it be if the Cabinet were enlarged to encompass powerful members of Congress? [9]

Even critics who believe in the need for reforms realize that improvements in the relations *between* the executive and legislative branches can come about only with improvements *within* the two branches. For example, they urge that Congress abandon the seniority rule, the filibuster, and other archaic procedures. They want the executive branch to be better organized, better staffed, and better led. Given such a combination of reforms (see Chapters 16 and 19), they believe that our government will be more efficient, effective, and responsible. But, as we have seen, changes within Congress and the executive branch are hard to bring about.

REFORMING THE CONSTITUTION

Other reformers believe that all these efforts to build a bridge between Congress and the President, even if they could be achieved, do not go far enough or deep enough. Tinkering with the machinery is not enough, these critics say; what we need is a *basic remodeling* of the governmental system. Such a remodeling, they grant, would call for sweeping changes in our Con-

---

8 Corwin, *The President: Office and Powers*, p. 362.
9 See Fenno, *The President's Cabinet*, cited above, which warns of the tendency of Cabinet-oriented reform proposals "to underemphasize the diversity and the fragmentation of political power" in the American governmental system.

stitution. Many plans have been suggested, but generally they fall into two types.

One plan for constitutional reform would make the President and his Cabinet *responsible to Congress* by giving Congress the power to oust the chief executive and to elect a new one. This plan is precisely the one considered on several occasions by the framers in 1787, and finally rejected. It would make the President almost wholly dependent on Congress. Because most Americans do not want to reduce the President to the role of a mere agent of the legislature, this plan has won little support. It smacks too much of the rickety parliamentary regimes that are believed to have weakened democracy in Europe. A faction-ridden Congress, it is felt, would continually want to hire and fire Presidents, giving us hair-trigger government.

A second plan cuts much deeper. It provides that whenever Congress voted lack of confidence in the President (or turned down an important administration bill), the chief executive could *dissolve Congress.* The legislators would thereupon run for re-election. Since an election would occur only when Congress and the chief executive were at odds over some vital issue or program, the results of the election could be considered a mandate for the government to follow. If the President's opponents won out, he would resign, and Congress could choose his successor. If the President was upheld by the people, his program would go through. There are various versions of this plan—but the essential idea is the *power of dissolution of Congress,* enabling elections to revolve around great issues instead of being held at prescribed intervals.[10]

Clearly this suggested scheme bears the earmarks of parliamentary government—especially that of Great Britain. There the Prime Minister and his cabinet members hold seats in Parliament: if they lose a vote of confidence on some issue, all the members of the House of Commons run for re-election in their constituencies, and the next government is composed of the leaders of the party that wins most of the seats in the election. In Britain this system has produced strong and stable government—yet one that is sensitive to deep shifts in public opinion. To import such a system, Americans would need to adopt electoral changes and probably reduce the power of the Senate.

The advocates of this system—which is usually called "cabinet" or "parliamentary government"—believe that it meets the basic problem of popular control of government. Cabinet government, they say, forces the rulers to keep a sharp eye cocked for changes in popular feeling. Thus the *people*—not the leaders—reign supreme. Government, moreover, is no longer divided internally. If President and Congress differ, an election is called and the people make the decision on the matter in dispute. This does not mean, it is said, that elections would take place too often. Politicians do not like to run for

---

[10] For three important versions of the plan, see W. Y. Elliott, *The Need for Constitutional Reform* (Whittlesey House, 1935), pp. 27-40; Henry Hazlitt, *A New Constitution Now* (Whittlesey House, 1942); and T. K. Finletter, *Can Representative Government Do the Job?* (Reynal & Hitchcock, 1945).

office, and both the chief executive and the congressmen would make every effort to compromise. Only on the most vital issues would the voters intervene. Government perforce would become alert and united without losing strength and stability.

COULD CABINET GOVERNMENT DO THE JOB?

Advocates of cabinet government admit that pushing through the necessary constitutional amendments would be a herculean task. A vast campaign of education would be needed, and even if most Americans were won over to the cause, thousands of politicians and groups with vested interests in the present system would stand in the way. Ratification of sweeping changes by legislatures or conventions in three-quarters of the states would be most unlikely. Nevertheless, the suggestions must be examined on their merits, regardless of their chances of adoption. They must be tested in terms of their own goals of effective, responsible, and democratic government.

Critics of cabinet government say this: To be sure, the plan would bring President and Congress into closer relationship. But at what price? Let us suppose, they argue, that a newly elected President and Congress clashed on some important issue or program. The President would let it be known that he would dissolve Congress and force another election unless the legislators went along with the White House. One of two things might then happen. Congress might give in to the President, in which case the price would be letting the chief executive have his way against the wishes of the other elected branch of government. Or—more likely—Congress might accept the challenge and an election would be called. If the President's opponents gained a majority of the seats in the election, he would resign and Congress would appoint a new chief executive. If his supporters won a majority, the new Congress and the old President could go ahead on the basis of his original program.

Everything turns, say the critics of cabinet government, on the outcome of these elections. And they feel that the outcome in every case would be defeat for the President. Why? Because Congress would accept the President's challenge only when it was sure of support back home. Most congressmen are well entrenched in their districts; they would be re-elected on the same basis as now—on the basis of personality, past favors to constituents, relations with local group and party leaders, and the like. Hence the outcome would not depend simply on the national issue that touched off the battle.

If the critics are right, the implications are clear. Cabinet government unquestionably would be weak and unstable, for if a majority of congressmen hostile to the President won the election they would return to Washington eager to select a new chief executive more responsive to their views. Minority blocs would virtually take over the government. The new President necessarily would be a mediator, a compromiser, a straddler—perhaps only a political cipher. Whatever way the wind blew, he would have to trim sail if he wanted to keep his job. He would be a follower, not a leader.

Yet the times seem to call for vigorous leadership, for strong executive control, not for instability, intrigue, and balance-of-power bargaining. Cabinet government would establish a link between White House and Capitol Hill, but the price—government impotence—seems too high. Is there any other way to unify our government and to make it both effective and responsible? We will return to this basic question in Chapter 21.

Is the President Becoming too Powerful?

How much power *should* the President have? This question is hard to answer because we cannot be sure what powers the President *does* have. The Constitution, as we have seen, is somewhat vague on the matter. It seems to grant the President a broad executive power without defining that power. Some scholars point out that the Constitution vests "the executive power of the United States" in the President but gives Congress only the legislative power "herein granted." They argue that the President has wide powers to protect the public interest in emergencies without specific legal authority or even at the cost of overriding existing laws. Despite considerable controversy over the matter, and the Supreme Court's rebuff of President Truman's attempt to exert "inherent powers" (see pp. 540-545), there seems to be a kind of "inherent power" in the Presidency, vast but undefined, that an aggressive President could exploit in time of crisis. The President also has a good deal of undefined power as the chief maker of foreign policy—a situation that has advantages in a crisis, but that makes it difficult to define presidential power.

THEORIES OF PRESIDENTIAL POWER

Presidents have had different ideas about their job. Two of them have given their views with great frankness. Theodore Roosevelt wrote in his *Autobiography:*

> The most important factor in getting the right spirit in my Administration, next to the insistence upon courage, honesty, and a genuine democracy of desire to serve the plain people was my insistence upon the theory that the executive power was limited only by specific restrictions and prohibitions appearing in the Constitution or imposed by the Congress under its Constitutional powers. My view was that every executive officer, and above all every executive officer in high position, was a steward of the people bound actively and affirmatively to do all he could for the people, and not to content himself with the negative merit of keeping his talents undamaged in a napkin. I declined to adopt the view that what was imperatively necessary for the Nation could not be done by the President unless he could find some specific authorization to do it. . . . Under this interpretation of executive power I did and caused to be done many things not previously done by the President and

the heads of the Departments. I did not usurp power, but I did greatly broaden the use of executive power.[11]

This has been called the *stewardship* theory of Presidential power. William Howard Taft, on the other hand, took a rather narrowly *constitutional* view of Presidential power. He wrote in 1916:

> The true view of the Executive functions is, as I conceive it, that the President can exercise no power which cannot be fairly and reasonably traced to some specific grant of power or justly implied and included within such express grant as proper and necessary to its exercise. Such specific grant must be either in the Federal Constitution or in an act of Congress passed in pursuance thereof. There is no undefined residuum of power which he can exercise because it seems to him to be in the public interest. . . .[12]

Franklin D. Roosevelt's conception of his powers—sometimes called the *prerogative theory*—was that the President in the face of emergencies had the same power that John Locke once argued that kings had—the power, in Locke's words, "to act according to discretion for the public good, without the prescription of the law and sometimes even against it." [13] The destroyer deal (see page 441), for example, violated several laws.

IS THE PRESIDENT POWERFUL ENOUGH?

Now for the other side of the ledger. The President's power is so great that it is easy to forget all the limits on his freedom. We have seen that as chief administrator and as chief legislator:

The President must share *policy-making* power with congressmen, administrators, and others.

He must share his *treaty-making* power with the Senate.

He must share his *appointing* power with congressmen, especially senators.

His power to *dismiss* agency heads is limited.

He is powerful in his *party,* but by no means all-powerful, particularly at the lower echelons.

Above all, the President is held in leash by the political situation in which he operates. No matter how strong a leader he may be, he is not a free agent. Not only must he deal with key congressmen, Cabinet members, important bureaucrats, the Vice President, party chiefs, and perhaps even leaders of the opposition party. He must also cope with the great political forces operating around the White House—public opinion in all its complexity, pressures from

---

[11] T. R. Roosevelt, *An Autobiography* (Macmillan, 1913), pp. 388-389.
[12] W. H. Taft, *Our Chief Magistrate and His Powers* (Columbia Univ. Press, 1916), p. 139.
[13] E. S. Corwin, *The Constitution and What It Means Today,* 10th ed. (Princeton Univ. Press, 1948), pp. 84-85.

organized interests, demands from his own party. He must negotiate endlessly among individuals and among interests. Always he must act—but without stepping on too many toes. Always the fierce light of public opinion, magnified by press, radio, and television, beats on the White House. Truly, the President has the toughest job on earth.

In recent years a severe curb has been put on the President's power: he has been made ineligible for a third term. Although the framers provided for indefinite re-eligibility, Washington quit after two terms and set a precedent that Presidents followed for a century and a half. By the time Coolidge turned down a chance to run again in 1928, the tradition against a consecutive third term had acquired virtually the force of a constitutional provision. In 1940, however, Franklin Roosevelt challenged this unwritten law and sought a third term. His victory in effect "repealed" the tradition, but the repeal was not to last long. In 1951 the thirty-sixth state ratified the Twenty-second Amendment, which now bars the President from being elected for more than two terms. It will be interesting to see if this change will survive should an immensely popular President want a third term some day. But in any event, the amendment will probably weaken Presidents during their second term, because powerful political leaders in Congress and in the administration will feel less obliged to support a man they know will be out of power on a certain date.

PROBLEM AND PROSPECTS

Have we come to the point where we are willing to accept the President as master of our fate and fortunes in time of crisis? Certainly we have rejected the concept of rigid checks on the chief executive, especially during times of crisis. For example, in June 1950, a few days after North Korean troops invaded South Korea, President Truman, acting on his own, ordered American forces to resist aggression. Equally significant, the few senators who criticized him for not going first to Congress found no support except in the extreme isolationist press. Today more than ever before, the President, as Woodrow Wilson once said, "is at liberty, both in law and conscience, to be as big a man as he can."

The growth of presidential power is not the result of White House conspiracies. It stems from social changes, economic crises, wars, the rise of political parties, the frequent failure of Congress to act effectively in the face of national problems, the deep popular demand for leadership and action. Today, more than ever before, continually recurring and deepening wars and economic dislocations demand drastic and far-reaching action by the man in the White House.

How dangerous is the tendency toward "one-man rule" in time of crisis? So far the danger has not been great. Perhaps we have been lucky. The great wartime leaders of the United States—Lincoln, Wilson, F.D.R.—were democrats in the best sense. They did not want power for power's sake, but simply as a means of overcoming national peril. Aside from one or two lapses, they maintained the basic democratic institutions of civil liberties and free elections. We may not always be so lucky. Some day we may elect a President who in time of crisis would find some pretext to postpone elections or stifle free speech. Indeed, we may elect a man who would deliberately create an emergency for the very purpose of suppressing the opposition.

The problem will grow more sinister if the twentieth century continues to be a time of endless emergencies, as seems likely. But one thing seems sure: We cannot eliminate the threat by trying to cut the President down to size. To do this would be to blunt the very weapon—Presidential power—that has served us so well in past emergencies. Nor should we try to raise Congress into full rivalry with the President, for that would give us divided government, which may be intolerable in time of crisis. A thoughtful student of the problem, generally satisfied with the workings of the office, has advised us, "Leave Your Presidency Alone!" [14]

The problem has two edges: On the one hand we must see to it that the President is our servant, not our master, that he leads us only in the direction we wish to go. On the other hand we need to help the President. He must have enough authority to do his job.[15] He must be free of some of the obstacles that now confront him. Above all, he needs the wise counsel of men who take a broad, national point of view, who can both guide him and sustain him. He cannot always find such associates in the Cabinet, for the members, though men of his choosing, seldom have national prestige of their own. He cannot often find them in Congress, because even congressmen of the same party have their own political loyalties and responsibilities. He cannot easily find them in his own party, because our parties tend to create sectional rather than national leaders.

The need, in essence, is for *responsible leadership*. The Presidency can be a vast reservoir of leadership, as Franklin D. Roosevelt realized. "The Presidency is not merely an administrative office," he said. "That is the least of it. It is more than an engineering job, efficient or inefficient. It is pre-eminently a place of moral leadership. All our great Presidents were leaders of thought at times when certain historic ideas in the life of the nation had to be clarified. . . . That is what the office is—a superb opportunity for reapplying, applying in new conditions, the simple rules of human conduct to which we always go back. Without leadership alert and sensitive to change, we are all bogged up or lose our way."

How can we win responsible leadership? We will come to grips with this question after we have looked in the next two chapters at our other national policy-makers.

---

[14] Rossiter, *The American Presidency*, p. 161.
[15] Louis Brownlow, *The President and the Presidency* (Public Administration Service, 1949), pp. 114-115.

*Eisenhower
and the Presidency*

When Dwight D. Eisenhower took office in January 1953, he brought to the White House a fresh approach to the Presidency after a generation of New Deal-Fair Deal leadership. He had ideas about changing the administrative organization of the Presidency. Feeling that Roosevelt and Truman had interfered too much in the business of Congress, he hoped to close the gap between the executive and legislative branches. On the other hand, he was less interested than his two predecessors in being a strong party leader. The new President was well trained to serve as commander in chief, and his middle-of-the-road policies and pleasing personality boded well for his future role as chief of state.

The Presidency itself is a great institution and a great tradition; it cannot easily be changed. In some respects Eisenhower changed the office to his liking. But, as the following recapitulation shows, in other respects the office changed *him*.[16]

EISENHOWER AS CHIEF ADMINISTRATOR

In his capacity as chief administrator, the President brought about some well-received changes. Feeling that his predecessors' methods had been disorderly and hit-or-miss, he installed the military form of staff, in which directions are supposed to flow in an orderly manner from the chief executive on down, and a chief of staff (or operations officer) sees to it that the directions are carried out. Eisenhower appointed Sherman Adams, a former governor of New Hampshire, as the Assistant to the President— in effect, a powerful chief of staff overseeing the White House and top government operations.

The President tried two other innovations. He resolved to make his Cabinet a real "team" that would work together harmoniously and take some of the burdens off the President. He also asked Vice President Nixon to serve as a leader of the executive branch, taking on important assignments and helping to smooth the Administration's relations with Congress.

In many respects all these changes worked well. Adams took an immense burden off the President's shoulders, allowing him more time for reflection and relaxation. Vice President Nixon was widely credited with able handling of a great variety of administrative, diplomatic, and legislative tasks. The Cabinet performed, at least outwardly, with more harmony than under the Roosevelt administrations (when Cabinet officers sometimes attacked one another openly in the newspapers). Agendas for meetings were more carefully prepared than in the past. These improvements were especially valu-

---

[16] This section is based in part on Robert J. Donovan, *Eisenhower: The Inside Story* (Harper, 1956), a revealing and "semi-official" treatment based on interviews with Administration leaders. See also Marquis Childs, *Eisenhower: Captive Hero* (Harcourt, Brace, 1958.)

able during the President's illnesses, when the top direction of government seemed to continue without major difficulty.

There was another side to the story. Democrats, and even some Republicans, complained that Adams was taking over too much power, making too many decisions, almost supplanting the real President. Some agency chiefs complained that they could not get through to the President; they felt deprived of direct and vigorous presidential support. The Cabinet never came to serve as an important policy-making body, nor was Nixon able to serve as a real substitute when his chief was ill.

In 1958 Adams resigned following charges that he had been friendly to favor-seekers in Washington. The next year Secretary of State Dulles quit because of ill health. Deprived of the two men to whom he had delegated wide powers, Eisenhower was now much more on his own: He was forced to take firmer command of his Administration and even exchanged visits with the ruler of Russia. Less was heard of the "team"; Americans seemed pleased at the revival of presidential influence.

EISENHOWER AS CHIEF LEGISLATOR

The new President brought to his office in 1953 a genuine regard for Congress and a respect for the tradition of governmental checks and balances. At his first Cabinet meeting in the White House, he urged Administration leaders to cooperate with Congress. He even invited all 531 members of Senate and House to a series of luncheons. He made overtures to Senator Robert A. Taft and Taft's strong supporters on the "Hill." For a time Eisenhower seemed to feel that this friendly approach would be enough to insure cooperation between the executive and legislative branches.

But soon disillusionment set in. Congress, though Republican-controlled, was soon opposing the Administration in many time-honored ways—investigating it, holding up presidential appointments (in the Senate), cutting down requested appropriations, voting down White House measures. Even worse for the President, Senator Joseph R. McCarthy attacked him for breaking his promises to "clean up the mess in Washington" and made headlines with his probes of alleged communists and security risks in the executive branch.

The President also had to deal with the proposed Bricker amendment, which would have curtailed presidential power over foreign relations. Secretary of State John Foster Dulles and other Administration leaders flatly opposed it. At first Eisenhower tried to resort to compromise, but compromise did not work. Then he tried to exert gentle pressure through conferences with legislative leaders. But this did little good, either. Nobody can "deliver" the Senate, warned Vice President Nixon.

Perhaps the most revealing example of the Administration's early difficulties involved its struggle with Representative Daniel Reed over excess-profits legislation.

EISENHOWER AND REED—A CASE STUDY

As chairman of the Ways and Means Committee of the House of Representatives, Reed headed the committee responsible for framing national tax policy. He had become chairman not because his tax views necessarily represented those of the Administration, of Congress, or of his committee, but because he had been in the House for 34 consecutive years and had climbed up the seniority ladder rung after rung. Representing a conservative Republican district in rural upstate New York, his views on tax policy differed sharply from those of the Republican President, who had won sweeping nationwide support in his first bid for office. The dispute typified many of the historic aspects of presidential-congressional conflict.

Herblock in *The Washington Post*

"He's one of my young-uns. What about it?"

This is how matters stood in the spring of 1953: Reed wanted to see the federal excess-profits tax expire on June 30, 1953, as had previously been scheduled by Congress. This tax, he argued, hurt business—especially small business—and for years the Republicans had been promising to cut taxes when they took office. President Eisenhower and other Administration leaders agreed that the tax was "bad," but they did not want the tax to expire until December 31, 1953. They had three reasons: (1) the Republicans had promised to balance the budget as well as cut taxes, and a deficit was looming; (2) Administration leaders feared it would be politically unwise to drop a tax on corporations before taxes on individuals could be cut; and (3) the government could not afford the loss in revenue—about $800 million—if EPT were not extended.

Accordingly, the Administration asked Congress for legislation extending EPT by six months. Representative Reed said "no." Deciding that they could get nowhere with Reed, Administration leaders decided on a new tack. The Rules Committee of the House (see pp. 387-388) not only controlled the right of way for bills reported out from other committees but could send its own measures to the floor of the House. Would the Rules Committee be willing to ignore the Ways and Means Committee and send its own EPT extension bill into the House? Speaker Martin quickly investigated and discovered that all the Republican members except one or two would go along with a new bill. By the skillful use of patronage, one more member was won over to the Administration's cause.

A one-time All-American football player and wrestling champion, who looked the part, Reed was furious when he heard of Martin's plans. He resolved to fight to the end. Appearing before the Rules Committee, he shouted that the Committee's action would destroy the "foundations of our legislative system." But a majority of the Rules Committee, anxious to support the President and the Speaker, voted to report their own EPT extension to the House.

Seemingly, the Eisenhower Administration had won the battle. Many representatives, however, were disturbed over the bypassing of the Ways and Means Committee. Moreover, an acrimonious fight over the Rules Committee's powers seemed likely to break out on the floor. Seeking to avoid such a fight, Martin gained assurances from members of the Ways and Means Committee that if no further action was taken on the Rules Committee bill, these members would sign a discharge petition, if necessary (see page 382), to bring the EPT bill out of Reed's committee. When Reed heard of this move, he knew his battle was lost. Grudgingly, he called a meeting of Ways and Means. When a member moved for consideration of EPT, the chairman, dogged to the end, ruled him out of order. By a majority vote, the committee then overruled Reed and promptly reported out the Administration's EPT extension bill.

EISENHOWER TAKES THE OFFENSIVE

His experience with congressional leaders like Bricker and Reed, and the failure of much of his program in Congress, convinced the President that he must exert stronger leadership over legislation. At the start of the 1954 session of Congress, he announced that he was "unalterably opposed" to the Bricker amendment. He vigorously defended Administration officials against Senator McCarthy's accusations (although he did not attack the senator openly by name). Most important, he told Republican congressional leaders that the time had come for them to act on their campaign pledges. He put pressure on the leaders. When one of them suggested that an independent Congress should not be pushed too far, the President shot back that he would carry the fight into the open if he had to.

Eisenhower continued to press for his program during the rest of his first term, but two events intervened. One was the Democratic capture of Congress in the fall of 1954, and the other was the failure of his health. Paradoxically, however, the President got along better with the Democratic Congresses of 1955-61 than he had with the previous Republican Congress.

Democratic control to some extent isolated Republicans who had thwarted the President, and McCarthy and other committee chiefs lost their chairmanships. But the cooperation between Eisenhower and the Democrats had its complications too, for in the 1956 and 1958 elections both the Administration and the Democrats claimed credit for the same bills or blamed the other side for the mistakes, so that the average voter had trouble discovering who was responsible for what.

Toward the end of his second term the President took somewhat stronger personal leadership in pressing for his legislative program. He also wielded his veto power freely against some measures passed by the Democratic Congress. Perhaps he had come to the same conclusion as had many former Presidents— that unless they take up the reins of legislative leadership, the government will bog down in confusion and inaction.

EISENHOWER AS PARTY CHIEF

When the new President took his oath of office, Senator Robert A. Taft was still leader of the more conservative and isolationist wing of the Republican party. The senator from Ohio had many loyal followers on the Hill, including many of the Republican committee chiefs. Taft and his supporters pledged to cooperate with the President, but they became extremely disturbed by some of Eisenhower's early actions; for example, by his appointment of a labor-union chief as Secretary of Labor.

For his part, the President was upset by the failure of the Taft wing to support his program. So distressed did he become over the division within the Republican party, that during 1953 he contemplated the possibility of forming a third party—one that would be essentially "his" party, representing his own brand of middle-of-the-road domestic and international policy.[17] But then his mind turned to the failure of earlier third-party movements, such as the Progressives led by Theodore Roosevelt. He decided that his best hope was to keep trying to give the Republican party "a new viewpoint and a new complexion."

Accordingly, the President resumed his role as party chief with new vigor. He had once remarked that the man in the White House was "President of all the people," and that he did not intend to use his office as an agency in partisan elections. Faced with the congressional elections of 1954, he changed his mind and plunged into probably the most active political campaign that any President has ever waged in a midterm election. He called openly for a Republican Congress and stumped the country speaking for Republican candidates. Although the Democrats still won control of Congress, some observers felt that their margin would have been larger

---

[17] Donovan, *op. cit.,* pp. 151-153.

had it not been for the President's intervention. In 1956 and 1958, the President again "lent his coattails" (as far as his health permitted) to Republican candidates in their national and state campaigns.

Eisenhower had learned that the President must be party leader as well as administrative and legislative leader. Otherwise the government would lack the propulsive, coordinating force it needs to produce results. And somehow the President had to combine his party leadership with his leadership of all the people as commander in chief and chief of state. Faced with a Democratic Congress during most of his Presidency, Eisenhower showed his willingness to deal with the Democrats while continuing to serve as Republican chief. But the task of party leadership, difficult enough with his own party in power, proved one of the most galling and perplexing problems of the President's second term with Congress controlled by the opposite party.

The Bureaucrats

Government officials are people. We hear so much these days about arrogant bureaucrats and red tape artists that it is well to keep this fact in mind. The bureaucrat is the postman who just stuck your mail in the door, Miss Green who teaches sixth grade at P.S. 19, the cop directing traffic on Elm Street, the judge who lives down the way. He is the man fighting a forest fire in Wyoming, the diplomat negotiating a treaty in Argentina, the tax collector checking figures in New Orleans, the bureau chief hurrying to the White House, the scientist studying a rare disease at a great medical center. These are people with hopes and worries, ambitions and frustrations, abilities and failings—just like all the rest of us.

Flaying the bureaucrat is an old American custom, and to an extent is a wholesome one. And yet we need to remind ourselves that all large organizations, governmental or not, are run by bureaucrats. Bureaucracy is a characteristic form of modern organization. We hear much of the "dead hand of bureaucracy," but bureaucracy as a type is neutral. It can be efficient or inefficient, democratic or autocratic, alert or stagnant.[1] *Some* governmental bureaucracies—like *some* private ones—are on balance inefficient (although inefficiency is very hard to measure). Why, then, is the criticism of bureaucrats in government so loud and persistent? Partly because Americans have a deep-seated fear of big government, partly because public officials work in a goldfish bowl under the sharp eyes of congressmen, columnists, radio commentators, and lobbyists.

In this chapter we are mainly interested in the 2⅓ million people who make up the executive branch of the federal government. Certain facts about these 2⅓ million people need to be emphasized at the outset:

1. Only a small part of the 2⅓ million work in Washington. The great majority are employed in regional, field, and local offices scattered through-

---

[1] John Dickinson, "The Perennial Cry of Bureaucracy," *The Yale Review* (March 1935), pp. 448-463.

out the country. The picture of a huge bureaucratic horde concentrated in Washington is a false one.

2. More than half of these 2⅓ million civilian employees work for the Army, Navy, Air Force, or some other defense agency. Perhaps three-quarters of them are connected with the fighting of past, present, or future wars. The continuing world crisis has put its stamp on our bureaucracy.

3. Only a small part of the bureaucrats—perhaps 10 per cent—work for so-called welfare agencies, such as the Social Security Administration or the Rural Electrification Administration. The welfare state may be a major point of controversy in our party battles, but it has a minor place in today's big government. A much smaller proportion of government employees work in regulatory agencies, such as the Interstate Commerce Commission.

4. Federal employees do not run to any one type. They are not all Democrats, or all Republicans. They are not all college-educated. They are not all conservatives, or all liberals. They are as varied as the American people themselves. They come from all parts of the country, have a variety of religious faiths and political views, represent a great range of national origins.

5. Their work in government is equally varied. Not all these officials pound typewriters or stamp forms or issue regulations, as the newspaper cartoons would have us think. Over 15,000 different personnel skills—about two-thirds as many as are found in all private business—are represented in the federal government. Like Americans generally, most government workers are specialists in some occupation or profession. Unlike Americans as a whole, however, most federal employees are white-collar workers—stenographers, clerks, lawyers, office heads, inspectors, and the like.

How important are the bureaucrats? In a sense, of course, they are all-important. They are the core of big government. Without officials and employees government would be a collection of politicians and lawmakers —generals without armies. Government without a bureaucracy is unthinkable. So influential are the officials that sometimes the political heads seem insignificant. Alexander Pope said over 200 years ago:

> For forms of government let fools contest,
> Whate'er is best administer'd is best.

But this sentiment goes too far. *Forms of government* help shape the political world in which the administrator lives; they influence the kind of decisions made, and the way they are carried out. Administration in the United States is different from administration in Russia, Spain, or Borneo.

Actually we cannot separate administration from politics. The two are inextricably linked. Our job is not to put each in a separate sphere, but to see the interrelationship between the two. Our job is to ask questions: How is administration carried on? What kinds of problem do administrators face? What are their powers? How are they made responsible and accountable to the people? In short, *how can the bureaucrats do their jobs and yet remain our servants and not our masters?*

The Shape of Administration

Big government is complex government. The executive branch is a cluster of thirteen departments, twenty-three government corporations, and forty-four independent agencies, together embracing over 2000 bureaus, divisions, branches, offices, services, and other subunits. Five big agencies, the Departments of Army, Navy, and Air Force, the Post Office, and the Veterans Administration, tower over all the others. Most of the agencies are responsible to the President, but some are partly independent of him. Virtually all the agencies exist by act of Congress; the legislators could abolish them either by passing a new law or by withholding funds. The power of Congress to set up departments and agencies is implicit in the Constitution. The framers simply assumed—without actually specifying—that Congress might establish such functions and organizations as it saw fit.

In its first session in 1789, Congress created the Departments of Foreign Affairs (later changed to State), War, and Treasury. During the next 100 years the government grew slowly but fairly steadily. World War I brought a mushrooming of federal agencies, and many of these survived into the postwar years. World War II brought an even greater expansion, as the government mobilized armed forces of fifteen million men, fought a war on many fronts, and controlled large areas of the nation's economy. The executive branch shrank after World War II, but not back to its prewar size, and increased sharply again during the Korean war.

FORMAL ORGANIZATION

A soldier writes to his mother that he is a member of the first squad of the second platoon of Company B of the 1st Battalion of the 426th Regiment of the 95th Division of the III Corps of the Ninth Army. A friend of his works in the personnel office of the parts section of the Flint Division of the Buick Department of General Motors. A "government girl" in Washington tells her father that she is in the stenographic section of the administrative service of the Budget and Finance Division of the Bureau of Supplies and Accounts of the Department of the Navy in the Department of Defense.

Bigness means organization. The larger the number of people and the more complex job, the more highly organized an agency will be. In establishing a new agency, Congress may lay down a general structural plan in legislation, the President may give further shape to it in executive orders and in private instructions, and the head of the agency and his assistants will extend the organizational skeleton of the new agency down to small units. But the executive branch, as a whole, it has been said, grew up "without plan or design like the barns, shacks, silos, tool sheds, and garages of an old farm." Although different functions produce different types of organization, in general the main agencies of government are composed of departments, corpora-

PROPOSED TYPICAL ORGANIZATION OF A FEDERAL AGENCY

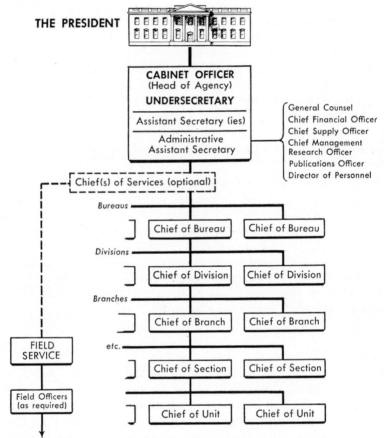

Coordination with state and local authorities as appropriate.

From Commission on Organization of the Executive Branch of the Government, *Concluding Report,* 1949, p. 10

Hoover Commission recommendation for departmental organization.

tions, independent agencies, and their subunits—bureaus, divisions, offices, and so on down the line—together with a network of regional and local offices.

The *departments* are headed by Secretaries (except Post Office, which is headed by the Postmaster General; and Justice, which is headed by the

Attorney General). These Secretaries also are Cabinet members (except for the Secretaries of the Army, Navy, and Air Force, who report to the President through their chief, the Secretary of Defense) and thus are directly responsible to the President. While the departments vary greatly in size, they have certain features in common. Often an undersecretary takes part of the administrative load off the Secretary's shoulders. One or more assistant secretaries direct major programs. Like the President, the Secretaries have personal assistants who help them in planning, budget, personnel, legal, public relations, and other staff functions. The departments are, of course, subdivided into bureaus and smaller units, but the basis of division may differ. The most common basis is *function;* for example, the Commerce Department is divided into the Census Bureau, the Patent Office, the Weather Bureau, and so on. Or the basis may be *clientele* (for example, the Bureau of Indian Affairs of the Interior Department), or *work processes* (for example, the Animal Husbandry Research Division of the Agriculture Department), or *area* (for example, the Alaskan Air Command of the Department of the Air Force).[2] The basis of organization of most departmental units—and indeed of the departments themselves—is mixed.

The score or more of *government corporations,* such as the Tennessee Valley Authority and the Federal Deposit Insurance Corporation, are "mongrel" organizations. A sort of cross between a business corporation and a regular government agency, the government corporation was designed to make possible a freedom of action and flexibility not always found in the regular federal agencies. For example, corporations have been free from control by annual appropriations by Congress and from certain regulations of the Budget Bureau and the Comptroller General. They also have had more leeway in using their own earnings as they pleased. And yet the fact that the government *owns* the corporations means that it retains basic control over their activities. Recently, Congress has deprived the corporations of much of their freedom, and they have taken on some of the character of regular departments—they are no longer free from the need to get annual congressional appropriations, for example. They remain, however, useful means of keeping certain government activities (especially financial) somewhat apart from the routine, congested, and centralized federal agencies and from excessive congressional and presidential control, particularly in time of emergency.

The *independent agencies* comprise many types of organization and many degrees of independence. Broadly speaking, all agencies that are not corporations and that do not fall under an executive department (such as Treasury or Interior) are called independent agencies. Many of these agencies, however, are no more independent of the President and Congress than are the executive departments themselves. The huge Veterans Administration is not represented in the Cabinet, for example, but its chief is directly responsible

---

[2] S. C. Wallace, *Federal Departmentalization* (Columbia Univ. Press, 1941), pp. 91 ff.

to the President. Their being outside the formal executive departments, however, does give them some measure of independence.

Another type of independent agency, however, really deserves the adjective. This is the *independent regulatory board* or *commission*—agencies like the Securities and Exchange Commission, the National Labor Relations Board, the Interstate Commerce Commission. Congress set up these boards mainly to keep them somewhat free from White House influence in exercising their quasi-*legislative* and quasi-*judicial* functions. Congress did not want the President, for example, to interfere in the ICC's setting of railroad rates or deciding whether its rules had been violated by railroad companies. Congress has protected their independence in several ways. The boards are headed by three or more commissioners with overlapping terms, they often have to be bipartisan in membership, and the President's power of removal is curbed. But this independence is limited. No agency can be completely separate from its governmental and political surroundings (nor should it be). And many of the boards have found that the more independence they have of the President, the more dependent they are on Congress or on the interests they regulate.[3]

Within the departments, corporations, and independent agencies are a host of subordinate units. The standard name for the largest subunit is the *bureau,* although sometimes it is called an office, administration, service, or what not. Bureaus are the working agencies of the federal government. In contrast to the big departments, which are often mere "holding companies" for a variety of agencies, the bureaus usually have fairly definite and clear-cut responsibilities, as do the Bureau of Customs and Bureau of Narcotics of the Treasury Department, the Bureau of Indian Affairs of the Interior Department, the Bureau of Motor Carriers of the ICC. Most bureaus are overshadowed by their mother agencies, but some of them, like the Federal Bureau of Investigation and the Bureau of Reclamation, enjoy a popular prestige and political position of their own. Below the bureaus are hundreds of branches, services, sections, and other units that perform even more specialized operations.

The *field service* of the federal government embraces a vast number of regional, state, county, and local units. The local post office is part of the field service, as is the local recruiting center or veterans office. As the action end of government, the field service runs into many vitally important problems. Ticklish questions of coordination constantly arise. How can cooperation be promoted between several federal offices in the region with overlapping duties but responsible to different departments in Washington? How far is it possible and desirable to depart from national regulations in meeting local situations? Which decisions should be made on the spot, and which should be referred to Washington? How much collaboration should be

---

3 See R. E. Cushman, *The Independent Regulatory Commissions* (Oxford Univ. Press, 1941), esp. Chapter 10.

tried with state and local governments? Washington administrators face problems, too: how far to decentralize, what decisions should be delegated to the field, what type of field organization is best suited to their needs (there are many types), how to combine local flexibility with national direction and responsibility.[4]

INFORMAL ORGANIZATION

All this elaborate organization of the executive branch gives order and system to administration. It assigns certain functions to certain units, places one official (or sometimes more) at the head of each unit and makes him responsible for its performance, allows both specialization and coordination, permits ready communication, and in general makes our far-flung administration somewhat controllable and manageable. But this formal organization is not all-important. Indeed, it can be highly misleading if taken too seriously. The detailed organization chart on the office wall of some administrator may represent hope and intention rather than reality.

Why? Because men and women are not standardized units. They differ in attitude, motive, ability, experience. And their very diversity leads to all sorts of complications. Relationships among officials in an agency may be based on *influence* rather than on legal authority. Leadership may be lodged not at the top but in a variety of places. A certain group of officials may have considerable power, while another group, with the same *formal* status, may have much less. The loyalties of some officials may cut across the formal aims of the agency.

Let us consider an imaginary but typical bureau. The bureau chief is an old-line administrator who has served through four presidential administrations. He is cautious and unimaginative. He has a rival in the person of an assistant to the Secretary who heads the whole department. Some officials in the bureau look to this assistant for leadership; they share his enthusiasm and support his plans, and they hope that he may take over the department some day and give them the power and position they feel they deserve. But the bureau chief has his own set of motives and attitudes; moreover, he enjoys the backing of a powerful bloc in Congress that will defend him if he is attacked. He has built a personal organization, made up of two or three division chiefs, an attorney, the personnel officer, and his own staff, and this personal following is intensely loyal to him.

This, perhaps, is an extreme case; but it shows how *informal* organization can have a major effect on administration. A subordinate official in an agency, for example, might be especially close to his chief simply because they went to the same college or play poker together, or because the subordinate knows how to ingratiate himself with his chief. A staff official may have tremendous influence, not because of his formal authority, but because his

---

[4] D. B. Truman, *Administrative Decentralization* (Univ. of Chicago Press, 1940).

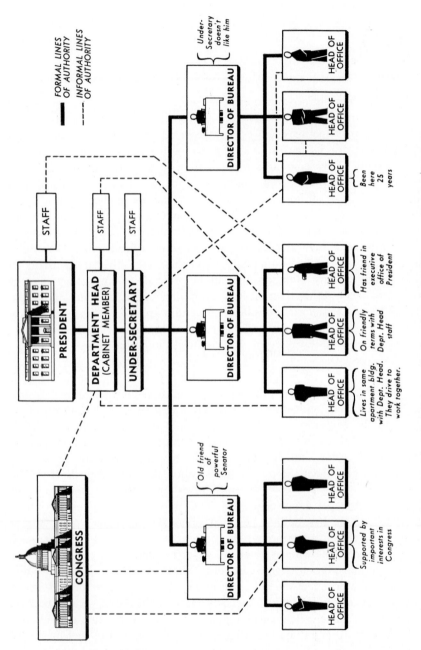

FORMAL LINES OF AUTHORITY

INFORMAL LINES OF AUTHORITY

PRESIDENT

STAFF

DEPARTMENT HEAD (CABINET MEMBER)

STAFF

UNDER-SECRETARY

STAFF

CONGRESS

DIRECTOR OF BUREAU

Old friend of powerful Senator

DIRECTOR OF BUREAU

DIRECTOR OF BUREAU

Under-Secretary doesn't like him

HEAD OF OFFICE

HEAD OF OFFICE

HEAD OF OFFICE

HEAD OF OFFICE

HEAD OF OFFICE

HEAD OF OFFICE

HEAD OF OFFICE

HEAD OF OFFICE

HEAD OF OFFICE

Supported by important interests in Congress

Lives in same apartment bldg. with Dept. Head. They drive to work together.

On friendly terms with Dept. Head staff

Has friend in executive office of President

Been here 25 years

FORMAL AND INFORMAL LINES OF A BUREAUCRATIC ORGANIZATION

476

experience, fairness, common sense, and general attractiveness lead men to turn to him for advice. In an agency headed by a chief who is weak, unimaginative, phlegmatic, and incompetent, a vacuum may develop that encourages others to try to take over. The private secretary of an official, through her charm, tact, and understanding of her boss' job and the politics of the agency, may gain great influence in an organization. The elevator man has no formal power at all, but he is a vital link in the informal communications network in the agency, and his rumor-mongering distinctly affects the morale of the employees.

Such informal organization and communication cutting across regular channels is inevitable to some degree in any organization, public or private. Even the Army, with all its hierarchy and regimentation, abounds with these elements. Is informal organization nevertheless an evil that has been allowed to develop too far?

Certainly it has its disadvantages. It may be a *disorganizing* force, in the sense that employees may not know who is really running the agency, what orders are to be followed, where the agency is trying to go. It may be a *demoralizing* force. Officials may come to feel that a group of "king's men" will receive quick promotions and other favors. Administrative decisions may hinge too much on personal factors and not enough on rules and tradition. Officials and subunits may work at cross purposes, responding to conflicting instructions or loyalties.

On the other hand, informal organization may be as beneficial as it is inevitable. In an agency that is unduly rigid in structure, it permits flexibility and vitality. It may give recognition to outstanding young administrators who have not yet risen very far in the formal hierarchy. It may allow more people to contribute to the agency's policies and planning, and thus raise agency morale. It may allow an astute administrator to bridge the artificial divisions, formal and informal, that always arise in an organization.[5] The wise agency chief tries not to suppress informal organization, but simply to turn it to good account.

SOME ADMINISTRATIVE CONCEPTS

Administration is a relatively young discipline and still unscientific in many respects. As a body of theory and experience, however, it has evolved a number of working concepts:

Unity of command. Every official should have a superior to whom he reports and from whom he takes orders. This principle of administration aims at bringing some order and unity into the actions of thousands of government employees. It is related to another concept, the *chain of command,*

---

[5] H. C. Mansfield and F. M. Marx, in *Elements of Public Administration,* F. M. Marx, ed. (Prentice-Hall, 1959), 2d ed., pp. 274-293.

which suggests a firm structure of authority running from the top down, and of responsibility, running from the bottom up. But as the practical workings of informal organization show, these principles are not—and cannot be— hard and fast. A subordinate cannot get all his instructions from his chief; he is influenced by other leaders, by his associates, by experts outside the agency, by his own background and personality. Nevertheless, unity of command is an important principle in assigning authority and responsibility.

Line and staff. Line, as we have seen in discussing the Presidency, con- sists of the pyramid of operating agencies. These agencies actually carry out specific jobs, such as preventing soil erosion or inspecting coal mines. The staff is the *advisory* agency, which does not issue orders on its own but acts *through the operating chiefs* and down the chain of command. In the Army, the staff might do intelligence work; in the Department of Agriculture, it might be responsible for personnel. Standard staff work involves helping the executive in his functions of planning, organizing, staffing, directing, coordi- nating, reporting, and budgeting (often described as POSDCORB). Once again, no easy distinction between line and staff is possible. Often staff units actually do control and command instead of merely advising. Some staff agencies, like the Budget Bureau, employ hundreds of persons and have operating as well as advisory tasks. Many line chiefs hold important advisory functions; a bureau chief may be the main adviser to a department head. Still, the line and staff concept is useful in understanding administrative organi- zation, especially on a large scale, as in the Army.

Span of control. How many persons can one man supervise effectively? A rule-of-thumb answer is three to fifteen. Much depends on the personality of the chief, the nature of the work, the size of the organization, the location of the subordinates (as in field offices), and many other factors. No matter how able a chief may be, a breaking point ultimately will be reached if he must supervise more and more subordinates. In practice, this principle is often violated. The Hoover Commission found that far too many officials report to the President, with the result that he could not effectively direct them.[6]

Decentralization. An administrator cannot make all the decisions him- self. He must delegate decisions and responsibilities, as well as action itself, to lower levels. One sign of an able administrator is the ability to prevent his own desk from becoming a bottleneck. But decentralization is difficult to achieve, for it may come into conflict with the principles of unity of command and span of control.

------

[6] Commission on Organization of the Executive Branch of the Government, *General Management of the Executive Branch* (Government Printing Office, 1949), p. 3.

Professionalism. Many of the most influential government figures are experts in some field of study, such as law or accounting, or in some field of administration, such as sanitation, building army camps, or operating new machines. Such professionals are indispensable to modern government, but their role poses certain questions. What should be the relation between the chief, holding broad responsibilities, and the expert? How can the professionals be geared into the operating program? How can their advice be evaluated? What if their suggestions clash with those of operating heads?

Leading the Team　These concepts suggest one of the chief goals of public administration: how to "make a *mesh* of things." The administrator, in short, must come to grips with the question that is central to democracy and central to this book: how to reconcile the demands of unity and diversity. He must lead a team made up of people with all sorts of skills, attitudes, and backgrounds; he must reach his goals without stifling the diversity and freedom that we prize in a democracy. In forming and leading a team, the administrator is both helped and handicapped by the ancient traditions and present practices of American administration.

BUILDING THE TEAM

The government administrator is not nearly so free in building his team as is the private businessman. Government has long followed prescribed methods of recruiting, examining, classifying, promoting, and dismissing personnel. These methods are largely a result of painful experience. For many years America had a notorious appointment system that was summed up in the slogan, "To the victor belong the spoils." When a new party came to power, its leaders and followers felt they had a right to take over desirable government jobs. The excuse was a double one. Parties should have patronage, it was said, to encourage members to work for the party, and to answer the people's demand for a new broom to sweep Washington clean. Men like Andrew Jackson argued, moreover, that a frequent turnover of officials would keep government democratic. Besides, they said, the duties of public officials were so plain and simple that any intelligent person could perform them.

Later in the century a sharp reaction set in against the spoils system. The job of government was becoming increasingly complex, and interested citizens, some of them organized in the National Civil Service Reform League, were agitating for reform. Presidents, too, were chafing under the pressures of hordes of job-seekers. Public opinion crystallized when President James A. Garfield was assassinated in 1881 by a disappointed office-seeker. Two years later Congress passed the Pendleton Act, which set up the beginnings of a merit system under a three-man bipartisan board, the Civil Service

Commission. The act placed certain types of employees under a new classified service, which could be entered only by passing a competitive examination. Congress put relatively few employees under the new merit system, but fortunately it gave the President power to expand the classified service. As a result of a series of executive orders over the years, about three-quarters of the federal employees today hold jobs that are covered by a merit system and protected from patronage.

Today the administrator must work closely with the Civil Service Commission in staffing his agency. With about 4000 employees of its own, the Commission acts as a central agency in recruiting, examining, and appointing government workers. It advertises for new employees, prepares and administers oral and written examinations throughout the country, and makes up a register of names of those who pass the tests. When an agency wishes to employ a person, the commission certifies to it three names taken from the top of the appropriate register. The administrator has some voice in the type of examination given, and he has some freedom of choice under the rule of three, but obviously his discretion is greatly limited.

The centralization of personnel direction in the Civil Service Commission disturbs administrators eager for freedom and flexibility in their agency operations. They charge that the Commission is entangled in red tape, uses old-fashioned personnel methods, and lacks initiative and imagination. Whatever its defects, the Civil Service Commission over the years has helped to keep most federal jobs out of the spoils system. Still designed to be nonpartisan, the Commission is composed of three members (no more than two of the same party) with six-year terms.

This is not to say, however, that appointment to the classified service is based on merit considerations alone. There is still a strong feeling in the United States that government jobs are a form of reward.[7] The best example of this feeling is *veterans' preference*. Today five points are automatically added to the examination grades of all veterans, and they receive other special considerations. Disabled veterans, their wives, and their widows, are also given special treatment. These provisions, supported by powerful veterans' groups in and out of Congress, have aroused much controversy. Some have charged that veterans' preference is a racket; others say that the government owes a debt to the ex-servicemen and that it can easily find able recruits among them. The Hoover Commission did not oppose veterans' preference, but it did favor a compromise policy that would give the administrator somewhat more leeway in making appointments. At any rate, veterans' preference is probably here to stay. It is not surprising that about half the federal employees today are veterans.

Hiring is only the first step in building the administrative team. The administrator must see that appointees get into the right positions, that they

[7] H. A. Simon, D. W. Smithburg, V. A. Thompson, *Public Administration* (Knopf, 1950), pp. 323-324.

are trained effectively, that their jobs are classified properly in terms of the nature and responsibility of the work. Here, too, the administrator shares his power with the Civil Service Commission. Around each of these fields, such as job classification, an elaborate procedure—indeed, virtually an administrative science—has grown up.

MANAGING THE TEAM

In directing his agency the good administrator is always conscious that he is directing people. As a practical psychologist he must remember that people's actions are influenced not merely by instructions from the top. He must also remember that:

People respond to many incentives. Chester I. Barnard, an outstanding businessman and author of a classic volume on administration, has listed some of these as material rewards (money), the chance for prestige or power, agreeable working conditions, pride of workmanship, happy relations with workmates, conformity to habitual practices, sense of taking part in something big, and patriotic or religious feeling.[8]

People respond to influences from outside the agency as well as from within. Government employees do not identify themselves wholly with the administrative unit to which they belong. They come to work as members of many groups—as southerners, veterans, Negroes, taxpayers, Catholics, and so on. The administrator faces the same problem of overlapping membership as the leader of a party or interest group.

People in administrative units tend to have a powerful feeling of solidarity and defensiveness. Most government workers are members of cohesive groups marked by excellent communication (that is, employees see one another throughout the working day), a sense of oneness, and a feeling of mutual protection. This in-group feeling has important practical effects. For example, the group may react in a hostile way to interference from outside the organization, particularly to attempts to reorganize it. At the same time, the desire of each person to have the respect and affection of his fellow workers is a big factor in promoting harmony, morale, and efficiency.

People—in the United States especially—have a mixed attitude toward authority. Generally government employees, like employees everywhere, will accept the orders of their superiors. But there are limits. Americans are individualists—they have their own opinions and they do not like to be pushed around. Much depends on the manner in which authority is exercised, and on the relations between administrator and employees.[9]

---

[8] C. I. Barnard, *The Functions of the Executive* (Harvard Univ. Press, 1938), pp. 142-148.
[9] Simon, Smithburg, and Thompson, *op. cit.*, pp. 70-71, 180-217.

To put the whole matter another way, the administrator finds that the morale and efficiency of his unit are affected by *informal* as well as *formal* organization. He must be *people*-minded, not simply *stereotype*-minded.[10] In directing his agency he must operate through informal channels of communication and organization as well as through formal channels. He ignores people's personalities—including their quirks and "bugs"—only at his peril.

On the other hand, the administrator has the benefit of certain powers or tools in running his unit. Much of his authority stems simply from his position as boss of the agency; his instructions are usually followed without question, and the agency is set up so that a stream of directions runs from the top to subordinate units. The administrator also has some power over promotions within the agency. Through this power he can reward able service and raise the ablest men and women to more responsible positions. Here, too, set procedures must be followed. Agencies are under pressure from the Civil Service Commission to give promotions only after examinations, some of which the Commission itself conducts. Promotions are based also on an elaborate system of efficiency ratings which are given employees by their supervisors and which can be appealed to boards of review if employees question the fairness of their ratings. Administrators may gain some flexibility through transfers of personnel to and from their agencies, although transfers must be handled carefully because of their relation to morale.

Finally, the administrator can discharge unsatisfactory employees. Despite a popular notion to the contrary, government workers *can* be fired. The process, however, is hedged in by many rules to prevent arbitrary dismissals. During their first six months of employment, new appointees are on probation, and they can easily be dropped at the end of the period (though very few are). After the probationary period, however, an employee can be removed only "for such cause as will promote the efficiency of the service." He must be furnished with a written statement of the charges against him and be given time to reply. Some inefficient employees have used cumbersome appeal procedures to protect their jobs. The Hoover Commission unearthed one case where a stenographer appealed to four separate boards, meanwhile hanging on to her job for seventeen months before she finally quit. But such cases are exceptional; more employees are removed for cause than is generally realized.

Administrators as Decision-Makers

A policeman stops a student who fails to bring his car to a full halt before crossing a highway. The student admits that he did not come to a full halt, but he argues that he did look both ways before entering the highway, and he did slow down enough so

---

[10] A. H. Leighton, *The Governing of Men* (Princeton Univ. Press, 1946), Chapter 3.

that he had to shift into second gear. The officer lets him off with a lecture and a warning. Why? The law requires that the student be arrested and pay a fine. But the officer knows that a full halt is not necessary at this particular corner, so long as the driver is reasonably careful.

Here is a simple example of administrative discretion and decision-making. The officer is not an automaton. He is an experienced man of good sense. In this case he exercised two functions basic in the administrative process: he established his own rule and he made a judicial decision. In his own way he was participating in *administrative legislation* and *administrative adjudication.*

The Constitution gives legislative powers to President and Congress, and judicial powers to the courts. Under today's big government some of these powers must be delegated to officials throughout the executive branch. Some officials have tremendous discretion, some have very little. Democratic government permits delegation of broad powers, but seeks to safeguard the manner in which those powers are exercised.

BIG DECISIONS

Every day in hundreds of ways federal bureaucrats make decisions that affect our jobs, our pocketbooks, our lives. We may or may not know about these decisions. The Board of Governors of the Federal Reserve Board issues a ruling that affects the size of the down payment we must make on a new car. The Rural Electrification Administration decides to bring electricity to farmers in one valley but not in another. The director of the Bureau of Labor Statistics formulates a new method of computing price indexes—one that may affect the government's anti-inflation policies. The Attorney General decides to prosecute a large corporation under the antitrust law. Officials in charge of civil service examinations change their methods of testing. Safety officials in the Civil Aeronautics Board issue a new and more stringent set of air safety regulations.

Wars and near-wars have vastly broadened the decision-making powers of administrative officials, especially in agencies involved in making war and peace. Obviously, the Secretary of State in dealing with foreign powers makes decisions that gravely affect the chances of peace or war. The Atomic Energy Commission and the Defense Department jointly or separately decide on crucial policies that bear on our capacity to win a war. If war comes, the fate of the nation hangs on decisions of commanders in the field. Many military decisions are secret, but some are public and become subjects of wide discussion.

To say that bureaucrats make important decisions, however, is not to say that they have a wide number of alternatives to choose from. An administrator may have been given broad discretion by both Congress and the President, and yet feel constricted by other forces. For an administrator, like a congressman or a President, works amid a complex set of political pressures. In making a key decision he must try to anticipate the attitudes of his own agency, of experts inside and outside the agency, of other agencies involved in the decision, of interest groups affected by the decision, of the press, of the attentive public as a whole,[11] of the party in power and the opposition party, of Congress and the President, perhaps even of foreign governments. He must take into account all kinds of complex organizational and psychological relationships.[12] To make things even more difficult, he often must act in a hurry and on the basis of incomplete knowledge.

ADMINISTRATIVE LAWMAKERS

Given these many influences and pressures, there is always the chance that bureaucrats may act irresponsibly, or at least may ignore the interests of the many for the benefit of the few. Congress has long realized that as governmental problems become more numerous and complex, administrators must make more and more important decisions. The lawmakers also know—or at least most of them do—that there is no easy way to reverse this trend. But Congress has sought to surround the decision-making process with safeguards, both because it is jealous of its own control over lawmaking and because it wants to prevent the abuse of delegated power. There is not much Congress can do in a formal and systematic way to regulate the decisions made by key officials who must face new and unprecedented problems—especially when those officials are acting under broad powers granted to the President. But in the cases of agencies that regulate and control private interests on a regular and long-term basis, an effort has been made to set up certain safeguards.

Well over 100 agencies have the power to issue rules and regulations affecting the public. Most of these agencies are *regulatory agencies,* like the Interstate Commerce Commission, which has powers over the nation's railroads, or the Federal Communications Commission, which polices the nation's radio and television waves. The most important regulatory functions have been placed in independent boards and commissions, but on occasion Congress has assigned them to line agencies such as the Department of Agriculture. Congress has a special interest in the regulatory agencies, for they must interpret the laws passed by Congress and fill them out to meet specific problems. For example, Congress has recognized the right of employees to "organize and bargain collectively through representatives of their own choosing." Such a general provision leads to a hundred new questions and definitions, such as the nature of unions, the rights of employers, the definition of unfair labor practices, the rights of nonunion employees, the scope of collective bargaining, and so on. And these all-important interpretations must be made by a *regulatory agency* —in this case the National Labor Relations Board.

---

[11] G. A. Almond, *The American People and Foreign Policy* (Harcourt, Brace, 1950), Chapter 7.

[12] See H. A. Simon, *Administrative Behavior* (Macmillan, 1949).

Safeguards against abuse of power are of several types:

1. The agencies interpret and enforce *laws of Congress,* and if they misinterpret a statute Congress can always amend it to make its intent more clear. The basic legislative power of House and Senate compels the agencies to identify the will of Congress and to interpret and apply laws as the congressmen would wish. Congress can exercise this control also through its powers of investigating and appropriating.

2. Congress has closely regulated the *procedure* to be followed by regulatory agencies. Under the Administrative Procedure Act of 1946, agencies must publicize their machinery and organization, must give advance information of proposed rules to interested persons, must allow such persons to present information and arguments, must allow parties appearing before the agency to be accompanied by counsel and to cross-examine witnesses.

3. Under certain conditions, rules made by regulatory agencies may be appealed to the courts.

4. Administrators in regulatory agencies, as in all agencies, are surrounded by informal political checks as well as formal ones. They must keep in mind the demands of professional ethics, the advice of experts, the attitudes of congressmen, President, interest groups, political parties, private persons, and so on. In the long run, these safeguards are the most important of all.

ADMINISTRATORS AS JUDGES

Among the hardest problems facing administrators are those that call for judgment and judiciousness in settling disputes or mediating among conflicting claims. The Secretary of Defense, for example, might have to reconcile the demands of two rival services, such as the Navy and Air Force. The Secretary of Agriculture might need to intervene in a conflict between two interest groups, such as growers and wholesalers of grain. A bureau chief might have to referee a jurisdictional squabble between two division heads. To umpire such disputes may call for the wisdom of Solomon, at the very least for fairness and understanding.

The regulatory agencies bear the main burden of making judicial decisions when disputes arise between two or more private interests, such as business groups, or between private interests and the government. Congress has delegated to the regulatory agencies power to make such decisions, a power that transforms the agencies into courts, the administrators into judges. They receive complaints, hold hearings, listen to witnesses and lawyers, study briefs, and make decisions, much like any other court.

Much of this judicial business is handled informally, through the voluntary settlement of cases at lower levels in an agency. The Interstate Commerce Commission, for example, arranged voluntary settlements of all but five out of 3500 complaint cases in one year. The National Labor Relations Board, even though it administers a very controversial law, made formal decisions in only 4 per cent of more than 12,000 cases involving unfair labor practices during the first four years of its existence.[13] Informal settlements of this sort make life a lot easier in the bureaucratic jumble of Washington. They dispose of disputes relatively quickly and inexpensively, and they take an immense burden off the courts. Moreover, they are handled by men who are experts in such technical areas as transportation, labor relations, and radio communication. And yet many persons—especially lawyers pleading cases before the regulatory agencies—have expressed concern over the extent of the judicial power vested in the agencies. They complain that the administrators violate due process of law by holding private and informal sessions, by failing to give interested parties an adequate hearing, by basing their decisions on insufficient evidence.

Partly in response to these complaints the Administrative Procedures Act of 1946 provided for broader judicial review of administrative decisions. The courts have always had the power to overturn administrative judgments on points of *law,* as in cases where an agency had exceeded its authority, or misinterpreted the law, or had simply been unfair. Under the 1946 act the courts seem to have acquired more authority to examine questions of *fact*—that is, to go over the mass of technical evidence examined by the agency. While this tendency has not gone very far, it points up the problem of maintaining the balance between judicial control and administrative efficiency and expertness. The 1946 law also provides for procedural safeguards, such as more formalized hearings and proper notice of action.

Finally, the act tackled another long-debated problem—the high concentration of both legislative and judicial power in regulatory agencies. This administrative absolutism, as some have called it, seems to run counter to the great doctrine of the separation of powers. The act provides that there should be a greater separation *within* regulatory agencies so that the same officials will not act as both judges and prosecutors. Thus officials who investigate cases and present them for action are not to have any part in deciding them. The act did not, however, provide that the agencies be divested of legislative or judicial duties. It could not. In an era of big government and big problems, Congress and the courts must delegate much of this job to the administrators—or else the job will not be done at all. Administrators will continue to act as lawmakers and judges as long as the functions of government are technical, complex, many-sided, and voluminous. And this means for a long time.

Those who worry about the concentration of judicial power in the agencies usually express the fear that administrators will do too much *prosecuting* and not enough impartial *judging*. Yet the opposite tendency may prevail. In some cases regulatory agencies become so occupied with umpiring disputes

---

[13] Attorney General's Committee on Administrative Procedure, *Final Report,* Senate Document 8, Seventy-seventh Congress, First Session (Washington, 1941), p. 35. For an admirable treatment of administrative action, see Emmette S. Redford, *Administration of National Economic Control* (Macmillan, 1952).

that they pay insufficient attention to prosecuting offenders. They tend to sit back and wait for complaints to be filed instead of taking the initiative in ferreting out violations of the law. They become "judicialized." Such a course may seem to be the safe thing to do; to some extent the regular courts have forced regulatory agencies to organize themselves mainly as judicial bodies. The result of this tendency may be inadequate protection of the very groups the regulatory agencies were set up to safeguard.

Administrators in Action—
Two Cases

We have seen something of the complex of pressures and loyalties amid which a bureaucrat must work. We have seen that the good administrator must have some of the qualities of the politician, the lawmaker, the judge, the expert, the team quarterback. Day after day he must make decisions that involve issues of policy, problems of organization, matters of law—and above all *people*. The following two cases, based on actual administrative experience, illustrate some of the painful choices that a bureaucrat may have to make, whether he is in Washington or in the field.

MR. BROWN'S DILEMMA

George Brown is chief of the Bureau of Erosion of the Department of Conservation.[14] He is still in his early forties; his appointment to the post was a result both of his ability and of luck. When the old bureau chief retired, the President wanted to bring in a new chief from outside the agency, but influential members of Congress pressed for the selection of an ex-senator who had represented a farm state. As a compromise, Brown, then a division head, was promoted to bureau chief. A graduate of a midwestern agricultural college, Brown is a career official in the federal service.

Early in March of Brown's second year in the new post, his boss, the Secretary of Conservation, summoned him and the other bureau heads to an important conference. The Secretary informed the group that he had just attended a Cabinet meeting, that the President had called for drastic economies wherever possible, and had specifically asked each department to effect at least a 10 per cent cut in spending in the coming fiscal year. The President, the Secretary reported, was convinced that there was a great popular demand for retrenchment.

Brown quickly calculated what this cutback would mean for his agency. For several years, the Bureau of Erosion had been spending about $45 million a year to help farmers protect their farmland. Could it get along on about $40 million, and where could savings be made? Returning to his office, Brown called a meeting of his personnel, budget, and management officials, together

---

[14] The persons and agencies (except for the Budget Bureau) in this case are fictitious, but the facts of the case are drawn from actual happenings in Washington.

with his four division chiefs. After several hours of discussion it was agreed that savings could be effected only by decreasing the scope of the program—which would involve ending the jobs of about 1200 of the Bureau's employees.

A few weeks later Mr. Brown presented a $40 million budget to Secretary Jones, who approved it and passed it on to the White House. The President went over the figures in a conference with the Director of the Budget, and a few weeks later the budget for the whole executive department, incorporating the Erosion Bureau's $40 million, was transmitted to Congress.

Meanwhile Brown was running into trouble. News of the proposed budget cut had leaked immediately to the personnel in the field. Nobody knew who would be dropped if the cut went through, and some of the abler officials were already looking around for other positions. Morale fell. Hearing of the cut, farmers' representatives in Washington notified local farm organizations throughout the country. Soon Brown began to receive letters asking that certain services be maintained. Members of the farm bloc in Congress were also becoming restless.

Shortly after the President's budget went to Congress, Representative Smith of Colorado asked Brown to see him. Smith was Chairman of the Agriculture Subcommittee of the House Appropriations Committee, and thus was a potent factor in congressional treatment of the budget. Brown immediately went up to the Hill. Smith began talking in an urgent tone. He said that he had consulted his fellow subcommittee members, both Democratic and Republican, and they all agreed that the Erosion Bureau's cut must not go through. The farmers needed the usual $45 million and even more. They would practically rise up in arms if the program were reduced. Members of Congress from agricultural areas, Smith went on, were under tremendous pressure. Leaders of farm groups in Washington were mobilizing the farmers everywhere. Besides, Smith said, the President was unfair in cracking down on the farm program; he didn't understand agricultural problems, and he was not cutting other expenses.

Then Smith came to the point. Brown, he said, must vigorously oppose the budget cut. Hearings on appropriations would commence in a few days and Brown as bureau chief would of course testify. At that time he must state that the cut would hurt the bureau and undermine its whole program. Brown would not have to volunteer this statement, Smith said, but just respond to leading questions put by the congressmen. Brown's testimony, he felt sure, would help clinch the argument against the cut because congressmen would respect the judgment of the administrator closest to the problem.

MR. BROWN'S DECISION

Brown returned to his office in a state of indecision. He was in an embarrassing position. He had submitted his estimates to the Secretary of Conservation and to the President, and it was his duty to back them up. An unwritten rule demanded, moreover, that agency heads would defend budget estimates submitted to Congress, whatever their personal feelings might be. The President had appointed him to his position, he reflected, and had a right to expect loyalty. On the other hand, he was on the spot with his own agency. The employees all expected their chief to look out for them. Brown had developed happy relations with "the field," and he squirmed at the thought of having to let over 1000 employees go. What would they think when they heard him defend the cut? Even more important, he wanted to maintain friendly relations with the farmers, the farm organizations, and the farm bloc in Congress.

Brown turned for advice to an old friend in the Bureau of the Budget. This friend urged him to defend the President's budget. He appealed to Brown's professional pride as an administrator and career servant, reminding him that every student of administration agreed that the chief executive must have central control of the budget, and that agency heads must subordinate their own interests to the executive program. As for the employees to be dropped— well, that was part of the game. A lot of them could get jobs in defense agencies; civil service would protect their status. Anyway, they would understand Brown's position. In a parting shot he mentioned that the President had Brown in mind for bigger things.

The next day Brown had lunch with a senator, wise and experienced in Washington ways, who had helped him get his start in the government. The senator was sympathetic. He understood Brown's perplexity, for many similar cases had arisen in the past. But there was no doubt about what Brown should do, the senator said. He should follow Representative Smith's plan, of course being as diplomatic as possible about it. This way he would protect his position with those who would be most important in the long run.

"After all," the senator said, "Presidents come and go, parties rise and fall, but Smith and those other congressmen will be here a long time, and so will these farm organizations. They can do a lot for you in future years. And remember one other thing—these people are elected representatives of the people. Constitutionally, Congress has the power to spend money as it sees fit. Why should you object if they want to spend an extra few million?"

Leaving the Senate Office Building, Brown realized that his dilemma was deeper than ever. The arguments on both sides were persuasive. He felt hopelessly divided in his loyalties and responsibilities. The President expected one thing of him. Congress (he was sure Smith reflected widespread feeling on Capitol Hill) expected another. As a career man and professional administrator, he sided with the President; as head of an agency, however, he wanted to protect his team. His future? Whatever decision he made, he was bound to alienate important people and interests. There was no way to compromise, because he would have to face a group of astute congressmen.

It was Brown's realization that the arguments in a sense canceled one another out, however, that in the end helped him make his decision. For he decided finally that the issue involved more than loyalties, ambitions, and programs. Ultimately it boiled down to two questions. First, to whom was he, Brown, legally and administratively responsible? Obviously to the chief executive who appointed him and who was accountable to the people for the actions of the Administration. And secondly, which course of action did he, Brown, feel was better for the welfare of all the people? Looking at the question this way, he felt the President was right in asking for economy. As a taxpayer himself, Brown knew of the strong sentiment for retrenchment. To be sure, Congress must make the final decision. But to make the decision, Brown reflected, Congress had to know the attitude of the Administration, and the Administration must speak with one voice for the majority of the people or it could hardly speak at all. Despite continued pressures and mixed feelings, Brown stuck to this decision.

ASSIGNMENT IN INDONESIA

In August 1945, shortly after the Japanese surrender, the Republic of Indonesia declared its independence from the Netherlands.[15] A difficult political situation immediately arose. The Dutch wanted to keep their rich islands; the Indonesians wanted their freedom—just as strongly as did Americans in 1776. For several months the Dutch and Indonesian forces skirmished, especially in Batavia, the capital. The United States, deeply interested in the area for economic and strategic reasons, followed a policy of neutrality.

Representing the United States in Batavia was a consul general who had served in the Indies for twelve years before the war. Sixty years old, he had enjoyed pleasant relations with Dutch officials before the war and tended to feel sympathetic toward their position. As an old hand he was experienced in Indonesian affairs but he tended to be somewhat prejudiced and set in his ways. In February 1946, the consul general was joined by a vice-consul, William Jones, who was sent out by the State Department to undertake economic analysis and reporting. At this time Washington had a particular need for full and accurate information on the economic situation in Indonesia to help in developing important foreign policies.

Jones was of a different stamp from his chief. A young economist, trained in American universities and in the State Department, he had studied the prewar pattern of colonialism and had developed strong sympathies for the nationalist cause. He had no established ties with the Foreign Service; indeed, his actual appointment was in the Foreign Service Reserve (see Chapter 23). While at the State Department, moreover, Jones had learned that there was some official concern over the consul general's pro-Dutch views.

Within a few months after his arrival, the new vice-consul was busy preparing economic reports on the Indonesian islands. His relations with his chief

---

[15] This case is drawn from an actual autobiographical account by the vice-consul involved, prepared for, and published by, the Committee on Public Administration Cases (Washington, 1950), under the title *Indonesian Assignment*.

were most cordial. But soon a difficult situation began to develop. To get complete information Jones needed to approach Indonesian as well as Dutch officials. But the consul general wanted him to see only the Dutch. He stressed the ticklish political situation that existed and warned Jones to move slowly. Eager to maintain friendly relations with his superior, Jones followed instructions, but he had an uneasy feeling that he was not doing a full job of reporting to Washington.

Some time later a confidential airgram arrived from the State Department requesting an extensive economic report on Indonesia, adding that "if possible, and with the utmost discretion, Dutch, Indonesian, and British sources should be consulted as far as feasible." Jones was elated to have the assignment, but puzzled about how he should proceed. Should he consult the Indonesian authorities?

Jones had several alternatives. He could consult the consul general, who would surely say "no"; this course would protect Jones' position in the Department and his friendly relations with his chief, but it would lessen the value of the report. Or he could go ahead with the report, inform the Department that he had not consulted the Indonesians, and let Washington specifically request such consultation if it was still desired. This was the safest course all around, but it would have meant a delayed report and perhaps a less satisfactory one. Finally, Jones could use the airgram to justify consultations with the Indonesians, at whatever risk to his relations with his chief and to Dutch-American relations.

Jones decided on the third course. Before doing so he spoke to a high Indonesian official, who assured him that he would receive useful material from the Republic and in confidence. Jones' decision proved a happy one. His talks with the Indonesians (as well as with the Dutch and British) were fruitful, and he was later commended by the State Department for the report he submitted. Yet he had to pay the price. His relations with the consul general cooled markedly—not a trivial matter in a small office thousands of miles from home. Nevertheless, Jones was satisfied with his decision. He felt that he had been loyal to his profession and to the interests of his country, though at the expense of loyalty to his superior. It is clear, however, that had Jones been a veteran career man, with family responsibilities, and with no particular sympathy for the Indonesians, his decision might have been very different.

Can We Control the Bureaucrats?

The foregoing case histories lead to three important generalizations:

1. Bureaucrats are people, not robots, and as people they are subject to many influences.

2. Bureaucrats do not respond merely to orders from the top but to a variety of motives stemming from their own personalities, formal and informal

organization and communication, their political attitudes, their educational and professional background, and others.

3. Bureaucrats are important in government. Some of them have tremendous discretion and make decisions of great significance—and the cumulative effect of all their policies and actions on our daily lives is enormous.

Put these three factors together and a crucial question arises. How can we keep this powerful bureaucracy responsible and responsive to the people? Bureaucrats are our servants—or should be—yet our picture of the bureaucrats implies that the people's wishes are by no means the only factor in giving marching orders to the bureaucracy. Let us look more closely at the problem of maintaining democratic control of bureaucratic administration.

BREAKS IN THE CHAIN OF COMMAND

Of all the 2⅓ million bureaucrats, the American people hire and fire only one—the President. The presidential office must be a clear and open channel between the people and the bureaucracy. Through this channel popular needs and expectations are converted into administrative action. Much depends on the sensitiveness of the bureaucracy to the President's—and hence to the people's—direction. Unfortunately, the chief executive does not fully control his own establishment. As the Hoover Commission discovered, lines of control are tangled and broken.

The formal organization of the agencies often does not provide clear-cut control. Harry Truman once showed visitors a huge chart on his office wall picturing well over 100 officials required by law to report to the chief executive alone; he complained, "I cannot even see all these men, let alone actually study what they are doing." Because of its lack of unity the Cabinet is not able to direct and coordinate the sprawling executive branch. Even the President's staff cannot give him all the help he needs in certain areas, such as control of personnel.

The chain of command is broken also at lower levels. Some subordinate officials have been given power by Congress to act independently of the White House. For example, the Army chief of engineers can plan public works without referring to the President. Some departments are simply holding companies for independent-minded bureaus that act on their own. Such a situation breeds all sorts of difficulties, including what Pendleton Herring has called "quiet sabotage by unsympathetic technicians and genteel blackmail by high policy officials." Simple communication and action become difficult. Harry Hopkins, who served as the President's "chief of staff" during World War II, once complained that after Mr. Roosevelt and Mr. Churchill and the high command made crucial decisions, months-long delays would ensue—"and then you start investigating and it takes you weeks to find out that the orders have been deliberately stalled on the desk of some commander or lieutenant colonel."

Failures of top control are especially serious in the military agencies. Americans have always feared the man on horseback; the Founding Fathers carefully put the Army and Navy under civilian control. Under conditions of modern war—whether of the atomic, bacteriological, or pushbutton type—the problem becomes even more urgent. On this score the Hoover Commission found that centralized civilian control of the military "scarcely exists." The weakest link, it reported, was between the Secretary of Defense and the service departments, the Army, Navy, and Air Force.

Another weak link in the chain of command involves the independent boards and commissions. Congress made these agencies semi-independent of the President so that they could pursue their regulatory activities without undue interference from the White House. Since the members have long, staggered terms, a new President must wait some time before he can install men of his own choice, for his power to fire commission members is usually limited. When President Roosevelt sought to remove William Humphrey, a conservative member of the Federal Trade Commission who hotly opposed the New Deal, the Supreme Court ruled in *Humphrey's Executor* v. *United States* that, by the terms of the act setting up the FTC, commissioners could be removed only for "inefficiency, neglect of duty, or malfeasance in office," not because of differences with the President over policy. In 1958 the Supreme Court, in *Wiener* v. *United States,* extended the Humphrey doctrine by holding that the President has no power to remove officers of quasi-judicial agencies unless specifically authorized to do so by Congress. There might be no serious problem if the independent boards had merely *judicial* functions, but as we have seen they also have important *lawmaking* and *administrative* powers.

Finally, central direction by the President runs into the basic political problem of pressures from *interest groups.* Some *bureaus* are known as *clientele agencies* because they perform services directly for certain group interests; examples might be the Bureau of Reclamation, the Army Engineers, Rural Electrification Administration, Veterans Administration, United States Maritime Administration. Close relations develop between interest group and agency. When the President, trying to enforce his idea of the general interest, seeks to control the agency, he comes into conflict with an organized interest and its narrower conception of the general interest. Agents for the group may appeal to members of Congress—especially those who represent districts where the organized interest is strong. Then a pitched battle may occur not only between President and interest group but between President and members of Congress. Armed with various weapons, including control of appropriations, the legislators often can hold their ground against the chief executive.

Is the bureaucrat an innocent bystander in these melées? Usually not. He often will line up with either the White House or Capitol Hill, choosing sides according to his own interests—and his own idea of the general interest. The bureaucracy is not a static force; it has political influence of its own. This influence is built on the public relations skills of the administrator and his staff, the nature and extent of the bureau's information program, relations with legislative and executive officials, and ultimately on the amount of support the bureau commands from interest groups and the attentive public. The government executive's concern for his agency's public relations, says F. M. Marx, "requires special internal organization, technical assistance within his own office, and much hard labor on his part in mingling socially with the right crowd, in building good will at his press conferences, and in cultivating his legislative contacts." [16] This does not mean that the publicity activities of the agencies are merely self-serving propaganda; despite charges to the contrary, most of the publicity is based on factual information about the agencies' work. It does mean that the large bureau finds public acceptance, interest-group backing, and a place in the web of government that give it a measure of political power of its own. [17]

REPAIRING THE BREAKS

After studying the executive branch, the Hoover Commission concluded that the President did not have sufficient control of his own establishment. "Definite authority at the top, a clear line of authority from top to bottom, and adequate staff aids . . . do not exist," said the Commission. "Authority is diffused, lines of authority are confused, staff services are insufficient. Consequently, responsibility and accountability are impaired." It warned that the critical state of world affairs required the government to speak and act with unity of purpose, and that if the executive branch worked at cross purposes within itself, the whole nation would suffer from disunity and from waste of funds.

To repair and strengthen the chain of command the Commission made many recommendations, including:

1. Regroup functions into major departments and agencies to promote more coherence and responsibility.

2. Give the President and department heads better staff services to help in controlling subordinate agencies. For example, the Commission favored setting up in the White House an Office of Personnel, headed by a director who would also be chairman of the Civil Service Commission, along with strengthening the Budget Bureau and other staff services.

3. In regulatory commissions, vest all administrative responsibility in the chairman. [18] Although this recommendation would not necessarily extend the President's control over the commissions, it would establish a stronger link between chief executive and commissions. The Hoover Commission urged also

---

[16] F. M. Marx, *Elements of Public Administration* (Prentice-Hall, 1946), p. 200.

[17] For a discerning study of this problem and related questions, see Simon, Smithburg, and Thompson, *Public Administration,* especially Chapters 18 and 19.

[18] Commission on Organization of the Executive Branch of the Government, *Regulatory Commissions* (Government Printing Office, 1949).

that a number of *executive* functions be transferred from the commissions to regular departments.

4. Grant the President power to propose plans for reorganization, which would go into effect unless both Senate and House disapproved them within a set period of time. And department heads, the Commission urged, should have broad authority to reorganize their own agencies as they saw fit.

Many of these proposals were not new. For years—in some cases decades —suggestions had been made for strengthening presidential control. Indeed, a Committee on Administrative Management, set up by President Roosevelt in 1936, went further in some respects than the Hoover Commission. For example, it proposed placing all personnel functions, including those held by the Civil Service Commission, under a civil service administrator responsible to the President, and it favored putting the nonjudicial activities of regulatory commissions into the executive departments.[19] Presidents Taft, Wilson, and Harding had also tried to achieve better organization and control in the executive branch.

What action has been taken on the Hoover Commission proposals? Decided progress has been made. The creation of the Department of Health, Education and Welfare in April 1953 was a milestone in the attempt to group separate agencies in departments under a Cabinet member directly responsible to the President. Rules and procedures have been adopted to grant department executives more authority to control and reorganize their own departments. The grouping of bureaus within departments has been somewhat improved. More administrative responsibility has been vested in chairmen of some of the regulatory commissions.

Yet in other respects progress has been very slow. One of the major recommendations of the Hoover Commission was that 65 agencies under the direct supervision of the President be consolidated into one-third of that number; aside from the one new Cabinet agency, little has been done. The President still does not have full power to reorganize his own office. Department heads, in the judgment of some observers, do not yet possess enough control over personnel policies and administration in their own organizations.

If the problem is so old, if there is wide agreement on general solutions, why are we still trying to apply first principles to the running of our administrative machinery? The answer lies in our system of *checks and balances*. The President is chief of the executive branch, but he is not its undisputed master. Congress too has control over the executive branch. It usually sets up the agencies. It usually determines, broadly, their organization (that is, whether a job shall be done by an independent commission or by a line agency). It tells them what their job will be. It provides the money. It establishes rules to guide bureaucrats in their work. It often reviews, formally (as in hearings) or in-

---

[19] *Administrative Management in the Government of the United States* (Government Printing Office, 1937).

formally, the actions bureaucrats take. And, as we have seen, it helps choose men for the jobs.[20]

To be sure, Congress shares these powers with the President, but the mere sharing implies divided control at the top. Moreover, it is not really *Congress* that helps run the bureaucracy but *individual members* of Congress and of committees. Since power in Congress is scattered and diffused, administrative control is split not between President and Congress but between the President (and his staff and immediate subordinates) on the one hand and a few dozen committees and a few hundred legislators on the other.

Congress *as a whole* might have every reason to strengthen the President's administrative control, for then it could pin responsibility squarely on him. But congressmen *as individuals* often resist greater central control. They wish to maintain their own influence over an agency, perhaps because that agency serves their constituents, or because they feel that they know its functions better than the President does (which often they do), or because of a general fear of presidential power. They can use their control over funds, investigations, appointments, and lawmaking to back up their wishes.

Consequently, congressmen often have failed to grant to the President power to reorganize the executive branch, or have granted that power grudgingly and in small doses. Indeed, a bill to give President Roosevelt broad reorganization powers in 1937 was dubbed the "dictator bill" and killed. And congressmen often try to make their pet agencies exempt from reorganizations. Nevertheless, Congress has given the President power to "reduce, coordinate, consolidate, and reorganize"—and even to abolish—a large number of agencies, subject, however, to congressional veto. Under the most recent reorganization act, the President submits plans to Congress, where they may be debated but not amended. The plan may be killed by either house if a majority of the entire membership (not simply a majority of those on the floor) vote adversely. Shortly after taking office, President Eisenhower asked Congress to continue the act and Congress complied.

Under the several reorganization plans that have been passed in the last two decades, the President has considerably extended his control over administration. But no reorganization act can resolve the basic problem, which is our divided system of government. Under that system the chain of command will always end up not just in the White House, but in a variety of places on Capitol Hill as well.

LOYALTY TO WHOM?

Reorganization is essentially a matter of *formal structure*. It tries to put the right men and the right jobs in the right place under presidential supervision. This is important, but it is not the whole problem. Bureaucrats have many loyalties, sometimes conflicting ones. The big job is to strengthen their

---

[20] Charles S. Hyneman, *Bureaucracy in a Democracy* (Harper, 1950), pp. 77-203.

loyalty to broad popular goals, to responsible leaders, to their own sense of integrity and workmanship. What kinds of loyalty are involved?

One is *party loyalty*. That the bureaucrats, at least those at the lower levels, should be politically neutral has long been accepted policy in this country. Not only has civil service largely overcome the patronage system, but the Hatch Acts of 1939 and 1940 extended the idea of neutrality by forbidding the bureaucrats to "take any active part in political management or in political campaigns." The aim has been both to prevent the building of a gigantic machine of federal officeholders and to protect the bureaucrats against having to donate money to parties or candidates. The laws allow them to discuss politics in private and to vote, but little else.

Is it a good idea to neutralize the bureaucrats politically? At a time when we are trying to broaden interest in democratic discussion and action, is it wise to try to isolate 2⅓ million people in a political vacuum, insulated against the rough-and-tumble of political agitation and participation? Which officials, moreover, should be "political" and which neutral? Department heads, of course, are expected to change as Presidents and parties rise and fall, but what about chiefs of bureaus, divisions, and other units?

What about the conflict of loyalties between *President* and *Congress?* As we have seen in the case of Mr. Brown, this conflict is severe. The President is chief of the executive branch; Congress has the fundamental lawmaking power. Inevitably the bureaucrat must be responsible to both. The situation is immensely complicated by the fact that it is not Congress as a whole but powerful individual congressmen with whom the bureaucrat must deal, and these congressmen often differ over administrative policy.

What about the bureaucrat's loyalties and responsibilities to *interest groups?* His activities impinge on all sorts of groups, some in a favorable, others perhaps in an unfavorable, way. These groups have many interests; it is hard to discover just at what point the bureaucrat's help to one group, like veterans or farmers, becomes harmful to another group, like taxpayers or consumers. Obviously, a bureaucrat is confronted in acute form with this question: What is the general interest in a society that embraces many interests? And what is the relation of that interest to the interest of the popular majority that won the last election and claims the right through newly elected leaders to tell the bureaucrats what to do?

Finally, what about loyalty to the highest *traditions of government service* —traditions of responsibility, initiative, efficiency? Perhaps the most serious loyalty problem is right here. Bureaucracies, whether governmental or business, tend to be routinized, cautious, and heavy-handed. They are often marked by inertia and red tape. A vast amount of paper-shuffling takes the place of direct dealing with real people. Procedures become clumsy and burdensome. Some bureaucrats stake out private preserves and beat off all interlopers. Even their language—as revealed in instructions to the public and to employees— becomes impersonal and obscure. As a result of this "gobbledygook," as one observer has remarked, a simple sentence like "I love you" becomes "Complete assurance of maximum affection is hereby implied." [21] Of all the problems of loyalty, this may be the hardest to solve. Big government inevitably means big bureaucracies and some of the faults that are summed up in the term "red tape." [22]

This last question can be turned right around—what are we the people doing to make bureaucrats loyal to the ideals of public service and to the public interest? Not much. Consider governmental salaries. The pay at lower levels compares favorably with that of private industry, but many a governmental executive with thousands of employees and the most exacting duties receives a third or a half of what he could get in business. Or think of the brickbats that we shower on government officials. Able bureaucrats have fled Washington because they could not stand the intemperate attacks (many of them emanating from Congress) directed against both their public and private life. The bureaucrat has very little "job security." If he fails to please the many political leaders and groups to whom he is responsible, or if there is a change of President or party, his usefulness in his agency may come to an end.

Herblock in *The Washington Post*

"What do you suppose keeps them away?"

Valiant efforts have been made to promote initiative, vigor, imagination, professional standards, and *esprit de corps* in the federal service, and the efforts are continuing. Recently, the Second Hoover Commission recommended the establishment of a senior civil service group that would have special and separate status, with high rank and pay. This group would be politically neutral, immune from the cross-fire of politicians inside and outside the government. This idea of a senior civil service has been hailed as a means of providing a pool of topflight men with high morale who would be able to work effectively in any agency and under any President. The idea of a senior civil service has been criticized because it sets up a special class with special privileges, because political or administrative neutrality is neither

---

[21] Rudolf Flesch, "More About Gobbledygook," *Public Administration Review,* Vol. 5 (1945), pp. 240-245.

[22] For another type of loyalty required of the bureaucrat—loyalty to country and Constitution—see Chapter 6.

possible nor desirable, and because it would not fit well with the American tradition or practice of public administration.

In any event, the problem is a challenging one, involving better working conditions, higher salaries (there has been a notable improvement in this respect in the last decade or two), greater recognition of services beyond the call of ordinary duty, and higher status.

The Judges

F oreigners are often amazed at the great power Americans give their judges, especially federal judges. In 1848, the French aristocrat Alexis de Tocqueville wrote, "If I were asked where I place the American aristocracy, I should reply without hesitation . . . that it occupies the judicial bench and bar. . . . Scarcely any political question arises in the United States that is not resolved sooner or later into a judicial question." [1] A century later the English laborite Harold Laski observed, "The respect in which the federal courts and, above all, the Supreme Court are held is hardly surpassed by the influence they exert on the life of the United States." [2]

Why do American federal judges have great influence and prestige? One reason is their power to exercise judicial review—that is, to interpret the Constitution. Only a constitutional amendment—and the judges would interpret the amendment—or the Supreme Court itself can modify the Court's constitutional doctrine. Mr. Justice Frankfurter put it tersely some years ago, "The Supreme Court is the Constitution."

When the judges interpret the Constitution, they are making policy decisions. Though the arguments will be clothed in constitutional terminology, the judges must resolve important social, economic, and political issues. Should the government regulate the economic market place? Should the activities of totalitarian political parties be restricted? Defeated at the polls or in the legislative halls, individuals may carry this kind of issue to the judicial chambers through the device of the lawsuit. "We are very quiet there," said Justice Holmes of the Supreme Court, "but it is the quiet of a storm centre."

The significance of judicial review, however, should not cause us to overlook the other important functions of judges. In addition, they serve as impartial tribunals for the settlement of legal controversies. They interpret

---

[1] Alexis de Tocqueville, *Democracy in America,* 2 vols. Phillips Bradley (ed.) (Knopf, 1946), I, 278, 180.
[2] Harold J. Laski, *The American Democracy* (Viking, 1948), p. 110.

the laws, determine the facts, apply the law to the facts, and see to it that the laws are enforced. Did Jones have a fair trial? Did Smith violate the terms of his contract with Brown? Is an elevator operator in a New York office building entitled to the minimum wages established by the Fair Labor Standards Act? Did the Ajax Corporation violate the antitrust laws? Must a bus company pay the hospital bills for one of its passengers who was assaulted by a fellow passenger? Answering these questions is the daily business of judges. In settling peacefully the innumerable controversies that arise among individuals and between individuals and the government, judges play as notable a role as when they help to shape the grand outlines of American politics.

The Shape of Federal Justice

The authority of federal judges, like that of congressmen and Presidents, is derived ultimately from the Constitution. But unlike congressmen and Presidents, federal judges receive very little power directly from that document. All the authority of federal judges except the original jurisdiction of the Supreme Court (see page 502) is given to them by Congress. The Constitution in Article III merely sets the outside limits. Congress determines which, if any, federal court is to exercise some or all of the judicial authority of the United States.

The purpose of the framers of the Constitution in delegating judicial power to the central government was to enable it to maintain its supremacy, to meet its national responsibilities, and to provide tribunals for cases where state judges might not be appropriate. Therefore, they gave to the national courts the power to hear and decide cases in law and equity if:

1. They arise under the Constitution, a federal law, or a treaty.
2. They arise under admiralty and maritime laws.
3. They arise because of a dispute involving land claimed under titles granted by two or more states.
4. The United States is a party to the case.
5. A state is a party to the case (but not including suits commenced or prosecuted against a state by an individual or a foreign nation).
6. They are between citizens of different states.
7. They affect the accredited representatives of a foreign nation.

THE ORGANIZATION OF FEDERAL COURTS

The Constitution provides only for one Supreme Court, leaving it up to Congress to ordain and establish inferior federal courts. (The Constitution also allows Congress to determine the size of the Supreme Court as well as of lower courts.) A Supreme Court is a logical necessity if the national government is to have the power to frame laws superior to those of the states. The lack of such a tribunal to maintain national supremacy, to insure uniform interpretation of national legislation, and to resolve conflicts among the states was one of the glaring deficiencies of the central government under the Articles of Confederation.

The framers did not feel that a complete system of *lower* courts was indispensable to an effective federal system. Hence they avoided that controversial issue and left the decision up to Congress. As a result, the structure as well as the authority of the national judiciary is largely controlled by Congress. The First Congress divided the nation into districts and created lower national courts for each district. That decision, though often supplemented, has never been seriously questioned. Today the hierarchy of the national courts consists of *district courts, courts of appeals,* and one *Supreme Court.*

The Supreme Court is the most glamorous and venerated court in the country—the national symbol of justice. Its members are known to the public, its decisions headlined in the press. It has the last word in interpreting the meaning of the Constitution and of federal laws; it is potentially the court of ultimate appeal for cases falling within the competence of national courts; it supervises the administration of justice by the federal courts. But the workhorses of the federal judiciary are the 86 district courts within the states, the district court in the District of Columbia, and the territorial district court in Puerto Rico. Each state has at least one district court; the larger states have as many as the demands of judicial business and the pressure of politics require (though no state has more than four). Each district court is composed of at least one judge, but there may be as many as eighteen. District judges normally sit separately and hold court by themselves. There are 241 district judgeships, all filled by the President with the consent of the Senate; all district judges, except those of the territorial courts, hold office during good behavior.

District courts are trial courts of *original jurisdiction.* They are the only federal courts that regularly employ grand (indicting) and petit (trial) juries. Many of the cases tried before district judges involve citizens of different states, and the judges apply the appropriate state laws. Otherwise, district judges are concerned with federal laws. For example, they hear and decide cases involving crimes against the United States, suits under the national revenue, postal, patent, copyright, trademark, and civil-rights laws. The federal bankruptcy laws often place these judges in business by making them responsible for the management of bankrupt concerns.

District judges are assisted by clerks, bailiffs, stenographers, law clerks, court reporters, probation officers, and United States commissioners. All these persons are appointed by the judges. The commissioners, who serve for four-year terms and are paid from fees, handle some of the preliminaries. For example, they issue warrants for arrests, and often hear the evidence to determine whether an arrested person should be held for action by the grand jury. If so, the commissioner may set the bail. A United States marshal,

questions, however, the litigant disappointed by the state decision has only the right to petition the Supreme Court to issue *a writ of certiorari* (pronounced ser-shee-o-rar′-e), ordering the state court to hand up the records of the case. But the Court does not have to grant the writ unless at least four justices feel that the case is of sufficient public importance to require their attention.

The Supreme Court has the same discretion in determining which cases coming up from the federal courts of appeals it shall review. Only if a court of appeals strikes down a state law because it is contrary to a federal law, treaty, or the Constitution, does a person disappointed by a decision of the court of appeals have the *right* to a Supreme Court review. Of course any disappointed litigant may petition the High Court for a writ of certiorari, but in most cases his petition will be rejected. The Supreme Court turns down about 80 per cent of the petitions it receives, selecting for review only those cases that involve issues of significant public interest. Thus it is not enough that Jones thinks he should have won the case against Smith.

The Supreme Court usually selects for review cases in which there seems to be a conflict between the rulings of the courts of appeals, or cases in which the lower courts seem to have departed from sound methods of judicial proceeding or which involve questions of considerable public importance. If the High Court had to review all cases from the courts of appeals and all cases involving federal questions from the highest state courts, it would still be deciding cases today that originated in the 1920's. The discretion enjoyed by the Supreme Court justices also enables them to select those issues that they feel are most significant and timely, and to duck those issues they do not wish to meet.

HOW THE SUPREME COURT OPERATES

At high noon on the days when the Supreme Court is in session, the eight associate justices and the Chief Justice, dressed in their judicial robes, file into the Court. As they take their seats—arranged according to seniority, with the Chief Justice in the center—the clerk of the Court introduces them as "the Honorable Chief Justice and Associate Justices of the Supreme Court of the United States." Though he concludes "May God save the United States," this is traditional—not editorial. Those present in the chambers then sit down, the counsel taking their places along tables in front of the bench, the attorneys for the Department of Justice, dressed in morning clothes, at the right. Counsel for each side is limited to a one-hour argument—in some cases even less—and the Court scrupulously enforces the time limits. Lawyers before the Court use a lectern to which two lights are attached. A white light flashes five minutes before time is up; when the red light goes on the lawyer must stop instantly even in the middle of a word.[6] The justices freely interrupt

---

[6] Henry J. Abraham, *Courts and Judges* (Oxford Univ. Press, 1959), p. 25.

the lawyers to ask questions, to inquire for more information. Sometimes, to the annoyance of the attorneys, the justices talk among themselves. The entire procedure is formally informal and designed to bring out the facts and issues in the case as quickly as possible. Although forensic flourishes are not unknown, oratory is discouraged and arguments before the High Court are usually matter-of-fact and direct. Eloquence is less important than soundness. After two hours of argument, the Court takes a half-hour out for lunch, finally adjourning for the day at 4:30 P.M.

The cases that come before this most famous court in the world fall into three main categories: (1) Cases involving citizens or companies of different states. Here the Supreme Court is concerned to see that the federal courts have applied the state laws fairly. These decisions rarely reach the headlines. (2) Cases involving interpretation of a federal law. (3) Cases involving a question of constitutional power. These last two types are the cases that make the Court famous—or infamous.

The justices are in session from the first Monday in October through June. In their gleaming Corinthian palace, they listen to oral arguments for two weeks and then adjourn for two weeks to consider the cases and write their opinions. Six justices must participate in each decision, and cases are decided by a majority. In the event of a tie vote, the decision of the lower court is sustained, although the case may be re-argued.

Each Friday the justices meet in conference. During the week they have heard the oral arguments, read and studied the briefs, and examined the petitions. Before the conference, each justice receives a list of the cases that will be discussed. Each brings to the meeting a red leather book (carefully locked) in which the cases and the votes of the justices are recorded. The Friday conferences are highly secret affairs; what goes on in these meetings has to be gleaned from the infrequent comments of members of the Court. The Chief Justice presides; it is in these closed sessions that he has an opportunity to influence his colleagues. Chief Justice Hughes ran these conferences like a stern taskmaster, keeping the justices talking to the point, moving the discussion along, and doing his best to work out compromises. Frowning on dissents, he tried to achieve a unanimous vote in order to give greater weight to Court decisions. Chief Justice Stone, on the other hand, perhaps influenced by his New England town-meeting background, encouraged each justice to state his own point of view, and let the discussion wander as it would.[7]

Although the procedure varies, these conferences are marked by informality and vigorous give-and-take. The Chief Justice usually opens the discussion by briefly stating the facts, summarizing the questions of law, and making suggestions for disposing of the case. He then asks each member of the Court, in order of seniority, to give his views and conclusions. After full discussion a vote is taken, with the least senior justice voting first.

---

[7] John P. Frank, *Marble Palace: The Supreme Court in American Life* (Knopf, 1958), p. 81.

The decision itself is of vital interest to the parties concerned, but the grounds on which it is made are often more important to the general public. Except for routine cases that can be disposed of by well-settled principles of law, the High Court always announces the reasons for each decision. If the Chief Justice is not among the majority, the senior justice must write the *Opinion for the Court* himself or else assign the task to one of his colleagues. This opinion is then circulated for comments and suggestions. Often a justice may agree with the majority on the decision but differ on the reasoning. He may then write his own opinion, which is known as a *concurring opinion.* Justices who are among the minority normally select one of their number to write a *dissenting opinion,* although each dissenter is free to write his own opinion. Dissenting opinions have no force in disposing of the case or as precedents, but they are not futile gestures. "A dissent in a court of last resort," wrote Chief Justice Hughes, "is an appeal to the brooding spirit of the law, to the intelligence of a future day when a later decision may possibly correct the error into which the dissenting judge believes the court to have been betrayed. . . . Nor is this appeal always in vain. In a number of cases dissenting opinions have in time become the law." [8]

Supreme Court opinions usually state the facts, present the issues, give the reasoning, and announce the decision. The Court's opinion on the ruling of law is binding on all lower federal courts and, when pertinent, on all state courts. Sometimes the justices wander off in their opinions and talk about issues not involved in the case before them. Chief Justice John Marshall, for example, in the case of *McCulloch* v. *Maryland* (see Chapter 4), stated that he thought the national government could tax the states. Since the question actually before the Court was whether the states could tax the federal government, Marshall's remark was *obiter dictum*—that is, reasoning and ruling on an issue not before the Court. *Obiter dicta* often provide valuable clues to the views of the justices; they are not, however, binding on other courts.

The Judges—Guardians of the Constitution

Judicial review is an American contribution to the art of government, though an independent judiciary is a means of enforcing constitutional limitations in all free governments. If an Englishman or an American is thrown into prison without cause, either can appeal to the courts of his respective country for protection. When Parliament passes a law, however, no English judge has the authority to declare it null and void because *he believes* it to violate the English constitution. Not the courts but Parliament is the guardian of the English constitution. But in the United States the courts, ultimately the Supreme Court, are the

[8] Charles Evans Hughes, "The Supreme Court of the United States: Its Foundation, Methods and Achievements," *American Bar Association Journal* (April 1930).

keepers of the constitutional conscience—not Congress and not the President. How did the judges get this tremendous responsibility?

The Constitution itself says nothing about who should be the final arbiter of disputes that might arise over its meaning. It does not specifically grant such power to the Supreme Court. Whether the members of the Convention of 1787 intended to bestow on the courts the power of judicial review is a question that has long been debated. There is little doubt that the framers intended the Supreme Court to have the power to declare *state* legislation unconstitutional, but whether they intended to give it the same power over *national* legislation is not clear. Professor Edward S. Corwin, an outstanding authority on the American Constitution, has concluded that unquestionably "the framers anticipated some sort of judicial review. . . . But it is equally without question that the ideas generally current in 1787 were far from presaging the present vast role of the Court." [9] Why, then, did the framers not specifically provide for judicial review? Probably because they believed the power rested upon certain general provisions that made specific statement unnecessary.

Certainly Alexander Hamilton intended the Supreme Court to have the power to set aside congressional legislation. He favored, as he said in *Federalist No. 78,* a strong and independent judiciary as a check upon the majority, as an "excellent barrier to the encroachments and oppressions of the representative body." He wanted judges appointed for life to protect private rights against "the occasional ill humors in society" that might lead the Congress to pass laws interfering with the propertied minority.

Not all Americans in the eighteenth century looked so kindly upon the courts. During the conflict with England the patriots invoked the doctrine that the courts should refuse to enforce the laws of Parliament that were against "natural equity" and the English constitution. But after the Revolution, when some state judges dared to void acts of the state legislatures on the grounds of conflict with a "higher law," there was widespread protest. Only a few persons thought of the courts as instruments to enforce constitutional limitations in behalf of the liberties of the people. Most of those who favored judicial review hoped to check the power of popular majorities.

The First Congress adopted—without much debate—the Judiciary Act of 1789, in which it was assumed that the Supreme Court had the power to refuse to enforce congressional legislation that the justices believed to be unconstitutional. Early in its history the Supreme Court did in several cases review acts of Congress, and in 1794 it apparently even declared an act of Congress invalid, but little attention was paid to this incident.

---

[9] Edward S. Corwin, "The Constitution as Instrument and as Symbol," *The American Political Science Review* (1936), p. 1078.

The Federalists—the men who wrote the Constitution and controlled the national government until 1801—generally supported the courts and favored judicial review, but their opponents, the Jeffersonian Republicans, were less enthusiastic. In 1798 and 1799 Jefferson and Madison (the latter by this time had left the Federalist party) came very close in the Virginia and Kentucky Resolutions to arguing that the state legislatures and not the Supreme Court had the ultimate power to interpret the Constitution. This would seem to imply that the Supreme Court did not even have the final authority to review *state* legislation, something about which there had been little doubt.

When the Jeffersonians defeated the Federalists in the elections of 1800, it was still undecided whether the Supreme Court would actually exercise the power of judicial review. "The idea was in the air, the ingredients to support a doctrine of judicial review were at hand, and a few precedents could even be cited"; nevertheless, judicial review was not an established power. Then in 1803 came the case of *Marbury* v. *Madison,* a case intimately related to the political struggles between the Federalists and the Jeffersonians.

THE CASE OF *MARBURY V. MADISON*

The elections of 1800 marked the rise to power of the Jeffersonian Republicans. President John Adams and his fellow Federalists did not take their defeat easily; indeed, they were greatly alarmed at what they considered to be the "enthronement of the rabble." But there was nothing much they could do about it before leaving office—or was there? The Constitution gives the President, with the consent of the Senate, the power to appoint federal judges to hold office during "good behavior"—virtually for life. If the judiciary should be manned by good Federalists, reasoned Adams and his party followers, they could stave off the worst consequences of Jefferson's victory. These Federalists were not motivated solely by partisan purposes; for some time they had contemplated reform of the judicial structure. But between their defeat in November 1800 and the expiration of their terms on March 4, 1801, they worked with renewed zeal.

By the end of February 1801 the Federalist lame-duck Congress had created dozens of new federal judicial posts. By March 3, Adams had appointed, and the Senate had confirmed, deserving Federalists to all these new positions. Adams signed the commissions and turned them over to John Marshall, the Secretary of State, to be sealed and delivered. Marshall had just received his own commission as Chief Justice of the United States, but he was continuing to serve as Secretary of State until Adams' term expired. Working right up to nine o'clock on the evening of March 3, Marshall sealed but was unable to deliver all the commissions. The important ones were taken care of, however, and only those for the justices of the peace for the District of Columbia were left undelivered. It was late and the

Chief Justice had a big day ahead: he was going to administer the presidential oath of office to his distant cousin and political enemy Thomas Jefferson. He retired to his lodgings and left the commissions to be delivered by his successor.

Jefferson was highly aroused by this Federalist packing of the judiciary. When he discovered that some of the commissions had not been delivered, he told the new Secretary of State, James Madison, to hold up seventeen of those still in his possession. Jefferson could see no reason why the District needed so many justices of the peace, especially Federalist justices.

Among the commissions that were not delivered was one for William Marbury. After waiting in vain, Marbury decided to seek action from the courts. Searching through the statute books, he came across Section 13 of the Judiciary Act of 1789, which authorized the Supreme Court "to issue writs of mandamus, in cases warranted by the principles and usages of law, to . . . persons holding office, under the authority of the United States." *A writ of mandamus* is a court order directing an official to perform a nondiscretionary or ministerial act. Delivering a commission is a ministerial act; the Secretary of State is a person holding office under the authority of the United States; so why not, thought Marbury, ask the Supreme Court to issue a writ of mandamus to force Madison to deliver the commission? He and his companions went directly to the Supreme Court and, citing Section 13, they so asked.

What could Marshall do? If the Court issued the mandamus, Madison and Jefferson would probably ignore it. The Court would be powerless, and its prestige, already low, might suffer a fatal blow. On the other hand, by refusing to issue the mandamus, the judges would appear to vindicate the Republican party's claim that the Court had no authority to interfere with the executive. Would Marshall issue the mandamus? Most people thought so; angry Republicans talked of impeachment.

On February 24, 1803, five dignified gentlemen in judicial robes took their seats in a small, dingy room in the basement of the Capitol.

JOHN MARSHALL'S DECISION

The first part of the opinion was as expected. Marbury was entitled to his commission, said Marshall, and Madison should have delivered it to him; a writ of mandamus could be issued by the proper court against even such an august officer as the Secretary of State.

Then came the surprise. Although Section 13 of the Judiciary Act purports to give the Supreme Court original jurisdiction in just such cases, this section, said Marshall, *is contrary to Article III of the Constitution.* This article gives the Supreme Court original jurisdiction in *only* those cases in which an ambassador or other foreign minister is affected or in which a state is a party. This is a case of original jurisdiction, but Marbury is neither a state nor a foreign minister. If we follow Section 13, wrote Marshall, we have jurisdiction; if we follow the Constitution we have no jurisdiction.

Then, in characteristic fashion, Marshall stated the question in such a way that the answer was obvious—namely, should the Supreme Court enforce an unconstitutional law? Of course not, he concluded; the Constitution is the supreme and binding law, and the courts cannot enforce any action of Congress that conflicts with it.

The real question remained unanswered. Congress, in passing the law, and the President, in signing it, had also read the Constitution, and according to *their* interpretation (which was also reasonable) Section 13 was compatible with Article III. Where did the *Supreme Court* get the right to say they were wrong? Why should the *Supreme Court's* interpretation of the Constitution be preferred to that of Congress and the President?

Marshall, paralleling Hamilton's argument in *Federalist No. 78,* reasoned that the Constitution is law, that judges—not legislators or executives—interpret law; therefore, the judges should interpret the Constitution. "If two laws conflict with each other, the courts must decide on the operation of each," he said. Obviously the Constitution is to be preferred to any ordinary act of Congress.

Case dismissed.

Jefferson fumed. For one thing, Marshall had said that a court with the proper jurisdiction could issue a writ of mandamus even against the Secretary of State, the President's right-hand man. But there was little Jefferson could do about it, for there was not even a specific court order that he could refuse to obey. Thus in a single stroke Marshall had given the Republicans a lecture for failing to perform their duties, and had gone a long way toward acquiring for the Supreme Court the power of judicial review of acts of Congress—all in a manner that made it difficult for the Republicans to retaliate.

Marbury v. *Madison* is a masterpiece of judicial strategy. Marshall, contrary to modern canons of judicial interpretation, went out of his way to declare Section 13 unconstitutional. He could have interpreted the section to mean that the Supreme Court could issue writs of mandamus in those cases in which it did have jurisdiction. He could have interpreted Article III to mean that Congress could add to, though not subtract from, the original jurisdiction that the Constitution gives to the Supreme Court. He could have dismissed the case for want of jurisdiction without discussing Marbury's right to his commission. But none of these would have suited his purpose. Jefferson and his fellow Republicans had been threatening to use the impeachment powers to remove Federalist partisans from the federal bench. Marshall was fearful for the Supreme Court's future, and he felt unless the Court spoke out it would become subordinate to the President and Congress.

Marshall's decision, important as it was, did not by itself necessarily establish for the Supreme Court the power to review and declare unconstitutional acts of the Congress. *Marbury* v. *Madison* could have meant simply that the Supreme Court had the right to interpret the scope of *its own* powers under Article III, but that Congress and the President had the authority to interpret their own powers under Articles I and II, respectively. However, Marshall's decision has not been interpreted by court or country in this way (though it was not until the Dred Scott case in 1857 that another act of Congress was declared unconstitutional). Had Marshall not spoken when he did, the Court might not have been able to assume the power of judicial review. The vital precedent had been created. Here we have a classic example of constitutional development through judicial interpretation. There is no specific authorization in the Constitution for the Supreme Court's power to declare congressional enactments null and void; yet today it is a vital part of our constitutional system.

The Supreme Court in American History

The importance of the Supreme Court in shaping the contours and policies of the American Republic has been hardly less than that of Congress and the President. A story of over 170 years cannot be told briefly without distortion. Yet we can see the rhythm of the law by highlighting the general attitudes of the most prominent of the more than ninety men who have served on the High Bench.[10]

THE FORMATIVE PERIOD: JOHN MARSHALL AND ROGER B. TANEY

Until John Marshall became Chief Justice in 1801, the Supreme Court had been a minor branch of the federal government. During the first ten years of its history, three Chief Justices came and departed without finding the position of sufficient importance to challenge their talents. Then came Marshall, a leading Federalist lawyer. During his 34 years as Chief Justice, he elevated the judiciary to a position of importance coordinate with that of Congress and the President.

After 1811 a majority of his fellow justices were nominally Jeffersonians, but Marshall's strong personality and intellect, combined with the fundamentally conservative character of the men appointed to serve with him, enabled the Chief Justice to dominate the Supreme Court to an extent never since equaled. Under his leadership the Court "struck blow after blow in support of the doctrine that the United States was a sovereign nation and not a mere confederacy of sovereign states." [11] Marshall, representing a political party whose views grew less popular with the passage of each year, continued

10 J. R. Schmidhauser, "The Justices of the Supreme Court: A Collective Portrait," *Midwest Journal of Political Science* (February 1959), pp. 1-57.

11 Alfred H. Kelley and Winfred A. Harbison, *The American Constitution*, revised edition (Norton, 1955), p. 272.

to uphold the authority of the national government and to protect the rights of property. His classic opinions for the Court in *Marbury* v. *Madison, Mc-Culloch* v. *Maryland, Gibbons* v. *Ogden,* and *Cohens* v. *Virginia* remain among the most influential opinions ever handed down by any court.

Roger B. Taney (pronounced "Tawney"), Marshall's successor, also started his political life as a Federalist, but he became an ardent supporter of Andrew Jackson, whom he served as Attorney General and as Secretary of the Treasury. When Jackson appointed Taney to the High Bench in 1835, only two men remained from the great days of the Marshall Court, and under Taney the ideas of Jacksonian democracy began to work their way into the Court's opinions. The break between the Marshall and Taney Courts is often exaggerated. Taney and his colleagues were just as devoted to the protection of property as was the Marshall Court. The Taney Court was concerned especially with property rights in land and slavery. And Taney did not differ with Marshall on the supremacy of the national government. Nevertheless, there were important differences between the dominant spirit of the Taney Court and that of its predecessor. In a limited retreat from Marshall's nationalism, the Supreme Court now began to stress the power of the states. The Taney Court was more inclined than its predecessor to recognize the rights of legislative majorities to regulate the uses of private property (especially property that was given special privilege by the states).

It is unfortunate that Taney's *Dred Scott* decision toward the end of his twenty-nine years as Chief Justice has obscured his many earlier constructive opinions. The Dred Scott case is now generally recognized as a misguided attempt by the Supreme Court to interfere in a political controversy in order to resolve the issue of slavery. The majority opinion—that the national government did not have the power to exclude slavery from the territories—merely aggravated the conflict and did the Court itself a grave disservice.

CIVIL WAR AND RECONSTRUCTION

During the decade in which Salmon P. Chase presided over the Supreme Court, 1864-1874, the Court tried to avoid the cross fire between President Johnson and the Radical Republicans in Congress. The Radical Republicans were in control, and they rode roughshod over those who got in their way. Nevertheless, the Chase Court declared ten acts of Congress unconstitutional, as contrasted with the two acts that had been held void in the preceding eighty-four years.

The High Court could not, however, insulate itself from the rough and tumble of postwar party politics, as the *Legal Tender Cases* made clear. To pay for the Civil War, Congress authorized the Treasury to issue greenbacks (paper currency), and it taxed state bank notes out of existence. The right of Congress to authorize paper currency not redeemable in gold or silver was vigorously challenged, and in 1870 (*Hepburn* v. *Griswold*) a bare

majority of Supreme Court justices declared the Legal Tender Act unconstitutional. President Grant, however, had an opportunity to appoint two new
justices, and soon (in 1871) the Supreme Court reversed its decision of the
previous year and upheld the Legal Tender Act.[12] President Grant's appointees "voted the right way."

The primary concern of the Supreme Court during the Chief Justiceship of Morrison R. Waite, 1874-1888, was to re-establish the equilibrium
between the states and the national government that had been upset by the
Civil War and Reconstruction. In the name of the federal system, the Court
nullified the Fourteenth Amendment as a constitutional prop for a positive
national program of protection for civil rights. At the same time the Court,
despite the bitter dissent of a minority, refused to expand its own powers
by using the due process clause to judge the reasonableness of state regulation
of business enterprise. The Supreme Court should not become, said the
Court, "a perpetual censor upon all legislation of the States." [13]

THE SUPREME COURT BECOMES A SUPERLEGISLATURE

Between the Civil War and the New Deal, Republicans were in the
White House for all but sixteen years. Regardless of party affiliation, most
of the Presidents and influential senators believed in the existence of un-
alterable economic laws beyond the sphere of governmental control. They
looked with suspicion on any proposal that interfered with the rights of men
to invest their capital or to hire workers, deeming such suggestions dangerous,
socialistic, populistic, and anarchistic. These were the men who selected most
of the members of the Supreme Court.

The appointment of Melville Fuller as Chief Justice in 1888 marked the
beginning of a new period in the Court's history. Between 1888 and 1937
the Supreme Court became "an aristocracy of the robe and twisted the due
process clause into a moat around all forms of private property." The Supreme
Court became a censor of legislation which, in the justices' opinions, un-
reasonably interfered with the use of private property. The Court also gave
such a restrictive interpretation of congressional power over interstate commerce that effective federal regulation of the economy was forestalled. The
Court, by interpretation, took the teeth out of the Sherman Antitrust and
Interstate Commerce Commission laws, and vetoed all attempts by Congress
to outlaw child labor.

In 1895 the Supreme Court demonstrated, perhaps too clearly, its concept of itself as the protector of property against the "revolutionaries." By
a five-to-four decision, the Court, reversing an old and theretofore unquestioned precedent, made it impossible for the federal government to levy an
income tax. Justice Field, in a concurring opinion, brought to the surface

---

[12] *Legal Tender Cases* (1871).
[13] *Slaughter-House Cases* (1873).

the majority's feelings about such dangerous experiments. The income tax was an assault on capital, he wrote, "it will be but the stepping stone to others, larger and more sweeping, till our political contests will become a war of the poor against the rich; a war constantly growing in intensity and bitterness." [14] In 1913 the Sixteenth Amendment was ratified reversing this decision.

The Supreme Court's assumption of power as a superlegislature was contested by a minority of the Supreme Court justices. Justice Oliver Wendell Holmes spent many of his thirty years on the Court (1902-1932) protesting against his colleagues' habit of writing their own economic predilections into the Constitution. Although he was not Chief Justice and was often in dissent, Holmes became the most famous member of the Court. Though he himself was a conservative with little faith in social reform by legislation, with Olympian detachment he refused to let his own social views become the measure of a law's constitutionality. In 1916 Louis D. Brandeis, appointed by President Wilson, joined with Holmes in protesting the major direction of the Supreme Court's opinions and in exposing the reasons behind the reasons of the Court majority. Brandeis' constitutional and social philosophy was radically different from that of Holmes, but it often produced the same results. When Harlan Fiske Stone became a member of the Court in 1925, he joined with the two dissenters, and "Holmes, Brandeis, and Stone dissenting" became a familiar phrase in the law reports.

THE NEW DEAL AND AFTER

Charles Evans Hughes was a majestic-looking man, the very model of a model Chief Justice. He was a liberal-conservative who used his great talents to guide the Supreme Court during the stormy period (1930-1941) when it collided with the New Deal (see page 536). The Hughes Court was split into fairly consistent conservative and liberal blocs. Four of the justices—Sutherland, Van Devanter, Butler, and McReynolds—held views that reflected the conservative political attitudes dominant in the times when they were appointed. Showing no reluctance to veto legislation that ran counter to their own economic and social attitudes, they looked upon the New Deal as an unconstitutional and dangerous interference with the rights of property and the constitutional system. On the other hand, Justices Brandeis, Stone, and Cardozo (the distinguished jurist who replaced Holmes in 1932), though they found constitutional objections to some New Deal legislation, could find nothing in the Constitution that prevented the national government from doing what was necessary and proper to fight the depression. Chief Justice Hughes and Justice Owen Roberts, both Hoover appointees, held the balance of power. They wavered, then joined the conservatives in ruling that much of the New Deal was unconstitutional.

---

[14] *Pollock* v. *Farmers' Loan and Trust Co.*

President Roosevelt counterattacked vigorously. After the smoke of battle had cleared, it was found that Justice Roberts and the Chief Justice had altered their positions. Moreover the conservatives—who had held on all during Roosevelt's first term—now began to leave the Court. By 1939 a liberal majority controlled the Supreme Court, and by 1941 all the old guard had been replaced by Roosevelt appointees. The "New Court," as it was called after 1937, soon knocked down the barriers that its predecessors had erected against social and economic reform. The Holmes, Brandeis, and Stone dissents became the ruling doctrine of the Court. The "New Court" returned to Marshall's broad construction of Congress' power over interstate commerce, and to the doctrine that the Fourteenth Amendment was not intended to give the Supreme Court justices "carte blanche to embody [their] economic or moral beliefs in its prohibitions."

Though tolerant of governmental regulation of business enterprise, the "New Court" became increasingly intolerant of any attempt to restrict civil liberties, especially attempts by the state governments. Between 1937 and 1946 the Supreme Court handed down many important decisions protecting the civil liberties of individuals.

Harlan Fiske Stone's elevation to the chief justiceship by President Roosevelt in 1941 did not mark any basic change in the Court's doctrines. By that date eight of the nine members of the Court were Roosevelt appointees. Many critics of the New Deal accused the President of creating a rubber-stamp court. To be sure, all his appointees shared the general political position symbolized by the New Deal, and none of them agreed with the constitutional doctrines of Sutherland or McReynolds. But they were far from united. In fact, more dissenting opinions were penned after 1940 than at any previous time in the Court's history. In many cases as many as five justices felt impelled to write separate opinions, often sharply attacking one another's views. The dissents reflected divergent constitutional attitudes among the men who were rapidly tailoring constitutional construction to the facts of the twentieth century, an adjustment that had been opposed by the old Court. The justices, most of whom had previously been active in politics, discussed the philosophical and political premises of their decisions to a much greater extent than had any of their predecessors.

THE VINSON COURT—A PASSIVE PERIOD

Under the leadership of Chief Justice Fred M. Vinson (1946-1953) the Supreme Court continued to sanction governmental regulations of business, labor, and agriculture. The Court pushed forward in behalf of civil rights for minority groups, but in the face of the tensions of the Cold War the Court retreated from the strong civil-liberties stand it had espoused under Chief Justice Stone. The High Court construed the Smith Act to ease the way for the Department of Justice to prosecute communists; it refused to consider cases challenging the right of congressional committees to interrogate private citizens about their political views; and it dodged constitutional questions raised by loyalty-security programs. In short, the Supreme Court deferred to the judgment of Congress and the state legislatures that national security required some sacrifice of civil liberties.

THE WARREN COURT—
CIVIL LIBERTIES TO THE FORE

In 1953 President Eisenhower made his first appointment to the Supreme Court when he selected Earl Warren, the governor of California and former Republican vice-presidential candidate, to fill the vacancy caused by the death of Chief Justice Vinson. (By 1960 five members of the Court were Eisenhower appointees, but just as in the case of the Roosevelt and Truman selections, the men picked by Eisenhower often differ with one another.)

Even if it does nothing else, the Warren Court's place in history is secure —it will be enough to say that this court took the final step to make the Constitution color-blind. Furthermore, since 1956, after the nation had already repudiated the excesses of what came to be known as McCarthyism, the Court returned to its earlier strong civil-liberties position. Although generally avoiding a ruling of unconstitutionality, the Supreme Court has construed statutes to maximize individual freedom. The Smith Act was reinterpreted to require for conviction substantial evidence of actual advocacy of violence; federal loyalty-security regulations were narrowly construed; passport laws were read to mean that the Secretary of State could not withhold a passport because of the applicant's political beliefs; the military's jurisdiction to try civilians was curtailed; and Congress' power to expatriate was limited.

Chief Justice Warren, Justice Brennan, another Eisenhower selection, and two Roosevelt appointees, Black and Douglas, make up a fairly consistent civil-liberties bloc. These four votes are sufficient to exercise the Court's discretionary reviewing authority in order to bring civil-liberties cases before it, but the civil libertarians need the vote of one more justice to control the decisions. At the other extreme stands Justice Clark, a Truman appointee, who consistently supports national security regulations. So far, it looks as though Clark has the better chance of winning the support of the two most recent selections, Whittaker and Stewart, than does the Warren bloc. This leaves as the "swing men" Frankfurter, chosen by Roosevelt, and Harlan, appointed by Eisenhower. Frankfurter and Harlan, especially the former, are impressed by what they consider to be the essentially undemocratic character of judicial review and usually hold that judges should defer to legislatures since these popularly elected and politically responsive officials have the major responsibility for balancing conflicting values. However, on occasion they vote with the civil-liberties bloc, especially if they can do it without having to interpose a constitutional veto.

With the Supreme Court so evenly balanced on many issues, reflecting the division of opinion within the nation itself, the next several appointments will be of crucial significance in the constant and continuous process of determining what the Constitution will mean tomorrow.

Judges as Technicians   The Constitution does not require judges to be lawyers. Yet all Supreme Court justices, as well as other federal judges, have been members of the bar. No businessman, farmer, or labor leader has ever served on any federal court. The reason is not hard to uncover. Although ignorance of the law is no excuse for the wrongdoer, knowledge of the law is a professional mystery, a technical subject that can be mastered only after long study.

What kind of law do federal judges apply? Where do they find it? [15]

THE LAW

Sometimes judges apply *constitutional law*. Since the Constitution contains only 7000 words and can be read in a half-hour or so, it might be assumed that any person could learn constitutional law after a little study. But even the Constitution has become a possession of the specialists, and to read the document itself sheds little light on constitutional law. Indeed, Professor T. R. Powell, one of Harvard's most distinguished teachers, is reported to have warned his students not to read the Constitution because it would "confuse their minds." Constitutional law is full of phrases like "the clear and present danger rule" and "separate but equal doctrine" that are not to be found in the written words of the Constitution. They come from the decisions of the Supreme Court. Constitutional law, in other words, consists of statements about the interpretation of the Constitution that have been given Supreme Court sanction. Constitutional law is applied in a relatively small number of cases.

In many instances it is *statutory law* that controls the judges' decisions. This is law formulated by the legislature, although it also includes treaties and executive orders; it is law that comes from authoritative and specific law-making sources. The legislature has no choice but to state the rules in general terms, for it cannot anticipate all the questions that will arise over their meaning. Even the most specific law must be applied to an infinite variety of concrete situations. The initial interpretation is often made by an administrator, but the final interpretation, short of an actual change in the law, is made by the judges.

Again, intelligence alone is not enough to interpret even the simplest of laws. The law must be interpreted according to the application of legal principles. In general, judges try to discover legislative intent—what the legislators

---

[15] See Epilogue to find out where the lay citizen can look up the law.

intended to do. When possible this is done by studying the words of the statute in question. Sometimes, however, judges must look to legislative journals, legislative debates, and committee hearings for clues to the intention of the legislators. A layman might try to consult the men who drafted, introduced, or considered the bill in committee, for they might seem to be the most informative and reliable source of legislative intent. But according to the judges' rules, which in large part they make themselves, this is not permissible.

What happens if there is no statutory law governing a case that comes before a court? What if the legislature has not formalized any rule to apply to the dispute? Then the judges must apply the *common law*. Common law is judge-made law. It has an ancient lineage reaching back through centuries of judicial decisions. It originated in England in the twelfth century when royal judges began traveling around the country settling disputes in each locality according to prevailing custom. Gradually these principles became the same for the entire nation. The common law continues to develop according to the rule of *stare decisis,* which means, "let the decision stand." *Stare decisis* requires that once a rule has been established by a court, it shall be followed in all similar cases. It makes the decisions of judges of superior courts binding not only on all subordinate courts in the same judicial system, but also on their own successors.

The American common law began to branch off from the English system in the seventeenth century. Today we have 49 separate common-law systems, or 50, counting the federal interpretation of state law. (In Louisiana the legal system is based on the other great western legal tradition, the *civil law*. The civil law gives more emphasis to codes of lawgivers and less to past judicial decisions. In Louisiana the civil law has been greatly influenced by and intermingled with the common law.) There is no federal common law. Whenever federal judges have to decide disputes between citizens of two states and there is no applicable state statute, they apply the common law as interpreted by the state courts. But when there is no state interpretation, federal judges strike out for themselves. The common law governs many disputes, and even where it has been superseded by statute, the statutory law is usually a modification and codification of the old common-law rules and is normally interpreted according to the common-law tradition.

Federal judges also apply *equity*. Like common law, equity is a system of judge-made law that had its origins in England. Early in the development of the common law, it was discovered that in certain circumstances the common law did not insure justice. Under the common law, for example, a person whose property rights are about to be injured has no choice but to wait until the injury has taken place and then to seek money damages. But the injury may do irreparable harm for which money damages cannot provide adequate compensation. Accordingly another set of rules was worked out to be used where the law was inadequate. Under equity, a person may go to a judge, show why the common-law remedy is inadequate, and ask for equitable relief—an injunction, for example, to prevent an act that threatens irreparable harm. If the wrongdoer persists, he may be punished for contempt of court.

Admiralty and maritime law is also applied by federal judges. This is a highly complex and technical body of rules applicable to cases arising in connection with shipping and water-borne commerce on the high seas and, by decision of the Supreme Court,[16] on the navigable waters of the United States.

A relatively new kind of law that has become increasingly prominent in the decisions of federal judges is *administrative law*. Congress has, within the last several decades, delegated to administrators and administrative agencies so much rule-making authority that today there is, in volume, more administrative than statutory law. Administrative law consists of the rules and regulations issued by administrative agencies that deal with the operations of the government or that determine private rights. An example is the Federal Trade Commission regulation that forbids interstate advertisers to use the word "free" in such a way as to mislead the reader. The rules and decisions of administrators may be reviewed by federal judges, and judges are often called upon to determine whether the administrators have acted properly and within their authority.

Law may also be classified as *criminal* or *civil*. Criminal law, which is almost entirely statutory, defines crimes against the public order and provides for punishment. Government has the primary responsibility for enforcing this type of law. The great body of criminal law is enacted by states and is enforced by state officials in the state courts, but the criminal business of federal judges is by no means negligible, and it is growing. The Constitution insists upon certain minimum procedures in the trial of criminal cases (see Chapter 8), and these procedures have been supplemented by law. The Supreme Court, as supervisor of the administration of justice in the federal courts, has adopted other rules that federal judges must follow.

Civil law governs the relations between individuals and defines their legal rights. For example: Jones, who has a trademark for "Atomic Pills," discovers that Smith is advertising "Atomic Tablets" in national magazines. If Jones wishes to protect his trademark, he may proceed against Smith before a federal judge. But the government can also be a party to a civil action. During World War II the federal courts did a brisk business in cases initiated by the Office of Price Administration to enforce price control regulations. Under the Sherman Antitrust Act, the federal government may initiate civil as well as criminal action to prevent violations of the law.

The Constitution says little about the procedure to be followed in civil

---

16 *The Genesee Chief* (1852).

cases, though it does require that suits at common law involving $20 or more be tried before a jury. This pertains, however, only to suits under the common law, and even in these suits the parties may, and frequently do, waive the right to trial before a jury. Congress has given to the federal courts authority to determine their own rules of civil procedure.

THE SCOPE OF JUDICIAL POWER

Some people seem to think that judges roam around the country ferreting out injustice. Perhaps they visualize a judge reading through the morning paper, looking for evidence of law violations or for legislation passed by Congress that he should declare unconstitutional. This is not the way judges operate. They have only *judicial power*—the power "to decide and pronounce a judgment and carry it into effect between persons . . . who bring a case before [them] for decision." [17] The Supreme Court has steadfastly refused to permit the constitutional courts to exercise any nonjudicial functions. These courts cannot make any decisions "not binding on the parties or subject to later . . . alteration by administrative action." Hence, the Supreme Court will not give any advisory opinions to Congress or the President; it will act, and permit other constitutional courts to act, only when it is presented with a controversy over which it has jurisdiction.

Not all disputes are within the scope of judicial power. Judges decide only *justiciable* disputes, those that grow out of actual cases and that are capable of settlement by legal methods. A rabid Dodger fan might engage in a violent dispute with a booster of the Cardinals, but no judge will use his judicial authority to determine which is the better team. Not even all governmental questions or constitutional problems are justiciable. For example, judges will not determine which government of a foreign state should be recognized by the United States. The Constitution gives this authority to the President, and judges will not question his decision. Similarly, the Supreme Court has ruled that some claims of unconstitutionality raise political and not justiciable questions. What does the Court mean by "political"? It means an issue that requires knowledge of a nonlegal character, that requires the use of techniques not suitable for a court, or that the Constitution addresses to the political branch of government. Examples of political questions are: Which of two competing state governments is the proper one? What is a republican form of state government? Has a constitutional amendment been ratified within a reasonable time after it was proposed? Are congressional districts properly drawn? [18]

Judges will not use their power unless the controversy is a real one. Two people cannot trump up a suit merely to contest the actions of the legislature. For example, in 1889 a man named Wellman tried to purchase a railway

---

[17] Justice Miller, *Constitution* 314, quoted by Justice Day for Supreme Court in *Muskrat* v. *United States* (1911).

[18] *Luther* v. *Borden* (1849); *Coleman* v. *Miller* (1939); and *Colegrove* v. *Green* (1946).

ticket the day after the Michigan legislature had fixed the rates. The ticket agent refused to sell a ticket at the new rate and Wellman brought suit. During the trial Wellman made no attempt to contest the railway company's testimony. It became clear that Wellman wanted the railway company to win; he made no attempt to present fully the facts in the case. The Supreme Court said, however, "It was never thought that, by means of a friendly suit, a party beaten in the legislature could transfer to the courts an inquiry as to the constitutionality of a legislative act." [19] (This, of course, is exactly what is done in a nonfriendly suit. In such cases, however, the two parties have an interest in getting the full facts before the Court.)

Can anybody challenge a law? Not unless he has "sustained or is immediately in danger of sustaining a direct injury. It is not sufficient that he has merely a general interest common to all members of the public." [20] Furthermore, the injury must be substantial. In 1921 Congress passed a law providing for federal grants to the states to help reduce maternal and infant mortality. When a Miss Frothingham heard about the law she was indignant. It was, she thought, clearly unconstitutional, for this activity was reserved to the states and beyond the power of the national government. She instructed her attorneys to seek an injunction to prevent Secretary of the Treasury Mellon from disbursing money in accordance with the law. Did she have the right to maintain the suit? Yes, her lawyers argued, because if the unconstitutional appropriations were made it would increase the burden of future taxes and thereby take her property without due process of the law. The Supreme Court decided, however, that Miss Frothingham's interest in the money in the Federal Treasury was too minute, and the effects of appropriation on future taxation too remote and uncertain, to give her any standing to contest the act. [21]

Judges are careful to decide only what is necessary to dispose of the case before them, especially when the constitutionality of an act of Congress is in question. The Supreme Court has frequently shown extreme reluctance to rule on constitutional questions. As Mr. Justice Brandeis wrote: "It is not the habit of the court to decide questions of a constitutional nature unless absolutely necessary to a decision of the case. . . . The Court will not 'formulate a rule of constitutional law broader than is required by the precise facts to which it is applied. . . .' The Court will not pass upon a constitutional question although properly presented by the record, if there is also present some other ground upon which the case may be disposed of. . . . [I]t is a cardinal principle that this Court will first ascertain whether a construction of the statute is fairly possible by which the question [of constitutionality] may be avoided." [22]

Judges do not always remain strictly within the limits set by these restrictions. At times the Supreme Court justices, despite their professed reluctance

---

[19] *Chicago & Grand Trunk Railway Co.* v. *Wellman* (1892).
[20] *Ex parte Levitt* (1937).
[21] *Frothingham* v. *Mellon* (1923).
[22] Concurring opinion in *Ashwander* v. *T.V.A.* (1936).

to do so, have had little hesitancy about striking down laws of Congress. Disputes have been trumped up entirely for the purpose of getting a Court decision; the Dred Scott case, for example, appears to have been a dispute of this kind. Other cases have been presented in which it is questionable whether the parties actually stood in an adverse relationship. Despite these breaches, the judges generally are careful to stay within their proper field of operations.

Laymen are often impatient with what they consider to be legal technicalities. But judges are not free agents with the power to right any and all wrongs according to their own sense of justice. "We do not sit," wrote Justice Frankfurter in the Terminiello case, "like a kadi under a tree dispensing justice according to considerations of individual expediency. . . ." In the long run, a court's violation of the settled rules of judicial procedure would probably lead to more uncertainty, to more abuse of judicial power, and to more delay than does the slow but inexorable movement of justice. "Some of these rules," Justice Frankfurter has admitted, ". . . may well appear overrefined or evasive to the laity. But they have the support not only of the profoundest wisdom. They have been vindicated, in conspicuous instances of disregard, by the painful lessons of our constitutional history." The rules restricting judges are designed to prevent them from interfering in matters beyond their competence and to confine them to the functions for which they were established.

Judges as Politicians

Do judges make law? 'Course they do. Made some myself," remarked Jeremiah Smith, former judge of the New Hampshire Supreme Court.[23] Today such statements raise few judicial eyebrows. But just a few generations ago, such frankness would have shocked many of the leading gentlemen of the bench and bar. Despite glaring evidence to the contrary and the realistic statements of outstanding judges and lawyers, the orthodox position was that judges *discovered* but never made laws. According to this orthodoxy, the judges' own views of public policy were irrelevant, since their only function was to apply the rule or principle applicable to the case before them. Judging, it was insisted, was solely a matter of knowledge of the law, and the personal values of the judges did not enter into the picture. According to the "discovery" theory of the law, a judge is bound by the rule of *stare decisis*. A judge merely *discovers* the right precedents; and when there are no precedents, he extends the old principles.

HOW JUDGES MAKE LAW

In deciding most cases, however, it is easy enough to find precedents to support a preconceived decision. There are competing principles, each of which might appropriately support a decision. In choosing between them, the

---

[23] Quoted in Paul H. Freund, *On Understanding the Supreme Court* (Little, Brown, 1950), p. 3.

judge acts very much like a legislator. The judge also has a range of choice when he interprets statutory law, for many statutes are so hastily and poorly drawn that they give no clear guide to legislative intent. But even carefully drafted legislation does not seriously restrict the judge. Although judges profess to search for legislative intent, how is one to discover the intention of all the congressmen and the President who make the law? Legislative intention is, as Professor Max Radin has written, "a transparent and absurd fiction." [24] Even where legislative history affords clear guides to the intent of the legislators, James M. Landis has pointed out, "strong judges prefer to override the intent of the legislature in order to make law according to their own views." [25] According to Judge Learned Hand, one of America's great jurists, the words of a statute that a judge must construe are "empty vessels into which he can pour nearly anything he will."

How judges make law is well illustrated by an example that is extreme but not unique. In 1890, Congress passed the Sherman Antitrust Law, declaring, "Every contract in restraint of trade and commerce among the several States is illegal." But the legislators left it to the judges to determine the concrete meaning of this law. In order to discover, for example, whether the law outlaws contracts pertaining to *manufacturing* that ultimately will restrain interstate commerce, one must look not to the words of the law or even to legislative history, but to the decisions of the Supreme Court. This was the question in *United States* v. *E. C. Knight Co.* (1895), the first case under the Sherman Act to come before the High Tribunal. The government had asked the Court to set aside a contract among a group of companies that gave them control over the refining of 98 per cent of the sugar in the United States. But a majority of the Supreme Court justices declared that the act did not outlaw such a contract. The sugar companies, they said, had restrained manufacturing —not commerce—and the restraint of commerce that might result was indirect. By this interpretation the Supreme Court took the heart out of the Sherman Antitrust Law, though the rationale of the Knight case was undercut by the Supreme Court a few years later. In 1911 the Court further "amended" the Sherman Act by ruling that, despite the words of the statute, Congress had intended to make illegal only "unreasonable contracts." [26]

The Supreme Court acts even more clearly as a lawmaker in interpreting the Constitution than in interpreting statutes. Yet the old "discovery theory" insisted that the power of judicial review was merely the power to follow the obvious intent of the Constitution. In 1936 Mr. Justice Roberts, speaking for the Court, fell back on this orthodox doctrine, frequently referred to as the theory of mechanical jurisprudence, to answer those who were criticizing the justices for writing their own value preferences into the Constitution. He wrote:

---

[24] Max Radin, "Statutory Interpretation," *Harvard Law Review* (April 1930), pp. 863-885.
[25] James M. Landis, "Statutory Interpretation," *Harvard Law Review* (April 1930), pp. 886-893.
[26] *United States* v. *American Tobacco Co.*

It is sometimes said that the court assumes a power to overrule or control the action of the people's representatives. This is a misconception. . . . When an act of Congress is appropriately challenged in the courts . . . the judicial branch . . . has only one duty,—to lay the article of the Constitution which is involved beside the statute which is challenged and to decide whether the latter squares with the former. All the Court does, or can do, is to announce its considered judgment upon the question. . . . The court neither approves nor condemns any legislative policy.[27]

Professor Roscoe Pound has called this explanation of the judicial process "the slot machine theory." Although it has been discredited, echoes of the doctrine are still frequently heard. As late as 1958 Chief Justice Warren, who on other occasions has acknowledged the judges' creative role in balancing conflicting values, fell back on mechanical jurisprudence when he wrote:

When it appears that an Act of Congress conflicts with one of the provisions [of the Constitution], we have no choice but to enforce the paramount commands of the Constitution. . . . We cannot push back the limits of the Constitution merely to accommodate challenged legislation. . . . We do well to approach this task cautiously. . . . But the ordeal of judgment cannot be shirked.[28]

Mechanical jurisprudence ignores the fact that the judges must choose which of the several meanings of the Constitution shall be adopted. It rests on the false assumption that the Constitution has a single, clear, precise meaning and that laws come already tagged with labels of "unconstitutionality." Of course no one argues that unconstitutional laws should be enforced or that judges should refrain from voiding a measure when it clearly conflicts with the Constitution. But in the very cases in which Roberts and Warren described their function as merely enforcing the clear commands of the Constitution, other Supreme Court justices were equally convinced that the particular laws in question did not conflict with the Constitution. True, the meaning of many parts of the Constitution is obvious and can be interpreted by a mechanical process. If Congress passed a law extending the term of United States senators beyond six years, its unconstitutionality would be apparent to everyone. If constitutional interpretation amounted only to this, judges would have no special claim as guardians of the Constitution. But it is not the specifically worded clauses of the Constitution that present questions of interpretation. Rather it is those open-ended clauses, those few words whose meaning cannot be interpreted solely with a dictionary. Judges have few external guides, for example, in trying to determine the meaning of due process or the First Amendment.

In giving specific meaning to ambiguous provisions of the Constitution,

---

[27] *United States* v. *Butler.*
[28] *Trop* v. *Dulles.*

Supreme Court justices are not seriously restricted by the doctrine of *stare decisis*.[29] The doctrine is even less controlling in the field of constitutional than in the field of statutory interpretation. The legislature can correct judicial errors of statutory interpretation, but only the Supreme Court or a constitutional amendment can alter the Court's "erroneous" construction of the Constitution. Justices are, therefore, less hesitant to overrule decisions on constitutional matters. Even when they do not wish to repudiate openly an earlier doctrine, it is easy to "distinguish" each new case from the old ones and thus permit a new ruling. Justice Harlan told a group of students, "I want to say to you young gentlemen that if we [the Supreme Court] don't like an act of Congress, we don't have much trouble to find grounds for declaring it unconstitutional." [30]

To recognize the facts of judicial life—that the judges often write their own views into law, that, in the words of Max Lerner, "judicial decisions are not babies brought by constitutional storks"—is not to criticize the judges. Nor is it to say that there are no limits to the judges' discretion. They are restricted, as we have seen, by precedent, by legal principles and procedures, by the severe discipline of the law itself, and by other techniques designed to offset their own political opinions. Those who insist that the law is only a reflection of the personal biases of the judges are as extreme as those who insist that these biases have no effect on the law.

ACTIVISTS VERSUS SELF-RESTRAINERS

Not all judges are convinced of the possibility or of the desirability of achieving objectivity, or of withdrawing from the field of policymaking. These judges, roughly characterized as "judicial activists," insist that political choice is inevitable and inherent in judging, and that judges should make no false pretense of objectivity. Rather, they should recognize that they are making policy, and they should consciously exercise their judicial power to achieve social justice.

The judicial "self-restrainers" take another view. They recognize the judge's difficulty in rising above his own biases, but they insist that objectivity is the goal that he should aim for. As the people's *political* representatives, the legislators and executives, they argue, have the chief responsibility for working out the accommodation of interests that is the essence of legislation. The self-restrainers insist that judges must be very careful to avoid injecting their own wishes into the judicial process, since it is not their responsibility to determine

---

[29] Justice William O. Douglas, *"Stare Decisis," Columbia Law Review* (June 1949), pp. 735-758.

[30] Quoted by E. S. Corwin, *Constitutional Revolution, Ltd.* (Claremont and Associated Colleges, 1941), p. 38. For a more recent treatment of the extent and limitations of judicial power, see John P. Roche, "Judicial Self-Restraint," *The American Political Science Review* (September 1955), pp. 762-772, and Frank, *Marble Palace,* pp. 20-41.

public policy. Judges should be especially hesitant to check the full play of the democratic process. As Justice Stone wrote in his dissenting opinion in the Butler case, "Courts are not the only agency of government that must be assumed to have the capacity to govern," and "The only check upon our own exercise of power is our own sense of self-restraint. For removal of unwise laws from the statute books appeal lies not to the courts but to the ballot and to the process of democratic government."

Some people take a position midway between the activists and the self-restrainers. They believe that judges should not invalidate economic and social laws affecting property rights, but should have full authority to void laws restricting civil liberties, such as free speech. Their argument for this compromise position goes like this: The majority should not be stopped from experimenting with social and economic arrangements. If mistakes are made, new majorities will arise to correct them. But majorities should not be permitted to tamper with basic liberties. For if they go too far, the very instruments for publicizing and correcting the mistakes—such as free speech and free press—will not be able to operate effectively. The Constitution does not embody any particular economic theory, and legislative majorities are free to adopt any they wish. But the Constitution *is* committed to the political theory of free debate, and it is the judges' special responsibility to prevent legislative tampering with the democratic processes.

These divergent views about the proper role of the judiciary have been formulated more explicitly in the recent opinions of the Supreme Court than they were when the "discovery theory" was prevalent. Yet judges cannot be fitted into neat categories; accusations that the judges are being influenced by their own political beliefs often stem from a dislike of the Court's opinions rather than from disagreement over the proper scope of the judiciary. Prior to 1937, when the Supreme Court majority was announcing constitutional doctrines that protected the business community, supporters of these doctrines insisted that the justices were merely applying the clear dictates of the Constitution. On the other hand, those who disliked the conservative tenor of the doctrines accused the justices of usurping the legislative function, of making their own partisan views the measure of constitutionality. From 1937 to the present, the shoe has been on the other foot. Those who dislike the decisions sustaining government regulation of the economy and striking down laws supporting racial segregation have accused the justices of being "New Dealers," "partisan politicians," and "incompetent judges." Those who like the decisions and approve of the new doctrines insist that the justices have merely returned to the true meaning of the Constitution.

Judges must make choices among conflicting values. By the very nature of their duties, judges—especially those on the Supreme Court—are forced into the storm center of politics and policymaking. What problems does this fact raise for democratic government?

Judges and Democratic Government

Judges are at one and the same time legal technicians and, in the broad sense, politicians. As legal technicians, it is their legal competence that controls their decisions; as policymakers it is their political attitude that counts. As impartial dispensers of equal justice under the law, judges should not be dependent on the pleasure of the executive, the legislature, or the parties to a case. As determiners of basic public policy, judges should be politically responsible and publicly accountable. As legal experts applying legal principles to the solution of justiciable controversies, judges should be above politics. As policymakers, judges should be—and inevitably are—in politics.

The Constitution takes into account the confusion occasioned by the blending of these dual and inextricably related functions in the person of a judge. In some of its provisions it looks to the independence of the judiciary: judges are appointed by the President with the consent of the Senate to serve for life terms; Congress is forbidden to decrease their salaries during their term of service. On the other hand, judges are made dependent on Congress for the money they need to operate, and for their authority to hear and decide cases. Congress creates the inferior courts, determines the size of all courts, and may remove judges by impeachment and conviction.

HOW INDEPENDENT SHOULD THE JUDGES BE?

This relation between courts, Congress, and the President is the familiar pattern of separation of powers, and checks and balances. The principle of separation of powers, however, is more vital for the independence of the judiciary than it is for the other branches. Many who urge the consolidation of legislative and executive powers in the same agency still insist on an independent judiciary. In the first place, it is an ancient and seldom-questioned maxim of justice that no man be trusted as both prosecutor and judge. The active enforcement of the law, the investigation of crimes, and the prosecution of wrongdoers are executive functions. If judges depended on the pleasure of the executive, then two incompatible functions would be consolidated in the same agency. Secondly, "a government of laws and not of men" is one in which public officials as well as private individuals operate under and in accordance with the law. To check the illegal actions of these officials requires an appeal to an independent judiciary.

Judges must also be free to apply the law impartially, even against the most popular person in a community or in favor of the most hated. Sometimes justice requires a judge to favor a person who has aroused the active hostility of his neighbors or to rule against one who has a strong popular following. He must have the independence to apply the law fearlessly—especially when the community has been swept by emotions that make it intolerant of restrained action. Independence is always a matter of degree, and even if the judges' sole duty were to serve as legal experts, complete isolation from the community and lack of all popular control would not be desirable. Yet few would question the value of an independent judiciary when judges are thought of as *legal technicians.*

But if few people have ever seriously questioned the arrangements that give national judges great independence, many, including Presidents Jefferson, Jackson, Lincoln, and both Roosevelts, have tilted with the defenders of *judicial review.* Although most people admit the necessity of having independent judges, some have questioned the need to give these independent judges the power to veto the desires of the majority as expressed through their elected representatives. All agree that an unconstitutional law should not be enforced. The question remains, *is the Supreme Court's interpretation of constitutionality to be preferred to that of Congress or the President?*

The most important parts of the Constitution, as we have noted, are vague and leave room for difference of opinion. Of the three branches of government, it is argued, the Supreme Court is the least responsive to the public will. If the Constitution is supreme because it is an expression of the people's ideas, then those agents who most directly represent those ideas have the best right to interpret the Constitution. Why should five men (i.e., a majority of the Court) holding office for life have the power to tell Congress and the President, elected by the people, what they may or may not do?

Other opponents of judicial review have pointed out that John Marshall's logic in *Marbury* v. *Madison* could be turned against him. Confronted with a Supreme Court decision that he considered unconstitutional, a President might reason that his duty would be to follow the Constitution and to refuse to enforce the Court's decision.

But despite the persistent attacks on judicial review, most Americans continue to hold it as a desirable feature of our governmental system. Generally speaking, Americans have never been willing to put full trust in the majority. An independent judiciary with the power of judicial review has been the major institutional sign of this fear of unchecked legislative and popular majorities. The belief in judicial review reflects and rests on the belief that the Constitution, like natural law, contains certain fundamental principles that no majority should tamper with. It is argued that the independence of judges from temporary majorities is their strength in protecting these rights, not their weakness. Justice Jackson phrased it, in a somewhat different context, this way, "One's right to life, liberty, and property, to free speech, a free press, freedom of worship and assembly, and other fundamental rights may not be submitted to vote; they depend on the outcome of no election." [31]

But just how independent in fact are the judges? Are they so independent that given also their power of interpreting the Constitution and the laws, they

[31] *West Virginia State Board of Education* v. *Barnette* (1943).

are the masters of the majority? For the moment, yes; in the long—and not so very long—run, no.

**"THE CONSTITUTION IS
WHAT MOST OF US SAY IT IS"**

The most important way in which political majorities have brought their weight to bear on the judiciary is through the selection of judges by the popularly elected President and senators. Political considerations have been of crucial significance in the selection of federal judges, particularly for the lower federal courts. By the rule of senatorial courtesy, the senators of a state, provided they are of the same party as the President, have a veto over all judicial appointments to the district courts within that state. In practice, the senators often send the President a list from which he is requested to nominate one for Senate confirmation, and this list seldom includes a member of the opposing political party.

Nor have party considerations been ignored, though they are of much less importance, in the naming of Supreme Court justices. Here the determining factors are the basic social, economic, and judicial attitudes of the individual. Every President since Washington has felt that his responsibilities demanded that he nominate to the Supreme Court men who could be depended on to make the "right" decisions, meaning decisions compatible with the views of the popularly elected President. President Theodore Roosevelt voiced this attitude in a letter to Senator Lodge about Judge Holmes of the Massachusetts Supreme Judicial Court, whom he was considering for the United States Supreme Court. Roosevelt wrote:

> In the ordinary and low sense which we attach to the words "partisan" and "politician," a judge of the Supreme Court should be neither. But in the higher sense, in the proper sense, he is not in my judgment fitted for the position unless he is a party man, a constructive statesman, constantly keeping in mind his adherence to the principles and policies under which this nation has been built up. . . . Now I should like to know that Judge Holmes was in entire sympathy with our views, that is with your views and mine. . . . I should hold myself guilty of an irreparable wrong to the nation if I should [appoint] any man who was not absolutely sane and sound on the great national policies for which we stand in public life.[32]

Presidents have occasionally been disappointed in the men they have appointed to the Supreme Court. Once on the bench, some justices have departed from the "sound policies" that the Presidents expected them to support. But by and large, through their selection of the personnel of the federal judiciary, Presidents and Senates have *eventually* been able to bring the Court's

---

[32] Henry Cabot Lodge, *Selections from the Correspondence of Theodore Roosevelt and Henry Cabot Lodge* (Scribner's, 1925), I, 518-519.

decisions into line with the general attitudes of contemporary political ma-jorities.

The difficulty, however, is that the judge's life tenure often keeps him in office long after the political climate has changed, and he continues to represent views of the era in which he was appointed. Some justices have even stayed on the Court to prevent incumbent Presidents from appointing successors. Chief Justice Taft, for example, feared to resign lest the "radical" Hoover be allowed to appoint someone in his place. In 1929 he wrote, "I am older and slower and less acute and more confused. However, as long as things continue as they are, and I am able to answer in my place, I must stay on the court in order to prevent the Bolsheviki from getting control. . . ." [33]

In most cases the Court's tardiness in adjusting to changing political climates is the normal result of the long tenure of the justices. Jefferson, for instance, became President only to discover that the judiciary was entirely manned by Federalists who represented the doctrines Jefferson had just defeated in the election. Many of these Federalist judges had no scruples against using their power to attack Jefferson's political doctrines.

Faced with this opposition, Jefferson and his followers tried to use the impeachment power to modernize the judiciary. Although judges hold office during good behavior, they may be impeached for "treason, bribery, or other high crimes and misdemeanors." Despite his belief in the doctrine of strict construction, Jefferson wished to interpret liberally the impeachment clause and to develop it as a device for keeping the judiciary in line with current views. The Federalist judges had not committed treason, high crimes, or misdemeanors, though some of them were guilty of conduct unbecoming a judge and of using their positions for frankly partisan purposes. Yet Jefferson felt that judges who held political views not in harmony with those of the political majority should not be permitted to thwart the wishes of the people and should be subject to some kind of political control. As a result, his supporters in the House of Representatives impeached Justice Chase, and Chief Justice Marshall was apparently to be next on the list. Although Chase had been an intemperate Federalist partisan, he had committed no crimes, and the Senate refused to sustain the impeachment charge. Since that date, impeachment has never been used to remove judges except, in a very few cases, for criminal or patently unethical practices.

Congressional control over the structure and jurisdiction of the federal courts has been used more successfully to influence the course of judicial decisions. Although thwarted in their attempts to impeach the judges, the Jeffersonians abolished the circuit courts that the Federalist Congress had created just prior to leaving office. In 1869 the Radical Republicans in Congress used its constitutional power to alter the Supreme Court's appellate jurisdiction in

---

[33] Letter to Horace Taft, November 14, 1929, quoted by H. F. Pringle, *The Life and Times of William Howard Taft* (Farrar & Rinehart, 1939), II, 967.

order to snatch from the Court a case it was about to review involving legislation of dubious constitutionality (*Ex parte McCardle*).

They also reduced the size of the Court to prevent President Johnson from filling two vacancies. After Johnson left the White House, Congress increased the size of the Court to permit Grant to select two justices. As we have seen, Grant selected men who made it possible to reverse the Supreme Court invalidation of the Legal Tender Act. Historians are still debating whether Grant packed the Court. Certainly he was not unaware that his two appointees shared his sentiments about the desirability of reversing the earlier decision.

F.D.R. VERSUS THE "NINE OLD MEN"

President Franklin D. Roosevelt's battle with the Supreme Court is a more dramatic attempt by a political leader to influence the course of judicial decisions. President Roosevelt took office on March 4, 1933, in the midst of the Great Depression. Under his leadership, Congress passed in quick succession a series of important laws designed to give Americans a "New Deal." By 1935 these measures began to come before the Supreme Court. In the next sixteen months the Supreme Court invalidated eight out of the ten measures that came before it. Despite the Supreme Court's judgment that the New Deal was unconstitutional, in 1936 Franklin D. Roosevelt won an overwhelming victory at the polls. An irresistible force seemed to be moving toward an immovable object. One or the other would have to give way.

Early in 1937, as the conflict between the President and the Supreme Court was approaching its climax, a variety of proposals were put forward to limit the judges' power. One suggested amendment would require a two-thirds vote of the justices before the Supreme Court could declare acts of Congress unconstitutional; another would permit Congress to override Supreme Court decisions by a two-thirds vote. But President Roosevelt decided that it would be impossible to secure ratification of such a constitutional amendment or, at any rate, that it would take too long. On February 5, 1937, he presented to Congress his own program to reorganize the federal judiciary. The most significant recommendation was that the President be given the right to appoint an additional justice for each member of the Court over the age of seventy who chose not to retire after ten years' service. The maximum size of the Supreme Court was to be set at fifteen. The ostensible purpose of the recommendation was to make the Supreme Court more efficient so that it could keep up with its work. The real purpose was obvious. The President wished to modernize the Supreme Court by "packing" it.

Clearly the Supreme Court, dominated by very conservative justices, was blocking the program endorsed by a majority of the voters. But the electorate that had given that program an overwhelming vote of confidence was less enthusiastic about the President's attack on the Supreme Court. Opponents of the New Deal were able to mobilize opinion against the President by capitalizing on the symbol of the Supreme Court as the inviolable guardian of the Constitution standing above the noisome sea of politics. The President was accused of wanting to be a dictator and, like Hitler and Mussolini, to subjugate the judiciary to his own will. Many persons who agreed with the President that something should be done to restrict the power of the Supreme Court could not accept the method he suggested. Others believed that while the President's proposal would be an expedient solution to the immediate problem, its ultimate result would be to weaken an important instrument for protecting individual liberties.

Yet the President was not without resources. Although many could not agree on what should be done, they could not deny that Supreme Court justices were blocking legislation endorsed by the electorate. The President had the support of powerful groups, but the Supreme Court itself dealt the final blow to the President's program to "pack" the Court. It simply reversed its direction. Between March and June 1937, in the midst of the debate over the President's proposal, the High Court upheld a state minimum wage law, the Farm Mortgage Act, the amended Railway Labor Act, the Wagner Act, the Social Security Act. Justice Roberts and Chief Justice Hughes, who theretofore had voted with the conservatives, switched their support to the liberals.[34] Here was the famous "switch in time that saved nine." No longer did the Supreme Court stand in the way of social and economic legislation. The President's reform proposal was rendered superfluous, as far as the immediate crisis was concerned, and it was defeated in Congress.

Did the Supreme Court follow the election returns? There is no way of knowing why Justice Roberts and the Chief Justice changed their position. But they could hardly have been blind to the 1936 election returns. They might well have interpreted these returns to mean that if the Supreme Court persisted in denying to the national and state governments the power that a majority of the people wanted them to exercise, it might be the Supreme Court and not the New Deal that would have been destroyed.

THE SUPREME COURT UNDER FIRE—1957-60

The most recent attempt to alter the course of judicially made policies stems from the Supreme Court's pro-civil liberties decisions. After its 1954 School Segregation Decisions, southern Democrats opened a furious attack on the Court, but most northern conservatives, though disturbed by the Supreme Court's failure to interpose any objections to legislative regulation of business enterprises, refrained from joining these denunciations. Southern Democrats,

---

[34] Merlo J. Pusey in his biography, *Charles Evans Hughes*, 2 vols. (Macmillan, 1951), Chapters 69-71, argues that Hughes did not change his position. But see E. S. Corwin's review of this book for contrary position, *The American Political Science Review* (December 1952), pp. 1167-1175.

despite the sound and fury of their comments, were making no headway. So long as the Court was merely taking on defenders of racial segregation, it was in little danger of retaliatory action.

But in 1956 when the Court took a more positive civil-liberties stand in behalf of so-called political defendants, many security-minded congressmen were added to its list of vocal critics. In August 1958 the chief justices of thirty-six state supreme courts rebuked the Supreme Court for paying too little attention to the rights of states. Early in 1959 the American Bar Association's House of Delegates threw its considerable prestige into the fray by adopting a critical report charging the Supreme Court with deciding cases "in such a manner to encourage or increase communist activity." In Congress dozens of proposals have been introduced "to do something about the Supreme Court." [35] These vary from impeachment resolutions to suggestions that the Constitution be amended to make justices elective, to bills depriving the Court of jurisdiction to hear cases involving threats to national security.

Southern Democrats have let their Republican allies carry the attack by playing down the issue of segregation. None of the anti-Court bills given serious congressional consideration would directly affect the Supreme Court's decisions dealing with racial segregation. But the attack has served the southern Democrats' purposes by giving credence to their charges of "judicial tyranny."

Although, as we have seen, attacks on the Supreme Court are not novel, this most recent controversy is unprecedented because for the first time *conservative* congressmen are mounting the offensive. In 1937 it was a New Deal President versus the Supreme Court—today it is a conservative faction of Congress versus the Supreme Court. Many of those who in 1936 were roundly denouncing President Roosevelt for trying to influence the work of the Supreme Court are now among the most active proponents of anti-Court legislation. On the other hand, many liberals who felt that President Roosevelt was justified in attacking the Court in 1937 today accuse the conservative critics of trying to undermine our constitutional system.

Defenders of the Court have been able through careful parliamentary maneuvering to avert substantial anti-Court legislation, and the elections of 1958 resulted in the defeat of some of the Court's most outspoken critics. But in 1937, although the President's plan to "pack" the Court was defeated, the Court altered its interpretation of the Constitution. Hence the full impact of the most recent controversy over the Supreme Court is not to be measured only by the fate of "anti-Court" or "corrective" legislation. The Supreme Court will be able to make its civil-liberties decisions stick only to the extent that these decisions are supported by a considerable portion of the electorate.

---

[35] See R. J. Steamer, "Statesmanship or Craftsmanship—Current Controversy Over the Supreme Court," *Western Political Quarterly* (June 1958), pp. 265 ff.; Sheldon D. Elliott, "Court-Curbing Proposals in Congress," *Notre Dame Lawyer* (August 1958), p. 597.

The main thrust of judicial policies cannot remain too far outside the main channels of American public life.

True, the Constitution is what the judges say it is. But ultimately the Constitution is what the people want it to be. The American democratic system has reached a pragmatic compromise between the desire for the independence of the judges and the desire to provide political checks on their policymaking activities. Judges have no armies or police to execute their laws. They have no authority to levy taxes to support their activities. In the long run they must adapt themselves to the nature and demands of government by the people. Ultimately the power they enjoy rests upon their retention of public support. No better criterion for determining the power of a government official has ever been invented.

How Can We Control
Our Leaders?

or the last six chapters we have been talking about "those guys in Washington," the people who are usually blamed for "the mess" there—whatever "mess" may exist at the moment. These are the men who rule us. But we in turn rule them. This two-way relationship between the people and their leaders is both the glory and the perplexity of democratic government. There is more to democracy, however, than this simple relationship between the governors and the governed. Self-government is also a complex of crisscrossing and interacting connections among all the groups that make up the people and all the leaders who represent the groups.

Sometimes we forget that the men in Washington—President, congressmen, judges, administrators—are *representatives*. They are leaders of *groups* (see Chapter 12), some small, some large, some very noisy, some hardly audible. We say that "the President wants the immigration laws revised but Senator So-and-So doesn't." This is just a shorthand way of saying that "some Americans, including the President, want the immigration laws revised; but other Americans, including Senator X, do not." It is not simply a private fight between the President and a senator in Washington. Politics is a running battle in which every one of us is caught up directly or indirectly.

What our leaders do, in short, depends in large part on the attitudes and activities of people throughout the country. It works the other way, too. The attitudes and activities of leaders help shape those of private citizens. This is as it should be in "government by the people."

By this time we have some idea of how self-government works. We have seen how the several parts operate—how congressmen, presidents, bureaucrats, judges, party leaders, interest-group spokesmen, and most of the rest of the people enter into the political process. Now let us put all these parts together and see what happens when the country is suddenly faced with an urgent political problem—in this case, a serious strike that took place in 1952. The parenthetical comments refer back to some of the aspects of the process described in preceding pages.

The Steel Strike of 1952

On November 1, 1951, the United Steel Workers of America, CIO, notified the steel industry that they wished to discuss new provisions to go into effect when their contract expired at the end of the year. For six weeks labor and management bargained. The union asked for wage increases, fringe benefits, a guaranteed annual wage, and a union shop. Management offered a small wage increase and refused to consider a union shop. It became obvious that no agreement would be reached. On December 17, 1951, President Philip Murray of the Steel Workers called a strike for the last day of the month.

A steel strike is damaging at any time. During the winter of 1952 it would have been perilous. American troops in Korea were fighting with weapons made largely of steel. America was supplying munitions for most of the rest of the United Nations forces there. The nation was rearming as the "cold war" intensified, and had adopted wage and price controls to forestall inflation. Now a serious strike loomed. What should be done? Who should do it?

On December 22 the President of the United States referred the dispute to the Wage Stabilization Board. Composed of representatives of labor, management, and the public, this board was responsible for insuring that wage increases would not jeopardize the nation's anti-inflation program. It also could make recommendations for wage settlements. The union agreed to postpone the strike until the board could hold a hearing and make its recommendations. (The *threat* of a strike is often as effective as a strike itself.)

The board held hearings and deliberated for two months. Representatives of union and management argued their cases. Charge was met by countercharge. Each side accused the other of distorting the facts and attempting to mislead the public. On March 20, 1952, the board recommended immediate benefits of around twenty cents an hour, with increases to total about twenty-six cents an hour by the end of the year. It also recommended a union shop (see page 649). The industry members of the board violently dissented. So did many congressmen and most newspapers. The public members had failed to represent the public and had sold out to labor, some businessmen charged. (Note the characteristic tendency of each group to identify its idea of the public interest as the only good one and to accuse the opposition of looking out only for its own special interest. Defining the "public interest" was of course the point of the dispute.)

The steel executives rejected the board's recommendations, insisting that they would agree only to the 13.7 cent "package" that had been recom-

[handwritten marginal note: This steel strike bad because needed ammunition at Korea — Wage increase feared would lead to inflation]

mended by the industry members of the board. Labor, on the other hand, was willing to accept the board's recommendations.

But wages were only one side of the problem. What about the price of steel? The Office of Price Stabilization had authority to bar or permit a price increase. Steel spokesmen said that they would need a price increase of twelve dollars a ton to pay for the recommended wage increase. Labor maintained that steel profits were so high the industry could pay the wage increase with only a slight increase in price—no more than $2.86 a ton that the price stabilization law automatically permitted. Price officials agreed with labor. It was clear that the workers would readily get their whole wage increase if management could get its price increase. But the labor officials refused to back up the steel heads' demands for higher steel prices.

The national nominating conventions were approaching and the presidential election would take place a few months later. Industry heads charged the Truman Administration with selling the public out in order to buy labor's votes. Labor and administration leaders accused the steel companies of seeking big profits at the expense of the workers and the public. Management argued that wage increases would cause inflation; labor contended that price increases would cause inflation. A fight for public support was under way. (Elections come so frequently in the United States that any important and protracted dispute among major groups becomes an election issue.)

By April no agreement was in sight. Labor prepared to use its classic weapon to enforce its demands. A strike was called for April 8. (It would be interesting to discover how this decision was made within the union—the division, if any, among union officials on the advisability of calling a strike—how concerned they were over the reaction of various nonlabor groups to the strike. In times of crisis interest-group organizations keep their affairs to themselves. Chances are that the crisis produced great unity in the union and a willingness to follow the leadership.)

In the White House the President was seeking advice. The Secretary of Defense warned that "a work stoppage in the steel industry will result immediately in serious curtailment of production of essential weapons and munitions of all kinds." Political and labor advisers went over various lines of action. Memos and reports were channeled to the President's desk. Some advised the President to use the Taft-Hartley Act and seek a court injunction preventing the union from striking for another eighty days. (In an election year a Democratic President would be reluctant to resort to legislation that was anathema to most labor leaders.) Some argued that the President should order price-stabilization officials to grant steel price increases and thus settle the whole issue. Others in the Administration held that this would wreck the economy and benefit industry at the expense of the "public." (Advice from all the experts—but the *President* had to make the decision. He alone was the elected representative and ultimately it was his responsibility. Failure to act would have been just as significant a decision as action itself.)

On April 8 the President by executive order instructed the Secretary of Commerce to take possession of the steel companies. The steel workers could not strike against the government. (The steel heads were still actually managing the industry, but the *symbolic* situation had changed). At the same time the President went to Congress and the country. To Congress he sent a message explaining why he had felt compelled to act and asking for congressional guidance. He defended his authority to act on the grounds that as chief executive and commander in chief he had the inherent power to act in an emergency and then to report to Congress on his action. (Note the President's use of several of his constitutional and extraconstitutional powers; the President was acting here as chief of state.) The President received little support in Congress.

That night President Truman made a nationwide radio address. He reviewed the course of the dispute and blamed the steel industry for failing to abide by the recommendations of the Wage Stabilization Board. The steel executives, he said, had made "outrageous" demands for price increases and were "recklessly forcing a shutdown of the steel mills." His opponents rose to the challenge. The next night a steel executive speaking for all the companies made a nationwide radio and television address. "Happily," he said, "we still live in a country where a private citizen may look the President in the eye and tell him that he was wrong." He charged that the President was playing election politics, that the Wage Stabilization Board was partisan, that the President "takes at least two thirds" of steel profits in taxes. "Is your boy making $1.70 an hour in Korea?" he asked. (Note the use by both sides of propaganda techniques such as name-calling and transfer, and the ingenious *personalization* of the issues—that is, *Mr. Truman* takes the taxes.)

The country—or at least the informed part of it—began to debate constitutional issues. (Political controversy often becomes clothed in legal terminology, and judges are expected to place immediate controversy in more long-range terms.) Both sides cited their authorities. Industry spokesmen, lawyers, Republican leaders, and most editorial writers and radio commentators held that the President had exceeded his authority. Defenders of the President pointed to historical examples. The Supreme Court had never addressed itself directly to the inherent powers of the President; so there were few clues in the law books. (One of the important aspects of the whole debate was that both sides assumed without arguing that if Congress had authorized the seizure there would be no doubt of its constitutionality. The idea that *any* branch of the national government could authorize such a seizure would have been hotly denied by many only fifteen years before.[1])

The steel companies turned to the courts as well as to the people. They went into the United States District Court to seek an injunction against the Secretary of Commerce to prevent the government from continuing to control steel. On April 29 Federal Judge Pine granted the injunction requested by

---

[1] For a detailed treatment of this legal action and its background see Alan F. Westin, *The Anatomy of a Constitutional Law Case* (Macmillan, 1958).

the steel companies, accepting their arguments that they were suffering irreparable damage and that the President had no authority to take over steel in an emergency. But before the strike could be resumed by the workers, the Court of Appeals stayed Judge Pine's order until the Supreme Court had had an opportunity to rule on the case.

Now attention was focused on the Supreme Court. Newspapers reported the give-and-take between the attorneys and the justices. Prominent among the steel companies' attorneys was the distinguished John W. Davis, onetime Democratic nominee for President. (Could the government's $12,000-a-year attorneys compete successfully with $50,000-a-year corporation lawyers?) All nine justices had been appointed by Democratic Presidents, four by President Truman. Those who were critical of the Roosevelt-Truman appointees thought that they never could be counted on to stand up against the President. But on June 2 the Court ruled, six to three, against the presidential action. (Appointing members of the Court obviously does not give the President a group of "yes-men.") This notable case was *Youngstown Co. v. Sawyer.*

Six of the justices agreed that the injunction should be issued, but they could not agree why. Justice Black asserted that the President had no inherent authority to seize private property even during an emergency—at least this particular emergency. Justices Frankfurter and Burton stressed the fact that Congress had withheld from the President the power of seizure when it passed the Taft-Hartley Act. Justice Clark held that Congress had laid down specific procedures and that the President must follow these procedures. Many questions remained unanswered, but the Court had given its official support to the steel companies and to all those who felt that the President had gone too far. (Only a minority of congressmen had supported the President; the majority believed that he should have used the Taft-Hartley Act. Thus both a majority of Congress and the Supreme Court majority represented groups different from those represented by the President.)

On June 2 the plants were returned to their private owners. Immediately the workers struck. The nation's steel furnaces were banked. Collective bargaining was resumed, while each side jockeyed for public support. Discussion of the steel strike quickly merged into talk about the approaching party conventions. The Republicans nominated General Eisenhower and adopted a platform endorsing the principle of the union shop. (Republican leaders, seeking majority support in the coming election, knew that they could not risk antagonizing broad segments of labor.) On July 22 the Army's largest shell-making plant closed. Now the Democrats were assembling in their convention in Chicago. Before leaving for Chicago, President Truman called both sides to the White House. He took a firm line. The situation was desperate, he said, and a settlement must be reached. (Whatever his legal authority, a President can wield tremendous moral authority as leader of the nation.)

A new contract was announced on July 24. The workers received a raise of sixteen cents an hour, fringe benefits worth another 5.4 cents, and a modified union-shop contract. Steel received a price increase of $5.20 per ton for carbon steel. On signing the contract, the president of United States Steel called Murray "a great leader, an honest man and a great American," and Murray said equally nice things about the president of United States Steel. (After a crisis, rival groups "shake hands" in the manner of boxers after a championship bout.)

The strike was over, but its consequences were felt in many ways—in the election in the fall, in the economic situation, in war production, in constitutional doctrine, in popular attitudes. The significance of the episode for the study of American government is worth noting. Who was responsible for dealing with the crisis—the President? Congress? The courts? The union or the industry? Republicans or Democrats? Obviously all of these. But who's ultimately in charge here?

Rule by Concurrent Majority

The story of the steel strike, as the parenthetical comments suggest, illustrates many of the processes of democratic government in the United States—the role of President, congressmen, and judges, of parties and interest groups, of opinion leaders and followers, of economic power and military crisis, of old constitutional powers and new social legislation. The story suggests, too, the interrelationship of these forces; the events of the strike, like most events in a large and complex democratic system, were a tangle of individuals, interests, institutions, and ideas. But perhaps the story's most important lesson for us as students of American politics is that the *checks and balances* built into our government by the framers of the Constitution are still vital forces despite all the changes that have taken place in the past 170 years. And these checks and balances still sharply limit our leaders.

This system of limiting our leaders' power was described in Chapter 3. It may be useful, following our excursion through the highways and byways of American government and politics, to review it here. The framers sought to limit the powers of the national government in order to prevent arbitrary rule. They did so by granting it only limited power, by dividing up that power among the different branches of government, and by making the different branches of government responsible to different groups of people. "Ambition" was to "counteract ambition." [2] A popular majority could take control of the whole government only with great difficulty, if at all. Power was inextricably mingled and blended throughout the various branches of government.

The framers planned well. The system of intermingled powers and conflicting loyalties that they set up is still very much alive today. To be sure, some things have been changed. Senators are now directly elected by the voters, and

---

[2] *Federalist No. 51.*

our leaders clash differences of opinion this

Presidents virtually so. But the basic arrangement endures. President, senators, representatives, and judges are chosen by different electorates. Their terms of office vary. Their responsibilities and loyalties differ. And, as almost every newspaper tells us, their interests and ambitions often clash.

Consider the practical effects of this arrangement. It makes straight majority rule impossible. If, for example, a simple majority of the voters should elect a President, he would face powerful minorities entrenched in Congress, the Supreme Court, even the bureaucracy. Even if a majority of the voters should elect a President *and* a Congress, these minorities would still exist. Witness what happened to Franklin D. Roosevelt's programs after he was re-elected in 1936 with 62 per cent of the two-party vote. The Democratic party held 76 of the 96 seats in the Senate, and 333 of the 435 seats in the House. And yet, as we have seen, when Mr. Roosevelt tried to pack the Supreme Court, his court reform bill was beaten in the Senate. When he tried to assert control of the executive branch, Congress balked at his administrative reorganization bill. When he tried to purge anti-New Deal Democrats in Congress, he failed more often than he succeeded.

How, then, can government govern? How do we get things done? If the majority does not rule, who does? The answer is that we are governed by *shifting coalitions of minorities* rather than by *simple majorities.* Consequently, our government *can act only with the consent of the several major interests in society.* What are these interests? Most of them are economic, such as the big farm, labor, and business interests. Some are sectional, such as West and South. Some are religious, such as Catholics and Protestants. Some are national-origin, such as the Irish and the Italians. Each of these major interests has a voice in government actions. Each has some kind of modified veto over those actions.

This doctrine of *concurrent majority rule*—that is, rule by all the major interests and not by a simple majority of the people—has long been part of American political theory. A century ago John C. Calhoun stated the theory in extreme form. Calhoun wanted to safeguard the diversity of the American nation. He wanted to protect minority rights against the unchecked rule of numerical majorities. Calhoun, of course, had good reason to support such a theory. He was desperately anxious to prevent the North from oppressing the planter interests in the South. But the fact that he represented a minority interest made the theory no less impressive.

CONCURRENT MAJORITY RULE TODAY

Our system of concurrent majority rule today is not so extreme as Calhoun would have wanted. Very few single interests, if any, hold a complete and final veto over the rest of the community. But the main features of the system are with us, and the system shows itself in every one of our major governmental and political institutions. Minority blocs in Congress strengthen their power through their control of committees, the filibuster in the Senate, and other devices for obstructing the majority. Business is done by trading votes (logrolling) among the main interest groups involved. Powerful minorities show their hand also in the Supreme Court, in the bureaucracy, and even in the Cabinet. Even a candidate for President cannot be nominated if he has antagonized some minority group, such as Negroes, Catholics, or farmers.

Above all, our system of concurrent majority rule reveals itself in our *party system*. Neither major party stands for a definite ideology or program. Both major parties follow shifting courses and straddle important issues as they seek to pick up votes from this group and that. Both parties appeal to every major interest. Both parties attract all types of people—labor, businessmen, farmers, old people, young people, reformers, standpatters, rich, poor, upper class, middle class, working class, Negro, Irish, and so on. Whatever issue becomes popular, whatever group becomes powerful, both parties adapt their principles and move in to catch what votes they can. Unlike the ideological parties of Europe, American parties are mainly concerned not with expounding programs but with getting enough votes to win office.

Courtesy *Des Moines Register & Tribune* and Interlandi

"Gad, when I think of the power the people have . . . it just isn't fair. . . ."

Government by concurrent majority rule, in short, is a sort of "broker rule." Brokers act essentially as go-betweens; likewise broker rule is a system of government in which leaders mediate between interest groups, veering now right, now left, as political pressures rise and fall. Instead of acting for a firm, united party majority with a fairly set program, either liberal or conservative, the government tries to satisfy virtually all minority groups by giving them a voice in decisions and a veto over actions. In the pushing and hauling of political groups, the government does a sort of delicate balancing act. Its condition is always one of unstable equilibrium.

THE SYSTEM DEFENDED

Broker rule has its supporters. Many thoughtful Americans believe that government by concurrent majorities is the price we pay—and not a very large price—for the maintenance of unity in a great, sprawling, diverse nation such as ours. Their arguments go something like this:

Arguments for:

1. The system protects minorities. Broker rule does not hurt interest groups of any size because by definition it acts only with their support—or at least their acquiescence. At the same time the system defends individual rights, which often find expression in minority action.[3]

2. Broker rule safeguards our diversity. Our varied nationality, religious, economic, and ideological groups are both the pride and strength of America. Our system of government should reflect the rich diversity of our group life. "The very multiplicity of interests," Merle Fainsod has said, "their freedom to maneuver and combine, and the open character of the society in which newly felt demands may always find organizational expression insure against the possibility of a frozen society and the rise of centers of intransigence within it." In short, our society is *pluralistic;* should our government not be pluralistic too?

3. Broker rule tames down the extremists on both sides by giving them a stake in government—and by giving them favors from government. By thus absorbing groups on the right and left, the system minimizes conflict and hardship.[4]

4. Broker rule permits a dynamic, flexible political system just as laissez faire encourages a competitive, dynamic economy. Power is not concentrated at the top, but is distributed throughout society. Everyone—not just a few key people—gets a chance to take part in the job of running the government.

5. Clearly, broker rule is the price of unity. It prevents our political parties from becoming hopelessly divided on ideological grounds, because each party embraces a diversity of interests stretching across the political spectrum. The parties serve as unifying agents. When they fail to do so, the nation is likely to become involved in civil war, as it did in 1861. "A federal nation," says one historian, "is safe so long as the parties are undogmatic and contain members with many contradictory views. But when the people begin to divide according to reason, with all the voters in one party who believe one way, the federal structure is strained."[5]

"How can we control our leaders?" Supporters of broker rule answer the question this way: Give our leaders limited power under the Constitution. Give them the means to check one another. Give them the ambition to check one another. Make them responsible to different combinations of voters—especially to shifting combinations of minority groups. Make it difficult for them to represent a simple majority of the people, at least for any length of time. Above all, prevent them from governing through a strong party representing an organized majority.

---

[3] Pendleton Herring, *The Politics of Democracy* (Norton, 1940), pp. 92-94.
[4] Herbert Agar, *Pursuit of Happiness* (Houghton Mifflin, 1938), p. 198.
[5] Herbert Agar, *The Price of Union* (Houghton Mifflin, 1950), pp. 689-690.

BROKER RULE CRITICIZED

Many Americans dislike certain features of broker or concurrent majority rule. They complain:

1. Broker rule is unrepresentative. True, it tends to give every big minority interest a voice in decisions. But leaders of organized interests are often not truly representative of the members of those groups. And what about the millions of Americans not organized in vocal, self-seeking groups? Does not broker rule ignore them?

2. Broker rule results in parties that do not stand for much of anything. The choice between them is often one between Tweedledum and Tweedledee. If people think that their parties will not take strong stands on important issues, they may begin to suspect that democratic government evades problems instead of solving them. If this suspicion hardens into conviction, they may turn to extremist leaders and parties, especially in time of social conflict and economic depression.

3. Broker rule may be all very well for a laissez-faire economy and a loose social organization, such as we had in the nineteenth century. But the world today is putting heavy demands on government, and these demands cannot be met by a polity of pressure groups. According to some observers, "the expanding responsibilities of modern government have brought about so extensive an interlacing of governmental action with the country's economic and social life that the need for coordinated and coherent programs, legislative as well as administrative, has become paramount." [6] The shifting, unstable alliances of minority interests cannot do the job of translating nationwide policies into firm decisions and actions.

4. Broker rule does *not* protect diversity. Heterogeneity, minority interests, and individual rights thrive best in a society that is productive, stable, and secure. A depression-ridden, frightened society cannot afford—or at least does not tolerate—diversity. Only positive action can keep the nation productive and strong. If democratic government cannot act, people may turn in frustration to more drastic solutions. In short, strong—not weak—government is necessary to safeguard democracy, which in turn protects diversity. [7]

5. Nor does broker rule lead to unity in the long run. On the contrary, by responding to pressures it sets group against group, section against section. Broker rule does not achieve genuine unity, but only temporary agreements and fleeting coalitions. By responding to minority pressures so readily, it fails to achieve a basic consensus of a majority of the people, and such a consensus is the only basis of real unity.

---

[6] "Toward a More Responsible Two-Party System," A Report of the Committee on Political Parties of the American Political Science Association, *The American Political Science Review,* Vol. XLIV (1950), Pt. 2, p. 31.

[7] See Max Lerner, *It Is Later Than You Think* (Viking, 1938).

Naturally enough, most supporters of broker rule do not seek major changes in the American system. Some of them might want improvements here and there to gain more efficiency in normal times and more stability in times of crisis, but on the whole they are glad to stand pat.

Not so the opponents of broker rule. Some of them urge *constitutional reform* designed to bring President and Congress into closer collaboration (see Chapter 18). By allowing the Chief Executive to dissolve the legislature and appeal to the country, the two branches would be compelled to work together. Other opponents of broker rule take a different tack. Constitutional reform leading to cabinet government, they fear, might bring instability. Even if it united President and Congress, it might fail to elicit teamwork from the other two sets of national leaders, namely bureaucrats and judges. The only hope, according to this argument, is party reform.

Party Reform:
Pros and Cons

Those who wish to improve our governmental system by working through our political party system believe that the essential structure of our national *government* cannot—and need not—be changed, but that our *political organization* must—and can—be improved.

Their reasoning runs as follows: The framers devised not only *governmental* checks and balances. They planned (as we have seen) for *political* checks and balances, also. Consequently any real attempt to unify and brace our governmental system must attack the problem in the political area, not the governmental. All the structural and mechanical reforms in the world are futile if our rulers continue to respond to shifting and conflicting groups of voters. Reorganizing the government—whether through mere tinkering or through basic constitutional changes—will do no good unless it is accompanied by political reorganization reaching deep down into the grass roots. Given such reorganization, our eighteenth-century government could effectively face the problems of the twentieth.

WANTED: MORE RESPONSIBLE PARTIES

The crux of the problem, according to this argument, lies in the make-up of our parties.[8] They are, as we saw in Chapter 13, loose associations of state and local groups, lacking in effective national machinery or real national cohesion. National and state party organizations are virtually independent of each other. Leadership is diffused. And yet the *potential* of our political parties is

---

[8] The arguments for party government described here are taken largely from "Toward a More Responsible Two-Party System," A Report of the Committee on Political Parties (E. E. Schattschneider, ed.) of the American Political Science Association, *The American Political Science Review*, Vol. XLIV (1950), No. 3, Pt. 2.

tremendous. They can be whatever the people want them to be; no constitutional amendments need be passed, no basic governmental institutions changed. And this is the time that the party potential must be realized. For today, the government must draw up and enact a broad range of social, economic, and military policy. Strong parties are needed to help formulate, coordinate, and develop popular support for these vital programs.

To party reformers the issue is *responsibility*. They maintain that parties should be more representative of the general public and of their own members. Parties should be less responsive to pressures from organized minority groups and local politicos, and more concerned with developing positive policies reflecting a broad national consensus of party membership. The party in power must be responsible for enacting the policies on which it won election. It must be willing to discipline its members in office—especially those in Congress—if they desert the party platform. All this goes for the opposition party, too. It must act as the critic of the party in power, constantly developing and presenting alternative policies. It must serve as a strong and united loyal opposition.

Several specific proposals have been made for enhancing party responsibility:

1. *Build up and improve the national party organization.* The national convention should continue as the party's main organ, but it should become more representative and more active. It should meet every year or two instead of every four years, as at present. A new party council of about fifty members should serve as the full-time governing organ of the party. The council would plan party strategy, interpret the platform, and run the organization. Above all—in the case of the party in power—it would take responsibility for pushing through the party platform—a task that involves coordinating the whole party, national, regional, state, and local.

2. *Make the party platform mean something.* Today no one takes party platforms very seriously. They are collections of pious hopes and vague promises. A newly nominated presidential candidate may interpret his party's platform as freely as he wishes during the campaign and later. Party platforms, it is proposed, should be drawn up at least every other year to keep them abreast of the times. State and local platforms should be consistent with the national platform. A broad range of groups within the party, including congressmen, should take part in platform-making, and the adopted platform should be binding on all members.

3. *Strengthen the party in Congress.* Advocates of more responsible parties see Congress as the graveyard of party hopes and party pledges. Congressional party organization, they suggest, should be tightened up. The separate leadership groups in both the Senate and the House should be merged into one responsible leadership committee for each party in each chamber. These four committees would submit proposed policies to the party members and would direct the legislative program. The caucus should meet more often, and

its decisions should carry greater weight. Party rebels should be prevented from serving as chairmen of important committees, even if it means violating the seniority rule. At any rate, the power of individual chairmen, of the House Rules Committee, and of senatorial filibusters should be curbed.

4. *Develop party activity at the grass roots.* Supporters of stronger national parties believe that the problem is largely one of political participation. They know, for example, that the only way to make congressmen more responsible to the party is to make the party mean more to the congressmen. The local party, with the full support of national party leaders, should build a strong democratic organization to carry the burden of congressional campaigns. Local party groups should meet more frequently to discuss and initiate policy. Party membership should be made more meaningful by imposing certain obligations on all members, such as paying dues and taking part in party activities. In return, party members would be assured of party policies that reflected their views and party leaders who would act on those views. Democracy within the parties would be invigorated by more widespread participation in party debate and action.

5. *Reform our electoral machinery.* The electoral-college method of electing the President allots all the electoral votes of a state to the candidate who wins the most popular votes, no matter how small his margin may be. Such a

"Relax—they only think about us at election time."

Herblock in
The Washington Post

system fosters one-party monopoly in certain sections of the country, especially in the South. The electoral college should be modified to give all sections a real voice in presidential elections. Nominating procedures that weaken party cohesiveness, such as the open primary and cross-filing, should be abandoned. Barriers to voting should be lifted. Voting should be made as easy as possible through such means as permanent registration and the short ballot (see Chapter 14).

THE PRICE OF PARTY RESPONSIBILITY

So much for the specific proposals for enhancing party responsibility. We still must face the question: Would party responsibility lead to a more democratic system of government? Would it give us greater control over our leaders?

The party reformers answer "yes." They believe that an invigorated party system would forge a stronger link between the people and the government. The men in power would be the leaders of the majority party. They would be bound by the wishes of the party rank and file, as embodied in the platform. If they ignored basic party policy, they would risk losing the support of sections of the party, and perhaps the next election as well. Thus the millions of party members would not only *sustain* the government, they would also *constrain* it, by forcing it to abide by its mandate at the previous election. The opposition party would serve as another check on the rulers. By holding out alternative policies and by continuously criticizing the government, the opposition would strive to win over a majority of the voters at the next election. The opposition party, like the party in power, would act as a responsible organization.

Not all political scientists agree with this diagnosis or with the proposed cure. Some say these proposals underestimate the present extent of party responsibility. They cite cases where the parties have presented clear alternatives to the voters. They fear, too, that more discipline in the parties would cut down party competition in certain areas, for the national leaders of a strong party might enforce doctrines that were unpopular in certain localities (for example, racial equality in the South).[9] Not party discipline but *party competition* is the great need, according to this view. "Our parties are big and clumsy and loosely hung together," says Professor Ruth C. Silva, "because our country is big and clumsy and loosely hung together." Nevertheless, virtually all students of the problem agree that in a democracy party responsibility is an important goal, however it is achieved.

Notice the difference between the party-reform approach and the concurrent-majority approach. Advocates of party reform stress responsibility and accountability to the *popular majority* that has won an election. They value *strict majority rule*—the idea that when a majority of the people vote a set of party leaders into power, the new government represents that majority and is

9 Julius Turner, "Responsible Parties: A Dissent from the Floor," *The American Political Science Review* (March 1951), pp. 143-152.

responsible for enacting its wishes into law. In short, the victorious leaders have no obligation to respect the wishes of the unsuccessful popular minority. Broker rule, on the other hand, shuns strict majority action. In its allegiance to rule by a concurrent majority, it stresses representation of people with diverse views. Under broker rule various minorities or combinations of minorities use governmental machinery to achieve their aims. They work through now one branch of government, now another. Both parties and all major interest groups have a voice in every major governmental action. The government acts not for a relatively solid and identifiable group of voters ranged on one side of the fence, but for all sorts of groups and for both parties.

Many Americans fear the strict majority rule sought by the party reformers. They believe that the majority holds in it the seeds of tyranny. They feel that a realignment of parties (which would be necessary under a system of strict majority rule) would hustle all the conservatives into one party, all the liberals and radicals into the other. The result would be extremism, whatever party was in power. Broker rule, they suggest, minimizes conflict by absorbing forces on the right and left. Majority rule would result in violent wrenches in the whole society as first one party, then the other, came to power. And neither party would be really representative of the people as a whole. Far better, they say, for each party to be a cross section of all important viewpoints, interests, and sections. This is the price of unity.

The party reformers deny all this. They maintain that majority rule must be safe because the majority, by definition, must embrace a tremendous variety of attitudes and interests. A simple, nationwide, popular majority is the least dangerous kind of backing for a ruling group, they say. It forces the leaders to act in the interests of a tremendous diversity of voters. Thus a popular majority—and hence a government based on the majority party—carries built-in checks and balances.[10] Minorities—not majorities—tend to be extremist. Majority rule, the party reformers add, is not prone to violate minority rights. They point to Great Britain as an example of a system of party government and majority rule that has fully protected the rights of minorities.

Opponents of majority rule fear that the majority, acting rashly, may make fatal mistakes. The present governmental system, with all its hesitations and delays, forces the rulers to think twice before acting. Government based on a party majority, they say, would command such strength in the White House and Congress that it could act rashly. Party reformers answer that the great need of the day is *action*. It is better, they say, to run the risk of making a few mistakes than to make the fatal error of not acting at all. Broker rule means that government can do little until all powerful interests in both parties have been appeased by compromises and concessions. Majority rule enables government to move ahead once a consensus has been achieved among a majority of the people. And a strong and responsible party, they conclude, is the

---

[10] H. S. Commager, *Majority Rule and Minority Rights* (Oxford Univ. Press, 1943), pp. 57 ff.

vital agent both in achieving that consensus and in organizing our divided government for rapid and effective action.

Needed: Responsible Leaders

This matter of the urgency of action deserves a few more words. But first a summary of the main points that have been presented in this chapter so far:

1. The steel strike of 1952 illustrated that our national leaders in Washington hold conflicting beliefs and loyalties and respond to conflicting alignments of voters.

2. The conflicts in Washington do not happen by chance; they are simply another example of our political system at work. The framers carefully planned a system of checks and balances with *different officials* responding to *different political forces.*

3. Our system is not one of strict majority rule but one of *concurrent majority rule* or "broker rule," which allows *combinations of minorities* to govern.

4. Broker rule is defended on the grounds that it produces flexible government, prevents extremism, protects diversity. It is attacked on the grounds that it results in weak government, disunity, inefficiency, and irresponsibility.

5. The chief alternative to broker rule is *majority rule;* supporters of this system, stressing the need for more *responsible* leadership, feel that the only way to strengthen our government is through a more *centralized* and *responsible party system.*

6. Critics of majority rule combined with a stronger party system fear that these would enable the party in power to tyrannize over the minority and would end up in rash, extremist government.

Each proposal, as this chapter has shown, has much to recommend it. But can we let the matter drop here? Is there no choice between the different paths? The answer depends largely on one's diagnosis of the main ills of the American system of government. The chief question one can raise about that system is: *In a time of deep and drawn-out crisis, can our government act boldly and positively and persistently over a long period of time, commanding a reliable source of popular support and a steady flow of governmental power?* In short, can our government *govern?*

WHAT KIND OF LEADERSHIP?

Arnold J. Toynbee, the famous English historian, has concluded that "the ultimate criterion and the fundamental cause of the breakdowns which precede disintegrations is an outbreak of *internal discords* through which societies forfeit their faculty of self-determination." [11] When groups in a community fail

---

[11] Arnold J. Toynbee, *A Study of History,* abridgement by D. C. Somervell (Oxford Univ. Press, 1947), p. 365. Italics supplied.

to resolve their differences, the community may disintegrate. Such a result has been called *stasis*. The threat of *stasis* may be especially grave in the United States, for our governmental system, as we have seen, is particularly subject to deadlock. During prolonged military or economic emergency, hostility among persons and groups might be reflected in a government ridden by warring blocs unable to agree on a program of action.

If, then, the great weakness of American government seems to be its failure to overcome internal divisions and to face the challenge of threats at home or abroad, what can be done? The answer seems to be: *"Provide for effective and responsible leadership."* Effective leadership can do several important things. First, it can rise above disputes and find areas of *agreement*. Second, it can *educate* and *persuade* people. And third, because effective leadership can do both these things, it can spur men and governments to *action*.

But leadership must be *responsible,* too. In a democracy men have a deep, almost instinctive fear of the man on horseback. And quite rightly. "One-man rule" and democracy are obviously incompatible. On the other hand, democracy not only can afford leadership—it *needs* leadership. "Without leadership alert and sensitive to change," Franklin D. Roosevelt said, "we are all bogged up or lose our way." By the same token, however, leadership must meet the tests of responsibility. These tests are crude but clear. Does the leader keep in touch with the rank and file even when he is ahead of his followers in his thinking and planning? Does he observe the basic rules of the game, such as the maintenance of civil liberties and free elections? Is he working, ultimately, for the interests of his nation or party as a whole, or merely for the interests of himself and his immediate coterie?

The American system of government makes effective and responsible leadership very difficult. Because of the factors discussed in Chapter 18, it is to the Presidency that we turn for such leadership, for only this office has the necessary constitutional, political, and administrative resources to lead the nation. Yet the President, as we have seen, is constantly hamstrung by minority groups operating in key places in Congress, the courts, and the bureaucracy. Some Presidents have been overcome by these groups. Others have exerted leadership despite them. But the danger, as we have seen, is that the President may violate constitutional provisions or political understandings. Lincoln's early conduct of the war without Congress, and Franklin D. Roosevelt's blunt threats to enact legislation on his own, are cases in point.

THE ART OF BEING GOVERNED

How, then, can we gain responsible yet effective leadership? Surely not by standing still. Our present system seems to hobble our leaders without effectively controlling and channeling the flow of needed power. What about the two basic courses outlined in this chapter and in Chapter 18?

The first basic course—constitutional or governmental reform—might strengthen responsible leadership, but we cannot be sure of this. The minor governmental changes, such as a question hour, might improve communication and understanding between Capitol and White House, but it is hard to see how they would allow more presidential leadership or hold it more responsible. The more sweeping proposals, involving constitutional changes, might make the President more responsible to Congress, but they might tie him too closely to the legislative apron strings.

There remains the second alternative: stronger parties. The preceding discussion of party reform centered largely on the possibilities of achieving more coordination and responsibility in our national government. These are important goals, but another role that a rejuvenated party system might play is to allow the President the power and discretion he must have as a leader, and yet to set some limits to his power. For a stronger majority party would play a more important part in electing the President, in furnishing popular support to him in office, and in compelling the different governmental agencies and political factions in Washington to pull together as a team. In doing so, the majority party (the one that polled the most electoral votes at the previous presidential election) would become more indispensable to the President and thus might be in a position to erect a "go slow" sign when the President seemed to go too fast for his followers. More particularly, the party might surround the President with other nationally minded party leaders, much as the British Prime Minister is surrounded by powerful party leaders who have posts in his cabinet.

In essence, this approach calls for more emphasis on *majority rule.* It means tying the President more tightly to the majority that elected him or sustains him, and freeing him from the fetters that minority groups fasten on him in Congress and elsewhere. Under a real system of majority rule the President must heed the party rank and file and consult its leaders before taking important steps. But he need not gain the support of *every* important minority before acting. In this sense presidential leadership and presidential responsibility to the majority party represent a sort of golden mean between Calhoun's concurrent-majority rule on the one hand and caesaristic, irresponsible leadership on the other. The President may still need to educate his popular majority, to render articulate their indistinct feelings, but he must abide by the majority program, however broadly conceived. The majority, in short, must be not only the basis of presidential *power* but also the source of presidential *containment.*

Whichever of these two courses one may choose, the problem of responsible leadership puts the basic question of this chapter—"How can we control our leaders?"—in a different light. That question cannot be solved by loading down our leaders with all kinds of checks and shackles. Such a procedure is self-defeating, for it renders leadership powerless to meet the economic, political, social, and military challenges of our time. We can rule our rulers best by making vigorous use of our civil liberties and free elections, by insisting that our leaders consult with the rank and file, and by holding our leaders ultimately responsible for their actions—and also by allowing our leaders to *act*. A successful democracy involves both the art of governing and the art of being governed.

PART **6**

Big Government in Action

A PROBLEM GUIDE

In Part Six we come to the *action* end of our political system— what government actually *does*. In these six chapters we shall explore the tremendous number and variety of federal functions, ranging from crucial foreign-policy decisions to the more routine domestic tasks, such as regulating interstate commerce. As we study these functions, we shall see that they raise anew all the five major sets of problems that we have explored in this book. These problems, originally listed above on pages 1-2, are worth reviewing here to see how they relate to the functions of the national government.

First, *the challenge to democratic government.* Do federal functions—the tasks that are finally carried out by Washington officials and others—prove the communist argument that demo-

cratic government serves mainly a few capitalistic interests rather than the people as a whole? Do the actual operations of government suggest that a democratic system cannot effectively perform the big tasks of strengthening and stabilizing the economy, aiding the underprivileged, promoting peace between business and labor, coping with farm problems, and the like? Chapters 25, 26, and 27 provide the factual background necessary for considering such questions.

Second, *the problem of constitutional government.* Because of the anarchical balance-of-power relation among nations, our leaders must be able to move quickly to head off crisis or to meet it head on. They must have power to mobilize and manage our armed forces without getting the consent of the voters, or even the consent of the legislators,

559

and sometimes without announcing their plans ahead of time. Under such conditions, what happens to our traditional constitutional processes of open debate and slow, deliberative action? Foreign and military programs require unity of purpose and action. Can we afford, then, the traditional splintering of power between the executive and legislative branches, the traditional supremacy of civilian over military leaders? These and related problems are most sharply raised in Chapters 22, 23, and 24.

Third, *the problem of individual rights.* This set of problems is not put as squarely in Part Six as in earlier chapters. But the increasing role of the federal government does raise the basic question of whether big government narrows or broadens individual liberty and initiative. Are we witnessing "creeping socialism" that may deprive Americans of their traditional rights against government? Or can federal functions, such as aid to education, help *expand* liberty? Such questions are implicit in Chapters 25, 26, and 27.

Fourth, *the problem of popular representation.* For whom does the federal government perform its immense variety of tasks? Does it serve major needs of the people as a whole, or does it actually operate on behalf of hundreds of special interests? Does federal regulation of interest groups such as business or labor—regulation ostensibly undertaken for the general welfare—actually turn out to be protection of that group at the expense of the public interest? The material in Chapters 25 and 26 raises such questions. The problem of whether our fiscal machinery—raising, lending, spending money, and so forth—is capable of serving the interests of the whole nation is taken up in Chapter 27.

Fifth, *the problem of responsible leadership.* The officials administering federal functions have great discretion and power. Do the people as a whole, acting through elected civilian officials, have adequate control over bureaucrats, technicians, military men? In matters of foreign and military policy, should federal officials be responsible to the people as a whole through *bipartisan* procedures, or to the party in power favoring foreign policies endorsed by a majority of the people, or to various organized minorities or interest groups? Or—the other side of the same coin—does our governmental system allow our leaders enough power to act quickly and comprehensively when such action is needed, at the same time holding those leaders ultimately responsible to the people for their performance in office?

CHAPTER 22

Foreign Policy:
Politics and Problems

One momentous fact dominates foreign-policy making in this country: The United States exists in a world of sovereign and independent nations. There is no world government that can guarantee to each of them its life, liberty, or property. There is little formal machinery for settling disputes. In contrast to the ordered relations of people *within* nations, the relations *among* nations tremble in a state of semianarchy. World order rests on a precarious balance-of-power system and on a mere handful of international rules and customs.

Some day the present system of sovereign states may come to an end. A single nation may conquer the world and impose, as Hitler tried to do, a "new order" directed from one supercapital. Or the peoples of the world may some day join hands and establish a world government capable of making and enforcing law for everyone everywhere. But these are future possibilities, not present-day realities. For good or for ill, the present system of sovereign independent states is the international framework in which the United States must strive to achieve its objectives.

What are these objectives? Have they changed significantly over the eighteen decades of our national existence? Who determines the objectives and the general means of reaching them? What role is played by organized interests, political parties, public opinion as a whole? What is the role of the United Nations in our foreign-policy making? How democratic is the procedure of making foreign policy in the United States?

The United States in a Changing World

The chief objective of American foreign policy has been to safeguard the security of the United States. Given the nature of the world we live in, our objective could be none other than this. To be sure, American politicians have often preferred to speak

561

in high moral terms about "safeguarding world peace" and "helping our little brown brothers" rather than to talk the blunt language of power politics. But beneath the high-flown rhetoric the central purpose has been fairly consistent.

We have not always achieved this objective. In a complex and turbulent world, the means of achieving maximum national security without war have sometimes been beyond the capabilities of our rulers and diplomats. To make things more difficult, the world about us, and the United States itself, have been in a process of constant change. What are some of the major forces at work?

SECURITY IN THE NINETEENTH CENTURY

In his famous *Farewell Address,* George Washington said: "Europe has a set of primary interests, which to us have none, or a very remote relation. Hence she must be engaged in frequent controversies, the causes of which are essentially foreign to our concerns. Hence, therefore, it must be unwise in us to implicate ourselves, by artificial ties, in the ordinary vicissitudes of her politics, or the ordinary combinations or collisions of her friendships or enmities." Quoted over the years by thousands of politicians, these words keynoted American foreign-policy making for decades.

During a good part of the nineteenth century this formula of "minding our own business" worked fairly well—not because American officials had some special knack of "keeping out of foreign entanglements," but because Americans "were the beneficiaries of a world balance of power which was unique and temporary but was confused in most American minds (when they were aware of it all) with the unchanging pattern of the cosmos." [1] The factors in that balance were threefold: Britannia ruled the waves, Europe was stable, and our oceans shielded us from attack.

The British navy controlled strategic sea lanes from Gibraltar to Hong Kong. And Britain stood between our virtually undefended shores and the other major powers. Any threat by a continental nation to the United States was a threat to Britain. At the same time, the European countries could neither permit Britain to regain control over her former colonies, nor allow any nation to threaten South America, because such action would upset the balance of power. That balance rested on a diffusion of military strength and on an elaborate network of treaties and understandings. Shaky though the structure was, it endured for a century.

The United States was not insulated completely from international power politics, of course. Americans fought a war with Britain at the beginning of the nineteenth century and a war with Spain at the end of it. We had frequent brushes with other great powers. We fought a war with Mexico. President Lincoln and Secretary of State Seward had their hands full trying to prevent

---

[1] F. L. Schuman, *International Politics*, 4th ed. (McGraw-Hill, 1948), p. 769.

foreign intervention during the Civil War. There were disputes with England over fisheries and boundaries, with France over her adventures in Mexico, with Germany and England over Venezuela. And yet the essential security of the United States was not seriously threatened in the hundred years after 1815.

Then, in the chaotic years after 1914, the relatively stable world of the nineteenth century came tumbling down around us.

SECURITY IN THE MID-TWENTIETH CENTURY

It is impossible to review here the past eventful fifty years. It is important, however, to survey the strange new world with which American foreign-policy makers must somehow cope.

Europe is no longer the pivot of world politics. Britain, France, Italy, and Germany are still important powers, but they are highly vulnerable to both economic and military stress. Dominating world politics are two superpowers, the United States of America and the Union of Soviet Socialist Republics. This new polarization of power has tended to pull the other nations into the orbits of the giants.

This sharp division between immense power blocs is perilous enough in itself. But along with it—and greatly intensifying it—is an ideological split. The new religion of communism stands as a challenge to believers in democracy and the values of democracy. Russian propaganda asserts that democracy in the West is actually rule by imperialistic, warmongering militarists and profiteers who would drown the world in blood for their own selfish ends. The Voice of America proclaims that communism in practice means rule by a self-elected elite, tyranny over the many, slave-labor camps, secret trials, mass purges, and ultimately war. The conflict between the Soviet Union and the non-communist nations is more than a traditional power struggle between nations; it is also a battle for the minds of men.

Another fact of international politics, which may be more significant in the long run, is the "awakening" of the peoples of Asia, the Middle East, and Africa. Nearly two billion people live in these lands. For centuries they have for the most part accepted squalor, hunger, and sickness as inevitable conditions of life. In the nineteenth century many of them were introduced to western ideas of liberty, equality, and progress, and western technical and scientific methods. Today that introduction is bearing fruit in national movements, reforms, and revolutions. India, Burma, and other countries have won their independence. Communists rule China. Japan is once again a sovereign nation. Other countries in Asia, the Middle East, and Africa are convulsed by social ferment, rebellion, and strife.

The superpowers have not ignored the explosive potentialities of this "revolution of rising expectations." The Soviet Union has been quick to take advantage of mass unrest and social revolution, and communism has a powerful appeal for people who feel they have nothing to lose but their chains. The democracies have been slower in sensing the profound consequences of the end of colonialism. But for defensive reasons, if no other, the United States and its allies have been forced to give economic and military aid to the governments in these areas and to step up their propaganda against Soviet communism. All this is a far cry from the day when American activities took place in sleepy consulates and embassies handling trivial duties that brought Americans into contact with a tiny fraction of the native population.

Finally, the world has seen immense technological changes in the past half-century. While ideologies have been tearing the world apart, technology has tended to make it one. The techniques of communications, transportation, and war have brought the continents of the world closer together than were the thirteen states of the Union in 1790. Techniques of war have been revolutionized. Russian rockets located on the northern shore of Europe can lay waste the industrial areas of the United States. Giant American airplanes can take off from Texas, drop hydrogen bombs deep in the heart of Europe, and land at British bases. Our geographical isolation, which, along with our powerful friends, once gave us a "cushion of time and distance," is no longer. Even the Arctic has become a strategic frontier.

NEW TIMES, NEW PROBLEMS

Such is the world that our foreign-policy makers look out on. A world sharply split geographically and ideologically but closely knit technologically. A world in which tens of millions of people are demanding a larger role. A world in which the decisive events of our times are those that affect our relations with other nations.

Has our thinking kept pace with these vast changes? In the nineteenth century a policy of isolationism worked, and twentieth-century America inherited a deep belief in "no foreign entanglements" as the best means of safeguarding our national security. Then, with shocking suddenness, national security seemed to demand that the United States play a positive and active part on the world stage. Slowly, grudgingly, almost belatedly, Americans, led by such men as Woodrow Wilson, Henry Stimson, Franklin D. Roosevelt, Cordell Hull, Wendell Willkie, Arthur Vandenberg, Harry S. Truman, Dwight D. Eisenhower, stirred themselves into action. Doubtless the world situation will continue to change, and new conditions will demand new thinking and new techniques.

Recently, our foreign policies have become increasingly linked with our domestic policies. The issue of federal protection of civil rights, for example, is sometimes discussed simply as a question of domestic politics or states' rights. But in the perspective of world politics the problem takes on a new dimension. The United States spends billions of dollars trying to win the friendship of the colored peoples in Africa and Asia. At the same time every denial of civil rights to Negroes is seized upon by our enemies to create ill will against the United States in these areas. Or take "domestic" economic matters. A high level of production not only supplies Americans with goods, it helps sustain our economic and military power abroad. A depression in this country dislocates the economies of other nations, vindicates communist predictions of "capitalist doom," causes political turmoil abroad as well as at home.

The makers of foreign policy in the United States must face all these facts of international politics. As if these were not difficult enough, they must also face the uncertainties and complexities of American politics at home. For example, in planning some new policy toward a foreign nation, American officials must consider not only the political situation in that nation, the attitude of our allies, the reaction of Soviet Russia and her satellites, and the effect on western military strength; they must also consider the attitude of the opposition party in this country and of the interest groups concerned (including the national-origin groups) and the state of public opinion. No wonder foreign-policy making is the most challenging and critical job facing Americans and their rulers today.

Who Makes Foreign Policy?

It is the awesome responsibility of those who formulate our foreign policy to determine the basic objectives vital to our national interests and to formulate programs to achieve these objectives. The chief instruments of these foreign-policy makers are military force, economic power, propaganda, and negotiation. They must determine what particular combination of these instruments should be brought into play.

Who is it that makes our foreign policy? The answer, of course, is the elected representatives of the people—namely Congress and the President. In earlier chapters of this book we discussed the roles of these representatives in foreign-policy making, and we shall return to them in later pages. But first we must look at the other officials who help the President make foreign policy.

THE PRESIDENT'S RIGHT-HAND MAN

The Constitution scatters responsibility for foreign-policy making among President, Senate, and the House of Representatives. But the initiative rests with the President. The President's role depends not only on his great constitutional powers, but also on his political influence, the attitudes of congressmen, and the very nature of foreign-policy making. But the job is too big for the President to perform without help.

The President's chief adviser is the *Secretary of State*, the most important member of the President's Cabinet and chief of the Department of State. The Secretary of State is politically important too. Many people who cannot identify any other member of the Cabinet know his name. The influence of the Secretary of State is suggested by the names of many famous American foreign policies or actions—the Hay Open Door Policy, the Kellogg Pact, the Stimson Doctrine, the Hull Reciprocal Trade Program, the Marshall Plan.

Officially the Secretary of State helps the President to make decisions. In actual practice the Secretary formulates a great deal of foreign policy himself and then secures the President's backing. According to Secretary of State Cordell Hull, "with the present immense network and mass of details involved in conducting our foreign relations, the President finds it impossible to keep familiar with more than the principal acts of the State Department. The Secretary of State must do the rest." But just how much influence the Secretary exercises depends largely on the President's personal desires. Presidents Harding, Coolidge, Hoover, and Eisenhower turned over to their Secretaries almost full responsibility for making important policy decisions. Other Presidents have taken a more active part; indeed, at times they have been their own Secretaries of State. Wilson and both Roosevelts are examples. Even so, important decisions on foreign policy are so numerous that both President and Secretary of State must usually play important roles.

The Secretary has a large department to administer. He receives many visits in Washington from foreign diplomats. He attends important international conferences and usually heads our delegation in the General Assembly of the United Nations. He makes key statements on foreign policy, sometimes speaking directly to the people. He visits other nations to confer with chiefs of state and foreign ministers. He deals directly with our ambassadors and ministers in other countries. As a leading member of the Cabinet, he may have a hand in shaping general administration policy.

In all these activities the Secretary of State serves as the President's "right-hand man." But he must also command support in Congress. Unless he enjoys congressional confidence, the foreign policies proposed by the President may have rough going on Capitol Hill. For this reason one of the Secretary's top assistants is assigned to keep congressmen in touch with the Secretary's policies and to serve as a channel of communication between the legislators and the Secretary. Broadly speaking, however, the Secretary is at the mercy of power relationships in Washington—the relations between President and Congress, the political strength of the President, the attitudes of key congressmen, all reflecting the temper of the country.

THE PRESIDENT'S LEFT-HAND MEN

Decades ago, the President needed to call only on the Secretary of State for advice in determining foreign-policy aims and formulating programs and policies. But today foreign policy is intimately related to every phase of governmental activity—finance, transportation, agriculture, commerce, and of course military activity. Suppose, for example, the President needed to make a decision on a matter of international trade. The specialized knowledge and expert help he would need are scattered throughout the executive structure, in the Departments of the Treasury, Commerce, Labor, and Agriculture, in the Federal Trade Commission, and in the United States Tariff Commission. The first Hoover Commission Task Force on Foreign Affairs pointed out that if the President wished to review United States policies toward Brazil, he would find the financial data in the Treasury, trade and commerce data in the State and Commerce departments and in the Tariff Commission, agricultural information in the Department of Agriculture, and military data in the Department of Defense.

At least 46 federal agencies are concerned in one way or another with foreign policy, and virtually all of them are called upon to furnish advice and make decisions. Sometimes these decisions are of great importance. It was the Secretary of the Treasury and not the Secretary of State, for example, who played the leading role in negotiating the Bretton Woods agreement to establish the International Bank for Reconstruction and Development and The International Monetary Fund. The Greek-Turkish aid program was developed with the advice of the heads of the Departments of Agriculture, State, Treasury, Labor, and Defense, the public health agencies, and others. In one sense the entire executive structure serves as the President's left hand in making foreign policy.

Next to the State Department, however, the Defense Department is the chief source of advice on foreign policy. Since the main goal of American foreign policy is maximum security for the United States, military factors are involved in almost every major foreign-policy decision. It is not surprising that military men and military agencies have a strong voice in shaping that policy. Moreover, the line between military and foreign policy is often hard to draw, for foreign policy makes little sense unless it is coordinated with military policy. The military were in direct control of occupied areas such as Japan, and have guided the development of the North Atlantic Treaty Organization. Generals are assigned to important diplomatic positions, are given command of international military forces, and are called upon to testify before Congress and to speak to the people on controversial foreign policies. The influence of a MacArthur, a Marshall, a Ridgeway, or a Radford on foreign policy is incalculable.

LINKING RIGHT AND LEFT— THE NATIONAL SECURITY COUNCIL

At ten o'clock every Thursday morning, about fifteen men file into the Cabinet Room in the West Wing of the White House. They carry papers marked "top secret." It is time for the meeting of the *National Security Council*, one of the most powerful and most secret of all governmental agencies, and one of the chief shapers of foreign policy.[2]

---

[2] The National Security Council's operations have been described by two who have served as Special Assistant to the President for National Security Affairs. See Dillon Anderson, "The President and National Security," *Atlantic* (January 1956), pp. 42-46, and Robert Cutler, "The Development of the National Security Council," *Foreign Affairs* (April 1956), pp. 440-458.

The President presides at council meetings, since it is he who must make the decisions. The council merely recommends. The other statutory members are the Vice President, Secretary of State, Secretary of Defense, and Director of the Office of Civil and Defense Mobilization. The Chairman of the Joint Chiefs of Staff and the Director of Central Intelligence are always there as advisers, and in recent years the President has asked the Secretary of the Treasury and Director of the Bureau of the Budget to serve. In addition, the President frequently requests other officials, such as the Attorney General and the Director of United States Information Agency, to sit in on the meetings. The Special Assistant to the President for National Security Affairs is there, as is the Executive Secretary of the council staff.

The council has the awesome responsibility of helping the President integrate foreign, military, economic, fiscal, internal security, and psychological policies that affect national security. Members of the council are expected to act not merely as representatives of their departments "but as a collegiate body seeking over-all policies rather than compromises of agencies' positions." Only as the director of the Central Intelligence Agency, however, does the council have any formal legal duty as a unit. Its main job is to assist the President in balancing our foreign risks and commitments against our domestic and military strength.

The Planning Board of the National Security Council insures that the busy men who make up the council are prepared for the weekly meetings. This board, which meets at least three times a week with the Special Assistant to the President for National Security Affairs presiding, consists of representatives at the assistant-secretary level of each of the agencies represented on the council. Members of this central staff agency are nominated by the departments concerned but hold their appointments from the President. The Planning Board's main responsibility is to prepare the policy papers to be discussed at council meetings.

To integrate security policy is one thing; to carry out this policy in an integrated manner is another. Council decisions, when initialed by the President, become official policies that the State Department is supposed to translate into foreign policy, the Joint Chiefs of Staff into strategic plans, and so on. To insure that the detailed operational programs of each agency are properly coordinated is the task of the *Operations Coordinating Board.* This board, consisting of high-ranking officers, periodically reports to the National Security Council.

The membership of the Vice President on the National Security Council is an interesting feature of this agency. The council gains from the Vice President's knowledge of attitudes on Capitol Hill; the Vice President keeps in touch with day-to-day developments in top policy-making—a matter of the utmost importance if he should suddenly succeed to the Presidency. How well the plan is working out cannot easily be estimated. Vice President Nixon played an active role in this respect; on the other hand, as we have seen, our political system makes it likely that the President and Vice President will have major differences over policy. If the President were to run into trouble working with the Security Council, he might tend to lean more heavily on the head of the Bureau of the Budget, whom he appoints personally.

The intermeshing of the executive departments at the top level for foreign policy is only one step in unifying the executive structure. The telephone, the lunch table, the cocktail lounge are still useful instruments of coordination. Of the formal methods, one of the most important is the interdepartmental committee, of which there are about 30 with over 140 subcommittees.

INTELLIGENCE AND FOREIGN POLICY

What is the significance of yesterday's election in Istanbul? How many trained infantrymen are there in Hungary? What is the morale of the Romanian peasants? What should we do about communist pressures on Berlin—send a diplomatic note, seek a resolution in the United Nations, use military power, propaganda, or something else? Before policy-makers can answer such questions, they must know a great deal about other countries—their probable reactions to a particular policy, their strengths and weaknesses, and—if possible—their strategic plans and intentions. Moreover, the makers of foreign policy must be familiar with the geographical and physical structure of the nations of the world; with the people—their numbers, skills, age distributions; the status of their arts, technology, engineering, and sciences; and their political and social systems.

Clearly, policy-makers must have detailed information in order to anticipate problems before they arise. They must be able to counter the moves of other nations, and have some idea of the direction in which they are going to move. They need, in other words, "high-level foreign-policy intelligence." Those who gather and analyze this material are among the most important assistants to the policy leaders. The term "intelligence work" conjures up visions of spies and undercover agents, but at least 95 per cent of the information comes from open sources. Yet secret intelligence often supplies the crucial data.

Intelligence work involves two operations: surveillance and research. Surveillance is the close and systematic observation of developments the world over. Research is the "attempt to establish meaningful patterns out of what was observed in the past and attempts to get meaning out of what appears to be going on now." [3]

Many agencies of the government are engaged in intelligence work. [4] The National Security Agency specializes in communication and intelligence; one of its chief tasks is cryptanalysis, making and breaking codes. The State De-

---

[3] Sherman Kent, *Strategic Intelligence* (Princeton Univ. Press, 1949), esp. p. 4.

[4] For detailed discussion, see Harry H. Ransom, *Central Intelligence and National Security* (Harvard Univ. Press, 1958).

partment gathers information through its missions abroad and interprets it in its intelligence divisions; the military branches have their own intelligence services, as do the Foreign Agricultural Service, the Bureau of Foreign Commerce (Department of Commerce), the Office of International Finance (Treasury), the Atomic Energy Commission, and others. But each of these agencies is primarily interested in gathering information within its own particular field of activity. When all the bits of information gathered by the many agencies are pieced together, they often reveal what is not evident when they are viewed separately.

In the past, American intelligence work has often been inadequate. Each department has gathered and analyzed its own information, often duplicating work done elsewhere and failing to take advantage of available material. On occasion American policy-makers have been caught by surprise and forced to improvise policies to meet situations for which they could have been forewarned by proper intelligence. Even when good intelligence work has been done, and when it has been evaluated by experienced intelligence men, it has not always been disseminated to those responsible for making the decisions.

To correct these deficiencies the Central Intelligence Agency was established to serve directly under the National Security Council. This highly secret agency is not required to report its activities to Congress or to the public, and its appropriations are secretly split up throughout the budget so that not even congressmen know how much it spends. The agency makes recommendations to the Security Council for improving the government's intelligence services, correlates and evaluates intelligence, provides for its distribution, supplements the work of the other intelligence agencies when necessary, and collects secret intelligence abroad. It is not a police agency; it does not catch spies or do "counter-intelligence" work. These are the responsibility of the FBI, the National Security Agency, and others.

The various interdepartmental committees, the National Security Council, the Central Intelligence Agency, are all attempts to improve the executive machinery for the formulation of foreign policy. The problem is tremendous. All the information and all the ramifications must be considered so that the influence and power of the United States can be effectively directed to secure its objectives. The final solution is still to be found. Policy-makers are constantly forced to meet problems as they arise and are so immersed in everyday affairs that they hardly have time to think ahead to meet tomorrow's contingencies. Decisions often have to be made so fast that the elaborate machinery is short-circuited. But the executive structure is probably better organized to meet its responsibilities now than it has ever been in the past.

PRESIDENT AND CONGRESS—FRIENDS OR FOES?

The President is the star performer in the making of foreign policy. But everybody in the executive department gets into the act. The co-star is Congress, and, like all co-stars, Congress and the President vie with each other for top billing.

The frictions produced by the American system of checks and balances are nowhere more obvious or potentially disastrous than in the field of foreign relations.[5] The President and his advisers often lack faith in the capacity of Congress to act wisely and responsibly. Congressmen suspect the President and Secretary of State of siding with foreigners and ignoring American interests. The State Department has no powerful interest group to help it win friends and influence congressmen, as does the Agriculture Department, for example. The State Department supports programs that cost money and require sacrifices for what seems, superficially at least, only to benefit other nations. As a result the President and Congress are often at odds with each other. The delay, confusion, and disunity produced by these interbranch struggles can be dangerous in a time of international tension.

Who speaks for the United States? What are our intentions? Will we meet our obligations? Our friends, it is said, hesitate to depend on our pledges. They fear that they will be forgotten in the midst of congressional-executive infight-

[5] Daniel S. Cheever and H. Field Haviland, Jr., *American Foreign Policy and the Separation of Powers* (Harvard Univ. Press, 1952).

From "Suggested Reforms to Improve U.S. Foreign Policy Machinery," *Strengthening Our Foreign Policy,* Public Affairs Pamphlet No. 189, pp. 14-15. A report by a study group of the Woodrow Wilson Foundation. Reproduced by permission of Public Affairs Committee, Inc., New York, N.Y.

HIGHLIGHTS OF SUGGESTED REFORMS

CONSTITUTIONAL

PROPOSED TREATY

TREATIES TO BE RATIFIED BY MAJORITY OF BOTH HOUSES INSTEAD OF 2/3 VOTE OF THE SENATE.

BILL

PRESIDENT EMPOWERED TO VETO ITEMS OF BILL WITHOUT REJECTING IT ENTIRELY.

CONGRESSIONAL EXECUTIVE

FOREIGN POLICY PROGRAM SHOULD BE PRESENTED IN GENERAL PACKAGE BILLS AS FAR AS POSSIBLE.

STATE DEPT

SECRETARY OF STATE MIGHT APPEAR PERSONALLY BEFORE BOTH HOUSES AND ANSWER QUESTIONS.

3,000,000 2,500,000 3,000,000 2,500,000

DIVIDE ELECTORAL VOTES IN PROPORTION TO TOTAL NUMBER OF VOTES CAST.

CONGRESSIONAL PROCEDURE

MORE INFORMAL CONFERENCES BETWEEN PRESIDENT, SECRETARY OF STATE AND CONGRESSMEN.

EXECUTIVE

DEPT. OF STATE

EXPAND STATE DEPT. CONTROL OVER OPERATING FUNCTIONS LIKE INFORMATION, COORDINATION OF FOREIGN FINANCIAL & MILITARY AID.

SPECIAL INTERESTS

PARTY PLATFORM

STRONG PARTY DISCIPLINE TO MAINTAIN AND SUPPORT CONTINUITY OF FOREIGN POLICY.

Illustrations by Graphics Institute

ing. Our enemies overlook our warnings, assuming that congressional-executive conflict will make American action too little and too late. Negotiations with other nations are difficult because no one can speak with assurance. Neither the legislators nor the President and his advisers have enough power to make policies for themselves, but each side has enough authority to thwart policies proposed by the other. Periods of presidential domination alternate with periods of congressional rebellion. One close student of foreign affairs has said, "The constitutional separation of powers . . . together with the stalemate in Russo-American diplomatic relations, have brought about the paradox that the traditional diplomatic techniques of persuasion, pressure, and bargaining are applied by the executive branch of the American Government in its relations with Congress rather than with foreign powers." [6]

Recognizing the urgency of the problem, some would take the bull by the horns and give the President a free hand in shaping foreign policy. Partnership is manifestly impossible, it is pointed out, and the legislative branch cannot operate with necessary speed, flexibility, secrecy, and expertness. Since the President can, he should be given the job. Furthermore, he is responsible to a nationwide electorate; he is not so much at the mercy of local and sectional feeling as are most congressmen.

Constitutional aspects aside, this argument overlooks a crucial difficulty. Foreign policy is so closely related to domestic policy that to free the President's hand in directing the former would be to give him tremendous power over the latter. Foreign policy demands money, organization, and manpower. And ultimately it may demand the sacrifice of American lives. If the President were able to make these commitments unchecked, his policies, both domestic and foreign, might be more sensible, but they might not be more responsible. Americans would hesitate to turn over such sweeping powers to one elected official and a few other officials appointed by him.

Few will deny, however, that the chief executive must have the initiative. What should be the role of Congress? There is much that Congress can do. It can provide the arena for the discussion of basic policies. It can educate both the people and the officials, and perhaps create wider understanding. It can mediate between the people and the experts, introducing the experts to the people's preferences and the people to the experts' knowledge.

Nevertheless, it serves no purpose to ignore the cardinal defects of the presidential-congressional conflict. And that conflict is not the result of "bad" people in Congress or White House, or of simple misunderstanding, or of failure to experiment. It is the result of both the system of checks and balances imposed by the Constitution and the political disunities of the American people (see Chapter 21). A glance at the politics of foreign-policy making will perhaps make this clear.

---

[6] Hans J. Morgenthau, "Conduct of American Foreign Policy," *Parliamentary Affairs* (Winter 1949), p. 155.

The Politics
of Foreign-Policy Making

Under government by the people, foreign-policy making cannot
be divorced from public opinions,
from the pressures of interest groups, from the operations of political parties.
Those who attack the idea of democratic government in general find particular
reason to decry popular control of foreign relations. The people, they say, are
especially ignorant, selfish, fickle, narrow-minded, and impetuous in their
attitudes toward foreign nations. These critics can find evidence to support their
position. But government by the people assumes that the people can make the
ultimate decisions, that ultimately they can choose the "right" course of action,
that at the very least they can tell "when the shoe pinches."

PUBLIC OPINION AND FOREIGN POLICY

Public opinion ordinarily is less concerned with foreign than with
domestic policy. Despite the overwhelming importance of foreign affairs, opinion surveys regularly confirm Cottrell and Eberhart's finding, "a third of the
people live in a world that psychologically does not include foreign affairs. As
for the other two-thirds . . . only a minority of the people can be considered
actively conversant with contemporary world problems." [7] The hard core of
chronic know-nothings that we noted in Chapter 11 is even larger in respect to
foreign affairs. Public opinion polls show that over 30 per cent of the voters
have never heard or read about the important issues of American foreign
policy. Approximately 45 per cent have heard or read about the issues, but they
have only an elementary knowledge of them. Only 25 per cent of the electorate
consistently has any knowledge about foreign policy. [8] In 1948, during the
Berlin blockade, the Survey Research Center found that 37 per cent of the
people did not even know of any trouble in Berlin. During the Berlin crisis in
1959 a *New York Times* survey showed that many people did not even know
that Berlin was located inside East Germany. [9] As late as 1950 only 60 per
cent of the people in one poll could give any answer other than "don't know"
to the question, "Will you tell me what the United Nations organization is?"
In February 1953 only 41 per cent of a national cross section of adults was
able to give any approximately correct answer to the question: "Can you tell
me what is the main job of the State Department in Washington?" [10] The less
than 25 per cent of the public considered informed about international affairs
compares with about 30 per cent considered informed on domestic affairs.

---

[7] Leonard S. Cottrell, Jr. and Sylvia Eberhart, *American Opinion on World Affairs in the
Atomic Age* (Princeton Univ. Press, 1948), p. 14.
[8] Martin Kriesberg, "Dark Areas of Ignorance," Chapter 2 in Lester Markel and others,
Public Opinion and Foreign Policy (Harper, 1949).
[9] *The New York Times*, March 22, 1959, Part IV, p. 8.
[10] William A. Scott and Stephen B. Withey, *The United States and the United Nations*
(Manhattan, 1958), pp. 32, 176.

Why are so many people indifferent or uninformed? A hundred years of effortless security have left their mark on American attitudes. The feeling still persists that what happens outside the boundaries of the United States is of less importance than what happens inside. We still tend to exaggerate the importance of our geographic isolation. Most Americans learn their geography from American-centered Mercator-projection maps whose distortions confirm their feeling that the United States lives in a world of its own. Some people still feel that diplomacy and foreign affairs have only to do with the squabbles of far-off Europeans.

Foreign affairs are more remote than domestic problems. People have more first-hand information about inflation than about Chinese communism. The worker in the factory and the boss in the front office know what labor-management relations are about, and they have strong opinions on the subject. They are less concerned about the consequences of revolt in Tibet. Not only are the issues of foreign policy more remote, they are highly complex.

Many people, uninformed and uninterested, react to foreign-policy issues on the basis of moods that have no intellectual structure or factual content.[11] These mood reactions are unstable; optimism gives way to pessimism, idealism to cynicism. So long as there is no glaring threat to American interests, the public mood is one of withdrawal from international affairs; but the moment danger appears, the mood shifts to a demand for full-scale intervention. Then, as the danger *appears* to subside, the mood shifts back to withdrawal.

The ordinary voter oversimplifies the problems of foreign politics. He tends to reduce all issues to the one issue that is most urgent at the moment. He thinks of the participants in terms of heroes and villains. He favors quick and easy remedies—fire the Secretary of State, lower trade barriers, get rid of Khrushchev, and all will be well.

The "expert" and the "informed citizen" are also subject to mood responses and oversimplification, but as the level of interest and information rises, the degree of sophistication increases.

Popular indifference toward international politics means that the official policy-makers often have to dramatize the issues in order to arouse public support for their programs. On the other hand, in periods of public excitement, fear of rash public opinion causes policy-makers to be overcautious. To secure American participation in the United Nations, for example, the State Department carried on an intensive publicity campaign, and in so doing gave many people the impression that the United Nations would insure peace and order in the world. To arouse public support for the Truman Doctrine, people were told of the looming "crisis." But then officials had to spend their energies cooling down public opinion to ease demands for hasty action. This overselling of policies may lead to a "giddy-ap and whoa" approach to foreign relations.

The instability of public moods makes it difficult for official policy-makers

---

[11]This material is drawn from Gabriel A. Almond, *The American People and Foreign Policy* (Harcourt, Brace, 1950).

to plan ahead, to take the long view after full consideration of the military, political, diplomatic, psychological, and other subtle factors involved in every major decision. The unorganized general public does not, of course, make foreign policy. Yet public opinion determines the broad limits within which others make the decisions. Public attitudes—the political climate in general— determine the political possibilities open to the policy-makers. The President and the congressional leaders know that, at a minimum, they must not arouse widespread public hostility to their proposals. At times they have to secure active public support for programs that call for large expenditures of money or for commitments that involve risk of grave danger. Even when the public plays a negative role in the making of foreign policy, that role may still be important. The people have effective ways of making their attitudes felt both at election time and between elections.

Congressmen are constantly alert to popular feeling. The Department of State makes a systematic effort to uncover public attitudes and to discover what groups are concerned with particular issues. Experts in the Division of Public Studies read public opinion polls, resolutions and publications of organized groups, ninety or more newspapers, and sixty or more magazines. Each noon the Secretary of State and his hundred top advisers receive a summary of opinions expressed in these media during the preceding 24 hours. The Division publishes weekly and monthly summaries of the state of public opinion. Another Division, Public Services, sends representatives to conventions of various organizations in order to sound out public opinion, receives and answers several hundred letters a day, and publishes an analysis of the mail on foreign policy. These activities are, however, more likely to tell the State Department what the opinion leaders and interest-group leaders are thinking than what the so-called "average citizen" has on his mind.

The State Department also does its best to inform the public of the policies of the United States and the reasons behind them. The Assistant Secretary for Public Affairs supervises an extensive program designed to keep the American public informed. The Secretary himself frequently holds press conferences. The Public Service Division issues a long list of informative pamphlets, periodicals, and books. The State Department sends speakers out to clubs and other organizations. On important issues the President himself takes a hand, and through radio and TV addresses, messages to Congress, and public speeches tries to "educate" the public. Despite all these efforts, however, evidence indicates that the word just does not get through, at least directly, to people who are indifferent and uninformed about international politics. But it does get through to those who are already interested, and these interested groups are important in the process of opinion formation.

The way in which public opinion conditions the making of our foreign policy, and conversely the way in which officials mold public opinion, are dramatically illustrated by the events of the late 1930's. By 1937 President Roosevelt and his advisers had become convinced that Germany, Italy, and

Japan threatened American security. They believed that the power of the United States had to be thrown behind England and France if the aggressors were to be prevented from controlling the Eurasian Continent. They hoped that a strong stand by the United States would swing the balance of power in favor of the democracies and deter the aggressors. In October 1937, President Roosevelt made his famous "quarantine the aggressor" speech in which he cautiously stated his position. But the public response, both inside and outside congressional chambers, was hostile. Most Americans still seemed to cling to the doctrines of nonintervention, neutrality, and freedom from entangling alliances. The people insisted upon neutrality laws that tied the executive's hands in the hope that if war came in Europe, we could stay out. So the President proceeded to move cautiously. Aided by the unfolding of events in Europe, he began to "educate" the public to support a more vigorous program. As public opinion became more favorable, the President gradually used the powers of his office to give as much aid and comfort to the democracies as public opinion would tolerate. But even as late as 1941, just prior to Pearl Harbor, public opinion was sharply divided. A large and vocal part of the population opposed the President's program. He had to move without the vigor and dispatch that many observers thought the crisis called for. The division of public opinion also obscured the intentions of the United States. Japanese and German leaders misjudged the significance of this division. They thought it meant that we would not have the unity needed to fight a war.

In Chapter 11 we noted that the American public is composed of hundreds of smaller publics, and that what we call "public opinion" is the complex interrelation and interaction of hundreds of interests, organized and unorganized. If the unorganized American public is indifferent to foreign politics, the same cannot be said of the organized publics and their spokesmen.

ORGANIZED INTERESTS AND FOREIGN POLICY

The indifference of the general public makes it easier for the interested special publics to influence foreign policy. The special publics exert the greatest influence on Congress. By using all the familiar devices—letter-writing campaigns, advice to congressmen, testimony before committees, and publicity and public relations—the special-interest groups are highly effective in molding foreign policy.

The staff members of the organized groups and the opinion leaders sprinkled through society—the priests and preachers, newspaper, radio, and TV commentators, teachers and public speakers—form an elite, an attentive public whose support is actively sought by the official policy-makers. State Department officials and the officials of the major interest groups often work together. The Department of State maintains relations with over four hundred national citizens' organizations, consulting with them and sending them materials and background information.

What groups are most interested in foreign affairs? First of all there is a small, but very influential, group of citizens' organizations devoted to increasing the public's knowledge and understanding of international politics. These organizations do not agitate for the adoption of particular policies, but they do provide information and stimulate the discussion of issues. Many of them issue their own publications, and in their meetings they bring together influential citizens and public officials. The Council on Foreign Relations, the Foreign Policy Association, and the Foundation for Foreign Affairs are examples of organizations that have assumed such leadership responsibility. Other citizen organizations operate in much the same manner, although they are not exclusively concerned with foreign affairs. The League of Women Voters, for example, takes stands on particular issues and carries on campaigns to raise the level of citizen understanding.

Foreign policies so affect the domestic scene that inevitably the major interest groups of agriculture, labor, and business are closely involved. The big interest groups may represent such a wide cross section of the general public, however, that they speak for broad national interests. Pacifist, patriotic, and veterans' organizations are also closely concerned with foreign policy. The patriotic and veterans' groups, for example, support large military appropriations whereas the pacifists oppose them. Farm, labor, and business interests have heavy economic stakes in foreign policy. Developments abroad affect businessmen's profits, farmers' markets, workers' jobs and wages.

Religious and national-origin publics are particularly interested in certain phases of foreign policy. These groups have intense feelings about some issues, and they are often strategically located to affect the outcome of elections.[12] Policy-makers are highly conscious of the wishes of these articulate groups. Many Americans of Irish origin, reflecting feelings aroused by English-Irish relations, are hostile toward Anglo-American cooperation. Many Americans of German origin voted against Roosevelt in 1940 because of his strong stand against Germany.[13] The attitude of Roman Catholics has been a significant factor in shaping American policy toward Spain both during the Spanish Civil War and after World War II. American policy toward Israel has been intimately affected by the pressures of American Zionists.

PARTIES AND FOREIGN POLICY

Parties, as such, do not play a major role in shaping foreign policy. There are two reasons: First, many Americans would prefer to keep foreign policy out of politics; party politics, they say, should "stop at the water's edge." Second, parties take even less clear and candid stands on foreign policy than they do on domestic policy. All the party weaknesses discussed earlier in this book

---

[12] Thomas A. Bailey, *The Man in the Street* (Macmillan, 1948).
[13] Samuel Lubell, "Who Votes Isolationist and Why," *Harper's Magazine,* April 1951.

operate in full measure in foreign-policy making. Party platforms often obscure the issues instead of highlighting them; many congressmen fail to follow even a very general party "line"; and the parties fail to discipline even the most outspoken rebels.

On the other hand, congressional voting does indicate that on some foreign-policy issues significant differences exist between the major parties. Speaking very generally, congressional Democrats, especially northern Democrats, are more likely to support commitment of American troops and resources to back up our European allies, American participation in international organizations, proposals for foreign aid, and large military appropriations; and they give first priority to European rather than to Asiatic defense against communism. Republicans, on the other hand, tend to look with suspicion on foreign-aid programs, oppose tariff reductions, regard more skeptically American participation in international organizations, view our European allies more critically, are more reluctant to support large military appropriations except during "all-out" war, and favor the use of American power in Asia rather than in Europe.[14] Of course striking exceptions may be found to these tendencies; certain Republicans are far more internationally minded than some Democrats.

Sectional and economic interests, however, easily disrupt these rough party lines.[15] A case in point is the action of a Democratic senator from a midwestern border state in connection with appropriations for the European Recovery Program. In this case the Democratic President and the Democratic party platform both stood behind large-scale help to Europe. The senator, however, moved to amend the measure to require that $1½ billion of the appropriation be devoted to the purchase of agricultural products. Although this amendment might have aided the American farmer, impartial observers agreed that it would reduce the effectiveness of the aid to Europe. Three major farm lobbies opposed the amendment because they objected to mixing farm and foreign policy, but 32 senators—all from predominantly farm states—supported it.

Should parties be concerned with foreign policy? At the end of World War II sentiment grew stronger for a "bipartisan approach" to foreign policy. An ambiguous term, bipartisanship seems to mean (1) collaboration between the executive and the congressional foreign-policy leaders of both parties; (2) support of foreign policies by both parties in Congress; (3) withdrawal of foreign-policy issues from debate in political campaigns. In general, bipartisanship is an attempt to remove the issues of foreign policy from partisan politics. In its defense, it is argued that despite the internal differences that divide Americans, they all share a common interest with respect to other nations.

---

[14] See R. A. Dahl, *Congress and Foreign Policy* (Harcourt, Brace, 1950), pp. 229, 284-287. See also, Ralph H. Smuckler, "The Region of Isolationism," *The American Political Science Review* (June 1953), pp. 386-401.

[15] See H. Bradford Westerfield, *Foreign Policy and Party Politics* (Yale Univ. Press, 1955), pp. 32-52, for discussion of sectional differences within parties.

During times of national danger we readily unite behind policies necessary to preserve the national well-being, and such unity is needed to support our foreign policies. American foreign policy, it is asserted, was ineffective following World War I because it became entangled in the partisan struggle between Democrats and Republicans.

Between 1942 and 1950, the leaders of the two parties, both in and outside of Congress, worked closely together on foreign policy. Once policies were agreed upon, they received broad support from both parties in Congress and were not seriously debated in the political campaigns. Democrats supported the policies largely out of loyalty to the Democratic Administration, and the Republicans at least partly because of their respect for Senator Vandenberg, the Republican foreign-policy spokesman. For the most part, the bipartisan policy was limited to programs calling for American participation in the United Nations and to policies of economic and military support for our European friends. Policy with respect to the Far East, however, won little bipartisan support.

After 1950, bipartisanship began to break down. The problems of the Far East took over the stage. During the 1952 elections the Republicans bitterly attacked the Truman Administration's Korean policies and made foreign policy a central issue. However, with the election of President Eisenhower, the bipartisan approach tended to reappear. Except for the first two years of his first term, the Congress was controlled by Democrats, whose support the President needed to gain legislation and appropriations. Although Democrats complained that Secretary of State Dulles failed to consult them and that Congress was being asked merely to rubber-stamp executive policies, in the face of Soviet pressures both parties pledged their support to the President. With the elevation of Christian Herter to Secretary of State, and with the Berlin crisis, bipartisanship seems to have been re-established, at least in a formal sense.

Is a Democratic Foreign Policy Possible?

Over a century ago, de Tocqueville wrote that democracies were decidedly inferior to other types of governments in the conduct of their foreign relations. "Foreign politics," he observed, "demand scarcely any of these qualities which are peculiar to a democracy; they require, on the contrary, the perfect use of almost all those in which it is deficient. . . . [A] democracy can only with great difficulty regulate the details of an important undertaking, persevere in a fixed design, and work out its execution in spite of serious obstacles. It cannot combine its measures with secrecy or await their consequences with patience." [16] More

---

[16] Alexis de Tocqueville, *Democracy in America*, The Henry Reeve text (Knopf, 1946), Vol. 1, pp. 234-235.

recent observers have expressed somewhat similar misgivings over the handling of foreign relations in the American democracy. Hans Morgenthau, for example, has observed that policy-makers "either . . . must sacrifice what they consider good policy upon the altar of public opinion, or they must by devious means gain support for policies whose true nature is concealed from the public." [17] How serious is this criticism? What role does the general electorate play in the making of foreign policy?

HOW MUCH POPULAR CONTROL?

Democratic foreign-policy making does not require that a general election be held before every decision is made. Everyone cannot be an expert; the people as a whole cannot actively take part in drawing up policy. "In the case of foreign affairs," it has been said, "where the given elements in a situation consist largely of the attitudes and intentions of foreign communities, to expect a very high level of information on the part of the electorate is utopian." [18] But it is equally unrealistic to conclude that the policy-makers can or should ignore the electorate. Foreign policies that commit American manpower and resources will have little success if Americans, through ignorance, apathy, or downright opposition, refuse to back them up. The electorate cannot fashion policy, but the voters can set limits to the policies they are willing to support.

The people, too, have a positive responsibility to keep themselves informed on foreign issues. No matter how able the top officials, foreign policy cannot be formulated over the long run without the support of an informed electorate. Undoubtedly we need better ways of spreading information, of enlarging the opportunities for discussion.

Granting all this, however, the basic trouble in the United States is perhaps not so much democracy or democrats but our particular set of institutional arrangements. Weak parties, strongly organized interests, halting legislative procedures—these difficulties disrupt democratic control of foreign policies in the same way that they threaten effective popular control of domestic policies. Indeed, some thoughtful observers believe that our governmental and political weaknesses in the foreign-policy area are far more serious than in the domestic. We do not enjoy the margin for error, the opportunity to improvise, in fast-moving international crises, they argue, that we enjoy in internal affairs.

PRESIDENTIAL LEADERSHIP

In the face of these difficulties Americans have evolved two methods of achieving effective national action in foreign affairs. One is to vest wide powers in the President. The framers of the Constitution gave the chief executive a

[17] Morgenthau, "Conduct of American Foreign Policy," p. 147.
[18] Max Beloff, *Foreign Policy and the Democratic Process* (The Johns Hopkins Press, 1955), p. 58.

paramount role in foreign relations, as we have seen, and with the passage of time he has taken on new powers, such as frequent resort to executive agreements. This method has advantages. The President can act swiftly and decisively. He can see the more general interest above the clamor of the crowd and the tugging of special interests. He must face the people in elections, but not so often that he feels the need to follow public opinion instead of leading it. But there are disadvantages too. The President may bear responsibilities that are a tremendous load for one man. In a time of crisis—a time when he may see factors that most of the people do not see—the President may have to withhold information, or at least his own true opinions, from the people. Many of those who approved President Roosevelt's course in the year or two before Pearl Harbor would agree that the President, "when confronted by an apathetic public and a critical foreign menace, felt compelled to deceive the people into an awareness of their peril."

To what extent should the President be a leader in shaping our foreign policy? To what extent a follower? These questions go to the heart of democratic government. One answer, as we noted in Chapter 21, is that the President should act as leader of the majority party and should be responsible to that party. But again, institutional arrangements for party rule are lacking in this country. This brings us to the second method of evading the weaknesses of the American system of government.

BIPARTISANSHIP AND RESPONSIBILITY

The second method of evading the weaknesses of our government in foreign-policy making is *bipartisanship*. Although bipartisanship means different things to different people, it is essentially an arrangement by which Administration leaders consult with minority party leaders before making important decisions, *and by which both parties share responsibility for those decisions and their consequences.*

Bipartisanship has enormous appeal. In this era of chronic crisis, it seems to symbolize a people standing shoulder to shoulder as they face their enemies abroad. It provides more continuity of policy, and it insures that a wider variety of leaders and interests are consulted in foreign-policy making. Psychologically, it helps to satisfy the instinct of people to turn to one another for reassurance as they shrink from the dark and disjointed world outside. Its motto—"Partisan politics stops at the water's edge"—is comforting to the many Americans worried about disunity at home.

But the idea of bipartisanship has come under sharp attack. Critics charge that bipartisanship denies a basic tenet of democracy—the right of a people to choose between alternative lines of action. According to this argument, in a free society men should be allowed and even encouraged to differ. The need in a democracy is not to stifle differences, or to ignore them, or to elude them. The need is to express the differences in a meaningful way, to find the will of the majority, to permit the government to act and the opposition to oppose. This is where parties come in. They present alternatives. Because they want to win as many votes as possible, parties find common denominators in the views of millions of people. Because we have a two-party system, each party distills the essence of agreement from a medley of conflicting opinions. The party that wins a majority takes office. The losing party has the equally important job of furnishing opposition.

Thus parties—and partisanship—are vital to democracy. "Why should we abandon them at the water's edge?" ask the opponents of bipartisanship. Certainly not because Americans are agreed on foreign policy. The nation abounds with differences, as recent crises have made clear. Surely not because we hope to show a united front to our enemies. We cannot deceive them with a pretense of agreement. With their trained observers stationed in Washington and throughout the country, they know our differences as well as we do. Besides, our party divisions should be something to flaunt with pride—not something to be slammed into the closet whenever foreigners seem to be looking at us.

Even more serious, the critics conclude, bipartisanship erodes responsibility. A great virtue of partisan government is that the men in office can be held to account simply because they hold authority. But when the leaders of both parties have their hands on the tiller, responsibility fades. After things go badly politicians begin the grand game of passing the buck. The leaders of each party maintain that it was the other gang that really steered the ship onto the rocks. Instead of a sober consideration of alternative courses of action, there is a frantic hunt for scapegoats.

Despite these criticisms, Americans will probably continue to resort to bipartisan arrangements in foreign-policy making. The reason is clear. Our constitutional system encourages bipartisanship. The two-thirds requirement for ratification of treaties forces the President to rely on the support of the minority party. Moreover, in a time of international tension and crisis, democracies must *act*. Any device that will permit action without violating constitutional forms is indispensable. Bipartisanship permits action. So does broad presidential power. These methods may flout democratic ideals of responsibility and popular control, but they seem to be part of the price we must pay for living in a chaotic world of sovereign nations.

Conducting Foreign Relations

High-level foreign-policy leaders are concerned mainly with the key issues of state. They work at the top of a governmental iceberg, and the organization below them is wide and deep. The day-by-day administration, the handling of routine problems, and the decisions that do not immediately involve great discretion are in the hands of others. These thousands of men and women greatly influence high-level policies by gathering and evaluating data and by making the scores of little decisions out of which the big ones are often compounded. The President, Congress, the Secretary of State, and the people depend on these officials for information and advice, and for the execution of policy once it has been determined. What finally emerges as a policy decision is the product of many minds.

The Role of the State Department

Who handles the day-by-day routine? The key agency is of course the State Department. This department has six traditional duties. (1) It must provide the President with the *information* he needs to conduct international relations. The department, through its missions abroad, collects data on political and economic events, sorts and analyzes them, sends some to other interested departments, and some to Central Intelligence. (2) The department assists the President in the *formulation and implementation of policy.* It evaluates the information, makes recommendations to the President, the National Security Council, and others, or it makes decisions in the name of the President. (3) The department has the primary responsibility for *representing* the United States in our dealings with other nations and international organizations. Messages to and from other nations are routed through the department. (4) The department has the primary but not exclusive responsibility for carrying on *negotiations* with other nations and international organizations. Only 25 per cent of the United States representatives in 390 recent international meetings were from the Department of State, but in most cases the heads of the delegations were State Department men. (5) The department has the *operating responsibility for technical and economic assistance* programs administered by the International Cooperation Administration (now part of the State Department). (6) A final function of the department is to *coordinate* the activities of the many groups, agencies, and interdepartmental committees that participate in the formulation and execution of foreign policy.

ORGANIZATION

The general organization of the Department of State is determined by its two major activities: one to advise on the formulation of policy; the other to handle the day-by-day relations of the United States with other nations and international organizations. For many years the department was able to handle its duties with a small staff. But with the steady growth of new activities, the organization gradually became unwieldy. In an attempt to improve its organization, the department has been reorganized eight times since January 1944. Though many critics still insist that the more it changes the more it stays the same, the department is now probably better organized to handle the problems of a major world power.

The policy-making and advisory activities of the department are centered in a team of high-ranking officers. At the top is, of course, the Secretary. Second in command is the Under Secretary, who serves as Acting Secretary during the Secretary's frequent absences. Two Deputy Under Secretaries assist in the running of the department and in giving advice, as does the Counselor, who serves as a senior adviser and assists in negotiations. An Under Secretary for Economic Affairs is responsible for the development of foreign economic policy and coordinates mutual relief programs. The Assistant Secretary for Policy Planning represents the department on the Planning Board of the National Security Council and assists the Secretary in the formulation of long-range policy. The existence of an Assistant Secretary for Public Affairs and an Assistant Secretary for Congressional Relations points up the department's concern with internal politics.

The actual operations are centered in the department's bureaus. Six bureaus are organized along functional lines: one for international organizations, one for economic affairs, one for security and consular affairs, one for personnel and housekeeping matters, one for public affairs, and one for intelligence and research. The International Cooperation Administration functions as a semiautonomous unit within the department; its director reports directly to the Secretary, and it maintains its own staff. This administration handles economic and technical assistance and coordinates military-aid programs. It works on the assumption that we can use our productive power to help build the strength of nations whose security and stability are vital to our own and who share our determination to stop aggression.

The five *geographic* offices have become the pivot of the department's operations. Each embraces a varying number of country desks. The "desk man," a specialist on a particular country, receives copies of all communications from our representatives in that country, and through him instructions are sent to these representatives. The desk man is expected to have a thorough understanding of his country. The geographic offices have their own staffs of economists, geographers, and other specialists.

What should be the function of the Department of State? Should it limit its activities to the *making* of policy but leave its *execution* to others? This is more or less the official view of the State Department. Except for the traditional agencies of diplomacy and the recently designated task of economic and technical assistance, the *instruments* of policy are operated by others—for example, military force and military assistance by the Department of Defense, and information programs by the United States Information Agency. A first Hoover Commission Task Force recommended that the department, in addition to representation, reporting, and negotiation, should "concentrate on the task of obtaining definition of proposed objectives, of formulating proposed policies, . . . and of recommending the choice and timing of the use of various instruments to carry out foreign policies. . . ." [1] As far as *operations* are concerned, however, the first Hoover Commission suggested that the department merely assist and supervise other departments to assure that they were using their respective instruments to achieve approved policy objectives. Not all students agree with the commission,[2] and the second Hoover Commission hedged on this point.[3] It is doubtful if any clean-cut division of responsibility can be established. Whatever the State Department's role, foreign affairs touch so many interests and activities that inevitably some of them will be handled outside the State Department.

THE STATE DEPARTMENT'S PARTNERS

To list the other agencies that manage some phase of our foreign policy would take many pages. A brief description of the activities of a few of the chief agencies will give some idea of the complexity and scope of our relations with other nations. Since military power is one of the chief instruments of foreign policy, some of the most important programs are administered in the Defense Department. An Assistant Secretary of Defense for International Security Affairs coordinates within the department all politico-military matters. He administers the military assistance programs, supervises the Department of

---

[1] Commission on Organization of the Executive Branch of the Government, *Task Force Report on Foreign Affairs* (Government Printing Office, 1949), p. 15.

[2] For example, The Brookings Institution, *The Administration of Foreign Affairs and Overseas Operations* (1951), p. xix. Also Arthur W. Macmahon, *Administration in Foreign Affairs* (Univ. of Alabama Press, 1953), pp. 94 ff.

[3] Commission on Organization of the Executive Branch of the Government, *Overseas Economic Operations, A Report to the Congress* (Government Printing Office, 1955), p. 42.

Defense activities in the National Security Council, and helps the Secretary develop military policy that relates to foreign relations.

The *United States Information Agency* was established in 1953 to take over from the State Department the responsibility for managing an important instrument of foreign policy—propaganda. The agency, under the guidance of the Secretary of State and the National Security Council, has control over all facets of our informational programs and maintains field offices in eighty-one foreign countries. The Voice of America broadcasts are well known, but they are only a part of an elaborate program of explaining American foreign policies to people abroad. It was during World War II that the United States for the first time seriously began to use propaganda as an instrument of policy. Under the Office of War Information, an independent agency, propaganda was used in order to soften enemy morale and gain the support of neutral countries. All kinds of propaganda, "white" (objective and balanced), "black" (slanted), and "gray" (mixed), were used. Today the emphasis is on the use of *white* propaganda. In addition to radio broadcasts, the United States maintains libraries in foreign countries containing books and magazines about this country and its culture and conducts an elaborate program to help foreign students come to the United States for their education. Democracies in general and the United States in particular have been reluctant to establish propaganda bureaus, but the success of the Soviet Union in painting the United States as a country dominated by capitalist warmongers has forced us to engage in "campaigns of truth." The propaganda instrument is especially important in gaining the support of peoples in colonial areas where programs must be designed in terms of local idea-systems. The American effort has been criticized for failing to provide materials that are sufficiently meaningful to peoples of different cultures.

The *Department of the Treasury* has become increasingly important in the international relations of the United States because of the key role played by fiscal activities in world affairs. It has chief responsibility for all foreign financial, monetary, and exchange activities of the government. The Office of International Finance makes reports and recommendations on the economic and financial aspects of international treaties and agreements. It also administers the frozen funds of other nations in this country and the laws prohibiting certain transactions with communist countries.

At least eight separate bureaus in the *Department of Commerce* are concerned with foreign activities. The most important is the Bureau of Foreign Commerce, which promotes American interests in connection with exports and imports, works to reduce barriers to international trade, and represents the department in economic negotiations with other countries. The Commerce Department has a major role in United States foreign economic activities and is represented on many interdepartmental economic committees. It has primary responsibility for the administration of export and import controls on all except agricultural commodities.

The *Department of Agriculture,* in addition to furnishing advice on top policy, has certain operational responsibilities. The Foreign Agricultural Service assists in agricultural phases of foreign assistance programs.

Americans Overseas

American diplomacy is older than the United States. Even before the Revolution, Benjamin Franklin was sent as our representative to France by the Continental Congress. Today the United States maintains 78 embassies, 3 legations, and approximately 198 consular posts in more than 80 nations.

During our early years as a nation, the caliber of our overseas representation was high. Men like John Adams, Thomas Jefferson, and James Monroe served American interests in foreign capitals. But following the War of 1812 diplomatic posts were in the main used to reward persons for political activities. High diplomatic assignments were given to wealthy men who had contributed to the campaigns of victorious presidents. Since the salaries of diplomats were small and their expenses large, only men of independent means could afford to take posts in the more important nations. The *consular* offices were in particular demand because of "the fees that went into the consul's pocket; at big ports such as Hamburg and London, the yearly plunder often exceeded the salary of the President of the United States." [4] Various minor reforms were made, but it was not until 1924 that a modern career service was established. In that year the Rogers Act consolidated the diplomatic and consular service and provided for a Foreign Service of the United States established on a career basis. The service was further modernized and reorganized in 1946, 1949, and 1954.

The elaborate protocol surrounding diplomacy gives an unwarranted impression of daintiness and mystery to the profession. Historical and popular novelists make out that diplomacy is the work of adroit and gallant heroes, voluptuous heroines, and scheming diplomats. Of course some diplomats are handsome and adept at making pretty compliments to beautiful ladies, but diplomacy is, as an experienced diplomat has written, a "grim business . . . a laborious business, singularly free from glamour and mystery."

THE AMERICAN FOREIGN SERVICE

The American Foreign Service is the eyes and ears of the United States. Although a part of the State Department, the service represents the entire government and performs jobs for many other agencies. Almost 90 per cent of its reports go to departments other than State. Its main duties are to carry out foreign policy as expressed in the directives of the Secretary of State, gather

---

[4] J. Rives Childs, *American Foreign Service* (Holt, 1948), p. 6.

"The U.S. Embassy?
Just follow us, we're
on our way there
right now."

data for American policy-makers, protect Americans and American interests in foreign countries, and cultivate friendly relations with foreign peoples. Although theoretically the service is only an instrument to assist policy leaders, its influence on policy is reflected in the quip, "foreign policy is made on the cables."

The Foreign Service is composed of officers, reserve officers, and staff.[5] At the core of the service are the Foreign Service officers, comparable to the officers of the Regular Army in the military services. It is a select, specially trained body of men and women who are expected to take an assignment at any place in the world on short notice. There are approximately 3000 such officers; in most years over 250 junior officers are appointed. They have their own training school, the Foreign Service Institute, where new officers and their wives are briefed and where experienced officers get advanced instruction. Offi-

---

[5] See Epilogue for discussion of method of appointment and preparation for entering the Foreign Service.

cers have either diplomatic or consular duties and provide the general direction of our missions abroad. As a small elite group, the Foreign Service has a high *esprit de corps.*

The Foreign Service is one of the most respected and most criticized branches of the national government. Recently the criticism seemed to outweigh the respect, and the service's morale suffered accordingly. Henry M. Wriston, chairman of a distinguished committee appointed in 1954 by the Secretary of State to study the service, stated that it "was dying at the bottom, they were resigning in the middle, and it was withering away at the top." [6] In loyalty-security hearings, officers were asked to justify remarks sometimes taken out of context from confidential reports made years ago to their superiors. Often the recommendations of yesterday were evaluated by the hindsight of today. Critics accused the service of being infiltrated by communist sympathizers; others charged that it was dominated by a high-society elite who were still under the impression that diplomacy was the business of "gentlemen." It is more important, said the critics, that our diplomats understand the social and economic problems of the Chinese peasant, for example, than to know how to behave at a fashionable cocktail party. The charges about communist infiltration were undoubtedly overdrawn, as were claims that the service was preoccupied with genteel manners. The latter charges probably stemmed in part from the conventional stereotype of a diplomat. Still, most of the personnel of the service did come from the same general social background—a fact that cut down on the effectiveness of their reporting, for every reporter, no matter how objective he tries to be, selects and evaluates what he sees on the basis of his own attitudes and "picture of the world."

Prior to 1954 most stateside positions within the Department of State were held by civil service employees whose salary and retirement systems were less favorable than those of the Foreign Service but who had no obligation to serve outside the United States. Since the Foreign Service was small, there was little opportunity to bring officers back for a tour of duty in Washington. Consequently, it was charged that they had lost contact with American domestic conditions. At the same time, the civil service employees with little or no service abroad often failed to understand other nations, appreciate foreign conditions, or sympathize with the job of the men working abroad. Friction occurred between the two groups: the Foreign Service officers felt that their system of selection and obligation to serve abroad made them an elite corps, the civil service employees felt that the Foreign Service officers were limited in viewpoint and got excessively high salaries, sometimes for doing the same kind of job assigned to civil service people. [7]

Between 1949 and 1954 five commissions or special committees studied

[6] Quoted by Dorothy Fosdick, "For the Foreign Service—Help Wanted," *The New York Times Magazine,* November 20, 1955, p. 13.

[7] The Commission on Organization of the Executive Branch of the Government, *Foreign Affairs* (Government Printing Office, 1949), p. 62.

Complaints about F. S. being elite — come...

the Foreign Service. All recommended that there should be a single service to staff both overseas and Washington positions, all persons being obliged to serve where needed. The most recent group to endorse this proposal was the Secretary of State's Public Committee on Personnel, popularly known after the name of its chairman as the Wriston Committee, which was appointed after the attacks on the loyalty of the Foreign Service had led to a decline in morale and to loss of public confidence. The committee also recommended that the service avoid selecting so many of its men from the Harvard-Yale-Princeton axis, use more imagination in recruiting young men, and improve its training program.[8]

Finally, in 1954, Congress authorized an expansion of the service to bring within the Foreign Service most of the State Department's policy positions. Holders of these positions wherever qualified were given a chance to accept a Foreign Service commission, carrying with it both a higher salary and the obligation to serve abroad. It was hoped that this expansion of the Foreign Service would give Foreign Service officers a stateside assignment at least after every six-year tour abroad.[9]

Except for clerical, custodial, and administrative jobs, key positions in the State Department are now held by members of the Foreign Service. The Foreign Service Reserve, really misnamed, permits the Secretary to appoint a few specialists to serve for a temporary period. Foreign Service Staff now consists of technical, clerical, and custodial personnel lower than officer rank. Steps are also being taken, in compliance with the other recommendations of the Wriston Committee, to recruit more men and women from colleges, to make the examinations less costly, and to place less emphasis on "personality" and "foreign service characteristics."

OPERATIONS OVERSEAS

The United States has diplomatic missions in the capital cities of almost all nations with which we carry on relations. In addition, we maintain permanent missions at the North Atlantic Treaty Organization, European regional organizations, and the United Nations. The heads of these missions, designated by the President with the consent of the Senate, hold the ranks of ambassador, minister, or chargé d'affaires. Historically, ambassadors were sent to the larger and more important countries, but now we maintain embassies (each headed by an ambassador) in many smaller countries. Over 60 per cent of the chiefs of missions are now Foreign Service officers, although the major diplomatic posts are still filled by political appointees, many of whom have little knowledge of foreign affairs. In fact recently the United States was repre-

---

[8] Report of the Secretary of State's Public Committee on Personnel, *Toward A Stronger Foreign Service,* Department of State Publication 5458 (Government Printing Office, 1954).

[9] For a recent treatment of personnel in the service, see James L. McCamy and Alessandro Corradini, "The People of the State Department and Foreign Service," *The American Political Science Review* (December 1954), pp. 1067-1082.

sented in France, Italy, Germany, Belgium, the Netherlands, Norway, Turkey, Japan, Korea, Burma, Thailand, Vietnam, and Indonesia by ambassadors none of whom could speak the native language.[10]

Diplomatic missions located in capital cities are chiefly concerned with political and economic relations between governments. Consular offices, though part of the Foreign Service, are largely concerned with the activities of individuals. Consuls are not official representatives of one government to another, but serve as public agents to promote the commercial interests and protect the citizens of their own state. Their powers and privileges are determined by arrangement with the countries concerned. Consular officers are ranked in descending order: consul general, consul, vice-consul, and consular agents. The latter are not members of the Foreign Service, and operate in less important places.

In order to get a better idea of the many duties of the Foreign Service, let us look at the activities of a typical American mission.

AMERICANS IN PARIS

Right off the Place de la Concorde stands an imposing building with the Stars and Stripes flying from the top of the portico overlooking the circular driveway. This is the American Embassy in Paris, the largest American mission in the world. This mission operates out of seven office buildings, spends over $15 million a year, and employs 2485 people. (Only part of these people make up the mission to France; the others make up the mission to NATO.) In addition, fifteen departments and agencies have smaller American missions attached to the embassy. The ambassador is the ranking American representative in France and is responsible for the coordination of all American officials in Paris.

The work of the embassy is divided into four major sections: political, administrative, economic, and consular. The political section, presided over by Foreign Service officers, keeps the Department of State informed on developments in the internal and foreign politics of the French government. It reports and analyzes, for example, debates in the French Assembly, election results, French public opinion, and decisions of the French Cabinet. These officers usually handle routine negotiations with the French government and transmit notes received from the French Ministry of Foreign Affairs to the Department of State. The political section reviews all messages from the Department of State and makes the necessary inquiries or gathers the information requested by the department.

The economic section, directed by an economic counselor, keeps the ambassador and the department informed of important economic developments in France. This section reviews all messages touching upon matters of eco-

---

10 William J. Lederer and Eugene Burdick, *The Ugly American* (Norton, 1958), p. 273.

nomic policy, represents the mission in economic negotiations, and keeps close contact with the French finance minister, the minister of national economy, the Bank of France, and other French officials responsible for economic policy. Liaison is also maintained with French businessmen and labor leaders. The scope of the economic section's work is suggested by the names of its operating units: wartime and emergency economic problems, civil aviation, telecommunications, commercial finance and statistics, agriculture, petroleum, commercial policy.

Since Paris is the economic as well as the political capital of France, there is no separate consular office; the consular section is part of the embassy. This section coordinates the activities of the various consular offices throughout France, which provide Americans in France the same services as do secretaries of chambers of commerce, justices of the peace, notaries public, commissioners of immigration and naturalization, and Veterans Administration officials. It examines applicants for admission to the United States, issues permits to exporters of goods destined for the United States, enforces maritime and health laws, administers customs laws, takes care of estates of American citizens who die abroad, and collects information for American business and agriculture.

Attached to the embassy are various kinds of specialist. Information and cultural relations specialists of the United States Information Agency issue a magazine known as *U.S.A.*, which contains materials not available through commercial press agencies. This publication is distributed to every newspaper in France, to leading officials, libraries, schools, and universities. A weekly bulletin is published containing general background information on the United States, such as *Political Parties in the United States, American Views on Economic Reconstruction*. A financial bulletin is issued weekly for distribution to French financial newspapers. Radio broadcasts are arranged, speakers' tours organized, a reference library operated, and information and cultural centers maintained throughout France. The cultural relations attaché tries to stimulate interest in American education, literature, the arts, and to encourage an exchange between French and American teachers, artists, and cultural leaders.

Military and naval attachés send reports direct to the Defense Department; indeed, about half of the Americans attached to the embassy are either military men or civilian officials of the Defense Department. Other departments send representatives to the mission to gather special materials or perform particular tasks. Just under a third of the Americans are actually employees of the State Department. In short, the American Embassy in Paris mirrors the diversity of interests and jobs found in the executive branch in Washington. In miniature, the embassy is a duplicate of the federal executive structure.

OTHER AMERICANS OVERSEAS

The Foreign Service has competitors. Of the over 85,000 Americans employed abroad, exclusive of the armed services, only about one out of 15 are

Foreign Service personnel. Prior to 1939 the Departments of Commerce, Agriculture, Treasury, and others had their own overseas staff. In that year, however, the principle was established that there should be but one foreign service, and that all American employees in a foreign country should be responsible to the chief of mission. Services of the Commerce and Agriculture Departments were merged with those of the Foreign Service. During the war, however, many agencies set up their own offices. The diplomatic missions in many cases were overshadowed, and friction and lack of coordination resulted. The American ambassador in England was not even kept informed of various matters affecting Anglo-American relations, and was all but superseded by the American lend-lease expediter.

After World War II many of these agencies were abolished and some of their duties and personnel were assigned to diplomatic and consular missions. But as postwar programs developed, the principle that the United States should have but one overseas arm was again violated and separate overseas missions were frequently established; for example, the United States Information Agency has its own staff, as do the economic assistance agencies (most of which are classified as Foreign Service Staff). Again friction and waste of effort developed.

According to an executive order of the President, the chief of the diplomatic mission is the ranking American in each foreign country and the coordinator of all overseas programs. In terms of official protocol, even the Vice President and the Secretary of State are junior to the ambassador when they visit the country of his mission; only the President takes precedence. But the ambassador's control is often nominal, as overseas personnel continue to deal directly with their superiors in Washington. Despite the contrary recommendations of the first Hoover Commission, the overseas representation of the United States was further splintered when agricultural attachés were in effect detached from diplomatic missions. Other agencies are also pressing for greater control over their attachés.

The second Hoover Commission reported that as a result of these independent overseas personnel systems, "The United States frequently speaks with numerous, often conflicting voices; its representatives can be played off one against the other by foreign officials, and its manifold policies and programs can be misconstrued." [11] The Commission urged "remedial measures . . . to strengthen the position of our Chief of Diplomatic Mission in each country" through assignment of overseas personnel of all United States agencies (except the military) under a single unified foreign service system, and for the integration of all separate field missions and overseas personnel of these agencies into the regular organizational units of the embassy, subject to the authority and control of the Ambassador or Minister.

---

[11] Commission on Organization of the Executive Branch of the Government, *Overseas Economic Operations* (Government Printing Office, 1955), p. 46.

The incorporation of the International Cooperation Administration as a semiautonomous unit of the State Department is a step in the direction of the Hoover Commission's recommendations. Still, the expansion of the Foreign Service by its integration with key personnel of the State Department will probably be all the integration that the Foreign Service can undertake for several years. And the pressure for separate establishments continues. It is likely that the United States Information Agency, for example, will establish its own overseas career service." [12]

Conducting Foreign Relations— Three Case Studies

Foreign policy is not made according to any set formula. A great deal depends on the nature of the issue, the speed with which the problem arises, the personality of the President, the political situation, and the accidents of history. Sometimes Congress initiates policy; more often it is the President, the Secretary of State, the Joint Chiefs of Staff, or an ambassador. Each problem calls for new decisions; each decision creates new problems. The initiative is sometimes in the hands of our government, but unfortunately it is more often in the hands of other governments. To search for the origins of any particular policy, to isolate the critical areas, to focus on the alternatives is not our purpose here. In the following cases we shall merely suggest the way in which the machinery works.

THE MARSHALL PLAN

In 1947 all Europe was in dire need of economic assistance. Much was already being done by the United States through the various branches of the government. But it seemed likely that unless a greater and broader program was adopted, European economies would be subject to such stresses and strains that the situation would become highly unstable. On March 8, 1947, Under Secretaries Acheson and Clayton discussed the emergency with the President. On May 8, Acheson in a speech at Cleveland, Mississippi, outlined the situation. This was the Administration's trial balloon to sound out public and congressional opinion. The department, meanwhile, consulted Senator Vandenberg, who warned that a carefully prepared long-range program had to be worked out. The State Department's policy planning staff advised that European nations should take the initiative and work out the plan. Secretary of State Marshall approved, but insisted that all Europe, including Russia, be included in the program. Meanwhile the State Department experts published a study on *The Development of the Foreign Reconstruction Policy of the United States.*

---

[12] Robert E. Elder, "A Career Service for U.S.I.A.?" *Foreign Service Journal* (February 1956), pp. 26 ff.

On June 5, the Secretary made a commencement address at Harvard University. Instead of an "as I look at your bright and shining faces" speech, Secretary Marshall took advantage of the opportunity to make a major policy statement. He described the serious situation in Europe, and the need for American help. But the initiative, he said, must come from Europe. The United States should aid in the drafting of a European recovery program and later support such a program.

The U.S.S.R. and her satellites refused to participate but the other European nations "seized the proposal with both hands." Soon sixteen nations met in Paris and formed the Committee of European Economic Cooperation. Within the United States, groups of specialists, calling on consultants and experts outside the government, made reports covering every phase of European recovery. The State Department studied these reports, and advised the President. Congress was not in session, but on November 10 Secretary Marshall appeared before a joint session of the Senate Foreign Relations Committee and the House Committee on Foreign Affairs. He outlined a program calling for an appropriation of over $6 billion for the first fifteen months of the program, which was to run for four years.

President Truman then called a special session of Congress. The legislators were presented with a proposed bill by the State Department, and Administration officials made numerous appearances before committees and addresses to the public. Three special committees, composed of over 350 State Department employees, were set up in the department to work out the details of the program.

Congressmen had their own ideas. Many of them were unconvinced that such vast expenditures were needed to protect American national interests. Then, on February 23-25, 1948, the communist coup in Czechoslovakia startled the world. Congress quickly approved the legislation, but not without amendments. The House included Franco Spain in the program, contrary to the wishes of the President and the Department of State, but aid to Spain was defeated in conference committee.

The Foreign Assistance Act of 1948 was passed on April 3. The next step was to secure the appropriations. The chairman of the House Committee on Appropriations was interested in saving money, and despite the fact that the House had previously approved the program, he recommended and the House approved a billion-dollar reduction in the program. Senator Vandenberg used his great prestige to have the amount restored, and except for the fact that the money was authorized for only a year instead of fifteen months, the final program was substantially as requested. The administration of the program was vested, however, not in the Department of State, but in a separate Economic Cooperation Administration.

The Marshall Plan was initiated by the President and the State Department, but approved by Congress, both houses of which were controlled by the opposite party to that of the chief executive. The leaders of the State Department and of Congress worked closely together, consulting on the details and collaborating in securing approval. Not all decisions, however, require congressional approval or permit public discussion, as the following cases indicate.

A DECISION NOT TO GO TO WAR [13]

On March 20, 1954, General Paul Ely, then French Chief of Staff, arrived in Washington to tell the President, Secretary of State Dulles, and Chairman of the Joint Chiefs of Staff Admiral Arthur W. Radford that unless the United States intervened Indo-China would be lost to the communists.

Some time immediately thereafter—the exact date is unknown—the National Security Council was called into special session. There Admiral Radford, Vice President Nixon, and Secretary Dulles agreed that Indo-China must not be allowed to fall into communist hands lest it set off a "falling row of dominoes" across all Southeast Asia. The Council decided that if necessary the United States should intervene, provided it could obtain the support of its allies and the French would grant Indo-China its independence. A policy paper was prepared, initialed "D.D.E." by the President to make it official.

The President had the constitutional power to put this policy into effect, but, as we have noted, President Eisenhower usually refused to make any major foreign-policy commitment without prior congressional approval. So on April 3, 1954, eight congressmen, the foreign-policy leaders of both parties, were called to a secret conference with Secretary Dulles. When they entered the State Department's fifth-floor conference room they found present Admiral Radford and several high Defense Department officials. The Secretary told the congressmen that the President wanted a joint resolution from Congress permitting the President to use air and naval power in Indo-China. (Constitutionally, the President as commander in chief already had this power.) Admiral Radford warned the congressmen that French forces under siege in Dienbienphu could not hold out much longer and that the fall of Indo-China would endanger all of Southwest Asia. If Congress passed the resolution, the Admiral said, the Navy and Air Force would be used for a single strike to attempt to break the siege.

The congressmen, both Republicans and Democrats, asked, "Would this mean war?" Would communist China intervene on the other side? Radford, who long believed that a showdown with the Chinese communists was inevitable and who felt that the sooner it came the better, minced no words: "Yes." Would land forces have to be used? No one could say for sure. As the talk continued, only Senator Knowland, Republican Senate leader, supported Dulles and Radford, and it became clear to the congressmen that the other Chiefs of Staff did not agree with Radford. Dulles, moreover, had not con-

---

[13] The materials on the Indo-China decision are drawn from Chalmers M. Roberts, "The Day We Didn't Go to War," *The Reporter* (September 14, 1954), pp. 31-35.

sulted our allies; he explained that it would take too long and that emergency action was needed if Dienbienphu was to be saved. Finally the congressmen told Dulles that before they would try to get a joint resolution from Congress, which would in effect commit the nation to war, the Secretary should first line up the Allies. Even Knowland now was cool to intervention.

Within a week Dulles had talked with the diplomatic representatives in Washington of Britain, France, Australia, New Zealand, the Philippines, Thailand, and the three Associated States of Indo-China. Dulles urged these nations to be ready at the time of U.S. military action with a statement defending our intervention and warning the Chinese communists against entering the war. Messages flashed back and forth. Our allies were opposed.

Dulles flew to London to talk personally with Prime Minister Churchill and Foreign Secretary Anthony Eden, but he could find little enthusiasm for American plans. Nor were the British any more ready to favor American military intervention after Dulles proposed the creation of a Southeast Asia Treaty Organization to serve as the vehicle for "united action." When Dulles returned to Washington and called for a drafting meeting on April 20 to set up SEATO, London instructed the British Ambassador not to attend.

A few days later Dulles flew back to Paris. The situation was more alarming than ever; when Radford arrived in Paris he told Dulles that only a massive air attack could save Dienbienphu. On April 24 Dulles and Radford informed Eden that if the Allies would agree, the President was prepared to go to Congress the next day, ask for a joint resolution, and then set the military strike for April 28. Under Secretary of State Walter Bedell Smith, who also supported intervention, gave the same proposal to the French Ambassador in Washington.

Eden balked. He said that coming on the eve of the Geneva Conference—which had been called in part to discuss means to end the seven-year Indo-China war—American military action would be disastrous. He was convinced it would lead to the use of ground troops and the spread of fighting to Communist China. Eden agreed, however, to carry the matter before the English Cabinet. But on Saturday, April 24, word came from the British Cabinet: "No support." On the following Tuesday, Churchill told the House of Commons that the British government was not prepared to undertake any military action in Indo-China. Reluctantly, Dulles concluded that the United States would not intervene. Dienbienphu fell, and eventually an agreement was reached to end the Indo-China war.

QUEMOY AND MATSU—THE FIRST ROUND [14]

Until September 3, 1954, few Americans had heard of the small islands of Quemoy and Matsu, which lie just off the Chinese mainland. Yet twice, in 1954 and 1958, we came close to a shooting war with the Chinese communists

---

[14] These materials are drawn from Stewart Alsop, "The Story Behind Quemoy: How We Drifted Close to War," *The Saturday Evening Post*, December 13, 1958, pp. 26 ff.

over these two islands. The story of our involvement began long before 1954 and is still far from over. Here we are concerned only with one of the many decisions—that of September 1954—made by the United States not to force a showdown.

These small islands, all military experts agree, are indefensible and hence not vital to the defense of Formosa, the headquarters of our ally, Nationalist China. Their only advantages are to serve as bases in staging small guerrilla attacks against the mainland or to serve as stepping stones in the event of an invasion of the mainland. But they have symbolic importance—their abandonment under communist pressures might encourage the communists to try seizing more territory by military threats, and might lead our Asiatic allies to doubt our willingness to defend them in time of need. Then too, the loss of these offshore islands would make "official" what is already recognized—namely, that the Nationalist Chinese retain no serious hope of returning to power on the mainland.

For a long time, our European allies have strongly urged that these off-shore islands be abandoned because they are not worth an all-out war, or even the risk of such a war. On the other hand, our Nationalist Chinese ally demands that these islands be protected. In the 1952 elections, the Republicans had been bitterly critical of the Truman Administration's Far Eastern policies and had charged, among other things, that the Democrats had failed to support Chiang. Hence the political victory of Republicans was generally taken as a sign that the United States would take a more active role in the Nationalist China-Red China struggle.

As his first official act, President Eisenhower withdrew the Seventh Fleet from its patrol of the Formosa Straits, and thus "unleashed Chiang." Democrats charged that the President and Secretary Dulles had made a "grandstand play," to make it appear that the Republicans had a more dynamic "liberation" policy, but that the "unleashing" amounted to nothing. Dulles defended the action as psychological warfare to make the communists more willing to settle the Korean War. Apparently this is all the Eisenhower Administration intended, for immediately after Chiang was publicly "unleashed," he was just as quickly but more quietly "released" when he was forced to agree not to use any equipment supplied by the United States for any attacks on the mainland.

In Formosa, however, the American Military Advisory Group took the unleashing order as a signal to step up their work. MAG, whose mission was to help strengthen the Nationalist military forces, encouraged Chiang to build up his forces on Quemoy and to replace the expendable guerrillas with first-line troops. By 1954, over 80,000 Nationalist troops were in place on Quemoy. To the military men in Formosa this seemed like a perfectly obvious step, but it was a step that was to have grave political consequences.

Also at work on the offshore islands were American intelligence agents; operating under the cover of Western Enterprises, Inc., these agents equipped and trained guerrillas for raids on the mainland. But early in 1954 these agents were withdrawn and U.S. military officers, who had previously been discouraged from going to the offshore islands, appeared openly in uniform to help train the Nationalist troops.

On September 3, 1954, the Chinese communists opened an artillery barrage, and two American officers were killed. What should the United States do? The President was vacationing in Denver and Secretary Dulles was in Manila organizing SEATO. The Pentagon was the first official agency to react. Seeing the shelling as a probable prelude to the invasion of Quemoy, the Joint Chiefs made two recommendations to the President. The first, unanimously supported by all the Joint Chiefs, and quickly approved by the President, gave Chiang's air force permission to bomb military objectives just across from Quemoy.

The second recommendation by the Joint Chiefs was far more portentous. It was to force a showdown. The Chiefs proposed that Chiang be allowed to bomb targets far inland, backed up by the pledge that if Red China launched a retaliatory assault on Quemoy or Formosa, American naval and air forces would join the battle, even using nuclear bombs if needed. But the Joint Chiefs were not united; General Matthew Ridgway, Chief of Staff of the Army, believed that action could not be limited to sea and air strikes and that to force a showdown would lead to an all-out war.

Ridgway found allies in Robert Bowie, Chief of the State Department's Policy Planning Staff, and General Walter B. Smith, the Under Secretary of State. When they heard of the Joint Chiefs' proposal, "their hair stood on end in horror." Smith immediately called the President, his old chief, and pointed out to him that a decision that might lead to global destruction should not be made lightly. The President agreed and scheduled a meeting of the National Security Council in Denver for September 12, the day Secretary Dulles was to return.

Dulles, who was hurrying back to the United States, had cabled to the military two questions: Can Quemoy be defended against all-out assault? Are Quemoy and the other offshore islands essential to the defense of Formosa? The answer that came back to both questions was "No."

When Dulles' plane landed on the West Coast for refueling, it was boarded by Bowie, who had flown out in order to ride back with Dulles and convince him of what Bowie thought was the folly of the Radford proposal. Bowie was especially worried because Radford had the active support of the Assistant Secretary of State for Far Eastern Affairs, Walter Robertson.

When the National Security Council assembled in the officers' club of Lowry Air Force Base, there was still doubt as to which side Dulles would favor. But the Secretary argued that we should not make any commitment to Chiang that would in effect allow him to determine whether or not the United States went to war against Communist China, and that American forces should intervene only in the event the attack on the offshore islands was clearly a prelude to the attack on Formosa. The President agreed.

Eventually the United States signed a treaty with Nationalist China to defend Formosa and the Pescadores, and the President secured from Congress a resolution pledging the United States to defend Formosa and the Pescadores, but purposely leaving vague the question of Quemoy and Matsu. Efforts to persuade Chiang to evacuate his forces from the offshore islands failed, but in April 1955 the Red Chinese stopped their bombardments of Quemoy. For three years all was quiet. Then in 1958 the bombardments started again, lasting for another six months. When the next flare-up will come, no one knows. But apparently the basic policy of the United States stems from the decision made in the fall of 1954—to defend the offshore islands with American military force only if they prove militarily essential to the protection of Formosa and the Pescadores.

The United States and the United Nations

The United States is an international joiner. Today it belongs to all the most important world organizations, and its representatives attend all major international conferences. The story of how the United States failed to join the League of Nations but took the leading role in the formation of the United Nations is well known. But not so many people realize that the international organization, and the international conference, are major weapons of American diplomacy. In addition to the United Nations and its related agencies, the United States is a member of well over two hundred international organizations of various types. The United States joins with other nations to carry on functions that can be best handled on an international basis. Slowly but inevitably certain functions are being transferred from the national to the international level.

In its own hemisphere the United States is a member of the *Organization of American States,* a regional organization of the nations of North and South America. Under its auspices Inter-American Conferences meet about once every five years, and special conferences meet more frequently to consider special problems. Foreign ministers' meetings convene whenever necessary to consider urgent questions and to consult on threats to the security of the Western Hemisphere. A council forms a continuing group between meetings of conferences and foreign ministers. The famous Pan-American Union serves as a central administrative unit. There are also several specialized organizations, including the Inter-American Economic and Social Council and the Inter-American Cultural Council.

THE UNITED NATIONS

The United States maintains a permanent diplomatic mission at the headquarters of the United Nations, the most important international organization to which we belong. This mission is headed by a chief holding the rank of ambassador, and includes three other leading diplomats, all appointed by the President with the advice and consent of the Senate. In addition, the President with the consent of the Senate appoints five representatives to the General Assembly, who serve for the duration of a particular session. The chief of the mission is responsible for coordinating the actions of our many delegates to other divisions of the U.N. Within the Department of State, a separate Bureau of International Organization Affairs coordinates American policies and activities with other federal agencies, helps to prepare instructions to our representatives, serves as technical adviser to them, spreads information to the public and the department regarding the United Nations, and assumes general responsibility for American participation.

MAJOR UNITED NATIONS AGENCIES

The United Nations is an organization designed to bring nations together to maintain international peace and security, to develop friendly relations, to achieve international cooperation in solving world problems, to promote and encourage respect for human rights, and to harmonize the actions of nations in attaining these common goals. Although basically an association of nations, the United Nations is an international legal personality with the power to make treaties and competence to claim reparations for injury to its agents. It maintains its own legal staff, operates its own headquarters, and has its own flag. The major United Nations organs are the Security Council, the General Assembly, the Social and Economic Council, the Trusteeship Council, the Secretariat, and the International Court of Justice.

The *Security Council* consists of five permanent members—Nationalist China, the Soviet Union, France, Great Britain, and the United States—plus six nonpermanent members elected by the General Assembly for two-year terms and ineligible for immediate re-election. Its chief function is to preserve and maintain international peace, and it has wide authority to take steps necessary to maintain world security. All the members of the United Nations are pledged by its charter to accept the decisions of the Security Council and to resolve their disputes by peaceful methods.

The Security Council, acting in behalf of all member nations, carries on discussions, makes investigations and recommendations, and even has authority to enforce its decisions. It may call upon nations to apply sanctions, including military force. It was originally intended that member nations would make armed forces available that the Security Council could use whenever it felt they were needed. Disputes between the Soviet bloc and the free nations have made it impossible to carry out these provisions. Nevertheless, nations are pledged to supply the military power that the Security Council requires to secure the peace. The Council has, of course, only as much power to enforce its decisions as the nations composing the United Nations are willing to supply.

Each member of the Security Council appoints a representative whose full-time job is to serve on the Council, which meets in continuous session. Council sessions are dramatic events. The representatives, behind the placards bearing the names of their countries, sit around the now famous curved table. Behind the representatives are their advisers. Under the kleig lights the delegates carry on their debates in five languages. The chairmanship of the Council rotates monthly among the national representatives.

Each member of the Council has one vote. Decisions on *procedural* matters require the approval of *any* seven members. Decisions on *substantive* issues must have the approval of seven nations, but any one of the five permanent members can *veto* the decision. A substantive issue has been defined to include any contemplated action, even as small as calling for a report or hearing a witness. And the veto applies to a vote on whether a question is to be regarded as procedural or substantive. When a permanent member *abstains* from voting, however, it is not counted as a veto.

This big-power veto has hit the headlines because of its frequent use by the Soviet Union. Many students of world affairs believe that the veto is only a reflection of the realities of the situation. In the present world of sovereign nations no great power can be induced except by armed might to act contrary to its own wishes on matters it considers essential. With or without the formal power of veto, the Security Council can maintain peace and security only if the big powers cooperate. The veto does, nevertheless, permit a nation to block collective action without expending its resources. The Soviet Union has been able by a veto to stop activities that would not have been worth preventing by force or other diplomatic measures. It was only the Soviet Union's absence from the Security Council that enabled that body to organize United Nations armed forces readily in the face of aggression against the Republic of Korea. At the same time it was the determination of the United States to act against North Korean aggression that gave substance to the Security Council's decision.

Although the United States originally insisted upon the veto so that we would not be forced to accept decisions we thought contrary to our national interest, the Soviet use of the veto has caused our government to "re-think" its position. In general, the view of the American government today is that the veto should be retained to prevent the use of force by the Council against the wishes of a permanent member, but that it should be abolished as applied to the *procedures* for the settlement of disputes not involving military force.

Despite the Soviet Union's obstreperous tactics, the Council has in its short period of existence demonstrated its usefulness as a diplomatic force. It has had a part in mitigating disputes between Russia and Iran, India and Pakistan, the Netherlands and Indonesia, Israel and the Arab world. The most spectacular move was the decision to use force to stop the aggression of the communists of North Korea and China. On June 24, 1950, North Korean armies attacked the Republic of Korea, a regime established under United Nations auspices. The United States promptly responded by sending in air and naval forces. On June 25 the Security Council (the Soviet Union was absent) called on the North Koreans to withdraw their invasion forces. On July 7 the Council—the Soviet Union still being absent—made the United States its agent to direct and organize United Nations forces in the area. Although the United States furnished the bulk of the troops, over thirty nations supplied men and munitions. For the first time, an international army had been organized under the command of an international organization to maintain the peace and security of the world. The independence of the Korean Republic was maintained and aggression was stopped. Again in 1956-57, the United Nations furnished a military force to police the Suez Canal.

The *General Assembly* is composed of all the 82 member nations of the United Nations. Each nation has one vote, and not more than five representatives. The Assembly can make investigations and recommendations on any questions except those currently before the Council or matters that are "essentially within the domestic jurisdiction of any state." The latter limitation is easier to state than to define, for the distinction between domestic and foreign affairs is elusive. The Assembly's decisions are only recommendations, since enforcement action is a responsibility of the Security Council. But a nation that votes in favor of a General Assembly decision is likely to heed its own recommendation.

Decisions of the Assembly require only a two-thirds vote even on important questions. The conflict between the Soviet Union and the other big powers, and the Soviet's use of the veto, have forced many issues that the Council has failed to act on to be referred to the General Assembly. The

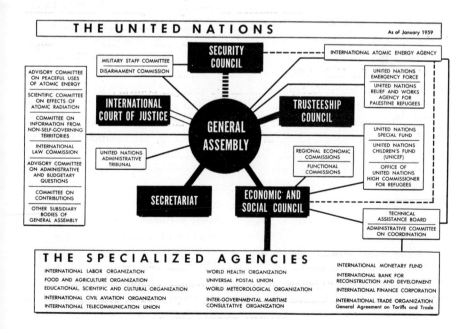

THE UNITED NATIONS   As of January 1959

SECURITY COUNCIL

MILITARY STAFF COMMITTEE
DISARMAMENT COMMISSION

INTERNATIONAL ATOMIC ENERGY AGENCY

ADVISORY COMMITTEE ON PEACEFUL USES OF ATOMIC ENERGY

SCIENTIFIC COMMITTEE ON EFFECTS OF ATOMIC RADIATION

COMMITTEE ON INFORMATION FROM NON-SELF-GOVERNING TERRITORIES

INTERNATIONAL LAW COMMISSION

ADVISORY COMMITTEE ON ADMINISTRATIVE AND BUDGETARY QUESTIONS

COMMITTEE ON CONTRIBUTIONS

OTHER SUBSIDIARY BODIES OF GENERAL ASSEMBLY

INTERNATIONAL COURT OF JUSTICE

UNITED NATIONS ADMINISTRATIVE TRIBUNAL

GENERAL ASSEMBLY

TRUSTEESHIP COUNCIL

REGIONAL ECONOMIC COMMISSIONS
FUNCTIONAL COMMISSIONS

UNITED NATIONS EMERGENCY FORCE
UNITED NATIONS RELIEF AND WORKS AGENCY FOR PALESTINE REFUGEES
UNITED NATIONS SPECIAL FUND
UNITED NATIONS CHILDREN'S FUND (UNICEF)
OFFICE OF UNITED NATIONS HIGH COMMISSIONER FOR REFUGEES

SECRETARIAT

ECONOMIC AND SOCIAL COUNCIL

TECHNICAL ASSISTANCE BOARD
ADMINISTRATIVE COMMITTEE ON COORDINATION

THE SPECIALIZED AGENCIES

INTERNATIONAL LABOR ORGANIZATION
FOOD AND AGRICULTURE ORGANIZATION
EDUCATIONAL, SCIENTIFIC AND CULTURAL ORGANIZATION
INTERNATIONAL CIVIL AVIATION ORGANIZATION
INTERNATIONAL TELECOMMUNICATION UNION

WORLD HEALTH ORGANIZATION
UNIVERSAL POSTAL UNION
WORLD METEOROLOGICAL ORGANIZATION
INTER-GOVERNMENTAL MARITIME CONSULTATIVE ORGANIZATION

INTERNATIONAL MONETARY FUND
INTERNATIONAL BANK FOR RECONSTRUCTION AND DEVELOPMENT
INTERNATIONAL FINANCE CORPORATION
INTERNATIONAL TRADE ORGANIZATION
General Agreement on Tariffs and Trade

Assembly has taken over some of the Council's functions of maintaining peace and security.

In addition to these deliberative, investigating, and recommending activities, the Assembly has supervisory responsibilities over all other organs of the United Nations except for the Security Council and the International Court of Justice. Both the Council and Secretary General make annual reports to the Assembly; the Economic and Social Council and the Trusteeship Council operate under its authority.

The Assembly draws up the budget and apportions United Nations expenses among the members. It elects new member nations and the Secretary General on the recommendations of the Security Council, and shares with the Council the election of judges to the International Court of Justice. By itself it elects the nonpermanent members of the Security Council, all members of the Economic and Social Council, and some of the members of the Trusteeship Council. The Assembly shares with the Council responsibility for proposing amendments to the charter and the authority to call a general conference to review the charter.

The General Assembly meets in regular annual sessions on the third Tuesday in September and in such special sessions as are called by the Security Council or by a majority of the members of the United Nations. Each session a president is chosen, generally from the small or middle powers, along with seven vice-presidents. Much of the business is carried on in committees. English, French, Spanish, Chinese, and Russian are the official languages; the first three are "working languages."

The General Assembly, the "town meeting of the world," has, among other things, adopted and presented for national signatures a convention outlawing genocide—"the destruction of national, ethnic, racial, or religious groups"—adopted The Universal Declaration of Human Rights, established a system of relief for Palestinian refugees, provided for the feeding and medical care of nearly five million children, administered a large-scale antituberculosis project, established a program to provide technical assistance to backward nations, and assisted in the settlement of disputes and resistance to aggression. An example of the latter is the General Assembly's action in recommending sanctions against Communist China because of its intervention and aggression against the Republic of Korea. The Assembly also played a prominent role in the settlement of the Lebanon crisis of 1958.

MORE SPECIALIZED AGENCIES

The Economic and Social Council is less spectacular than either the Security Council or the General Assembly, but in many ways its work offers the most promise for developing an orderly and peaceful world community. This council consists of eighteen nations elected by the General Assembly. Its job is to promote and coordinate activities designed to provide higher standards of living; solve international economic, social, and health programs; promote international cultural and educational cooperation; and encourage universal respect for and observance of human rights. The council has established fact-finding and consulting commissions through which international conferences are held, draft conventions are prepared, and recommendations are made to the General Assembly.

The Economic and Social Council is the United Nations' point of contact with the specialized agencies that have been established by agreements among most governments. Some of these agencies were established many years before the United Nations was organized; a great many have been created since that time. They include such agencies as the Universal Postal Union, International Labor Organization, Food and Agricultural Organization, World Health Organization, United Nations Educational, Scientific and Cultural Organization. Each of these specialized agencies has its own charter, budget, staff, and the like. In some cases the specialized agencies include representatives from private organizations as well as governmental representatives.

The United Nations Educational, Scientific and Cultural Organization, more generally known as UNESCO, is one of the more active specialized agencies. Composed of 81 member nations, it has the responsibility of promoting peace and security through educational, scientific, and cultural cooperation. "Since wars begin in the minds of men," its preamble states, "it is in the minds of men that the defences of peace must be constructed." UNESCO functions in member nations through national commissions. The United States National Commission for UNESCO consists of one hundred members representing various types of private organizations, and includes local, state, and federal officials. The National Commission advises our delegation to the UNESCO General Conference and sponsors projects designed to advance mutual knowledge, diffuse information, and increase popular education.

By bringing people of various nations together to work on critically important tasks, UNESCO and the other specialized agencies of the United Nations are helping to build a sense of community among the peoples of the world. As more and more functions are taken over by the international community, all people will have concrete evidence that we live in one world, that the economic prosperity of one nation is tied to the prosperity of other nations, and that the health and security of the people of the world can be protected only by international cooperation.

The *Trusteeship Council* of the United Nations supervises the administration of territories held in trust until the people who live in them "become of age" and can govern themselves. The council, composed of six trustee and six nontrustee nations, is responsible to the General Assembly for general supervision of trustee powers to insure that they meet their charter obligations to the 200 million people living in territories that are not fully self-governing.

The *Secretariat,* administered by the Secretary General, provides an international civil service to staff and operate the United Nations agencies. The

Secretary General, however, is more than the director of this civil service; as the chief administrative officer of the United Nations, he is the only person who stands for the United Nations as a whole, and he has certain political responsibilities. Authorized to bring to the Security Council's attention any matter that in his opinion may threaten peace, he can direct world attention to world issues. The Security Council, meeting in private session, recommends the candidate for the Secretary-Generalship to the General Assembly. The appointment of a candidate requires only a majority vote of the nations present in the Assembly. The charter itself specifies no term of office, but the General Assembly has made five years the normal term. The Secretary General appoints the staff under regulations prescribed by the Assembly. Members of the staff retain their citizenship, but they are prohibited from seeking instructions from any government since they function as an international civil service.

The *International Court of Justice* is the United Nations' judicial branch. It provides a judicial forum for the settlement of disputes between *nations*. It has jurisdiction over disputes only when the parties to the case give their consent. Some 34 states have signed the optional clause, and have thus agreed in advance to submit to the court certain types of legal dispute. The court (unlike the United States Supreme Court) also renders advisory opinions when so requested by the General Assembly or the Security Council. The court is composed of fifteen judges who have a term of nine years; no more than two of the judges may be nationals of the same state.

The United Nations' failure to solve each and every dispute among the nations of the world, and its inability to resolve the conflict between the East and West, have caused some Americans to become disillusioned. Part of their disillusionment stems from their failure to understand the nature of the organization. The United Nations is essentially the collective name of some 82 nations that have organized themselves in order to facilitate cooperation. It is a diplomatic technique that simplifies the problem of multilateral consultation. The United Nations, unlike the United States of America, is not an entity separate and above its member states. Its power is the power of the nations of the world. What the United Nations can do is what the member nations want to do.

The United Nations is a useful organization for diplomatic consultation. It provides techniques and machinery for discussion, for working out joint plans of action, and for establishing international machinery to handle worldwide problems. As such it has been a useful device by which the United States has been able to carry on its relations with the other nations of the world. But the United Nations, like every other agency of international politics, is affected by the fact that the world is divided into separate national sovereignties.

CHAPTER **24**

To Provide
for the Common Defense

At 8:15 on the morning of August 6, 1945, an A-bomb hurtled down toward the city of Hiroshima. At this moment there were 340,000 people living there. One minute later only 280,000 were left alive; of these, 31,000 more were to die from injuries. A total of 91,000 men, women, and children were killed by this single bomb; tens of thousands more were injured and maimed. This was a small bomb. Two days later an "improved model" was dropped on Nagasaki.

Seven years later in the Central Pacific, a deserted island was destroyed by a fusion-type bomb—the hydrogen bomb. Spectacular as the reports were, seven years of living with atomic weapons had exhausted the supply of superlatives, and many thought that the fusion bomb had introduced nothing new except a larger area of death. But it had done far more than that. The hydrogen bomb, with its associated fallout and radiation, added a dimension of destruction to atomic weapons as great as these weapons had added to more conventional techniques.[1] Today, intercontinental missiles can carry these fusion bombs to any place in the world.

We live in a world in which literally hundreds of millions could be killed in a single night.[2] An attack on 50 of our most important cities would produce at least 10 to 15 million dead, 15 to 20 million injured from blast and heat, and 25 to 35 million casualties from fall-out—a total of 65 million dead and injured Americans, one out of every three of us. Winston Churchill has warned that it may no longer be possible "for nations to fight each other and survive

---

[1] Bernard Brodie, "Strategy Hits a Dead End," *Harper's* (October 1955), p. 34.

[2] See testimony of Lt. Gen. James M. Gavin, Chief of Research and Development, Department of the Army, before Subcommittee on Air Force of Senate Committee on Military Affairs, May 25, 1956, reported in *The New York Times,* June 29, 1956; and Special Studies Report II of Rockefeller Brothers Fund, *International Security: The Military Aspect* (Doubleday, 1958), p. 9.

as nations, or even for armies to fight a battle and have at the end of it enough men on either side to fight another." [3] The age of absolute weapons has arrived.

To some, the fact that men are able to destroy their fellow men by the millions brings the hope that they will forego such a foolish venture. To others, it means that modern civilization is doomed. But all agree that the United States must pay a high price to maintain security in a world of absolute weapons. Not only is the United States open to attack every minute of the day and night, but in any major war we would undoubtedly be the prime target. No longer will we have a year or two to mobilize our military might while our traditional allies hold the enemy from our shores. If an all-out thermonuclear war comes, it will be too late to start to build up our military strength. What, then, are the elements of a defense program?

First and foremost we have to be powerful enough not only to win the next war but to avoid it. We need military power of such proportions that any potential aggressor would be reluctant to attack the United States or its allies. This military power must be ready at a moment's notice to strike a stupendous retaliatory blow.

Second, in addition to massive retaliatory forces, we need mobile units for limited wars, to resist aggressions of a local nature, and to achieve objectives in situations where it would be suicidal to use major nuclear weapons. As the influential Rockefeller Brothers report pointed out, "We can no longer rely on our capability to deliver crushing retaliation on the Soviet homeland as the deterrent to *all* types of aggression. For with the growth of the Soviet capability to inflict a massive blow on the United States, there exists the great

---

[3] Paraphrase of Churchill by Roger Hilsman, *Military Policy and National Security,* William W. Kaufman (ed.) (Princeton Univ. Press, 1956), p. 44.

U. S. and U. S. S. R. — 1958 PRODUCTION COMPARED

(U. S. output equals 100)

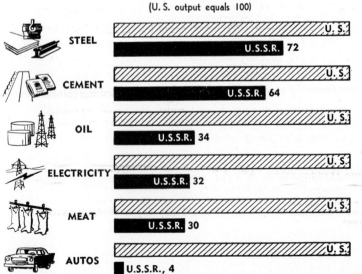

	U.S.	U.S.S.R.
STEEL	100	72
CEMENT	100	64
OIL	100	34
ELECTRICITY	100	32
MEAT	100	30
AUTOS	100	4

American military power includes more than combat forces; it comprises also our industrial and agricultural resources.

Source: E. I. du Pont de Nemours & Co.

danger that the Soviet Union will seek to use its nuclear striking force as a shield behind which to expand by more limited means." [4]

Third, not only must we have powerful offensive forces, but also strong defenses at home to complement our deterrent military power. If we make an inviting target, the enemy may be persuaded to believe that he could knock us out in a single blow and destroy our ability to retaliate.

Friends and Neighbors

Our power includes that of other nations whose security is inextricably interwoven with our own. Over 300 million intelligent and productive people make up our Western European allies. They produce over 65 million tons of steel a year and they possess the second strongest navy in the world; they have bases, plants, airports, and a great military and industrial potential. Unless it is firmly defended, however, this great potential could fall overnight before a military thrust by the communist world. Moreover, the United States would lose military bases needed to carry the fighting to the enemy.

One of the most important links in the American defense effort is the North Atlantic Treaty among the United States, Canada, United Kingdom, France, Italy, Belgium, Denmark, Iceland, Luxembourg, the Netherlands, Norway, Portugal, Greece, Turkey, and West Germany. These nations have agreed "by means of continuous and effective self-help and mutual aid" to develop their own capacities to resist armed attack. Each nation has pledged itself to regard an attack on any member of the treaty community as an attack on all.

The North Atlantic Treaty is more than a scrap of paper,[5] for a permanent defense organization has been established to give it real meaning. A North Atlantic Council composed of top cabinet officers—foreign, defense, and finance ministers—meets intermittently, and a board of permanent representatives works continuously in Paris on long-range strategic matters. There is also an International Staff under the direction of a Secretary General who serves as vice-chairman of the council. The staff provides technical services, prepares reports, and insures that the council's decisions are carried out. A Military Committee of the top military leaders meets frequently, and there is a permanent group of military men, the Standing Group, located in Washington. France, the United Kingdom, and the United States, as well as regional military committees, are all represented in the Standing Group. Financial, economic, and military production committees round out the North Atlantic Treaty Organization, popularly known as NATO.

NATO has at its disposal several military commands, of which the best known is the Supreme Headquarters, Allied Powers, Europe (SHAPE) under

---

[4] The "Rockefeller Report," *op. cit.,* p. 13.

[5] Department of State Publication 4630, *North Atlantic Treaty Organization, Its Development and Significance,* 1952.

the direction of an American commander. Although the United States is not required by the terms of the treaty to provide military assistance, it has taken the lead in supplying troops and munitions for NATO forces. In addition, the United States furnishes machines, tools, and technical assistance to its allies in order to increase their ability to contribute to mutual defense.

The Southeast Asia Treaty Organization, popularly known as SEATO, forms another link in the American defense system. The United States, France, the United Kingdom, Australia, New Zealand, the Philippines, Pakistan, and Thailand are pledged to consider as a threat to their own security communist aggression against any member nation or against Cambodia, Laos, or South Vietnam, and to meet the common danger in accord with their own constitutional processes. In case of nonmilitary aggression or attacks by noncommunist nations, these nations have agreed to consult on common action. Each nation maintains a permanent representative in Bangkok, Thailand, the permanent headquarters of SEATO. The council, composed of foreign ministers, is the governing body and meets at irregular intervals.

Through the Rio Pact (The Inter-American Treaty of Reciprocal Assistance), the United States has joined with its southern neighbors in a multilateral treaty of mutual help. To the north, the United States has a defensive alliance with Canada that predates World War II and recognizes that the two countries are a strategic entity. We also have bilateral agreements of mutual defense and assistance with Nationalist China, Korea, Japan, and the Philippines.

Politicians, Bureaucrats, and Armed Forces

Both the President and Congress are responsible for the common defense, and both have the powers needed to discharge that responsibility. Congress controls the purse; the President directs the sword. Congress declares war; the President runs it. Congress appropriates the money and determines the size, structure, and organization of the fighting forces; the President is the commander in chief of these forces.

Although Congress, President, State Department, and National Security Council make over-all policy and integrate our national security programs, the day-by-day work of developing and executing our military policy is the job of the Department of Defense.

PENTAGONIA

The world's largest office building, the famed Pentagon, is the headquarters of the United States Defense Department, a department so big that in comparison it makes even the American Telephone and Telegraph Company look like a small-town business. The Department spends over $40 billion a year, 10 per cent of the entire nation's gross annual product. At work in the Pentagon are 21,000 civilians and 10,000 soldiers. Over 170 security officers prowl the corridors to guard the restricted areas in which the nation's military plans are made. This vast building is a communications center that is in constant touch with our armed forces throughout the world.

Prior to 1947 there were two separate military departments, War and Navy. But the lack of coordination between them during World War II led to demands for unification. In 1947 the Air Force, already an autonomous unit within the War Department, was made an independent unit, and the three military departments—Army, Navy, Air Force—were placed under the "general supervision" of the Secretary of Defense.

The Unification Act of 1947, a hesitant first step, was a bundle of compromises between the Army, which favored a tightly integrated department, and the Navy, which wanted a loosely federated structure. It also reflected compromises between congressmen who felt that disunity and interservice rivalries were undermining our defense efforts, and, on the other hand, congressmen who feared that a unified defense establishment would defy civilian control and smother dissenting views.

The 1947 act had not been long in operation before it became apparent that the Department of Defense, which was supposed to be the nation's sword, looked more like a pitchfork.[6] All that the 1947 act had really accomplished was to bring the military services under a common organization chart. But instead of having moved from two military departments to one, we had ended up with three. Despite further centralizing moves, congressional amendments in 1949, and presidential directives in 1953, each service retained considerable autonomy and the Defense Department was unable to develop an integrated military program.

In 1958, when headlines featured factional struggles among military services while the Russians were sending up sputniks, President Eisenhower came forward with Defense Department reorganization proposals. He urged Congress to appropriate all funds to the Secretary of Defense rather than to the separate military departments, and to give the Secretary full control over the armed services, including the authority to transfer or abolish combatant functions and to establish direct lines of command between his office and operational forces in the field. The President recommended that a Director of Defense Research and Engineering be appointed to operate directly under the Secretary of Defense with the same rank as the service civilian secretaries and with power to coordinate development-of-weapons systems. The President also asked that the Joint Chiefs of Staff be strengthened by giving its Chairman a vote, that the staff of the Joint Chiefs of Staff be enlarged, and that each service chief be allowed to delegate his command duties so that he could devote most of his time to the work of the Joint Chiefs.

---

[6] See Carnegie Corporation of New York, *Quarterly* (October 1958), p. 1.

The President's plan to unify further the Defense Department by increasing the authority of the Secretary of Defense and by centralizing the Joint Chiefs was subjected to heavy congressional fire. Many congressmen, fearful of creating a "Prussian-type" military establishment, argued that instead of

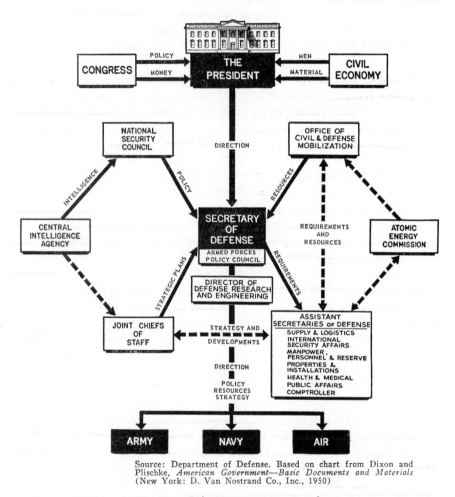

Source: Department of Defense. Based on chart from Dixon and Plischke, *American Government—Basic Documents and Materials* (New York: D. Van Nostrand Co., Inc., 1950)

Relations among national security agencies.

concentrating greater authority in the Defense Secretary, what was needed was a cleaning out of the large number of assistant secretaries of defense and assistants to the assistant secretaries that had been spawned in the Defense Secretary's office. They contended that with layer upon layer of civilian staffs, with so many initials to obtain on every action, and with so much red tape, nothing was getting done.

Other critics of the President's recommendations charged that the problems of the Defense Department did not grow primarily out of faulty organization but out of second-rate personnel. The average tenure of the top civilian political officials in the Defense Department has been only about eighteen months. Among the civilian leaders in one service were "a former school prexy, . . . a small furniture company president . . . ; another small company president; . . . a banker from a little midwest town; . . . a playboy from the West Coast." [7] This was the group in charge of the largest business in the world.

President Eisenhower felt so strongly about his proposals for Defense Department reorganization that he used the prestige and influence of his office to campaign in their behalf. In the end, the Defense Department Reorganization Act of 1958 gave the President most of what he wanted. Congress, however, refused to approve the appropriation of funds to the Secretary of Defense. Furthermore, at the prompting of the Naval Air Force, Marine Corps, and National Guard (who, as Professor Ivan Hinderaker has pointed out, live in constant fear that somebody will abolish them), [8] Congress insisted that the Secretary of Defense notify the House and Senate armed services committees if he contemplates any major change in combatant functions. If within 30 days either committee disapproves, each chamber has another 40 days to stop the order from taking effect.

Congress also refused to repeal a provision, which President Eisenhower called "legalized insubordination," authorizing a secretary of a military department or a member of the Joint Chiefs to make any recommendations he wishes to Congress about Defense Department matters even if contrary to Defense Department policy. Eisenhower's view, as that of other Presidents, is that he is the commander in chief, that the Secretary of Defense is his deputy, and that it is the duty of all military men to support before Congress and the country the agreed-on policies of the Defense Department regardless of their own judgment.

On the other hand, congressmen who appropriate the money believe they are entitled to know what the professional military men think about official recommendations. Hence they refused to alter this legal right of high-ranking officers to take their case to Congress.

Despite all the reorganization, each of the three military departments still exists as a separate organization with its own civilian secretary, under secretary, assistant secretaries, and military chiefs. Only the Secretary of Defense has Cabinet rank, and only he regularly sits with the National Security Council, but his ability to control the three departments still depends in large part on his influence with the President and Congress.

---

[7] An anonymous official quoted by William R. Kintner and others, *Forging a New Sword: A Study of the Department of Defense* (Harper, 1958), p. 71.

[8] Ivan Hinderaker, "The Eisenhower Administration: The Last Years," in *American Government Annual, 1959-1960* (Holt, 1959), p. 82.

The *Armed Forces Policy Council* constitutes the Defense Department's "little cabinet." It is composed of the department secretary, deputy secretary, the three civilian secretaries of the military departments, and the Director of Defense, Research and Engineering, the Chairman of the Joint Chiefs of Staff, and the chief of staff of each of the services. It advises the Secretary on matters of broad policy.

The *Joint Chiefs of Staff* serve as the principal military advisers to the President, the National Security Council, and the Secretary of Defense. They comprise the military heads of the three armed services, the commandant of the Marine Corps—whenever a matter comes up directly concerning the Marine Corps—and a chairman, all appointed by the President with the consent of the Senate for a two-year term, and eligible in peacetime for only one reappointment. Behind double steel doors in the Pentagon the Joint Chiefs shape strategic plans, work out joint supply programs, review major supply and personnel requirements, formulate programs for joint training, make recommendations to the Secretary of Defense on the establishment of unified commands in strategic areas, and provide American representation on the military commissions of the United Nations, NATO, and SEATO.

The Chairman of the Joint Chiefs takes precedence over all other military officers. He presides over the meetings of the Joint Chiefs, prepares the agenda, directs the staff, and informs the Secretary of Defense and the President of issues on which the Joint Chiefs have been unable to reach agreement.

It is too early to assess the impact of the Defense Reorganization Act of 1958 on the operations of the Joint Chiefs of Staff, but many students of defense policies do not believe it will basically alter the pattern of interservice rivalries. Each chief continues to wear two hats, one as chief of his own armed service and the other as a member of the Joint Chiefs. His life-long loyalties are to his own service, and it is difficult for him to see military priorities except in terms of the missions of the service for which he is primarily responsible.

In the past, the Joint Chiefs have been unable to develop united strategies or to agree on the allocation of resources. There is more to disputes among military services, however, than mere professional jealousies. The technological revolution in warfare has rendered obsolete existing concepts about military missions. In the past, it made sense to divide command over land, sea, and air forces, but today "technology makes a mockery of such distinctions." [9] Under the impact of ever-changing military technology and the outmoding of traditional divisions of roles and missions, each service supports a concept that enables it to claim a decisive role, each "seeks to control weapons which

---

[9] Henry A. Kissinger, *Nuclear Weapons and Foreign Policy* (Doubleday, 1958), p. 228.

will enable it to carry out that role virtually independently of operations of other services." [10]

The Army, for example, argues that missiles are a form of artillery and should be developed by the Army. The Air Force insists they are merely an extension of the airplane and should be developed by the Air Force. The Navy argues that it needs to develop missiles for its submarines. The artificial division of military missions among the services also leads to many other disputes. For example, the Air Force opposes the diversion of airplanes to serve as an airlift for the Army on the grounds that planes are most needed for strategic and tactical purposes. But the Army wants planes so that it can rapidly move its forces to theaters of combat.

Frequently interservice rivalries break out in the Congress and the press. Quasi-official organizations such as the Association of the United States Army, the Navy League, and the Air Force Association lobby openly in behalf of their particular service. Behind the scenes the military men themselves are active. The President, as we have mentioned, has tried to keep interservice disputes inside the administration. But the military commander who feels deeply that administration policy threatens the national security is in something of a quandary. He is taught to respect civilian supremacy and to obey his civilian superiors. But which civilian superiors? The President as commander in chief? Or should he—as he has a legal right to do—report to Congress, which is after all also a civilian superior? A few officers, such as General James M. Gavin, former chief of the Army missile program, resolve the dilemma of conflicting loyalties to President, Congress, and conscience by resigning so that they will be free to carry their views to the nation. More commonly, military men who wish to express dissents from official policy get their views to Congress by resorting to the normal Washington practice of "leaking" information to the press. Furthermore, when before congressional committees it is not difficult for officers to support only in a formal sense policies of the Defense Department, and to get their real views across.[11]

The inability of the Joint Chiefs to resolve interservice differences and to develop strategic policies has led many to advocate their replacement by a single chief of staff, the complete integration of all military into a single branch, and the reassignment of forces in terms of *strategic missions* rather than means of locomotion. Although such a system has had the support of many high-ranking Army and some Air Force officers, it is opposed by most Navy officers and most congressmen. Nevertheless, there has been a trend toward centralization, and few believe that the Reorganization Act of 1958 is the last word.

---

[10] Kintner, *op. cit.,* p. 172.
[11] Edward L. Katzenback, "Should Our Military Leaders Speak Up?" *The New York Times Magazine,* April 15, 1956.

*Military Policy
in the Nuclear Age*

During the first years of the atomic age, no basic changes in military strategies seemed to be called for. Our atomic monopoly reinforced our traditional policy of not maintaining large standing armies. Even after the Soviet Union exploded its first atomic bomb, the situation was not seriously altered. We believed that our technological superiority would keep us ahead of the Soviets for many years to come, and that from our overseas bases we could rain down hundreds of bombs in the event of attack. At the same time, our defense system would reduce the enemy's ability to deliver these expensive weapons to American targets. Although wars would be terribly costly, it was still possible to talk about "winning" such wars.

Then, on October 4, 1957, the Moscow radio announced that the Soviet Union had placed in orbit the first earth satellite. The space age was born and the military implications were terrifyingly clear. The Soviet Union had beaten us to the punch and was perfecting the intercontinental missile. Not only that, but the Soviet Union had an ample supply of nuclear weapons. A balance of terror suddenly loomed. The enemy had sufficient power to destroy us, and the fact that we could do the same to him provided little comfort to Americans. It has become clear that air-atomic weapons cannot be used except under extreme provocation and—we hope—the rarest circumstances.

WHAT MILITARY STRATEGY FOR AMERICA?

All agree that a strong air-atomic arm is central to our policy of deterring the Soviets from starting a major war. It would be dangerous to relax even after massing sufficient retaliatory power to destroy the enemy, for he might achieve a technological breakthrough giving him a temporary advantage, such as a system to stop missiles or reduce the dangers of radiation.

Army spokesmen, however, as well as many students of foreign policy, have been critical of the tendency to place so much emphasis on massive weapons at the expense of mobile tactical forces capable of being used in "limited wars." They contend that the desire to balance the national government's budget by reducing the Army and relying on relatively less expensive air-atomic power has left us dangerously exposed to local aggressions. Neither the United States nor the Soviet Union, they argue, is likely to start a thermonuclear war of mass destruction, since such a war would lead to their own extermination. Such a war is "morally, politically and practically unjustifiable." Furthermore, these critics argue, to rely only on massive retaliation and weapons of mass destruction actually increases the likelihood of all-out war. For if the Soviet Union is led to believe that these are our only weapons and that we plan to use them, the Russians might be tempted to shoot first, especially while they have a temporary missile superiority. But even more likely, leaders of the Soviet Union know that the United States will not let loose a catastrophic conflict merely to prevent localized aggressions such as those in Korea in 1950 or Laos in 1959. The risk of unleashing an all-out war would be too great, and it would bring down on the United States the disapproval of the entire world. Nor, according to this view, is air-atomic power suitable to stop Soviet conquest of Western Europe, because its use would also destroy our allies. Hence, the Army and others argue, we must spend more on forces that can be used restrictively in order to prevent the communists from nibbling at the edge of the free world.[12]

Herblock in *The Washington Post and Times-Herald.*

"No fair—I can't afford a gun."

Our weaknesses in "limited-war" forces was demonstrated by our intervention in Lebanon during the summer of 1958. Although we faced no military opposition, American capacity to deploy quickly conventional military forces was strained to capacity.[13] Our nuclear weapons were of little use; even if we had decided politically to use them, they would have endangered our own troops and our allies as much as the enemy. Yet in 1960 limited-war forces were further cut back.

Air Force spokesmen and most Navy men, on the other hand, contend that to slow down the build-up of our air-atomic weapons at the present time would be dangerous. They argue that we have not as yet achieved decisive superiority; and until we do, the Soviet Union will be tempted, despite the risks, to take advantage of any superiority it might gain. The Soviets have intercontinental missiles and a formidable air defense, so that an all-out effort

[12] Army Staff Paper, *The New York Times,* June 24, 1956, Section 1, p. 46. See also General Matthew B. Ridgway, *Soldier* (Harper, 1956), pp. 295-361. The same view has been expressed by General Ridgway's successor as Army Chief of Staff, General Maxwell D. Taylor, before many congressional committees; see, for example, the statement reported in *Army Navy Air Force Journal* (April 1959), pp. 1 ff. Kissinger's book cited above has been influential in presenting the point of view of those who believe we should strengthen our limited-warfare forces.

[13] Peter Braestroup, "Limited Wars and the Lessons of Lebanon," *The Reporter* (April 3, 1958), pp. 25-27.

is needed to overcome their missile superiority. Until we catch up, we must depend on our strategic airpower and atomic submarines, and not divert any resources to limited-war forces.

Some spokesmen for airpower—but not necessarily for the Air Force—argue that mass armies are obsolete, that airpower can be used for limited conflicts, and that by concentrating on airpower and missiles we will be able to get more defense for less money—"More bang for the buck," as this policy is sometimes popularly known. They believe it is foolish to commit our forces to peripheral small-scale wars—"brushfires"—and that we need only have the ability to retaliate massively if the enemy starts trouble. Here is a good example of how military and foreign policy are interrelated. A policy of placing main reliance on massive retaliation, for example, makes allies less important than does a policy of maintaining forces able to resist invasion without resorting to mass destruction.

Differences among military leaders are not, it should be stressed, of the "either-or" kind. Rather, they are differences of emphasis and priority. All agree that the nation has to be prepared for all kinds of war—limited, middle-size, and all-out nuclear mass destruction.

THE FIRST LINE OF DEFENSE

A large force ready for action is the first element in a security program. But the standing force can be too large as well as too small. To support a combat force of eleven or twelve million men for a long time might create such a drain on our resources of materials and manpower that the whole economy would be weakened, and other programs essential to security would be impaired. The problem is to maintain an adequate defense force for an indefinite period at a steady level, and to "guard against the tendency to let defenses sink or rise depending upon each breeze that blows from the Kremlin." As General Marshall said, "We must keep a durable layer of military protection that would survive the alternate moods of public alarm or complacency."

The first line of our national defense consists of the Army, the United States Navy, the Marine Corps, the United States Air Force, and the Coast Guard.

The United States Air Force, like the other services, has both offensive and defensive responsibilities. Its primary strategic mission is to be ready on a few hours' notice to strike a retaliatory blow at the enemy. This is the job of the Strategic Air Command, which recently has received the most financial support. The Air Defense Command is charged with providing the air defense of the United States. The Tactical Air Command provides tactical air support to our ground and naval forces.

The Army has to be prepared to defend the United States and our overseas allies, seize and hold bases, and invade enemy territory. It has the primary responsibility for all land operations, including airborne attack and antiaircraft activity. Army divisions are now deployed overseas as well as in the United States.

The Navy's mission is to seek out and destroy enemy naval forces and to gain control of the seas, including the air above and water below. The Coast Guard, which in peacetime is under the jurisdiction of the Treasury Department, becomes part of the Navy in time of emergency. Also a part of the Navy, but a complete unit in itself, is the Marine Corps, which holds itself in its traditional state of readiness to be deployed from the "halls of Montezuma to the shores of Tripoli."

In the past, our nation's practice was to rely on a small standing force that would be joined in an emergency by all able-bodied men. The sturdy farmer could be called to snatch his musket from the mantelpiece and rush to the battlefield. Today, however, our armed forces are a complex organization of trained specialists. It takes many months, even years, to train a man to serve with the modern fighting machine. A stout heart and a straight-shooting gun are not enough. The time lag between the decision to create a large military organization and its actual existence as a fighting unit can be fatal.

SECOND LINE OF DEFENSE— THE READY RESERVES

Today, standing behind the combat forces is a second line of defense, the Ready Reserves, consisting of the National Guard, the Army, Navy, Air Force, and Coast Guard Reserves. In a thermonuclear war these reserves would probably be of restricted use, but in a limited war such as that in Korea, these reserves could be called to duty by the President. These reserve personnel take part in weekly drills and attend summer camps so that they will be ready to serve with a minimum of additional training.

An important component of the Ready Reserves is the National Guard, composed of the organized militias of the states.[14] Except when called into federal service, the Guard is under the command of the governors of the respective states. The governors commission the officers, and through their adjutant generals supervise the training of the militias. The national government, however, provides most of the money for their training and equipment, and has established minimum standards.

A state-controlled militia is an established tradition. In fact, in 1787 the states insisted on the adoption of the Second Amendment to prohibit the national government from depriving them of the right to maintain their own militias. During the War of 1812 some states would not even let their militias be used outside their own boundaries. Today, however, the national government exercises far-reaching supervision over the National Guard. Congress has the authority to call state militias into federal service, and it has given the

---

[14] See W. H. Riker, *Soldiers of the States: The Role of the National Guard in American Democracy* (Public Affairs Press, 1957).

President power to call the National Guard into immediate federal service. Once this is done, the Guard becomes an integral part of the national fighting forces subject only to such limitations as Congress may impose.

The chief purpose of the Guard today is to provide a trained reserve for the national military forces. Its service to the states is less important, for the state police have taken over many of its former duties. For this reason, and because the states have not always done a good job of training, it has been suggested that the National Guard be "federalized" and combined with the organized reserves to provide one reserve unit as an integral part of the federal defense establishment. Every such proposal, however, has drawn little support and much opposition in Congress.

Behind the Ready Reserves are the Standby Reserves, which consist merely of a pool of men who have completed their military duty—active and reserve—and who are not liable for any further service except during war or major emergency.

THE DRAFT

Despite the improvements in pay and other benefits, Congress has found it necessary to continue the draft both to secure men for the Army, the only branch that presently uses inductees, and to stimulate voluntary enlistments in the other armed forces. Although Congress establishes the top limits to the size of the armed forces and sets the broad standards to be used in selecting men for military duty, the actual administration of the draft act is a joint function of federal, state, and local governments. The Director of the Selective Service System, operating directly under the President, sets broad policies. In each state the President appoints, on the recommendation of the governor, a director of selective service who coordinates the activities of the county draft boards. These boards consist of three or more civilian residents of the county who are responsible for registering, examining, classifying, selecting, and delivering specified numbers of men to the armed forces for induction. The local board's decisions are subject to review by appeal boards established at the state and national level.

Although all men between the ages of 18 and 25 are liable for induction, only about half of all these young men are likely to be called for military service of any kind. All must register with their local draft board at age 18, but of those who register 45 per cent do not meet the minimum mental and physical standards.[15] Of those who qualified, many are entitled to deferments—for example, college students. Although deferment extends liability for military duty to age 35, only about 100,000 men are needed yearly for induction and men over 26 are called only after almost the entire manpower pool is exhausted, a most unlikely contingency.

---

[15] Report of Senate Committee on Armed Forces to accompany H.R. 2260, 86 Cong. 1 Sess. Senate Report 96, 1959, in *U.S. Code Congressional and Administrative News* (West Publishing Company, 1959), No. 5, April 20, 1959, p. 612.

Here is the sequence of inductions:

1. Delinquents (under the selective service laws) over 19, with the oldest first.
2. Volunteers under 26.
3. Nonfathers between 19 and 26, with the oldest first.
4. Fathers between 19 and 26, with the oldest first.
5. Registrants over 26, with the youngest first.
6. Registrants between 18½ and 19, with the oldest first.

No local board has so far found it necessary to reach below the third category. Although most qualified nonfathers have to meet their military obligation, the large number who are disqualified and the deferment of fathers means that the Universal Military Service and Training Act is somewhat less than universal in application.

"There are," as John Graham has pointed out, "about sixty ways for a young man to fulfill his military obligation." [16] One of the most common ways is to be drafted and serve for two years, followed by another two years in the Ready Reserves with evening and summer training. Many men prefer, however, to enlist directly in the Ready Reserves, since they are required to spend only six months on active duty followed by three years of weekly and summer training in the Ready Reserves. The Reserve Officer Training Corps programs in 300 universities and colleges also enable college students to meet part of their military obligation by taking advanced work. In fact, Advanced ROTC furnishes the bulk of the officers of our armed forces; in 1957, 22,388 officers came from ROTC as against 1319 from the military academies.[17] Graduates of Advanced ROTC receive commissions and after a period of required active duty keep themselves prepared by weekly and summer duty; a good many of them become career officers. (For a full description of choices of fulfilling military obligation, see Epilogue.)

Such, then, are the fighting forces of the United States—large combat forces and a second line of defense of trained reserves. But no matter how large our armed forces, they must be equipped with the most advanced military weapons. For these weapons we depend on science and industry.

Science and Security

When the atomic bomb was dropped on Hiroshima, few could any longer doubt that science had become a decisive element in a defense program. Wars are fought and won in large measure in a nation's scientific laboratories.

The nature of war has been altered by the invention of the proximity fuse, the snorkel submarine, radar, sonar, and the guided missile. The scientist's con-

---

[16] John Graham, *The Universal Military Obligation* (The Fund for the Republic, 1958), p. 5.

[17] Gene M. Lyons and John W. Masland, *Education and Military Leadership: A Study of the ROTC* (Princeton Univ. Press, 1958).

tribution to the war effort during World War II is well known. But what is not so well known is that the scientists drew "heavily on the accumulated stockpile of fundamental scientific knowledge that was all but exhausted when fighting stopped." [18] Further advance will depend upon the extension of fundamental scientific knowledge, on what is sometimes called "pure science." Such science is not preoccupied with finding more powerful explosives or better devices to guide missiles, but with unlocking the mysteries of the world in which we live.

It is essential, therefore, to create the conditions under which scientific inquiry can best operate. Hitler's misunderstanding of the importance of scientific research led him to expel from Germany those who did not conform to the "New Order." Our own preoccupation with *applied* science, and particularly with applications that have military significance, has tended to exhaust our fund of scientific knowledge without replenishing it. For this reason the government has established a National Science Foundation, which through scholarships and other forms of assistance helps to train scientists without regard to the immediate military value of their possible contributions.

The military departments themselves have tapped the knowledge and skill of scientists in commercial laboratories and universities. This problem of integrating scientific and military knowledge is an essential but difficult task. Military men, like other professionals, tend to be cautious in adopting new techniques. In the past, almost every new weapon of war—gunpowder, submarine, tank, airplane, proximity fuse—had to be pushed on the military by civilians.

Should scientific knowledge be kept secret, or disseminated as widely as possible? Some scientific knowledge must be kept secret. Yet to stamp every new research finding "top secret" in the interests of national security would be disastrous, for scientific progress depends on the wide sharing of information. Many scientists—men whose patriotism is beyond doubt—have questioned whether we are not losing more than we gain by our excessive concern over secrecy.[19] Moreover, the withholding of information sometimes deprives the policy-planners themselves of essential knowledge. One atomic scientist has written, "The most fateful step, which has permitted the Soviet Union to achieve its present atomic strength, was not the betrayal of our secrets by May, Fuchs, and Greenglass, but the decision of American political and military leaders in 1945 to give to the Soviet Union control over the parts of Czechoslovakia and Germany in which important uranium ore deposits were known to exist. . . . Perhaps, if the atomic bomb development in the United States had not been surrounded with such extreme secrecy, those responsible for the drawing of the demarcation line would have known better what they were giving away. . . ." [20]

---

[18] Vannevar Bush, *Modern Arms and Free Men* (Simon & Schuster, 1949), p. 27.

[19] Walter Gellhorn, *Security, Loyalty, and Science* (Cornell Univ. Press, 1950), Chapters 2, 4.

[20] Eugene Rabinowitch, "Atomic Spy Trials: Heretical Afterthoughts," *Bulletin of the Atomic Scientists* (May 1951), p. 140.

Protecting the Home Front— Civil Defense

The United States will probably not be as lucky in any future war as it has been in the past. An attack on the American mainland is now technically possible; and in case of a full-scale war, our factories, transportation centers, atomic plants, and other vital installations will be prime targets. The defense circle cannot be closed without an adequate program for defending the home base. Until 1953, when the Soviet Union exploded their H-bomb, the military tended to neglect defensive power on the theory that the best defense is a good offense. More attention is now paid, however, to strengthening the Continental Air Command and developing an early-warning system. The Continental Air Command operates on a 24-hour alert, instantly ready to send planes into the air. A "crash" program is underway to develop three radar lines across Canada. Warning of an enemy attack is vital both to defend the home base and to unleash our retaliatory power. The radar lines are supplemented by 13,000 Ground Observer Corps stations manned by civilian volunteers who watch for enemy bombers sneaking in under the radar signals.

Even the best warning systems cannot guarantee more than six hours notice at most and, with the development of intercontinental missiles, perhaps no more than 15 minutes. Even the finest defense will not be able to prevent some of the enemy bombers and missiles from getting through. The most optimistic estimate is that 30 per cent of the bombers approaching the United States could be stopped. A more realistic figure is perhaps half that. Missiles would be even harder to destroy.

Civil defense means "the protection of the home front by civilians acting under civilian authority to minimize casualties and war damage and preserve maximum civilian support of the war effort." The functions of civil defense may be grouped under four general categories: "(1) measures designed to prevent enemy attack; (2) measures designed to reduce the effects of an enemy attack; (3) services that will alleviate the damage of an enemy attack; and (4) general measures pertaining to the over-all program." [21] Civilian activity designed to prevent enemy attack is limited to camouflage programs, blackout measures, and aircraft observation. The main task is to be prepared with plans and organizations to keep community life going if an attack comes. Air-raid warning; dispersion of vital facilities; evacuation; emergency medical, health, rescue, salvage, fire-fighting, and decontamination services; education; and intelligence are some of the key jobs.

The industrial power of the United States is concentrated in the area north of the Ohio and east of the Mississippi, and along the West Coast. And many of our basic industries are in the coastal cities, which are particularly

---

[21] Carey Brewer, "Civil Defense in the United States: Federal, State and Local," *Public Affairs Bulletin* 92 (The Library of Congress, Legislative Reference Service), p. 4.

vulnerable to attack. We could decentralize industry and create duplicate facilities dispersed throughout the United States. But large-scale decentralization is not feasible. There is strong political opposition. Decentralization itself would require the expenditure of enormous quantities of manpower, resources, and facilities. In some cases, it would result in lower productivity. Accordingly, air-raid shelters must be built, millions of citizens must be trained to fight fires and to aid in the evacuation of wounded persons, medical supplies must be stockpiled, emergency communications networks must be created. Until 1958, most civil defense preparations were limited to a "run for the hills" strategy, but recently more attention has been paid to "duck and cover" tactics.

Americans have been reluctant to face up to the necessity for civil defense. Not until the Korean conflict was any progress made, and organization and training are still in their infancy. As late as 1960 nothing had happened to alter a 1955 *New York Times* survey of our major cities, the primary targets of the enemy, which showed that Chicago is "helpless," Bostonians have "almost no chance of survival," Cleveland is a "sitting duck," Seattle is "not ready," Fort Worth "woefully unprepared." [22] Civil defense has been retarded by an attitude of "It can't happen here," and perhaps even more by an attitude that if it does happen, advance preparation will do little good since millions will be killed anyway. Although the Office of Civil and Defense Mobilization has reported, "There is no certainty that any nation can survive an all-out nuclear attack," [23] it has also pointed out that an effective defense will save the lives of millions of Americans. Furthermore, a strong defense may discourage attack, and along with our offensive power must be considered part of our policy of deterrence. [24]

ADMINISTRATION OF CIVIL DEFENSE

The responsibility for civil defense programs is shared by federal, state, and local governments. The Director of the Office of Civil and Defense Mobilization—with the advice of a twelve-member advisory council of national, state, and local officials and an eighteen-man coordinating board of national officials—controls the federal effort and also administers disaster relief. The Office of Civil and Defense Mobilization provides 50 per cent of the costs of mutual-aid facilities and personnel, coordinates plans of state and local governments, provides training and educational materials, and prepares national programs. Most of the states have adopted civil defense programs, although most of them are inadequate. Local governments have the job of providing on-the-spot services.

The basic principles behind the civil defense program are to use existing

---

22 *The New York Times,* June 12, 1955.
23 *The New York Times,* April 18, 1956.
24 See Klaus Knorr, "Passive Air Defense for the United States," *Military Policy and National Security,* William W. Kaufman (ed.) (Princeton Univ. Press, 1956), pp. 75-101.

agencies and levels of government and to encourage self-help at every level. These principles have come in for increasing criticism. The overlapping and duplication of American governmental units causes real problems. In some metropolitan areas, for example, fire-fighting equipment is under the jurisdiction of twenty to fifty separate municipalities. Many state governments, the Commission on Intergovernmental Relations, and a special citizens commission on civil defense have all recommended that the national government should assume the primary responsibility for civil defense, and they have criticized the self-help principle as inadequate.[25] Some congressmen have argued that a crash program be adopted to strengthen this weakest link in our defense program.

Security and Liberty

So long as the United States exists in a world of sovereign, independent nations, it must look to its defenses. As we have seen, this means large standing military forces, adequately trained reserves, the application of scientific and other knowledge to military problems, a strong and stable economy, an alert and trained citizen body, and powerful allies.

NOT BY POWER ALONE

To fail to do what is necessary to provide for the common defense would be disastrous. But it would be equally disastrous to depend solely on military power to provide security. Not even the United States has sufficient resources, even if the people had the stomach for it, to control the destinies of the international community. Politics is conflict, but it is also cooperation, and power must be used to help build the kind of world community in which armies and tanks will one day be archaic.

What should be the role of the military in a democratic society? A fear of the military is deeply rooted in American traditions. The framers of the Constitution, recognizing that military domination was incompatible with free government, wove into the Constitution several precautions. The President, an elected officer, is commander in chief of the armed forces. With the Senate's consent, he commissions all officers; Congress makes the rules for the governance of the military services; and appropriations for the Army are limited to a two-year period. Congress has supplemented these precautions by requiring that the Secretary of Defense and the heads of the military departments be civilians, and by devising elaborate procedures to prevent the military from controlling the selection of men for West Point, Annapolis, and the Air Force Academy.

In the past, professional military men were largely ignored. During time

---

[25] *The New York Times,* January 4, 1956, Part 4, p. 1.

of peace, their recommendations were shrugged off, or the generals were accused of wanting war. A career in the armed services was not attractive. The military mind was stereotyped as conservative, stodgy, and concerned mainly with protocol. Failure to heed the words of our professional soldiers, sailors, and airmen has cost us much. Certain it is that in the future what they have to say will be given serious consideration. At the other extreme there is the danger of elevating them into positions where what they have to say is accepted uncritically. This would be disastrous both for the preservation of liberty and for the promotion of security.

War and defense today, more than ever before, are too important and too complex to leave to the generals. As we have seen, security programs require the talents of the bureaucrat, social scientist, natural scientist, labor leader, engineer, industrialist, and all other professionals. What the military expert knows must be meshed with what others know. But he may not know enough to be trusted with the running of our defense program.

MILITARISM VERSUS DEMOCRACY

Maintaining civilian supremacy over the military today is harder than ever. There is no longer a clear separation between military and civilian spheres of activity. As national security problems are brought to the fore, the generals, often reluctantly, are called upon to pass judgment on issues that in the past have not been thought to be within the scope of their competence. At the same time, their civilian superiors find it more difficult to secure the information they need to exercise control. In many cases it is the military who decide what information must remain top secret. Congressmen and the general public are at a disadvantage in exercising effective supremacy over the military.

The dangers to liberty arising from the garrison state—a nation that is constantly prepared for total war and that is organized to exert its military might—were recognized by Alexander Hamilton when he wrote: "Safety from external danger is the most powerful director of national conduct. Even the ardent love of liberty will after a time give way to its dictates. The violent destruction of life and property incident to war, the continual effort and alarm attendant on a state of continual danger, will compel nations the most attached to liberty to resort for repose and security to institutions which have a tendency to destroy their civil and political rights. To be more safe, they at length become willing to run the risk of being less free." [26]

Professor Harold D. Lasswell has summarized the impact of militarization upon individual freedom as follows: "To militarize is to governmentalize. It is also to centralize. To centralize is to enhance the effective control of the executive over decisions, and thereby to reduce the control exercised by courts

---

[26] *Federalist No. 8,* The Modern Library edition (Random House, 1937), p. 42. For a recent treatment of the problem, see Samuel P. Huntington, "Civilian Control and the Constitution," *The American Political Science Review* (September 1956), pp. 676-699.

and legislatures. To centralize is to enhance the role of the military in the allocation of national resources. Continuing fear of external attack sustains an atmosphere of distrust that finds expression in spy hunts directed against fellow officials and fellow citizens. Outspoken criticism of official measures launched for the national defense is more and more resented as unpatriotic and subversive of the common good. The community at large, therefore, acquiesces in denials of freedom that go beyond the technical requirements of military security." [27]

The threat of militarization comes not only from the military, however. As John McCloy wrote in dissent to one of the recommendations of the Hoover Commission's task force on security organization, "I doubt whether we need fear the men in uniform in this regard [seeking unfettered power] any more than the man or men in civil clothes to whom we have given far greater authority. Indeed, as many examples as there are of authority usurped by generals or admirals, I believe history records as many instances of usurpation on the part of civilians with at least as many disastrous results." [28]

The United States has been fortunate. It has never developed a military caste. Its generals and admirals have demonstrated statesmanlike qualities, including respect for civilian authority. American soldiers have been imbued with democratic principles of civilian supremacy. Now that the skills required of military men are so varied, it becomes all the more necessary to educate them not only to be good soldiers but also to be good democrats. For it is by "civilizing" the military that much can be done to prevent militarizing the civilians.[29]

---

[27] Harold D. Lasswell, "Does the Garrison State Threaten Civil Rights?" *Civil Rights in America,* The *Annals* of the American Academy of Political and Social Science (May 1951), p. 111.

[28] *Task Force Report on National Security Organization,* p. 59.

[29] For a different interpretation see Samuel P. Huntington, *The Soldier and the State* (Harvard Univ. Press, 1957), especially Chapter 17.

CHAPTER **25**

Government as Regulator

It is impossible to draw a sharp line between the activities of the national government in waging war and peace on the one hand and its so-called domestic functions on the other. The two are inextricably intertwined. The foreign policies administered by the State Department have a direct impact on American businessmen and farmers. Fighting a war mobilizes both the nation's economy and the whole peacetime bureaucracy. Our foreign economic policies directly affect employment, wages, prices, and taxes at home. This book discusses domestic activities separately from foreign affairs only for purposes of convenience.

Americans have always been quick to criticize their country's foreign policy, but no one has ever seriously questioned that foreign policy must be made by the *national government.* Even the most waspish critic of bureaucratic inefficiency has never urged that foreign affairs be turned over to businessmen, for example, or that the job of defending the country against attack be turned over to the state governments. Everyone agrees that the national government must manage the relations of Americans with other peoples.

But when it comes to the dealings of Americans with *one another*—that is a different matter. On domestic questions people differ not only over *what* policies should be adopted, but also over *whether* government should act at all, and if so, *which* government. And even if they agree that government should act, the dispute shifts to new grounds of controversy: How far should government go? What kinds of control or procedure should it use? Should it act as the *partner* of business, labor, or farmers—or as their *boss?* And so the debate rages on and on—in editorial pages, over the air, in legislative chambers, and on the platform.

This chapter and the next two will describe the functions of our national government and also consider some of the answers that are given to such questions. These three chapters will also describe federal functions *that illustrate a major technique of governmental control or intervention.* In this chapter we

628

shall explore the national government's major *regulatory* functions—regulatory in the narrow sense of trying to limit the activities of private groups, to prevent "bad" practices, to restrict one interest from interfering with the rights of others (as defined, of course, by the politicians in power). This is government in a somewhat negative or restrictive sense. In the next chapter we shall turn to some of the newer welfare functions of government. And in Chapter 27 we shall survey the more positive role of the national government—that is, its *active intervention in the economy* at strategic points to strengthen it, stabilize it, and reform it.

A traditional type of governmental regulation is of course the regulation of human behavior to *prevent crime.* In the United States such regulation has been largely the job of state and local governments. The national government has been concerned with crime prevention mainly in connection with such activities as delivering mail or collecting taxes. Increasingly in recent years, however, fighting crime has become an important national function. The Department of Justice, which employs the services of the highly efficient Federal Bureau of Investigation and other agencies, has the main responsibility for investigating crime and prosecuting criminals. The Secret Service in the Treasury Department has special crime-fighting responsibilities, such as investigating counterfeiting. Other members of the "federal police" are postal inspectors, narcotics agents, treasury inspectors, and border patrols. Under the kind of cooperative federalism described in Chapter 5, these federal officials work closely with state and local police. Paradoxically, though law enforcement of this sort is one of the most ancient functions of government, it is a relatively new responsibility of the national government. Since crime has become a big interstate business, however, the national government will probably become more and more involved in policing the country. For example, after the Kefauver committee publicized the power of huge crime syndicates a few years ago, it recommended a number of measures, such as enlarging the rackets squad in the Justice Department and the fraud squad in the Bureau of Internal Revenue, and barring interstate transportation of punch boards and roulette wheels.

The main regulatory task of the national government, however, is not crime-prevention, but the policing of powerful interest groups, such as business and labor. But two words of caution before we take up these regulatory functions: First, government is not the only regulating agency. Regulatory control is also exercised by families, friends, church, and the over-all social environment, as we saw in earlier chapters. Second, the type of activity described in this chapter is only one type of regulation. Government also acts as a regulating agency in some of its newer functions, as we shall see later.

Regulating Business   Businessmen today operate in a complex web of national, state, and local laws. It was not always thus. Business has never been altogether free of restrictive legislation, of course, but during much of the latter part of the nineteenth century our national policy was to leave business alone. Most of the nation's leaders, and the country at large, believed broadly in laissez faire —or hands off. Given their head, businessmen set about developing a nation that was enormously rich in natural resources. The heroes of the 1870's and 1880's were not politicians but business magnates—the Rockefellers, Morgans, Carnegies, and Fricks. "From rags to riches" became the nation's motto.

Then, toward the end of the century, a reaction set in. Sharp depressions rocked the nation's economy and threw men out of work. Millions of people, including workers and farmers, labored long hours in factory and field for little money. "Muckrakers" revealed that some of the most famous business leaders had indulged in shoddy practices and corrupt deals, taking a "public-be-damned" attitude. A demand for government regulation of business sprang up, and a series of national and state laws were passed to correct specific abuses. These laws followed no methodical plan or philosophy; rather, they were adopted on the pragmatic assumption that each problem could be handled as it arose.

ANTITRUST POLICY: BACKGROUND

We Americans have mixed feelings about big business. On the one hand we are easily impressed by bigness—the tallest skyscraper, the largest football stadium, the biggest corporation—and the efficiency and power that seem to go with bigness. On the other hand, we like to believe that our economic system functions best under conditions of fair competition among small business-men. This mixed attitude has been reflected in our attempts to prevent monopoly and restraint of trade.

The popular clamor for government control late in the nineteenth century culminated in attacks on monopoly. The trust-busters argued that little business was being squeezed out by huge trusts in oil, sugar, whisky, steel, and other commodities. In 1890 Congress responded to this sentiment by passing the famous Sherman Antitrust Act. Designed to foster competition and stop the growth of private monopolies, this act made clear its intention "to protect trade and commerce against unlawful restraints and monopolies." Henceforth, persons making contracts, combinations, or conspiracies in restraint of trade in interstate and foreign commerce could be sued for damages, required to stop their illegal practices, and subjected to criminal penalties.

Presidents Cleveland and McKinley showed little interest in enforcing the Sherman Act. Indeed, a Supreme Court decision in the Sugar Trust Case (1895) considerably limited the scope of the act by ruling that a sugar-refining company which produced 98 per cent of the sugar used in the United States was primarily engaged in *manufacturing* rather than *commerce,* and hence could not be regulated by the national government.[1] But in 1901 Theodore Roosevelt became President. Wielding a "big stick," he responded to the growing sentiment against the "giant octopus" of monopoly. Yet even Roosevelt talked more than he acted. Like most Americans he had conflicting attitudes toward bigness. Mr. Dooley, the Chicago bartender-philosopher, poked fun at Roosevelt's vacillation by pretending to quote him as saying: "Th' trusts are heejoous monsthers built up be th'enlightened intherprise iv th'men that have done so much to advance progress in our beloved country. On wan hand I wud stamp thim undher fut; on th'other hand not so fast." During the Taft and Wilson Administrations the trusts were prosecuted more vigorously, and court rulings gave the rather vague provisions of the act more definite meaning. Certain consolidations were permitted unless a clear intent to monopolize was proved. Voting trusts, pools, and some collusive practices were sharply curbed.

"THIS HURTS ME MORE THAN IT DOES YOU."

A typical cartoon of a half-century ago against the "trusts."

The Clayton Act in 1914 further clarified antitrust policy. It outlawed specific abuses affecting interstate commerce, such as charging different prices to different buyers, the granting of rebates, and the making of false statements about competitors in order to take business away from them. Corporations were prohibited from acquiring stock (amended in 1950 to include assets) in competing concerns if such acquisitions substantially lessened interstate competition, and interlocking directorates in large corporations were banned. Labor had been enraged by a Supreme Court ruling that applied the Sherman Act to a union boycott against the products of a nonunion manufacturer; the Clayton Act exempted labor from the 1890 act and was greeted by unions as their Magna Carta. Later legislation exempted various business activities from the Sherman Act.

Antitrust activity languished in the 1920's. Times were prosperous; the Republican administrations were actively pro-business; and the Department of Justice, charged with enforcing the Sherman Act, paid little attention to it.

---

[1] *United States* v. *E. C. Knight Co.* See Chapter 20.

anti-trust is federal

During the Depression popular resentment mounted against big business as abuses were revealed. At first the Roosevelt Administration tried a new method of industrial self-government under the National Industrial Recovery Act of 1933, which tried to promote cooperation among businessmen by allowing them to work out codes of fair competition. This was virtually a suspension of antitrust policy. The NIRA, however, was invalidated by the Supreme Court in 1935.

Subsequent years saw a revival of trust-busting. In the late 1930's a well-publicized committee of congressmen and New Deal experts, the Temporary National Economic Committee, made an elaborate investigation of economic concentration and monopoly. It unanimously urged that enforcement be strengthened "to cope with the gigantic aggregations of capital which have become so dominant in our economic life." Under the leadership of Thurman Arnold, a former Yale professor, the antitrust division of the Justice Department was given a larger staff to commence trust-busting in earnest. In one year, 1940, the government instituted 345 suits; of the 280 suits that were terminated, the government won 265. Antitrust activity flagged during World War II but was revived during the postwar years. During the Eisenhower Administration the antitrust division continued to be active, and it seems evident that "vigorous antitrust enforcement has become a bipartisan policy." [2]

The main burden of measuring business practices by the antitrust yardstick falls to the federal courts. In hammering out the extent of permissible corporate power consistent with antitrust laws, the judges over the years have found these factors to be relevant: "the number of firms in the market; their effective size from the standpoint of technological development, and from the standpoint of competition with substitute materials and foreign trade; national security interests in the maintenance of strong productive facilities, and maximum scientific research and development; together with the public interest in lowered costs and uninterrupted production." [3] As an example of how the courts apply such tests, in an important case in 1957 the Supreme Court held that Du Pont threatened to monopolize the market for automobile fabrics and finishes because of Du Pont's control over stock ownership in General Motors, with its consequent power to bar sales of competing fabric and finish manufacturers. [4]

BIGNESS—CURSE OR BLESSING?

The attitude of the antitrust division during the Roosevelt-Truman, and to a lesser extent the Eisenhower, years has been well expressed by Justice William O. Douglas in a Supreme Court dissenting opinion: "Size is the measure of the power of a handful of men over our economy. That power can

---

[2] Merle Fainsod, Lincoln Gordon, and J. C. Palamountain, Jr., *Government and the American Economy* (Norton, 1959), p. 616.

[3] *U.S.* v. *Aluminum Co. of America.*

[4] *U.S.* v. *E. I. du Pont de Nemours & Co.*

be utilized with lightning speed. It can be benign or it can be dangerous. The philosophy of the Sherman Act is that it should not exist. For all power tends to develop into a government in itself. Power that controls the economy should be in the hands of elected representatives of the people, not in the hands of an industrial oligarchy. Industrial power should be decentralized. It should be scattered into many hands so that the fortunes of the people will not be dependent on the whim or caprice, the political prejudices, the emotional stability, of a few self-appointed men." [5]

What success have we had with our antitrust policies? After a half-century of experience observers are still not sure. Some believe that antitrust laws have curbed monopolistic tendencies and have forced business to keep its house in order. It has become difficult, for example, for rival manufacturers to agree to restrict output in order to maintain prices. Other students of monopoly believe that antitrust action has had little effect on monopoly. Have the antitrust laws been successful in preventing concentration? Economists, business, and government officials argue at length over the answer. A few years ago the Federal Trade Commission reported that a recent increase in mergers by large concerns constituted a menace to competition. Others hold that the economy is more competitive today than in the past.

Should bigness as such be outlawed? Yes, say some Americans, taking the view of Justice Douglas. Others, like David E. Lilienthal, former Chairman of the Atomic Energy Commission, say no. Lilienthal believes that "in Big Business we have more than an efficient way to produce and distribute basic commodities, and to strengthen the Nation's security; we have a social institution that promotes human freedom and individualism." [6] Rather than outlaw bigness, Lilienthal would encourage it, since he believes that big business makes several positive contributions: it stimulates competition in ideas, products, and services; through research it develops more and better products; it strengthens constructive labor-management relations; it produces greater stability of employment; it increases industrial output; it promotes conservation of natural resources; and it creates new opportunities for independent and small businessmen. Any danger that big business will abuse its power has been reduced to manageable proportions, argues Lilienthal, by the expanded role of government in economic affairs in recent years.

Who controls the large corporations? In a classic study, Berle and Means showed that corporation ownership has been divorced from corporation control.[7] The ownership of stock in large corporations is widely dispersed, leaving control in the hands of a small group of managers. To whom are these

---

[5] *United States* v. *Columbia Steel Co.* (1948).

[6] D. E. Lilienthal, *Big Business: a New Era* (Harper, 1952), p. ix.

[7] A. A. Berle, Jr. and Gardiner C. Means, *The Modern Corporation and Private Property* (Macmillan, 1932). For an interesting picture of the "checks and balances" in the American economy that, in the author's opinion, tend to prevent excessive concentration of power, see J. K. Galbraith, *American Capitalism, The Concept of Countervailing Power* (Houghton Mifflin, 1952).

managers responsible? If they are not truly responsible to the owners, should they be made more responsible to all the people through the national government? Although this problem does not directly relate to the monopoly problem, it touches on the whole role of the national government in regulating business.

Most Americans believe in vigorous but fair and open competition. In a simple economy, competition virtually enforces itself; buyers and sellers know one another and follow the old principle of *caveat emptor*—let the buyer beware. By the turn of the century, however, the American business economy was becoming so large and impersonal that a demand arose for the government to police competition. Big business was especially suspect for its trade practices; the same Congress that passed the Clayton Act in 1914 also enacted the Federal Trade Commission Act. When Wilson was campaigning for election, he had said that one vice of the trusts was their tendency to stop men of genuine ability but limited capital from making their way under the competitive system. The new act was a sort of "Magna Carta" for businessmen opposed to unfair and injurious methods of competition.

Because our industrial life is so diverse, Congress put enforcement of the law in the hands of a five-member Federal Trade Commission, an independent regulatory board whose job is to apply the act to specific practices. As its membership slowly changed (the term of office is seven years), the FTC's conception of its job changed too. In the 1920's the commission exercised its powers rather mildly, but more recently it has taken a stricter view toward business practices, and has been given new responsibilities by Congress. Today the FTC exercises a wide range of powers. For example, it can outlaw:

1. *Misrepresentation.* A businessman who sells in interstate commerce must not sell rebuilt or second-hand products as new. Watches cannot be branded "Made in U.S.A." if the movements come from Switzerland. An attempt to issue a film called "The Love Pirate" two years later as "The She Tiger" was branded unfair.

2. *Tying contracts.* The Radio Corporation of America was forbidden to require radio manufacturers to buy from RCA all vacuum tubes needed for first use in radio sets. On the other hand, when the General Motors Corporation required its Buick and Chevrolet agents to use only GM replacement parts in repair work, an FTC ban on this practice was overturned by the Supreme Court.

3. *Misbranding.* Putting misleading names on products sold in interstate commerce, and using deceptive containers, is illegal. A coat made of cheap fur cannot be described as made of beaver. A physical culture outfit that advertised its courses as starting "new inches of massive power pushing out your chest" and as banishing constipation, skin blotches, etc., etc., was ordered to desist.

More recently, the maker of Gosewich's Odorless Garlic Tablets was ordered to drop the word "Garlic" because the FTC found the pills contained no substantial amount of garlic.

4. *Price discrimination.* It is unfair to sell below cost in an effort to destroy weaker competitors and thus secure a monopoly position. This practice had been a favorite one with the "robber barons" of old.

5. *Monopolistic practices.* There are a host of these—buying up supplies in order to stifle competition, conspiring to set uniform selling prices and conditions, harassing competitors (such as by bribing their employees or bringing vexatious law suits), and selling below cost in order to hinder competition. The FTC works closely with the Justice Department in trying to curb practices that improperly restrain trade among the states.)

6. *Dangerous practices.* The FTC, for example, can regulate the interstate marketing of apparel to bar the use of highly flammable materials.

Some of the FTC's decisions have had a profound effect on our whole system of trade. Take the case of "Pittsburgh plus." For years steel producers had a friendly arrangement—called the basing point system—whereby the same prices were charged to all steel fabricators throughout the country no matter where they were located and where their steel came from. For example, if you were a Chicago fabricator buying steel from a Chicago mill, you would have to pay a Pittsburgh base price plus transportation charges from Pittsburgh even though no transportation was involved. The FTC watched this collusive arrangement in steel and other industries, such as cement, and then held hearings that lasted for three years. On the basis of almost 100,000 pages of oral testimony and exhibits, the FTC in 1943 issued a cease and desist order against the basing point system in the cement industry. The case went to the Supreme Court, which in 1948—eleven years after the FTC investigation first got under way—upheld the commission's action. Even this decision did not end the story. Supporters of the basing point system carried the battle to Congress, where bills were introduced to legalize the system, and they have exerted pressure on the Federal Trade Commission to modify its stand.

Another trade practice that affects us all is *re-sale price maintenance.* You may have noticed that the makers of nationally advertised brand-name products often set the prices you pay at the drugstore or corner grocery. Manufacturers of such products sometimes require retailers to sign a contract insuring that these prices will be charged. What if some retailers do not wish to sign such a contract? To guard against such holdouts, manufacturers in recent decades have induced most of the states to pass "Fair Trade Acts" legalizing re-sale price maintenance—that is, requiring (in most cases) that when such a contract has gone into effect in a certain state it becomes binding on *all* retailers of the product in that state, including both signers of the contract and *non-signers.* These are state laws applying only to *intra*state commerce.

Then, in 1937, business groups persuaded Congress to pass the Miller-

Tydings amendment as a rider to an appropriation act. This amendment legalized re-sale price maintenance for *inter*state commerce where states had approved it for intrastate commerce. President Roosevelt denounced the rider method (see page 418) but signed the bill. In 1950, however, the Supreme Court ruled that Congress had not intended the amendment to apply to non-signers engaged in interstate commerce who hence could not be compelled to charge the required prices. For a time "cut-rate" establishments—that is, highly competitive ones—had a field day; but other business groups, alarmed by the decision, induced Congress to pass a law (the McGuire Act) permitting the control of nonsigners' prices in states that have price maintenance laws. Since state judges have become increasingly hostile to state re-sale price maintenance laws, however, small business groups have been seeking a stronger measure from Congress.

POLICING THE MONEY MARKET

The American economy rests on a vast system of investment and credit. Our resources could not have been developed had people not been willing to invest money in factories and machinery. The credit system—the "economic promises men live by"—has helped make possible enormous investments and the development of the economy. Before World War I there were hardly half a million investors in this country, but during the war and the 1920's millions of little people began to buy securities. Investment trusts and brokerage houses mushroomed.

For many years individual states had tried to cope with some of the abuses of the money markets, such as outright swindling. But it took the stock-market crash of 1929 and the collapse of the rosy hopes of millions of investors to bring vigorous national action. Investigation during the Depression revealed that abuses had been many and varied. Worthless or questionable securities had been unloaded on the public through various kinds of fraud. Insiders had used confidential information to arrange deals for themselves at the expense of thousands of fleeced lambs. Investment bankers had sponsored stock issues that created unsound corporate structures. An enormous amount of speculating on margin (buying stocks on credit) had helped precipitate the 1929 crash. Pools, rigging the market, and preferred lists were other means of manipulating the money markets. More specifically, there was the wash sale, whereby one speculator agrees to sell a stock, and another agrees to buy it, at a point higher than it normally would command, in order to give the impression of a stronger market for the stock. There was the matched order, whereby two innocent brokers are hired, one to sell a stock and another to buy, to give the appearance of an active market for the stock.

The Federal Securities Act of 1933 and the Securities Exchange Act of 1934 were passed in response to wide bitterness and disillusionment over "Wall Street" practices. The 1933 act required the registration of all issues of stocks, bonds, or other securities offered in interstate commerce or by mail, along with a registration statement providing full information for potential investors. The 1934 act regulated the buying and selling of securities on exchanges throughout the country. To administer both acts Congress established the Securities and Exchange Commission, an independent regulatory board of five men with five-year terms. All firms having securities listed must file regular reports with the SEC and with the exchanges. The main objective of these acts is to give full publicity to stock-market transactions, but they also outlaw manipulation and other unsavory practices of the past. The SEC even has the power to impose new trading rules on exchanges.

The commission has special powers over *public utility holding companies* —corporations that control networks of operating companies. Formerly, holding companies could escape regulation by incorporating in one state to take control of operating companies in another. Many abuses developed, such as siphoning funds from operating utilities into holding companies. There was also a problem of concentration. An investigation revealed that thirteen large holding-company groups controlled three-fourths of the entire privately owned electric utility industry, and over 40 per cent was concentrated in the hands of the three largest groups. To meet this problem, Congress in 1935 passed the Public Utility Holding Act. Not only must holding companies register full information with the SEC, but many of their transactions, such as issuing and buying securities, may be made only with the commission's consent. Congress also required the holding companies to get rid of their extraneous operating companies and to confine themselves each to a single integrated system.

Transportation and Communication

In August 1787, the framers of the Constitution were debating how much power they should give the new national government to regulate commerce. One day, as a relief from their labors, they junketed to the banks of the Delaware River to watch John Fitch demonstrate his sensational steamboat. "As we look back, it seems that Fitch and the Founding Fathers were working at different parts of one unfolding problem." While Fitch's experiment would bring the states into closer economic relations, the Framers were granting Congress power to "regulate commerce with foreign nations, and among the several States. . . ." [8] Today Congress has virtually complete power to regulate interstate commerce.

National power over interstate commerce is a far more powerful weapon today than the framers could have expected. For today that power extends to hundreds of thousands of miles of railways, to waterborne commerce, to motor and air transportation. Congress controls not only the movement of persons, things, and words from state to state; it also has broad powers over the conduct of industries that *affect* interstate commerce.

---

[8] Charles Fairman, *American Constitutional Decisions* (Holt, 1948), p. 173.

RAILROAD POLITICS

It is hard for us today to realize how deeply the railroads were involved in the politics of the late nineteenth century. To many Americans of that time the railroads were ogres intent on ruining the little man. Farmers had especially bitter grievances. They charged that railroads extorted outrageously high rates, conspired with one another to prevent competition, discriminated against certain localities and individuals, corrupted state officials, evaded taxes, watered their capital, and stole the money that farmers had invested in railroad construction. Angry and desperate, the farmers turned to political action. The powerful Grange movement, which swept the West in the 1870's and 1880's, was a response to the tactics of railroads as well as to monopoly, middlemen, and the "money power" of eastern financiers.

The Grange movement helped secure a number of state laws regulating the railroads. The railroads fought the new laws through appeals to the courts, evasion, and propaganda. For a time the Supreme Court allowed the states to regulate, within their boundaries, the rates of carriers engaged in interstate commerce. But in 1886 the Court in the *Wabash* decision held that states could not regulate transportation within their state boundaries that constituted a part of commerce among the states. A void was created that only the national government could fill. Now shippers and small businessmen joined the farmers in demanding that Congress do something about the abuses inflicted by the railroads.

The result was the Interstate Commerce Act of 1887, which ordered carriers to publicize their rates and to give advance notice of proposed increases. Special rates, rebates, and other methods of discrimination were illegalized. In order to enforce competition, pooling was forbidden, as was the old trick of charging more for a short haul over a line (where there might be no competition) than for a long haul. The act also set up the Interstate Commerce Commission, the first independent regulatory commission established by Congress and a landmark in the development of systematic national regulation of business. Composed initially of five men holding six-year terms, this body was given limited power to enforce the new law.

The act of 1887 was only a modest beginning, and for its first two decades of life the ICC had little weight. Although the act had given the commission no power to set blanket rates, supposedly the agency did have authority to find individual rates to be unreasonable and to modify them. A series of Supreme Court decisions stripped ICC of its authority over these rates, however, as well as control of the long and short haul and of pooling. By 1897 the ICC was formally complaining that it was powerless to protect the people, and railroad users were becoming disturbed. As a result of popular pressure during Theodore Roosevelt's Administration, Congress in 1906 passed the Hepburn Act, which explicitly granted rate-making power to the commission and broadened its jurisdiction to include express companies, sleeping-car companies, and other railroad facilities. In the following years a steady stream of laws bolstered the power and scope of the commission.

Today the commission regulates not only railroads but also motor carriers, certain domestic water carriers, and pipe lines. Its functions are varied. The ICC has wide powers to fix rates for various types of carriers, to prevent undue discrimination in rates, and to require carriers to provide adequate facilities and reasonable service, such as through routes. Carriers must obtain permission from the commission in order to engage in transportation. The ICC has control over mergers among railroads and among motor carriers, and over the issuance of securities by these carriers. It regulates safety standards and methods. In exercising these powers the commission has considerable discretion. It has filled out the general terms of congressional statutes by hundreds of decisions over the years—enough cases to fill over 300 printed volumes.

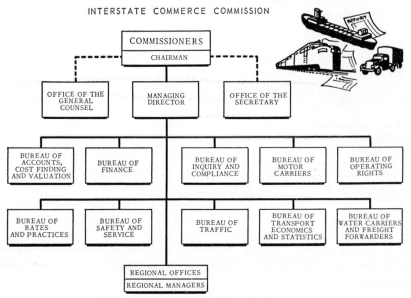

U.S. Government Organization Manual, 1959-60, p. 624.

Today the ICC is a large agency composed of eleven commissioners (now holding seven-year terms) and a staff of over 2000. It is organized into ten bureaus, including the important Bureaus of Motor Carriers, Traffic, Transport Economics and Statistics, Valuation, Safety and Service, Water Carriers and Freight Forwarders, and into numerous field offices. The eleven members are divided into five divisions, each of which specializes in certain types of cases. When the parties consent, individual commissioners will handle cases. As in other independent commissions, trial examiners do the great bulk of the hearing work, research, and initial reports. Many disputes are disposed of informally.

The ICC's most difficult and important job is rate-making. In the Transportation Act of 1920, Congress established a rule under which the commission was to set such rates that the railroads would earn, assuming "honest, efficient and economical management," an income equal to a fair return on their property. The commission's job was thus twofold: to determine the value of the railways and to decide what would be a fair return. Neither task is an easy one. Many factors enter into the valuation of property, and the railroads and the consumers naturally differ on what constitutes a fair return. Alternating periods of depression and prosperity put a heavy strain on rate structures; wars, whether hot or cold, mean heavier traffic but also higher costs. Finally, rate-making is greatly complicated by the fact that over the last three decades railroads have faced increasing competition from bus lines, truck lines, air lines, and even pipe lines and ship lines.

WHO SHALL HAUL WHAT?

For decades the railroads had little inland competition except for boats plying lakes, rivers, and canals. The railroad was transportation king. In the 1920's, however, the picture changed. Buses and trucks began to handle passengers and freight on a tremendous scale. And the infant air industry showed signs of growing out of its swaddling clothes. In recent years the railroads have been in distress—so much so that Congress in the Transportation Act of 1958 authorized the ICC to guarantee (up to a total of $500 million) loans made to railroads for maintaining and improving their systems, and also made it easier for the railroads to abandon local services on which they were losing money.

Thus transportation was becoming a more complex industry than ever, and so were transportation problems. One of the most pressing questions was that of *coordination*. It was clear that left to themselves the different carriers—railroads, motor, and air—might patch together an inefficient and poorly planned transportation system. This was one area where free competition seemed undesirable. Congress in 1935 gave the ICC power to regulate motor carriers operating between states. Today the commission regulates motor carriers in much the same way as it regulates railroads; it can, for example, require certain standards of service, establish systems of records and reports, and set safety requirements. The ICC's transportation authority was further broadened by the Transportation Act of 1940, which extended its regulatory power to water carriers in domestic service (such as ships operating on canals or rivers).

Congress has not, however, established an integrated system of transportation regulation. It has concentrated the regulation of railroads, buses, trucks, and some water carriers in the ICC, but it has put the regulation of two vital segments of transportation—air and transoceanic—into the hands of other agencies.

In 1936 Congress established the United States Maritime Commission and gave it wide regulatory powers over *ocean carriers* as well as important operating and promotional functions (see Chapter 26). A five-man independent board, the commission had power to consider complaints of shippers or passengers alleging discrimination by ocean carriers in forwarding freight or furnishing docks or other facilities in ports. It could approve, disapprove, or modify cooperative working agreements among shipping companies. In some respects this commission's problems were even more difficult than those of the ICC, for our ships must compete with foreign lines that often can operate at lower cost. In 1949 the first Hoover Commission recommended that the managerial responsibilities of the independent Maritime Commission be put in a line department under the President. The following year President Truman abolished the commission and distributed its functions between two new agencies, the Federal Maritime Board and a Maritime Administration. While both these agencies are located in the Department of Commerce under an under secretary, the Maritime Board retains its status of an independent agency because of the judicial decisions it must make in regulating ocean carriers.

Regulation of air transportation is in the hands of still other agencies— the Civil Aeronautics Board and the Federal Aviation Agency. The Board is an independent agency composed of five members which grants licenses to airlines to engage in interstate and foreign transportation. It regulates rates charged the public for air transportation, establishes rates for the carriage of mail by air carriers, authorizes and pays subsidies to certain carriers, and regulates mergers and competitive practices of air carriers. The Board also investigates accidents involving civil aircraft and determines their cause. The Federal Aviation Agency, under the control of an administrator (but not of the Board) enforces safety regulations in the manufacture and operation of aircraft. It develops and evaluates systems to improve air navigation facilities and even builds and maintains certain facilities such as emergency landing fields. This agency also administers the Federal Airport grants-in-aid for the development of public airports.

Through all this elaborate machinery the federal government has a good deal of influence over the question of "who shall haul what?" Yet there is still little basic plan. For one thing, Congress has never declared a broad and definite transportation policy. It has preferred to deal with problems in a piecemeal, pragmatic fashion as they arose. In the second place—and partly as a result of the lack of basic policy—the administrative machinery for direction of transportation is broken up. As agencies largely independent of a central directing force such as the President, the regulatory boards and commissions often go their own way. There is some virtue in this freedom, however. Our transportation system is still in a somewhat changing and fluid situation, and rigid controls might restrict initiative and progress.

Some believe, however, that a unified transportation policy is vitally needed, especially in the present era of international crisis, and that the first step must be the creation of a single, over-all transportation agency. Two members of the first Hoover Commission, for example, called for the integration of the various forms of transportation into an efficient, economical, and progressive national system so that the government could follow a "consistent and balanced policy among competing forms of transportation." [9] Such a policy will be hard to achieve, however, as long as government must both *regulate* transportation and *promote* it, in wartime as well as in peacetime.

PATROLLING THE AIR WAVES

Nowhere is regulation more necessary than in the field of radio and television. Without a strong umpire, broadcasters would quickly become involved in a tussle for wave lengths on the limited broadcasting spectrum. Yet nowhere is regulation more difficult. Not only are there the ordinary problems of regulation—problems of concentration of control, licensing and withholding of licenses, technical standards, and the like—but regulation also touches on the delicate problem of censorship versus freedom of the air. Moreover, regulation means not merely adjusting the claims of rival broadcasters, but also mediating between commercial broadcasting and alternative uses, such as ship-to-shore radio services, amateur broadcasting, police and aviation communication, and educational broadcasting.

The need for regulation of radio broadcasting was well demonstrated in 1926. For several years the Secretary of Commerce had been allocating radio frequencies under an old law. In 1926, a Chicago station dissatisfied with its assigned frequency jumped its wave length. When the Secretary of Commerce tried to penalize the station for this action, it appealed to the courts and won its case. As soon as word spread that the Secretary lacked authority to exact penalties, a wild scramble took place for favorable wave lengths and greater power. Out of the ensuing chaos rose a strong public demand for congressional action. The Radio Act of 1927 gave authority to a new Federal Radio Commission to police the industry.

Today the act is administered by the Federal Communications Commission, an independent regulatory board of seven men holding staggered seven-year terms. In addition to regulating the radio and television industry, the FCC licenses operators and prescribes their qualifications, inspects radio and television installations, and monitors the radio and television spectrum, among other services. The commission's main job, of course, is allocating frequencies and licensing broadcasting stations. In handling applications for licenses the commission must decide whether a license to a particular applicant would be consistent with the public convenience, interest, or necessity. It must make its grants in such a way as to provide services throughout the nation. Licenses are good for three years and may be renewed; this provision enables the FCC to keep a periodic check on the activities of broadcasting stations.

---

[9] Commission on Organization of the Executive Branch of the Government, *Regulatory Commissions* (Government Printing Office, 1949), pp. 19-22.

The FCC has the ticklish task of *policing* the broadcasters without *censoring* them. On the one hand the Communications Act of 1934 specifies that nothing therein shall be understood to give the commission the power to interfere with the right of free speech by radio and television. The commission has stated that it has no power to make regulations governing the content of programs. On the other hand, in considering applications for the renewal of licenses it takes into account the content and character of a broadcaster's past programs. The commission also has power to suspend the license of any operator who is proved to have transmitted profane or obscene words on the air waves.

Despite these ambiguities, the FCC has a good record of guarding the freedom of the air. It tries to enforce the statutory requirement that if a station's facilities are made available to one candidate for a public office they must be opened to all candidates for that office on the same terms. The commission has, perhaps, guarded freedom of the air more zealously than have individual broadcasters.

The advent of television re-emphasized all the problems facing the FCC. One of these is the place of education in the broadcasting system. The central question has been how to divide TV time between commercial and educational purposes. Quite naturally, the commercial broadcasters are happier with programs that bring in revenue than they are with unsponsored educational programs. Television, with its enormous powers both to inform and misinform, has greatly underlined the problem. The FCC has tried to encourage educational features, but progress has been slow. There has been some discussion of furthering radio and television education by requiring radio and television companies to devote a certain portion of their facilities to education. Another suggestion has been to set up either a privately endowed or government-owned and -operated network. Disclosures recently of the rigging of television quiz shows and of other questionable video practices aroused demands for closer government regulation of television. FCC officials contended, however, that Congress had not given the agency power to police the content or handling of television shows. The television industry declared that it did not need regulation from government—it could police itself. What role should government have? The problem is a vital one, involving not only the maintenance of free speech but its vigor and scope.

The FCC also regulates interstate telephone and telegraph. It has power to fix reasonable rates, prescribe standards of service, control mergers and expansion or curtailment of service, and to undertake other activities typical of the modern independent commissions that regulate transportation and communication agencies. The FCC does not face such difficult issues in this area as in radio and television, but the problem of mergers has been a difficult one. For example, it was only with the permission of the FCC that two competing telegraph companies, Western Union and Postal Telegraph, could combine to form one company in 1943.

Labor   **A**s we have seen, governmental regulation of business has been essentially *restrictive*. Most of the laws and rules have served to curb certain business practices and channel the dynamic force of private enterprise into socially useful channels. But regulation cuts two ways. In the case of American workers, most laws in recent decades have tended not to *restrict* labor but to *confer rights* and *opportunities* on it. Actually, many labor laws do not touch labor directly; instead, they regulate its relations with employers, including contract provisions.

Most business leaders would probably like to see government return to its old hands-off policy (though with certain exceptions, noted in the next chapter). But not labor leaders. For if governmental regulation were to be wiped out, they fear that business would impose far stricter regulations of its own—longer working hours, for example.

LABOR AND THE GOVERNMENT

Labor has not always looked on government with a friendly eye. Traditionally, workers have viewed federal and state judges with particular suspicion. Steeped in the common law, judges tended to follow the *conspiracy doctrine*—the idea that men must not combine to injure others. Since organized labor's traditional weapon has been the strike, this doctrine could be used by antiunion judges to prevent workers from acting effectively. Some judges freely issued injunctions against strikes, boycotts, and other kinds of union activities. Moreover, the courts often *interpreted* laws in a way that hurt labor. As we saw earlier in this chapter, the Supreme Court turned the Sherman Antitrust

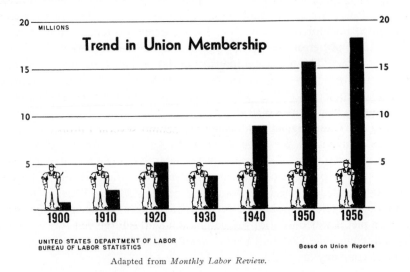

Trend in Union Membership

UNITED STATES DEPARTMENT OF LABOR
BUREAU OF LABOR STATISTICS   Based on Union Reports

Adapted from *Monthly Labor Review.*

Act against labor, even though the workers thought it had been passed to curb business combinations rather than their own unions. Finally, the courts held unconstitutional a number of acts designed to improve the worker's lot. Perhaps the most famous example was the Supreme Court's invalidation of a New York law limiting employment in bakeries to sixty hours a week and ten hours a day, on the grounds that the law interfered with freedom of contract and therefore violated the due process clause of the Fourteenth Amendment.[10]

But during the first half of this century governmental protection and promotion were gradually extended over the whole range of labor activity and organization. This change was the result of two basic political developments— labor's growing political power, and the awareness of millions of Americans in all walks of life that a healthy and secure nation depends in large measure on a healthy and secure labor force. Both these developments were reflected in the election of pro-labor Presidents, such as Wilson and the two Roosevelts, and of friendly legislators in Senate and House and the state capitols.

Labor's basic struggle was for the *right to organize.* For many decades trade unions had been held lawful by acts of state legislatures, but here again the courts had chipped away at this right by legalizing certain antiunion devices. The most notorious was the yellow-dog contract, by which antiunion employers, before they would hire a new worker, made him promise not to join a labor organization. If labor organizers later tried to unionize the worker, the employer, on the basis of yellow-dog contracts, could apply for injunctions from the courts to stop the organizers. This was a great stumbling block in the path of American unions. Chafing under this restriction, labor in 1932 secured the passage of the Norris-La Guardia Act, which made yellow-dog contracts unenforceable in federal courts. Granting labor the right to organize, the act also drastically limited the issuance of labor injunctions in other respects.

By 1932 labor had won other kinds of protection from the federal government. Almost a century before, in 1840, the government had established the ten-hour day in its navy yards, and later Congress shortened the working day of governmental employees to eight hours and required the eight-hour day for railroad employees and for seamen. Nevertheless, progress was slow, partly because of the courts. In 1918 the Supreme Court invalidated a national law prohibiting the interstate transportation of goods produced by child labor, and a constitutional amendment to give Congress this power had not got very far. By 1932 the United States still lagged far behind several European countries in the protection afforded to labor.

A NEW DEAL FOR LABOR

In 1932, on the eve of the Roosevelt Administration, the AFL was down to barely two million members—partly a result of unemployment during the Great Depression. Its political influence was small. But the new Administration

---

[10] *Lochner* v. *New York* (1905).

was sympathetic toward labor. During the 1930's organized labor rose to a position of tremendous economic and political power. Under the New Deal, labor achieved both an array of protective legislation and governmental help in its campaign to organize the unorganized. The CIO split off from the AFL and unionized a number of vital industries, such as steel, automobiles, and rubber, but the AFL itself re-formed its ranks and became larger and stronger than ever.

The National Industrial Recovery Act of 1933 laid the stage for the New Deal's labor policies. This act was essentially a means of giving business a shot in the arm by allowing industries to work out codes of fair competition. Such codes, however, involved labor standards, such as wages, hours, and child labor, and the unions were given a part in the code-making process. Moreover, Section 7a of the act contained the famous provision that "employees shall have the right to organize and bargain collectively through representatives of their own choosing, and shall be free from the interference, restraint, or coercion of employers of labor, or their agents, in the designation of such representatives or in self-organization or in other concerted activities for the purpose of collective bargaining or other mutual aid or protection." Under the stimulus of the NRA and the subsequent upturn in business, the unions blossomed. New members flocked into unions and violent organizational strikes occurred in many parts of the country.

The NRA was short-lived, for the Supreme Court declared the act unconstitutional in 1935. But the New Deal Congress, determined to maintain national protection and encouragement of labor, passed a series of acts in the next few years that amounted to a sort of NRA for labor. These acts embraced:

Public contracts. The Walsh-Healey Act of 1936 requires that all national government supply contracts in excess of $10,000 must provide that no worker employed under such contracts shall be paid less than the prevailing minimum wage as determined by the Secretary of Labor and overtime for all work in excess of eight hours per day or forty hours per week; that convict labor will not be used; and that child labor (boys under sixteen and girls under eighteen) will not be employed.

Wages and hours. The Fair Labor Standards Act of 1938 went much further. It set a maximum work-week of 44 hours, to be successively reduced to 42 and then to 40 hours, for all employees engaged in interstate commerce, or in the production of goods for interstate commerce (with certain major exemptions). Employees could work beyond these limits only if paid at 1½ times the regular rate. Minimum wages were set at 25 cents an hour, but were to rise by jumps to 40 cents. In 1949 the minimum was raised to 75 cents an hour, and in 1956 to $1.00 an hour. Not only did the Supreme Court uphold the constitutionality of the Fair Labor Standards Act, but in later decisions it broadened the scope of the act.

Today about 24 million workers are protected under this act, including most workers in factories and mining, transportation and communications. But millions are still not covered. In addition to those who are not engaged in interstate commerce, Congress has exempted agricultural workers, most employees in the retail and service trades, immediate processors of agricultural commodities, outside salesmen, seamen, and others.

The Fair Labor Standards and Walsh-Healey acts are administered by the Wage and Hour and Public Contracts Divisions of the Department of Labor; these two divisions are jointly administered by a head appointed by the President (with the consent of the Senate). They maintain a crew of inspectors who check business firms to insure compliance with the law, but their administrator has frequently asked Congress for more funds to permit more intensive inspection.

Child labor. The Fair Labor Standards Act prohibited child labor (under sixteen years of age or under eighteen in hazardous occupations) in industries that engage in, or that produce goods for, interstate commerce. These provisions are enforced by the Wage and Hour Division and the Bureau of Labor Standards (in the Labor Department).

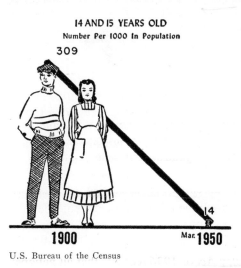

14 AND 15 YEARS OLD
Number Per 1000 In Population
309
1900   Mar. **1950**
U.S. Bureau of the Census
Children in the labor force.

Labor relations. Section 7a of the NRA was resurrected in the National Labor Relations Act, which was passed in 1935 only two months after the Supreme Court struck down the former act. In the preamble, the Wagner Act (so called after its chief sponsor, Senator Robert Wagner of New York) declared that workers in industries affecting interstate commerce (with certain exceptions) should have the right to organize and bargain collectively, and that inequality in bargaining power between employers and workers led to industrial strife and economic instability. The act made five types of action unfair for employers to practice: (1) interfering with workers in their attempts to organize unions or bargain collectively; (2) supporting company unions (unions set up and dominated by the employer); (3) discriminating against membership in unions; (4) firing or otherwise victimizing an employee for having taken action under the act; (5) refusing to bargain with union representatives. The act was intended to prevent open-shop employers from using violence, espionage, propaganda, and community pressure to resist unionization of their plants.

The Wagner Act also set up machinery to decide contests over what union should represent a given group of employees. Such conflicts—which became numerous and bitter when the CIO broke away from the AFL in the mid-1930's—were to be settled by secret ballot and majority rule. To administer the act a board of three members, holding overlapping terms of five years each, was set up. Under the act, the National Labor Relations Board (NLRB), an independent regulatory commission, has the ticklish job of determining the appropriate bargaining unit—that is, whether the employees may organize by plant, by craft, or on some other basis. The board operates largely through regional officers, who investigate charges of unfair labor practices and may issue formal complaints, and through trial examiners, who hold hearings and submit reports to the board in Washington.

STRIKING A BALANCE

From the start the Wagner Act was a center of controversy. It strengthened the unions and helped them seize greater economic and political power. In 1936 a committee of eminent attorneys declared that the measure was unconstitutional. Taking heart from this "opinion," many corporations simply ignored NLRB decisions. Unions, unwilling to wait for the slow-moving procedures of the law, organized a series of violent strikes, including the much-criticized sit-down strikes. In April 1937, during President Roosevelt's campaign to pack the Supreme Court, the Court by a five-to-four vote upheld the constitutionality of the Wagner Act.[11] The fight then shifted to Congress, where senators and representatives attacked the NLRB through denunciations, investigations, and slashes in its appropriations.

What had caused all this uproar? Three things: First, from the outset the board applied vigorously the prolabor provisions of the act. For example, the act prohibited the employer from interfering with employee unionization; the board interpreted this to mean that employers could not even make public statements advising workers not to join unions. Such rulings raised a storm of protest from employers. Second, the board got caught in the struggle between the AFL and CIO. Whichever way it decided certain representation cases, it was bound to antagonize one labor faction or the other. Some of these cases, moreover, were highly consequential; in one decision the board designated the CIO Longshoremen's Union as the bargaining agent for all West Coast ports, although the AFL claimed majority support of employees in particular companies. Third, the purpose of the act was widely misunderstood. Employers and editorial writers solemnly charged the measure and the board with being biased in favor of labor, when the very aim of the act had been to improve the workers' bargaining power.

The heat of the controversy was heightened by criticism of several union practices. These practices were not new, but now that labor was achieving greater power they came in for more public attention. One was featherbedding.

---

[11] *National Labor Relations Board* v. *Jones & Laughlin Steel Corp.*

Faced with labor-saving devices that cut down on the number of workers needed to do a given job, some unions demanded that the original number of workers be paid, even if they had nothing to do and merely stood around. For example, James C. Petrillo, head of the AFL Musicians' Union, barred his members from making records, taking part in television broadcasts, or making transcriptions that could be played over the radio. Then there was the charge that unions were in the hands of dictators. Some union leaders stayed in office for years, even decades; some received exorbitant salaries (for example, Petrillo, $46,000 a year). To be sure, many union leaders had no more dictatorial control over their unions than did many business executives over their enterprises, but, as we saw in Chapter 12, people's attitudes toward labor leaders are often hostile. And unions are supposed to be run in a democratic manner. Moreover, protected by the *closed shop* (an establishment where only union members can be hired), some union heads seemed to have as much power to discipline members as had the more ruthless employers of old. And a few unions were out-and-out rackets. Investigations revealed intimate connections between certain union leaders and the underworld.

Most unions continued to be run honestly and democratically. Nevertheless, public opinion, fed by antiunion propaganda, seemed to swing against labor after World War II. Not only labor excesses but a wave of great industry-wide strikes intensified demands in Congress for a law that would equalize the obligations of labor and management. In 1946 the Republicans won majorities in House and Senate, paving the way for modification of the Wagner Act.

THE TAFT-HARTLEY ACT

The upshot was the Labor-Management Relations Act of 1947, commonly called the Taft-Hartley Act after its sponsors. This act, which applies with certain exceptions to industries affecting interstate commerce:

    1. Outlawed the closed shop, and permitted the *union shop* (under which newly employed workers must join the union within a stated time period) only under certain conditions.

    2. Required unions to file affidavits that their officers are not communists, if such unions want to secure federal action on complaints against employers.

    3. Outlawed jurisdictional strikes (strikes arising from disputes between unions over which has the right to do a job), secondary boycotts, political expenditures by unions in connection with federal elections, excessive union dues or fees, and strikes by federal employees.

    4. Made it an unfair labor practice for unions to refuse to bargain with employers.

    5. Permitted employers and unions to sue each other for violation of contracts in federal courts.

    6. Allowed the use of the labor injunction on a limited scale, reversing the policy set by the Norris-La Guardia Act.

7. Revamped the National Labor Relations Board, increasing its membership to five and strengthening the semi-independent position of the board's general counsel.

Organized labor greeted the new measure as a "slave-labor" act and vowed that it would use its political power to wipe the act from the statute books. Senator Taft saw the bill as "an extraordinary reversal along the right lines toward equalizing the power of labor unions and employers." Most observers recognized the measure as neither a slave-labor act nor as a cure-all. While acknowledging the seriousness of some labor practices, they expressed fears that the Taft-Hartley Act, despite its conservative sponsorship, may have pushed the government too far into the hitherto voluntary area of collective bargaining.

THE LABOR REFORM ACT OF 1959

During the late 1950's public attention focused less on relations between union and management and more on the internal affairs of unions. A Senate "rackets" committee investigating labor activities found in some unions glaring cases of corruption, dictatorial control by a few bosses, loose financial practices, and other deplorable practices. Heavily publicized, the committee's disclosures aroused popular demand for reform. At the same time, businessmen and others, with the backing of the Eisenhower Administration, wanted new restrictions on labor's use of the boycott and picketing. Union leaders hotly opposed reform on the grounds that it would harass good unions and have no effect on the bad ones. After two years of deadlock over the issue, Congress in 1959 passed the Labor Reform Act of 1959, which:

1. Requires labor organizations to file comprehensive reports with the Secretary of Labor on all financial transactions and on the workings of its constitution and bylaws.
2. Under a "bill of rights" section, grants union members the unqualified right to vote in union elections by secret ballot, to speak up freely in union meetings, to get open hearings in discipline cases, and to sue in federal courts if they feel that they are not getting fair play under union rules.
3. Requires secret elections at least every three years for local union officers and at least every five years for national union officers, and bars from union office ex-convicts, embezzlers of union funds, communists, and any union leader with conflicting business interests.
4. Plugs loopholes in the Taft-Hartley Act's provisions against the secondary boycott. For example, the new act outlaws the "hot cargo" weapon used by unions like the Teamsters to refuse to handle cargoes to or from firms involved in labor disputes.
5. Outlaws organizational picketing if the employer has validly recognized another union, or if the employer had held an NLRB election within the preceding year.

KEEPING LABOR-MANAGEMENT PEACE

The Federal Mediation and Conciliation Service, with mediators located in eight regional offices, stands ready to help settle labor-management disputes in any industry affecting interstate commerce (except railroads and airlines, which are covered by the Railway Labor Act), either on request of one of the parties to the dispute or whenever the dispute threatens to cause a substantial interruption of interstate commerce. Through tact and persuasion the trouble-shooters of the Federal Mediation and Conciliation Service induce unions to call off strikes and persuade employers to make concessions. The service has no power to dictate terms; the parties to the dispute are free to ignore the conciliators and their suggestions. If mediation fails, the parties may ask the service to assist in the selection of an arbitrator; under this arrangement the parties agree in advance to accept the arbitrator's decision.

The Taft-Hartley Act also set up new machinery for handling disputes affecting an entire industry, or a major part of it, where a stoppage would threaten the national health or safety. When such a strike breaks out, the following steps are authorized:

1. The President appoints a special board to investigate and report the facts.
2. The President may then instruct the Attorney General to seek in a federal court an eighty-day injunction against the strike.
3. The court grants this injunction if it agrees that the national health or safety is endangered.
4. If the parties have not settled the strike within the eighty days, the board informs the President of the employer's last offer of settlement.
5. The NLRB takes a secret vote among the employees to see if they will accept the employer's last offer.
6. If no settlement is reached, the injunction expires, and the President reports to Congress with such recommendations as he may wish to make.

How successful has the Taft-Hartley Act been in helping keep labor peace? It has been invoked several times against strikes in vital sectors of the economy, such as atomic energy, coal, shipping, and telephone service, sometimes successfully, sometimes not. On one occasion an injunction was issued ordering John L. Lewis to send his coal miners back to work. Lewis sent out the order, but the miners stayed off the job. The government asked the court for a contempt of court citation against the miners' leader, but the court held that Lewis had done his best. Neither President Truman nor Eisenhower made use of the act in the 1952 or 1956 steel strikes, but the latter invoked its provisions in waterfront and steel disputes in 1959.

Resources   Following the Civil War, the nation's enormous resources underwent a period of feverish development. The General Land Office of the federal government handed our western riches—lands, forests, minerals—to thousands of individuals and corporations. At the time, our resources seemed inexhaustible. But as the years passed, people began to demand that the government act to protect the public interest and to curb some of the worst abuses of exploitation. Well before the end of the century, Yellowstone National Park had been created and many million acres of forest reservation had been set aside.

The conservation movement found a champion in Theodore Roosevelt. The "Rough Rider" had lived in the West as a young man and had come to cherish its scenic beauties and its wild life. On assuming office he told Congress that "forest and water problems are perhaps the most vital internal problems of the United States." With the help of Gifford Pinchot, another conservation zealot and chief of the Forestry Bureau, Roosevelt drew the nation's attention to conservation problems and greatly enlarged public coal, oil, phosphate, and forest reserves. In the years since Roosevelt's Square Deal, the federal government not only has continued to protect and enlarge public reserves of forest land and other resources: it also has extended regulation over *private* exploitation of the nation's riches.

OIL

The conservation of oil is becoming a particularly important problem. Oil can easily be wasted. It can be produced in such a way as to give quick profits to a few operators, while leaving underground millions of barrels that

WHAT FEDERAL LANDS ARE USED FOR

Principal use	Number of acres	Principal use	Number of acres
Forests and wildlife	186.3 million	Reclamation and irrigation	8.8 million
Grazing	169.6 million	Flood control and navigation	3.2 million
Military (except airfields)	15.2 million	Industrial uses, including atomic energy	1.8 million
Airfields	2.0 million	Power development	1.5 million
Parks and historic sites	15.0 million	Sites for hospitals, offices, storage, housing, other purposes	1.7 million

TOTAL LAND OWNED BY THE GOVERNMENT IN THE U.S. — 405.1 million acres OR 21.3% of entire country

Reprinted from *U.S. News & World Report*, an independent weekly news magazine published at Washington. Copyright 1955 U.S. News Publishing Corporation

GOVERNMENT OWNS NEARLY HALF
OF ALL LAND IN THE WEST

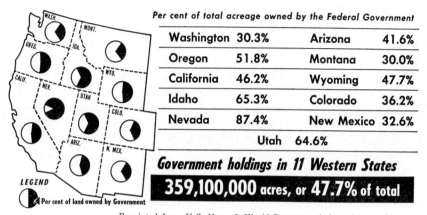

Per cent of total acreage owned by the Federal Government

Washington	30.3%	Arizona	41.6%
Oregon	51.8%	Montana	30.0%
California	46.2%	Wyoming	47.7%
Idaho	65.3%	Colorado	36.2%
Nevada	87.4%	New Mexico	32.6%
Utah	64.6%		

Government holdings in 11 Western States
359,100,000 acres, or 47.7% of total

LEGEND

● Per cent of land owned by Government

Reprinted from *U.S. News & World Report,* an independent weekly news magazine published at Washington. Copyright 1955 U.S. News Publishing Corporation

can be recovered only by costly processes. Moreover, oil can be wasted by burning, running off into the ground, or by uncontrolled blowing off of gas. Our reserves are still vast but by no means limitless. Since oil is a vitally urgent mineral in war as well as in peace, the federal goverment has been drawn into the problem.

During the Depression, hundreds of new wells were opened up, and prices dropped to fantastically low levels. Individual states attempted to stabilize the industry and conserve oil by restricting production, but they had little success. The National Industrial Recovery Act gave the President power to regulate the industry, including authority to prohibit the interstate transportation of oil produced in excess of quotas set by state law. In 1935, however, the Supreme Court invalidated the oil-control section of NRA on the grounds that the President's power to stop the shipment of "hot oil" (oil produced above the quota) was an unconstitutional delegation of legislative power.[12] Congress then passed a new measure directly forbidding the shipment in interstate commerce of oil produced in excess of state quotas. The President had authority to suspend this embargo on oil if he found a lack of balance between supply and demand. Congress also authorized an interstate compact among the big producing states, and this was soon drawn up and ratified by Texas, Oklahoma, and other oil-producing states.

Some conservationists believe that the federal government has not done enough to conserve oil. Proposals have been made for tougher federal laws requiring and enforcing rigid standards of conservation. Representatives of the oil states, however, have resisted further federal control. Indeed, they have

---

[12] *Panama Refining Co.* v. *Ryan.*

gained a tax subsidy through the "depletion allowance" which exempts part of the income of oil and gas producers from the federal income tax. As our oil resources become depleted, political disputes between conservationists and producers may grow more bitter. Consumers of oil and gasoline may also be drawn more closely into oil politics.

In recent years a political struggle has taken place over ownership of the rich oil deposits off the shore of the United States between low-water mark and the three-mile limit. The Supreme Court has ruled that the national government has a paramount interest in this offshore oil. In 1946 President Truman vetoed an act of Congress handing over ownership of the oil to the several states bordering the ocean. In 1952, however, offshore oil became an election issue, and the following year Congress passed and President Eisenhower signed a bill giving those states title to submerged lands and resources within their "historic" boundaries while confirming federal ownership of submerged lands of the continental shelf beyond state boundaries. Democrats denounced the act as a "giveaway"; Republicans replied that it was merely part of their program of "restoring more power to the states." The issues are complex, involving the views of states-righters and conservationists and the struggles of oil companies and state governments for control of the oil. Since the oil off the coasts of Texas and Louisiana alone has been valued at $27 billion, the controversy is likely to continue for some time. The Supreme Court has recently been presented with the issue as to whether the "historic" boundaries of Texas and Louisiana give these states control over oil beyond the three-mile limit.

WATER AND OTHER RESOURCES

Water is both a vital resource in itself (see Chapter 26) and also a source of electric power. In 1920 Congress passed the Federal Water Power Act to regulate the use of water power on public lands and navigable streams. A Federal Power Commission, composed of the Secretaries of Agriculture, Interior, and War, was set up. Ten years later the FPC was converted into a new independent regulatory commission, with five full-time members holding five-year terms, and its powers were broadened. The major job of the commission is to protect the rights of the American people in the water-power potential of navigable streams. Private companies can build dams and other hydroelectric facilities only after receiving a license from the FPC, which grants such licenses only if the projects fit into a comprehensive plan for developing the waterway for use of water power, development of navigation, recreation, and other beneficial purposes.

The commission not only regulates rates, services, and securities, but under the Federal Power Act of 1935 it has jurisdiction over all public utilities engaged in selling or sending electricity across state boundaries. Here, too, the FPC has power to fix just and reasonable rates, and its approval is required for selling or merging facilities and buying or selling securities. The FPC is a sort of ICC for electricity. It also has some voice in the development of power facilities by other federal agencies, such as the Army.

Natural gas, an increasingly important commodity in recent years, has also been subject to regulation by the Federal Power Commission. The Natural Gas Act of 1938 requires that natural-gas companies selling in interstate commerce must obtain licenses from the commission. The FPC also has power to fix reasonable rates. Since natural gas is a relatively young industry, the commission was involved in the scramble of private companies for authorization to build new pipe lines to urban areas in the North and East. It has sought to protect the welfare of the consumer and to prevent the overbuilding of pipe lines to one community.

In recent years, independent natural-gas producers have tried to gain exemption from federal regulation. Arguing that such regulation was unnecessary and discriminatory, they persuaded Congress to pass an exemption measure in 1956. President Eisenhower had been expected to sign the bill; but during debate in the upper chamber, a senator announced that he could not vote for the bill because a lawyer working for its passage had given $2500 to the senator's campaign manager. The President vetoed the bill because of what he called the "arrogant tactics" of gas-and-oil lobbyists. Supporters of exemption indicated, however, that they would again introduce the bill in a subsequent session of Congress.

The Politics of Regulation

Karl Marx, the theorist of "capitalist decay," maintained that the long-run interests of all capitalists were the same. He argued that the proletariat had a similar unity of interest, and that eventually the exploiting class would give way to a government of the workers. Relations among the new proletarian rulers would be so harmonious that eventually the state would just wither away.

A look at the American economy today is enough to dispel the idea of a united group of businessmen facing a united group of workers. To be sure, there is conflict between businessmen and workers. But such conflict is obscured by a vast complex of antagonistic interests operating *within* economic groups. The American political scene reflects not only the struggle of employer against worker, but also the struggles of consumer against producer, of businessmen against businessmen, of labor against labor, of section against section. And all these interests are intertwined and interlocked in such a way as to make the whole picture very complex indeed.

THE CLASH OF INTERESTS

Earlier (see Chapter 12) we noted some of the characteristics and weapons of the larger economic interests. Here it might be well to look more closely at the competition among interest groups in the light of the problem of governmental regulation.

Some of the sharpest contests take place within the world of business. Consider, for example, the railroad interests. Early attempts to regulate the railroads reflected chiefly a struggle between the railroads and consumers. But other interests more and more were drawn into the struggle—for example, financial control groups, railroad investors, railroad equipment and supply industries. Later, the railroads began to meet intense competition from other forms of transportation, and railroad politics became even more intricate than before.

Today a political battle constantly simmers between railroad carriers and the trucking business, and occasionally this battle erupts in full-page advertisements in leading newspapers. The railroads argue that the trucking business offers unfair competition. The fact that government builds and maintains the nation's highways, they protest, means that motor transportation is subsidized, while the railroads must provide their own facilities. The truckers reply that they contribute heavily to highway maintenance through gasoline and other taxes—and so the battle rages. The railroads also complain of the subsidies granted airlines and water shippers.

The internal rivalries of labor also affect the politics of regulation. Labor, as we saw in Chapter 12, is by no means a unified, monolithic body; it is a cluster of unions of all kinds, sizes, and interests, along with many unorganized workers. The cleavages that develop within the ranks of organized labor were dramatically revealed in the 1930's when the CIO broke away from the AFL. But less conspicuous rivalries are also important. One of these is between workers employed in rival industries. For example, the Railroad Brotherhoods and the Teamsters' Union (mainly truck drivers) often clash on national transportation policy simply because industrially these two groups compete with one another. Sometimes, of course, unions ignore such competitive situations. Ford, General Motors, and Chrysler may compete in selling cars, but this rivalry has little effect on the solidarity of the United Auto Workers Union, which embraces workers from all three corporations.

The struggle of the interests influences also regulatory *procedures*. Recently, for example, the Civil Aeronautics Board decided to formulate a plan for federally subsidized local air service for seven midwestern states that were facing a transportation crisis because of contraction of railroad services. So many airlines, mayors, presidents of Chambers of Commerce, and others were affected by the plan that there were almost a hundred parties to the case and almost 200 witnesses testified before one of the Board's examiners. This expert, after reading through pleadings, transcripts, exhibits, and briefs that, piled up, were five and a half feet high, announced his plan for air service for the area—in two volumes totaling 658 pages. More exceptions and briefs were filed by the interests affected. Then the case went before the Civil Aeronautics Board and took on more of a political atmosphere, for sixteen senators, twenty-two representatives, and three governors testified along with spokesmen for the airlines concerned. The Board finally announced its decision at the end of 1958—well over three years after the need for action became apparent.[13]

WASHINGTON BATTLEGROUND

Indeed, Congress more than any other branch of government mirrors the efforts of interest groups to gain or evade federal regulation. Many members of Congress represent states or districts dominated by one or two economic interests—for example, "silver" senators and "cotton" representatives. Other members of Congress—especially those from heavily populated areas—are more concerned with the interests of consumers. When the consumer feels that he is being pinched by excessive rates, when a transportation industry believes that it cannot make a fair profit on present charges, when little businessmen think that they are being squeezed out by the big fellows, their complaints are quickly followed—indeed, sometimes aroused by—outcries in the halls of Congress.

Congress has delegated to the regulatory agencies the big job of mediating the claims of conflicting interests. Most of these regulatory agencies are *independent regulatory boards*—the ICC, FTC, FCC, SEC, NLRB, and others. This is not accidental. Congress has put the regulatory function in the hands of agencies somewhat independent of elected officials, and especially independent of the President (see Chapter 19). As a practical matter this procedure was not necessary. Regulatory functions can be—and are—effectively and fairly handled by line agencies in regular federal departments. For example, the Packers and Stockyards Act of 1921, which seeks to protect farmers against arbitrary charges and other unfair practices, is administered by the Bureau of Animal Industry in the Department of Agriculture. And wages and hours are administered by a line agency headed by an administrator and lodged in the Labor Department. Nevertheless Congress has generally preferred to keep the President from dominating the regulatory agencies. It has given board members long, staggered terms; it has limited the President's power to remove members; and it has usually required that members must be selected from both parties.

As a result, the regulatory commissions have been somewhat insulated from partisan politics and partisan control. But they have not been kept out of politics; no agency making important decisions can be. A commission ultimately reflects prevailing sentiment, as did the FTC in its probusiness decisions during the 1920's. A commission is inevitably influenced by new members; if a President appoints a series of consumer-conscious commissioners, the decisions of the agency will respect consumer interests. And, as we have seen,

---

[13] Condensed from a case study in Louis J. Hector, "The New Critique of the Regulatory Agency," remarks before Section of Administrative Law, American Bar Association, August 25, 1959.

the regulatory agencies are influenced by Congress, which allots them funds, investigates them, and shares in the making of appointments.

The lake cargo coal rate controversy in the 1920's is an example of the exposure of regulatory agencies to political rough and tumble. In this case the ICC was caught in the cross fire between coal operators in the northern coal fields and those in the southern. Each group wanted to supply lake cargo coal and to gain preferential freight rates to Lake Erie ports. The fight became so "intense as to lead to direct political interference with the rate-making process. Appointments were made and rejected with a view to swaying the decision of the Commission." [14] The commission was divided; finally the railroads themselves worked out a compromise.

The conflict between the AFL and CIO, before they merged in 1955, closely affected regulatory politics. The passage of the Wages and Hours Act was gravely imperiled by the AFL's fear that it was essentially a CIO bill and would mainly help CIO members. More important, the NLRB ran head-on into AFL-CIO jurisdictional rivalry in attempting to determine the appropriate bargaining unit. When the President nominated new board appointees, they were carefully scrutinized by each labor organization to see if they had leanings to the other side. During its early years the NLRB was greatly handicapped by the need to follow a cautious policy of neutrality between the two labor groups. The reunion of AFL and CIO may mean that government labor agencies will be less vulnerable to the struggles between those two organizations, but the rivalries among individual unions will certainly be reflected on the Washington battleground.

To be sure, some regulatory agencies have protected themselves from political cross currents better than others. The ICC, for example, is often cited as one of the most judicial and independent agencies in Washington. Yet such an agency may become highly political in another sense—namely, of being overly protective of the industry it is designed to regulate. The ICC, though it is rarely charged with showing favoritism for one railroad over another, is often accused of favoring railroads over other forms of transportation. Whether this charge is true or not, the capture of a regulatory agency by the regulated interests is not unknown in Washington.

---

[14] Merle Fainsod and Lincoln Gordon, *Government and the American Economy* (Norton, 1941), p. 272. See H. C. Mansfield, *The Lake Cargo Coal Rate Controversy* (Columbia Univ. Press, 1932) for the full account.

LEGISLATIVE

Senate   House

Architect of the Capitol

General Accounting Office

Government Printing Offi

Library of Congress

United States Botanic Gar

THE CONGRESS

EXECUTIVE

Executive Office of the Preside

The White House Office

Bureau of the Budget

Council of Economic Advisers

National Aeronautics and Space Council

National Security Council

Office of Civil and Defense Mobilization

President's Advisory Committee on Government Organization

THE PRESIDENT

THE CONSTITUTION

JUDICIAL

United States Courts of Appeals

District Courts of the United Sta

United States Court of Claims

United States Court of Customs Patent Appeal

United States Customs Court

Territorial Courts

**THE
SUPREME COURT**
of the United States

Note: This chart, adapted from U.S. Government Organization Manual,
seeks to show only the more important agencies of the Federal Government.

Government as Promoter

In recent years we have heard a great deal about the welfare state. Politicians have charged that spendthrifts in Washington have been trying to buy votes through give-away programs. Supporters of federal subsidies—which we will call here "promotion"—have denounced their opponents as heartless skinflints who would put dollars before human lives. In the heat of the argument, certain facts are sometimes ignored.

In the first place, governmental promotion is by no means a recent development in the United States. In his first annual address to Congress, President Washington called for a tariff to protect business. In his famous *Report on the Subject of Manufactures* in 1791, Secretary of the Treasury Alexander Hamilton proposed that government help develop business by giving bounties to new enterprises. Henry Clay's American System was a plan in the first part of the last century for federally subsidized roads and waterways, a strengthened banking system, and tariff protection. Parts of these ambitious programs were carried out during the first half of the nineteenth century, and after the Civil War the Republican party bestowed special-interest subsidies on businessmen, farmers, veterans and other groups.

In the second place, almost all special-interest groups have at one time or another benefited directly from government aid. During much of the nation's history, business has been the main recipient of help from Washington; today farmers and veterans seem to have preference. Governmental promotion can be used to help any group. The main questions are: Who shall be aided? In what way? And to what extent? The politics of promotion revolves around these questions.

Although we are using the term *promotion* to mean something different from *regulation, it is impossible to make a sharp distinction between the two activities.* Regulation means setting restraints on individuals and groups, directly compelling them to take, or not to take, certain actions. Promotion means encouraging, strengthening, safeguarding, or advancing the interests of

659

particular persons, groups, industries, or sectors of the economy. In the case of either regulation or promotion the aim may be the benefit of one group or of the whole nation. Similarly, promotion can be used to *regulate* interests as well as to help them, as the following pages will show. Promotion savors a little more of the carrot, regulation of the stick, but often either one, or a combination, can be used to carry out a purpose of government.

Federal promotion is an expensive operation. In a recent year the national government gave veterans $4.7 billion, farmers $1.7 billion, newspapers and magazines (through mail charges far below actual cost) over $250 million, road-users almost $750 million, and needy people over $1.5 billion, aside from grants to foreign countries of over $4 billion. Let us see just where this money goes, and why.

Helping Businessmen   **I**n the broadest sense, government assists business by maintaining an orderly legal and economic system. A government that protects private property and enforces contracts enables businessmen to operate in a stable situation where agreements can be enforced. A government that helps promote a prosperous economy enables businessmen to enjoy a large volume of sales and good profits. A high or low tariff can have considerable effect on the profits of individual concerns. The kind of monetary system established by government—for example, "tight" or "easy" money—is of direct interest to businessmen (see Chapter 27).

Aside from such obvious aids to business, the national government supplies a number of specific services, and assists individual sectors of business.

THE DEPARTMENT OF COMMERCE

Occupying one of the largest office buildings in the world, the Department of Commerce in Washington is the nation's "service center for business." The Secretary of Commerce is usually a person with a business background who is also prominent in the party in power. Under his direction the department assists business in many ways. For example, the Bureau of Foreign Commerce and the Office of Business Economics report on business activities and prospects at home and abroad. The National Bureau of Standards makes scientific investigations and tries to standardize units of weight and measurement.

The *Census Bureau* has been called the greatest fact-finding and figure-counting agency in the world. The Constitution requires that a national census be taken every ten years, and the results of this census, and of others in between, supply businessmen with valuable information on business and agricultural activity, incomes, occupations, employment, housing, home ownership, governmental finances, crime, and many other matters. Its findings are presented in bulky volumes published by the Government Printing Office. Per-

haps the most valuable of these, especially for businessmen, is the annual *Statistical Abstract of the United States.* The Census Bureau employs over 4000 permanent workers and 100,000 during census-taking.

Another historic bureau now in the Commerce Department is the *Patent Office.* The first article of the Constitution authorizes Congress to secure to authors and inventors for a limited period "the exclusive right to their respective writings and discoveries." A patent, conferring the right of exclusive use of an invention for seventeen years, is a valuable property right. On receiving an application for a patent right, the Patent Office must study its records to see if any prior patent might be infringed and if the invention is sufficiently original and useful to be patentable; meanwhile the applicant marks his product "Patent Pending." Since decisions of the Patent Office directly involve legal rights, its rulings may be appealed to a board of appeals in the Patent Office and then to the Court of Customs and Patent Appeals or to a federal district court. Some cases go even to the Supreme Court. Although most patent problems are technical, patent policy also involves such broad problems as the stimulation of invention and the threat of monopoly and economic concentration.

Two other promotional services in the Department of Commerce are:

The Weather Bureau. We still like to quote Mark Twain, who is reported to have said that "Everybody talks about the weather but nobody does anything about it." Actually, the United States Weather Bureau not only tries to forecast the weather, but, working with private agencies, also attempts to do

From *U.S. Government Organization Manual,* 1959-60, p. 608.

DEPARTMENT OF COMMERCE

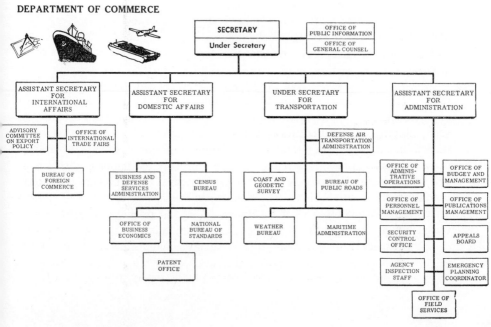

something about it. Staffed with over 8000 employees, this agency makes forecasts on the basis of data funneled in by its 300 field stations in this country and overseas. Formerly the bureau's services were used mostly by farmers, but today they are used by airlines, the resort business, and by other industries. Such experiments as seeding clouds to induce rain and the use of electronic computers suggest that the Weather Bureau may have an even greater role for both civilian and military activities in days to come.

The Coast and Geodetic Survey. This bureau charts the nation's coast-lines, lake and river beds, and the ocean tides and currents along routes of commerce. Its maps and charts are used by air and sea navigators, engineers, fishermen, and others.

AIDS TO TRANSPORTATION

Of all the aid that government has bestowed on business, the *transportation industry* has had the lion's share. Part of this heavy promotion of transportation has been due to historic circumstance; part to transportation politics; part to deliberate national policy.

Railroads led the way in gaining subsidies. During the second half of the nineteenth century the national government gave huge land grants to the railroads, which were by that time spanning the continent. During the years 1862-1866 alone over 100 million acres of land were given away by Congress to the railroad builders. Later, as we have seen (see Chapter 25), public opinion turned against the railway magnates, and promotion was followed by regulation. In the 1930's, however, the government lent money to railroads weakened by the depression to help them meet costs and maintain equipment. It has been estimated that the grand total of all types of aid (including loans) given to railroads by national, state, and local governments amounts to almost a billion and a half dollars.[1] In recent years, as railroads have declined in the face of air and highway transportation, they have received additional federally supported grants.

Shipping also has a lengthy history of government aid. In its very first session in 1789 Congress provided that only ships built in the United States and belonging to American citizens could register under the American flag, and such shipping was favored through discriminatory tonnage taxes and customs duties. In effect the important coastal trade was fenced off for American-owned ships. At times during the nineteenth century the national government subsidized steamship companies by means of grants to carry mail. But these mail subsidies invariably led to scandalous inefficiency and corruption and provoked long arguments over the propriety of giving public money to private businessmen. When World War I caught the nation with a severe shortage of shipping, however, the problem arose of having enough ships for emergencies.

---

[1] *Public Aids to Transportation* (Federal Coordinator of Transportation, 1940), I, 13.

Between the two world wars Congress passed a series of acts designed to aid and strengthen the shipping industry. In 1936 it abandoned the mail subsidy system, which had led to further scandals, in favor of direct subsidies.

In these days of international tension, the federal government is responsible for keeping alive a merchant marine that could quickly be converted into a wartime fleet. The Federal Maritime Administration in the Department of Commerce administers a subsidy program designed to enable American shipbuilders and shipping companies to compete with those of foreign nations. This agency subsidizes both the building and operating of ships. It finances the construction of vessels in American shipyards, and sells these vessels for an amount equal to the estimated cost of building the ships in foreign yards. It pays shipping companies the amounts by which certain items of their expenses, such as wages, exceed those of foreign competitors. The administration's other promotional functions include accepting obsolete vessels in exchange for credit on the purchase of new ones, administering a federal ship mortgage insurance fund, and managing construction reserve funds for American shipowners. The Maritime Administration also has sizable regulatory functions, as noted in Chapter 25.

Air traffic is playing a bigger role in transportation than ever before. To back up its military air arm, the United States government encourages civil aviation with large subsidies. The chief method of helping air carriers financially is through fixing rates for carrying air mail. In setting these rates the Civil Aeronautics Board considers the need of each air carrier for enough revenues from mail and other sources to enable it to maintain air transportation as needed for commerce, the postal service, and national defense. The board also has regulatory functions (see Chapter 25). Most of the promotional activity is conducted by the Federal Aviation Agency. The FAA, operating through a large field staff, administers the Federal Airport Act of 1946, which provides for the construction of a nationwide system of civil airports through federal aid to states and municipalities. The FAA also operates an extensive system of federal airways, and conducts research projects designed to benefit civil aviation in general.

Highways enjoy by far the largest federal transportation promotion. Ever since 1916 the national government has given financial support to the states, but the Federal Highway Act of 1956 increased the amount of aid manyfold. The states do the planning, estimate the costs, and get the construction done. In order to receive federal support, however, states must submit their plans and have their work inspected by the Department of Commerce's Bureau of Public Roads. All federally backed highways must meet certain standards governing engineering of the road, employment conditions for construction workers, and weight and load conditions for trucks using the roads.

The federal government participates in three road-building programs. Most important is the National System of Interstate and Defense Highways, known as the Interstate System, which is to be built during the next 13 years.

When finished it will consist of 41,000 miles of superhighways linking almost all cities over 50,000. All but 7000 miles will be of at least four lanes, grades are to be no more than a three-foot rise per 100 feet, there will be a limited number of entry roads, and the number of signs, roadside stands, or filling stations on the right of way will be regulated. Although some of these super-highways will use existing roads, most will be built along new rights of way. The federal government will pay 90 per cent of the costs, securing most of the money from user taxes—gasoline, tires, trucks—which are to be placed in a trust fund earmarked for that purpose. Funds will be distributed among the states according to a formula that gives greater weight to population than has been given in other federal-aid highway programs. No federal money may be used for toll roads, bridges, or tunnels, although these may be part of the Interstate System. In 1959 Congress offered any state a bonus of one-half of one per cent of the total cost of a project if it would agree to restrict billboards along interstate highways in accordance with national standards.

The national government has also stepped up its traditional aid for the construction and rebuilding of existing primary, secondary, and urban roads. For this program, the federal government continues to match state appropriations on a fifty-fifty basis. These roads provide access to the interstate highways, permit farmers to get their products to the market, and help reduce traffic congestion in cities.

Finally, the national government is accelerating its own program of constructing roads that give access to federally owned lands and public domains, such as national parks and military reservations.

All told, national and state governments are expected to spend in the next decade $50 billion to rebuild or construct about 750,000 miles of highways and streets, making it the largest nondefense public construction program in our history.

UNCLE SAM, MONEYLENDER

The second Hoover Commission reported, "There are 104 agencies, instrumentalities, or entities of the Federal Government engaged in lending, guaranteeing, or insuring activities. They employ about 40,000 people. The Government has an investment of about $16.9 billion in these entities and they are authorized to call on the Treasury for about $14.1 billion of additional funds." [2]

The national government's first ventures in moneylending date from the establishment of the Federal Reserve System in 1913. Following World War I federal credit was used to strengthen rural banks facing the postwar agricultural depression. In 1932, during the Great Depression, Congress carried government lending much further by setting up the Reconstruction Finance Cor-

---

[2] Citizens Committee for the Hoover Report, *Digest and Analyses of The Nineteen Hoover Commission Reports* (Citizens Committee for the Hoover Report, 1955), p. 38.

poration in response to President Hoover's recommendation. Starting as an emergency agency, the RFC proved so successful that it survived to help meet the recession of 1939 and the defense needs of World War II. As its authority was gradually extended, it began to lend not only to banks and other financial institutions but also to business firms in general, mining companies, and reclamation projects. Its loans were used to expand plant capacity, pay teachers' salaries, and for other rather specialized purposes.

In 1953 Congress abolished the RFC but created a Small Business Administration to replace it. The new agency has a narrower scope than the RFC. Its revolving fund of $650 million is used mainly for loans to small businesses that cannot acquire private credit. No more than $350,000 may be lent to any one business. Funds are also made available to help small concerns secure government contracts, and for disaster loans.

Courtesy *The Chicago Tribune* and Parrish

The big-hearted donor—a critical view.

The national government also lends, guarantees, or insures in order to promote public housing and slum clearance, keep the costs of home mortgages down, support farm insurance programs, help veterans to get started in business, keep farm prices up, help build ships, and accomplish other tasks that Congress considers to be in the general welfare.

Aiding Farmers

Nowhere is the diversity of American life more apparent than in agriculture. American farmers grow an amazing variety of crops. There are big farmers employing scores of workers on hundreds of acres of land; there are "family-sized" farmers operating farms of 100 to 200 acres with the help of one or two hired hands; there are tenant farmers working other men's farms for a share of the produce and profits; there are, finally, millions of farm laborers, many of whom move on from farm to farm as the seasons change.

Other important facts are these:

American farming is highly mechanized. The average farmer in this country is not "the man with a hoe." He uses a complex array of equipment —sixteen-ton rice combines, air-driven hoes, tractor-towed self-tying hay balers. Some farms, however, have very little machinery.

American farming is enormously productive. Mainly because of climate, geography, machinery, and know-how, our farmers have met both a large part of our huge domestic needs and a heavy foreign demand.

American farming is highly sensitive to world developments. A war in Europe, a depression at home, even changes in the supply-and-demand situation in Canada or Australia or Latin America have an immediate effect on agricultural stability in this country.

At home, farmers find that the *prices* they *receive* for their products tend to be highly *flexible,* rising and falling in a competitive market, while the prices they *pay* for goods—prices administered by corporations and influenced by union demands—tend to be *rigid.*

All these facts closely affect the relation of government to agriculture.

THE GROWTH OF FEDERAL AID

The main agricultural role of the federal government during much of the nineteenth century was to dispose of broad stretches of public land. In effect, the government gave this land away, charging only a dollar or two an acre. But giving away land was not as simple as it might seem. Speculators bought up huge tracts and sold them at high profits. Moreover, many Americans were opposed to a free-and-easy land policy. In 1862, however, Congress passed the Homestead Act, which was designed to encourage the family farmer and discourage the speculator by giving 160 acres of public land to each settler willing to occupy the land for at least five years. In the same year Congress granted large tracts of land for the establishment of state colleges, and set up a Department of Agriculture (which, however, did not become a full-fledged department with Cabinet rank until 1889).

Other promotional activities were launched during the latter part of the century. The federal government set up agricultural experiment stations, encouraged the development of farm cooperatives, fought the spread of animal diseases and insect pests, and undertook conservation and reclamation programs. In 1916 Congress passed a Federal Farm Loan Act to provide credit for farmers.

Thus even before World War I the government was directly involved in agriculture, and the war and postwar years speeded up the trend. World War I created a boom for the farmers, and prices of food, cotton, and farm land skyrocketed. Farmers borrowed money, bought land and machinery, and produced more meat and crops. In 1920 the bubble burst. Prices plummeted and millions of farmers were left with surplus land, unpaid-for machinery, high taxes, and burdensome debts. Inevitably they turned to Washington for help. In response to a bipartisan demand, Congress passed measures to *police the trading in contracts for future delivery of agricultural commodities,* to *encourage agricultural cooperatives,* and to *ease credit facilities.* But these steps

did little to lighten what was becoming an agricultural depression. The farm bloc in Congress pressed for an equalization fee plan, under which the government would buy up farm products for sale abroad in order to raise prices at home. But this plan, as embodied in the McNary-Haugen bill, was twice vetoed by President Coolidge. The government did, however, provide loans to enable farmers to hold surpluses off the market.

The Great Depression simply intensified agricultural stagnation. Demand for farm produce fell, and so did prices. Once again, farmers began to "raise less corn and more hell," as Populist leaders had urged them to do decades before. They organized protest demonstrations, burned or dumped their products, and defied courts that ordered mortgaged farms to be foreclosed and sold. When the Roosevelt Administration took office in March 1933, the new President and Congress acted swiftly. In two months an almost revolutionary new farm measure—the Agricultural Adjustment Act—was drawn up and passed.

The new act was a complicated piece of legislation, but its chief objective was simple—to raise farm prices to help the farmer and to stimulate the whole economy. Experience had clearly shown that the more the farmer produced, the greater were his surpluses and the lower the prices he got for his goods. The new act was intended to induce farmers to *cut down production* to a level low enough to force prices to rise. But how could the farmers be induced to decrease production? The answer was: pay them to do it. So in return for cash bounties several million farmers voluntarily cut down production, plowed under part of their crops, and killed sows and pigs. Results were quickly forthcoming. Farm production decreased, prices rose, and farm income increased by over a third.

To pay for the cash benefits, the 1933 act levied a tax on processors of farm commodities, such as millers and meat packers. This provision proved to be the act's Achilles' heel, for in 1936 the Supreme Court found the measure unconstitutional on the grounds that the taxes were not levies to finance government but levies on one group to give benefits to another, and that Congress had entered a field reserved for state action under the Tenth Amendment.[3]

RECENT FARM POLICY

Stunned by this decision, the Administration set about formulating a new farm program. This time the strategy was to tie a control plan to *soil conservation.* Drought and dust storms had dramatized the need for soil conservation, and it was reasoned that the Supreme Court would not veto an act directed toward this purpose provided no processing tax was involved. Furthermore, the government could build on experience, for a soil erosion act in 1935 had authorized that farmers be paid out of general Treasury funds for taking land out of

---

[3] *United States* v. *Butler.*

production in order to conserve soil. Accordingly, Congress in 1936 enacted the Soil Conservation and Domestic Allotment Act. Half a billion dollars was appropriated to pay farmers for adopting good conservation methods, such as cutting down on soil-depleting crops like wheat, corn, and cotton, and growing more grasses and legumes that replenish the soil.

This act helped stabilize prices and production, but it could not cope with the immensity of the problem. Faced with continuing surpluses and low prices —and with increased political agitation in farm regions—Congress passed a new Agricultural Adjustment Act in 1938. This measure was somewhat similar to the ill-fated 1933 act, except that it carefully avoided the processing tax. Control of production was achieved by these steps: First, if in any year forecasts indicated a heavy production of basic farm commodities and a possible price break, producers of the crop involved would be asked in a referendum if they favored setting limits on production. Second, if two-thirds of the voting farmers supported limitations, each county was to be allotted a certain number of acres for the crop; in turn, each farmer was allotted a maximum acreage for growing crops under the plan. Third, if the farmer wished to grow more than his allotment, he could do so, but he would be subject to a fine if he marketed his excess production during a time of surplus conditions. Fourth, on controlled crops the farmer would receive government loans; the government would then store the surplus crops until a time of scarcity, at which point the farmer might sell them at stable prices and pay back his loan. The essential idea was an ever-normal granary plan that would store surplus crops in time of high production and release them in years of shortage. This approach is still one of the pillars of our agricultural policy.

World War II brought an abrupt change in farm policy. The problem in the years 1942-45 was not to restrict production but to meet the immense needs of our armed forces, our allies, and our civilian population. Following the war the old problem of surpluses turned up once again, and the government resumed its stabilization program. The Eisenhower Administration ran into thorny farm problems as soon as it took office in 1953. Huge surpluses of wheat, cotton, and other farm commodities were piling up, and farmers felt caught in a squeeze between rising production and falling commodity prices. On the one hand, the Administration wanted to reduce federal control of agriculture and to cut down the cost to taxpayers of buying up and storing farm produce. On the other hand, the Republicans feared to take any action that might jeopardize farm income lest they alienate the millions of farmers who might have a balance-of-power role in the 1954 and 1956 elections. Agriculture officials hoped to establish a system of farm supports that would be more flexibly related to production, but many farmers were more interested in firm price support than in flexibility.

In 1954, following a study by farm representatives and Agriculture Department experts, the Eisenhower Administration proposed a somewhat new farm program. A system of *flexible* price supports was set up for the basic or

staple commodities at a sliding scale of 82½ to 90 per cent of parity. Huge quantities of wheat, cotton, milk solids, and other products were set aside for disaster relief, school aid, and other purposes that would not impair the home market for farm goods. Democrats denounced the new program as inadequate and resolved to substitute their own plan after they won control of Congress later in the year.

The farm economy weakened in 1954 and 1955, and the battle over farm policy came to a head in the 1956 session of Congress. First the Democrats passed a bill to return to the *rigid* price supports of 90 per cent that President Eisenhower had persuaded the preceding Congress to drop. The President vetoed this bill, and the Democrats, holding only a small majority in the House, were unable to override his veto. The Democrats in the Senate failed to push through a long-term extension of the 90 per cent formula. With the 1956 campaigns rapidly approaching, leaders of both parties decided that some sort of compromise was the safest policy. An act was passed embodying an old conservation idea in the new form of a "soil bank." Under this plan the government pays farmers for taking certain types of land out of production. Following the 1956 elections, farm policy sharply split the Republican Administration and the Democratic Congress. The President vetoed a Democratic bill to freeze existing price supports and acreage allotments. Democratic leaders ignored the Administration's recommendations. In the end, a compromise bill was adopted—the Agricultural Act of 1958—that represented a retreat from high rigid supports. It required a gradual lowering of supports for rice and cotton and ended the acreage-reserve feature of the soil-bank program; but it granted more funds to the long-range conservation reserve part of the soil bank in order to take more land permanently out of corn production.

As the 1960's began, there was growing evidence that farm policy would need major reshaping early in the new decade. The productivity of American farmers has shot up so far and fast that although in 1958 the total number of acres planted was the smallest in forty years, the total crop output was much the highest in our history. Other portentous facts were the continuing decline of the small farm, the restiveness in the cities over the high cost of food, and soaring farm surpluses, which at the end of 1959 amounted to more than $9 billion and were costing a billion dollars a year simply to store.

Governmental control of farm production and marketing today involves essentially these elements:

Acreage allotments. Government experts regularly estimate the probable demand for staple commodities like cotton, wheat, and rice. Then, using an elaborate system that takes into account the past and present characteristics of each farm, they break down the national acreage allotments into individual allotments.

Conservation reserves. This is the long-term phase of the soil bank in which lands are taken out of production for three to fifteen years. The farmers

who agree to plant their land in grass or trees receive from the government most of the costs of planting and a "reasonable annual return." No grazing on this land is to be permitted. It is estimated that expenditures for the soil bank will reach $2 billion a year.

Benefit payments. These are grants to farmers to secure their cooperation in acreage reserves and conservation programs, in order to induce them to plan production in the light of the national and international situation and the needs of soil conservation.

Commodity loans. The average farmer, operating without government assistance, would have to sell his crops at prevailing prices as soon as they were harvested, for he would need cash to meet out-of-pocket expenses. Commodity loans from the government, however, enable the farmer to store his crops until he can sell them at a good price. By discouraging farm commodities from flooding into the market after each harvest, these loans encourage orderly marketing and eliminate sharp price changes.

Marketing quotas. These limits on what the farmer may market supplement the acreage allotments. When production becomes high and a price

"It looks as if we'll have a good corn crop too."

Herblock in *The Washington Post and Times-Herald.*

collapse threatens, farmers by a two-thirds vote may approve the establishment of marketing quotas. Each producer is alloted his share; he pays a penalty if he markets more than his share.

Price support. In its price-support program, the government buys up commodities when it appears that excess production may cause prices to fall below a certain minimum. This policy does for farmers what the Wages and Hours Act does for labor—it puts a floor under income.

FARM POLICY: PROS AND CONS

These farm policies have aroused sharp controversy. Defenders point to three undeniable facts: American farmers as a group are better off today than ever before in history; working and living conditions on the farm have been vastly improved; farm production is high and yet relatively stable. These facts are important, they say, not only for the farmers but also for the economic and military security of all Americans. Admitting that the machinery of administration is somewhat cumbersome, they stress the democratic nature of the program—for example, the way farmers can vote on marketing quotas. Finally they point out that while the program has been expensive in terms of dollars, the cost has been low considering the tremendous benefits that have accrued to the farmers.

Opponents of the farm program believe that it involves a tragic paradox. On the one hand, they point out, the government under its price-support program has been buying up farm products, storing them, and then selling them for fertilizer and even destroying them or letting them rot. On the other hand, millions of Americans—not to mention tens of millions of foreigners—need more potatoes and eggs and wheat than they now consume. Artificial price supports may help the farmer, but they certainly pinch the consumer. The present policies, these critics say, have created a sort of Frankenstein's monster of surpluses that the government hardly knows what to do with. So far, at least, production-control measures have not been sufficient to prevent large surpluses. And present policy, it is said, tends to freeze existing agricultural activity and render it less adaptable to changing conditions.

LONG-TERM FARM PROBLEMS

To what extent should the federal government subsidize farmers, and in what manner? This key issue is summed up in the word *parity.* Farmers demand that their income should be roughly equal to the income of other sections of the population. Parity, they argue, means that the products the farmer sells should bring him a return roughly equal to the cost of the products that he buys. But what should parity amount to? Farmers feel that during the 1920's they were not receiving a fair income, for their costs were high while farm prices were low. The fairest ratio between farm and other prices, they say, was

achieved in the period 1909 to 1914. One of the main efforts of farmers' organizations has been to induce Congress to use the 1909-14 yardstick in establishing price supports and other controls.

Quotas, allotments, benefit payments, price supports—these and other devices have given the farmer a large measure of stability and even prosperity. But basic long-term problems persist. One is the constant increase in agricultural technology and productivity, with the possibility of long-term farm surpluses. Another problem is rural poverty. Half of the nation's farms produce only 10 per cent of the farm products. Many farmers till substandard land, lack equipment and expertness, and live in deplorable conditions. At the opposite pole are farm operators who own thousands of acres and make a good deal of money, and at the same time are receiving federal subsidies. A special problem is the lack of housing, medical, and educational facilities for the families of migratory workers.[4] But the basic problem is this: How can we give farmers—influenced as they are by faraway events—a measure of security in an unstable economy and an unstable world?

Farming is more than an occupation or a livelihood; it is a way of life. Despite the movement of millions of Americans from country to city, many people still cling to farming even when it seems almost impossible to earn a living from the land. Partly because of his wish to stay close to the soil, partly because of the very nature of agriculture, the farmer is in a vulnerable position. Compare his difficulties with those of a businessman. When demand for his products falls, the businessman can retrench. He lets some of his workers off, cuts down on his orders for materials, decreases his output, and thus reduces his expenses. But most of the farmer's expenses continue at the same level no matter what the state of the market is. There is little he can do to cut back. So when the price of wheat, for example, drops from $1 a bushel to 50 cents, the farmer tries to grow more wheat to make the same income. Result: next year, if conditions remain the same, wheat may be down to 25 cents a bushel. Nor can farmers get together to agree to reduce production—they are too numerous and widely scattered.

What the first New Deal agricultural program tried to do for farmers was essentially what businessmen have done without governmental aid. Although plowing under corn and killing little pigs made dramatic newspaper headlines, the same thing was being done throughout the country by private businessmen. Millions of automobiles, washing machines, houses, radios were not plowed under but were simply not produced. The first AAA was an attempt to fight agricultural depression by reducing production. Since then we have been moving, though haltingly, in the general direction of meeting the farm problem by increasing consumption, by creating new demand, by swinging farm production toward commodities for which there is a good market.

---

[4] See Carey McWilliams, *Ill Fares the Land* (Little, Brown, 1942).

From a strictly economic viewpoint, of course, we could just let farm prices drop indefinitely until the market had eliminated all farmers who could not make a go of it at prevailing prices. But farming is a *political* as well as an economic matter. Farmers are politically potent in Washington and in the state capitals. And the people as a whole, though they may grumble about the cost of farm produce, want to protect the farmer's economic position and way of life.

THE DEPARTMENT OF AGRICULTURE

Administering the complex controls described above is the job of the Department of Agriculture, one of the largest and most influential civilian agencies in Washington. This is the farmer's agency; the department makes no bones about protecting his interests and promoting his welfare. The Secretary of Agriculture is usually a man from a farming state who has the respect of the leading farm organizations (see Chapter 12). Indeed, the political influence of the department in Washington is rooted in the power of the farm interests. The department also works closely with the farm bloc and the agricultural committees in Congress.[5]

Aside from price and production controls, the Department of Agriculture is responsible for many other activities:

Research. The department is one of the world's great research agencies. Its Agricultural Research Service employs about 18,000 people, among them internationally known scientists. The department's laboratories have helped to develop remarkable methods for combating animal and plant diseases, overcoming the scourges of insects, improving the yield and quality of crops, making soils more productive, and improving the breeding of hogs, cattle, and other domestic animals.

Education and information. For over ninety years the federal government has helped sponsor and finance state agricultural colleges, and some of the most significant educational and research activities are conducted at these institutions. The Department of Agriculture carries on an extensive information program in Washington and in the field. For example, it employs several thousand county demonstration agents to improve home and community living. Its experts in nutrition and home economics seek to induce farm people to use more nourishing types of food, and to buy more wisely for home and farm.

Soil conservation. The department's Soil Conservation Service, employing over 14,000 people, teaches farmers how to maintain the productivity of the soil, demonstrates erosion-control methods, develops water facilities, and buys and develops land worn out by wind, rain, and bad farming or grazing prac-

---

[5] See J. M. Gaus and L. O. Wolcott, *Public Administration and the United States Department of Agriculture* (Public Administration Service, 1940).

tices. This service works closely with the Forest Service and the Interior Department's Reclamation Bureau, as well as with state agencies and local soil-conservation districts.

Rural rehabilitation. The department also tries to help tenant farmers, sharecroppers, and farm workers, many of whom live in rural slums. The Farmers Home Administration—once the Farm Security Administration, a New Deal agency of the 1930's—makes easy, forty-year loans to grubstake such farmers in the purchase of farms and equipment of their own. In some cases outright grants are provided. The Farmers Home Administration has helped to improve the lot of the marginal farm, but the only hope for lasting improvement may involve resettlement programs to move people off substandard farms.

Rural electrification. Twenty years ago most farmers lacked many of the conveniences enjoyed by their city brethren. Many were without adequate telephone facilities and few had electricity. In 1935 the Rural Electrification Administration, now in the Department of Agriculture, started making low-interest loans to governmental bodies and cooperatives for the construction of electric generation and transmission facilities and for the purchase of electrical appliances. By January 1959, there were 1030 REA-financed power systems covering 1,426,000 miles of line and serving 4,590,000 consumers. Since 1950 REA has been making loans to extend rural telephone facilities and by January 1959 money had been allocated to bring new or improved service to 1,100,234 rural families. Other farm families have been indirectly benefited by the availability of REA credit, for it has stimulated private utilities to expand their facilities.

Farm credit. Most farmers have an acute need for loans at reasonable interest rates. Federal land banks in leading farm centers make farm-improvement loans to members of local farm associations. Intermediate credit banks lend to livestock companies, credit associations, and similar institutions. Production credit services provide short-term loans secured on the farmer's products. These and other credit activities are coordinated by the Farm Credit Administration. This independent agency, which is not part of the Department of Agriculture, is governed by a board of thirteen members, twelve of whom are appointed for a six-year term by the President with the advice and consent of the Senate on the basis of nominations by the various organizations especially concerned with farm credit. The thirteenth member serves at the pleasure of the Secretary of Agriculture. The board appoints a governor (until all government capital is retired from the various institutions supervised by the Farm Credit Administration, the President's approval of the board's choice is necessary) who is the chief administrative officer of the agency. The purpose of this rather elaborate organization is to give farmers more of a voice in the agricultural credit system. The hope is that all government capital will ultimately be withdrawn so that the borrowers themselves will own the institutions of farm credit.

Social Welfare **T**here is nothing new—as the foregoing pages have shown—in the idea of governmental aid to certain sectors of the economy or to certain groups of people. For at least 160 years we have had a "welfare state," to some degree. This is certainly true of social services. As far back as colonial times, parishes and counties undertook poor relief, and later on the states set up hospitals, asylums, and other institutions. Nevertheless, until recent years American government—especially the national government—lagged far behind other countries in furnishing social services. The situation was paradoxical. On the one hand the federal government gave huge bounties to railroads, farmers, veterans, and other groups. On the other, Washington ignored the dire need of millions of "ill-housed, ill-clad, ill-nourished" Americans.

One reason for this paradox is that America has traditionally been a land of opportunity. The millions of acres of free land, the enormous resources, the technical advances—all helped take care of the people who otherwise might

AMERICA'S LOWER-INCOME FAMILIES

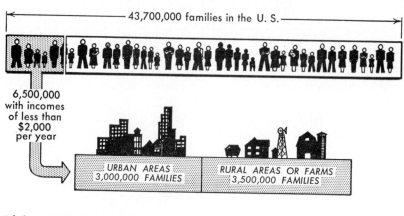

|← 43,700,000 families in the U. S. →|

6,500,000
with incomes
of less than
$2,000
per year

URBAN AREAS
3,000,000 FAMILIES

RURAL AREAS OR FARMS
3,500,000 FAMILIES

Of these 6,500,000 families:

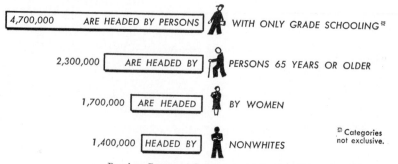

4,700,000 ARE HEADED BY PERSONS WITH ONLY GRADE SCHOOLING *

2,300,000 ARE HEADED BY PERSONS 65 YEARS OR OLDER

1,700,000 ARE HEADED BY WOMEN

1,400,000 HEADED BY NONWHITES

* Categories
not exclusive.

Based on Bureau of Census reports, April and December 1958.

not have made a go of it. Then, too, Americans have traditionally subscribed to a philosophy of rugged individualism and devil take the hindmost. If a man failed to get ahead, people said, it was his own fault. Rather grudgingly the state governments—mainly during the early twentieth century—extended relief to needy groups, especially old people, blind persons, and orphans. But government aid was limited, and private charity was relied on to supply most social services.

Then the nation was struck by the Great Depression. Unemployment mounted to sickening heights; in the early 1930's between ten and fifteen million men were without work. Bread lines, soup kitchens, private charity, meager state and local programs—these were pitifully inadequate gestures. In 1932 the federal government began making loans to states and localities for public relief. The Roosevelt Administration established a series of relief programs designed to boost the economy by increasing purchasing power. Directed by Harry Hopkins, the famous WPA—Works Progress Administration—spent billions of dollars on local projects. The Public Works Administration, under Secretary of the Interior Harold Ickes, undertook more permanent projects—dams and roads and bridges.

Before long a reaction set in to the makeshift manner in which relief was being administered. People grew critical of useless leaf-raking projects—popularly called "boondoggles"—and of the cost and waste of the relief program. Some wanted to go back to the dole—simple handouts of food or cash by the government. But others argued for a well-planned, long-term program that would foster both the security and self-respect of the people aided. Progress was slow. The first federal attempt at an extensive security program—the Railroad Retirement Act of 1934—was declared unconstitutional by the Supreme Court.[6] Insurance companies and even certain labor groups were hostile to extensive social security programs. But over the last two decades the national government has built a social security program that has come to be widely accepted by the American people.

Broadly speaking, the program is based on the assumption that society must take care of old people, the unemployed, and the helpless. For such people are in any event a cost charged against the rest of the community. Old people are a good example. In the past, when large families were common, much of the cost of social security for the aged was borne by the family itself. The family was often large enough to bear this burden without too much difficulty, for a century ago it might be composed of father and mother, six to ten children, a grandmother, Aunt Susie, and Uncle George. Today the typical family in an urban society will consist of mother and father and two children living in a small house. It is impossible to let relatives move in. Some primitive societies kill off excess and helpless people, or let them starve. Some communities today put them in poorhouses at the expense of the rest of the citizens.

---

[6] *Railroad Retirement Board* v. *Alton Railroad Company* (1935).

Most modern democratic societies have governmental security systems that try to plan ahead and make provision for needy people in a fair and orderly fashion.

The foundation of the social-welfare system in the United States is the Social Security Act, passed by Congress in 1935 after elaborate study, and since then frequently amended and supplemented. Today the national government's social security activities consist of two different kinds of program—financial grants to the states for *assistance* to needy persons, and unemployment and old-age *insurance*.

The *unemployment insurance system* is operated jointly by the national and state governments. Until Congress acted, many states were reluctant to establish their own unemployment insurance programs for fear that the cost would place their businessmen at a competitive disadvantage with industries in states that had no such programs. Then, in 1935, Congress eliminated this source of reluctance by levying on all employers of eight persons (since amended to four) or more a 3 per cent payroll tax on the first $3000 paid each year to each employee. If an employer contributes to a state unemployment program that meets federal standards, he may deduct from his federal payroll tax all that he pays to the state fund, provided it is no more than 90 per cent of his federal tax. A state could stay out of the program, but none has done so because the national government levies the payroll tax in any event, and the money cannot be used by the state's unemployed unless the state adopts a plan satisfactory to Washington.

The national government helps defray the administrative costs of the programs, but each state administers its own program. Programs vary in eligibility requirements, the amount paid, the period of payment, and in other respects. All states levy a tax upon employers; Alaska, Alabama, and New Jersey also collect from employees. Almost half the states cover firms with fewer than four workers, and since 1954 Congress has extended unemployment benefits to federal civilian employees. These employees receive the same amounts and are governed by the same conditions as if their employer were subject to state law. In 1958 Congress extended these same benefits to all servicemen discharged since 1958. Payments to federal employees and ex-servicemen are made through state employment security agncies, but the federal government reimburses the states for payments made. (The national government supplemented the program to insure that unemployed Korean veterans received at least $26 per week of total unemployment up to $676 over one period, but veterans otherwise had to comply with requirements of state laws.) Altogether, about 50 million workers earn some credits toward unemployment payments. The major groups not covered by unemployment insurance are self-employed workers, agricultural employees, domestics, and—in half the

HOW THE SOCIAL SECURITY SYSTEM FUNCTIONS

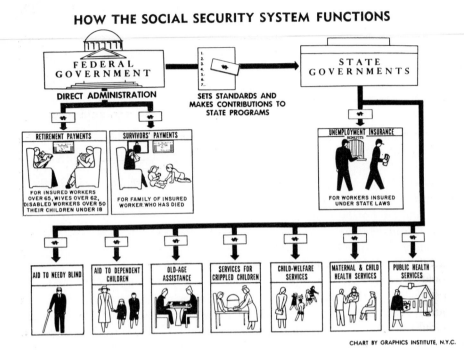

CHART BY GRAPHICS INSTITUTE, N.Y.C.

states—employees of firms that have fewer than four workers. Railway workers are covered under a separate system administered by the Federal Railroad Retirement Board. During the 1958 depression many jobless persons exhausted their unemployment benefits, so Congress authorized emergency loans to states in order to allow them to extend the period of payment. About 20 states took advantage of these laws.

The money collected by each state is deposited to that state's account in the United States Treasury. From this fund each state pays benefits to workers who report to state public employment agencies and are willing and *able* to work, but for whom there are no jobs. Each state sets its own scale of benefits and determines who is eligible to receive them. In most states, to be eligible a person must be able to work. Indeed, if a worker is drawing benefits and becomes ill, he is no longer entitled to payments. Although states have *workmen's compensation* programs that pay disability benefits to some workers for industrial accidents or occupational diseases, these programs give no protection to those who are unable to work because of illness or accidents suffered off the job. Only four states—Rhode Island, California, New Jersey, and New York—pay unemployment compensation or workmen's compensation to workers who are unemployed because of nonoccupational illness or injury. The recent amendment to old-age insurance (see below) giving benefits to permanently disabled workers over fifty will help some of these workers.

Federal-state cooperation meets local demands and keeps the program flexible. It also has disadvantages. Benefits vary considerably. Recently the

average weekly benefit ranged from $38.51 in Nebraska to $20.57 in Arkansas (the *average* national weekly benefit was $30.08). The number of weeks for which benefits were paid varied between 30 and 16. Administrative services in some states have proved unduly inefficient and expensive. In some states "chiselers" are able to collect payments where jobs are available, and even while holding jobs. In other states the test of unemployment is so stiff that unemployed persons find it difficult to get benefits. Because of the state-federal arrangement, administrators have sometimes had difficulty in locating jobs and steering workers to them. However, the Bureau of Employment Security in the Department of Labor, which administers the federal part of the program, does attempt to coordinate the states' efforts to place jobless workers.

Old-age and survivors insurance, unlike unemployment insurance, is run solely by the national government. By 1935 it had become clear that old age was a problem that required national action. For some time the percentage of old people in the population had been steadily increasing. Persons over sixty-five now number twelve million; their percentage of the whole population has quadrupled in the last 100 years. This social and economic problem was affecting politics, too. By 1935 the Townsend movement, clamoring for "thirty dollars every Thursday" for the aged, had reached formidable proportions. The Social Security Act was in part a move to head off this political force.

The act of 1935 established a nationwide contributory retirement system under which payments to retired workers are made out of a fund built up from money collected equally from employers and employees through payroll taxes. Payments vary according to the earnings of the employee and the length of time his salary has been taxed. Since this is an *insurance* program, the plan pays for itself, except for the cost of administration, which the federal government assumes.

In 1939, old-age insurance was broadened to *old-age* and *survivors insurance,* so that not only the wage-earner but the whole family benefits. Under present rates, employers and employees each pay 3 per cent on the employee's income up to $4800 a year; a self-employed person pays 4½ per cent on his income up to $4800. The rate is scheduled to rise gradually so that by 1969 it will be 4¼ per cent for each employer and employee and 6¾ per cent for self-employed persons.

Today the system, as amended in 1956 and 1958, pays men sixty-five or over and women sixty-two or over monthly retirement benefits which vary from $33 to $254, in accordance with the worker's contributions and the number of persons in his family entitled to secondary benefits. (If the insured has a wife sixty-two or over or a dependent husband sixty-five or over, dependent children under eighteen, or disabled children whatever their age, the family receives additional benefits.) Permanently disabled workers may retire and draw their benefits when they are only fifty years old. Full benefits are paid to men between sixty-five and seventy-two and women between sixty-two and seventy-two only if they are not earning more than $1200 a year from jobs

covered by social security. Income from dividends, interests, rents, and annuities is not counted, but by a complicated formula a worker loses part or all of his retirement benefits, depending upon his earnings, if he continues to work. After age seventy-two, however, a person is entitled to his retirement benefits regardless of his wages. Survivors' benefits for wives, dependent parents, children under eighteen, and disabled children include a lump sum of money and monthly payments. Benefits are subject to change by Congress, which has been liberalizing them since the system was started in 1939.

The old-age and survivors insurance program now covers almost all workers, either on a mandatory or permissive basis. The only major professions not covered are doctors, whose spokesmen have opposed participation, and public employees who have their own special retirement systems. Approximately 70 million workers participate, and over 11 million are now drawing benefits. The fact that social security has been broadened extensively under both the Truman and Eisenhower administrations suggests that the basic system is now outside the arena of party battle.

PUBLIC ASSISTANCE

Eventually, it is hoped, social insurance will reduce the need for public assistance. But there will probably always be people who cannot support themselves. Some are not eligible for payments under the insurance programs, some cannot get along on the monthly payments, and some are physically handicapped.

The states have the primary responsibility for public assistance to needy persons. They initiate and administer the programs, but the national government helps. It makes yearly grants to the states to help support four specific groups—needy aged, needy blind, needy persons who are permanently and totally disabled, and children who are in need because of the death, abandonment, or physical or mental incapacity of a parent. Unlike the insurance programs, this public assistance is essentially a charity service, for the recipients of benefits make no contributions.

Federal assistance is given to the states on certain conditions. The states must contribute some of the money, they must establish a single state agency to administer or supervise the program, and other details must meet federal minimum standards. In certain programs, Washington contributes from 60 to 75 per cent of the money. The average individual old-age assistance monthly payment varies from state to state, depending on local standards, but the average is a little over $61.00.

In addition to these four programs, which are designed to assist non-institutionalized needy persons, federal grants are also available to enable states to extend their services to crippled children, health services to mothers and children, and child welfare services, especially in the rural regions. The Children's Bureau of the Social Security Administration approves state programs

and distributes federal money in accordance with each state's contribution, its number of live births, its need for help, and its rural child population.

THE PEOPLE'S HEALTH

Security also is affected by the health of the population. No one is more insecure than a worker who is laid up in a hospital for months, or who is incapacitated for years by a chronic illness. Moreover, sickness is a drain on the strength and efficiency of the whole nation. The main cause of absenteeism from work is illness; every year the nation loses over four million man-years of work through ill health alone, the equivalent of over $25 billion. Finally, bad health saps our military strength. During World War II five million men were found to be physically or mentally unfit for military service. The Women's Army Corps rejected over one-third of the young women who volunteered for service. Fifteen per cent of the draftees examined between July 1950 and June 1951 were rejected for solely medical reasons.

For many years the federal government has been trying to do something about the nation's health. According to the second Hoover Commission, twenty-six federal departments and agencies administer one or more health activities. The national government gives some kind of direct medical care to thirty million people (most of them veterans) and employs about 10 per cent of the doctors, 9 per cent of the dentists, and 6 per cent of the nurses. Thirteen per cent of all hospital beds are in institutions operated by the national government, and 7 per cent of the total number of patients admitted each year enter these hospitals.[7] In addition, the national government makes grants to the states to construct hospitals and research facilities and to maintain medical programs, including maternal and child welfare services. The national government also directly supports research in its own and private facilities and has special programs to meet problems such as cancer, venereal diseases, tuberculosis, mental illness, and heart disease.

Much of the responsibility for these programs rests with the Public Health Service, headed by a surgeon general and lodged in the Department of Health, Education and Welfare. The Health Service operates several dozen general hospitals, quarantine stations, outpatient clinics, and dispensaries. The service licenses the manufacture and interstate sale of serums, toxins, vaccines, and similar products. Perhaps most important for the long run, it carries on research through its national institutes of health. Scientists in these institutes, working closely with experts in nongovernmental laboratories, study the cause and cure of a number of serious diseases. Fellowships for research are given to scientists and physicians. The service also administers grants to the states and local communities to support their research programs.

---

[7] *Digests and Analyses of the Nineteen Hoover Commission Reports* (Citizens Committee for the Hoover Report, 1955), p. 22.

Another national health agency, which resorts to *regulation* rather than subsidy, is the *Food and Drug Administration,* also located in the Health, Education and Welfare Department. Intense popular concern over injurious food and drugs dates from early in the century, when Upton Sinclair and other muckrakers exposed the filthy practices in slaughterhouses and the evil effects of adulterated foods. Congress passed the Pure Food and Drug Act in 1906, has strengthened it in later amendments, and has passed other laws covering tea, milk, and caustic poisons. The Food and Drug Administration polices the misbranding, false labeling, and adulteration of foods, drugs, cosmetics, and therapeutic devices destined for interstate shipment. Its agents inspect sanitary conditions in factories and the processing, packaging, and labeling of products covered by the law. They keep drugstores under surveillance to prevent the dispensation of dangerous drugs without prescriptions, engage in research to evaluate the safety of goods, drugs, and cosmetics, and make studies in order to formulate definitions and standards that will promote honest and accurate labeling of foods. Before new drugs may be placed on sale in the interstate market, the Food and Drug Administration must give its approval and be assured that the drug is safe, effective, and fairly labeled.

One of the most hotly debated subjects in recent years has been the national government's role in helping to pay for the costs of hospital and medical services. Some have proposed—the Truman Administration, for example— that the social security system be expanded to provide for a *national system of medical care insurance.* The heart of such proposals is a scheme for *compulsory prepaid* federal insurance. The national government would match, out of its general funds, money raised by states through payroll taxes on employers and employees. People would choose their own doctors, but doctors' bills would be paid out of the insurance fund.

Proposals for federally imposed medical insurance have stirred up a hornet's nest of controversy. Leading the opposition is the American Medical Association, representing most of the nation's doctors, which calls these proposals "socialized medicine." The AMA argues that (1) tremendous strides have been made in improving the nation's health under the present system; (2) the plan would bring politics into the traditionally private doctor-patient relationship; (3) standards might be lowered; (4) the program would be expensive and wasteful; and (5) private plans such as Blue Cross and Blue Shield are covering more and more people.

Republican party platforms have expressly opposed compulsory federal health insurance. President Eisenhower at one point suggested that the national government should help private insurance companies lower their rates by insuring them against major losses, much as is done in the case of housing loans. But this proposal, too, is opposed by the American Medical Association. Recently, agitation for governmental action to help finance cost of illness has, for the moment at least, died down, but it remains a potential political issue.

DEPARTMENT OF LABOR

The Labor Department was set up in 1913 (after having been a part of the Department of Commerce and Labor for ten years) as a frankly pro-labor agency. Its purpose, according to the act that established it, is "to foster, promote, and develop the welfare of the wage earners of the United States. . . ." The Secretary of Labor and leading officials have traditionally been chosen either from the ranks of labor, or from groups friendly to labor. This may be one reason that the Labor Department is one of the smallest and weakest departments. It has seemed inappropriate to put general welfare functions under such a special service type of department. Moreover, the former split between AFL and CIO weakened the interest group which, if united, would be a powerful force for strengthening the department.

The Hoover Commission in 1949 concluded that the Labor Department had "lost much of its significance." The commission recommended that the Bureau of Employment Security, the Selective Service System, and several other agencies be transferred to it.[8] At the same time the commission advised that a new department, headed by a Cabinet officer, take over the main welfare functions.[9] The first proposal, however, did not get far. The Bureau of Employment Security, however, was transferred to the Labor Department.

Today the Labor Department is still not as strong as the commission wished, but some of its bureaus do play a notable role in government. One of these is the *Bureau of Labor Statistics,* set up in 1885 to collect information on hours, wages, jobs, living costs, strikes, accidents, and other labor matters. Today the bureau does a remarkably comprehensive job, and its findings are used throughout the government. Its reports on prices, based on checks of literally thousands of stores, are essential to inflation-control programs. It makes up the complex cost-of-living index, which is economically and politically important today because wages under many union contracts are tied to this index. The *Women's Bureau* makes studies of such problems as hours and wages of women workers, equal pay, and working conditions. The *Office of International Labor Affairs* assists in the participation of the United States in the International Labor Organization and other world agencies and it helps administer international training and technical programs.

Other Promotional Activities

The Departments of Commerce, Agriculture, Labor, and Health, Education and Welfare are obvi-

---

[8] Commission on Organization of the Executive Branch of the Government, *Department of Labor* (Government Printing Office, 1949), pp. 4, 9.

[9] Commission on Organization of the Executive Branch of the Government, *Social Security and Education* (Government Printing Office, 1949), pp. 7-12.

ously *clientele* agencies that cater to special groups, large and small. A two-way relationship exists between such agencies and their clients. The bureaucrats serve certain of the needs of the groups; the groups give popular support to the agencies' programs. When Congress is considering annual appropriations for these agencies, representatives of interested groups often appear before House or Senate committees to defend the agency concerned and the work performed.

It is not surprising that in the pushing and hauling of national politics other groups besides businessmen, farmers, and workers try to enlist the aid of the federal government.

WHEN JOHNNY COMES MARCHING HOME

Caring for veterans is one of the oldest federal activities. Ever since the Revolution, voters have felt an obligation to reward returning soldiers with money, land, and other benefits. And for much of this time powerful veterans' groups (see Chapter 12) have backed up ex-servicemen's claims by mobilizing political support. Moreover, many ex-servicemen have been disabled during their war service and have needed special attention.

There are over 22 million American veterans. The Veterans Administration, an independent agency operating directly under the President, spends more money than any other federal civilian agency. It employs more persons (by latest count about 172,000) than any other civilian agency except the Post Office Department.

Here are the major benefits that the VA administers:

Medical and hospital benefits. It operates 173 hospitals and uses other facilities for 110,000 or more patients per day, about half of whom are being treated for mental illness. Any veteran of any war who is suffering from a service-connected disability or one made worse by service is entitled to free medical care. If beds are available, veterans with nonservice disabilities may receive treatment if they will state under oath that they are unable to pay for private treatment.

Educational benefits. Generally considered to be a highly successful program, this system was inaugurated by the Servicemen's Readjustment Act of 1944—the GI Bill of Rights—which provided generous grants to veterans for education or training. By the time this program expired on July 25, 1956, more than 7,800,000 veterans had enrolled for some kind of training; 2,300,000 of them attended college. The success of this program as an investment in the veteran's welfare and as a general enrichment of the nation's human resources led to the continuation of the program for Korean veterans, who are entitled to one and one-half days of education or training for each day they served during the Korean war, with maximum training limited to 36 months. The government grants the veteran a monthly allowance from which he pays for tuition, fees, books, and living costs, with benefits going up to $160 a month

for those with more than one dependent. The VA also provides vocational training to help veterans disabled as a result of World War II or the Korean conflict to overcome their handicaps and become self-sufficient.

GI loans. Veterans of both World War II and Korea are assisted by the VA in borrowing money to build homes, buy farms, or go into business. The VA guarantees the lender that the loan will be repaid if the veteran defaults. This guarantee enables veterans to borrow more money and at lower rates than they could otherwise. Over a million GI loans, most of them for homes, have been made, and the veterans have an excellent record of paying up.

Compensation and pensions. Veterans suffering from disabilities connected with war or peacetime service are entitled to monthly compensation. The rates for wartime service—including Korea—range from $17 to $181 a month, depending on the degree of disability. Additional payments are made for certain serious disabilities, such as blindness or loss of limbs. *Needy* veterans of World War I and II or Korea receive pensions if they are permanently and totally disabled for nonservice-connected reasons. Almost three million veterans are now receiving compensation or pensions.

Insurance. The VA administers several insurance programs for veterans and also for those presently on active duty. These insurance programs enable veterans to get coverage for considerably less than they could through regular sources. The program is huge. Veterans life insurance serves about seven million men; insurance outstanding amounts to over $44 billion.

In addition to the above programs, veterans are entitled to special privileges in securing government employment, help in getting readjusted to civilian employment, mustering-out allowances, and other benefits.

Behind the VA stand the American Legion, Veterans of Foreign Wars, and other ex-servicemen's groups. "The pressures of veterans' groups on this agency are virtually continuous," McKean has said.[10] It is often hard to tell whether a VA proposal to expand veterans' services originates with the agency or with some veterans' organization. It is certain that veterans' groups defend the VA against any attempt to slash its appropriations or to trim its offices. Actually, the huge medical program for veterans and their families is an example of "socialized medicine," for the doctors are employed by the national government, and the services are provided free. Yet the veterans are so powerful politically, and the idea of helping veterans is so popular generally, that few politicians are heard denouncing this particular form of socialism!

HOUSING PROGRAMS

The problem of poor housing is an old one, but the federal government's entrance into this field is relatively recent. For a long time housing was re-

---

[10] D. D. McKean, *Party and Pressure Politics* (Houghton Mifflin, 1949), p. 519.

garded as a strictly private concern; and for a long time after that it was considered a matter only for state and local action, if any. Local government, however, was unable to cope with slums (both city and rural), crowded conditions, and poor sanitation. The depression that hit the country in 1929 intensified a housing situation that was already critical. The housing problem has been aggravated by the growing population and the even faster growth of family units. Smaller families mean that the same population requires a greater number of separate housing units.

At first, during the early 1930's, the federal government did little more than bail out impoverished homeowners. Under government auspices, home loan banks were set up to furnish credit to local banks engaged in financing homes, and a Home Owners' Loan Corporation was established to make long-term loans to hard-up homeowners. A Federal Housing Administration was created to insure loans made by lending institutions in order to promote the building of low-rent dwellings. Even more important, in 1937 the United States Housing Authority (now called Public Housing Administration) was set up to lend money to state or local housing authorities for building low-rent housing and clearing slums.

So far the government had not directly engaged in building; it had simply stimulated construction or demolition through financial incentives. During World War II government housing agencies did build several hundred thousand units, but only to meet emergency conditions near military posts and war plants. After the war, the housing situation was worse than ever. Returning veterans looked vainly for homes; thousands of young married couples had to live with their in-laws. The government renewed its program of financial aid to private enterprise by lending to home buyers, builders, and others. Then, in response to a strong demand for more direct and positive action, legislation was proposed for governmental construction of low-cost housing for low- and middle-income groups.

There followed a long and bitter legislative battle. Real-estate and building interests, declaring that the legislation was socialistic and wasteful, mobilized lobbies in Washington. Supporters of the bill were also active. The legislation quickly passed the Senate, but was held up in the House for four years. Following the Democratic victory in 1948—won partly through support of social services—a law was passed in the summer of 1949 providing for 810,000 new housing units. Under the legislation the national government itself does not build dwellings; its chief role is to give and lend money to local housing authorities so that low-income families can rent adequate housing at a rate they could afford (estimated at not over $30 a month), but less than actual cost. Construction and operation are undertaken by local housing authorities, but Congress has tied several conditions to the program—for example, the units are available only to American citizens (except for families of certain servicemen).

The 1949 Housing Act was rather a hollow victory for proponents of

low-cost public housing, however, for in subsequent years Congress appropriated money for only a fraction of the 810,000 authorized units. In the election year of 1956, however, Congress authorized 70,000 low-rent public housing units over the ensuing two years and liberalized loan terms on federally guaranteed mortgages for financing home improvements, single-family home purchases, and rental housing. As another election year neared, pro-housing members of Congress—mainly urban Democrats—tried to expand the housing programs, but Eisenhower was opposed. In any event, it seems likely that future political battles will revolve around *how much* the federal government will help subsidize housing, rather than *whether* it will at all.

In 1937 President Roosevelt declared that one-third of the nation was "ill-housed, ill-clad, ill-nourished." Is the nation any better housed now than it was then? Millions of new houses have been built in the intervening years, but millions of dwellings have become obsolete, too. The worst problem is the plight of certain groups. Housing conditions are generally better among white families than among Negro, among city people than among country, among northerners than among southerners. As late as 1947 only one-fifth of the nation's farm houses had both bath and toilet facilities, and over half lacked running water. Housing for some people, such as migratory workers, was atrocious. Although private building was at a peak during the late 1950's, and housing conditions improved, housing remains one of our major social problems.

EDUCATION

Unequal facilities are found in the vital area of education. The amount of money spent on school children varies from well over $100 per pupil per year in some states to well under $50 in others. Compared with a national average of 5 per cent, five states count 12 to 18 per cent of their 25-to-34-year-old population as functionally illiterate—that is, people with less than five years of schooling. In these five states, about 48 per cent of the young men called for service during the Korean war were rejected because they failed to pass the Armed Forces Qualifications Test. The over-all national average was approximately 19 per cent.[11] In 1950, more than 33 per cent of the white adult Americans, but only 13 per cent of the nonwhites, had at least four years of high school. There has been a vast improvement in the scope, at least, of public education in the last half-century. Yet 9½ million adult Americans, according to the 1950 census, had received less than five years of elementary schooling. To add to the challenge, the school-age population is going through a tremendous expansion.

Education is essentially a function of state and local governments; but the federal government has long been indirectly involved in education through its aid to land-grant colleges, its research activities, and its rehabilitation pro-

---

[11] *Annual Report of the U.S. Department of Health, Education and Welfare, 1954* (Government Printing Office, 1954), p. 176.

grams for veterans. Recently, the federal government has been spending over $2.5 billion a year on education, most of it for veterans. The activities are remarkably broad and varied. At the elementary and secondary level the federal government aids the school lunch program (by providing perishable foods acquired under farm price support operations), helps on problems of curriculum, and educates Indians and others. The federal government helps to construct and operate schools in local districts that have been flooded by new pupils from military bases or other federal installations. At the level of higher education it provides research grants to colleges and universities, operates special educational projects (such as the famed Howard University, the extension service of the Department of Agriculture, and the military academies), gives annual grants for agricultural and mechanical arts education at land-grant colleges, and offers special education and training for the public services. Other activities include on-farm training and education in nonmilitary subjects for members of the armed services. Although these activities are administered by a variety of agencies, many of them, including vocational education and assistance to land-grant colleges, are centralized in the Office of Education in the Department of Health, Education and Welfare.

Is the federal government doing enough for education? Many observers have urged Washington to make large grants-in-aid to the states to help hard-pressed local districts build and operate the schools needed to educate our growing population. These proposals, however, have run into heavy opposition stemming mainly from three sources: fear that the federal government might try to dictate what should be taught in public schools; a dispute over whether parochial schools should be eligible for benefits; and wide differences over whether federal money should be given to school districts that practice racial segregation.

Although the Eisenhower Administration at first minimized the part that the national government should play in providing educational services, the President later told Congress: "Youth—our greatest resource—is being seriously neglected in a vital respect. The Nation as a whole is not preparing teachers or building schools fast enough to keep up with the increase in our population." In 1955 Eisenhower sponsored the White House Conference on Education, attended by representatives of educators and parents, the first such meeting to be held. On the basis of the conference's recommendations, President Eisenhower submitted to Congress a plan authorizing $1.6 billion in federal school grants, spread over four years, in order to build 23,000 new classrooms annually. In the House a number of representatives argued that federal funds would lead to federal control of schools, including, ultimately, "thought-control" of the children. They joined with pro-civil-rights congressmen to vote an amendment to the bill banning help to school districts that continued to defy the Supreme Courts School Segregation decision. This amendment so inflamed southern congressmen that, together with many who

opposed any kind of federal aid, they mustered a majority to defeat the measure.

School aid was dead—but not for long. In 1957 Russia dramatized its educational and scientific achievements by sending aloft her first Sputnik. A year later, after a hard look at the state of American education, Congress passed the National Defense Education Act of 1958, authorizing the spending of $900 million over the next four years, mainly to improve the teaching of science. The law provides for:

Student loans. Undergraduates preparing in science, mathematics, engineering, modern foreign languages, or teacher education have a priority in receiving low-interest loans. To encourage students to take up primary or secondary school teaching, one tenth of the loan is forgiven for each year of teaching, up to a total of half the loan. The colleges administer the loans and put up one dollar for every nine granted by the government.

Postgraduate fellowships. A few fellowships are available at universities undertaking new or expanded graduate programs approved by the Office of Education. The university receives a grant for each fellow it trains.

Grants to high schools. The act authorizes grants to high schools and private schools to help them secure better equipment for the teaching of science, mathematics, and languages, and for developing new teaching techniques, such as the use of television.

Loyalty oath and disclaimer affidavit. Each student receiving a loan or grant, in addition to swearing a positive oath of loyalty, must execute an affidavit stating that he "does not believe in, and is not a member of and does not support any organization that believes and teaches the overthrow of the United States Government by force or violence or by any illegal or unconstitutional methods. . . ." Educators have strongly opposed this requirement on the grounds that it is unnecessary and implies that students are disloyal unless they expurgate themselves by oath. But Congress refused by a close vote to remove the provision in its 1959 session after members had argued that loyalty affidavits were appropriate for a defense education act.

The new program was widely hailed as a good start, but it did nothing, of course, to meet the shortage of classrooms. At the beginning of 1960 the public schools were short 195,000 teachers and 140,000 classrooms; there were over a million and a half more children than the schools had room for. The United States was maintaining an "educational deficit" estimated at between $6 and $9 billion a year. In view of this critical situation and the tremendous financial resources of the federal government, federal aid to education is likely to be a sharp political issue during the 1960's. Federal aid to school construction is still a focus of attention. A bolder proposal, urged by the President's Commission on Higher Education in 1947, favored federal subsidization of two years of college training for all worthy students.

The Politics of Promotion—   **E**verybody who comes to this
                    A Case Study   town," a Washington official once
                                    complained, "seems to want his
own group subsidized and every other group regulated." Big government, with
its power to disburse billions of dollars, is pressured by any group that needs
help or that can think up some reason to jump on the gravy-train. And once a
group receives federal help, it fights to keep it. Moreover, it plumps for the
regulation of other groups. Even those who most dislike interference from
Washington often favor new acts that will restrict other people's activities.

This tendency is inevitable—and desirable. So long as we have a responsible government and a free society, people will go right on agitating for
governmental help. The important question is not whether people demand help;
it is whether government is able to sift out and give priority to those demands
that are genuinely related to the general welfare. As an example of the politics
of government promotion in just one area, federal administration of water
resources is worth a brief glance.

WATER RESOURCES

Water is a vital resource. Not only does it supply power, but it provides
avenues of transportation, irrigates the land, and offers recreational opportunities. Water can also be a menace; it erodes land and floods cities and
farms. People with special needs for water have long turned to the federal
government for help. Today the government spends over a billion dollars a
year managing the nation's water resources. The Army Corps of Engineers,
one of the oldest federal agencies, is responsible for improving navigational
facilities in rivers and harbors. The Bureau of Reclamation in the Department
of the Interior was established in 1902 to promote irrigation in the dry states
of the West. The Federal Power Commission, the Department of Agriculture,
the Fish and Wildlife Service (Interior Department), the Public Health Service, and several other federal agencies have a keen interest in rivers and their
uses.

If each of these agencies supervised different rivers, things might be
simpler. But this of course is impossible. "The same river can provide irrigation, supply a constant flow for navigation, cause floods, generate electrical
energy, provide a habitat for fish and wildlife, and at the same time absorb
the pollution of factories and mines." [12] Rivers, in short, have many uses.
And that is just what causes all the trouble.

Dozens of groups maintain lobbies in Washington and the state capitals
to press their interests in the nation's water resources. One of the most power-

---

[12] Robert de Roos and A. A. Maass, "The Lobby that Can't Be Licked," *Harper's Magazine* (August 1949), p. 22.

ful is the National Rivers and Harbors Congress, a sort of holding company
of lobbies, which is mainly interested in navigation, harbor development, and
flood control. Composed of contractors, state and local officials, and representatives of groups benefiting from river and harbor improvements, the
congress works closely with other groups, such as intercoastal canal associations and flood-control organizations. Farmers and livestock producers interested in irrigation and reclamation have their organizations, too. The National
Reclamation Association has connections with farmers' groups and livestock
marketing associations. Both the supporters and opponents of new dams to

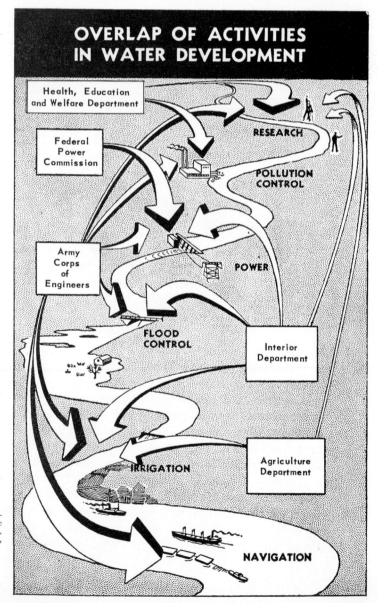

OVERLAP OF ACTIVITIES IN WATER DEVELOPMENT

Health, Education and Welfare Department

Federal Power Commission

RESEARCH

POLLUTION CONTROL

Army Corps of Engineers

POWER

FLOOD CONTROL

Interior Department

IRRIGATION

Agriculture Department

NAVIGATION

From Commission on Or-
ganization of the Executive
Branch of the Government,
Concluding Report, 1949,
p. 28

generate public power have organized for political action. Associations of lumbermen, fish and game clubs, bird lovers—even dude ranchers—are interested in the development of water resources. And each group puts its own interest first.

Some of these groups do better than just maintaining a lobby in Washington. The chairman of the flood-control committee of the House of Representatives also served as vice-president of both the National Rivers and Harbors Congress and of the Mississippi Valley Flood Control Association. Other members of the so-called rivers and harbors bloc have high seniority on congressional committees handling navigation, flood control, and harbor improvement. Reclamation interests are not so well entrenched as their downriver neighbors, but congressional committees handling irrigation and reclamation have been dominated by representatives of arid and semiarid areas.

"Well, Clambertson, a fine botch you've made of the Department of Rivers and Highways!"

Ed Fisher in *The Saturday Review*

Perhaps even more important, the interested groups maintain strong connections with federal officials both in Washington and in the field. As clientele agencies, the Reclamation Bureau, the Corps of Engineers, and other water-resource agencies naturally wish to keep the good will of their "clients." Actually a triangular relationship links bureau, clients, and interested congressmen. The Corps of Engineers, for example, has power to pass on the desirability of hundreds of projects in congressional districts throughout the nation.

Similar triangular relationships prevail among labor agencies, trade unions, and the labor bloc in Congress, among farm agencies, farm organizations, and the farm bloc in Congress, and so on. How can the national interest be isolated from the special-interest demands mirrored—and magnified—in the national government? The President, as a national leader, is in a position

to give priority to the general welfare. But can he do it? The Missouri Valley is a case in point.

MISSOURI VALLEY DEVELOPMENT

In this broad valley, covering about one-sixth of the nation's land area, a sharp cleavage exists between people in the semiarid regions of the upper valley and those of the more populated areas in the lower part. The former wish to exploit the river's water for irrigation, the latter want it for navigation—and each group fears that there is not enough water for all. Navigation interests, railroads, public power supporters, public power opponents, farmers—all these and many other groups are in the fight. And the same splits reveal themselves in Washington—the Reclamation Bureau, the Fish and Wildlife Service, and other agencies of the Interior Department lining up on one side, and the Corps of Engineers on the other. However, as a result of the threat that a Missouri Valley Authority might be established (see Chapter 27) the agencies arranged a "shotgun marriage" and divided the river among them.

Clearly, makeshift solutions of this sort are inadequate. What we must do is recognize that water resources serve *many purposes,* and then coordinate the activities of all the agencies concerned in one comprehensive program of development. Again and again, experts have urged that the development of each river basin be planned as a whole, instead of being left to a patchwork of plans by separate agencies for separate purposes. Such a procedure, said the President's Water Resources Policy Commission in 1950, "will assure the most harmonious development of the water resources of the basin, enabling them to make their greatest contribution to the welfare of the people." [13] Since a river basin is an integrated, nondivisible unit, the committee recommended the motto, "One river, one plan."

The Hoover Commission has recommended that the development of our water resources be consolidated in a new Water Development and Use Service in the Department of the Interior. Army engineers who could be spared from military duties would be assigned to the Interior Department.[14] Actually, only a few army officers would be involved, since over 90 per cent of the army staff for river projects are civilian engineers. But the proposal ran head on into opposition from local interests, congressmen, and the Corps of Engineers.

Again we must see the problem in broad perspective. Promotional politics in water resource development is comparable to promotional politics in other areas. The triangular relationship among businessmen receiving subsidies, agencies handing out subsidies, and interested congressmen raises the same problems. It is pointless to denounce selfish interests or "kept" congressmen or en-

---

[13] President's Water Resources Policy Commission, *A Water Policy for the American People* (Government Printing Office, 1950), Vol. I, p. 9.
[14] Commission on Organization of the Executive Branch of the Government, *Reorganization of the Department of the Interior* (Government Printing Office, 1949), p. 35.

trenched bureaucrats. The individuals and groups concerned will protect what they consider their interests as long as this is a free country. The real questions are: How can we plan our federal promotional activities so that the public interest is safeguarded? To what extent should local interests be promoted? In short, how can we maintain a balance between the national good and local interests?

THE EISENHOWER ADMINISTRATION

AND HELL'S CANYON DEVELOPMENT

The Eisenhower Administration, with new leadership in the Interior Department, brought a fresh approach to these questions. The new policy in developing electric power from the nation's rivers, it was announced, called for the heightened participation of state and local committees and private citizens. This approach was dubbed by the Administration as a "partnership policy." Many Americans hailed the idea of putting more control in local hands. But others continued to ask the old questions: Would this move really satisfy the groups concerned? Would it establish proper balance between the "national," more general interest and the local, more special interest? Or would it simply help local groups who might—through charging high power rates, for example— promote their interests at the expense of the rest of the nation's consumers and taxpayers?

The dispute over Hell's Canyon illustrates the Eisenhower Administration's shift in policy. Hell's Canyon, a deeply eroded reach of the Snake River on the Idaho-Oregon border, is one of the greatest unexploited sources of power and water in the country. How can we best use these resources? The issue was whether the development and operation of Hell's Canyon was to be carried out by the federal government in line with a comprehensive, multipurpose plan for the whole Columbia River, or by a privately owned electric utility company with a less ambitious development plan. The Truman Administration had favored the federal program. The local utility, the Idaho Power Company, applied to the Federal Power Commission for permission to go ahead with its own development program, against opposition from the Department of the Interior.[15]

So matters stood when the Eisenhower Administration came to office in January 1953. The Interior Department, now under Republican leadership, soon withdrew its opposition to private development. The Idaho Power Company renewed its application to the FPC, whose examiner, after conducting hearings, recommended that the company be granted its license, although he found the federal plan superior to the company's plan in several respects. The commission then accepted the company's proposal and in July 1955 issued its license.

---

[15] This case study is based chiefly on Roy F. Bessey, "The Political Issues of the Hell's Canyon Controversy," *The Western Political Quarterly* (September 1956), pp. 676-690.

Meantime, however, widespread opposition to the company's plan had sprung up. Labor groups, public power associations, fish and wildlife associations, Rural Electrification Administration cooperatives, farm organizations, and Democratic leaders in the area and in Congress complained that the company's plan was too limited, that the power would cost too much, that comprehensive development of the Columbia valley would be stunted, and that above all the plan was a simple "giveaway."

President Eisenhower's re-election in 1956 seemed to some a national endorsement of the "partnership policy," but others disagreed. Many Democratic candidates in the area—most notably Senator Wayne Morse of Oregon —defeated their opponents partly on the Hell's Canyon issue. Meantime the private companies went ahead with the Hell's Canyon project.

The Hell's Canyon story suggests that much more is at stake than the simple question of "partnership" between the government and private businessmen. Other vital issues were the best means of resource development from an engineering and economic standpoint, the overlapping of responsibilities of federal and state agencies, the dependence of political leaders on experts who themselves differed on technical matters, the representation or misrepresentation of the maze of local and regional interests cutting across state boundaries, and ultimately the question of who was responsible—federal, state, or private officials, or some combination of these—for intelligent action. In short, we have come right back to our basic question: How do we distill a general interest out of the medley of local, regional, and national interests involved?

CHAPTER **27**

Government as Manager

In the last two chapters we have been looking into two of the methods by which government influences society —regulation and promotion. Through regulation, government lays down the rules controlling what men may and may not do. Through promotion, government directly or indirectly advances the interests of certain groups. We have discovered that regulation and promotion are not really distinct approaches, for promotion may be used for regulatory purposes, regulation for promotional. The same government agency—indeed the same law—may embody both approaches. Many promotional laws, as we have seen, have built-in regulations that must be observed before benefits may be enjoyed.

There is a third method by which government influences society: *direct management* or *control*. These terms are used here in two senses. One is the *direct operation* or *management* of *enterprise*. The Post Office is a good example. Presumably the government could allow a private company to handle the mail, and it could regulate that company in the public interest, or subsidize it, or do both. Instead, the government itself took over the job long ago. The second sense in which the terms are used involves *control of the economy*. Government has come to intervene in the economy in so many ways, with such broad powers and effective instruments of control, that our political rulers are to a real extent our economic rulers as well.

Governmental management is no more recent a development in the United States than governmental regulation or promotion. What *is* new is the tremendous *increase* in governmental management during the last decade or two. All over the world, in both democratic and totalitarian countries, governments have come to direct national economies and to take over operating areas hitherto reserved for private enterprise. The trend has not been so pronounced in the United States as in Britain, Soviet Russia, Sweden, or Australia, but it has clearly shown up here too.

Some call this trend "socialism." Others call it a drift toward the "welfare

state." But let us ignore this name-calling—at least for the moment—and examine just what is happening. What enterprises does our federal government directly operate? With what success? To what extent does government manage the economy as a whole? What methods does it use? What political and governmental problems does this kind of management raise?

Managing Enterprises

Americans have a curiously mixed attitude toward governmental management. On the one hand, almost all of us stolidly and unquestioningly accept the fact that the federal government fights wars, runs some hospitals and public utilities, operates parks, delivers mail, manages a huge insurance system, and during emergencies takes over private enterprises such as coal mines and railroads. On the other hand, most of us oppose governmental operation of enterprise, and we can think up pretty good reasons to support our views. We dislike socialism—but we seem willing to accept it if it comes in little chunks.

Actually, most Americans approach the question of governmental ownership on a practical, matter-of-fact basis. Nobody seriously objects to the government's management of the armed forces. Few would want the government to take over the retail stores on Main Street. It is in the vast area between these extremes that disagreements arise. In general, we feel that most enterprises should be owned and managed privately, and that the burden of proof is on those who wish to extend governmental control. Even so, the national government in recent decades has assumed direct control of important economic activities.

Is there a trend away from direct management in the United States? The Eisenhower Administration, opposing in principle federal operation of enterprises, closed down a number of federal establishments that were competing with private enterprise. But other forces work in the opposite direction—for example, technology. The Russian success in landing a rocket on the moon in 1959 climaxed an intensive program of exploring space that has compelled the United States to look to its own position in the race for space. The agency responsible for catching up with the Soviets in this race is the National Aeronautics and Space Administration, which is now busy building additional launching facilities capable of handling both liquid- and solid-fueled rockets; electronic tracking systems; telemetry data receiving and recording systems; range operation and control systems; and a long-range radar tracking net. The space agency has been given this vast assignment simply because no private enterprise could undertake it.

The types of enterprise operated by the national government range from the Forest Service to the Government Printing Office to the Hoover Dam. The national government, according to the Director of the Budget, owns 19,771 business enterprises with assets of $11.86 billion, employing 258,425 people.

And this report does not include the Post Office.[1] A review of all these activities is impossible here. Case studies of the Post Office, the Tennessee Valley Authority, and the Atomic Energy Commission will suggest some of the major problems involved.

WORLD'S BIGGEST BUSINESS

The United States Post Office likes to call itself the biggest single business in the world. It is the largest nonmilitary department of the national government, and its 500,000 employees account for almost one-quarter of the entire federal civil service. It handles over 40 billion pieces of mail every year; supervises over 38,000 post offices; operates more than 10,000 trucks; and has gross receipts in excess of $2.5 billion a year. Aside from delivering mail, it operates a postal savings system and a money-order service. It contracts for ship, rail, air, and truck transportation at a cost of many million dollars a year.

At the head of the postal service is the Postmaster General. His is a historic office; Benjamin Franklin served for twenty years as British postmaster general for the colonies, and for two years during the Revolution he ran the post-office system for the independent states.[2] The Post Office achieved Cabinet rank in 1829. For many years, however, the "PMG" has been more important politically than administratively, for it was long traditional for the President to appoint to the post the national chairman of his own party. The reason for putting a politician in this post is obvious: the PMG had thousands of patronage jobs to parcel out to the loyal party workers. Over the years, however, postal employees have gradually been brought under civil service. While perhaps 20,000 jobs are still political appointments (including some top officials and first-, second-, and third-class postmasters), postal patronage is not what it used to be.

The postal service, a business agency, has only its headquarters in Washington. All but a tiny fraction of its employees work in the field. Assisting the Postmaster General are a deputy and four assistant postmasters general, and beneath them are a host of officials supervising operations in the field. Local post offices come in all sizes. Some are enormous, like that in New York with its 100 substations. The smallest are branch offices run in retail stores by small merchants. In between are the stations run by fourth-class postmasters—almost half the total number—who are appointed by the PMG partly on a civil service, partly on a political basis. First-, second-, and third-class postmasters are appointed by the President with Senate approval; these are prize patronage plums. But appointees now have to pass competitive examinations and, if they win permanent appointments, they may never be dismissed for political reasons.

Here is a gigantic experiment in socialism. How well has the experiment

---

[1] *U.S. Code Congressional and Administrative News* (West Publishing Company, 1956), No. 9, p. i, June 1956.
[2] See R. L. Butler, *Doctor Franklin: Postmaster General* (Doubleday Doran, 1928).

worked? In 1949 the Hoover Commission made some severe criticisms of the Post Office. The administrative structure, it said, was obsolete and overcentralized. A maze of old-fashioned practices had stifled progress. Though a business-type establishment, the Post Office lacked the flexibility essential to good business operation. Rate-making machinery was inadequate and concealed subsidies to carriers. There were still too many political appointments. Most important, the service was losing money—up to $500 million a year.[3] Ludicrous tangles resulted from the failure to decentralize. In one case, the bough of a tree dropped through a post-office roof, and the postmaster had to write to Washington for authorization to fix it; he could not act on his own. In another case, a postmaster was not allowed to buy a badly needed tow truck from army surplus even though he offered to do so at his own expense.

The Hoover Commission report was a damaging indictment, but the Post Office had some answers ready. One reason it loses money is that it has to provide services below cost. Government officials, including congressmen, have the franking privilege under which they send official mail free. More important, a huge volume of printed matter is carried at a very low rate. The airlines are in effect subsidized at rates fixed by the CAB (see Chapter 26); rail shipping rates are not set by the Post Office but by the ICC. Postal authorities figured that of the total deficit in a recent year, one-sixth was lost in carrying free mail, one-half in carrying second-class mail, one-sixth in subsidizing the airlines.

Is it really feasible to apply ordinary dollars-and-cents profit standards to a government enterprise? If an efficient business firm took over our mail service, it might make a profit—but at what cost to the public? The farmer on a remote hillside would no longer, perhaps, enjoy rural free delivery. Newspapers and magazines would cost much more to distribute, and some might go out of existence. A cut in the air subsidy might impair the nation's military strength.

Nevertheless, many of the Hoover Commission's criticisms could not be refuted, and attempts have been made to improve operations. A reorganization plan for the Post Office has been proposed that would give it more departmental autonomy. An advisory board, representing interested public groups, has been set up. Certain postal rates have been increased. There is little immediate prospect, however, that the Post Office will get out of the red. Attempts to run services at cost invariably arouse the opposition of groups who benefit from present below-cost services.

HARNESSING A RIVER: THE TVA

During World War I, in order to produce nitrogen for explosives, the federal government bought a good deal of land, a dam, a powerhouse, and

---

[3] Commission on Organization of the Executive Branch of the Government, *The Post Office* (Government Printing Office, 1949).

other facilities at Muscle Shoals, on the Tennessee River. After the war people began to ask what the government should do with this property. Some wanted to sell it to private interests. Others, led by a man of great vision and integrity, Senator George W. Norris, a Republican from Nebraska, urged that the federal government assume responsibility for developing the whole Tennessee Valley.[4] After years of controversy, Congress in May 1933 passed a comprehensive act to improve the navigability of the Tennessee, to provide for flood control, reforestation, agricultural and industrial development, and the national defense. A *government corporation,* called the Tennessee Valley Authority and headed by a board of three men, was set up. The TVA had a big job: to develop the physical, social, and economic resources of the whole Tennessee Valley, covering more than 40,000 square miles.

The TVA's achievements have been remarkable. Today it operates over a score of dams on the Tennessee and its tributaries. It produces a vast quantity of electricity, much of which is used for defense activities, such as making atomic energy, explosives, and aluminum. It manufactures and sells fertilizers. The Tennessee is now navigable for 630 miles, and no damaging floods have swept the area since the elaborate storage system was completed. Water pollution has been reduced, malaria all but wiped out, hillsides reforested, fish and wildlife fostered, recreation areas developed. But TVA's main impact has been on the people of the valley. They benefited directly from the low electricity rates, cheap fertilizer, flood control, and construction jobs. Moreover, TVA experts have taught them how to conserve soil, use machinery, diversify their farming, improve their education and health.

All this would suggest that the TVA experiment has turned out very well indeed. And much of the early criticism of valley socialism has in fact disappeared. Nevertheless, a good many people are still asking questions. Some, for example, criticize the TVA's financial policies. Originally the agency was viewed as a yardstick against which private utilities would be measured. As things have turned out, the average kilowatt-hour price of TVA electricity is 1.5 cents, about half the average cost for the rest of the country. But critics of TVA charge that this is not a fair yardstick, because TVA's rates do not include all the expenses that a comparable private utility would have to pay. They argue, for example, that TVA pays far less in taxation than private utilities (TVA does make some payments to local governments in lieu of taxes) and can borrow money at a lower rate of interest. Furthermore, they declare, too small a portion of the original investment was assessed to electric power, and the TVA has not returned from its sale of electricity enough funds to repay the original investment.

The real truth has been shrouded in a confusion of charges, counter-charges, and fancy figure-juggling, but it does seem clear that the yardstick

---

[4] See *Fighting Liberal, The Autobiography of George W. Norris* (Macmillan, 1945), esp. pp. 245-267.

idea has not worked out very well. Here again we see the difficulty of judging public enterprise in terms of private-enterprise standards. On the other hand, there seem to be wide agreements on the following:

1. The Tennessee Valley Authority has been run efficiently and honestly, although management by a three-man board has raised serious problems.
2. Politics, in the narrow sense of party patronage and spoils, has been kept out of the agency.
3. The people in the Valley have benefited enormously from TVA's work. (Average per capita income rose from $148 in 1933 to $797 in 1947 as compared with an increase in the same period from $368 to $1323 for the whole country.)
4. The Tennessee Valley Authority has cost a good deal of money, and much of it from the national treasury, but TVA has strengthened national defense and the whole economy.

TVA has also made a major contribution to the science of government, and has developed interesting new methods of cooperating with state and local officials. It has shown that the federal government can decentralize and still do its job. Above all, it has dramatized the enormous possibilities of *unified regional development*. It has proved the truth of the first Hoover Commission's judgment that "A plan for the development of a river basin cannot be devised by adding together the special studies and the separate recommendations of unifunctional agencies concerned, respectively, with navigation, flood control, irrigation, land drainage, pollution abatement, power development, domestic and industrial water supply, fishing, and recreation. These varied and sometimes conflicting purposes must be put together and integrated in a single plan of development." [5]

Will there be more TVA's? No one can say, but two obstacles may stand in the way of other unified valley authorities. One is the opposition of special interests in the valleys and of key officials in Washington, as mentioned in the previous chapter. The other is the fear that if further regional authorities are created, a problem will arise of coordinating the different authorities. It is possible that future authorities—if any are created—might operate under the general supervision of the Department of the Interior.

ATOMIC ENERGY FOR PEACE

The main business of the Atomic Energy Commission is to build and stockpile atomic bombs. This is a supremely important job; yet the peacetime aspects of atomic energy may in the long run be even more significant. The Atomic Energy Act of 1946, which established the commission, has been called "perhaps the most radical law ever enacted in the United States"—one

---

[5] Commission on Organization of the Executive Branch of the Government, *Reorganization of the Department of the Interior* (Government Printing Office, 1949), p. 28.

NATIONAL ATOMIC ENERGY COMMISSION

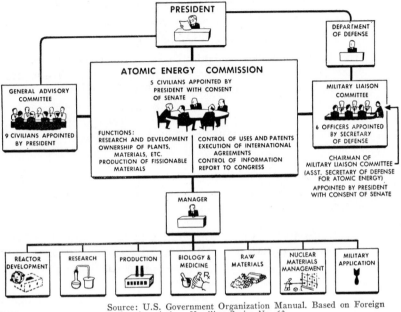

Source: U.S. Government Organization Manual. Based on Foreign Policy Association, *Headline Series No. 63*

that virtually set up "an island of socialism in the midst of a free enterprise economy." [6] How did a conservative Congress happen to pass such a measure?

In 1945, Congress found itself in the remarkable position of being able to provide in advance for the rational control of a gigantic new resource— atomic energy. Some voices were raised in favor of private control. But most congressmen decided that the opportunity was too precious to surrender. Scientists testified that the use of fissionable and radioactive materials would lead to further significant discoveries, which in time would create numberless and unpredictable problems. Without some kind of central control and planning, chaos would set in. So certain was Congress of the need for government development that, in the end, it socialized atomic energy with virtually no discussion at all.

Legislative battles did break out, however, over several provisions of the bill. Civilian versus military control was the most controversial issue. As first introduced, the atomic energy bill explicitly provided that members of the proposed Atomic Energy Commission might be officers of the Army or Navy. Shortly a new type of pressure group sprang into action—atomic scientists. Many of them had chafed under military control during the war, and they feared that such control might be authoritarian, militaristic, and harmful to the spirit of free, scientific inquiry. The scientists organized citizens' committees, testified before Congress, made speeches, put out propaganda, and lobbied on

---

[6] J. R. Newman, "America's Most Radical Law," *Harper's Magazine* (May 1947), p. 436.

Capitol Hill. Partly as a result of this skillful political action, the bill was changed. The commission would be entirely civilian, but it would be advised on military matters by a military liaison committee.

Another battle raged over the handling of patents. In handing over atomic energy to governmental control, the bill gave the new commission unprecedented power over patents. The AEC might, for example, abrogate existing patent rights in areas apparently remote from the field of atomic energy. Business organizations complained that this provision interfered with the traditional patent system, but to no avail. Other issues involved secrecy of information and research. While the act restricted the dissemination of data, it did allow broad freedom of research. The commission was given the job of stimulating, promoting, and coordinating scientific research in atomic energy and all its applications.

The act was finally passed in the summer of 1946. Since then, the AEC has taken as its primary concern the main purpose of the measure—"assuring the common defense and security." Its operations are shrouded in secrecy, but we do know that it owns huge installations at Hanford, Washington, and Oak Ridge, Tennessee, and elsewhere, that larger atomic bombs and hydrogen bombs are being made and at a faster rate, that the AEC contracts with private companies and universities for research and operations, and that basic work is going ahead on peacetime uses of atomic energy.

Obviously it will be a long time before we can evaluate this experiment in governmental management. For the long-range tests is not its success in making bigger and better bombs, but, in the words of Congress, its success in "improving the public welfare, increasing the standard of living, strengthening free competition in private enterprise, and promoting world peace." The AEC is conducting vast research operations through its research centers, such as Argonne and Brookhaven National Laboratories, and in its proving and testing grounds at Los Alamos, Las Vegas, and in the Pacific.

As industry makes increasing use of atomic energy, government and private enterprise are bound to come into sharper conflict. Atomic energy is fraught with a heavy public interest. Even aside from our common stake in its successful development and exploitation, there are such problems as conflict stemming from overlapping federal and state safety codes, the extent of permissible competition among private atomic enterprises, the impact of atomic energy on other sources of power, and the effects on the economy of the location of atomic facilities. The AEC's decision to concentrate the bulk of its atomic installations in the Ohio Valley, for example, stimulated the whole economy of that region and caused a major shift of population. In 1954 Congress modified the security provisions of the act to promote wider understanding of nuclear energy, and it encouraged private industry to enter the field by liberalizing the act's patent provisions. The extent to which atomic energy should be made part of the normal pattern of American enterprise is bound to be an increasingly sharp political problem during coming years.

So much for our three case studies in the direct management of enterprises by the national government. Now let us turn to an even more important role of the government as manager—the indirect *fiscal* management of the whole economy through taxing, spending, investment, and other economic methods.

Raising the Money   **B**ig government is expensive. In 1958 federal, state, and local governments spent $134.9 billion. This is between one-fourth and one-third of the income of all Americans; in short, our governments spend about 30 cents of every dollar we earn. The national government is the biggest spender of all. In recent years Washington has spent about three times as much as all state and local governments combined.

Where does all this money come from? The federal government gets most of its funds from taxes, and the rest from loans, commercial revenues from governmental enterprises, income from special fees and fines, and from grants and gifts.

LEVYING TAXES

"In this world," Benjamin Franklin once said, "nothing is certain but death and taxes." Tax-collecting is one of the oldest activities of government. Indeed, one of the few contacts that many people in earlier societies had with government was through the tax-collector. He was the dread figure who symbolized the demands and authority of some far-off ruler. Putting power over taxation into the hands of the people was a landmark in the rise of self-government. "No taxation without representation" has been the war cry not only of early Americans but, in effect, of people in countries the world over.

The new Constitution in 1787 clearly provided that Congress "shall have power to lay and collect taxes, duties, imposts, and excises." But duties and excise taxes had to be levied uniformly throughout the United States; direct taxes had to be apportioned among the states according to population; and no tax could be levied on articles exported from any state. Except during the Civil War, the federal government for a century relied on the tariff for most of its revenue. This hidden tax—which many people falsely thought to be a tax on foreigners—fluctuated with the rise and fall of trade and tariff levels. Congress supplemented these taxes with *excise taxes* on the manufacture or sale of certain goods. In 1894 an *income tax* law was enacted (such a tax had been used during the Civil War, but given up shortly afterwards). The 1894 tax was not very drastic—only 2 per cent on all incomes over $4000—but it seemed a portent of worse things to come. The next year, in *Pollock* v. *Farmers Loan and Trust Co.,* the Supreme Court held the tax measure unconstitutional on the ground that it was a direct tax and therefore had to be apportioned among the states according to population. Twenty years later, in 1915, the Sixteenth

Amendment was adopted authorizing Congress "to lay and collect taxes on incomes, from whatever source derived, without apportionment among the several States, and without regard to any census or enumeration."

Raising money is only one objective of taxation; *regulation* is almost as important. In a broad sense, all taxation regulates human behavior; for example, a graduated income tax has a leveling influence on incomes, and a tariff act affects foreign trade. More specifically, Congress has used its taxing power to prevent or regulate certain practices. Years ago Congress laid a 10 per cent tax on the circulation of notes by state banks, immediately putting an end to such issues. Certain professional gamblers are now required to secure a federal license and pay a tax of 10 per cent on their receipts. Congress maintains a prohibitively heavy tax on sawed-off shotguns. The Supreme Court has in the past invalidated regulation by taxation when the regulation itself was held to be unconstitutional.[7] Today, however, the Court is likely to sustain taxation for regulatory purposes, especially if it can be tied to the other great constitutional power, control over interstate commerce.

Today the federal tax cake looks something like this:

Income taxes on individuals. Levies on the income of individuals account for over one-half of the federal government's tax revenue. Originally a low rate, the income tax was greatly increased during World War I and went to new heights during World War II and the Korean war. One advantage of in-

---

[7] See, for example, the child labor tax case, *Bailey* v. *Drexel Furniture Co.* (1922).

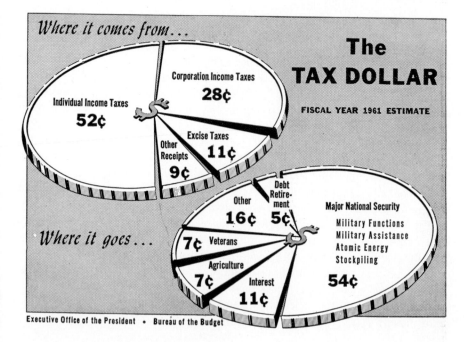

Where it comes from...

The TAX DOLLAR

FISCAL YEAR 1961 ESTIMATE

Individual Income Taxes
52¢

Corporation Income Taxes
28¢

Excise Taxes
11¢

Other Receipts
9¢

Where it goes...

Other
16¢

Debt Retirement
5¢

Veterans
7¢

Agriculture
7¢

Interest
11¢

Major National Security
Military Functions
Military Assistance
Atomic Energy
Stockpiling
54¢

Executive Office of the President • Bureau of the Budget

come taxes is their flexibility. Rates can be raised and lowered, exemptions can be permitted, and the individual's ability to pay can be taken into account. The federal government—and most of the states—also levy *estate, inheritance,* and *gift* taxes.

Income taxes on corporations. These account for over one-fourth of the national government's tax dollar. As late as 1942 corporate income taxes amounted to more than individual, but returns from the latter increased relatively more rapidly during World War II.

Excise taxes. Federal excise taxes yield about one-tenth of tax returns. Most of it comes from liquor, with tobacco second. *Manufacturers' excise taxes* are levied on the manufacture of automobiles, gasoline, electric power, and so on. *Retailers' excise taxes* hit luxury items such as furs and jewelry. Miscellaneous excise taxes include those on tickets to amusements, telephone and telegraph facilities, and a surprising variety of other goods.

Customs duties. Though no longer the main source of federal income, these taxes are far from negligible. The annual yield runs to about half a billion dollars. While other tax returns have increased by several hundred per cent, however, customs returns have been fairly stable in recent years. The reason, of course, is that the revenue aspect of tariffs is far less important today than their relation to broad political and economic issues at home and abroad.

THE POLITICS AND MACHINERY OF TAXATION

When a young law assistant once commiserated with Justice Holmes on the taxes he had to pay, the old man replied, "With taxes I buy civilization." Most of us are less philosophical. We complain that our tax load is too heavy and that someone else is not carrying his fair share. People with large incomes naturally grumble about income taxes as high as 70 per cent or even more. Low-income people point out that even a low tax may deprive them of the necessities of life. People in the middle-income brackets feel that their plight is worst of all: their incomes are not high but their taxes are.

What is the best type of tax? Some say the graduated *income tax,* because it is relatively easy to collect, it hits hardest those who are most able to pay, and it hardly touches those at the bottom of the income ladder. Others argue that *excise taxes* are the fairest, because they are paid by people who are actually spending money for goods—especially luxury goods—and thus obviously have money to spare. Furthermore, by discouraging people from buying expensive goods, excise taxes have a desirable deflationary effect in time of rising prices. On the other hand, excise taxes are more expensive to collect than income taxes, and in some cases, such as the tax on tobacco, they may

hit the poor hardest. Most controversial of all taxes is the *general sales tax,* which resembles the excise tax except that it is levied against the sales of all goods. Labor and liberal organizations denounce this form of tax as regressive—that is, it hurts the poor man more than the rich man, because the former uses all his earnings to buy goods, while the latter may devote more of his income to buying personal services or to savings. Proponents of the sales tax stress its anti-inflationary effect and point to its successful use in a number of states.

A recent tax bill illustrated the wide impact of taxes on a variety of individuals and groups. Testifying on proposed tax changes before a congressional committee, 138 witnesses expressed their views, and scores of briefs were submitted. The printed testimony covered more than 1600 pages. Business representatives opposed new taxes on corporations. Small businessmen complained that existing taxes favored big business. Spokesmen for tobacco-growers, transportation interests, the wine and spirits industry, movies, the legitimate theater, candy-makers, telephone companies, and bowling-alley proprietors argued that the proposed tax would discriminate against them. Labor demanded a lighter burden for low-income groups, higher taxes on business. Unorganized workers and consumers, however, were not represented.

Courtesy *Minneapolis Star* and Justus

Under our form of federalism the taxpayer supports three levels of government.

Although the Constitution provides that all revenue bills must be initiated in the House of Representatives, it is usually the *President* who originates tax legislation. With the help of tax experts on his staff and in the Treasury Department, he draws up a tax program designed to meet the government's revenue needs for the coming fiscal year. Often the representatives of interest groups are consulted while the bill is being formulated. Then the President submits his tax program to Congress, often along with his budget message. The powerful House Ways and Means Committee next holds hearings on the bill; administration spokesmen, headed by the Secretary of the Treasury, usually lead off the parade of witnesses, followed by representatives of interested groups, taxation experts, and others. Following committee consideration, tax measures go through Congress in much the same manner as other bills. Although the Senate cannot

initiate tax legislation, it refuses to take a back seat on tax matters. It often differs with the House, and forces extensive changes of bills coming from the lower chamber. Sometimes Congress refuses to follow the President's recommendations, and works out a tax measure largely on its own.

The Treasury Department has the job of collecting the taxes levied by Congress. One of the original departments set up in 1789, and headed by the second highest-ranking Secretary, this department today is a large agency employing about 76,000 people. The actual tax-collecting job falls mainly to the huge Internal Revenue Service. Sixty-four district directors are located throughout the country, and taxes are paid into district offices rather than directly to Washington. The Service takes in $40 to $50 billion a year at a cost of less than 50 cents for each $100 in returns. Customs are collected by the Treasury Department's Bureau of Customs, which maintains ports of entry, inspects the discharge of cargo, assesses the value of merchandise, and, through the services of the United States Coast Guard, prevents smuggling.

UNCLE SAM, BORROWER

When an individual person is suddenly faced with expenses too heavy to meet out of his regular income, he may have to borrow money. The same is true of government. During military and economic crises, the federal government has gone heavily in debt. It borrowed $23 billion during World War I, about $13 billion more during the 1930's, and over $200 billion more during World War II. Between crises, the government has tried to pay off its debts, but progress has been slow. By 1960 the federal public debt was about $285 billion.

Borrowing costs money. The federal government can borrow at a low rate—recently about 5 per cent—because no security is safer than a government bond. Nevertheless the public federal debt is so huge today that the interest alone is costing over nine billion dollars a year. The size of the debt itself and of the interest payments alarm many Americans. How long can we allow the debt to grow at this staggering rate? Two considerations must be kept in mind. In the first place, the government owes most of the money to its own people (rather than to foreign governments or persons); in a sense, we all owe the money to one another. Second, the economic strength and resources of the country are more significant than the size of the public debt. As we shall see later in this chapter, more borrowing may actually improve the country's economic position. Still, it is discouraging that we have failed to pay off the debt in the years between wars and depressions. The debt was reduced by about $25 billion after World War II, but then it began to go up again.

How does the government borrow money? The Constitution says that Congress may "borrow money on the credit of the United States"; it puts no limit on either the extent or the method of borrowing. Under congressional

authorization the Treasury Department sells securities to banks, corporations, and individuals. Usually these securities take the form of long-term bonds or short-term treasury notes. Some bonds may be cashed in any time; others not until their maturity dates. Because the United States government backs up these bonds they are in great demand, especially by banks and investment companies. However, the government, particularly in time of war, likes to induce as many individual persons as possible to buy bonds, because individuals who buy bonds have that much less money to purchase goods, and thus will contribute less to inflationary pressures. This is why famous athletes and movie stars are enlisted to help out in well-publicized bond drives. If voluntary methods fail, the government could always require purchases by making compulsory deductions from wages and salaries.

A third source of federal funds consists of *administrative* and *commercial revenues*. The fee paid to the State Department for a passport, the fine paid by a criminal, are administrative revenues that account for a portion—though a very small portion—of federal income. More important are the funds paid to the federal government in exchange for direct services—payments to the Post Office for stamps, to the Park Service for recreation, to the Government Printing Office for pamphlets.

Finally, some public-spirited people actually *give* money or property to the government! Mr. Justice Holmes, who didn't mind taxes, left the government almost his entire estate when he died. But gifts, needless to say, are an infinitesimal source of federal revenue.

Spending the Money **A**ll the billions of dollars the government takes in are funneled into the Treasury and then rapidly move out through hundreds of channels to points throughout the nation and, indeed, throughout the world. Nothing reflects the rise of big government more clearly than the change in the amount and methods of its spending. As recently as 1932 the federal government spent only $4 billion, about $30 per capita. In 1960 the respective figures were $80 billion and $444. The machinery for spending has changed, too. Spending at one time was loosely administered. Records show, for example, that in an early year of the Republic one Nicholas Johnson, a Navy agent of Newburyport, Massachusetts, was handed several thousand dollars to supply "Capt. Brown for recruiting his Crew." [8] Today Mr. Johnson would have to make out detailed forms and wait for a government check.

Where does the money go? Most of it, of course, for national defense. The 79.8-billion-dollar budget estimated for the fiscal year 1961 allots about 54 per cent to the military services; 7 per cent to agricultural programs; 11 per cent to interest on the national debt; 7 per cent to veterans; and 21 per cent

---

[8] L. D. White, *The Federalists* (Macmillan, 1948), p. 341.

for all other services. Interesting changes have taken place even in the last two decades. In 1939 total expenditures of the federal government amounted to $9 billion. Of this, national defense took about $1 billion, interest less than $1 billion, and veterans about $600 million. It is hard to realize today that as recently as 1939 most federal expenses were for domestic relief and welfare functions. Significantly, in 1939 we spent only about 0.5 per cent of the budget on international activities. The proportion has risen manyfold as we have faced up to our global responsibilities.

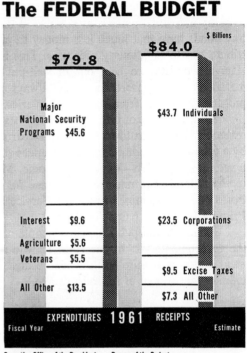

The FEDERAL BUDGET

The sheer fact of spending $80 billion a year is most significant of all. Years ago, federal revenues and outlays were so small that national taxing and spending had little impact on the over-all economy. But today the federal government cannot drain billions of dollars from certain areas of the economy and pump them back into other areas without having a profound effect on the economy of the nation and of the world at large. This problem will be considered later in the chapter. First we must see how the federal budget is drawn up and made into law.

FORMULATING THE BUDGET

The power to spend is one of the basic powers granted to Congress in the Constitution. The Supreme Court has put very few limitations on that authority —so few, indeed, that some observers fear that Congress might use its vast spending powers to bribe the states into following its lead by grants-in-aid, thus undermining the federal system.[9] Today, while Congress must authorize the spending of funds, the *initiation* of appropriations has come to be essentially an executive function. Indeed, under the Budget and Accounting Act of 1921, the President is formally responsible for preparing an executive budget; the act was designed to fix responsibility on the chief executive and to

---

[9] See, for example, E. S. Corwin, *The Twilight of the Supreme Court* (Yale Univ. Press, 1934).

put an end to a situation where budget-making had become highly disorganized and decentralized throughout the executive establishment.

The first step in preparing a budget is for the various departments and agencies to estimate their needs for the future. This process starts very early;

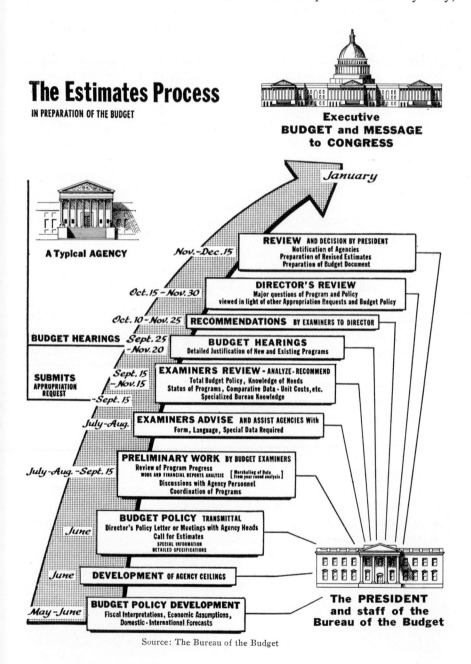

The Estimates Process

IN PREPARATION OF THE BUDGET

Executive
BUDGET and MESSAGE
to CONGRESS

January

A Typical AGENCY

Nov.–Dec.15
REVIEW AND DECISION BY PRESIDENT
Notification of Agencies
Preparation of Revised Estimates
Preparation of Budget Document

Oct.15 – Nov. 30
DIRECTOR'S REVIEW
Major questions of Program and Policy
viewed in light of other Appropriation Requests and Budget Policy

Oct. 10 – Nov. 25
RECOMMENDATIONS BY EXAMINERS TO DIRECTOR

BUDGET HEARINGS *Sept. 25 – Nov. 20*
BUDGET HEARINGS
Detailed Justification of New and Existing Programs

SUBMITS APPROPRIATION REQUEST
Sept. 15 – Nov. 15
– Sept. 15
EXAMINERS REVIEW - ANALYZE- RECOMMEND
Total Budget Policy, Knowledge of Needs
Status of Programs, Comparative Data - Unit Costs, etc.
Specialized Bureau Knowledge

July–Aug.
EXAMINERS ADVISE AND ASSIST AGENCIES With
Form, Language, Special Data Required

July–Aug. –Sept. 15
PRELIMINARY WORK BY BUDGET EXAMINERS
Review of Program Progress
WORK AND FINANCIAL REPORTS ANALYSIS [Marshaling of Data from year round analysis]
Discussions with Agency Personnel
Coordination of Programs

June
BUDGET POLICY TRANSMITTAL
Director's Policy Letter or Meetings with Agency Heads
Call for Estimates
SPECIAL INFORMATION
DETAILED SPECIFICATIONS

June
DEVELOPMENT OF AGENCY CEILINGS

May –June
BUDGET POLICY DEVELOPMENT
Fiscal Interpretations, Economic Assumptions,
Domestic - International Forecasts

**The PRESIDENT
and staff of the
Bureau of the Budget**

Source: The Bureau of the Budget

while Congress is debating the consolidated budget for the fiscal year immediately ahead, the agencies are making budget estimates for the year following. (The fiscal year runs half a year ahead of the calendar year, from July 1 through the subsequent June 30. Thus fiscal year 1961 starts July 1, 1960, and ends June 30, 1961.) The estimating job is handled largely by budget officers working under the direction of the agency chief and heads of subordinate units. The agency officials must take into account not only their needs as they see them, but also the over-all presidential program and the probable reactions of Congress.[10] Departmental budgets are highly detailed, including estimates on expected needs for personnel, supplies, office space, and the like.

In the next phase of budget-making, the scene shifts to the Budget Bureau. A staff agency of the President, the bureau scrutinizes each agency budget to see if it is in accord with the President's budget plans. This job is done by experienced budget examiners who usually have a long acquaintance with a particular agency, and can look over its requests with a sharp eye for accuracy, economy, and good program planning. Hearings are then held to give agency spokesmen a chance to clarify and defend their estimated needs. The Director of the Budget and his aides, who make the final decision, sometimes prune the agencies' requests rather severely.

Once again the scene shifts—this time to the White House. For months the budget director has been conferring with the chief executive and has been trying to keep the agencies below the budget ceilings set by the President. Finally—it is probably December by now—the director arrives at the White House with a single consolidated set of estimates of both revenue and expenditures, the product of perhaps a year's work. The President has reserved a day or two for a final review of the budget, and the two men check the consolidated figures. The budget director also helps the President prepare a budget message that will stress key aspects of the budget and tie it in with broad national plans. By January, soon after Congress convenes, the budget and the message are ready for the legislature and the people.

THE LEGISLATIVE GANTLET

After it has been formally presented to Congress, the President's budget goes first to the Appropriations Committee of the House of Representatives. This committee operates through nine subcommittees, each of which considers appropriations for a particular department or group of agencies. Agency representatives are invited before the subcommittees to defend their requests in formal hearings. The subcommittees have their own staff assistants who help in examining the budgets. Following the hearings, the subcommittee and its staff work out legislative schedules embodying the agency budgets as modified by the legislators. The full Appropriations Committee goes over the subcom-

---

[10] See Chapter 19 for an example of the considerations that may enter at this stage.

mittee reports and schedules and incorporates them, perhaps with further changes, into appropriations bills.

The Appropriations Committee submits each bill to the House, which debates it for two or three days, amends it, and passes it. The bill then goes to the Senate, which refers it to the Senate Appropriations Committee. Smaller than its counterpart in the House, this committee usually concentrates on controversial items and even allows agency spokesmen to appeal for the restoration of funds slashed in the House.[11] Debate in the Senate may be freer and more general than in the lower chamber. Differences between the two houses are resolved in conference committee. Finally, the President must either accept or veto the whole appropriations measure; since he cannot veto individual items, he almost always signs the measure.

All this is the formal procedure, and it looks like a sensible, efficient— though somewhat cumbersome—arrangement. Actually, the whole treatment of an appropriations bill is inevitably dominated by the conflicting positions of President, bureaucrats, and congressmen. The President may be trying to finance a broad program that he has promised the nation to carry out. The bureaucrats are committed to their own projects, and they are supported by the groups that will benefit. The congressmen have all kinds of interests. They may be eager to push through a project that will benefit their constituents, hamstring an agency that they oppose, prove themselves watchdogs of the Treasury, or ingratiate themselves with the President, an influential Cabinet member, or a powerful interest group.

Politics is, of course, both desirable and inevitable in the handling of any legislation, including appropriations measures. Unfortunately, however, such bills are subjected to a type of political pulling and hauling that raises hob with orderly responsible fiscal policy. The reasons are twofold. First, despite improvement in recent years, the appropriations are *highly detailed*. This condition both helps and hurts the legislator: it helps him to accomplish specific objectives, but it also immerses him in such a flood of detail that he is often unable to look at the appropriations situation in broad perspective. (If a congressman were to spend an hour studying each million dollars of expenditures, it would take him over twenty years to go over the annual budget!) Second, the committees and subcommittees handling appropriations are often manned by legislators who are out of touch with the general needs of the country. These legislators enjoy long seniority, and because of the seniority rule they rise to positions of great influence on the committees. To be sure, the committee and subcommittee chairmen are members of the majority party in Congress. But the majority, as we have seen, has little internal cohesion or discipline. And when the President and the congressional majority are of different parties, the confusion, irresponsibility, and delay are compounded.

---

[11] See A. W. Macmahon, "Congressional Oversight Over Administration: The Power of the Purse," *Political Science Quarterly* (June, September 1943), pp. 161-190, 380-414.

What can be done? Both the first and second Hoover Commissions made recommendations to improve the handling of budgets in both the executive and legislative branches. The first Hoover Commission recommended that the "whole budgetary concept of the Federal Government should be refashioned by the adoption of a budget based upon functions, activities, and projects." [12] This is called a *performance* or *program budget*. The idea is simple. Instead of concentrating on things to be acquired, such as personnel and supplies, the commission said, the budget should focus attention on the *general character and relative importance of the work to be done, or service to be rendered*. For example, the commission noted that a naval hospital was receiving allotments from twelve different Navy appropriations titles, such as Bureau of Ships and Bureau of Ordnance; under a performance budget the total appropriations for this hospital would be compared with those for previous years and with those for other hospitals. Since fiscal year 1951 some budgetary statements from the executive branch have been couched in performance terms.

Although some congressmen criticized performance budgeting, the second Hoover Commission also recommended its use, but suggested "a review of performance by organizational units where these do not coincide with performance budget classifications." [13] This commission also recommended that agencies should formulate their budget requests in terms of estimated costs of goods and services actually to be received during a year instead of in terms of estimated obligations to be incurred. Perhaps the most drastic recommendation was that Congress make appropriations on an annual accrued expenditure basis. For example, instead of authorizing the Navy to spend $150 million for a ship over a four-year period, each year Congress should appropriate only the amount the Navy would need for actual goods and services to be received during the year. The commission argued that under the existing system Congress does not have a clear picture of how much money an agency is actually going to spend. Many agencies even have money left over from previous years' appropriations.

Some of the members of the Hoover Commission dissented, holding that the recommended procedures might be suitable for a business where profits are the main concern but would be harmful to many government agencies whose main job is service. Congress refused to make its own appropriations on an annual accrued expenditure basis, but in 1956 it did enact legislation adopting other of the Hoover Commission recommendations, directing that executive budget requests be stated in performance terms, that they be formulated on the basis of costs, and that agencies show how much they will need for the goods and services actually to be received during the year. It will take four or five years for these reforms to be put into effect and whether they will be effective remains to be seen.

---

[12] Commission on Organization of the Executive Branch of the Government, *Budgeting and Accounting* (Government Printing Office, 1949), pp. 8-12.
[13] Commission on Organization of the Executive Branch of the Government, *Budget and Accounting* (Government Printing Office, 1955), p. 13.

Some congressmen have tried to improve their own procedures. The Legislative Reorganization Act of 1946 provided for a *legislative budget* designed to emphasize the budgetary forest instead of the trees. The act authorized the members of the appropriations and revenue committees of House and Senate to meet jointly early each calendar year in order to map out a broad budgetary program and to set appropriations ceilings for the coming year in relation to expected income. The plan, in short, was to set an overall framework within which executive requests might be studied. This laudable plan has been tried but it has not worked, partly because the four committees have been too busy with their regular tasks, and partly because individual congressmen are prone to go their own way on individual budgetary items.

CHECKING UP ON EXPENDITURES

After Congress has appropriated money, it reserves the right to check up on the way the money is spent. Under the Budget and Accounting Act of 1921 the *General Accounting Office* does the national government's accounting job. The GAO is headed by a Comptroller General, who is appointed by the President with the approval of the Senate. The Comptroller General enjoys some measure of independence, however, for his term of office is fifteen years, he is ineligible for reappointment, and he can be removed only for specific cause by a joint resolution of Congress.

The Comptroller General was originally intended to operate as an independent auditor serving as an arm of Congress to guard against improper and unauthorized expenditures. But as time went on he was swamped by a gigantic *accounting* job that forced him to handle administrative matters in the executive branch even though he was not responsible to the chief executive. At the same time, over-all management in the executive branch suffered, because day-to-day accounting, an important instrument of administrative control, had been placed in a separate agency. Prior to 1949 the GAO imposed rigid requirements on the agencies, maintained detailed accounting records that frequently duplicated agency records, and brought tons of papers to Washington to check laboriously for irregularities.

In recent years, partly in response to recommendations of the Hoover Commissions, improvements have been made. The GAO now uses spot sampling methods to check vouchers, and makes its audits in the field rather than in Washington. Although the Comptroller General still has the authority to disallow expenditures, his approval is no longer needed prior to the disbursement of funds. Being relieved of personal responsibility for payments that may subsequently be disallowed (provided they have acted in good faith and with reasonable diligence), disbursing officers have been encouraged to make their own decisions about the legality of expenditures. Moreover, in 1950 Congress gave the departments and agencies, subject to supervision of the GAO, the responsibility and authority to set up their own internal accounting operations. Both the first and second Hoover Commissions urged that the executive de-

partments be given even greater authority.[14] These new procedures presumably will allow the Comptroller General to spend more time carrying out the vital legislative function of scrutinizing administrative fiscal practices, of making sure that laws governing appropriations are being correctly interpreted, of checking on the efficiency of accounting and other administrative practices —and of reporting on all these to Congress.

It might seem that accounting is a technical matter that could be settled without much argument. On the contrary, accounting is a political problem, too, for it reflects two struggles that go on in Washington. One is the attempt of Congress as a whole to maintain as much control as possible over the still mushrooming bureaucratic machine. The other is the struggle of individual legislators in Washington to keep a system that checks individual administrative payments.

Managing Money   **T**oday's economy is essentially a money economy. Instead of using a system of barter—like that of South Sea islanders who swap fruit for beads—"civilized" peoples exchange commodities through a vast system of money and credit. We have seen the tremendous role the federal government plays in this system, simply because it gets and spends $70 or $80 billion a year. But aside from its role as the biggest buyer and seller of goods and

---

[14] Commission on Organization of the Executive Branch of the Government, *Budgeting and Accounting* (Government Printing Office, 1949), pp. 39, 47 ff; see also Commission on Organization of the Executive Branch of the Government, *Budgeting and Accounting* (Government Printing Office, 1955), pp. 29 ff.

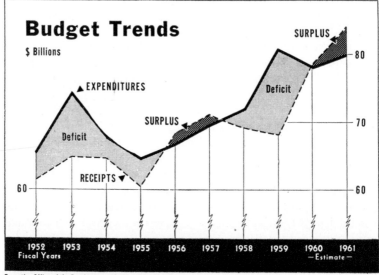

Executive Office of the President • Bureau of the Budget

services, the federal government has a more direct impact on our money economy. First, it manufactures money. Second, it regulates the value of money. Third, it controls the nation's credit system.

Manufacturing money is the easiest of these jobs. The Bureau of Engraving and Printing in the Treasury Department, using carefully designed plates and special types of paper, turns out millions of dollars of bills, bonds, and postage stamps every week. This "folding-money" is fed into general circulation through the Treasury and the Federal Reserve banks. The Bureau of the Mint in Philadelphia, Denver, and San Francisco (also under the Treasury) coins the silver dollars, half-dollars, quarters, and dimes, the nickel-copper nickels, and the copper and iron pennies that together make up about one-twentieth of the country's cash.

In itself, this money is only so much paper and metal. How does the government maintain its value?

THE CURRENCY SYSTEM

The Constitution gives the federal government the right to manage the nation's money system. Under the old Articles of Confederation, the national currency had consisted mainly of almost worthless paper money, and the individual states had maintained separate currencies. To correct this monetary hodgepodge, the Constitution of 1787 carefully vested in Congress authority to coin money and to regulate its value, and it carefully withheld this power from the states. Thanks partly to Secretary of the Treasury Hamilton, the early Americans scrapped the confusing British system of guineas, pounds, shillings, and pence, and adopted a decimal system.

The new government manufactured coins from two precious metals, gold and silver, which had intrinsic value of their own. Fifteen ounces of coined silver were exchangeable for one ounce of coined gold. This *bimetallic* monetary standard was then quite common among commercial nations. But the trouble with this system was that the relative values of gold and silver on the open market (for use in wedding rings, gold teeth, silverware, and so on) fluctuated as supply and demand rose and fell. For example, the discovery of gold in California made gold much cheaper and drove silver out of circulation. After striving for many years to keep both gold and silver coins in circulation, Congress in 1900 established the gold dollar of 23.22 grains of pure gold as the standard unit of value. This was the famous gold standard, under which all money was maintained on a parity with the yellow metal.

Of course, the country had not been using only metal currency all this time. Coin is hard to handle and expensive to ship in big quantities. In 1791 Congress chartered a national bank with power to issue bank notes. These notes were not legal tender—that is, no person was forced to accept them in payment of a debt—they were simply a convenience. During the Civil War, however, the federal government needed unprecedented sums of money, and it had trouble borrowing enough funds. So Congress issued new notes known as

"greenbacks," with no metal to back them up, and these were made legal tender. After a long and bitter battle in the courts, the Supreme Court in the *Legal Tender Cases* in 1884 held that Congress did have the right to issue unbacked legal-tender notes.

The Great Depression beginning in 1929 affected our monetary arrangements just as it did other sectors of the economy. Under the gold standard any lawful money could be redeemed in gold, individuals could freely trade in that metal, and gold reserves backed up all other money. But the depression forced many depositors to withdraw their gold from the banks. The decline in bank reserves imperiled the whole banking and credit system. In 1933 the gold standard was abandoned. In a series of rapid moves, private possession of gold was outlawed, coinage of gold was ended, holders of gold were compelled to turn it in to the government in exchange for other currency, and the value of the gold dollar was reduced to about 59 cents.

Today the United States is on the "gold standard" in the limited sense that the money and credit supply is backed up in part with a huge store of gold at Fort Knox, Kentucky, and the unit of monetary value is defined in terms of gold. But all the currency of the United States—Federal Reserve Notes, Silver Certificates, silver dollars, and subsidiary coins—are legal tender and cannot be freely exchanged for gold. (A few United States Notes, Treasury Notes, Federal Bank Notes, and National Bank Notes are still outstanding but they are being retired.) In short, the money of the United States is freely redeemable only for other money of the United States.

Money makes up only a part of the circulating medium and is less important to our economy than *credit*. In the expansion and contraction of credit, the most important institutions are the nation's banks and the Federal Reserve System.

BANKS AND LENDING INSTITUTIONS

Although banking is a private business, it is subject to close governmental supervision. There are over 14,000 banks in the United States; 5000 are chartered by the national government, the others by the states. The national banks, however, have almost 50 per cent of all bank deposits in their custody. The Comptroller of the Currency in the Department of Treasury supervises their operations. Each national bank must file reports on its financial condition at least three times a year, and must permit bank examiners to inspect its books at least twice a year—at unannounced times.

Although state authorities have the primary responsibility to supervise state-chartered banks, most of these banks are also subject to federal regulation, since their deposits are insured by the Federal Deposit Insurance Corporation. All national banks must participate in this program, and state banks that meet approved standards are permitted to do so. All but a few hundred of the 14,000 commercial bank and trust companies in the United States have their deposits insured by the FDIC, as do some of the 529 mutual savings

banks. The FDIC routinely examines banks that are not members of the Federal Reserve System (see below) and establishes rules designed to keep them solvent. In case of an insolvent member bank, the FDIC takes over its management and pays off each depositor up to $10,000.

The Federal Savings and Loan Insurance Corporation, operating under the supervision of the Federal Home Loan Bank Board, protects investors in federal savings and loan associations and those state-chartered institutions approved for participation. Like the FDIC, it guarantees savings up to $10,000 for each account.

The national government also promotes the establishment of *credit unions,* associations of persons having a common bond of occupation or residence who may secure a federal charter and receive assistance from the Bureau of Federal Credit Unions in the Department of Health, Education and Welfare. These unions, which now number over 7500, encourage members to deposit excess funds which may then be lent to other members at relatively low interest rates.

CREDIT AND POLITICS

In many nations a central bank owned and operated by the national government determines general monetary policies. The Constitution does not specifically authorize the national government to create such a bank—indeed, it says nothing at all about banking. But Alexander Hamilton believed some such institution was necessary; and in 1791, on his initiative, the United States Bank was incorporated by the national government and given a twenty-year charter. The United States Bank was partly private and partly public; the national government owned only a minority of the shares and had only a minority voice in its management. Jefferson and his supporters opposed the bank on monetary, political, and constitutional grounds. Nevertheless, President Madison found it necessary to have the bank rechartered for another twenty years in 1816, after the Jeffersonians had refused to do so in 1811.

In 1819 the Supreme Court in *McCulloch* v. *Maryland* (see Chapter 4) upheld the constitutionality of the bank as a necessary and proper way for the national government to establish a uniform currency and to care for the property of the United States. During Jackson's administration the bank issue was reopened again and dominated the political scene. Headed by the formidable Nicholas Biddle, the Second United States Bank became extremely unpopular in the rural West when it carried out wholesale foreclosures of mortgaged farm land. The bank came to symbolize the financial and political power of vested interests. Jackson seized on this issue. After vetoing Senator Henry Clay's bill to recharter the bank, he won re-election despite the efforts of Biddle and other of the bank's friends. After his re-election he decided to withdraw government funds from the bank and thus destroy it even before its old charter expired. When his Secretary of the Treasury refused to withdraw the funds, Jackson fired him and hired another Secretary who would. And when

Clay put a resolution of censure through the Senate, Jackson mobilized his supporters and had the resolution expunged.

After the bank closed its doors in 1836, state banks, which had previously been restrained by the Second United States Bank, embarked on an orgy of issuing notes that often could not be redeemed. A military crisis forced a housecleaning. To stabilize an economy beset with war demands and to support the desires of the "dear money" groups, Congress in 1863 authorized the chartering of national banks. These are privately owned corporations not to be confused with a central bank or an institution like the United States Bank. State banks were permitted to continue in business, but a 10 per cent federal tax on their notes quickly drove state bank notes out of existence.

The struggle over bank policy was in part a struggle over cheap versus dear money. Those who possess money and who are creditors naturally want to maintain, and if possible increase, its value. Those who do not have much money, and especially those who owe money, want to cheapen it. This struggle reached bitter proportions during the decades following the Civil War. Faced with low farm prices and entangled in debt, farmers campaigned for printing more paper money and thus cheapening the dollar. William Jennings Bryan waged a long fight to restore free coinage of silver at the rate of sixteen ounces of silver to one ounce of gold. As a candidate for President, however, he was beaten by both McKinley and Taft.

The national bank system created during the Civil War was stable—indeed, so stable that it was inflexible. Financial crises during the late nineteenth century and in 1907 revealed an unhappy tendency of banks to restrict their loans, and of national banks to contract their issuance of notes, just at the times when an *expansion* of money was needed. In order to furnish an elastic currency, and for other reasons, Congress established the Federal Reserve System in 1913.

THE FEDERAL RESERVE SYSTEM

The Act of 1913 was a compromise. Some wanted a strong central bank, but many feared, just as the Jacksonians had eighty years before, that this would centralize control over currency in too few hands. So a system was established that gives us a modified central banking program with considerable decentralization.

The country is divided into twelve Federal Reserve Districts, in each of which there is a Federal Reserve Bank (most Federal Reserve Banks have branches). Each Federal Reserve Bank is owned by member banks. All national banks must join the system, and state banks that meet standards are permitted to do so. Today approximately 6500 of the more than 14,000 banks are members of the Federal Reserve System; these are the largest banks in the country and have around 75 per cent of total deposits.

Each Federal Reserve Bank is headed by a board of directors, six elected by the member banks, and three appointed by the Board of Governors (see

immediately below) in Washington. Three of the directors elected by the member banks must be bankers, and three must be active in business and industry. The three directors appointed by the Board of Governors may not have any financial interest in, and may not work for, any bank. The Board of Governors designates one of its appointees to be chairman of the board of directors and this board in turn selects a president to serve as its chief executive officer.

A seven-man Board of Governors sitting in Washington supervises the entire system. These men are selected by the President with the consent of the Senate for fourteen-year terms, and the President designates the chairman. The Board of Governors, advised by the Federal Advisory Council composed of a member from each Federal Reserve district that meets in Washington at least four times a year, determines general monetary and credit policies. It has four major weapons to tighten or loosen the financial activities of the nation's banks and, in turn, of the whole economy. They are:

1. Increase or decrease within legal limits the reserves that member banks must maintain against their deposits in the Federal Reserve Bank.

2. Raise or lower the rediscount rate charged by Federal Reserve Banks to member banks. The rediscount rate is the price member banks must pay to get cash from the Federal Reserve Banks for acceptable commercial notes that the banks hold.

3. Through the Open Market Committee (composed of all members of the Board of Governors and five representatives of the Reserve Banks) sell or buy government securities and certain other bills of exchanges, bank acceptances, and so on.

4. Exercise direct control over the credit that may be extended in order to purchase securities (called "margin requirements"). From time to time Congress has given the Board of Governors temporary authority to fix terms of consumer credit.

Through these and other devices, the Board of Governors may affect the flow of circulating medium by tightening or loosening credit. For example, if inflation is threatening, the board can dampen down the economy by raising member bank reserve requirements (thus cutting down on the cash they have available for lending), by raising rediscount rates (thus forcing member banks to raise the rates for which they will lend money), by selling government securities in the open market (thus absorbing funds from the economy), and by raising margin requirements (thus reducing credit available to bid up the prices of securities).

The Federal Reserve Banks also serve as depositories for government funds, clear checks and transfer funds among member banks, and may in case of economic emergency even lend money directly to businesses.

The Board of Governors is intentionally isolated from the direct influence of the executive and is supposed to use its own judgment in making monetary decisions. However, the Treasury Department also has a good bit of influence

HIGHLIGHTS OF THE FEDERAL RESERVE SYSTEM

STRUCTURE

BOARD OF GOVERNORS

FEDERAL RESERVE BANKS

MEMBER BANKS

Chairman and 6 other members appointed for 14 year terms by President of U.S. Supervise operations of the 12 Federal Reserve Banks. Fix (within limits set by Congress) share of member banks' total deposits they must keep with their FRB as a reserve against these deposits.

OPEN MARKET COMMITTEE

Board of Governors plus 5 of the 12 FRB presidents. Buys and sells U.S. Bonds and other obligations on the open market.

One Federal Reserve Bank for each of 12 districts. Each FRB has 9 directors: 6 chosen by member banks, 3 (including chairman) by Board of Governors. Each FRB holds the reserve of its members. Also issues currency (Federal Reserve Notes) backed by gold certificates, U.S. Bonds, commercial and agricultural paper.

All national banks must join the System. State-chartered commercial banks can join too. Members must buy stock in their district FRB, keep their legal reserve balance on deposit there.

FUNCTIONS

A. Influences the Supply of Money and Credit

To INCREASE supply

1. Lowers the % of cash (reserve) the members must put up against their deposits. Members can then use excess funds to extend credit.

2. Buys U.S. Govt. securities in open market. This provides member banks with additional reserve funds.

3. Lowers discount rate it charges members for loans. Makes it profitable for members, in turn, to make more loans.

To DECREASE supply

1. Increases the reserve requirement. Member banks put up additional money by calling loans, selling investments.

2. Sells U.S. Govt. securities, draining deposits from member banks.

3. Raises discount rate. This causes banks to be reluctant to lend additional amounts of money.

B. Provides special services for the Federal Government

1. Maintains an orderly market in Federal securities.

2. Acts as Treasury's banker, and helps issue and redeem its bonds.

3. Sets amount of down payment that must be made by buyers of stock market securities.

C. Provides services for Member Banks and the Public

1. Furnishes elastic supply of currency for circulation.

2. Safeguards, keeps track of members' reserve balances.

3. Settles up for checks drawn on members or received by them.

4. Supplies credit by discounts, loans, security purchases.

From *A Visual History of the United States,* by Harold U. Faulkner & Graphics Institute; Abelard-Schuman

over the flow of credit, and at times Treasury officials and the Board of Governors have worked at cross-purposes. The Treasury may wish to pay a low interest on government securities at a time when the Board of Governors is moving to raise interest rates in order to damp inflation. Despite the Board's formal independence, the President's influence and prestige are at times difficult for the Board to withstand.

Understandably enough, money and credit policies are always a target of political pressures. One of the most influential groups in Washington, for example, has been the silver lobby, which works hand in hand with the silver bloc in Congress. Yet the situation has changed in at least one important respect from the past. Money and banking in today's battles figure less as isolated policies and more as parts of over-all economic strategy. Monetary policy has become but one phase, one weapon, used to combat depression, control inflation, foster full employment and high national income. The crucial political issue today, in short, is what should the government do to keep the economy sound?

Managing the Economy

So far, we have seen how the national government directly manages certain economic activities, such as the post office and TVA, how it raises and spends billions of dollars a year, and how it controls currency, banking, and credit (although the banks themselves are legally under private control). We have observed the political and governmental processes that shape the way in which government operates these controls.

Does the government have the same direct control over the national economy that it has, say, over the post office and national forests? No. Only if we had a socialized economy administered from Washington would we have a managed economy in that sense. Actually we have—and, one hopes, will always have—an economy in which a great deal of power is left to private individuals and enterprises. And yet the government keeps a firm hand on all the gears and levers that control the general direction in which the economy will move and the rate at which it will travel. These gears and levers are marked taxes, spending, credit, and the like.

If these levers were operated in a haphazard, whimsical way, they might have no effect at all on the economy. Or else they might have a catastrophic effect—as if a ship captain were to order full speed ahead and a sharp turn to the starboard at one and the same time. Operated in a carefully synchronized manner, however, they can help keep the economy on an even keel.

It is only rather recently that Americans have recognized the part that government *could* play in stabilizing and invigorating the economy. (There are still differences of opinion over the part that it *should* play.) The slow development of our understanding, the political struggle over the question of whether the federal government should take responsibility for full employment, the

enactment of the Employment Act of 1946—these are fascinating episodes in the trend toward over-all control of the economy by the federal government.

Austerity is a hard teacher. The depression of the 1930's had a tremendous impact on American thinking about the role of government in economic matters. We had had long, severe depressions before—for example, in the 1870's and 1890's. But by 1929 the United States had become a rich and powerful nation, and prosperity seemed here to stay. Then the Great Depression struck. Millions of unemployed, falling prices and income, plummeting production—all added up to mass misery. "One vivid, gruesome moment of those dark days we shall never forget," wrote one observer. "We saw a crowd of some fifty men fighting over a barrel of garbage which had been set outside the back door of a restaurant. American citizens fighting for scraps of food like animals!" [15]

During the "dismal thirties" many ideas were put forward to end the depression. There were schemes for printing paper money, for huge public works, for "hot money" that would decline in value if not spent, for sharing the work or sharing the profits, for wholesale changes in the banking and credit system, to name a few.[16] Some of the proposals were nostrums; others had real merit. As we saw in the last chapter, the Hoover Administration, after waiting for some time for the economy to recover by itself, tried to stimulate the economy through such devices as the RFC. The New Deal intensified and widened the attack on depression through the NRA, AAA, PWA, WPA, social security, and wages-and-hours legislation.

But still the depression hung on. Faint stirrings of recovery showed themselves in the mid-1930's, but the recession of 1937-1938 indicated that we were by no means out of the woods. Eight or nine million people were jobless in 1939. Then came the war, and unemployment was cured—for a while. Millions of people had more income, more security, a higher standard of living. Lord Beveridge in England posed a question that bothered many thoughtful Americans: "Unemployment has been practically abolished twice in the lives of most of us—in the last war and in this war. Why does war solve the problem of unemployment which is so insoluble in peace?" [17] Worried that the economy might collapse after the war, literally thousands of people came up with plans to insure jobs for all.

These plans were infinitely varied, but two approaches to the problem of mass unemployment were particularly important. Many businessmen and newspaper editors and some economists believed that the main reason for the persistence of the depression had been the New Deal's hostility to business. If

---

[15] Quoted in F. L. Allen, *Since Yesterday* (Harper, 1940), p. 64.

[16] The remainder of this chapter is drawn largely from S. K. Bailey, *Congress Makes a Law* (Columbia Univ. Press, 1950).

[17] W. H. Beveridge, *The Pillars of Security* (Macmillan, 1943), p. 51.

only the government had left the economy alone, they argued, recovery would have come much sooner. They urged the government to cut down on spending, lower taxes, reduce the national debt, curb the power of labor, and generally to leave business alone except for traditional regulation and aids to certain businesses. Give private enterprise a chance, they urged, and the problem of economic stagnation and unemployment would be solved in short order.

Another large group, made up of economists, labor representatives, government officials, and others, took a very different tack. They said that the trouble with the New Deal was not that it had done too much, but that it had done too little. The thinking of this group was deeply influenced by the work of John Maynard Keynes, a world-famous English economist who had advised the British government on economic matters and had run a large insurance company in England. In visits to the United States during the 1930's, Keynes warned that if people do not consume enough or invest enough, national income will fall. The way to increase national income is either to spend money on consumption goods (such as clothes or food or automobiles) or on investment goods (steel mills and dock facilities) or on both. Finally—and this was the dynamite in the proposition—*government must do the spending and investing if private enterprise by itself would not or could not.* The Keynesian approach was tied in with related concepts involving governmental influence on public works, wages, prices, credit, taxation, and the like.

These two approaches dominated the efforts of Congress to grapple with the problem of unemployment after World War II. The story of the Full Employment bill of 1946 is the story of how the national government came to assume a large measure of responsibility for maintaining employment. It suggests that full employment is a political as well as an economic problem.

THE EMPLOYMENT ACT OF 1946

The story of the Employment Act of 1946 is amazingly complex; we can review it only in broad outline.[18] Supporting the idea of full-employment legislation were a group of government officials, the head of the National Farmers Union (which, it will be recalled, represents smaller farmers), some economists who were more or less Keynesian in their thinking, a number of United States senators, representatives of organized labor, and members of several Senate committee staffs. During the war, members of this group had been impressed by two things: the powerful impact on employment of heavy government spending, and the possibility that the bottom might drop out of the economy when federal spending decreased after the war. A bill was drafted that began, "It is the policy of the United States to foster free competitive enterprise. . . . All Americans able to work and seeking work have the right to a useful and remunerative job in the industries or shops or offices or farms or mines of the nation." In a bid for as much support as possible, the bill was

---

[18] For the full history of the bill, see Bailey, *Congress Makes a Law.*

introduced not by one Democratic senator but by four, from New York, Utah, Wyoming, and Montana. Supporters of the bill, mainly representatives of liberal and labor organizations, proceeded to line up congressional backing, arouse public interest, and win over members of business, farm, and veterans groups.

The bill had relatively easy going in the Senate. The four Democratic senators were joined by four Republicans, thus providing bipartisan support. Of sixty-seven witnesses who testified before the committee considering the bill, only four were strongly opposed to the measure. In the Senate debate, supporters argued that the bill was neither left-wing nor radical, but that it would actually strengthen the free-enterprise system. Liberals in both parties joined forces to beat down hostile amendments, although some changes were made to appease the opposition. The bill passed the Senate, 71-10.

But the opposition was mobilizing outside the Senate. This bill, argued its opponents, would not work. It might kill initiative. Government spending would undermine business confidence. It would lead to inflation. It might bring socialism or even communism. The National Association of Manufacturers circulated criticisms of the bill to its 16,000 members and to a much wider mailing list. Chambers of Commerce in states and localities sprang into action. The American Farm Bureau Federation put heavy pressure on key members of Congress.

The bill had a hard time in the House. First of all, it was sent to an unfriendly committee. President Truman appealed to leading members of the committee on the basis of party loyalty, but he made little progress. The Administration itself was divided. The House committee finally submitted a weak bill that was hardly more than a pious whisper that the government had some sort of interest in maintaining employment. Composed largely of conservative members, the Rules Committee made certain that either this weak bill would be passed, or no bill at all. The House was split three ways among those who wanted no bill, those who wanted a strong bill, and those who wanted a weak bill. The weak bill won out.

But at least the measure had been kept alive, and a final compromise was reached in conference committee on a measure that had some teeth to it. Passed in February 1946, the bill declared:

> It is the continuing policy and responsibility of the Federal Government to use all practicable means consistent with its needs and obligations and other essential considerations of national policy, with the assistance and co-operation of industry, agriculture, labor, and State and local governments, to coordinate and utilize all its plans, functions, and resources for the purpose of creating and maintaining, in a manner calculated to foster and promote free competitive enterprise and the general welfare, conditions under which there will be afforded useful employment, for those able, willing, and seeking to work, and to promote maximum employment, production, and purchasing power.

If this declaration sounds like double talk, the reason may be that the bill had to be built on a series of compromises. In effect, the bill made the federal government responsible for acting in the face of rising unemployment instead of relying wholly on nongovernmental forces. Equally important, the act established machinery to carry out that responsibility. It created:

The Council of Economic Advisers. Part of the President's staff organization, this council studies and tries to forecast economic trends, assesses the contribution of federal programs to maximum employment, and recommends to the President "national economic policies to foster and promote free competition, to avoid economic fluctuations or to diminish the effects thereof, and to maintain employment, production, and purchasing power."

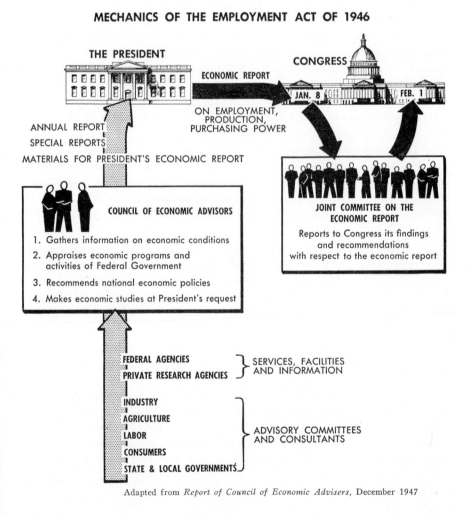

MECHANICS OF THE EMPLOYMENT ACT OF 1946

THE PRESIDENT

CONGRESS

ECONOMIC REPORT

JAN. 8   FEB. 1

ON EMPLOYMENT,
PRODUCTION,
PURCHASING POWER

ANNUAL REPORT
SPECIAL REPORTS
MATERIALS FOR PRESIDENT'S ECONOMIC REPORT

COUNCIL OF ECONOMIC ADVISORS

1. Gathers information on economic conditions
2. Appraises economic programs and activities of Federal Government
3. Recommends national economic policies
4. Makes economic studies at President's request

JOINT COMMITTEE ON THE
ECONOMIC REPORT

Reports to Congress its findings
and recommendations
with respect to the economic report

FEDERAL AGENCIES
PRIVATE RESEARCH AGENCIES } SERVICES, FACILITIES
AND INFORMATION

INDUSTRY
AGRICULTURE
LABOR
CONSUMERS
STATE & LOCAL GOVERNMENTS } ADVISORY COMMITTEES
AND CONSULTANTS

Adapted from *Report of Council of Economic Advisers,* December 1947

The Economic Report of the President. The President must submit to Congress every January an economic report based on the data and forecasts of the council. The report must include a program for carrying out the policy of the act, and recommendations for legislation if the President sees fit.

Joint Committee on the Economic Report. This is a committee of Congress authorized by the act. Composed of seven senators and seven representatives, it must report early in each year its findings and proposals in respect to presidential recommendations.

How has the Employment Act of 1946 worked out in practice? So far, of course, it has faced no stern test, because employment and income have generally been high since 1946. The nation's chief problem has been inflation, not depression. The economic reports of the council and of the President have received a good deal of publicity and probably have had considerable educational value. The council itself has operated in a somewhat different manner from that originally contemplated. Instead of being an independent agency acting entirely objectively and nonpolitically, the council has tended to become subordinate to the President. Indeed, the chairman of the council has been a sort of personal economic adviser to the chief executive. On the other hand, the council has not, as some feared, propagandized for radical philosophies. It has frequently consulted with businessmen and has stressed the role of private enterprise in maintaining employment.

The difficulties lie much more in the legislative and political parts of the act. The Joint Committee on the Economic Report has not played a major role. It has had little time to act, and its members have usually been busy with more pressing legislative duties. The committee has little influence over the really important committees, such as those that handle taxing or spending. The council itself has said: [19]

> Early experience under the Employment Act of 1946 has brought into sharp focus the practical difficulties which lie between the initiation of a national economic policy and the adoption of that policy by the Congress. Our American democracy will yield only slowly to the need for the deliberate formulation and integration of national policies in the interest of sustained prosperity.

The problem, in short, is not one of economic know-how. Hard experience and the work of both economists and men of affairs have taught us a lot about the workings and management of the national economy. The problem is not unwillingness to accept governmental responsibility for maintaining employment. The Act of 1946 specifically recognizes that responsibility. The problem is whether a governmental system such as ours can act effectively when action is needed. The true test would come if our economy took a serious turn downward after the high level of prosperity we have enjoyed for two decades.

---

[19] Council of Economic Advisers, *Third Annual Report to the President* (Government Printing Office, 1948), p. 12.

Challenge and Opportunity

Toward the end of Chapter 1, we stated the totalitarian challenge to democracy, and we invited you to formulate your answer to that challenge as you read this book. We have reserved the statement of our own answer till now. You may wish to compare our answer with your own.

Is democratic government unrealistic? The antidemocrats charge that man is irrational and selfish, hence incapable of governing himself. But because men are *not always* rational, it does not follow that they are *never* rational. The use of reason is still the best method for arriving at the truth, and the truth is still the best basis for action. And if men are selfish, if human nature is so bad, that is all the more reason for not trusting any one man or single group of men with irresponsible power. It is all the more reason for preserving *democratic* government, which prevents any narrow clique from monopolizing power. "Sometimes it is said that man cannot be trusted with the government of himself," Jefferson once said. "Can he, then, be trusted with the government of others?" Or to quote one of the world's great contemporary theologians, Reinhold Niebuhr, "Man's capacity for justice makes democracy possible; but man's inclination to injustice makes democracy necessary."

Democratic government, moreover, is best designed to bring out the rational and the good in man. If men are denied any voice in directing their own affairs, they are deprived of the one experience that is most likely to make them social, rational, and responsible persons.

Nor are we impressed by the charge that, since the average man is too poorly informed to make intelligent judgments on governmental matters, democratic government means mediocre government. Democratic theory does not require that the voters as a whole make *all* the decisions. It does require that those who make the decisions must, over the long run, please the majority of the people. And the great number of people are fully capable of making over-all judgments on the general course of the nation. They are

capable, as A. D. Lindsay has said, to tell when their shoes are pinching. "No doubt," Lindsay concedes, "the ordinary voter has the vaguest ideas as to what legislative or administrative reform will stop the pinching of his shoes. . . . But for all that, only he, the ordinary man, can tell whether the shoe pinches and where; and without that knowledge the wisest statesman cannot make good laws."

Indeed, this idea of leaving government in the hands of "the best" is self-defeating. Who are the best? Authoritarians talk about government by the best, the supermen, the party elite. But they themselves disagree on who are the best—the Politburo, or Nordics, or the upper class, or the working class, or Anglo-Saxon whites, or the intellectuals, or businessmen. The fact is that good government requires many talents, and talents are not monopolized by any one individual or group. A brilliant physicist may be an innocent about politics; an All-American football player is the best in his business, but by himself he might make a botch of foreign policy. Even if we limited political power to the most highly educated groups, those who should most clearly see the general good, what assurance do we have that they will *seek* the general good? None whatsoever. Where power is restricted to the few, those few define the good in terms of their own narrow interests. In the long run, the best can be found in equal measure among all groups. By giving political power to all people, we allow men and women of real talents, regardless of group or origin, the best opportunity of rising to the top of the political ladder and governing intelligently in behalf of the great number of people.

True, it is easier to defend democratic government in general than it is to defend a particular democratic government. Certainly this is true of the American governmental system. Throughout this book we have raised sharp questions about the caliber of our government measured in terms of the first five basic questions listed at the start of Part One. But none of these problems is insuperable, and perhaps not even critical; indeed, other students of government might express somewhat less concern over them than we have in this book. Consider, for example, the problems of representation and responsibility. We believe that fairer representation in the nation's legislatures and more clear-cut party responsibility would bring about a stronger democratic system and a more efficient and effective government. But there is another whole side to the problem, as Chapter 21 suggests. In any case, there are no failings in the American system that cannot be resolved through traditional processes of constitutional and political change.

Democratic government is not perfect, in America or anywhere else. But defense of democratic government does not require proof of its perfection. Sir Winston Churchill, a former British prime minister and a member of the rich and wellborn, summed it all up when he said, "Democracy is the worst form of government except for any other that has ever been tried."

It is well to keep in mind, though, that government by the people needs thinkers and doers, leaders who can heed the injunction, "Think as men of

action, act as men of thought." So in the remainder of this last chapter we shall suggest some of the ways in which you can put your knowledge and your belief in democratic government to good use.

Needed: *100,000,000 Politicians*

College men and women do not need to be told how important it is for them to take part in politics. Since grade school, they have had this sermon dinned into their ears. Nor do they agree with Boss Plunkitt that "if you have been to college, so much the worse for you" in the rough-and-tumble of American politics. They do not feel the need to "unlearn" all they learned in college. The question is, have they learned enough?

Playing an effective part in politics depends on more than good will and interest in community affairs. It demands a good deal of political know-how. It would be pleasant to be able to say about political activity that "there's nothing to it—just learn as you go." But this would not be true. American political mechanics are a complex affair—far more complex, for example, than those in Great Britain.

Many of the procedures of American politics discussed above may seem dull and difficult. So they are, until you suddenly come face to face with them in a real situation. Registration requirements, for example, seem dull matters, until someone publicly challenges your right to vote. Getting out the vote on election day seems a remote problem—until you find yourself in campaign headquarters at 2 A.M. waiting tensely for the last wards to report in. Limitations on campaign spending seem unimportant—until the opposition accuses your candidate of trying to buy the election.

PLUNGING IN

The first step is to find the name of the local chairman of your party. Someone will know at city hall or at the court house. Calling on the chairman to tell him that you would like to help out in the campaign is the next step. Chances are that he will give you a warm welcome.

Voting lists must be checked, letters stamped, leaflets distributed, meetings arranged, publicity sent out, posters put up. Special skills will come in handy. Anyone in the advertising business can help with radio or newspaper publicity. Amateur sign painters will have ample occasion to make use of their talents. A good money-raiser can help meet the problems of campaign expenses—usually the worst headache of all. Typists, from the hunt-and-peck variety on up, are needed (with their typewriters). Good organizers are required to direct doorbell-ringing, an art and a science in itself. Cars and drivers are wanted for the countless errands that must be run.

One of the most important jobs in a political campaign is to get

people registered to vote. Registration, you will recall (Chapter 14), falls into two types: permanent and periodic. How does one go about getting people registered? At best, it is a chore. First, one must find names and addresses of those not registered. One way to do this is to check city directories or police lists against registration lists. Another, and more common, practice is to check the membership lists of organizations such as the American Legion or a labor union for names not on the voting lists. Then the unregistered person must be approached by mail, over the phone, or, best of all, in his home.

The unregistered voter is often an apathetic citizen. He may not see much point in voting. He will probably not know when the registration period comes. He may ask questions: Will they ask me how old I am? Will they make me take a reading test? Do I have to pay anything? How long do I have to live in the area? Answers to these questions—almost always they can be reassuring ones—will be expected of anyone taking part in a registration drive. In many cases, transportation and baby-sitters also must be provided.

Another highly important job in political campaigning is to get people to vote on election day. The most effective work here is usually done by party committees and candidates. Workers are stationed at every polling booth to check off the names of persons as they vote. Then "checkers" send hourly reports to people at party headquarters, who begin telephoning voters who have not shown up. Other party workers drive voters to the polls. The success of the whole operation depends on good timing, carefully checked lists, and efficient communication and transportation.

The heart of registration and voting drives lies in approaching the individual voter in person, but the approach is much more effective if it comes as part of a general drive. This is especially true of registration drives. A nonpartisan, community-wide program is often the most fruitful procedure. The drive is carried on through the press, radio, television, posters, civic groups, trade unions, veterans' organizations, window displays, churches, schools, door-to-door canvassing, rallies—even sky-writing! In some communities police cars have carried "get-out-the-vote" signs, "vote-mobiles" have toured the area with sample voting machines or sample ballots, and REGISTER TO VOTE has been stenciled on the sidewalks.

Much of this work would be simple drudgery under any other circumstances. In the heat of a campaign, however, it takes on an aura of the dramatic. Volunteers are part of a team engaged in a keen struggle. Party headquarters is always crowded; the phone seems always to be ringing. Crisis follows crisis. Candidates dash in to make arrangements for coming meetings, rush out to speak at the Odd Fellows' barbecue. Rumors flow thick and fast. A few of them are even true.

Taking part in party politics is a rewarding business. Perhaps the biggest satisfaction comes on election day. The blinders have been taken off; the

names on the ballot are those of flesh-and-blood persons. Politics has taken on a new dimension. At this stage you can feel that you are no longer an outsider, but an insider in party affairs. You have learned something of the rules and gimmicks of the political game.

After the election, what then? We will be told on all sides that "politics is now adjourned." But politics is never adjourned. It is a year-round business —at least for the professionals. The only question is whether they will have the game all to themselves.

KEEPING AT IT

Vitally important decisions are made between elections. New members are added to local party committees, precinct captains are selected, perhaps new chairmen are elected. Members of state committees and delegates to conventions are chosen. Plans are made for registration drives, election of candidates to national conventions, future campaigns. These activities determine the shape of politics in the elections ahead. Obviously, running a party, like running a war, is too important to be left to the professionals. The period between elections is the ideal time for public-spirited citizens to make their influence felt in the party councils—an influence that will be all the greater because important party decisions are made by relatively few persons.

In most cases party workers will have no trouble gaining a foothold in the party organization. Occasionally, the old-line leaders may try to close out newcomers to keep the organization as their private preserve. They should not be allowed to succeed without a struggle. If necessary, one can often work with another part of the organization, or join or form auxiliary groups like the Young Democrats or Young Republicans.

Our mental picture of a local party leader is usually one of a ruthless boss, complete with cigar, jowls, and a taste for "honest graft." In real life the party leader usually turns out to be an amiable, honest individual who holds his position as a result of working hard and doing countless favors. Of course, unscrupulous bosses are to be found. But one should not be discouraged from taking part in politics because the local party organization seems to be controlled by a disreputable group. It is far easier to clean the organization from within than from without. Party bosses can ignore the criticism of outsiders, but they cannot resist those who outwork and outvote them within their own domain.

Let there be fair warning. Anyone going into party politics with illusions about the way the parties operate is likely to be in for a shock. On the local level, organization is often stagnant, if not moribund. Committees rarely meet and attendance is poor. Where the local organization is energetic and influential, it is usually because a leader has infused some life into it. His reward is to be called the local "boss"—whether or not he is serving private rather than public needs.

The South is spoken of slightingly as a one-party area, but in many parts of the North only one effective party organization can be found. A rival party may exist in name, but not in fact. Often, especially in the cities, one party organization is the "captive" of the other. It exists on crumbs of patronage handed out by the dominant organization, which is willing to pay for token opposition in order to prevent real competition. Real party rivalry cannot be expected in a situation like this.

Most disillusioning of all is the inglorious nature of local party operations. Any hope that men have banded together for the sake of grand principles may quickly evaporate. The main reason for party activity often turns out to be the "cohesive power of public plunder." Doubtless local politics has been purified a bit since the days of the "muckrakers," but in all too many cases, city and county organizations still are occupied with personalities and petty business rather than with the real needs of the community.

This is disconcerting to the good citizen who has gone to party headquarters to stay. The local problems worrying him concern schools for his children, lower taxes, better roads, faster snow removal in winter, a new library building. He has only one consolation, but it is a big one. The greater the need for improving the character of local politics, the larger the opportunity for him and his fellows to pitch in and do something.

"You're the boss," Mr. Edward J. Flynn of the Bronx told us reassuringly. But he added an important proviso. We're the boss only if we are willing to dirty our hands a bit at the grass roots of party politics. Never was the need greater than today.

Running for Office

For those interested in making a career of politics there are few set rules. Generalizations about the road to election-day victories are risky; the exceptions to the rules are legion. But before entering politics, the individual would be wise to reflect on his assets and liabilities. If he is sensitive to criticism, excessively shy, if he dislikes "good fellowship" and wants to lead a quiet, peaceful life, the chances are against his being successful—or at least happy—in politics. On the other hand, if he enjoys working with others, likes to speak, and can look forward without fear to countless dinners of cold peas and roast beef, then politics offers an exciting and rewarding career.

"One who enters politics must realize that he is to live dangerously," a candidate has said. "In business, the line between the red and the black divides anxiety and comfort, but a businessman can survive a bad year; in politics .1 per cent of one's biennial gross vote can mean the difference between prosperity and ruin." [1]

---

[1] Stimson Bullitt, *To Be a Politician* (Doubleday, 1959), p. 53.

Hugh D. Scott, Jr., a senator, former chairman of the Republican National Committee, and an experienced politician, believes that the following traits are helpful to politically active men and women:

1. Be politically informed.

2. Integrity is the most valuable tool of the trade. Despite cynicism about politics, a dishonest politician is almost always exposed sooner or later.

3. "Patience is a prime political virtue," says Mr. Scott after observing that he had spent "twenty years or so of being stopped several times a day by people with something on their mind, of having my lapels seized firmly or my sleeve tugged by someone who wants something done that he feels I may be able to do, of long interviews with people with a grievance, a petition, a plan, an invention, or just a two-way ball-bearing tongue."

4. Courtesy—"on Ballot Boulevard there's no market at all for the sour stuff."

5. Gregariousness.

6. Hard work. "To know your neighborhood and to help your neighbors is a 365-day-a-year job."

7. A sense of humor. Freshman members of Congress are warned by their elders "Don't violate Rule Six." And what is Rule Six? "Don't take yourself too seriously." And Rules One to Five? "Don't take yourself too seriously." A sense of proportion, a sense of humor.

8. Courage.[2]

Politics does not offer much in the way of job security. It is, therefore, helpful if the aspiring politician has some other source of income. In American politics this has often been the case. Lawyers have more of an opportunity to combine politics and business than do doctors, teachers, workers, and others. The young graduate from law school is forbidden by the ethics of his profession to advertise, but he can run for office. If he wins, he will make valuable contacts. If he loses, he can return to the practice of law with a name that is better known to the public.

Insurance and farming are other professions that may be readily combined with politics. But one need not be a lawyer, insurance man, or farmer to enter politics. The avenues to public office are many, and the halls of Congress and the offices of the executive departments are filled with men and women who came into politics from every conceivable background and occupation.

---

[2] From Hugh D. Scott, Jr., *How to Go into Politics* (John Day, 1949), pp. 26 ff.

Here are some of the do's and don't's of politics.

1. Be a joiner. Try to join as great a variety of organizations as possible. By working for the Community Chest, becoming active in the union, the chamber of commerce, the service club, the lodges, and in church work, the candidate makes his name familiar, wins friends, and learns the skills of his trade.

2. Be one of the boys and avoid snobbish mannerisms, but be colorful.

3. Learn to remember names and faces, but don't be effusive.

4. Ignore unfriendly attacks. "Never get into an argument with a newspaper or a preacher; the newspaper always has the last word with its readers, and the preacher always calls on Heaven as witness that he is right." [3]

5. Know your facts.

6. "Don't overestimate the people's knowledge or underestimate their intelligence."

7. Remember that a nice personality and a mastery of all the do's and don't's of politics are no substitute for intelligence, integrity, and conviction.

A Career in the Civil Service

Political work often leads to appointive as well as elective public positions. Lawyers who have come to the aid of their party are sometimes in line for judgeships, and others may be appointed to places in state or local government. But today more and more of the positions in the federal administrative structure are open to qualified nonpoliticians. These positions offer much to those who have a desire for public service—but little liking for politics—or for people who have administrative talents. The government needs all kinds of people with all kinds of skills. These positions offer reasonable compensation, considerable security, and an exciting challenge. How does one become a bureaucrat?

Men and women may apply for commissions as officers in the armed forces. Young men between the ages of 17 and 22 can apply for admission to West Point, Annapolis, or the Air Force Academy, and on graduation will receive commissions in the Regular Army, Navy, or Air Force. Candidates for these positions must pass stiff physical and mental examinations. Congressmen, senators, the President, and the Vice President have the authority to appoint candidates who meet the qualifications. Information on entrance can be obtained from any congressman. The Secretaries of Army, Navy, and Air Force can also select cadets from among honor graduates

---

[3] *Ibid.*, p. 32. See also Harold Gauer, *How To Win in Politics* (Humphries, 1946), and E. E. Schattschneider, Victor Jones, Stephen K. Bailey, *A Guide to the Study of Public Affairs* (Sloane, 1952), a citizens' manual.

of military schools. Sons of men and women killed in the armed services of the United States are given some preferential treatment.

Some Military Choices Open to College-Age Youths

ARMY

Programs for Enlisted Men

REGULAR ARMY ENLISTMENT
Age Limits: 17 to 34
You may enlist for your choice of 3, 4, 5 or 6 years, or indefinitely. If you are a qualified high school graduate, you may choose your own field of training. This is the enlistment usually chosen by men who wish to make their career in the Army. A special 2-year enlistment is open to Selective Service registrants between the ages of 18½ and 26.

ARMY ENLISTED RESERVE
Age Limits: 17 to 26
If you are qualified and have not been ordered to report for induction you may enlist in the Reserve for 6 years, subject to the requirement that during the early part of that period you will perform 2 years of active service.

ARMY 6-MONTH RESERVE
Age Limits: 18½ to 25
You may enlist in the Reserve for a 6-year period, take 6 months of active duty for training and serve the remainder of the enlistment in the Ready Reserve. Students may delay entry on active duty up to 1 year to complete high school.

ARMY NATIONAL GUARD
Age Limits: 17 to 35
1. *Ages 17 to 18½*—You may enlist in an organized unit and incur an 8-year reserve obligation including 6 months of active duty for training. If you start the 6-months training *before* age 18½ (with up to 1 year's delay permitted for completing high school), you follow with 3 years in the Ready Reserve and then become eligible for transfer to the Standby Reserve for the remainder of the 8 years. If you start the 6-months training *after* age 18½ (except where you were permitted to delay beyond 18½, as above) you will serve a total of 6 years in the Ready Reserve, including the 6 months of active duty and any other prior Ready Reserve service, and then become eligible for transfer to the Standby Reserve for the remainder of the 8 years.

2. *Ages 18½ to 25*—You may enlist in an organized unit for a 6-year period, take 6 months of active duty for training and serve the remainder in the Ready Reserve. Students may delay entry on active duty up to one year to complete high school.

Programs for Officer Candidates

U. S. MILITARY ACADEMY (WEST POINT)
Age Limits: 17 to 22
The United States Military Academy offers you a 4-year college/military course. Graduates are commissioned as Regular Army second lieutenants. Entrance is largely by Congressional appointment and examinations. Enlisted personnel of the Regular and Reserve components may compete for nomination for a limited number of Executive appointments. Physical and mental requirements are rigid. Applicants should be interested in the military service as a career.

ARMY RESERVE OFFICERS TRAINING CORPS (ROTC)
Age Limits: 14 to 24
Under this program you receive part-time military training in one of the colleges or universities having ROTC units. Upon graduation some are selected and offered Regular Army commissions; all others are commissioned as Reserve Army second lieutenants and are required to perform 2 years active duty within a 6-year obligation, or 6 months active duty for training within an 8-year obligation, dependent upon the needs of the Army. Graduates cannot receive a commission prior to age 21 or after reaching age 28.

ARMY OFFICER CANDIDATE SCHOOL (OCS)
Age Limits: 18 to 28
To qualify for this program you must become a warrant officer or enlisted man in the Regular Army, Army Reserve, or National Guard, and must possess a high school diploma or equivalent education. On successful completion of a 22-week training course, you will be commissioned as a Reserve Army second lieutenant, and may be required to perform 2 years active duty in commissioned status.

AIR FORCE

Programs for Enlisted Men

REGULAR AIR FORCE ENLISTMENT
Age Limits: 17 to 34
You may enlist for your choice of 4 or 6 years, and you may select a specified field for technical training depending upon your aptitude, education, and needs of the Air Force. This is the enlistment usually chosen by men who wish a career in the Air Force.

AIR FORCE 6-MONTH RESERVE
Age Limits: 18½ to 25
You may enlist in the Reserve for a 6-year period, take 6 months of active duty for training and serve the remainder of the enlistment in the Ready Reserve. Men are enlisted into these programs on a highly selective basis.

AIR NATIONAL GUARD
Age Limits: 17 to 35
The Air National Guard units are organized within the States and Territories and, when not in the service of the United States, are subject to the control of Governors.

1. *Ages 17 to 18½*—You may enlist in an organized unit, take 11 weeks of active duty training followed by satisfactory participation in the Ready Reserve until age 28, *or* you may take 6 months of active duty training followed by 7½ years in the Ready Reserve.

2. *Ages 18½ to 25*—You may enlist in an organized unit and incur a 6-year reserve obligation, take 11 weeks active duty for basic training plus additional active duty for training as available, and serve the remainder of the 6 years in the Ready Reserve.

Programs for Officer Candidates

U. S. AIR FORCE ACADEMY
Age Limits: 17 to 22

The United States Air Force Academy offers you a 4-year college/aviation course. Graduates are commissioned as Regular Air Force second lieutenants. Entrance is largely by Congressional appointment and examination. Enlisted personnel of the Regular and Reserve components may compete for nominations for a limited number of Executive appointments. Flight physical and mental requirements are rigid. Applicants should be interested in the Air Force as a career.

AIR FORCE RESERVE OFFICER TRAINING CORPS (AFROTC)
Age Limits: 14 to 24

Under this program you will receive part-time aviation training in one of the colleges or universities having AFROTC units. In your last 2 years you may choose flight or ground training. (Emphasis is placed on acceptance of men who are qualified for and are interested in entering flight training after graduation.) Upon graduation you will be commissioned as a Reserve Air Force second lieutenant and will be required to perform 3 years active duty if in the nonflying program, or 5 years active duty if in the flying program. You cannot qualify for a commission prior to age 18 or after age 27.

AIR FORCE OFFICER CANDIDATE SCHOOL
Age Limits: 20½ to 26½

To qualify for this program you must be an enlisted man in the Regular Air Force, Air Force Reserve or National Guard. You must possess a high school diploma or equivalent education. Upon successful completion of a 6-month training course, you will be commissioned as a Reserve Air Force second lieutenant, and may be required to serve 3 years active or reserve duty in commissioned status.

AIR FORCE AVIATION CADET
Age Limits: 19 to 26½

If you have a high school diploma you may apply for this program. (Men who have had at least two years of college are preferred.) The training program is approximately 14 months for pilots and 1 year for navigators. Upon graduation you will be commissioned as a Reserve Air Force second lieutenant. You will be required to perform 5 years active duty.

AIR NATIONAL GUARD AVIATION CADET PROGRAM
Age Limits: 19 to 26½

To qualify for this program you must enlist in the Air National Guard and possess a high school diploma or equivalent education. Air National Guard Aviation Cadets are sent to the Air Force flying schools and are given the same training as regular Air Force cadets. At the end of approximately 18 months of training, they are returned to their ANG units as second lieutenants and holders of appropriate aeronautical ratings as pilots or navigators.

NAVY

Programs for Enlisted Men

REGULAR NAVY ENLISTMENT
Age Limits: 17 to 31

You may enlist for your choice of 4 or 6 years, with the exception that if you are 17 years of age you may enlist for a period ending on the day prior to your 21st birthday. If you are a qualified graduate of a high school or a 4-year vocational school you may enlist for training in special fields. This is the enlistment usually chosen by men who wish to make their career in the Navy.

NAVY ENLISTED RESERVE
Age Limits: 17 to 31

If you are qualified and have not been ordered to report for induction you may enlist in the Reserve for 6 years, subject to the requirement that during the early part of that period you will perform 2 years of active service.

Programs for Officer Candidates

U. S. NAVAL ACADEMY (ANNAPOLIS)
Age Limits: 17 to 22

The United States Naval Academy offers you a 4-year college/naval course. Graduates are commissioned as Regular Navy ensigns or Regular Marine Corps second lieutenants. Entrance is largely by Congressional appointment and examinations. Enlisted personnel of the Regular and Reserve components may compete for nomination for a limited number of Executive appointments. Physical and mental requirements are rigid. Applicants should be interested in making the service a career.

NAVAL RESERVE OFFICERS TRAINING CORPS (NROTC) REGULAR
Age Limits: 17 to 21

If you are accepted for this program you receive 4 years of Navy-subsidized education including part-time naval training in one of the colleges or universities having NROTC units. Upon graduation you will be commissioned as a Regular Navy ensign or a Regular Marine Corps second lieutenant according to your choice of training. You will be required to perform at least 4 years active duty.

NAVAL RESERVE OFFICERS TRAINING CORPS (NROTC) CONTRACT
Age Limits: 17 to 21

Under this program you receive part-time naval training in one of the colleges or universities having NROTC units. Upon graduation you will be commissioned as a Naval Reserve ensign or a Reserve Marine Corps second lieutenant according to your choice of training. You will be required to perform 2 years active duty.

NAVY OFFICER CANDIDATE SCHOOL (OCS)
Age Limits: 19 to 33½

This is a program open to you only if you are a college graduate. Upon successful completion of 4 months intensive naval training you will be commissioned as a Naval Reserve ensign. You will be required to perform 3 years active duty.

NAVY RESERVE OFFICER CANDIDATE (ROC)
Age Limits: 17 to 25

To qualify for this program you must become a member of the Naval Reserve and be enrolled in an accredited college or university. Initial enrollment is restricted to men in the freshmen, sophomore, or junior year. You will take two 8-week Navy training courses during two separate summers. Upon graduation you will be commissioned as a Naval Reserve ensign. You will be required to perform 3 years active duty.

NAVAL AVIATION CADET
Age Limits: 18 to 25

To qualify for this program you must have had at least 2 years of college or 60 semester credit hours. Following approximately 18 months of naval aviation training (pre-flight, basic, and advanced), you will be commissioned as a Naval Reserve ensign or a Reserve Marine Corps second lieutenant. You will be required to serve approximately 2½ years active duty (total training and active duty time required is 4 years).

NAVAL AVIATION OFFICER CANDIDATE
Age Limits: 19 to 26

To qualify for this program you must be a college graduate. After successful completion of approximately 4 months of indoctrination training, you will be commissioned as a Naval Reserve ensign. Approximately 14 months additional basic and advanced flight training will follow in officer status, and you will then be required to perform 3½ years active duty as a naval aviator (total training and active duty time required is approximately 5 years).

MARINE CORPS

Programs for Enlisted Men

REGULAR MARINE CORPS ENLISTMENT
Age Limits: 17 to 28

You may enlist for your choice of 3, 4, or 6 years. You will be enlisted for general duty, but, on completion of recruit training, you may be assigned duties in accordance with your education, skills, prior training, physical capabilities, preferences, and the needs of the Marine Corps. This is the enlistment usually chosen by men who wish to make their career in the Marine Corps.

MARINE CORPS ENLISTED RESERVE
Age Limits: 17 to 26

If you are qualified and have not been ordered to report for induction you may enlist in the Reserve for 6 years, subject to the requirement that during the early part of that period you will perform 2 years of active service.

MARINE CORPS 6-MONTH RESERVE
Age Limits: 18½ to 25

You may enlist in the Reserve for a 6-year period, take 6 months active duty for training and serve the remainder of the enlistment in the Ready Reserve.

You may be assigned to either ground or aviation training.

Programs for Officer Candidates

MARINE CORPS OFFICER CANDIDATE COURSE
(GROUND OR AVIATION)
Age Limits: 20 to 26

To qualify for either the Ground or Aviation program you must be a senior or a graduate of an accredited college or university. On completion of a 10-week training course you will be commissioned as a Reserve Marine Corps second lieutenant and be required to perform 3 years active duty.

MARINE CORPS PLATOON LEADERS CLASS
(GROUND OR AVIATION)
Age Limits: 17 to 25

Under either the Ground or Aviation program you must take two 6-week summer training courses while attending a college or university. On graduation you will be commissioned as either a Reserve Marine Corps second lieutenant or, if qualified, as a Regular Marine Corps second lieutenant. You will be required to perform 3 years active duty.

COAST GUARD

Programs for Enlisted Men

REGULAR COAST GUARD ENLISTMENT
Age Limits: 17 to 26

Under this program you will be enlisted for a period of 4 years. After completion of basic training consideration will be given to assigning you to existing Coast Guard Stations near your home whenever possible. If you are a qualified graduate of a high school or a 4-year vocational school you may enlist for training in special fields. This is the program usually chosen by men who wish to make their career in the Coast Guard.

COAST GUARD ENLISTED RESERVE
Age Limits: 17 to 26

If you are qualified and have not been ordered to report for induction you may enlist in the Reserve for 6 years, subject to the requirement that during the early part of that period you will perform 2 years active service.

COAST GUARD 6-MONTH RESERVE
Age Limits: 18½ to 21

You may enlist in the Reserve for a 6-year period,

take 6 months active duty for training and serve the remainder of the enlistment in the Ready Reserve.

Programs for Officer Candidates

U. S. COAST GUARD ACADEMY
Age Limits: 17 to 22

The United States Coast Guard Academy offers you a 4-year college/naval course. You will be commissioned as a Regular Coast Guard ensign. Entrance is by nationwide competitive examination. Physical and mental requirements are rigid. Applicants should be interested in the Coast Guard as a career.

COAST GUARD OFFICER CANDIDATE SCHOOL (OCS)
Age Limits: 21 to 26

Under this program you must be a college graduate or within 4 months of graduation at the time of application. On completion of a 17-week training course you will be commissioned as a Reserve Coast Guard ensign and required to perform 3 years of active duty as part of a 6-year obligation. If, at the time of appointment, your services are not required on active duty, you will serve on active duty for training for a period of 6 consecutive months followed by 7½ years in an appropriate Reserve unit.

How does one go about getting a position in one of the civilian agencies of government? There are now approximately 2⅓ million civilian positions in the federal government. Only 537 of these are filled by election—namely, 437 representatives, 100 senators, the President, and the Vice President. To secure one of these positions it is necessary to go into politics. The same is generally true of an appointment to the Supreme Court or an inferior federal court, district attorneyship, or appointment as a first-, second-, or third-class postmaster, or a Cabinet member. These and other such positions are filled by presidential appointment with the consent of the Senate.

But well over 80 per cent of the positions in the executive branch are open to qualified citizens regardless of their politics, except that they must be loyal to the United States and not be fascists or communists. Most of these positions are filled through civil service examinations. Veterans receive preference on these examinations, which are held throughout the United States at the various regional headquarters of the Civil Service Commission. If one does not live in a city with a Civil Service Regional Headquarters, information can be secured from the Civil Service Secretary at the local post office.

Only about 10 per cent of these positions are in Washington. The rest are scattered throughout the world. Unlike English practice, American civil service examinations are for particular kinds of jobs. Positions calling for professional training are filled through unassembled examinations. Such examinations are not examinations in the usual sense, but questionnaires that enable the Civil Service Commission and the appointing agencies to learn the competence and experience of the individual.

Civil service jobs are now graded in a general schedule of 18 grades with salaries going up in steps from $2960 to $17,500. The work normally involves a 5-day, 40-hour week with annual vacations of from 13 to 26 days and generous sick leave. Low-cost life insurance is available, employees are entitled to unemployment compensation, and there is an attractive retirement system. The Hatch Act protects civil servants from being obligated to contribute to political funds, but it also bars them from participating in any partisan political activity.

TYPES OF JOB

The positions open are so many and varied that only a few can be mentioned here. Engineers, physicists, chemists, and other technical personnel are recruited through specially designed unassembled examinations. The *Federal Service Entrance Examination* is of special interest to college graduates who wish to enter the career civil service and work up to high-level assignments. This new examination is designed to recruit upwards of 5000 college-caliber people each year, and its purpose is not just to fill particular

jobs, but to secure talented persons who have the ability to mature on the job. This is a move in the direction of English civil service recruitment concepts.

The Federal Service Entrance Examination is open continuously. Following are examples of the fields in which positions are filled: general administration, economics and other social sciences, communications, library science, information and records management, statistics, personnel management. Appointments are made for college graduates at a minimum beginning salary of $4040 (Grade GS-5). Those with a year's graduate study are eligible for Grade GS-7 positions, with starting salaries of $4980.

To qualify for the Federal Service Entrance Examination, a person (1) must have completed a four-year college course, or have three years experience in responsible work, or have a combination of education and experience; (2) must pass a written test of general abilities; (3) must be rated satisfactory in an oral interview; (4) must submit satisfactory references; (5) must be a United States citizen of undoubted loyalty; (6) must be physically able to perform the duties of the position. College seniors may take the examination and may receive provisional appointments which permit them to enter on duty after graduation. To apply for these positions, obtain Card Form 5000-AB from any post office, civil service office, or college placement bureau. The examinations are given every few months at cities throughout the nation.

Of special interest to persons of unusual ability are the management internships (formerly known as Junior Management Assistant) that are offered by some of the agencies. These agencies have specially planned programs that give varied work assignments and training designed to develop persons of unusual promise. In order to obtain one of these internships, in addition to passing the Federal Service Entrance Examination the candidate must also pass a more comprehensive written test on either administrative problems or public affairs, and must demonstrate in an oral interview that he has the personal qualities required for higher managerial positions.

There is always room in the civil service for persons with secretarial skills. Men and women with college training or comparable experience and secretarial skills often get into the service as secretaries and then quickly move up to administrative positions. Persons who wish to go from agency to agency to look for civil-service positions should secure Form 57 from the Civil Service Commission and fill it out before going job-hunting. Completing this form is required procedure, and to fill it out before seeing appointing officers will save much time. Several federal agencies have their own personnel systems and are not covered by regular civil service rules. The TVA, the FBI, the Armed Forces Security Agency, and the Central Intelligence Agency, for example, recruit and hire their own employees. The FBI appoints its special agents from among physically and mentally eligible lawyers (those who have graduated from an accredited law school) and accountants (with at least three years' experience). G-men receive a starting

salary of $6505 and after a probationary period are given raises and permanent appointments.

In addition to opportunities in the federal service, many attractive positions are open in state and municipal public service. Since each year the states and cities improve the conditions of their public service, opportunities are becoming more attractive for able people.

Although positions with the United Nations are difficult to secure because the American quota is usually filled, the effort may be worth while, for service with the United Nations offers many advantages in pay and other benefits, in addition to the satisfaction of working for the community of mankind.

Entering the Foreign Service

The Foreign Service has attractions for many people. In some ways it is the glamor service of the federal government, but, as we noted in Chapter 23, much of the work is routine, and life can be dull and even unpleasant in some posts. Yet the Service has many advantages.

In order to be eligible to take the Foreign Service Officer examinations one must: (1) be at least 20 and under 31 years of age; (2) be a citizen of the United States for at least 10 years; (3) not be married to an alien. Examinations for these positions are written, oral, and physical. The written examination is usually held in June and December in approximately fifty cities within the United States, and at any American diplomatic or consulate post that candidates residing abroad may designate. The oral examinations are held in Washington, at certain regional centers in the United States, and certain posts abroad. Persons who wish to take the examinations may receive applications from the Board of Examiners for the Foreign Service, Department of State, Washington 25, D.C.; these applications should be completed at least six weeks before the date set for the examination.

FOREIGN SERVICE EXAMINATIONS

Taking a full day to complete, the written examination is composed of three parts. The first part is an English Expression test (90 minutes) intended to examine the candidate's ability to apply the basic principles of rhetoric and usage; ability to organize ideas in logical order; and "sensitivity to the appropriateness of a piece of writing for a particular situation and a particular audience." [4] The second part is a General Ability test (90 minutes) designed to measure the candidate's basic learning skills—ability to read, to analyze, and to interpret data in a variety of forms, and to make

---

[4] "Analysis of the Written Examination for Foreign Service Officer Candidates," *Foreign Service News Letter*, No. 113, July 15, 1956, p. 4.

simple mathematical deductions. The third part (2 hours) is a General Background test consisting of 50 per cent social studies, 25 per cent humanities, and 25 per cent science questions.

The oral examination is designed to test qualities such as appearance, manner, diction, and personality. The Service uses the oral interview to eliminate candidates who are "shy, aggressive, boorish, unable to defend their views, who give evidence of low standards of conduct, and who show a lack of knowledge of the United States." To test this last quality, natives of one section of the country are often questioned on other sections. Factual knowledge is given less weight than "ability to form thoughtful opinions based on the facts at the candidates' disposal, to organize his views logically, and to speak clearly and understandably." While the examinations are exacting, they are less so than formerly, and the number of positions open has recently been increased.

SERVICE ABROAD

The President, with the consent of the Senate, appoints successful candidates as Foreign Service officers (since 1956, most of them at Class 8). The salaries in this class range from $4730 to $5885; moreover, officers may work themselves up the scale until they get to the top class, where the salaries are $18,700. In addition, career officers may be appointed as ambassadors and ministers at higher salaries, up to $20,000. While abroad, salaries are supplemented by quarters allowances; officers receive from 13 to 26 days of annual leave; and after two years abroad they are entitled to home leave in the United States with pay and travel expenses for their families. Unless an officer is promoted within a maximum period in each class, except for the top two classes, he must retire.

Before foreign assignment, Foreign Service officers are trained at the Foreign Service Institute, and throughout their careers they continue special studies. There is no one method of preparation for the Foreign Service, but persons interested in taking the examination should, while in college, learn to write clear and correct English, master a foreign language, and take enough social science, humanities, and science courses to be able to pass the examinations.

A Last Word

Some of you have no interest in learning about political or administrative jobs. Your future lies elsewhere. Even so, you can and should have a political career—in the party of your choice. As we have seen, our parties badly need strengthening at every level. The country needs more *party* politicians to hunt out good candidates and help elect them, drive workers to the polls on election day, spread the party gospel, and remind the officeholders of their responsibilities to the people.

Every individual in a democracy contributes to its success or failure. Those who, because of ignorance or indifference, try to stay on the side lines nevertheless influence the course of events, negative and destructive though their influence may be. If the 180 million Americans are to keep their free government, it will be mainly because of the activities of the people as a whole. Leaders dedicated to the principles of free government and leaders with vision and courage are essential, but it is from the private citizens that the leaders are recruited. The standards and values of the people determine broadly the type of leadership they get.

"Fourscore and seven years ago," said Abraham Lincoln in the midst of a crucial struggle, "our fathers brought forth on this continent a new nation, conceived in liberty, and dedicated to the proposition that all men are created equal." Lincoln saw that struggle as a test of whether government of the *people,* by the *people,* for the *people* could endure. Eighty years later another President, Franklin D. Roosevelt, could report in the midst of another great war that "the state of this Nation is good—the heart of this Nation is sound—the spirit of this Nation is strong—the faith of this Nation is eternal." Government by the people has met and mastered many crises. How well will it meet the tests to come?

Keeping Informed: Bibliography

Newspapers, radio, and television are important sources of information, but the person who depends solely on these sources will have an imperfect picture of the world around him. They give only a disconnected story of the sensational—the newsworthy—events. They tell little of the whys and wherefores. The successful negotiation of a hundred collective bargaining contracts during a day goes unnoticed while public attention is focused on the one case in which negotiations break down.

To some extent magazines supplement the news. Some give background information; others digest the weekly events for those too busy to read the daily papers. *Time* and *Newsweek* with their clipped and dramatic reporting of the week's events are major sources of information for many citizens. The weekly *U.S. News & World Report* presents the news in attractive form, and is especially aimed toward influential members of the business community. While *Time, Newsweek,* and *U.S. News & World Report* are "right of center," *The Nation, The New Leader,* and *The New Republic* are militantly liberal journals of opinion which report the week's events from left of center; the *National Review* discusses events from the conservative point of view. Though these last four have, compared to the others, only a relatively small circulation, their audience includes many leaders of opinion —clergymen, teachers, lawyers, public officials, and the like. *The Reporter,* also liberal in tone, gives less attention to the news of the week and more to extended discussion of issues of contemporary significance, especially in Washington and abroad.

Among the monthly magazines, *Harper's Magazine, Atlantic Monthly,* and *Fortune,* have relatively small audiences but great influence, since they are read by strategically placed individuals. The first two are more "liberal" in tone than *Fortune,* but all three attempt to present a balanced diet. *Fortune* features materials of interest to businessmen, but it covers all phases of American society. By far the largest-circulation monthly is *The Reader's Digest,* read each month by millions of persons. In addition to features

written by its own staff members, *The Reader's Digest* selects and abridges articles that appear in other magazines. It has "conservative" leanings.

Magazines of general circulation contain useful material, but they do not go deeply into particular questions. Where do you find a law? How do you look up a court decision? Where can you find information on the United Nations? How do you find out how your congressman has voted? What are some good books on the U.S.S.R.? Many aids and services have been designed to make such information readily available.

Important information-dispensing centers are the more than 7500 public libraries and the many hundreds of private libraries that are open to the public. In the periodical room can be found, in addition to magazines of general interest, many specialized journals such as the *The American Political Science Review.* The articles in these and many other periodicals are indexed by subject and author in the *Reader's Guide to Periodical Literature.* Another useful index to materials on public affairs is the *Bulletin of the Public Affairs Information Service.* This *Bulletin* is published monthly and indexed cumulatively at the end of the year; it contains references not only to articles, but also to books, government documents, and pamphlets on economic and public affairs. These indexes will help you locate available materials on most subjects. The card catalogue in the library will reveal the books that are available there. You can learn something about an author's credentials and the opinion of informed persons about a particular book in *The Book Review Digest.*

In the reference room one of the most useful volumes is the *United States Government Organization Manual,* an annual publication. The *Manual,* which can be obtained from the Superintendent of Documents, Government Printing Office, covers the authority, organization, and functions of all branches of the government. It has up-to-date organization charts, tells which individuals hold the higher executive positions, and gives a brief description of the work of each unit of government. If you want to know, for example, who heads the Bureau of Mines in the Department of the Interior, and what that bureau does, the *Manual* is the place to look. The *Congressional Directory,* published each year, has some of the materials found in the *Manual,* and it includes autobiographical sketches of members of Congress, lists of congressional committees and committee assignments, election statistics for the last several congressional elections, and maps of congressional districts. The *Directory* is the place to find out the name of your congressman, a short sketch of his life, what committees he is on, and the boundaries of the district he represents.

Of special interest to persons interested in public affairs is *The Encyclopedia of the Social Sciences,* which contains articles on various topics—political parties, sovereignty, representation, John Locke, for example—that are among the best short treatments to be found. In *Current Biography* you can find materials and background information on men in the news, and *Facts on File* provides a quick reference to current events.

If you are interested in statistical information, consult the *Statistical Abstract of the United States,* published yearly by the Commerce Department. Many arguments can be readily settled by resorting to this volume. The reference librarian will be able to point out other useful tools for getting information.

Where can you find a *law?* We often hear people talk about some statute without having seen it. Where can the actual text be found?

The laws of the United States as passed by Congress are first printed individually and are known as *slip laws.* Each law has a number; the Taft-Hartley Act, for example, is known as Public Law 101, Eightieth Congress, First Session. At the end of each year the laws are collected and published by the Government Printing Office under the title of *United States Statutes at Large.* Each year's collection is separately numbered, though there are two separate parts for each number. Part One contains *public laws,* that is, laws affecting the people generally or having to do with governmental organization. Part Two contains *private* laws, those having to do with particular groups or individuals. The laws in the *Statutes at Large* are listed chronologically, each law constituting a separate chapter. The Taft-Hartley Act, for example, is Chapter 120 of Volume 61, on page 136. (It is cited as follows: 61 Stat. 136.)

The *Statutes at Large* are useful for research, but they include many laws of only specialized interest, such as rivers and harbors appropriations. Furthermore, many of the measures modify earlier legislation and are themselves modified by later legislation. To find *current* laws on a topic it is best to go to the *United States Code,* which contains the public laws of the United States that are in force at the present time. The last codification was in 1946, but each year the *Code* is supplemented by a volume that brings the subject up to date. The laws are arranged according to fifty titles, each title is divided into sections, and each section into paragraphs that are numbered consecutively for each title. The fifty titles cover such subjects as Congress, Title 2; Army, Title 10; Bankruptcy, Title 11; Labor, Title 29; and so on. The *Code* is cited by title and paragraph. The citation of the Taft-Hartley Act, for example, is 29 U. S. C. 141 ff.

The *Code,* like the *Statutes at Large,* is printed by the Government Printing Office, but there are also commercially published editions known as *United States Code Annotated* (U. S. C. A.) and the *Federal Code Annotated* (F. C. A.). These annotated editions include notes on judicial interpretations of the law as well as the law itself. If available, they are more useful than the *Code* itself.

Where can you find the rules and regulations issued by the President and the executive agencies? Every day except Sunday and Monday the government publishes *The Federal Register,* which contains executive orders, regulations, and proclamations issued by the President, as well as the orders and regulations promulgated by the executive agencies (including the independent

regulatory commissions). These administrative rules and regulations are collected, codified, and kept up to date in the *Code of Federal Regulations,* organized on the same plan as the *United States Code.*

The laws as they finally appear on the statute books give, however, only part of the story. Where do you find out what went on before the laws were passed or why certain laws were not passed? This information can, in part, be found in one of the most edifying and interesting items of American letters—the *Congressional Record.* The *Record* is issued every day Congress is in session, and is bound and indexed at the end of each session. It contains everything that is said on the floors of the two chambers, plus a lot that is not said. Congress freely gives its consent to requests of its members "to revise and extend their remarks," which is a polite way of saying that congressmen are permitted to include in the *Record* statements that they did not make before the Congress. These speeches are then reprinted and distributed to the folks back home. Congressmen, with the unanimous consent of their colleagues, also place in the *Record* poems, articles, letters, editorials, and other materials they find interesting. Each day's *Record* is now accompanied by a *Daily Digest* that highlights the events on both the floor of Congress and in committees.

Action on specific items can be traced by searching through the index. An easier method is to use the *Digest of Public General Bills* published by the Legislative Reference Service, which gives a brief summary of all public bills and their progress in the legislative mills.

There are several commercial services that provide convenient references to congressional activities. *The Congressional Quarterly News Reports*: *Weekly Log* contains voting records, legislative action, reports on lobbying, and other materials about Congress in action. This is the best source for materials on lobbying activity. The materials are indexed and collected in an *Annual Almanac*. The *United States Code*: *Congressional and Administrative News,* and the *Congressional Index* also provide ready reference to congressional activity.

Since most of the real work of Congress is done in committees, the reports of these committees and the printed records of hearings are important sources of information. The hearings and reports can be found in any of the over 500 depository libraries in the United States (libraries that receive most publications issued by the Government Printing Office) and the more important ones are in most libraries.

Congress is not the only branch of the federal government that keeps a record of its work. All the other agencies have their own publications, describing their work and supplying the citizen with general and specialized information. These can be obtained from the Superintendent of Documents, Government Printing Office, Washington 25, D.C., at a nominal price. They are indexed in the *Monthly Catalogue of United States Government Publications*. W. P. Leidy, *A Popular Guide to Government Publications* (1953)

is an annotated bibliography of 2500 of the most popular Government Printing Office titles.

Where can you find the reports of the federal judiciary? Legal bibliography is a complex subject, but the law is too important to leave to lawyers. The decisions of the Supreme Court are published by the government in numbered volumes known as the *United States Reports*. Cases are cited by volume and page number, e.g., *Illinois ex rel McCollum* v. *Board of Education,* 333 U. S. 203 (1948) means that this case can be found in the 333rd volume of the *United States Reports* on page 203 and that the opinion was handed down in 1948. Decisions of the Court prior to 1875 are cited by the name of the Supreme Court reporter. Thus, *Marbury* v. *Madison,* 1 Cranch 137 (1803) can be found in the first volume of Cranch's Supreme Court reports on page 137; the opinion was announced in 1803. Two other editions of Supreme Court opinions are commercially published and each has its own form of citation. Some of the federal district court rulings are now commercially published in volumes known as the *Federal Supplement*. Those of the federal courts of appeals are now also published by the same commercial publisher in volumes known as the *Federal Reporter*. These reports are not available in many general libraries, but in many communities a special law library, usually located in the court house, contains the reports of the cases plus other materials needed by lawyers in their professional work.

Selected Bibliography

This bibliography makes no pretense of including even all the good books pertinent to the American experiment in government by the people. Its purpose is to provide an *initial* guide to the literature. With few exceptions the rich periodical literature is not mentioned. A number of books which in the opinion of the authors are of special importance to the general reader have been starred.

PART ONE: DEMOCRATIC GOVERNMENT IN AMERICA

GENERAL SOURCES

C. S. Hyneman, *The Study of Politics; The Present State of American Political Science* (1959). Survey of current research, problems, methods, and data.

R. Young, ed., *Approaches to the Study of Politics* (1958). Essays on the methodology of political science.

B. Crick, *The American Science of Politics: Its Origins and Conditions* (1959). Critical study of American political science.

* R. M. MacIver, *The Web of Government* (1947). Analysis of government.

H. Finer, *Theory and Practice of Modern Government,* abr. ed. (1954). Description of political institutions of modern government.

C. E. Merriam, *Systematic Politics* (1945).

A. F. Bentley, *The Process of Government* (1908; reprinted 1949). Seminal study in methodology and systematic treatment of the role of interest groups in the political process.

* D. B. Truman, *The Governmental Process* (1951). Builds on Bentley's work; analysis of political interests and public opinion.

D. Easton, *The Political System* (1953). Analysis of theoretical structure of political science; need to develop systematic causal theory.

E. Voegelin, *The New Science of Politics* (1952). Attack on positivism and liberalism and defense of thesis that political science must rest on Greek and Christian philosophy.

K. Lowenstein, *Political Power and the Governmental Process* (1957). Power viewed as the central concept of politics and government.

I. Howe, *Politics and the Novel* (1957). Politics in and related to contemporary novels.

GENERAL TREATMENTS
OF AMERICAN GOVERNMENT AND SOCIETY

J. K. Galbraith, *The Affluent Society* (1958). Study of American economy challenging many present assumptions.

* M. Lerner, *America as a Civilization: Life and Thought in the United States Today* (1957). Wide-ranging study of American pluralism.

J. Barzun, *The House of Intellect* (1959). Critical analysis of American culture.

M. Beloff, *The American Federal Government* (1959). Critical analysis by noted British scholar.

A. de Tocqueville, *Democracy in America* (Phillips Bradley edition, 1946, 2 vols.; first published in 1835). Classic study of American government.

J. Bryce, *The American Commonwealth* (1888, 2 vols.). Ranks with de Tocqueville; more descriptive and less analytical.

D. W. Brogan, *Politics in America* (1954). Special emphasis on party system.

H. J. Laski, *The American Democracy* (1948). Provocative interpretation by another English political scientist.

V. O. Packard, *The Status Seekers* (1959). Popular analysis of class in American society.

W. H. Whyte, Jr., *The Organization Man* (1956). The impact of bureaucracy on the individual in American society.

M. Einaudi, *The Roosevelt Revolution* (1959). Impact of the New Deal on American society and government.

* C. A. Beard, *The Republic* (1943). Comments by distinguished scholar presented in the form of dialogues between Beard and his friends.

* G. Myrdal, *An American Dilemma* (1944). Monumental study of American society with special attention to the problems of Negro-white relationships.

R. M. Williams, *American Society* (1951). Sociological interpretation.

J. F. Dewhurst and associates, *America's Needs and Resources: A New Survey* (1955). Survey of basic trends—for example, capital requirements, income—in the decade 1950-1960.

AMERICAN POLITICAL THOUGHT

A. T. Mason and R. H. Leach, *In Quest of Freedom: American Political Thought and Practice* (1959).

* V. L. Parrington, *Main Currents in American Thought* (1927-1930). Interpretation of American literature, including the writings of the major political theorists and practitioners.

R. H. Gabriel, *The Course of American Democratic Thought,* 2nd ed. (1956). Interpretation of democratic thought from 1815 to present.

R. Hofstadter, *The American Political Tradition and the Men Who Made It* (1948). Study of the ideology of American statesmen, emphasizing the basic agreement underlying their political conflicts.

L. Hartz, *The Liberal Tradition in America: An Interpretation of American Political Thought since the Revolution* (1955). Emphasizes uniqueness of American liberal tradition.

F. G. Wilson, *The American Political Mind* (1949). Traces the development of American thought.

H. S. Commager, *The American Mind* (1950). An interpretation of American thought and character since the 1880's.

C. L. Rossiter, *Seedtime of the Republic* (1953). Political ideas of the men who founded the Republic.

W. F. Craven, *The Legend of the Founding Fathers* (1956). Emphasizes contributions of the Puritans.

C. E. Merriam, *A History of American Political Theories* (1903; reissued, 1936). Standard classic.

R. A. Dahl, *A Preface to Democratic Theory* (1956). Constructs model of

democracy and finds Madisonian and populistic models inadequate.

F. A. Hermens, *The Representative Republic* (1958). Defense of indirect democracy.

S. M. Lipset, M. A. Trow, and J. S. Coleman, *Union Democracy: The Inside Politics of the International Typographical Union* (1956). Conditions of democratic and oligarchical control of voluntary organizations.

J. S. Mill, *Representative Government* (1882). One of the most important books on foundations and problems of democracy.

C. L. Becker, *Modern Democracy* (1941). Study accenting the economic basis of democracy and the discrepancy between the ideal and the actual.

C. J. Friedrich, *The New Image of the Common Man* (enl. ed., 1950). Defense of the belief that the common man is better able to govern than the uncommon man.

R. B. Perry, *Puritanism and Democracy* (1944). Study of two American ideals; has been called a "Thesaurus of democratic thought and an arsenal of democratic defense."

R. Niebuhr, *The Children of Light and the Children of Darkness* (1944). Short defense of democracy by one of America's leading theologians.

* A. D. Lindsay, *The Modern Democratic State* (1943). Statement of the nature of democracy, its development, its essence, and defense of it, by an English scholar.

W. Lippmann, *Essays in the Public Philosophy* (1956). Antimajoritarian, Burkean defense of democracy.

J. H. Hallowell, *The Moral Foundation of Democracy* (1954). Statement that democracy depends upon Hebraic-Greek-Christian tradition.

D. Spitz, *Patterns of Anti-democratic Thought* (1949). Refutation of the major critics of democracy from the "Right."

J. R. Pennock, *Liberal Democracy* (1950). Defense of democracy, major threats to it, and the limitations on the majority in democratic government.

W. Kendall, *John Locke and the Doctrine of Majority-Rule* (1941). Written by an exponent of the absolute majority rule principle.

H. S. Commager, *Majority Rule and Minority Rights* (1943). Defense of majority rule principle and attack on the limitations of judicial review.

CONSTITUTIONALISM

W. H. Hamilton, "Constitutionalism," *Encyclopedia of the Social Sciences,* Vol. 9.

C. H. McIlwain, *Constitutionalism: Ancient and Modern* (rev. ed., 1947). Papers and essays by distinguished scholar showing the evolution of the concept of limited government.

F. D. Wormuth, *The Origins of Modern Constitutionalism* (1949). Examination of the origins and developments of constitutional limitations—separation of powers, checks and balances, judicial review, and so on.

F. M. Watkins, *The Political Tradition of the West* (1948). Traces development of modern liberalism.

C. J. Friedrich, *Constitutional Government and Democracy* (rev. ed., 1950). Analysis of relations between democracy and constitutionalism; covers all major contemporary constitutional governments.

PART TWO: THE RULES AND HOW THEY GREW

REVOLUTION AND CONFEDERATION

D. J. Boorstin, *The Americans; the Colonial Experience* (1958). Emphasis on colonial uniqueness and its influence on the development of the American character.

J. C. Miller, *Origins of the American Revolution* (1943).

J. F. Jameson, *The American Revolution Considered as a Social Movement* (1926).

C. L. Becker, *The Declaration of Independence,* new ed. (1942).

E. Dumbauld, *The Declaration of Independence and What It Means Today* (1950). A phrase-by-phrase explanation

of the Declaration, placing it in the context of the days in which it was written.

A. C. McLaughlin, *The Confederation and the Constitution, 1783-1789* (1905). Standard work.

M. Jensen, *The New Nation* (1950). Study of the Confederation, contains sharp criticism of the "chaos and patriots-to-the-rescue" interpretation.

E. P. Douglass, *Rebels and Democrats* (1955). A study of the democratic forces at work during the Revolution.

THE CONSTITUTIONAL CONVENTION

W. U. Solberg, *The Federal Convention and the Formation of the Union of the American States* (1958). Documentary account.

M. Farrand, *The Records of the Federal Convention of 1787,* 4 vols. (rev. ed., 1937).

A. T. Prescott, *Drafting the Federal Constitution* (1941). Rearrangement of the debates in the Constitutional Convention according to topics.

J. Elliot, *The Debates in the Several Conventions on the Adoption of the Federal Constitution* (1835-1846, 2nd ed., 5 vols.). Contains the debates in the state ratifying conventions.

* J. Jay, J. Madison, and A. Hamilton, *The Federalist* (1788-1789). Basic source material, classic exposition of Constitution.

C. A. Beard, *An Economic Interpretation of the Constitution of the United States* (1913). Caused a popular furor and has had a strong influence on historians and political scientists.

R. E. Brown, *Charles Beard and the Constitution: A Critical Analysis of "An Economic Interpretation of the Constitution"* (1956).

F. McDonald, *We the People: The Economic Origins of the Constitution* (1958). Examination of Beard's thesis; concludes that economic interpretation is inadequate.

B. F. Wright, *Consensus and Continuity, 1776-1787* (1958). Another criticism of Beard, with emphasis on consensus among the framers.

J. A. Smith, *The Spirit of American Government* (1911). Spirited statement of

thesis that the Constitution is the platform of an antidemocratic movement.

C. Warren, *The Making of the Constitution* (1937). Disputes the Beard thesis, contains day-by-day account of the activities of the delegates.

C. Van Doren, *The Great Rehearsal* (1948). Popularly written account of the Constitutional Convention.

W. W. Crosskey, *Politics and the Constitution,* 2 vols. (1953). Argument that framers intended to create a unitary system.

THE LIVING CONSTITUTION

C. H. Pritchett, *The American Constitution* (1959). General treatment of our constitutional system.

J. M. Smith and P. L. Murphy, eds., *Liberty and Justice; A Historical Record of American Constitutional Development* (1958). Collection of documents.

* E. S. Corwin, *The Constitution and What It Means Today,* 12th ed. (1958). Phrase-by-phrase explanation.

E. S. Corwin and J. W. Peltason, *Understanding the Constitution* (1958). More elementary phrase-by-phrase explanation.

C. B. Swisher, *The Growth of Constitutional Power in the United States* (1946). The Constitution as symbol, as limitation, and as grant of power.

A. N. Holcombe, *Our More Perfect Union* (1950). Defense of American constitutional principles as expounded by Madison and other Founding Fathers.

E. S. Corwin, ed., *The Constitution of the United States of America: Analysis and Interpretation* (revised and annotated, 1952). Senate Doc. 170, 82 Cong., 2 Sess., 1953.

L. B. Orfield, *Amending the Federal Constitution* (1942). Leading book on the subject.

C. E. Merriam, *The Written Constitution and the Unwritten Attitude* (1931). Emphasizes the impact of urbanism and political parties on constitutional system.

W. B. Munro, *The Makers of the Unwritten Constitution* (1930). Biographical essays on some of the persons who have shaped our constitutional tradition.

W. O. Douglas, *We the Judges* (1956). Comparison of Indian and American law with survey of American developments.

FEDERALISM

J. R. Schmidhauser, *The Supreme Court as Final Arbiter in Federal-State Relations, 1789-1957* (1958). Study of the Supreme Court as "umpire of the federal system."

J. J. Kilpatrick, *The Sovereign States* (1957). Presentation of states'-rights position.

A. Maass, ed., *Area and Power* (1959). Theoretical analysis of areal division of powers.

R. L. Roettinger, *The Supreme Court and State Police Power: A Study of Federalism* (1957).

A. W. Macmahon, ed., *Federalism: Mature and Emergent* (1955). Symposium dealing with federalism throughout the world.

J. P. Clark, *The Rise of a New Federalism* (1938). Pioneering discussion of the several varieties of federal-state cooperation.

G. C. S. Benson, *The New Centralization* (1941). Interpretation of the changing nature of federal-state relations.

Commission on Intergovernmental Relations, *A Report to the President for Transmittal to Congress* (1955). Recommendations, and survey of national-state relations with emphasis on financial aspects; generally known by name of its chairman as the "Kestnbaum Report."

————, *Reports of Study Committees*

(1955). Fifteen publications of reports of staff and subcommittees.

W. Anderson, *The Nation and the States, Rivals or Partners?* (1955). History and present status, by senior political scientist and member of Commission on Intergovernmental Relations.

L. D. White, *The States and the Nation* (1953). Another distinguished political scientist's interpretation with somewhat different emphasis from Anderson's.

V. V. Thursby, *Interstate Cooperation: A Study of the Interstate Compact* (1952).

R. H. Leach and R. S. Sugg, Jr., *The Administration of Interstate Compacts* (1959). Review of administrative machinery and case studies of several compacts.

House Committee on Governmental Operations, *Reports on Federal-State-Local Relations, Federal Grants-in-Aid,* 85 Cong., 2 Sess., 1958.

V. O. Key, Jr., *The Administration of Federal Grants to States* (1937). Administration of the grant system.

W. Anderson and W. D. Durfee, Jr., *Intergovernmental Fiscal Relations* (1956).

Council of State Governments, *Federal-State Relations,* Sen. Doc. No. 81, 81 Cong., 1 Sess., 1949. Report to the Hoover Commission.

J. W. Fesler, *Area and Administration* (1949). Lectures on problems arising from functional and regional administration.

PART THREE: CIVIL LIBERTIES AND CITIZENSHIP

FREEDOM OF RELIGION

U.S. Department of Health, Education and Welfare, *The State and the Non-Public School* (1958).

F. W. O'Brien, *Justice Reed and the First Amendment: The Religion Clauses* (1958).

A. W. Johnson and F. H. Yost, *Separation of Church and State in the United States* (rev. ed., 1948). Theory and development of American law.

J. M. O'Neill, *Religion and Education under the Constitution* (1949).

A. P. Stokes, *Church and State in the United States* (1950, 3 vols.). Encyclopedic source material.

C. Bay, *The Structure of Freedom* (1958). Concept of freedom in light of the behavioral sciences.

G. W. Spicer, *The Supreme Court and Fundamental Freedoms* (1959). Analysis of the Court as guardian of civil liberties.

M. R. Konvitz and C. Rossiter, eds., *Aspects of Liberty* (1959). Essays presented to R. E. Cushman on various aspects of civil liberty.

M. R. Konvitz, *Fundamental Liberties of a Free People* (1957). Discussion of religion, speech, press, and association.

R. Pound, *The Development of Constitutional Guarantees of Liberty* (1957).

Noted American legal scholar analyzes the circumstances giving rise to guarantees of liberty in England and America.

A. H. Kelly, ed., *Foundations of Freedom: in the American Constitution* (1958). Articles on problems of national security and constitutional liberties.

R. E. Cushman, *Civil Liberties in the United States* (1956). Summary of laws and court rulings.

T. I. Emerson and D. Haber, *Political and Civil Rights in the United States* (2 vols., 2 ed., 1958). Comprehensive collection of civil liberty materials.

L. Pfeffer, *The Liberties of an American* (1956). General discussion of Supreme Court cases dealing with civil liberties.

American Civil Liberties Union, *Annual Reports*. The state of civil liberties in the United States.

A. Meiklejohn, *Free Speech and Its Relation to Self-government* (1948). Attack on "clear and present danger doctrine" and defense of the absolute right of political speech.

* L. Hand, *The Bill of Rights* (1958). Famous judge's statement of need for judicial self-restraint in the area of civil liberties.

* W. O. Douglas, *The Right of the People* (1958). Defense of judicial activism with regard to civil liberties by a Supreme Court justice.

* J. S. Mill, *Essay on Liberty* (1859; many editions). Famous defense of free speech.

Z. Chafee, *Free Speech in the United States* (rev. ed., 1941). Most comprehensive study of restrictions on speech during and after World War I; discussion of dangers inherent in sedition laws.

J. R. Wiggins, *Freedom or Secrecy?* (1959). Attack on governmental secrecy by a newspaperman.

E. E. Smead, *Freedom of Speech by Radio and Television* (1959). Special problems of freedom in these areas.

W. Gellhorn, *Individual Freedom and Governmental Restraints* (1956). Recent governmental developments encroaching on freedom of the individual.

Commission on the Freedom of the Press, *A Free and Responsible Press* (1947). Critical report on media of mass communication, emphasizes dangers of irresponsible economic control.

H. Brucker, *Freedom of Information* (1949). Discussion of problems; dissent from some of criticisms and recommendations of Commission on the Freedom of the Press.

W. E. Hocking, *Freedom of the Press* (1947). By leading American philosopher.

W. L. Chenery, *Freedom of the Press* (1955). By an editor.

J. M. Smith, *Freedom's Fetters* (1956). Study of Alien and Sedition Laws.

R. A. Horn, *Groups and the Constitution* (1956). Constitutional rights of groups; their role in constitutional development.

S. L. Morrison, *Freedom in Contemporary Society* (1956). Discussion of political, economic, and academic freedom.

THE BATTLE AGAINST SUBVERSIVE CONDUCT AND SEDITIOUS SPEECH

Commission on Government Security, *Report* (1957). Study of the internal security program; popularly known as the "Wright Report."

H. M. Hyman, *To Try Men's Souls: Loyalty Tests in American History* (1959). Historical background.

J. H. Schoar, *Loyalty in America* (1957). Analysis of the concept of loyalty.

R. S. Brown, *Loyalty and Security; Employment Tests in the United States* (1958). Critical study of loyalty and security programs.

S. Hook, *Political Power and Personal Freedom: Critical Studies in Democracy, Communism, and Civil Rights* (1959).

S. H. Stouffer, *Communism, Conformity and Civil Liberties* (1955). Survey of American attitudes.

H. D. Lasswell, *National Security and Individual Freedom* (1950). Pressures created by cold war, with recommendations.

H. W. Chase, *Security and Liberty* (1955). Legislative and judicial handling of native communists, 1947-1955.

W. Gellhorn, *The States and Subversion* (1952). Symposium dealing with activities of six states.

M. Grodzins, *The Loyal and the Disloyal* (1956). Discussion of factors that make men loyal.

E. Bontecou, *The Federal Loyalty-Security Program* (1953). Coverage through 1952.

W. Gellhorn, *Security, Loyalty, and Science* (1950). Critical discussion of important phase of security program.

J. L. O'Brian, *National Security and Individual Freedom* (1955). Critical evaluation of our security programs.

T. I. Cook, *Democratic Rights versus Communist Activity* (1954). Defends view that it is consistent with democratic principles and practices to make communist political activity illegal.

Subcommittee on Constitutional Rights of Senate Judiciary Committee, *Hearings, Security and Constitutional Rights,* 84 Cong., 2 Sess., 1955. Testimony of officials who administer programs and of witnesses critical of the programs.

Senate Judiciary Committee, *The Communist Party of the United States,* 84 Cong., 2 Sess., Senate Doc. No. 117, 1956. "A Handbook on Operations of Communist Party."

J. E. Hoover, *Masters of Deceit: The Story of Communism in America and How to Fight It* (1958). By the Director of the FBI.

————, *Subversive Influence in the Educational Process,* Report, 82 Cong., 1 Sess., Jan. 2, 1953 (Committee print).

A. Yarmolinsky, *Case Studies in Personnel Security* (1955). Series of security-loyalty cases.

Association of the Bar of the City of New York, Special Committee on Federal Loyalty-Security Program, *The Federal Loyalty-Security Program* (1956). Critical report by this influential body.

EQUALITY UNDER THE LAW

C. Vann Woodward, *The Strange Career of Jim Crow* (1955). Account of the growth of segregation laws.

Southern School News. Periodic reports on desegregation in public schools.

Race Relations Law Reporter. Periodic presentation of court cases, legislation, orders, regulations.

M. M. Tumin and Others, *Desegregation: Resistance and Readiness* (1958). Study of attitudes toward the Negro and desegregation.

A. P. Blaustein and C. C. Ferguson, Jr., *Desegregation and the Law* (1957). Legal aspects of desegregation.

D. Shoemaker and others, *With All Deliberate Speed* (1957). Journalist's report on progress of school integration or lack of it to date.

V. T. Blossom, *It Has Happened Here* (1959). Former Superintendent of Little Rock schools discusses explosive situation there.

H. S. Ashmore, *Epitaph for Dixie* (1958). Presentation of the "middle ground" in the race controversy.

B. Hays, *A Southern Moderate Speaks* (1959). Discussion of the race issue by former congressman from the Little Rock area.

A. S. Miller, *Racial Discrimination and Private Education: A Legal Analysis* (1957).

P. McCauley and E. D. Ball, eds., *Southern Schools: Progress and Problems* (1959).

W. Peters, *The Southern Temper* (1959). The progress of desegregation.

C. E. Vose, *Caucasians Only* (1959). Comprehensive discussion of Supreme Court's decisions on restrictive covenants.

C. Abrams, *Forbidden Neighbors: A Study of Prejudice in Housing* (1955).

U.S. President's Committee on Civil Rights, *To Secure These Rights* (1947).

U.S. Commission on Civil Rights, *Report* (1959). Findings and recommendations of Commission created by the Civil Rights Act of 1957.

M. R. Konvitz, *The Constitution and Civil Rights* (1947). Study of civil rights in employment and accommodation in public places.

R. L. Hale, *Freedom through Law* (1952). Public control of private power.

M. R. Konvitz, ed., *Law and Social Action* (1951). Essays on infringement of civil rights by private groups.

M. Berger, *Equality by Statute* (1952). Review of case law and analysis of work of the New York Commission against Discrimination, set in a broad social science framework.

J. ten Broek and others, *Prejudice, War, and the Constitution* (1954). Origins, politics, and legality of Japanese–American evacuations in World War II.

M. Grodzins, *Americans Betrayed: Politics and the Japanese Evacuation* (1949). Treats what many considered a violation of civil liberties during World War II.

RIGHTS TO LIFE, LIBERTY, AND PROPERTY

E. S. Corwin, *Liberty against Government* (1948). Essays on the growth and decline of substantive due process.

B. F. Wright, *The Contract Clause of the Constitution* (1938). Standard source.

D. Fellman, *The Defendant's Rights* (1958). Survey of cases and decisions on the rights of the accused from arrest to imprisonment.

H. Mannheim, *Criminal Justice and Social Reconstruction* (1946). Survey of recent developments, suggestions for practical reform.

J. Frank, *Courts on Trial* (1950). By a late federal circuit judge, criticism of court procedures, especially jury trials.

F. H. Heller, *The Sixth Amendment* (1951). Origin and contemporary application of procedural guarantees of this amendment.

W. M. Beaney, *Right to Counsel in American Courts* (1955). Survey of law and decisions.

E. N. Griswold, *The Fifth Amendment Today* (1955). Dean of the Harvard Law School writes about self-incrimination clause.

R. E. Edwards, *The Fourteenth Amendment and Civil Liberty* (1955). Pamphlet describing application of some civil rights as restrictions on states via Fourteenth Amendment.

IMMIGRATION AND CITIZENSHIP

E. P. Hutchinson, *Immigrants and Their Children, 1850-1950* (1956). Demographic study of the foreign-born in our population.

O. Handlin, *The Uprooted* (1952). Moving history of immigration from the perspective of the immigrants.

———, *Race and Nationality in American Life* (1957).

R. A. Diving, *American Immigration Policy, 1924-1952* (1957).

E. Lowenstein, *The Alien and Migration Law* (1958).

President's Commission on Immigration and Naturalization, *Whom Shall We Welcome* (1952). Report of commission appointed by President Truman, critical of Immigration and Nationality Act of 1952.

M. R. Konvitz, *Civil Rights in Immigration* (1953). Critical study of legislation relating to admission, exclusion, deportation, and naturalization of immigrants.

PART FOUR: THE PEOPLE IN POLITICS

VOTING AND VOTING BEHAVIOR

H. F. Gosnell, *Democracy, the Threshold of Freedom* (1948). Contains discussion of several theories of citizenship, and of the theoretical premises of the right to vote.

K. H. Porter, *A History of Suffrage in the United States* (1918). Single-volume history.

D. O. McGovney, *American Suffrage Medley* (1949). Survey of voting requirements; argument for constitutional amendment to secure national suffrage standards.

J. Higham, *Strangers in the Land* (1955). Antiforeignism in the United States.

R. E. Lane, *Political Life: How People Get Involved in Politics* (1958).

E. Burdick and A. J. Bradbeck, eds., *American Voting Behavior* (1956). Collection of essays.

S. M. Lipset and others, "The Psychology of Voting: An Analysis of Political Behavior," in G. Lindzey, ed., *Handbook of Social Psychology*, II (1954). Survey of data.

A. Kornhauser, A. J. Mayer, and H. L. Sheppard, *When Labor Votes: A Study of Auto Workers* (1956). Detroit auto workers in the 1952 presidential election.

L. Fuchs, *The Political Behavior of American Jews* (1956).

A. Campbell, G. Gurin, and W. E. Miller, *The Voter Decides* (1954). Study of the 1952 election based on data gathered by sampling.

A. Campbell and H. C. Cooper, *Group Differences in Attitudes and Votes* (1956). Study of the 1954 election based on a nationwide survey.

C. E. Merriam and H. F. Gosnell, *Non-voting* (1924). Pioneering study.

G. M. Connelly and H. H. Field, "The Non-Voter—Who He Is, What He Thinks," *Public Opinion Quarterly* (1944). Two excellent articles.

S. Lubell, *The Future of American Politics* (1951). Basic party and voting trends, interestingly presented.

———, *The Revolt of the Moderates* (1956). A more recent study by one who has spent much time talking with all kinds of voters in all kinds of places.

L. Harris, *Is There a Republican Majority?* (1954). Study of 1952 election by associate in the Roper polling organization.

J. K. Pollock, *Voting Behavior, a Case Study* (1939). Data drawn from Ann Arbor, Michigan.

D. Anderson and P. E. Davidson, *Ballots and the Democratic Class Struggle* (1943). Class and voting behavior.

L. H. Bean, *How to Predict Elections* (1948). Demonstration of use of statistics to project election trends and to study voting behavior.

P. F. Lazarsfeld, B. Berelson, and H. Gaudet, *The People's Choice* (1948). Demonstrates the technique of panel interviewing on "How the Voter Makes Up His Mind in a Presidential Campaign."

B. R. Berelson, P. F. Lazarsfeld, and W. N. McPhee, *Voting* (1954). 1948 voting in a New York community, with useful summary of findings of other voting studies.

H. L. Moon, *Balance of Power* (1948). The Negroes' use of political power.

* V. O. Key, Jr., *Southern Politics in State and Nation* (1949). The impact of the "Negro problem" on southern politics.

E. L. Tatum, *The Changed Political Thought of the Negro, 1915-1940* (1952). Causes and consequences of changing political allegiances of Negroes.

H. J. Abraham, *Compulsory Voting* (1955). An evaluation.

H. M. Bain and D. S. Hecock, *Ballot Position and Voter's Choice* (1957). Effect of candidate's position on the ballot on voting behavior.

INTEREST GROUPS

H. W. Ehrmann, *Interest Groups on Four Continents* (1958). Discussions of interest groups in several countries, including the United States.

D. C. Blaisdell, ed., "Unofficial Government, Pressure Groups and Lobbies," *The Annals,* September, 1958.

W. McCune, *Who's Behind Our Farm Policy* (1957). The politics of farm programs.

C. A. Beard, *The Economic Basis of Politics* (1922). The importance of economic interests in the political process.

Select Committee on Lobbying Activities of the House, *Hearings,* 81 Cong., 2 Sess., 1950. Important congressional investigation; materials on some major organizations.

———, *General Interim Report,* House Report 3138; Report and Recommendations on Federal Lobbying Act, House Report 3239, 81 Cong., 2 Sess., 1950. Recommendations for national legislation to control lobbyists more effectively.

D. C. Blaisdell, *Economic Power and Political Pressures* (1941). TNEC Monograph 26. Pioneering study.

S. Chase, *Democracy under Pressure* (1945). Critical analysis of the role of interest groups.

P. H. Odegard, *Pressure Politics: The Study of the Anti-saloon League* (1928). Standard source.

Senate Committee on Education and Labor, *Report No. 6,* 76 Cong., 1 Sess., 1939. Materials on the NAM and other employer associations.

E. Gruening, *The Public Pays* (1931). Critical study of propaganda activities of the electric power industry.

Federal Trade Commission, *Summary Report ... on Efforts by Associations ... of Electric and Gas Utilities to Influence Public Opinion,* Senate Doc. 92, 70 Cong., 1 Sess., 1934. Efforts of industry to defeat Public Utility Holding Company Act.

J. Gaer, *The First Round: The Story of the C.I.O. Political Action Committee* (1944). Contains facsimile examples of CIO pamphlets.

F. Calkins, *The C.I.O. and the Democratic Party* (1952). Five case studies in 1950 elections by research assistant of CIO-PAC.

O. M. Kile, *The Farm Bureau through Three Decades* (1948). The official history.

R. Baker, *The American Legion and American Foreign Policy* (1954). Recent analysis.

J. Gray and V. H. Bernstein, *The Inside Story of the Legion* (1948). Critical of the American Legion.

R. S. Jones, *A History of the American Legion* (1946). The official history.

D. Wecter, *When Johnny Comes Marching Home* (1944). Study of return of soldiers after Revolutionary, Civil, and First World wars.

O. Garceau, *The Political Life of the American Medical Association* (1941). Pioneering study of the political activities of America's doctors.

M. L. Rutherford, *The Influence of the American Bar Association on Public Opinion and Legislation* (1937). Story of politically active professions.

B. R. Twiss, *Lawyers and the Constitution* (1942). "How laissez faire came to the Supreme Court."

L. C. Kesselman, *The Social Politics of FEPC* (1948). "A Study in Reform Pressure Movements."

L. E. Ebersole, *Church Lobbying in the Nation's Capital* (1951). The religious lobbies—the causes for which they work, and the methods they use.

D. D. McKean, *Pressures on the Legislature of New Jersey* (1938). By a political scientist and former member of New Jersey legislature.

B. Zeller, *Pressure Politics in New York* (1937).

E. P. Herring, *Group Representation before Congress* (1929). Relations between interest groups and formal institutions of government.

E. E. Schattschneider, *Politics, Pressures, and the Tariff* (1935). Case study based on mass of evidence from hearings on the Smoot-Hawley tariff bill.

E. Latham, *The Group Basis of Politics* (1952). Interplay of group pressures in basing-point legislation.

F. W. Riggs, *Pressures on Congress: A Study of the Repeal of Chinese Exclusion* (1950). Informing case study.

E. P. Herring, *Public Administration and the Public Interest* (1936). Interaction between interest groups and administrative machinery.

J. Frank, *If Men Were Angels* (1942). Social, economic, and psychological factors in the working of administrative agencies.

A. Leiserson, *Administrative Regulation* (1942). Analysis of interest groups and regulatory agencies.

A. Maass, *Muddy Waters* (1951). Indictment of the Army Corps of Engineers as "The Lobby That Can't Be Licked."

PUBLIC OPINION

Two journals of special interest are: *International Journal of Opinion and Attitude Research* and *Public Opinion Quarterly.*

A. C. Dicey, *Law and Public Opinion in England* (1905).

G. Wallas, *Human Nature in Politics* (1919; first published in 1908). Marked a reaction from earlier over-rationalistic interpretations of politics and public opinion.

A. L. Lowell, *Public Opinion and Popular Government* (1913).

* W. Lippmann, *Public Opinion* (1922).

J. Dewey, *The Public and Its Problems* (1927).

A. O. Hero, *Opinion Leaders in American Communities* (1959). Effect of primary group communications on opinions.

S. Kelley, Jr., *Professional Public Relations and Political Power* (1956). Role of "Madison Avenue" in American politics.

B. Berelson and M. Janowitz, eds., *Reader in Public Opinion and Communication* (1951). Readings on all major phases of subject.

M. B. Smith, J. S. Bruner, and R. W. White, *Opinions and Personality* (1956).

PUBLIC OPINION POLLS

F. F. Stephan and P. J. McCarthy, *Sampling Opinions: An Analysis of Survey Procedure* (1958).

M. B. Parten, *Surveys, Polls, and Samples* (1950). Description of polling procedures.

F. Mosteller and others, *The Pre-Election Polls of 1948* (1949). Essays by experts who investigated the reasons for the 1948 polling fiasco.

L. Rogers, *The Pollsters* (1949). Criticism of procedures, and attack upon contribution of public opinion polls.

H. Cantril, ed., *Public Opinion: Directory of Polls, 1935-1946* (1951). Comprehensive collection of poll data.

MEDIA OF COMMUNICATION

S. D. Cater, *The Fourth Branch of Government* (1959). Critical evaluation of the relations of the press with the national government.

A. E. Rowse, *Slanted News: A Case Study of the Nixon and Stevenson Fund Stories* (1957).

A. O. Hero, *Mass Media and World Affairs* (1959). Study of mass media's influence on opinions toward foreign affairs.

P. F. Lazarsfeld, *Radio and the Printed Page* (1940). Role of radio described by outstanding authorities.

W. Schramm, *Mass Communications* (1949). Readings.

Z. Chafee, *Government and Mass Communications* (1947). Published under auspices of the Commission on Freedom of the Press.

F. L. Mott, *American Journalism* (1941). Standard history.

W. Lippmann, *Liberty and the News* (1920). Critical essay by one of America's famous journalists.

C. A. H. Thomson, *Television and Presidential Politics* (1956).

L. C. Ferguson and R. H. Smuckler, *Politics in the Press: An Analysis of Press Content in 1952 Senatorial Campaigns* (1954).

C. A. Siepmann, *Radio, Television and Society* (1950). Analysis of the problems of the role of radio and television in a free society.

L. White, *The American Radio* (1947). Comprehensive study that formed one of the reports of the Commission on Freedom of the Press.

L. C. Rosten, *Hollywood* (1941). Interpretation of social and political pressures.

R. A. Inglis, *Freedom of the Movies* (1947). Under the auspices of the Commission on Freedom of the Press.

POLITICAL PARTIES

* H. D. Lasswell, *Politics: Who Gets What, When, How* (1946; reissued in 1958). One of Lasswell's more popular treatments.

Eagleton Foundation, *Case Studies in Practical Politics*. Continuing series of studies of concrete political situations.

R. Michels, *Political Parties* (reprinted in 1949). Important sociological study of the oligarchical tendencies of European democratic political parties.

M. Ostrogorski, *Democracy and the Organization of Political Parties*, 2 vols. (1908). Early, classic interpretation of development of parties in the United States and England.

N. E. Cunningham, *The Jeffersonian Republicans: The Foundation of Party Organization, 1789-1801* (1957).

W. E. Binkley, *American Political Parties, Their Natural History*, 3rd ed. (1958). Stresses role of parties as coalitions of interest groups.

* F. J. Turner, *The Significance of Sections in American History* (1937). The importance of sectionalism in American politics was first projected by Turner at the beginning of the twentieth century.

A. N. Holcombe, *The Political Parties of Today* (1924), *The New Party Politics* (1933), *The Middle Classes in American Politics* (1940). Interpretation of American politics as moving from sectional to urban or "class" politics with the middle class holding the balance and preserving free government.

E. E. Schattschneider, *Party Government* (1942), *The Struggle for Party Government* (1948). Case for more centralized and disciplined parties by an outstanding scholar who has virtually developed a "school of thought" about American politics.

Committee on Political Parties of the American Political Science Association, *Toward a More Responsible Two Party System* (1950). By committee of 16 authorities under chairmanship of Professor Schattschneider; recommendations for strengthening the American party system.

E. P. Herring, *The Politics of Democracy* (1940). Interpretation and defense of present system; interpretations somewhat contrary to those of Schattschneider and the committee report mentioned above.

H. Agar, *The Price of Union* (1950). History stressing the thesis that loosely organized and undisciplined parties are essential to the preservation of the Union.

A. Ranney and W. Kendall, *The American Party System* (1956). Examination of American parties as instruments of democratic government; defense of existing party system.

A. Leiserson, *Parties and Politics, An Institutional and Behavioral Approach* (1958).

S. Neumann, ed., *Modern Political Parties* (1956). Discussions of the party systems in several nations, including the United States.

J. M. Redding, *Inside the Democratic Party* (1958). Lively account of the 1948 campaign by former publicity director of the Democratic National Committee.

D. Acheson, *A Democrat Looks at His Party* (1955). By a former Secretary of State.

H. S. Merrill, *Bourbon Leader: Grover Cleveland and the Democratic Party* (1957).

R. V. Remini, *Martin Van Buren and the Making of the Democratic Party* (1959).

A. Larson, *A Republican Looks At His Party* (1956). Member of the "liberal" wing of the Republican Party.

H. P. Nash, Jr., *Third Parties in American Politics* (1958). Their role and history.

M. Stedman and S. Stedman, *Discontent at the Polls* (1950). Incisive account of legal, political, and other aspects of third parties.

R. L. Morlan, *Political Prairie Fire: The Non-Partisan League, 1915-1922* (1958).

H. A. Bone, *Party Committees and National Politics* (1958). Study of national party organization, including Senate and House campaign committees.

K. A. Porter and D. B. Johnson, *National Party Platforms, 1940-1956* (1956).

LEADERSHIP

R. G. Tugwell, *The Art of Politics* (1958). Studies of three politicians: F. D. Roosevelt, La Guardia, and Luis Morin.

* A. M. Schlesinger, Jr., *The Age of Roosevelt:* Vol. I., *The Crisis of the Old Order* (1958); Vol. II., *The Coming of the New Deal* (1959). Studies by leading historian.

R. H. Rovere, *Senator Joe McCarthy* (1959). Critical biography of the late senator.

J. M. Burns, *Roosevelt: The Lion and the Fox* (1956). Problems and practices of FDR as a democratic leader.

E. Roper, *You and Your Leaders: Their Actions and Your Reactions, 1936-1956* (1957). Study of nine recent American political leaders and the public attitudes toward them; by a leading American pollster.

H. Lasswell, *Psychopathology and Politics* (1930), and *Power and Personality* (1948). Through use of interviews, observations, and psychological techniques Lasswell has developed a typology of political leaders and related their public careers to their psychological characteristics.

H. H. Gerth and C. W. Mills, tr. and ed., *From Max Weber: Essays in Sociology* (1946). Essays by famous German sociologist, pioneering student of leadership.

W. F. Whyte, *Street Corner Society* (1943). Close study of informal leadership.

A. W. Gouldner, ed., *Studies in Leadership* (1950). Essays on apathy and various kinds of leadership.

ELECTIONS

F. D. Ogden, *The Poll Tax in the South* (1958). Its history and present status.

C. A. M. Ewing, *Primary Elections in the South* (1953). Statistical study.

C. E. Merriam and L. Overacker, *Primary Elections* (1928). Standard source.

J. B. Johnson, *Registration for Voting in the United States,* rev. ed. (1946). Survey of methods used.

R. M. Scammon, *America Votes,* 3 vols. (1956, 1958, and 1960). Most compre-

hensive collection of recent election statistics, to be kept up to date with additional volumes every two years.

L. Wilmerding, *The Electoral College* (1958). Critical analysis of its operation and of proposals for change.

Subcommitee of the Senate Committee on the Judiciary, *Hearings, Nomination and Election of President and Vice-President*, 84 Cong., 1 Sess. Testimony on several proposals to alter electoral college.

P. T. David and others, *Presidential Nominating Politics in 1952* (1954). Five-vol.

report undertaken by over 150 political scientists.

R. V. Peel and T. C. Donnelly, *The 1928 Campaign* (1931), *The 1932 Campaign* (1935). Accounts of two campaigns from nomination to election.

J. B. Shannon, *Money and Politics* (1959). American and Norwegian experience.

A. Heard, *Money and Politics* (1956). Study of campaign finance.

M. Moos, *Politics, Presidents, and Coattails* (1953). Study of congressional elections, emphasizing interaction of presidential and congressional elections.

PART FIVE: POLICY-MAKERS FOR THE PEOPLE

THE LEGISLATIVE PROCESS

J. C. Wahlke and H. Eulau, eds., *Legislative Behavior: A Reader in Theory and Research* (1959). Studies of several aspects of legislative behavior.

T. V. Smith, *The Legislative Way of Life* (1940). Defense of the legislature by an ex-congressman, ex-state legislator, philosopher, and political scientist.

H. F. Gosnell, *Democracy, the Threshold of Freedom* (1948). Contains discussion of the functions of representatives and representative assemblies.

A. de Grazia, *Public and Republic* (1951). History of who represents what and how.

CONGRESS

* W. Wilson, *Congressional Government* (1885). Classic interpretation.

F. M. Riddick, *The United States Congress* (1949). Authoritative discussion of organizational and procedural aspects.

D. B. Truman, *The Congressional Party: A Case Study* (1959). The party system in Congress, analyzed through studies of roll calls.

R. A. Young, *The American Congress* (1958). Discussion of the functions of Congress and how it performs them; with a guide to future research.

———, *Congressional Politics in the Second World War* (1956). Analysis of congressional behavior reflecting the pattern of politics during the war years.

E. S. Griffith, *Congress: Its Contemporary Role* (1951). Favorable assessment of

operation of Congress, by Director of its Legislative Reference Service.

D. Acheson, *A Citizen Looks at Congress* (1957). Former Secretary of State reviews problems and weaknesses.

J. Burnham, *Congress and the American Tradition* (1959). Congress viewed as losing its rightful authority.

G. B. Galloway, *The Legislative Process in Congress* (1953). Organization, procedures, and problems by political scientist who played leading role in reorganization of Congress in 1946; sequel to his earlier *Congress at the Crossroads*.

Joint Committee on Organization of the Congress, *Organization of Congress,* Senate Report 1011, 79 Cong., 2 Sess., 1946. Favorable report on Reorganization Act.

T. L. McDonald, *The Wagner Housing Act: A Case Study of the Legislative Process* (1957).

M. E. Ridgeway, *The Missouri Basin's Pick-Sloan Plan* (1955). "A Case Study in Congressional Policy Determination."

L. H. Chamberlain, *The President, Congress, and Legislation* (1946). Study of roles of the President and Congress in lawmaking; a different view is given in the following book.

J. M. Burns, *Congress on Trial* (1949). Description of the politics of lawmaking; presentation of view that the fundamental defect arises from the nature of the party system.

S. K. Bailey, *Congress Makes a Law* (1950). Detailed account of the enactment of the Employment Act of 1946 and analysis of the forces interacting in, on, and through Congress.

S. K. Bailey and H. Samuel, *Congress at Work* (1952). Series of brief case studies exploring all aspects of Congress at work.

* B. M. Gross, *The Legislative Struggle* (1953). Probing analysis of Congress as the battleground of interest struggles.

H. B. Westerfield, *Foreign Policy and Party Politics* (1955). Congressional voting and role of parties.

G. L. Grassmuck, *Sectional Biases in Congress on Foreign Policy* (1951). Statistical study of congressional behavior.

R. A. Dahl, *Congress and Foreign Policy* (1950). Evaluation of Congress' role in the making of foreign policy; suggestions for improving its functioning.

J. Turner, *Party and Constituency* (1952). Measurement of relative impact of parties and constituencies upon congressional voting behavior.

W. S. White, *Citadel: The Story of the United States Senate* (1956). Readable account of the Senate with emphasis on the "unwritten rules."

G. H. Haynes, *The Senate of the United States,* 2 vols. (1938).

F. L. Burdette, *Filibustering in the Senate* (1940). Standard source.

R. J. Dangerfield, *In Defense of the Senate: A Study in Treaty-Making* (1933). Evidence that Senate's obstruction is less serious than usually thought.

K. Colegrove, *The American Senate and World Peace* (1944). Criticism of two-thirds treaty requirement.

J. P. Harris, *The Advice and Consent of the Senate* (1953). "A Study of the Confirmation of Appointments by the United States Senate."

A. Drury, *Advise and Consent* (1959). Novel dealing with the same subject.

COMMITTEES

E. E. Dennison, *The Senate Foreign Relations Committee* (1942).

A. C. F. Westphal, *The House Committee on Foreign Affairs* (1942).

G. Y. Steiner, *The Congressional Conference Committee: Seventieth to Eightieth Congress* (1951). Case study of the operations of this important committee.

Congressional investigations are covered in:

M. N. McGeary, *The Development of Congressional Investigative Power* (1940).

R. K. Carr, *The House Un-American Activities Committee* (1952). Balanced discussion.

T. Taylor, *Grand Inquest* (1955). Critical study of congressional investigations.

A. Barth, *Government by Investigation* (1955). Critical.

THE PRESIDENT

W. Binkley, *The Man in the White House* (1959). The growth of the Presidency and the many facets of the office.

* C. Rossiter, *The American Presidency* (1956). Analysis of the growth and uses of the Presidency.

G. A. Schubert, Jr., *The Presidency in the Courts* (1957). Study of the Supreme Court's interpretation of the office and powers.

E. S. Corwin, *The President: Office and Powers,* rev. ed. (1948). Comprehensive discussion of the historical and constitutional development.

——— and L. W. Koenig, *The Presidency Today* (1956).

S. Hyman, *The American President* (1954). Interpretive study.

H. J. Laski, *The American Presidency* (1940). Dynamics of the Presidency by famous British political scientist.

P. Herring, *Presidential Leadership* (1940). Analysis of the interrelations among the President, party, and Congress; defense of the presidential system.

M. W. Childs, *Eisenhower—Captive Hero: A Critical Study of the General and the President* (1958). Readable biographical account of the man and his administration.

R. J. Donovan, *The Inside Story* (1956). Taken from notes on the Eisenhower Cabinet meetings; gives picture of this and other aspects of the Eisenhower Administration.

J. Hart, *The American Presidency in Action, 1789* (1948). Study of the formative years.

L. D. White, *The Federalists* (1948), *The Jeffersonians* (1951), *The Jacksonians* (1955), and *The Republican Era, 1869-*

1901 (1958). Cover the early years and emphasize the administrative organization of the Executive.

W. Wilson, *Constitutional Government in the United States* (reprinted 1921). Written before he became President; indicates Wilson's concept of the role and responsibility of the office.

W. H. Taft, *Our Chief Magistrate and His Powers* (1916). Presents a much more limited concept of the Presidency.

C. L. Rossiter, *The Supreme Court and the Commander in Chief* (1951). How the Supreme Court has interpreted the President's status and authority as commander in chief.

L. W. Koenig, *The Presidency and the Crisis* (1944). Scope of presidential emergency powers.

I. G. Williams, *The Rise of the Vice-Presidency* (1956). History and role.

E. W. Wough, *Second Consul: The Vice Presidency—Our Greatest Political Problem* (1956). History and analysis of the office.

L. C. Hatch, *A History of the Vice-Presidency of the United States* (1934). Standard source.

R. C. Silva, *Presidential Succession* (1951). Study of "history, interpretation, statutory development, and practical application of the provisions ... for presidential succession."

PRESIDENT AS ADMINISTRATOR

R. F. Fenno, Jr., *The President's Cabinet* (1959). Analysis of cabinets from Wilson to Eisenhower.

E. H. Hobbs, *Behind the President* (1954). Study of the agencies working directly under the President.

The President's Committee on Administrative Management, *Reports ... with Studies of Administrative Management in the Federal Government* (1937). Influential studies; primary source for understanding the problems of "high-level" governmental administration.

The Commission on the Organization of the Executive Branch of the Government, *General Management of the Executive Branch;* and *Concluding Report* (1949 and 1955). Attempt to strengthen Presidency as central agency of administration.

H. M. Somers, *Presidential Agency: OWMR* (1950). Problems of coordinating administrative agencies; suggestions for strengthening the Presidency.

PUBLIC ADMINISTRATION

W. Wilson, "The Study of Administration," *Political Science Quarterly,* June 1887. Classic essay marking the beginning of the modern study of administration.

F. J. Goodnow, *Politics and Administration* (1900). Another pioneering volume; attempt to isolate administration from politics as separate branch of study.

These works of the early pioneers contrast with those of modern writers mentioned below. The early students tended to divide policy and administration into separable categories.

* C. S. Hyneman, *Bureaucracy in a Democracy* (1950). Study of the control and role of the bureaucracy with special attention to the question of legislative and executive responsibilities.

J. D. Millett, *Government and Public Administration: The Quest for Responsible Performance* (1959). The control of bureaucracy.

C. N. Parkinson, *Parkinson's Law* (1957). The "laws" of bureaucratic expansion.

J. G. March and H. A. Simon, *Organizations* (1958). Study of the theory of organizations.

P. Selznick, *Leadership in Administration: A Sociological Interpretation* (1957). Study of leadership in administrative organizations.

J. Ahmad, *The Expert and the Administrator* (1959). Roles and problems of the specialist in administrative organizations.

F. M. Marx, *The Administrative State* (1957). Comparative study of bureaucracy.

E. S. Redford, *Public Administration and Policy Formation* (1956). "Studies in Oil, Gas, Banking, River Development, and Corporate Investigation."

* P. H. Appleby, *Policy and Administration* (1949). Interpretations of the dynamic aspects of administration; the interrelations between policy and administration.

———, *Morality and Administration in Democratic Government* (1952). How to promote "public interest" against demands of "special interests."

H. A. Simon, *Administrative Behavior* (1950). "A Study of Decision-Making Processes in Administrative Organization."

P. M. Blau, *The Dynamics of Bureaucracy* (1955). Interpersonal relationships of civil servants.

D. Waldo, *The Administrative State* (1948). The theory of American public administration; survey of the various "schools" of thought.

R. K. Merton and others, *Reader in Bureaucracy* (1951). Collection of articles by authorities in sociology and political science.

FEDERAL ADMINISTRATIVE STRUCTURE

O. Kraines, *Congress and the Challenge of Big Government* (1958). History of the first congressional investigation into administrative structure and organization.

General Services Administration, *United States Government Organization Manual,* published annually. Contains descriptions of legislative, judicial, and executive branches—their organization and functions, organization charts of the major agencies, select lists of government publications, and other information.

L. M. Short, *The Development of National Administrative Organization in the United States* (1923). Standard history.

S. C. Wallace, *Federal Departmentalization* (1941). Critical analysis of the theories of federal departmentalization.

W. S. Sayre, ed., *The Federal Government Service: Its Character, Prestige, and Problems* (1955). An American Assembly Symposium.

In addition to the Reports and Studies of the Committee on Administrative Management, other reorganization literature includes:

L. Meriam and L. K. Schmeckebier, *Reorganization of the National Government* (1939). Critical discussion of the Reports of the President's Committee on Administrative Management.

Commission on Organization of the Executive Branch of the Government (the Hoover Commission), *Reports and Task*

Force Reports (1949 and 1954). Especially those on personnel and civil service.

B. D. Nash and C. Lynde, *A Hook in Leviathan* (1950). Work of the Hoover Commission.

L. W. Koenig, ed., "The Hoover Commission: A Symposium," *American Political Science Review,* October 1949. Critical review.

H. Emmerich, *Essays on Federal Reorganization* (1950). Discussion of reorganization, stressing it as a continuous process.

REGULATORY ADMINISTRATION

B. Schwartz, *The Professor and the Commissions* (1959). Story of congressional investigation of regulatory commissions and trials and tribulations of a former committee counsel.

E. Latham, *The Politics of Railroad Coordination, 1933-1936* (1959). Politics of railroad regulation during the first years of the New Deal.

E. Freund, *Administrative Powers over Persons and Property* (1928). Investigation that brought to light the extent to which "policy-power" had been conferred upon administrators.

J. M. Landis, *The Administrative Process* (1938). Insightful analysis.

R. E. Cushman, *The Independent Regulatory Commissions* (1941). General discussion of the independent regulatory commissions.

M. H. Bernstein, *Regulating Business by Independent Commissions* (1955). Critical study of politics of regulation.

PUBLIC PERSONNEL MANAGEMENT

P. Van Riper, *History of the United States Civil Service* (1959). History of public employment in the United States; emphasis on the period since the beginning of civil service reform.

H. E. Kaplov, *The Law of Civil Service* (1958).

E. Ginzburg and J. K. Anderson, *Manpower for Government—A Decade Forecast* (1959). Sees the federal government in a poor competitive position unless public employment is made more attractive.

S. B. Sweeney, ed., *Education for Administrative Careers in Government Service*

(1958). Problems of training public administrators.

P. T. David and R. Pollock, *Executives in Government: Central Issues of Federal Personnel Administration* (1957). Problems of recruiting and keeping high-level personnel.

M. H. Bernstein, *The Job of the Federal Executive* (1958). Description of the work of top career and political executives; problems of keeping able men in government.

O. G. Stahl, *Public Personnel Administration,* 4th ed. (1956). General discussion.

W. S. Carpenter, *The Unfinished Business of Civil Service Reform* (1952). Discussion of failure "to reconcile the merit system with a method of positive administrative control by the responsible executive."

THE JUDGES

See also the titles listed under "The Living Constitution," p. 752.

* B. N. Cardozo, *The Nature of the Judicial Process* (1921). One of the American classics in legal theory.

J. Frank, *Law and the Modern Mind* (1930). Discussion of the various factors, especially psychological, that affect men, including judges.

F. Frankfurter, *Law and Politics* (1939). Articles, book reviews, occasional papers written before the author became a Justice.

S. P. Simpson and J. Stone, *Case and Readings on Law and Society* (1948). Selection of materials ranging from the Code of Hammurabi to United Nations Commission on Atomic Energy.

J. W. Peltason, *Federal Courts in the Political Process* (1955).

J. W. Hurst, *The Growth of American Law* (1950). Discussion of the role of legislatures, courts, constitution-makers, the Bar, and the executives in development of American law.

L. Mayers, *The American Legal System* (1955). Comprehensive description of legal machinery.

THE SUPREME COURT

J. P. Frank, *Marble Palace: The Supreme Court in American Life* (1958). Organization and work of the Court.

A. T. Mason, *The Supreme Court from Taft to Warren* (1958). Interpretative history.

C. B. Swisher, *The Supreme Court in Its Modern Role* (1958).

B. Schwartz, *The Supreme Court* (1957). Analysis of the work of the Court, especially since 1937.

G. G. Haines, *The Role of the Supreme Court in American Government and Politics, 1789-1835* (1944). Detailed history of the formative years.

T. R. Powell, *Vagaries and Varieties in Constitutional Interpretation* (1955). Survey of Supreme Court behavior in "deed and work."

W. Hurst, ed., *Supreme Court and Supreme Law* (1954). Symposium by distinguished scholars.

* C. P. Curtis, *Lions under the Throne* (1947). Interpretation of role of courts in the American system.

P. A. Freund, *On Understanding the Supreme Court* (1950). Interpretive lectures with comments on the Supreme Court and Supreme Court commentators.

O. J. Roberts, *The Court and the Constitution* (1951). Critical discussion of recent Court decisions by former member of the Court.

C. M. Ewing, *The Judges of the Supreme Court, 1789-1937* (1938). Information about the men who have served on the High Court.

C. H. Pritchett, *The Roosevelt Court* (1948). Survey of the Court from 1937 to 1947 with statistical charts on each Justice's "batting average" on particular issues.

————, *Civil Liberties and the Vinson Court* (1954). Continuation of earlier volume during period 1946-1953.

————, *The Political Offender and the Warren Court* (1959). Analysis of Warren Court reaction to anticommunist legislation.

Senate Committee on Judiciary, *Hearings, Reorganization of the Federal Judiciary,* 79 Cong., 2 Sess. (1937). Verbatim testimony of the many people who appeared for and against President Roosevelt's Court Plan.

J. Alsop and T. Catledge, *The 168 Days*

(1938). Account of the "Supreme Court Battle of 1937."

Senate Committee on the Judiciary, *Hearings* of Subcommittee to Investigate the Administration of the Internal Security Act and Other Internal Security Laws, 85 Cong., 1 and 2 Sess. (1957 and 1958). Hearings on the Jenner Bill, which would have curbed the power of the Supreme Court in security cases; rich source of data on public reactions to the Court's decisions.

V. G. Rosenblum, *Law as a Political Instrument* (1955). Exploration of the Supreme Court's policy-making role.

JUDICIAL REVIEW

E. McWhinney, *Judicial Review in the English-Speaking World* (1956). Comparative study.

A. F. Westin, *The Anatomy of a Constitutional Law Case* (1958). Case study of *Youngstown Sheet and Tube Co. v. Sawyer,* "The Steel Seizure Decision."

C. Warren, *The Supreme Court in United States History,* rev. ed., 2 vols. (1932). Standard history, sympathetic to the Court's use of judicial review.

H. J. Abraham, *Courts and Judges* (1959). "An Introduction to the Judicial Process."

C. G. Haines, *The American Doctrine of Judicial Supremacy,* 2nd ed. (1932). Balanced investigation of the role of the Supreme Court and its use of judicial review.

R. K. Carr, *The Supreme Court and Judicial Review* (1942). Among other things, discusses *Marbury* v. *Madison, McCullough* v. *Maryland.*

E. S. Corwin, *The Doctrine of Judicial Review* (1914). Essays including famous article on *Marbury* v. *Madison.*

———, *Court over Constitution,* 2nd ed. (1942). In terms of its subtitle, "A Study of Judicial Review as an Instrument of Government."

R. H. Jackson, *The Struggle for Judicial Supremacy* (1941). Critical discussion of Supreme Court, especially its activities during the New Deal period.

F. V. Cahill, Jr., *Judicial Legislation* (1952). Analytical survey of modern American jurisprudence, stressing the problem of right of the judiciary to

review acts of other levels of government.

JUDICIAL BIOGRAPHY

A. Dunham and P. B. Kurland, eds., *Mr. Justice* (1956). Essays on nine justices.

E. C. Gerhart, *America's Advocate: Robert H. Jackson* (1958).

M. D. Howe, *Justice Oliver Wendell Holmes: The Shaping Years, 1841-1870* (1957).

A. T. Mason, *Harlan Fiske Stone* (1956).

S. J. Konefsky, *The Legacy of Holmes and Brandeis* (1957). Study of the constitutional philosophy of two outstanding justices.

V. Countryman, *Douglas and the Supreme Court: A Selection of His Opinions* (1959). Contains a biographical sketch of Douglas.

A. J. Beveridge, *The Life of John Marshall,* 4 vols. (1916-1919). History; has become the prototype of judicial biography.

W. M. Jones, ed., *Chief Justice John Marshall: A Reappraisal* (1956). Symposium on the occasion of Marshall's bicentennial.

C. P. Smith, *James Wilson, Founding Father* (1956).

D. G. Morgan, *Justice William Johnson: The First Dissenter* (1954).

C. B. Swisher, *Roger B. Taney* (1935).

C. Fairman, *Mr. Justice Miller and the Supreme Court* (1939). Contains account of the Court's work and Reconstruction politics during the critical years, 1860-1890.

C. B. Swisher, *Stephen J. Field, Craftsman of the Law* (1930). Biography of a Justice who had much to do with the development of substantive due process.

W. L. King, *Melville Weston Fuller, Chief Justice of the United States* (1950). Study of a moderately able Justice and outstanding Chief Justice; informative on the internal working of the Court.

Max Lerner, ed., *The Mind and Faith of Justice Holmes* (1943). Collection of Justice Holmes' speeches, essays, letters, and judicial opinions, with introduction and notes by the editor.

A. T. Mason, *Brandeis: A Free Man's Life* (1946).

S. Hendel, *Charles Evans Hughes and the Supreme Court* (1951).

M. J. Pusey, *Charles Evans Hughes,* 2 vols. (1951). Biography.

H. F. Pringle, *The Life and Times of William Howard Taft,* 2 vols. (1939). Biography of former President and Chief Justice.

F. J. Paschal, *Mr. Justice Sutherland* (1951).

G. S. Hellman, *Benjamin N. Cardozo* (1940).

S. J. Konefsky, *The Constitutional World of Mr. Justice Frankfurter* (1949). Collection of opinions with introductory notes by editor.

C. Williams, *Hugo L. Black* (1950).

J. P. Frank, *Mr. Justice Black* (1949). By leading legal thinker.

PART SIX: BIG GOVERNMENT IN ACTION

JOURNALS AND ANNUALS

World Politics, published quarterly by the Institute of International Affairs, approaches the subject more in the framework of social science and less in terms of history and current policy than do some of the other journals.

Foreign Affairs, published quarterly by the Council of Foreign Affairs, contains articles by scholars and practicing diplomats, and emphasizes the substantive aspect of current policy and diplomatic history.

World Organization, published quarterly by the World Peace Foundation; survey of the activities of the several international organizations; articles by various authorities on world politics.

Orbis: A Quarterly Journal of World Affairs, published by the Foreign Policy Research Institute of the University of Pennsylvania.

The American Journal of International Law, published quarterly by The American Society of International Law; the professional journal for those interested in legal aspects of international affairs.

Foreign Policy Reports, published twice a month by the Foreign Policy Association; extended treatment of particular topics of current significance.

Foreign Policy Bulletins, published weekly by the Foreign Policy Association; shorter and more popularly written than the *Reports* mentioned above.

The United Nations Bulletin, published every two weeks by the United Nations Department of Public Information.

The Department of State Bulletin, issued weekly; articles explaining United States policy, speeches by officials, and documents such as treaties and executive agreements.

Foreign Policy Briefs, biweekly news sheet issued by State Department giving reports on current affairs.

Foreign Service Journal, unofficial "house organ" containing articles and reports of Foreign Service published by The American Foreign Service Institute.

Current Developments in U.S. Foreign Policy, published monthly by The Brookings Institution and supplemented by a yearly survey entitled *Major Problems of U.S. Foreign Policy.*

The United States in World Affairs, annual survey edited by R. P. Stebbins and the Research Staff of the Council on Foreign Relations.

Documents on American Foreign Relations, annual collection published by World Peace Foundation presented under editorship of R. Dennett and R. K. Turner.

Yearbook of the United Nations, annual survey published by the United Nations.

C. Eagleton and R. V. Swift, eds., *Annual Review of United Nations Affairs.*

INTERNATIONAL POLITICS

Here are just a few of the many general studies of international politics that provide the framework for understanding American foreign policy:

J. H. Herz, *International Politics in the Atomic Age* (1959). Problem of applicability of traditional concepts to present conditions.

S. Hoffmann, *Contemporary Theories in International Relations* (1960).

M. A. Kaplan, *System and Process in International Politics* (1957). Systematic theoretical analysis of international politics.

H. J. Mackinder, *Democratic Ideals and Reality* (1919; republished, 1942). Seminal study of what is too narrowly called "geopolitics."

* E. H. Carr, *The Twenty Years' Crisis 1919-1939* (1940). Discussion of trends and forces in world politics; has had important impact on students of international politics.

H. Sprout and M. Sprout, eds., *Foundations of National Power,* rev. ed. (1951). Readings on major factors that determine power and policy; notes by the editors.

G. Kirk and others, *The Changing Environment of International Relations* (1956). Lectures by experts.

AMERICAN FOREIGN POLICY

Department of State, *American Foreign Policy, 1950-1955,* Department of State Publication 6446 (1958).

* H. S. Kissinger, *Nuclear Weapons and Foreign Policy* (1957). Influential discussion of the strategic impact of nuclear technology and defense of policy of "limited nuclear war."

T. K. Finletter, *Foreign Policy: The Next Phase* (1958). Criticism of America's militarily oriented policy and call for new thinking.

K. Knorr, ed., *NATO and American Security* (1959). Readings.

Rockefeller Brothers Fund, *Foreign Economic Policy in the Twentieth Century* (1958). Discussion of economic aspects of American policy.

D. G. Acheson, *Power and Diplomacy* (1958). Criticism of recent American policy.

G. F. Kennan, *American Diplomacy: 1900-1950* (1951). By former Director of State Department's Policy Planning Staff; important as background of American policy of containment; has famous article, "The Sources of Soviet Conduct."

————, *The Realities of American Foreign Policy* (1954).

————, *Russia, the Atom and the West* (1958). Kennan's argument for disengagement in Central Europe.

S. F. Bemis, *A Diplomatic History of the United States* (1950), *American Secretaries of State and Their Diplomacy* (1957), and *A Short History of American Foreign Policy and Diplomacy* (1959).

J. W. Pratt, *A History of United States Foreign Policy* (1955).

W. A. Reitzel, M. A. Kaplan, and C. G. Coblentz, *United States Foreign Policy, 1945-1955* (1956). Brookings study in a historical-topical analysis of American policy.

T. A. Bailey, *A Diplomatic History of the American People,* 4th ed. (1950). Lively account emphasizing the role of public opinion and interest groups.

E. Lefever, *Ethics and United States Foreign Policy* (1957).

D. Perkins, *The American Approach to Foreign Policy* (1952). Topical historical analysis of principles and parties in American foreign policy.

J. W. Wiggins and H. Schoeck, eds., *Foreign Aid Re-examined: A Critical Appraisal* (1958). Views by social scientists.

W. J. Lederer and E. Burdick, *The Ugly American* (1958). Novel portraying the weakness of the American approach to the peoples and problems of Southeast Asia.

N. J. Spykman, *America's Strategy in World Politics* (1942). Geopolitical analysis of American policy.

H. J. Morgenthau, *In Defense of the National Interest* (1951). Critical evaluation of American foreign policy since end of World War II.

F. Tannenbaum, *The American Tradition in Foreign Policy* (1955). Opposes "realpolitik" basis of interpretation.

L. B. Pearson, *Democracy in World Politics* (1955). By Nobel Prizewinner, leader of the Canadian Liberal Party.

C. B. Marshall, *The Limits of Foreign Policy* (1954).

T. I. Cook and M. Moos, *Power through Purpose* (1934). "The Realism of Idealism as a Basis for Foreign Policy."

L. J. Halle, *Civilization and Foreign Policy* (1955). By a former State Department official.

HOW FOREIGN POLICY IS MADE

R. E. Elder, *The Policy Machine* (1959). Description of policy-making process in the State Department and related agencies.

P. W. Buck and M. Travis, Jr., eds., *Control of Foreign Relations in Modern Nations* (1957). Study of the machinery and methods of making and executing policy in several nations, including the U.S.

H. N. Carroll, *The House of Representatives and Foreign Affairs* (1958).

C. V. Crabb, Jr., *Bipartisan Foreign Policy: Myth or Reality* (1957). The virtues and hazards of bipartisanship.

H. B. Westerfield, *Foreign Policy and Party Politics* (1955). Role of the parties and bipartisanship in Congress.

E. Plischke, *Summit Diplomacy: Personal Diplomacy of the President of the United States* (1959). Study of history and techniques used.

B. C. Cohen, *The Political Process and Foreign Policy: The Making of the Japanese Peace* (1957). Case study.

H. H. Ransom, *Central Intelligence and National Security* (1958). Study of the organization and procedures of American intelligence agencies.

* R. Hilsman, *Strategic Intelligence and National Decisions* (1956). Discussion of the place of strategic intelligence in decision-making; more critical than above volume.

A. Vagts, *Defense and Diplomacy: The Soldier and the Conduct of Foreign Relations* (1956). Role of the military in American foreign policy from a historical perspective.

M. Beloff, *Foreign Policy and the Democratic Process* (1955). By noted British scholar.

H. M. Wriston, *Diplomacy in a Democracy* (1956). Discussion of the problems of foreign policy in a democracy.

S. Huddleston, *Popular Diplomacy and War* (1954). Critical comments about the impact of mass opinion on diplomacy.

* G. A. Almond, *The American People and Foreign Policy* (1950). Analysis of the effect of public, interest groups, and opinion leaders in shaping foreign policy.

A. W. Macmahon, *Administration in Foreign Affairs* (1953).

J. L. McCamy, *The Administration of American Foreign Affairs* (1950). Critical evaluation of the machinery for the making and administering of foreign policy.

W. Y. Elliott, *United States Foreign Policy* (1953). Report of a study group, with recommendations for improving organizational procedures.

J. J. McCloy, *The Challenge to American Foreign Policy* (1953). Brief discussion of problems of making and executing foreign policy, special attention to problem of civil-military relations, by former U.S. High Commissioner for Germany.

T. V. Kalijarvi and C. E. Merrow, eds., "Congress and Foreign Relations," *The Annals,* September 1953. A symposium.

D. S. Cheever and H. F. Haviland, Jr., *American Foreign Policy and the Separation of Powers* (1952). Survey of constitutional arrangements, case studies, and recommendations for improving machinery of government.

W. Y. Elliott and others, *The Political Economy of American Foreign Policy* (1955). Policy recommendations.

H. B. Price, *The Marshall Plan and Its Meaning* (1955). Evaluation and history.

W. L. Thorp, *Trade, Aid, or What?* (1953). "A Report on International Economic Policy."

G. H. Stuart, *The Department of State* (1949). Comprehensive history.

Report of the Secretary of State's Public Committee on Personnel, *Toward A Stronger Foreign Service* (1954). The important Wriston Report, which resulted in major organizational changes in Foreign Service.

Commission on Organization of the Executive Branch of the Government, *Report on Overseas Economic Operations and Task Force Report* (1955).

V. M. Barnett, Jr., ed., *The Representation of the U.S. Abroad* (1956). Study papers for a meeting of the American Assembly.

Commission on the Organization of the Government, *Task Force Report on the Organization of the Government for the Conduct of Foreign Affairs* (1949). Prepared under direction of H. H. Bundy and J. G. Rogers; generally con-

sidered one of the better Task Force Reports.

E. W. Barrett, *Truth Is Our Weapon* (1953). Defense of American information programs.

THE U.N. AND WORLD ORGANIZATION

S. S. Goodspeed, *The Nature and Function of International Organization* (1959).

L. M. Goodrich, *The United Nations* (1959). Introduction to its origins, structure, and functions.

R. E. Asher and others, *The United Nations and Promotion of the General Welfare* (1957). Account of the U.N. and related agencies.

W. A. Scott and S. B. Withey, *The United States and the United Nations: The Public View, 1945-1955* (1958). American attitudes toward the organization as revealed in opinion polls.

L. M. Goodrich, *Korea: A Study of United States Policy in the United Nations* (1956).

R. E. Riggs, *Politics in the United Nations: A Study of United States Influence in the General Assembly* (1958). Study of the extent of American influence and the techniques used.

G. Clark and L. B. Sohn, *World Peace Through World Law* (1958). Outlines program for strengthening the U.N.

I. L. Claude, Jr., *Swords into Ploughshares* (1956). Analysis of the problems of international organizations.

J. Lague, *The Great Debate on Charter Reform: A Proposal for a Strong U.N.* (1958).

F. S. C. Northrup, *The Taming of the Nations* (1953). "A Study of the Cultural Basis of International Policy."

C. M. Eichelberger, *UN: The First Ten Years* (1955). By one who helped prepare first American draft and believes U.N. to be a success.

C. Manly, *The UN Record* (1955). By severe critic who believes U.N. to be a failure and an instrument of subversion.

L. M. Goodrich and A. P. Simons, *The United Nations and the Maintenance of International Peace and Security* (1955). Appraisal of activity.

United Nations, *Everyman's United Nations* (1953). Handbook on the U.N. and its related agencies.

D. Sterling, *United Nations, N.Y.* (1953). Story of the work of the U.N. Secretariat.

W. H. C. Laves and C. A. Thomson, *UNESCO: Purposes, Progress, Prospects* (1957). Account of the organization's first ten years.

L. W. Holborn, *The International Refugee Organization* (1956). Comprehensive report.

C. G. Fenwick, *The Inter-American Regional System* (1949).

Commission to Study the Organization of Peace, A. N. Holcombe, Chairman, *Organizing Peace in the Nuclear Age* (1959). Discussions of the international control of atomic energy.

P. C. Jessup and H. J. Taubenfeld, *Controls for Outer Space and the Antarctic Analogy* (1959). Examination of the problems and possibilities of international control of outer space.

WAR AND NATIONAL DEFENSE

W. R. Kintner and others, *Forging a New Sword* (1958). Study of Defense Department and recommendations for improving its operations.

E. M. Emme, ed., *The Impact of Air Power: National Security and World Politics* (1959). Collection of readings on all aspects of air power and strategy.

* W. Millis, *Arms and Men* (1956). History of American military institutions.

W. Millis, H. C. Mansfield, and H. Stein, *Arms and the State: Civil-military Elements in National Policy* (1958). Relations of military and civilian factors in the making of recent American policy.

T. W. Stanley, *American Defense and National Security* (1956). Organization of government for defense.

J. M. Gavin, *War and Peace in the Space Age* (1958). Critical evaluation of American military policy by a former Army Chief of Research and Development.

E. S. Furniss, Jr., ed., *American Military Power* (1957). Readings on current problems.

W. W. Kaufmann, ed., *Military Policy and National Security* (1956). Essays on current problems.

R. G. Hubler, *SAC: The Strategic Air Command* (1958). Popular account of

its history, functions, and the controversy surrounding it.

E. S. Corwin, *Total War and the Constitution* (1947). Impact of war and defense requirements upon constitutional system.

E. Huzar, *The Purse and the Sword* (1950). Study of "the control of the Army by Congress through military appropriations."

H. and M. Sprout, *The Rise of American Naval Power, 1776-1918* (1939), and *Toward a New Order of Sea Power, 1918-1922* (1940). Relations among naval policy, domestic politics, and foreign policy.

D. O. Smith, *U.S. Military Doctrine* (1955). By an Air Force general.

SCIENCE, SCIENTISTS,
AND NATIONAL SECURITY

* V. Bush, *Modern Arms and Free Men* (1949). Head of Office of Scientific Research and Development during World War II discusses the relations between new weapons and modern warfare and the conditions under which science can make its best contribution to national security.

W. Gellhorn, *Security, Loyalty, and Science* (1950). Presents the view that national security and scientific development are being jeopardized by overzealous concern for security and secrecy.

Bulletin of Atomic Scientists, published monthly; articles on science and international security.

H. D. Smyth, *Atomic Energy for Military Purposes* (1946). First official report.

J. R. Newman and B. S. Miller, *The Control of Atomic Energy* (1948). Discussion of political control.

W. L. Laurence, *The Hell Bomb* (1951). The Hydrogen Bomb—its implications, and recommendations for American policy toward its use; by *The New York Times'* science editor.

R. E. Lapp, *Atoms and People* (1956). The atomic world of the future, by a physicist.

WARS, MILITARY, AND CIVILIANS

S. P. Huntington, *The Soldier and the State* (1957). Study of civil-military relations in the United States.

J. W. Spanier, *The Truman-MacArthur Controversy and the Korean War* (1959). Case study of civil-military relationships in wartime.

Senate Committee on Armed Services and Committee on Foreign Relations, *Hearings, Military Situation in Far East,* 82 Cong., 1 Sess. (1951). MacArthur hearings contain materials on how decisions are made, the relations among the President, his military, and his civilian advisers.

L. Smith, *American Democracy and Military Power* (1951). Survey of democratic theory, constitutional law, and administrative practices, and evaluation of their adequacy to preserve civilian control of the armed forces.

A. A. Ekirch, Jr., *The Civilian and the Military* (1956). Survey of American tradition and discussion of contemporary application.

H. D. Lasswell, *National Security and Individual Freedom* (1950). Recommendations as to how to avoid the "garrison state."

GOVERNMENT AND THE ECONOMY

T. C. Cochran, *The American Business System* (1957). Interpretative history since 1900.

L. M. Hacker, *American Capitalism* (1957). Role of capitalism in American society.

C. B. Hoover, *The Economy, Liberty and the State* (1959). Study of the relation of the state to the economy in several nations, including the U.S.

H. K. Girvetz, *From Wealth to Welfare* (1950). Interpretation of the forces that have led to the welfare state.

N. J. Ware, *Wealth and Welfare* (1949). Brief history of the evolution of our economic system.

J. K. Galbraith, *American Capitalism* (1952). Role of government, business, and labor in modern American competitive economy, "the concept of countervailing power."

* R. A. Dahl and C. E. Lindblom, *Politics, Economics and Welfare* (1953). Patterns of economic and political power; suggests new theoretical approaches.

Although the several writers vary considerably in their beliefs, the following

are just a few of the many books that in general support the thesis "the less government the better."

H. Spencer, *The Man versus the State* (T. Beale edition, 1916). Classic statement of belief in limited government by one of the most influential men of the late nineteenth century.

F. A. Hayek, *The Road to Serfdom* (1944). Attack on governmental planning.

F. H. Knight, *Freedom and Reform* (1947). By outstanding economists.

* H. C. Simons, *Economic Policy for a Free Society* (1947). Devoted to the thesis that capital and labor monopolies must be destroyed so that free enterprise can be re-established.

J. A. Schumpeter, *Capitalism, Socialism, and Democracy* (1950). Defense of the entrepreneur.

Disagreeing with views in above volumes, the following authors believe that government should perform certain welfare functions, regulate the economy for full employment, and act positively to preserve a free society.

H. Finer, *Road to Reaction* (1945). Vigorous answer to Hayek.

* J. M. Clark, *Alternative to Serfdom* (1948). Comments on the role of government; less faith in planning than the above author.

K. Mannheim, *Freedom, Power, and Democratic Planning* (1950). By famous sociologist.

GOVERNMENT AND BUSINESS

H. J. Levin, ed., *Business Organization and Public Policy* (1958). Readings on government's relation to business.

M. E. Dimock, *Business and Government*, 3rd ed. (1957). Survey of government-business relations.

D. F. Pegrum, *Public Regulation of Business* (1959).

M. G. Glaeser, *Public Utilities in American Capitalism* (1957). Study of problems and policies of regulation.

J. Bauer, *Transforming Public Utility Regulations* (1950). Recommendations for improving regulatory activities.

S. N. Whitney, *Anti-trust Policies: American Experience in Twenty Industries,* 2

vols. (1958). Analysis of the effectiveness of antitrust action.

J. W. Burns, *A Study of Anti-trust Laws* (1958). Greater emphasis on legal aspects than the above volume.

W. Adams and H. M. Gray, *Monopoly in America* (1956). Evidence to support argument that governmental policy in recent years tends to promote monopoly.

D. Lynch, *The Concentration of Economic Power* (1946). Summary of the hearings and reports of the Temporary National Economic Committee (TNEC).

A. D. H. Kaplan, *Big Enterprise in a Competitive System* (1954).

J. Scoville and N. Sargent, *Fact and Fancy in the T.N.E.C. Monographs* (1942). Critical review of TNEC reports prepared under auspices of NAM.

D. E. Lilienthal, *Big Business: A New Era* (1952). Argues for an affirmative program to help develop big business and discussion of its contributions.

C. D. Edwards, *Maintaining Competition* (1949). Recommendations for a governmental policy.

E. S. Redford, *Administration of National Economic Controls* (1952). Analysis of process by which policy is made and instruments through which it is executed.

I. L. Sharfman, *The Interstate Commerce Commission,* 4 vols. (1931-1937). Comprehensive study of the oldest federal regulatory agency.

J. M. Edelman, *The Licensing of Radio Services in the U.S., 1927 to 1947* (1950). Study in administrative formulation of policy.

* A. A. Berle and G. C. Means, *The Modern Corporation and Private Property* (1933). Analysis of the growth of large industry, the separation between ownership and control, and problems of social control.

R. E. Lane, *The Regulation of Businessmen* (1954). Responses of businessmen to regulation.

T. W. Arnold, *The Folklore of Capitalism* (1937). Mythology of business and trust-busting, with emphasis on its futility, by man who subsequently became an active trust-buster.

D. R. Fuller, *Government Financing of Private Enterprise* (1948).

The Commission on Organization of the Executive Branch of the Government, *Department of Commerce* (1949).

GOVERNMENT AND AGRICULTURE

M. R. Benedict, *Farm Policies of the United States, 1790-1950* (1953). Origins and development of governmental policy.

M. R. Benedict and O. C. Stine, *The Agricultural Commodity Program: Two Decades of Experience* (1956). Farm program discussed in terms of specific commodities.

M. R. Benedict, *Can We Solve the Farm Problem? An Analysis of Federal Aid to Agriculture* (1955).

W. W. Cochrane, *Farm Prices, Myth and Reality* (1958). Emphasis on problems of commercial agriculture.

L. Soth, *Farm Trouble* (1957). Discussion of farm problems, especially those of the marginal farmer.

R. M. Christenson, *The Brannan Plan: Farm Politics and Policy* (1959). Study of farm politics as focused on the Brannan Plan controversy.

C. M. Hardin, *The Politics of Agriculture* (1952). Taking field of soil conservation, author develops methods to describe the political process.

Commission on Organization of the Executive Branch of the Government, *Department of Agriculture;* and *Task Force Report on Agricultural Activities* (1949).

G. Baker, *The County Agent* (1939). Traces the work of this link between government and the farmer from 1911 to 1939.

C. McWilliams, *Factories in the Field* (1939). Story of migratory farm workers in California.

President's Commission on Migratory Labor, *Report, Migratory Labor in American Agriculture* (1951). Latest study of this social problem.

CONSERVATION

Popular discussions that deal with general problems are:

M. W. Straus, *Why Not Survive?* (1955).

F. Osborn, *Our Plundered Planet* (1948).

W. Vogt, *Road to Survival* (1948).

G. Pinchot, *Breaking New Ground* (1947). Autobiography of a crusader for conservation.

Other important works include:

H. Jarrett, ed., *Perspectives on Conservation: Essays on America's Natural Resources* (1958).

M. Clawson and B. Held, *The Federal Lands: Their Use and Management* (1957).

R. M. Robbins, *Our Landed Heritage* (1942). History of public land policies.

E. F. Renshow, *Toward Responsible Government: An Economic Appraisal of Federal Investment in the Water Resources Program* (1957). Critical of the program.

President's Water Resources Policy Commission, *A Water Policy for the American People; Ten Rivers in America's Future; Water Resources Law* (1950). Primary source of information, presentation of program with supporting data.

J. W. Fesler, ed., "Government and Water Resources," *American Political Science Review*, September 1950. Symposium.

L. H. Gulick, *American Forest Policy* (1951). Survey of current policy and description of administrative techniques.

W. B. Greeley, *Forests and Men* (1951). Former Chief of the Forest Service discusses problems and programs.

President's Materials Policy Commission, *Resources for Freedom* (1952). With five supporting volumes, one of the most significant studies of resources and public policy in recent years.

N. I. Wengert, *Natural Resources and the Political Struggle* (1955). History and politics of conservation.

C. McKinley, *Uncle Sam in the Pacific Northwest* (1952). Detailed study of federal government's program for management of natural resources in the area.

B. Lyons, *Tomorrow's Birthright: A Political and Economic Interpretation of Our Natural Resources* (1955). Discussion of the politics and economics of conservation.

P. W. Bidwell, *Raw Materials: A Study of American Policy* (1958).

E. Ginzburg, *Human Resources: The Wealth of a Nation* (1958).

THE LABOR MOVEMENT

J. G. Rayback, *A History of American Labor* (1959).

J. R. Commons and others, *History of Labor in the United States,* 4 vols. (1935). One of the best labor histories covering period before the New Deal.

H. A. Millis and R. Montgomery, *Organized Labor* (1945). Another outstanding labor history.

L. L. Lorwin, *The American Federation of Labor* (1933). Standard history written before development of CIO and events of 1930's and 1940's.

R. A. Lester, *As Unions Mature: An Analysis of the Evolution of American Unionism* (1958). Background and current problems.

S. Lens, *The Crisis of American Labor* (1959). Current issues and problems.

"American Labor Problems" in *Current History,* June 1959.

C. W. Mills, *The New Men of Power* (1948). Study of the leaders of organized labor, by a sociologist.

M. Karson, *American Labor and Politics, 1900-1918* (1958).

M. Derber and E. Young, eds., *Labor and the New Deal* (1957). Essays on various aspects of labor during the New Deal.

P. Taft, *The Structure and Government of Labor Unions* (1954).

M. M. Kampelman, *The Communist Party vs. the CIO: A Study of Power Politics* (1957). Study of attempted communist infiltration and union counteraction.

L. E. H. Chamberlin and others, *Labor Unions and Public Policy* (1958). Critical of the power unions now have.

C. E. Lindblom, *Unions and Capitalism* (1949). Questions the compatibility of unions and capitalism.

F. Tannenbaum, *A Philosophy of Labor* (1951). Interpretation of unions as a conservative force in modern capitalistic society.

GOVERNMENT LABOR POLICY

S. Petro, *Power Unlimited: The Corruption of Union Leadership* (1959). Interpretation and summary of the McClellan Committee disclosures.

P. Sultan, *Right to Work Laws: A Study of Conflict* (1958). Balanced discussion of their background and arguments on both sides of the fence.

U.S. Department of Labor, *Federal Labor Laws and Agencies,* Bulletin No. 123, August 1950, periodically revised. Provides quick reference to laws and regulations.

H. A. Millis and E. C. Brown, *From the Wagner Act to Taft-Hartley* (1950). Labor policy from the New Deal to Taft-Hartley.

J. H. Leek, *Government and Labor in the United States* (1952). "Survey of legislation, administration, and major court decisions."

R. N. Baldwin and C. B. Randall, *Civil Liberties and Industrial Conflict* (1938).

H. David, *The History of the Haymarket Affair* (1936). Story of a *cause célèbre.*

SOCIAL SECURITY

J. G. Turnhill, *et al., Economic and Social Security: Public and Private Measures Against Economic Insecurity* (1957). General treatment of problems and policies.

E. M. Burns, *Social Security and Public Policy* (1956). General survey emphasizing problems.

Rockefeller Brothers Fund, *The Challenge to America: Its Economic and Social Aspects* (1958). Sections on problems of economic and social security.

J. D. Hagan and F. A. J. Ianni, *American Social Legislation* (1957). Appraisal of problems and alternatives; sociological emphasis.

National Association of Social Workers, *The Social Welfare Year Book,* annual collection of articles.

A. Larson, *Know Your Social Security* (1955). By former Under Secretary of Department of Health, Education and Welfare.

HEALTH INSURANCE

G. Rosen, *A History of Public Health* (1958). General review of programs through several centuries.

H. S. Mustard, *An Introduction to Public Health* (1953).

U.S. Department of Health, Education and Welfare, *Annual Report,* useful information on current problems.

The President's Commission on the Health Needs of the Nation, *Building America's Health,* 5 vols. (1953). Findings of fact and recommendations of action needed to meet the nation's health requirements.

H. E. Livingston, *National Health Insurance,* Public Affairs Bulletin 85, Legislative Reference Service (1950).

O. R. Ewing, *The Nation's Health—A Ten Year Program* (1948). Former administrator of Federal Security Agency presents summary of existing conditions, program for compulsory health insurance, federal aid to build hospitals and to educate doctors.

EDUCATION

* Rockefeller Brothers Fund, *The Pursuit of Excellence: Education and the Future of America* (1958). Study of needs, problems, and philosophy.

Senate Committee on Labor and Public Welfare, 85 Cong., 2nd S., *The National Defense Education Act of 1958* (1958). Summary and analysis of the law.

H. P. Allen, *The Federal Government and Education* (1950). Study made for the Hoover Commission of federal activities in field of education.

S. E. Harris, *How Shall We Pay for Education?* (1948).

U.S. President's Committee for the White House Conference on Education, *Report to the President* (1956).

President's Commission on Higher Education, *Higher Education for American Democracy* (1947).

C. V. Kidd, *American Universities and Federal Research* (1959). Input of federal funds.

HOUSING

R. M. Fisher, *Twenty Years of Public Housing: Economic Aspects of the Federal Program* (1959). History of federal policy and activities.

G. H. Beyer, *Housing: A Factual Analysis* (1958). Technical information as well as information on governmental policy.

Housing and Home Finance Agency, *Annual Report,* valuable factual data.

Joint (Congressional) Committee on Housing, *Final Majority Report,* Housing Study and Investigation, House Report 1564, 80 Cong., 2 Sess. (1949).

FEDERAL POLICEMEN

J. N. Markis, *The Silent Investigators* (1959). Account of the U.S. Postal Inspection service.

B. Smith, *Police Systems in the United States,* rev. ed. (1949). General discussion of all police systems; special chapters on federal agencies.

M. Lowenthal, *The Federal Bureau of Investigation* (1950). Criticism of the FBI.

D. Whitehead, *The F.B.I. Story* (1956). Readable, sympathetic, and wide-ranging account.

A. C. Millspaugh, *Crime Control by the National Government* (1937).

GOVERNMENT AS MANAGER

D. K. Price, *Government and Science* (1954). Shows major role of government in scientific activity.

Commission on Organization of the Executive Branch of the Government, *Report on Federal Business Enterprises;* and *Report on the Post Office* (1949 and 1955).

M. Thomas and R. M. Northrop, *Atomic Energy and Congress* (1956).

J. R. Newman and B. S. Miller, *The Control of Atomic Energy* (1948).

G. R. Clapp, *The TVA: An Approach to the Development of a Region* (1955). By former chairman.

D. E. Lilienthal, *TVA: Democracy on the March,* rev. ed. (1953). Defense by former director of TVA as major instrument of grass-roots democracy.

C. H. Pritchett, *The Tennessee Valley Authority: A Study in Public Administration* (1943). Standard study of TVA administration.

P. Selznick, *TVA and the Grass Roots* (1949). Sociological interpretation.

BIG GOVERNMENT:
ITS PROBLEMS AND ITS LIMITS

L. H. Kimmel, *Federal Budget and Fiscal Policy, 1789-1958* (1959). General survey of policies and procedures.

P. J. Strayer, *Fiscal Policy and Politics* (1958).

J. Burkhead, *Government Budgeting* (1956). Description of the budgetary process.

Commission on the Organization of the Executive Department, *Report on Budgeting and Accounting;* and *Task Force Report on Fiscal, Budgeting, and Accounting Activities* (1949 and 1955). Contains discussion of organizational problems.

P. H. Douglas, *Economy in the National Government* (1952). By U.S. senator; includes critical comments on budget and appropriation process.

A. Smithies, *The Budgetary Process in the United States* (1955). Surveys role of federal budget.

Bureau of the Budget, *The Federal Budget in Brief;* published annually, summary of budget; many illustrations.

G. L. Bach, *Inflation: A Study in Economics, Ethics and Politics* (1958).

* J. M. Keynes, *The General Theory of Employment, Interest, and Money* (1936). One of the most influential books of modern times; interpretation of economics that calls for governmental fiscal and monetary policy and public works to offset unemployment.

W. E. Upjohn Institute for Community Research, *Public Works and Employment* (1956). Impact of public works on local unemployment.

A. Hart, *The Economics of Illusion* (1949). Criticism of Keynesian economics.

R. Blough, *The Federal Taxing Process* (1952). The forces at work and institutions involved in the taxing process.

R. E. Paul, *Taxation in the United States* (1954). By former high Treasury official.

H. C. Simons, *Federal Tax Reform* (1950). By distinguished anti-Keynesian economist.

S. Ratner, *American Taxation* (1942). "Its History as a Social Force in Democracy."

G. L. Bach, *Federal Reserve Policy-Making* (1950).

E. W. and D. L. Kemmerer, *The ABC of the Federal Reserve System,* rev. ed. (1950).

Senate Committee on Banking and Currency, *Federal Reserve Policy and Economic Stability, 1951-1957,* study prepared by A. Achinstein, Senate Report No. 2500, 85 Cong., 2 Sess. (1958).

The several reports resulting from the Employment Act of 1946 are primary sources for the whole problem of governmental fiscal and monetary policy. These include the President's Economic Report to the Congress, Report of the Council of Economic Advisers, and Reports and Hearings of the Joint Congressional Committee on Economic Report. These are issued regularly.

EPILOGUE: CHALLENGE AND OPPORTUNITY

POLITICS AND YOU

*S. Bullitt, *To Be a Politician* (1959). An intellectual reflects on his experience in the world of "practical politics."

R. E. Merriam and R. M. Goetz, *Going Into Politics* (1957). "A Guide for Citizens."

S. A. Mitchell, *Elm St. Politics* (1959). Former Chairman of Democratic National Committee discusses the role of "amateurs" in politics and outlines how a citizen can become active in politics.

H. D. Scott, Jr., *How to Go Into Politics* (1949). By former chairman of Republican National Committee and member of Congress.

P. P. Van Riper, *Handbook of Practical Politics* (1951). Materials drawn from many sources "to familiarize citizens with concrete ways . . . of carrying on effective political activity on the local and state levels."

National Municipal League, *The Citizen Association: How to Organize and Run It* (1953), and *The Citizen Association: How to Win Civic Campaigns* (1953).

J. E. McLean, *Politics Is What You Make It* (1952). Pamphlet with information and suggestions on how to be an effective citizen-politician.

M. Tallman, *Dictionary of Civics and Government* (1953).

E. E. Schattschneider, V. Jones, and S. Bailey, *A Guide to the Study of Public Affairs* (1952). Practical guides to gathering political information.

A Selective Bibliography of Current Research on American Government

This is a selective list of articles relevant to the study of American government that have appeared in some of the professional political science journals between 1957 and September 1959. These articles will be of special interest to students planning to major in political science, but they will give any student an idea of the kind of work being done by "professionals" and how they report to their fellow political scientists.

The journals covered are:

The American Political Science Review (APSR)—the official journal of the American Political Science Association.

The Journal of Politics (JP)—the journal of the Southern Political Science Association.

Midwest Journal of Politics (MJPS)—the journal of the Midwest Conference of Political Scientists.

Political Science Quarterly (PSQ)—the journal of the Academy of Political Science of Columbia University.

The Review of Politics (RP)—published by Notre Dame University.

The Western Political Quarterly (WPQ)—the journal of the Western Political Science Association.

PART ONE: DEMOCRATIC GOVERNMENT IN AMERICA

GENERAL

Albert Somit and others, "The Effect of the Introductory Political Science Course on Student Attitudes Toward Personal Political Participation," *APSR,* Dec. 58, p. 1129.

William H. Harbold and Dell G. Hitchner, "Some Reflections on Method In the Study of Politics," *WPQ,* Dec. 58, p. 753.

Robert G. McCloskey, with comments by Martin Diamond and John P. Roche, "American Political Theory in Study of Politics," *APSR,* March and June 57, p. 115, 130, and 484.

Frank J. Sorauf, "The Public Interest Reconsidered," *JP,* Nov. 57, p. 616.

DEMOCRACY

Christopher Dawson, "The Birth of Democracy," *RP,* Jan. 57, p. 48.

Marvin Meyers, "The Basic Democrat: A Version of Tocqueville," *PSQ,* March 57, p. 50.

C. W. Cassinelli, "The Consent of the Governed," *WPQ,* June 59, p. 391.

Seymour M. Lipset, "Some Social Requisites of Democracy: Economic Development and Political Legitimacy," *APSR,* March 59, p. 69.

W. Hayward Rogers, "Some Methodological Difficulties in Anthony Down's *An Economic Theory of Democracy,*" *APSR,* June 59, p. 483.

Douglas N. Morgan, "A Postscript to Professor Dahl's *Preface,*" *APSR,* Dec. 57, p. 1040; and rejoinder by Dahl, p. 1053.

Neal Riemer, "Two Conceptions of the Genius of American Politics," *JP,* Nov. 58, p. 695.

Harry V. Jaffa, "Value Consensus in Democracy: The Issue in the Lincoln-Douglas Debates," *APSR,* Sept. 58, p. 745.

Samuel P. Huntington, "Conservatism as an Ideology," *APSR,* June 57, p. 454; and comment by Murry N. Rothbard, Sept. 57, p. 784.

H. Malcolm MacDonald, "The Revival of Conservative Thought," *JP*, Feb. 57, p. 66.

Louis Hartz, "The Coming of Age of America," *APSR*, June 57, p. 474.

Andrew Hacker and Samuel Du Bois

Cook, Exchange on "Liberal Democracy and Social Control," *APSR*, Dec. 57, p. 1027.

David Spitz, "On The Abuses of Power in Democratic States," *MJPS*, Nov. 57, p. 225.

PART TWO: THE RULES AND HOW THEY GREW

John C. Livingston, "Alexander Hamilton and the American Tradition," *MJPS*, Nov. 57, p. 209.

Cecelia M. Kenyon, "Alexander Hamilton: Rousseau of the Right," *PSQ*, June 58, p. 161.

Bernard Wishy, "John Locke and the Spirit of '78," *PSQ*, Sept. 58, p. 413.

Martin Diamond, "Democracy and 'The Federalist,' A Reconsideration of the Framers' Intent," *APSR*, March 59, p. 52.

Ralph Ketcham, "Notes on James Madison's Sources for the Tenth Federalist Paper," *MJPS*, May 57, p. 20.

Morton J. Frisch, "John Marshall's Philos-

ophy of Constitutional Republicanism," *RP*, Jan. 58, p. 34.

William S. Livingston, "Emigration as a Theoretical Doctrine During the American Revolution," *JP*, Nov. 57, p. 591.

G. Homer Durban, "WICHE: An Experiment in Interstate Cooperation and Regional Planning," *WPQ*, Sept. 57, p. 692 (study of the Western Interstate Commission for Higher Education).

Reed L. Frischknecht, "State Extension Services and the Administration of Farm Prices and Income Support Programs: A Case Study in Federal-State Relations," *WPQ*, June 57, p. 416.

Gordon B. Dodds, "Arizona, Oregon, and The Nation," *WPQ*, June 57, p. 398.

PART THREE: CIVIL LIBERTIES AND CITIZENSHIP

Claudius O. Johnson, "The Status of Freedom of Expression Under the Smith Act," *WPQ*, Sept. 58, p. 469.

Dalmas H. Nelson, "Political Expression under the Hatch Act and the Problem of Statutory Ambiguity," *MJPS*, Feb. 58, p. 76.

Milton Greenberg, "Loyalty Oaths: An Appraisal of the Legal Issues," *JP*, Aug. 58, p. 487.

Cornelius P. Cotter and J. Malcolm Smith. "An American Paradox: The Emergency Detention Act of 1950," *JP*, Feb. 57, p. 20.

Guy B. Johnson, "Freedom, Equality, and Segregation," *RP*, April 58, p. 147.

Carl B. Swisher, "Dred Scott One Hundred Years After," *JP*, May 57, p. 167.

Samuel Krislov, "Constituency versus Constitutionalism: The Desegregation Issue and Tensions and Aspirations of Southern Attorneys General," *MJPS*, Feb. 59, p. 750.

Walter F. Murphy, "Private Education With Public Funds?" *JP*, Nov. 58, p. 635.

———, "The South Counterattacks: The Anti-NAACP Laws," *WPQ*, June 59, p. 371.

Herbert Garfinkel, "Social Science Evidence and the School Segregation Cases," *JP*, Feb. 59, p. 37.

John H. Fenton and Kenneth N. Vines, "Negro Registration in Louisiana," *APSR*, Sept. 57, p. 704.

Joseph L. Bernd and Lynwood M. Holland, "Recent Restrictions Upon Negro Suffrage: The Case of Georgia," *JP*, Aug. 59, p. 487.

David Fellman, "Cruel and Unusual Punishments," *JP*, Feb. 57, p. 34.

Frederick T. Moore, "Criminal Jurisdiction in Overseas Areas," *JP*, May 59, p. 276.

Francis E. Rourke, "Secrecy in American Bureaucracy," *PSQ*, Dec. 57, p. 540.

PART FOUR: THE PEOPLE IN POLITICS

VOTING AND VOTING BEHAVIOR

Angus Campbell and Warren E. Miller, "The Motivational Basis of Straight and Split Ticket Voting," *APSR*, June 57, p. 293.

Donald E. Stokes, Angus Campbell, and Warren E. Miller, "Components of Electoral Decision," *APSR*, June 59, p. 567.

Warren E. Miller, "The Socio-Economic Analysis of Political Behavior," *MJPS*, Aug. 58, p. 239.

James W. Prothro and others, "Two Party Voting in the South: Class vs. Party Identification," *APSR*, March 58, p. 131.

Daniel M. Ogden, Jr., "A Voting-Behavior Approach to Split-Ticket Voting in 1952," *WPQ*, Sept. 58, p. 481.

William A. Glaser, "Intention and Voting Turnout," *APSR*, Dec. 58, p. 1030.

James C. Davies, "A Note on Political Motivation," *WPQ*, June 59, p. 410.

Oscar Glantz, "Unitary Political Behavior and Differential Political Motivation," *WPQ*, Dec. 57, p. 833.

M. Brewster Smith, "Opinions, Personality, and Political Behavior," and "Comments" by Alexander L. George, *APSR*, March 58, p. 1.

James G. March, "Measurement Concepts in the Theory of Influence," *JP*, May 57, p. 202.

John R. Schmidhauser, "The Political Behavior of Older Persons: A Discussion of Some Frontiers in Research," *WPQ*, March 58, p. 113.

Charles Press, "Voting Statistics and Presidential Coattails," *APSR*, Dec. 58, p. 1041.

D. H. Mendel, Jr., "The Japanese Voter and Political Action," *WPQ*, Dec. 57, p. 847.

Robert E. Lane, "The Fear of Equality," *APSR*, March 59, p. 35.

Felix E. Oppenheim, "An Analysis of Political Control: Actual and Potential," *JP*, Aug. 58, p. 515.

Harold L. Sheppard and Nicholas A. Masters, "The Political Attitudes and Preferences of Union Members," *APSR*, June 59, p. 437.

Richard M. Scammon, "Voting for President in the Larger Metropolitan Areas, 1952-1956," *MJPS*, Nov. 57, p. 370.

Oliver P. Williams, "The Commodity Credit Corporation and the 1948 Presidential Elections," *MJPS*, Aug. 57, p. 111.

Herbert McClosky, "Conservatism and Personality," *APSR*, March 58, p. 27.

Wilmore Kendall, "Comment on McClosky," *APSR*, June 58, p. 506.

Morton J. Frisch, "Comment on McClosky," *APSR*, Dec. 58, p. 1108.

Herbert McClosky, "Rejoinder to Kendall and Frisch," *APSR*, Dec. 1958, p. 1111.

Robert M. Rosenzweig, "The Politician and the Career in Politics," *MJPS*, Aug. 57, p. 163.

Albert Somit and Joseph Tanenhaus, "The Veteran in the Electoral Process: The House of Representatives," *JP*, May 57, p. 184.

INTEREST GROUPS, PUBLIC OPINION, AND CAMPAIGNS

Lester W. Milbrath, "The Political Party Activity of Washington Lobbyists," *JP*, May 58, p. 339.

Clement E. Vose, "The National Consumers League and the Brandeis Brief," *MJPS*, Nov. 57, p. 267.

James P. Shenton, "The Coughlin Movement and the New Deal," *PSQ*, Sept. 58, p. 352.

Victor C. Ferkiss, "Populist Influences on American Fascism," *WPQ*, June 57, p. 350.

Grant McConnell, "The Spirit of Private Government," *APSR*, Sept. 58, p. 754.

Robert A. Dahl, "Business and Politics: A Critical Appraisal of Political Science," *APSR*, March 59, p. 1.

Joseph A. Schlesinger, "Lawyers and American Politics: A Clarified View," *MJPS*, May 57, p. 26.

Vaughn Davis Bornet, "The Communist Party in the Presidential Elections of 1928," *WPQ*, Sept. 58, p. 514.

Richard F. Schier, "Political Fund Raising and the Small Contributor: A Case Study," *WPQ*, March 58, p. 104.

Eric L. McKitrick, "The Study of Corruption," *PSQ*, Dec. 57, p. 502.

Robert J. Pitchell, "The Influence of Professional Campaign Management Firms in Partisan Elections in California," *WPQ*, June 58, p. 278.

Raymond Fielding, "Mirror of Discontent: The *March of Time* and Its Politically Controversial Film Issues," *WPQ*, March 59, p. 141.

Beo. M. Christenson, "The Power of the Press: The Use of 'The Toledo Blade,'" *MJPS*, Aug. 59, p. 227.

POLITICAL PARTIES

V. O. Key, Jr., "Secular Realignment and the Party System," *JP*, May 59, p. 198.

Howard J. McMurray, "The Responsible Majority—Some Reflections on Political Parties," *WPQ*, June 58, p. 175.

Murray S. Stedman, Jr., "American Political Parties as a Conservative Force," *WPQ*, June 57, p. 392.

Avery Leiserson, "The Place of Parties in the Study of Politics," *APSR*, Dec. 57, p. 943.

Frank J. Sorauf, "Patronage and Party," *MJPS*, May 59, p. 115.

Robert J. Golembiewski, "A Taxonomic Approach to State Political Party Strength," *WPQ*, Sept. 58, p. 494.

William G. Carleton, "The Revolution in the Presidential Nominating Convention," *PSQ*, June 57, p. 224.

William J. Gore and Robert L. Peabody, "The Functions of the Political Campaign: A Case Study," *WPQ*, March 58, p. 55.

Frank H. Jonas, "The Art of Political Dynamiting," *WPQ*, June 57, p. 374 (story of use of "scatological propaganda" in a Utah campaign).

John G. Grumm, "Theories of Electoral Systems," *MJPS*, Nov. 58, p. 357.

Robert J. Pitchell, "The Electoral System and Voting Behavior: The Case of California's Cross-Filing," *WPQ*, June 59, p. 459.

Ralph M. Goldman, "Hubert Humphrey's S. J. 152: A New Proposal for Electoral College Reform," *MJPS*, Feb. 58, p. 89.

Morris S. Ogul, "Residence Requirements as Barriers to Voting in Presidential Elections," *MJPS*, Aug. 59, p. 254.

Roger H. Marz, "The Democratic Digest: A Content Analysis," *APSR*, Sept. 57, p. 696.

H. B. Mayo, "A Note on the Alleged Duty to Vote," *JP*, May 59, p. 319.

Donald H. Ackerman, Jr., "Significance of Congressional Races with Identical Candidates in Successive District Elections," *MJPS*, Aug. 57, p. 173.

PART FIVE: POLICY-MAKERS FOR THE PEOPLE

CONGRESS

Floyd M. Riddick, annual analysis of work of Congress in March issue of *The Western Political Quarterly.*

George B. Galloway, "Precedents Established in the First Congress," *WPQ*, Sept. 58, p. 454.

————, "Leadership in the House of Representatives," *WPQ*, June 59, p. 417.

Edward J. Heubel, "Congressional Resistance to Reform: The House Adopts a Code for Investigating Committees," *MJPS*, Nov. 57, p. 313.

William H. Riker, "The Paradox of Voting and Congressional Rules for Voting on Amendments," *APSR*, June 58, p. 349.

Howard E. Shuman, "Senate Rules and the Civil Rights Bill: A Case Study," *APSR*, Dec. 57, p. 955.

Neal A. Maxwell, "The Conference of Western Senators," *WPQ*, Dec. 57, p. 902.

Ralph K. Huitt, "The Morse Committee Assignment Controversy: A Study in Senate Norms," *APSR*, June 57, p. 313.

George Goodwin, Jr., "The Seniority System in Congress," *APSR*, June 59, p. 412.

Robert Ash Wallace, "Congressional Control of the Budget," *MJPS*, May 59, p. 151.

Charles D. Farris, "A Method of Determining Ideological Groupings in the Congress," *JP*, May 58, p. 308.

Murray G. Lawson, "The Foreign-Born in Congress, 1789-1949: A Statistical Summary," *APSR*, Dec. 57, p. 1183.

George M. Belknap, "A Method of Analyzing Legislative Behavior," *MJPS*, Nov. 58, p. 377.

Lawrence H. Fuchs, "The World Federation Resolution: A Case Study in Congressional Decision-Making," *MJPS*, Aug. 57, p. 151.

Robert E. Elder, "The Foreign Affairs Division of the Legislative Reference Service: Organization and Functions of a Professional Staff," *WPQ*, March 57, p. 169.

THE PRESIDENCY AND ADMINISTRATION

Marion D. Irish, "The Organization Man in the Presidency," *JP*, May 58, p. 259.

Marshall E. Dimock, "Woodrow Wilson as Legislative Leader," *JP*, Feb. 57, p. 3.

Don W. Driggs, "The President as Chief Educator on Foreign Affairs," *WPQ*, Dec. 58, p. 813.

Lucius Wilmerding, Jr., "Presidential Inability," *PSQ*, June 57, p. 161.

Richard F. Fenno, Jr., "President-Cabinet Relations: A Pattern and A Case Study," *APSR*, June 58, p. 388.

Felix A. Nigro, "The Warren Case," *WPQ*, Dec. 58, p. 835. (Battle over President Coolidge's unsuccessful attempt to secure Senate confirmation of Charles Warren as Attorney General.)

Charles E. Gilbert, "The Framework of Administrative Responsibility," *JP*, Aug. 59, p. 371.

Glendon A. Schubert, Jr., " 'The Public Interest' in Administrative Decision-Making: Theorem, Theosophy, or Theory?" *APSR*, June 57, p. 346.

Arch Dotson, "Fundamental Approaches to Administrative Responsibility," *WPQ*, Sept. 57, p. 701.

J. Malcolm Smith and Cornelius P. Cotter, "Administrative Accountability: Reporting to Congress," *WPQ*, March 57, p. 405.

Cornelius P. Cotter and J. Malcolm Smith, "Administrative Responsibility: Congressional Prescription of Interagency Relationship," *WPQ*, Dec. 57, p. 765.

James W. Fesler, "Administrative Literature and the Second Hoover Commission Reports," *APSR*, March 57, p. 135.

Paul H. Nitze, "The Role of the Learned Man in Government," *RP*, July 58, p. 275.

Francis E. Rourke, "The Politics of Administrative Organization: A Case History," *JP*, Aug. 57, p. 461.

Norman K. Keiser, "Public Responsibility and Federal Advisory Groups: A Case Study," *WPQ*, Jan. 58, p. 251. (Business Advisory Group and Department of Commerce.)

Elma M. Saletan, "Administrative Trustification," *WPQ*, Dec. 58, p. 857. (Use of advisory groups.)

Wallace Mendelson, "Mr. Justice Frankfurter on Administrative Law," *JP*, Aug. 57, p. 441.

THE FEDERAL COURTS

David Fellman, "Constitutional Law in . . . . . ," in each March issue of *APSR;* a summary of decisions and bibliography of the literature.

Joseph O. Losos, "The Supreme Court and Its Critics: Is the Court Moving Left?" *RP*, July 59, p. 495.

Wallace Mendelson, "The Court Must Not Be Curbed: A Reply to Mr. Byrnes," *JP*, Feb. 57, p. 81.

Robert J. Steamer, "Statesmanship or Craftsmanship: Current Conflict Over the Supreme Court," *WPQ*, June 58, p. 265.

John R. Schmidhauser, "The Justices of the Supreme Court: A Collective Portrait," *MJPS*, Feb. 59, p. 1.

Chester A. Newland, "Legal Periodicals and the U.S. Supreme Court," *MJPS*, Feb. 59, p. 58.

Fred Kort, "Predicting Supreme Court Decisions Mathematically: A Quantitative Analysis of the 'Right To Counsel Cases,' " *APSR*, March 57, p. 1.

Franklin M. Fisher, "The Mathematical Analysis of Supreme Court Decisions: The Use and Abuse of Quantitative Methods," *APSR*, June 58, p. 321. (Reply by Kort, p. 339.)

Glendon A. Schubert, "The Study of Judicial Decision-Making as an Aspect of Political Behavior," *APSR*, Dec. 58, p. 1007. (Game theory and judicial behavior.)

John P. Roche, "Political Science and Science Fiction," *APSR*, Dec. 58, p. 1026. (A response to Schubert.)

Wallace Mendelson, "Mr. Justice Frankfurter on the Distribution of Judicial Power in the United States," *MJPS*, Feb. 58, p. 40.

Glendon A. Schubert, "The Theory of 'The Public Interest' in Judicial Decisionmaking," *MJPS*, Feb. 58, p. 1.

Kenneth W. Treacy, "The Olmstead Case, 1778-1809," *WPQ*, Sept. 57, p. 675. (An early conflict between state and national courts.)

Albert A. Mavrinac, "From *Lochner* to *Brown vs. Topeka:* The Court and Conflicting Concepts of the Political Process," *APSR*, Sept. 58, p. 641.

Alan F. Westin, "The Supreme Court and Group Conflict: Thoughts on Seeing Burke Put Through the Mill," *APSR*, Sept. 58, p. 665. (Response to the Mavrinac article.)

Rita W. Cooley, "The Office of United States Marshal," *WPQ*, March 59, p. 123.

Walter F. Murphy, "Civil Liberties and the Japanese American Cases: A Study in the Uses of *Stare Decisis*," *WPQ*, March 58, p. 3.

PART SIX: BIG GOVERNMENT IN ACTION

Robert E. Elder, "The Public Studies Division of the Department of State: Public Opinion Analysts in the Formulation and Conduct of American Foreign Policy," *WPQ*, Dec. 57, p. 783.

Urban Whitaker, "Is the United States a Second Rate Power?" *WPQ*, June 58, p. 195.

Paul L. Beckett, *"Ad Astra Per Aspera:* Meditations on the Ecology of Technical Assistance Administration," *WPQ*, Sept. 58, p. 437.

Virginia L. Snitow, "The Mushroom Cloud," WPQ, Dec. 58, p. 875.

Neil D. Houghton, "The Challenge to Political Scientists in Recent American Foreign Policy: Scholarship or Indoctrination?" *APSR*, Sept. 58, p. 678.

H. Field Haviland, Jr., "Foreign Aid and the Foreign Policy Process," *APSR*, Sept. 58, p. 689.

Roger Hilsman, "Congressional-Executive Relations and the Foreign Policy Consensus," *APSR*, Sept. 58, p. 725.

Stephen D. Kertesz, "Reflections on Soviet and American Negotiating Behavior," *RP*, Jan. 57, p. 3.

Lawrence H. Fuchs, "Minority Groups and Foreign Policy," *PSQ*, June 59, p. 161.

Doris A. Graber, "The Truman and Eisenhower Doctrines in the Light of the Doctrine of Non-Intervention," *PSQ*, Sept. 58, p. 321.

William C. Mallalieu, "The Origin of the Marshall Plan: A Study in Policy Formation and National Leadership," *PSQ*, Dec. 58, p. 481.

Jahangir Amuzegar, "Point Four: Performance and Prospect," *PSQ*, Dec. 58, p. 530.

Richard N. Swift, "United States Leadership in the United Nations," *WPQ*, June 58, p. 183.

Charles M. Hardin, "American Agriculture," *RP*, April 58, p. 196.

Edward F. Renshaw, "Reclamation and the American Sugar Policy: A Case of Compounding Resource Misallocation," *WPQ*, Dec. 57, p. 858.

James L. Potts, "The Relation of the Income Tax to Democracy in the United States," *WPQ*, Dec. 57, p. 911.

Constitution
of the United States

We the People of the United States, in Order to form a more perfect Union, establish Justice, insure domestic Tranquillity, provide for the common defence, promote the general Welfare, and secure the Blessings of Liberty to ourselves and our Posterity, do ordain and establish this Constitution for the United States of America.

ARTICLE I

Section. 1. All legislative Powers herein granted shall be vested in a Congress of the United States, which shall consist of a Senate and House of Representatives.

Section. 2. The House of Representatives shall be composed of Members chosen every second Year by the People of the several States, and the Electors in each State shall have the Qualifications requisite for Electors of the most numerous Branch of the State Legislature.

No Person shall be a Representative who shall not have attained to the age of twenty five Years, and been seven Years a Citizen of the United States, and who shall not, when elected, be an Inhabitant of that State in which he shall be chosen.

Representatives and direct Taxes shall be apportioned among the several States which may be included within this Union, according to their respective Numbers, *which shall be determined by adding to the whole Number of free Persons, including those bound to Service for a Term of Years, and excluding Indians not taxed, three fifths of all other persons.*[1] The actual Enumeration shall be made within three Years after the first Meeting of the Congress of the United States, and within every subsequent Term of ten Years, in such Manner as they shall by Law direct. The Number of Representatives shall not exceed one for every thirty Thousand, but each State shall have at Least one Representative; and until such enumeration shall be made, the State of New Hampshire shall be entitled to chuse three, Massachusetts eight, Rhode-Island and Providence Plantations one, Connecticut five, New-York six, New Jersey four, Pennsylvania eight, Delaware one, Maryland six, Virginia ten, North Carolina five, South Carolina five, and Georgia three.

When vacancies happen in the Representation from any State, the Executive Authority thereof shall issue Writs of Election to fill such Vacancies.

The House of Representatives shall chuse their Speaker and other Officers; and shall have the sole Power of Impeachment.

Section. 3. The Senate of the United States shall be composed of two Senators from each State, *chosen by the Legislature thereof,*[2] for six Years; and each Senator shall have one Vote.

Immediately after they shall be assembled in Consequence of the first Election, they shall be divided as equally as may be into three Classes. The Seats of the Senators of the first Class shall be vacated at the Expiration of the second Year, of the second Class at the Expiration of the fourth Year, and of the third Class at the Expiration of the sixth Year, so that one third may be chosen every second Year; *and if Vacancies happen by Resignation, or otherwise, during the Recess of the Legislature of any State, the Executive thereof may make temporary Appointments until the next Meeting of the Legislature, which shall then fill such Vacancies.*[3]

No Person shall be a Senator who shall not

---

[1] Throughout, italics are used to indicate passages altered by subsequent amendments. In this instance, for example, see 14th Amendment.

[2] See 17th Amendment.
[3] *Ibid.*

have attained to the Age of thirty Years, and been nine Years a Citizen of the United States, and who shall not, when elected, be an Inhabitant of that State for which he shall be chosen.

The Vice President of the United States shall be President of the Senate, but shall have no Vote, unless they be equally divided.

The Senate shall chuse their other Officers, and also a President pro tempore, in the Absence of the Vice President, or when he shall exercise the Office of President of the United States.

The Senate shall have the sole Power to try all Impeachments. When sitting for that Purpose, they shall be on Oath or Affirmation. When the President of the United States is tried, the Chief Justice shall preside: And no Person shall be convicted without the Concurrence of two thirds of the Members present.

Judgment in Cases of Impeachment shall not extend further than to removal from Office, and disqualification to hold and enjoy any Office of honor, Trust or Profit under the United States: but the Party convicted shall nevertheless be liable and subject to Indictment, Trial, Judgment and Punishment, according to Law.

Section. 4. The Times, Places and Manner of holding Elections for Senators and Representatives, shall be prescribed in each State by the Legislature thereof; but the Congress may at any time by Law make or alter such Regulations, except as to the Places of chusing Senators.

The Congress shall assemble at least once in every Year, and such Meeting shall be on the first Monday in December, unless they shall by Law appoint a different Day.[4]

Section. 5. Each House shall be the Judge of the Elections, Returns and Qualifications of its own Members, and a Majority of each shall constitute a Quorum to do Business; but a smaller Number may adjourn from day to day, and may be authorized to compel the Attendance of absent Members, in such Manner, and under such Penalties as each House may provide.

Each House may determine the Rules of its Proceedings, punish its Members for disorderly Behaviour, and, with the Concurrence of two thirds, expel a Member.

Each House shall keep a Journal of its Proceedings, and from time to time publish the same, excepting such Parts as may in their Judgment require Secrecy; and the Yeas and Nays of the Members of either House on any question shall, at the Desire of one fifth of those Present, be entered on the Journal.

Neither House, during the Session of Congress, shall, without the Consent of the other, adjourn for more than three days, nor to any other Place than that in which the two Houses shall be sitting.

---

[4] See 20th Amendment.

Section. 6. The Senators and Representatives shall receive a Compensation for their Services, to be ascertained by Law, and paid out of the Treasury of the United States. They shall in all Cases, except Treason, Felony and Breach of the Peace, be privileged from Arrest during their Attendance at the Session of their respective Houses, and in going to and returning from the same; and for any Speech or Debate in either House, they shall not be questioned in any other Place.

No Senator or Representative shall, during the Time for which he was elected, be appointed to any civil Office under the Authority of the United States, which shall have been created, or the Emoluments whereof shall have been encreased during such time; and no Person holding any Office under the United States, shall be a Member of either House during his Continuance in Office.

Section. 7. All Bills for raising Revenue shall originate in the House of Representatives; but the Senate may propose or concur with Amendments as on other Bills.

Every Bill which shall have passed the House of Representatives and the Senate, shall, before it become a Law, be presented to the President of the United States; if he approve he shall sign it, but if not he shall return it, with his Objections to that House in which it shall have originated, who shall enter the Objections at large on their Journal, and proceed to reconsider it. If after such Reconsideration two thirds of that House shall agree to pass the Bill, it shall be sent, together with the Objections, to the other House, by which it shall likewise be reconsidered, and if approved by two thirds of that House, it shall become a Law. But in all such Cases the Votes of both Houses shall be determined by yeas and Nays, and the Names of the Persons voting for and against the Bill shall be entered on the Journal of each House respectively. If any Bill shall not be returned by the President within ten Days (Sundays excepted) after it shall have been presented to him, the Same shall be a Law, in like Manner as if he had signed it, unless Congress by their Adjournment prevent its Return, in which Case it shall not be a Law.

Every Order, Resolution, or Vote to which the Concurrence of the Senate and House of Representatives may be necessary (except on a question of Adjournment) shall be presented to the President of the United States; and before the Same shall take Effect, shall be approved by him, or being disapproved by him, shall be repassed by two thirds of the Senate and House of Representatives, according to the Rules and Limitations prescribed in the Case of a Bill.

Section. 8. The Congress shall have Power To lay and collect Taxes, Duties, Imposts and Excises, to pay the Debts and provide for the common Defence and general Welfare of the United States; but all Duties, Imposts and

Excises shall be uniform throughout the United States;

To borrow Money on the credit of the United States;

To regulate Commerce with foreign Nations, and among the several States, and with the Indian Tribes;

To establish an uniform Rule of Naturalization, and uniform Laws on the subject of Bankruptcies throughout the United States;

To coin Money, regulate the Value thereof, and of foreign Coin, and fix the Standard of Weights and Measures;

To provide for the Punishment of counterfeiting the Securities and current Coin of the United States;

To establish Post Offices and post Roads;

To promote the Progress of Science and useful Arts, by securing for limited Times to Authors and Inventors the exclusive Right to their respective Writings and Discoveries;

To constitute Tribunals inferior to the Supreme Court;

To define and punish Piracies and Felonies committed on the high Seas, and Offences against the Law of Nations;

To declare War, grant Letters of Marque and Reprisal, and make Rules concerning Captures on Land and Water;

To raise and support Armies, but no Appropriation of Money to that Use shall be for a longer Term than two Years;

To provide and maintain a Navy;

To make Rules for the Government and Regulation of the land and naval Forces;

To provide for calling forth the Militia to execute the Laws of the Union, suppress Insurrections and repel Invasions;

To provide for organizing, arming, and disciplining, the Militia, and for governing such Part of them as may be employed in the Service of the United States, reserving to the States respectively, the Appointment of the Officers, and the Authority of training the Militia according to the discipline prescribed by Congress;

To exercise exclusive Legislation in all Cases whatsoever, over such District (not exceeding ten Miles square) as may, by Cession of particular States, and the Acceptance of Congress, become the Seat of the Government of the United States, and to exercise like Authority over all Places purchased by the Consent of the Legislature of the State in which the Same shall be, for the Erection of Forts, Magazines, Arsenals, dock-Yards, and other needful Buildings;—And

To make all Laws which shall be necessary and proper for carrying into Execution the foregoing Powers, and all other Powers vested by this Constitution in the Government of the United States, or in any Department or Officer thereof.

Section. 9. The Migration or Importation of such Persons as any of the States now existing shall think proper to admit, shall not be prohibited by the Congress prior to the Year one thousand eight hundred and eight, but a Tax or duty may be imposed on such Importation, not exceeding ten dollars for each Person.

The Privilege of the Writ of Habeas Corpus shall not be suspended, unless when in Cases of Rebellion or Invasion the public Safety may require it.

No Bill of Attainder or ex post facto Law shall be passed.

No Capitation, or other direct, Tax shall be laid, unless in Proportion to the Census or Enumeration herein before directed to be taken.

No Tax or Duty shall be laid on Articles exported from any State.

No Preference shall be given by any Regulation of Commerce or Revenue to the Ports of one State over those of another: nor shall Vessels bound to, or from, one State, be obliged to enter, clear or pay Duties in another.

No Money shall be drawn from the Treasury, but in Consequence of Appropriations made by Law; and a regular Statement and Account of the Receipts and Expenditures of all public Money shall be published from time to time.

No title of Nobility shall be granted by the United States: And no Person holding any Office of Profit or Trust under them, shall, without the Consent of the Congress, accept of any present, Emolument, Office, or Title, of any kind whatever, from any King, Prince, or foreign State.

Section. 10. No State shall enter into any Treaty, Alliance, or Confederation; grant Letters of Marque and Reprisal; coin Money; emit Bills of Credit; make any Thing but gold and silver Coin a Tender in Payment of Debts; pass any Bill of Attainder, ex post facto Law, or Law impairing the Obligation of Contracts, or Grant any Title of Nobility.

No State shall, without the Consent of the Congress, lay any Imposts or Duties on Imports or Exports, except what may be absolutely necessary for executing its inspection Laws: and the net Produce of all Duties and Imposts, laid by any State on Imports or Exports, shall be for the Use of the Treasury of the United States; and all such Laws shall be subject to the Revision and Controul of the Congress.

No State shall, without the Consent of Congress, lay any Duty of Tonnage, keep Troops, or Ships of War in time of Peace, enter into any Agreement or Compact with another State, or with a foreign Power, or engage in War, unless actually invaded, or in such imminent Danger as will not admit of delay.

ARTICLE II

Section. 1. The executive Power shall be vested in a President of the United States of

America. He shall hold his Office during the Term of four Years, and, together with the Vice President, chosen for the same Term, be elected, as follows

Each State shall appoint, in such Manner as the Legislature thereof may direct, a Number of Electors, equal to the whole Number of Senators and Representatives to which the State may be entitled in the Congress: but no Senator or Representative, or Person holding an Office of Trust or Profit under the United States, shall be appointed an Elector.

The Electors shall meet in their respective States, and vote by Ballot for two Persons, of whom one at least shall not be an Inhabitant of the same State with themselves. And they shall make a List of all the Persons voted for, and of the Number of Votes for each; which List they shall sign and certify, and transmit sealed to the Seat of the Government of the United States, directed to the President of the Senate. The President of the Senate shall, in the Presence of the Senate and House of Representatives, open all the Certificates, and the Votes shall then be counted. The Person having the greatest Number of Votes shall be the President, if such Number be a Majority of the whole Number of Electors appointed; and if there be more than one who have such Majority, and have an equal Number of Votes, then the House of Representatives shall immediately chuse by Ballot one of them for President; and if no Person have a Majority, then from the five highest on the List the said House shall in like Manner chuse the President. But in chusing the President, the Votes shall be taken by States, the Representation from each State having one Vote; A quorum for this purpose shall consist of a Member or Members from two thirds of the States, and a Majority of all the States shall be necessary to a Choice. In every Case, after the Choice of the President, the Person having the greatest Number of Votes of the Electors shall be the Vice President. But if there should remain two or more who have equal Votes, the Senate shall chuse from them by Ballot the Vice President.[5]

The Congress may determine the Time of chusing the Electors, and the Day on which they shall give their Votes; which Day shall be the same throughout the United States.

No Person except a natural born Citizen, or a Citizen of the United States, at the time of the Adoption of this Constitution, shall be eligible to the Office of President; neither shall any Person be eligible to that Office who shall not have attained to the Age of thirty five Years, and been fourteen Years a Resident within the United States.

In Case of the Removal of the President from Office, or of his Death, Resignation, or Inability to discharge the Powers and Duties of the said Office, the Same shall devolve on the Vice President, and the Congress may by Law provide for the Case of Removal, Death, Resignation or Inability, both of the President and Vice President, declaring what Officer shall then act as President, and such Officer shall act accordingly, until the Disability be removed, or a President shall be elected.

The President shall, at stated Times, receive for his Services, a Compensation which shall neither be encreased nor diminished during the Period for which he shall have been elected, and he shall not receive within that Period any other Emolument from the United States, or any of them.

Before he enter on the Execution of his Office, he shall take the following Oath or Affirmation:—"I do solemnly swear (or affirm) that I will faithfully execute the Office of President of the United States, and will to the best of my Ability, preserve, protect and defend the Constitution of the United States."

Section. 2. The President shall be Commander in Chief of the Army and Navy of the United States, and of the Militia of the several States, when called into the actual service of the United States; he may require the Opinion, in writing, of the principal Officer in each of the executive Departments, upon any Subject relating to the Duties of their respective Offices, and he shall have Power to grant Reprieves and Pardons for Offences against the United States, except in Cases of Impeachment.

He shall have Power, by and with the Advice and Consent of the Senate, to make Treaties, provided two thirds of the Senators present concur; and he shall nominate, and by and with the Advice and Consent of the Senate, shall appoint Ambassadors, other public Ministers and Consuls, Judges of the supreme Court, and all other Officers of the United States, whose Appointments are not herein otherwise provided for, and which shall be established by Law: but the Congress may by Law vest the Appointment of such inferior Officers, as they think proper, in the President alone, in the Courts of Law, or in the Heads of Departments.

The President shall have Power to fill up all Vacancies that may happen during the Recess of the Senate, by granting Commissions which shall expire at the End of their next Session.

Section. 3. He shall from time to time give to the Congress Information of the State of the Union, and recommend to their Consideration such Measures as he shall judge necessary and expedient; he may, on extraordinary Occasions, convene both Houses, or either of them, and in Case of Disagreement between them, with Respect to the Time of Adjournment, he may adjourn them to such Time as he shall think proper; he shall receive Ambassadors and other public Ministers; he shall take Care that the Laws be faithfully executed, and shall Commission all the Officers of the United States.

---

[5] Superseded by the 12th Amendment.

Section. 4. The President, Vice President and all civil Officers of the United States, shall be removed from Office on Impeachment for, and Conviction of, Treason, Bribery, or other high Crimes and Misdemeanors.

ARTICLE III

Section. 1. The judicial Power of the United States, shall be vested in one supreme Court, and in such inferior Courts as the Congress may from time to time ordain and establish. The Judges, both of the supreme and inferior Courts, shall hold their Offices during good Behavior, and shall, at stated Times, receive for their Services, a Compensation, which shall not be diminished during their Continuance in Office.

Section. 2. The judicial Power shall extend to all Cases, in Law and Equity, arising under this Constitution, the Laws of the United States, and Treaties made, or which shall be made, under their Authority;—to all Cases affecting Ambassadors, other public Ministers and Consuls;—to all Cases of admiralty and maritime Jurisdiction;—to Controversies to which the United States shall be a Party;—to Controversies between two or more States;—*between a State and Citizens of another State;* 6—between Citizens of different States; —between Citizens of the same State claiming Lands under Grants of different States, *and between a State, or the Citizens thereof, and foreign States, Citizens or Subjects.*7

In all cases affecting Ambassadors, other public Ministers and Consuls, and those in which a State shall be Party, the supreme Court shall have original Jurisdiction. In all the other Cases before mentioned, the supreme Court shall have appellate Jurisdiction, both as to Law and Fact, with such Exceptions, and under such Regulations as the Congress shall make.

The Trial of all Crimes, except in Cases of Impeachment, shall be by Jury; and such Trial shall be held in the State where the said Crimes shall have been committed; but when not committed within any State, the Trial shall be at such Place or Places as the Congress may by Law have directed.

Section. 3. Treason against the United States, shall consist only in levying War against them, or in adhering to their Enemies, giving them Aid and Comfort. No Person shall be convicted of Treason unless on the Testimony of two Witnesses to the same overt Act, or on Confession in open Court.

The Congress shall have Power to declare the Punishment of Treason, but no Attainder of Treason shall work Corruption of Blood, or Forfeiture except during the Life of the Person attainted.

ARTICLE IV

Section. 1. Full Faith and Credit shall be given in each State to the public Acts, Records, and judicial Proceedings of every other State. And the Congress may by general Laws prescribe the Manner in which such Acts, Records and Proceedings shall be proved, and the Effect therof.

Section. 2. The Citizens of each State shall be entitled to all Privileges and Immunities of Citizens in the several States.

A Person charged in any State with Treason, Felony, or other Crime, who shall flee from Justice, and be found in another State, shall on Demand of the executive Authority of the State from which he fled, be delivered up, to be removed to the State having Jurisdiction of the Crime.

*No Person held to Service or Labour in one State, under the Laws thereof, escaping into another, shall, in Consequence of any Law or Regulation therein, be discharged from such Service or Labour, but shall be delivered up on Claim of the Party to whom such Service or Labour may be due.*8

Section. 3. New States may be admitted by the Congress into this Union; but no new State shall be formed or erected within the Jurisdiction of any other State; nor any State be formed by the Junction of two or more States, or Parts of States, without the Consent of the Legislatures of the States concerned as well as of the Congress.

The Congress shall have Power to dispose of and make all needful Rules and Regulations respecting the Territory or other Property belonging to the United States; and nothing in this Constitution shall be so construed as to Prejudice any claims of the United States, or of any particular State.

Section. 4. The United States shall guarantee to every State in this Union a Republican Form of Government, and shall protect each of them against Invasion; and on Application of the Legislature, or of the Executive (when the Legislature cannot be convened) against domestic Violence.

ARTICLE V

The Congress, whenever two thirds of both Houses shall deem it necessary, shall propose Amendments to this Constitution, or, on the Application of the Legislatures of two thirds of the several States, shall call a Convention for proposing Amendments, which, in either Case, shall be valid to all Intents and Pur-

---

6 See the 11th Amendment.
7 *Ibid.*

8 See 13th Amendment.

poses, as Part of this Constitution, when ratified by the Legislatures of three fourths of the several States, or by Conventions in three fourths thereof, as the one or the other Mode of Ratification may be proposed by the Congress; Provided that no Amendment which may be made prior to the Year One thousand eight hundred and eight shall in any Manner affect the first and fourth Clauses in the Ninth Section of the first Article; and that no State, without its Consent, shall be deprived of its equal Suffrage in the Senate.

ARTICLE VI

All Debts contracted and Engagements entered into, before the Adoption of this Constitution, shall be as valid against the United States under this Constitution, as under the Confederation.

This Constitution, and the Laws of the United States which shall be made in Pursuance thereof; and all Treaties made, or which shall be made, under the Authority of the United States, shall be the supreme Law of the Land; and the Judges in every State shall be bound thereby, any Thing in the Constitution or Laws of any State to the Contrary notwithstanding.

The Senators and Representatives before mentioned, and the Members of the several State Legislatures, and all executive and judicial Officers, both of the United States and of the several States, shall be bound by Oath or Affirmation, to support this Constitution; but no religious Test shall ever be required as a Qualification to any Office or public Trust under the United States.

ARTICLE VII

The Ratification of the Conventions of nine States, shall be sufficient for the Establishment of this Constitution between the States so ratifying the Same.

DONE in Convention by the Unanimous Consent of the States present the Seventeenth Day of September in the Year of our Lord one thousand seven hundred and Eighty seven and of the Independence of the United States of America the Twelfth In witness whereof We have hereunto subscribed our Names.

.   .   .

ARTICLES IN ADDITION TO, AND AMENDMENT OF, THE CONSTITUTION OF THE UNITED STATES OF AMERICA, PROPOSED BY CONGRESS, AND RATIFIED BY THE SEVERAL STATES, PURSUANT TO THE FIFTH ARTICLE OF THE ORIGINAL CONSTITUTION.

AMENDMENT I

[Ratification of the first ten amendments was completed December 15, 1791]

Congress shall make no law respecting an establishment of religion, or prohibiting the free exercise thereof; or abridging the freedom of speech, or of the press; or the right of the people peaceably to assemble, and to petition the Government for a redress of grievances.

AMENDMENT II

A well regulated Militia, being necessary to the security of a free State, the right of the people to keep and bear Arms, shall not be infringed.

AMENDMENT III

No Soldier shall, in time of peace be quartered in any house, without the consent of the Owner, nor in time of war, but in a manner to be prescribed by law.

AMENDMENT IV

The right of the people to be secure in their persons, houses, papers, and effects, against unreasonable searches and seizures, shall not be violated, and no Warrants shall issue, but upon probable cause, supported by Oath or affirmation, and particularly describing the place to be searched, and the persons or things to be seized.

AMENDMENT V

No person shall be held to answer for a capital, or otherwise infamous crime, unless on a presentment or indictment of a Grand Jury, except in cases arising in the land or naval forces, or in the Militia, when in actual service in time of War or public danger; nor shall any person be subject for the same offence to be twice put in jeopardy of life or limb; nor shall be compelled in any criminal case to be a witness against himself, nor be deprived of life, liberty, or property, without due process of law; nor shall private property be taken for public use, without just compensation.

AMENDMENT VI

In all criminal prosecutions, the accused shall enjoy the right to a speedy and public trial, by an impartial jury of the State and district wherein the crime shall have been committed, which district shall have been previously ascertained by law, and to be in-

formed of the nature and cause of the accusation; to be confronted with the witness against him; to have compulsory process for obtaining witness in his favor, and to have the Assistance of Counsel for his defence.

AMENDMENT VII

In Suits at common law, where the value in controversy shall exceed twenty dollars, the right of trial by jury shall be preserved, and no fact tried by a jury, shall be otherwise re-examined in any Court of the United States, than according to the rules of the common law.

AMENDMENT VIII

Excessive bail shall not be required, nor excessive fines imposed, nor cruel and unusual punishments inflicted.

AMENDMENT IX

The enumeration in the Constitution, of certain rights, shall not be construed to deny or disparage others retained by the people.

AMENDMENT X

The powers not delegated to the United States by the Constitution, nor prohibited by it to the States, are reserved to the States respectively, or to the people.

AMENDMENT XI

[January 8, 1798]

The Judicial power of the United States shall not be construed to extend to any suit in law or equity, commenced or prosecuted against one of the United States by Citizens of another State, or by Citizens or Subjects of any Foreign State.

AMENDMENT XII

[September 25, 1804]

The Electors shall meet in their respective states and vote by ballot for President and Vice-President, one of whom, at least, shall not be an inhabitant of the same state with themselves; they shall name in their ballots the person voted for as President, and in distinct ballots the person voted for as Vice-President, and they shall make distinct lists of all persons voted for as President, and of all persons voted for as Vice-President, and of the number of votes for each, which lists

they shall sign and certify, and transmit sealed to the seat of the government of the United States, directed to the President of the Senate; —The President of the Senate shall, in the presence of Senate and House of Representatives, open all the certificates and the votes shall then be counted;—The person having the greatest number of votes for President, shall be the President, if such number be a majority of the whole number of Electors appointed; and if no person have such majority, then from the persons having the highest numbers not exceeding three on the list of those voted for as President, the House of Representatives shall choose immediately, by ballot, the President. But in choosing the President, the votes shall be taken by states, the representation from each state having one vote; a quorum for this purpose shall consist of a member or members from two-thirds of the states, and a majority of all the states shall be necessary to a choice. And if the House of Representatives shall not choose a President whenever the right of choice shall devolve upon them, *before the fourth day of March next following,*[9] then the Vice-President shall act as President, as in the case of the death or other constitutional disability of the President.—The person having the greatest number of votes as Vice-President, shall be the Vice-President, if such number be a majority of the whole number of Electors appointed, and if no person have a majority, then from the two highest numbers on the list, the Senate shall choose the Vice-President; a quorum for the purpose shall consist of two-thirds of the whole number of Senators, and a majority of the whole number shall be necessary to a choice. But no person constitutionally ineligible to the office of President shall be eligible to that of Vice-President of the United States.

AMENDMENT XIII

[December 18, 1865]

Section 1. Neither slavery nor involuntary servitude, except as a punishment for crime whereof the party shall have been duly convicted, shall exist within the United States, or any place subject to their jurisdiction.

Section 2. Congress shall have power to enforce this article by appropriate legislation.

AMENDMENT XIV

[July 28, 1868]

Section 1. All persons born or naturalized in the United States, and subject to the jurisdiction thereof, are citizens of the United States and of the State wherein they reside. No State shall make or enforce any law which

---

[9] Altered by the 20th Amendment.

shall abridge the privileges or immunities of citizens of the United States; nor shall any state deprive any person of life, liberty, or property, without due process of law; nor deny to any person within its jurisdiction the equal protection of the laws.

Section 2. Representatives shall be apportioned among the several States according to their respective numbers, counting the whole number of persons in each State, excluding Indians not taxed. But when the right to vote at any election for the choice of electors for President and Vice President of the United States, Representatives in Congress, the Executive and Judicial officers of a State, or the members of the Legislature thereof, is denied to any of the male inhabitants of such State, being twenty-one years of age, and citizens of the United States, or in any way abridged, except for participation in rebellion, or other crime, the basis of representation therein shall be reduced in the proportion which the number of such male citizens shall bear to the whole number of male citizens twenty-one years of age in such State.

Section 3. No person shall be a Senator or Representative in Congress, or elector of President and Vice President, or hold any office, civil or military, under the United States, or under any State, who, having previously taken an oath, as a member of Congress, or as an officer of the United States, or as a member of any State legislature, or as an executive or judicial officer of any State, to support the Constitution of the United States, shall have engaged in insurrection or rebellion against the same, or given aid or comfort to the enemies thereof. But Congress may by a vote of two-thirds of each House, remove such disability.

Section 4. The validity of the public debt of the United States, authorized by law, including debts incurred for payment of pensions and bounties for services in suppressing insurrection or rebellion, shall not be questioned. But neither the United States nor any State shall assume or pay any debt or obligation incurred in aid of insurrection or rebellion against the United States, or any claim for the loss or emancipation of any slave; but all such debts, obligations and claims shall be held illegal and void.

Section 5. The Congress shall have power to enforce, by appropriate legislation, the provisions of this article.

AMENDMENT XV

[March 30, 1870]

Section 1. The right of citizens of the United States to vote shall not be denied or abridged by the United States or by any State on account of race, color, or previous condition of servitude.

Section 2. The Congress shall have power to enforce this article by appropriate legislation.

AMENDMENT XVI

[February 25, 1913]

The Congress shall have power to lay and collect taxes on incomes, from whatever source derived, without apportionment among the several States, and without regard to any census or enumeration.

AMENDMENT XVII

[May 31, 1913]

The Senate of the United States shall be composed of two Senators from each State, elected by the people thereof, for six years; and each Senator shall have one vote. The electors in each State shall have the qualifications requisite for electors of the most numerous branch of the State legislatures.

When vacancies happen in the representation of any State in the Senate, the executive authority of such State shall issue writs of election to fill such vacancies: *Provided,* That the legislature of any State may empower the executive thereof to make temporary appointments until the people fill the vacancies by election as the legislature may direct.

This amendment shall not be so construed as to affect the election or term of any Senator chosen before it becomes valid as part of the Constitution.

AMENDMENT XVIII

[January 29, 1919]

Section 1. *After one year from the ratification of this article the manufacture, sale, or transportation of intoxicating liquors within, the importation thereof into, or the exportation thereof from the United States and all territory subject to the jurisdiction thereof for beverage purposes is hereby prohibited.*

Sec. 2. *The Congress and the several States shall have concurrent power to enforce this article by appropriate legislation.*

Sec. 3. *This article shall be inoperative unless it shall have been ratified as an amendment to the Constitution by the legislatures of the several States, as provided in the Constitution, within seven years from the date of the submission hereof to the States by the Congress.*[10]

AMENDMENT XIX

[August 26, 1920]

The right of citizens of the United States to vote shall not be denied or abridged by the

---

[10] Repealed by the 21st Amendment.

United States or by any State on account of sex.

Congress shall have power to enforce this article by appropriate legislation.

AMENDMENT XX

[February 6, 1933]

Section 1. The terms of the President and Vice President shall end at noon on the 20th day of January, and the terms of Senators and Representatives at noon on the 3d day of January, of the years in which such terms would have ended if this article had not been ratified; and the terms of their successors shall then begin.

Sec. 2. The Congress shall assemble at least once in every year, and such meeting shall begin at noon on the 3d day of January, unless they shall by law appoint a different day.

Sec. 3. If, at the time fixed for the beginning of the term of the President, the President elect shall have died, the Vice President elect shall become President. If a President shall not have been chosen before the time fixed for the beginning of his term, or if the President elect shall have failed to qualify, then the Vice President elect shall act as President until a President shall have qualified; and the Congress may by law provide for the case wherein neither a President elect nor a Vice President elect shall have qualified, declaring who shall then act as President, or the manner in which one who is to act shall be selected, and such person shall act accordingly until a President or Vice President shall have qualified.

Sec. 4. The Congress may by law provide for the case of the death of any of the persons from whom the House of Representatives may choose a President whenever the right of choice shall have devolved upon them, and for the case of the death of any of the persons from whom the Senate may choose a Vice President whenever the right of choice shall have devolved upon them.

Sec. 5. Sections 1 and 2 shall take effect on the 15th day of October following the ratification of this article.

Sec. 6. This article shall be inoperative un-less it shall have been ratified as an amendment to the Constitution by the legislatures of three-fourths of the several States within seven years from the date of its submission.

AMENDMENT XXI

[December 5, 1933]

Section 1. The eighteenth article of amendment to the Constitution of the United States is hereby repealed.

Sec. 2. The transportation or importation into any State, Territory, or possession of the United States for delivery or use therein of intoxicating liquors, in violation of the laws thereof, is hereby prohibited.

Sec. 3. This article shall be inoperative unless it shall have been ratified as an amendment to the Constitution by conventions in the several States, as provided in the Constitution, within seven years from the date of the submission hereof to the States by the Congress.

AMENDMENT XXII

[February 26, 1951]

Section 1. No person shall be elected to the office of the President more than twice, and no person who has held the office of President, or acted as President, for more than two years of a term to which some other person was elected President shall be elected to the office of President more than once. But this Article shall not apply to any person holding the office of President when this Article was proposed by the Congress, and shall not prevent any person who may be holding the office of President, or acting as President, during the term within which this Article becomes operative from holding the office of President or acting as President during the remainder of such term.

Sec. 2. This article shall be inoperative unless it shall have been ratified as an amendment to the Constitution by the legislatures of three-fourths of the several States within seven years from the date of its submission to the States by the Congress.

Index